STAN LEE PRESENTS:

THE ESSENTIAL X-MEN

VOLUME 2

UNCANNY X-MEN #120-144

SSENTIAL X-MEN® VOL. II Originally published in magazine form as UNCANNY X-MEN #'s 120-144. Published by MARVEL COMICS; 387 PARK AVEN
OUTH, NEW YORK, N.Y. 10016. Copyright © 1979, 1980, 1981, 1997 Marvel Characters, Inc. All rights reserved. X-MEN (including all prominent charac
atured in this issue and the distinctive likenesses thereof) is a trademark of MARVEL CHARACTERS, INC. No part of this book may be printed or reprodu
any manner without the written permission of the publisher. Printed in the U.S.A. 2nd Printing   ISBN #0-7851-0298-1. GST #R127032852.

P. 256 #134 CO-PLOT & SCRIPT - CHRIS CLAREMONT, CO-PLOT & PENCILER - JOHN BYRNE, INKER - TERRY AUSTIN, LETTERER - TOM ORZECHOWSKI, EDITOR - JIM SALICRUP

P. 274 #135 CO-PLOT & SCRIPT - CHRIS CLAREMONT, CO-PLOT & PENCILER - JOHN BYRNE, INKER - TERRY AUSTIN, LETTERER - TOM ORZECHOWSKI, EDITOR - JIM SALICRUP

P. 292 #136 CO-PLOT & SCRIPT - CHRIS CLAREMONT, CO-PLOT & PENCILER - JOHN BYRNE, INKER - TERRY AUSTIN, LETTERER - TOM ORZECHOWSKI, EDITOR - JIM SALICRUP

P. 310 #137 CO-PLOT & SCRIPT - CHRIS CLAREMONT, CO-PLOT & PENCILER - JOHN BYRNE, INKER - TERRY AUSTIN, LETTERER - TOM ORZECHOWSKI, EDITOR - JIM SALICRUP

P. 346 #138 CO-PLOT & SCRIPT - CHRIS CLAREMONT, CO-PLOT & PENCILER - JOHN BYRNE, INKER - TERRY AUSTIN, LETTERER - TOM ORZECHOWSKI, EDITOR - LOUISE JONES

P. 366 #139 CO-PLOT & SCRIPT - CHRIS CLAREMONT, CO-PLOT & PENCILER - JOHN BYRNE, INKER - TERRY AUSTIN, LETTERER - TOM ORZECHOWSKI, EDITOR - LOUISE JONES

P. 389 #140 CO-PLOT & SCRIPT - CHRIS CLAREMONT, CO-PLOT & PENCILER - JOHN BYRNE, INKER - TERRY AUSTIN, LETTERER - TOM ORZECHOWSKI, EDITOR - LOUISE JONES

P. 412 #141 CO-PLOT & SCRIPT - CHRIS CLAREMONT, CO-PLOT & PENCILER - JOHN BYRNE, INKER - TERRY AUSTIN, LETTERER - TOM ORZECHOWSKI, EDITOR - LOUISE JONES

P. 436 #142 CO-PLOT & SCRIPT - CHRIS CLAREMONT, CO-PLOT & PENCILER - JOHN BYRNE, INKER - TERRY AUSTIN, LETTERER - TOM ORZECHOWSKI, EDITOR - LOUISE JONES

P. 458 #143 CO-PLOT & SCRIPT - CHRIS CLAREMONT, CO-PLOT & PENCILER - JOHN BYRNE, INKER - TERRY AUSTIN, LETTERER - TOM ORZECHOWSKI, EDITOR - LOUISE JONES

P. 481 #144 WRITER - CHRIS CLAREMONT, PENCILER - BRENT ANDERSON, INKER - JOSEF RUBINSTEIN, LETTERER - TOM ORZECHOWSKI, EDITOR - LOUISE JONES

REPRINT CREDITS

PAUL TUTRONE - REPRINT ASSISTANT EDITOR

JOE ANDREANI - REPRINT EDITOR

BOB HARRAS - EDITOR IN CHIEF

JOHN BYRNE - NEW COVER ART

CHRIS LICHTNER - COVER COLORS AND SEPARATIONS

CAROLINE "MISTRESS" WELLS - DESIGN

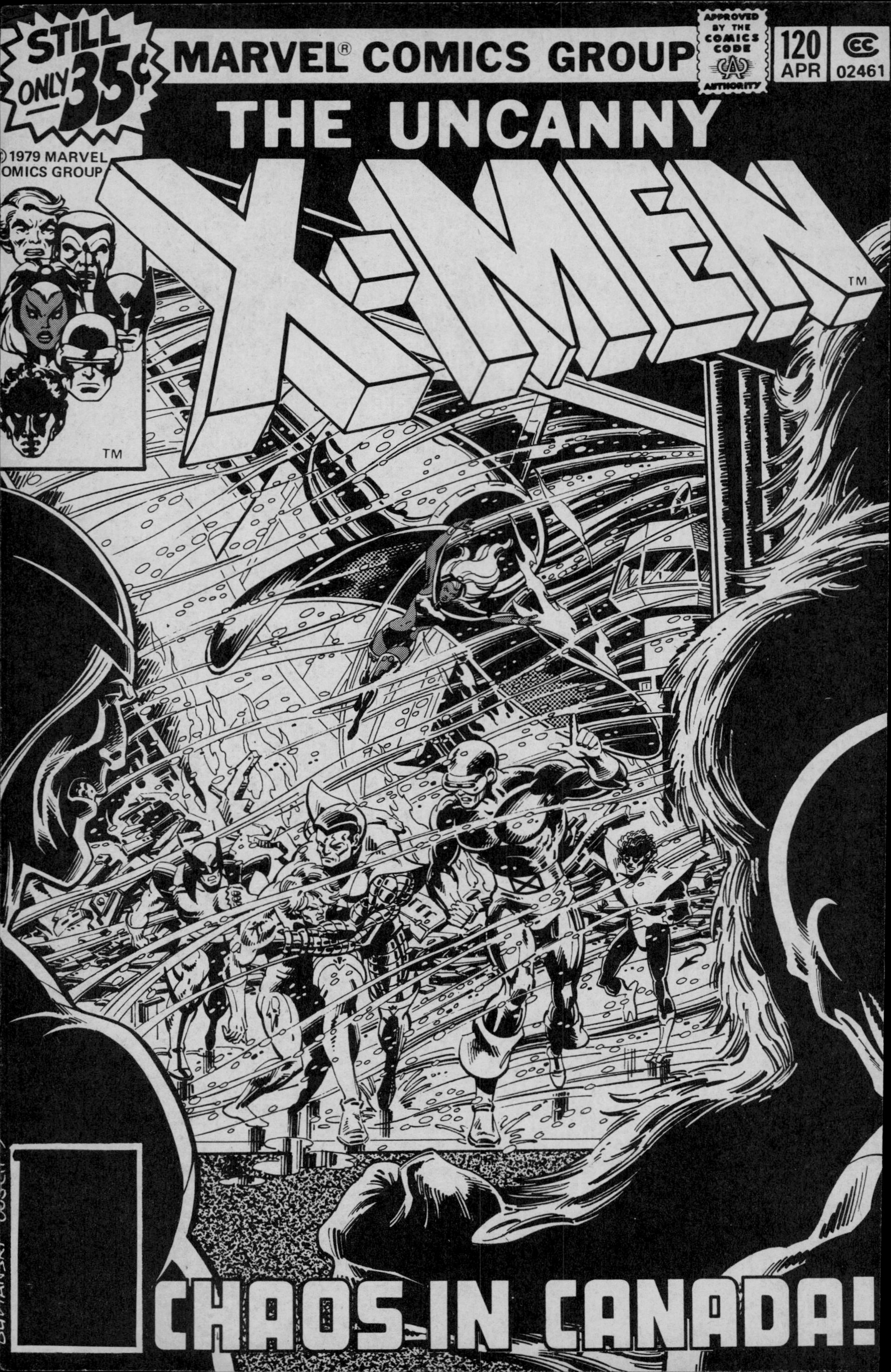
STILL ONLY 35¢
MARVEL® COMICS GROUP
APPROVED BY THE COMICS CODE AUTHORITY
120 APR
CC 02461
THE UNCANNY
© 1979 MARVEL COMICS GROUP
X-MEN™
TM
CHAOS IN CANADA!

Cyclops. Storm. Banshee. Nightcrawler. Wolverine. Colossus. Children of the atom, students of Charles Xavier, MUTANTS––feared and hated by the world they have sworn to protect. These are the STRANGEST heroes of all!

Stan Lee PRESENTS: THE UNCANNY X-MEN!™

CHRIS CLAREMONT & JOHN BYRNE AUTHOR/CO-PLOTTERS/PENCILER * TERRY AUSTIN INKER | TOM ORZECHOWSKI, letterer GLYNIS WEIN, colorist | ROGER STERN EDITOR | JIM SHOOTER EDITOR-IN-CHIEF

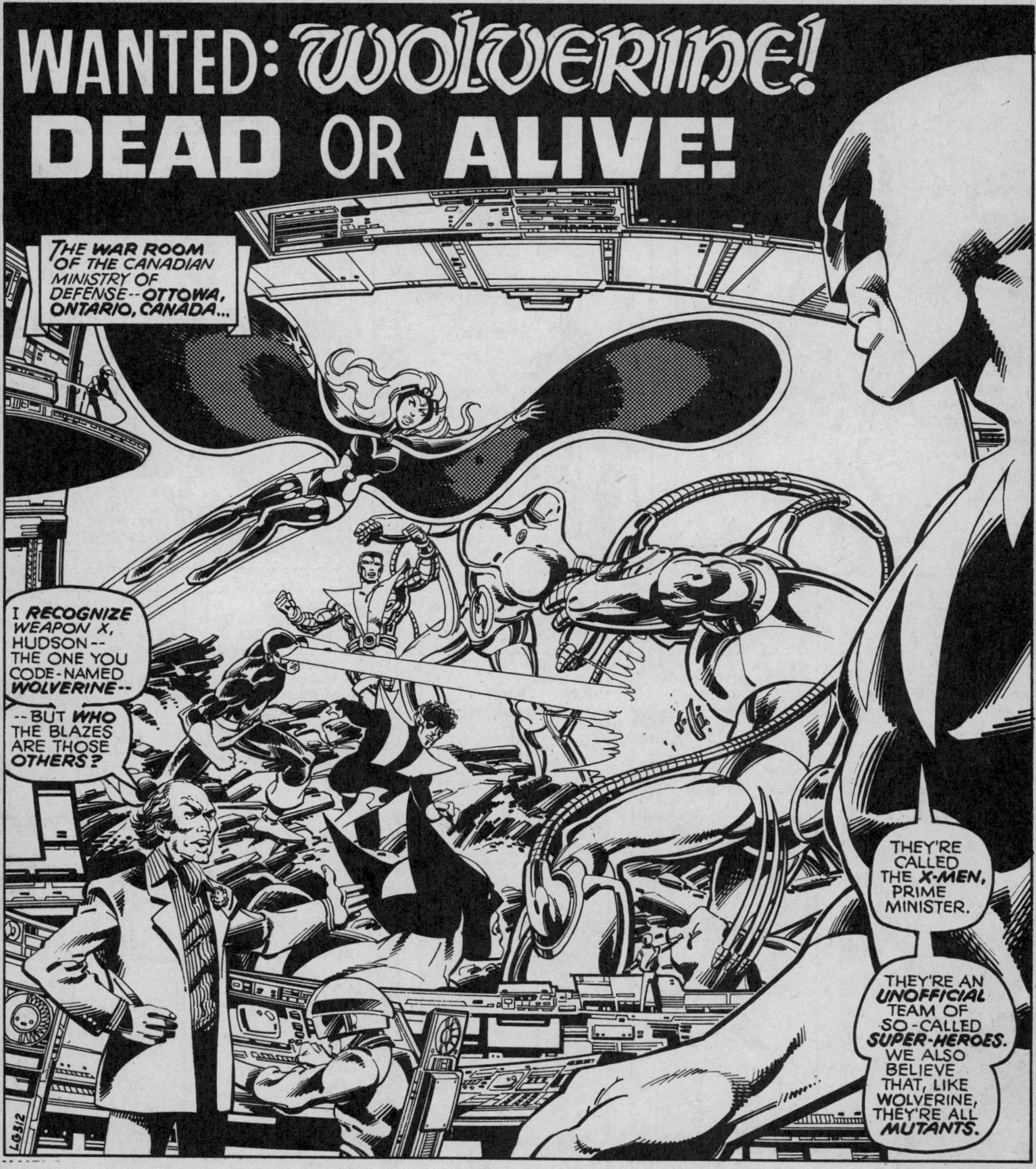
WANTED: WOLVERINE!
DEAD OR ALIVE!
THE WAR ROOM OF THE CANADIAN MINISTRY OF DEFENSE--OTTOWA, ONTARIO, CANADA...
I RECOGNIZE WEAPON X, HUDSON-- THE ONE YOU CODE-NAMED WOLVERINE--
--BUT WHO THE BLAZES ARE THOSE OTHERS?
THEY'RE CALLED THE X-MEN, PRIME MINISTER.
THEY'RE AN UNOFFICIAL TEAM OF SO-CALLED SUPER-HEROES. WE ALSO BELIEVE THAT, LIKE WOLVERINE, THEY'RE ALL MUTANTS.

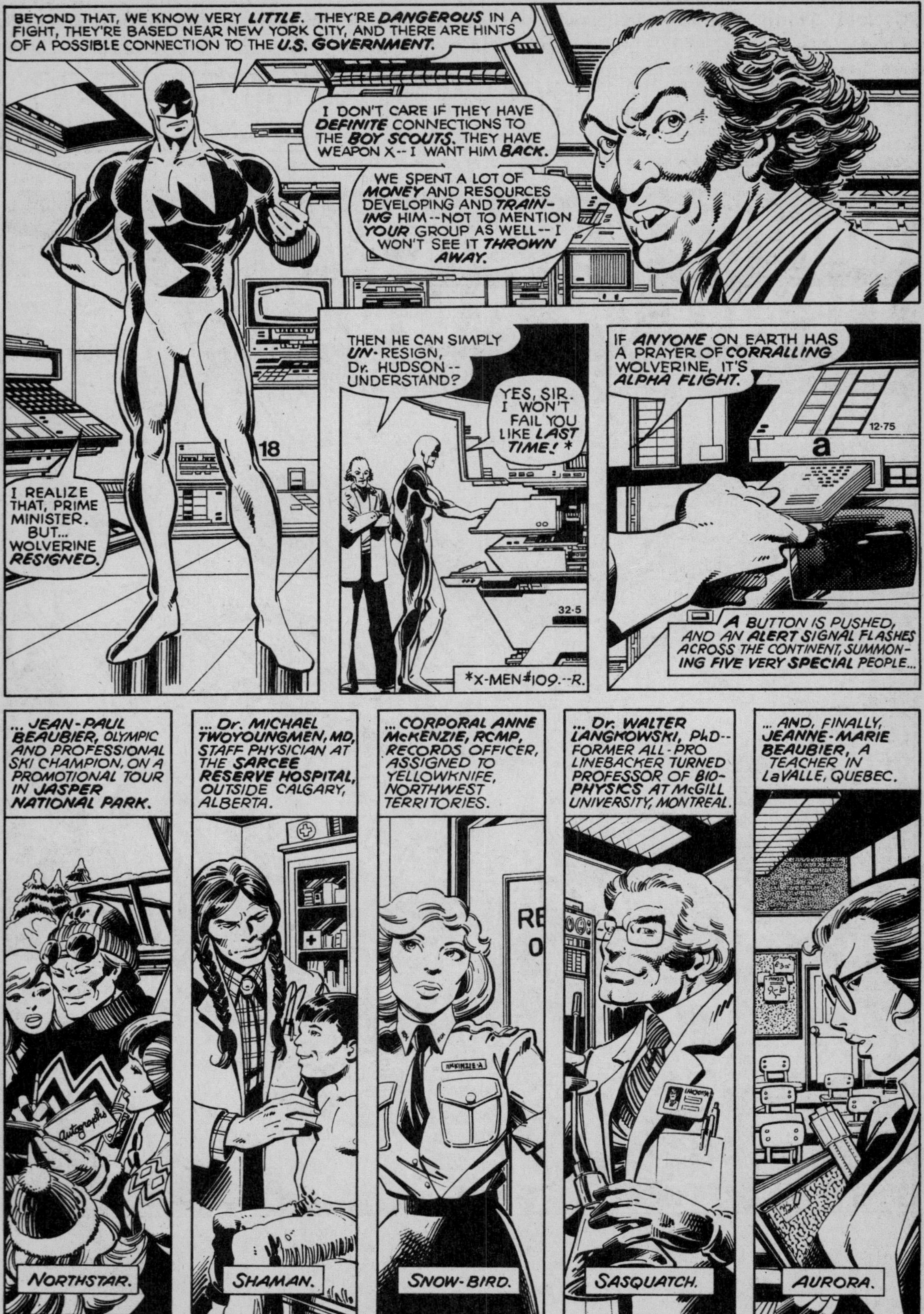
BEYOND THAT, WE KNOW VERY LITTLE. THEY'RE DANGEROUS IN A FIGHT, THEY'RE BASED NEAR NEW YORK CITY, AND THERE ARE HINTS OF A POSSIBLE CONNECTION TO THE U.S. GOVERNMENT.
I DON'T CARE IF THEY HAVE DEFINITE CONNECTIONS TO THE BOY SCOUTS. THEY HAVE WEAPON X-- I WANT HIM BACK.
WE SPENT A LOT OF MONEY AND RESOURCES DEVELOPING AND TRAINING HIM --NOT TO MENTION YOUR GROUP AS WELL-- I WON'T SEE IT THROWN AWAY.
I REALIZE THAT, PRIME MINISTER. BUT... WOLVERINE RESIGNED.
THEN HE CAN SIMPLY UN-RESIGN, Dr. HUDSON -- UNDERSTAND?
YES, SIR. I WON'T FAIL YOU LIKE LAST TIME! *
*X-MEN #109.--R.
IF ANYONE ON EARTH HAS A PRAYER OF CORRALLING WOLVERINE, IT'S ALPHA FLIGHT.
A BUTTON IS PUSHED, AND AN ALERT SIGNAL FLASHES ACROSS THE CONTINENT, SUMMONING FIVE VERY SPECIAL PEOPLE...
... JEAN-PAUL BEAUBIER, OLYMPIC AND PROFESSIONAL SKI CHAMPION, ON A PROMOTIONAL TOUR IN JASPER NATIONAL PARK.
Autographs
NORTHSTAR.
... Dr. MICHAEL TWOYOUNGMEN, MD, STAFF PHYSICIAN AT THE SARCEE RESERVE HOSPITAL, OUTSIDE CALGARY, ALBERTA.
SHAMAN.
... CORPORAL ANNE McKENZIE, RCMP, RECORDS OFFICER, ASSIGNED TO YELLOWKNIFE, NORTHWEST TERRITORIES.
SNOW-BIRD.
... Dr. WALTER LANGKOWSKI, PhD-- FORMER ALL-PRO LINEBACKER TURNED PROFESSOR OF BIO-PHYSICS AT McGILL UNIVERSITY, MONTREAL.
SASQUATCH.
... AND, FINALLY, JEANNE-MARIE BEAUBIER, A TEACHER IN LaVALLE, QUEBEC.
AURORA.

HALF-A-WORLD AWAY, HOWEVER, THE X-MEN KNOW NOTHING OF THIS AS THEY PREPARE TO LEAVE JAPAN...

...ON WHAT THEY HOPE IS THE LAST LEG OF THEIR SEEMINGLY ENDLESS JOURNEY HOME FROM THE SAVAGE LAND. *

*BEGUN IN X-MEN #116.--R.

SAYONARA, MY FRIEND... AND THANK YOU FOR ALL THE HELP YOU GAVE ME. AND JAPAN.

I WAS... PROUD TO FIGHT BY YOUR SIDE, AND WOULD BE HONORED TO DO SO AGAIN. FAREWELL.

THE FEELING'S MUTUAL, SHIRO. AND REMEMBER-- IF YOU'RE EVER IN THE STATES-- --OUR HOME IS YOURS.

DONE WITH THE CEREMONIES, ARE WE, LADDIE?

THAT WE ARE, BANSHEE--AND ABOUT TIME, TOO. C'MON, PEOPLE, LET'S BOARD THAT PLANE.

WAIT A MOMENT, CYCLOPS! WHERE'S WOLVERINE?!

FOR THAT ANSWER, WE NEED LOOK NO FURTHER THAN THE LIMOUSINE OF SHIRO YASHIDA--SUNFIRE-- PARKED JUST BEYOND THE BARRIER FENCE.

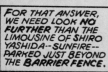

IT HAS ONE OCCUPANT...

"...SHIRO'S COUSIN, MARIKO.

I LIKE THE X-MEN.

TAP! TAP!

I WILL MISS THEM, ESPECIALLY-- WHAT'S THAT?!

SOMEONE OUTSIDE-- BUT WHO?

WHIRRR

≧?!?≦

<A WHITE CHRYSAN-THE-MUM ???>

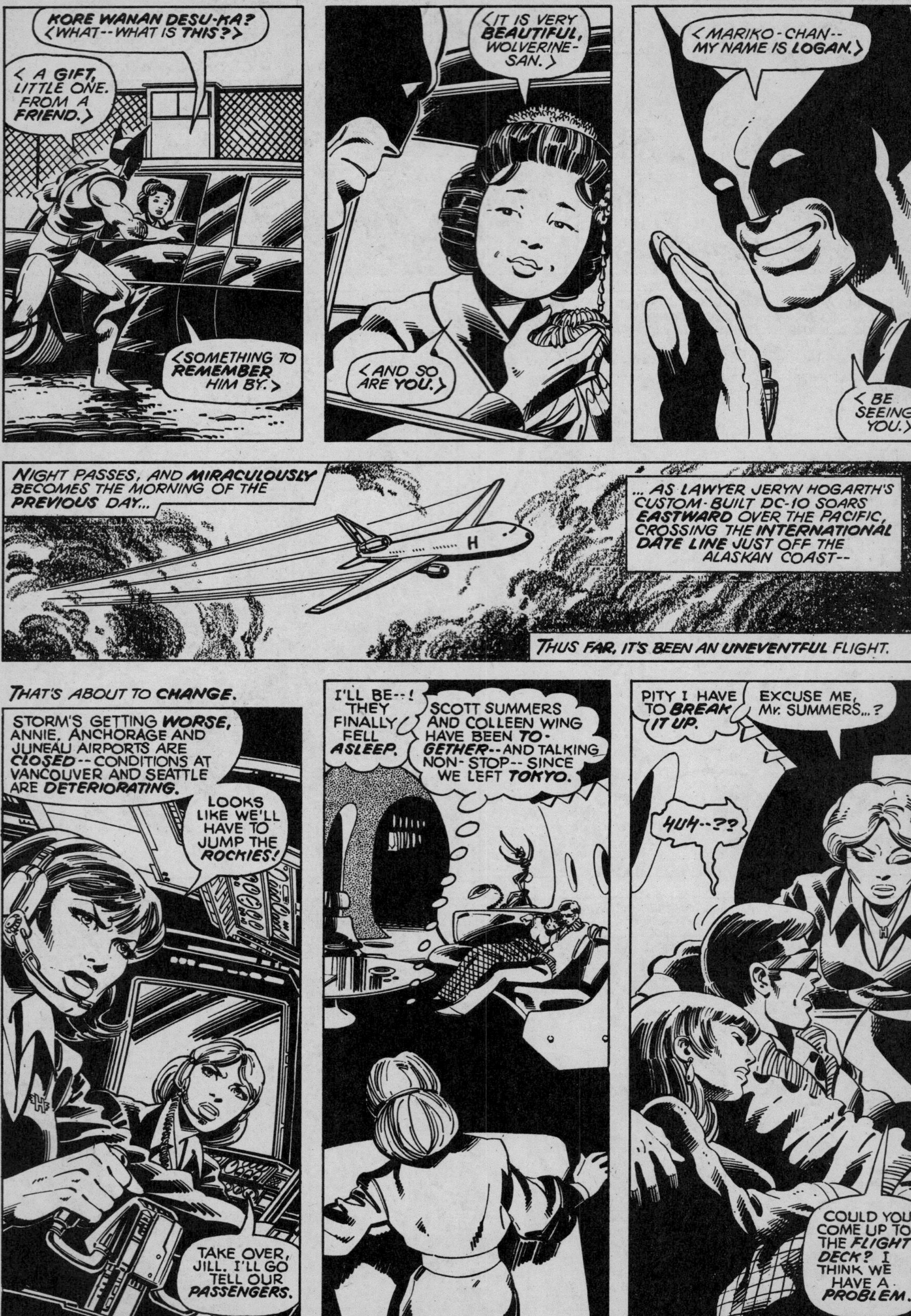

KORE WANAN DESU-KA? <WHAT--WHAT IS THIS?>
< A GIFT, LITTLE ONE. FROM A FRIEND.>
<SOMETHING TO REMEMBER HIM BY.>
<IT IS VERY BEAUTIFUL, WOLVERINE-SAN.>
<AND SO ARE YOU.>
< MARIKO-CHAN-- MY NAME IS LOGAN.>
< BE SEEING YOU.>
NIGHT PASSES, AND MIRACULOUSLY BECOMES THE MORNING OF THE PREVIOUS DAY...
... AS LAWYER JERYN HOGARTH'S CUSTOM-BUILT DC-10 SOARS EASTWARD OVER THE PACIFIC, CROSSING THE INTERNATIONAL DATE LINE JUST OFF THE ALASKAN COAST--
H
THUS FAR, IT'S BEEN AN UNEVENTFUL FLIGHT.
THAT'S ABOUT TO CHANGE.
STORM'S GETTING WORSE, ANNIE. ANCHORAGE AND JUNEAU AIRPORTS ARE CLOSED--CONDITIONS AT VANCOUVER AND SEATTLE ARE DETERIORATING.
LOOKS LIKE WE'LL HAVE TO JUMP THE ROCKIES!
TAKE OVER, JILL. I'LL GO TELL OUR PASSENGERS.
I'LL BE--! THEY FINALLY FELL ASLEEP.
SCOTT SUMMERS AND COLLEEN WING HAVE BEEN TO-GETHER--AND TALKING NON-STOP--SINCE WE LEFT TOKYO.
PITY I HAVE TO BREAK IT UP.
EXCUSE ME, Mr. SUMMERS...?
HUH--??
COULD YOU COME UP TO THE FLIGHT DECK? I THINK WE HAVE A PROBLEM.

WHAT'S WRONG?

THE FORECAST WAS FOR *CLEAR* WEATHER ALL THE WAY TO NEW YORK, BUT AN HOUR AGO, THIS *FREAK BLIZZARD* BLEW UP FROM NOWHERE. IT'S SHUT DOWN EVERY *AIRPORT* WEST OF THE ROCKIES.

WE *CHANGED* OUR COURSE FOR SAN FRANCISCO, AND THE STORM MOVED TO *CUT US OFF.* WE VECTORED FOR HAWAII, AND IT *CLOSED IN* AROUND US.

Hmmm. DEFINITELY NOT YOUR *NORMAL* STORM.

SCOTT, I SENSE A... *WRONGNESS* ABOUT US.

I WAS JUST ABOUT TO CALL YOU, ORORO. WE'VE RUN INTO SOME VERY *SINGLE-MINDED* WEATHER. CAN YOU DO *SOMETHING* ABOUT IT?

I CAN *TRY.*

SHE *GESTURES...*

....HER EYES BECOMING POOLS OF *COBALT FIRE* AS SHE REACHES OUT WITH MIND AND BODY AND *SOUL*...

...TO *GENTLY SHAPE* THE ELEMENTS TO HER *WILL.*

CYCLOPS-- THE STORM *RESISTS* ME!

SOME *OUTSIDE* FORCE-- AN INTELLIGENCE-- *CONTROLS* IT!

FOR THE LOVE OF HEAVEN, SUMMERS-- *NO MORE!* THE *STRAIN* IS STARTING TO TEAR THE PLANE *APART!*

THAT'S *ENOUGH,* ORORO. SOMEONE'S OBVIOUSLY GOING TO A LOT OF *TROUBLE* TO CAPTURE US. AND *I,* FOR ONE, AM CURIOUS TO FIND OUT *WHY.*

THE HOURS PASS, THE *WORLD* AROUND THE DC-10 REDUCED TO A *HORIZONLESS COCOON* OF CLOUDS...

... AS THE FREAK BLIZZARD *HERDS* IT EAST ACROSS THE *YUKON,* THEN SOUTH INTO THE PROVINCE OF *ALBERTA.*

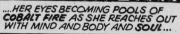

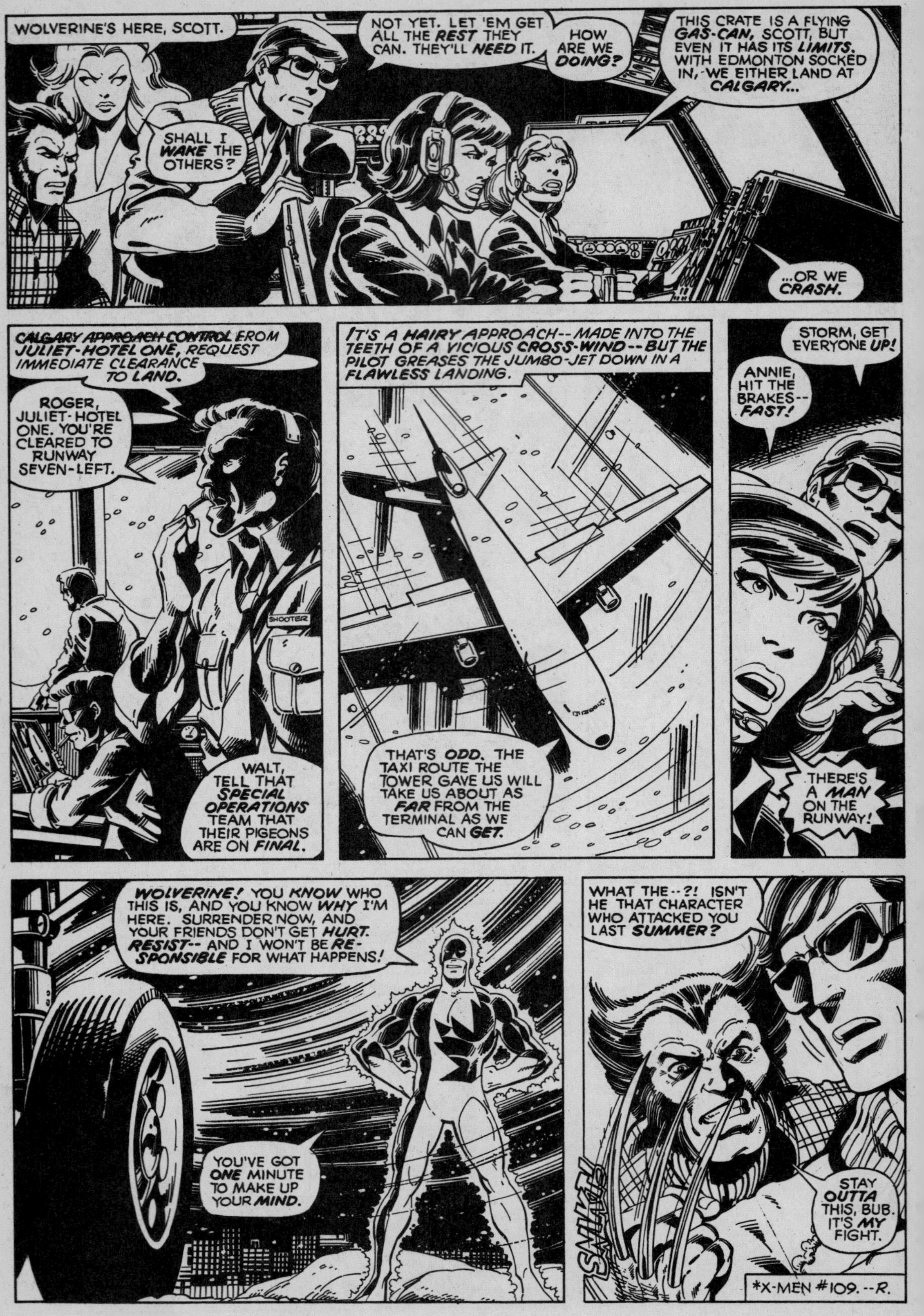

WOLVERINE'S HERE, SCOTT.
SHALL I WAKE THE OTHERS?
NOT YET. LET 'EM GET ALL THE REST THEY CAN. THEY'LL NEED IT.
HOW ARE WE DOING?
THIS CRATE IS A FLYING GAS-CAN, SCOTT, BUT EVEN IT HAS ITS LIMITS. WITH EDMONTON SOCKED IN, WE EITHER LAND AT CALGARY...
...OR WE CRASH.
CALGARY APPROACH CONTROL FROM JULIET-HOTEL ONE, REQUEST IMMEDIATE CLEARANCE TO LAND.
ROGER, JULIET-HOTEL ONE. YOU'RE CLEARED TO RUNWAY SEVEN-LEFT.
SHOOTER
WALT, TELL THAT SPECIAL OPERATIONS TEAM THAT THEIR PIGEONS ARE ON FINAL.
IT'S A HAIRY APPROACH-- MADE INTO THE TEETH OF A VICIOUS CROSS-WIND--BUT THE PILOT GREASES THE JUMBO-JET DOWN IN A FLAWLESS LANDING.
THAT'S ODD. THE TAXI ROUTE THE TOWER GAVE US WILL TAKE US ABOUT AS FAR FROM THE TERMINAL AS WE CAN GET.
STORM, GET EVERYONE UP!
ANNIE, HIT THE BRAKES-- FAST!
THERE'S A MAN ON THE RUNWAY!
WOLVERINE! YOU KNOW WHO THIS IS, AND YOU KNOW WHY I'M HERE. SURRENDER NOW, AND YOUR FRIENDS DON'T GET HURT. RESIST-- AND I WON'T BE RE-SPONSIBLE FOR WHAT HAPPENS!
YOU'VE GOT ONE MINUTE TO MAKE UP YOUR MIND.
WHAT THE--?! ISN'T HE THAT CHARACTER WHO ATTACKED YOU LAST SUMMER?
STAY OUTTA THIS, BUB. IT'S MY FIGHT.
*X-MEN #109. --R.

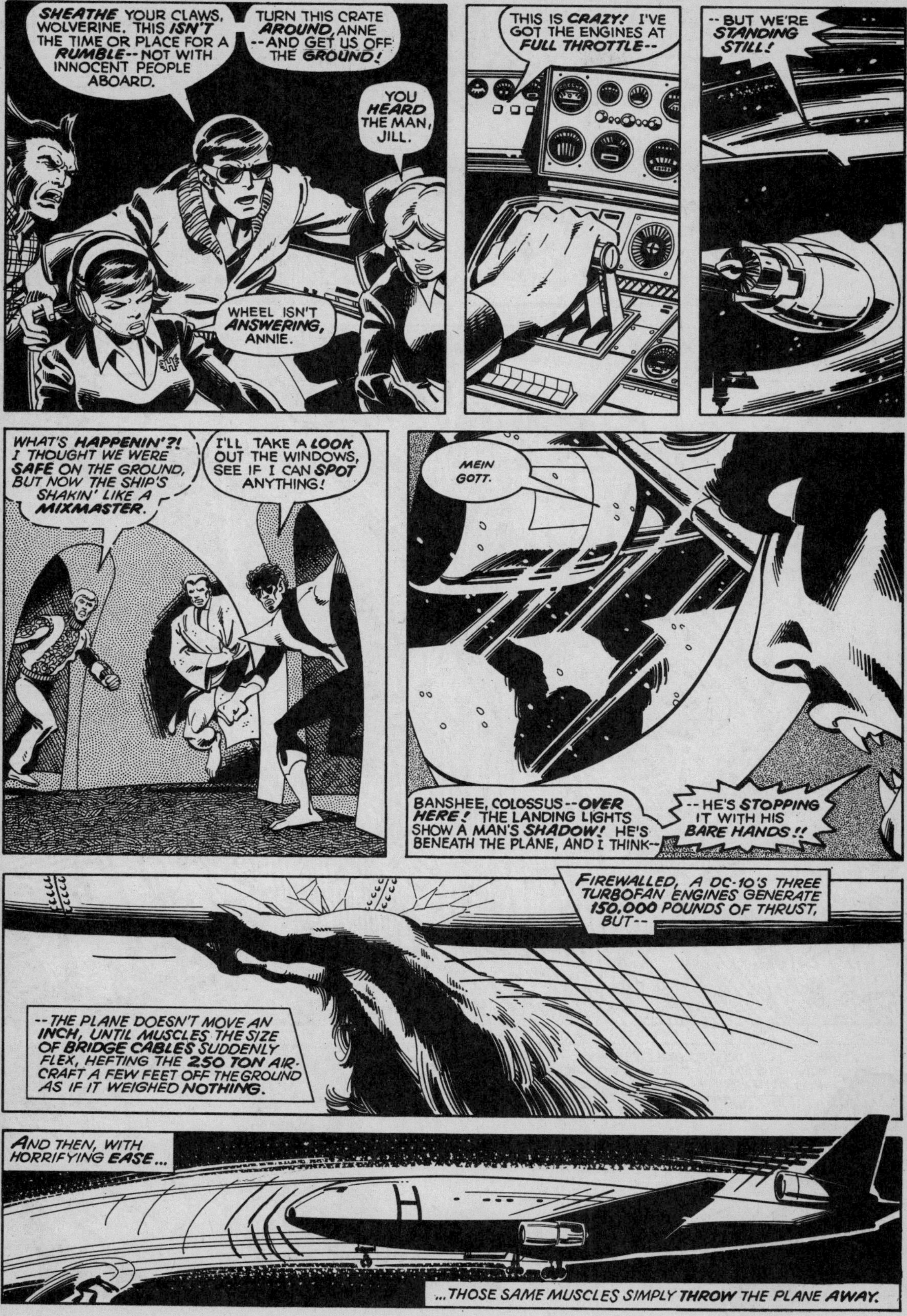
SHEATHE YOUR CLAWS, WOLVERINE. THIS ISN'T THE TIME OR PLACE FOR A RUMBLE-- NOT WITH INNOCENT PEOPLE ABOARD.
TURN THIS CRATE AROUND, ANNE --AND GET US OFF THE GROUND!
YOU HEARD THE MAN, JILL.
WHEEL ISN'T ANSWERING, ANNIE.
THIS IS CRAZY! I'VE GOT THE ENGINES AT FULL THROTTLE--
--BUT WE'RE STANDING STILL!
WHAT'S HAPPENIN'?! I THOUGHT WE WERE SAFE ON THE GROUND, BUT NOW THE SHIP'S SHAKIN' LIKE A MIXMASTER.
I'LL TAKE A LOOK OUT THE WINDOWS, SEE IF I CAN SPOT ANYTHING!
MEIN GOTT.
BANSHEE, COLOSSUS--OVER HERE! THE LANDING LIGHTS SHOW A MAN'S SHADOW! HE'S BENEATH THE PLANE, AND I THINK--
--HE'S STOPPING IT WITH HIS BARE HANDS!!
FIREWALLED, A DC-10'S THREE TURBOFAN ENGINES GENERATE 150,000 POUNDS OF THRUST, BUT--
--THE PLANE DOESN'T MOVE AN INCH, UNTIL MUSCLES THE SIZE OF BRIDGE CABLES SUDDENLY FLEX, HEFTING THE 250 TON AIRCRAFT A FEW FEET OFF THE GROUND AS IF IT WEIGHED NOTHING.
AND THEN, WITH HORRIFYING EASE...
...THOSE SAME MUSCLES SIMPLY THROW THE PLANE AWAY.

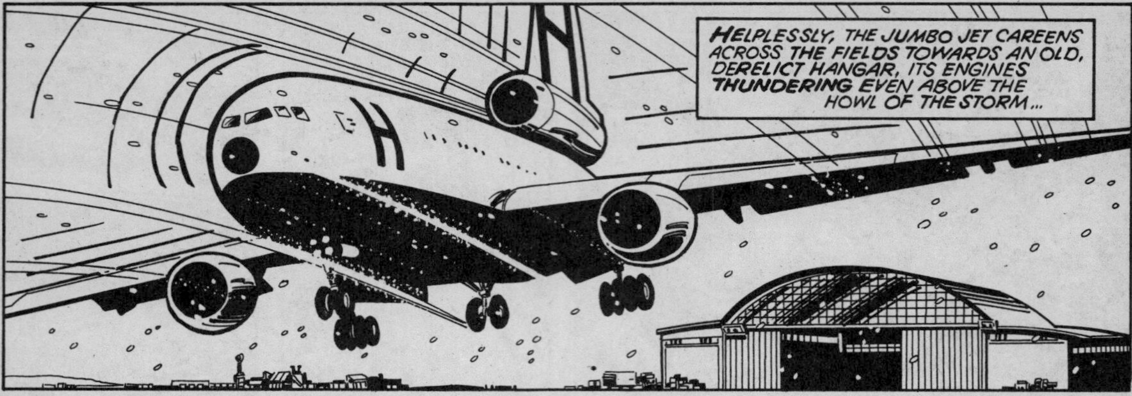
HELPLESSLY, THE JUMBO JET CAREENS ACROSS THE FIELDS TOWARDS AN OLD, DERELICT HANGAR, ITS ENGINES THUNDERING EVEN ABOVE THE HOWL OF THE STORM...

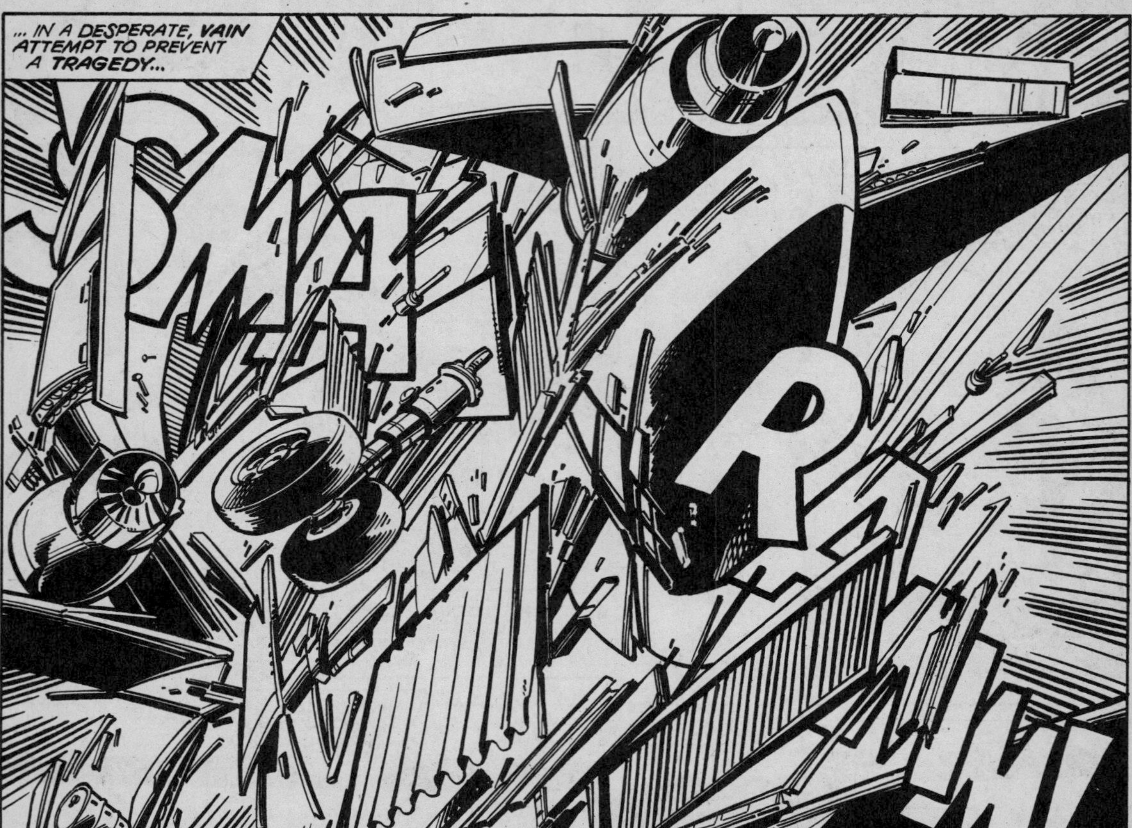
...IN A DESPERATE, VAIN ATTEMPT TO PREVENT A TRAGEDY...
SMA-R-M!

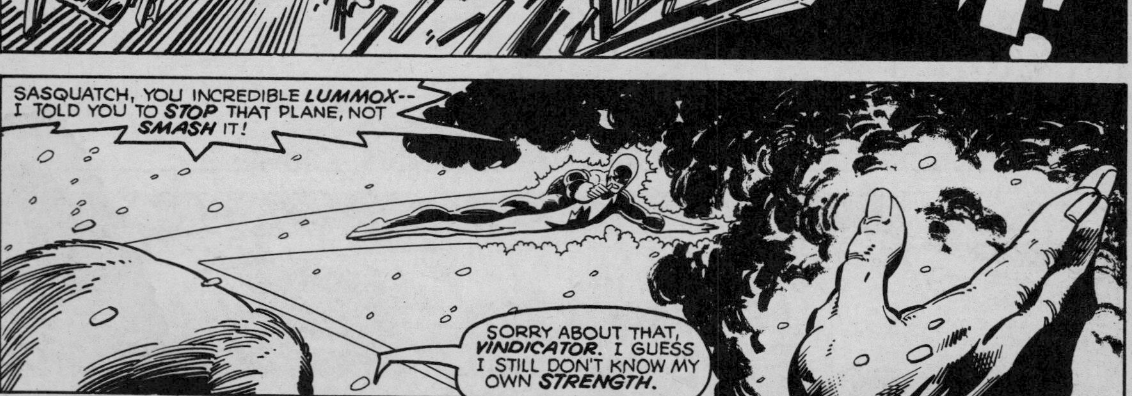
SASQUATCH, YOU INCREDIBLE LUMMOX-- I TOLD YOU TO STOP THAT PLANE, NOT SMASH IT!
SORRY ABOUT THAT, VINDICATOR. I GUESS I STILL DON'T KNOW MY OWN STRENGTH.

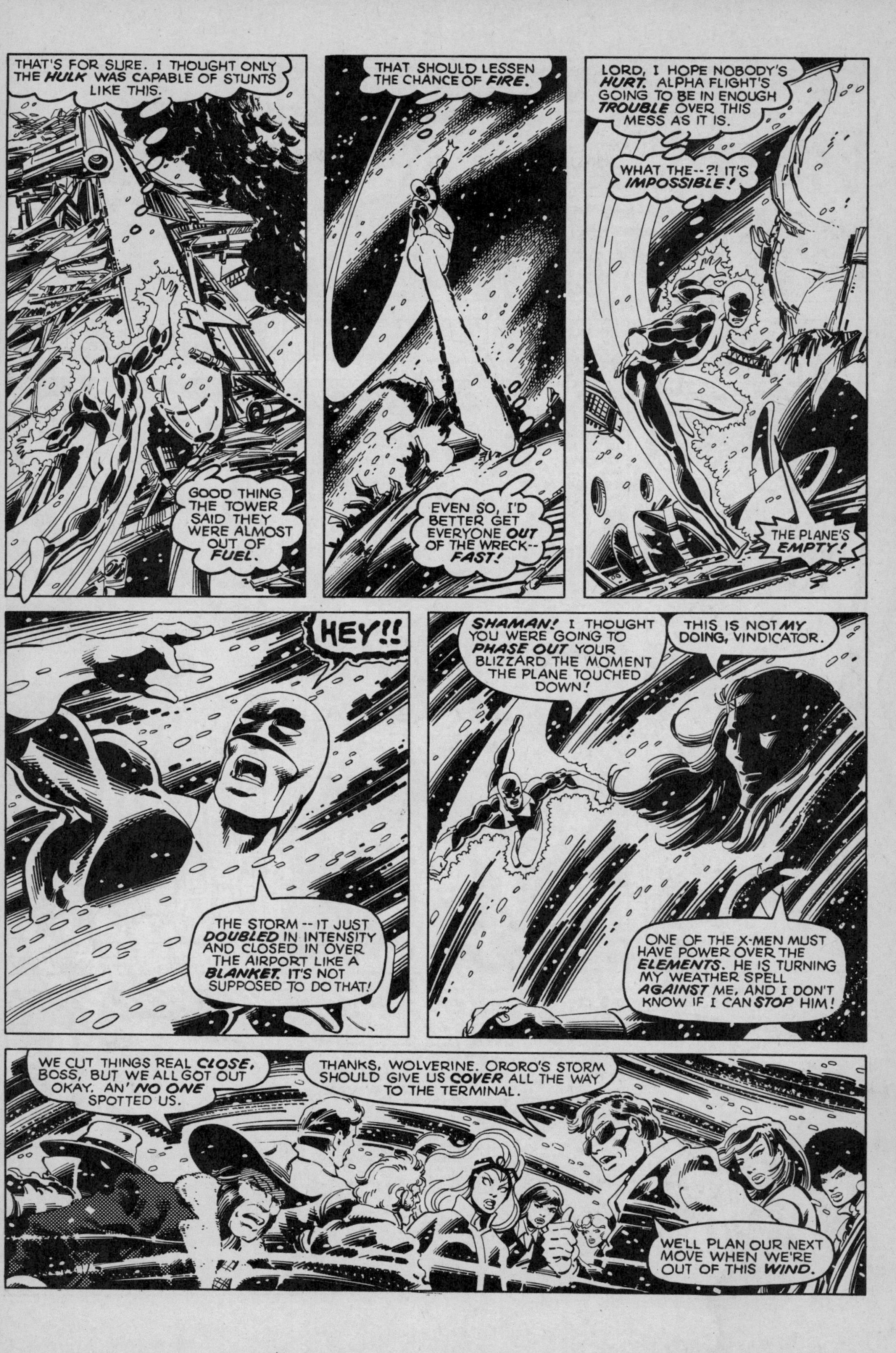
THAT'S FOR SURE. I THOUGHT ONLY THE HULK WAS CAPABLE OF STUNTS LIKE THIS.
GOOD THING THE TOWER SAID THEY WERE ALMOST OUT OF FUEL.
THAT SHOULD LESSEN THE CHANCE OF FIRE.
EVEN SO, I'D BETTER GET EVERYONE OUT OF THE WRECK-- FAST!
LORD, I HOPE NOBODY'S HURT. ALPHA FLIGHT'S GOING TO BE IN ENOUGH TROUBLE OVER THIS MESS AS IT IS.
WHAT THE--?! IT'S IMPOSSIBLE!
THE PLANE'S EMPTY!
HEY!!
THE STORM -- IT JUST DOUBLED IN INTENSITY AND CLOSED IN OVER THE AIRPORT LIKE A BLANKET. IT'S NOT SUPPOSED TO DO THAT!
SHAMAN! I THOUGHT YOU WERE GOING TO PHASE OUT YOUR BLIZZARD THE MOMENT THE PLANE TOUCHED DOWN!
THIS IS NOT MY DOING, VINDICATOR.
ONE OF THE X-MEN MUST HAVE POWER OVER THE ELEMENTS. HE IS TURNING MY WEATHER SPELL AGAINST ME, AND I DON'T KNOW IF I CAN STOP HIM!
WE CUT THINGS REAL CLOSE, BOSS, BUT WE ALL GOT OUT OKAY. AN' NO ONE SPOTTED US.
THANKS, WOLVERINE. ORORO'S STORM SHOULD GIVE US COVER ALL THE WAY TO THE TERMINAL.
WE'LL PLAN OUR NEXT MOVE WHEN WE'RE OUT OF THIS WIND.

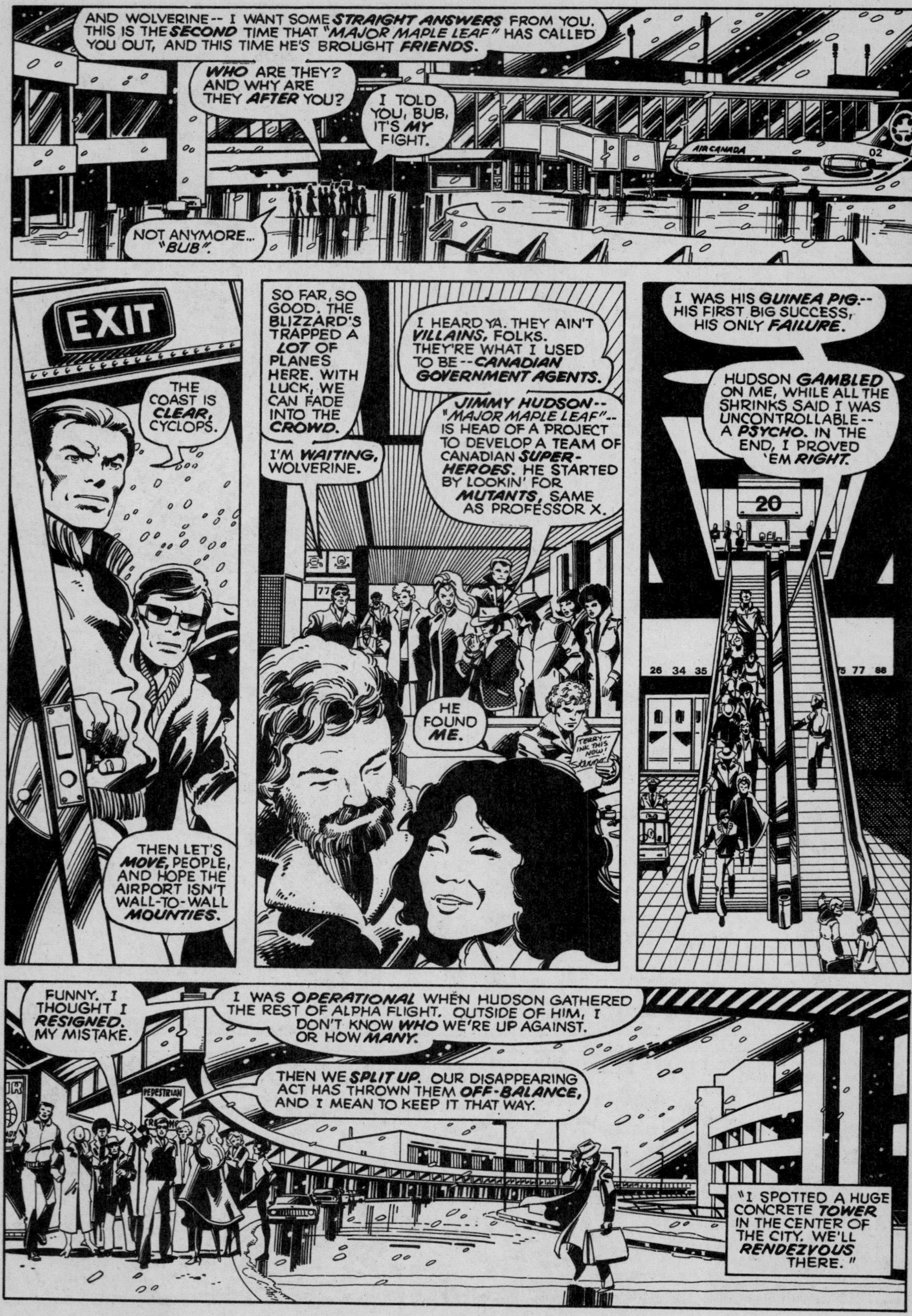
AND WOLVERINE-- I WANT SOME STRAIGHT ANSWERS FROM YOU. THIS IS THE SECOND TIME THAT "MAJOR MAPLE LEAF" HAS CALLED YOU OUT, AND THIS TIME HE'S BROUGHT FRIENDS.
WHO ARE THEY? AND WHY ARE THEY AFTER YOU?
I TOLD YOU, BUB, IT'S MY FIGHT.
NOT ANYMORE... "BUB".
AIR CANADA
EXIT
THE COAST IS CLEAR, CYCLOPS.
THEN LET'S MOVE, PEOPLE, AND HOPE THE AIRPORT ISN'T WALL-TO-WALL MOUNTIES.
SO FAR, SO GOOD. THE BLIZZARD'S TRAPPED A LOT OF PLANES HERE. WITH LUCK, WE CAN FADE INTO THE CROWD.
I'M WAITING, WOLVERINE.
I HEARD YA. THEY AIN'T VILLAINS, FOLKS. THEY'RE WHAT I USED TO BE--CANADIAN GOVERNMENT AGENTS.
JIMMY HUDSON-- "MAJOR MAPLE LEAF"-- IS HEAD OF A PROJECT TO DEVELOP A TEAM OF CANADIAN SUPER-HEROES. HE STARTED BY LOOKIN' FOR MUTANTS, SAME AS PROFESSOR X.
HE FOUND ME.
I WAS HIS GUINEA PIG-- HIS FIRST BIG SUCCESS, HIS ONLY FAILURE.
HUDSON GAMBLED ON ME, WHILE ALL THE SHRINKS SAID I WAS UNCONTROLLABLE-- A PSYCHO. IN THE END, I PROVED 'EM RIGHT.
20
26 34 35
75 77 88
FUNNY. I THOUGHT I RESIGNED. MY MISTAKE.
I WAS OPERATIONAL WHEN HUDSON GATHERED THE REST OF ALPHA FLIGHT. OUTSIDE OF HIM, I DON'T KNOW WHO WE'RE UP AGAINST. OR HOW MANY.
THEN WE SPLIT UP. OUR DISAPPEARING ACT HAS THROWN THEM OFF-BALANCE, AND I MEAN TO KEEP IT THAT WAY.
PEDESTRIAN X
"I SPOTTED A HUGE CONCRETE TOWER IN THE CENTER OF THE CITY. WE'LL RENDEZVOUS THERE."

NOT MUCH LATER, IN A WET, SNOW-STREWN SIDE STREET...

I THINK I'M LEARNING THE *LIMITS* OF MY TELEPORTING TALENT. COLLEEN WING SAID THE CITY WAS ABOUT *SEVEN* MILES FROM THE AIRPORT...

...AND I MADE IT IN *THREE* "JUMPS."

SO THIS IS *CALGARY,* hm? NOT MUCH TO *LOOK* AT--BUT THEN, WHAT CITY *IS* WHEN YOU'RE ON THE RUN?

I HAVEN'T FELT LIKE THIS SINCE *WINZELDORF*--AND I DON'T MUCH LIKE IT. I CAME IN *FRIENDSHIP* THAT NIGHT, AND THE VILLAGERS CALLED ME *DEMON*--AND TRIED TO BURN ME AT THE STAKE. *

ACH! WHAT AM I THINKING?! THAT IS ALL PAST... THINGS ARE *DIFFERENT* NOW...

*GIANT-SIZED X-MEN #1--*ROG.

ARE THEY, KURT WAGNER? STAND WHERE YOU ARE, X-MAN, AND YOU WILL NOT BE *HARMED!*

WAS--?!?

NO SHADOWS NEARBY--MUST TELEPORT--!

MY-- EYES!!

SUDDENLY, NIGHTCRAWLER IS ENVELOPED IN PURE, ELEMENTAL *LIGHT.*

FOR A MOMENT, HE'S TOO *STUNNED* TO MOVE OR *THINK*...

...AND IN THAT MOMENT, HE IS *LOST.*

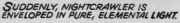

‹HE IS *UNCONSCIOUS,* SISTER--ONE DOWN, FIVE TO GO.›

‹YOU HIT HIM VERY *HARD,* BROTHER. I HOPE HE ISN'T *HURT.*›

‹DESPITE HIS *APPEARANCE,* HE IS LIKE *US*--A *MUTANT.* I DON'T LIKE HUNTING MY OWN *KIND.*›

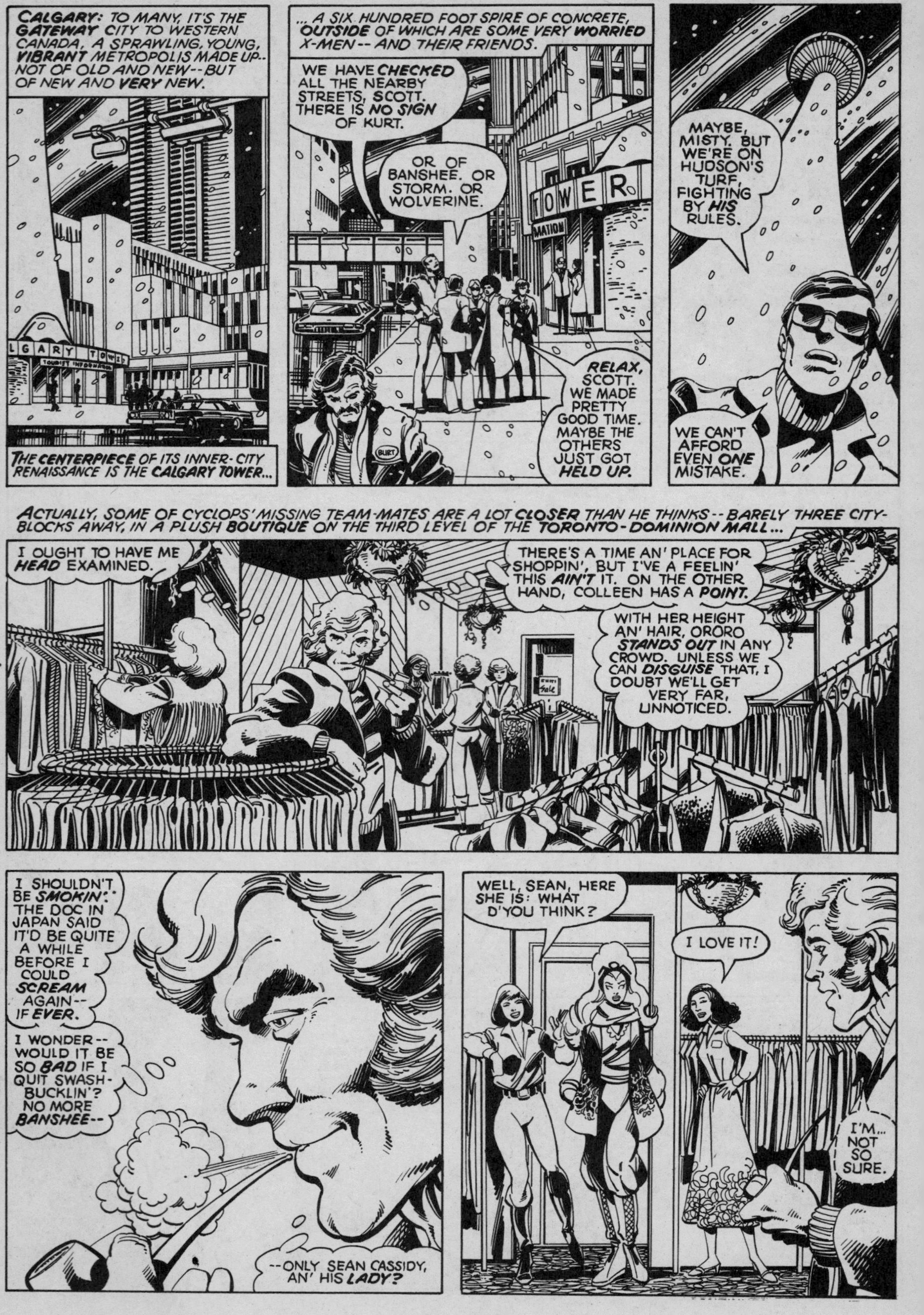
CALGARY: TO MANY, IT'S THE GATEWAY CITY TO WESTERN CANADA, A SPRAWLING, YOUNG, VIBRANT METROPOLIS MADE UP-- NOT OF OLD AND NEW-- BUT OF NEW AND VERY NEW.
THE CENTERPIECE OF ITS INNER-CITY RENAISSANCE IS THE CALGARY TOWER...
...A SIX HUNDRED FOOT SPIRE OF CONCRETE, OUTSIDE OF WHICH ARE SOME VERY WORRIED X-MEN -- AND THEIR FRIENDS.
WE HAVE CHECKED ALL THE NEARBY STREETS, SCOTT. THERE IS NO SIGN OF KURT.
OR OF BANSHEE. OR STORM. OR WOLVERINE.
TOWER
RELAX, SCOTT. WE MADE PRETTY GOOD TIME. MAYBE THE OTHERS JUST GOT HELD UP.
MAYBE, MISTY. BUT WE'RE ON HUDSON'S TURF, FIGHTING BY HIS RULES.
WE CAN'T AFFORD EVEN ONE MISTAKE.
ACTUALLY, SOME OF CYCLOPS' MISSING TEAM-MATES ARE A LOT CLOSER THAN HE THINKS -- BARELY THREE CITY-BLOCKS AWAY, IN A PLUSH BOUTIQUE ON THE THIRD LEVEL OF THE TORONTO-DOMINION MALL...
I OUGHT TO HAVE ME HEAD EXAMINED.
THERE'S A TIME AN' PLACE FOR SHOPPIN', BUT I'VE A FEELIN' THIS AIN'T IT. ON THE OTHER HAND, COLLEEN HAS A POINT.
WITH HER HEIGHT AN' HAIR, ORORO STANDS OUT IN ANY CROWD. UNLESS WE CAN DISGUISE THAT, I DOUBT WE'LL GET VERY FAR, UNNOTICED.
I SHOULDN'T BE SMOKIN'. THE DOC IN JAPAN SAID IT'D BE QUITE A WHILE BEFORE I COULD SCREAM AGAIN-- IF EVER.
I WONDER-- WOULD IT BE SO BAD IF I QUIT SWASH-BUCKLIN'? NO MORE BANSHEE--
--ONLY SEAN CASSIDY, AN' HIS LADY?
WELL, SEAN, HERE SHE IS: WHAT D'YOU THINK?
I LOVE IT!
I'M... NOT SO SURE.

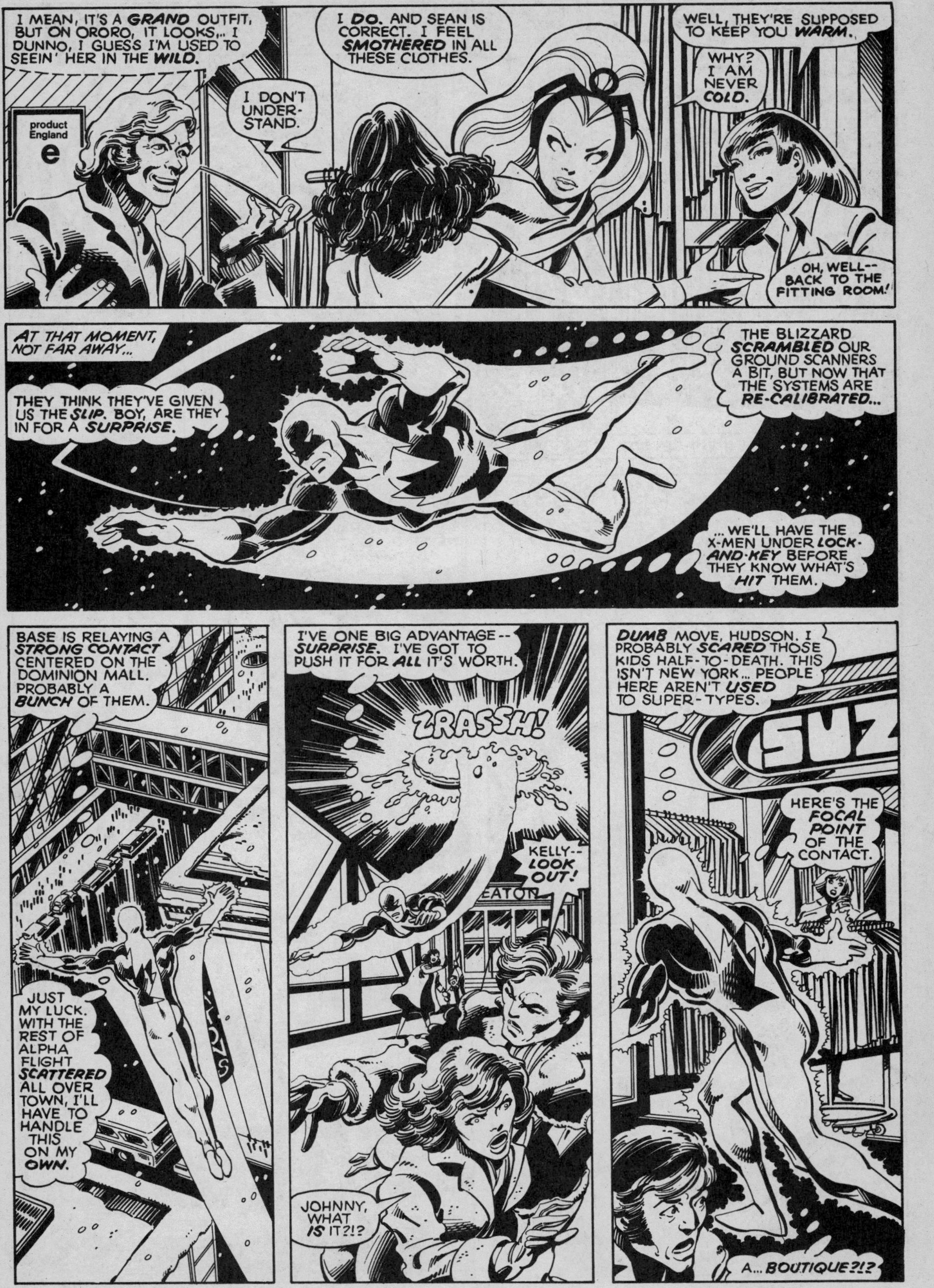
I MEAN, IT'S A GRAND OUTFIT, BUT ON ORORO, IT LOOKS,.. I DUNNO, I GUESS I'M USED TO SEEIN' HER IN THE WILD.
I DON'T UNDER-STAND.
I DO. AND SEAN IS CORRECT. I FEEL SMOTHERED IN ALL THESE CLOTHES.
WELL, THEY'RE SUPPOSED TO KEEP YOU WARM.
WHY? I AM NEVER COLD.
OH, WELL-- BACK TO THE FITTING ROOM!
product England
e
AT THAT MOMENT, NOT FAR AWAY...
THEY THINK THEY'VE GIVEN US THE SLIP. BOY, ARE THEY IN FOR A SURPRISE.
THE BLIZZARD SCRAMBLED OUR GROUND SCANNERS A BIT, BUT NOW THAT THE SYSTEMS ARE RE-CALIBRATED...
...WE'LL HAVE THE X-MEN UNDER LOCK-AND-KEY BEFORE THEY KNOW WHAT'S HIT THEM.
BASE IS RELAYING A STRONG CONTACT CENTERED ON THE DOMINION MALL. PROBABLY A BUNCH OF THEM.
JUST MY LUCK. WITH THE REST OF ALPHA FLIGHT SCATTERED ALL OVER TOWN, I'LL HAVE TO HANDLE THIS ON MY OWN.
I'VE ONE BIG ADVANTAGE -- SURPRISE. I'VE GOT TO PUSH IT FOR ALL IT'S WORTH.
ZRASSH!
EATON
KELLY-- LOOK OUT!
JOHNNY, WHAT IS IT?!?
DUMB MOVE, HUDSON. I PROBABLY SCARED THOSE KIDS HALF-TO-DEATH. THIS ISN'T NEW YORK... PEOPLE HERE AREN'T USED TO SUPER-TYPES.
SUZ
HERE'S THE FOCAL POINT OF THE CONTACT.
A... BOUTIQUE?!?

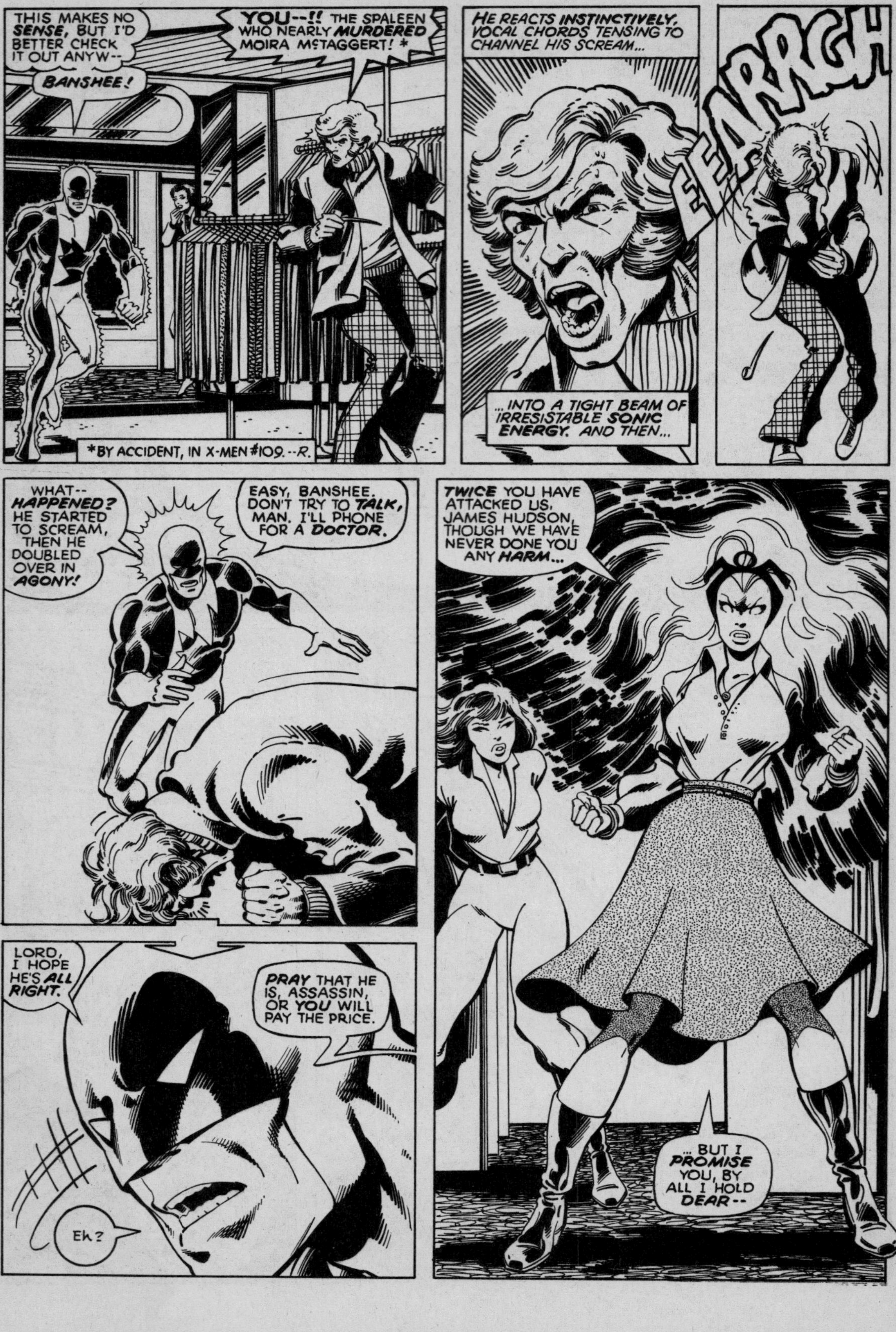
THIS MAKES NO SENSE, BUT I'D BETTER CHECK IT OUT ANYW--
BANSHEE!
YOU--!! THE SPALEEN WHO NEARLY MURDERED MOIRA McTAGGERT! *
*BY ACCIDENT, IN X-MEN #109.--R.
HE REACTS INSTINCTIVELY, VOCAL CHORDS TENSING TO CHANNEL HIS SCREAM...
...INTO A TIGHT BEAM OF IRRESISTABLE SONIC ENERGY. AND THEN...
EEARRGH
WHAT-- HAPPENED? HE STARTED TO SCREAM, THEN HE DOUBLED OVER IN AGONY!
EASY, BANSHEE. DON'T TRY TO TALK, MAN. I'LL PHONE FOR A DOCTOR.
LORD, I HOPE HE'S ALL RIGHT.
PRAY THAT HE IS, ASSASSIN, OR YOU WILL PAY THE PRICE.
Eh?
TWICE YOU HAVE ATTACKED US, JAMES HUDSON, THOUGH WE HAVE NEVER DONE YOU ANY HARM...
...BUT I PROMISE YOU, BY ALL I HOLD DEAR--

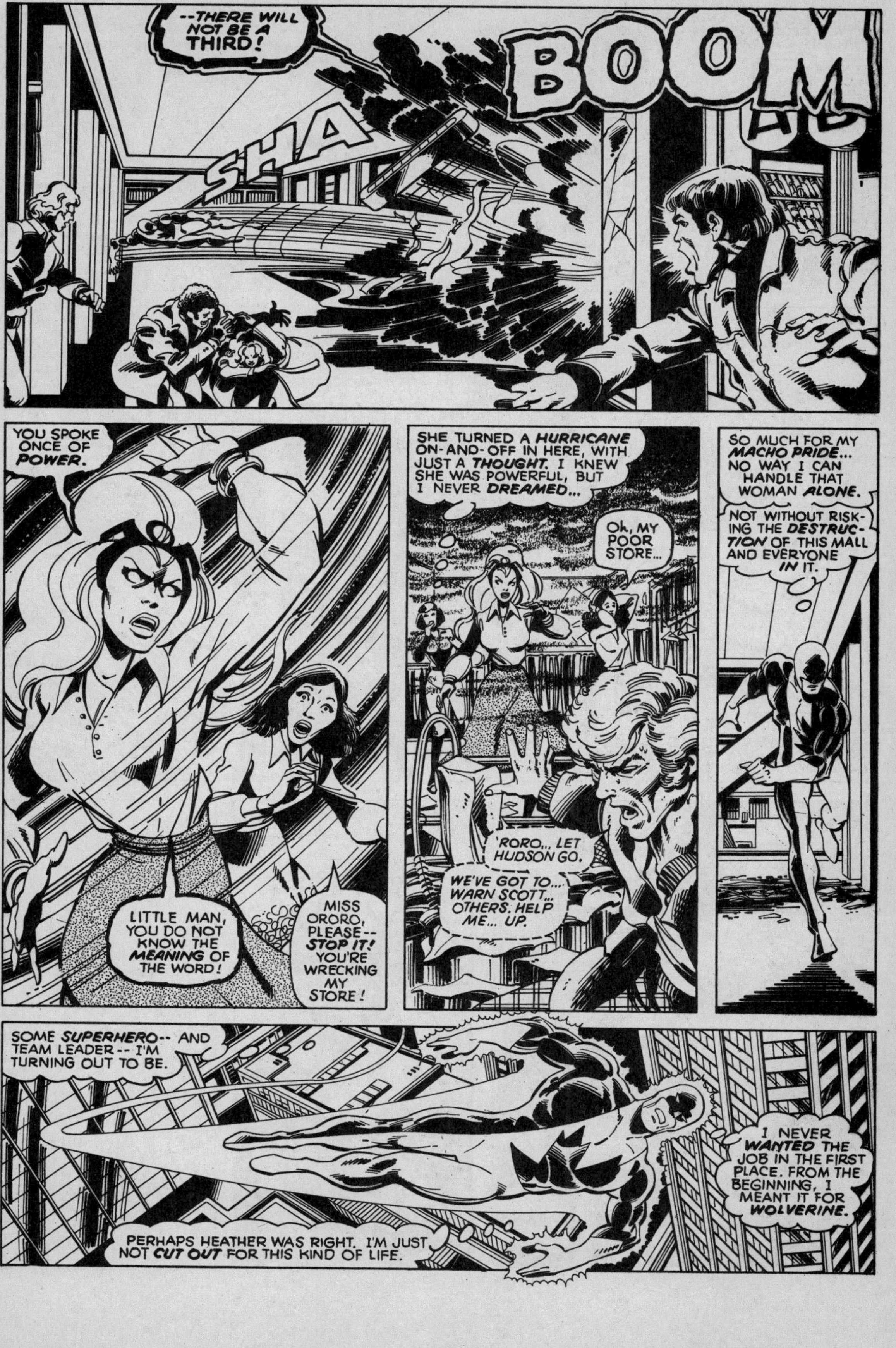
--THERE WILL NOT BE A THIRD!
BOOOM
SHA
YOU SPOKE ONCE OF POWER.
LITTLE MAN, YOU DO NOT KNOW THE MEANING OF THE WORD!
MISS ORORO, PLEASE-- STOP IT! YOU'RE WRECKING MY STORE!
SHE TURNED A HURRICANE ON-AND-OFF IN HERE, WITH JUST A THOUGHT. I KNEW SHE WAS POWERFUL, BUT I NEVER DREAMED...
Oh, MY POOR STORE...
'RORO... LET HUDSON GO.
WE'VE GOT TO... WARN SCOTT... OTHERS. HELP ME... UP.
SO MUCH FOR MY MACHO PRIDE... NO WAY I CAN HANDLE THAT WOMAN ALONE.
NOT WITHOUT RISKING THE DESTRUCTION OF THIS MALL AND EVERYONE IN IT.
SOME SUPERHERO-- AND TEAM LEADER-- I'M TURNING OUT TO BE.
I NEVER WANTED THE JOB IN THE FIRST PLACE. FROM THE BEGINNING, I MEANT IT FOR WOLVERINE.
PERHAPS HEATHER WAS RIGHT. I'M JUST NOT CUT OUT FOR THIS KIND OF LIFE.

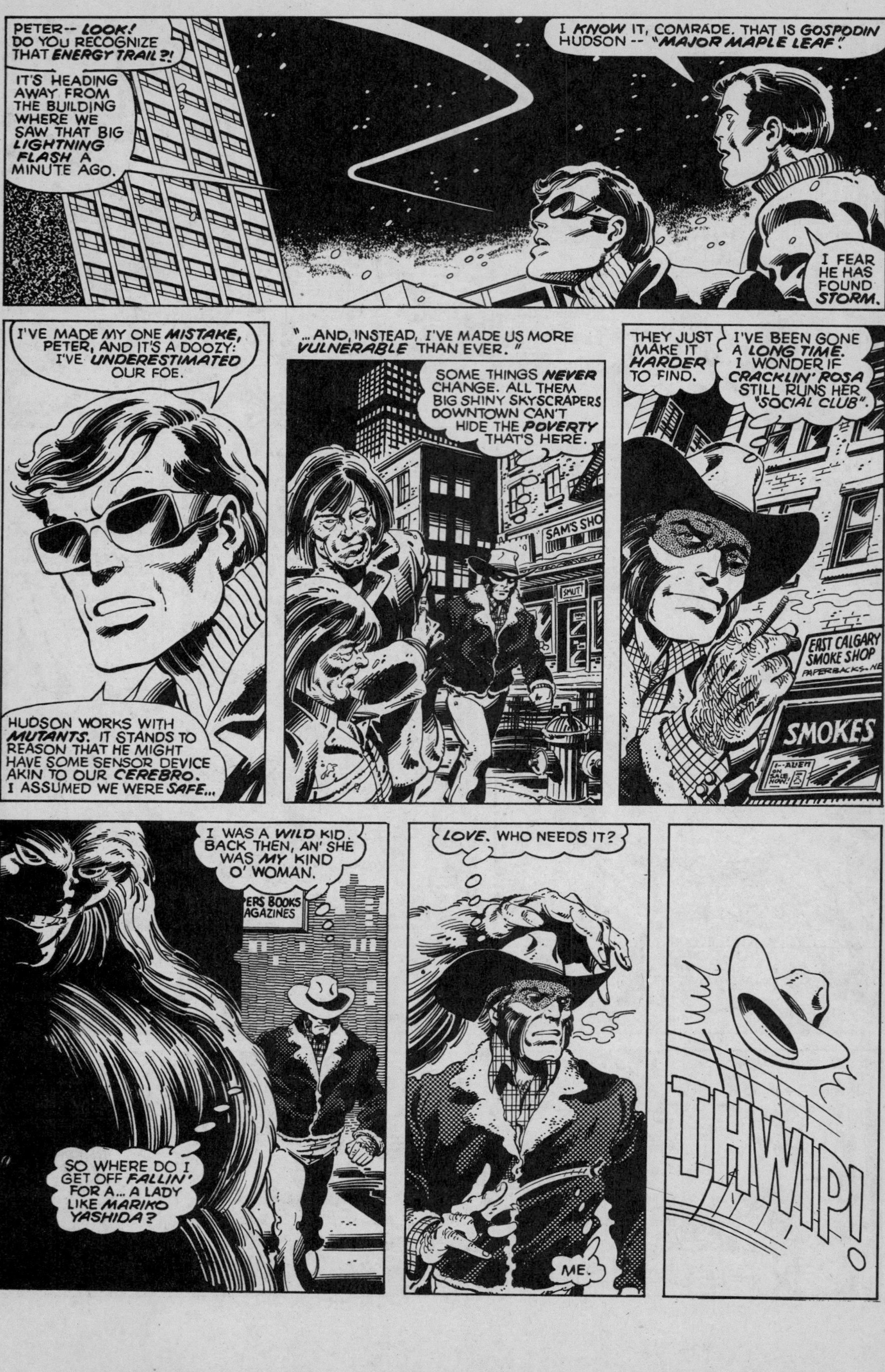
PETER-- LOOK! DO YOU RECOGNIZE THAT ENERGY TRAIL?!
IT'S HEADING AWAY FROM THE BUILDING WHERE WE SAW THAT BIG LIGHTNING FLASH A MINUTE AGO.
I KNOW IT, COMRADE. THAT IS GOSPODIN HUDSON -- "MAJOR MAPLE LEAF!"
I FEAR HE HAS FOUND STORM.
I'VE MADE MY ONE MISTAKE, PETER, AND IT'S A DOOZY: I'VE UNDERESTIMATED OUR FOE.
HUDSON WORKS WITH MUTANTS. IT STANDS TO REASON THAT HE MIGHT HAVE SOME SENSOR DEVICE AKIN TO OUR CEREBRO. I ASSUMED WE WERE SAFE...
"...AND, INSTEAD, I'VE MADE US MORE VULNERABLE THAN EVER."
SOME THINGS NEVER CHANGE. ALL THEM BIG SHINY SKYSCRAPERS DOWNTOWN CAN'T HIDE THE POVERTY THAT'S HERE.
SAM'S SHO
SMUT
THEY JUST MAKE IT HARDER TO FIND.
I'VE BEEN GONE A LONG TIME. I WONDER IF CRACKLIN' ROSA STILL RUNS HER "SOCIAL CLUB".
EAST CALGARY SMOKE SHOP
PAPERBACKS-NE
SMOKES
I WAS A WILD KID. BACK THEN, AN' SHE WAS MY KIND O' WOMAN.
PERS BOOKS
AGAZINES
SO WHERE DO I GET OFF FALLIN' FOR A... A LADY LIKE MARIKO YASHIDA?
LOVE. WHO NEEDS IT?
ME.
THWIP!

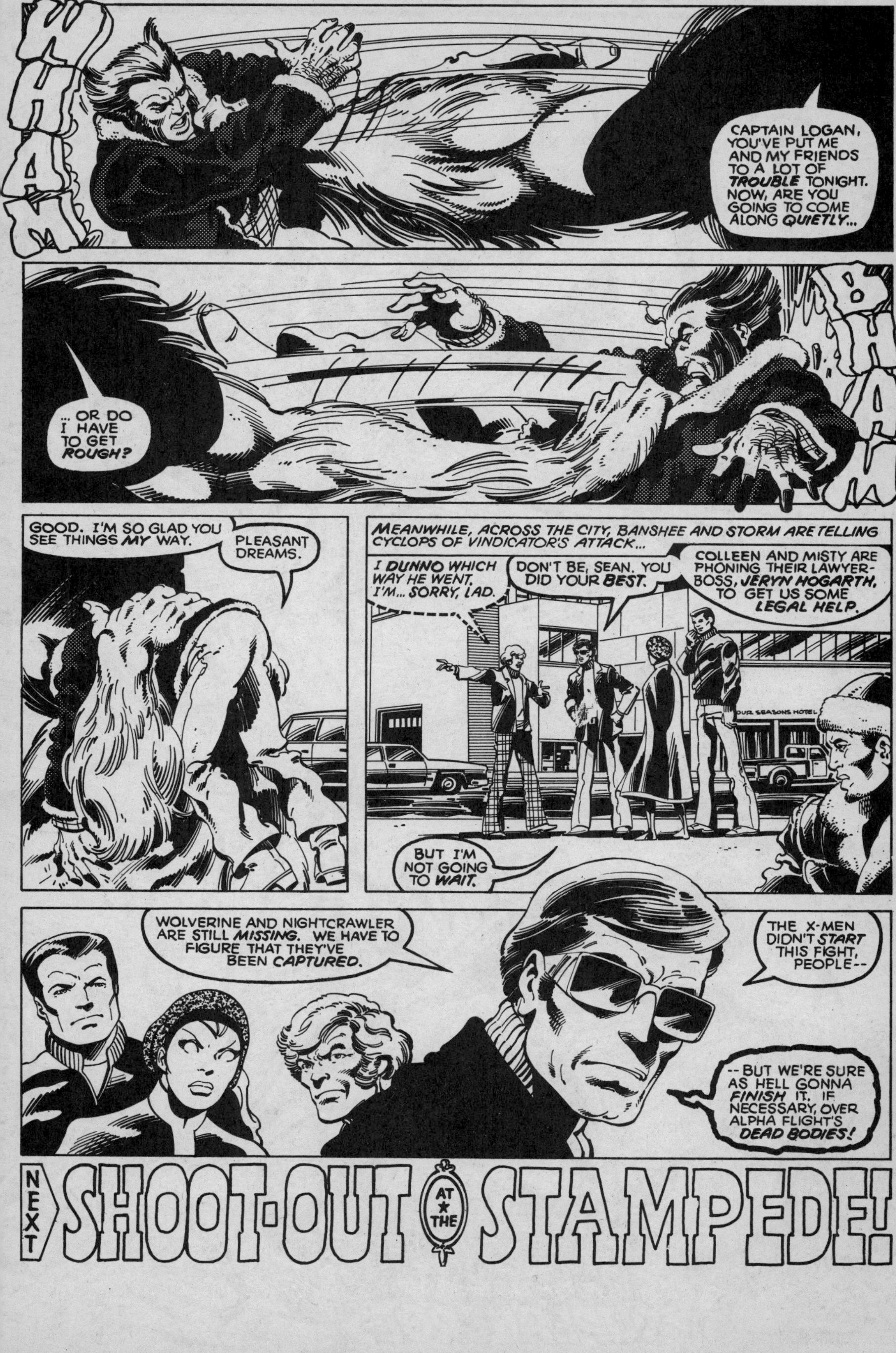
WHAM
CAPTAIN LOGAN, YOU'VE PUT ME AND MY FRIENDS TO A LOT OF TROUBLE TONIGHT. NOW, ARE YOU GOING TO COME ALONG QUIETLY...
...OR DO I HAVE TO GET ROUGH?
BHAM
GOOD. I'M SO GLAD YOU SEE THINGS MY WAY.
PLEASANT DREAMS.
MEANWHILE, ACROSS THE CITY, BANSHEE AND STORM ARE TELLING CYCLOPS OF VINDICATOR'S ATTACK...
I DUNNO WHICH WAY HE WENT. I'M... SORRY, LAD.
DON'T BE, SEAN. YOU DID YOUR BEST.
COLLEEN AND MISTY ARE PHONING THEIR LAWYER-BOSS, JERYN HOGARTH, TO GET US SOME LEGAL HELP.
OUR SEASONS HOTEL
BUT I'M NOT GOING TO WAIT.
WOLVERINE AND NIGHTCRAWLER ARE STILL MISSING. WE HAVE TO FIGURE THAT THEY'VE BEEN CAPTURED.
THE X-MEN DIDN'T START THIS FIGHT, PEOPLE--
--BUT WE'RE SURE AS HELL GONNA FINISH IT. IF NECESSARY, OVER ALPHA FLIGHT'S DEAD BODIES!
NEXT SHOOT-OUT AT THE STAMPEDE!

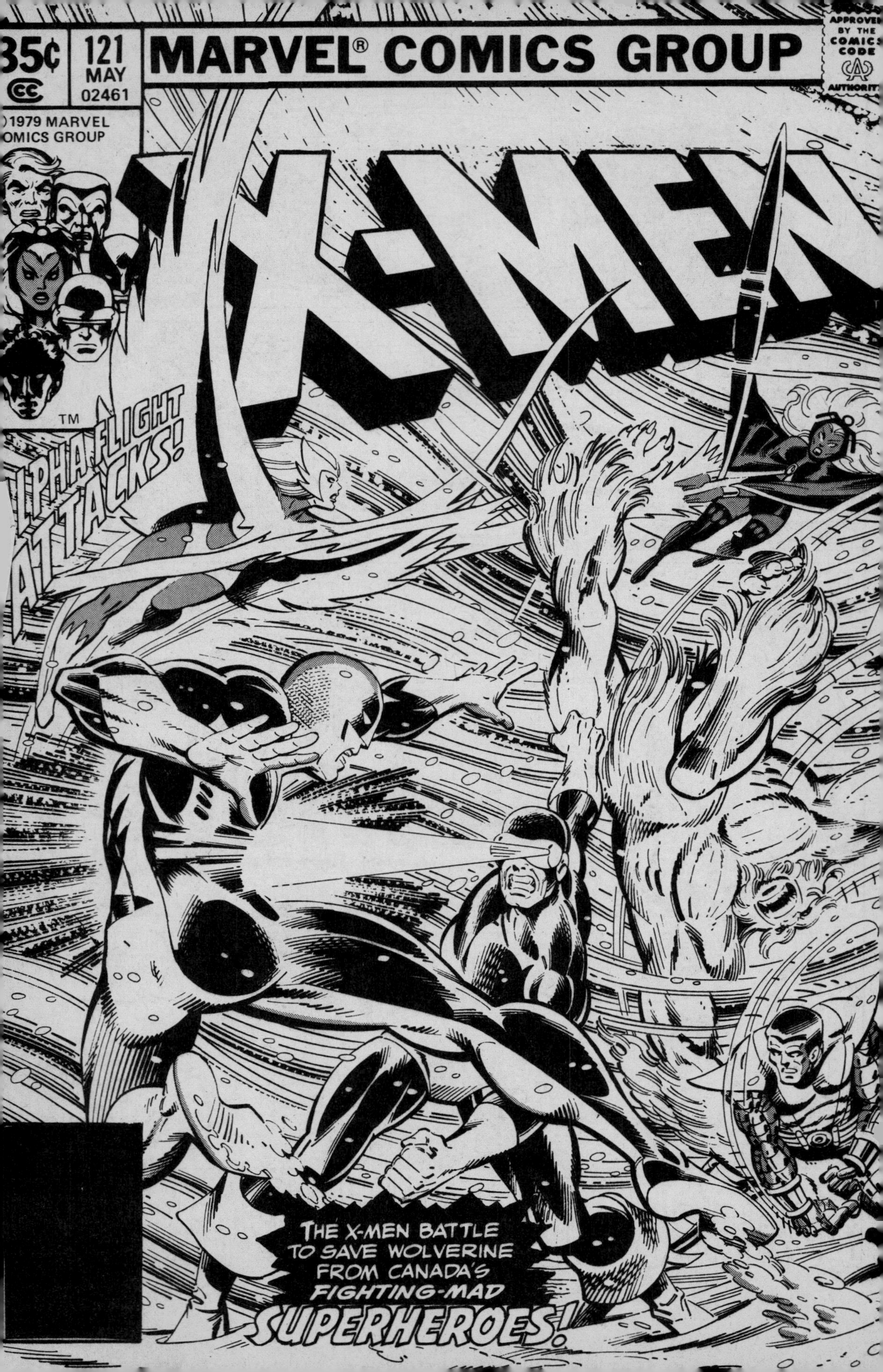
35¢
121
MAY
02461
MARVEL® COMICS GROUP
APPROVED BY THE COMICS CODE AUTHORITY
©1979 MARVEL COMICS GROUP
X-MEN
TM
LPHA FLIGHT ATTACKS!
THE X-MEN BATTLE TO SAVE WOLVERINE FROM CANADA'S FIGHTING-MAD SUPERHEROES!

Cyclops. Storm. Banshee. Nightcrawler. Wolverine. Colossus. Children of the atom, students of Charles Xavier, MUTANTS——feared and hated by the world they have sworn to protect. These are the STRANGEST heroes of all!

Stan Lee PRESENTS: THE UNCANNY X-MEN!™

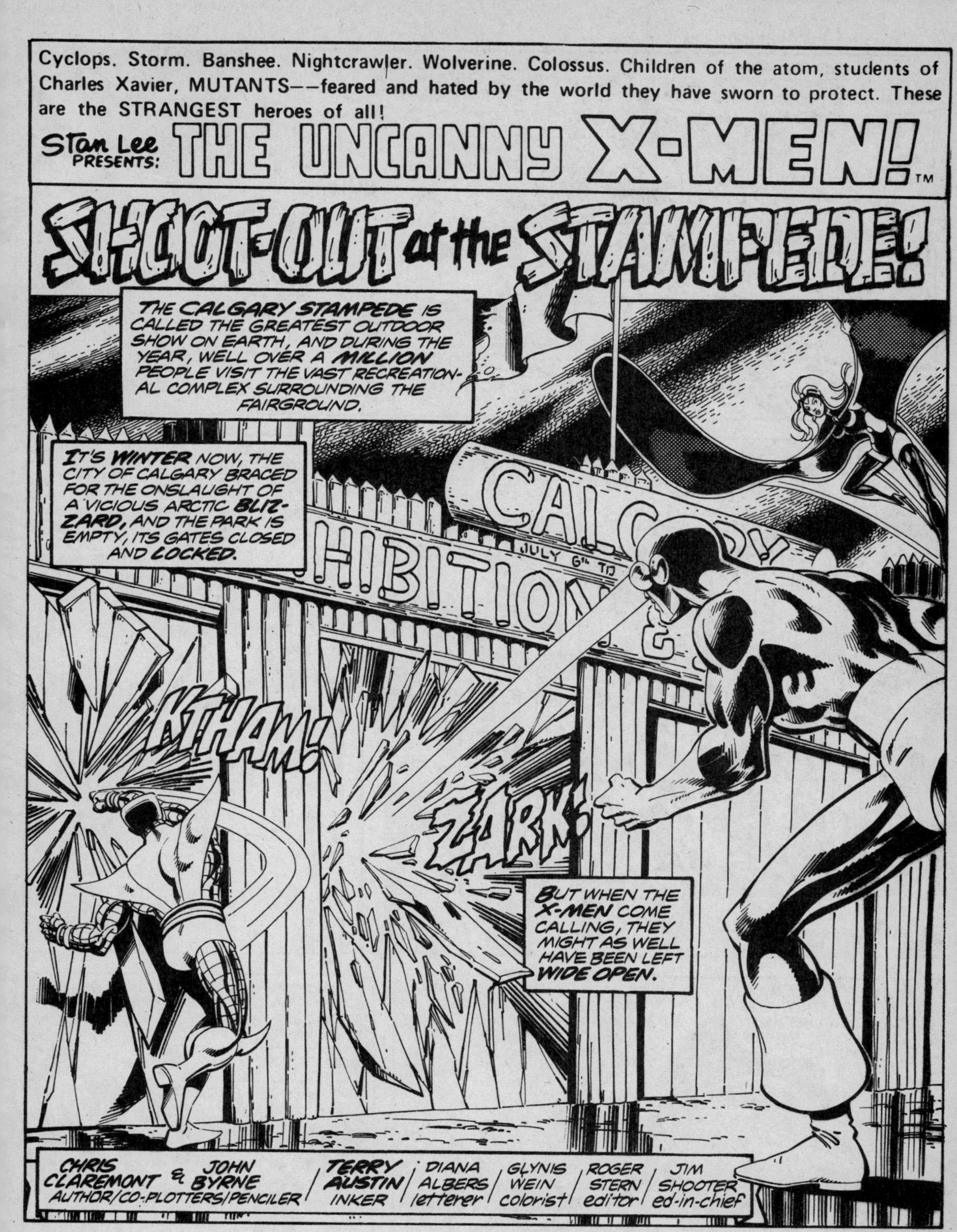
SHOOT-OUT at the STAMPEDE!
THE CALGARY STAMPEDE IS CALLED THE GREATEST OUTDOOR SHOW ON EARTH, AND DURING THE YEAR, WELL OVER A MILLION PEOPLE VISIT THE VAST RECREATIONAL COMPLEX SURROUNDING THE FAIRGROUND.
IT'S WINTER NOW, THE CITY OF CALGARY BRACED FOR THE ONSLAUGHT OF A VICIOUS ARCTIC BLIZZARD, AND THE PARK IS EMPTY, ITS GATES CLOSED AND LOCKED.
CALGARY
HIBITION
JULY 6th TO
KTHAM!
ZARK!
BUT WHEN THE X-MEN COME CALLING, THEY MIGHT AS WELL HAVE BEEN LEFT WIDE OPEN.
CHRIS CLAREMONT & JOHN BYRNE AUTHOR/CO-PLOTTERS/PENCILER
TERRY AUSTIN INKER
DIANA ALBERS letterer
GLYNIS WEIN colorist
ROGER STERN editor
JIM SHOOTER ed-in-chief

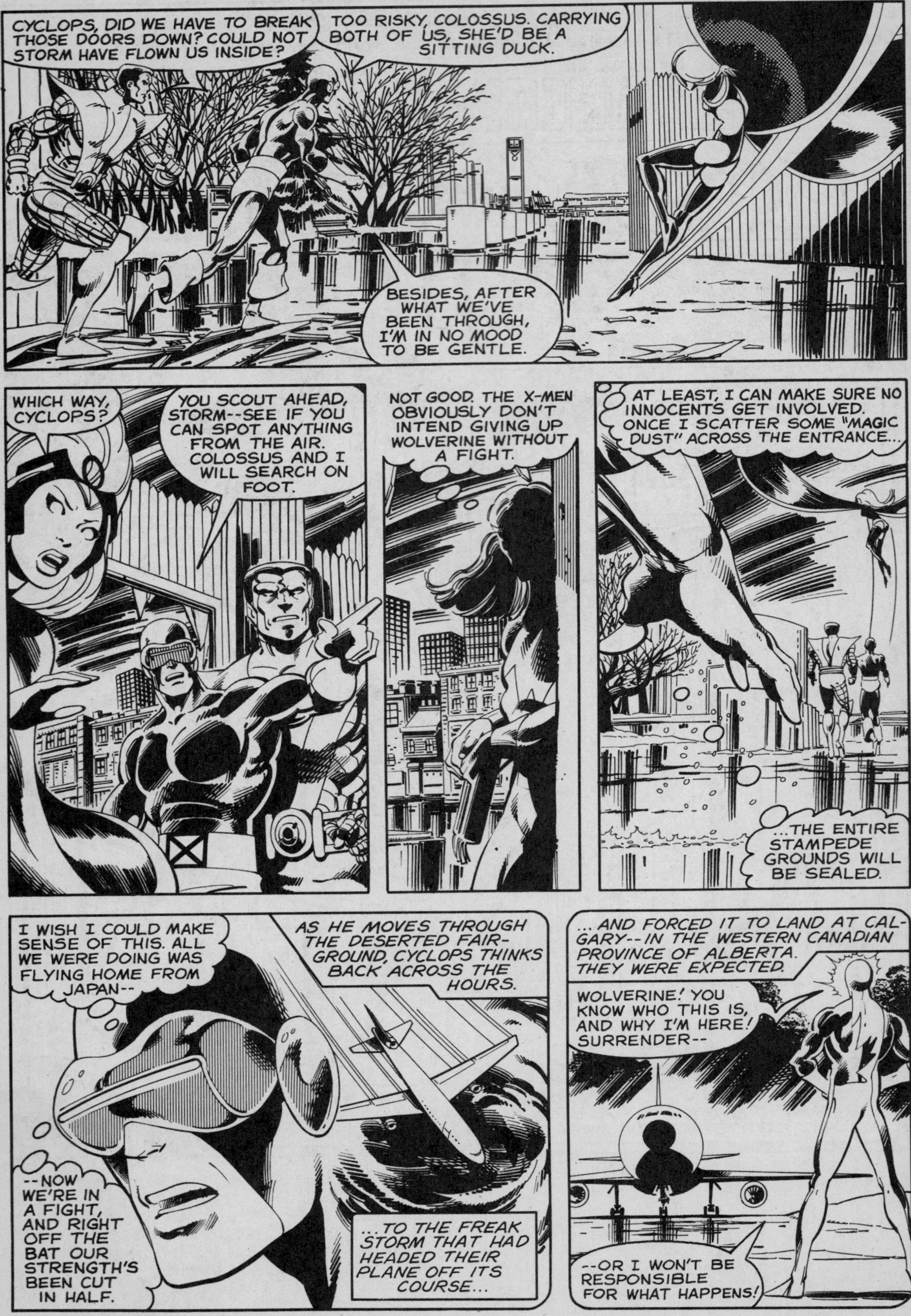

CYCLOPS, DID WE HAVE TO BREAK THOSE DOORS DOWN? COULD NOT STORM HAVE FLOWN US INSIDE?
TOO RISKY, COLOSSUS. CARRYING BOTH OF US, SHE'D BE A SITTING DUCK.
BESIDES, AFTER WHAT WE'VE BEEN THROUGH, I'M IN NO MOOD TO BE GENTLE.
WHICH WAY, CYCLOPS?
YOU SCOUT AHEAD, STORM--SEE IF YOU CAN SPOT ANYTHING FROM THE AIR. COLOSSUS AND I WILL SEARCH ON FOOT.
NOT GOOD. THE X-MEN OBVIOUSLY DON'T INTEND GIVING UP WOLVERINE WITHOUT A FIGHT.
AT LEAST, I CAN MAKE SURE NO INNOCENTS GET INVOLVED. ONCE I SCATTER SOME "MAGIC DUST" ACROSS THE ENTRANCE...
...THE ENTIRE STAMPEDE GROUNDS WILL BE SEALED.
I WISH I COULD MAKE SENSE OF THIS. ALL WE WERE DOING WAS FLYING HOME FROM JAPAN--
AS HE MOVES THROUGH THE DESERTED FAIR-GROUND, CYCLOPS THINKS BACK ACROSS THE HOURS.
--NOW WE'RE IN A FIGHT, AND RIGHT OFF THE BAT OUR STRENGTH'S BEEN CUT IN HALF.
...TO THE FREAK STORM THAT HAD HEADED THEIR PLANE OFF ITS COURSE...
... AND FORCED IT TO LAND AT CAL-GARY--IN THE WESTERN CANADIAN PROVINCE OF ALBERTA. THEY WERE EXPECTED.
WOLVERINE! YOU KNOW WHO THIS IS, AND WHY I'M HERE! SURRENDER--
--OR I WON'T BE RESPONSIBLE FOR WHAT HAPPENS!

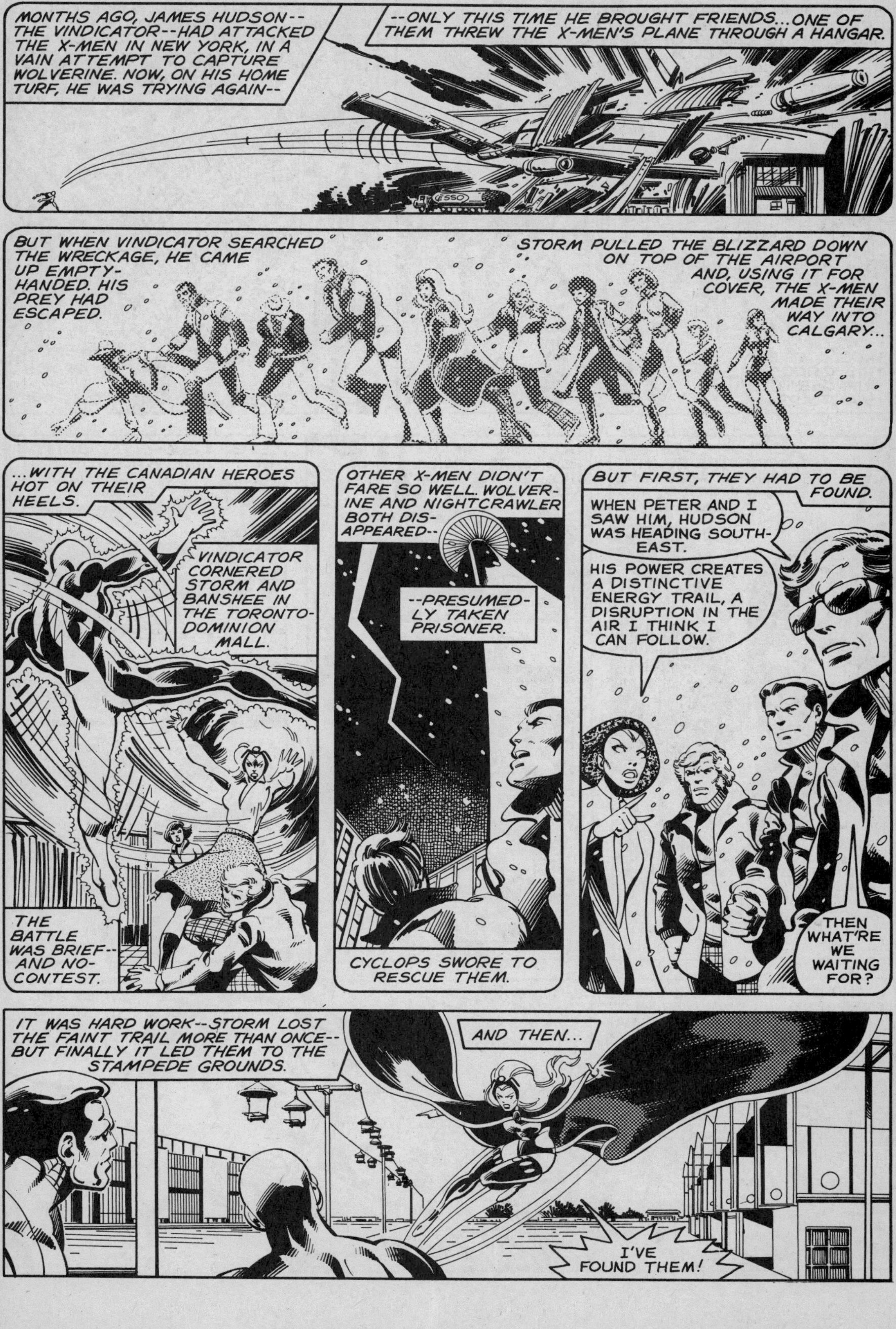

MONTHS AGO, JAMES HUDSON--THE VINDICATOR--HAD ATTACKED THE X-MEN IN NEW YORK, IN A VAIN ATTEMPT TO CAPTURE WOLVERINE. NOW, ON HIS HOME TURF, HE WAS TRYING AGAIN--
--ONLY THIS TIME HE BROUGHT FRIENDS...ONE OF THEM THREW THE X-MEN'S PLANE THROUGH A HANGAR.
ESSO
BUT WHEN VINDICATOR SEARCHED THE WRECKAGE, HE CAME UP EMPTY-HANDED. HIS PREY HAD ESCAPED.
STORM PULLED THE BLIZZARD DOWN ON TOP OF THE AIRPORT AND, USING IT FOR COVER, THE X-MEN MADE THEIR WAY INTO CALGARY...
...WITH THE CANADIAN HEROES HOT ON THEIR HEELS.
VINDICATOR CORNERED STORM AND BANSHEE IN THE TORONTO-DOMINION MALL.
THE BATTLE WAS BRIEF--AND NO-CONTEST.
OTHER X-MEN DIDN'T FARE SO WELL. WOLVERINE AND NIGHTCRAWLER BOTH DISAPPEARED--
--PRESUMEDLY TAKEN PRISONER.
CYCLOPS SWORE TO RESCUE THEM.
BUT FIRST, THEY HAD TO BE FOUND.
WHEN PETER AND I SAW HIM, HUDSON WAS HEADING SOUTH-EAST.
HIS POWER CREATES A DISTINCTIVE ENERGY TRAIL, A DISRUPTION IN THE AIR I THINK I CAN FOLLOW.
THEN WHAT'RE WE WAITING FOR?
IT WAS HARD WORK--STORM LOST THE FAINT TRAIL MORE THAN ONCE--BUT FINALLY IT LED THEM TO THE STAMPEDE GROUNDS.
AND THEN...
I'VE FOUND THEM!

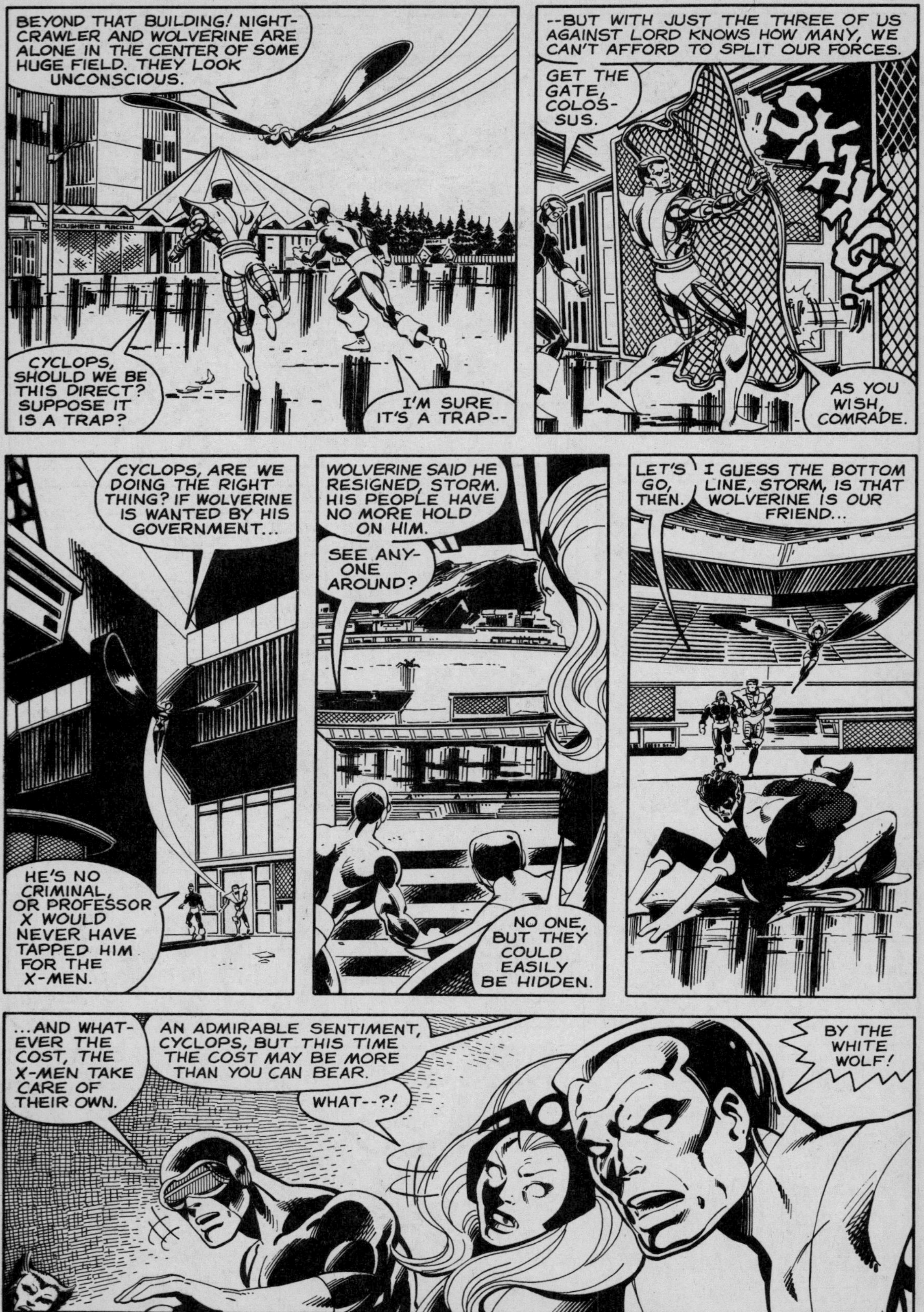
BEYOND THAT BUILDING! NIGHT-CRAWLER AND WOLVERINE ARE ALONE IN THE CENTER OF SOME HUGE FIELD. THEY LOOK UNCONSCIOUS.
THOROUGHBRED RACING
CYCLOPS, SHOULD WE BE THIS DIRECT? SUPPOSE IT IS A TRAP?
I'M SURE IT'S A TRAP--
--BUT WITH JUST THE THREE OF US AGAINST LORD KNOWS HOW MANY, WE CAN'T AFFORD TO SPLIT OUR FORCES.
GET THE GATE, COLOS-SUS.
SKANG!
AS YOU WISH, COMRADE.
CYCLOPS, ARE WE DOING THE RIGHT THING? IF WOLVERINE IS WANTED BY HIS GOVERNMENT...
HE'S NO CRIMINAL, OR PROFESSOR X WOULD NEVER HAVE TAPPED HIM FOR THE X-MEN.
WOLVERINE SAID HE RESIGNED, STORM. HIS PEOPLE HAVE NO MORE HOLD ON HIM.
SEE ANY-ONE AROUND?
NO ONE, BUT THEY COULD EASILY BE HIDDEN.
LET'S GO, THEN.
I GUESS THE BOTTOM LINE, STORM, IS THAT WOLVERINE IS OUR FRIEND...
...AND WHAT-EVER THE COST, THE X-MEN TAKE CARE OF THEIR OWN.
AN ADMIRABLE SENTIMENT, CYCLOPS, BUT THIS TIME THE COST MAY BE MORE THAN YOU CAN BEAR.
WHAT--?!
BY THE WHITE WOLF!

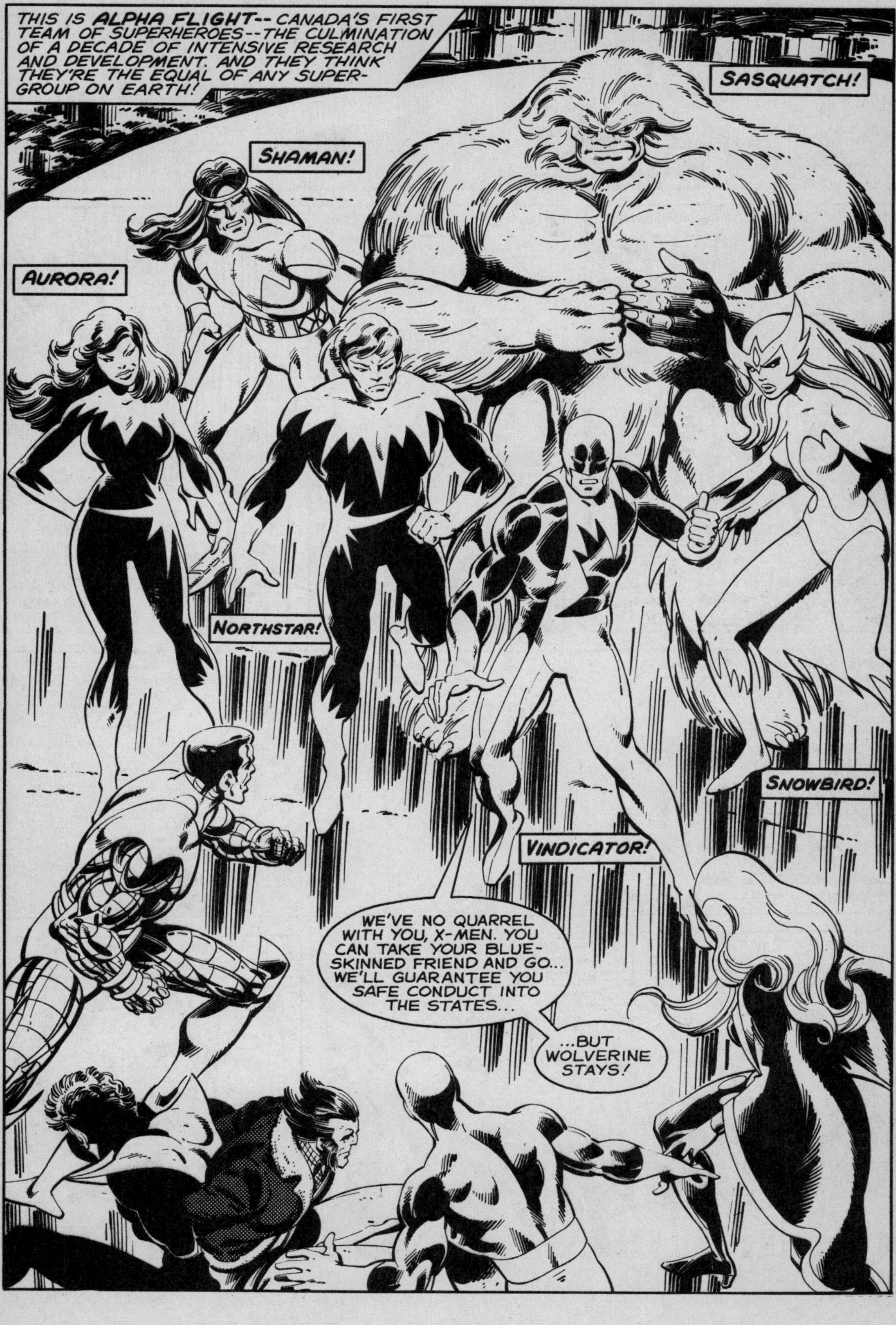
THIS IS ALPHA FLIGHT-- CANADA'S FIRST TEAM OF SUPERHEROES--THE CULMINATION OF A DECADE OF INTENSIVE RESEARCH AND DEVELOPMENT. AND THEY THINK THEY'RE THE EQUAL OF ANY SUPER-GROUP ON EARTH!
SASQUATCH!
SHAMAN!
AURORA!
NORTHSTAR!
SNOWBIRD!
VINDICATOR!
WE'VE NO QUARREL WITH YOU, X-MEN. YOU CAN TAKE YOUR BLUE-SKINNED FRIEND AND GO... WE'LL GUARANTEE YOU SAFE CONDUCT INTO THE STATES...
...BUT WOLVERINE STAYS!

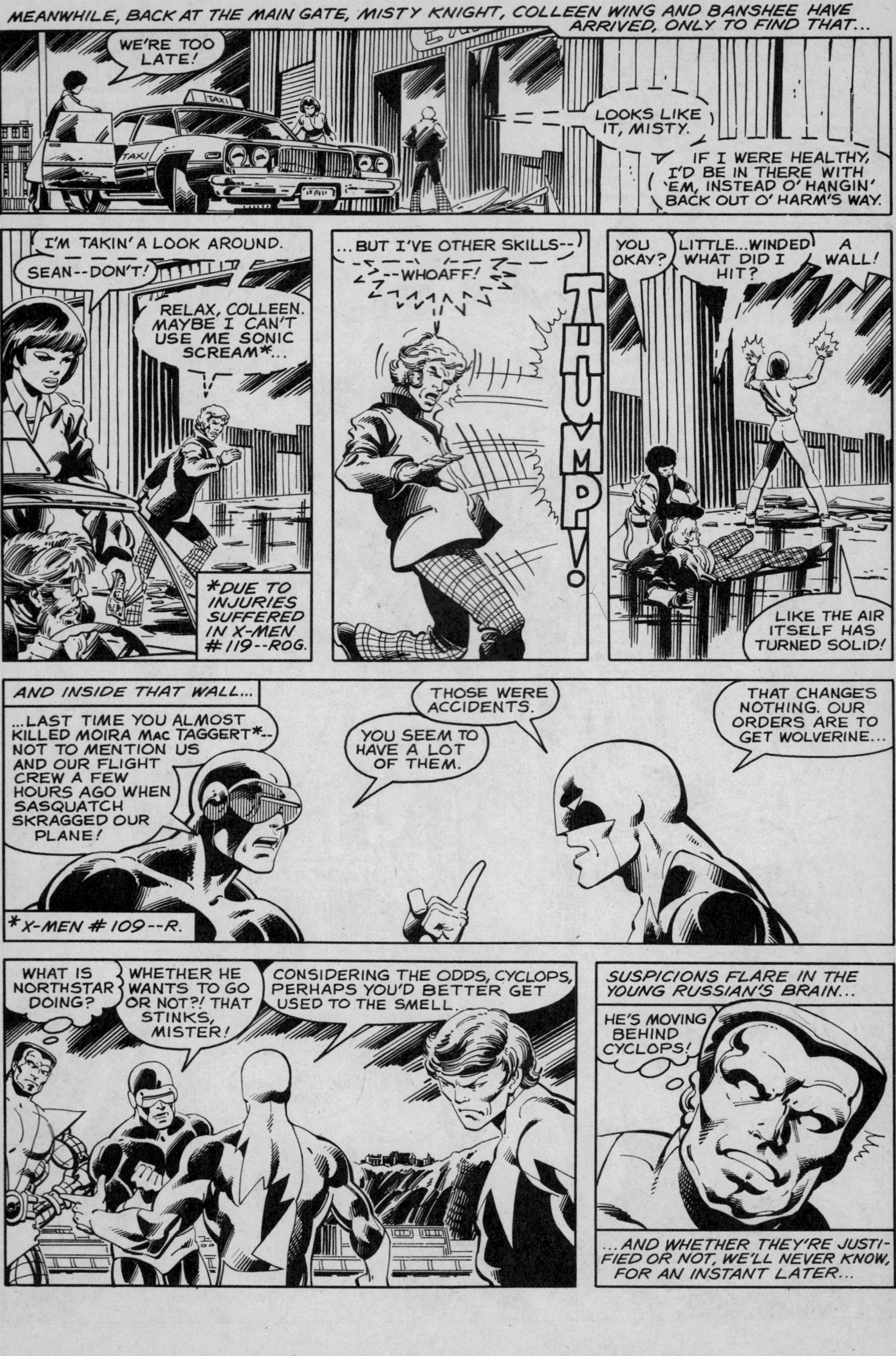
MEANWHILE, BACK AT THE MAIN GATE, MISTY KNIGHT, COLLEEN WING AND BANSHEE HAVE ARRIVED, ONLY TO FIND THAT...
WE'RE TOO LATE!
TAXI
LOOKS LIKE IT, MISTY.
IF I WERE HEALTHY, I'D BE IN THERE WITH 'EM, INSTEAD O' HANGIN' BACK OUT O' HARM'S WAY.
I'M TAKIN' A LOOK AROUND.
SEAN--DON'T!
RELAX, COLLEEN. MAYBE I CAN'T USE ME SONIC SCREAM*...
*DUE TO INJURIES SUFFERED IN X-MEN #119--ROG.
...BUT I'VE OTHER SKILLS--
--WHOAFF!
THUMP!
YOU OKAY?
LITTLE...WINDED WHAT DID I HIT?
A WALL!
LIKE THE AIR ITSELF HAS TURNED SOLID!
AND INSIDE THAT WALL...
...LAST TIME YOU ALMOST KILLED MOIRA MacTAGGERT*--NOT TO MENTION US AND OUR FLIGHT CREW A FEW HOURS AGO WHEN SASQUATCH SKRAGGED OUR PLANE!
THOSE WERE ACCIDENTS.
YOU SEEM TO HAVE A LOT OF THEM.
THAT CHANGES NOTHING. OUR ORDERS ARE TO GET WOLVERINE...
*X-MEN #109--R.
WHAT IS NORTHSTAR DOING?
WHETHER HE WANTS TO GO OR NOT?! THAT STINKS, MISTER!
CONSIDERING THE ODDS, CYCLOPS, PERHAPS YOU'D BETTER GET USED TO THE SMELL.
SUSPICIONS FLARE IN THE YOUNG RUSSIAN'S BRAIN...
HE'S MOVING BEHIND CYCLOPS!
...AND WHETHER THEY'RE JUSTIFIED OR NOT, WE'LL NEVER KNOW, FOR AN INSTANT LATER...

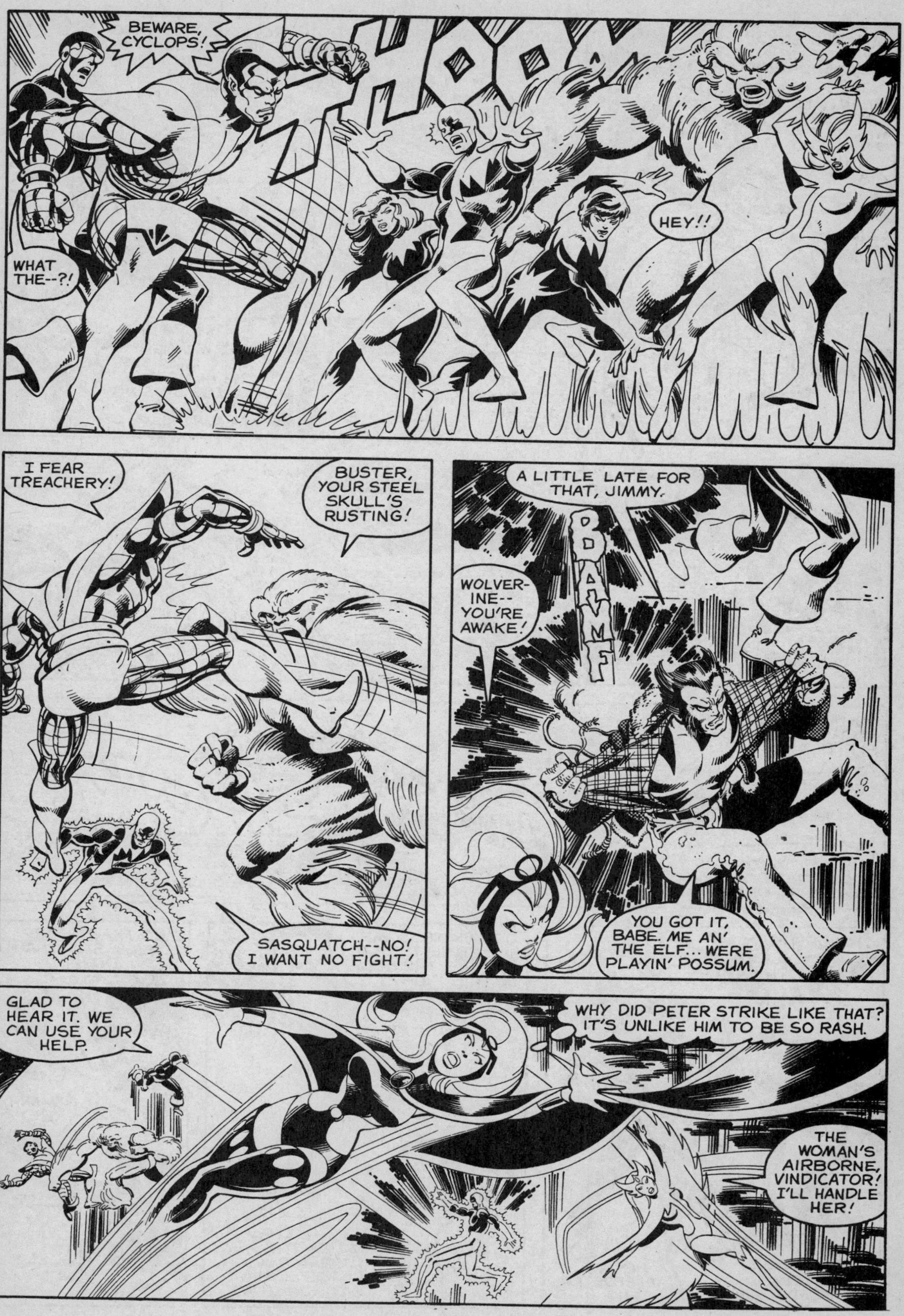
BEWARE, CYCLOPS!
WHAT THE--?!
THOOM
HEY!!
I FEAR TREACHERY!
BUSTER, YOUR STEEL SKULL'S RUSTING!
SASQUATCH--NO! I WANT NO FIGHT!
A LITTLE LATE FOR THAT, JIMMY.
BAMF
WOLVERINE-- YOU'RE AWAKE!
YOU GOT IT, BABE. ME AN' THE ELF... WERE PLAYIN' POSSUM.
GLAD TO HEAR IT. WE CAN USE YOUR HELP.
WHY DID PETER STRIKE LIKE THAT? IT'S UNLIKE HIM TO BE SO RASH.
THE WOMAN'S AIRBORNE, VINDICATOR! I'LL HANDLE HER!

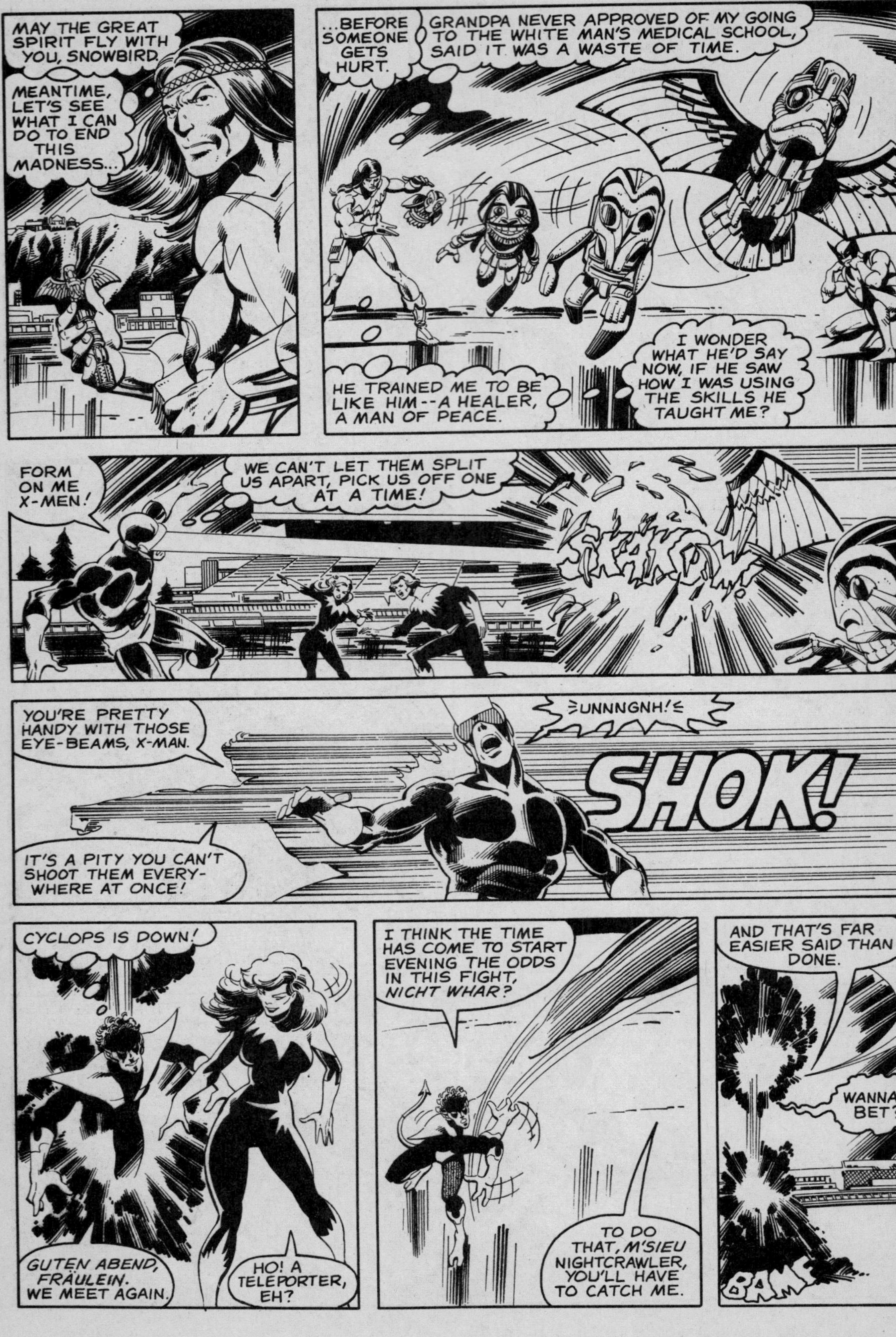
MAY THE GREAT SPIRIT FLY WITH YOU, SNOWBIRD.
MEANTIME, LET'S SEE WHAT I CAN DO TO END THIS MADNESS...
...BEFORE SOMEONE GETS HURT.
GRANDPA NEVER APPROVED OF MY GOING TO THE WHITE MAN'S MEDICAL SCHOOL, SAID IT WAS A WASTE OF TIME.
HE TRAINED ME TO BE LIKE HIM--A HEALER, A MAN OF PEACE.
I WONDER WHAT HE'D SAY NOW, IF HE SAW HOW I WAS USING THE SKILLS HE TAUGHT ME?
FORM ON ME X-MEN!
WE CAN'T LET THEM SPLIT US APART, PICK US OFF ONE AT A TIME!
YOU'RE PRETTY HANDY WITH THOSE EYE-BEAMS, X-MAN.
UNNNGNH!
SHOK!
IT'S A PITY YOU CAN'T SHOOT THEM EVERY-WHERE AT ONCE!
CYCLOPS IS DOWN!
GUTEN ABEND, FRÄULEIN. WE MEET AGAIN.
HO! A TELEPORTER, EH?
I THINK THE TIME HAS COME TO START EVENING THE ODDS IN THIS FIGHT, NICHT WHAR?
TO DO THAT, M'SIEU NIGHTCRAWLER, YOU'LL HAVE TO CATCH ME.
AND THAT'S FAR EASIER SAID THAN DONE.
WANNA BET?
BAM

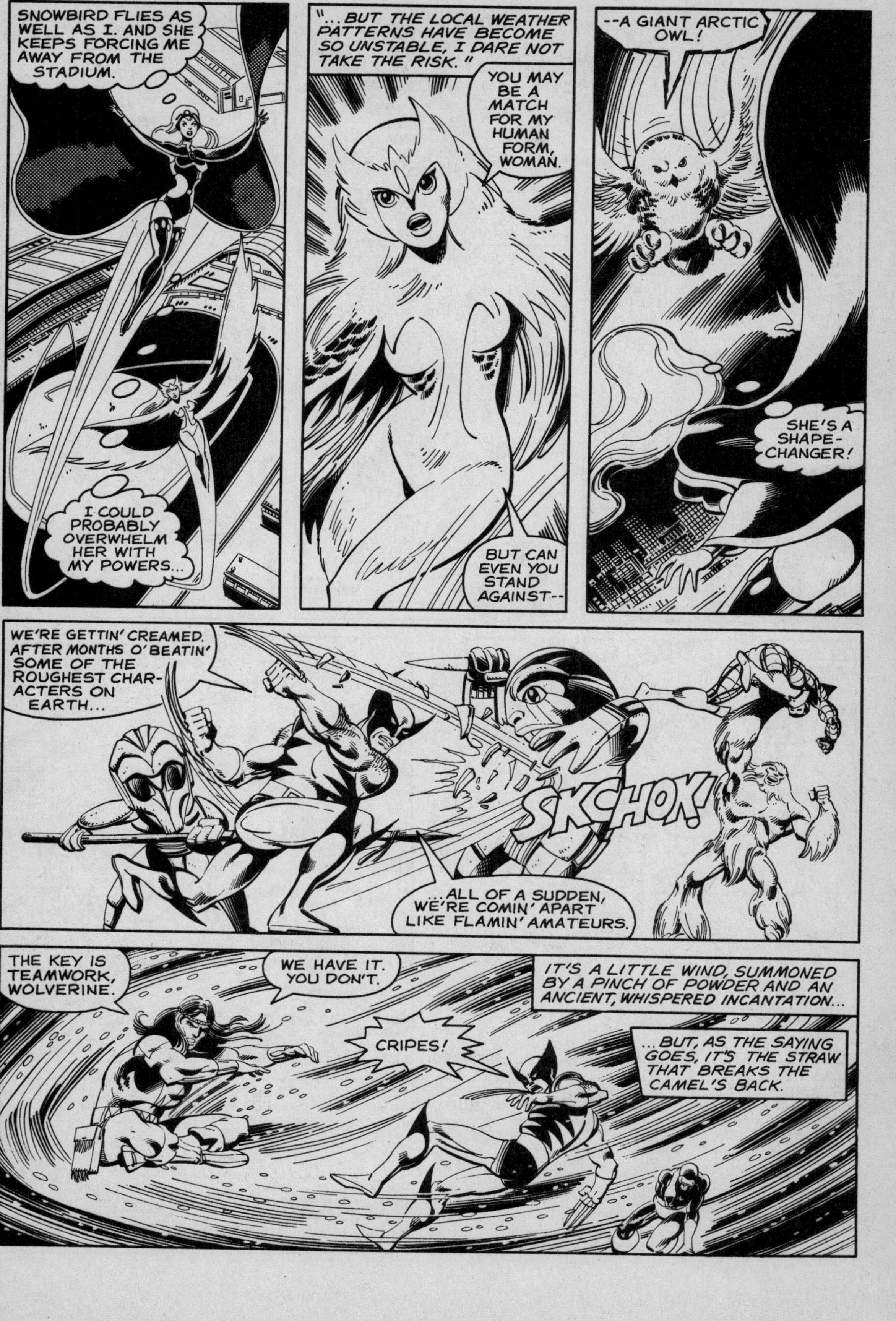
SNOWBIRD FLIES AS WELL AS I. AND SHE KEEPS FORCING ME AWAY FROM THE STADIUM.
I COULD PROBABLY OVERWHELM HER WITH MY POWERS...
"...BUT THE LOCAL WEATHER PATTERNS HAVE BECOME SO UNSTABLE, I DARE NOT TAKE THE RISK."
YOU MAY BE A MATCH FOR MY HUMAN FORM, WOMAN.
BUT CAN EVEN YOU STAND AGAINST--
--A GIANT ARCTIC OWL!
SHE'S A SHAPE-CHANGER!
WE'RE GETTIN' CREAMED. AFTER MONTHS O' BEATIN' SOME OF THE ROUGHEST CHARACTERS ON EARTH...
SKCHOK!
...ALL OF A SUDDEN, WE'RE COMIN' APART LIKE FLAMIN' AMATEURS.
THE KEY IS TEAMWORK, WOLVERINE.
WE HAVE IT. YOU DON'T.
IT'S A LITTLE WIND, SUMMONED BY A PINCH OF POWDER AND AN ANCIENT, WHISPERED INCANTATION...
CRIPES!
...BUT, AS THE SAYING GOES, IT'S THE STRAW THAT BREAKS THE CAMEL'S BACK.

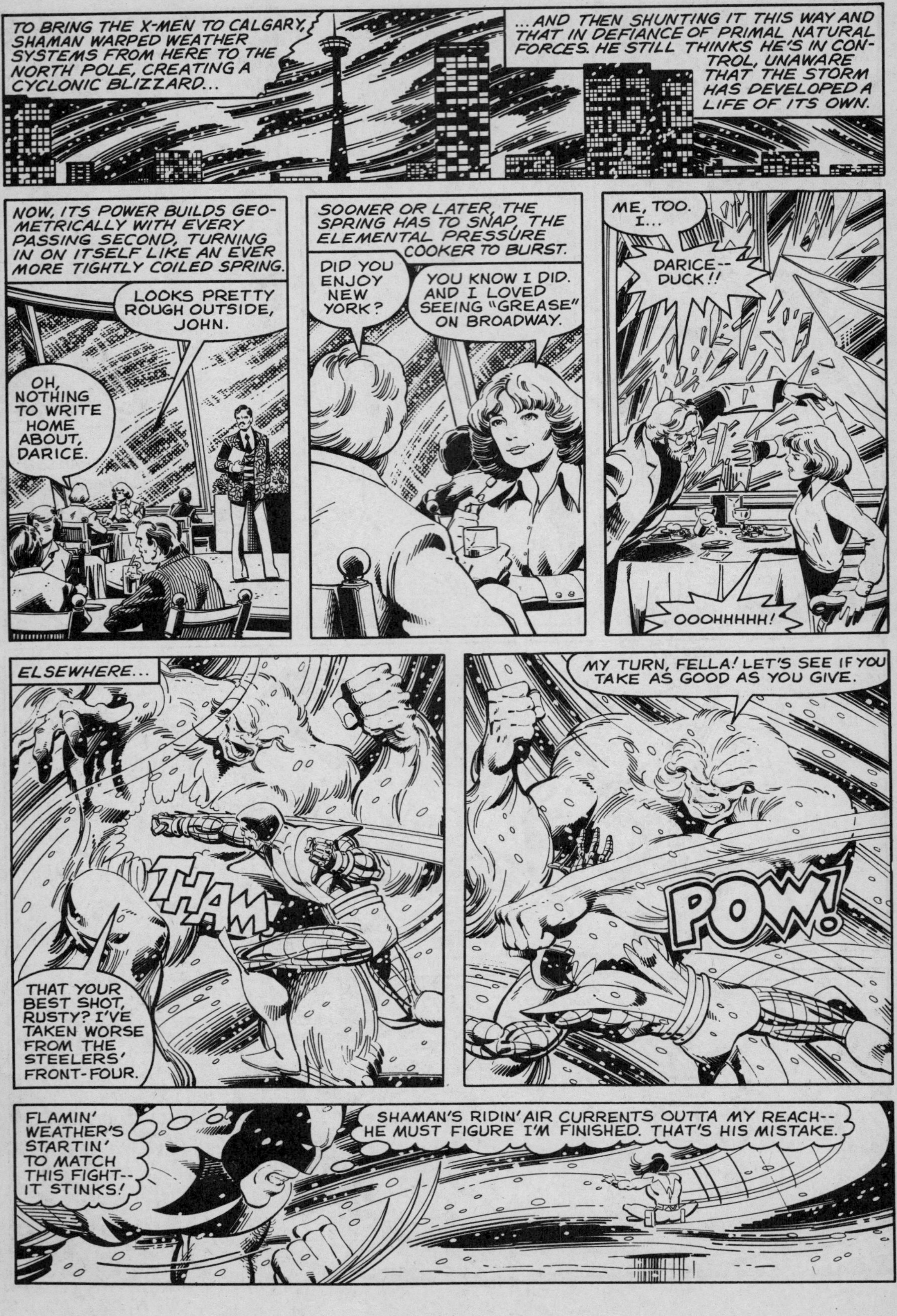
TO BRING THE X-MEN TO CALGARY, SHAMAN WARPED WEATHER SYSTEMS FROM HERE TO THE NORTH POLE, CREATING A CYCLONIC BLIZZARD...
...AND THEN SHUNTING IT THIS WAY AND THAT IN DEFIANCE OF PRIMAL NATURAL FORCES. HE STILL THINKS HE'S IN CONTROL, UNAWARE THAT THE STORM HAS DEVELOPED A LIFE OF ITS OWN.
NOW, ITS POWER BUILDS GEOMETRICALLY WITH EVERY PASSING SECOND, TURNING IN ON ITSELF LIKE AN EVER MORE TIGHTLY COILED SPRING.
LOOKS PRETTY ROUGH OUTSIDE, JOHN.
OH, NOTHING TO WRITE HOME ABOUT, DARICE.
SOONER OR LATER, THE SPRING HAS TO SNAP, THE ELEMENTAL PRESSURE COOKER TO BURST.
DID YOU ENJOY NEW YORK?
YOU KNOW I DID. AND I LOVED SEEING "GREASE" ON BROADWAY.
ME, TOO. I...
DARICE-- DUCK!!
OOOHHHHH!
ELSEWHERE...
THAM
THAT YOUR BEST SHOT, RUSTY? I'VE TAKEN WORSE FROM THE STEELERS' FRONT-FOUR.
MY TURN, FELLA! LET'S SEE IF YOU TAKE AS GOOD AS YOU GIVE.
POW!
FLAMIN' WEATHER'S STARTIN' TO MATCH THIS FIGHT-- IT STINKS!
SHAMAN'S RIDIN' AIR CURRENTS OUTTA MY REACH-- HE MUST FIGURE I'M FINISHED. THAT'S HIS MISTAKE.

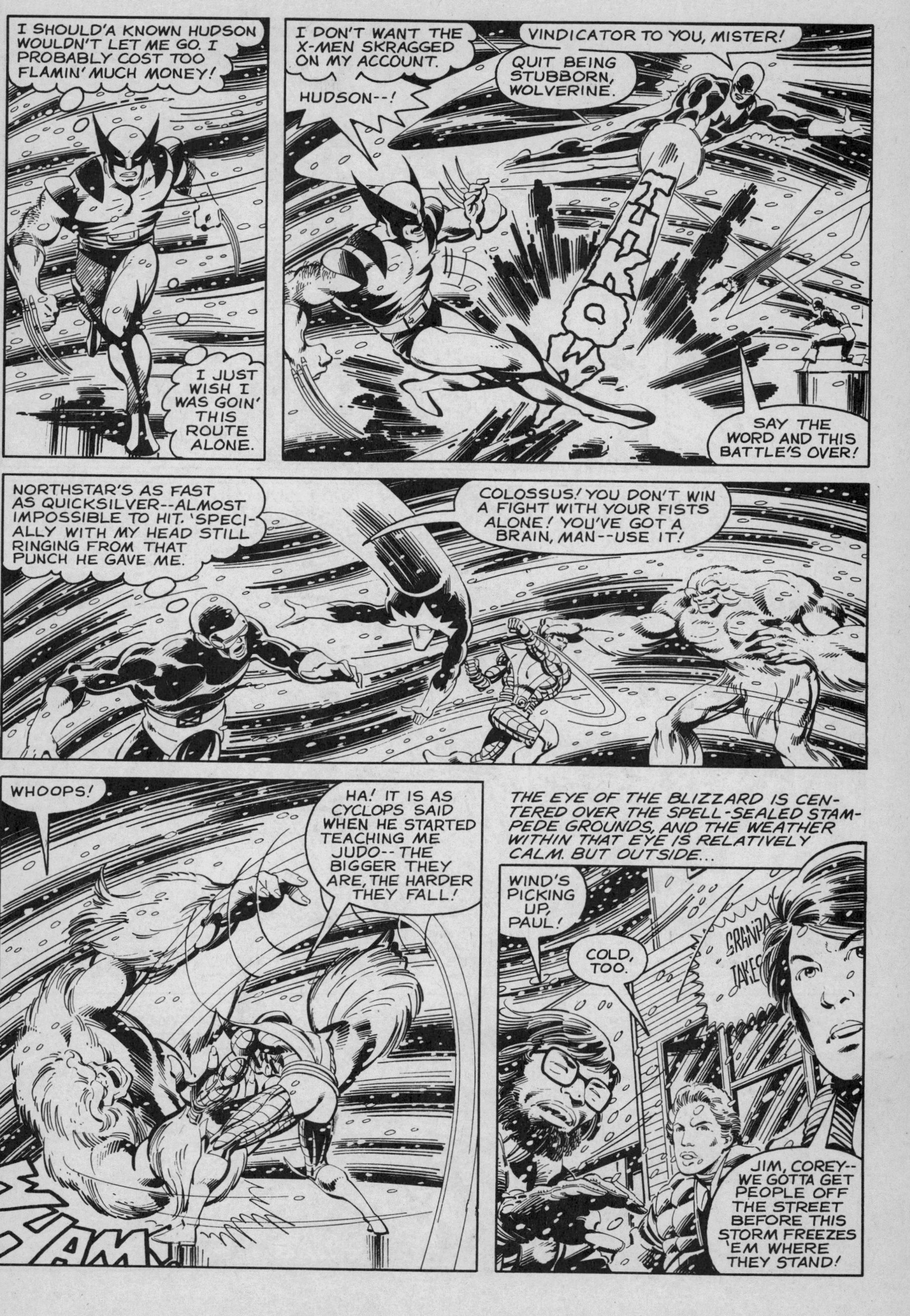
I SHOULD'A KNOWN HUDSON WOULDN'T LET ME GO. I PROBABLY COST TOO FLAMIN' MUCH MONEY!
I JUST WISH I WAS GOIN' THIS ROUTE ALONE.
I DON'T WANT THE X-MEN SKRAGGED ON MY ACCOUNT.
HUDSON--!
VINDICATOR TO YOU, MISTER!
QUIT BEING STUBBORN, WOLVERINE.
THOOM
SAY THE WORD AND THIS BATTLE'S OVER!
NORTHSTAR'S AS FAST AS QUICKSILVER--ALMOST IMPOSSIBLE TO HIT. 'SPECIALLY WITH MY HEAD STILL RINGING FROM THAT PUNCH HE GAVE ME.
COLOSSUS! YOU DON'T WIN A FIGHT WITH YOUR FISTS ALONE! YOU'VE GOT A BRAIN, MAN--USE IT!
WHOOPS!
HA! IT IS AS CYCLOPS SAID WHEN HE STARTED TEACHING ME JUDO--THE BIGGER THEY ARE, THE HARDER THEY FALL!
WHAM
THE EYE OF THE BLIZZARD IS CENTERED OVER THE SPELL-SEALED STAMPEDE GROUNDS, AND THE WEATHER WITHIN THAT EYE IS RELATIVELY CALM. BUT OUTSIDE...
WIND'S PICKING UP, PAUL!
COLD, TOO.
GRANPA JAKE'S
JIM, COREY--WE GOTTA GET PEOPLE OFF THE STREET BEFORE THIS STORM FREEZES 'EM WHERE THEY STAND!

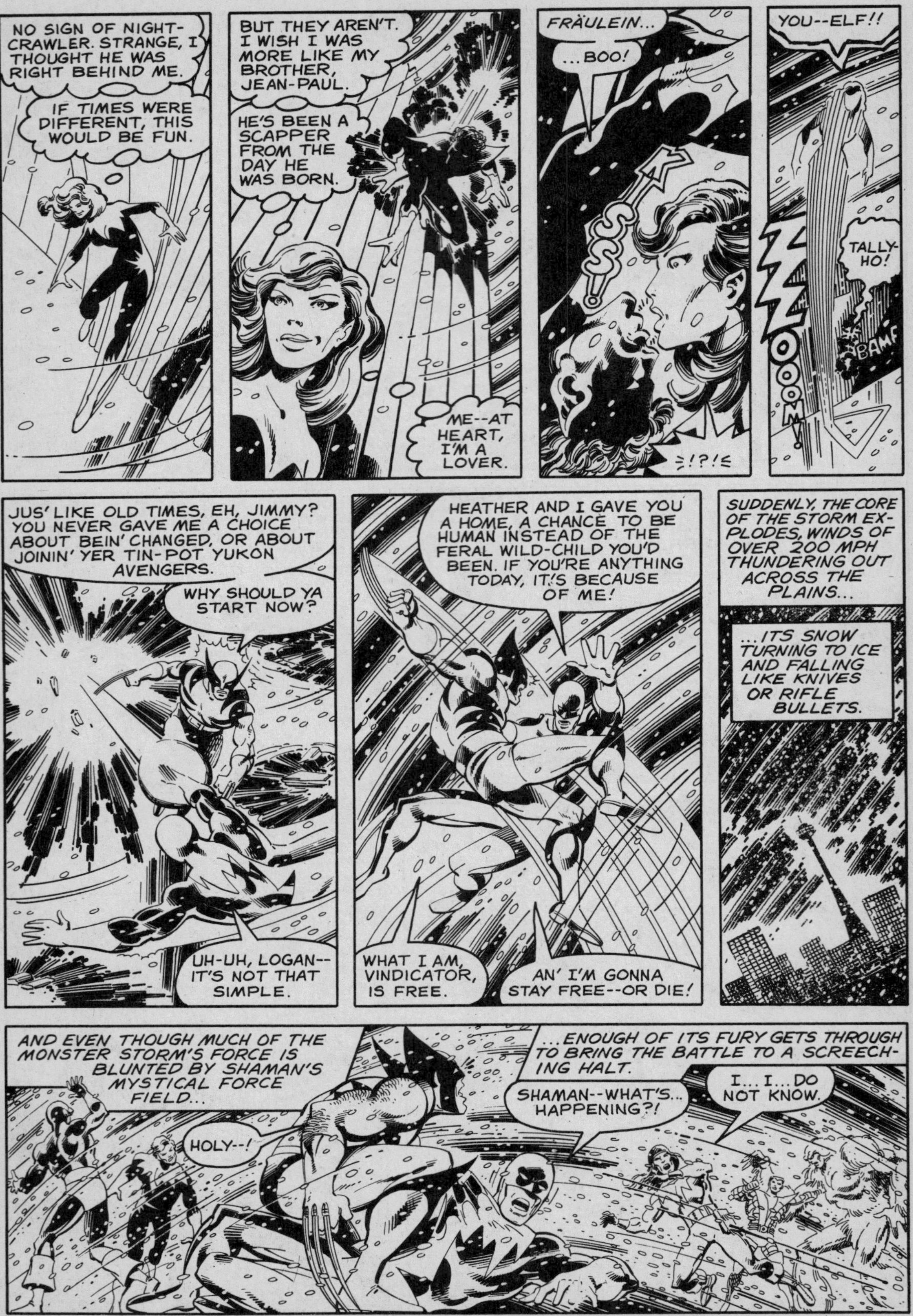
NO SIGN OF NIGHT-CRAWLER. STRANGE, I THOUGHT HE WAS RIGHT BEHIND ME.
IF TIMES WERE DIFFERENT, THIS WOULD BE FUN.
BUT THEY AREN'T. I WISH I WAS MORE LIKE MY BROTHER, JEAN-PAUL.
HE'S BEEN A SCAPPER FROM THE DAY HE WAS BORN.
ME--AT HEART, I'M A LOVER.
FRÄULEIN...
...BOO!
YOU--ELF!!
TALLY-HO!
JUS' LIKE OLD TIMES, EH, JIMMY? YOU NEVER GAVE ME A CHOICE ABOUT BEIN' CHANGED, OR ABOUT JOININ' YER TIN-POT YUKON AVENGERS.
WHY SHOULD YA START NOW?
UH-UH, LOGAN-- IT'S NOT THAT SIMPLE.
HEATHER AND I GAVE YOU A HOME, A CHANCE TO BE HUMAN INSTEAD OF THE FERAL WILD-CHILD YOU'D BEEN. IF YOU'RE ANYTHING TODAY, IT'S BECAUSE OF ME!
WHAT I AM, VINDICATOR, IS FREE.
AN' I'M GONNA STAY FREE--OR DIE!
SUDDENLY, THE CORE OF THE STORM EXPLODES, WINDS OF OVER 200 MPH THUNDERING OUT ACROSS THE PLAINS...
...ITS SNOW TURNING TO ICE AND FALLING LIKE KNIVES OR RIFLE BULLETS.
AND EVEN THOUGH MUCH OF THE MONSTER STORM'S FORCE IS BLUNTED BY SHAMAN'S MYSTICAL FORCE FIELD...
...ENOUGH OF ITS FURY GETS THROUGH TO BRING THE BATTLE TO A SCREECHING HALT.
HOLY--!
SHAMAN--WHAT'S... HAPPENING?!
I... I... DO NOT KNOW.

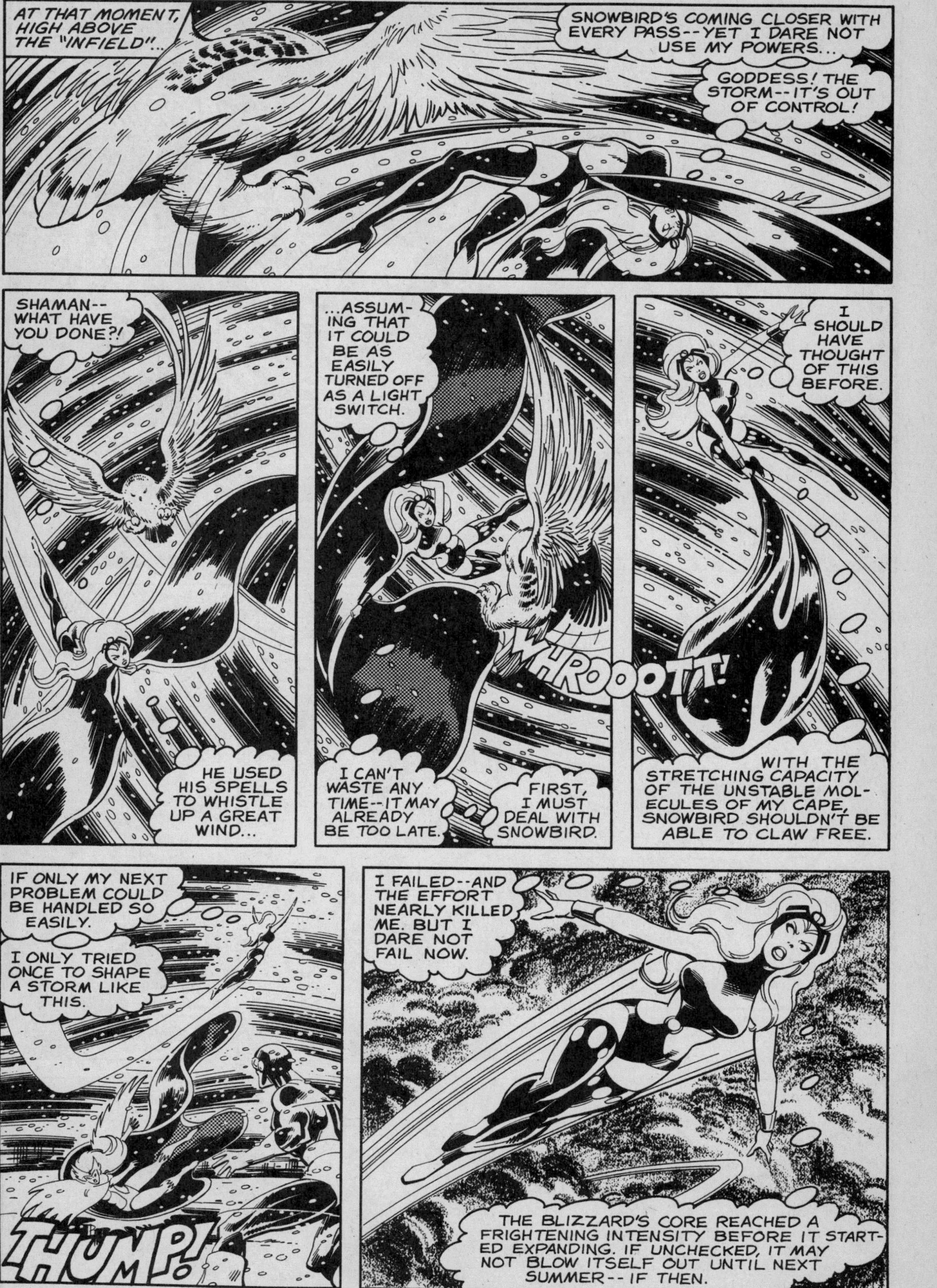
AT THAT MOMENT, HIGH ABOVE THE "INFIELD"...
SNOWBIRD'S COMING CLOSER WITH EVERY PASS--YET I DARE NOT USE MY POWERS...
GODDESS! THE STORM--IT'S OUT OF CONTROL!
SHAMAN-- WHAT HAVE YOU DONE?!
HE USED HIS SPELLS TO WHISTLE UP A GREAT WIND...
...ASSUMING THAT IT COULD BE AS EASILY TURNED OFF AS A LIGHT SWITCH.
I CAN'T WASTE ANY TIME--IT MAY ALREADY BE TOO LATE.
FIRST, I MUST DEAL WITH SNOWBIRD.
WHROOOTT!
I SHOULD HAVE THOUGHT OF THIS BEFORE.
WITH THE STRETCHING CAPACITY OF THE UNSTABLE MOLECULES OF MY CAPE, SNOWBIRD SHOULDN'T BE ABLE TO CLAW FREE.
IF ONLY MY NEXT PROBLEM COULD BE HANDLED SO EASILY.
I ONLY TRIED ONCE TO SHAPE A STORM LIKE THIS.
THUMP!
I FAILED--AND THE EFFORT NEARLY KILLED ME. BUT I DARE NOT FAIL NOW.
THE BLIZZARD'S CORE REACHED A FRIGHTENING INTENSITY BEFORE IT STARTED EXPANDING. IF UNCHECKED, IT MAY NOT BLOW ITSELF OUT UNTIL NEXT SUMMER-- IF THEN.

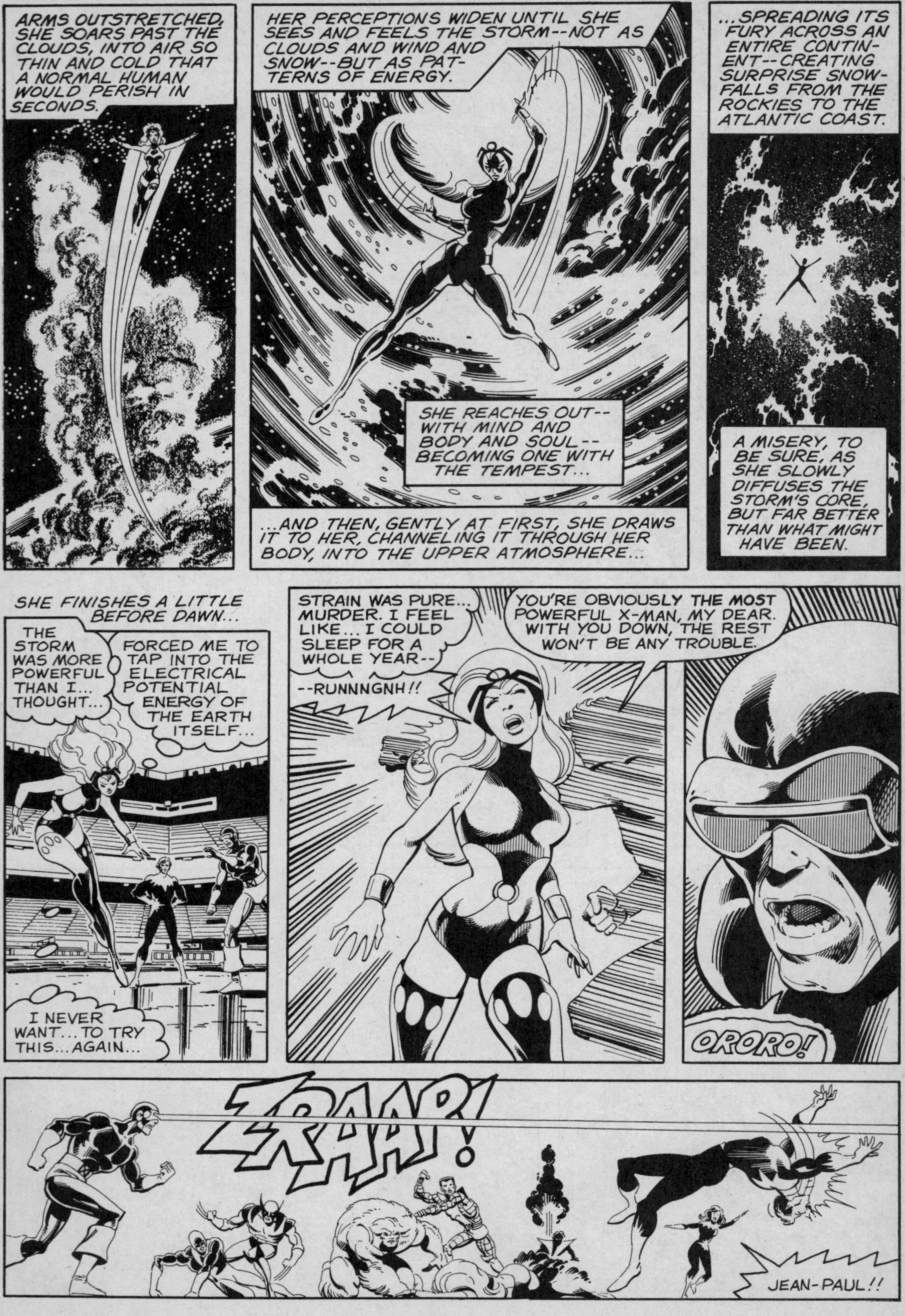
ARMS OUTSTRETCHED, SHE SOARS PAST THE CLOUDS, INTO AIR SO THIN AND COLD THAT A NORMAL HUMAN WOULD PERISH IN SECONDS.
HER PERCEPTIONS WIDEN UNTIL SHE SEES AND FEELS THE STORM--NOT AS CLOUDS AND WIND AND SNOW--BUT AS PATTERNS OF ENERGY.
SHE REACHES OUT--WITH MIND AND BODY AND SOUL--BECOMING ONE WITH THE TEMPEST...
...AND THEN, GENTLY AT FIRST, SHE DRAWS IT TO HER, CHANNELING IT THROUGH HER BODY, INTO THE UPPER ATMOSPHERE...
...SPREADING ITS FURY ACROSS AN ENTIRE CONTINENT--CREATING SURPRISE SNOWFALLS FROM THE ROCKIES TO THE ATLANTIC COAST.
A MISERY, TO BE SURE, AS SHE SLOWLY DIFFUSES THE STORM'S CORE, BUT FAR BETTER THAN WHAT MIGHT HAVE BEEN.
SHE FINISHES A LITTLE BEFORE DAWN...
THE STORM WAS MORE POWERFUL THAN I... THOUGHT...
FORCED ME TO TAP INTO THE ELECTRICAL POTENTIAL ENERGY OF THE EARTH ITSELF...
I NEVER WANT... TO TRY THIS... AGAIN...
STRAIN WAS PURE... MURDER. I FEEL LIKE... I COULD SLEEP FOR A WHOLE YEAR--
--RUNNNGNH!!
YOU'RE OBVIOUSLY THE MOST POWERFUL X-MAN, MY DEAR. WITH YOU DOWN, THE REST WON'T BE ANY TROUBLE.
ORORO!
ZRAAP!
JEAN-PAUL!!

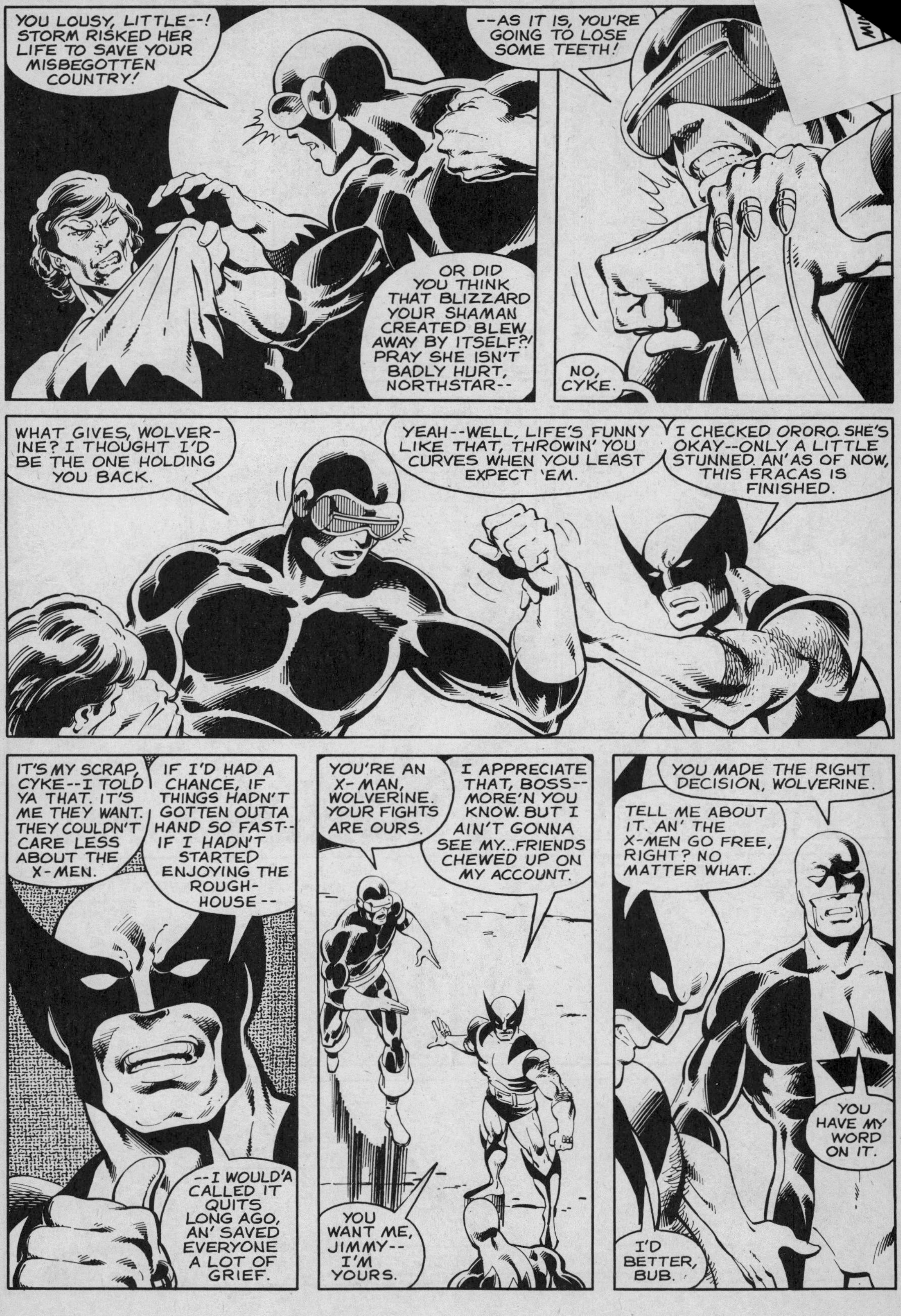
YOU LOUSY, LITTLE--! STORM RISKED HER LIFE TO SAVE YOUR MISBEGOTTEN COUNTRY!
OR DID YOU THINK THAT BLIZZARD YOUR SHAMAN CREATED BLEW AWAY BY ITSELF?! PRAY SHE ISN'T BADLY HURT, NORTHSTAR--
--AS IT IS, YOU'RE GOING TO LOSE SOME TEETH!
NO, CYKE.
WHAT GIVES, WOLVERINE? I THOUGHT I'D BE THE ONE HOLDING YOU BACK.
YEAH--WELL, LIFE'S FUNNY LIKE THAT, THROWIN' YOU CURVES WHEN YOU LEAST EXPECT 'EM.
I CHECKED ORORO. SHE'S OKAY--ONLY A LITTLE STUNNED. AN' AS OF NOW, THIS FRACAS IS FINISHED.
IT'S MY SCRAP, CYKE--I TOLD YA THAT. IT'S ME THEY WANT. THEY COULDN'T CARE LESS ABOUT THE X-MEN.
IF I'D HAD A CHANCE, IF THINGS HADN'T GOTTEN OUTTA HAND SO FAST--IF I HADN'T STARTED ENJOYING THE ROUGH-HOUSE--
--I WOULD'A CALLED IT QUITS LONG AGO, AN' SAVED EVERYONE A LOT OF GRIEF.
YOU'RE AN X-MAN, WOLVERINE. YOUR FIGHTS ARE OURS.
I APPRECIATE THAT, BOSS--MORE'N YOU KNOW. BUT I AIN'T GONNA SEE MY...FRIENDS CHEWED UP ON MY ACCOUNT.
YOU WANT ME, JIMMY--I'M YOURS.
YOU MADE THE RIGHT DECISION, WOLVERINE.
TELL ME ABOUT IT. AN' THE X-MEN GO FREE, RIGHT? NO MATTER WHAT.
YOU HAVE MY WORD ON IT.
I'D BETTER, BUB.

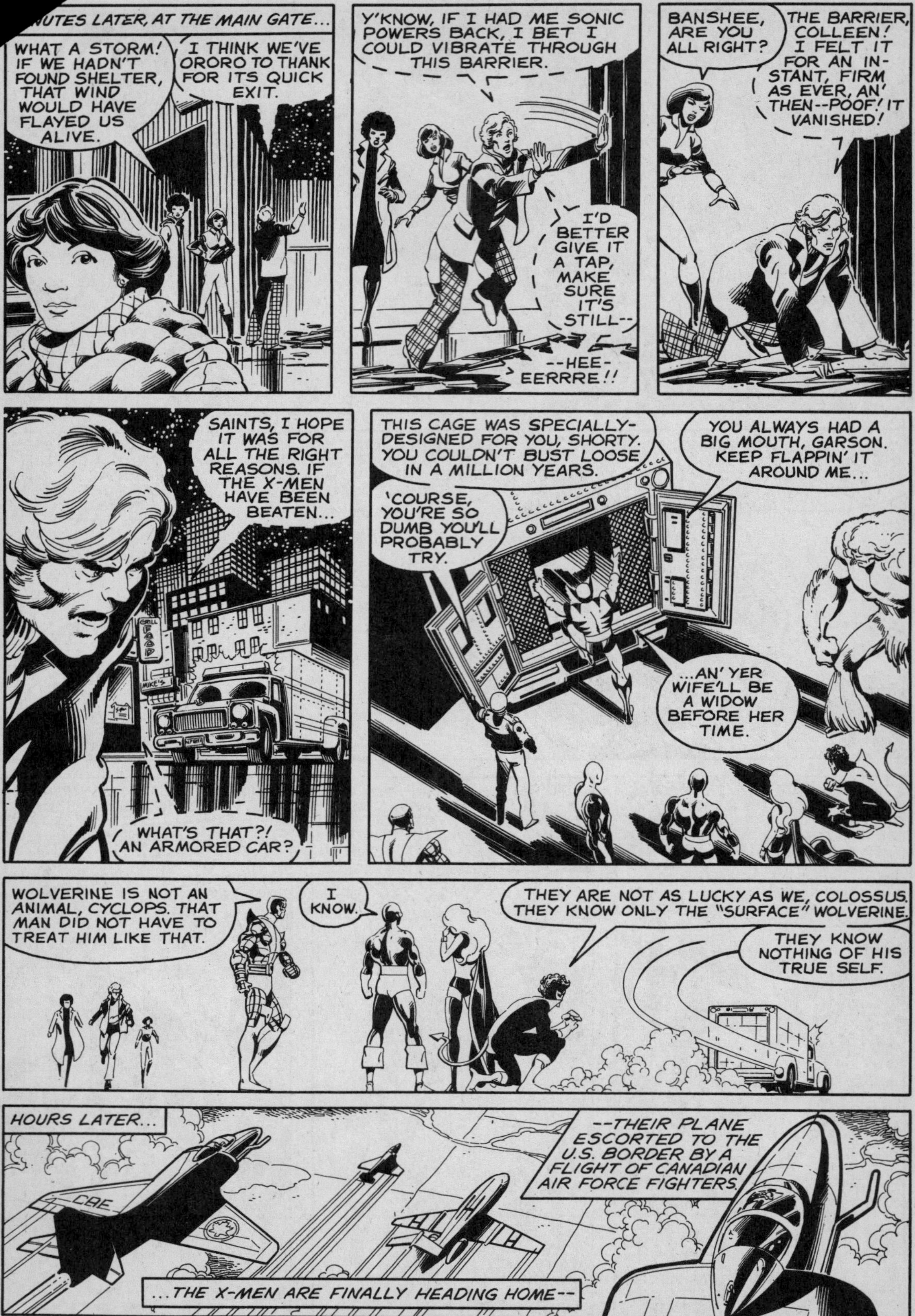
...NUTES LATER, AT THE MAIN GATE...
WHAT A STORM! IF WE HADN'T FOUND SHELTER, THAT WIND WOULD HAVE FLAYED US ALIVE.
I THINK WE'VE ORORO TO THANK FOR ITS QUICK EXIT.
Y'KNOW, IF I HAD ME SONIC POWERS BACK, I BET I COULD VIBRATE THROUGH THIS BARRIER.
I'D BETTER GIVE IT A TAP, MAKE SURE IT'S STILL--
--HEE-EERRRE!!
BANSHEE, ARE YOU ALL RIGHT?
THE BARRIER, COLLEEN! I FELT IT FOR AN IN-STANT, FIRM AS EVER, AN' THEN--POOF! IT VANISHED!
SAINTS, I HOPE IT WAS FOR ALL THE RIGHT REASONS. IF THE X-MEN HAVE BEEN BEATEN...
WHAT'S THAT?! AN ARMORED CAR?
THIS CAGE WAS SPECIALLY-DESIGNED FOR YOU, SHORTY. YOU COULDN'T BUST LOOSE IN A MILLION YEARS.
'COURSE, YOU'RE SO DUMB YOU'LL PROBABLY TRY.
YOU ALWAYS HAD A BIG MOUTH, GARSON. KEEP FLAPPIN' IT AROUND ME...
...AN' YER WIFE'LL BE A WIDOW BEFORE HER TIME.
WOLVERINE IS NOT AN ANIMAL, CYCLOPS. THAT MAN DID NOT HAVE TO TREAT HIM LIKE THAT.
I KNOW.
THEY ARE NOT AS LUCKY AS WE, COLOSSUS. THEY KNOW ONLY THE "SURFACE" WOLVERINE.
THEY KNOW NOTHING OF HIS TRUE SELF.
HOURS LATER...
--THEIR PLANE ESCORTED TO THE U.S. BORDER BY A FLIGHT OF CANADIAN AIR FORCE FIGHTERS.
...THE X-MEN ARE FINALLY HEADING HOME--

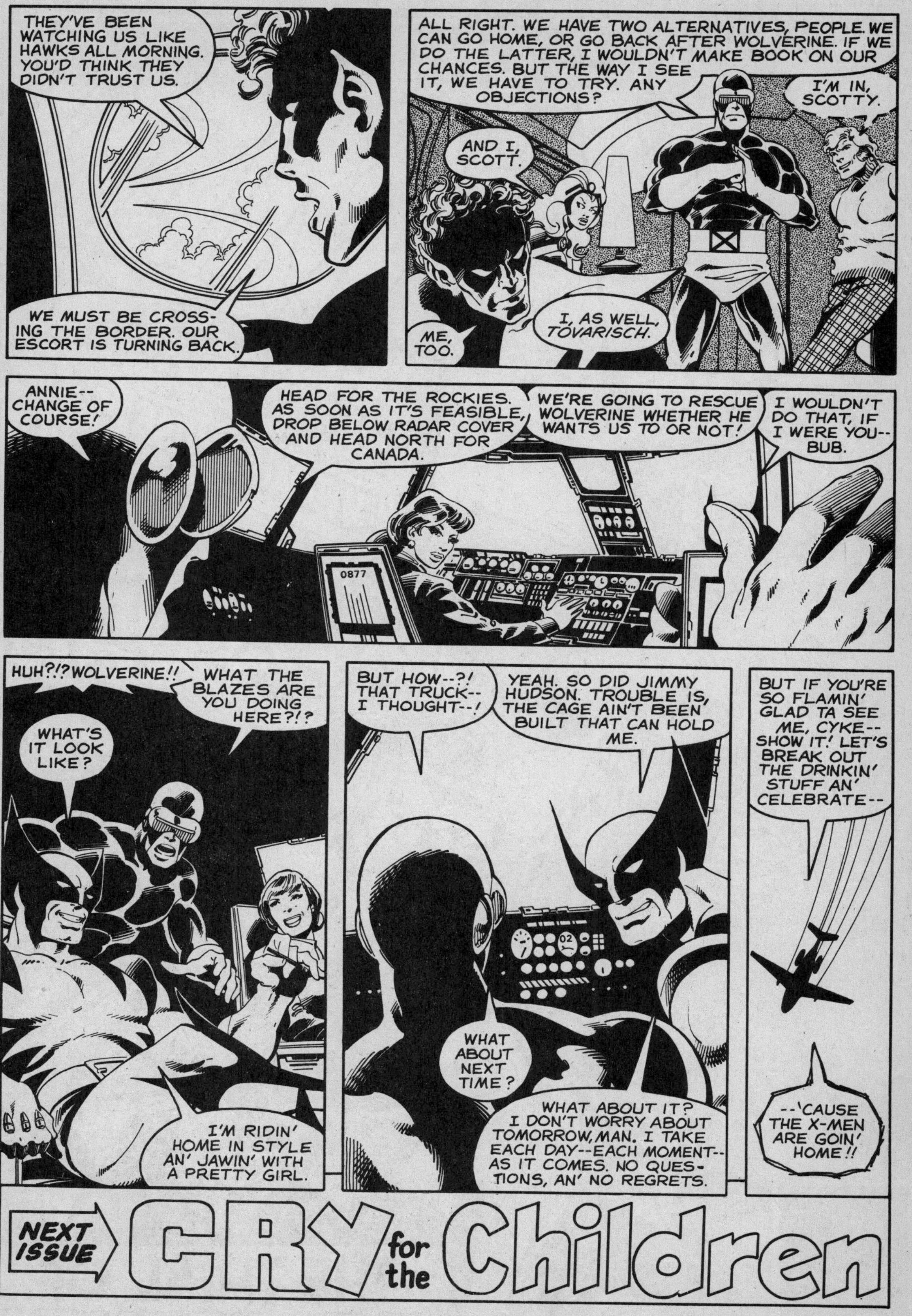
THEY'VE BEEN WATCHING US LIKE HAWKS ALL MORNING. YOU'D THINK THEY DIDN'T TRUST US.
WE MUST BE CROSSING THE BORDER. OUR ESCORT IS TURNING BACK.
ALL RIGHT. WE HAVE TWO ALTERNATIVES, PEOPLE. WE CAN GO HOME, OR GO BACK AFTER WOLVERINE. IF WE DO THE LATTER, I WOULDN'T MAKE BOOK ON OUR CHANCES. BUT THE WAY I SEE IT, WE HAVE TO TRY. ANY OBJECTIONS?
I'M IN, SCOTTY.
AND I, SCOTT.
I, AS WELL, TOVARISCH.
ME, TOO.
ANNIE-- CHANGE OF COURSE!
HEAD FOR THE ROCKIES. AS SOON AS IT'S FEASIBLE, DROP BELOW RADAR COVER AND HEAD NORTH FOR CANADA.
WE'RE GOING TO RESCUE WOLVERINE WHETHER HE WANTS US TO OR NOT!
I WOULDN'T DO THAT, IF I WERE YOU-- BUB.
0877
HUH?!? WOLVERINE!!
WHAT THE BLAZES ARE YOU DOING HERE?!?
WHAT'S IT LOOK LIKE?
I'M RIDIN' HOME IN STYLE AN' JAWIN' WITH A PRETTY GIRL.
BUT HOW--?! THAT TRUCK-- I THOUGHT--!
YEAH. SO DID JIMMY HUDSON. TROUBLE IS, THE CAGE AIN'T BEEN BUILT THAT CAN HOLD ME.
WHAT ABOUT NEXT TIME?
WHAT ABOUT IT? I DON'T WORRY ABOUT TOMORROW, MAN. I TAKE EACH DAY--EACH MOMENT-- AS IT COMES. NO QUESTIONS, AN' NO REGRETS.
BUT IF YOU'RE SO FLAMIN' GLAD TA SEE ME, CYKE-- SHOW IT! LET'S BREAK OUT THE DRINKIN' STUFF AN' CELEBRATE--
--'CAUSE THE X-MEN ARE GOIN' HOME!!
NEXT ISSUE
CRY for the Children

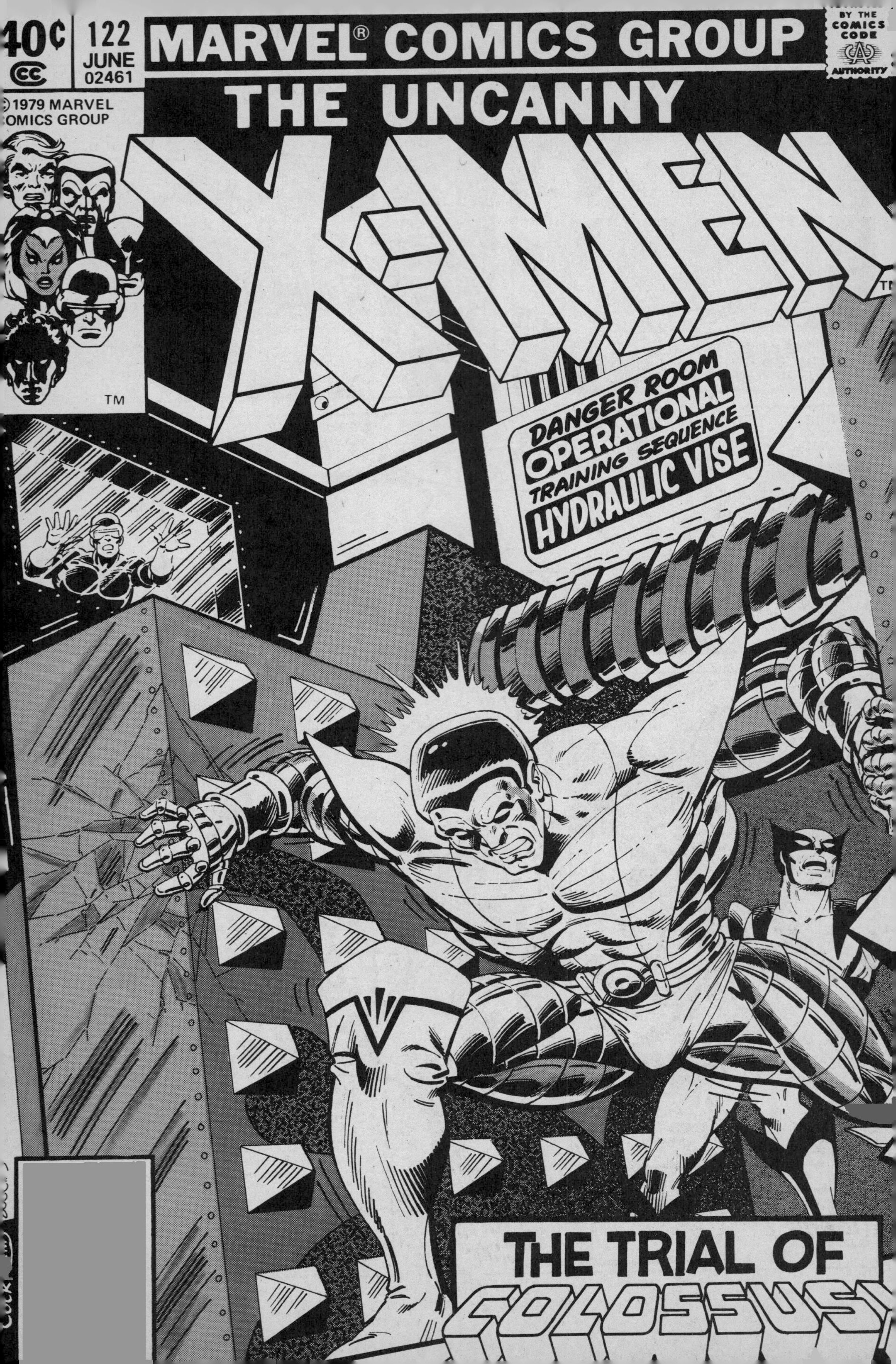

40¢
CC
122
JUNE
02461
MARVEL® COMICS GROUP
APPROVED BY THE COMICS CODE AUTHORITY
THE UNCANNY
X-MEN
©1979 MARVEL COMICS GROUP
TM
DANGER ROOM
OPERATIONAL
TRAINING SEQUENCE
HYDRAULIC VISE
THE TRIAL OF
COLOSSUS!

Cyclops. Storm. Banshee. Nightcrawler. Wolverine. Colossus. Children of the atom, students of Charles Xavier, MUTANTS––feared and hated by the world they have sworn to protect. These are the STRANGEST heroes of all!

Stan Lee PRESENTS: **THE UNCANNY X-MEN!**™

CHRIS CLAREMONT · JOHN BYRNE · TERRY AUSTIN | TOM ORZECHOWSKI, *letterer* | ROGER STERN * JIM SHOOTER
WRITER / CO-PLOTTERS / BREAKDOWNS · FINISHED ART | GLYNIS WEIN, *colorist* | *EDITOR* *EDITOR-IN-CHIEF*

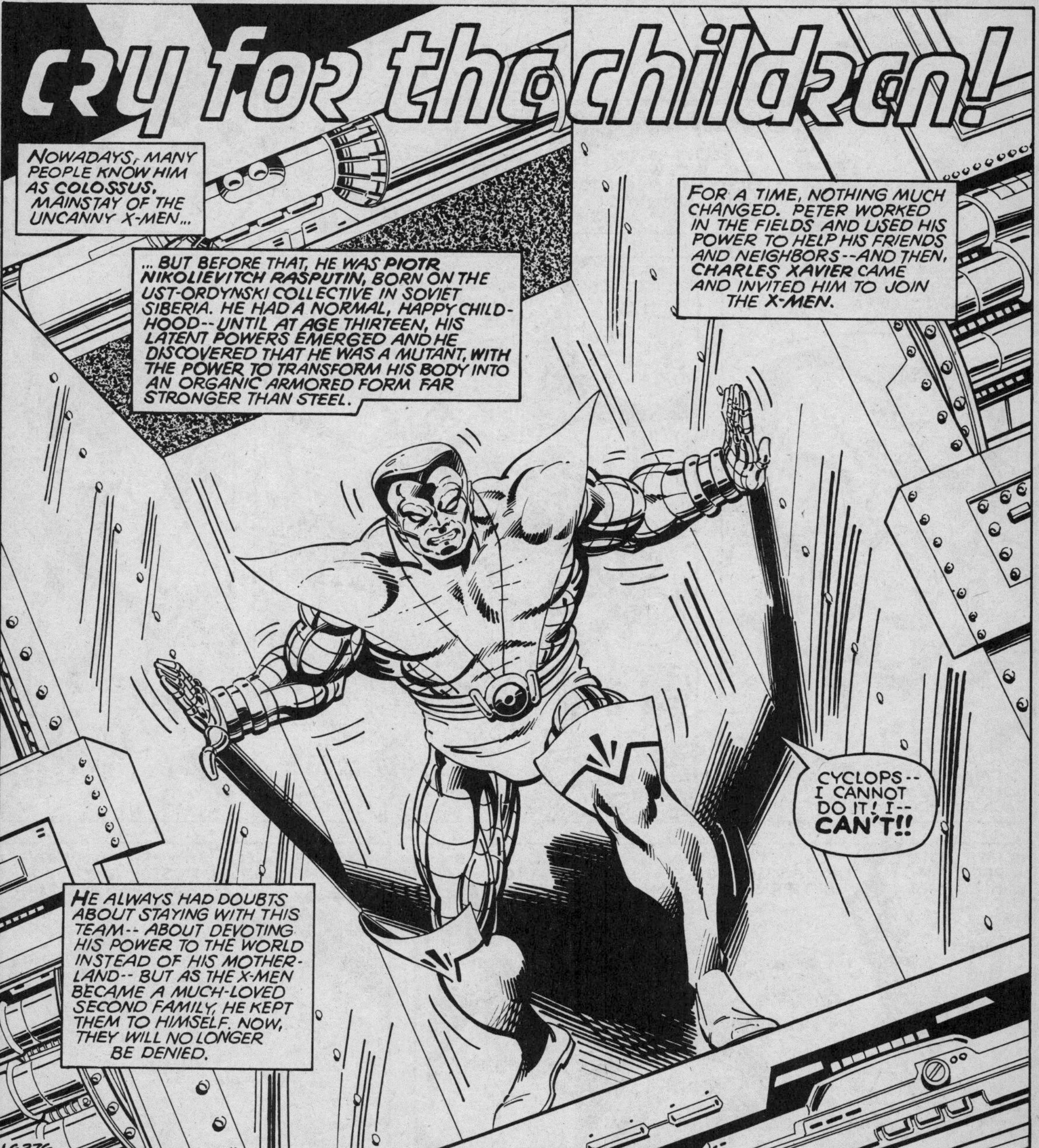
CRY FOR THE CHILDREN!
NOWADAYS, MANY PEOPLE KNOW HIM AS COLOSSUS, MAINSTAY OF THE UNCANNY X-MEN...
... BUT BEFORE THAT, HE WAS PIOTR NIKOLIEVITCH RASPUTIN, BORN ON THE UST-ORDYNSKI COLLECTIVE IN SOVIET SIBERIA. HE HAD A NORMAL, HAPPY CHILDHOOD-- UNTIL AT AGE THIRTEEN, HIS LATENT POWERS EMERGED AND HE DISCOVERED THAT HE WAS A MUTANT, WITH THE POWER TO TRANSFORM HIS BODY INTO AN ORGANIC ARMORED FORM FAR STRONGER THAN STEEL.
FOR A TIME, NOTHING MUCH CHANGED. PETER WORKED IN THE FIELDS AND USED HIS POWER TO HELP HIS FRIENDS AND NEIGHBORS--AND THEN, CHARLES XAVIER CAME AND INVITED HIM TO JOIN THE X-MEN.
CYCLOPS-- I CANNOT DO IT! I-- CAN'T!!
HE ALWAYS HAD DOUBTS ABOUT STAYING WITH THIS TEAM-- ABOUT DEVOTING HIS POWER TO THE WORLD INSTEAD OF HIS MOTHERLAND-- BUT AS THE X-MEN BECAME A MUCH-LOVED SECOND FAMILY, HE KEPT THEM TO HIMSELF. NOW, THEY WILL NO LONGER BE DENIED.
LG 376

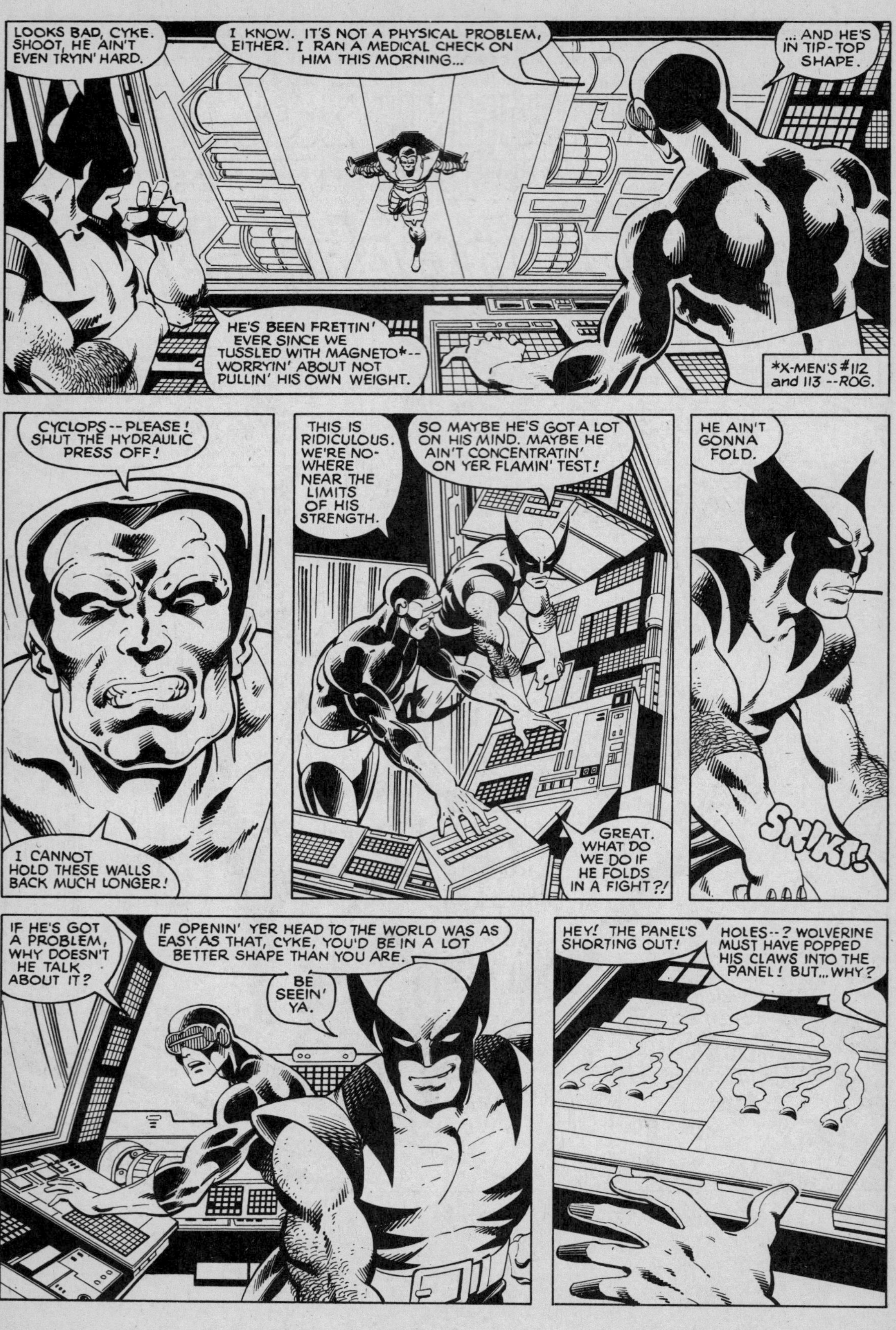

LOOKS BAD, CYKE. SHOOT, HE AIN'T EVEN TRYIN' HARD.
I KNOW. IT'S NOT A PHYSICAL PROBLEM, EITHER. I RAN A MEDICAL CHECK ON HIM THIS MORNING...
...AND HE'S IN TIP-TOP SHAPE.
HE'S BEEN FRETTIN' EVER SINCE WE TUSSLED WITH MAGNETO*-- WORRYIN' ABOUT NOT PULLIN' HIS OWN WEIGHT.
*X-MEN'S #112 and 113 --ROG.
CYCLOPS -- PLEASE! SHUT THE HYDRAULIC PRESS OFF!
I CANNOT HOLD THESE WALLS BACK MUCH LONGER!
THIS IS RIDICULOUS. WE'RE NO-WHERE NEAR THE LIMITS OF HIS STRENGTH.
SO MAYBE HE'S GOT A LOT ON HIS MIND. MAYBE HE AIN'T CONCENTRATIN' ON YER FLAMIN' TEST!
GREAT. WHAT DO WE DO IF HE FOLDS IN A FIGHT?!
HE AIN'T GONNA FOLD.
SNIKT!
IF HE'S GOT A PROBLEM, WHY DOESN'T HE TALK ABOUT IT?
IF OPENIN' YER HEAD TO THE WORLD WAS AS EASY AS THAT, CYKE, YOU'D BE IN A LOT BETTER SHAPE THAN YOU ARE.
BE SEEIN' YA.
HEY! THE PANEL'S SHORTING OUT!
HOLES--? WOLVERINE MUST HAVE POPPED HIS CLAWS INTO THE PANEL! BUT...WHY?

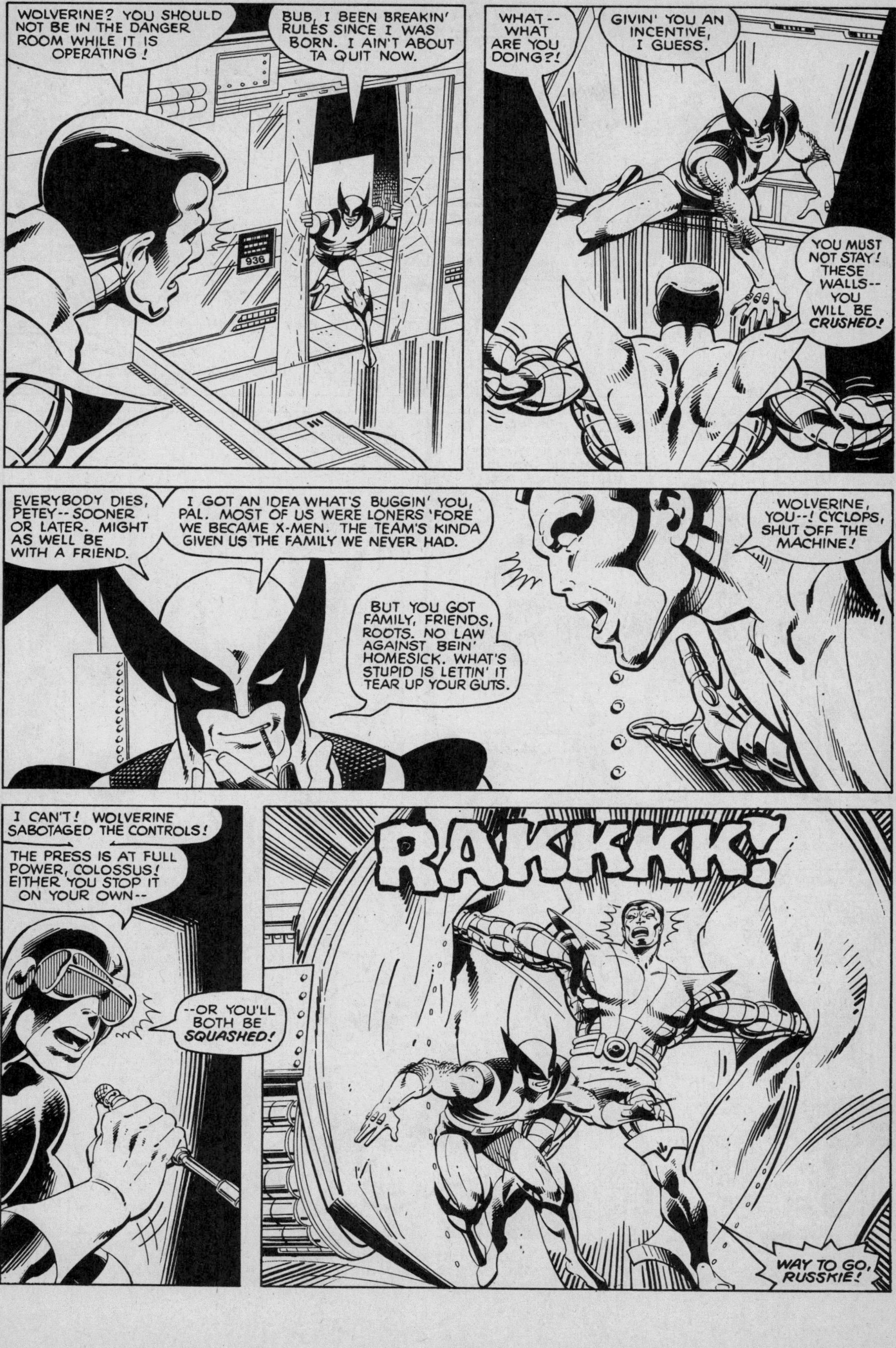
WOLVERINE? YOU SHOULD NOT BE IN THE DANGER ROOM WHILE IT IS OPERATING!
BUB, I BEEN BREAKIN' RULES SINCE I WAS BORN. I AIN'T ABOUT TA QUIT NOW.
936
WHAT-- WHAT ARE YOU DOING?!
GIVIN' YOU AN INCENTIVE, I GUESS.
YOU MUST NOT STAY! THESE WALLS-- YOU WILL BE CRUSHED!
EVERYBODY DIES, PETEY-- SOONER OR LATER. MIGHT AS WELL BE WITH A FRIEND.
I GOT AN IDEA WHAT'S BUGGIN' YOU, PAL. MOST OF US WERE LONERS 'FORE WE BECAME X-MEN. THE TEAM'S KINDA GIVEN US THE FAMILY WE NEVER HAD.
BUT YOU GOT FAMILY, FRIENDS, ROOTS. NO LAW AGAINST BEIN' HOMESICK. WHAT'S STUPID IS LETTIN' IT TEAR UP YOUR GUTS.
WOLVERINE, YOU--! CYCLOPS, SHUT OFF THE MACHINE!
I CAN'T! WOLVERINE SABOTAGED THE CONTROLS!
THE PRESS IS AT FULL POWER, COLOSSUS! EITHER YOU STOP IT ON YOUR OWN--
--OR YOU'LL BOTH BE SQUASHED!
RAKKKK!
WAY TO GO, RUSSKIE!

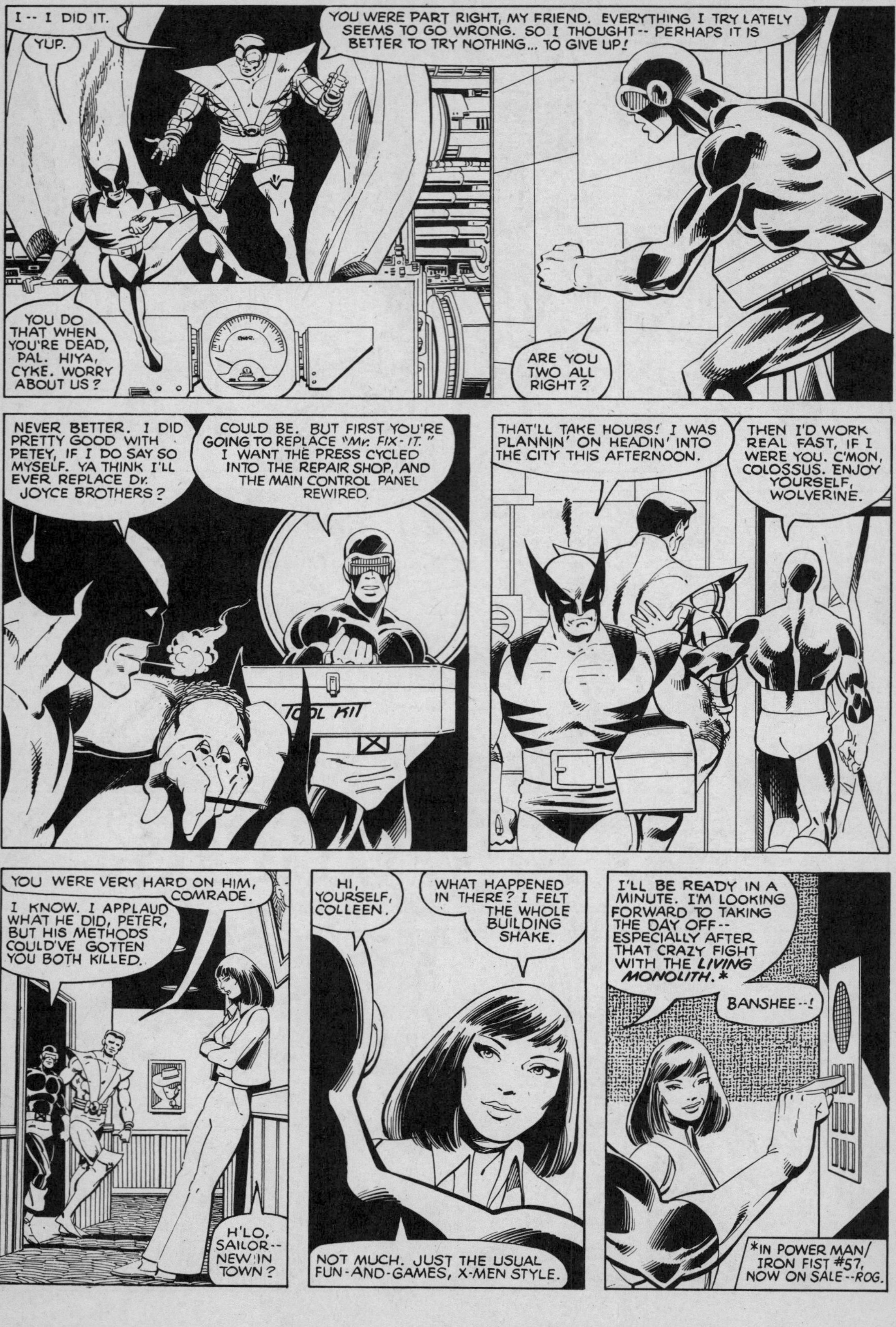
I -- I DID IT.
YUP.
YOU WERE PART RIGHT, MY FRIEND. EVERYTHING I TRY LATELY SEEMS TO GO WRONG. SO I THOUGHT -- PERHAPS IT IS BETTER TO TRY NOTHING... TO GIVE UP!
YOU DO THAT WHEN YOU'RE DEAD, PAL. HIYA, CYKE. WORRY ABOUT US?
ARE YOU TWO ALL RIGHT?
NEVER BETTER. I DID PRETTY GOOD WITH PETEY, IF I DO SAY SO MYSELF. YA THINK I'LL EVER REPLACE Dr. JOYCE BROTHERS?
COULD BE. BUT FIRST YOU'RE GOING TO REPLACE "Mr. FIX-IT." I WANT THE PRESS CYCLED INTO THE REPAIR SHOP, AND THE MAIN CONTROL PANEL REWIRED.
TOOL KIT
THAT'LL TAKE HOURS! I WAS PLANNIN' ON HEADIN' INTO THE CITY THIS AFTERNOON.
THEN I'D WORK REAL FAST, IF I WERE YOU. C'MON, COLOSSUS. ENJOY YOURSELF, WOLVERINE.
YOU WERE VERY HARD ON HIM, COMRADE.
I KNOW. I APPLAUD WHAT HE DID, PETER, BUT HIS METHODS COULD'VE GOTTEN YOU BOTH KILLED.
H'LO, SAILOR -- NEW IN TOWN?
HI, YOURSELF, COLLEEN.
WHAT HAPPENED IN THERE? I FELT THE WHOLE BUILDING SHAKE.
NOT MUCH. JUST THE USUAL FUN-AND-GAMES, X-MEN STYLE.
I'LL BE READY IN A MINUTE. I'M LOOKING FORWARD TO TAKING THE DAY OFF -- ESPECIALLY AFTER THAT CRAZY FIGHT WITH THE LIVING MONOLITH.*
BANSHEE --!
*IN POWER MAN/ IRON FIST #57, NOW ON SALE --ROG.

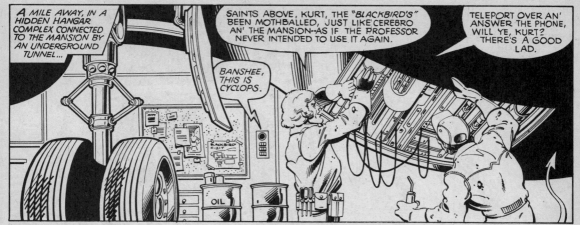

A MILE AWAY, IN A HIDDEN HANGAR COMPLEX CONNECTED TO THE MANSION BY AN UNDERGROUND TUNNEL...

SAINTS ABOVE, KURT, THE "BLACKBIRD'S" BEEN MOTHBALLED, JUST LIKE CEREBRO AN' THE MANSION--AS IF THE PROFESSOR NEVER INTENDED TO USE IT AGAIN.

TELEPORT OVER AN' ANSWER THE PHONE, WILL YE, KURT? THERE'S A GOOD LAD.

BANSHEE, THIS IS CYCLOPS.

X-WING RESTORATIONS-- APPRENTICE MECHANIC WAGNER SPEAKING. WHAT CAN I DO FOR YOU, FEARLESS LEADER?

THAT'S WHAT I LIKE, NIGHTCRAWLER-- A MAN WHO'S HAPPY IN HIS WORK. HOW'S IT GOING?

SLOWLY, I'M AFRAID. CONDITIONS HERE ARE AS BAD AS WE FOUND IN THE HOUSE. WHAT DO YOU THINK HAPPENED?

I DON'T KNOW.

SEAN, LISTEN UP. WOLVERINE MESSED UP THE DANGER ROOM MAIN CONTROL PANEL PRETTY BADLY.

CHECK THE CIRCUITS OUT WHEN HE'S DONE FIXING IT. I'D HELP HIM, BUT I'M DUE AT THE PHONE COMPANY.

NOT T' WORRY. I'LL GIVE HIM A HAND. YOU GO ENJOY YOURSELF, LAD. YE'VE MORE'N EARNED IT.

SOMETHING'S STILL BOTHERING YOU.

IS IT THAT OBVIOUS?

TO SOMEONE WHO CARES ABOUT YOU, SCOTT--YES.

IT'S PROFESSOR XAVIER. HE'S GONE... CLEARED OUT! PRINCESS LILANDRA, TOO. AND I CAN'T SHAKE THE FEELING THAT THEY'RE NOT COMING BACK.

AT THAT MOMENT, IN A FAR, DISTANT GALAXY...

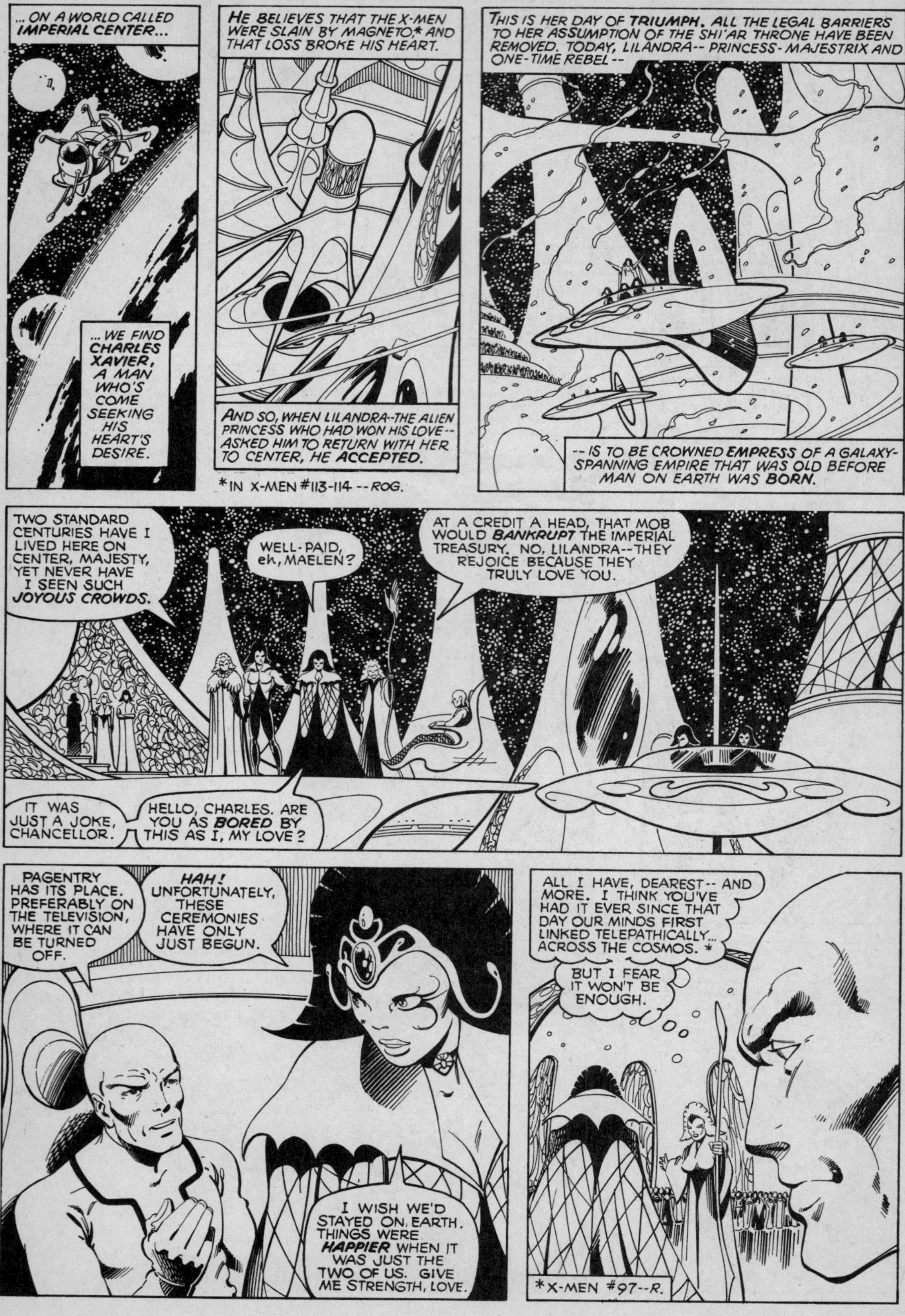
...ON A WORLD CALLED IMPERIAL CENTER...
...WE FIND CHARLES XAVIER, A MAN WHO'S COME SEEKING HIS HEART'S DESIRE.
HE BELIEVES THAT THE X-MEN WERE SLAIN BY MAGNETO,* AND THAT LOSS BROKE HIS HEART.
AND SO, WHEN LILANDRA--THE ALIEN PRINCESS WHO HAD WON HIS LOVE--ASKED HIM TO RETURN WITH HER TO CENTER, HE ACCEPTED.
*IN X-MEN #113-114 --ROG.
THIS IS HER DAY OF TRIUMPH. ALL THE LEGAL BARRIERS TO HER ASSUMPTION OF THE SHI'AR THRONE HAVE BEEN REMOVED. TODAY, LILANDRA-- PRINCESS-MAJESTRIX AND ONE-TIME REBEL--
--IS TO BE CROWNED EMPRESS OF A GALAXY-SPANNING EMPIRE THAT WAS OLD BEFORE MAN ON EARTH WAS BORN.
TWO STANDARD CENTURIES HAVE I LIVED HERE ON CENTER, MAJESTY, YET NEVER HAVE I SEEN SUCH JOYOUS CROWDS.
WELL-PAID, eh, MAELEN?
AT A CREDIT A HEAD, THAT MOB WOULD BANKRUPT THE IMPERIAL TREASURY. NO, LILANDRA--THEY REJOICE BECAUSE THEY TRULY LOVE YOU.
IT WAS JUST A JOKE, CHANCELLOR.
HELLO, CHARLES. ARE YOU AS BORED BY THIS AS I, MY LOVE?
PAGENTRY HAS ITS PLACE. PREFERABLY ON THE TELEVISION, WHERE IT CAN BE TURNED OFF.
HAH! UNFORTUNATELY, THESE CEREMONIES HAVE ONLY JUST BEGUN.
I WISH WE'D STAYED ON EARTH. THINGS WERE HAPPIER WHEN IT WAS JUST THE TWO OF US. GIVE ME STRENGTH, LOVE.
ALL I HAVE, DEAREST-- AND MORE. I THINK YOU'VE HAD IT EVER SINCE THAT DAY OUR MINDS FIRST LINKED TELEPATHICALLY... ACROSS THE COSMOS. *
BUT I FEAR IT WON'T BE ENOUGH.
*X-MEN #97--R.

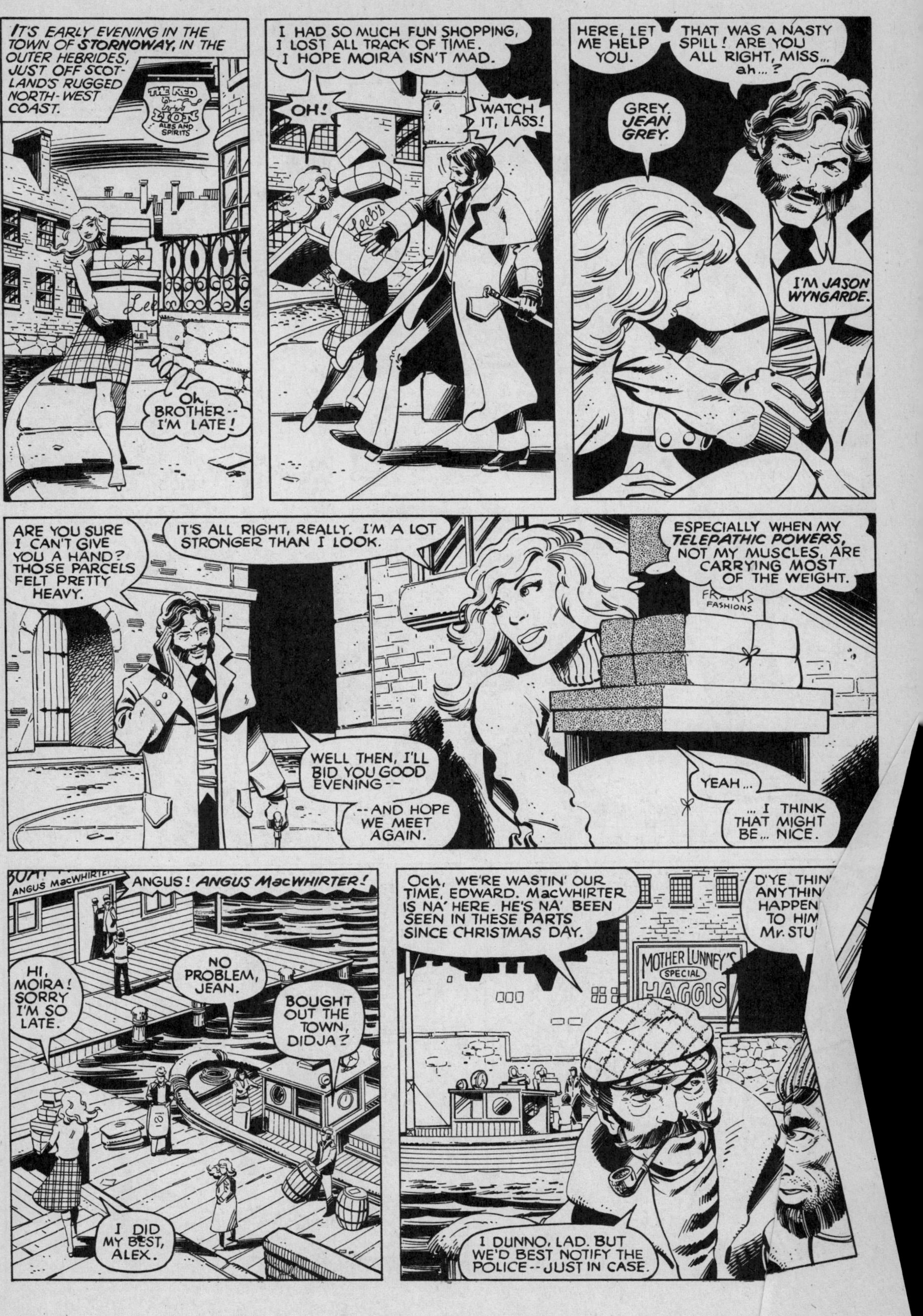
IT'S EARLY EVENING IN THE TOWN OF STORNOWAY, IN THE OUTER HEBRIDES, JUST OFF SCOTLAND'S RUGGED NORTH-WEST COAST.
THE RED LION ALES AND SPIRITS
Oh, BROTHER-- I'M LATE!
I HAD SO MUCH FUN SHOPPING, I LOST ALL TRACK OF TIME. I HOPE MOIRA ISN'T MAD.
OH!
WATCH IT, LASS!
HERE, LET ME HELP YOU.
THAT WAS A NASTY SPILL! ARE YOU ALL RIGHT, MISS... ah...?
GREY. JEAN GREY.
I'M JASON WYNGARDE.
ARE YOU SURE I CAN'T GIVE YOU A HAND? THOSE PARCELS FELT PRETTY HEAVY.
IT'S ALL RIGHT, REALLY. I'M A LOT STRONGER THAN I LOOK.
ESPECIALLY WHEN MY TELEPATHIC POWERS, NOT MY MUSCLES, ARE CARRYING MOST OF THE WEIGHT.
FRANKS FASHIONS
WELL THEN, I'LL BID YOU GOOD EVENING--
--AND HOPE WE MEET AGAIN.
YEAH...
...I THINK THAT MIGHT BE... NICE.
ANGUS MacWHIRTER
ANGUS! ANGUS MacWHIRTER!
HI, MOIRA! SORRY I'M SO LATE.
NO PROBLEM, JEAN.
BOUGHT OUT THE TOWN, DIDJA?
I DID MY BEST, ALEX.
Och, WE'RE WASTIN' OUR TIME, EDWARD. MacWHIRTER IS NA' HERE. HE'S NA' BEEN SEEN IN THESE PARTS SINCE CHRISTMAS DAY.
D'YE THIN ANYTHIN HAPPEN TO HIM Mr. STU
MOTHER LUNNEY'S SPECIAL HAGGIS
I DUNNO, LAD. BUT WE'D BEST NOTIFY THE POLICE--JUST IN CASE.

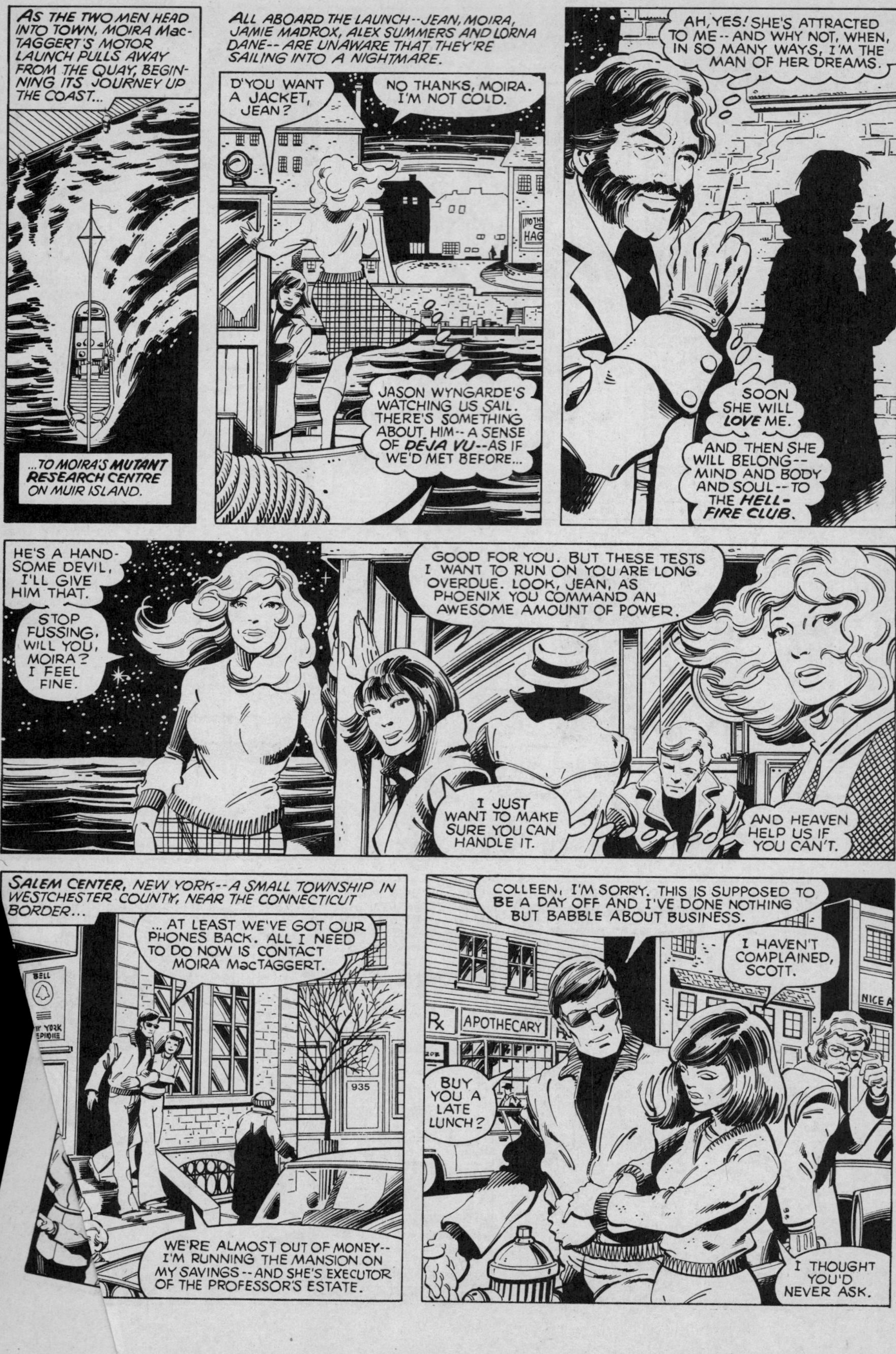
AS THE TWO MEN HEAD INTO TOWN, MOIRA MacTAGGERT'S MOTOR LAUNCH PULLS AWAY FROM THE QUAY, BEGINNING ITS JOURNEY UP THE COAST...
...TO MOIRA'S MUTANT RESEARCH CENTRE ON MUIR ISLAND.
ALL ABOARD THE LAUNCH--JEAN, MOIRA, JAMIE MADROX, ALEX SUMMERS AND LORNA DANE--ARE UNAWARE THAT THEY'RE SAILING INTO A NIGHTMARE.
D'YOU WANT A JACKET, JEAN?
NO THANKS, MOIRA. I'M NOT COLD.
JASON WYNGARDE'S WATCHING US SAIL. THERE'S SOMETHING ABOUT HIM--A SENSE OF DÉJA VU--AS IF WE'D MET BEFORE...
AH, YES! SHE'S ATTRACTED TO ME--AND WHY NOT, WHEN, IN SO MANY WAYS, I'M THE MAN OF HER DREAMS.
SOON SHE WILL LOVE ME.
AND THEN SHE WILL BELONG--MIND AND BODY AND SOUL--TO THE HELL-FIRE CLUB.
HE'S A HANDSOME DEVIL, I'LL GIVE HIM THAT.
STOP FUSSING, WILL YOU, MOIRA? I FEEL FINE.
GOOD FOR YOU. BUT THESE TESTS I WANT TO RUN ON YOU ARE LONG OVERDUE. LOOK, JEAN, AS PHOENIX YOU COMMAND AN AWESOME AMOUNT OF POWER.
I JUST WANT TO MAKE SURE YOU CAN HANDLE IT.
AND HEAVEN HELP US IF YOU CAN'T.
SALEM CENTER, NEW YORK--A SMALL TOWNSHIP IN WESTCHESTER COUNTY, NEAR THE CONNECTICUT BORDER...
...AT LEAST WE'VE GOT OUR PHONES BACK. ALL I NEED TO DO NOW IS CONTACT MOIRA MacTAGGERT.
935
WE'RE ALMOST OUT OF MONEY--I'M RUNNING THE MANSION ON MY SAVINGS--AND SHE'S EXECUTOR OF THE PROFESSOR'S ESTATE.
COLLEEN, I'M SORRY. THIS IS SUPPOSED TO BE A DAY OFF AND I'VE DONE NOTHING BUT BABBLE ABOUT BUSINESS.
I HAVEN'T COMPLAINED, SCOTT.
Rx APOTHECARY
BUY YOU A LATE LUNCH?
I THOUGHT YOU'D NEVER ASK.

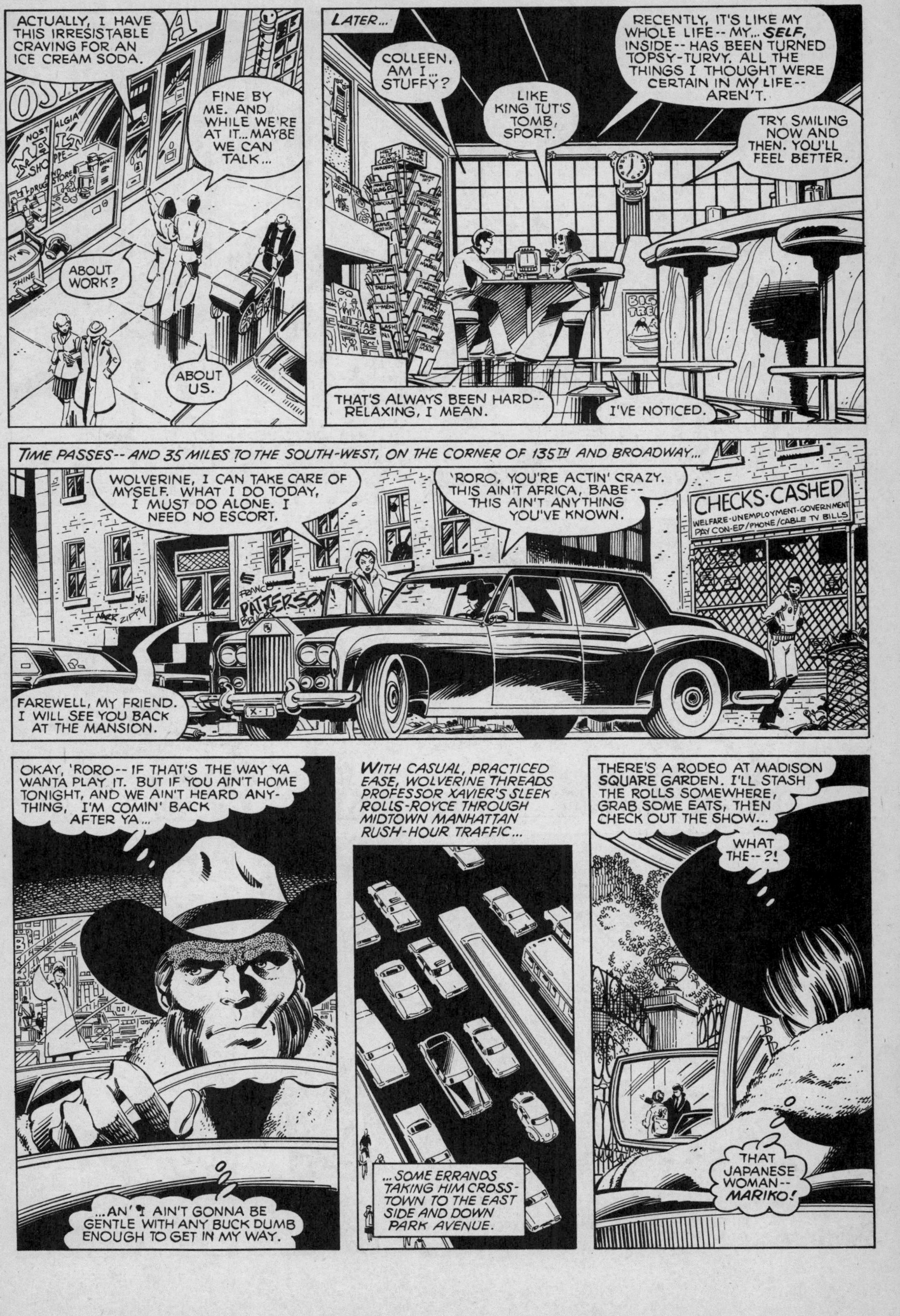
ACTUALLY, I HAVE THIS IRRESISTABLE CRAVING FOR AN ICE CREAM SODA.
FINE BY ME. AND WHILE WE'RE AT IT... MAYBE WE CAN TALK...
ABOUT WORK?
ABOUT US.
LATER...
COLLEEN, AM I... STUFFY?
LIKE KING TUT'S TOMB, SPORT.
RECENTLY, IT'S LIKE MY WHOLE LIFE-- MY... SELF, INSIDE-- HAS BEEN TURNED TOPSY-TURVY. ALL THE THINGS I THOUGHT WERE CERTAIN IN MY LIFE-- AREN'T.
TRY SMILING NOW AND THEN. YOU'LL FEEL BETTER.
THAT'S ALWAYS BEEN HARD-- RELAXING, I MEAN.
I'VE NOTICED.
TIME PASSES-- AND 35 MILES TO THE SOUTH-WEST, ON THE CORNER OF 135TH AND BROADWAY...
WOLVERINE, I CAN TAKE CARE OF MYSELF. WHAT I DO TODAY, I MUST DO ALONE. I NEED NO ESCORT.
'RORO, YOU'RE ACTIN' CRAZY. THIS AIN'T AFRICA, BABE-- THIS AIN'T ANYTHING YOU'VE KNOWN.
CHECKS·CASHED
WELFARE-UNEMPLOYMENT-GOVERNMENT
PAY CON-ED/PHONE/CABLE TV BILLS
FAREWELL, MY FRIEND. I WILL SEE YOU BACK AT THE MANSION.
OKAY, 'RORO-- IF THAT'S THE WAY YA WANTA PLAY IT. BUT IF YOU AIN'T HOME TONIGHT, AND WE AIN'T HEARD ANYTHING, I'M COMIN' BACK AFTER YA...
...AN' I AIN'T GONNA BE GENTLE WITH ANY BUCK DUMB ENOUGH TO GET IN MY WAY.
WITH CASUAL, PRACTICED EASE, WOLVERINE THREADS PROFESSOR XAVIER'S SLEEK ROLLS-ROYCE THROUGH MIDTOWN MANHATTAN RUSH-HOUR TRAFFIC...
...SOME ERRANDS TAKING HIM CROSS-TOWN TO THE EAST SIDE AND DOWN PARK AVENUE.
THERE'S A RODEO AT MADISON SQUARE GARDEN. I'LL STASH THE ROLLS SOMEWHERE, GRAB SOME EATS, THEN CHECK OUT THE SHOW...
WHAT THE--?!
THAT JAPANESE WOMAN-- MARIKO!

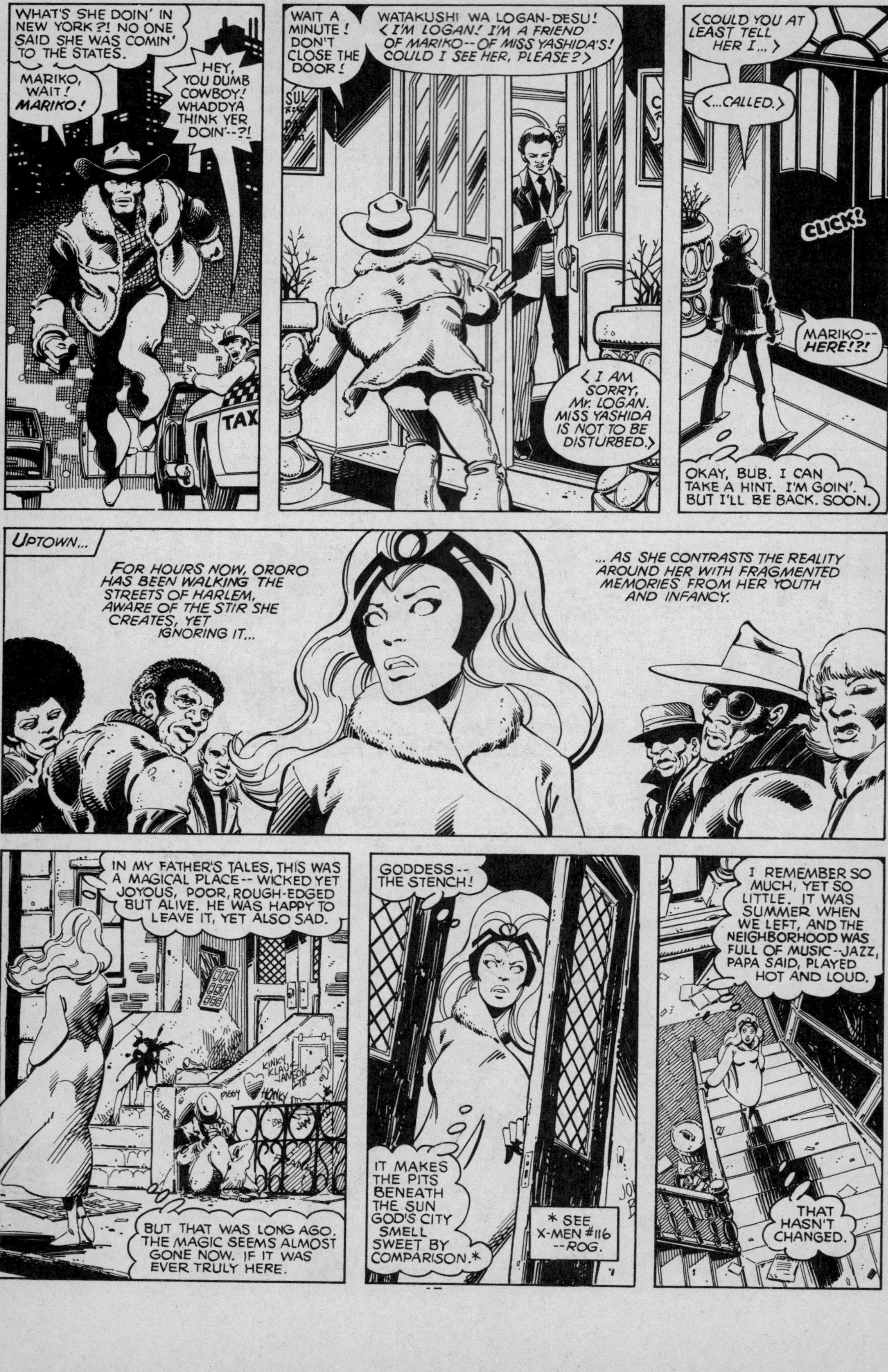
WHAT'S SHE DOIN' IN NEW YORK?! NO ONE SAID SHE WAS COMIN' TO THE STATES.
MARIKO, WAIT! MARIKO!
HEY, YOU DUMB COWBOY! WHADDYA THINK YER DOIN'--?!
TAX
WAIT A MINUTE! DON'T CLOSE THE DOOR!
WATAKUSHI WA LOGAN-DESU! <I'M LOGAN! I'M A FRIEND OF MARIKO--OF MISS YASHIDA'S! COULD I SEE HER, PLEASE?>
<I AM SORRY, Mr. LOGAN. MISS YASHIDA IS NOT TO BE DISTURBED.>
<COULD YOU AT LEAST TELL HER I...>
<...CALLED.>
CLICK!
MARIKO-- HERE!?!
OKAY, BUB. I CAN TAKE A HINT. I'M GOIN'. BUT I'LL BE BACK. SOON.
UPTOWN...
FOR HOURS NOW, ORORO HAS BEEN WALKING THE STREETS OF HARLEM, AWARE OF THE STIR SHE CREATES, YET IGNORING IT...
... AS SHE CONTRASTS THE REALITY AROUND HER WITH FRAGMENTED MEMORIES FROM HER YOUTH AND INFANCY.
IN MY FATHER'S TALES, THIS WAS A MAGICAL PLACE-- WICKED YET JOYOUS, POOR, ROUGH-EDGED BUT ALIVE. HE WAS HAPPY TO LEAVE IT, YET ALSO SAD.
KINKY KLAUS JANSON '78
PIGGY
HONKY
BUT THAT WAS LONG AGO. THE MAGIC SEEMS ALMOST GONE NOW. IF IT WAS EVER TRULY HERE.
GODDESS-- THE STENCH!
IT MAKES THE PITS BENEATH THE SUN GOD'S CITY SMELL SWEET BY COMPARISON.*
* SEE X-MEN #116 --ROG.
I REMEMBER SO MUCH, YET SO LITTLE. IT WAS SUMMER WHEN WE LEFT, AND THE NEIGHBORHOOD WAS FULL OF MUSIC--JAZZ, PAPA SAID, PLAYED HOT AND LOUD.
THAT HASN'T CHANGED.

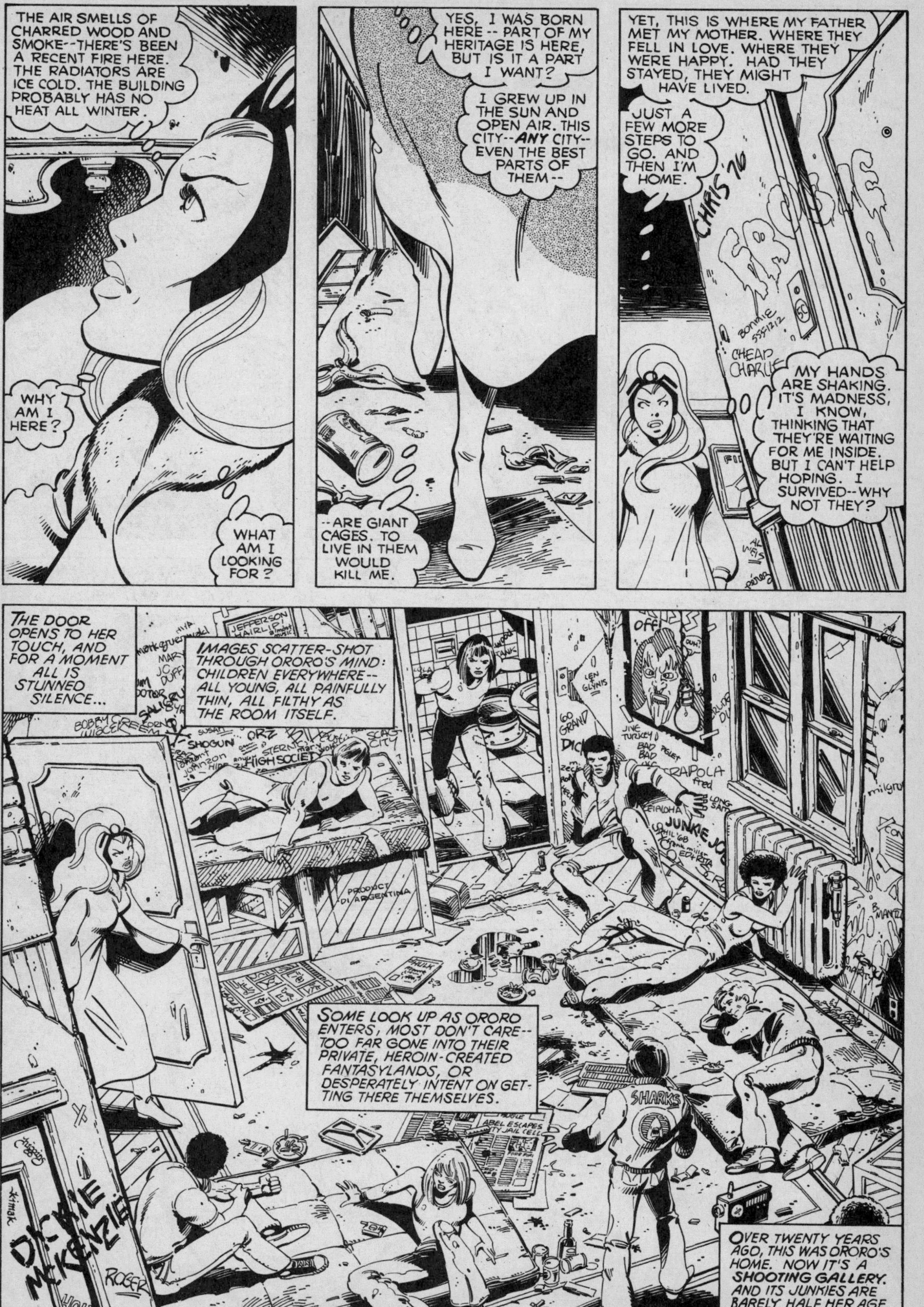
THE AIR SMELLS OF CHARRED WOOD AND SMOKE--THERE'S BEEN A RECENT FIRE HERE. THE RADIATORS ARE ICE COLD. THE BUILDING PROBABLY HAS NO HEAT ALL WINTER.
WHY AM I HERE?
WHAT AM I LOOKING FOR?
YES, I WAS BORN HERE -- PART OF MY HERITAGE IS HERE, BUT IS IT A PART I WANT?
I GREW UP IN THE SUN AND OPEN AIR. THIS CITY--ANY CITY--EVEN THE BEST PARTS OF THEM --
--ARE GIANT CAGES. TO LIVE IN THEM WOULD KILL ME.
YET, THIS IS WHERE MY FATHER MET MY MOTHER. WHERE THEY FELL IN LOVE. WHERE THEY WERE HAPPY. HAD THEY STAYED, THEY MIGHT HAVE LIVED.
JUST A FEW MORE STEPS TO GO. AND THEN I'M HOME.
MY HANDS ARE SHAKING. IT'S MADNESS, I KNOW, THINKING THAT THEY'RE WAITING FOR ME INSIDE. BUT I CAN'T HELP HOPING. I SURVIVED--WHY NOT THEY?
THE DOOR OPENS TO HER TOUCH, AND FOR A MOMENT ALL IS STUNNED SILENCE...
IMAGES SCATTER-SHOT THROUGH ORORO'S MIND: CHILDREN EVERYWHERE--ALL YOUNG, ALL PAINFULLY THIN, ALL FILTHY AS THE ROOM ITSELF.
SOME LOOK UP AS ORORO ENTERS, MOST DON'T CARE--TOO FAR GONE INTO THEIR PRIVATE, HEROIN-CREATED FANTASYLANDS, OR DESPERATELY INTENT ON GETTING THERE THEMSELVES.
OVER TWENTY YEARS AGO, THIS WAS ORORO'S HOME. NOW IT'S A SHOOTING GALLERY. AND ITS JUNKIES ARE BARELY HALF HER AGE.

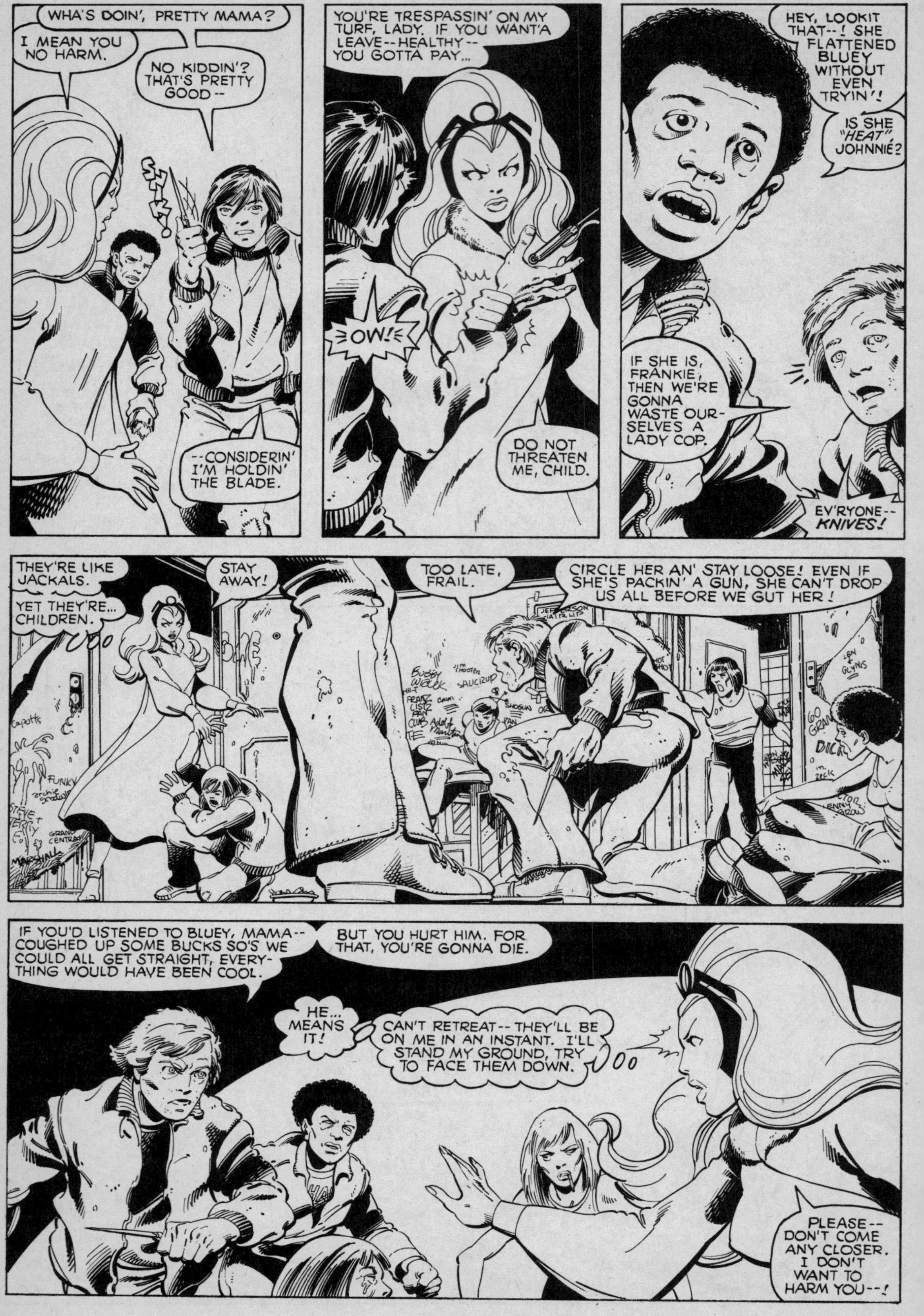
WHA'S DOIN', PRETTY MAMA?
I MEAN YOU NO HARM.
NO KIDDIN'? THAT'S PRETTY GOOD --
SHIK!
--CONSIDERIN' I'M HOLDIN' THE BLADE.
YOU'RE TRESPASSIN' ON MY TURF, LADY. IF YOU WANT'A LEAVE -- HEALTHY -- YOU GOTTA PAY...
OW!
DO NOT THREATEN ME, CHILD.
HEY, LOOKIT THAT--! SHE FLATTENED BLUEY WITHOUT EVEN TRYIN'!
IS SHE "HEAT," JOHNNIE?
IF SHE IS, FRANKIE, THEN WE'RE GONNA WASTE OURSELVES A LADY COP.
EV'RYONE-- KNIVES!
THEY'RE LIKE JACKALS.
YET THEY'RE... CHILDREN.
STAY AWAY!
TOO LATE, FRAIL.
CIRCLE HER AN' STAY LOOSE! EVEN IF SHE'S PACKIN' A GUN, SHE CAN'T DROP US ALL BEFORE WE GUT HER!
IF YOU'D LISTENED TO BLUEY, MAMA-- COUGHED UP SOME BUCKS SO'S WE COULD ALL GET STRAIGHT, EVERYTHING WOULD HAVE BEEN COOL.
BUT YOU HURT HIM. FOR THAT, YOU'RE GONNA DIE.
HE... MEANS IT!
CAN'T RETREAT-- THEY'LL BE ON ME IN AN INSTANT. I'LL STAND MY GROUND, TRY TO FACE THEM DOWN.
PLEASE-- DON'T COME ANY CLOSER. I DON'T WANT TO HARM YOU--!

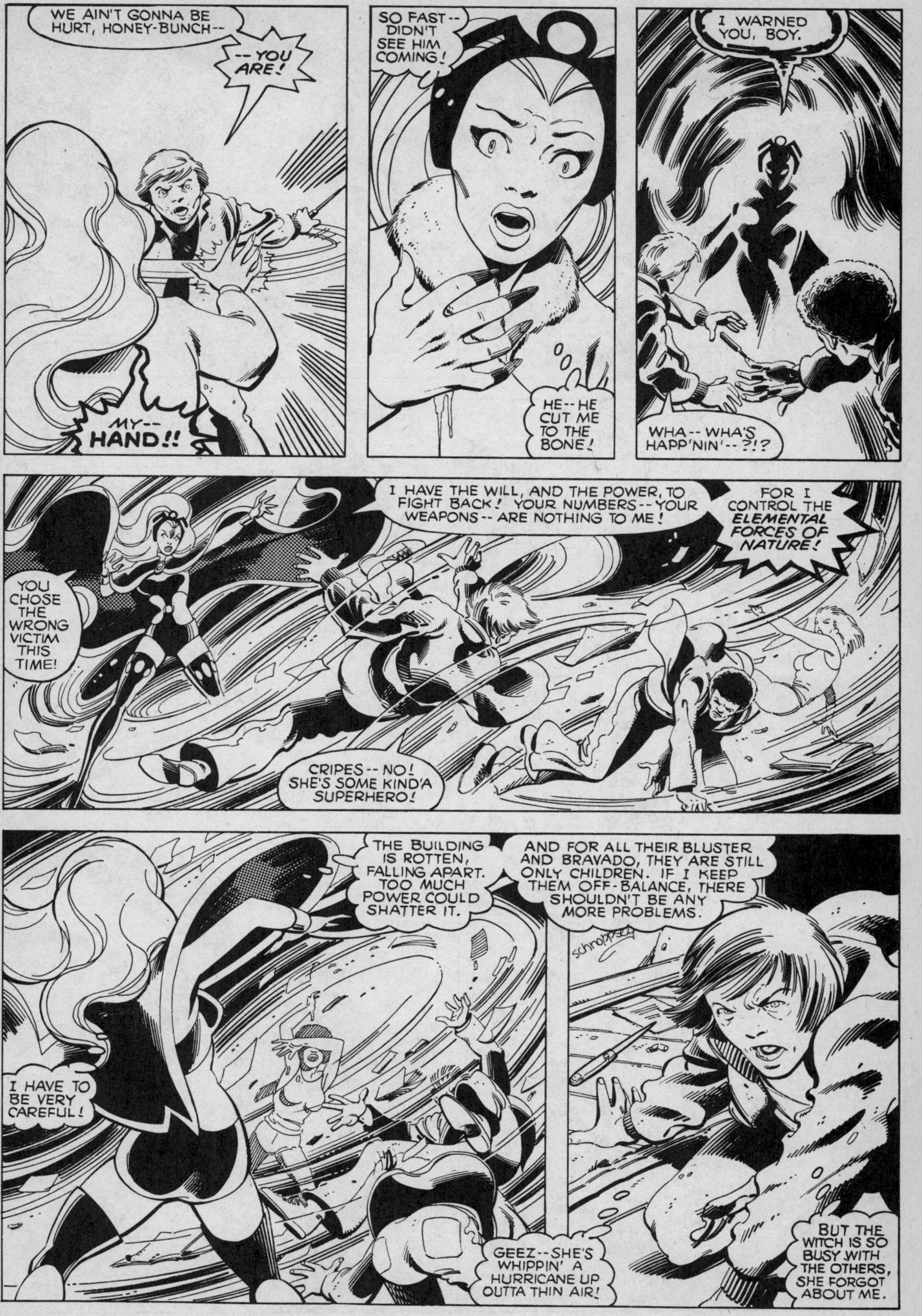
WE AIN'T GONNA BE HURT, HONEY-BUNCH--
--YOU ARE!
MY-- HAND!!
SO FAST-- DIDN'T SEE HIM COMING!
HE--HE CUT ME TO THE BONE!
I WARNED YOU, BOY.
WHA--WHA'S HAPP'NIN'--?!?
I HAVE THE WILL, AND THE POWER, TO FIGHT BACK! YOUR NUMBERS--YOUR WEAPONS--ARE NOTHING TO ME!
FOR I CONTROL THE ELEMENTAL FORCES OF NATURE!
YOU CHOSE THE WRONG VICTIM THIS TIME!
CRIPES--NO! SHE'S SOME KIND'A SUPERHERO!
THE BUILDING IS ROTTEN, FALLING APART. TOO MUCH POWER COULD SHATTER IT.
AND FOR ALL THEIR BLUSTER AND BRAVADO, THEY ARE STILL ONLY CHILDREN. IF I KEEP THEM OFF-BALANCE, THERE SHOULDN'T BE ANY MORE PROBLEMS.
I HAVE TO BE VERY CAREFUL!
GEEZ--SHE'S WHIPPIN' A HURRICANE UP OUTTA THIN AIR!
BUT THE WITCH IS SO BUSY WITH THE OTHERS, SHE FORGOT ABOUT ME.

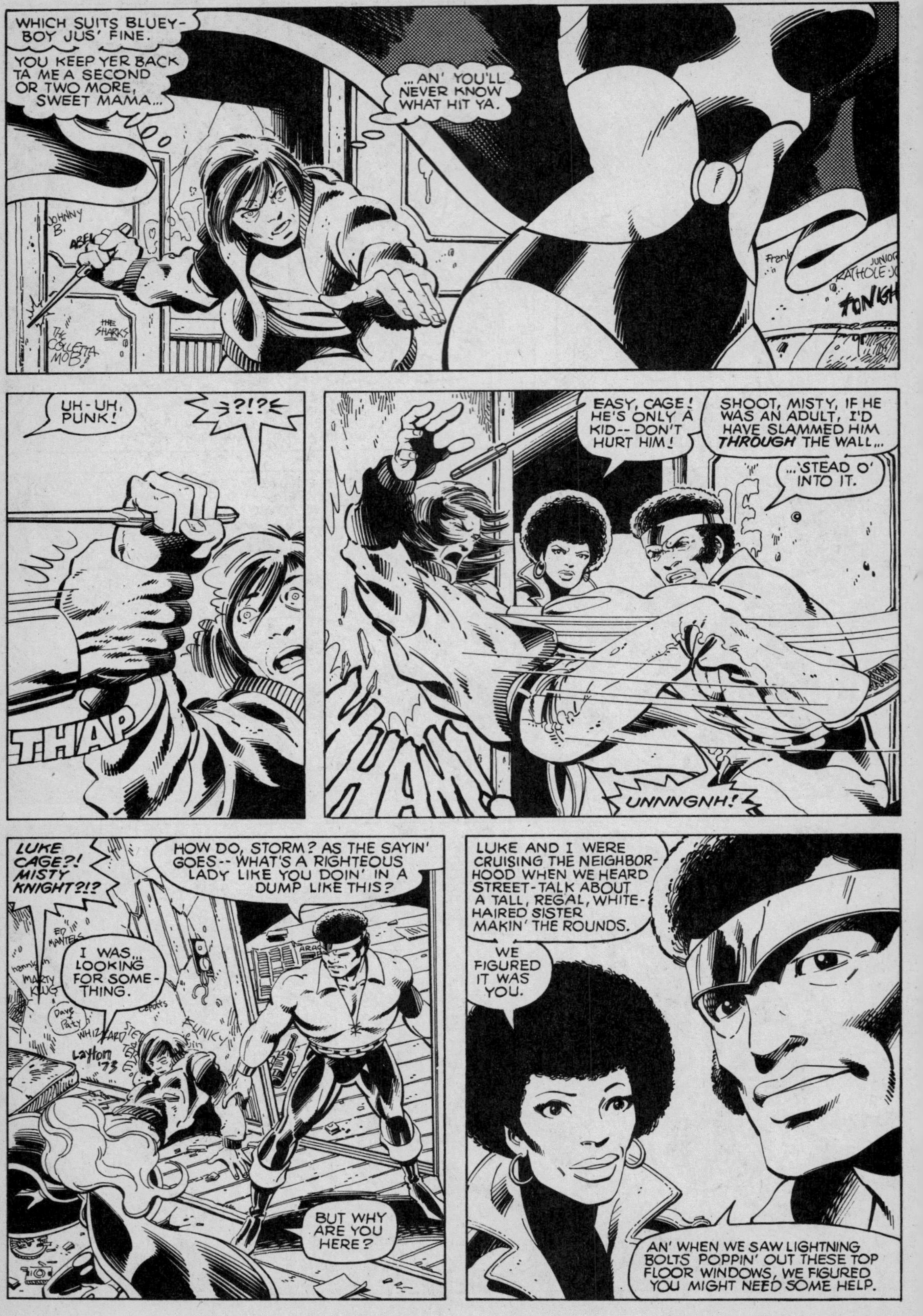
WHICH SUITS BLUEY-BOY JUS' FINE.
YOU KEEP YER BACK TA ME A SECOND OR TWO MORE, SWEET MAMA...
...AN' YOU'LL NEVER KNOW WHAT HIT YA.
UH-UH, PUNK!
?!?
THAP
EASY, CAGE! HE'S ONLY A KID-- DON'T HURT HIM!
SHOOT, MISTY, IF HE WAS AN ADULT, I'D HAVE SLAMMED HIM THROUGH THE WALL...
...'STEAD O' INTO IT.
WHAM
UNNNGNH!
LUKE CAGE?! MISTY KNIGHT?!?
HOW DO, STORM? AS THE SAYIN' GOES-- WHAT'S A RIGHTEOUS LADY LIKE YOU DOIN' IN A DUMP LIKE THIS?
I WAS... LOOKING FOR SOME-THING.
BUT WHY ARE YOU HERE?
LUKE AND I WERE CRUISING THE NEIGHBOR-HOOD WHEN WE HEARD STREET-TALK ABOUT A TALL, REGAL, WHITE-HAIRED SISTER MAKIN' THE ROUNDS.
WE FIGURED IT WAS YOU.
AN' WHEN WE SAW LIGHTNING BOLTS POPPIN' OUT THESE TOP FLOOR WINDOWS, WE FIGURED YOU MIGHT NEED SOME HELP.

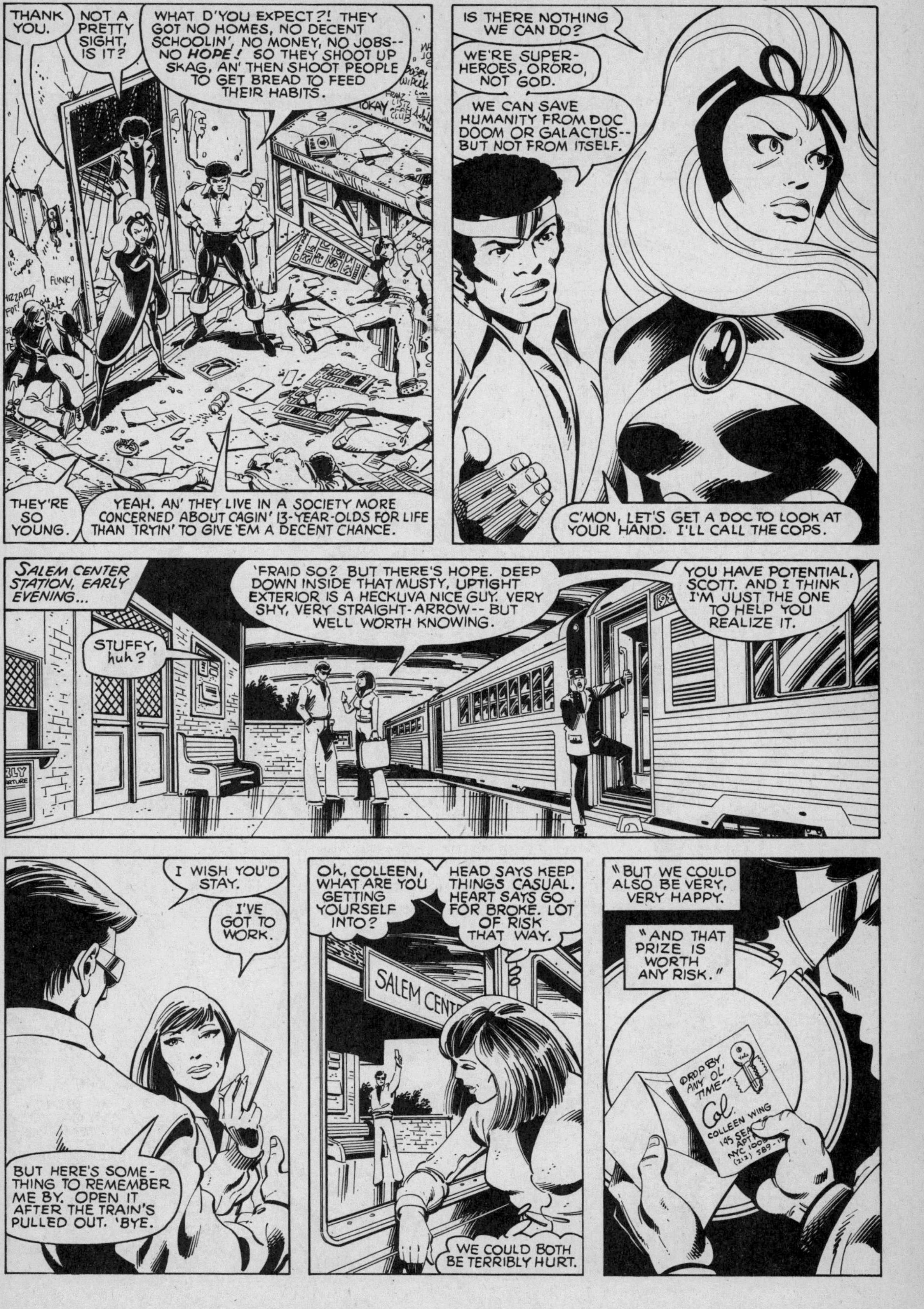
THANK YOU.
NOT A PRETTY SIGHT, IS IT?
WHAT D'YOU EXPECT?! THEY GOT NO HOMES, NO DECENT SCHOOLIN', NO MONEY, NO JOBS-- NO HOPE! SO THEY SHOOT UP SKAG, AN' THEN SHOOT PEOPLE TO GET BREAD TO FEED THEIR HABITS.
THEY'RE SO YOUNG.
YEAH. AN' THEY LIVE IN A SOCIETY MORE CONCERNED ABOUT CAGIN' 13-YEAR-OLDS FOR LIFE THAN TRYIN' TO GIVE 'EM A DECENT CHANCE.
IS THERE NOTHING WE CAN DO?
WE'RE SUPER-HEROES, ORORO, NOT GOD.
WE CAN SAVE HUMANITY FROM DOC DOOM OR GALACTUS-- BUT NOT FROM ITSELF.
C'MON, LET'S GET A DOC TO LOOK AT YOUR HAND. I'LL CALL THE COPS.
SALEM CENTER STATION, EARLY EVENING...
STUFFY, huh?
'FRAID SO? BUT THERE'S HOPE. DEEP DOWN INSIDE THAT MUSTY, UPTIGHT EXTERIOR IS A HECKUVA NICE GUY. VERY SHY, VERY STRAIGHT-ARROW-- BUT WELL WORTH KNOWING.
YOU HAVE POTENTIAL, SCOTT. AND I THINK I'M JUST THE ONE TO HELP YOU REALIZE IT.
I WISH YOU'D STAY.
I'VE GOT TO WORK.
BUT HERE'S SOMETHING TO REMEMBER ME BY. OPEN IT AFTER THE TRAIN'S PULLED OUT. 'BYE.
Oh, COLLEEN, WHAT ARE YOU GETTING YOURSELF INTO?
HEAD SAYS KEEP THINGS CASUAL. HEART SAYS GO FOR BROKE. LOT OF RISK THAT WAY.
SALEM CENTER
WE COULD BOTH BE TERRIBLY HURT.
"BUT WE COULD ALSO BE VERY, VERY HAPPY.
"AND THAT PRIZE IS WORTH ANY RISK."
DROP BY ANY OL' TIME--
Col.
COLLEEN WING

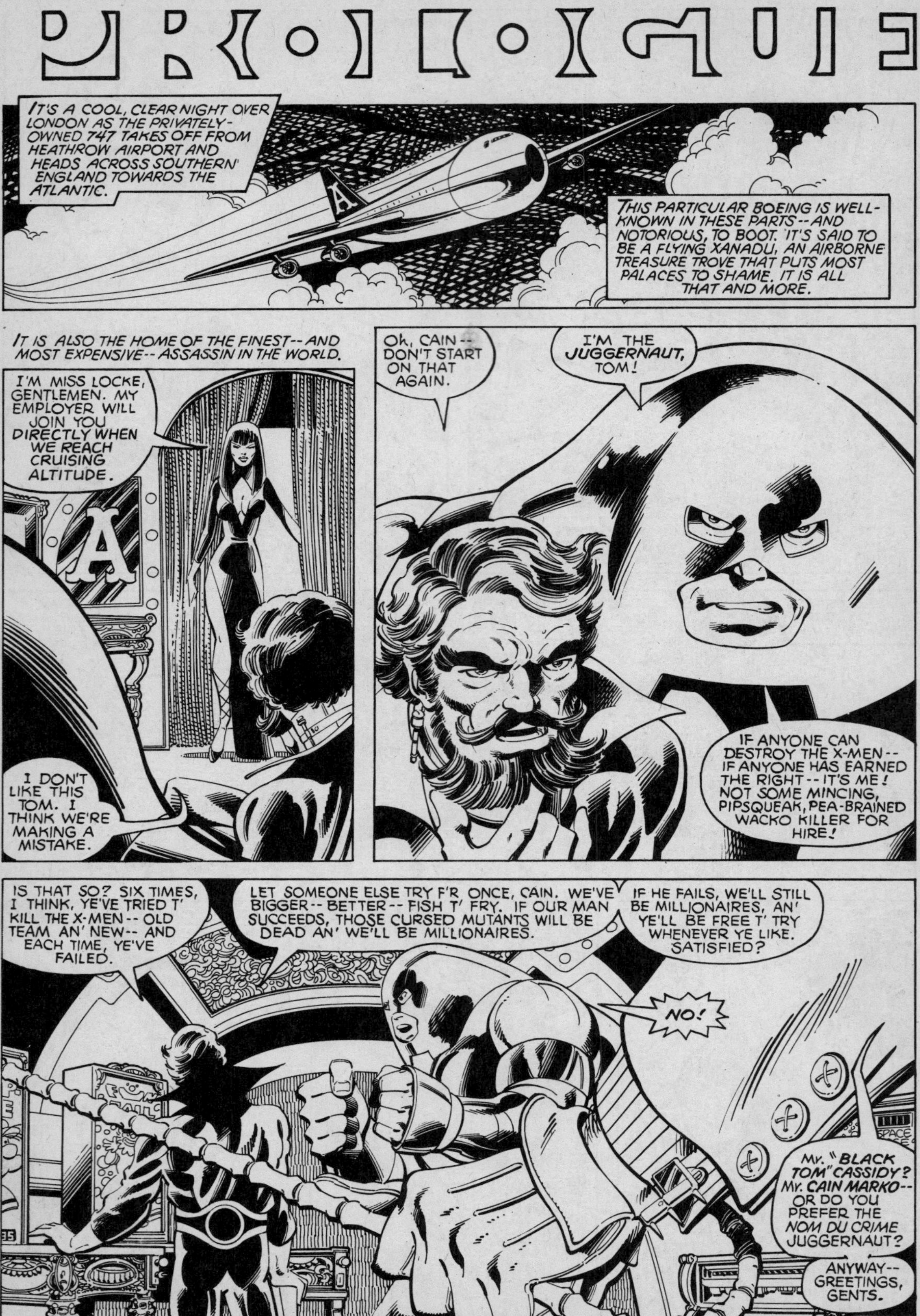
PROLOGUE
IT'S A COOL, CLEAR NIGHT OVER LONDON AS THE PRIVATELY-OWNED 747 TAKES OFF FROM HEATHROW AIRPORT AND HEADS ACROSS SOUTHERN ENGLAND TOWARDS THE ATLANTIC.
THIS PARTICULAR BOEING IS WELL-KNOWN IN THESE PARTS -- AND NOTORIOUS, TO BOOT. IT'S SAID TO BE A FLYING XANADU, AN AIRBORNE TREASURE TROVE THAT PUTS MOST PALACES TO SHAME. IT IS ALL THAT AND MORE.
IT IS ALSO THE HOME OF THE FINEST -- AND MOST EXPENSIVE -- ASSASSIN IN THE WORLD.
I'M MISS LOCKE, GENTLEMEN. MY EMPLOYER WILL JOIN YOU DIRECTLY WHEN WE REACH CRUISING ALTITUDE.
I DON'T LIKE THIS TOM. I THINK WE'RE MAKING A MISTAKE.
Oh, CAIN -- DON'T START ON THAT AGAIN.
I'M THE JUGGERNAUT, TOM!
IF ANYONE CAN DESTROY THE X-MEN -- IF ANYONE HAS EARNED THE RIGHT -- IT'S ME! NOT SOME MINCING, PIPSQUEAK, PEA-BRAINED WACKO KILLER FOR HIRE!
IS THAT SO? SIX TIMES, I THINK, YE'VE TRIED T' KILL THE X-MEN -- OLD TEAM AN' NEW -- AND EACH TIME, YE'VE FAILED.
LET SOMEONE ELSE TRY F'R ONCE, CAIN. WE'VE BIGGER -- BETTER -- FISH T' FRY. IF OUR MAN SUCCEEDS, THOSE CURSED MUTANTS WILL BE DEAD AN' WE'LL BE MILLIONAIRES.
IF HE FAILS, WE'LL STILL BE MILLIONAIRES, AN' YE'LL BE FREE T' TRY WHENEVER YE LIKE. SATISFIED?
NO!
Mr. "BLACK TOM" CASSIDY? Mr. CAIN MARKO -- OR DO YOU PREFER THE NOM DU CRIME JUGGERNAUT?
ANYWAY -- GREETINGS, GENTS.

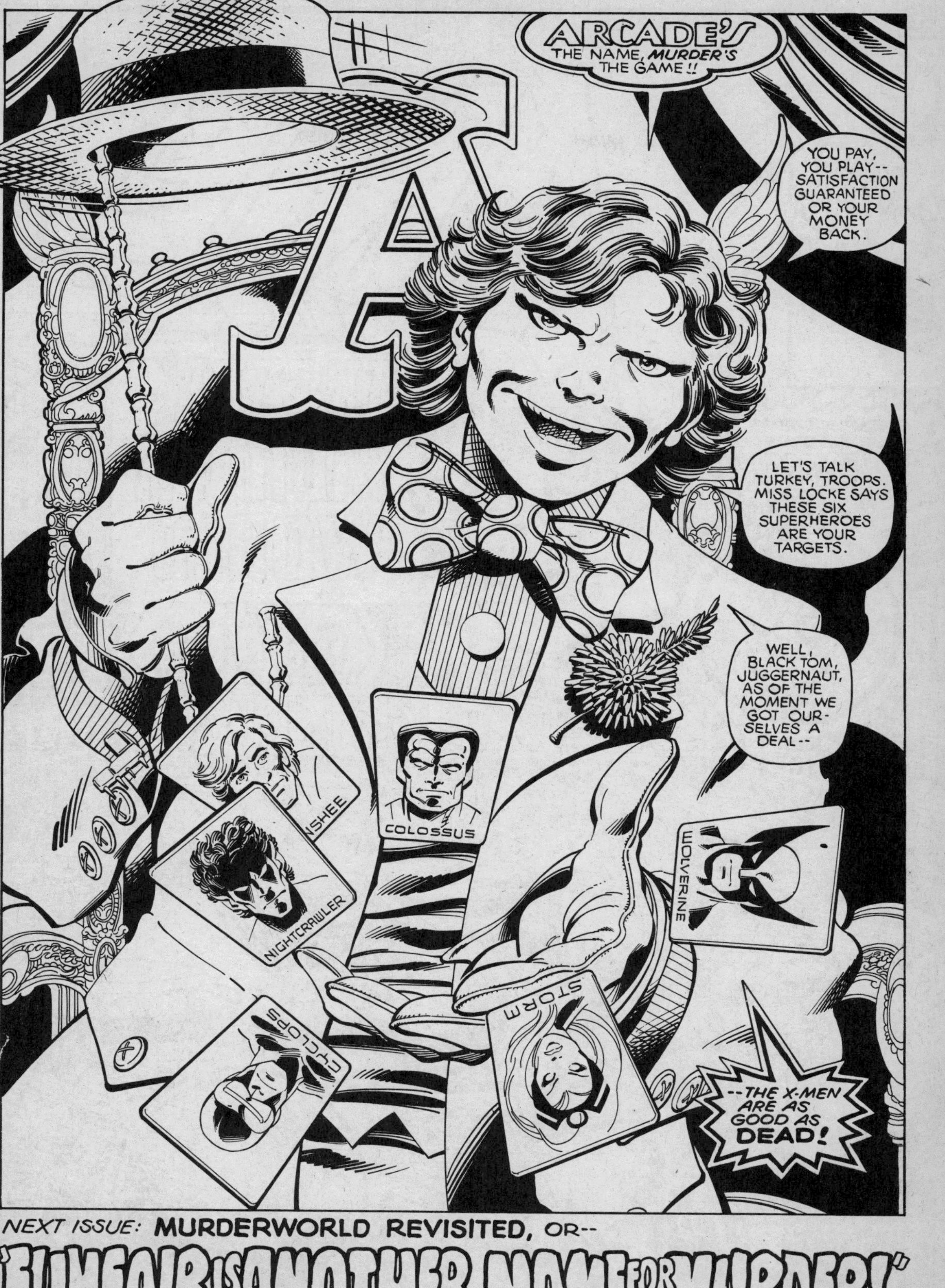
ARCADE'S THE NAME, MURDER'S THE GAME!!
YOU PAY, YOU PLAY-- SATISFACTION GUARANTEED OR YOUR MONEY BACK.
LET'S TALK TURKEY, TROOPS. MISS LOCKE SAYS THESE SIX SUPERHEROES ARE YOUR TARGETS.
WELL, BLACK TOM, JUGGERNAUT, AS OF THE MOMENT WE GOT OURSELVES A DEAL--
--THE X-MEN ARE AS GOOD AS DEAD!
COLOSSUS
NIGHTCRAWLER
WOLVERINE
STORM
CYCLOPS

NEXT ISSUE: **MURDERWORLD REVISITED,** *OR--*

"FUNFAIR IS ANOTHER NAME FOR MURDER!"

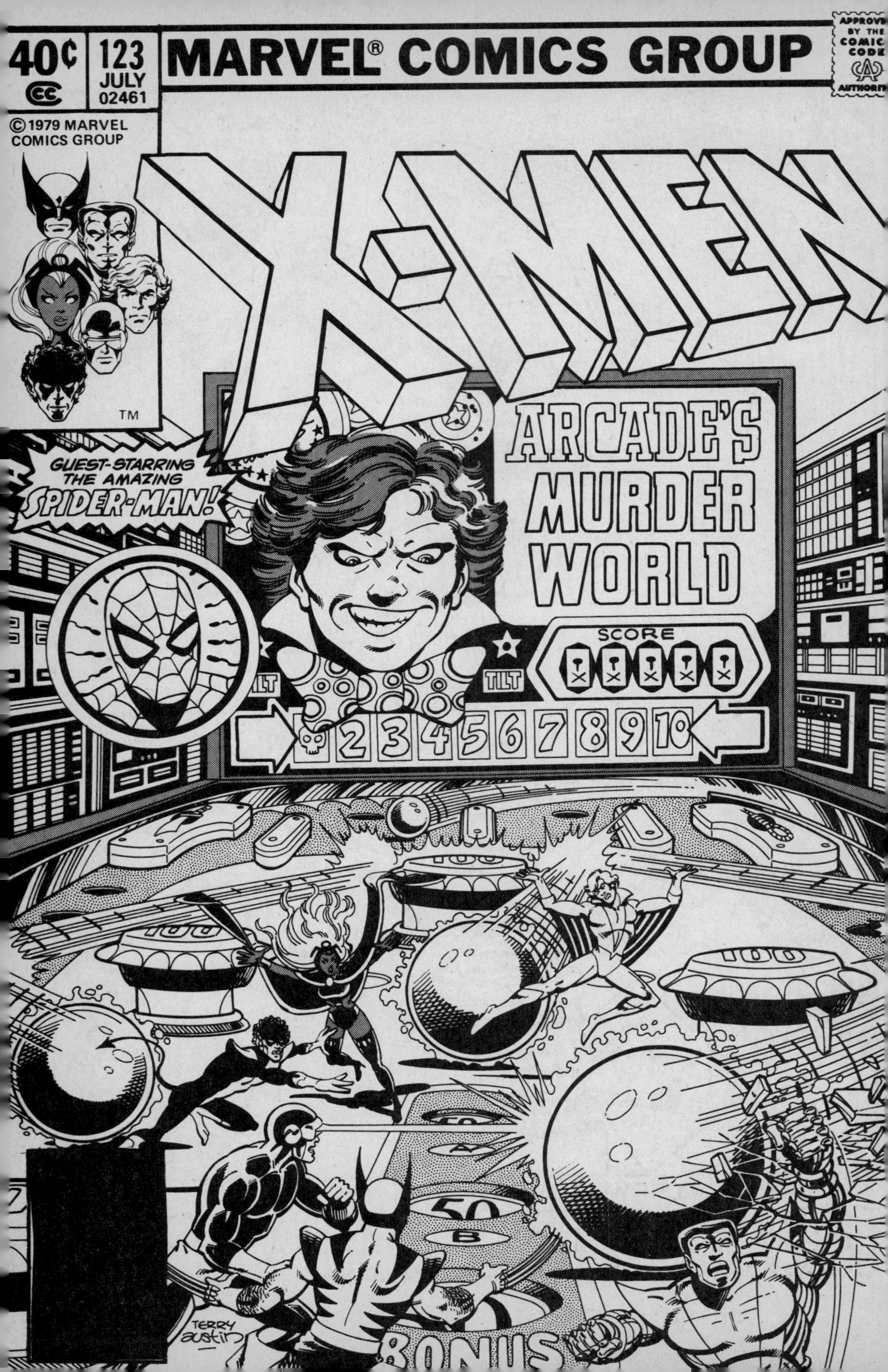
40¢
123
JULY
02461
MARVEL® COMICS GROUP
APPROVED BY THE COMICS CODE AUTHORITY
© 1979 MARVEL COMICS GROUP
TM
X-MEN
GUEST-STARRING THE AMAZING SPIDER-MAN!
ARCADE'S MURDER WORLD
SCORE
TILT
TILT
2 3 4 5 6 7 8 9 10
100
50
B
TERRY austin
BONUS

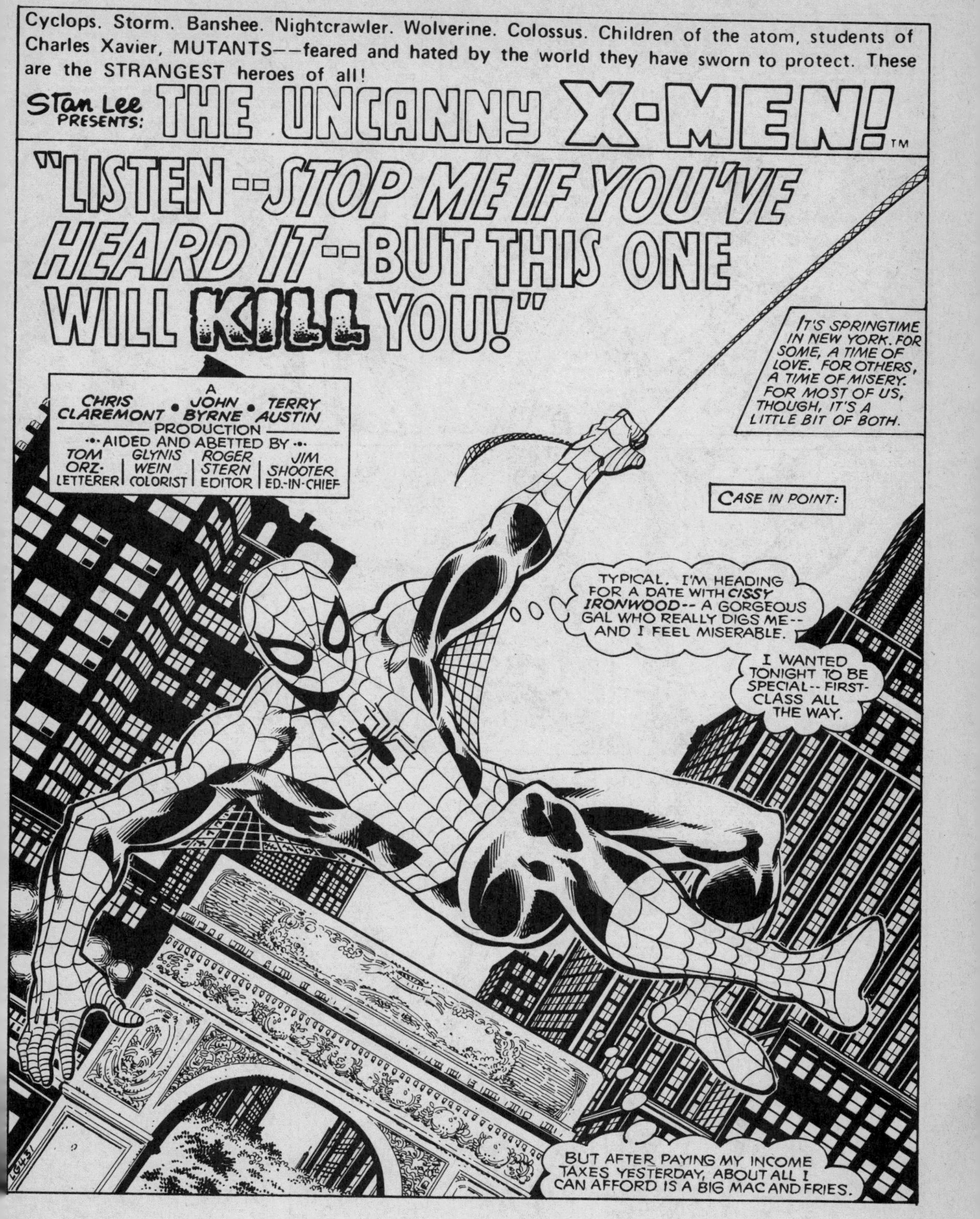
Cyclops. Storm. Banshee. Nightcrawler. Wolverine. Colossus. Children of the atom, students of Charles Xavier, MUTANTS--feared and hated by the world they have sworn to protect. These are the STRANGEST heroes of all!
STAN LEE PRESENTS: THE UNCANNY X-MEN!™
"LISTEN--STOP ME IF YOU'VE HEARD IT--BUT THIS ONE WILL KILL YOU!"
A CHRIS CLAREMONT • JOHN BYRNE • TERRY AUSTIN PRODUCTION
AIDED AND ABETTED BY
TOM ORZ-LETTERER | GLYNIS WEIN COLORIST | ROGER STERN EDITOR | JIM SHOOTER ED.-IN-CHIEF
IT'S SPRINGTIME IN NEW YORK. FOR SOME, A TIME OF LOVE. FOR OTHERS, A TIME OF MISERY. FOR MOST OF US, THOUGH, IT'S A LITTLE BIT OF BOTH.
CASE IN POINT:
TYPICAL. I'M HEADING FOR A DATE WITH CISSY IRONWOOD-- A GORGEOUS GAL WHO REALLY DIGS ME-- AND I FEEL MISERABLE.
I WANTED TONIGHT TO BE SPECIAL-- FIRST-CLASS ALL THE WAY.
BUT AFTER PAYING MY INCOME TAXES YESTERDAY, ABOUT ALL I CAN AFFORD IS A BIG MAC AND FRIES.

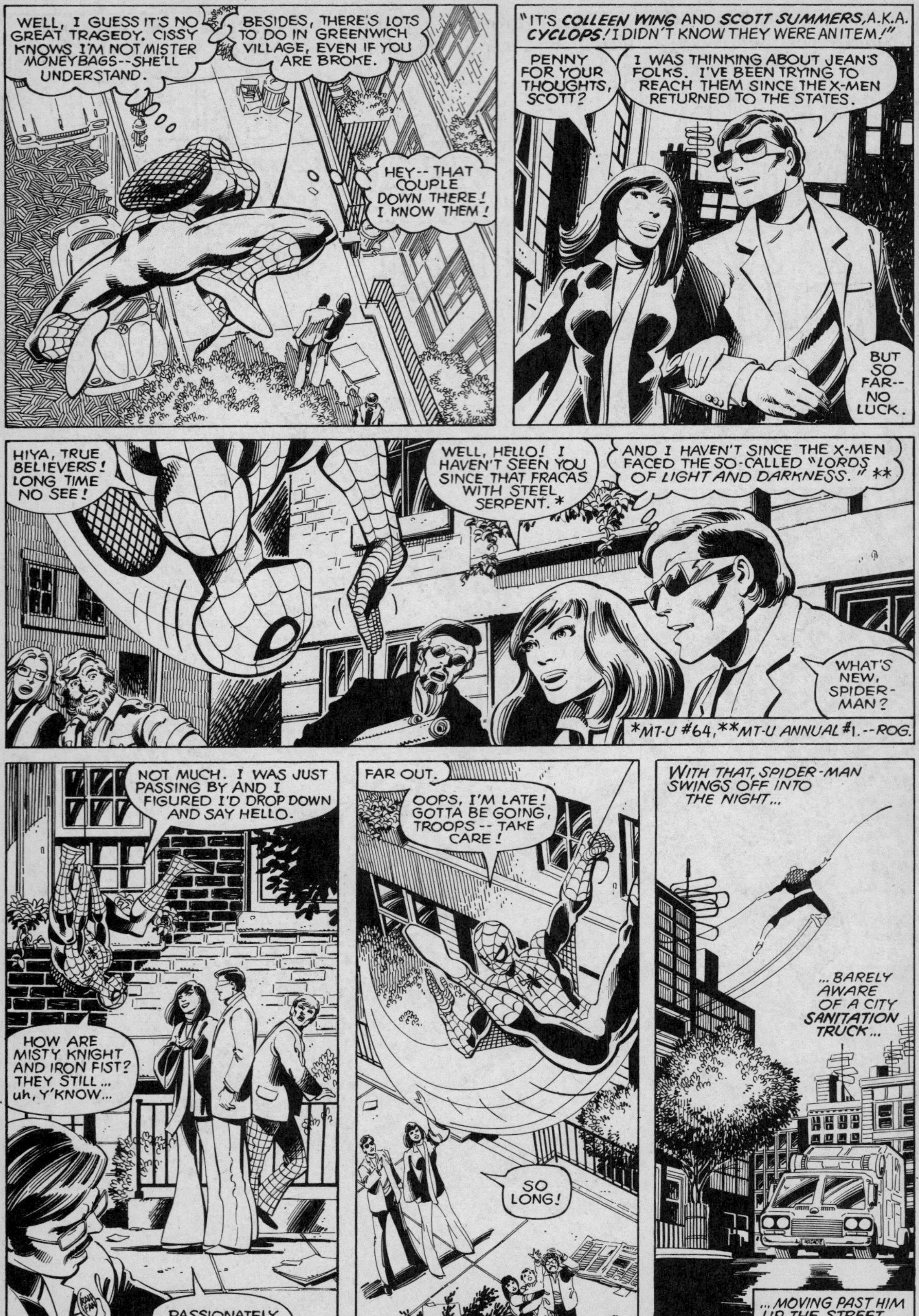
WELL, I GUESS IT'S NO GREAT TRAGEDY. CISSY KNOWS I'M NOT MISTER MONEYBAGS--SHE'LL UNDERSTAND.
BESIDES, THERE'S LOTS TO DO IN GREENWICH VILLAGE, EVEN IF YOU ARE BROKE.
HEY-- THAT COUPLE DOWN THERE! I KNOW THEM!
"IT'S COLLEEN WING AND SCOTT SUMMERS, A.K.A. CYCLOPS! I DIDN'T KNOW THEY WERE AN ITEM!"
PENNY FOR YOUR THOUGHTS, SCOTT?
I WAS THINKING ABOUT JEAN'S FOLKS. I'VE BEEN TRYING TO REACH THEM SINCE THE X-MEN RETURNED TO THE STATES.
BUT SO FAR-- NO LUCK.
HIYA, TRUE BELIEVERS! LONG TIME NO SEE!
WELL, HELLO! I HAVEN'T SEEN YOU SINCE THAT FRACAS WITH STEEL SERPENT.*
AND I HAVEN'T SINCE THE X-MEN FACED THE SO-CALLED "LORDS OF LIGHT AND DARKNESS." **
WHAT'S NEW, SPIDER-MAN?
*MT-U #64, **MT-U ANNUAL #1. --ROG.
NOT MUCH. I WAS JUST PASSING BY AND I FIGURED I'D DROP DOWN AND SAY HELLO.
HOW ARE MISTY KNIGHT AND IRON FIST? THEY STILL... uh, Y'KNOW...
PASSIONATELY.
FAR OUT.
OOPS, I'M LATE! GOTTA BE GOING, TROOPS -- TAKE CARE!
SO LONG!
WITH THAT, SPIDER-MAN SWINGS OFF INTO THE NIGHT...
...BARELY AWARE OF A CITY SANITATION TRUCK...
...MOVING PAST HIM UP THE STREET.

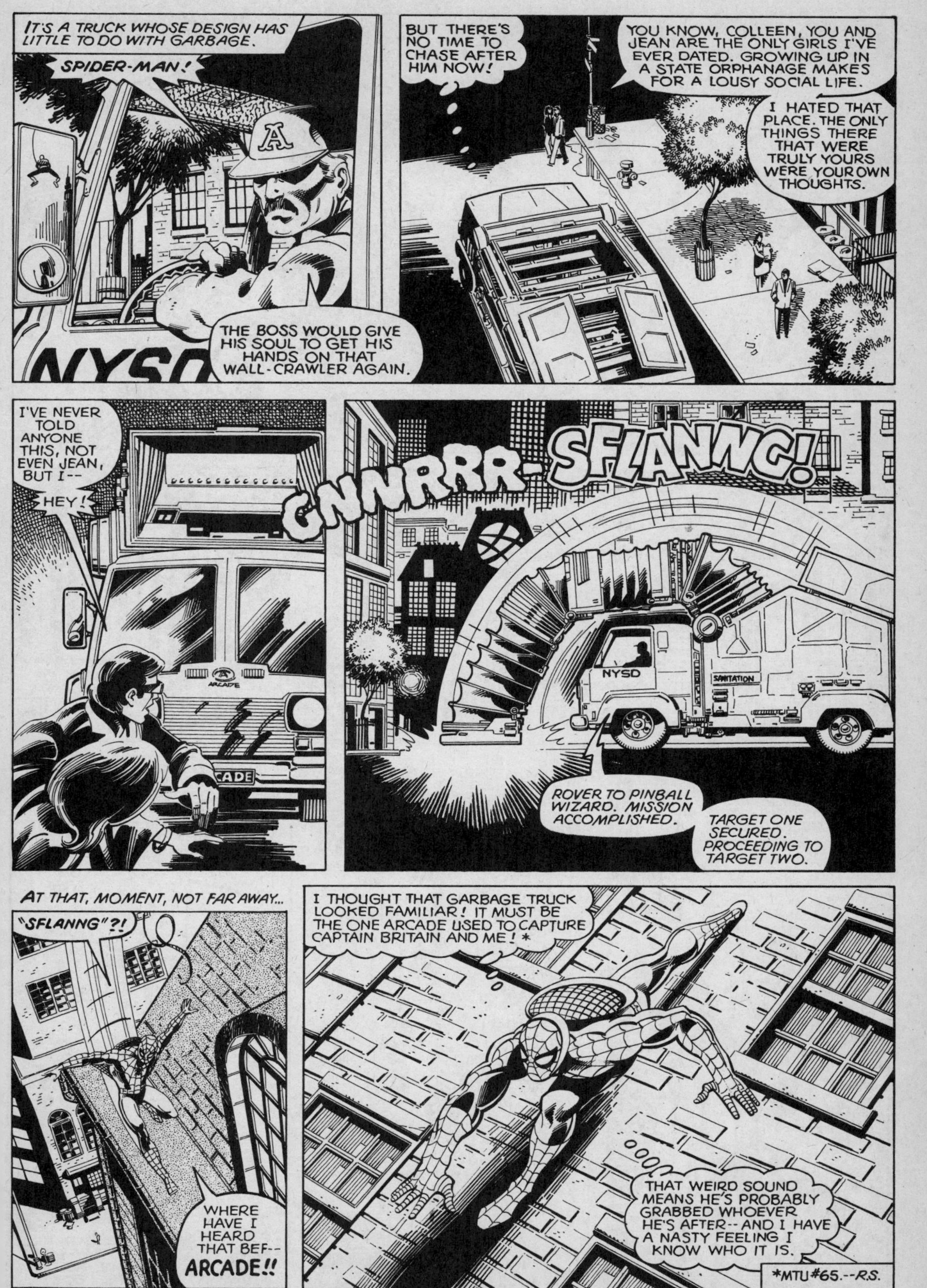
IT'S A TRUCK WHOSE DESIGN HAS LITTLE TO DO WITH GARBAGE.
SPIDER-MAN!
THE BOSS WOULD GIVE HIS SOUL TO GET HIS HANDS ON THAT WALL-CRAWLER AGAIN.
NYSD
BUT THERE'S NO TIME TO CHASE AFTER HIM NOW!
YOU KNOW, COLLEEN, YOU AND JEAN ARE THE ONLY GIRLS I'VE EVER DATED. GROWING UP IN A STATE ORPHANAGE MAKES FOR A LOUSY SOCIAL LIFE.
I HATED THAT PLACE. THE ONLY THINGS THERE THAT WERE TRULY YOURS WERE YOUR OWN THOUGHTS.
I'VE NEVER TOLD ANYONE THIS, NOT EVEN JEAN, BUT I--
HEY!
ARCADE
GNNRRR-SFLANNG!
NYSD
SANITATION
ROVER TO PINBALL WIZARD. MISSION ACCOMPLISHED.
TARGET ONE SECURED. PROCEEDING TO TARGET TWO.
AT THAT, MOMENT, NOT FAR AWAY...
"SFLANNG"?!
WHERE HAVE I HEARD THAT BEF-- ARCADE!!
I THOUGHT THAT GARBAGE TRUCK LOOKED FAMILIAR! IT MUST BE THE ONE ARCADE USED TO CAPTURE CAPTAIN BRITAIN AND ME! *
THAT WEIRD SOUND MEANS HE'S PROBABLY GRABBED WHOEVER HE'S AFTER-- AND I HAVE A NASTY FEELING I KNOW WHO IT IS.
*MTU #65.--R.S.

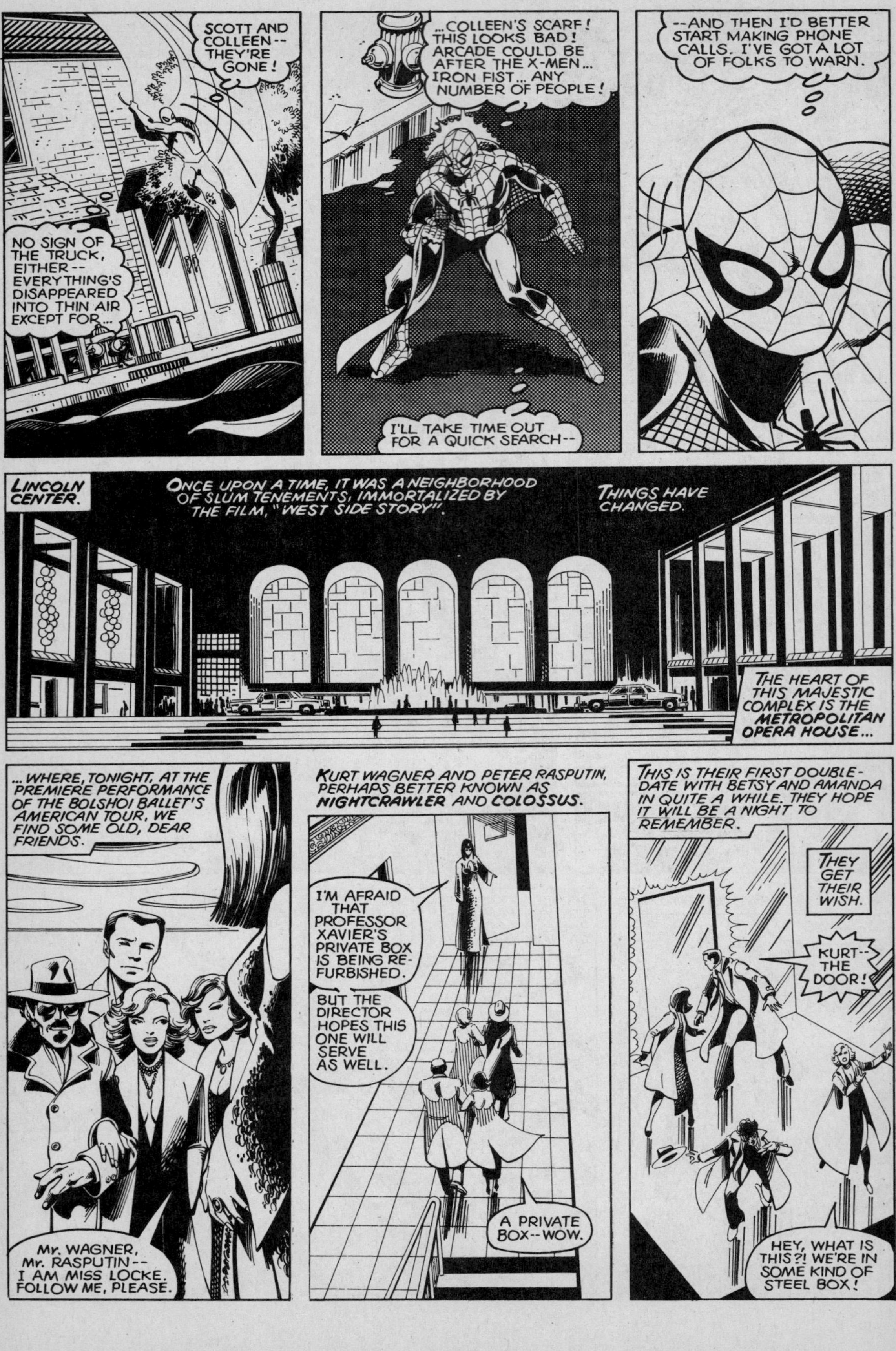

SCOTT AND COLLEEN-- THEY'RE GONE!
NO SIGN OF THE TRUCK, EITHER-- EVERYTHING'S DISAPPEARED INTO THIN AIR EXCEPT FOR...
...COLLEEN'S SCARF! THIS LOOKS BAD! ARCADE COULD BE AFTER THE X-MEN... IRON FIST... ANY NUMBER OF PEOPLE!
I'LL TAKE TIME OUT FOR A QUICK SEARCH--
--AND THEN I'D BETTER START MAKING PHONE CALLS. I'VE GOT A LOT OF FOLKS TO WARN.
LINCOLN CENTER.
ONCE UPON A TIME, IT WAS A NEIGHBORHOOD OF SLUM TENEMENTS, IMMORTALIZED BY THE FILM, "WEST SIDE STORY".
THINGS HAVE CHANGED.
THE HEART OF THIS MAJESTIC COMPLEX IS THE METROPOLITAN OPERA HOUSE...
...WHERE, TONIGHT, AT THE PREMIERE PERFORMANCE OF THE BOLSHOI BALLET'S AMERICAN TOUR, WE FIND SOME OLD, DEAR FRIENDS.
Mr. WAGNER, Mr. RASPUTIN-- I AM MISS LOCKE. FOLLOW ME, PLEASE.
KURT WAGNER AND PETER RASPUTIN, PERHAPS BETTER KNOWN AS NIGHTCRAWLER AND COLOSSUS.
I'M AFRAID THAT PROFESSOR XAVIER'S PRIVATE BOX IS BEING RE-FURBISHED.
BUT THE DIRECTOR HOPES THIS ONE WILL SERVE AS WELL.
A PRIVATE BOX--WOW.
THIS IS THEIR FIRST DOUBLE-DATE WITH BETSY AND AMANDA IN QUITE A WHILE. THEY HOPE IT WILL BE A NIGHT TO REMEMBER.
THEY GET THEIR WISH.
KURT-- THE DOOR!
HEY, WHAT IS THIS?! WE'RE IN SOME KIND OF STEEL BOX!

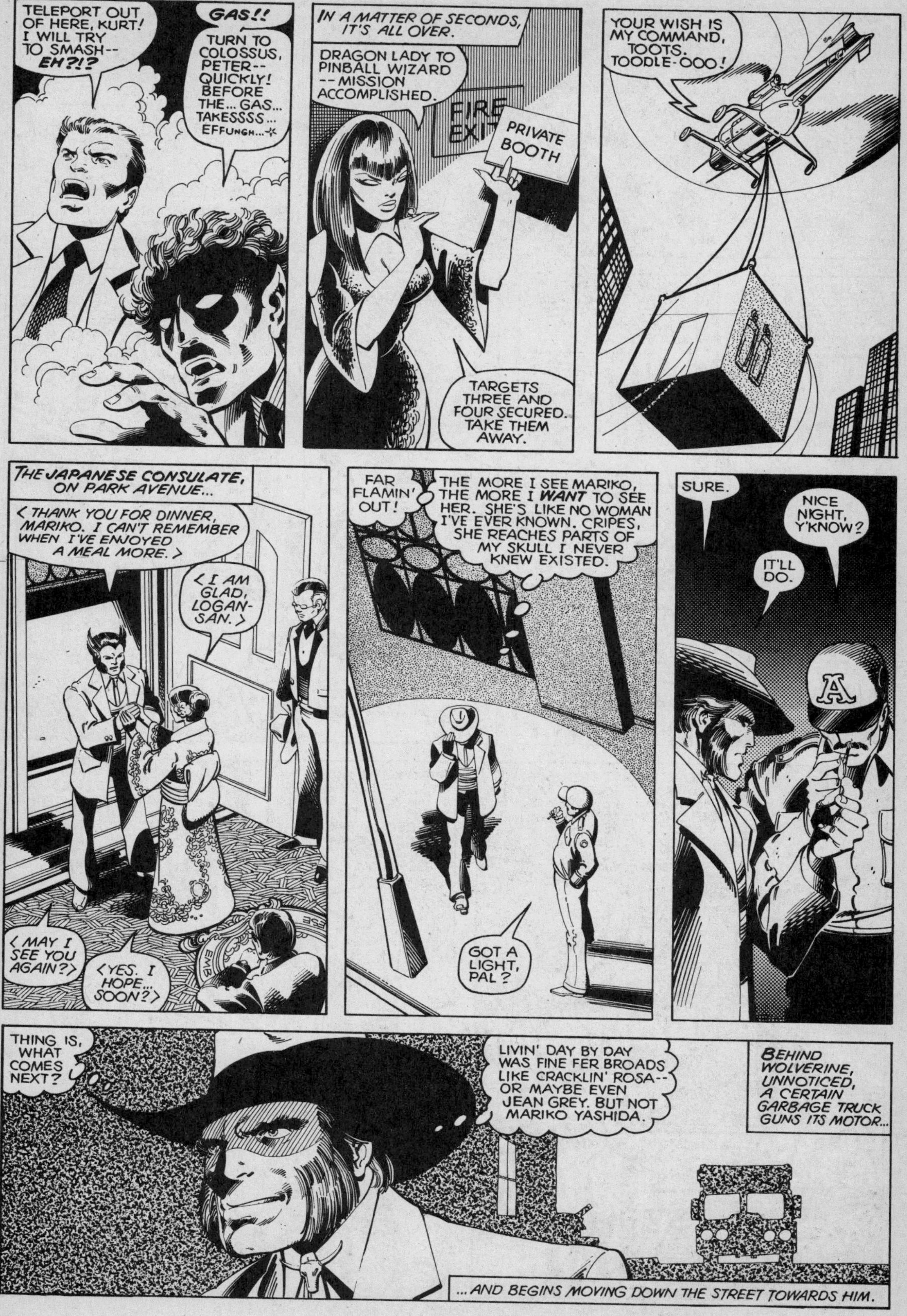

TELEPORT OUT OF HERE, KURT! I WILL TRY TO SMASH-- EH?!?
GAS!! TURN TO COLOSSUS, PETER-- QUICKLY! BEFORE THE... GAS... TAKESSSS... EFFUNGH...
IN A MATTER OF SECONDS, IT'S ALL OVER.
DRAGON LADY TO PINBALL WIZARD -- MISSION ACCOMPLISHED.
FIRE EXIT
PRIVATE BOOTH
TARGETS THREE AND FOUR SECURED. TAKE THEM AWAY.
YOUR WISH IS MY COMMAND, TOOTS. TOODLE-OOO!
THE JAPANESE CONSULATE, ON PARK AVENUE...
< THANK YOU FOR DINNER, MARIKO. I CAN'T REMEMBER WHEN I'VE ENJOYED A MEAL MORE. >
< I AM GLAD, LOGAN-SAN. >
< MAY I SEE YOU AGAIN? >
< YES. I HOPE... SOON? >
FAR FLAMIN' OUT!
THE MORE I SEE MARIKO, THE MORE I WANT TO SEE HER. SHE'S LIKE NO WOMAN I'VE EVER KNOWN. CRIPES, SHE REACHES PARTS OF MY SKULL I NEVER KNEW EXISTED.
GOT A LIGHT, PAL?
SURE.
NICE NIGHT, Y'KNOW?
IT'LL DO.
THING IS, WHAT COMES NEXT?
LIVIN' DAY BY DAY WAS FINE FER BROADS LIKE CRACKLIN' ROSA-- OR MAYBE EVEN JEAN GREY. BUT NOT MARIKO YASHIDA.
BEHIND WOLVERINE, UNNOTICED, A CERTAIN GARBAGE TRUCK GUNS ITS MOTOR...
...AND BEGINS MOVING DOWN THE STREET TOWARDS HIM.

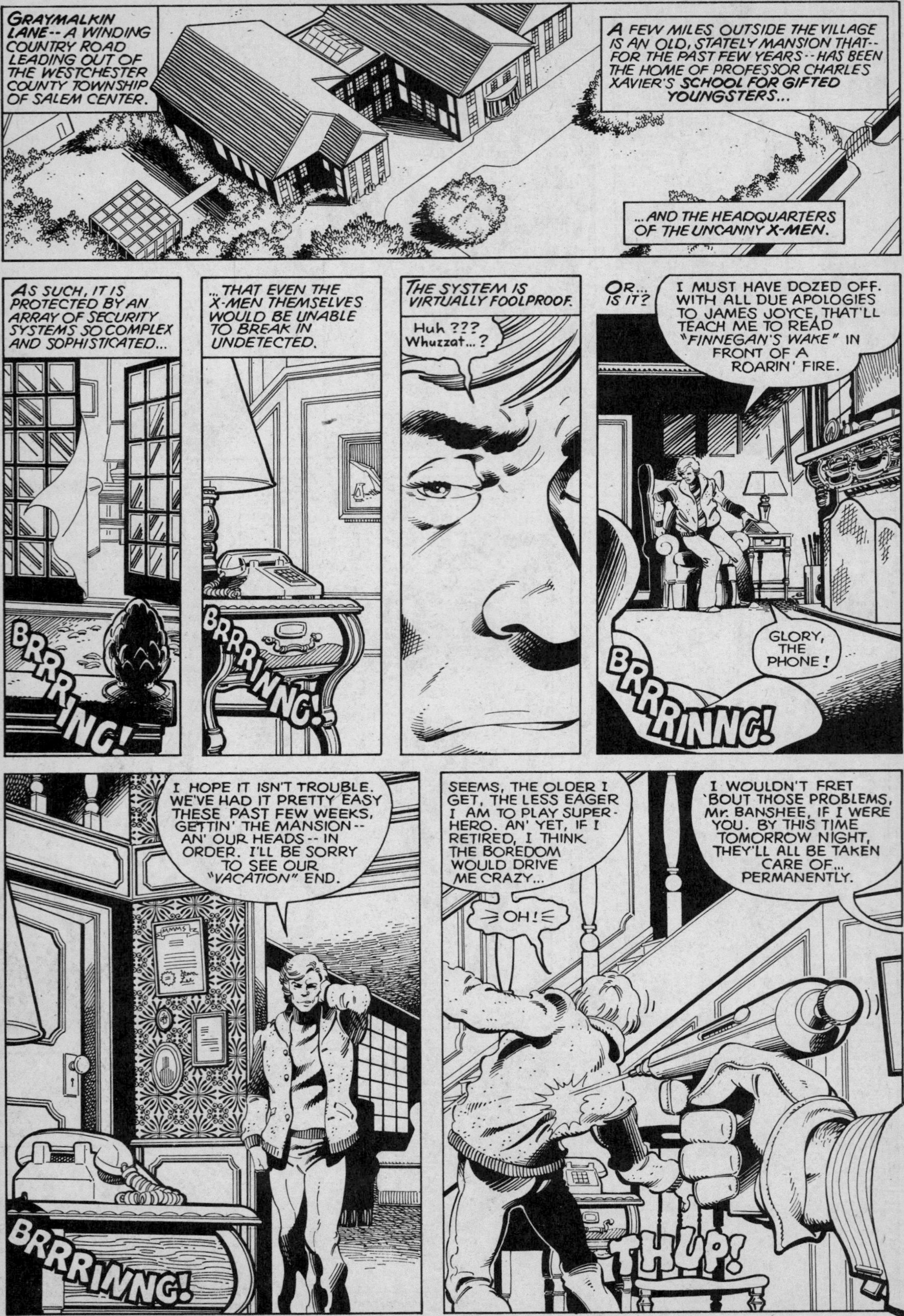
GRAYMALKIN LANE -- A WINDING COUNTRY ROAD LEADING OUT OF THE WESTCHESTER COUNTY TOWNSHIP OF SALEM CENTER.
A FEW MILES OUTSIDE THE VILLAGE IS AN OLD, STATELY MANSION THAT-- FOR THE PAST FEW YEARS -- HAS BEEN THE HOME OF PROFESSOR CHARLES XAVIER'S SCHOOL FOR GIFTED YOUNGSTERS...
...AND THE HEADQUARTERS OF THE UNCANNY X-MEN.
AS SUCH, IT IS PROTECTED BY AN ARRAY OF SECURITY SYSTEMS SO COMPLEX AND SOPHISTICATED...
BRRRING!
...THAT EVEN THE X-MEN THEMSELVES WOULD BE UNABLE TO BREAK IN UNDETECTED.
BRRRINNG!
THE SYSTEM IS VIRTUALLY FOOLPROOF.
Huh ??? Whuzzat...?
OR... IS IT?
I MUST HAVE DOZED OFF. WITH ALL DUE APOLOGIES TO JAMES JOYCE, THAT'LL TEACH ME TO READ "FINNEGAN'S WAKE" IN FRONT OF A ROARIN' FIRE.
GLORY, THE PHONE!
BRRRINNG!
I HOPE IT ISN'T TROUBLE. WE'VE HAD IT PRETTY EASY THESE PAST FEW WEEKS, GETTIN' THE MANSION -- AN' OUR HEADS -- IN ORDER. I'LL BE SORRY TO SEE OUR "VACATION" END.
BRRRINNG!
SEEMS, THE OLDER I GET, THE LESS EAGER I AM TO PLAY SUPER-HERO. AN' YET, IF I RETIRED, I THINK THE BOREDOM WOULD DRIVE ME CRAZY...
I WOULDN'T FRET 'BOUT THOSE PROBLEMS, Mr. BANSHEE, IF I WERE YOU. BY THIS TIME TOMORROW NIGHT, THEY'LL ALL BE TAKEN CARE OF... PERMANENTLY.
OH!
THUP!

SEAN, THE TELEPHONE-- WILL YOU ANSWER IT, PLEASE?

SEAN? BANSHEE?!

BRRRNNG!

DEVILS TAKE THE MAN, HE MUST HAVE GONE OUT.

IT NEVER FAILS. THAT INFERNAL DEVICE ALWAYS RINGS AT THE MOST INCONVENIENT TIMES.

BRRING!

I WISH SEAN HAD TOLD ME HE WAS LEAVING. I WOULD HAVE POSTPONED MY BATH.

BE STILL, I'M COM-- --UNNNGNH!

SLEEPY-BYE, HONEY- CHILE.

THUP!

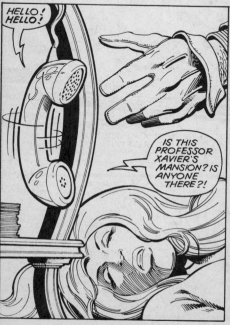

HELLO! HELLO!

IS THIS PROFESSOR XAVIER'S MANSION? IS ANYONE THERE?!

H'LO?

THANK HEAVEN I'M IN TIME. THIS IS SPIDER-MAN. SCOTT SUMMERS WAS KIDNAPPED TONIGHT BY A CRAZY ASSASSIN-FOR- HIRE NAMED ARCADE.

I THINK HE MAY BE GUNNING FOR THE X-MEN!

YOU GOT IT, WALL- CRAWLER. I AM GUNNIN' FOR THE X-MEN. TROUBLE IS, YOUR WARNIN' COMES A WEE BIT TOO LATE.

"AN' WHEN I'M DONE WITH THEM, SPIDEY..."

"...I'M COMIN' AFTER YOU. 'BYE NOW."

NOOOO!

SKRRRASH!

GEEZ.

TIME PASSES. AND SCOTT SUMMERS WAKES TO A STYGIAN DARKNESS...

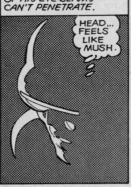

...THAT EVEN THE LIGHT OF HIS EYE BEAMS CAN'T PENETRATE.

HEAD... FEELS LIKE MUSH.

I REMEMBER BEING ATTACKED BY... A GARBAGE TRUCK? HIT BY SOME KIND OF NERVE GAS, KNOCKED OUT BEFORE I COULD FIRE AN OPTIC BLAST.

COLLEEN, IS SHE-- LIGHTS!

GOOD LORD!

THE X-MEN! WE'RE ALL IN UNIFORM...

...ALL SEALED INSIDE THESE LUCITE SPHERES. WHAT GOES ON HERE, ANYWAY?!

WE'RE IN SOME SORT OF TUNNEL. WE'D BETTER BUST OUT--FAST--BEFORE OUR UNKNOWN HOST MAKES HIS MOVE.

THEY ARE ALL AWAKE, ARCADE.

THANK YOU, MISS LOCKE. SYSTEMS UP-DATE, MISTER CHAMBERS?

ALL READINGS NOMINAL. YOU CAN START WHEN-EVER YOU'RE READY.

MY FRIEND, THAT'S JUST WHAT I WANTED TO HEAR.

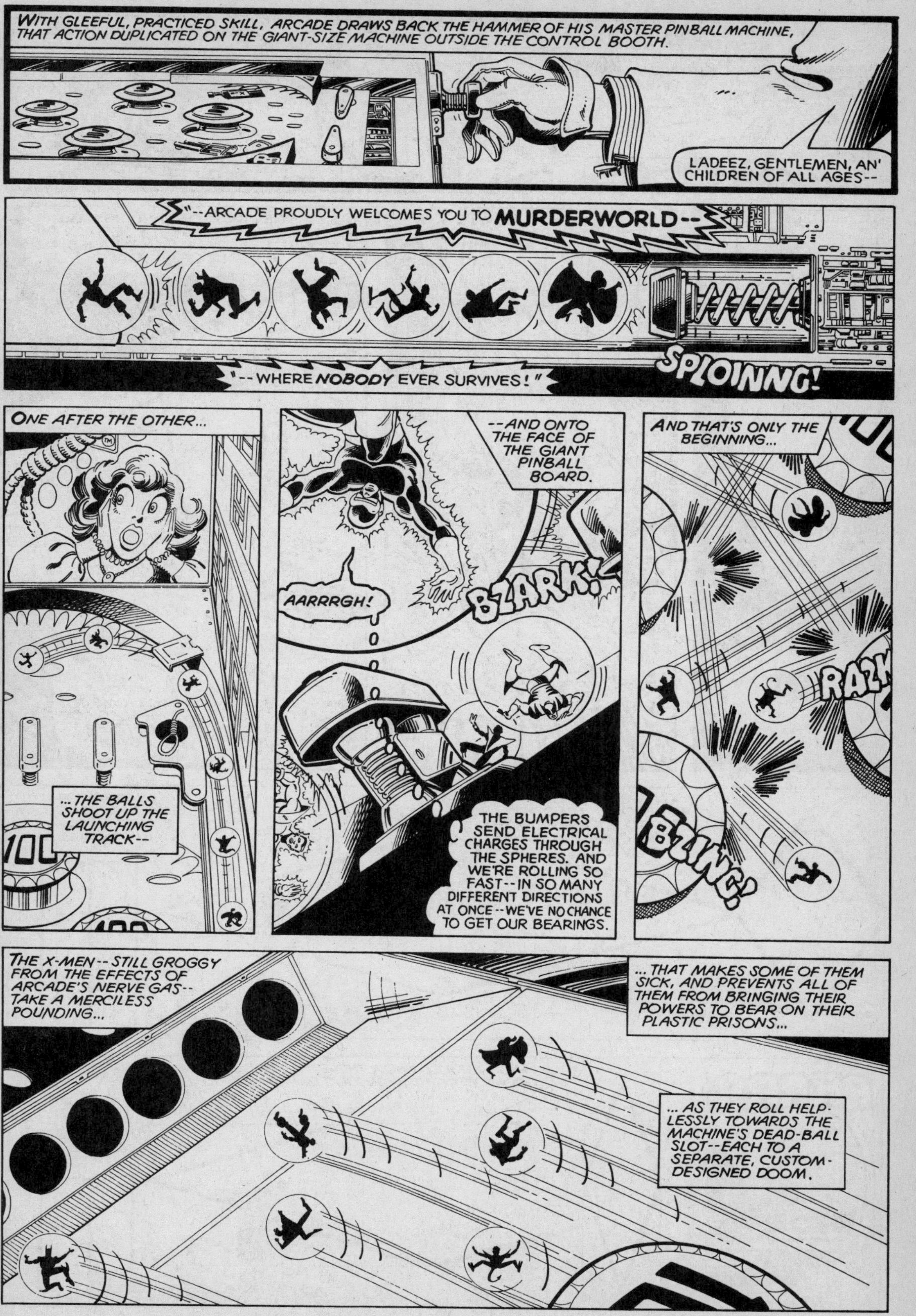
WITH GLEEFUL, PRACTICED SKILL, ARCADE DRAWS BACK THE HAMMER OF HIS MASTER PINBALL MACHINE, THAT ACTION DUPLICATED ON THE GIANT-SIZE MACHINE OUTSIDE THE CONTROL BOOTH.
LADEEZ, GENTLEMEN, AN' CHILDREN OF ALL AGES--
"--ARCADE PROUDLY WELCOMES YOU TO MURDERWORLD--
"--WHERE NOBODY EVER SURVIVES!"
SPLOINNG!
ONE AFTER THE OTHER...
...THE BALLS SHOOT UP THE LAUNCHING TRACK--
--AND ONTO THE FACE OF THE GIANT PINBALL BOARD.
AARRRGH!
BZARK!
THE BUMPERS SEND ELECTRICAL CHARGES THROUGH THE SPHERES. AND WE'RE ROLLING SO FAST--IN SO MANY DIFFERENT DIRECTIONS AT ONCE--WE'VE NO CHANCE TO GET OUR BEARINGS.
AND THAT'S ONLY THE BEGINNING...
BZING!
THE X-MEN--STILL GROGGY FROM THE EFFECTS OF ARCADE'S NERVE GAS--TAKE A MERCILESS POUNDING...
...THAT MAKES SOME OF THEM SICK, AND PREVENTS ALL OF THEM FROM BRINGING THEIR POWERS TO BEAR ON THEIR PLASTIC PRISONS...
...AS THEY ROLL HELPLESSLY TOWARDS THE MACHINE'S DEAD-BALL SLOT--EACH TO A SEPARATE, CUSTOM-DESIGNED DOOM.

WE'RE OFF AND RUNNIN', FOLKS, AND SO FAR, I'M NOT IMPRESSED. WHEN I TUSSLED WITH SPIDER-MAN, * HE BROKE FREE OF HIS PINBALL.

THE GAME'S STILL YOUNG --

*MTU #66--ROG.

"-- BUT IF THE X-MEN DON'T START GETTING THEIR ACT TOGETHER, IT'S GONNA BE OVER BEFORE IT'S BEGUN."

OW!

B-A-THUMP!

NOT THE GENTLEST OF LANDINGS, BUT MAYBE THAT'S JUST WHAT I NEEDED. THE MIXTURE OF FEAR AND PAIN CLEARED ALL THE COBWEBS OUT OF MY HEAD.

EXIT   EXIT   EXIT

I'M STILL NOT SURE WHAT'S GOING ON, BUT AT LEAST NOW I THINK I'VE GOT AN EVEN CHANCE.

HOW DO, CYCLOPS. WELCOME TO MY "LADY OR THE TIGER" ROOM.

YOU HAVE THREE DOORS -- ONE'S A WAY OUT... THE OTHER TWO LEAD TO HORRIBLE DEATHS. THE CHOICE IS YOURS.

THANKS.

MY PLEASURE. AND JUST TO GIVE YOU AN INCENTIVE TO MAKE UP YOUR MIND --

EXIT EXIT EXIT

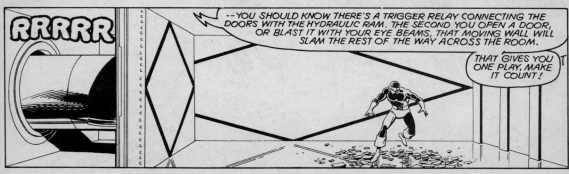

RRRRR

-- YOU SHOULD KNOW THERE'S A TRIGGER RELAY CONNECTING THE DOORS WITH THE HYDRAULIC RAM. THE SECOND YOU OPEN A DOOR, OR BLAST IT WITH YOUR EYE BEAMS, THAT MOVING WALL WILL SLAM THE REST OF THE WAY ACROSS THE ROOM.

THAT GIVES YOU ONE PLAY, MAKE IT COUNT!

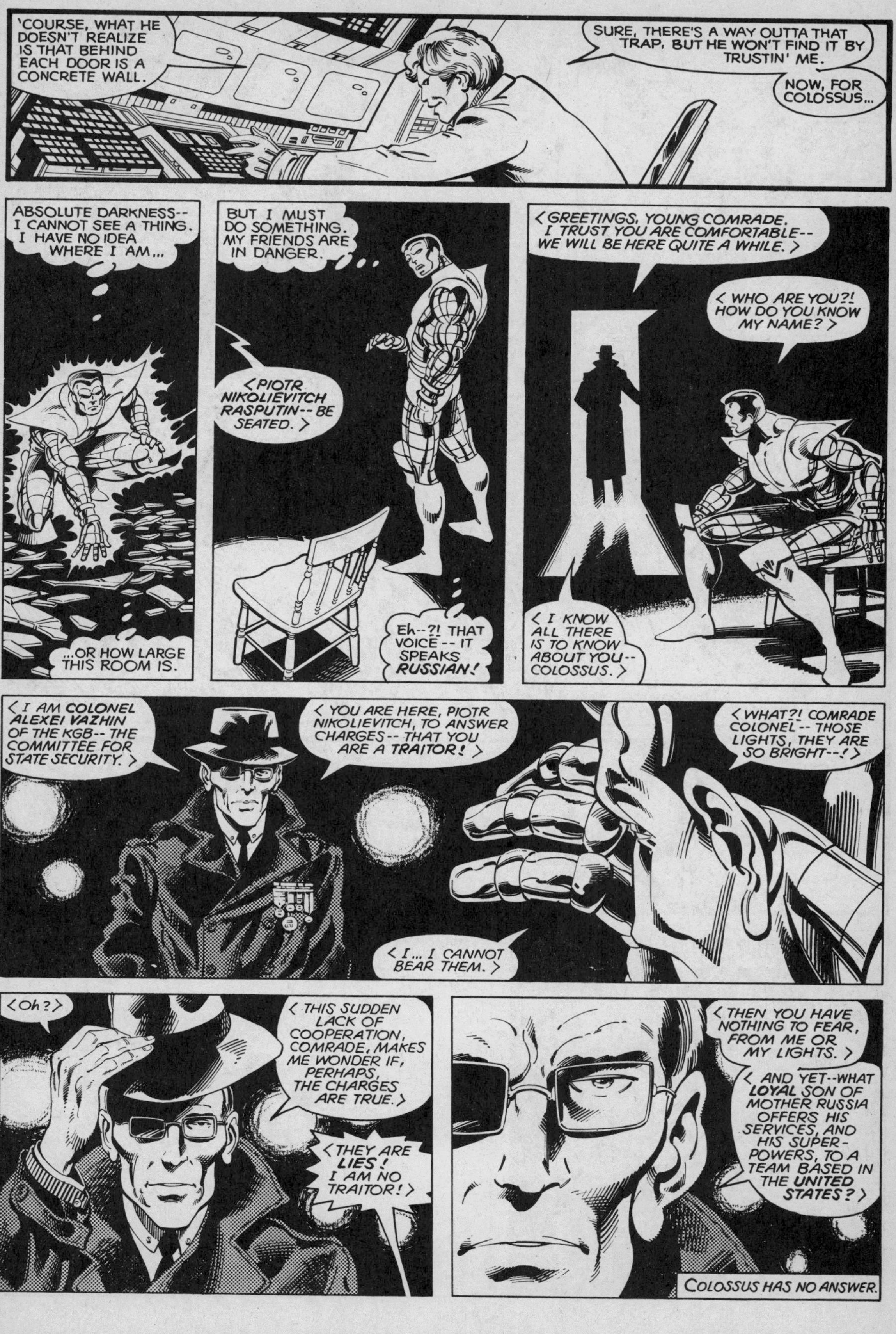

'COURSE, WHAT HE DOESN'T REALIZE IS THAT BEHIND EACH DOOR IS A CONCRETE WALL.
SURE, THERE'S A WAY OUTTA THAT TRAP, BUT HE WON'T FIND IT BY TRUSTIN' ME.
NOW, FOR COLOSSUS...
ABSOLUTE DARKNESS-- I CANNOT SEE A THING. I HAVE NO IDEA WHERE I AM...
...OR HOW LARGE THIS ROOM IS.
BUT I MUST DO SOMETHING. MY FRIENDS ARE IN DANGER.
< PIOTR NIKOLIEVITCH RASPUTIN-- BE SEATED. >
Eh--?! THAT VOICE -- IT SPEAKS RUSSIAN!
< GREETINGS, YOUNG COMRADE. I TRUST YOU ARE COMFORTABLE-- WE WILL BE HERE QUITE A WHILE. >
< WHO ARE YOU?! HOW DO YOU KNOW MY NAME? >
< I KNOW ALL THERE IS TO KNOW ABOUT YOU-- COLOSSUS. >
< I AM COLONEL ALEXEI VAZHIN OF THE KGB-- THE COMMITTEE FOR STATE SECURITY. >
< YOU ARE HERE, PIOTR NIKOLIEVITCH, TO ANSWER CHARGES-- THAT YOU ARE A TRAITOR! >
< WHAT?! COMRADE COLONEL-- THOSE LIGHTS, THEY ARE SO BRIGHT--! >
< I... I CANNOT BEAR THEM. >
<Oh?>
< THIS SUDDEN LACK OF COOPERATION, COMRADE, MAKES ME WONDER IF, PERHAPS, THE CHARGES ARE TRUE. >
< THEY ARE LIES! I AM NO TRAITOR! >
< THEN YOU HAVE NOTHING TO FEAR, FROM ME OR MY LIGHTS. >
< AND YET--WHAT LOYAL SON OF MOTHER RUSSIA OFFERS HIS SERVICES, AND HIS SUPER-POWERS, TO A TEAM BASED IN THE UNITED STATES? >
COLOSSUS HAS NO ANSWER.

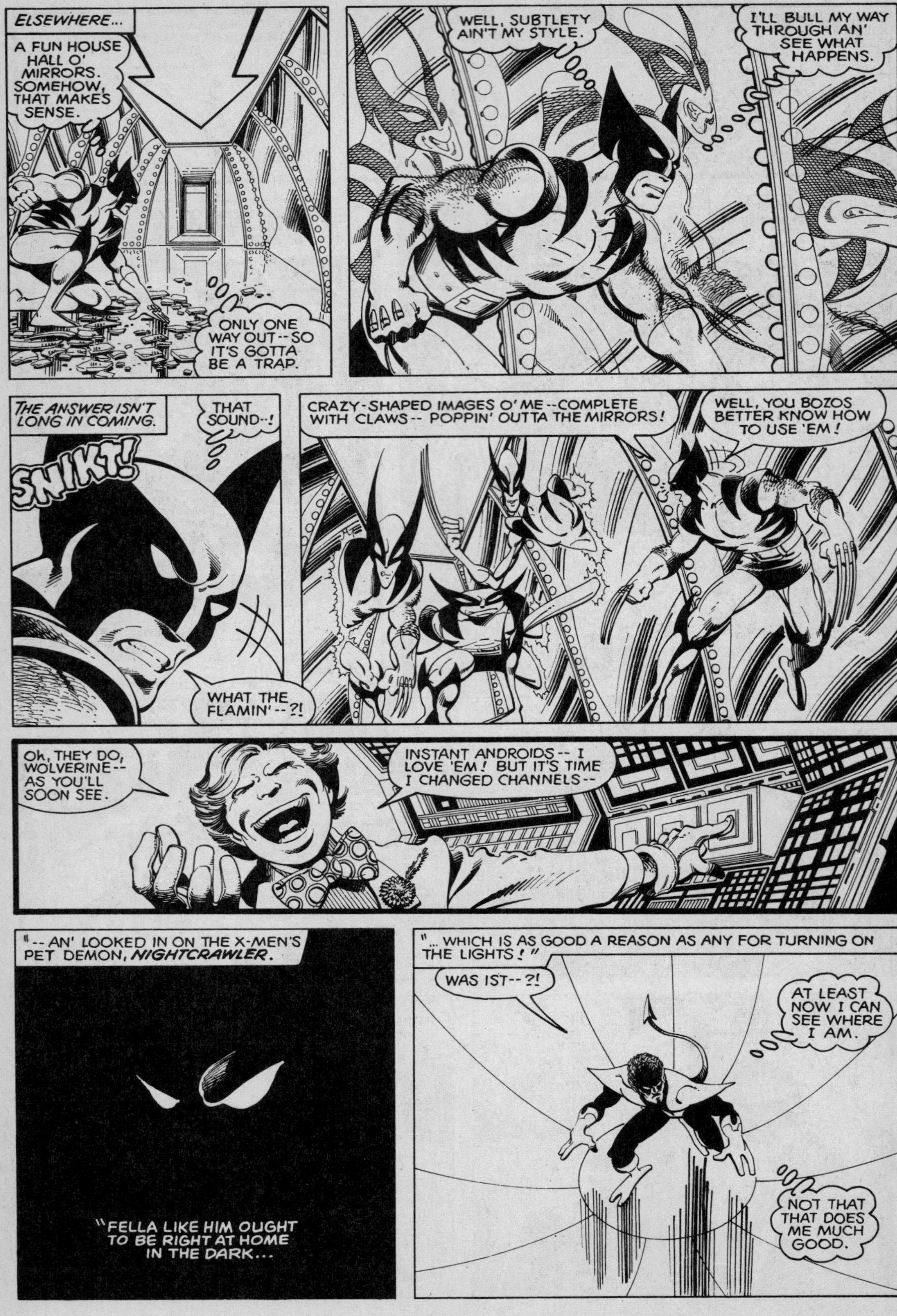
ELSEWHERE...
A FUN HOUSE HALL O' MIRRORS. SOMEHOW, THAT MAKES SENSE.
ONLY ONE WAY OUT--SO IT'S GOTTA BE A TRAP.
WELL, SUBTLETY AIN'T MY STYLE.
I'LL BULL MY WAY THROUGH AN' SEE WHAT HAPPENS.
THE ANSWER ISN'T LONG IN COMING.
THAT SOUND--!
SNIKT!
WHAT THE FLAMIN'--?!
CRAZY-SHAPED IMAGES O' ME--COMPLETE WITH CLAWS-- POPPIN' OUTTA THE MIRRORS!
WELL, YOU BOZOS BETTER KNOW HOW TO USE 'EM!
Oh, THEY DO, WOLVERINE-- AS YOU'LL SOON SEE.
INSTANT ANDROIDS-- I LOVE 'EM! BUT IT'S TIME I CHANGED CHANNELS--
"--AN' LOOKED IN ON THE X-MEN'S PET DEMON, NIGHTCRAWLER.
"FELLA LIKE HIM OUGHT TO BE RIGHT AT HOME IN THE DARK...
"...WHICH IS AS GOOD A REASON AS ANY FOR TURNING ON THE LIGHTS!"
WAS IST--?!
AT LEAST NOW I CAN SEE WHERE I AM.
NOT THAT THAT DOES ME MUCH GOOD.

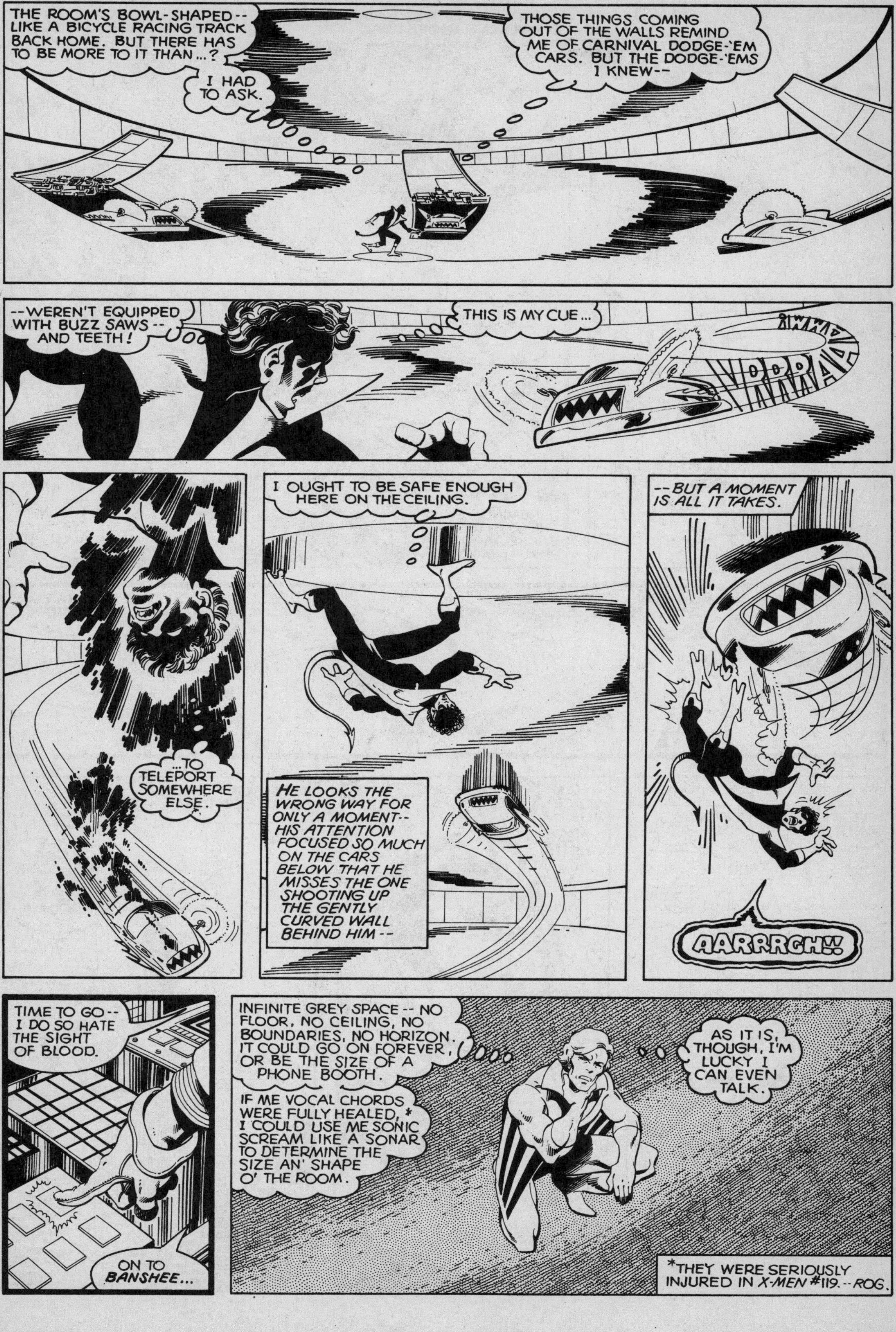

THE ROOM'S BOWL-SHAPED -- LIKE A BICYCLE RACING TRACK BACK HOME. BUT THERE HAS TO BE MORE TO IT THAN ...?
I HAD TO ASK.
THOSE THINGS COMING OUT OF THE WALLS REMIND ME OF CARNIVAL DODGE-'EM CARS. BUT THE DODGE-'EMS I KNEW--
--WEREN'T EQUIPPED WITH BUZZ SAWS -- AND TEETH!
THIS IS MY CUE...
...TO TELEPORT SOMEWHERE ELSE.
I OUGHT TO BE SAFE ENOUGH HERE ON THE CEILING.
HE LOOKS THE WRONG WAY FOR ONLY A MOMENT-- HIS ATTENTION FOCUSED SO MUCH ON THE CARS BELOW THAT HE MISSES THE ONE SHOOTING UP THE GENTLY CURVED WALL BEHIND HIM --
--BUT A MOMENT IS ALL IT TAKES.
AARRRGH!!
TIME TO GO -- I DO SO HATE THE SIGHT OF BLOOD.
ON TO BANSHEE...
INFINITE GREY SPACE -- NO FLOOR, NO CEILING, NO BOUNDARIES, NO HORIZON. IT COULD GO ON FOREVER, OR BE THE SIZE OF A PHONE BOOTH.
IF ME VOCAL CHORDS WERE FULLY HEALED, * I COULD USE ME SONIC SCREAM LIKE A SONAR TO DETERMINE THE SIZE AN' SHAPE O' THE ROOM.
AS IT IS, THOUGH, I'M LUCKY I CAN EVEN TALK.
*THEY WERE SERIOUSLY INJURED IN X-MEN #119. --ROG.

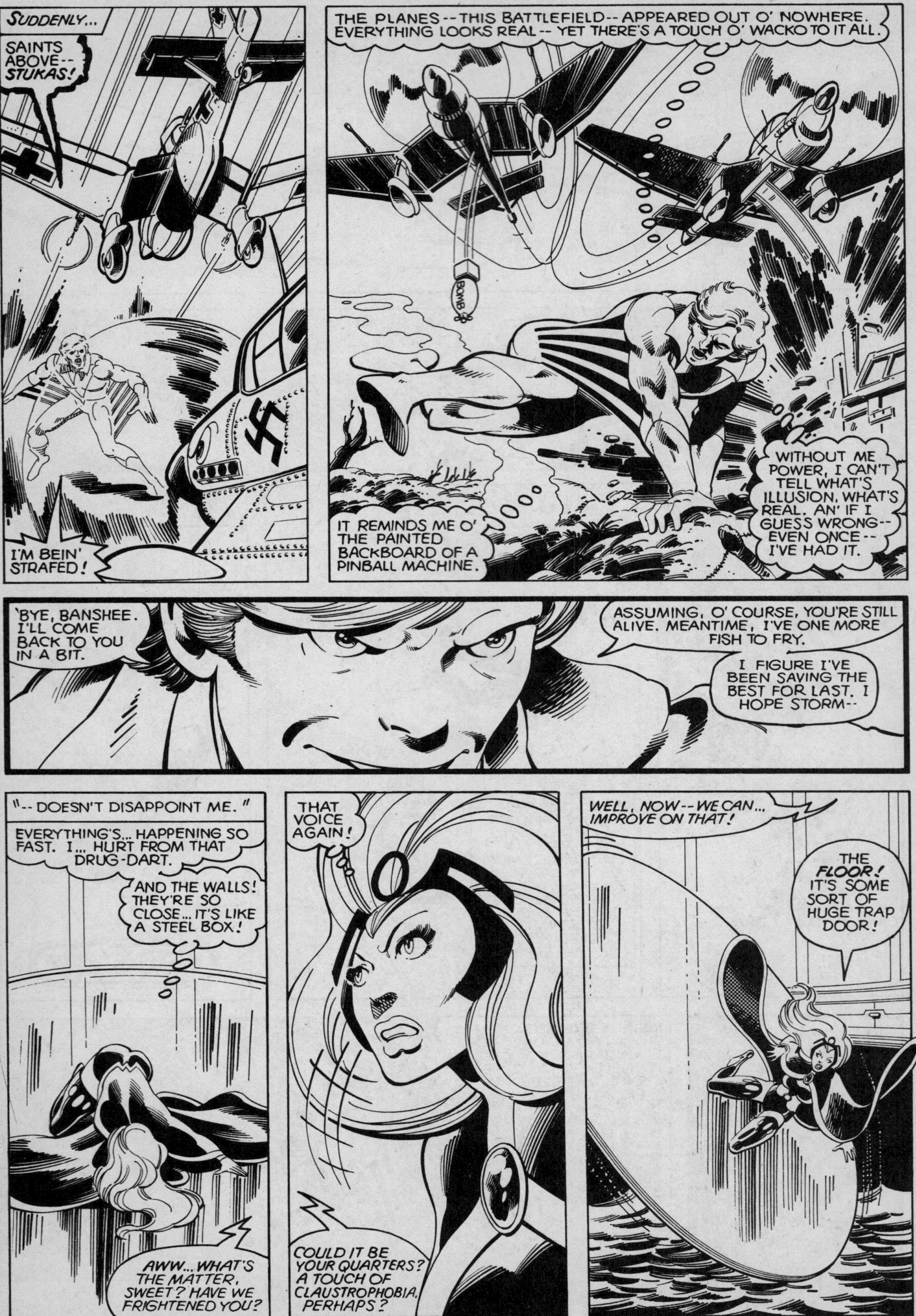

SUDDENLY...
SAINTS ABOVE-- STUKAS!
I'M BEIN' STRAFED!
THE PLANES--THIS BATTLEFIELD--APPEARED OUT O' NOWHERE. EVERYTHING LOOKS REAL--YET THERE'S A TOUCH O' WACKO TO IT ALL.
BOMB
IT REMINDS ME O' THE PAINTED BACKBOARD OF A PINBALL MACHINE.
WITHOUT ME POWER, I CAN'T TELL WHAT'S ILLUSION, WHAT'S REAL. AN' IF I GUESS WRONG--EVEN ONCE--I'VE HAD IT.
'BYE, BANSHEE. I'LL COME BACK TO YOU IN A BIT.
ASSUMING, O' COURSE, YOU'RE STILL ALIVE. MEANTIME, I'VE ONE MORE FISH TO FRY.
I FIGURE I'VE BEEN SAVING THE BEST FOR LAST. I HOPE STORM--
"--DOESN'T DISAPPOINT ME."
EVERYTHING'S... HAPPENING SO FAST. I... HURT FROM THAT DRUG-DART.
AND THE WALLS! THEY'RE SO CLOSE... IT'S LIKE A STEEL BOX!
AWW...WHAT'S THE MATTER, SWEET? HAVE WE FRIGHTENED YOU?
THAT VOICE AGAIN!
COULD IT BE YOUR QUARTERS? A TOUCH OF CLAUSTROPHOBIA, PERHAPS?
WELL, NOW--WE CAN... IMPROVE ON THAT!
THE FLOOR! IT'S SOME SORT OF HUGE TRAP DOOR!

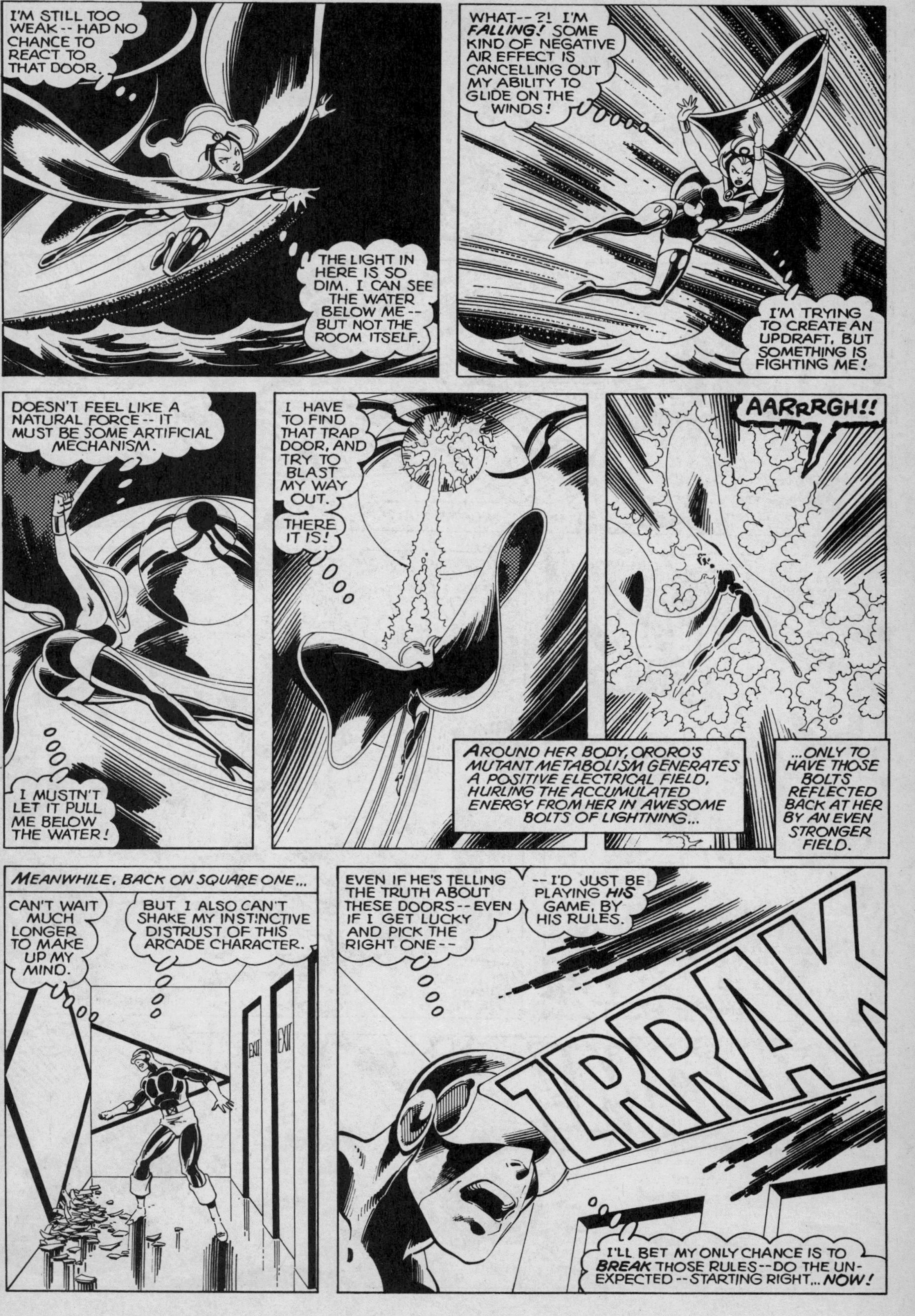
I'M STILL TOO WEAK -- HAD NO CHANCE TO REACT TO THAT DOOR.
THE LIGHT IN HERE IS SO DIM. I CAN SEE THE WATER BELOW ME -- BUT NOT THE ROOM ITSELF.
WHAT--?! I'M FALLING! SOME KIND OF NEGATIVE AIR EFFECT IS CANCELLING OUT MY ABILITY TO GLIDE ON THE WINDS!
I'M TRYING TO CREATE AN UPDRAFT, BUT SOMETHING IS FIGHTING ME!
DOESN'T FEEL LIKE A NATURAL FORCE -- IT MUST BE SOME ARTIFICIAL MECHANISM.
I MUSTN'T LET IT PULL ME BELOW THE WATER!
I HAVE TO FIND THAT TRAP DOOR, AND TRY TO BLAST MY WAY OUT.
THERE IT IS!
AARRRGH!!
AROUND HER BODY, ORORO'S MUTANT METABOLISM GENERATES A POSITIVE ELECTRICAL FIELD, HURLING THE ACCUMULATED ENERGY FROM HER IN AWESOME BOLTS OF LIGHTNING...
...ONLY TO HAVE THOSE BOLTS REFLECTED BACK AT HER BY AN EVEN STRONGER FIELD.
MEANWHILE, BACK ON SQUARE ONE...
CAN'T WAIT MUCH LONGER TO MAKE UP MY MIND.
BUT I ALSO CAN'T SHAKE MY INSTINCTIVE DISTRUST OF THIS ARCADE CHARACTER.
EXIT
EXIT
EVEN IF HE'S TELLING THE TRUTH ABOUT THESE DOORS -- EVEN IF I GET LUCKY AND PICK THE RIGHT ONE --
-- I'D JUST BE PLAYING HIS GAME, BY HIS RULES.
ZRRAK
I'LL BET MY ONLY CHANCE IS TO BREAK THOSE RULES -- DO THE UN-EXPECTED -- STARTING RIGHT... NOW!

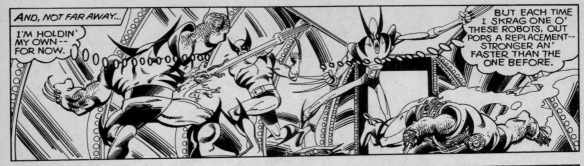

AND, NOT FAR AWAY...

I'M HOLDIN' MY OWN-- FOR NOW.

BUT EACH TIME I SKRAG ONE O' THESE ROBOTS, OUT POPS A REPLACEMENT-- STRONGER AN' FASTER THAN THE ONE BEFORE.

THEY'RE WORKIN' AS A TEAM, TOO-- HEMMIN' ME IN, KEEPIN' ME FROM SMASHIN' THE MIRRORS OR REACHIN' THE EXIT, WEARIN' ME DOWN!

SHZZKOW!

HUH--?! WHAT'S THAT?!

CYKE! I HATE TA SAY IT, BOSS, BUT FOR ONCE, I'M GLAD TA SEE YA.

LIKEWISE, WOLVERINE. YOU OKAY?

YUP.

YOUR OPTIC BLAST MUST'A ZAPPED THE MACHINERY-- THESE FLAKEY MIRRORS HAVE STOPPED GROWIN' ROBOTS. WHICH IS JUST FINE WITH ME.

C'MON. LET'S MAKE TRACKS BEFORE THIS FREAKED-OUT FUN HOUSE POPS ANY MORE SURPRISES.

WOLVERINE-- AHEAD OF YOU! SOMEONE'S IN THE SHADOWS!

NO SWEAT, I ALREADY GOT HIS SCENT. IT'S--

--UNNNGNH!!

KROM!

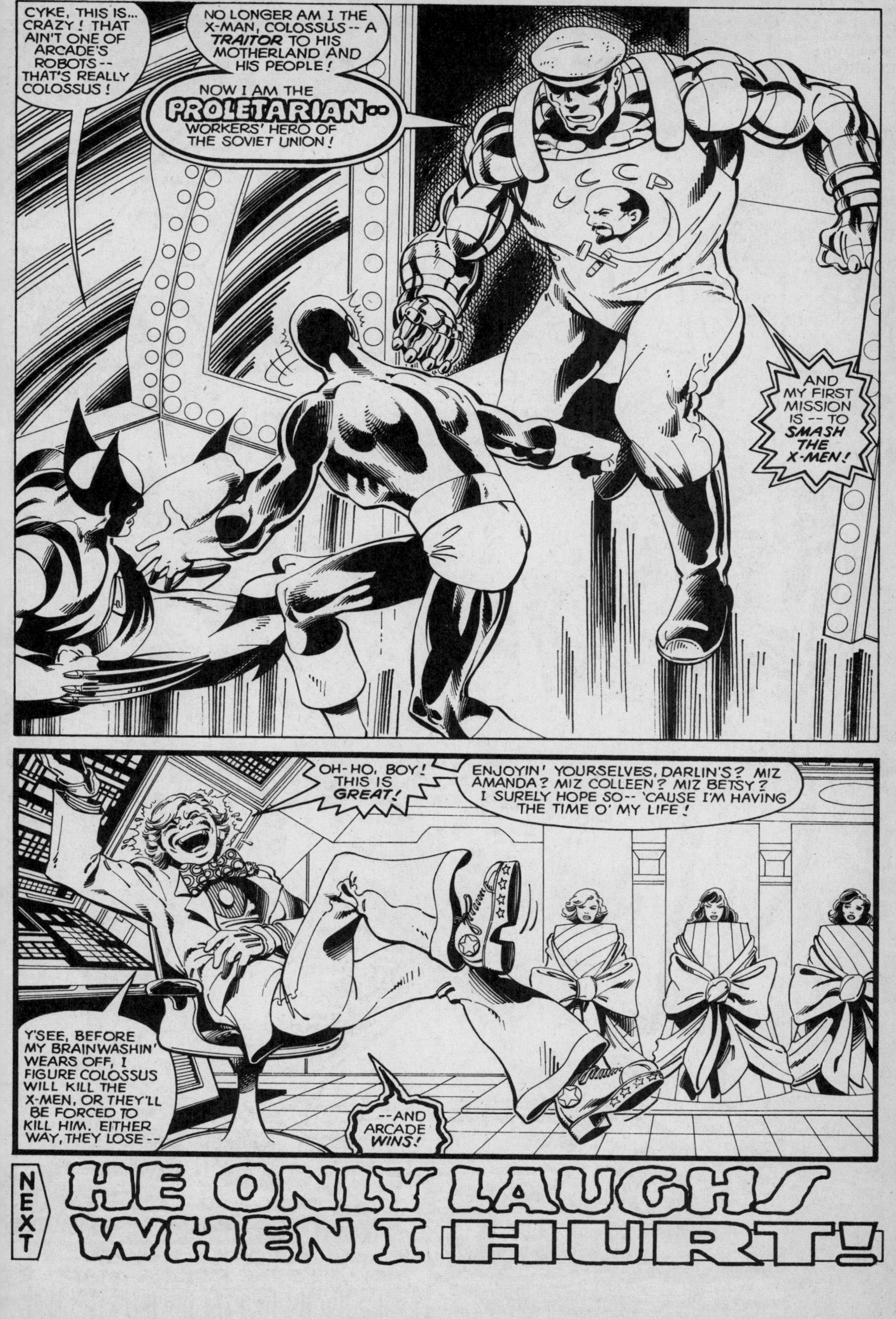
CYKE, THIS IS... CRAZY! THAT AIN'T ONE OF ARCADE'S ROBOTS -- THAT'S REALLY COLOSSUS!
NO LONGER AM I THE X-MAN, COLOSSUS -- A TRAITOR TO HIS MOTHERLAND AND HIS PEOPLE!
NOW I AM THE PROLETARIAN -- WORKERS' HERO OF THE SOVIET UNION!
AND MY FIRST MISSION IS -- TO SMASH THE X-MEN!
CCCP
OH-HO, BOY! THIS IS GREAT!
ENJOYIN' YOURSELVES, DARLIN'S? MIZ AMANDA? MIZ COLLEEN? MIZ BETSY? I SURELY HOPE SO-- 'CAUSE I'M HAVING THE TIME O' MY LIFE!
Y'SEE, BEFORE MY BRAINWASHIN' WEARS OFF, I FIGURE COLOSSUS WILL KILL THE X-MEN, OR THEY'LL BE FORCED TO KILL HIM. EITHER WAY, THEY LOSE --
--AND ARCADE WINS!

NEXT: HE ONLY LAUGHS WHEN I HURT!

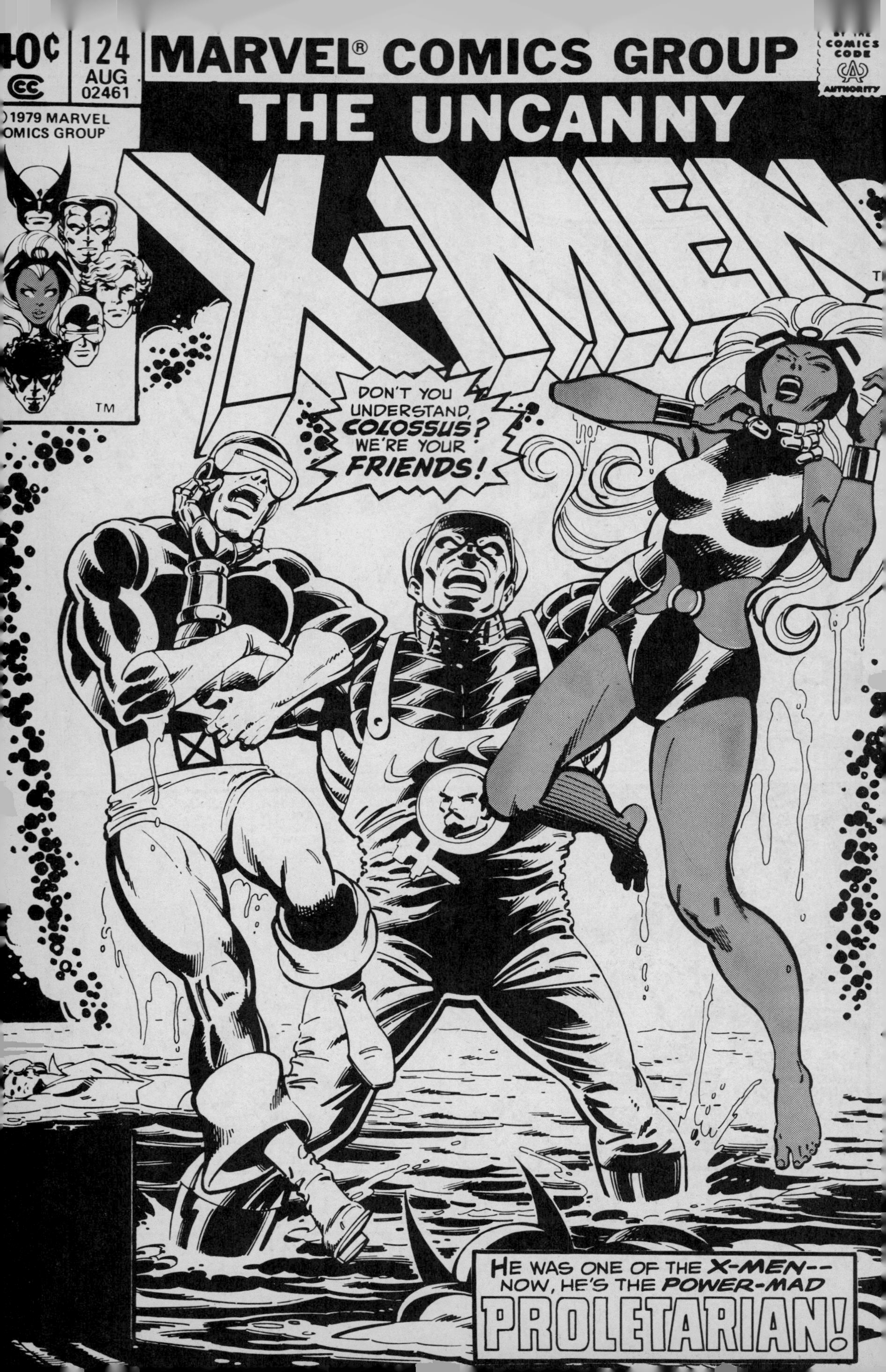

40¢
124
AUG
02461
MARVEL® COMICS GROUP
APPROVED BY THE COMICS CODE AUTHORITY
©1979 MARVEL COMICS GROUP
THE UNCANNY
X-MEN
DON'T YOU UNDERSTAND, COLOSSUS? WE'RE YOUR FRIENDS!
HE WAS ONE OF THE X-MEN-- NOW, HE'S THE POWER-MAD
PROLETARIAN!

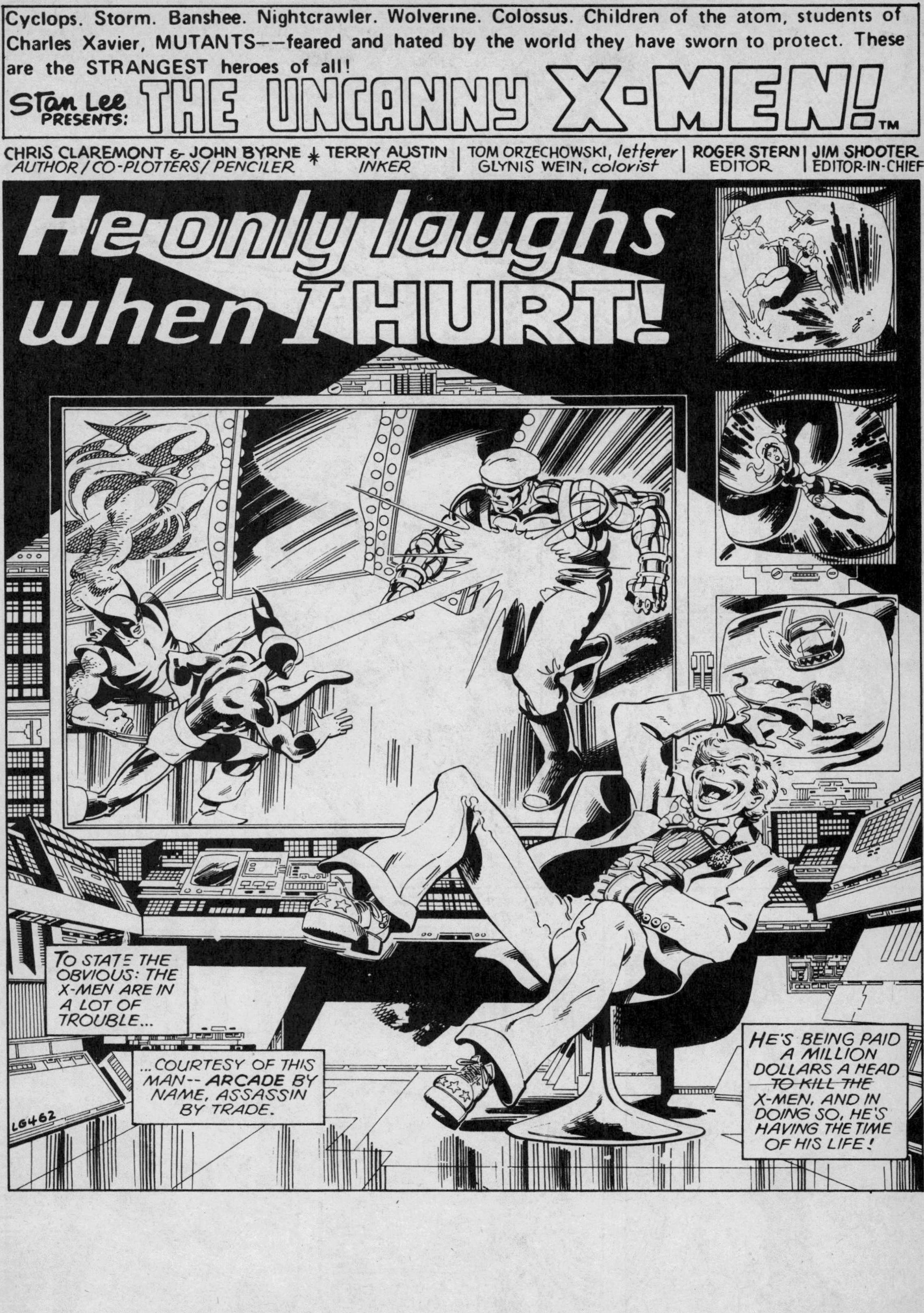

Cyclops. Storm. Banshee. Nightcrawler. Wolverine. Colossus. Children of the atom, students of Charles Xavier, MUTANTS--feared and hated by the world they have sworn to protect. These are the STRANGEST heroes of all!
Stan Lee PRESENTS: THE UNCANNY X-MEN!™
CHRIS CLAREMONT & JOHN BYRNE AUTHOR/CO-PLOTTERS/PENCILER ✱ TERRY AUSTIN INKER | TOM ORZECHOWSKI, letterer GLYNIS WEIN, colorist | ROGER STERN EDITOR | JIM SHOOTER EDITOR-IN-CHIEF
He only laughs when I HURT!
TO STATE THE OBVIOUS: THE X-MEN ARE IN A LOT OF TROUBLE...
...COURTESY OF THIS MAN-- ARCADE BY NAME, ASSASSIN BY TRADE.
HE'S BEING PAID A MILLION DOLLARS A HEAD TO KILL THE X-MEN, AND IN DOING SO, HE'S HAVING THE TIME OF HIS LIFE!
LG462

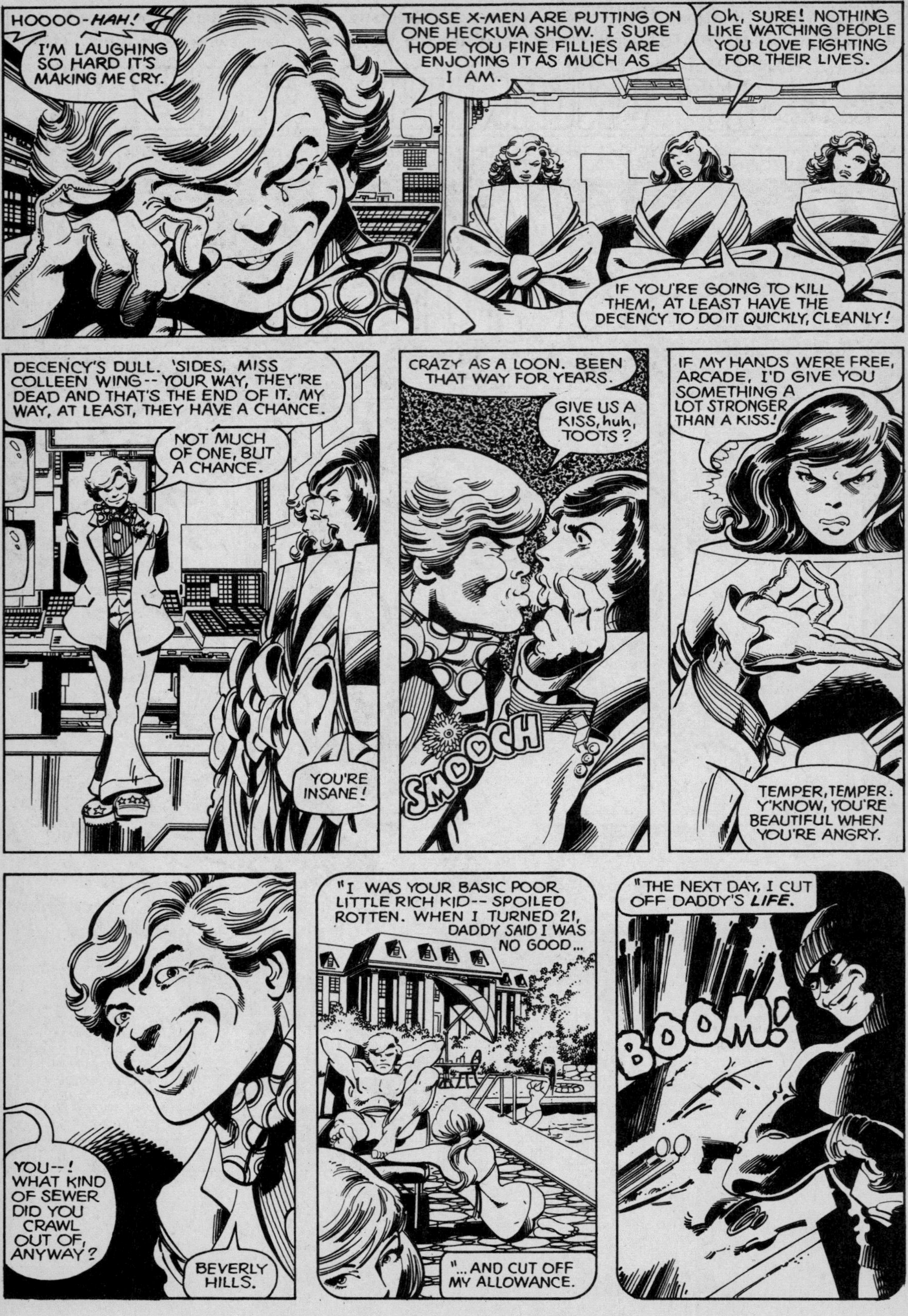
HOOOO-*HAH!*
I'M LAUGHING SO HARD IT'S MAKING ME CRY.
THOSE X-MEN ARE PUTTING ON ONE HECKUVA SHOW. I SURE HOPE YOU FINE FILLIES ARE ENJOYING IT AS MUCH AS I AM.
Oh, SURE! NOTHING LIKE WATCHING PEOPLE YOU LOVE FIGHTING FOR THEIR LIVES.
IF YOU'RE GOING TO KILL THEM, AT LEAST HAVE THE DECENCY TO DO IT QUICKLY, CLEANLY!
DECENCY'S DULL. 'SIDES, MISS COLLEEN WING -- YOUR WAY, THEY'RE DEAD AND THAT'S THE END OF IT. MY WAY, AT LEAST, THEY HAVE A CHANCE.
NOT MUCH OF ONE, BUT A CHANCE.
YOU'RE INSANE!
CRAZY AS A LOON. BEEN THAT WAY FOR YEARS.
GIVE US A KISS, huh, TOOTS?
SMOOCH
IF MY HANDS WERE FREE, ARCADE, I'D GIVE YOU SOMETHING A LOT STRONGER THAN A KISS!
TEMPER, TEMPER. Y'KNOW, YOU'RE BEAUTIFUL WHEN YOU'RE ANGRY.
YOU--! WHAT KIND OF SEWER DID YOU CRAWL OUT OF, ANYWAY?
BEVERLY HILLS.
"I WAS YOUR BASIC POOR LITTLE RICH KID-- SPOILED ROTTEN. WHEN I TURNED 21, DADDY SAID I WAS NO GOOD...
"...AND CUT OFF MY ALLOWANCE.
"THE NEXT DAY, I CUT OFF DADDY'S *LIFE*.
BOOM!

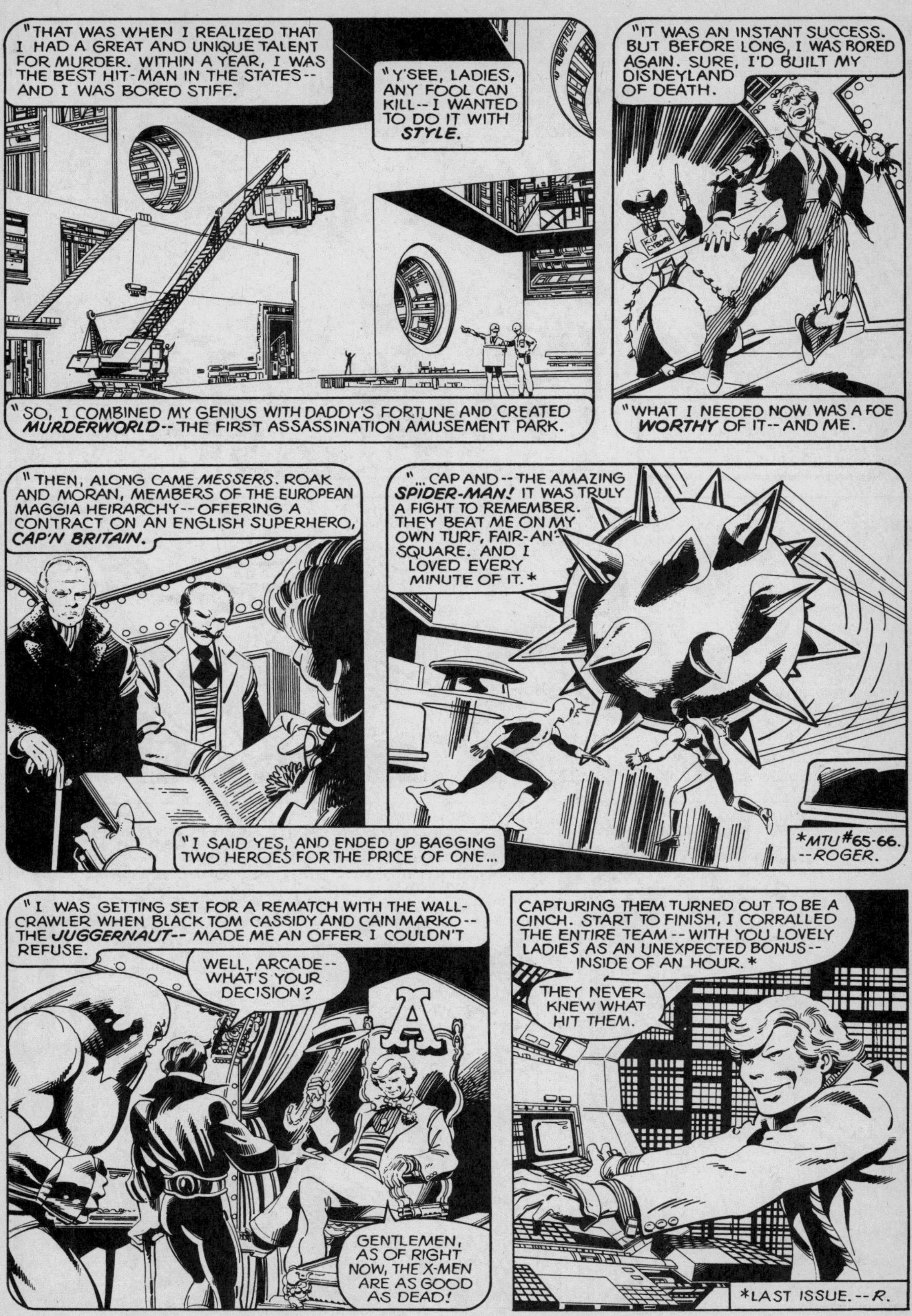
"THAT WAS WHEN I REALIZED THAT I HAD A GREAT AND UNIQUE TALENT FOR MURDER. WITHIN A YEAR, I WAS THE BEST HIT-MAN IN THE STATES-- AND I WAS BORED STIFF.
"Y'SEE, LADIES, ANY FOOL CAN KILL--I WANTED TO DO IT WITH STYLE.
"SO, I COMBINED MY GENIUS WITH DADDY'S FORTUNE AND CREATED MURDERWORLD-- THE FIRST ASSASSINATION AMUSEMENT PARK.
"IT WAS AN INSTANT SUCCESS. BUT BEFORE LONG, I WAS BORED AGAIN. SURE, I'D BUILT MY DISNEYLAND OF DEATH.
KID CYBORG
"WHAT I NEEDED NOW WAS A FOE WORTHY OF IT--AND ME.
"THEN, ALONG CAME MESSERS. ROAK AND MORAN, MEMBERS OF THE EUROPEAN MAGGIA HEIRARCHY--OFFERING A CONTRACT ON AN ENGLISH SUPERHERO, CAP'N BRITAIN.
"I SAID YES, AND ENDED UP BAGGING TWO HEROES FOR THE PRICE OF ONE...
"...CAP AND--THE AMAZING SPIDER-MAN! IT WAS TRULY A FIGHT TO REMEMBER. THEY BEAT ME ON MY OWN TURF, FAIR-AN'-SQUARE. AND I LOVED EVERY MINUTE OF IT.*
*MTU #65-66. --ROGER.
"I WAS GETTING SET FOR A REMATCH WITH THE WALL-CRAWLER WHEN BLACK TOM CASSIDY AND CAIN MARKO-- THE JUGGERNAUT-- MADE ME AN OFFER I COULDN'T REFUSE.
WELL, ARCADE-- WHAT'S YOUR DECISION?
A
GENTLEMEN, AS OF RIGHT NOW, THE X-MEN ARE AS GOOD AS DEAD!
CAPTURING THEM TURNED OUT TO BE A CINCH. START TO FINISH, I CORRALLED THE ENTIRE TEAM--WITH YOU LOVELY LADIES AS AN UNEXPECTED BONUS-- INSIDE OF AN HOUR.*
THEY NEVER KNEW WHAT HIT THEM.
*LAST ISSUE.--R.

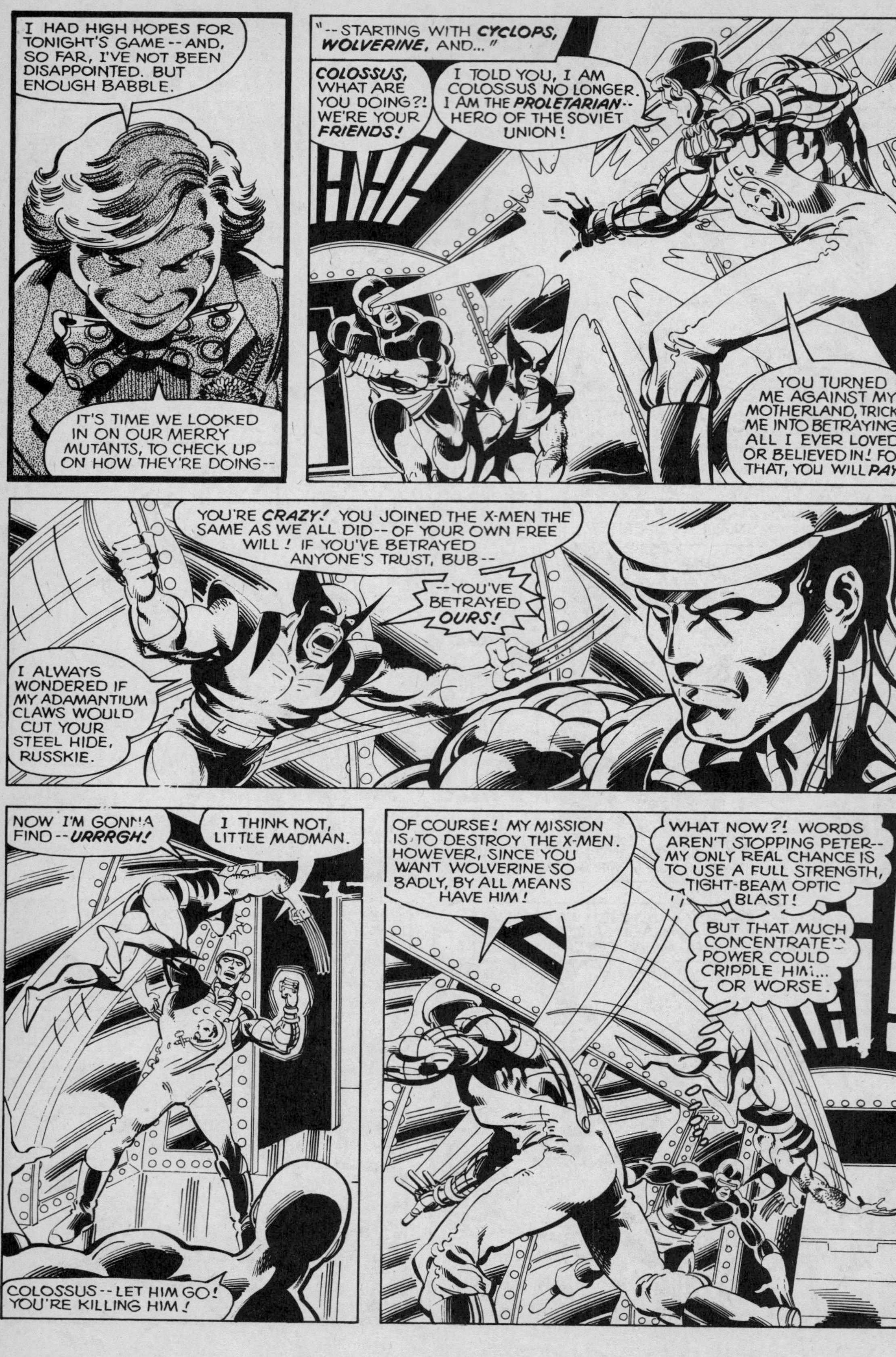
I HAD HIGH HOPES FOR TONIGHT'S GAME -- AND, SO FAR, I'VE NOT BEEN DISAPPOINTED. BUT ENOUGH BABBLE.
IT'S TIME WE LOOKED IN ON OUR MERRY MUTANTS, TO CHECK UP ON HOW THEY'RE DOING --
"-- STARTING WITH CYCLOPS, WOLVERINE, AND..."
COLOSSUS, WHAT ARE YOU DOING?! WE'RE YOUR FRIENDS!
I TOLD YOU, I AM COLOSSUS NO LONGER. I AM THE PROLETARIAN -- HERO OF THE SOVIET UNION!
YOU TURNED ME AGAINST MY MOTHERLAND, TRICKED ME INTO BETRAYING ALL I EVER LOVED OR BELIEVED IN! FOR THAT, YOU WILL PAY!
YOU'RE CRAZY! YOU JOINED THE X-MEN THE SAME AS WE ALL DID -- OF YOUR OWN FREE WILL! IF YOU'VE BETRAYED ANYONE'S TRUST, BUB --
-- YOU'VE BETRAYED OURS!
I ALWAYS WONDERED IF MY ADAMANTIUM CLAWS WOULD CUT YOUR STEEL HIDE, RUSSKIE.
NOW I'M GONNA FIND -- URRRGH!
I THINK NOT, LITTLE MADMAN.
COLOSSUS -- LET HIM GO! YOU'RE KILLING HIM!
OF COURSE! MY MISSION IS TO DESTROY THE X-MEN. HOWEVER, SINCE YOU WANT WOLVERINE SO BADLY, BY ALL MEANS HAVE HIM!
WHAT NOW?! WORDS AREN'T STOPPING PETER -- MY ONLY REAL CHANCE IS TO USE A FULL STRENGTH, TIGHT-BEAM OPTIC BLAST!
BUT THAT MUCH CONCENTRATED POWER COULD CRIPPLE HIM... OR WORSE.

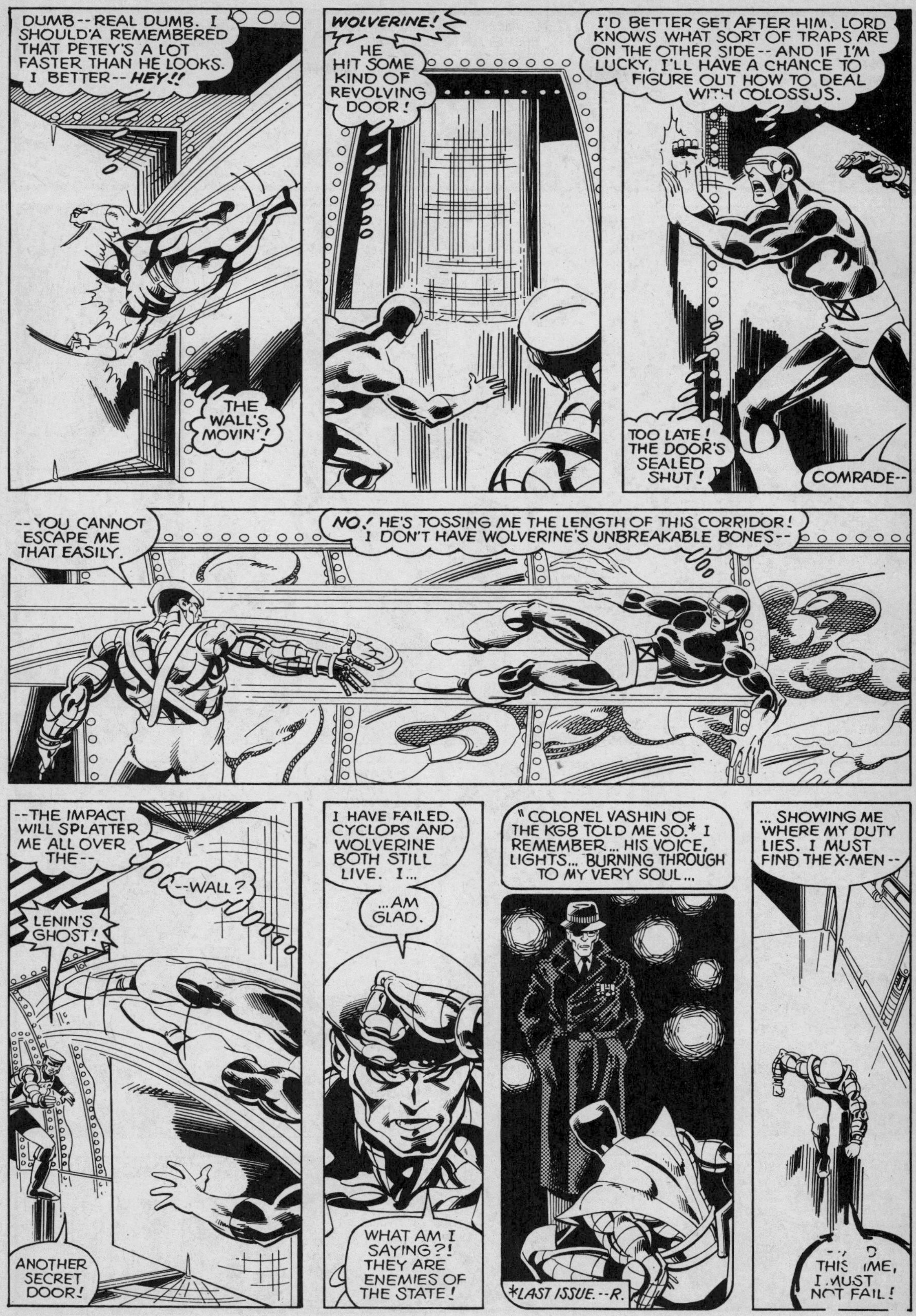
DUMB -- REAL DUMB. I SHOULD'A REMEMBERED THAT PETEY'S A LOT FASTER THAN HE LOOKS. I BETTER-- HEY!!
THE WALL'S MOVIN'!
WOLVERINE!
HE HIT SOME KIND OF REVOLVING DOOR!
I'D BETTER GET AFTER HIM. LORD KNOWS WHAT SORT OF TRAPS ARE ON THE OTHER SIDE -- AND IF I'M LUCKY, I'LL HAVE A CHANCE TO FIGURE OUT HOW TO DEAL WITH COLOSSUS.
TOO LATE! THE DOOR'S SEALED SHUT!
COMRADE--
-- YOU CANNOT ESCAPE ME THAT EASILY.
NO! HE'S TOSSING ME THE LENGTH OF THIS CORRIDOR! I DON'T HAVE WOLVERINE'S UNBREAKABLE BONES--
-- THE IMPACT WILL SPLATTER ME ALL OVER THE--
-- WALL?
LENIN'S GHOST!
ANOTHER SECRET DOOR!
I HAVE FAILED. CYCLOPS AND WOLVERINE BOTH STILL LIVE. I...
...AM GLAD.
WHAT AM I SAYING?! THEY ARE ENEMIES OF THE STATE!
"COLONEL VASHIN OF THE KGB TOLD ME SO.* I REMEMBER... HIS VOICE, LIGHTS... BURNING THROUGH TO MY VERY SOUL...
*LAST ISSUE. --R.
... SHOWING ME WHERE MY DUTY LIES. I MUST FIND THE X-MEN --
I MUST NOT FAIL!

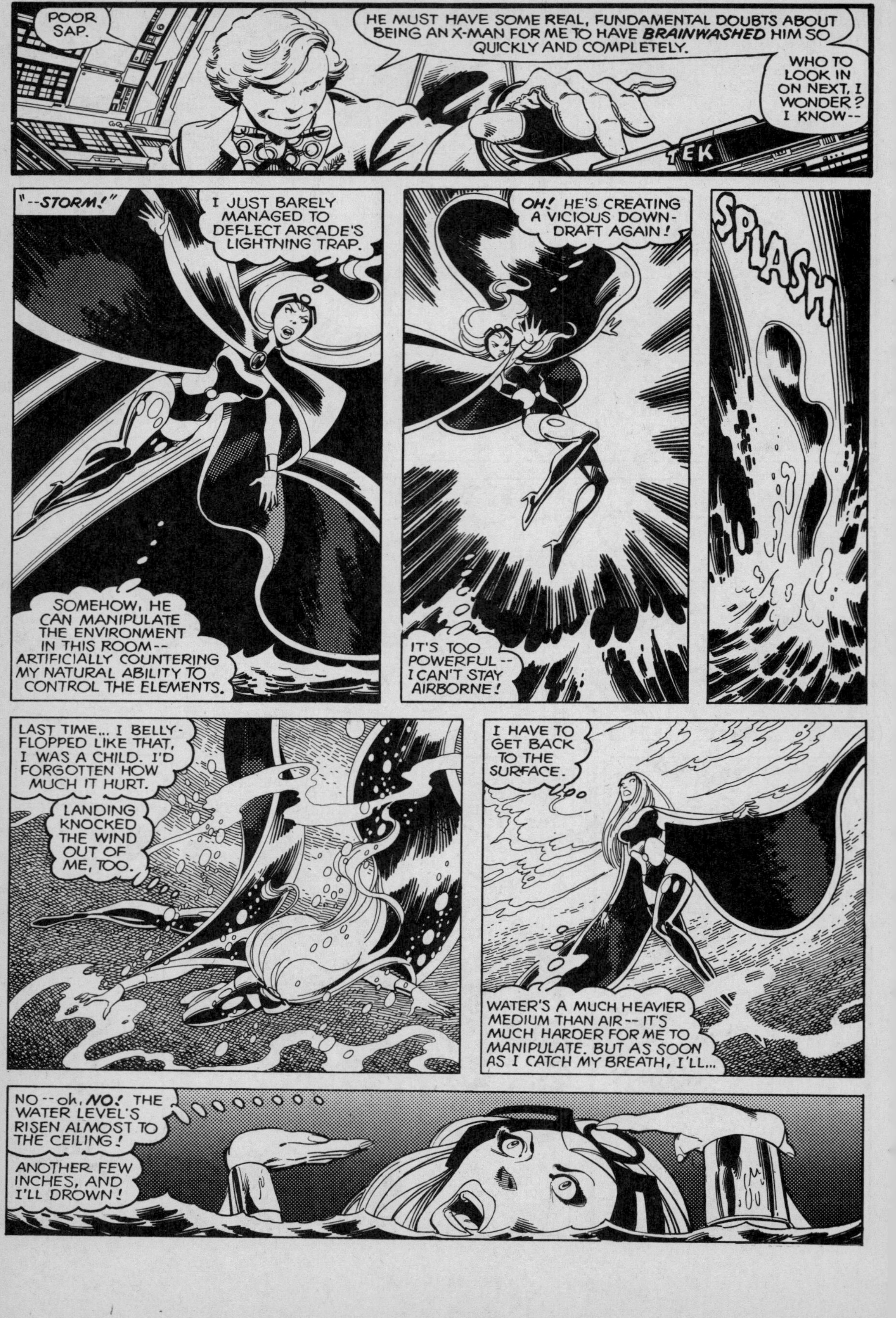
POOR SAP.
HE MUST HAVE SOME REAL, FUNDAMENTAL DOUBTS ABOUT BEING AN X-MAN FOR ME TO HAVE BRAINWASHED HIM SO QUICKLY AND COMPLETELY.
WHO TO LOOK IN ON NEXT, I WONDER? I KNOW--
TEK
"--STORM!"
I JUST BARELY MANAGED TO DEFLECT ARCADE'S LIGHTNING TRAP.
SOMEHOW, HE CAN MANIPULATE THE ENVIRONMENT IN THIS ROOM-- ARTIFICIALLY COUNTERING MY NATURAL ABILITY TO CONTROL THE ELEMENTS.
OH! HE'S CREATING A VICIOUS DOWN-DRAFT AGAIN!
IT'S TOO POWERFUL-- I CAN'T STAY AIRBORNE!
SPLASH
LAST TIME... I BELLY-FLOPPED LIKE THAT, I WAS A CHILD. I'D FORGOTTEN HOW MUCH IT HURT.
LANDING KNOCKED THE WIND OUT OF ME, TOO.
I HAVE TO GET BACK TO THE SURFACE.
WATER'S A MUCH HEAVIER MEDIUM THAN AIR-- IT'S MUCH HARDER FOR ME TO MANIPULATE. BUT AS SOON AS I CATCH MY BREATH, I'LL...
NO--oh, NO! THE WATER LEVEL'S RISEN ALMOST TO THE CEILING!
ANOTHER FEW INCHES, AND I'LL DROWN!

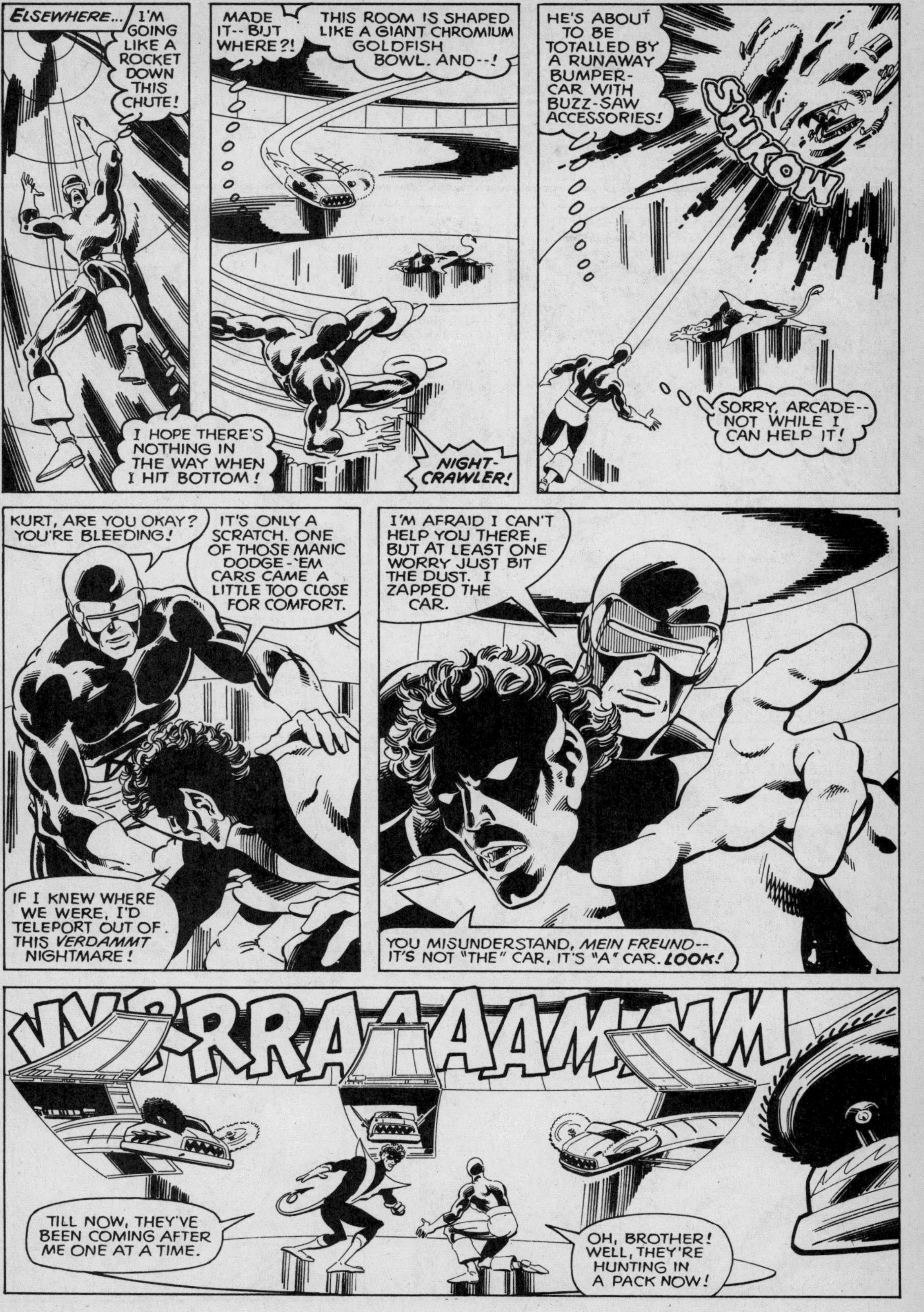
ELSEWHERE...
I'M GOING LIKE A ROCKET DOWN THIS CHUTE!
I HOPE THERE'S NOTHING IN THE WAY WHEN I HIT BOTTOM!
MADE IT-- BUT WHERE?!
THIS ROOM IS SHAPED LIKE A GIANT CHROMIUM GOLDFISH BOWL. AND--!
NIGHT-CRAWLER!
HE'S ABOUT TO BE TOTALLED BY A RUNAWAY BUMPER-CAR WITH BUZZ-SAW ACCESSORIES!
SHKOW
SORRY, ARCADE-- NOT WHILE I CAN HELP IT!
KURT, ARE YOU OKAY? YOU'RE BLEEDING!
IT'S ONLY A SCRATCH. ONE OF THOSE MANIC DODGE-'EM CARS CAME A LITTLE TOO CLOSE FOR COMFORT.
IF I KNEW WHERE WE WERE, I'D TELEPORT OUT OF THIS VERDAMMT NIGHTMARE!
I'M AFRAID I CAN'T HELP YOU THERE, BUT AT LEAST ONE WORRY JUST BIT THE DUST. I ZAPPED THE CAR.
YOU MISUNDERSTAND, MEIN FREUND-- IT'S NOT "THE" CAR, IT'S "A" CAR. LOOK!
VVRRRAAAAMMMM
TILL NOW, THEY'VE BEEN COMING AFTER ME ONE AT A TIME.
OH, BROTHER! WELL, THEY'RE HUNTING IN A PACK NOW!

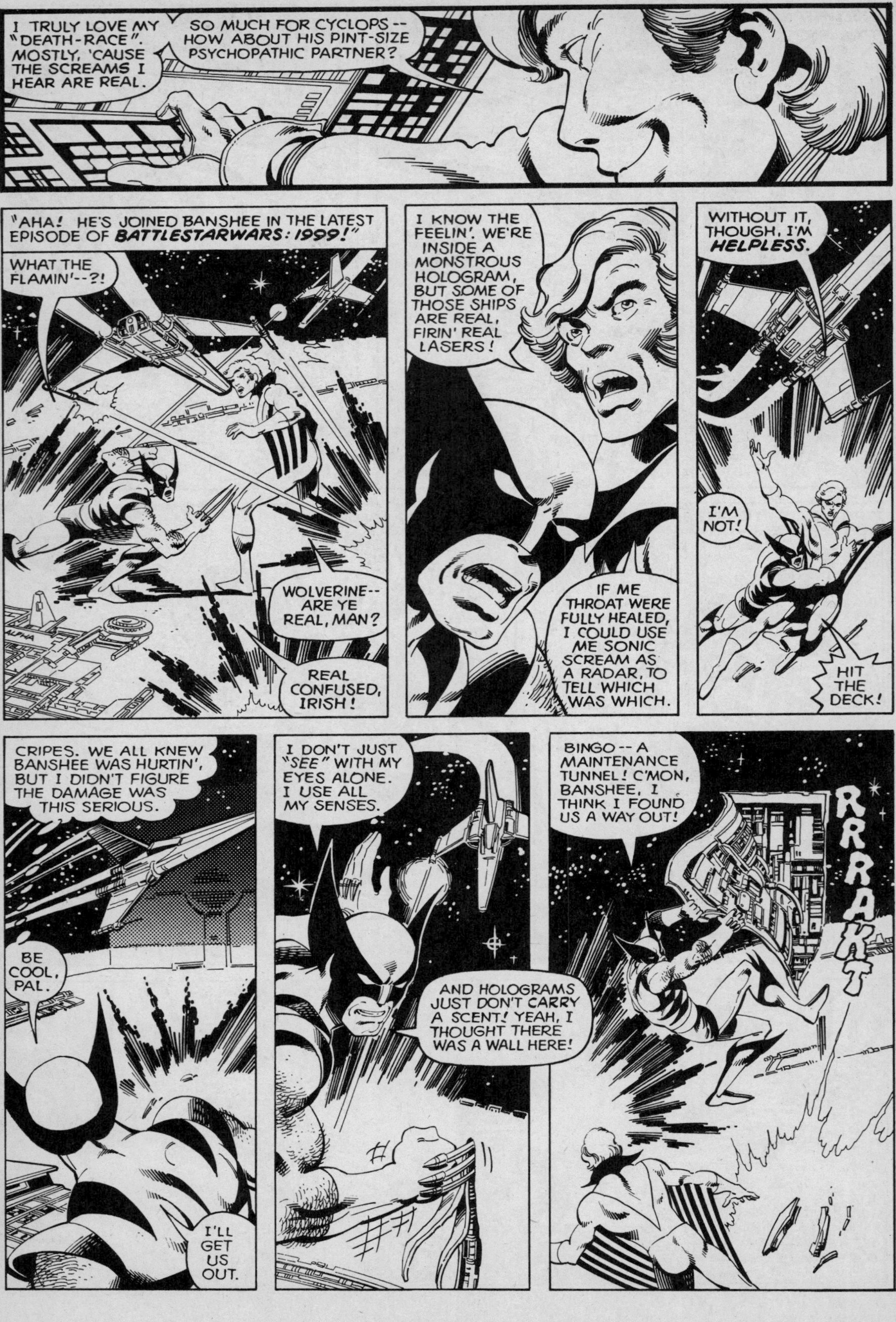
I TRULY LOVE MY "DEATH-RACE". MOSTLY, 'CAUSE THE SCREAMS I HEAR ARE REAL.
SO MUCH FOR CYCLOPS -- HOW ABOUT HIS PINT-SIZE PSYCHOPATHIC PARTNER?
"AHA! HE'S JOINED BANSHEE IN THE LATEST EPISODE OF BATTLESTARWARS: 1999!"
WHAT THE FLAMIN'--?!
WOLVERINE-- ARE YE REAL, MAN?
REAL CONFUSED, IRISH!
I KNOW THE FEELIN'. WE'RE INSIDE A MONSTROUS HOLOGRAM, BUT SOME OF THOSE SHIPS ARE REAL, FIRIN' REAL LASERS!
IF ME THROAT WERE FULLY HEALED, I COULD USE ME SONIC SCREAM AS A RADAR, TO TELL WHICH WAS WHICH.
WITHOUT IT, THOUGH, I'M HELPLESS.
I'M NOT!
HIT THE DECK!
CRIPES. WE ALL KNEW BANSHEE WAS HURTIN', BUT I DIDN'T FIGURE THE DAMAGE WAS THIS SERIOUS.
BE COOL, PAL.
I'LL GET US OUT.
I DON'T JUST "SEE" WITH MY EYES ALONE. I USE ALL MY SENSES.
AND HOLOGRAMS JUST DON'T CARRY A SCENT! YEAH, I THOUGHT THERE WAS A WALL HERE!
BINGO -- A MAINTENANCE TUNNEL! C'MON, BANSHEE, I THINK I FOUND US A WAY OUT!
RRRAKT

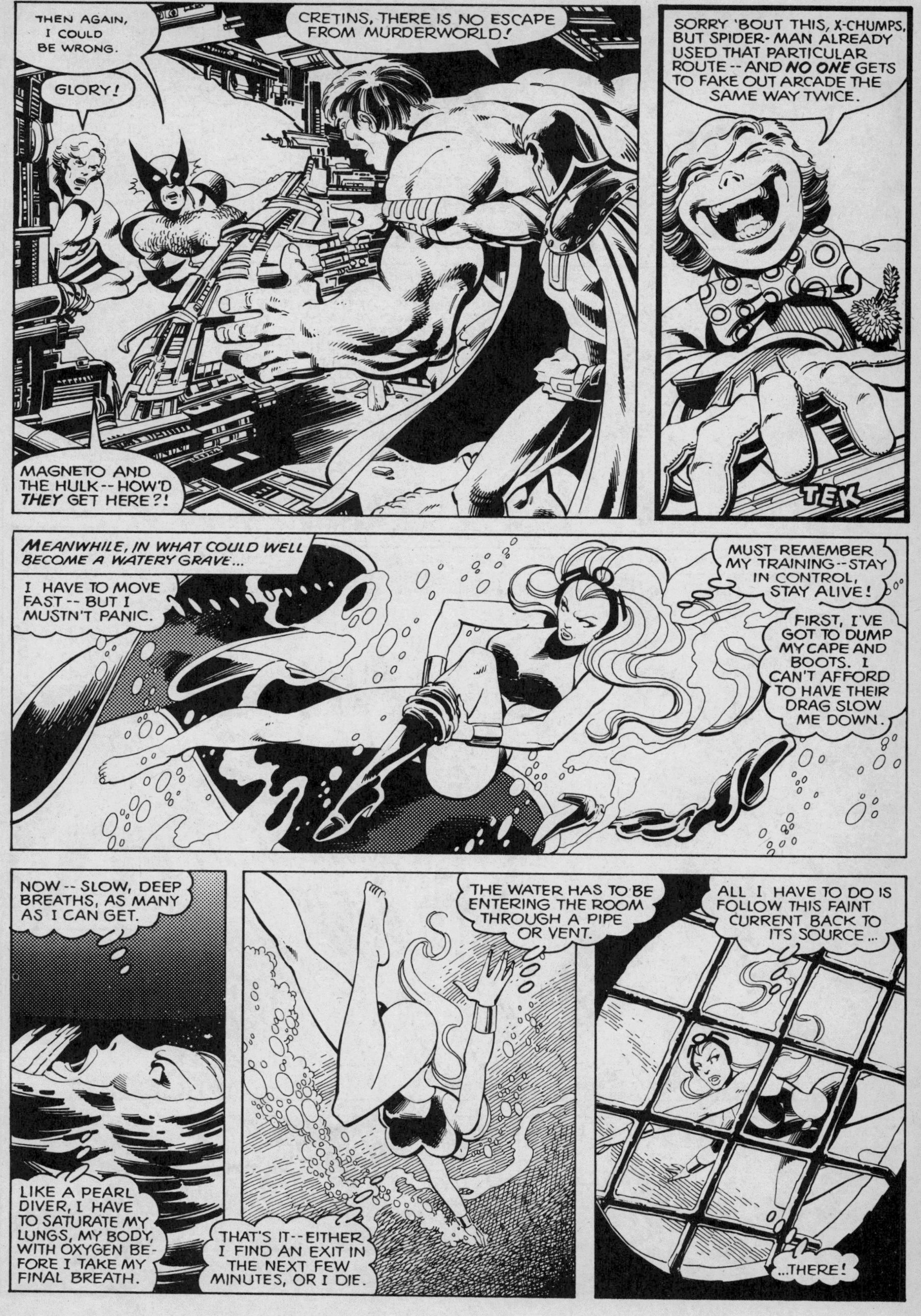

THEN AGAIN, I COULD BE WRONG.
GLORY!
CRETINS, THERE IS NO ESCAPE FROM MURDERWORLD!
MAGNETO AND THE HULK -- HOW'D THEY GET HERE?!
SORRY 'BOUT THIS, X-CHUMPS, BUT SPIDER-MAN ALREADY USED THAT PARTICULAR ROUTE -- AND NO ONE GETS TO FAKE OUT ARCADE THE SAME WAY TWICE.
TEK
MEANWHILE, IN WHAT COULD WELL BECOME A WATERY GRAVE...
I HAVE TO MOVE FAST -- BUT I MUSTN'T PANIC.
MUST REMEMBER MY TRAINING -- STAY IN CONTROL, STAY ALIVE!
FIRST, I'VE GOT TO DUMP MY CAPE AND BOOTS. I CAN'T AFFORD TO HAVE THEIR DRAG SLOW ME DOWN.
NOW -- SLOW, DEEP BREATHS, AS MANY AS I CAN GET.
LIKE A PEARL DIVER, I HAVE TO SATURATE MY LUNGS, MY BODY, WITH OXYGEN BEFORE I TAKE MY FINAL BREATH.
THE WATER HAS TO BE ENTERING THE ROOM THROUGH A PIPE OR VENT.
THAT'S IT -- EITHER I FIND AN EXIT IN THE NEXT FEW MINUTES, OR I DIE.
ALL I HAVE TO DO IS FOLLOW THIS FAINT CURRENT BACK TO ITS SOURCE...
...THERE!

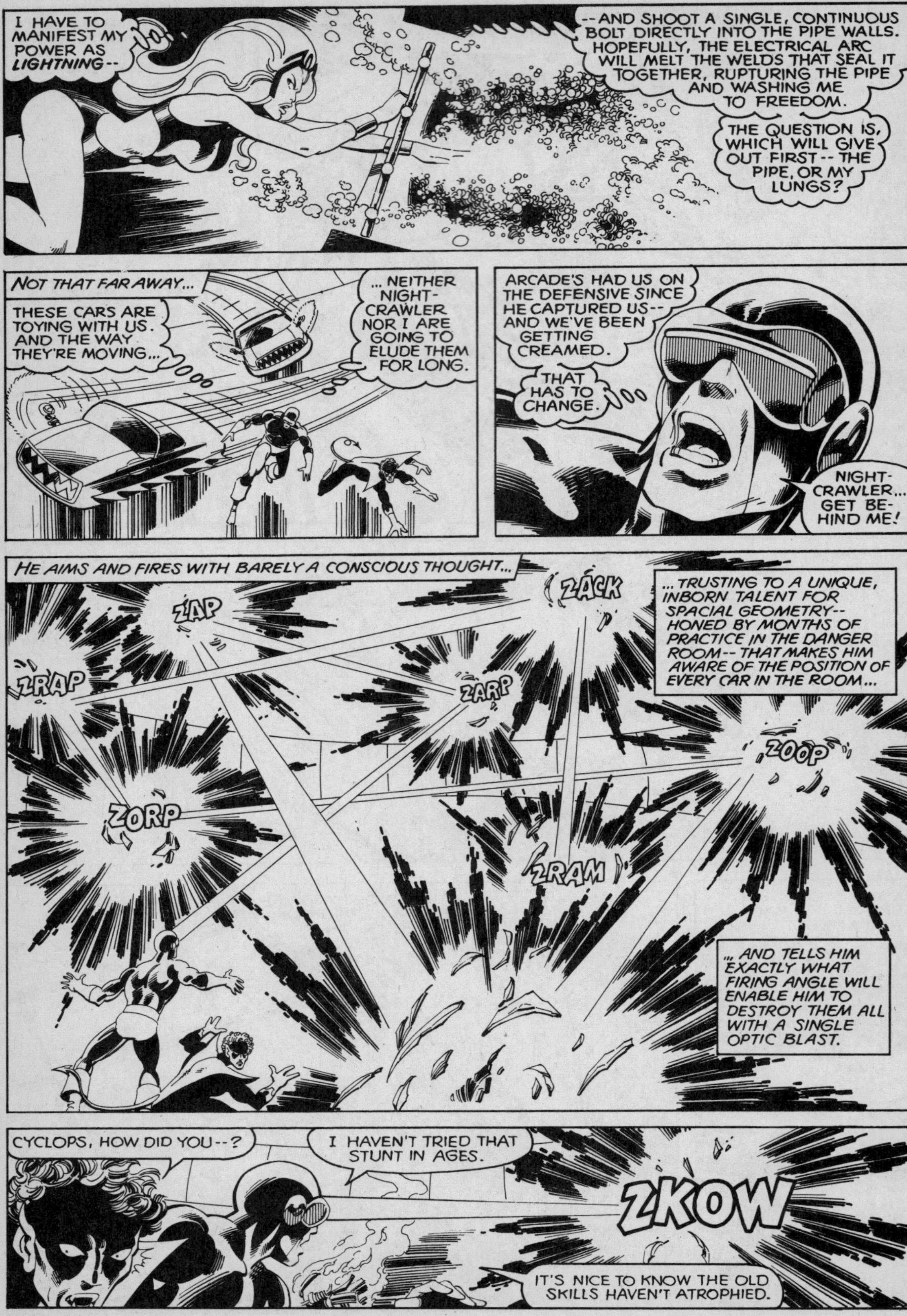

I HAVE TO MANIFEST MY POWER AS LIGHTNING--
--AND SHOOT A SINGLE, CONTINUOUS BOLT DIRECTLY INTO THE PIPE WALLS. HOPEFULLY, THE ELECTRICAL ARC WILL MELT THE WELDS THAT SEAL IT TOGETHER, RUPTURING THE PIPE AND WASHING ME TO FREEDOM.
THE QUESTION IS, WHICH WILL GIVE OUT FIRST -- THE PIPE, OR MY LUNGS?
NOT THAT FAR AWAY...
THESE CARS ARE TOYING WITH US. AND THE WAY THEY'RE MOVING...
... NEITHER NIGHT-CRAWLER NOR I ARE GOING TO ELUDE THEM FOR LONG.
ARCADE'S HAD US ON THE DEFENSIVE SINCE HE CAPTURED US-- AND WE'VE BEEN GETTING CREAMED.
THAT HAS TO CHANGE.
NIGHT-CRAWLER... GET BE-HIND ME!
HE AIMS AND FIRES WITH BARELY A CONSCIOUS THOUGHT...
...TRUSTING TO A UNIQUE, INBORN TALENT FOR SPACIAL GEOMETRY-- HONED BY MONTHS OF PRACTICE IN THE DANGER ROOM-- THAT MAKES HIM AWARE OF THE POSITION OF EVERY CAR IN THE ROOM...
ZAP
ZACK
ZRAP
ZARP
ZOOP
ZORP
ZRAM
... AND TELLS HIM EXACTLY WHAT FIRING ANGLE WILL ENABLE HIM TO DESTROY THEM ALL WITH A SINGLE OPTIC BLAST.
CYCLOPS, HOW DID YOU--?
I HAVEN'T TRIED THAT STUNT IN AGES.
ZKOW
IT'S NICE TO KNOW THE OLD SKILLS HAVEN'T ATROPHIED.

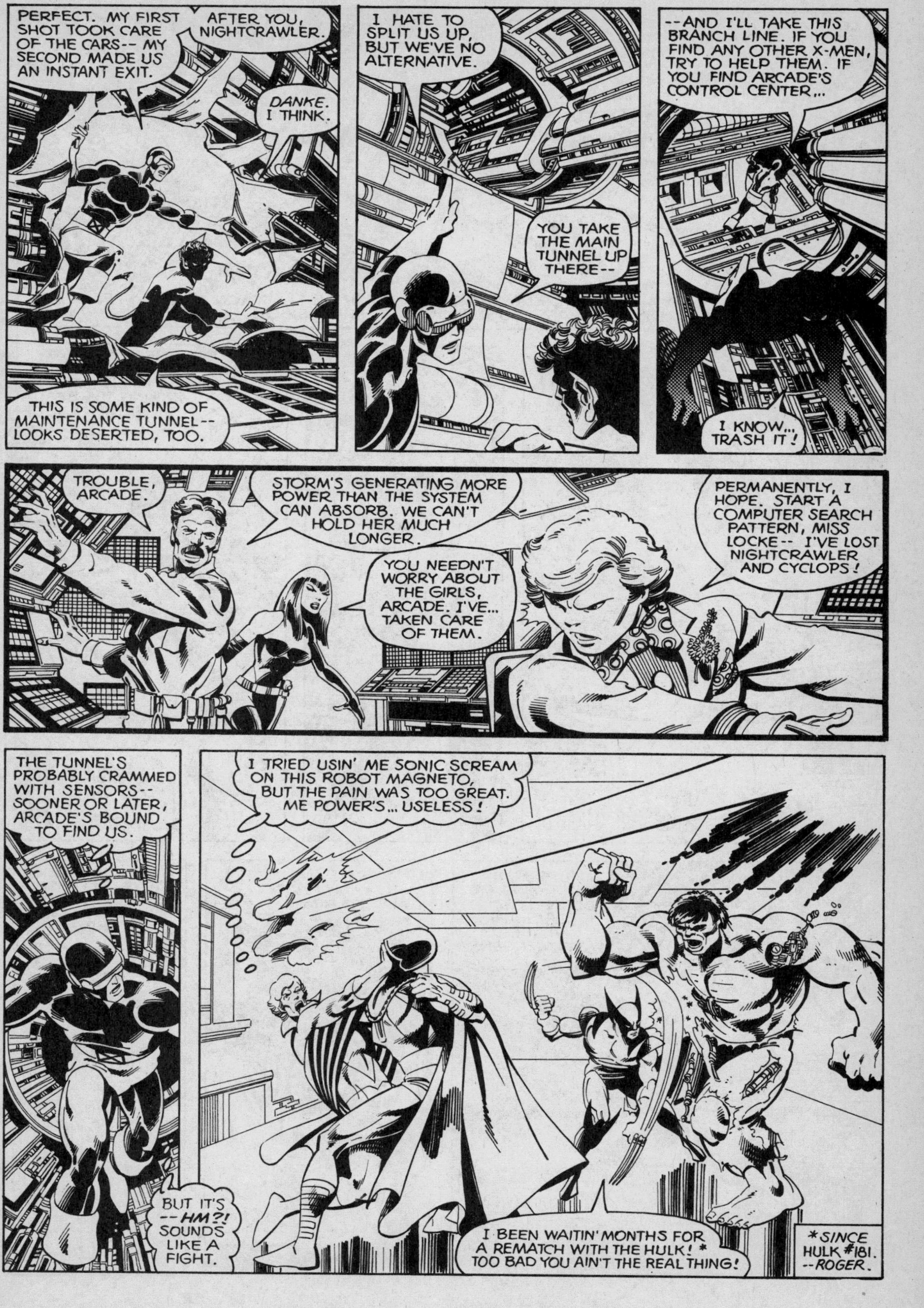
PERFECT. MY FIRST SHOT TOOK CARE OF THE CARS-- MY SECOND MADE US AN INSTANT EXIT.
AFTER YOU, NIGHTCRAWLER.
DANKE. I THINK.
THIS IS SOME KIND OF MAINTENANCE TUNNEL-- LOOKS DESERTED, TOO.
I HATE TO SPLIT US UP, BUT WE'VE NO ALTERNATIVE.
YOU TAKE THE MAIN TUNNEL UP THERE--
--AND I'LL TAKE THIS BRANCH LINE. IF YOU FIND ANY OTHER X-MEN, TRY TO HELP THEM. IF YOU FIND ARCADE'S CONTROL CENTER...
I KNOW... TRASH IT!
TROUBLE, ARCADE.
STORM'S GENERATING MORE POWER THAN THE SYSTEM CAN ABSORB. WE CAN'T HOLD HER MUCH LONGER.
YOU NEEDN'T WORRY ABOUT THE GIRLS, ARCADE. I'VE... TAKEN CARE OF THEM.
PERMANENTLY, I HOPE. START A COMPUTER SEARCH PATTERN, MISS LOCKE-- I'VE LOST NIGHTCRAWLER AND CYCLOPS!
THE TUNNEL'S PROBABLY CRAMMED WITH SENSORS-- SOONER OR LATER, ARCADE'S BOUND TO FIND US.
BUT IT'S --HM?! SOUNDS LIKE A FIGHT.
I TRIED USIN' ME SONIC SCREAM ON THIS ROBOT MAGNETO, BUT THE PAIN WAS TOO GREAT. ME POWER'S... USELESS!
I BEEN WAITIN' MONTHS FOR A REMATCH WITH THE HULK! * TOO BAD YOU AIN'T THE REAL THING!
*SINCE HULK #181. --ROGER.

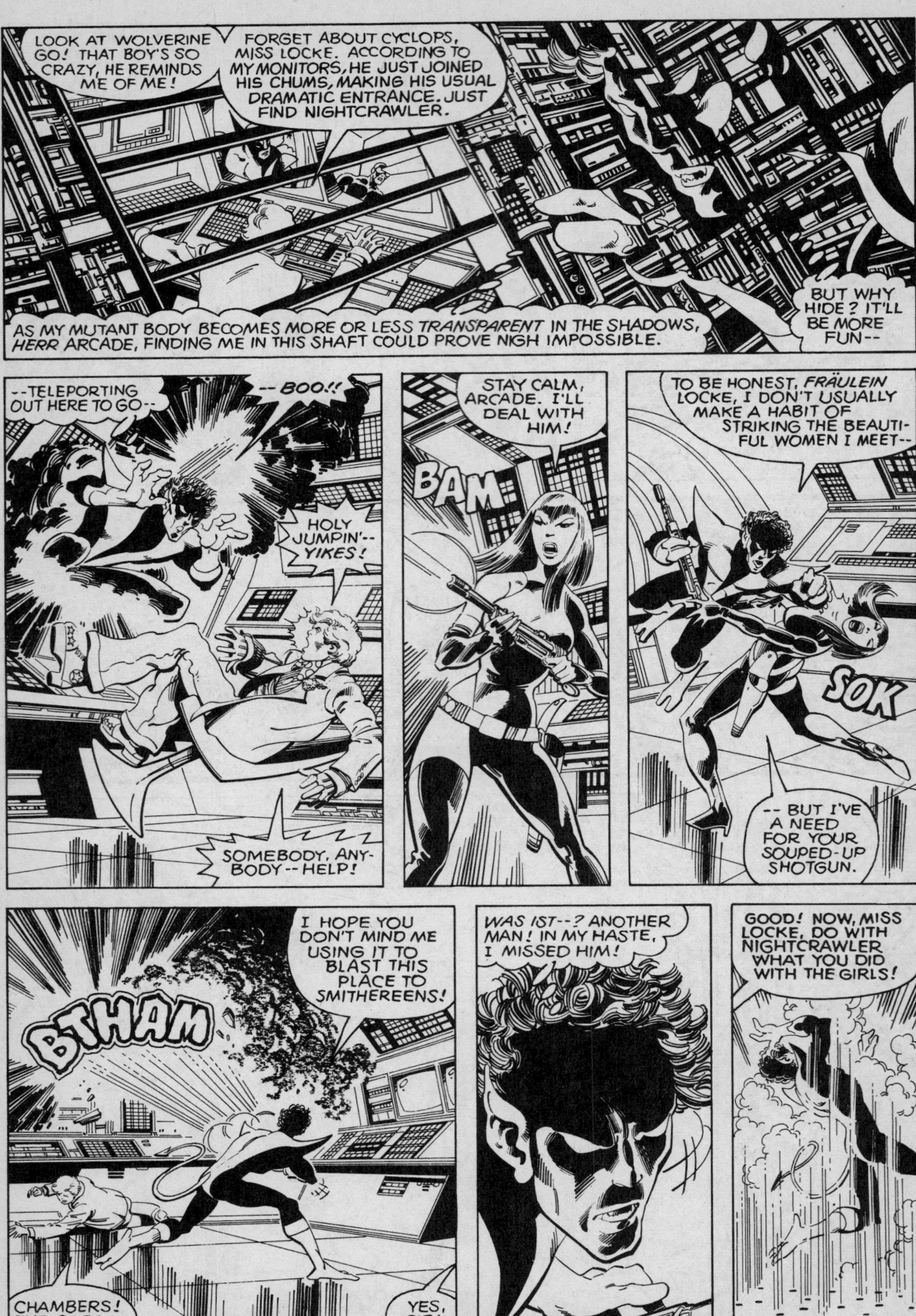
LOOK AT WOLVERINE GO! THAT BOY'S SO CRAZY, HE REMINDS ME OF ME!
FORGET ABOUT CYCLOPS, MISS LOCKE. ACCORDING TO MY MONITORS, HE JUST JOINED HIS CHUMS, MAKING HIS USUAL DRAMATIC ENTRANCE. JUST FIND NIGHTCRAWLER.
AS MY MUTANT BODY BECOMES MORE OR LESS TRANSPARENT IN THE SHADOWS, HERR ARCADE, FINDING ME IN THIS SHAFT COULD PROVE NIGH IMPOSSIBLE.
BUT WHY HIDE? IT'LL BE MORE FUN--
--TELEPORTING OUT HERE TO GO--
--BOO!!
HOLY JUMPIN'-- YIKES!
SOMEBODY, ANY-BODY--HELP!
STAY CALM, ARCADE. I'LL DEAL WITH HIM!
BAM
TO BE HONEST, FRÄULEIN LOCKE, I DON'T USUALLY MAKE A HABIT OF STRIKING THE BEAUTIFUL WOMEN I MEET--
SOK
--BUT I'VE A NEED FOR YOUR SOUPED-UP SHOTGUN.
I HOPE YOU DON'T MIND ME USING IT TO BLAST THIS PLACE TO SMITHEREENS!
BTHAM
CHAMBERS! THE GAS!
YES, SIR!
WAS IST--? ANOTHER MAN! IN MY HASTE, I MISSED HIM!
GOOD! NOW, MISS LOCKE, DO WITH NIGHTCRAWLER WHAT YOU DID WITH THE GIRLS!

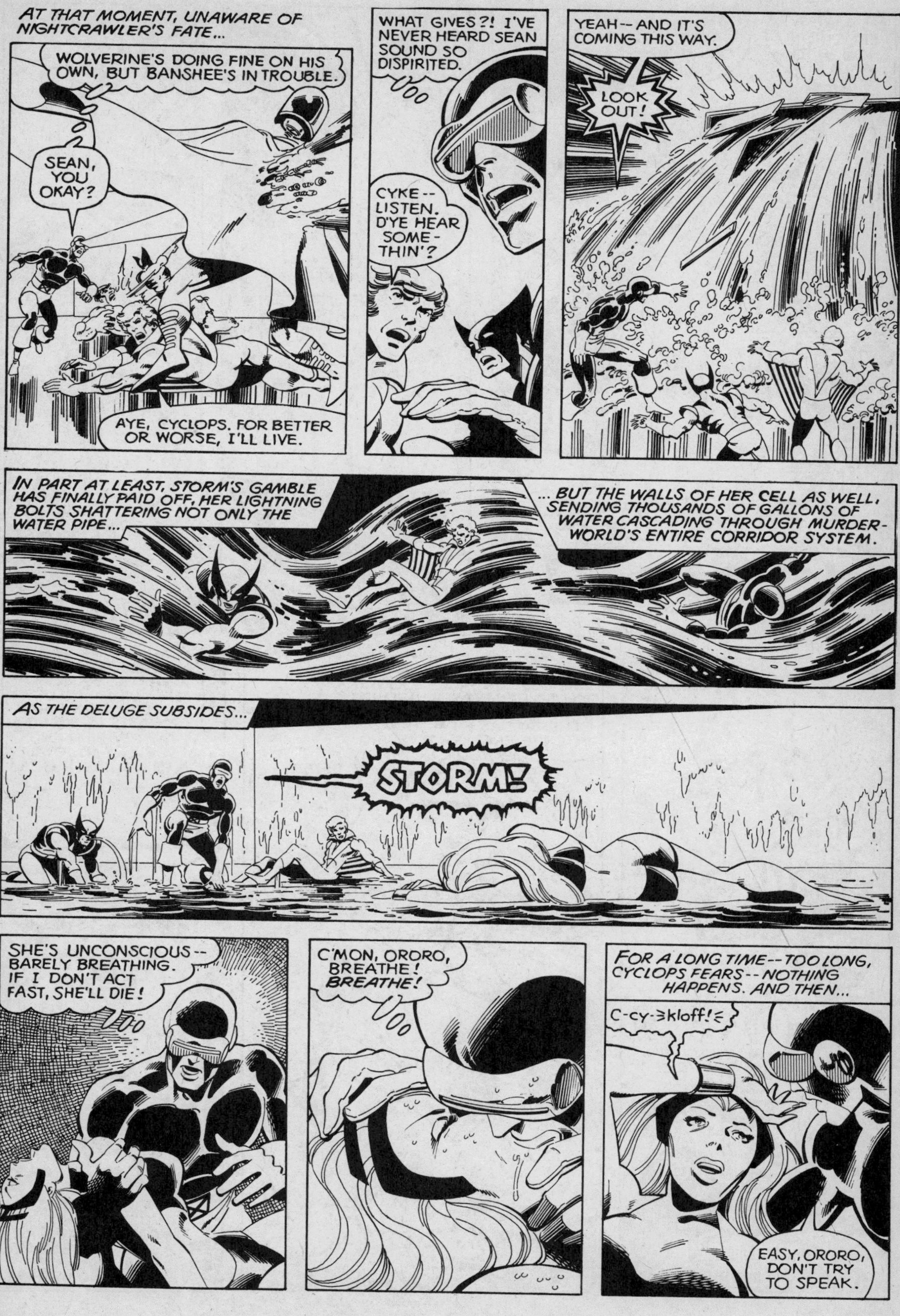
AT THAT MOMENT, UNAWARE OF NIGHTCRAWLER'S FATE...
WOLVERINE'S DOING FINE ON HIS OWN, BUT BANSHEE'S IN TROUBLE.
SEAN, YOU OKAY?
AYE, CYCLOPS. FOR BETTER OR WORSE, I'LL LIVE.
WHAT GIVES?! I'VE NEVER HEARD SEAN SOUND SO DISPIRITED.
CYKE -- LISTEN. D'YE HEAR SOME-THIN'?
YEAH -- AND IT'S COMING THIS WAY.
LOOK OUT!
IN PART AT LEAST, STORM'S GAMBLE HAS FINALLY PAID OFF, HER LIGHTNING BOLTS SHATTERING NOT ONLY THE WATER PIPE...
... BUT THE WALLS OF HER CELL AS WELL, SENDING THOUSANDS OF GALLONS OF WATER CASCADING THROUGH MURDER-WORLD'S ENTIRE CORRIDOR SYSTEM.
AS THE DELUGE SUBSIDES...
STORM!
SHE'S UNCONSCIOUS -- BARELY BREATHING. IF I DON'T ACT FAST, SHE'LL DIE!
C'MON, ORORO, BREATHE! BREATHE!
FOR A LONG TIME -- TOO LONG, CYCLOPS FEARS -- NOTHING HAPPENS. AND THEN...
C-cy-kloff!
EASY, ORORO, DON'T TRY TO SPEAK.

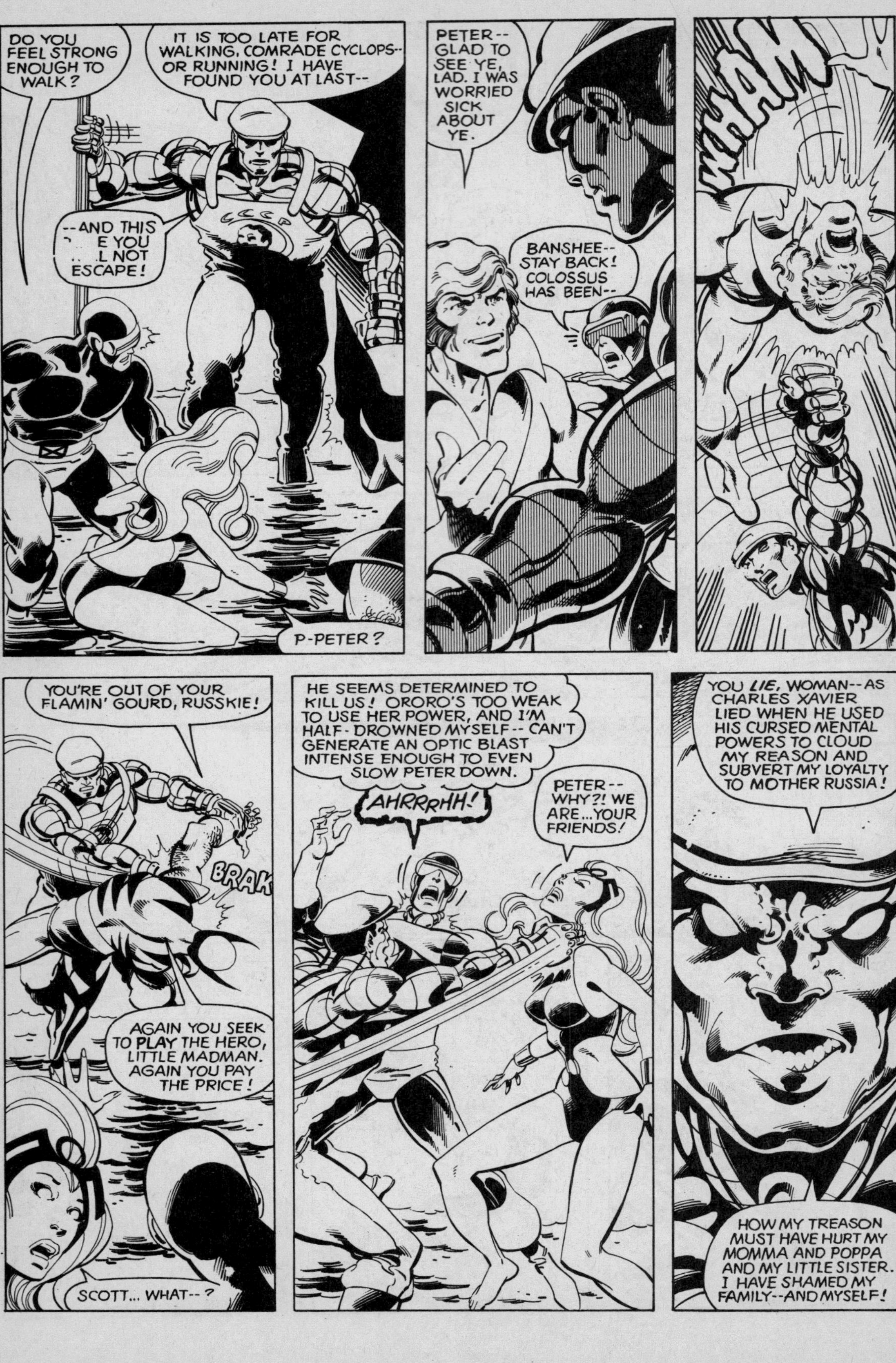
DO YOU FEEL STRONG ENOUGH TO WALK?
IT IS TOO LATE FOR WALKING, COMRADE CYCLOPS-- OR RUNNING! I HAVE FOUND YOU AT LAST--
--AND THIS E YOU L NOT ESCAPE!
P-PETER?
PETER-- GLAD TO SEE YE, LAD. I WAS WORRIED SICK ABOUT YE.
BANSHEE-- STAY BACK! COLOSSUS HAS BEEN--
WHAM
YOU'RE OUT OF YOUR FLAMIN' GOURD, RUSSKIE!
BRAK
AGAIN YOU SEEK TO PLAY THE HERO, LITTLE MADMAN. AGAIN YOU PAY THE PRICE!
SCOTT... WHAT--?
HE SEEMS DETERMINED TO KILL US! ORORO'S TOO WEAK TO USE HER POWER, AND I'M HALF-DROWNED MYSELF-- CAN'T GENERATE AN OPTIC BLAST INTENSE ENOUGH TO EVEN SLOW PETER DOWN.
AHRRRHH!
PETER-- WHY?! WE ARE...YOUR FRIENDS!
YOU LIE, WOMAN--AS CHARLES XAVIER LIED WHEN HE USED HIS CURSED MENTAL POWERS TO CLOUD MY REASON AND SUBVERT MY LOYALTY TO MOTHER RUSSIA!
HOW MY TREASON MUST HAVE HURT MY MOMMA AND POPPA AND MY LITTLE SISTER. I HAVE SHAMED MY FAMILY--AND MYSELF!

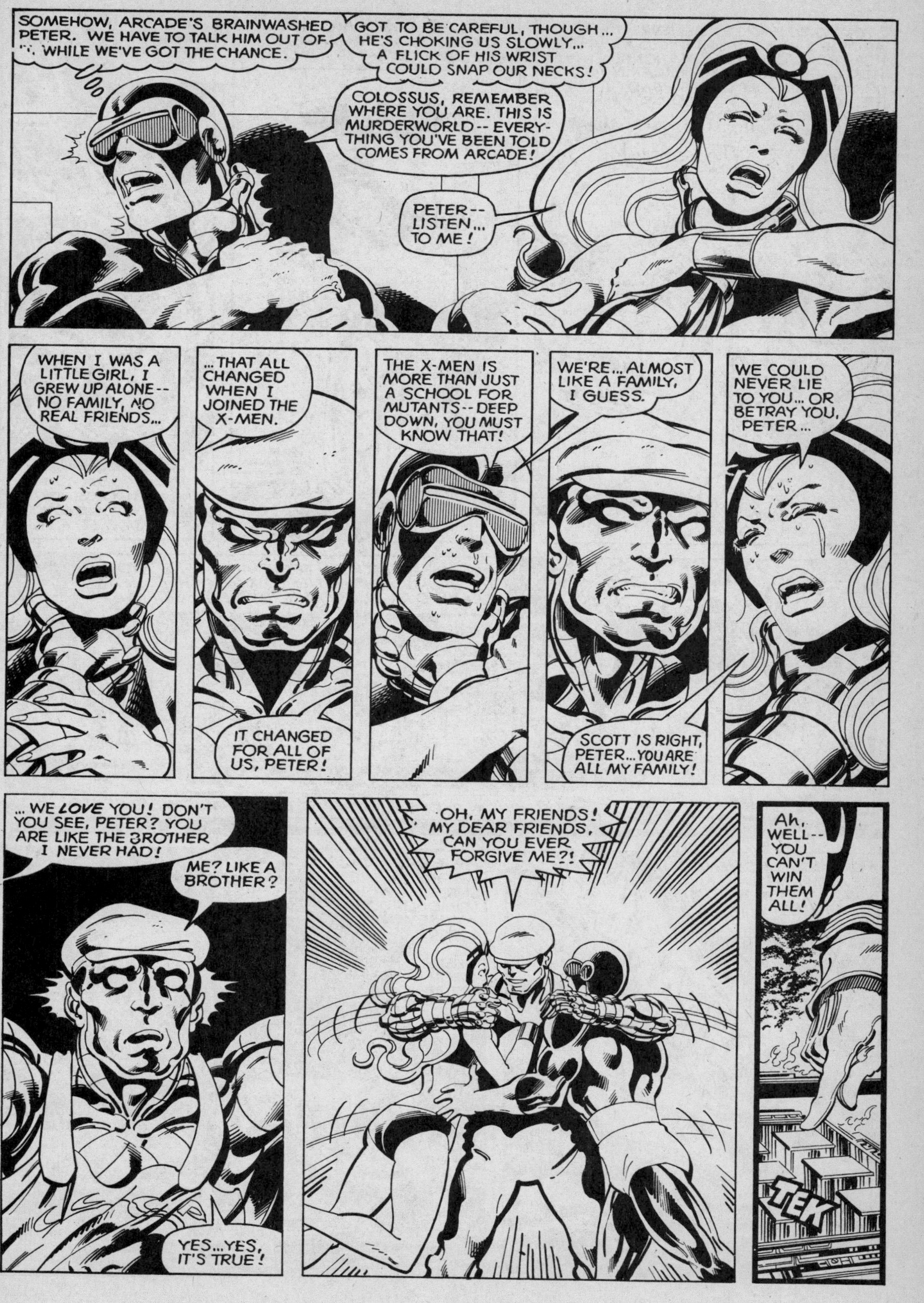
SOMEHOW, ARCADE'S BRAINWASHED PETER. WE HAVE TO TALK HIM OUT OF IT, WHILE WE'VE GOT THE CHANCE.
GOT TO BE CAREFUL, THOUGH... HE'S CHOKING US SLOWLY... A FLICK OF HIS WRIST COULD SNAP OUR NECKS!
COLOSSUS, REMEMBER WHERE YOU ARE. THIS IS MURDERWORLD -- EVERYTHING YOU'VE BEEN TOLD COMES FROM ARCADE!
PETER -- LISTEN... TO ME!
WHEN I WAS A LITTLE GIRL, I GREW UP ALONE -- NO FAMILY, NO REAL FRIENDS...
...THAT ALL CHANGED WHEN I JOINED THE X-MEN.
IT CHANGED FOR ALL OF US, PETER!
THE X-MEN IS MORE THAN JUST A SCHOOL FOR MUTANTS -- DEEP DOWN, YOU MUST KNOW THAT!
WE'RE... ALMOST LIKE A FAMILY, I GUESS.
SCOTT IS RIGHT, PETER... YOU ARE ALL MY FAMILY!
WE COULD NEVER LIE TO YOU... OR BETRAY YOU, PETER...
...WE LOVE YOU! DON'T YOU SEE, PETER? YOU ARE LIKE THE BROTHER I NEVER HAD!
ME? LIKE A BROTHER?
YES... YES, IT'S TRUE!
OH, MY FRIENDS! MY DEAR FRIENDS, CAN YOU EVER FORGIVE ME?!
Ah, WELL -- YOU CAN'T WIN THEM ALL!
TEK

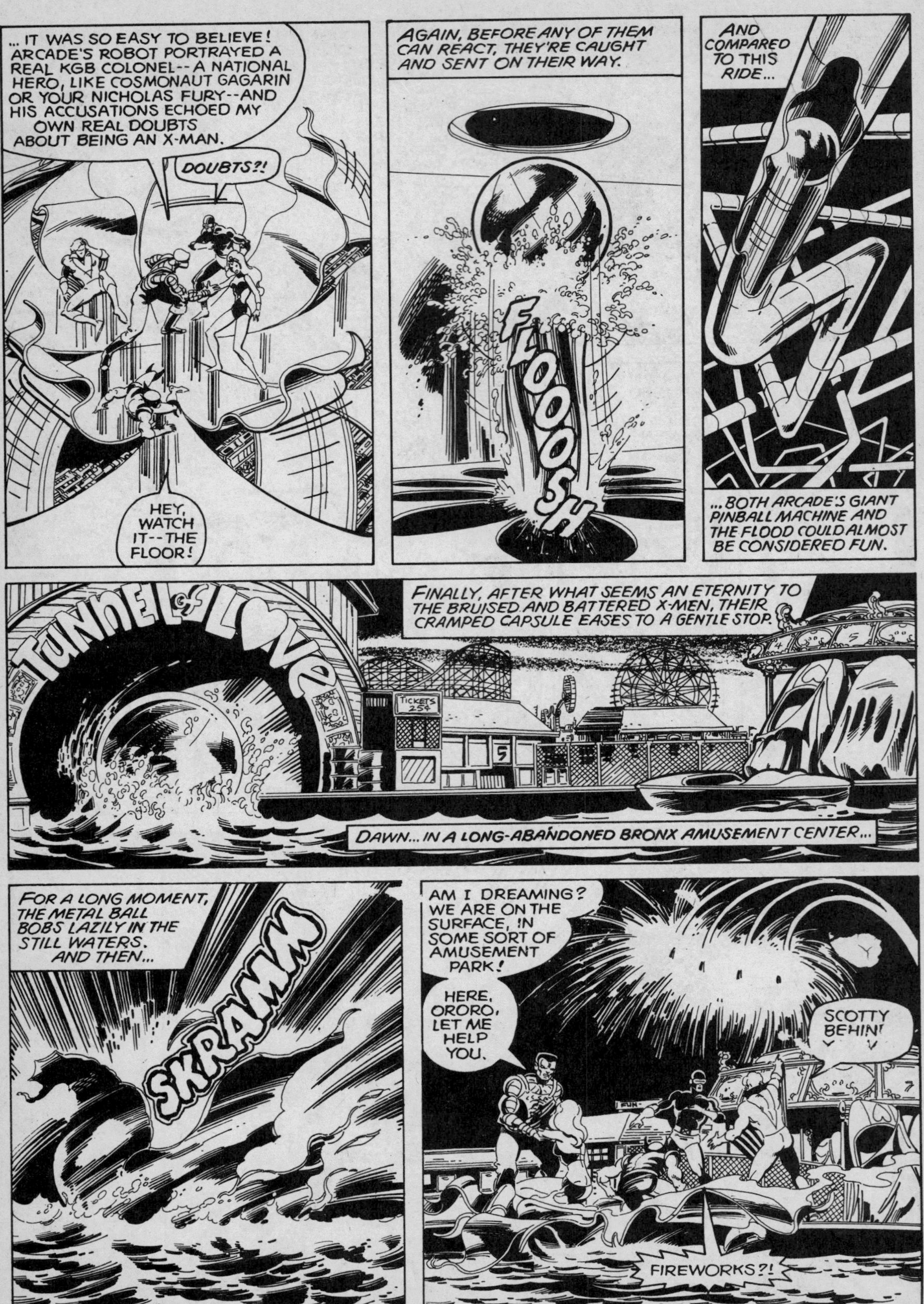
... IT WAS SO EASY TO BELIEVE! ARCADE'S ROBOT PORTRAYED A REAL KGB COLONEL-- A NATIONAL HERO, LIKE COSMONAUT GAGARIN OR YOUR NICHOLAS FURY--AND HIS ACCUSATIONS ECHOED MY OWN REAL DOUBTS ABOUT BEING AN X-MAN.
DOUBTS?!
HEY, WATCH IT--THE FLOOR!
AGAIN, BEFORE ANY OF THEM CAN REACT, THEY'RE CAUGHT AND SENT ON THEIR WAY.
FLOOOSH
AND COMPARED TO THIS RIDE...
...BOTH ARCADE'S GIANT PINBALL MACHINE AND THE FLOOD COULD ALMOST BE CONSIDERED FUN.
FINALLY, AFTER WHAT SEEMS AN ETERNITY TO THE BRUISED AND BATTERED X-MEN, THEIR CRAMPED CAPSULE EASES TO A GENTLE STOP.
TUNNEL of LOVE
TICKETS 25¢
DAWN... IN A LONG-ABANDONED BRONX AMUSEMENT CENTER...
FOR A LONG MOMENT, THE METAL BALL BOBS LAZILY IN THE STILL WATERS. AND THEN...
SKRAMM
AM I DREAMING? WE ARE ON THE SURFACE, IN SOME SORT OF AMUSEMENT PARK!
HERE, ORORO, LET ME HELP YOU.
SCOTTY BEHIN!
FUN
FIREWORKS?!

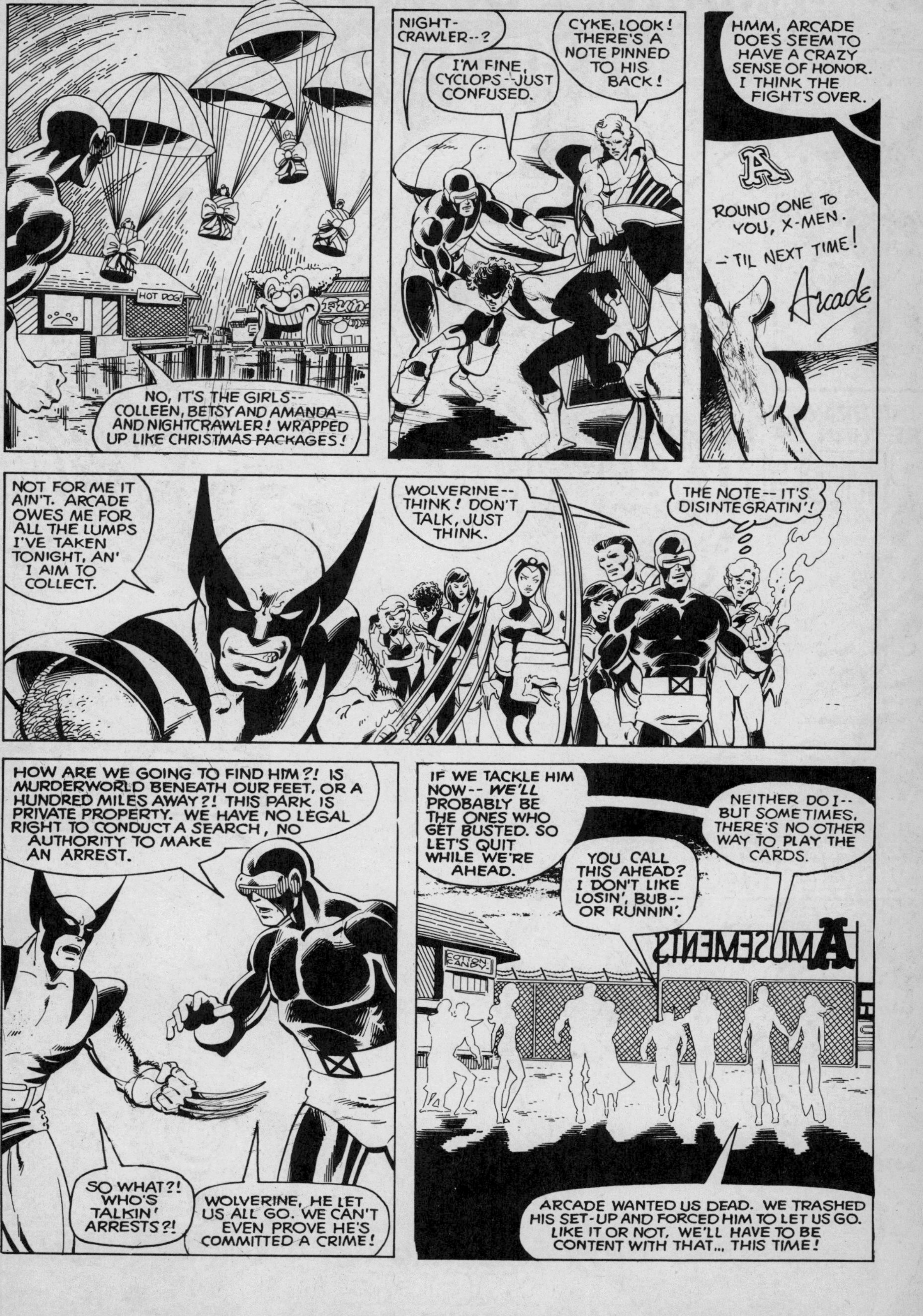
NO, IT'S THE GIRLS-- COLLEEN, BETSY AND AMANDA-- AND NIGHTCRAWLER! WRAPPED UP LIKE CHRISTMAS PACKAGES!
HOT DOG!
NIGHT-CRAWLER--?
I'M FINE, CYCLOPS--JUST CONFUSED.
CYKE, LOOK! THERE'S A NOTE PINNED TO HIS BACK!
HMM, ARCADE DOES SEEM TO HAVE A CRAZY SENSE OF HONOR. I THINK THE FIGHT'S OVER.
A
ROUND ONE TO YOU, X-MEN.
-'TIL NEXT TIME!
Arcade
NOT FOR ME IT AIN'T. ARCADE OWES ME FOR ALL THE LUMPS I'VE TAKEN TONIGHT, AN' I AIM TO COLLECT.
WOLVERINE-- THINK! DON'T TALK, JUST THINK.
THE NOTE-- IT'S DISINTEGRATIN'!
HOW ARE WE GOING TO FIND HIM?! IS MURDERWORLD BENEATH OUR FEET, OR A HUNDRED MILES AWAY?! THIS PARK IS PRIVATE PROPERTY. WE HAVE NO LEGAL RIGHT TO CONDUCT A SEARCH, NO AUTHORITY TO MAKE AN ARREST.
SO WHAT?! WHO'S TALKIN' ARRESTS?!
WOLVERINE, HE LET US ALL GO. WE CAN'T EVEN PROVE HE'S COMMITTED A CRIME!
IF WE TACKLE HIM NOW-- WE'LL PROBABLY BE THE ONES WHO GET BUSTED. SO LET'S QUIT WHILE WE'RE AHEAD.
YOU CALL THIS AHEAD? I DON'T LIKE LOSIN', BUB-- OR RUNNIN'.
NEITHER DO I-- BUT SOMETIMES, THERE'S NO OTHER WAY TO PLAY THE CARDS.
COTTON CANDY
AMUSEMENTS
ARCADE WANTED US DEAD. WE TRASHED HIS SET-UP AND FORCED HIM TO LET US GO. LIKE IT OR NOT, WE'LL HAVE TO BE CONTENT WITH THAT... THIS TIME!

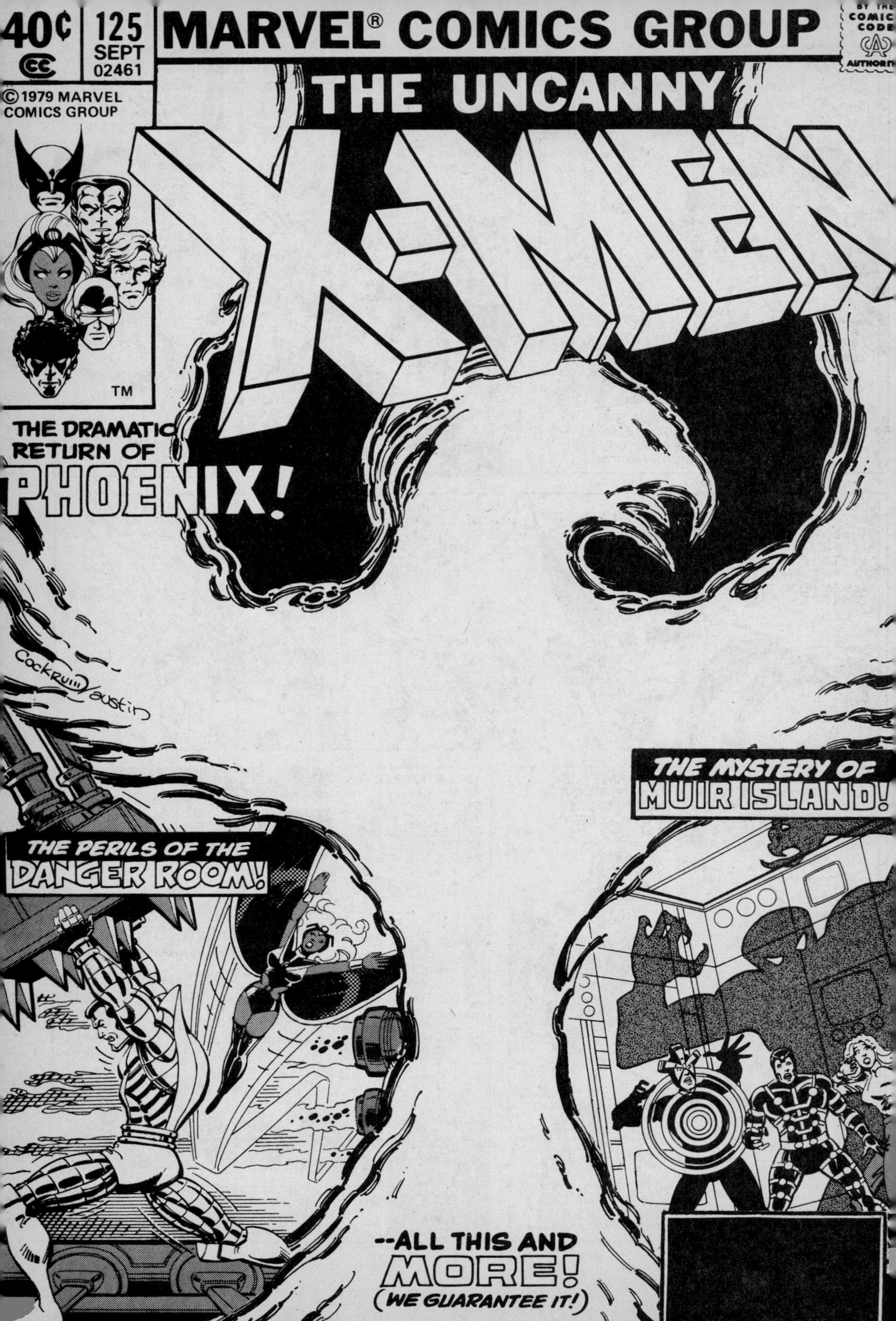
40¢
125
SEPT
02461
MARVEL® COMICS GROUP
©1979 MARVEL COMICS GROUP
THE UNCANNY
X-MEN
TM
THE DRAMATIC RETURN OF
PHOENIX!
Cockrum/austin
THE MYSTERY OF
MUIR ISLAND!
THE PERILS OF THE
DANGER ROOM!
--ALL THIS AND
MORE!
(WE GUARANTEE IT!)

Cyclops. Storm. Banshee. Nightcrawler. Wolverine. Colossus. Children of the atom, students of Charles Xavier, MUTANTS––feared and hated by the world they have sworn to protect. These are the STRANGEST heroes of all!

Stan Lee PRESENTS: THE UNCANNY X-MEN!™

CHRIS CLAREMONT, AUTHOR * JOHN BYRNE, PENCILER * TERRY AUSTIN, INKER | ORZECHOWSKI, letterer | GLYNIS WEIN, colorist | ROGER STERN, EDITOR * JIM SHOOTER, EDITOR-IN-CHIEF

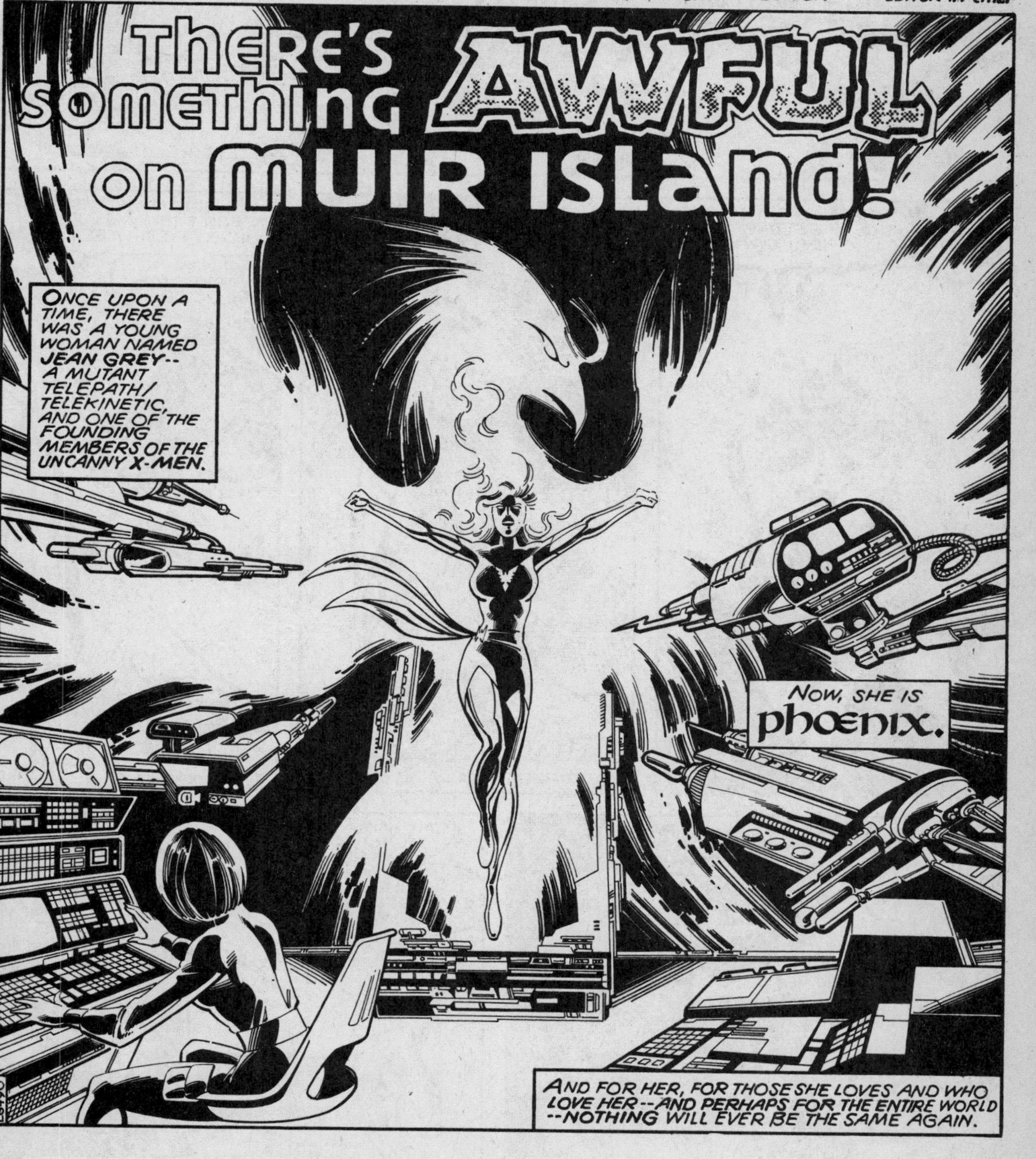

THERE'S SOMETHING AWFUL ON MUIR ISLAND!
ONCE UPON A TIME, THERE WAS A YOUNG WOMAN NAMED JEAN GREY-- A MUTANT TELEPATH/ TELEKINETIC, AND ONE OF THE FOUNDING MEMBERS OF THE UNCANNY X-MEN.
NOW, SHE IS PHOENIX.
AND FOR HER, FOR THOSE SHE LOVES AND WHO LOVE HER--AND PERHAPS FOR THE ENTIRE WORLD --NOTHING WILL EVER BE THE SAME AGAIN.

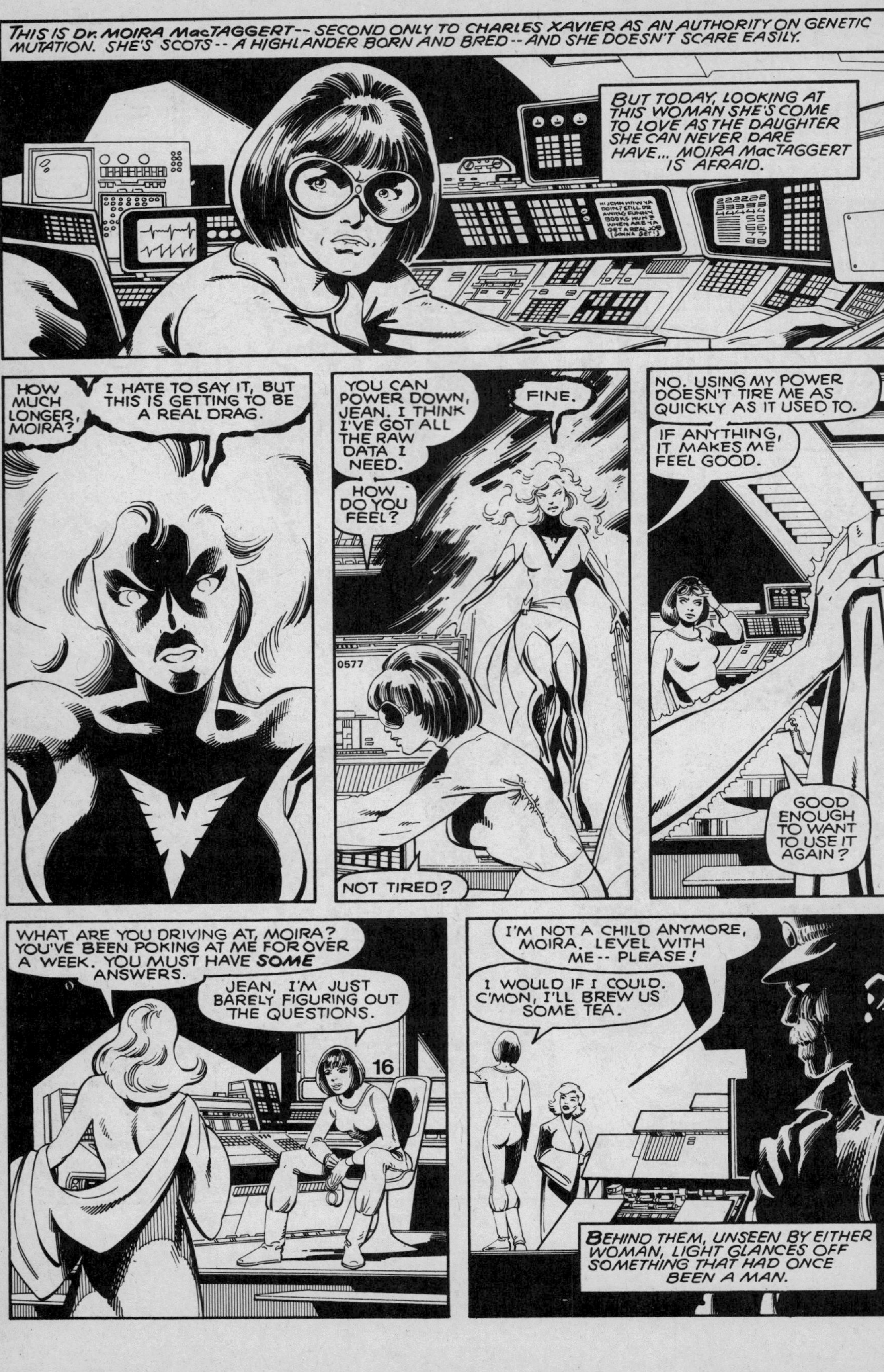
THIS IS Dr. MOIRA MacTAGGERT-- SECOND ONLY TO CHARLES XAVIER AS AN AUTHORITY ON GENETIC MUTATION. SHE'S SCOTS -- A HIGHLANDER BORN AND BRED -- AND SHE DOESN'T SCARE EASILY.
BUT TODAY, LOOKING AT THIS WOMAN SHE'S COME TO LOVE AS THE DAUGHTER SHE CAN NEVER DARE HAVE... MOIRA MacTAGGERT IS AFRAID.
HOW MUCH LONGER, MOIRA?
I HATE TO SAY IT, BUT THIS IS GETTING TO BE A REAL DRAG.
YOU CAN POWER DOWN, JEAN. I THINK I'VE GOT ALL THE RAW DATA I NEED.
FINE.
HOW DO YOU FEEL?
NOT TIRED?
NO. USING MY POWER DOESN'T TIRE ME AS QUICKLY AS IT USED TO.
IF ANYTHING, IT MAKES ME FEEL GOOD.
GOOD ENOUGH TO WANT TO USE IT AGAIN?
WHAT ARE YOU DRIVING AT, MOIRA? YOU'VE BEEN POKING AT ME FOR OVER A WEEK. YOU MUST HAVE SOME ANSWERS.
JEAN, I'M JUST BARELY FIGURING OUT THE QUESTIONS.
16
I'M NOT A CHILD ANYMORE, MOIRA. LEVEL WITH ME -- PLEASE!
I WOULD IF I COULD. C'MON, I'LL BREW US SOME TEA.
BEHIND THEM, UNSEEN BY EITHER WOMAN, LIGHT GLANCES OFF SOMETHING THAT HAD ONCE BEEN A MAN.

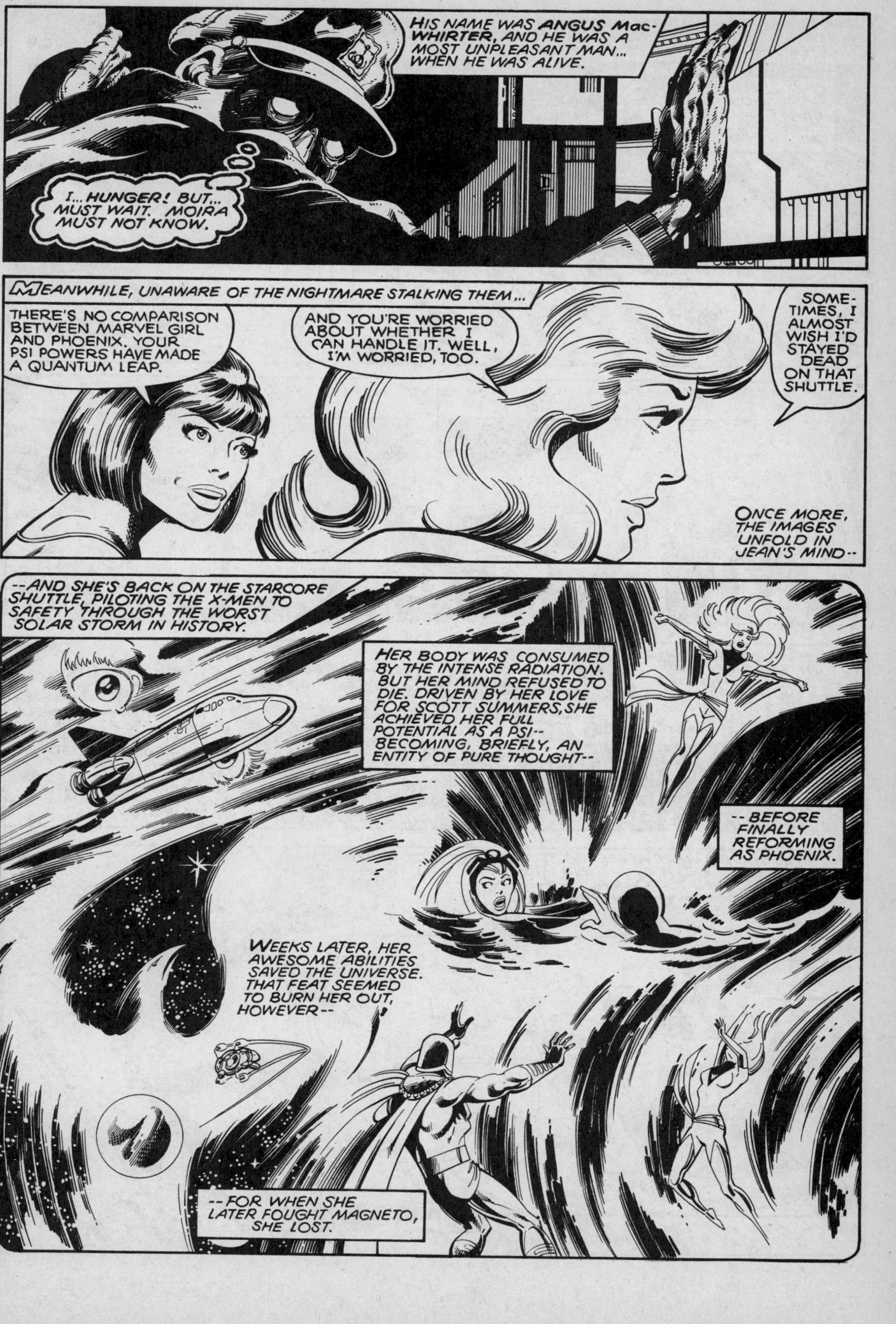
HIS NAME WAS ANGUS MacWHIRTER, AND HE WAS A MOST UNPLEASANT MAN... WHEN HE WAS ALIVE.
I... HUNGER! BUT... MUST WAIT. MOIRA MUST NOT KNOW.
MEANWHILE, UNAWARE OF THE NIGHTMARE STALKING THEM...
THERE'S NO COMPARISON BETWEEN MARVEL GIRL AND PHOENIX. YOUR PSI POWERS HAVE MADE A QUANTUM LEAP.
AND YOU'RE WORRIED ABOUT WHETHER I CAN HANDLE IT. WELL, I'M WORRIED, TOO.
SOMETIMES, I ALMOST WISH I'D STAYED DEAD ON THAT SHUTTLE.
ONCE MORE, THE IMAGES UNFOLD IN JEAN'S MIND--
--AND SHE'S BACK ON THE STARCORE SHUTTLE, PILOTING THE X-MEN TO SAFETY THROUGH THE WORST SOLAR STORM IN HISTORY.
HER BODY WAS CONSUMED BY THE INTENSE RADIATION. BUT HER MIND REFUSED TO DIE. DRIVEN BY HER LOVE FOR SCOTT SUMMERS, SHE ACHIEVED HER FULL POTENTIAL AS A PSI-- BECOMING, BRIEFLY, AN ENTITY OF PURE THOUGHT--
--BEFORE FINALLY REFORMING AS PHOENIX.
WEEKS LATER, HER AWESOME ABILITIES SAVED THE UNIVERSE. THAT FEAT SEEMED TO BURN HER OUT, HOWEVER--
--FOR WHEN SHE LATER FOUGHT MAGNETO, SHE LOST.

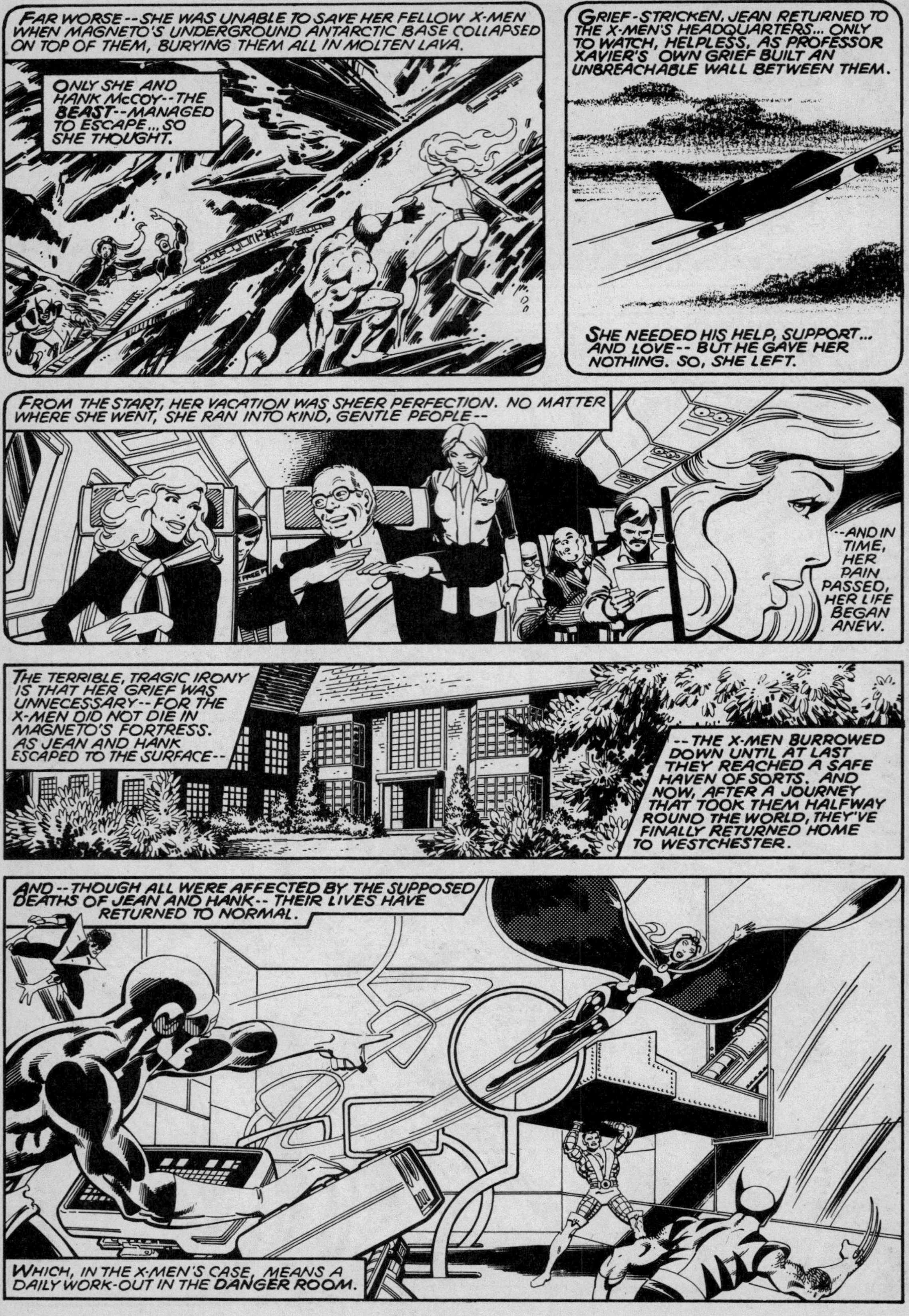
FAR WORSE--SHE WAS UNABLE TO SAVE HER FELLOW X-MEN WHEN MAGNETO'S UNDERGROUND ANTARCTIC BASE COLLAPSED ON TOP OF THEM, BURYING THEM ALL IN MOLTEN LAVA.
ONLY SHE AND HANK McCOY--THE BEAST--MANAGED TO ESCAPE... SO SHE THOUGHT.
GRIEF-STRICKEN, JEAN RETURNED TO THE X-MEN'S HEADQUARTERS... ONLY TO WATCH, HELPLESS, AS PROFESSOR XAVIER'S OWN GRIEF BUILT AN UNBREACHABLE WALL BETWEEN THEM.
SHE NEEDED HIS HELP, SUPPORT... AND LOVE-- BUT HE GAVE HER NOTHING. SO, SHE LEFT.
FROM THE START, HER VACATION WAS SHEER PERFECTION. NO MATTER WHERE SHE WENT, SHE RAN INTO KIND, GENTLE PEOPLE--
--AND IN TIME, HER PAIN PASSED, HER LIFE BEGAN ANEW.
THE TERRIBLE, TRAGIC IRONY IS THAT HER GRIEF WAS UNNECESSARY--FOR THE X-MEN DID NOT DIE IN MAGNETO'S FORTRESS. AS JEAN AND HANK ESCAPED TO THE SURFACE--
--THE X-MEN BURROWED DOWN UNTIL AT LAST THEY REACHED A SAFE HAVEN OF SORTS. AND NOW, AFTER A JOURNEY THAT TOOK THEM HALFWAY ROUND THE WORLD, THEY'VE FINALLY RETURNED HOME TO WESTCHESTER.
AND--THOUGH ALL WERE AFFECTED BY THE SUPPOSED DEATHS OF JEAN AND HANK-- THEIR LIVES HAVE RETURNED TO NORMAL.
WHICH, IN THE X-MEN'S CASE, MEANS A DAILY WORK-OUT IN THE DANGER ROOM.

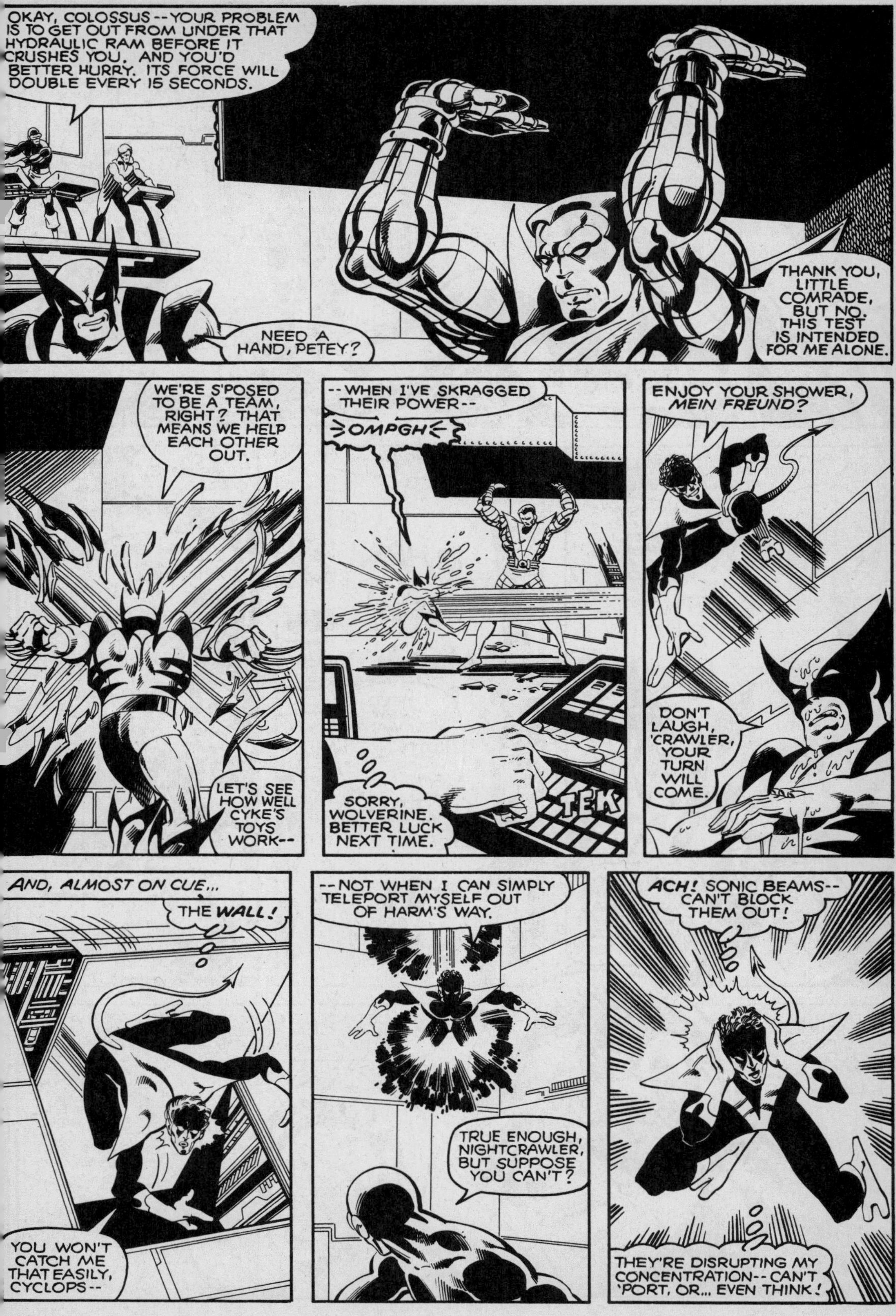
OKAY, COLOSSUS--YOUR PROBLEM IS TO GET OUT FROM UNDER THAT HYDRAULIC RAM BEFORE IT CRUSHES YOU. AND YOU'D BETTER HURRY. ITS FORCE WILL DOUBLE EVERY 15 SECONDS.
NEED A HAND, PETEY?
THANK YOU, LITTLE COMRADE, BUT NO. THIS TEST IS INTENDED FOR ME ALONE.
WE'RE S'POSED TO BE A TEAM, RIGHT? THAT MEANS WE HELP EACH OTHER OUT.
LET'S SEE HOW WELL CYKE'S TOYS WORK--
--WHEN I'VE SKRAGGED THEIR POWER--
OMPGH
SORRY, WOLVERINE. BETTER LUCK NEXT TIME.
TEK
ENJOY YOUR SHOWER, MEIN FREUND?
DON'T LAUGH, 'CRAWLER, YOUR TURN WILL COME.
AND, ALMOST ON CUE...
THE WALL!
YOU WON'T CATCH ME THAT EASILY, CYCLOPS--
--NOT WHEN I CAN SIMPLY TELEPORT MYSELF OUT OF HARM'S WAY.
TRUE ENOUGH, NIGHTCRAWLER, BUT SUPPOSE YOU CAN'T?
ACH! SONIC BEAMS-- CAN'T BLOCK THEM OUT!
THEY'RE DISRUPTING MY CONCENTRATION--CAN'T 'PORT, OR... EVEN THINK!

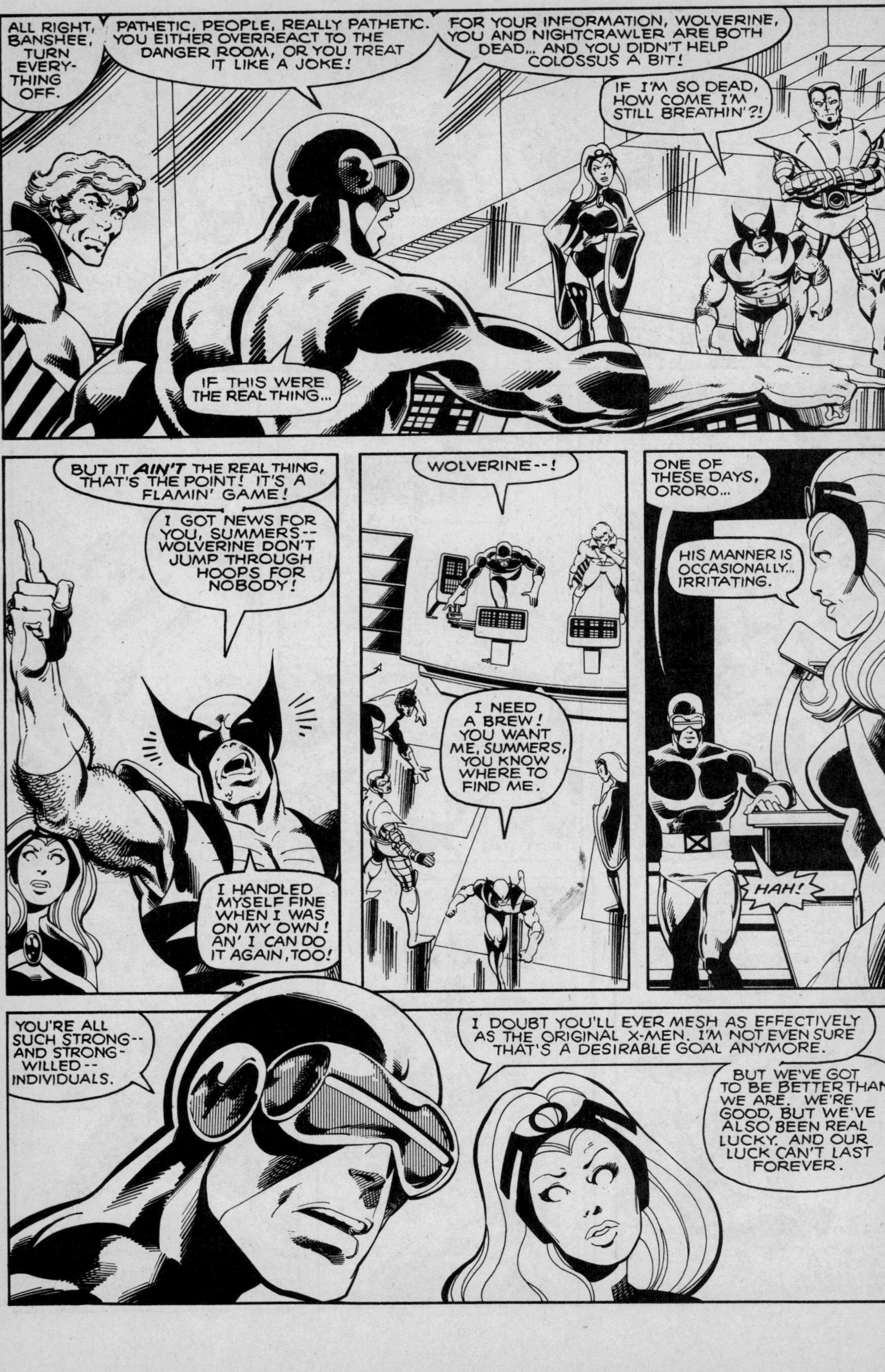
ALL RIGHT, BANSHEE, TURN EVERY-THING OFF.
PATHETIC, PEOPLE, REALLY PATHETIC. YOU EITHER OVERREACT TO THE DANGER ROOM, OR YOU TREAT IT LIKE A JOKE!
FOR YOUR INFORMATION, WOLVERINE, YOU AND NIGHTCRAWLER ARE BOTH DEAD... AND YOU DIDN'T HELP COLOSSUS A BIT!
IF I'M SO DEAD, HOW COME I'M STILL BREATHIN'?!
IF THIS WERE THE REAL THING...
BUT IT AIN'T THE REAL THING, THAT'S THE POINT! IT'S A FLAMIN' GAME!
I GOT NEWS FOR YOU, SUMMERS-- WOLVERINE DON'T JUMP THROUGH HOOPS FOR NOBODY!
I HANDLED MYSELF FINE WHEN I WAS ON MY OWN! AN' I CAN DO IT AGAIN, TOO!
WOLVERINE--!
I NEED A BREW! YOU WANT ME, SUMMERS, YOU KNOW WHERE TO FIND ME.
ONE OF THESE DAYS, ORORO...
HIS MANNER IS OCCASIONALLY... IRRITATING.
HAH!
YOU'RE ALL SUCH STRONG-- AND STRONG-WILLED-- INDIVIDUALS.
I DOUBT YOU'LL EVER MESH AS EFFECTIVELY AS THE ORIGINAL X-MEN. I'M NOT EVEN SURE THAT'S A DESIRABLE GOAL ANYMORE.
BUT WE'VE GOT TO BE BETTER THAN WE ARE. WE'RE GOOD, BUT WE'VE ALSO BEEN REAL LUCKY. AND OUR LUCK CAN'T LAST FOREVER.

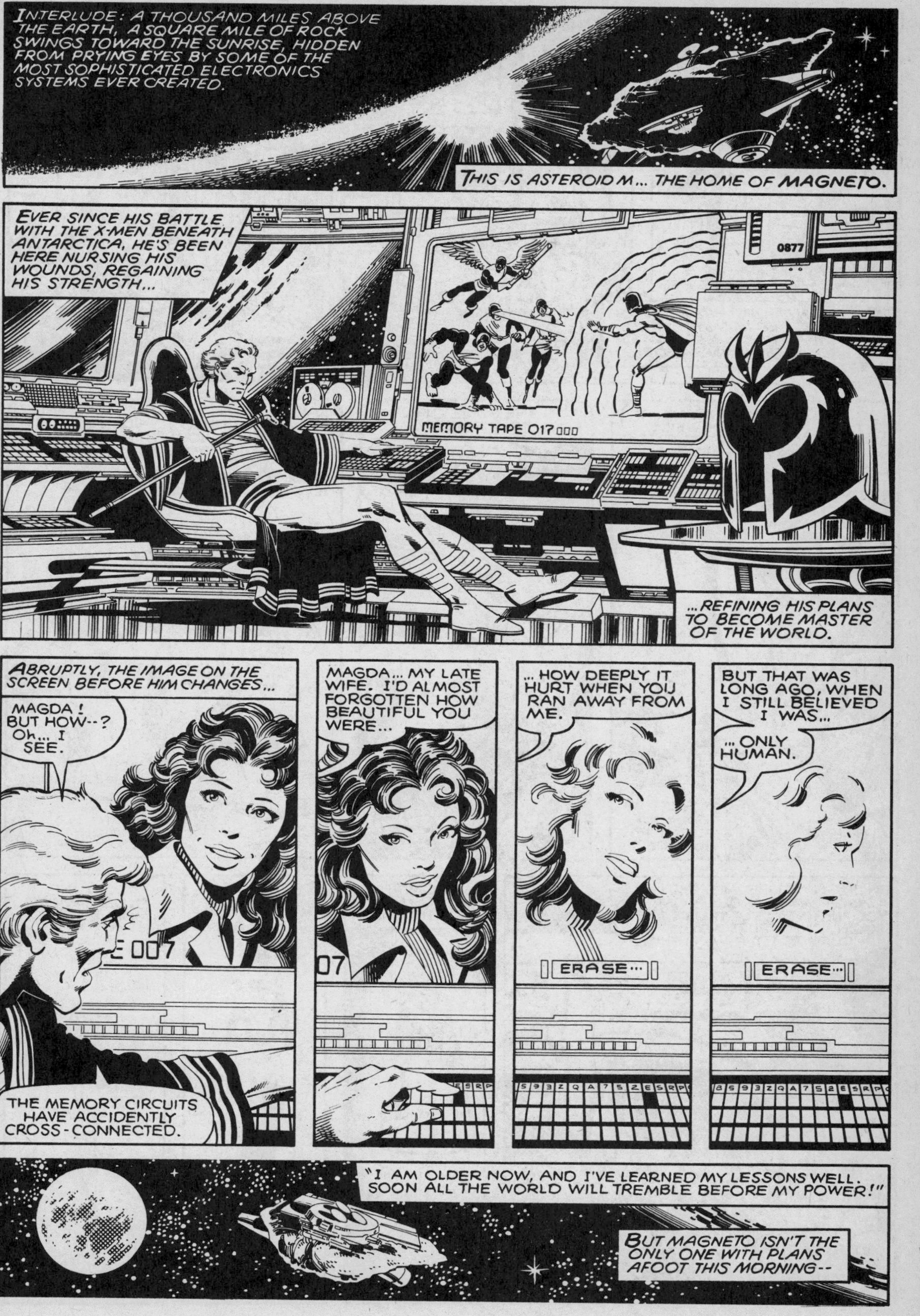
INTERLUDE: A THOUSAND MILES ABOVE THE EARTH, A SQUARE MILE OF ROCK SWINGS TOWARD THE SUNRISE, HIDDEN FROM PRYING EYES BY SOME OF THE MOST SOPHISTICATED ELECTRONICS SYSTEMS EVER CREATED.
THIS IS ASTEROID M... THE HOME OF MAGNETO.
EVER SINCE HIS BATTLE WITH THE X-MEN BENEATH ANTARCTICA, HE'S BEEN HERE NURSING HIS WOUNDS, REGAINING HIS STRENGTH...
0877
MEMORY TAPE 017
...REFINING HIS PLANS TO BECOME MASTER OF THE WORLD.
ABRUPTLY, THE IMAGE ON THE SCREEN BEFORE HIM CHANGES...
MAGDA! BUT HOW--? Oh... I SEE.
E 007
THE MEMORY CIRCUITS HAVE ACCIDENTLY CROSS-CONNECTED.
MAGDA... MY LATE WIFE. I'D ALMOST FORGOTTEN HOW BEAUTIFUL YOU WERE...
07
...HOW DEEPLY IT HURT WHEN YOU RAN AWAY FROM ME.
ERASE...
BUT THAT WAS LONG AGO, WHEN I STILL BELIEVED I WAS...
...ONLY HUMAN.
ERASE...
"I AM OLDER NOW, AND I'VE LEARNED MY LESSONS WELL. SOON ALL THE WORLD WILL TREMBLE BEFORE MY POWER!"
BUT MAGNETO ISN'T THE ONLY ONE WITH PLANS AFOOT THIS MORNING--

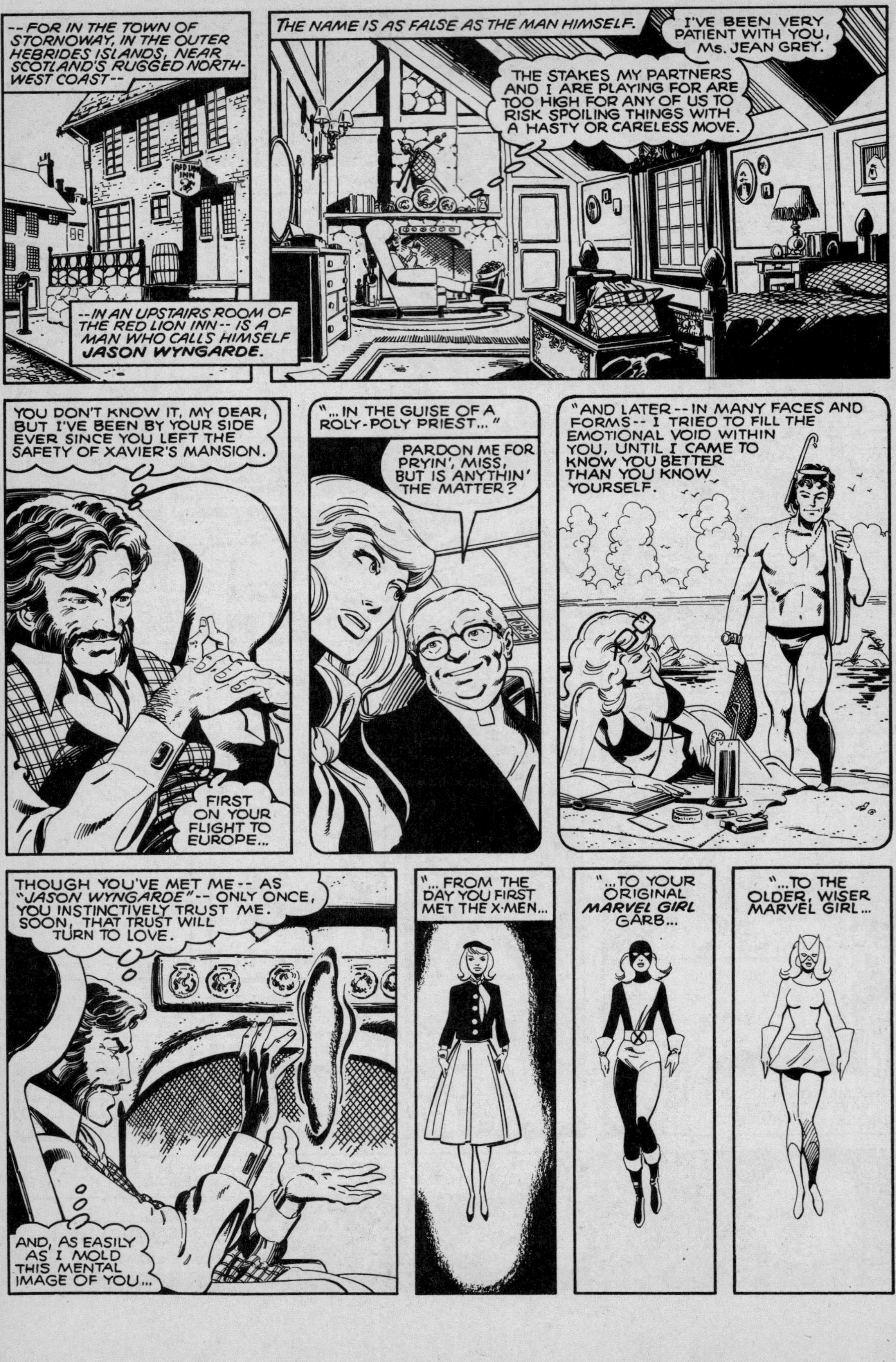

--FOR IN THE TOWN OF STORNOWAY, IN THE OUTER HEBRIDES ISLANDS, NEAR SCOTLAND'S RUGGED NORTH-WEST COAST--
RED LION INN
--IN AN UPSTAIRS ROOM OF THE RED LION INN-- IS A MAN WHO CALLS HIMSELF JASON WYNGARDE.
THE NAME IS AS FALSE AS THE MAN HIMSELF.
I'VE BEEN VERY PATIENT WITH YOU, Ms. JEAN GREY.
THE STAKES MY PARTNERS AND I ARE PLAYING FOR ARE TOO HIGH FOR ANY OF US TO RISK SPOILING THINGS WITH A HASTY OR CARELESS MOVE.
YOU DON'T KNOW IT, MY DEAR, BUT I'VE BEEN BY YOUR SIDE EVER SINCE YOU LEFT THE SAFETY OF XAVIER'S MANSION.
FIRST ON YOUR FLIGHT TO EUROPE...
"...IN THE GUISE OF A ROLY-POLY PRIEST..."
PARDON ME FOR PRYIN', MISS, BUT IS ANYTHIN' THE MATTER?
"AND LATER--IN MANY FACES AND FORMS--I TRIED TO FILL THE EMOTIONAL VOID WITHIN YOU, UNTIL I CAME TO KNOW YOU BETTER THAN YOU KNOW YOURSELF.
THOUGH YOU'VE MET ME--AS "JASON WYNGARDE"--ONLY ONCE, YOU INSTINCTIVELY TRUST ME. SOON, THAT TRUST WILL TURN TO LOVE.
AND, AS EASILY AS I MOLD THIS MENTAL IMAGE OF YOU...
"...FROM THE DAY YOU FIRST MET THE X-MEN...
"...TO YOUR ORIGINAL MARVEL GIRL GARB...
"...TO THE OLDER, WISER MARVEL GIRL...

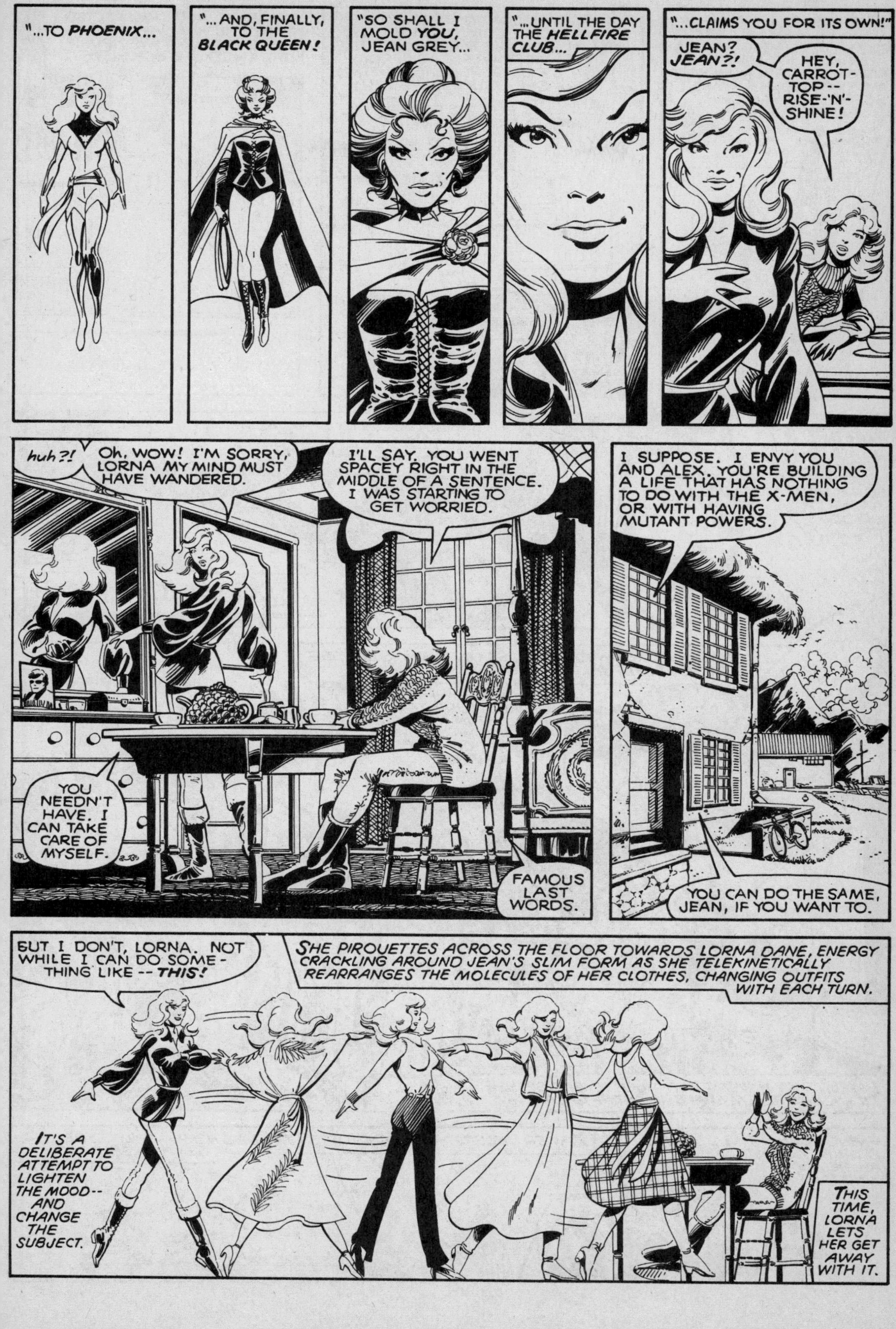
"...TO PHOENIX...
"...AND, FINALLY, TO THE BLACK QUEEN!
"SO SHALL I MOLD YOU, JEAN GREY...
"...UNTIL THE DAY THE HELLFIRE CLUB...
"...CLAIMS YOU FOR ITS OWN!"
JEAN? JEAN?!
HEY, CARROT-TOP-- RISE-'N'-SHINE!
huh?!
OH, WOW! I'M SORRY, LORNA MY MIND MUST HAVE WANDERED.
I'LL SAY. YOU WENT SPACEY RIGHT IN THE MIDDLE OF A SENTENCE. I WAS STARTING TO GET WORRIED.
YOU NEEDN'T HAVE. I CAN TAKE CARE OF MYSELF.
FAMOUS LAST WORDS.
I SUPPOSE. I ENVY YOU AND ALEX. YOU'RE BUILDING A LIFE THAT HAS NOTHING TO DO WITH THE X-MEN, OR WITH HAVING MUTANT POWERS.
YOU CAN DO THE SAME, JEAN, IF YOU WANT TO.
BUT I DON'T, LORNA. NOT WHILE I CAN DO SOME-THING LIKE -- THIS!
SHE PIROUETTES ACROSS THE FLOOR TOWARDS LORNA DANE, ENERGY CRACKLING AROUND JEAN'S SLIM FORM AS SHE TELEKINETICALLY REARRANGES THE MOLECULES OF HER CLOTHES, CHANGING OUTFITS WITH EACH TURN.
IT'S A DELIBERATE ATTEMPT TO LIGHTEN THE MOOD-- AND CHANGE THE SUBJECT.
THIS TIME, LORNA LETS HER GET AWAY WITH IT.

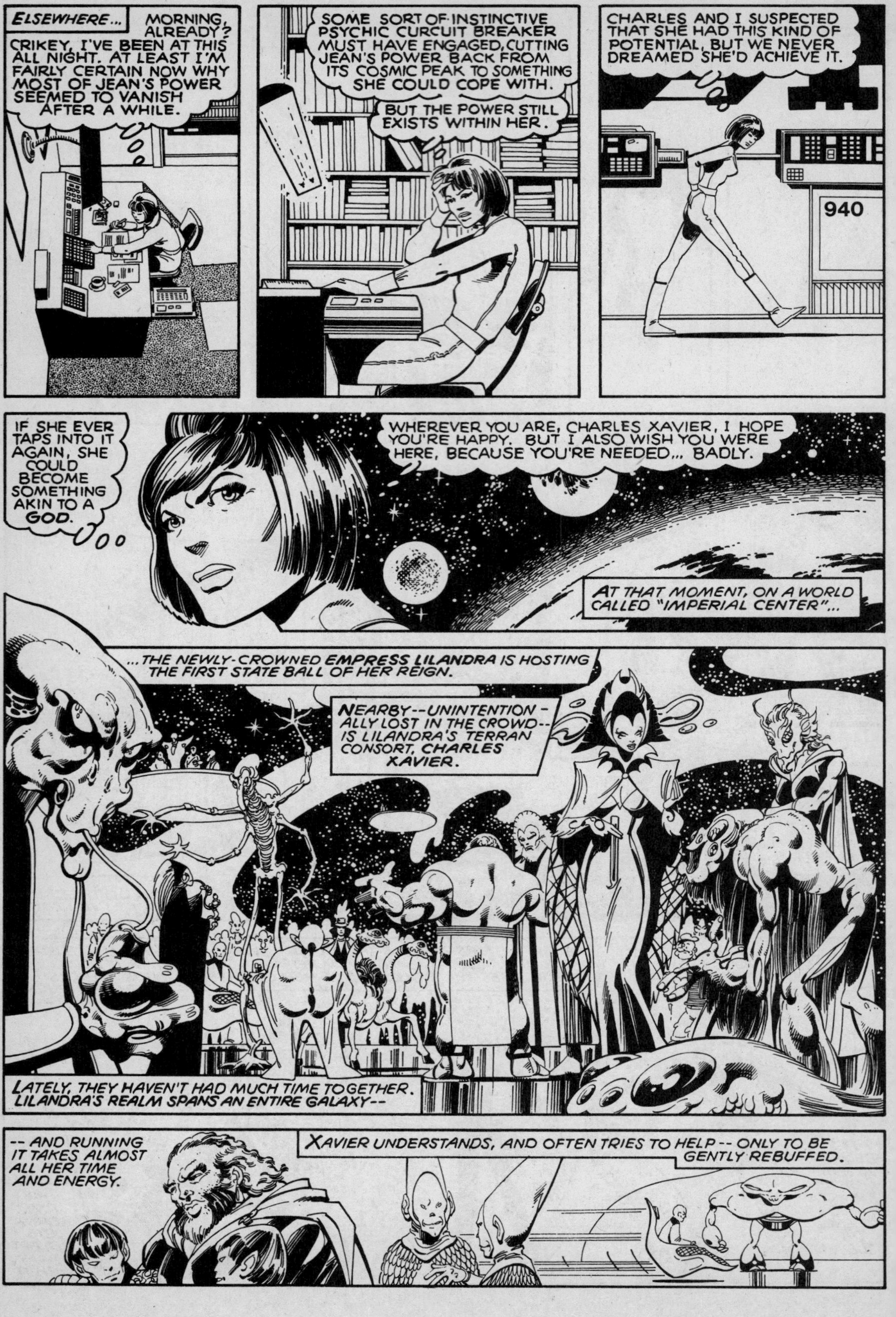
ELSEWHERE...
MORNING, ALREADY? CRIKEY, I'VE BEEN AT THIS ALL NIGHT. AT LEAST I'M FAIRLY CERTAIN NOW WHY MOST OF JEAN'S POWER SEEMED TO VANISH AFTER A WHILE.
SOME SORT OF INSTINCTIVE PSYCHIC CURCUIT BREAKER MUST HAVE ENGAGED, CUTTING JEAN'S POWER BACK FROM ITS COSMIC PEAK TO SOMETHING SHE COULD COPE WITH.
BUT THE POWER STILL EXISTS WITHIN HER.
CHARLES AND I SUSPECTED THAT SHE HAD THIS KIND OF POTENTIAL, BUT WE NEVER DREAMED SHE'D ACHIEVE IT.
940
IF SHE EVER TAPS INTO IT AGAIN, SHE COULD BECOME SOMETHING AKIN TO A GOD.
WHEREVER YOU ARE, CHARLES XAVIER, I HOPE YOU'RE HAPPY. BUT I ALSO WISH YOU WERE HERE, BECAUSE YOU'RE NEEDED... BADLY.
AT THAT MOMENT, ON A WORLD CALLED "IMPERIAL CENTER"...
...THE NEWLY-CROWNED EMPRESS LILANDRA IS HOSTING THE FIRST STATE BALL OF HER REIGN.
NEARBY--UNINTENTION-ALLY LOST IN THE CROWD--IS LILANDRA'S TERRAN CONSORT, CHARLES XAVIER.
LATELY, THEY HAVEN'T HAD MUCH TIME TOGETHER. LILANDRA'S REALM SPANS AN ENTIRE GALAXY--
--AND RUNNING IT TAKES ALMOST ALL HER TIME AND ENERGY.
XAVIER UNDERSTANDS, AND OFTEN TRIES TO HELP--ONLY TO BE GENTLY REBUFFED.

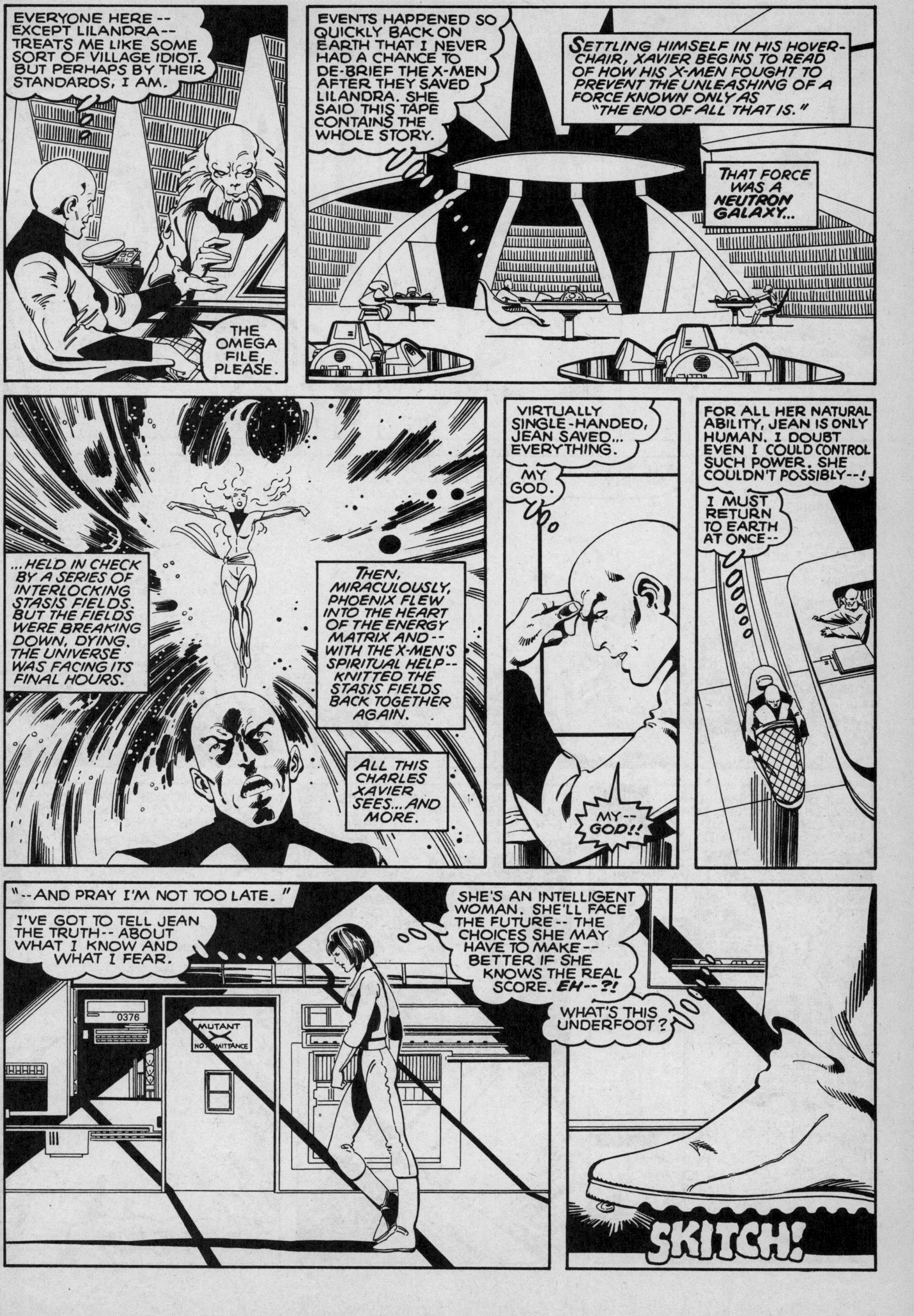

EVERYONE HERE -- EXCEPT LILANDRA -- TREATS ME LIKE SOME SORT OF VILLAGE IDIOT. BUT PERHAPS BY THEIR STANDARDS, I AM.
THE OMEGA FILE, PLEASE.
EVENTS HAPPENED SO QUICKLY BACK ON EARTH THAT I NEVER HAD A CHANCE TO DE-BRIEF THE X-MEN AFTER THEY SAVED LILANDRA. SHE SAID THIS TAPE CONTAINS THE WHOLE STORY.
SETTLING HIMSELF IN HIS HOVER-CHAIR, XAVIER BEGINS TO READ OF HOW HIS X-MEN FOUGHT TO PREVENT THE UNLEASHING OF A FORCE KNOWN ONLY AS "THE END OF ALL THAT IS."
THAT FORCE WAS A NEUTRON GALAXY...
...HELD IN CHECK BY A SERIES OF INTERLOCKING STASIS FIELDS. BUT THE FIELDS WERE BREAKING DOWN, DYING. THE UNIVERSE WAS FACING ITS FINAL HOURS.
THEN, MIRACULOUSLY, PHOENIX FLEW INTO THE HEART OF THE ENERGY MATRIX AND -- WITH THE X-MEN'S SPIRITUAL HELP -- KNITTED THE STASIS FIELDS BACK TOGETHER AGAIN.
ALL THIS CHARLES XAVIER SEES... AND MORE.
VIRTUALLY SINGLE-HANDED, JEAN SAVED... EVERYTHING.
MY GOD.
MY -- GOD!!
FOR ALL HER NATURAL ABILITY, JEAN IS ONLY HUMAN. I DOUBT EVEN I COULD CONTROL SUCH POWER. SHE COULDN'T POSSIBLY --!
I MUST RETURN TO EARTH AT ONCE --
"-- AND PRAY I'M NOT TOO LATE."
I'VE GOT TO TELL JEAN THE TRUTH -- ABOUT WHAT I KNOW AND WHAT I FEAR.
0376
MUTANT
NO ADMITTANCE
SHE'S AN INTELLIGENT WOMAN. SHE'LL FACE THE FUTURE -- THE CHOICES SHE MAY HAVE TO MAKE -- BETTER IF SHE KNOWS THE REAL SCORE. EH --?!
WHAT'S THIS UNDERFOOT?
SKITCH!

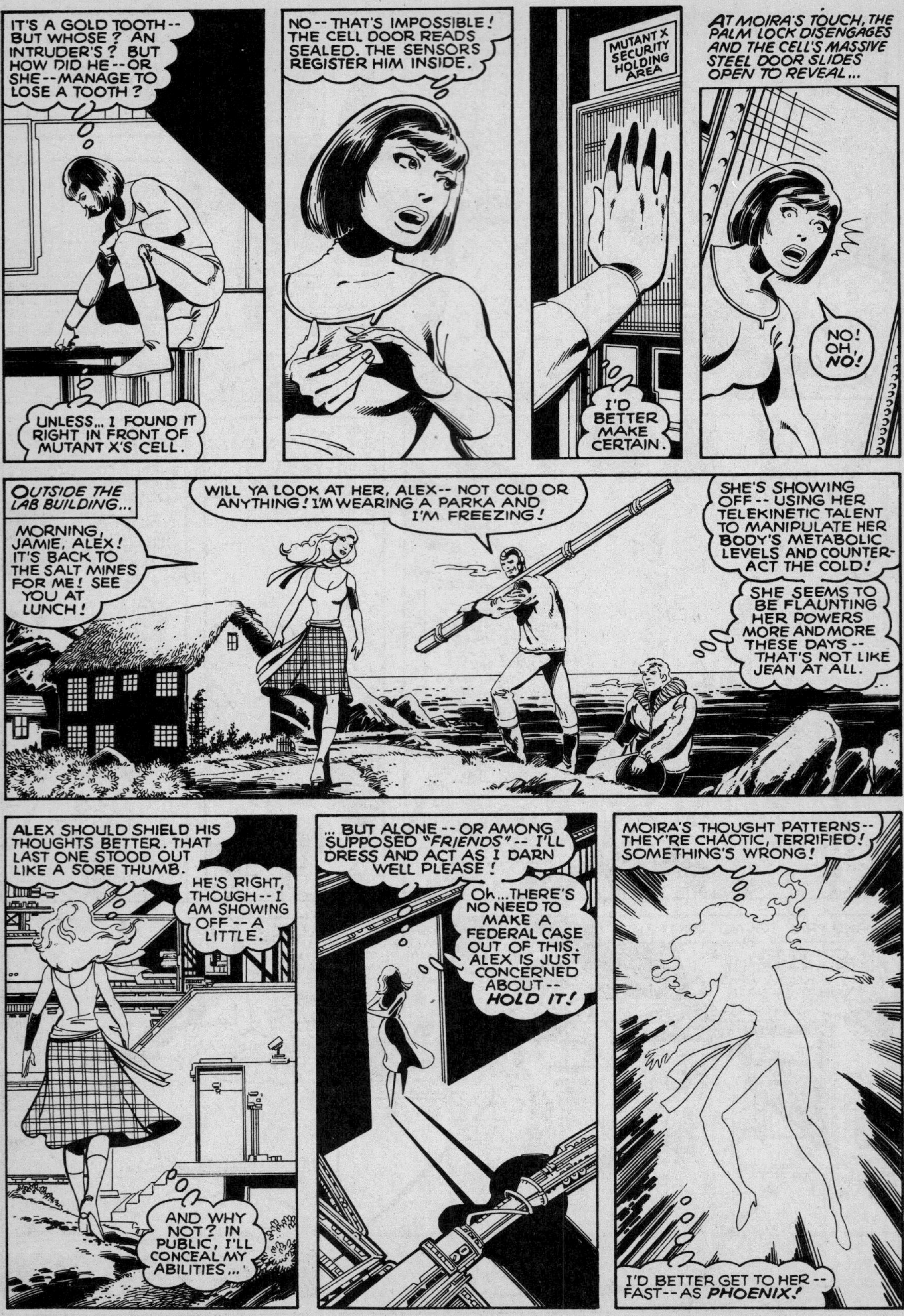
IT'S A GOLD TOOTH-- BUT WHOSE? AN INTRUDER'S? BUT HOW DID HE--OR SHE--MANAGE TO LOSE A TOOTH?
UNLESS... I FOUND IT RIGHT IN FRONT OF MUTANT X'S CELL.
NO--THAT'S IMPOSSIBLE! THE CELL DOOR READS SEALED. THE SENSORS REGISTER HIM INSIDE.
MUTANT X SECURITY HOLDING AREA
I'D BETTER MAKE CERTAIN.
AT MOIRA'S TOUCH, THE PALM LOCK DISENGAGES AND THE CELL'S MASSIVE STEEL DOOR SLIDES OPEN TO REVEAL...
NO! OH, NO!
OUTSIDE THE LAB BUILDING...
MORNING, JAMIE, ALEX! IT'S BACK TO THE SALT MINES FOR ME! SEE YOU AT LUNCH!
WILL YA LOOK AT HER, ALEX-- NOT COLD OR ANYTHING! I'M WEARING A PARKA AND I'M FREEZING!
SHE'S SHOWING OFF--USING HER TELEKINETIC TALENT TO MANIPULATE HER BODY'S METABOLIC LEVELS AND COUNTER-ACT THE COLD!
SHE SEEMS TO BE FLAUNTING HER POWERS MORE AND MORE THESE DAYS-- THAT'S NOT LIKE JEAN AT ALL.
ALEX SHOULD SHIELD HIS THOUGHTS BETTER. THAT LAST ONE STOOD OUT LIKE A SORE THUMB.
HE'S RIGHT, THOUGH--I AM SHOWING OFF--A LITTLE.
AND WHY NOT? IN PUBLIC, I'LL CONCEAL MY ABILITIES...
...BUT ALONE--OR AMONG SUPPOSED "FRIENDS"--I'LL DRESS AND ACT AS I DARN WELL PLEASE!
OH...THERE'S NO NEED TO MAKE A FEDERAL CASE OUT OF THIS. ALEX IS JUST CONCERNED ABOUT-- HOLD IT!
MOIRA'S THOUGHT PATTERNS-- THEY'RE CHAOTIC, TERRIFIED! SOMETHING'S WRONG!
I'D BETTER GET TO HER-- FAST--AS PHOENIX!

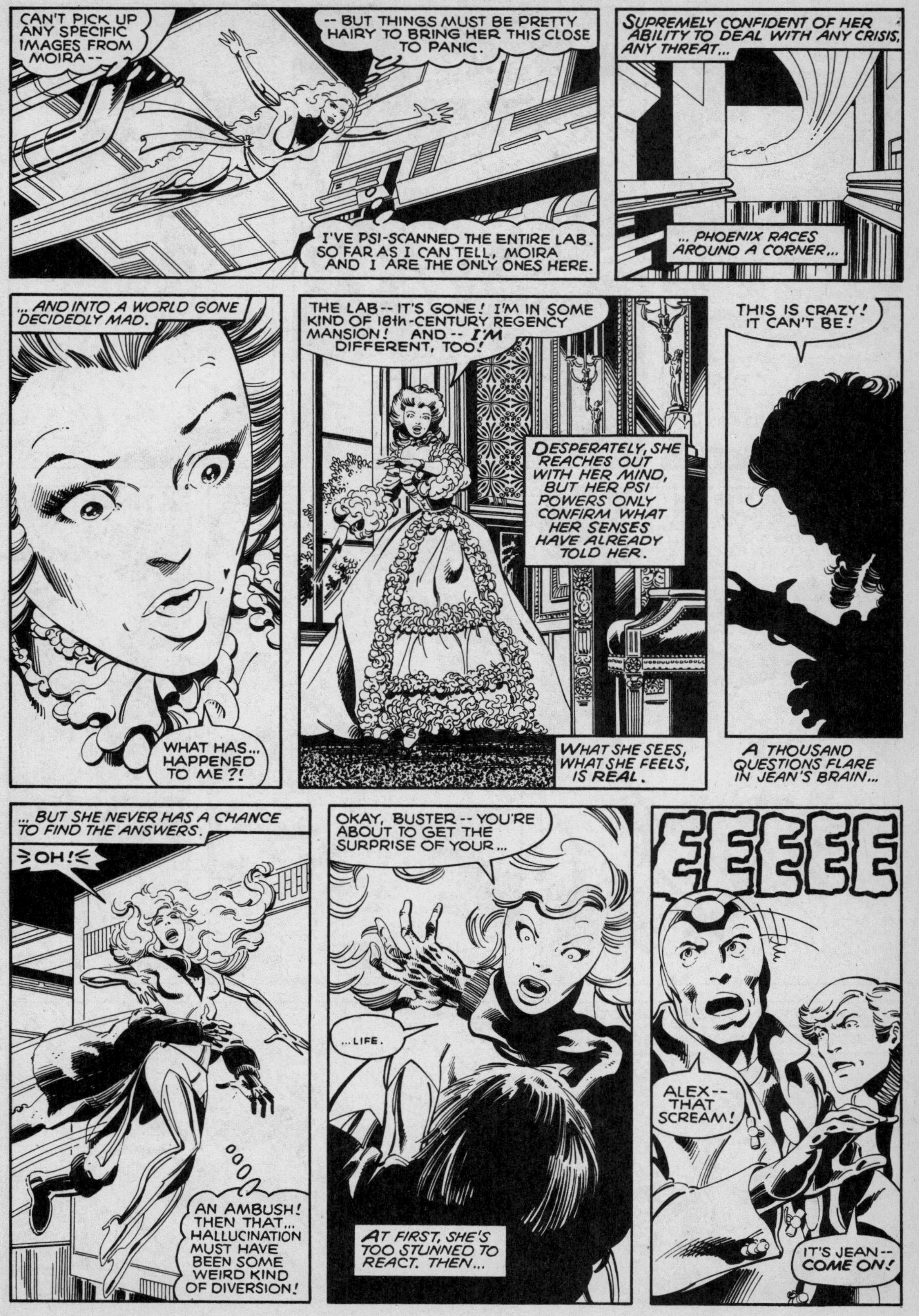
CAN'T PICK UP ANY SPECIFIC IMAGES FROM MOIRA --
-- BUT THINGS MUST BE PRETTY HAIRY TO BRING HER THIS CLOSE TO PANIC.
I'VE PSI-SCANNED THE ENTIRE LAB. SO FAR AS I CAN TELL, MOIRA AND I ARE THE ONLY ONES HERE.
SUPREMELY CONFIDENT OF HER ABILITY TO DEAL WITH ANY CRISIS, ANY THREAT...
... PHOENIX RACES AROUND A CORNER...
... AND INTO A WORLD GONE DECIDEDLY MAD.
WHAT HAS... HAPPENED TO ME?!
THE LAB -- IT'S GONE! I'M IN SOME KIND OF 18th-CENTURY REGENCY MANSION! AND -- I'M DIFFERENT, TOO!
DESPERATELY, SHE REACHES OUT WITH HER MIND, BUT HER PSI POWERS ONLY CONFIRM WHAT HER SENSES HAVE ALREADY TOLD HER.
WHAT SHE SEES, WHAT SHE FEELS, IS REAL.
THIS IS CRAZY! IT CAN'T BE!
A THOUSAND QUESTIONS FLARE IN JEAN'S BRAIN...
... BUT SHE NEVER HAS A CHANCE TO FIND THE ANSWERS.
OH!
OOO
AN AMBUSH! THEN THAT... HALLUCINATION MUST HAVE BEEN SOME WEIRD KIND OF DIVERSION!
OKAY, BUSTER -- YOU'RE ABOUT TO GET THE SURPRISE OF YOUR...
... LIFE.
AT FIRST, SHE'S TOO STUNNED TO REACT. THEN...
EEEEE
ALEX -- THAT SCREAM!
IT'S JEAN -- COME ON!

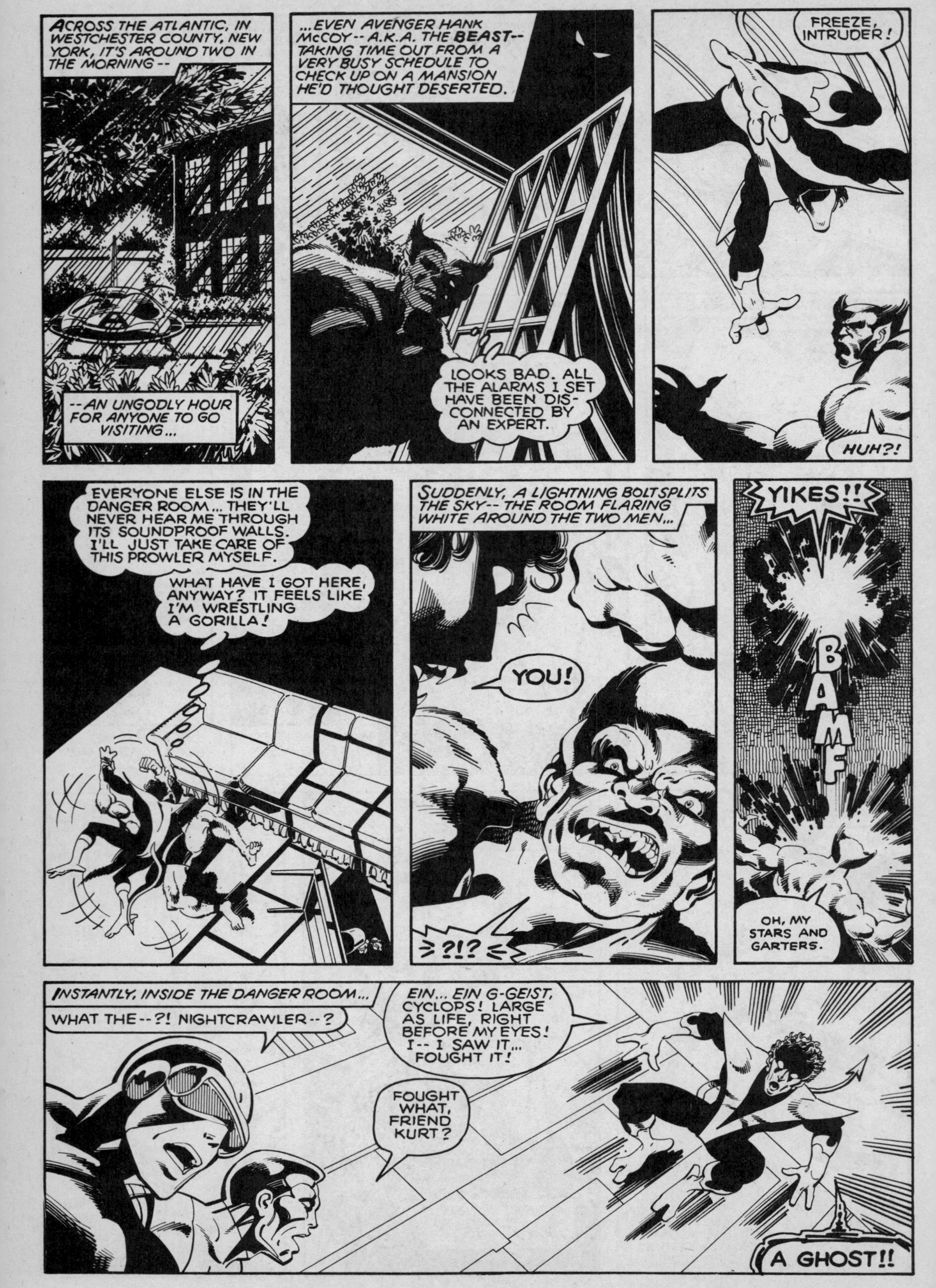
ACROSS THE ATLANTIC, IN WESTCHESTER COUNTY, NEW YORK, IT'S AROUND TWO IN THE MORNING --
-- AN UNGODLY HOUR FOR ANYONE TO GO VISITING...
...EVEN AVENGER HANK McCOY -- A.K.A. THE BEAST -- TAKING TIME OUT FROM A VERY BUSY SCHEDULE TO CHECK UP ON A MANSION HE'D THOUGHT DESERTED.
LOOKS BAD. ALL THE ALARMS I SET HAVE BEEN DISCONNECTED BY AN EXPERT.
FREEZE, INTRUDER!
HUH?!
EVERYONE ELSE IS IN THE DANGER ROOM... THEY'LL NEVER HEAR ME THROUGH ITS SOUNDPROOF WALLS. I'LL JUST TAKE CARE OF THIS PROWLER MYSELF.
WHAT HAVE I GOT HERE, ANYWAY? IT FEELS LIKE I'M WRESTLING A GORILLA!
SUDDENLY, A LIGHTNING BOLT SPLITS THE SKY -- THE ROOM FLARING WHITE AROUND THE TWO MEN...
YOU!
?!?
YIKES!!
BAMF
OH, MY STARS AND GARTERS.
INSTANTLY, INSIDE THE DANGER ROOM...
WHAT THE --?! NIGHTCRAWLER --?
EIN... EIN G-GEIST, CYCLOPS! LARGE AS LIFE, RIGHT BEFORE MY EYES! I-- I SAW IT... FOUGHT IT!
FOUGHT WHAT, FRIEND KURT?
A GHOST!!

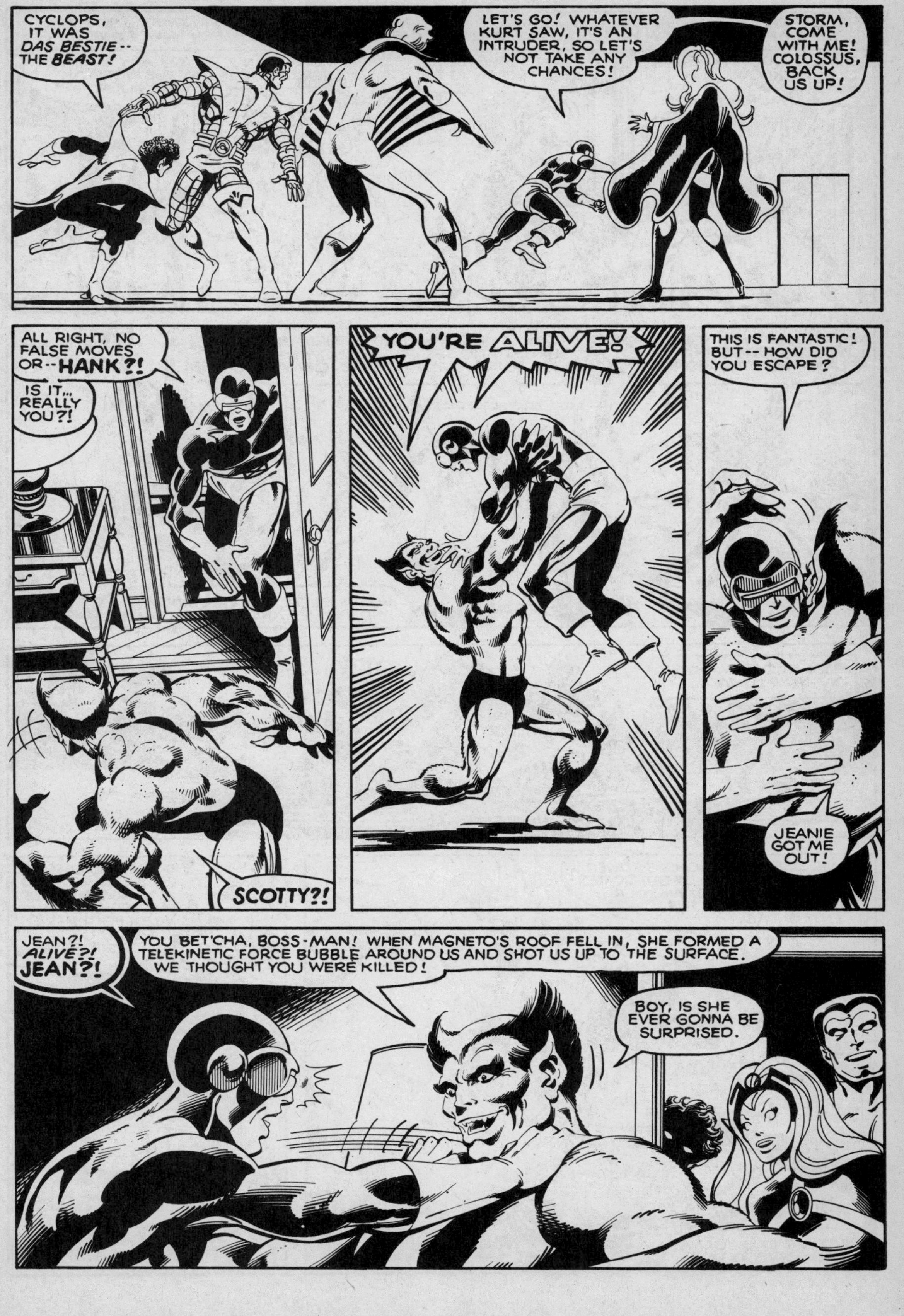
CYCLOPS, IT WAS *DAS BESTIE* -- THE **BEAST**!
LET'S GO! WHATEVER KURT SAW, IT'S AN INTRUDER, SO LET'S NOT TAKE ANY CHANCES!
STORM, COME WITH ME! COLOSSUS, BACK US UP!
ALL RIGHT, NO FALSE MOVES OR-- **HANK?!**
IS IT... REALLY YOU?!
SCOTTY?!
YOU'RE ALIVE!
THIS IS FANTASTIC! BUT-- HOW DID YOU ESCAPE?
JEANIE GOT ME OUT!
JEAN?! *ALIVE?!* **JEAN?!**
YOU BET'CHA, BOSS-MAN! WHEN MAGNETO'S ROOF FELL IN, SHE FORMED A TELEKINETIC FORCE BUBBLE AROUND US AND SHOT US UP TO THE SURFACE. WE THOUGHT YOU WERE KILLED!
BOY, IS SHE EVER GONNA BE SURPRISED.

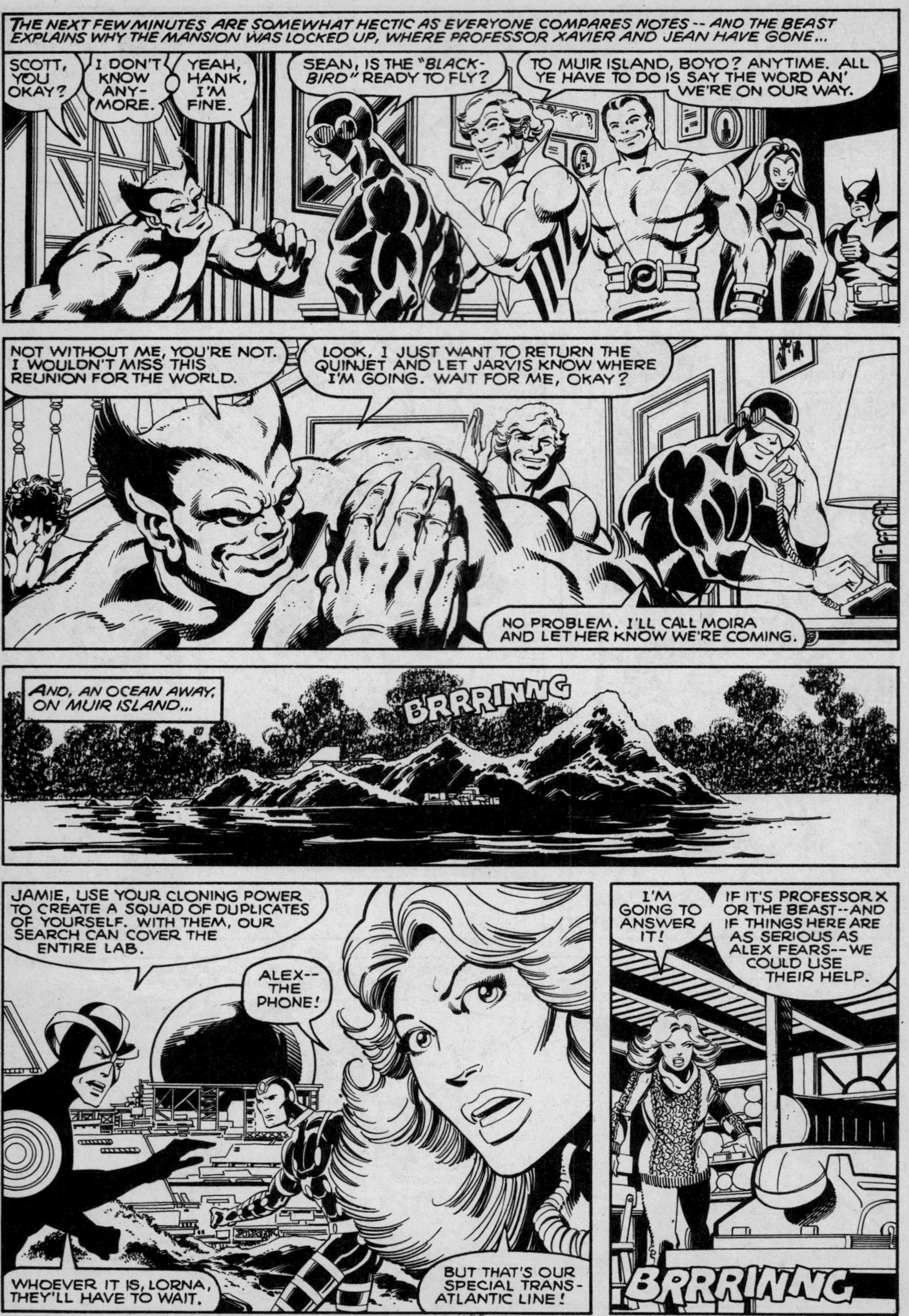
THE NEXT FEW MINUTES ARE SOMEWHAT HECTIC AS EVERYONE COMPARES NOTES -- AND THE BEAST EXPLAINS WHY THE MANSION WAS LOCKED UP, WHERE PROFESSOR XAVIER AND JEAN HAVE GONE...
SCOTT, YOU OKAY?
I DON'T KNOW ANYMORE.
YEAH, HANK, I'M FINE.
SEAN, IS THE "BLACKBIRD" READY TO FLY?
TO MUIR ISLAND, BOYO? ANYTIME. ALL YE HAVE TO DO IS SAY THE WORD AN' WE'RE ON OUR WAY.
NOT WITHOUT ME, YOU'RE NOT. I WOULDN'T MISS THIS REUNION FOR THE WORLD.
LOOK, I JUST WANT TO RETURN THE QUINJET AND LET JARVIS KNOW WHERE I'M GOING. WAIT FOR ME, OKAY?
NO PROBLEM. I'LL CALL MOIRA AND LET HER KNOW WE'RE COMING.
AND, AN OCEAN AWAY, ON MUIR ISLAND...
BRRRINNG
JAMIE, USE YOUR CLONING POWER TO CREATE A SQUAD OF DUPLICATES OF YOURSELF. WITH THEM, OUR SEARCH CAN COVER THE ENTIRE LAB.
ALEX-- THE PHONE!
WHOEVER IT IS, LORNA, THEY'LL HAVE TO WAIT.
BUT THAT'S OUR SPECIAL TRANS-ATLANTIC LINE!
I'M GOING TO ANSWER IT!
IF IT'S PROFESSOR X OR THE BEAST--AND IF THINGS HERE ARE AS SERIOUS AS ALEX FEARS--WE COULD USE THEIR HELP.
BRRRINNG

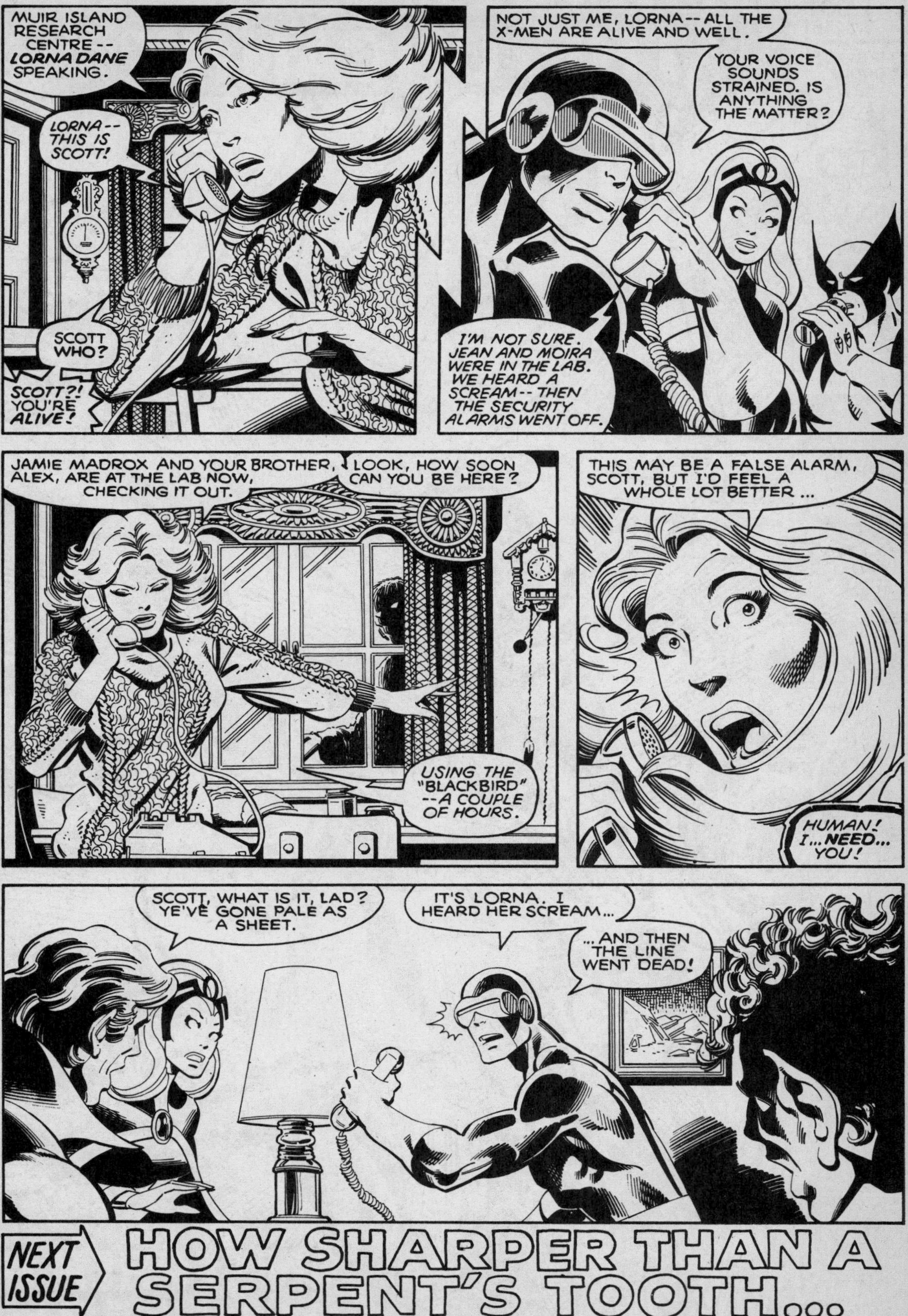

MUIR ISLAND RESEARCH CENTRE -- LORNA DANE SPEAKING.
LORNA -- THIS IS SCOTT!
SCOTT WHO?
SCOTT?! YOU'RE ALIVE!
NOT JUST ME, LORNA -- ALL THE X-MEN ARE ALIVE AND WELL.
YOUR VOICE SOUNDS STRAINED. IS ANYTHING THE MATTER?
I'M NOT SURE. JEAN AND MOIRA WERE IN THE LAB. WE HEARD A SCREAM -- THEN THE SECURITY ALARMS WENT OFF.
JAMIE MADROX AND YOUR BROTHER, ALEX, ARE AT THE LAB NOW, CHECKING IT OUT.
LOOK, HOW SOON CAN YOU BE HERE?
USING THE "BLACKBIRD" -- A COUPLE OF HOURS.
THIS MAY BE A FALSE ALARM, SCOTT, BUT I'D FEEL A WHOLE LOT BETTER ...
HUMAN! I... NEED... YOU!
SCOTT, WHAT IS IT, LAD? YE'VE GONE PALE AS A SHEET.
IT'S LORNA. I HEARD HER SCREAM...
... AND THEN THE LINE WENT DEAD!
NEXT ISSUE
HOW SHARPER THAN A SERPENT'S TOOTH...

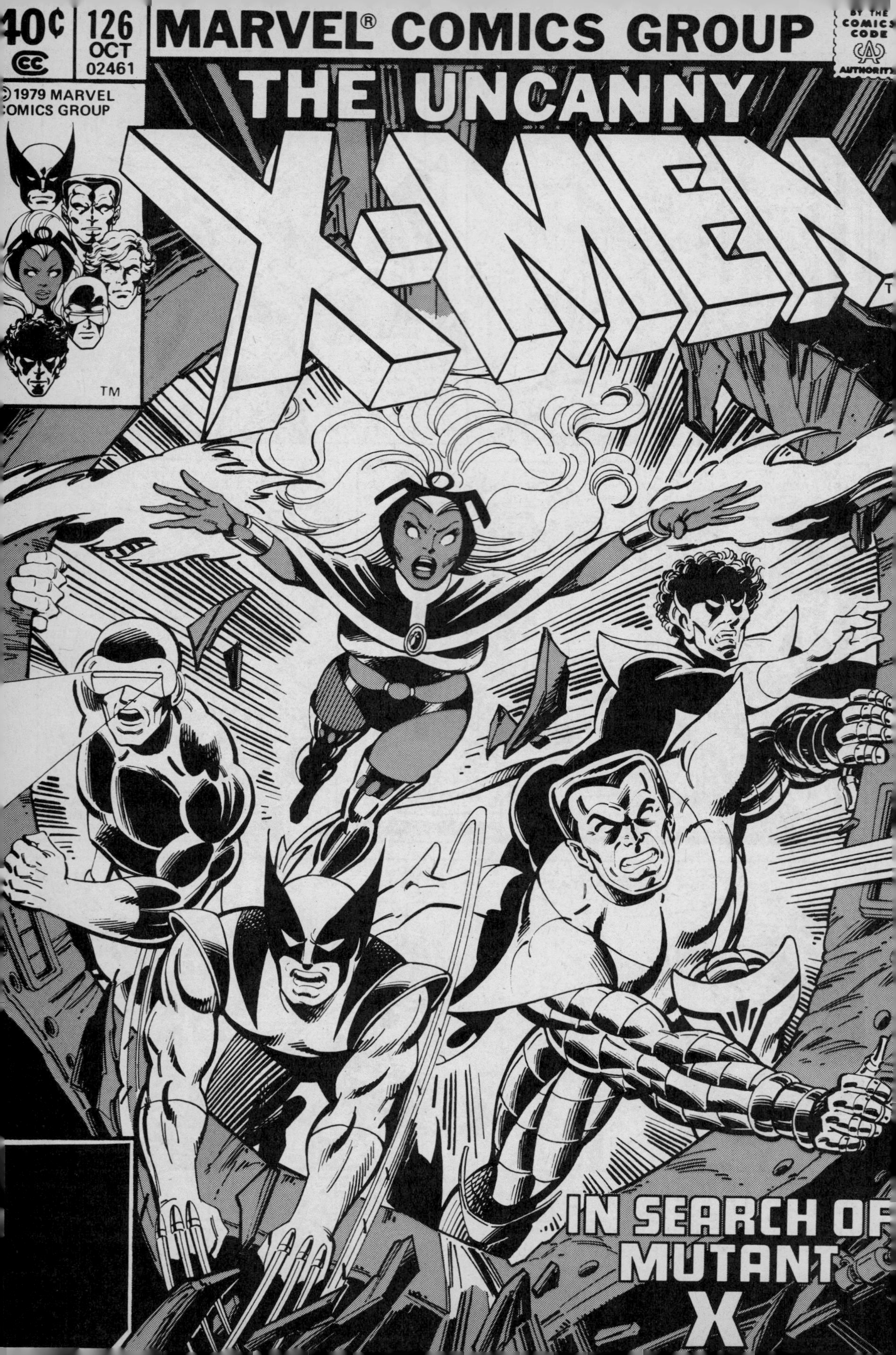

40¢
CC
126
OCT
02461
MARVEL® COMICS GROUP
BY THE COMICS CODE AUTHORITY
© 1979 MARVEL COMICS GROUP
THE UNCANNY
X-MEN
TM
IN SEARCH OF MUTANT X

Cyclops. Storm. Banshee. Nightcrawler. Wolverine. Colossus. Children of the atom, students of Charles Xavier, MUTANTS––feared and hated by the world they have sworn to protect. These are the STRANGEST heroes of all!

Stan Lee PRESENTS: THE UNCANNY X-MEN!™

CHRIS CLAREMONT AUTHOR | JOHN BYRNE PENCILER | TERRY AUSTIN INKER | TOM ORZECHOWSKI, letterer GLYNIS WEIN, colorist | ROGER STERN EDITOR | JIM SHOOTER Ed.-IN-CHIEF

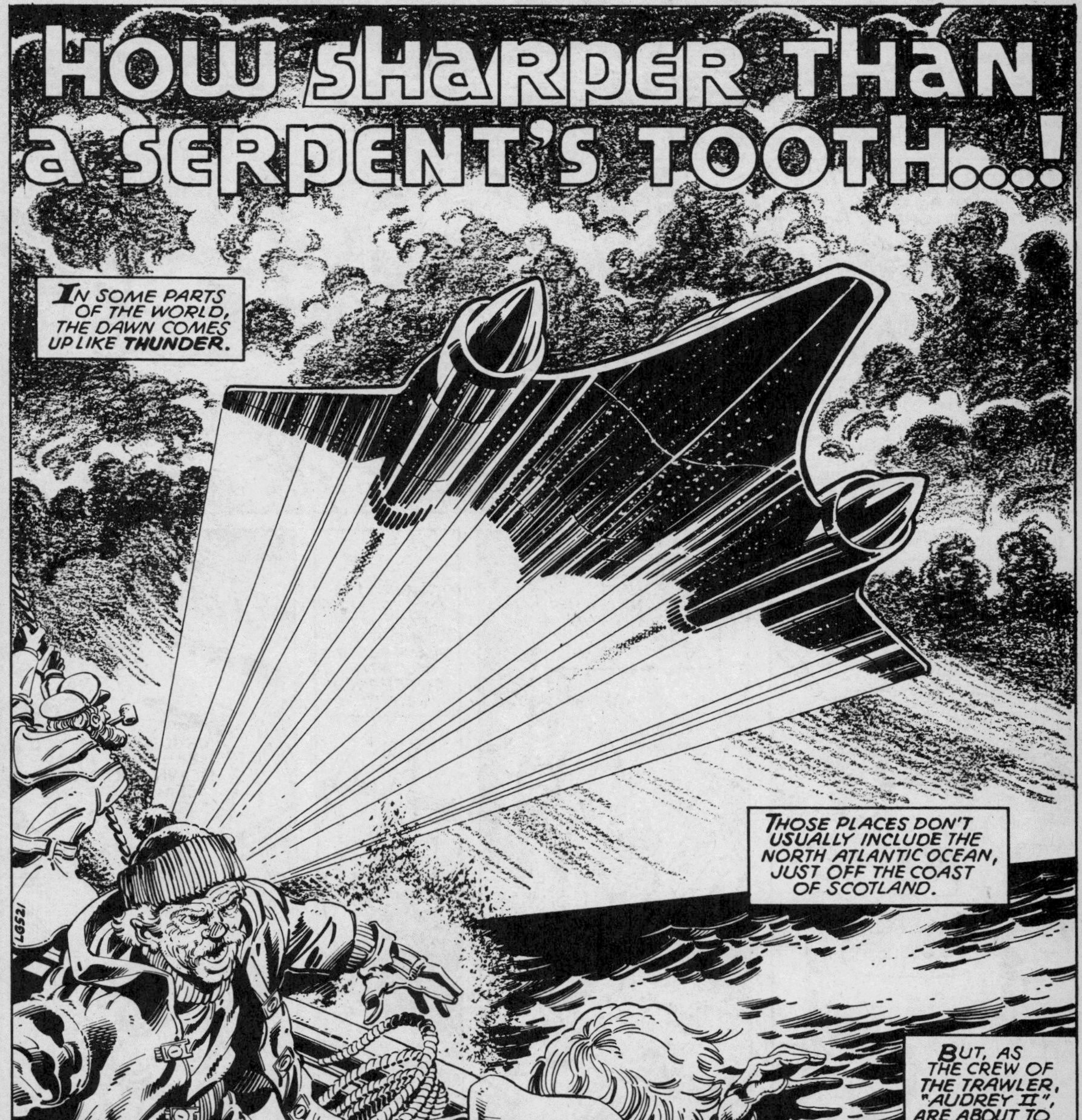
HOW SHARPER THAN A SERPENT'S TOOTH...!
IN SOME PARTS OF THE WORLD, THE DAWN COMES UP LIKE THUNDER.
THOSE PLACES DON'T USUALLY INCLUDE THE NORTH ATLANTIC OCEAN, JUST OFF THE COAST OF SCOTLAND.
BUT, AS THE CREW OF THE TRAWLER, "AUDREY II", ARE ABOUT TO DISCOVER, THIS MORNING IS DIFFERENT.

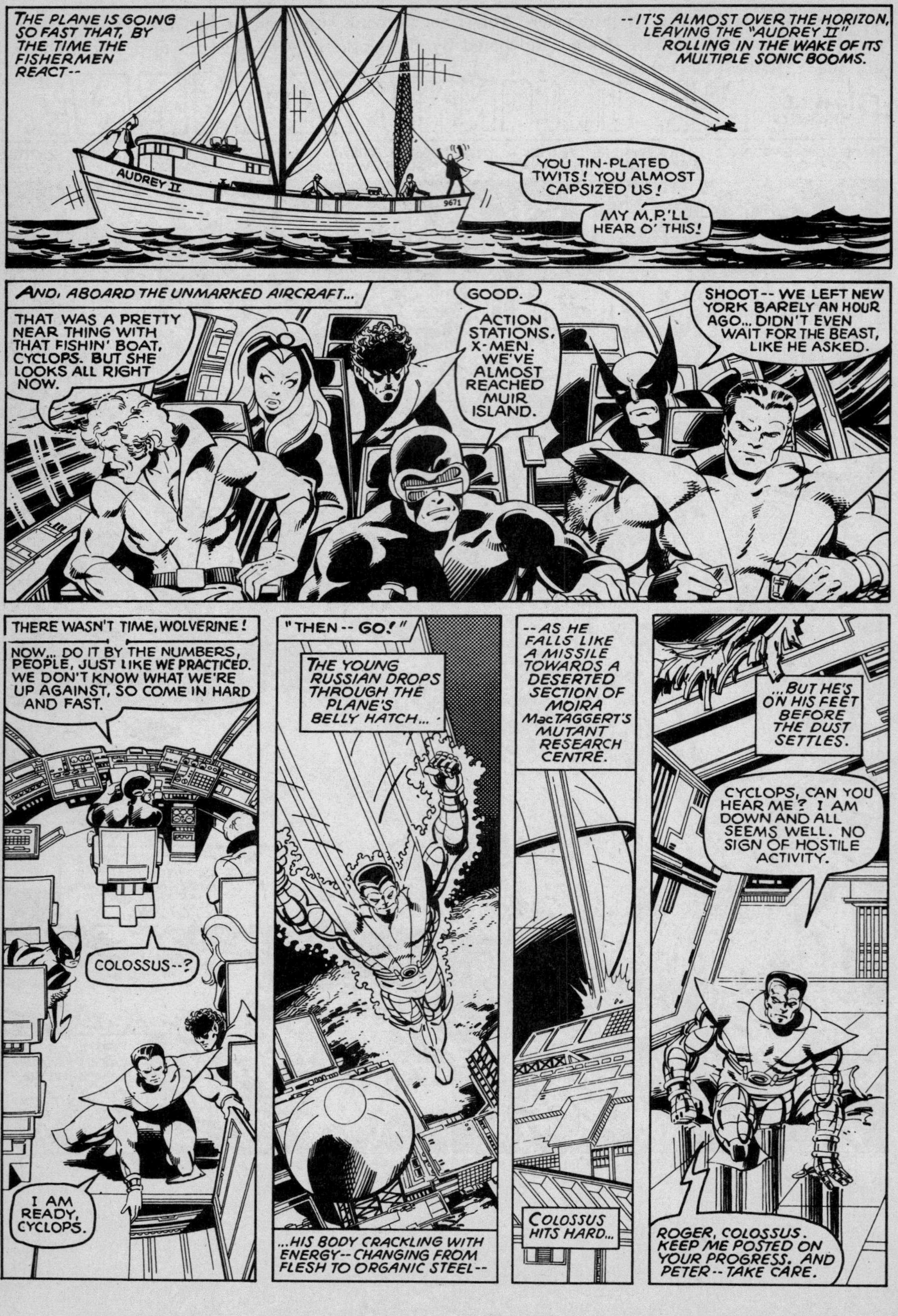
THE PLANE IS GOING SO FAST THAT, BY THE TIME THE FISHERMEN REACT--
--IT'S ALMOST OVER THE HORIZON, LEAVING THE "AUDREY II" ROLLING IN THE WAKE OF ITS MULTIPLE SONIC BOOMS.
AUDREY II
9671
YOU TIN-PLATED TWITS! YOU ALMOST CAPSIZED US!
MY M.P.'LL HEAR O' THIS!
AND, ABOARD THE UNMARKED AIRCRAFT...
THAT WAS A PRETTY NEAR THING WITH THAT FISHIN' BOAT, CYCLOPS. BUT SHE LOOKS ALL RIGHT NOW.
GOOD.
ACTION STATIONS, X-MEN. WE'VE ALMOST REACHED MUIR ISLAND.
SHOOT-- WE LEFT NEW YORK BARELY AN HOUR AGO... DIDN'T EVEN WAIT FOR THE BEAST, LIKE HE ASKED.
THERE WASN'T TIME, WOLVERINE!
NOW... DO IT BY THE NUMBERS, PEOPLE, JUST LIKE WE PRACTICED. WE DON'T KNOW WHAT WE'RE UP AGAINST, SO COME IN HARD AND FAST.
COLOSSUS--?
I AM READY, CYCLOPS.
"THEN -- GO!"
THE YOUNG RUSSIAN DROPS THROUGH THE PLANE'S BELLY HATCH...
...HIS BODY CRACKLING WITH ENERGY-- CHANGING FROM FLESH TO ORGANIC STEEL--
--AS HE FALLS LIKE A MISSILE TOWARDS A DESERTED SECTION OF MOIRA MacTAGGERT'S MUTANT RESEARCH CENTRE.
COLOSSUS HITS HARD...
...BUT HE'S ON HIS FEET BEFORE THE DUST SETTLES.
CYCLOPS, CAN YOU HEAR ME? I AM DOWN AND ALL SEEMS WELL. NO SIGN OF HOSTILE ACTIVITY.
ROGER, COLOSSUS. KEEP ME POSTED ON YOUR PROGRESS. AND PETER-- TAKE CARE.

CYCLOPS MAKES ANOTHER LOW PASS OVER THE ISLAND. THIS TIME, IT'S *STORM* AND *WOLVERINE'S* TURN TO BAIL OUT.

TAKE IT EASY, WILLYA, ORORO?!

YA LEFT MY STOMACH BACK ON THE FLAMIN' PLANE!

OUR FRIENDS HERE ARE IN DANGER, WOLVERINE. WE CANNOT AFFORD TO WASTE EVEN AN INSTANT.

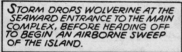
STORM DROPS WOLVERINE AT THE SEAWARD ENTRANCE TO THE MAIN COMPLEX, BEFORE HEADING OFF TO BEGIN AN AIRBORNE SWEEP OF THE ISLAND.

BEHIND HER, CYCLOPS DROPS THE PLANE INTO A PERFECT VERTICAL TOUCHDOWN ON THE LANDING PAD BEHIND THE LAB.

GET GOING, NIGHTCRAWLER. TELEPORT INTO THE RESIDENCE AND SEARCH IT FROM ATTIC TO CELLAR.

NOT TO WORRY, CYCLOPS! I'M--

BAMF

--ALREADY THERE!

WITH A FLASH OF BRIMSTONE, NIGHTCRAWLER DISAPPEARS FROM THE FLIGHT DECK, INSTANTLY MATERIALIZING IN THE LIVING ROOM OF MOIRA'S HOUSE.

YOU'RE PUSHIN' AWFUL HARD, CYCLOPS.

YOU DIDN'T HEAR LORNA DANE'S SCREAM OVER THE PHONE, SEAN-- I'VE NEVER HEARD SUCH RAW...TERROR-- AND THEN, A MOMENT LATER, THE LINE WENT DEAD.

THAT WAS OVER AN HOUR AGO.* A LOT CAN HAPPEN IN THAT MUCH TIME.

*LAST ISSUE FOR THE REST OF US. --ROG.

JUST BEFORE WE WERE CUT OFF, LORNA SAID THE LAB SECURITY ALARMS HAD SOUNDED, THAT JAMIE MADROX AND MY BROTHER, ALEX, HAD GONE TO CHECK THINGS OUT...

CYCLOPS, THIS IS NIGHTCRAWLER! COME AT ONCE! HURRY!

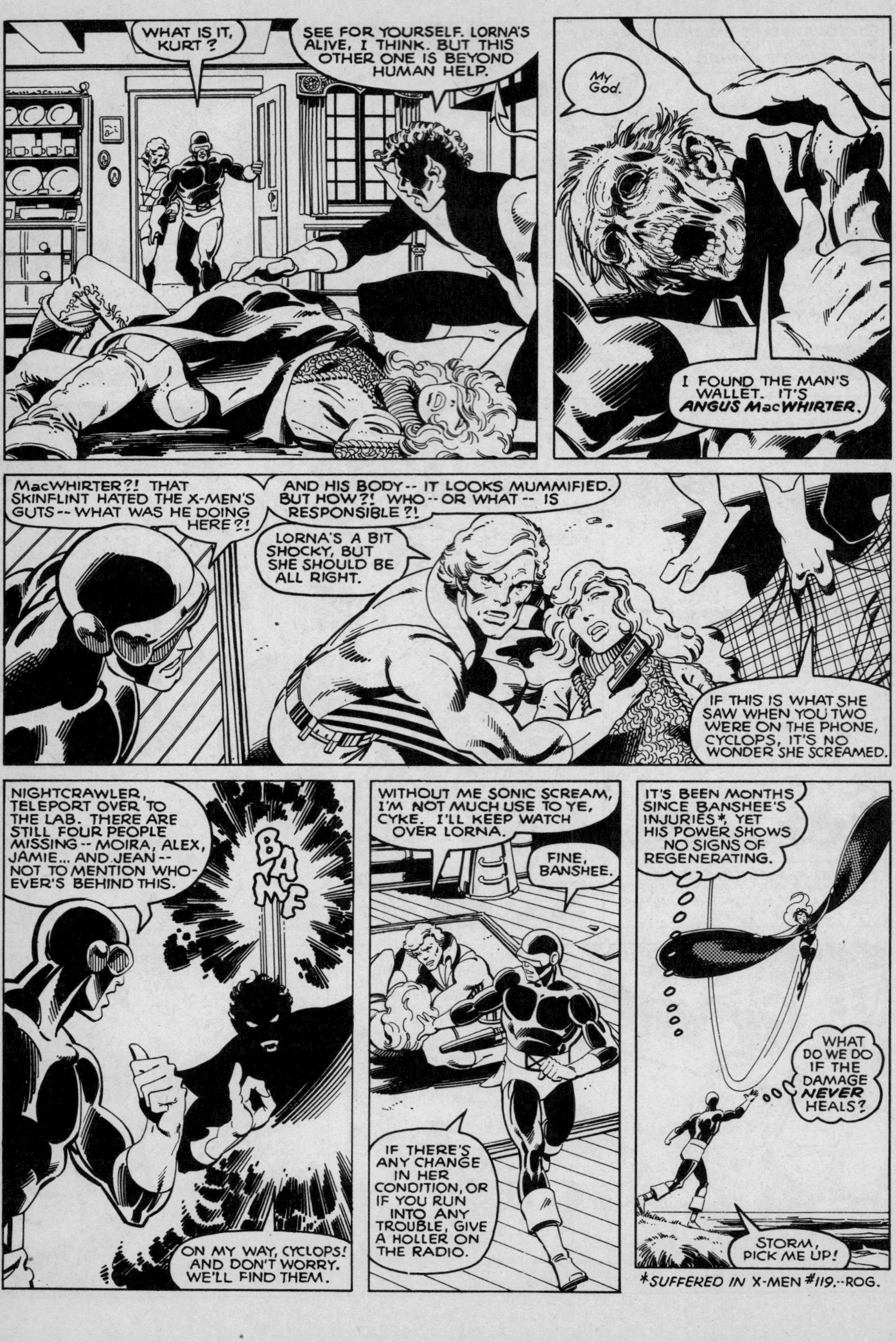
WHAT IS IT, KURT?
SEE FOR YOURSELF. LORNA'S ALIVE, I THINK. BUT THIS OTHER ONE IS BEYOND HUMAN HELP.
My God.
I FOUND THE MAN'S WALLET. IT'S ANGUS MacWHIRTER.
MacWHIRTER?! THAT SKINFLINT HATED THE X-MEN'S GUTS -- WHAT WAS HE DOING HERE?!
AND HIS BODY -- IT LOOKS MUMMIFIED. BUT HOW?! WHO -- OR WHAT -- IS RESPONSIBLE?!
LORNA'S A BIT SHOCKY, BUT SHE SHOULD BE ALL RIGHT.
IF THIS IS WHAT SHE SAW WHEN YOU TWO WERE ON THE PHONE, CYCLOPS, IT'S NO WONDER SHE SCREAMED.
NIGHTCRAWLER, TELEPORT OVER TO THE LAB. THERE ARE STILL FOUR PEOPLE MISSING -- MOIRA, ALEX, JAMIE... AND JEAN -- NOT TO MENTION WHO-EVER'S BEHIND THIS.
BAMF
ON MY WAY, CYCLOPS! AND DON'T WORRY. WE'LL FIND THEM.
WITHOUT ME SONIC SCREAM, I'M NOT MUCH USE TO YE, CYKE. I'LL KEEP WATCH OVER LORNA.
FINE, BANSHEE.
IF THERE'S ANY CHANGE IN HER CONDITION, OR IF YOU RUN INTO ANY TROUBLE, GIVE A HOLLER ON THE RADIO.
IT'S BEEN MONTHS SINCE BANSHEE'S INJURIES*, YET HIS POWER SHOWS NO SIGNS OF REGENERATING.
WHAT DO WE DO IF THE DAMAGE NEVER HEALS?
STORM, PICK ME UP!
*SUFFERED IN X-MEN #119.--ROG.

I'VE SCOUTED THE ENTIRE ISLAND FROM THE AIR, CYCLOPS. THERE ARE NO SIGNS OF ANY INTRUDERS... OR OF OUR FRIENDS.

HEAD FOR THE LAB, STORM. THAT'S WHERE I'M BETTING WE'LL FIND THEM.

AND, DEEP INSIDE THAT COMPLEX...

COMPLETE DARKNESS... NOT EVEN EMERGENCY LIGHTS!

FROM THE FUSE BOXES I'VE SEEN, EVERY CIRCUIT IN THE PLACE MUST HAVE OVERLOADED AND BLOWN AT ONCE.

BUT WHO HAS THE POWER TO DO THAT? LORNA? OR... MAGNETO!

YIKES!

SHZAK

FREEZE!

HAVOK!

DON'T SHOOT! IT'S ME, NIGHTCRAWLER!

SORRY, BUSTER -- NIGHTCRAWLER'S DEAD, AND I STOPPED BELIEVING IN GHOSTS LONG AGO. NOW, STEP OUT WHERE I CAN SEE YOU OR I'LL BURN YOU DOWN.

HE STILL THINKS WE'RE DEAD! AND THE CORRIDOR'S TOO DARK -- I BECOME NEAR-INVISIBLE IN THESE DEEP SHADOWS. I'D BETTER 'PORT OUT OF HERE AND GET CYCLOPS.

BUT BEFORE NIGHTCRAWLER CAN DO ANYTHING...

WHAT THE --?!

YOU MAY BE STRONG, PAL, BUT LET'S SEE THAT STRENGTH SAVE YOU --

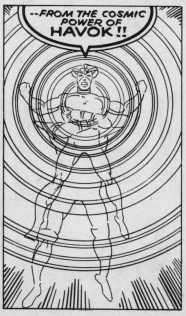

--FROM THE COSMIC POWER OF HAVOK!!

I HAVE FACED YOUR ENERGY BLASTS BEFORE, MY AMERICAN FRIEND -- AND WITHSTOOD THEM.

HUH?! COLOSSUS! YOU'RE ALIVE!!

I, AND ALL THE X-MEN, HAVOK. IT IS GOOD TO SEE YOU AGAIN.

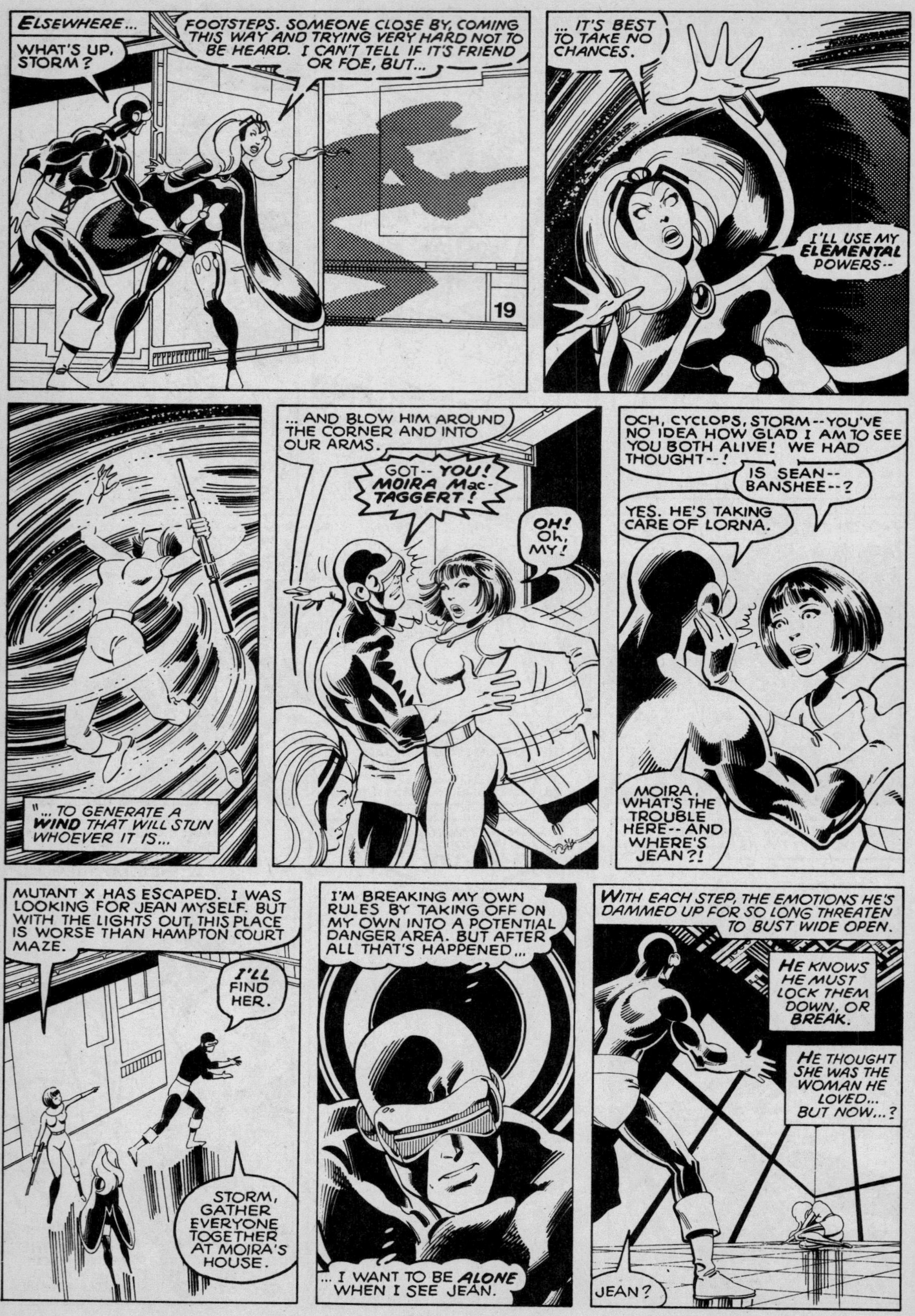
ELSEWHERE...
WHAT'S UP, STORM?
FOOTSTEPS. SOMEONE CLOSE BY, COMING THIS WAY AND TRYING VERY HARD NOT TO BE HEARD. I CAN'T TELL IF IT'S FRIEND OR FOE, BUT...
19
... IT'S BEST TO TAKE NO CHANCES.
I'LL USE MY ELEMENTAL POWERS--
"... TO GENERATE A WIND THAT WILL STUN WHOEVER IT IS...
... AND BLOW HIM AROUND THE CORNER AND INTO OUR ARMS.
GOT-- YOU! MOIRA MacTAGGERT!
OH! Oh, MY!
OCH, CYCLOPS, STORM--YOU'VE NO IDEA HOW GLAD I AM TO SEE YOU BOTH ALIVE! WE HAD THOUGHT--!
IS SEAN--BANSHEE--?
YES. HE'S TAKING CARE OF LORNA.
MOIRA, WHAT'S THE TROUBLE HERE--AND WHERE'S JEAN?!
MUTANT X HAS ESCAPED. I WAS LOOKING FOR JEAN MYSELF. BUT WITH THE LIGHTS OUT, THIS PLACE IS WORSE THAN HAMPTON COURT MAZE.
I'LL FIND HER.
STORM, GATHER EVERYONE TOGETHER AT MOIRA'S HOUSE.
I'M BREAKING MY OWN RULES BY TAKING OFF ON MY OWN INTO A POTENTIAL DANGER AREA. BUT AFTER ALL THAT'S HAPPENED...
... I WANT TO BE ALONE WHEN I SEE JEAN.
WITH EACH STEP, THE EMOTIONS HE'S DAMMED UP FOR SO LONG THREATEN TO BUST WIDE OPEN.
HE KNOWS HE MUST LOCK THEM DOWN, OR BREAK.
HE THOUGHT SHE WAS THE WOMAN HE LOVED... BUT NOW...?
JEAN?

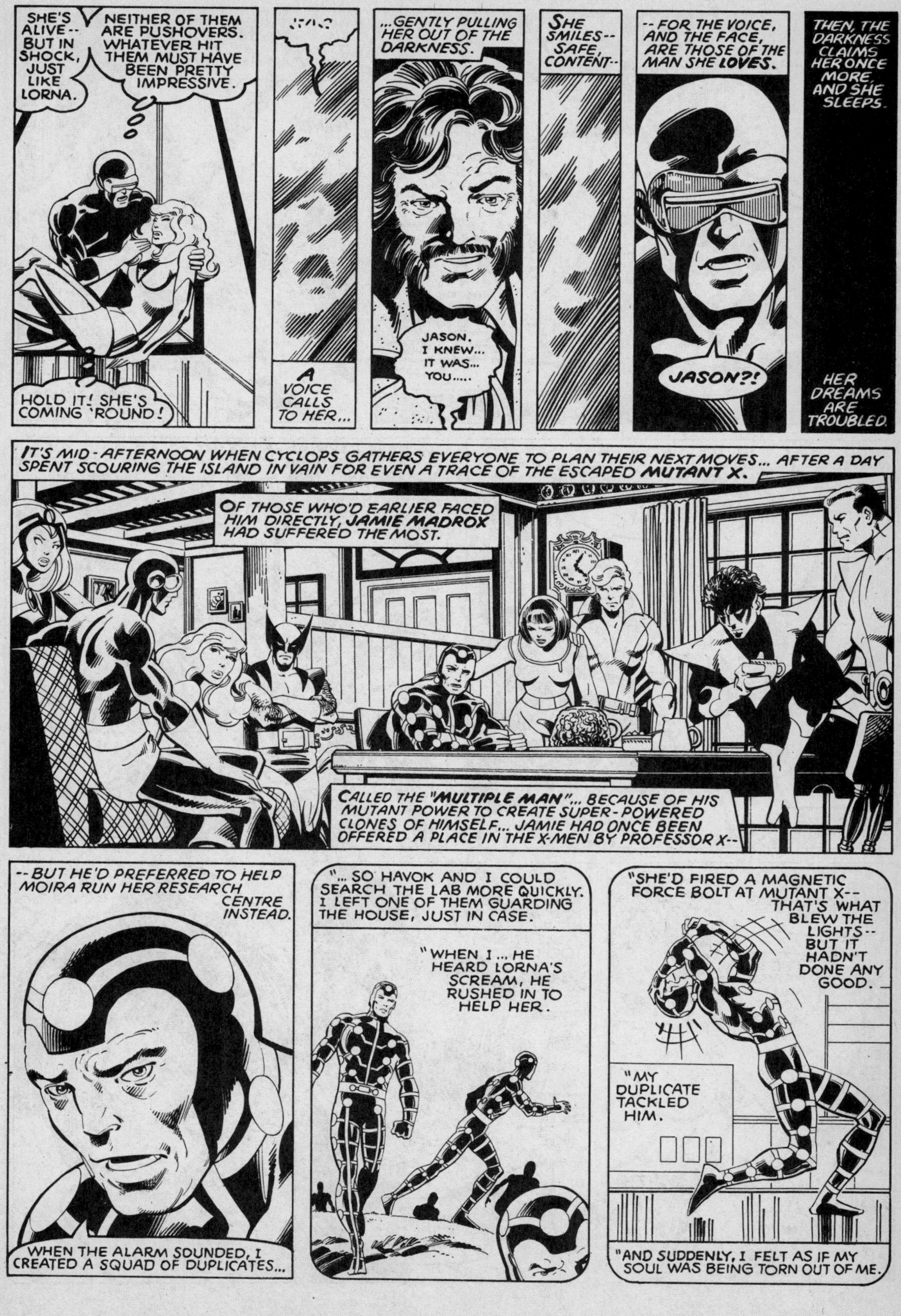
SHE'S ALIVE -- BUT IN SHOCK, JUST LIKE LORNA.
NEITHER OF THEM ARE PUSHOVERS. WHATEVER HIT THEM MUST HAVE BEEN PRETTY IMPRESSIVE.
HOLD IT! SHE'S COMING 'ROUND!
A VOICE CALLS TO HER...
...GENTLY PULLING HER OUT OF THE DARKNESS.
JASON. I KNEW... IT WAS... YOU.....
SHE SMILES-- SAFE, CONTENT--
-- FOR THE VOICE, AND THE FACE, ARE THOSE OF THE MAN SHE LOVES.
JASON?!
THEN, THE DARKNESS CLAIMS HER ONCE MORE, AND SHE SLEEPS.
HER DREAMS ARE TROUBLED.
IT'S MID-AFTERNOON WHEN CYCLOPS GATHERS EVERYONE TO PLAN THEIR NEXT MOVES... AFTER A DAY SPENT SCOURING THE ISLAND IN VAIN FOR EVEN A TRACE OF THE ESCAPED MUTANT X.
OF THOSE WHO'D EARLIER FACED HIM DIRECTLY, JAMIE MADROX HAD SUFFERED THE MOST.
CALLED THE "MULTIPLE MAN"... BECAUSE OF HIS MUTANT POWER TO CREATE SUPER-POWERED CLONES OF HIMSELF... JAMIE HAD ONCE BEEN OFFERED A PLACE IN THE X-MEN BY PROFESSOR X--
-- BUT HE'D PREFERRED TO HELP MOIRA RUN HER RESEARCH CENTRE INSTEAD.
WHEN THE ALARM SOUNDED, I CREATED A SQUAD OF DUPLICATES...
"... SO HAVOK AND I COULD SEARCH THE LAB MORE QUICKLY. I LEFT ONE OF THEM GUARDING THE HOUSE, JUST IN CASE.
"WHEN I ... HE HEARD LORNA'S SCREAM, HE RUSHED IN TO HELP HER.
"SHE'D FIRED A MAGNETIC FORCE BOLT AT MUTANT X-- THAT'S WHAT BLEW THE LIGHTS -- BUT IT HADN'T DONE ANY GOOD.
"MY DUPLICATE TACKLED HIM.
"AND SUDDENLY, I FELT AS IF MY SOUL WAS BEING TORN OUT OF ME.

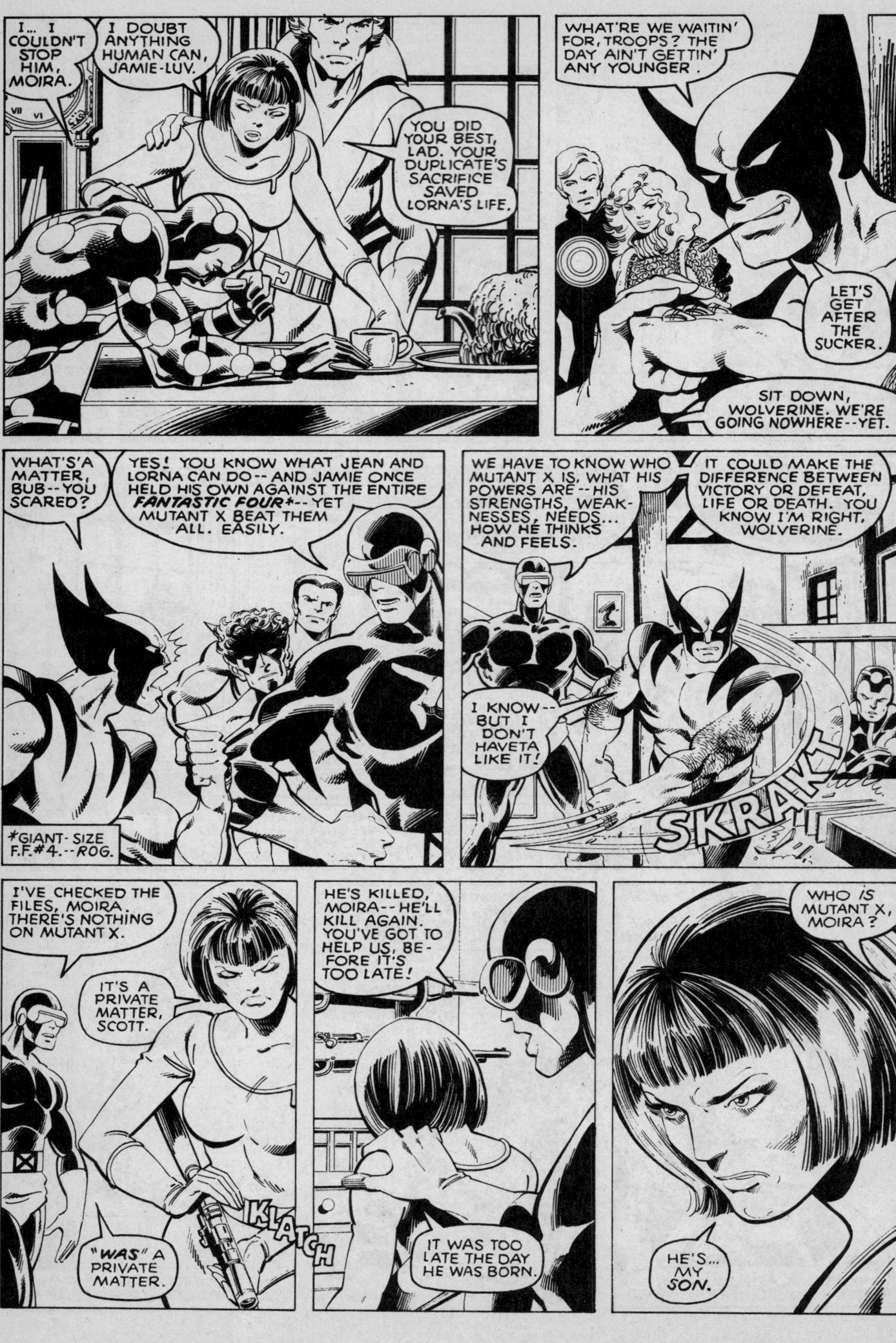
I... I COULDN'T STOP HIM, MOIRA.
I DOUBT ANYTHING HUMAN CAN, JAMIE-LUV.
YOU DID YOUR BEST, LAD. YOUR DUPLICATE'S SACRIFICE SAVED LORNA'S LIFE.
WHAT'RE WE WAITIN' FOR, TROOPS? THE DAY AIN'T GETTIN' ANY YOUNGER.
LET'S GET AFTER THE SUCKER.
SIT DOWN, WOLVERINE. WE'RE GOING NOWHERE--YET.
WHAT'S'A MATTER, BUB--YOU SCARED?
YES! YOU KNOW WHAT JEAN AND LORNA CAN DO--AND JAMIE ONCE HELD HIS OWN AGAINST THE ENTIRE FANTASTIC FOUR*--YET MUTANT X BEAT THEM ALL. EASILY.
*GIANT-SIZE F.F.#4.--ROG.
WE HAVE TO KNOW WHO MUTANT X IS, WHAT HIS POWERS ARE--HIS STRENGTHS, WEAKNESSES, NEEDS... HOW HE THINKS AND FEELS.
IT COULD MAKE THE DIFFERENCE BETWEEN VICTORY OR DEFEAT, LIFE OR DEATH. YOU KNOW I'M RIGHT, WOLVERINE.
I KNOW--BUT I DON'T HAVETA LIKE IT!
SKRAKT
I'VE CHECKED THE FILES, MOIRA. THERE'S NOTHING ON MUTANT X.
IT'S A PRIVATE MATTER, SCOTT.
"WAS" A PRIVATE MATTER.
KLATCH
HE'S KILLED, MOIRA--HE'LL KILL AGAIN. YOU'VE GOT TO HELP US, BEFORE IT'S TOO LATE!
IT WAS TOO LATE THE DAY HE WAS BORN.
WHO IS MUTANT X, MOIRA?
HE'S... MY SON.

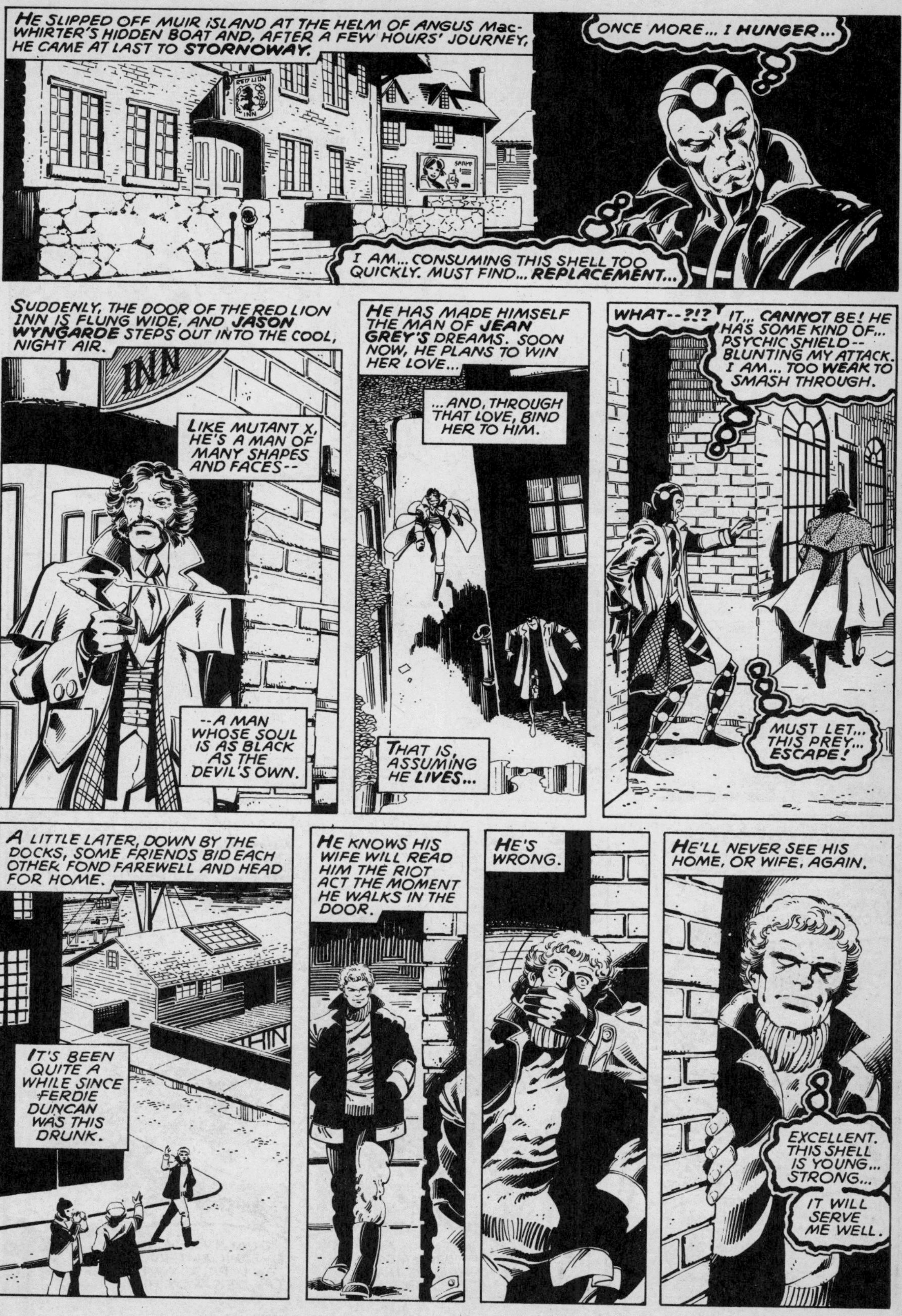
HE SLIPPED OFF MUIR ISLAND AT THE HELM OF ANGUS MacWHIRTER'S HIDDEN BOAT AND, AFTER A FEW HOURS' JOURNEY, HE CAME AT LAST TO STORNOWAY.
RED LION INN
ONCE MORE... I HUNGER...
I AM... CONSUMING THIS SHELL TOO QUICKLY. MUST FIND... REPLACEMENT...
SUDDENLY, THE DOOR OF THE RED LION INN IS FLUNG WIDE, AND JASON WYNGARDE STEPS OUT INTO THE COOL, NIGHT AIR.
INN
LIKE MUTANT X, HE'S A MAN OF MANY SHAPES AND FACES--
--A MAN WHOSE SOUL IS AS BLACK AS THE DEVIL'S OWN.
HE HAS MADE HIMSELF THE MAN OF JEAN GREY'S DREAMS. SOON NOW, HE PLANS TO WIN HER LOVE...
...AND, THROUGH THAT LOVE, BIND HER TO HIM.
THAT IS, ASSUMING HE LIVES...
WHAT--?!?
IT... CANNOT BE! HE HAS SOME KIND OF... PSYCHIC SHIELD--BLUNTING MY ATTACK. I AM... TOO WEAK TO SMASH THROUGH.
MUST LET... THIS PREY... ESCAPE!
A LITTLE LATER, DOWN BY THE DOCKS, SOME FRIENDS BID EACH OTHER FOND FAREWELL AND HEAD FOR HOME.
IT'S BEEN QUITE A WHILE SINCE FERDIE DUNCAN WAS THIS DRUNK.
HE KNOWS HIS WIFE WILL READ HIM THE RIOT ACT THE MOMENT HE WALKS IN THE DOOR.
HE'S WRONG.
HE'LL NEVER SEE HIS HOME, OR WIFE, AGAIN.
EXCELLENT. THIS SHELL IS YOUNG... STRONG...
IT WILL SERVE ME WELL.

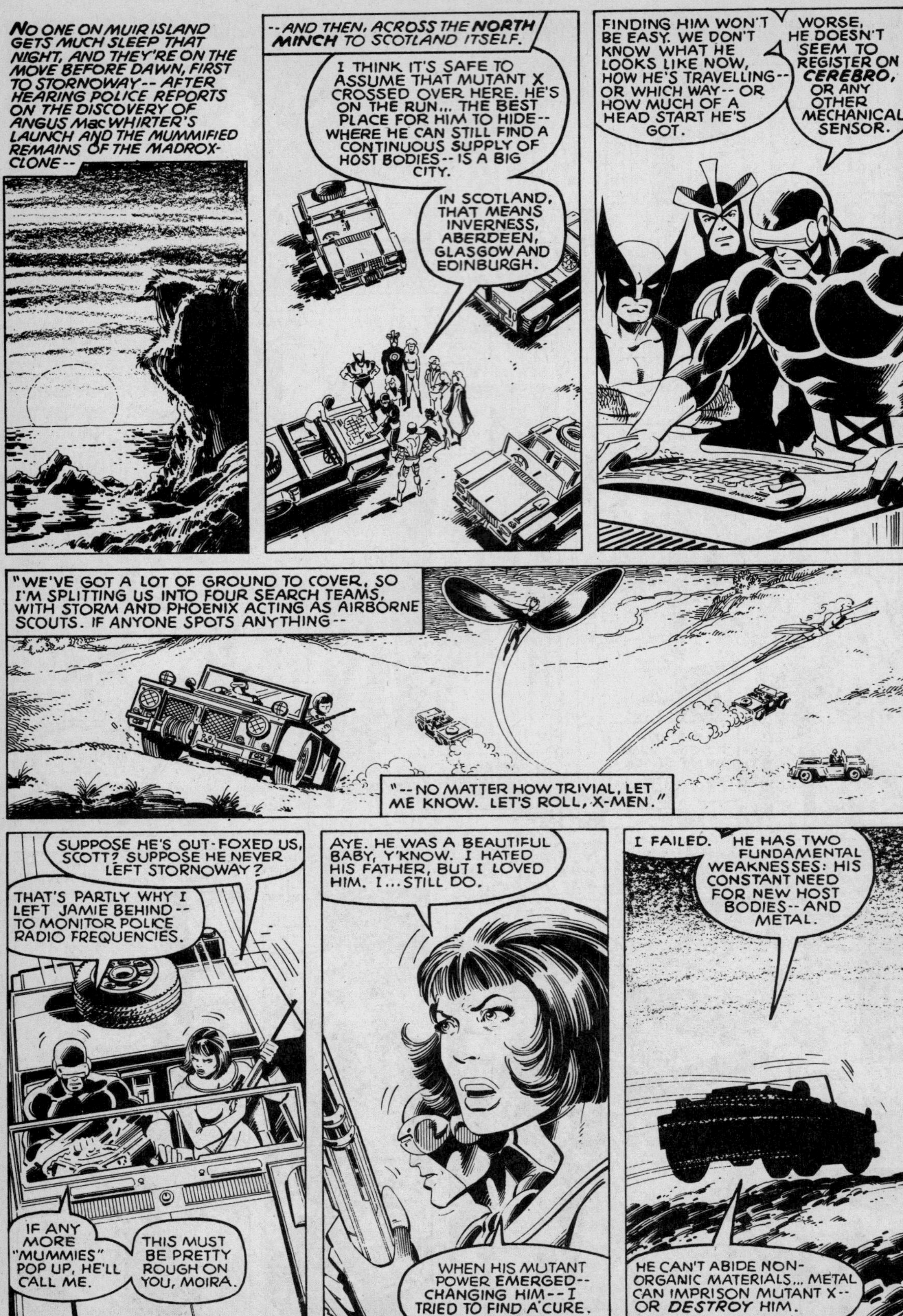
NO ONE ON MUIR ISLAND GETS MUCH SLEEP THAT NIGHT, AND THEY'RE ON THE MOVE BEFORE DAWN, FIRST TO STORNOWAY-- AFTER HEARING POLICE REPORTS ON THE DISCOVERY OF ANGUS MacWHIRTER'S LAUNCH AND THE MUMMIFIED REMAINS OF THE MADROX-CLONE--
--AND THEN, ACROSS THE NORTH MINCH TO SCOTLAND ITSELF.
I THINK IT'S SAFE TO ASSUME THAT MUTANT X CROSSED OVER HERE. HE'S ON THE RUN... THE BEST PLACE FOR HIM TO HIDE-- WHERE HE CAN STILL FIND A CONTINUOUS SUPPLY OF HOST BODIES-- IS A BIG CITY.
IN SCOTLAND, THAT MEANS INVERNESS, ABERDEEN, GLASGOW AND EDINBURGH.
FINDING HIM WON'T BE EASY. WE DON'T KNOW WHAT HE LOOKS LIKE NOW, HOW HE'S TRAVELLING-- OR WHICH WAY-- OR HOW MUCH OF A HEAD START HE'S GOT.
WORSE, HE DOESN'T SEEM TO REGISTER ON CEREBRO, OR ANY OTHER MECHANICAL SENSOR.
"WE'VE GOT A LOT OF GROUND TO COVER, SO I'M SPLITTING US INTO FOUR SEARCH TEAMS, WITH STORM AND PHOENIX ACTING AS AIRBORNE SCOUTS. IF ANYONE SPOTS ANYTHING--
"--NO MATTER HOW TRIVIAL, LET ME KNOW. LET'S ROLL, X-MEN."
SUPPOSE HE'S OUT-FOXED US, SCOTT? SUPPOSE HE NEVER LEFT STORNOWAY?
THAT'S PARTLY WHY I LEFT JAMIE BEHIND-- TO MONITOR POLICE RADIO FREQUENCIES.
IF ANY MORE "MUMMIES" POP UP, HE'LL CALL ME.
THIS MUST BE PRETTY ROUGH ON YOU, MOIRA.
AYE. HE WAS A BEAUTIFUL BABY, Y'KNOW. I HATED HIS FATHER, BUT I LOVED HIM. I... STILL DO.
WHEN HIS MUTANT POWER EMERGED-- CHANGING HIM-- I TRIED TO FIND A CURE.
I FAILED.
HE HAS TWO FUNDAMENTAL WEAKNESSES: HIS CONSTANT NEED FOR NEW HOST BODIES-- AND METAL.
HE CAN'T ABIDE NON-ORGANIC MATERIALS... METAL CAN IMPRISON MUTANT X-- OR DESTROY HIM.

I SHOULD HAVE MENTIONED TO SCOTT THAT MUTANT X SEEMS *INVISIBLE* TO MY TELEPATHIC POWERS, AS WELL.

I SHOULD HAVE TOLD HIM A LOT OF THINGS... BUT I... COULDN'T. THE VIBES I PICKED UP OFF HIM WERE SO CONFUSED... HE'S CHANGED... GROWN, TOO. I'M GLAD OF THAT, I THINK.

BUT... HOW WILL IT ALL AFFECT... US?

AT THAT MOMENT, ON A NEARBY HILLOCK...

THE X-MEN ARE OUT IN FORCE.

HEAVEN HELP WHOEVER THEY'RE AFTER.

IN SO MANY WAYS, PHOENIX IS THE MOST POWERFUL X-MAN... YET ALSO THE MOST *VULNERABLE.*

JASON WYNGARDE SMILES...

935

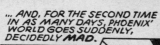

... AND, FOR THE SECOND TIME IN AS MANY DAYS, PHOENIX' WORLD GOES SUDDENLY, DECIDEDLY *MAD.*

OH, NO--IT'S HAPPENED AGAIN!

ONCE MORE, SHE FINDS HERSELF MYSTERI- OUSLY TRANSPORTED BACK TO THE 18TH CENTURY, TRANSFORMED THIS TIME INTO A NOBLE LADY RIDING TO THE HOUNDS... WITH JASON WYNGARDE BY HER SIDE.

SHE'S NEVER RIDDEN A HORSE IN HER LIFE, YET SHE HANDLES THE BIG BLACK STALLION BENEATH HER WITH PRACTICED EASE.

AND AS THE HORSES THUNDER ACROSS THE HEATHER, SHE FINDS HERSELF ACCEPTING THIS NEW REALITY-- *WELCOMING* IT. SHE IS LADY JEAN GREY-- THIS IS HER MANOR, THESE MEN HER GUESTS. ONE IS HER LOVE.

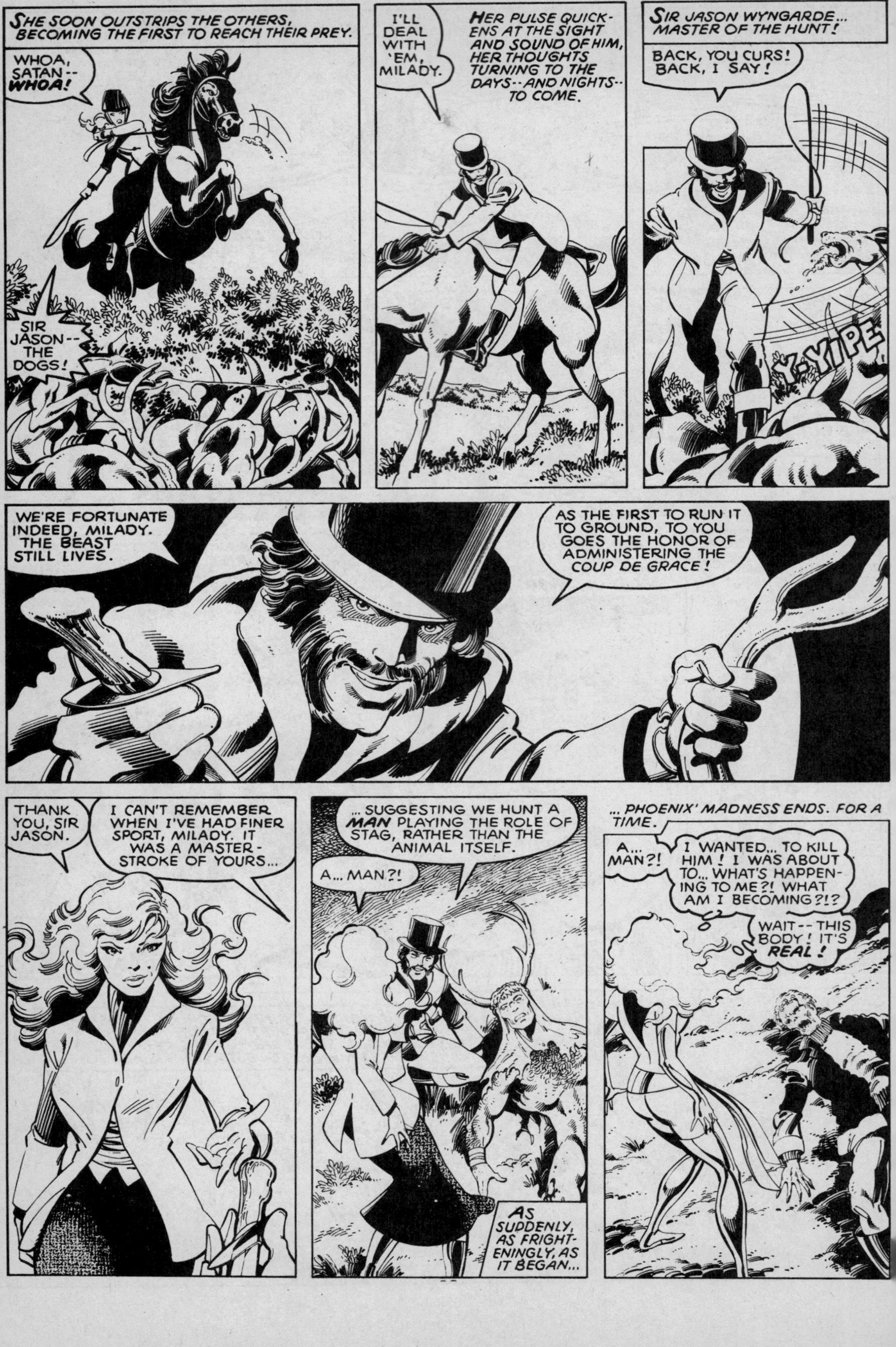
SHE SOON OUTSTRIPS THE OTHERS, BECOMING THE FIRST TO REACH THEIR PREY.
WHOA, SATAN -- WHOA!
SIR JASON -- THE DOGS!
I'LL DEAL WITH 'EM, MILADY.
HER PULSE QUICKENS AT THE SIGHT AND SOUND OF HIM, HER THOUGHTS TURNING TO THE DAYS -- AND NIGHTS -- TO COME.
SIR JASON WYNGARDE... MASTER OF THE HUNT!
BACK, YOU CURS! BACK, I SAY!
Y-YIPE
WE'RE FORTUNATE INDEED, MILADY. THE BEAST STILL LIVES.
AS THE FIRST TO RUN IT TO GROUND, TO YOU GOES THE HONOR OF ADMINISTERING THE COUP DE GRACE!
THANK YOU, SIR JASON.
I CAN'T REMEMBER WHEN I'VE HAD FINER SPORT, MILADY. IT WAS A MASTER-STROKE OF YOURS...
... SUGGESTING WE HUNT A MAN PLAYING THE ROLE OF STAG, RATHER THAN THE ANIMAL ITSELF.
A... MAN?!
AS SUDDENLY, AS FRIGHTENINGLY, AS IT BEGAN...
... PHOENIX' MADNESS ENDS. FOR A TIME.
A... MAN?!
I WANTED... TO KILL HIM! I WAS ABOUT TO... WHAT'S HAPPENING TO ME?! WHAT AM I BECOMING?!?
WAIT -- THIS BODY! IT'S REAL!

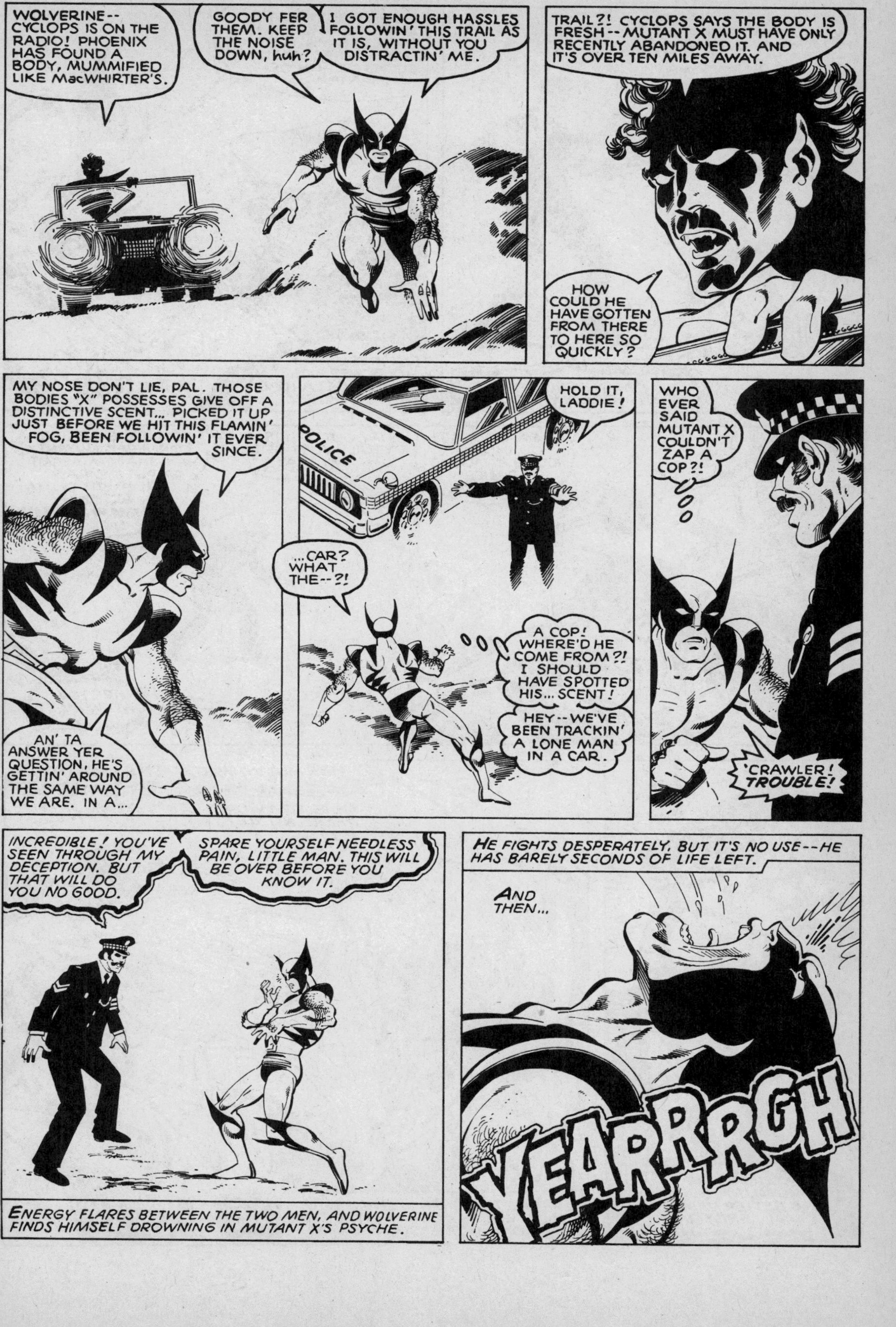
WOLVERINE-- CYCLOPS IS ON THE RADIO! PHOENIX HAS FOUND A BODY, MUMMIFIED LIKE MacWHIRTER'S.
GOODY FER THEM. KEEP THE NOISE DOWN, huh?
I GOT ENOUGH HASSLES FOLLOWIN' THIS TRAIL AS IT IS, WITHOUT YOU DISTRACTIN' ME.
TRAIL?! CYCLOPS SAYS THE BODY IS FRESH -- MUTANT X MUST HAVE ONLY RECENTLY ABANDONED IT. AND IT'S OVER TEN MILES AWAY.
HOW COULD HE HAVE GOTTEN FROM THERE TO HERE SO QUICKLY?
MY NOSE DON'T LIE, PAL. THOSE BODIES "X" POSSESSES GIVE OFF A DISTINCTIVE SCENT... PICKED IT UP JUST BEFORE WE HIT THIS FLAMIN' FOG, BEEN FOLLOWIN' IT EVER SINCE.
AN' TA ANSWER YER QUESTION, HE'S GETTIN' AROUND THE SAME WAY WE ARE. IN A...
POLICE
HOLD IT, LADDIE!
...CAR? WHAT THE--?!
A COP! WHERE'D HE COME FROM?! I SHOULD HAVE SPOTTED HIS... SCENT!
HEY--WE'VE BEEN TRACKIN' A LONE MAN IN A CAR.
WHO EVER SAID MUTANT X COULDN'T ZAP A COP?!
'CRAWLER! TROUBLE!
INCREDIBLE! YOU'VE SEEN THROUGH MY DECEPTION. BUT THAT WILL DO YOU NO GOOD.
SPARE YOURSELF NEEDLESS PAIN, LITTLE MAN. THIS WILL BE OVER BEFORE YOU KNOW IT.
ENERGY FLARES BETWEEN THE TWO MEN, AND WOLVERINE FINDS HIMSELF DROWNING IN MUTANT X'S PSYCHE.
HE FIGHTS DESPERATELY, BUT IT'S NO USE--HE HAS BARELY SECONDS OF LIFE LEFT.
AND THEN...
YEARRRGH

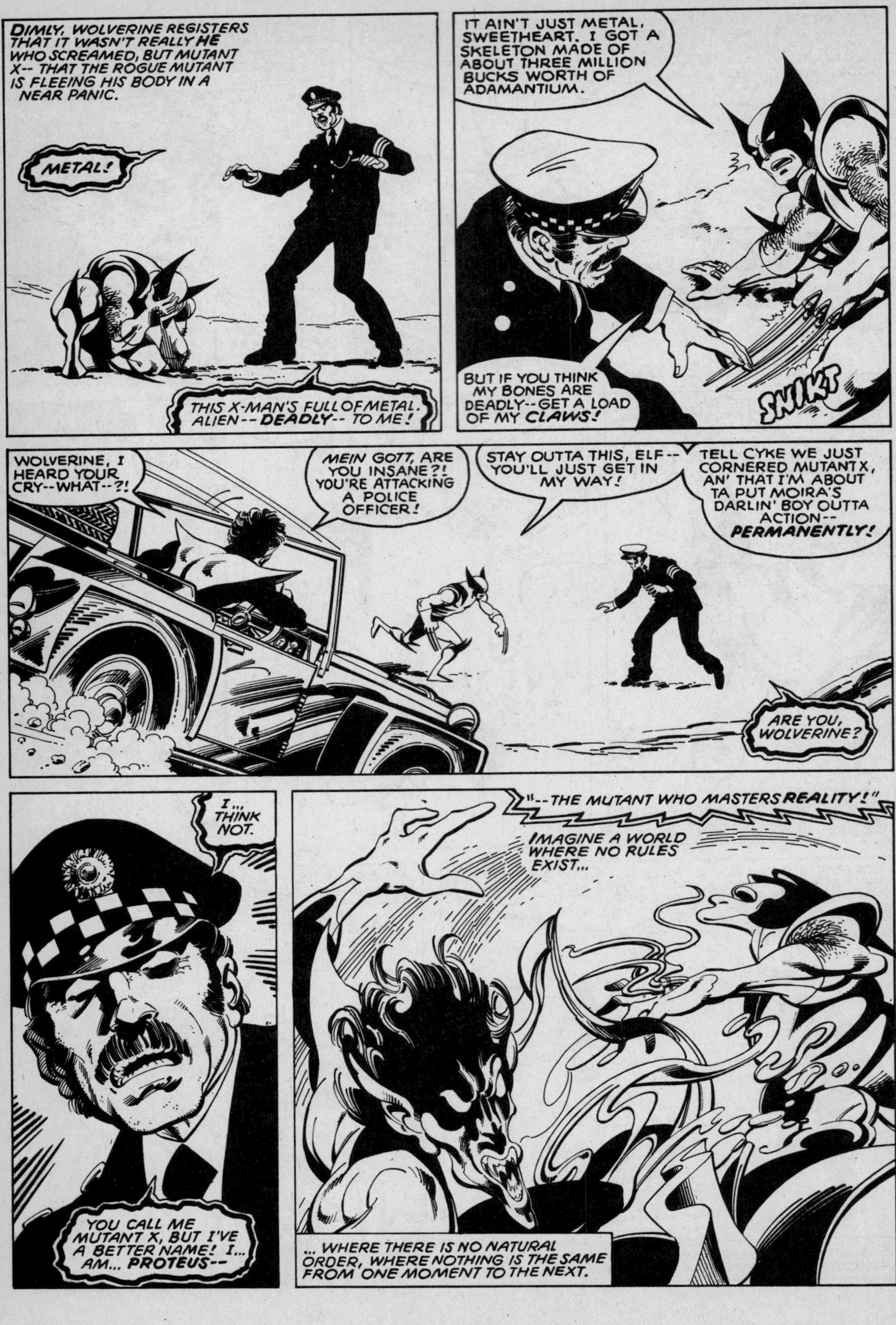

DIMLY, WOLVERINE REGISTERS THAT IT WASN'T REALLY HE WHO SCREAMED, BUT MUTANT X-- THAT THE ROGUE MUTANT IS FLEEING HIS BODY IN A NEAR PANIC.
METAL!
THIS X-MAN'S FULL OF METAL. ALIEN-- DEADLY-- TO ME!
IT AIN'T JUST METAL, SWEETHEART. I GOT A SKELETON MADE OF ABOUT THREE MILLION BUCKS WORTH OF ADAMANTIUM.
BUT IF YOU THINK MY BONES ARE DEADLY--GET A LOAD OF MY CLAWS!
SNIKT
WOLVERINE, I HEARD YOUR CRY--WHAT--?!
MEIN GOTT, ARE YOU INSANE?! YOU'RE ATTACKING A POLICE OFFICER!
STAY OUTTA THIS, ELF-- YOU'LL JUST GET IN MY WAY!
TELL CYKE WE JUST CORNERED MUTANT X, AN' THAT I'M ABOUT TA PUT MOIRA'S DARLIN' BOY OUTTA ACTION-- PERMANENTLY!
ARE YOU, WOLVERINE?
I... THINK NOT.
YOU CALL ME MUTANT X, BUT I'VE A BETTER NAME! I... AM... PROTEUS--
"--THE MUTANT WHO MASTERS REALITY!"
IMAGINE A WORLD WHERE NO RULES EXIST...
... WHERE THERE IS NO NATURAL ORDER, WHERE NOTHING IS THE SAME FROM ONE MOMENT TO THE NEXT.

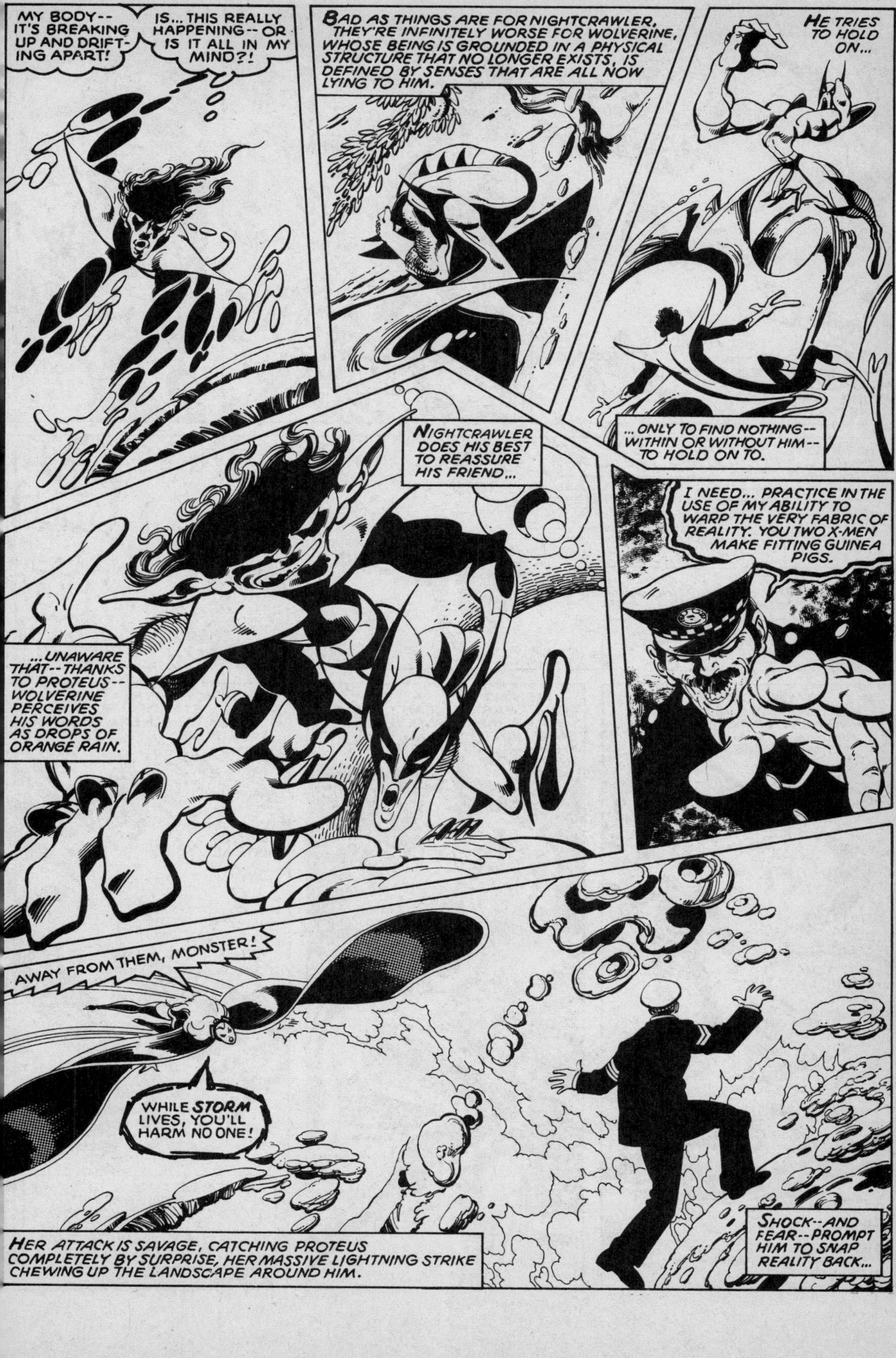
MY BODY-- IT'S BREAKING UP AND DRIFTING APART!
IS... THIS REALLY HAPPENING-- OR IS IT ALL IN MY MIND?!
BAD AS THINGS ARE FOR NIGHTCRAWLER, THEY'RE INFINITELY WORSE FOR WOLVERINE, WHOSE BEING IS GROUNDED IN A PHYSICAL STRUCTURE THAT NO LONGER EXISTS, IS DEFINED BY SENSES THAT ARE ALL NOW LYING TO HIM.
HE TRIES TO HOLD ON...
...ONLY TO FIND NOTHING-- WITHIN OR WITHOUT HIM-- TO HOLD ON TO.
NIGHTCRAWLER DOES HIS BEST TO REASSURE HIS FRIEND...
...UNAWARE THAT--THANKS TO PROTEUS-- WOLVERINE PERCEIVES HIS WORDS AS DROPS OF ORANGE RAIN.
I NEED... PRACTICE IN THE USE OF MY ABILITY TO WARP THE VERY FABRIC OF REALITY. YOU TWO X-MEN MAKE FITTING GUINEA PIGS.
AWAY FROM THEM, MONSTER!
WHILE STORM LIVES, YOU'LL HARM NO ONE!
HER ATTACK IS SAVAGE, CATCHING PROTEUS COMPLETELY BY SURPRISE, HER MASSIVE LIGHTNING STRIKE CHEWING UP THE LANDSCAPE AROUND HIM.
SHOCK--AND FEAR--PROMPT HIM TO SNAP REALITY BACK...

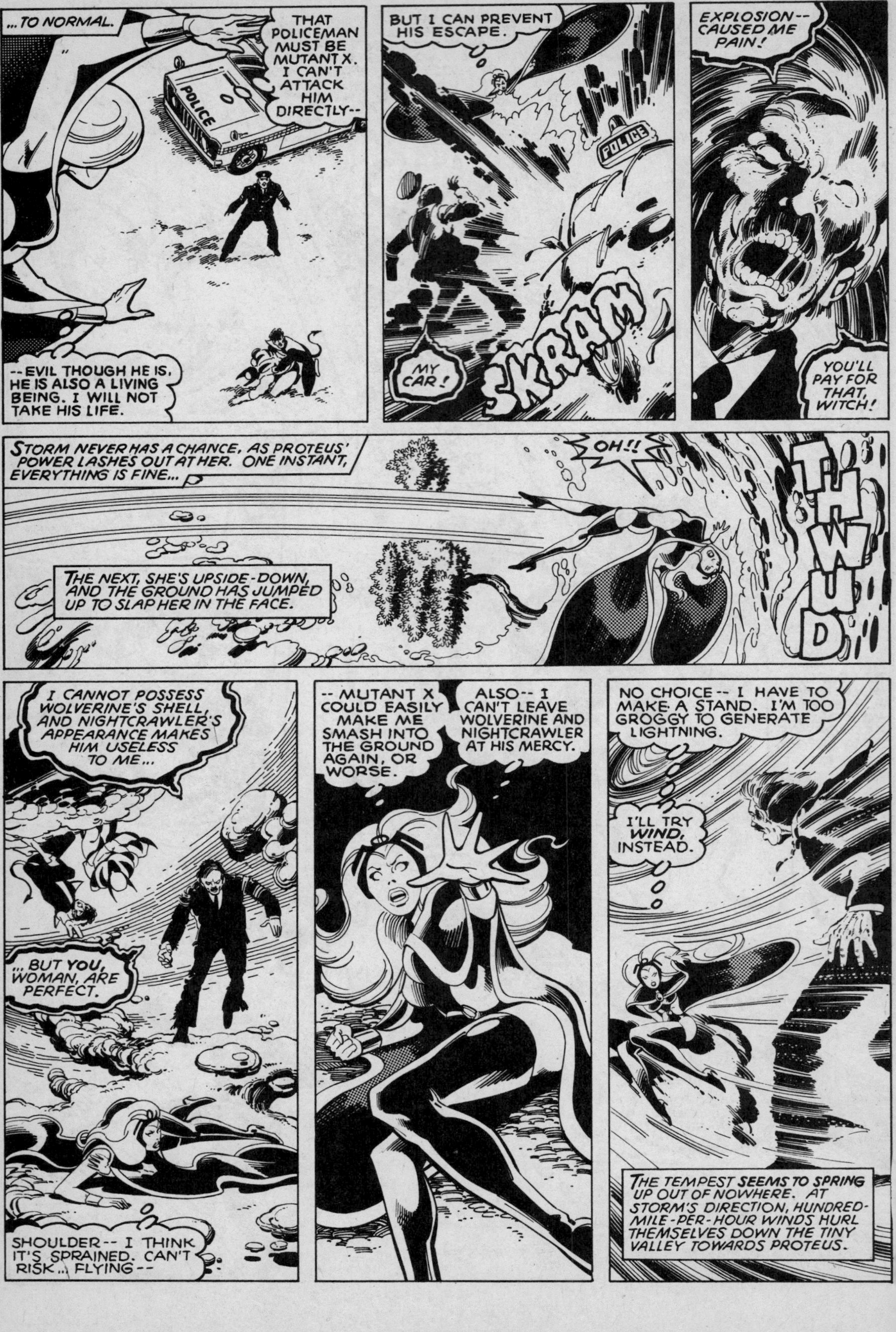
...TO NORMAL.
THAT POLICEMAN MUST BE MUTANT X. I CAN'T ATTACK HIM DIRECTLY--
POLICE
POLICE
--EVIL THOUGH HE IS, HE IS ALSO A LIVING BEING. I WILL NOT TAKE HIS LIFE.
BUT I CAN PREVENT HIS ESCAPE.
POLICE
MY CAR!
SKRAM
EXPLOSION-- CAUSED ME PAIN!
YOU'LL PAY FOR THAT, WITCH!
STORM NEVER HAS A CHANCE, AS PROTEUS' POWER LASHES OUT AT HER. ONE INSTANT, EVERYTHING IS FINE...
OH!!
THE NEXT, SHE'S UPSIDE-DOWN, AND THE GROUND HAS JUMPED UP TO SLAP HER IN THE FACE.
THWUD
I CANNOT POSSESS WOLVERINE'S SHELL, AND NIGHTCRAWLER'S APPEARANCE MAKES HIM USELESS TO ME...
...BUT YOU, WOMAN, ARE PERFECT.
SHOULDER-- I THINK IT'S SPRAINED. CAN'T RISK... FLYING--
--MUTANT X COULD EASILY MAKE ME SMASH INTO THE GROUND AGAIN, OR WORSE.
ALSO-- I CAN'T LEAVE WOLVERINE AND NIGHTCRAWLER AT HIS MERCY.
NO CHOICE -- I HAVE TO MAKE A STAND. I'M TOO GROGGY TO GENERATE LIGHTNING.
I'LL TRY WIND, INSTEAD.
THE TEMPEST SEEMS TO SPRING UP OUT OF NOWHERE. AT STORM'S DIRECTION, HUNDRED-MILE-PER-HOUR WINDS HURL THEMSELVES DOWN THE TINY VALLEY TOWARDS PROTEUS.

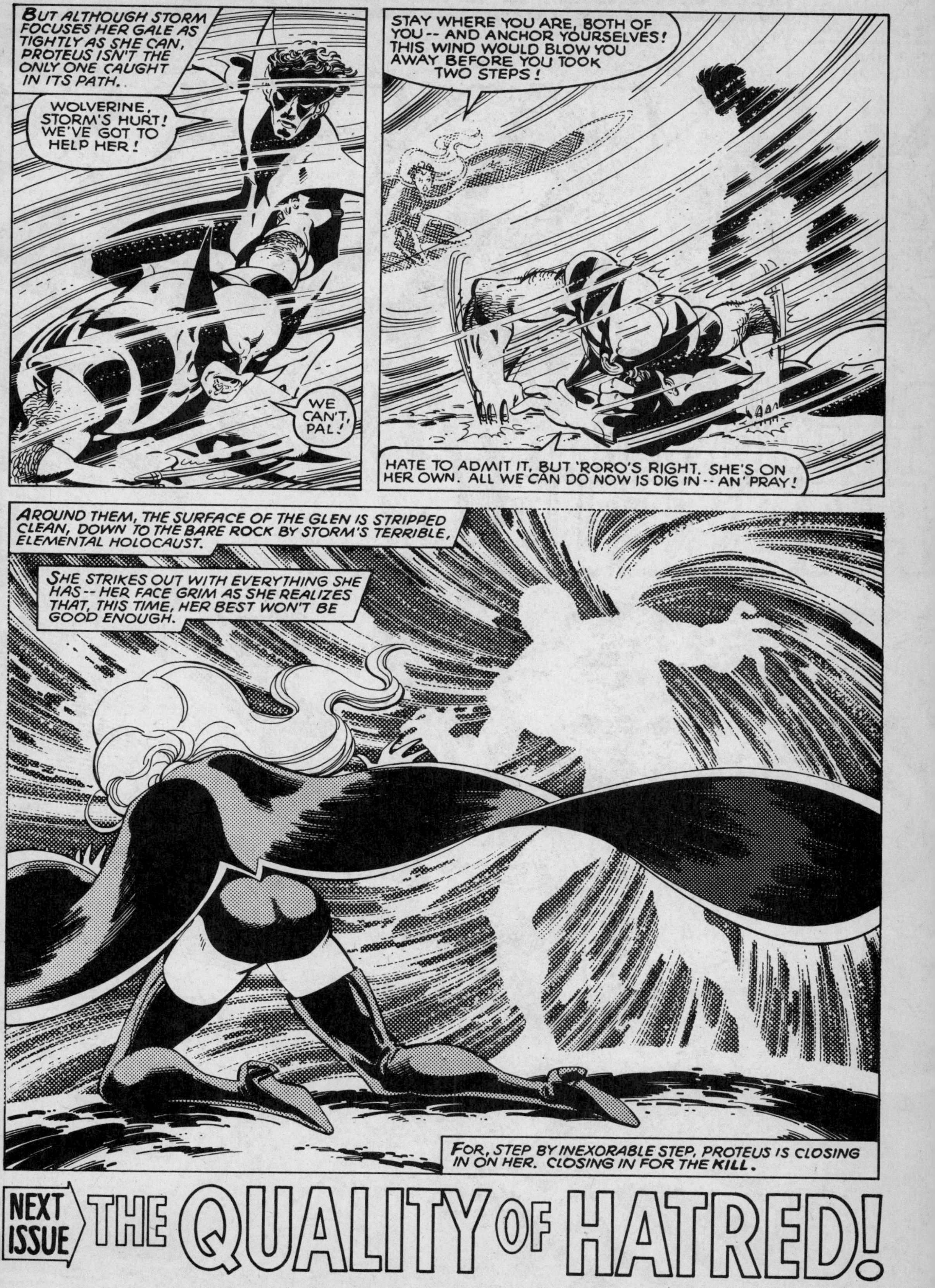
BUT ALTHOUGH STORM FOCUSES HER GALE AS TIGHTLY AS SHE CAN, PROTEUS ISN'T THE ONLY ONE CAUGHT IN ITS PATH.
WOLVERINE, STORM'S HURT! WE'VE GOT TO HELP HER!
WE CAN'T, PAL!
STAY WHERE YOU ARE, BOTH OF YOU -- AND ANCHOR YOURSELVES! THIS WIND WOULD BLOW YOU AWAY BEFORE YOU TOOK TWO STEPS!
HATE TO ADMIT IT, BUT 'RORO'S RIGHT. SHE'S ON HER OWN. ALL WE CAN DO NOW IS DIG IN -- AN' PRAY!
AROUND THEM, THE SURFACE OF THE GLEN IS STRIPPED CLEAN, DOWN TO THE BARE ROCK BY STORM'S TERRIBLE, ELEMENTAL HOLOCAUST.
SHE STRIKES OUT WITH EVERYTHING SHE HAS -- HER FACE GRIM AS SHE REALIZES THAT, THIS TIME, HER BEST WON'T BE GOOD ENOUGH.
FOR, STEP BY INEXORABLE STEP, PROTEUS IS CLOSING IN ON HER. CLOSING IN FOR THE KILL.
NEXT ISSUE
THE QUALITY OF HATRED!

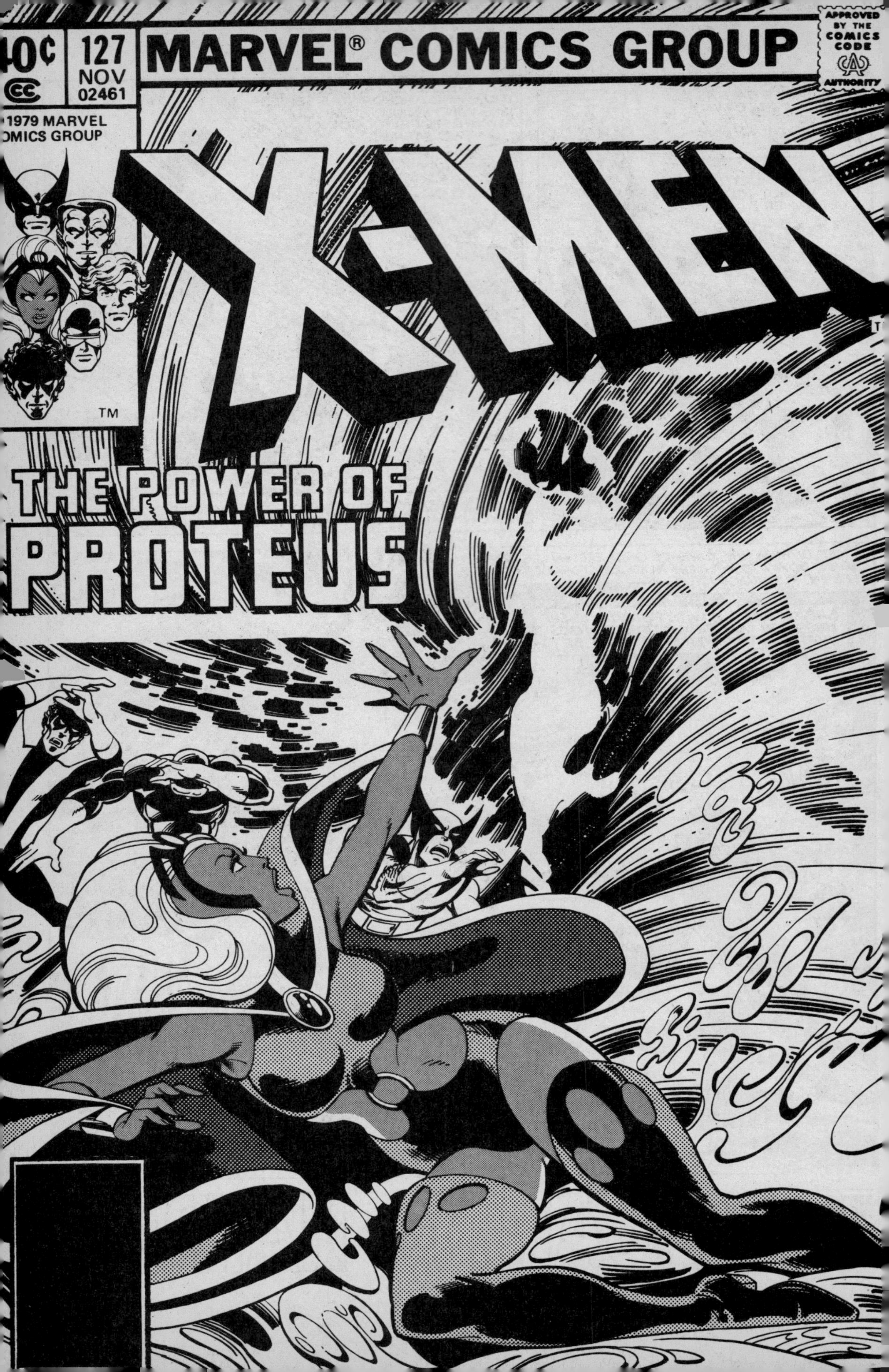
40¢
127
NOV
02461
MARVEL® COMICS GROUP
APPROVED BY THE COMICS CODE AUTHORITY
1979 MARVEL
OMICS GROUP
X-MEN
THE POWER OF
PROTEUS

Cyclops. Storm. Banshee. Nightcrawler. Wolverine. Colossus. Children of the atom, students of Charles Xavier, MUTANTS––feared and hated by the world they have sworn to protect. These are the STRANGEST heroes of all!

Stan Lee PRESENTS: THE UNCANNY X-MEN!™

CHRIS CLAREMONT ✱ JOHN BYRNE WRITER - PLOTTERS - PENCILER | TERRY AUSTIN INKER | TOM ORZECHOWSKI, *letterer* GLYNIS WEIN, *colorist* | ROGER STERN EDITOR | JIM SHOOTER *Ed.-IN-CHIEF*

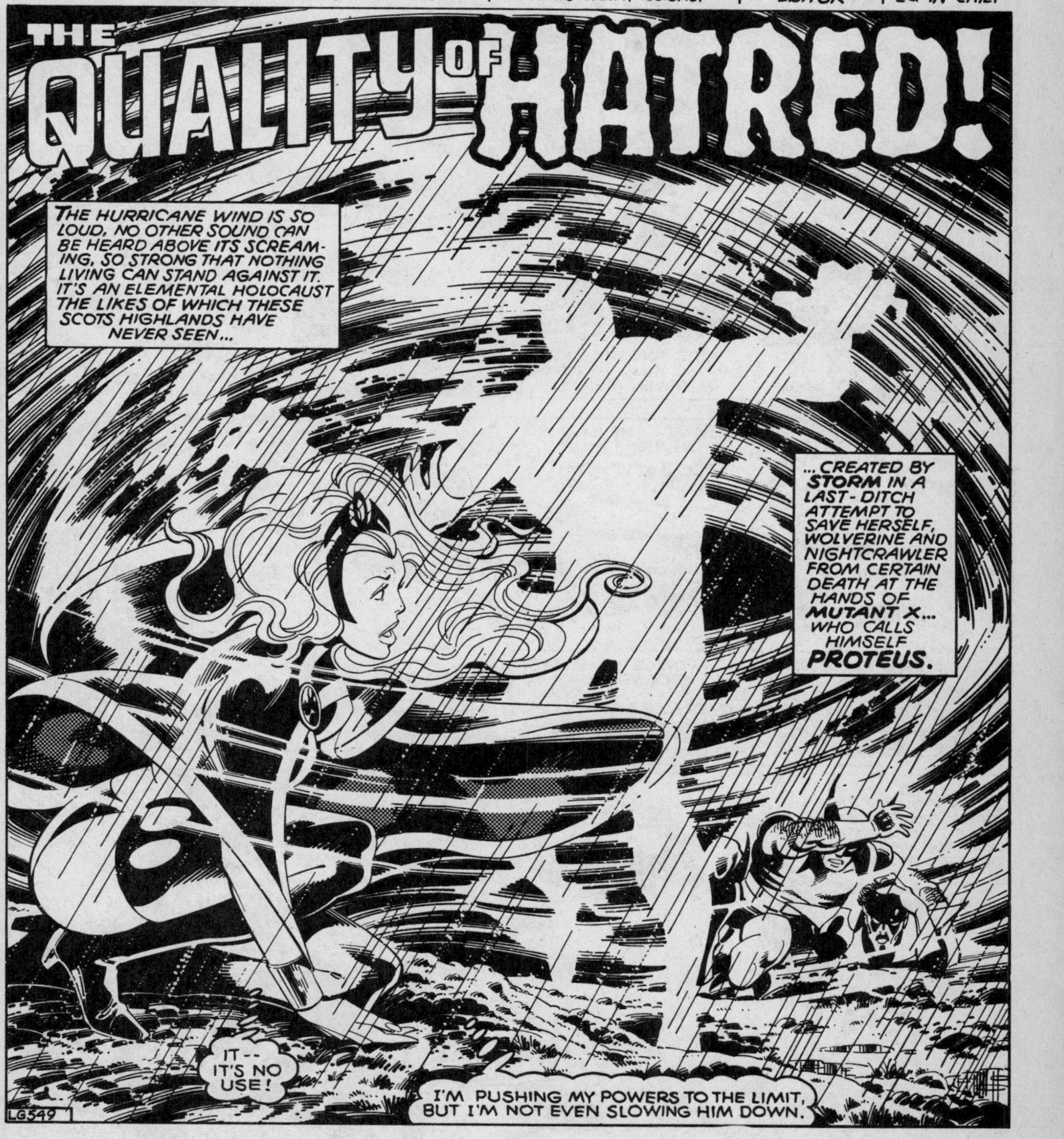
THE QUALITY OF HATRED!
THE HURRICANE WIND IS SO LOUD, NO OTHER SOUND CAN BE HEARD ABOVE ITS SCREAMING, SO STRONG THAT NOTHING LIVING CAN STAND AGAINST IT. IT'S AN ELEMENTAL HOLOCAUST THE LIKES OF WHICH THESE SCOTS HIGHLANDS HAVE NEVER SEEN...
...CREATED BY STORM IN A LAST-DITCH ATTEMPT TO SAVE HERSELF, WOLVERINE AND NIGHTCRAWLER FROM CERTAIN DEATH AT THE HANDS OF MUTANT X... WHO CALLS HIMSELF PROTEUS.
IT-- IT'S NO USE!
I'M PUSHING MY POWERS TO THE LIMIT, BUT I'M NOT EVEN SLOWING HIM DOWN.
LG549

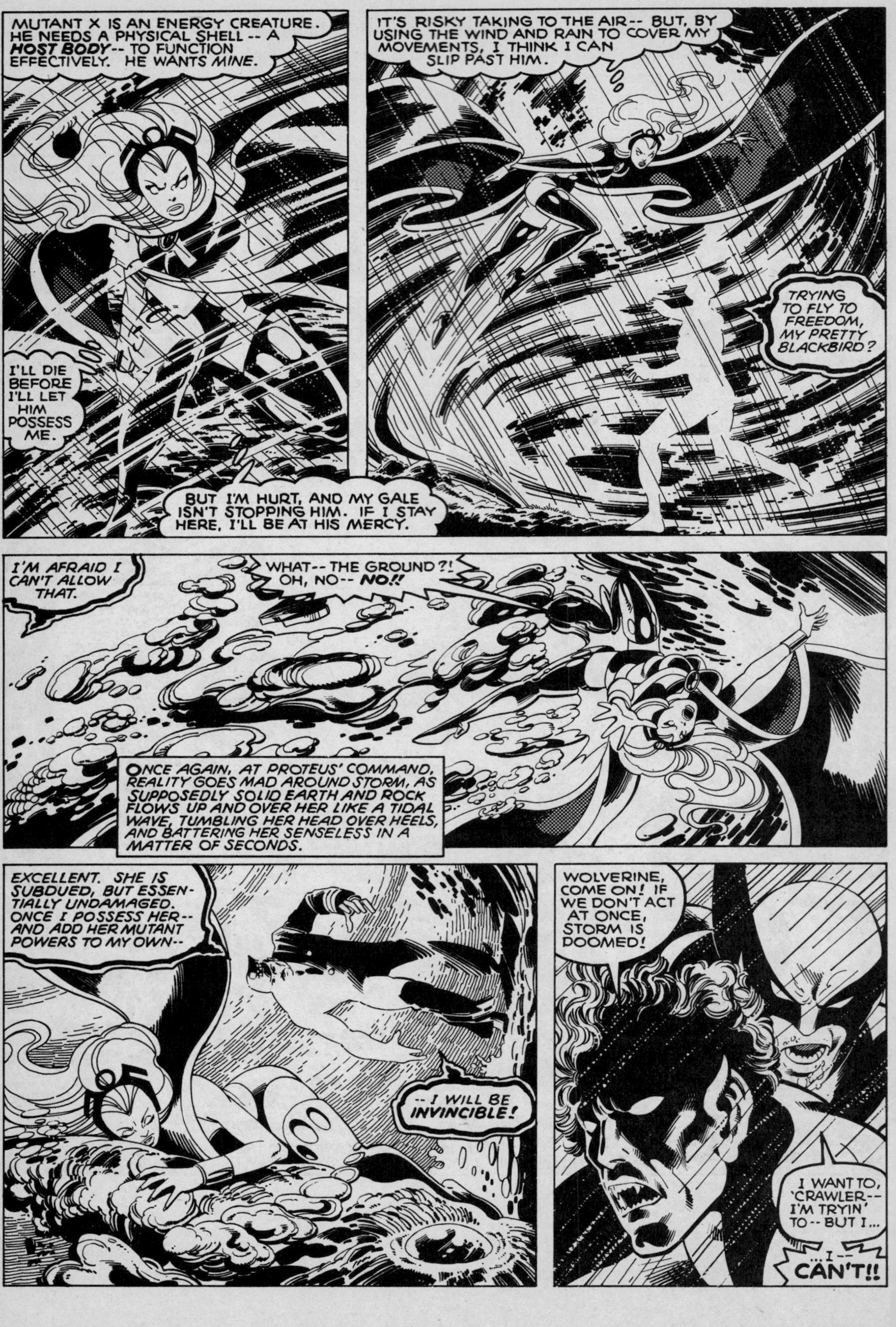
MUTANT X IS AN ENERGY CREATURE. HE NEEDS A PHYSICAL SHELL -- A HOST BODY -- TO FUNCTION EFFECTIVELY. HE WANTS MINE.
I'LL DIE BEFORE I'LL LET HIM POSSESS ME.
BUT I'M HURT, AND MY GALE ISN'T STOPPING HIM. IF I STAY HERE, I'LL BE AT HIS MERCY.
IT'S RISKY TAKING TO THE AIR -- BUT, BY USING THE WIND AND RAIN TO COVER MY MOVEMENTS, I THINK I CAN SLIP PAST HIM.
TRYING TO FLY TO FREEDOM, MY PRETTY BLACKBIRD?
I'M AFRAID I CAN'T ALLOW THAT.
WHAT -- THE GROUND?! OH, NO -- NO!!
ONCE AGAIN, AT PROTEUS' COMMAND, REALITY GOES MAD AROUND STORM, AS SUPPOSEDLY SOLID EARTH AND ROCK FLOWS UP AND OVER HER LIKE A TIDAL WAVE, TUMBLING HER HEAD OVER HEELS, AND BATTERING HER SENSELESS IN A MATTER OF SECONDS.
EXCELLENT. SHE IS SUBDUED, BUT ESSENTIALLY UNDAMAGED. ONCE I POSSESS HER -- AND ADD HER MUTANT POWERS TO MY OWN --
-- I WILL BE INVINCIBLE!
WOLVERINE, COME ON! IF WE DON'T ACT AT ONCE, STORM IS DOOMED!
I WANT TO, 'CRAWLER -- I'M TRYIN' TO -- BUT I...
... I -- CAN'T!!

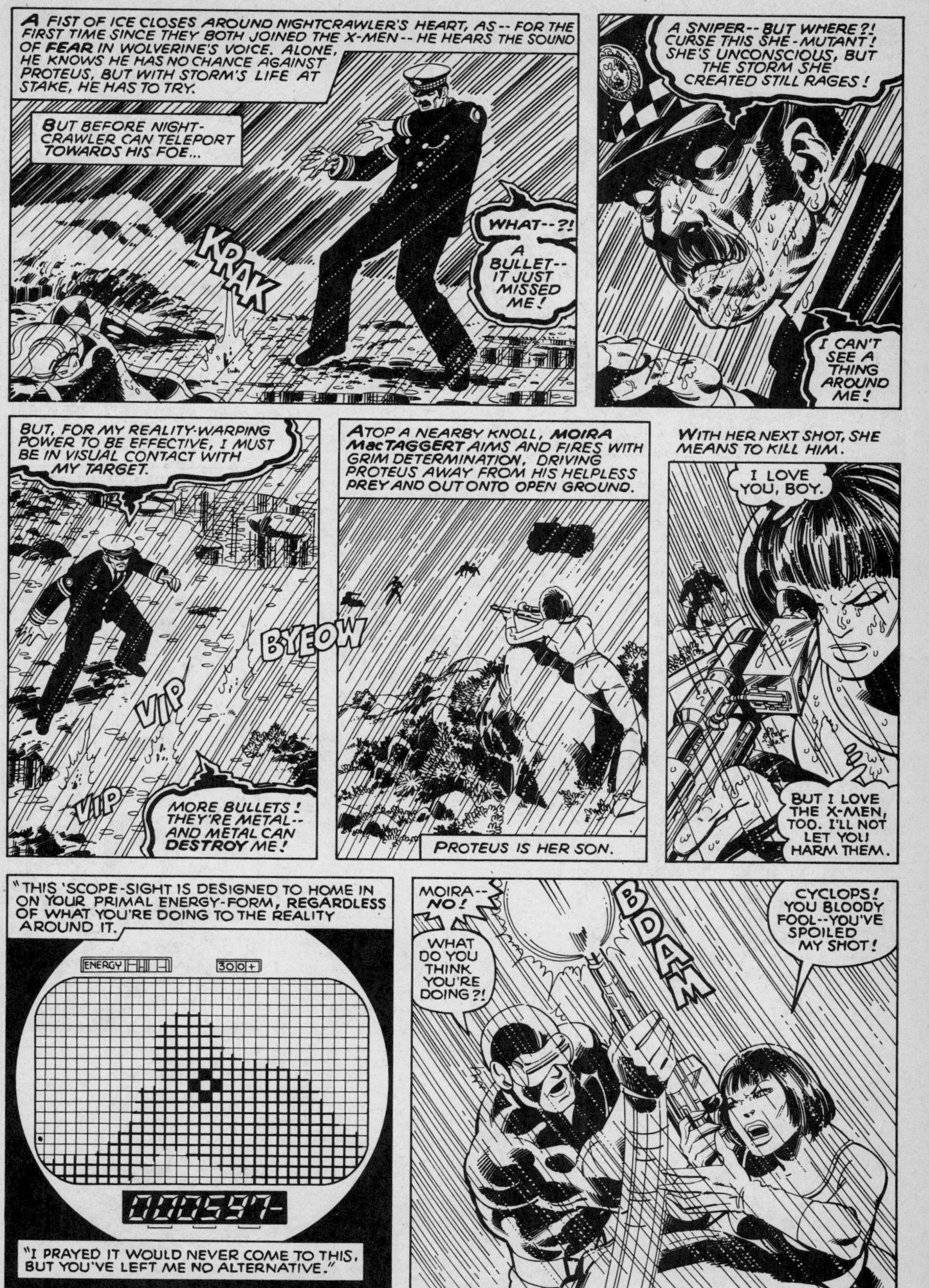

A FIST OF ICE CLOSES AROUND NIGHTCRAWLER'S HEART, AS -- FOR THE FIRST TIME SINCE THEY BOTH JOINED THE X-MEN -- HE HEARS THE SOUND OF FEAR IN WOLVERINE'S VOICE. ALONE, HE KNOWS HE HAS NO CHANCE AGAINST PROTEUS, BUT WITH STORM'S LIFE AT STAKE, HE HAS TO TRY.
BUT BEFORE NIGHT-CRAWLER CAN TELEPORT TOWARDS HIS FOE...
KRAK
WHAT--?! A BULLET-- IT JUST MISSED ME!
A SNIPER-- BUT WHERE?! CURSE THIS SHE-MUTANT! SHE'S UNCONSCIOUS, BUT THE STORM SHE CREATED STILL RAGES!
I CAN'T SEE A THING AROUND ME!
BUT, FOR MY REALITY-WARPING POWER TO BE EFFECTIVE, I MUST BE IN VISUAL CONTACT WITH MY TARGET.
BYEOW
VIP
VIP
MORE BULLETS! THEY'RE METAL-- AND METAL CAN DESTROY ME!
ATOP A NEARBY KNOLL, MOIRA MacTAGGERT AIMS AND FIRES WITH GRIM DETERMINATION, DRIVING PROTEUS AWAY FROM HIS HELPLESS PREY AND OUT ONTO OPEN GROUND.
PROTEUS IS HER SON.
WITH HER NEXT SHOT, SHE MEANS TO KILL HIM.
I LOVE YOU, BOY.
BUT I LOVE THE X-MEN, TOO. I'LL NOT LET YOU HARM THEM.
"THIS 'SCOPE-SIGHT IS DESIGNED TO HOME IN ON YOUR PRIMAL ENERGY-FORM, REGARDLESS OF WHAT YOU'RE DOING TO THE REALITY AROUND IT.
ENERGY
300+
000597-
"I PRAYED IT WOULD NEVER COME TO THIS, BUT YOU'VE LEFT ME NO ALTERNATIVE."
MOIRA-- NO!
WHAT DO YOU THINK YOU'RE DOING?!
BDAM
CYCLOPS! YOU BLOODY FOOL--YOU'VE SPOILED MY SHOT!

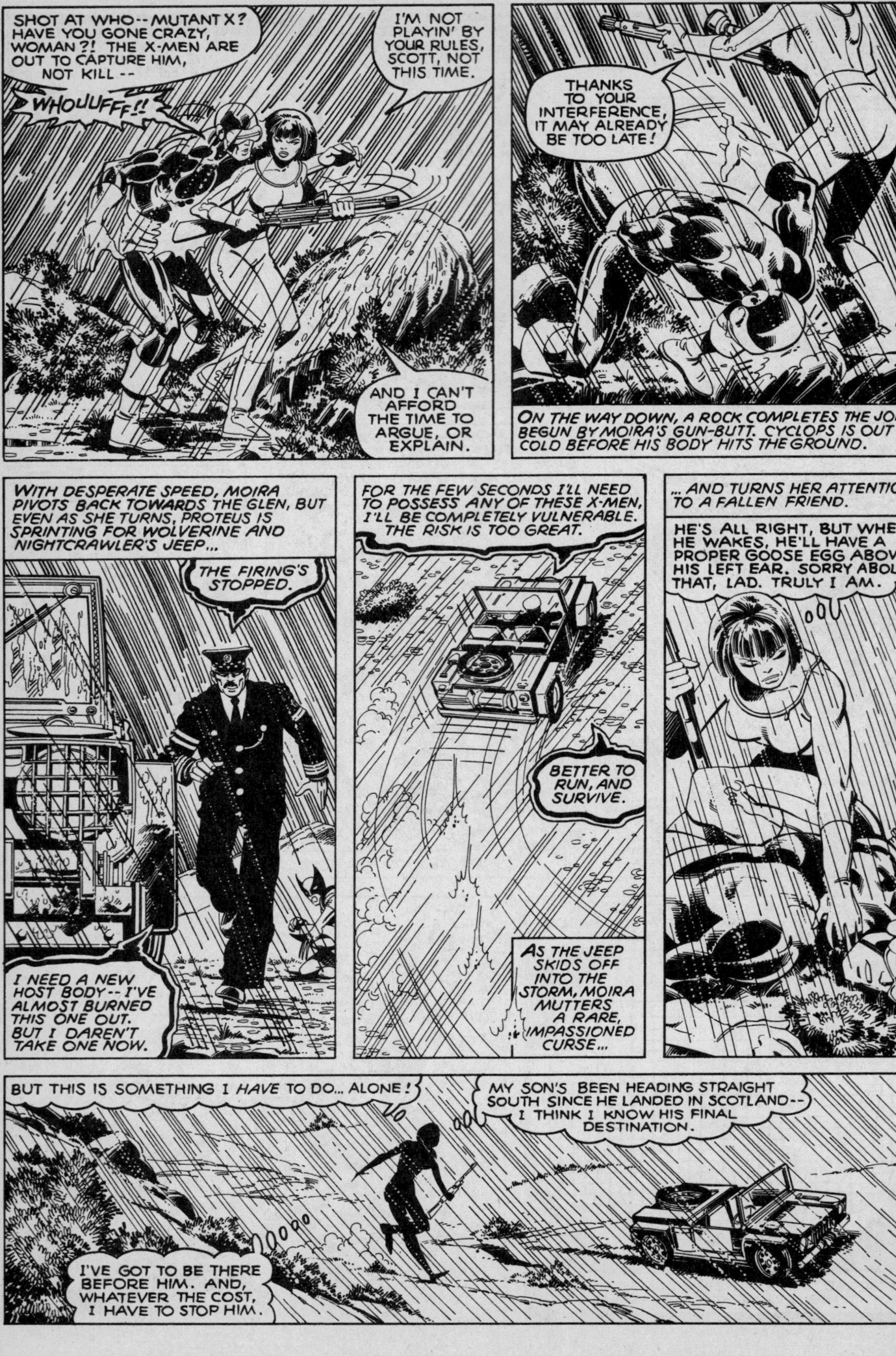
SHOT AT WHO-- MUTANT X? HAVE YOU GONE CRAZY, WOMAN?! THE X-MEN ARE OUT TO CAPTURE HIM, NOT KILL --
I'M NOT PLAYIN' BY YOUR RULES, SCOTT, NOT THIS TIME.
WHOUUFFF!!
AND I CAN'T AFFORD THE TIME TO ARGUE, OR EXPLAIN.
THANKS TO YOUR INTERFERENCE, IT MAY ALREADY BE TOO LATE!
ON THE WAY DOWN, A ROCK COMPLETES THE JOB BEGUN BY MOIRA'S GUN-BUTT. CYCLOPS IS OUT COLD BEFORE HIS BODY HITS THE GROUND.
WITH DESPERATE SPEED, MOIRA PIVOTS BACK TOWARDS THE GLEN, BUT EVEN AS SHE TURNS, PROTEUS IS SPRINTING FOR WOLVERINE AND NIGHTCRAWLER'S JEEP...
THE FIRING'S STOPPED.
I NEED A NEW HOST BODY -- I'VE ALMOST BURNED THIS ONE OUT. BUT I DAREN'T TAKE ONE NOW.
FOR THE FEW SECONDS I'LL NEED TO POSSESS ANY OF THESE X-MEN, I'LL BE COMPLETELY VULNERABLE. THE RISK IS TOO GREAT.
BETTER TO RUN, AND SURVIVE.
AS THE JEEP SKIDS OFF INTO THE STORM, MOIRA MUTTERS A RARE, IMPASSIONED CURSE...
... AND TURNS HER ATTENTION TO A FALLEN FRIEND.
HE'S ALL RIGHT, BUT WHEN HE WAKES, HE'LL HAVE A PROPER GOOSE EGG ABOVE HIS LEFT EAR. SORRY ABOUT THAT, LAD. TRULY I AM.
BUT THIS IS SOMETHING I HAVE TO DO... ALONE!
MY SON'S BEEN HEADING STRAIGHT SOUTH SINCE HE LANDED IN SCOTLAND -- I THINK I KNOW HIS FINAL DESTINATION.
I'VE GOT TO BE THERE BEFORE HIM. AND, WHATEVER THE COST, I HAVE TO STOP HIM.

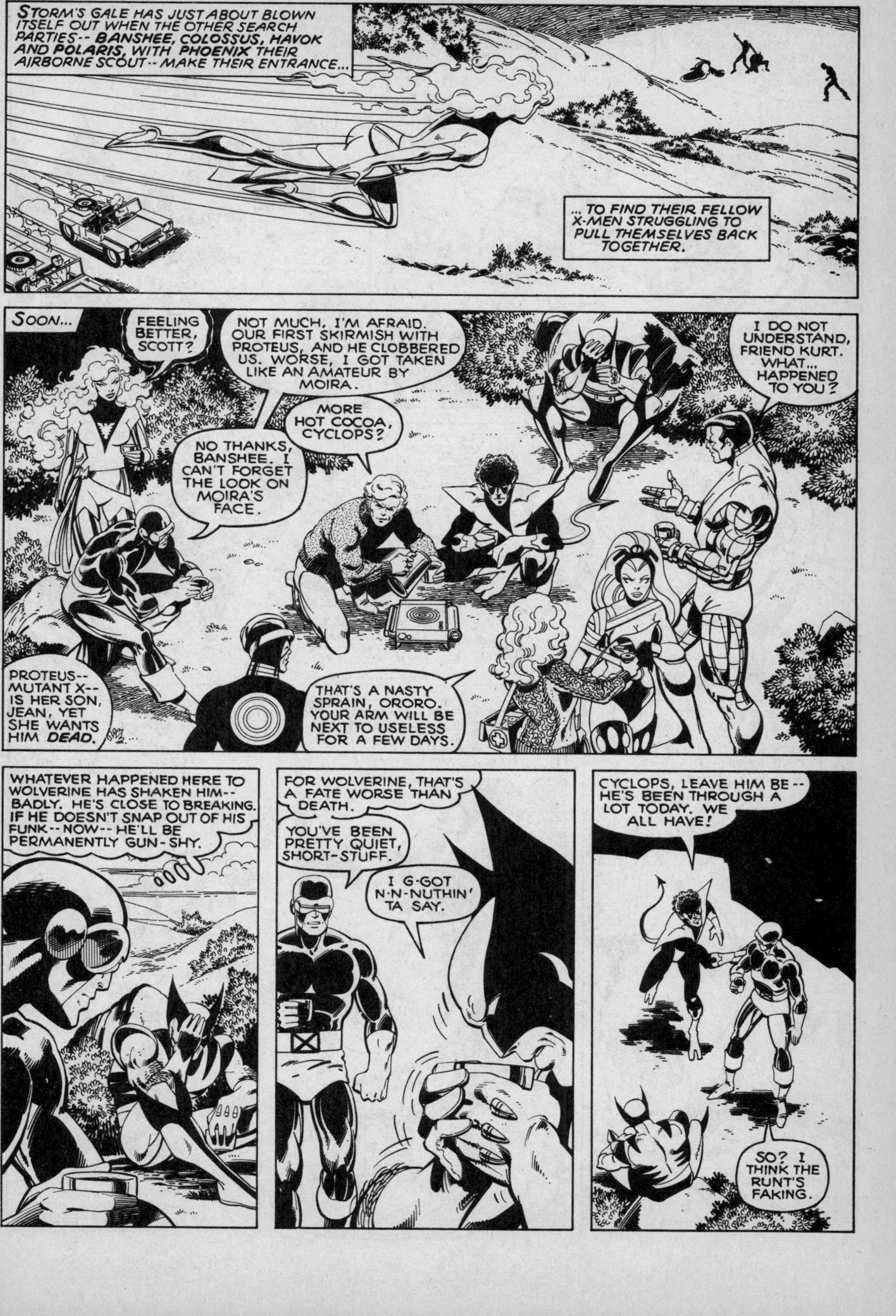
STORM'S GALE HAS JUST ABOUT BLOWN ITSELF OUT WHEN THE OTHER SEARCH PARTIES-- BANSHEE, COLOSSUS, HAVOK AND POLARIS, WITH PHOENIX THEIR AIRBORNE SCOUT-- MAKE THEIR ENTRANCE...
...TO FIND THEIR FELLOW X-MEN STRUGGLING TO PULL THEMSELVES BACK TOGETHER.
SOON...
FEELING BETTER, SCOTT?
NOT MUCH, I'M AFRAID. OUR FIRST SKIRMISH WITH PROTEUS, AND HE CLOBBERED US. WORSE, I GOT TAKEN LIKE AN AMATEUR BY MOIRA.
MORE HOT COCOA, CYCLOPS?
NO THANKS, BANSHEE. I CAN'T FORGET THE LOOK ON MOIRA'S FACE.
PROTEUS-- MUTANT X-- IS HER SON, JEAN, YET SHE WANTS HIM DEAD.
I DO NOT UNDERSTAND, FRIEND KURT. WHAT... HAPPENED TO YOU?
THAT'S A NASTY SPRAIN, ORORO. YOUR ARM WILL BE NEXT TO USELESS FOR A FEW DAYS.
WHATEVER HAPPENED HERE TO WOLVERINE HAS SHAKEN HIM-- BADLY. HE'S CLOSE TO BREAKING. IF HE DOESN'T SNAP OUT OF HIS FUNK-- NOW-- HE'LL BE PERMANENTLY GUN-SHY.
FOR WOLVERINE, THAT'S A FATE WORSE THAN DEATH.
YOU'VE BEEN PRETTY QUIET, SHORT-STUFF.
I G-GOT N-N-NUTHIN' TA SAY.
CYCLOPS, LEAVE HIM BE-- HE'S BEEN THROUGH A LOT TODAY. WE ALL HAVE!
SO? I THINK THE RUNT'S FAKING.

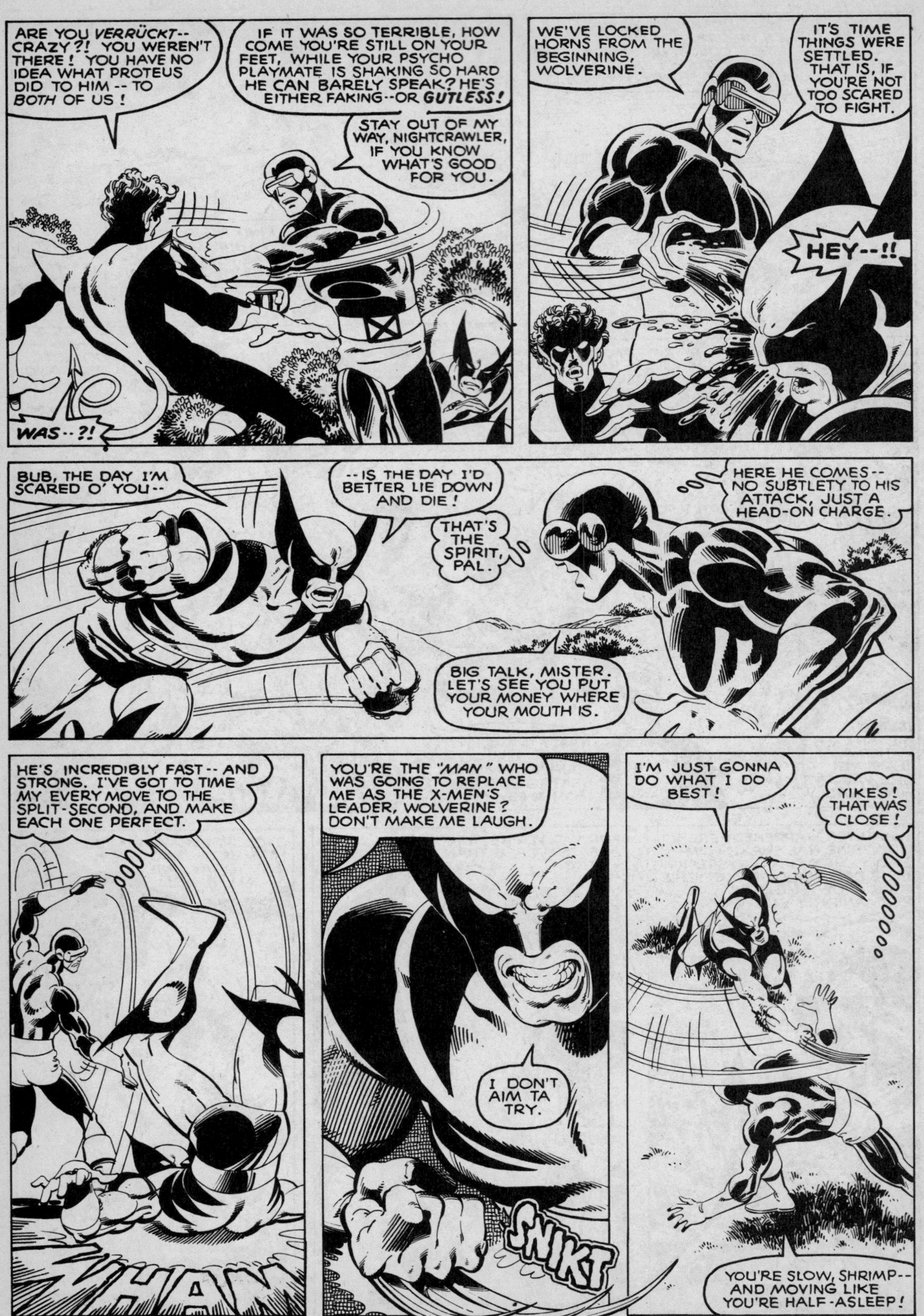
ARE YOU VERRÜCKT-- CRAZY?! YOU WEREN'T THERE! YOU HAVE NO IDEA WHAT PROTEUS DID TO HIM -- TO BOTH OF US!
IF IT WAS SO TERRIBLE, HOW COME YOU'RE STILL ON YOUR FEET, WHILE YOUR PSYCHO PLAYMATE IS SHAKING SO HARD HE CAN BARELY SPEAK? HE'S EITHER FAKING--OR GUTLESS!
STAY OUT OF MY WAY, NIGHTCRAWLER, IF YOU KNOW WHAT'S GOOD FOR YOU.
WAS--?!
WE'VE LOCKED HORNS FROM THE BEGINNING, WOLVERINE.
IT'S TIME THINGS WERE SETTLED. THAT IS, IF YOU'RE NOT TOO SCARED TO FIGHT.
HEY--!!
BUB, THE DAY I'M SCARED O' YOU--
--IS THE DAY I'D BETTER LIE DOWN AND DIE!
THAT'S THE SPIRIT, PAL.
HERE HE COMES-- NO SUBTLETY TO HIS ATTACK, JUST A HEAD-ON CHARGE.
BIG TALK, MISTER. LET'S SEE YOU PUT YOUR MONEY WHERE YOUR MOUTH IS.
HE'S INCREDIBLY FAST-- AND STRONG. I'VE GOT TO TIME MY EVERY MOVE TO THE SPLIT-SECOND, AND MAKE EACH ONE PERFECT.
WHAM
YOU'RE THE "MAN" WHO WAS GOING TO REPLACE ME AS THE X-MEN'S LEADER, WOLVERINE? DON'T MAKE ME LAUGH.
I DON'T AIM TA TRY.
SNIKT
I'M JUST GONNA DO WHAT I DO BEST!
YIKES! THAT WAS CLOSE!
YOU'RE SLOW, SHRIMP-- AND MOVING LIKE YOU'RE HALF-ASLEEP!

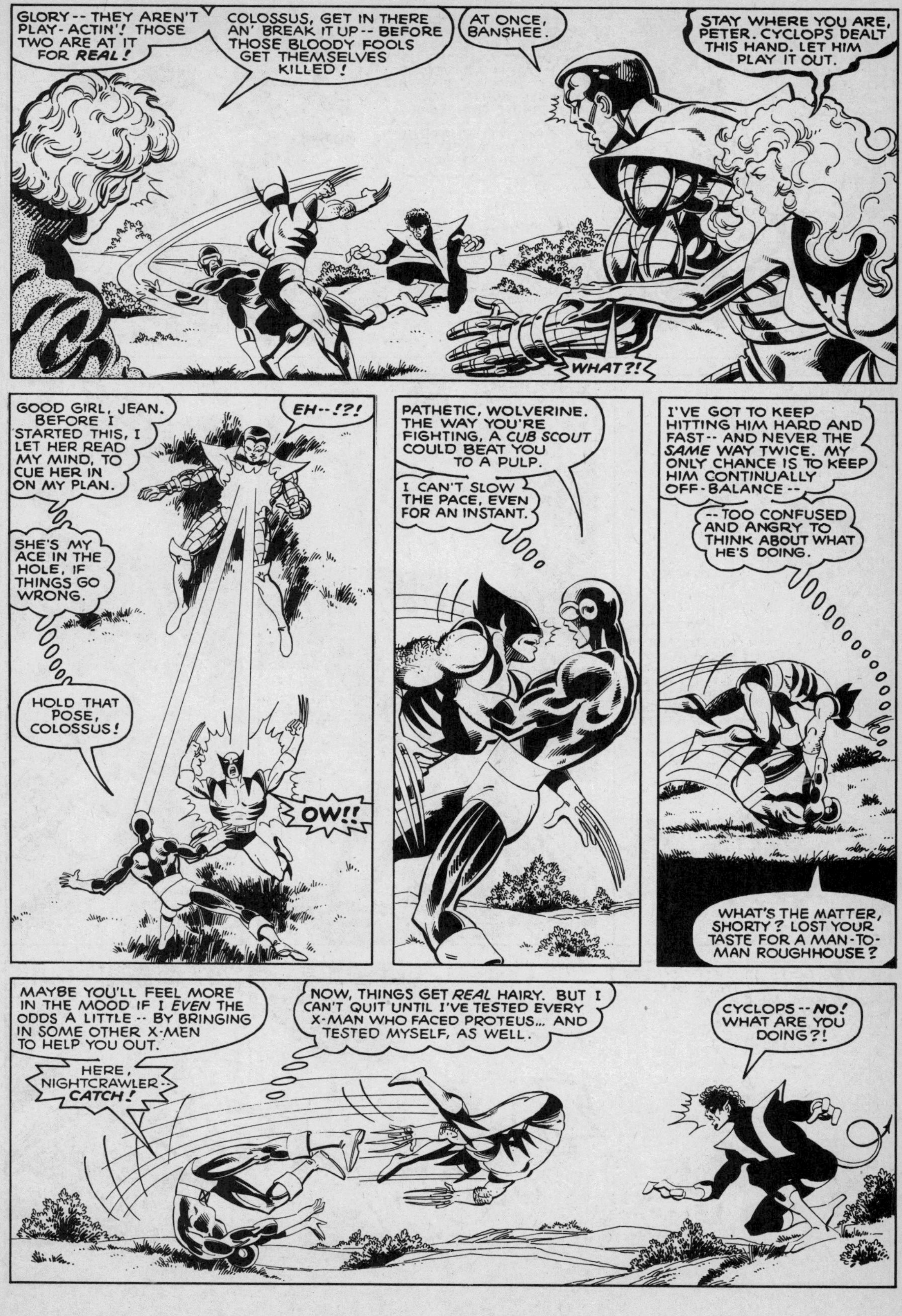
GLORY -- THEY AREN'T PLAY-ACTIN'! THOSE TWO ARE AT IT FOR **REAL**!
COLOSSUS, GET IN THERE AN' BREAK IT UP -- BEFORE THOSE BLOODY FOOLS GET THEMSELVES KILLED!
AT ONCE, BANSHEE.
STAY WHERE YOU ARE, PETER. CYCLOPS DEALT THIS HAND. LET HIM PLAY IT OUT.
WHAT?!
GOOD GIRL, JEAN. BEFORE I STARTED THIS, I LET HER READ MY MIND, TO CUE HER IN ON MY PLAN.
EH--!?!
SHE'S MY ACE IN THE HOLE, IF THINGS GO WRONG.
HOLD THAT POSE, COLOSSUS!
OW!!
PATHETIC, WOLVERINE. THE WAY YOU'RE FIGHTING, A *CUB SCOUT* COULD BEAT YOU TO A PULP.
I CAN'T SLOW THE PACE, EVEN FOR AN INSTANT.
I'VE GOT TO KEEP HITTING HIM HARD AND FAST -- AND NEVER THE *SAME* WAY TWICE. MY ONLY CHANCE IS TO KEEP HIM CONTINUALLY OFF-BALANCE --
-- TOO CONFUSED AND ANGRY TO THINK ABOUT WHAT HE'S DOING.
WHAT'S THE MATTER, SHORTY? LOST YOUR TASTE FOR A MAN-TO-MAN ROUGHHOUSE?
MAYBE YOU'LL FEEL MORE IN THE MOOD IF I *EVEN* THE ODDS A LITTLE -- BY BRINGING IN SOME OTHER X-MEN TO HELP YOU OUT.
HERE, NIGHTCRAWLER -- **CATCH!**
NOW, THINGS GET *REAL* HAIRY. BUT I CAN'T QUIT UNTIL I'VE TESTED EVERY X-MAN WHO FACED PROTEUS... AND TESTED MYSELF, AS WELL.
CYCLOPS -- **NO!** WHAT ARE YOU DOING?!

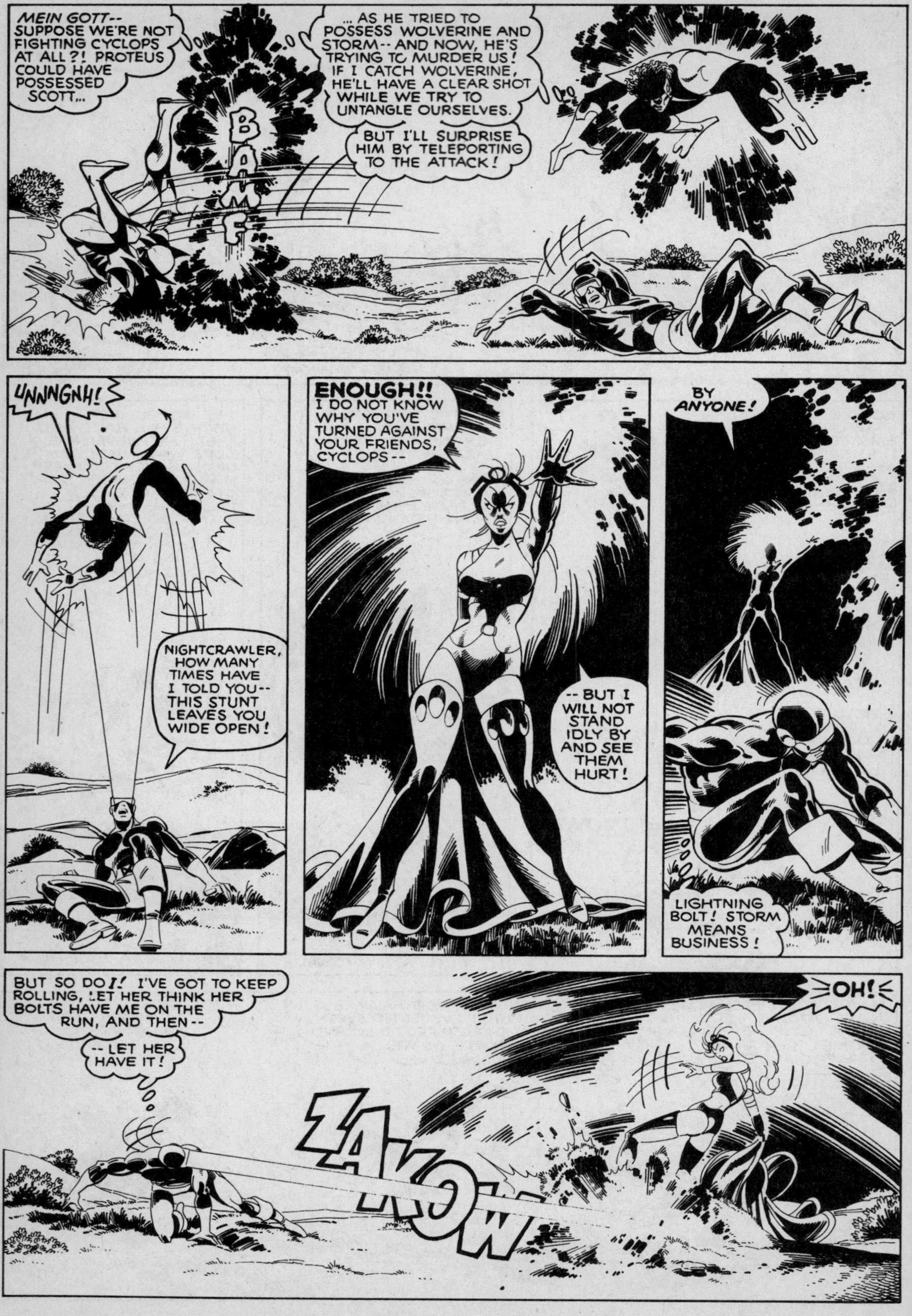
MEIN GOTT-- SUPPOSE WE'RE NOT FIGHTING CYCLOPS AT ALL?! PROTEUS COULD HAVE POSSESSED SCOTT...
...AS HE TRIED TO POSSESS WOLVERINE AND STORM-- AND NOW, HE'S TRYING TO MURDER US! IF I CATCH WOLVERINE, HE'LL HAVE A CLEAR SHOT WHILE WE TRY TO UNTANGLE OURSELVES.
BUT I'LL SURPRISE HIM BY TELEPORTING TO THE ATTACK!
BAMF
UNNNGNH!
NIGHTCRAWLER, HOW MANY TIMES HAVE I TOLD YOU-- THIS STUNT LEAVES YOU WIDE OPEN!
ENOUGH!! I DO NOT KNOW WHY YOU'VE TURNED AGAINST YOUR FRIENDS, CYCLOPS--
--BUT I WILL NOT STAND IDLY BY AND SEE THEM HURT!
BY ANYONE!
LIGHTNING BOLT! STORM MEANS BUSINESS!
BUT SO DO I! I'VE GOT TO KEEP ROLLING, LET HER THINK HER BOLTS HAVE ME ON THE RUN, AND THEN--
--LET HER HAVE IT!
ZAKOW
OH!

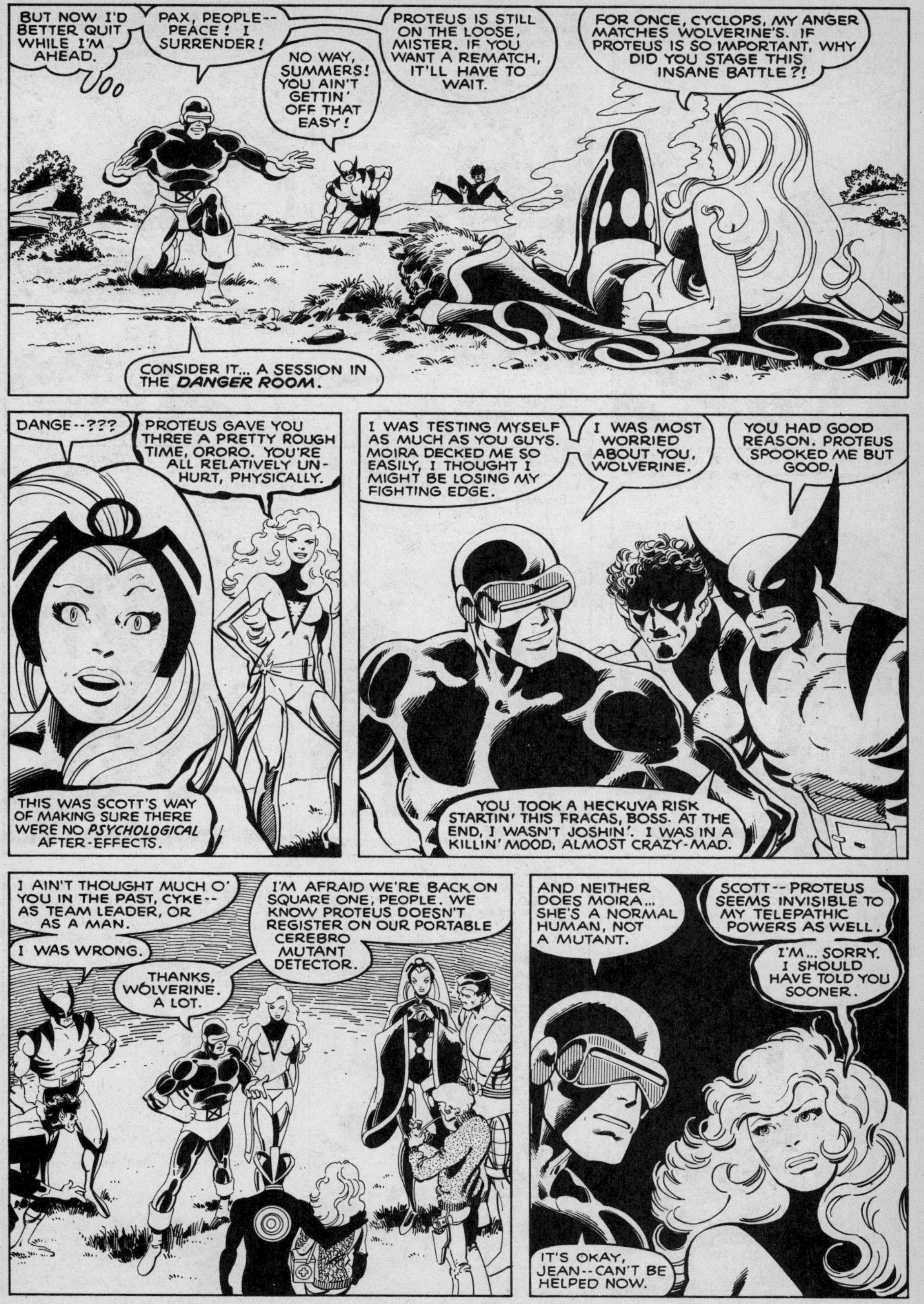
BUT NOW I'D BETTER QUIT WHILE I'M AHEAD.
PAX, PEOPLE-- PEACE! I SURRENDER!
NO WAY, SUMMERS! YOU AIN'T GETTIN' OFF THAT EASY!
PROTEUS IS STILL ON THE LOOSE, MISTER. IF YOU WANT A REMATCH, IT'LL HAVE TO WAIT.
FOR ONCE, CYCLOPS, MY ANGER MATCHES WOLVERINE'S. IF PROTEUS IS SO IMPORTANT, WHY DID YOU STAGE THIS INSANE BATTLE?!
OOO
CONSIDER IT... A SESSION IN THE DANGER ROOM.
DANGE--???
PROTEUS GAVE YOU THREE A PRETTY ROUGH TIME, ORORO. YOU'RE ALL RELATIVELY UNHURT, PHYSICALLY.
THIS WAS SCOTT'S WAY OF MAKING SURE THERE WERE NO PSYCHOLOGICAL AFTER-EFFECTS.
I WAS TESTING MYSELF AS MUCH AS YOU GUYS. MOIRA DECKED ME SO EASILY, I THOUGHT I MIGHT BE LOSING MY FIGHTING EDGE.
I WAS MOST WORRIED ABOUT YOU, WOLVERINE.
YOU HAD GOOD REASON. PROTEUS SPOOKED ME BUT GOOD.
YOU TOOK A HECKUVA RISK STARTIN' THIS FRACAS, BOSS. AT THE END, I WASN'T JOSHIN'. I WAS IN A KILLIN' MOOD, ALMOST CRAZY-MAD.
I AIN'T THOUGHT MUCH O' YOU IN THE PAST, CYKE-- AS TEAM LEADER, OR AS A MAN.
I WAS WRONG.
THANKS, WOLVERINE. A LOT.
I'M AFRAID WE'RE BACK ON SQUARE ONE, PEOPLE. WE KNOW PROTEUS DOESN'T REGISTER ON OUR PORTABLE CEREBRO MUTANT DETECTOR.
AND NEITHER DOES MOIRA... SHE'S A NORMAL HUMAN, NOT A MUTANT.
SCOTT--PROTEUS SEEMS INVISIBLE TO MY TELEPATHIC POWERS AS WELL.
I'M... SORRY. I SHOULD HAVE TOLD YOU SOONER.
IT'S OKAY, JEAN--CAN'T BE HELPED NOW.

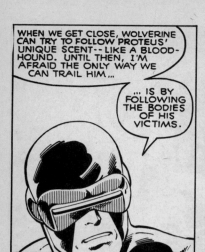

WHEN WE GET CLOSE, WOLVERINE CAN TRY TO FOLLOW PROTEUS' UNIQUE SCENT—LIKE A BLOODHOUND. UNTIL THEN, I'M AFRAID THE ONLY WAY WE CAN TRAIL HIM...

...IS BY FOLLOWING THE BODIES OF HIS VICTIMS.

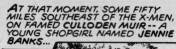

AT THAT MOMENT, SOME FIFTY MILES SOUTHEAST OF THE X-MEN, ON FAMED *CULLODEN MUIR*—A YOUNG SHOPGIRL NAMED *JENNIE BANKS*...

...IS MUTTERING ANGRILY OVER A FLAT TIRE.

OCH—BAD ENOUGH I'M IN A TEARING HURRY, BUT IT'S MORE'N A MILE TO THE NEAREST PETROL STATION, AN'—WHAT'S THAT?!

A POLICEMAN! I'M IN LUCK!

ANYTHING TH' MATTER, MISS?

NOT ANYMORE, I HOPE. I'VE LOST A TIRE—COULD YOU GIVE ME A HAND...

OH! NO—PLEASE, NO!!

DO NOT RESIST, LITTLE ONE. NOTHING CAN SAVE YOU NOW.

BEFORE SHE EVEN KNOWS WHAT'S HAPPENING...

...JENNIE BANKS IS DEAD, HER BODY ONLY A HOLLOW SHELL WHICH PROTEUS POSSESSES... DISCARDING THE OLD BODY AS EASILY AS AN OVERCOAT.

HE FEELS NO REMORSE FOR WHAT HE'S DONE. TO HIM, IT'S SIMPLY A MATTER OF SURVIVAL—THE STRONG PREYING ON THE WEAK.

THE X-MEN ARE HUNTING A POLICEMAN IN A STOLEN JEEP.

NOW, EVEN IF THEY FIND HIS BODY, THEY'LL HAVE NO IDEA WHAT NEW FORM I'M WEARING, OR WHAT VEHICLE I'M DRIVING, OR WHERE I'M GOING.

NO MATTER HOW HARD THEY TRY, THEY'LL ALWAYS REMAIN ONE STEP BEHIND ME. AND FOR ALL THEIR VAUNTED POWER, THEY CANNOT KEEP ME FROM FINDING AND DESTROYING THE "ONE-I-HATE."

EDINBURGH ZOO KM

AND WHEN HE IS NO MORE, IT WILL BE THE *X-MEN'S* TURN.

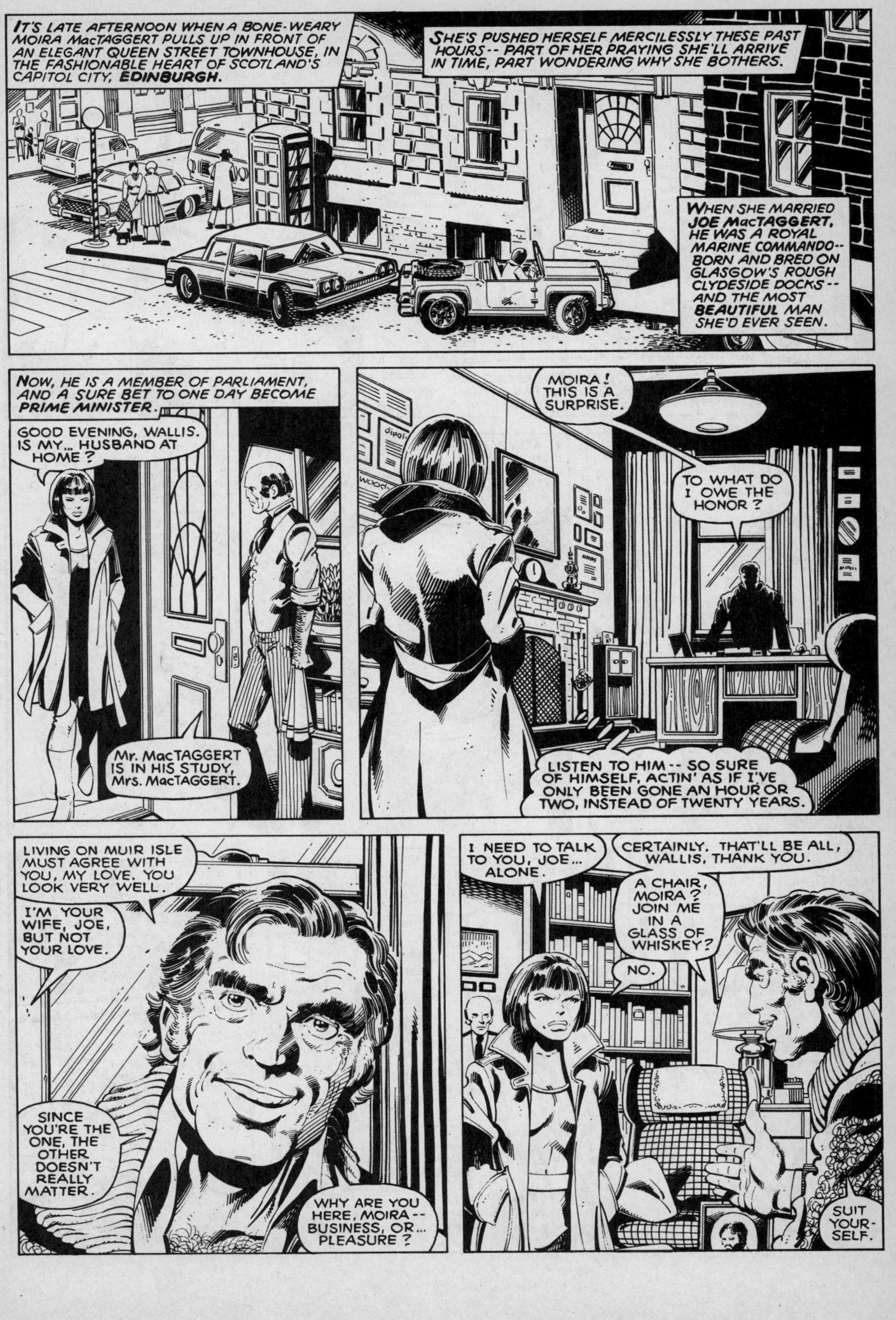
IT'S LATE AFTERNOON WHEN A BONE-WEARY MOIRA MacTAGGERT PULLS UP IN FRONT OF AN ELEGANT QUEEN STREET TOWNHOUSE, IN THE FASHIONABLE HEART OF SCOTLAND'S CAPITOL CITY, EDINBURGH.
SHE'S PUSHED HERSELF MERCILESSLY THESE PAST HOURS -- PART OF HER PRAYING SHE'LL ARRIVE IN TIME, PART WONDERING WHY SHE BOTHERS.
WHEN SHE MARRIED JOE MacTAGGERT, HE WAS A ROYAL MARINE COMMANDO-- BORN AND BRED ON GLASGOW'S ROUGH CLYDESIDE DOCKS -- AND THE MOST BEAUTIFUL MAN SHE'D EVER SEEN.
NOW, HE IS A MEMBER OF PARLIAMENT, AND A SURE BET TO ONE DAY BECOME PRIME MINISTER.
GOOD EVENING, WALLIS. IS MY... HUSBAND AT HOME?
Mr. MacTAGGERT IS IN HIS STUDY, Mrs. MacTAGGERT.
MOIRA! THIS IS A SURPRISE.
TO WHAT DO I OWE THE HONOR?
LISTEN TO HIM -- SO SURE OF HIMSELF, ACTIN' AS IF I'VE ONLY BEEN GONE AN HOUR OR TWO, INSTEAD OF TWENTY YEARS.
LIVING ON MUIR ISLE MUST AGREE WITH YOU, MY LOVE. YOU LOOK VERY WELL.
I'M YOUR WIFE, JOE, BUT NOT YOUR LOVE.
SINCE YOU'RE THE ONE, THE OTHER DOESN'T REALLY MATTER.
WHY ARE YOU HERE, MOIRA -- BUSINESS, OR... PLEASURE?
I NEED TO TALK TO YOU, JOE... ALONE.
CERTAINLY. THAT'LL BE ALL, WALLIS, THANK YOU.
A CHAIR, MOIRA? JOIN ME IN A GLASS OF WHISKEY?
NO.
SUIT YOURSELF.

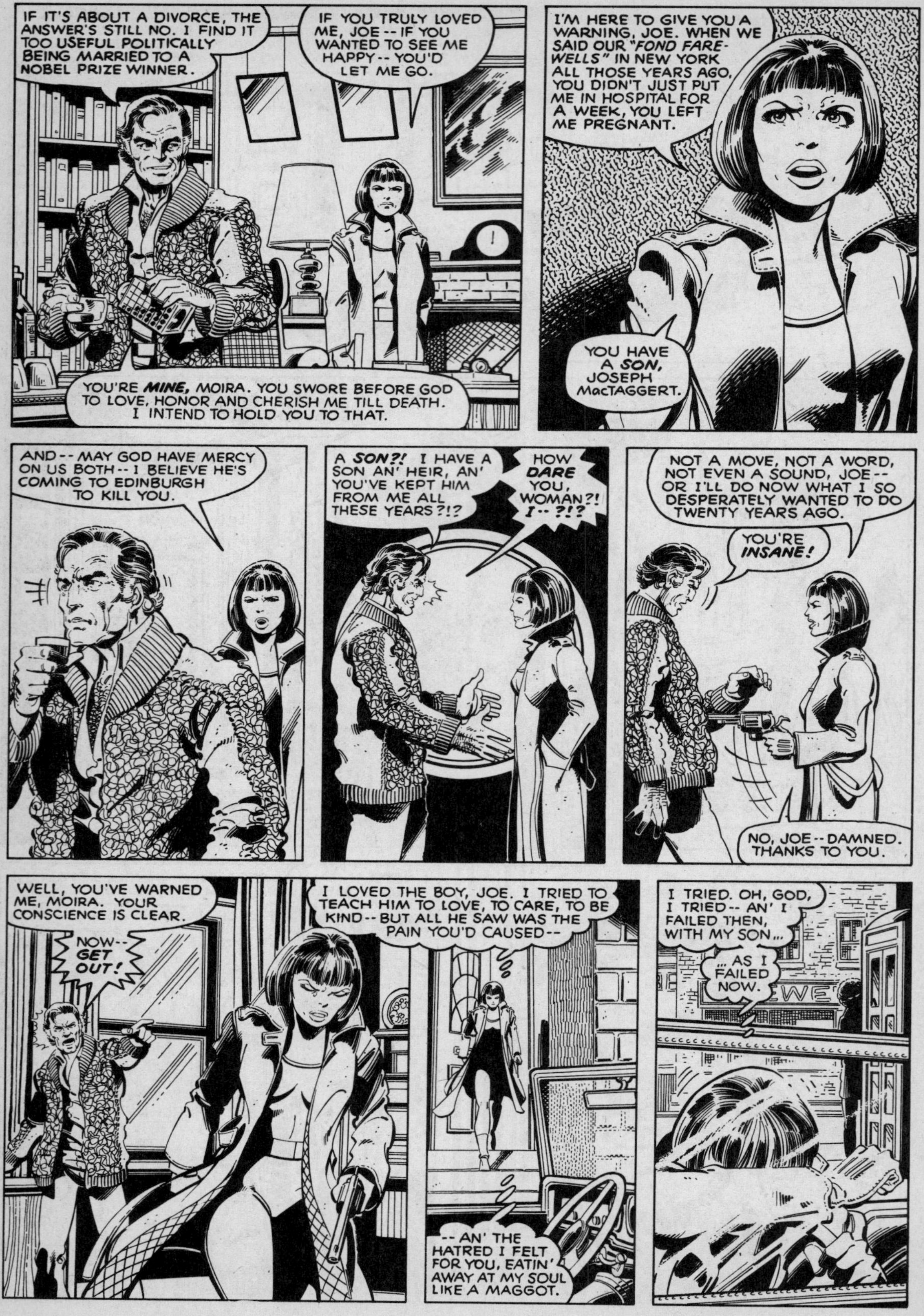
IF IT'S ABOUT A DIVORCE, THE ANSWER'S STILL NO. I FIND IT TOO USEFUL POLITICALLY BEING MARRIED TO A NOBEL PRIZE WINNER.
IF YOU TRULY LOVED ME, JOE -- IF YOU WANTED TO SEE ME HAPPY -- YOU'D LET ME GO.
YOU'RE MINE, MOIRA. YOU SWORE BEFORE GOD TO LOVE, HONOR AND CHERISH ME TILL DEATH. I INTEND TO HOLD YOU TO THAT.
I'M HERE TO GIVE YOU A WARNING, JOE. WHEN WE SAID OUR "FOND FARE-WELLS" IN NEW YORK ALL THOSE YEARS AGO, YOU DIDN'T JUST PUT ME IN HOSPITAL FOR A WEEK, YOU LEFT ME PREGNANT.
YOU HAVE A SON, JOSEPH MacTAGGERT.
AND -- MAY GOD HAVE MERCY ON US BOTH -- I BELIEVE HE'S COMING TO EDINBURGH TO KILL YOU.
A SON?! I HAVE A SON AN' HEIR, AN' YOU'VE KEPT HIM FROM ME ALL THESE YEARS?!?
HOW DARE YOU, WOMAN?! I -- ?!?
NOT A MOVE, NOT A WORD, NOT EVEN A SOUND, JOE -- OR I'LL DO NOW WHAT I SO DESPERATELY WANTED TO DO TWENTY YEARS AGO.
YOU'RE INSANE!
NO, JOE -- DAMNED. THANKS TO YOU.
WELL, YOU'VE WARNED ME, MOIRA. YOUR CONSCIENCE IS CLEAR.
NOW -- GET OUT!
I LOVED THE BOY, JOE. I TRIED TO TEACH HIM TO LOVE, TO CARE, TO BE KIND -- BUT ALL HE SAW WAS THE PAIN YOU'D CAUSED --
-- AN' THE HATRED I FELT FOR YOU, EATIN' AWAY AT MY SOUL LIKE A MAGGOT.
I TRIED. OH, GOD, I TRIED -- AN' I FAILED THEN, WITH MY SON...
...AS I FAILED NOW.

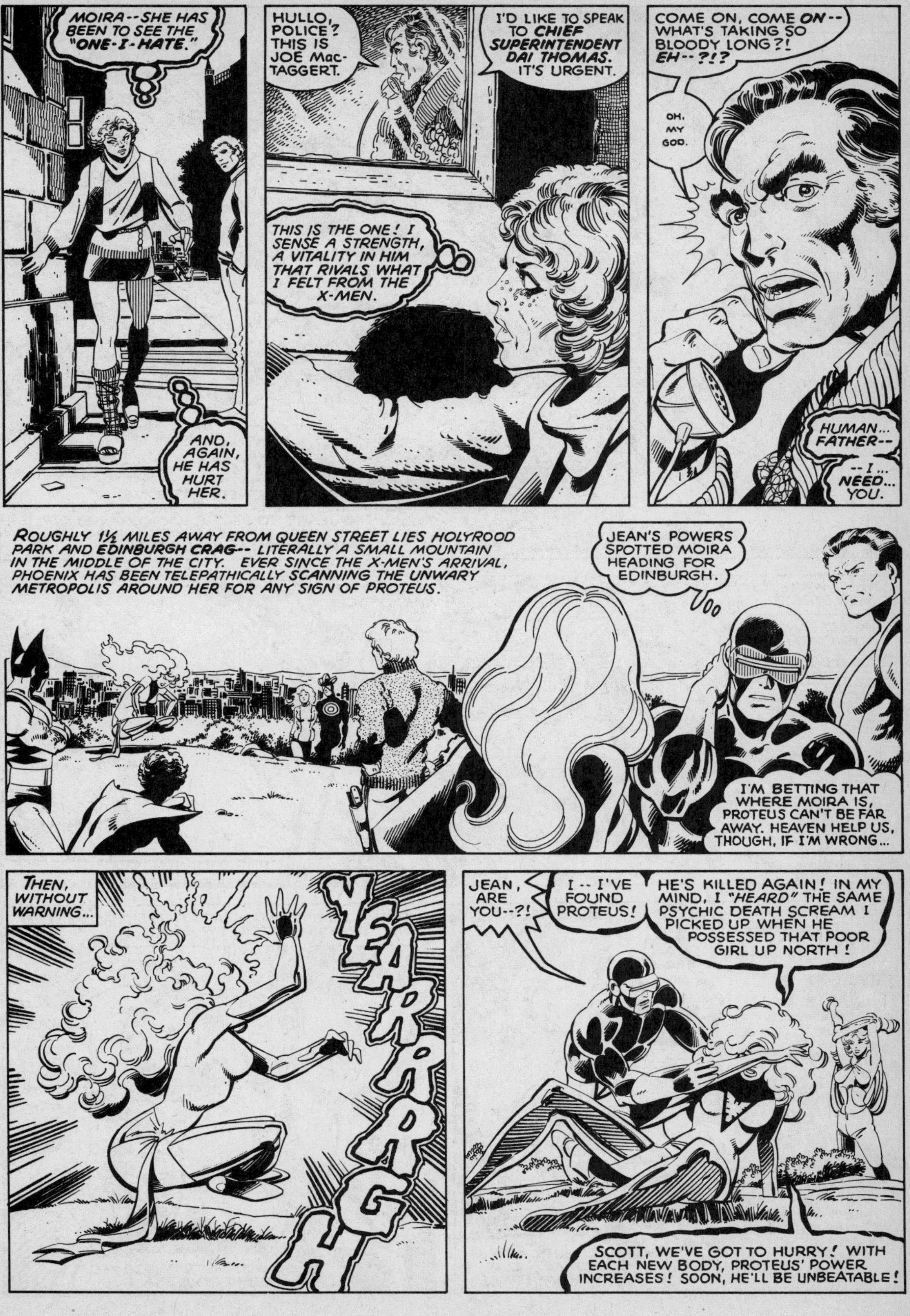
MOIRA--SHE HAS BEEN TO SEE THE "ONE-I-HATE."
AND, AGAIN, HE HAS HURT HER.
HULLO, POLICE? THIS IS JOE MacTAGGERT.
I'D LIKE TO SPEAK TO CHIEF SUPERINTENDENT DAI THOMAS. IT'S URGENT.
THIS IS THE ONE! I SENSE A STRENGTH, A VITALITY IN HIM THAT RIVALS WHAT I FELT FROM THE X-MEN.
COME ON, COME ON-- WHAT'S TAKING SO BLOODY LONG?! EH--?!?
OH, MY GOD.
HUMAN... FATHER--
--I... NEED... YOU.
ROUGHLY 1½ MILES AWAY FROM QUEEN STREET LIES HOLYROOD PARK AND EDINBURGH CRAG-- LITERALLY A SMALL MOUNTAIN IN THE MIDDLE OF THE CITY. EVER SINCE THE X-MEN'S ARRIVAL, PHOENIX HAS BEEN TELEPATHICALLY SCANNING THE UNWARY METROPOLIS AROUND HER FOR ANY SIGN OF PROTEUS.
JEAN'S POWERS SPOTTED MOIRA HEADING FOR EDINBURGH.
I'M BETTING THAT WHERE MOIRA IS, PROTEUS CAN'T BE FAR AWAY. HEAVEN HELP US, THOUGH, IF I'M WRONG...
THEN, WITHOUT WARNING...
YEARRRGH
JEAN, ARE YOU--?!
I -- I'VE FOUND PROTEUS!
HE'S KILLED AGAIN! IN MY MIND, I "HEARD" THE SAME PSYCHIC DEATH SCREAM I PICKED UP WHEN HE POSSESSED THAT POOR GIRL UP NORTH!
SCOTT, WE'VE GOT TO HURRY! WITH EACH NEW BODY, PROTEUS' POWER INCREASES! SOON, HE'LL BE UNBEATABLE!

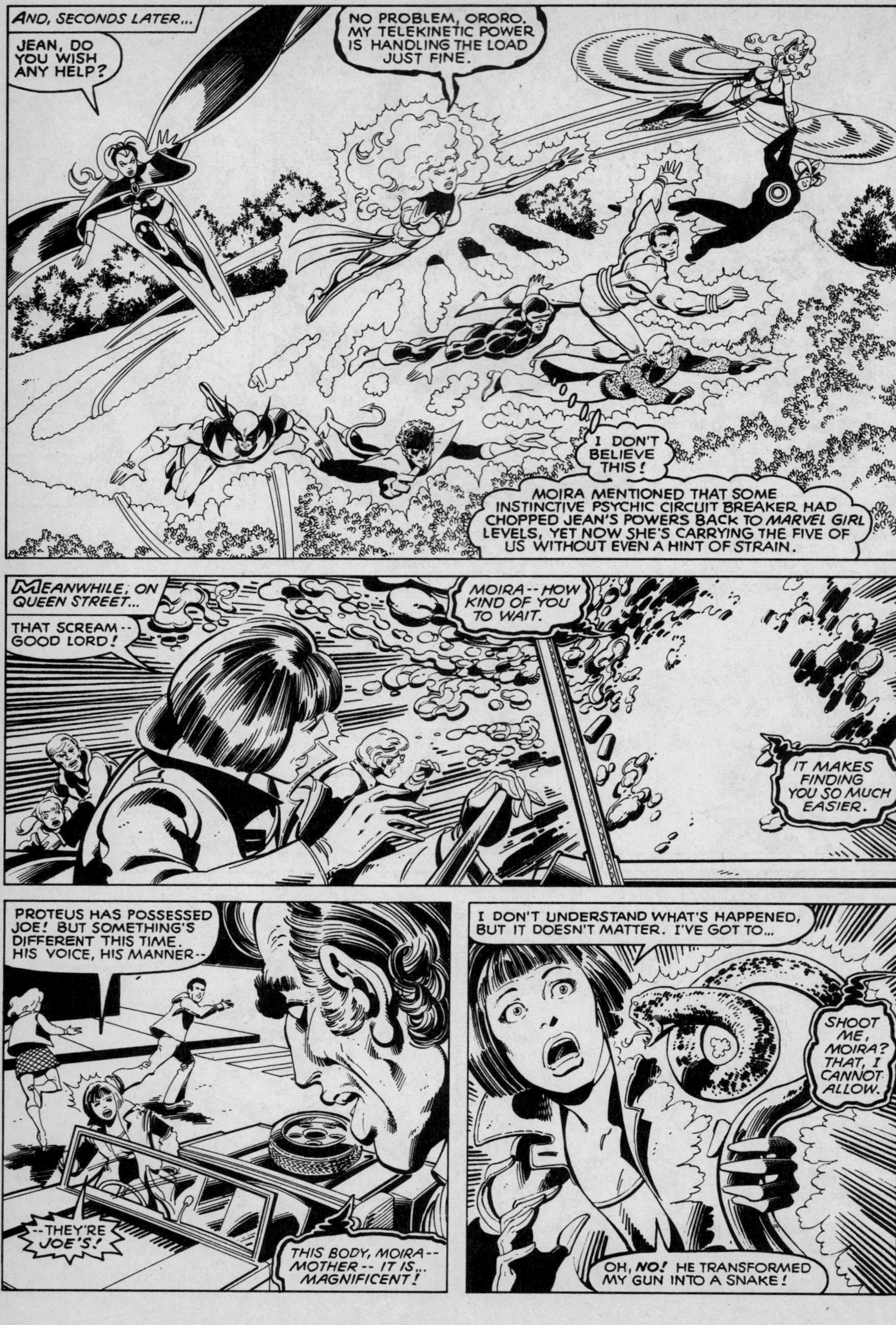
AND, SECONDS LATER...
JEAN, DO YOU WISH ANY HELP?
NO PROBLEM, ORORO. MY TELEKINETIC POWER IS HANDLING THE LOAD JUST FINE.
I DON'T BELIEVE THIS!
MOIRA MENTIONED THAT SOME INSTINCTIVE PSYCHIC CIRCUIT BREAKER HAD CHOPPED JEAN'S POWERS BACK TO MARVEL GIRL LEVELS, YET NOW SHE'S CARRYING THE FIVE OF US WITHOUT EVEN A HINT OF STRAIN.
MEANWHILE, ON QUEEN STREET...
THAT SCREAM -- GOOD LORD!
MOIRA -- HOW KIND OF YOU TO WAIT.
IT MAKES FINDING YOU SO MUCH EASIER.
PROTEUS HAS POSSESSED JOE! BUT SOMETHING'S DIFFERENT THIS TIME. HIS VOICE, HIS MANNER --
-- THEY'RE JOE'S!
THIS BODY, MOIRA -- MOTHER -- IT IS... MAGNIFICENT!
I DON'T UNDERSTAND WHAT'S HAPPENED, BUT IT DOESN'T MATTER. I'VE GOT TO...
SHOOT ME, MOIRA? THAT, I CANNOT ALLOW.
OH, NO! HE TRANSFORMED MY GUN INTO A SNAKE!

CONFUSED, MOIRA? ALLOW ME TO ENLIGHTEN YOU. WHEN I POSSESS PEOPLE, I ABSORB THEIR MEMORIES, THEIR EMOTIONS, AS WELL AS THEIR BODIES.

I KNOW ALL MY... FATHER KNEW, FEEL ALL HE FELT. NEVER HAVE I EXPERIENCED SUCH PASSION, SUCH RAW STRENGTH. THIS FORM WILL LAST ME A LONG TIME.

HE AND I ARE MUCH ALIKE, YOU KNOW. WHAT WE WANT, WE TAKE. AND WHAT WE TAKE, WE NEVER GIVE UP.

AND NOW, MOIRA, WHAT I -- WE -- WANT... IS YOU!

NOT FAR AWAY...

I'M PICKING UP MOIRA'S THOUGHTS, SCOTT.

SHE'S BADLY SCARED. PROTEUS IS AFTER HER!

THERE, CYKE! UP AHEAD!

THAT LIGHT SHOW HAS T'BE IT!

BLESSED SAINTS -- THE WOMAN I LOVE IS FIGHTIN' FOR HER LIFE AN', WITH ME SONIC SCREAM GONE,* I'M HELPLESS TO DO ANYTHIN' TO SAVE HER.

*DUE TO INJURIES SUFFERED IN X-MEN #119. -- DOC STERN.

POOR BANSHEE -- HE SOUNDS LIKE HE'S IN AGONY. MAYBE IT WOULD HAVE BEEN BETTER -- KINDER -- TO LEAVE HIM BEHIND.

COLOSSUS, YOU LEAD OFF THE ATTACK!

PROTEUS CAN'T STAND METAL, SO IN YOUR ARMORED FORM, YOU'LL HAVE THE BEST CHANCE OF GETTING TO HIM.

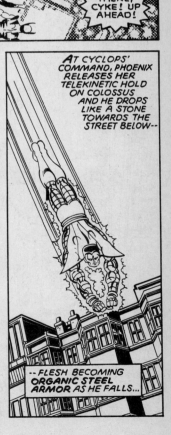

AT CYCLOPS' COMMAND, PHOENIX RELEASES HER TELEKINETIC HOLD ON COLOSSUS AND HE DROPS LIKE A STONE TOWARDS THE STREET BELOW--

--FLESH BECOMING ORGANIC STEEL ARMOR AS HE FALLS...

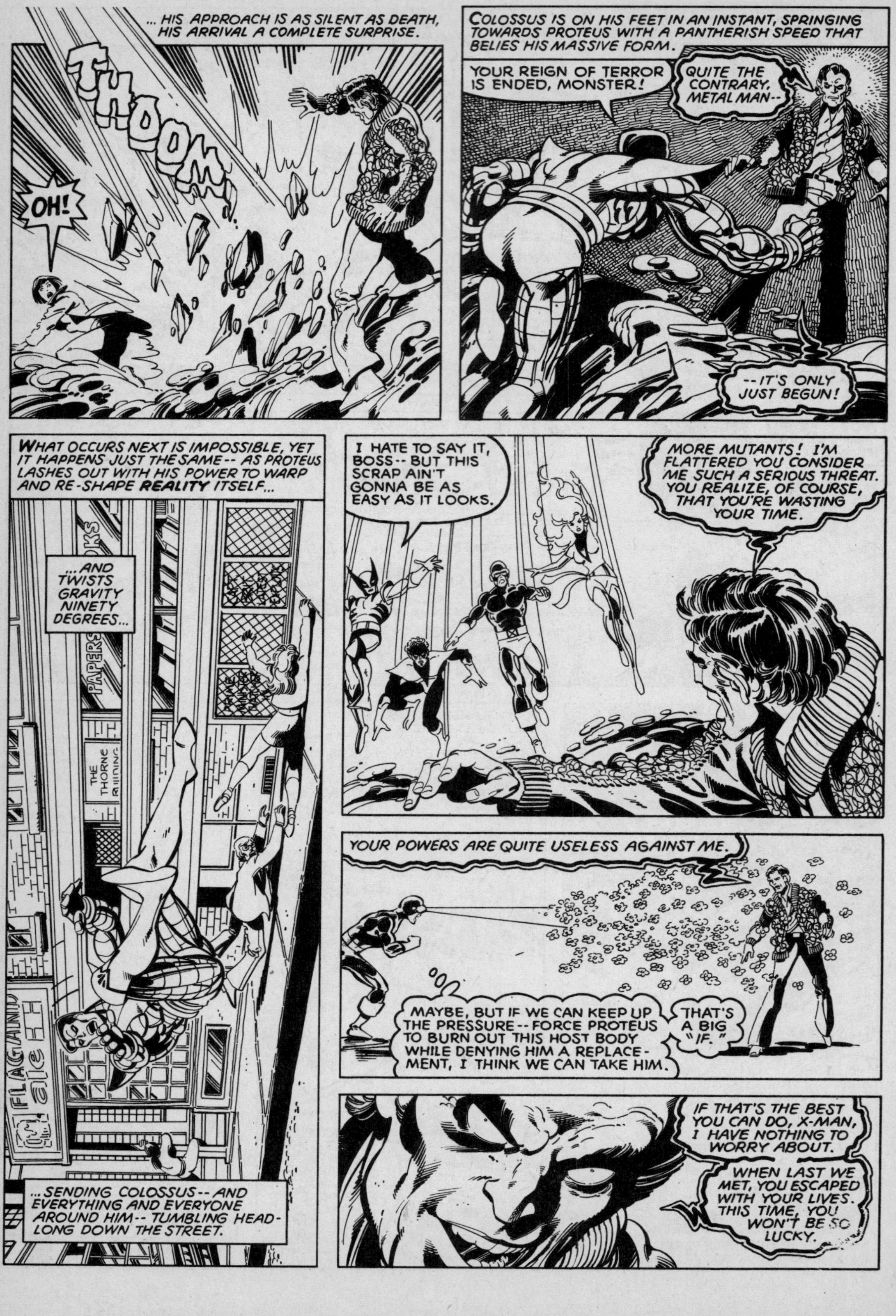

... HIS APPROACH IS AS SILENT AS DEATH, HIS ARRIVAL A COMPLETE SURPRISE.
THOOM
OH!
COLOSSUS IS ON HIS FEET IN AN INSTANT, SPRINGING TOWARDS PROTEUS WITH A PANTHERISH SPEED THAT BELIES HIS MASSIVE FORM.
YOUR REIGN OF TERROR IS ENDED, MONSTER!
QUITE THE CONTRARY, METAL MAN--
--IT'S ONLY JUST BEGUN!
WHAT OCCURS NEXT IS IMPOSSIBLE, YET IT HAPPENS JUST THE SAME-- AS PROTEUS LASHES OUT WITH HIS POWER TO WARP AND RE-SHAPE REALITY ITSELF...
...AND TWISTS GRAVITY NINETY DEGREES...
PAPERS
THE THORNE BUILDING
...SENDING COLOSSUS-- AND EVERYTHING AND EVERYONE AROUND HIM-- TUMBLING HEAD-LONG DOWN THE STREET.
I HATE TO SAY IT, BOSS-- BUT THIS SCRAP AIN'T GONNA BE AS EASY AS IT LOOKS.
MORE MUTANTS! I'M FLATTERED YOU CONSIDER ME SUCH A SERIOUS THREAT. YOU REALIZE, OF COURSE, THAT YOU'RE WASTING YOUR TIME.
YOUR POWERS ARE QUITE USELESS AGAINST ME.
MAYBE, BUT IF WE CAN KEEP UP THE PRESSURE-- FORCE PROTEUS TO BURN OUT THIS HOST BODY WHILE DENYING HIM A REPLACE-MENT, I THINK WE CAN TAKE HIM.
THAT'S A BIG "IF."
IF THAT'S THE BEST YOU CAN DO, X-MAN, I HAVE NOTHING TO WORRY ABOUT.
WHEN LAST WE MET, YOU ESCAPED WITH YOUR LIVES. THIS TIME, YOU WON'T BE SO LUCKY.

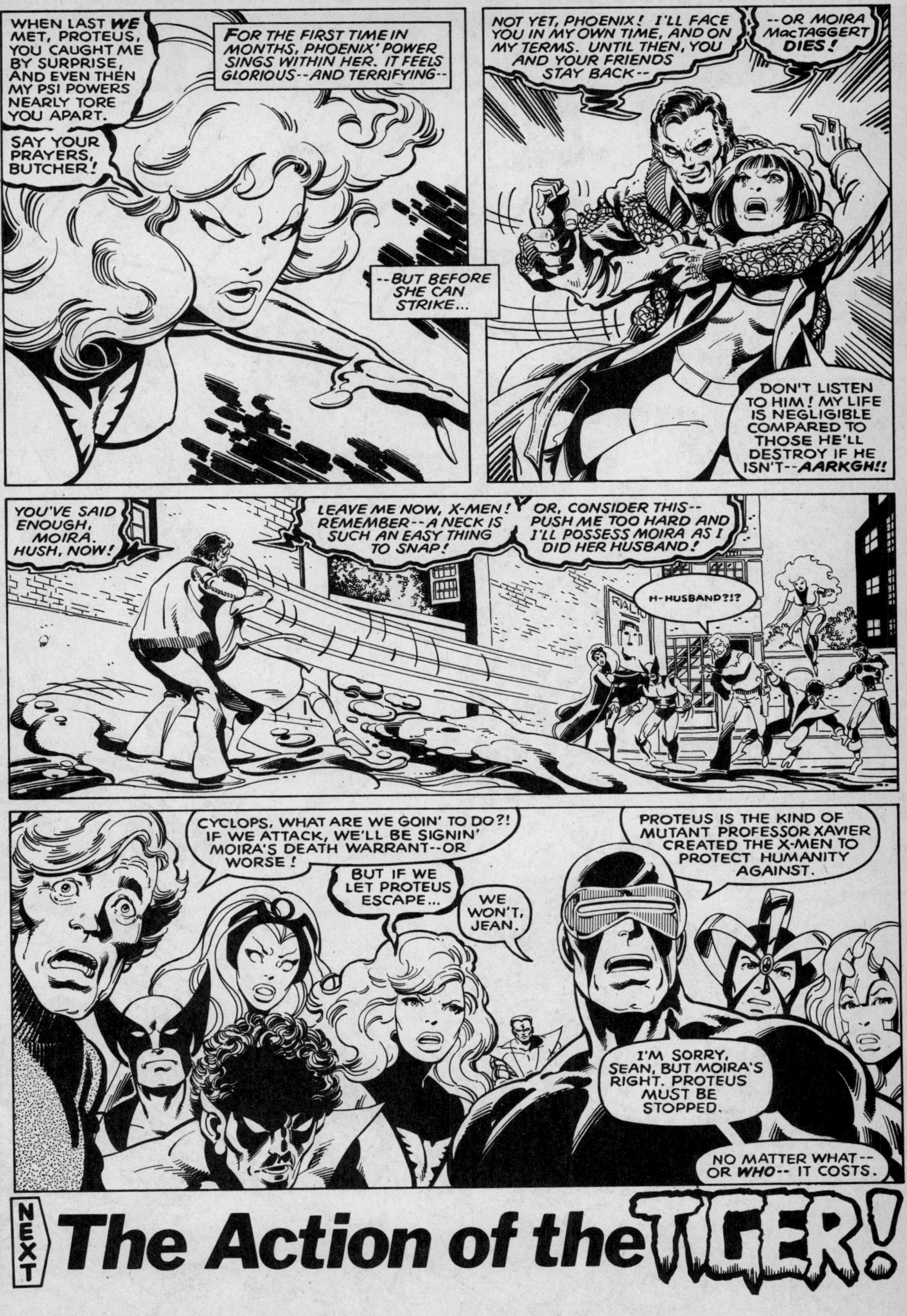
WHEN LAST WE MET, PROTEUS, YOU CAUGHT ME BY SURPRISE, AND EVEN THEN MY PSI POWERS NEARLY TORE YOU APART.
SAY YOUR PRAYERS, BUTCHER!
FOR THE FIRST TIME IN MONTHS, PHOENIX' POWER SINGS WITHIN HER. IT FEELS GLORIOUS--AND TERRIFYING--
--BUT BEFORE SHE CAN STRIKE...
NOT YET, PHOENIX! I'LL FACE YOU IN MY OWN TIME, AND ON MY TERMS. UNTIL THEN, YOU AND YOUR FRIENDS STAY BACK--
--OR MOIRA MacTAGGERT DIES!
DON'T LISTEN TO HIM! MY LIFE IS NEGLIGIBLE COMPARED TO THOSE HE'LL DESTROY IF HE ISN'T--AARKGH!!
YOU'VE SAID ENOUGH, MOIRA. HUSH, NOW!
LEAVE ME NOW, X-MEN! REMEMBER--A NECK IS SUCH AN EASY THING TO SNAP!
OR, CONSIDER THIS--PUSH ME TOO HARD AND I'LL POSSESS MOIRA AS I DID HER HUSBAND!
H-HUSBAND?!?
CYCLOPS, WHAT ARE WE GOIN' TO DO?! IF WE ATTACK, WE'LL BE SIGNIN' MOIRA'S DEATH WARRANT--OR WORSE!
BUT IF WE LET PROTEUS ESCAPE...
WE WON'T, JEAN.
PROTEUS IS THE KIND OF MUTANT PROFESSOR XAVIER CREATED THE X-MEN TO PROTECT HUMANITY AGAINST.
I'M SORRY, SEAN, BUT MOIRA'S RIGHT. PROTEUS MUST BE STOPPED.
NO MATTER WHAT--OR WHO--IT COSTS.
NEXT
The Action of the TIGER!

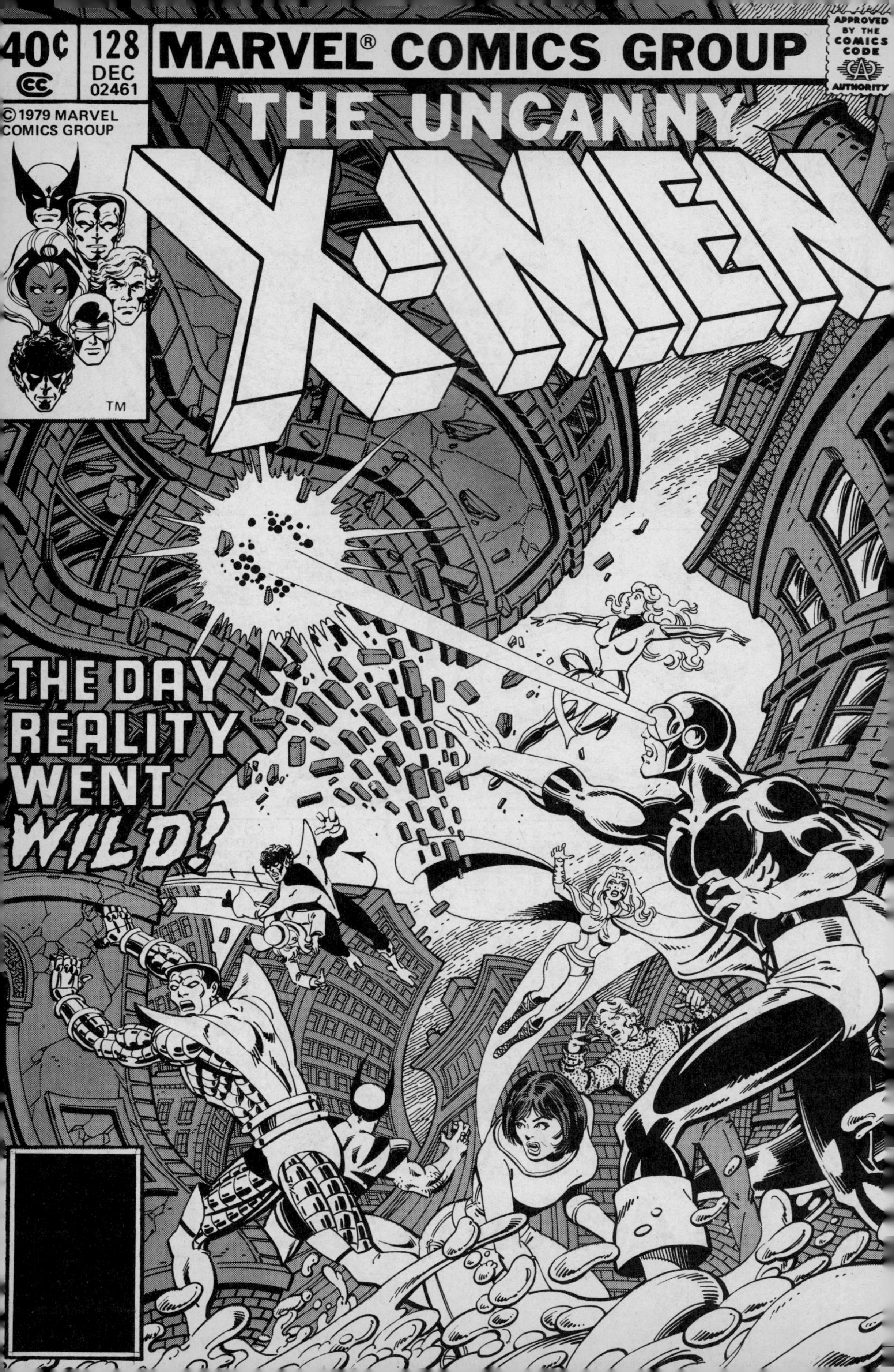

40¢
128
DEC
02461
MARVEL® COMICS GROUP
APPROVED BY THE COMICS CODE AUTHORITY
©1979 MARVEL COMICS GROUP
THE UNCANNY
X-MEN
TM
THE DAY REALITY WENT WILD!

Cyclops. Storm. Banshee. Nightcrawler. Wolverine. Colossus. Children of the atom, students of Charles Xavier, MUTANTS--feared and hated by the world they have sworn to protect. These are the STRANGEST heroes of all!

STAN LEE PRESENTS: THE UNCANNY X-MEN!™

CHRIS CLAREMONT ✱ JOHN BYRNE, AUTHOR - PLOTTERS - PENCILER | TERRY AUSTIN, INKER | TOM ORZECHOWSKI, letterer; GLYNIS WEIN, colorist | ROGER STERN, EDITOR | JIM SHOOTER, Ed.-IN-CHIEF

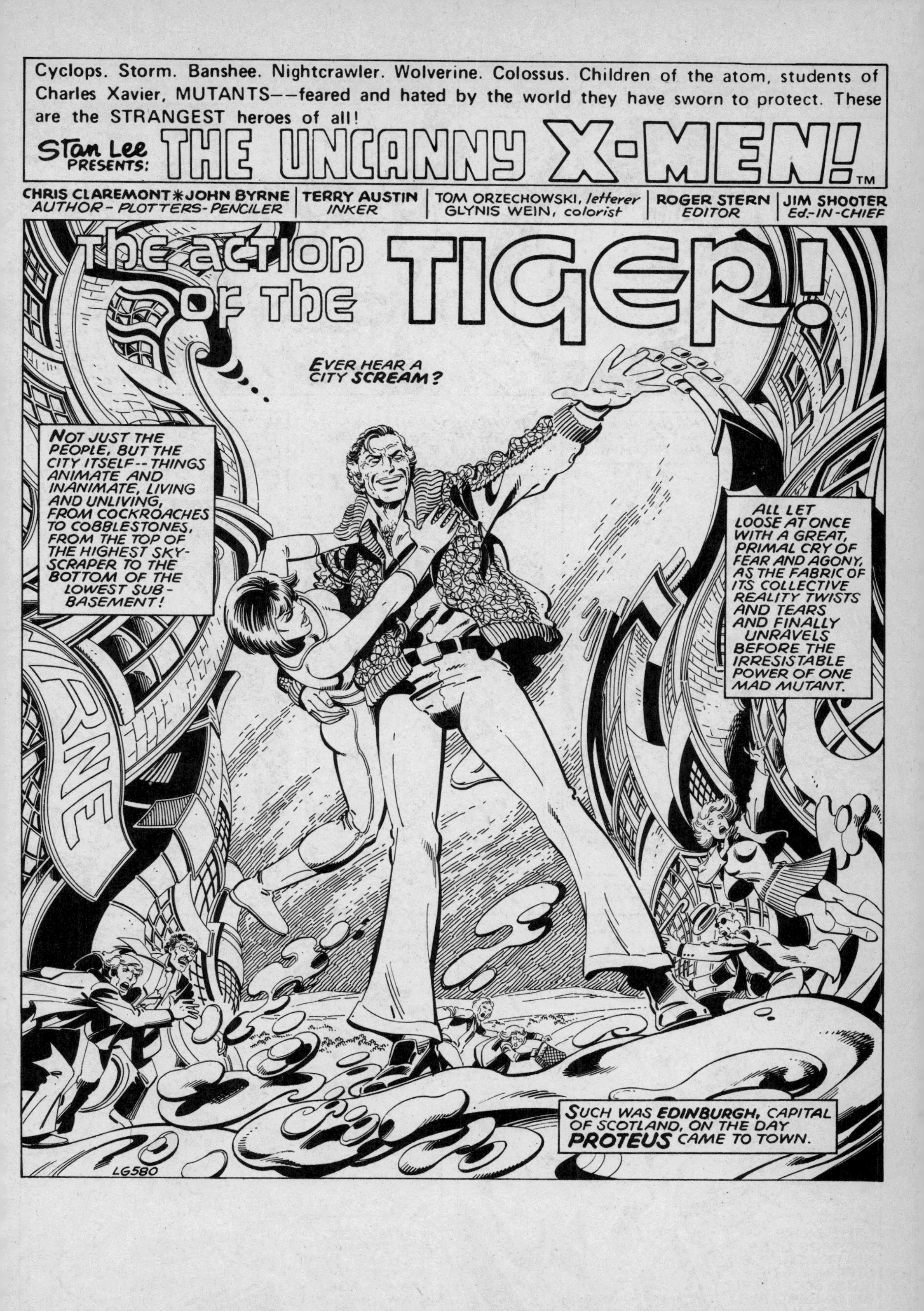
THE ACTION OF THE TIGER!
EVER HEAR A CITY SCREAM?
NOT JUST THE PEOPLE, BUT THE CITY ITSELF--THINGS ANIMATE AND INANIMATE, LIVING AND UNLIVING, FROM COCKROACHES TO COBBLESTONES, FROM THE TOP OF THE HIGHEST SKY-SCRAPER TO THE BOTTOM OF THE LOWEST SUB-BASEMENT!
ALL LET LOOSE AT ONCE WITH A GREAT, PRIMAL CRY OF FEAR AND AGONY, AS THE FABRIC OF ITS COLLECTIVE REALITY TWISTS AND TEARS AND FINALLY UNRAVELS BEFORE THE IRRESISTABLE POWER OF ONE MAD MUTANT.
SUCH WAS EDINBURGH, CAPITAL OF SCOTLAND, ON THE DAY PROTEUS CAME TO TOWN.
LG580

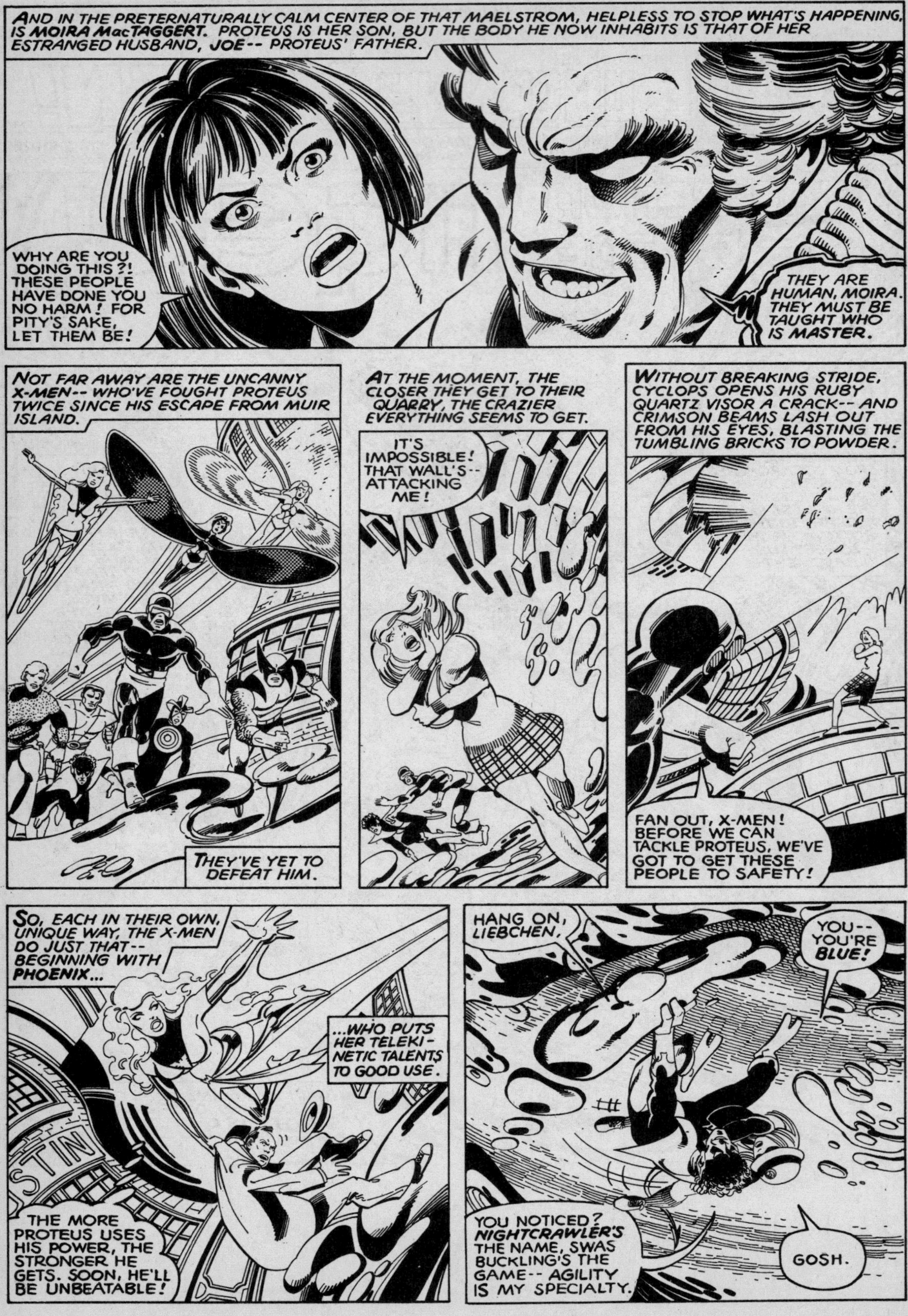

AND IN THE PRETERNATURALLY CALM CENTER OF THAT MAELSTROM, HELPLESS TO STOP WHAT'S HAPPENING, IS MOIRA MacTAGGERT. PROTEUS IS HER SON, BUT THE BODY HE NOW INHABITS IS THAT OF HER ESTRANGED HUSBAND, JOE-- PROTEUS' FATHER.
WHY ARE YOU DOING THIS?! THESE PEOPLE HAVE DONE YOU NO HARM! FOR PITY'S SAKE, LET THEM BE!
THEY ARE HUMAN, MOIRA. THEY MUST BE TAUGHT WHO IS MASTER.
NOT FAR AWAY ARE THE UNCANNY X-MEN-- WHO'VE FOUGHT PROTEUS TWICE SINCE HIS ESCAPE FROM MUIR ISLAND.
THEY'VE YET TO DEFEAT HIM.
AT THE MOMENT, THE CLOSER THEY GET TO THEIR QUARRY, THE CRAZIER EVERYTHING SEEMS TO GET.
IT'S IMPOSSIBLE! THAT WALL'S-- ATTACKING ME!
WITHOUT BREAKING STRIDE, CYCLOPS OPENS HIS RUBY QUARTZ VISOR A CRACK-- AND CRIMSON BEAMS LASH OUT FROM HIS EYES, BLASTING THE TUMBLING BRICKS TO POWDER.
FAN OUT, X-MEN! BEFORE WE CAN TACKLE PROTEUS, WE'VE GOT TO GET THESE PEOPLE TO SAFETY!
SO, EACH IN THEIR OWN, UNIQUE WAY, THE X-MEN DO JUST THAT-- BEGINNING WITH PHOENIX...
...WHO PUTS HER TELEKINETIC TALENTS TO GOOD USE.
THE MORE PROTEUS USES HIS POWER, THE STRONGER HE GETS. SOON, HE'LL BE UNBEATABLE!
HANG ON, LIEBCHEN.
YOU-- YOU'RE BLUE!
YOU NOTICED? NIGHTCRAWLER'S THE NAME, SWASHBUCKLING'S THE GAME-- AGILITY IS MY SPECIALTY.
GOSH.

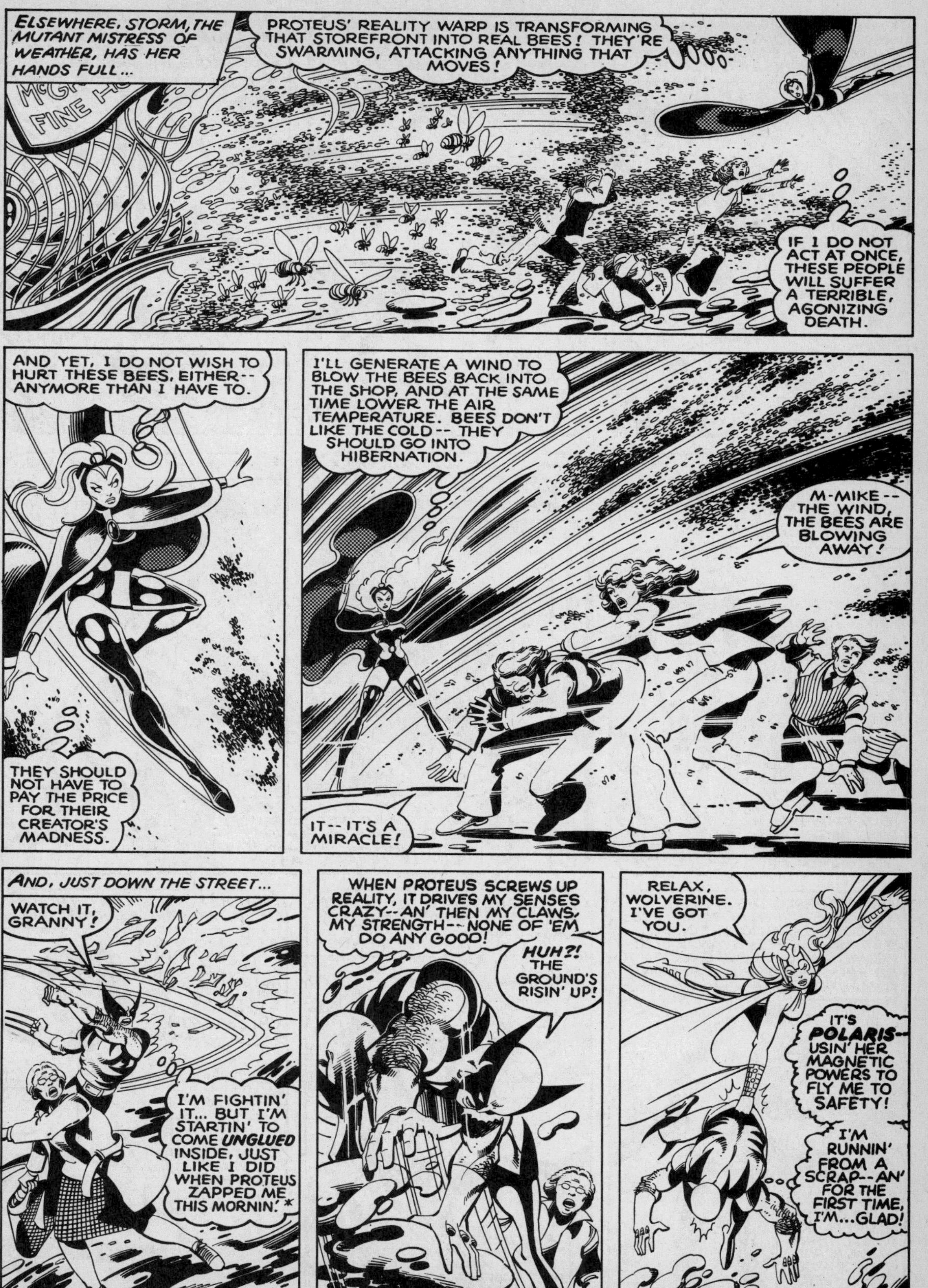
ELSEWHERE, STORM, THE MUTANT MISTRESS OF WEATHER, HAS HER HANDS FULL...
PROTEUS' REALITY WARP IS TRANSFORMING THAT STOREFRONT INTO REAL BEES! THEY'RE SWARMING, ATTACKING ANYTHING THAT MOVES!
IF I DO NOT ACT AT ONCE, THESE PEOPLE WILL SUFFER A TERRIBLE, AGONIZING DEATH.
AND YET, I DO NOT WISH TO HURT THESE BEES, EITHER-- ANYMORE THAN I HAVE TO.
THEY SHOULD NOT HAVE TO PAY THE PRICE FOR THEIR CREATOR'S MADNESS.
I'LL GENERATE A WIND TO BLOW THE BEES BACK INTO THE SHOP, AND AT THE SAME TIME LOWER THE AIR TEMPERATURE. BEES DON'T LIKE THE COLD-- THEY SHOULD GO INTO HIBERNATION.
M-MIKE-- THE WIND, THE BEES ARE BLOWING AWAY!
IT--IT'S A MIRACLE!
AND, JUST DOWN THE STREET...
WATCH IT, GRANNY!
I'M FIGHTIN' IT... BUT I'M STARTIN' TO COME UNGLUED INSIDE, JUST LIKE I DID WHEN PROTEUS ZAPPED ME THIS MORNIN'.*
*LAST ISSUE.--ROG.
WHEN PROTEUS SCREWS UP REALITY, IT DRIVES MY SENSES CRAZY--AN' THEN MY CLAWS, MY STRENGTH--NONE OF 'EM DO ANY GOOD!
HUH?! THE GROUND'S RISIN' UP!
RELAX, WOLVERINE. I'VE GOT YOU.
IT'S POLARIS-- USIN' HER MAGNETIC POWERS TO FLY ME TO SAFETY!
I'M RUNNIN' FROM A SCRAP--AN' FOR THE FIRST TIME, I'M...GLAD!

THERE'S NO RHYME OR REASON TO PROTEUS' ACTIONS. IF A WHIM STRIKES HIM, HE INDULGES IT. HE'S WAITED HALF HIS LIFE FOR THIS MOMENT...

...AND HE MEANS TO ENJOY HIMSELF.

FOR TEN YEARS, THE ONLY WORLD HE KNEW WAS A HOLDING CELL IN MOIRA'S MUIR ISLAND RESEARCH CENTRE. HE'D BE THERE STILL IF A BATTLE-ROYAL BETWEEN THE X-MEN AND THEIR ARCH-FOE, MAGNETO*..

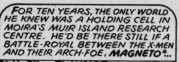
*X-MEN #104 —R.

...HADN'T BREACHED THE VANADIUM STEEL WALLS AND ESOTERIC ENERGY FIELDS THAT KEPT PROTEUS A PRISONER.

BUT WHEN HE FINALLY EMERGED, MAGNETO, THE X-MEN, AND ALL MOIRA'S OTHER MUTANT PATIENTS HAD LONG GONE.

AND WITHOUT THE CELL'S ENERGY FIELDS TO SUSTAIN HIM, HE SOON BEGAN TO BURN OUT HIS OWN NATURAL BODY.

TIME PASSED, AND MUTANT X-- THE FUTURE PROTEUS--REMAINED ALONE ON MUIR ISLAND. YET, SOMEHOW, HE SURVIVED...

...UNTIL THE DAY ANGUS MAC-WHIRTER ARRIVED TO PAY OFF AN OLD GRUDGE AGAINST THE X-MEN. HE'D PLANNED TO BLOW UP MOIRA'S LAB --

--BUT BY THEN, PROTEUS WAS RAVENOUS. MAcWHIRTER NEVER HAD A CHANCE.

HE ABSORBED THE MAN'S MEMORIES WHEN HE POSSESSED HIS BODY--AND SO HE FOUND THAT MacWHIRTER'S MINOR ELECTRONIC SKILLS WERE ENOUGH TO RE-PROGRAM THE LAB'S MAIN COMPUTER...

...TO SHOW HIS CELL AS SEALED TIGHT-- WHEN, IN FACT, IT WAS WIDE OPEN -- AND THEREBY COVER HIS ESCAPE.

BEFORE HE COULD SLIP OFF THE ISLAND, THOUGH, MOIRA RETURNED-- WITH FRIENDS.

AND PROTEUS DECIDED TO "FEED" ONCE MORE BEFORE HE LEFT. HE WOULD POSSESS THE MOST POWERFUL MUTANT PRESENT: JEAN GREY-- PHOENIX.

BUT AS HE CLOSED IN ON HIS UN-SUSPECTING PREY, MOIRA FOUND...

A GOLD TOOTH... LYING RIGHT IN FRONT OF MUTANT X'S CELL. BUT HOW-- UNLESS...?!

1277

FEARING WHAT SHE WOULD FIND...

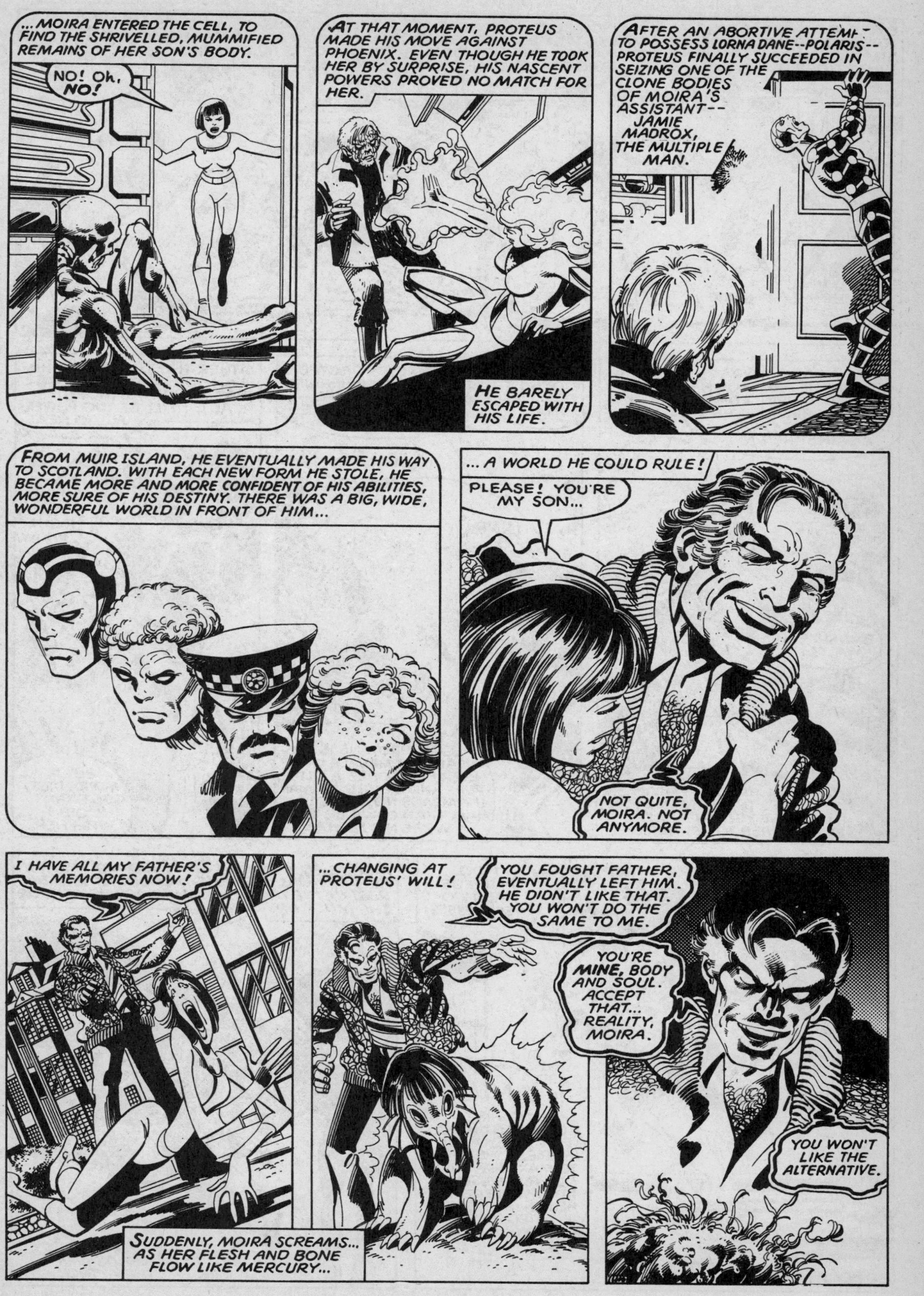
...MOIRA ENTERED THE CELL, TO FIND THE SHRIVELLED, MUMMIFIED REMAINS OF HER SON'S BODY.
NO! Oh, NO!
AT THAT MOMENT, PROTEUS MADE HIS MOVE AGAINST PHOENIX. EVEN THOUGH HE TOOK HER BY SURPRISE, HIS NASCENT POWERS PROVED NO MATCH FOR HER.
HE BARELY ESCAPED WITH HIS LIFE.
AFTER AN ABORTIVE ATTEMPT TO POSSESS LORNA DANE--POLARIS--PROTEUS FINALLY SUCCEEDED IN SEIZING ONE OF THE CLONE BODIES OF MOIRA'S ASSISTANT--JAMIE MADROX, THE MULTIPLE MAN.
FROM MUIR ISLAND, HE EVENTUALLY MADE HIS WAY TO SCOTLAND. WITH EACH NEW FORM HE STOLE, HE BECAME MORE AND MORE CONFIDENT OF HIS ABILITIES, MORE SURE OF HIS DESTINY. THERE WAS A BIG, WIDE, WONDERFUL WORLD IN FRONT OF HIM...
...A WORLD HE COULD RULE!
PLEASE! YOU'RE MY SON...
NOT QUITE, MOIRA. NOT ANYMORE.
I HAVE ALL MY FATHER'S MEMORIES NOW!
SUDDENLY, MOIRA SCREAMS... AS HER FLESH AND BONE FLOW LIKE MERCURY...
...CHANGING AT PROTEUS' WILL!
YOU FOUGHT FATHER, EVENTUALLY LEFT HIM. HE DIDN'T LIKE THAT. YOU WON'T DO THE SAME TO ME.
YOU'RE MINE, BODY AND SOUL. ACCEPT THAT... REALITY, MOIRA.
YOU WON'T LIKE THE ALTERNATIVE.

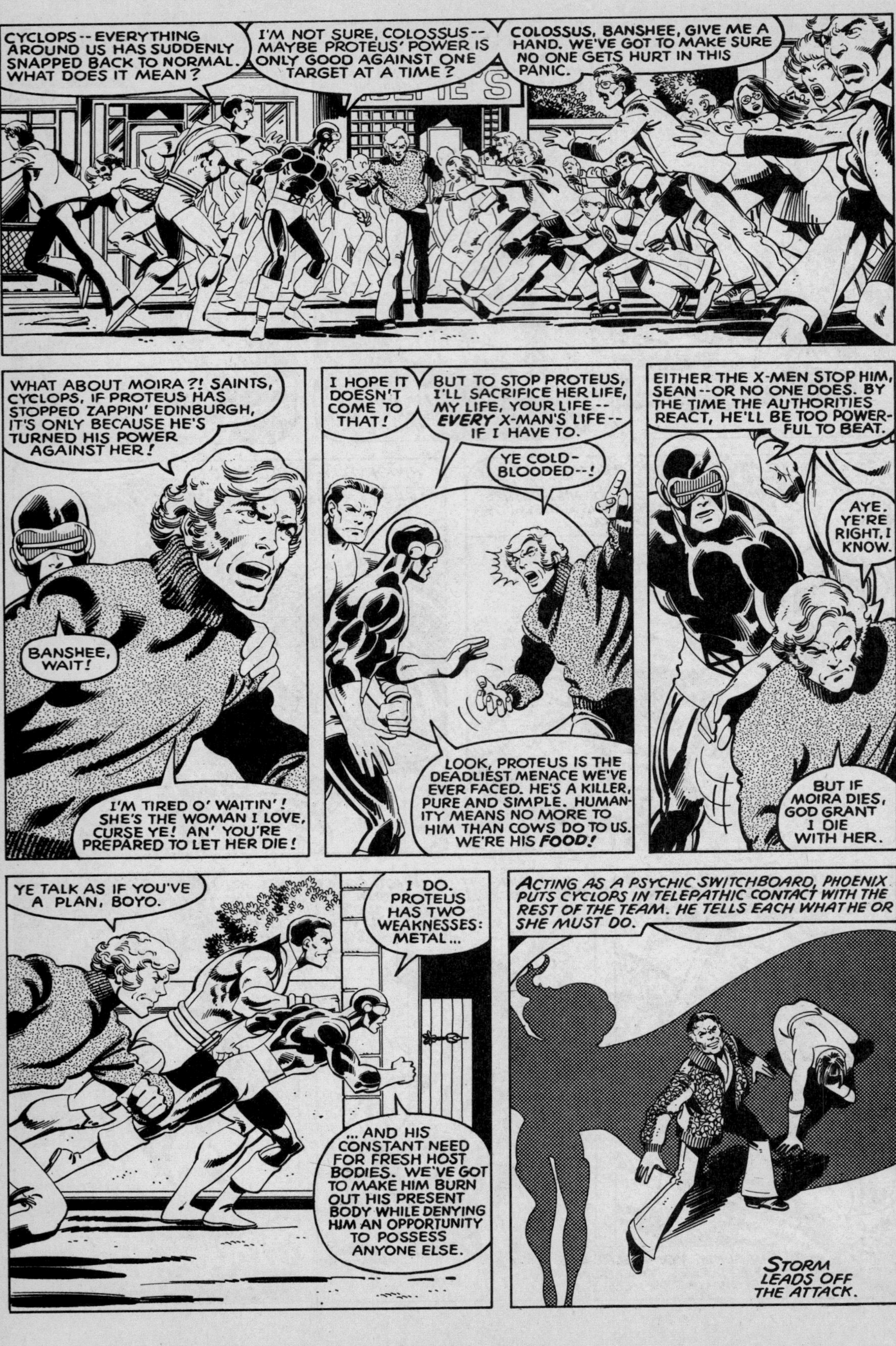
CYCLOPS -- EVERYTHING AROUND US HAS SUDDENLY SNAPPED BACK TO NORMAL. WHAT DOES IT MEAN?
I'M NOT SURE, COLOSSUS -- MAYBE PROTEUS' POWER IS ONLY GOOD AGAINST ONE TARGET AT A TIME?
COLOSSUS, BANSHEE, GIVE ME A HAND. WE'VE GOT TO MAKE SURE NO ONE GETS HURT IN THIS PANIC.
WHAT ABOUT MOIRA?! SAINTS, CYCLOPS, IF PROTEUS HAS STOPPED ZAPPIN' EDINBURGH, IT'S ONLY BECAUSE HE'S TURNED HIS POWER AGAINST HER!
BANSHEE, WAIT!
I'M TIRED O' WAITIN'! SHE'S THE WOMAN I LOVE, CURSE YE! AN' YOU'RE PREPARED TO LET HER DIE!
I HOPE IT DOESN'T COME TO THAT!
BUT TO STOP PROTEUS, I'LL SACRIFICE HER LIFE, MY LIFE, YOUR LIFE -- EVERY X-MAN'S LIFE -- IF I HAVE TO.
YE COLD-BLOODED --!
LOOK, PROTEUS IS THE DEADLIEST MENACE WE'VE EVER FACED. HE'S A KILLER, PURE AND SIMPLE. HUMANITY MEANS NO MORE TO HIM THAN COWS DO TO US. WE'RE HIS FOOD!
EITHER THE X-MEN STOP HIM, SEAN -- OR NO ONE DOES. BY THE TIME THE AUTHORITIES REACT, HE'LL BE TOO POWERFUL TO BEAT.
AYE. YE'RE RIGHT, I KNOW.
BUT IF MOIRA DIES, GOD GRANT I DIE WITH HER.
YE TALK AS IF YOU'VE A PLAN, BOYO.
I DO. PROTEUS HAS TWO WEAKNESSES: METAL...
... AND HIS CONSTANT NEED FOR FRESH HOST BODIES. WE'VE GOT TO MAKE HIM BURN OUT HIS PRESENT BODY WHILE DENYING HIM AN OPPORTUNITY TO POSSESS ANYONE ELSE.
ACTING AS A PSYCHIC SWITCHBOARD, PHOENIX PUTS CYCLOPS IN TELEPATHIC CONTACT WITH THE REST OF THE TEAM. HE TELLS EACH WHAT HE OR SHE MUST DO.
STORM LEADS OFF THE ATTACK.

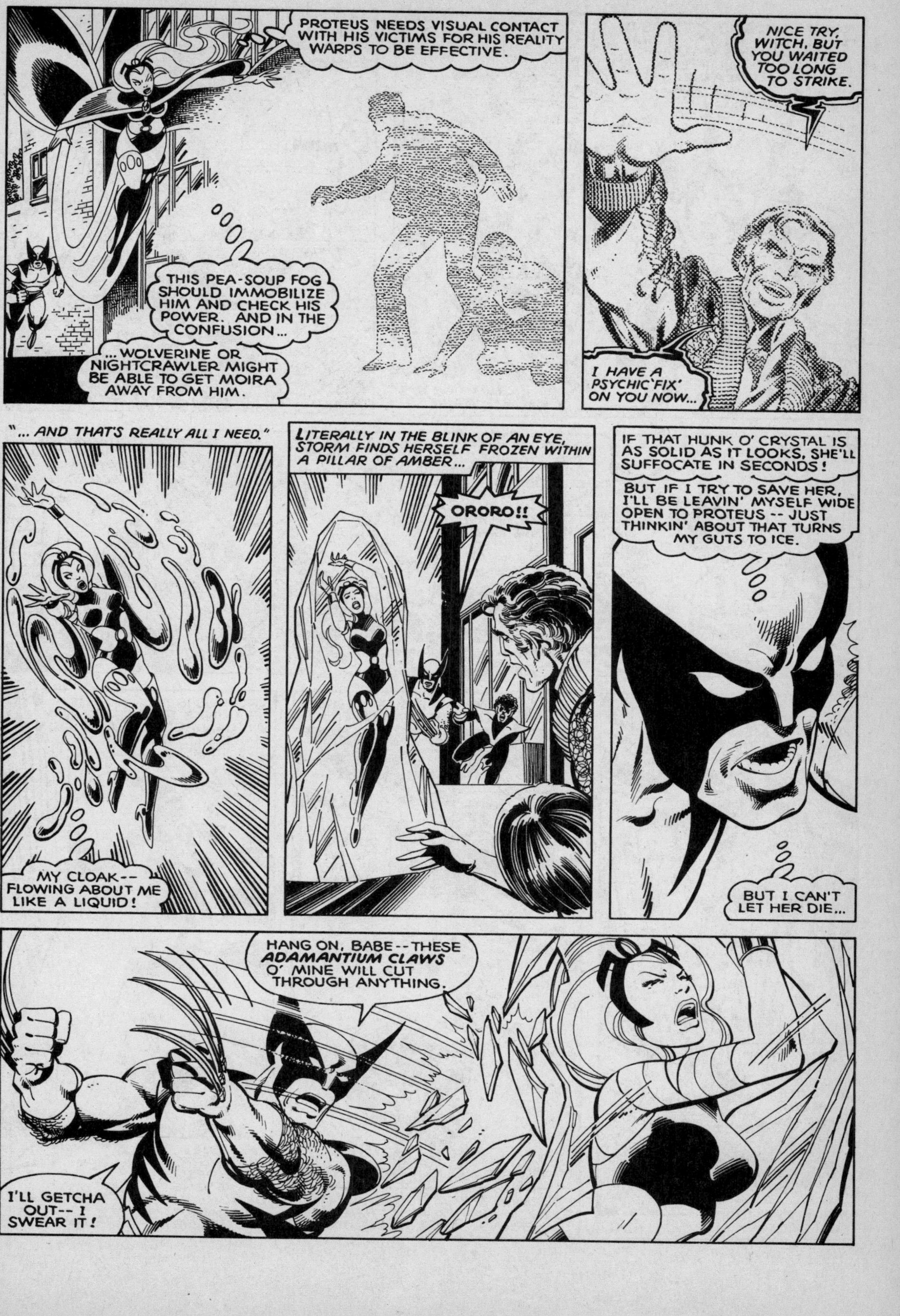
PROTEUS NEEDS VISUAL CONTACT WITH HIS VICTIMS FOR HIS REALITY WARPS TO BE EFFECTIVE.
THIS PEA-SOUP FOG SHOULD IMMOBILIZE HIM AND CHECK HIS POWER. AND IN THE CONFUSION...
...WOLVERINE OR NIGHTCRAWLER MIGHT BE ABLE TO GET MOIRA AWAY FROM HIM.
NICE TRY, WITCH, BUT YOU WAITED TOO LONG TO STRIKE.
I HAVE A PSYCHIC 'FIX' ON YOU NOW...
"... AND THAT'S REALLY ALL I NEED."
MY CLOAK-- FLOWING ABOUT ME LIKE A LIQUID!
LITERALLY IN THE BLINK OF AN EYE, STORM FINDS HERSELF FROZEN WITHIN A PILLAR OF AMBER...
ORORO!!
IF THAT HUNK O' CRYSTAL IS AS SOLID AS IT LOOKS, SHE'LL SUFFOCATE IN SECONDS!
BUT IF I TRY TO SAVE HER, I'LL BE LEAVIN' MYSELF WIDE OPEN TO PROTEUS -- JUST THINKIN' ABOUT THAT TURNS MY GUTS TO ICE.
BUT I CAN'T LET HER DIE...
HANG ON, BABE--THESE ADAMANTIUM CLAWS O' MINE WILL CUT THROUGH ANYTHING.
I'LL GETCHA OUT-- I SWEAR IT!

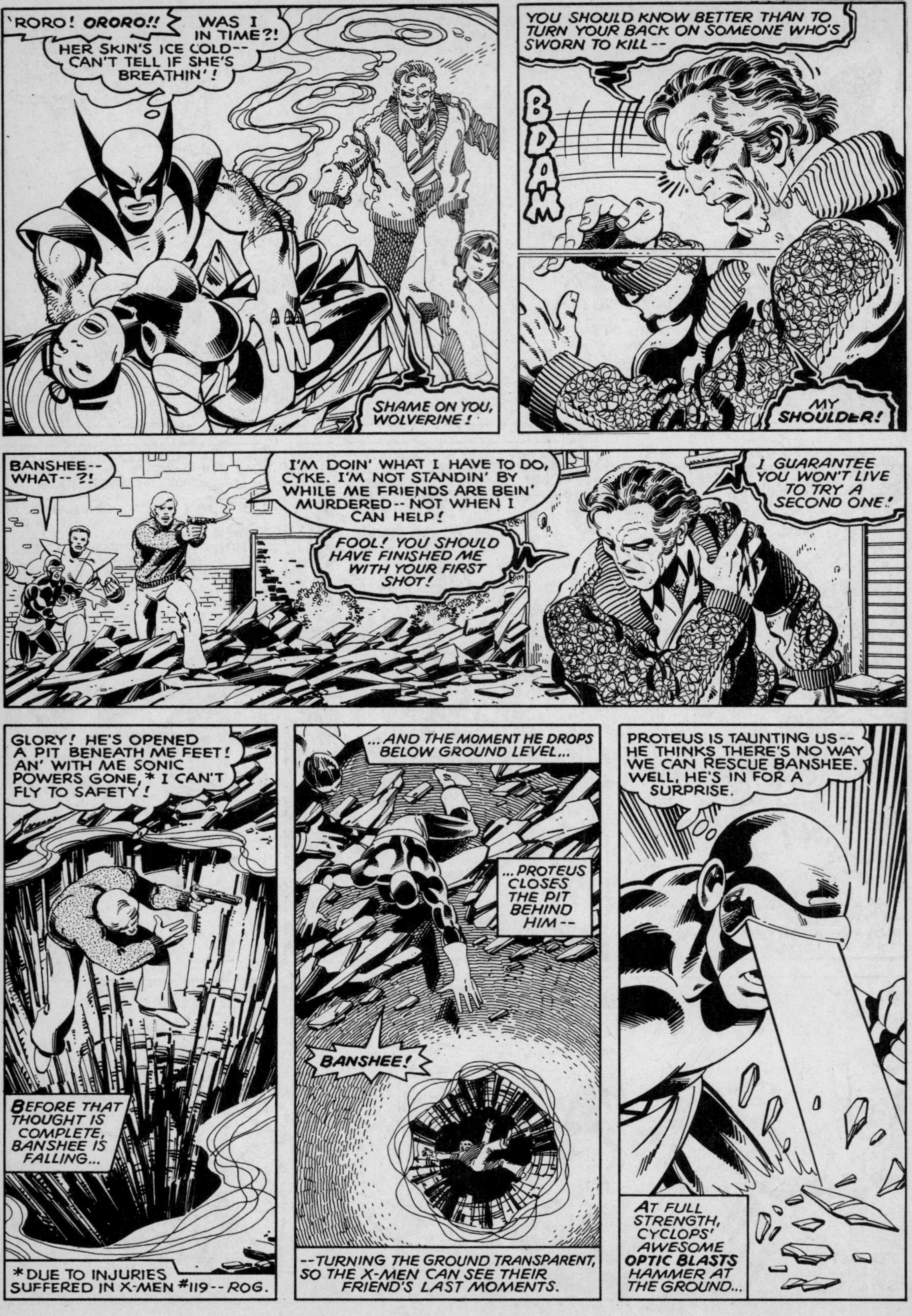
'RORO! ORORO!!
WAS I IN TIME?!
HER SKIN'S ICE COLD-- CAN'T TELL IF SHE'S BREATHIN'!
SHAME ON YOU, WOLVERINE!
YOU SHOULD KNOW BETTER THAN TO TURN YOUR BACK ON SOMEONE WHO'S SWORN TO KILL--
BDAM
MY SHOULDER!
BANSHEE-- WHAT-- ?!
I'M DOIN' WHAT I HAVE TO DO, CYKE. I'M NOT STANDIN' BY WHILE ME FRIENDS ARE BEIN' MURDERED-- NOT WHEN I CAN HELP!
FOOL! YOU SHOULD HAVE FINISHED ME WITH YOUR FIRST SHOT!
I GUARANTEE YOU WON'T LIVE TO TRY A SECOND ONE!
GLORY! HE'S OPENED A PIT BENEATH ME FEET! AN' WITH ME SONIC POWERS GONE,* I CAN'T FLY TO SAFETY!
BEFORE THAT THOUGHT IS COMPLETE, BANSHEE IS FALLING...
*DUE TO INJURIES SUFFERED IN X-MEN #119-- ROG.
...AND THE MOMENT HE DROPS BELOW GROUND LEVEL...
...PROTEUS CLOSES THE PIT BEHIND HIM--
BANSHEE!
--TURNING THE GROUND TRANSPARENT, SO THE X-MEN CAN SEE THEIR FRIEND'S LAST MOMENTS.
PROTEUS IS TAUNTING US-- HE THINKS THERE'S NO WAY WE CAN RESCUE BANSHEE. WELL, HE'S IN FOR A SURPRISE.
AT FULL STRENGTH, CYCLOPS' AWESOME OPTIC BLASTS HAMMER AT THE GROUND...

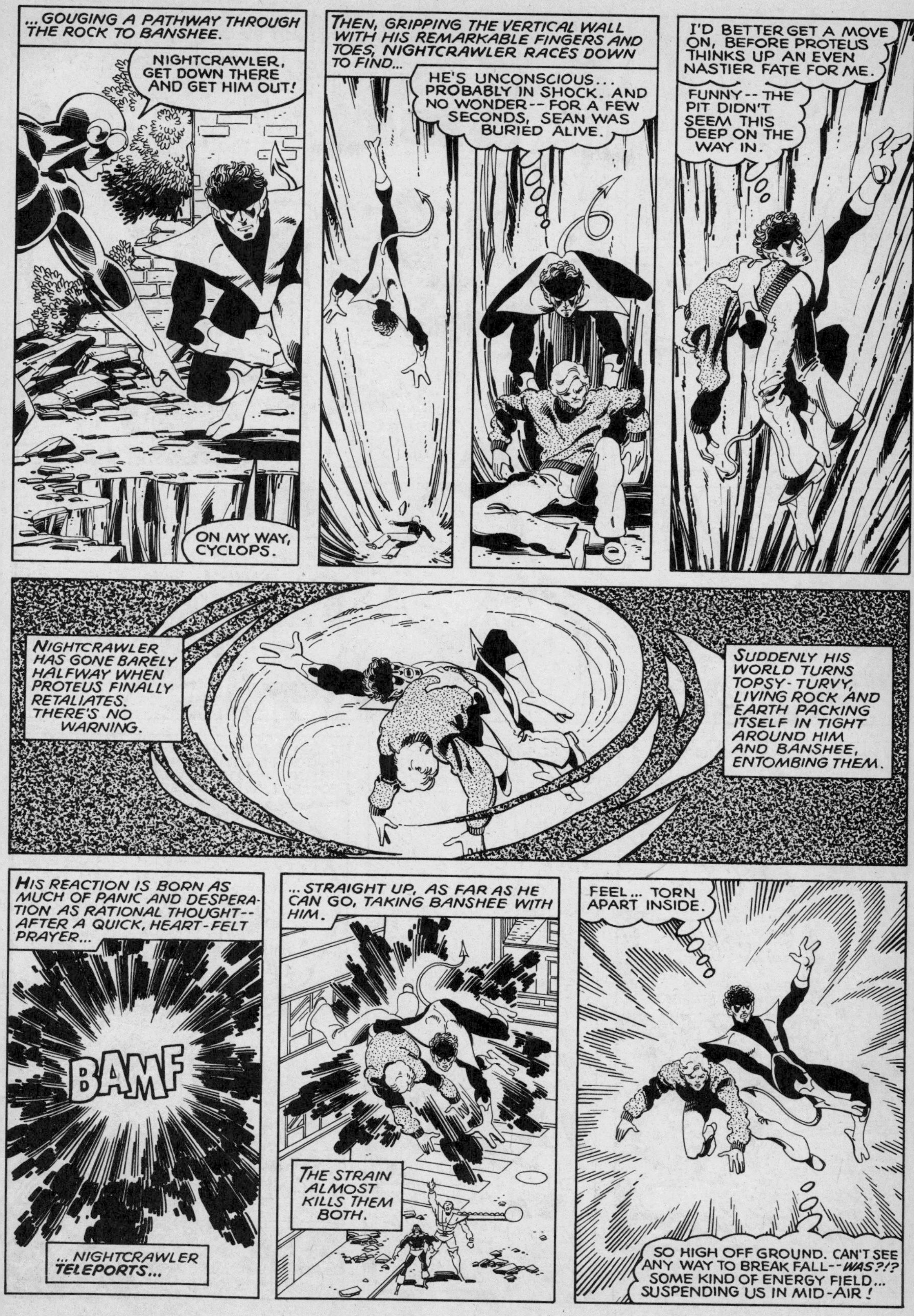
...GOUGING A PATHWAY THROUGH THE ROCK TO BANSHEE.
NIGHTCRAWLER, GET DOWN THERE AND GET HIM OUT!
ON MY WAY, CYCLOPS.
THEN, GRIPPING THE VERTICAL WALL WITH HIS REMARKABLE FINGERS AND TOES, NIGHTCRAWLER RACES DOWN TO FIND...
HE'S UNCONSCIOUS... PROBABLY IN SHOCK. AND NO WONDER-- FOR A FEW SECONDS, SEAN WAS BURIED ALIVE.
I'D BETTER GET A MOVE ON, BEFORE PROTEUS THINKS UP AN EVEN NASTIER FATE FOR ME.
FUNNY-- THE PIT DIDN'T SEEM THIS DEEP ON THE WAY IN.
NIGHTCRAWLER HAS GONE BARELY HALFWAY WHEN PROTEUS FINALLY RETALIATES. THERE'S NO WARNING.
SUDDENLY HIS WORLD TURNS TOPSY-TURVY, LIVING ROCK AND EARTH PACKING ITSELF IN TIGHT AROUND HIM AND BANSHEE, ENTOMBING THEM.
HIS REACTION IS BORN AS MUCH OF PANIC AND DESPERATION AS RATIONAL THOUGHT-- AFTER A QUICK, HEART-FELT PRAYER...
BAMF
...NIGHTCRAWLER TELEPORTS...
...STRAIGHT UP, AS FAR AS HE CAN GO, TAKING BANSHEE WITH HIM.
THE STRAIN ALMOST KILLS THEM BOTH.
FEEL... TORN APART INSIDE.
SO HIGH OFF GROUND. CAN'T SEE ANY WAY TO BREAK FALL--WAS?!? SOME KIND OF ENERGY FIELD... SUSPENDING US IN MID-AIR!

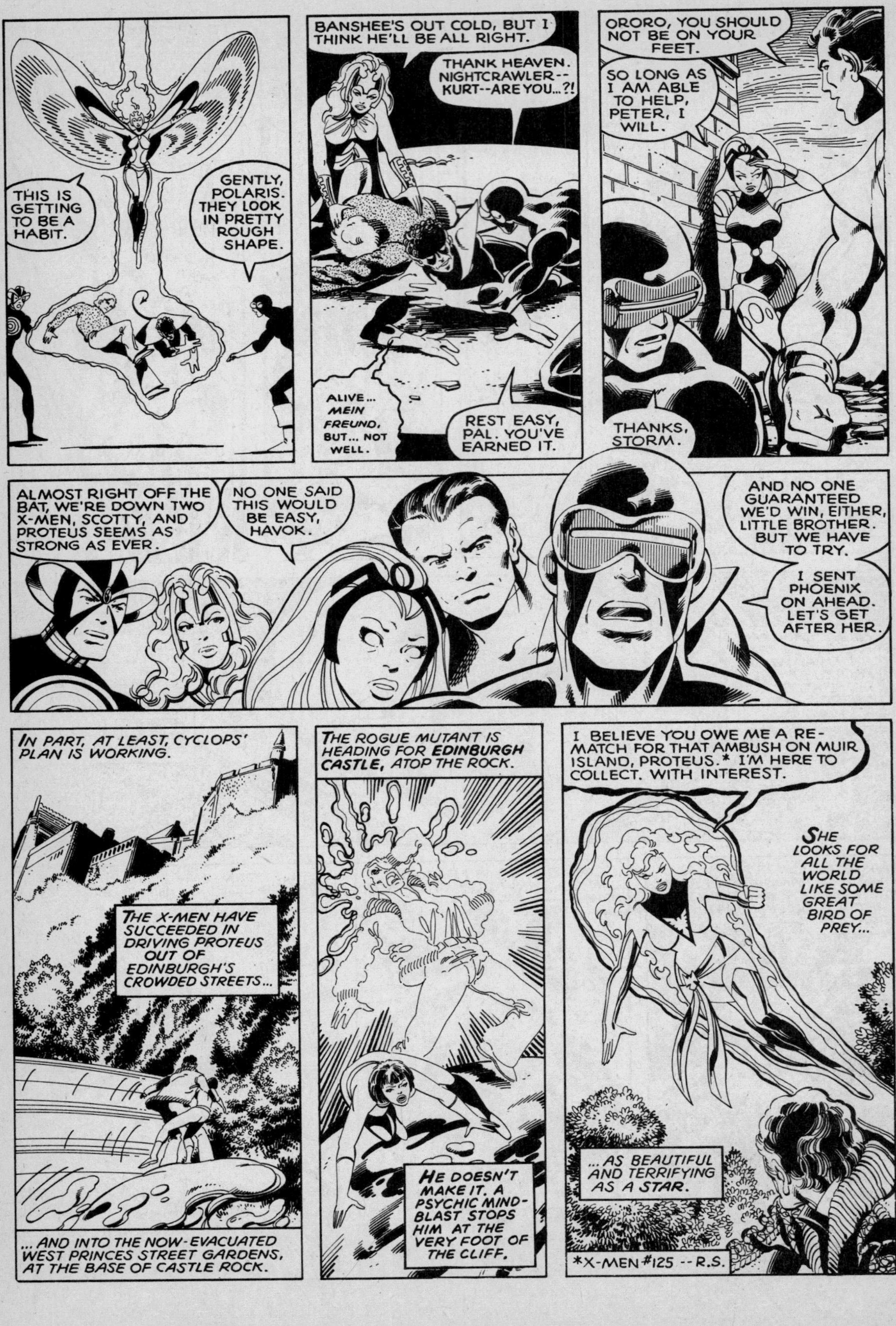
THIS IS GETTING TO BE A HABIT.
GENTLY, POLARIS. THEY LOOK IN PRETTY ROUGH SHAPE.
BANSHEE'S OUT COLD, BUT I THINK HE'LL BE ALL RIGHT.
THANK HEAVEN. NIGHTCRAWLER-- KURT--ARE YOU...?!
ALIVE... MEIN FREUND. BUT... NOT WELL.
REST EASY, PAL. YOU'VE EARNED IT.
ORORO, YOU SHOULD NOT BE ON YOUR FEET.
SO LONG AS I AM ABLE TO HELP, PETER, I WILL.
THANKS, STORM.
ALMOST RIGHT OFF THE BAT, WE'RE DOWN TWO X-MEN, SCOTTY, AND PROTEUS SEEMS AS STRONG AS EVER.
NO ONE SAID THIS WOULD BE EASY, HAVOK.
AND NO ONE GUARANTEED WE'D WIN, EITHER, LITTLE BROTHER. BUT WE HAVE TO TRY.
I SENT PHOENIX ON AHEAD. LET'S GET AFTER HER.
IN PART, AT LEAST, CYCLOPS' PLAN IS WORKING.
THE X-MEN HAVE SUCCEEDED IN DRIVING PROTEUS OUT OF EDINBURGH'S CROWDED STREETS...
...AND INTO THE NOW-EVACUATED WEST PRINCES STREET GARDENS, AT THE BASE OF CASTLE ROCK.
THE ROGUE MUTANT IS HEADING FOR EDINBURGH CASTLE, ATOP THE ROCK.
HE DOESN'T MAKE IT. A PSYCHIC MIND-BLAST STOPS HIM AT THE VERY FOOT OF THE CLIFF.
I BELIEVE YOU OWE ME A RE-MATCH FOR THAT AMBUSH ON MUIR ISLAND, PROTEUS.* I'M HERE TO COLLECT. WITH INTEREST.
SHE LOOKS FOR ALL THE WORLD LIKE SOME GREAT BIRD OF PREY...
...AS BEAUTIFUL AND TERRIFYING AS A STAR.
*X-MEN #125 -- R.S.

PROTEUS HARDLY HAS TIME TO REACT BEFORE SHE ATTACKS!

JEAN, WHAT'RE YOU DOIN'?

AGAIN AND AGAIN, PHOENIX LASHES OUT WITH A FEROCITY THAT SHOCKS MOIRA, HER POWER A SYMPHONY WITHIN HER...

... A SONG OF JOY THAT BUILDS TOO QUICKLY IN ITS CRESCENDO.

HE'S DOWN -- BUT HE'S NOT GIVIN' UP!

WAY TO GO, JEANIE!

IN A ROUGHHOUSE, BABE, YER MY KIND'A GAL.

Uh-oh -- MY GUTS ARE CHURNIN'! PROTEUS MUST BE FIGHTIN' BACK!

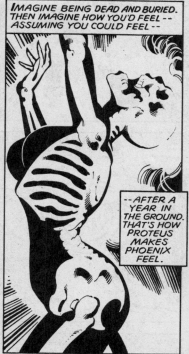

IMAGINE BEING DEAD AND BURIED. THEN IMAGINE HOW YOU'D FEEL -- ASSUMING YOU COULD FEEL --

-- AFTER A YEAR IN THE GROUND. THAT'S HOW PROTEUS MAKES PHOENIX FEEL.

HER SCREAM IS INDESCRIBABLE.

LEAVE HER ALONE!!

I LOVED THAT LADY, BUB!

AN' I'LL SEE YOU DEAD BEFORE I LET YOU HURT HER AGAIN!

AARRRGH

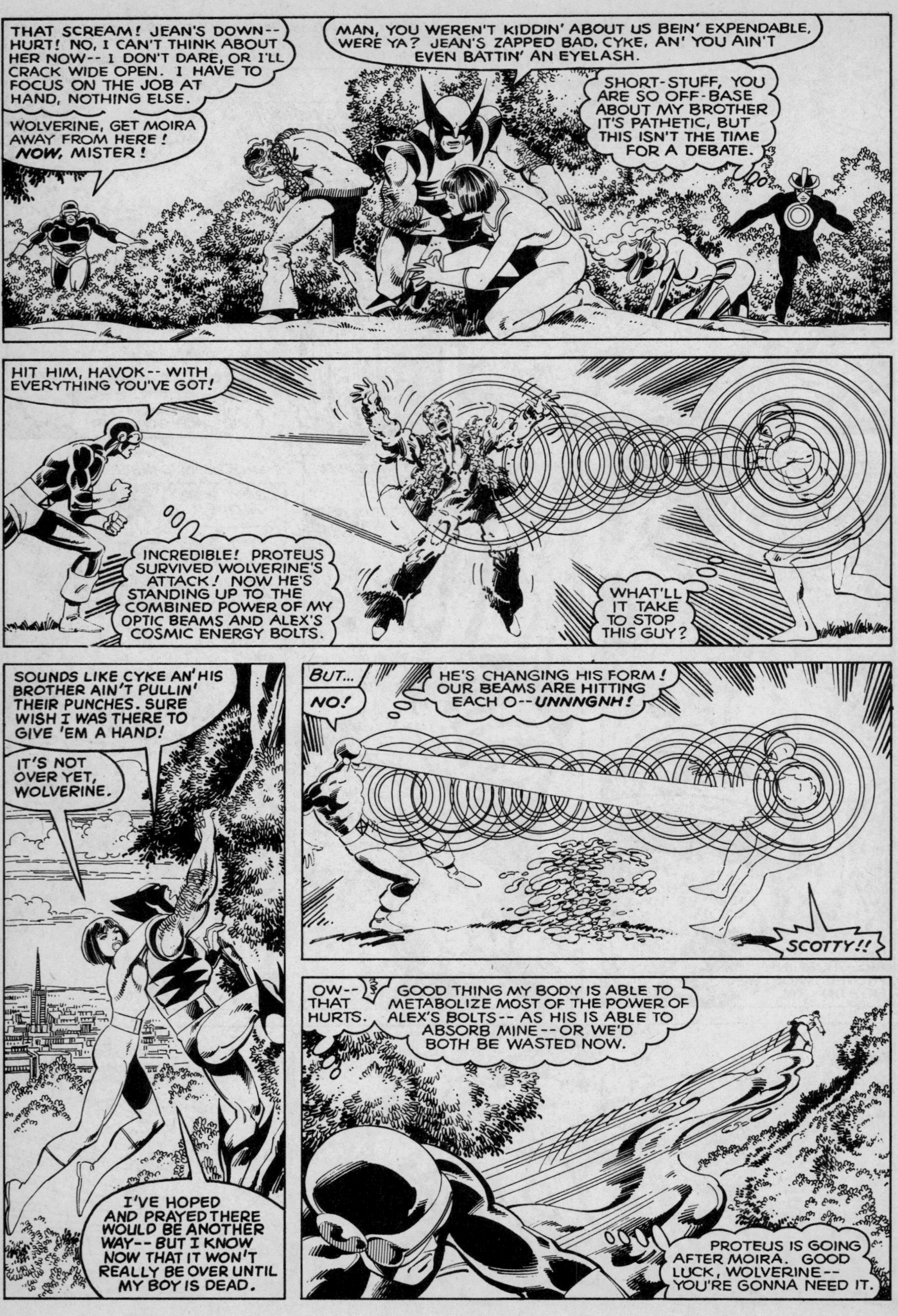
THAT SCREAM! JEAN'S DOWN-- HURT! NO, I CAN'T THINK ABOUT HER NOW-- I DON'T DARE, OR I'LL CRACK WIDE OPEN. I HAVE TO FOCUS ON THE JOB AT HAND, NOTHING ELSE.
WOLVERINE, GET MOIRA AWAY FROM HERE! NOW, MISTER!
MAN, YOU WEREN'T KIDDIN' ABOUT US BEIN' EXPENDABLE, WERE YA? JEAN'S ZAPPED BAD, CYKE, AN' YOU AIN'T EVEN BATTIN' AN EYELASH.
SHORT-STUFF, YOU ARE SO OFF-BASE ABOUT MY BROTHER IT'S PATHETIC, BUT THIS ISN'T THE TIME FOR A DEBATE.
HIT HIM, HAVOK-- WITH EVERYTHING YOU'VE GOT!
INCREDIBLE! PROTEUS SURVIVED WOLVERINE'S ATTACK! NOW HE'S STANDING UP TO THE COMBINED POWER OF MY OPTIC BEAMS AND ALEX'S COSMIC ENERGY BOLTS.
WHAT'LL IT TAKE TO STOP THIS GUY?
SOUNDS LIKE CYKE AN' HIS BROTHER AIN'T PULLIN' THEIR PUNCHES. SURE WISH I WAS THERE TO GIVE 'EM A HAND!
IT'S NOT OVER YET, WOLVERINE.
I'VE HOPED AND PRAYED THERE WOULD BE ANOTHER WAY-- BUT I KNOW NOW THAT IT WON'T REALLY BE OVER UNTIL MY BOY IS DEAD.
BUT...
NO!
HE'S CHANGING HIS FORM! OUR BEAMS ARE HITTING EACH O--UNNNGNH!
SCOTTY!!
OW-- THAT HURTS.
GOOD THING MY BODY IS ABLE TO METABOLIZE MOST OF THE POWER OF ALEX'S BOLTS-- AS HIS IS ABLE TO ABSORB MINE--OR WE'D BOTH BE WASTED NOW.
PROTEUS IS GOING AFTER MOIRA. GOOD LUCK, WOLVERINE-- YOU'RE GONNA NEED IT.

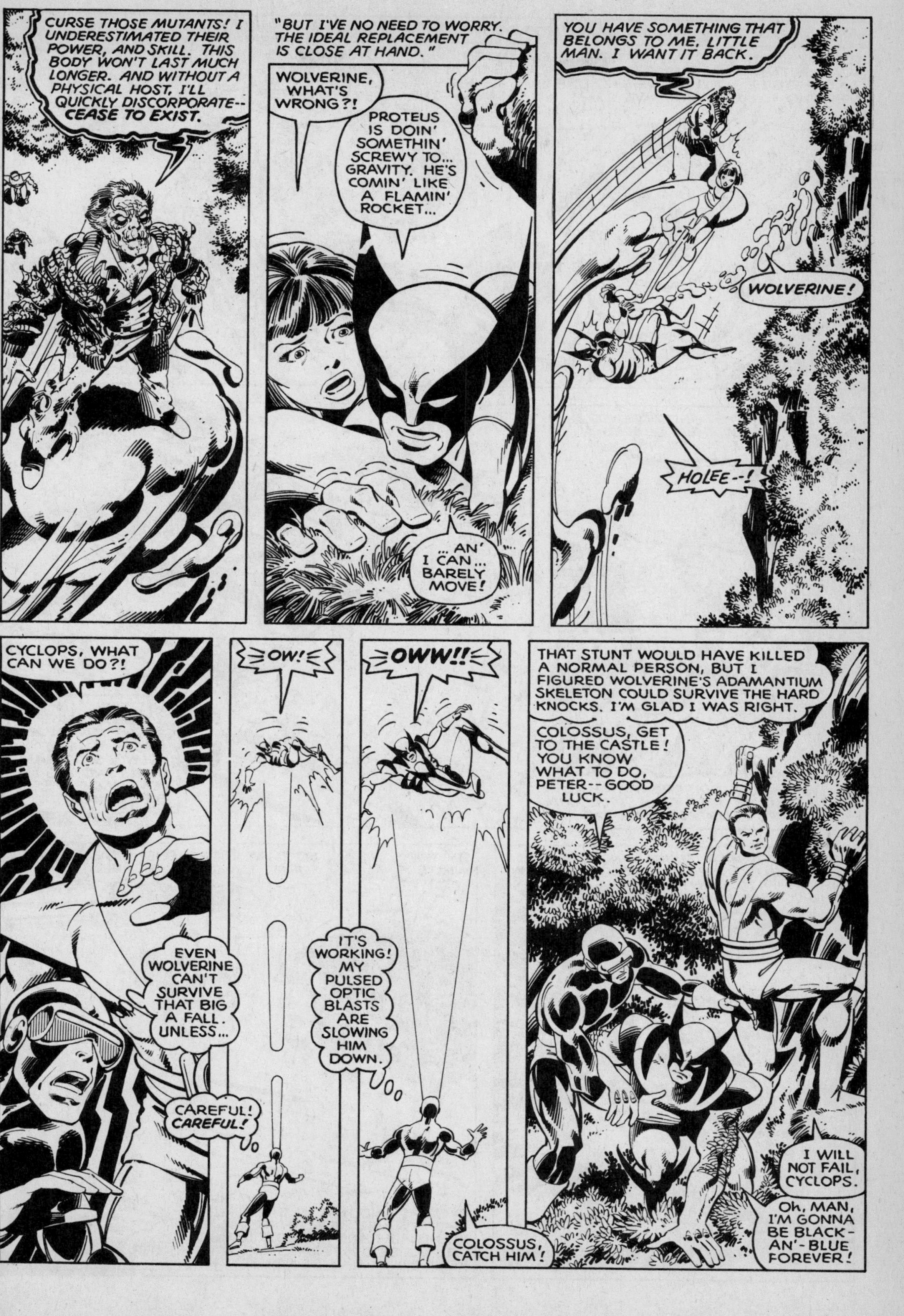
CURSE THOSE MUTANTS! I UNDERESTIMATED THEIR POWER, AND SKILL. THIS BODY WON'T LAST MUCH LONGER. AND WITHOUT A PHYSICAL HOST, I'LL QUICKLY DISCORPORATE-- CEASE TO EXIST.
"BUT I'VE NO NEED TO WORRY. THE IDEAL REPLACEMENT IS CLOSE AT HAND."
WOLVERINE, WHAT'S WRONG?!
PROTEUS IS DOIN' SOMETHIN' SCREWY TO... GRAVITY. HE'S COMIN' LIKE A FLAMIN' ROCKET...
... AN' I CAN... BARELY MOVE!
YOU HAVE SOMETHING THAT BELONGS TO ME, LITTLE MAN. I WANT IT BACK.
WOLVERINE!
HOLEE--!
CYCLOPS, WHAT CAN WE DO?!
EVEN WOLVERINE CAN'T SURVIVE THAT BIG A FALL. UNLESS...
CAREFUL! CAREFUL!
OW!
OWW!!
IT'S WORKING! MY PULSED OPTIC BLASTS ARE SLOWING HIM DOWN.
COLOSSUS, CATCH HIM!
THAT STUNT WOULD HAVE KILLED A NORMAL PERSON, BUT I FIGURED WOLVERINE'S ADAMANTIUM SKELETON COULD SURVIVE THE HARD KNOCKS. I'M GLAD I WAS RIGHT.
COLOSSUS, GET TO THE CASTLE! YOU KNOW WHAT TO DO, PETER--GOOD LUCK.
I WILL NOT FAIL, CYCLOPS.
Oh, MAN, I'M GONNA BE BLACK-AN'-BLUE FOREVER!

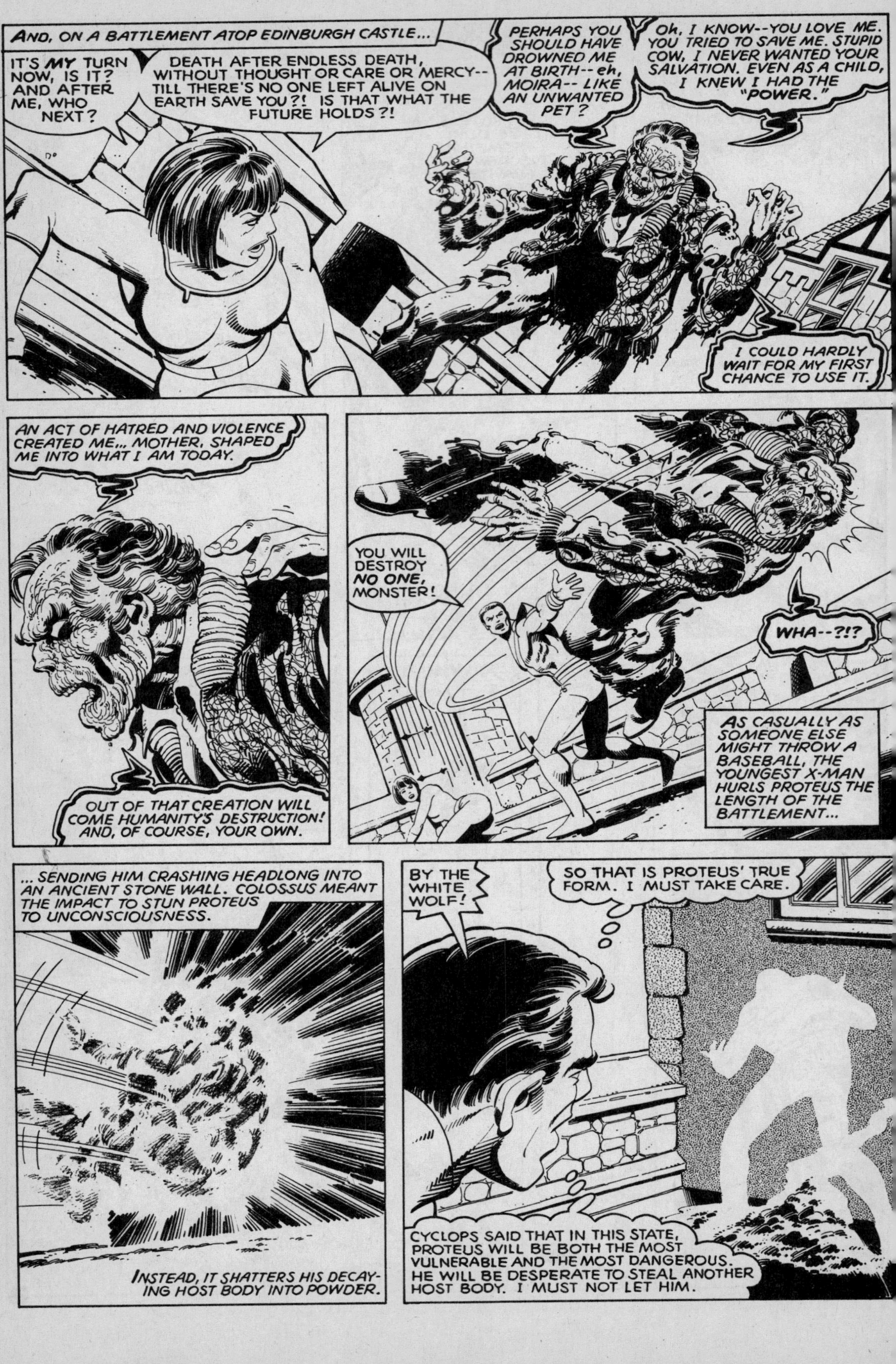
AND, ON A BATTLEMENT ATOP EDINBURGH CASTLE...
IT'S MY TURN NOW, IS IT? AND AFTER ME, WHO NEXT?
DEATH AFTER ENDLESS DEATH, WITHOUT THOUGHT OR CARE OR MERCY-- TILL THERE'S NO ONE LEFT ALIVE ON EARTH SAVE YOU?! IS THAT WHAT THE FUTURE HOLDS?!
PERHAPS YOU SHOULD HAVE DROWNED ME AT BIRTH-- eh, MOIRA-- LIKE AN UNWANTED PET?
Oh, I KNOW--YOU LOVE ME. YOU TRIED TO SAVE ME. STUPID COW, I NEVER WANTED YOUR SALVATION. EVEN AS A CHILD, I KNEW I HAD THE "POWER."
I COULD HARDLY WAIT FOR MY FIRST CHANCE TO USE IT.
AN ACT OF HATRED AND VIOLENCE CREATED ME... MOTHER, SHAPED ME INTO WHAT I AM TODAY.
OUT OF THAT CREATION WILL COME HUMANITY'S DESTRUCTION! AND, OF COURSE, YOUR OWN.
YOU WILL DESTROY NO ONE, MONSTER!
WHA--?!?
AS CASUALLY AS SOMEONE ELSE MIGHT THROW A BASEBALL, THE YOUNGEST X-MAN HURLS PROTEUS THE LENGTH OF THE BATTLEMENT...
... SENDING HIM CRASHING HEADLONG INTO AN ANCIENT STONE WALL. COLOSSUS MEANT THE IMPACT TO STUN PROTEUS TO UNCONSCIOUSNESS.
INSTEAD, IT SHATTERS HIS DECAYING HOST BODY INTO POWDER.
BY THE WHITE WOLF!
SO THAT IS PROTEUS' TRUE FORM. I MUST TAKE CARE.
CYCLOPS SAID THAT IN THIS STATE, PROTEUS WILL BE BOTH THE MOST VULNERABLE AND THE MOST DANGEROUS. HE WILL BE DESPERATE TO STEAL ANOTHER HOST BODY. I MUST NOT LET HIM.

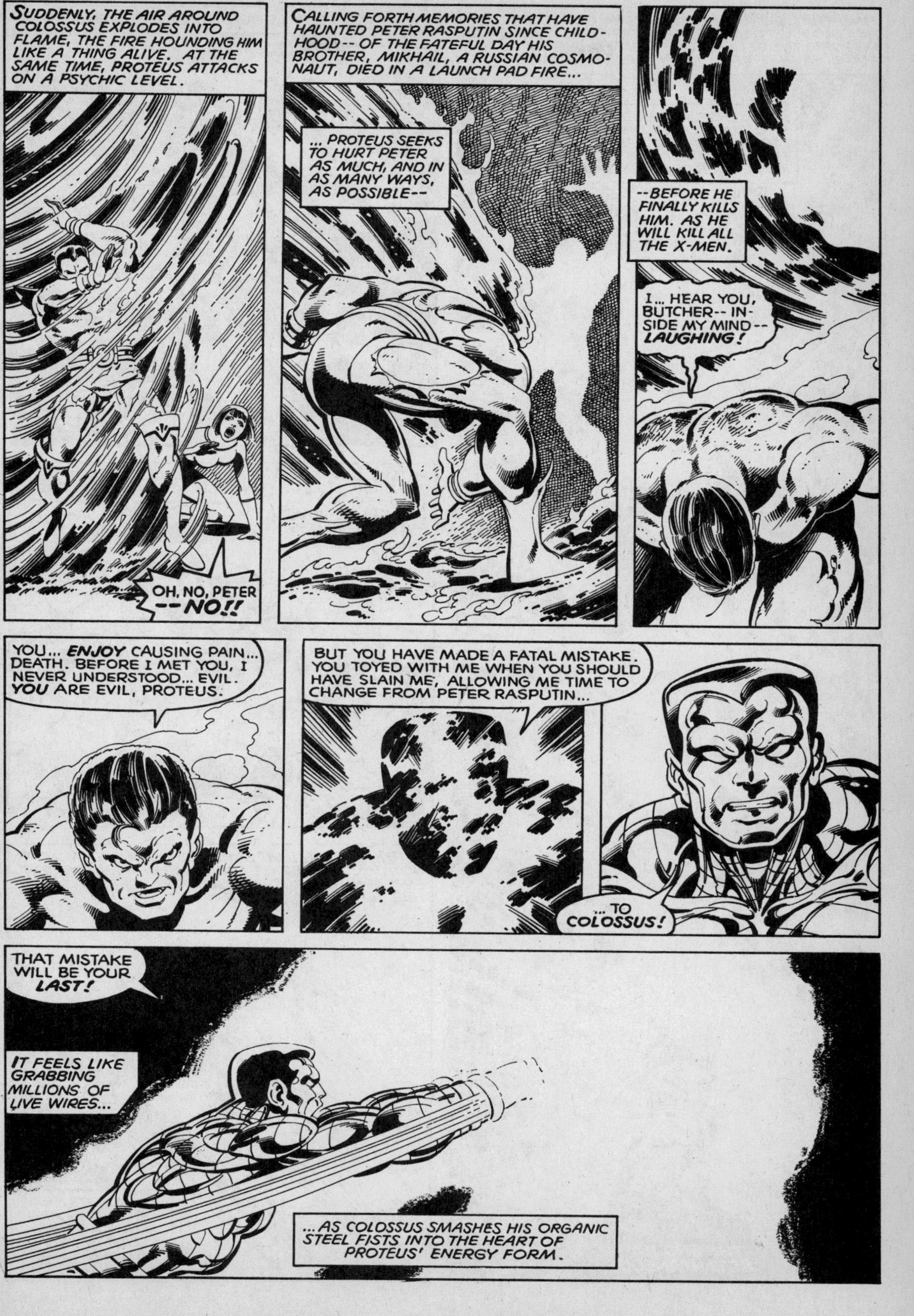
SUDDENLY, THE AIR AROUND COLOSSUS EXPLODES INTO FLAME, THE FIRE HOUNDING HIM LIKE A THING ALIVE. AT THE SAME TIME, PROTEUS ATTACKS ON A PSYCHIC LEVEL.
OH, NO, PETER --NO!!
CALLING FORTH MEMORIES THAT HAVE HAUNTED PETER RASPUTIN SINCE CHILDHOOD-- OF THE FATEFUL DAY HIS BROTHER, MIKHAIL, A RUSSIAN COSMONAUT, DIED IN A LAUNCH PAD FIRE...
... PROTEUS SEEKS TO HURT PETER AS MUCH, AND IN AS MANY WAYS, AS POSSIBLE--
--BEFORE HE FINALLY KILLS HIM. AS HE WILL KILL ALL THE X-MEN.
I... HEAR YOU, BUTCHER-- INSIDE MY MIND-- LAUGHING!
YOU... ENJOY CAUSING PAIN... DEATH. BEFORE I MET YOU, I NEVER UNDERSTOOD... EVIL. YOU ARE EVIL, PROTEUS.
BUT YOU HAVE MADE A FATAL MISTAKE. YOU TOYED WITH ME WHEN YOU SHOULD HAVE SLAIN ME, ALLOWING ME TIME TO CHANGE FROM PETER RASPUTIN...
... TO COLOSSUS!
THAT MISTAKE WILL BE YOUR LAST!
IT FEELS LIKE GRABBING MILLIONS OF LIVE WIRES...
...AS COLOSSUS SMASHES HIS ORGANIC STEEL FISTS INTO THE HEART OF PROTEUS' ENERGY FORM.

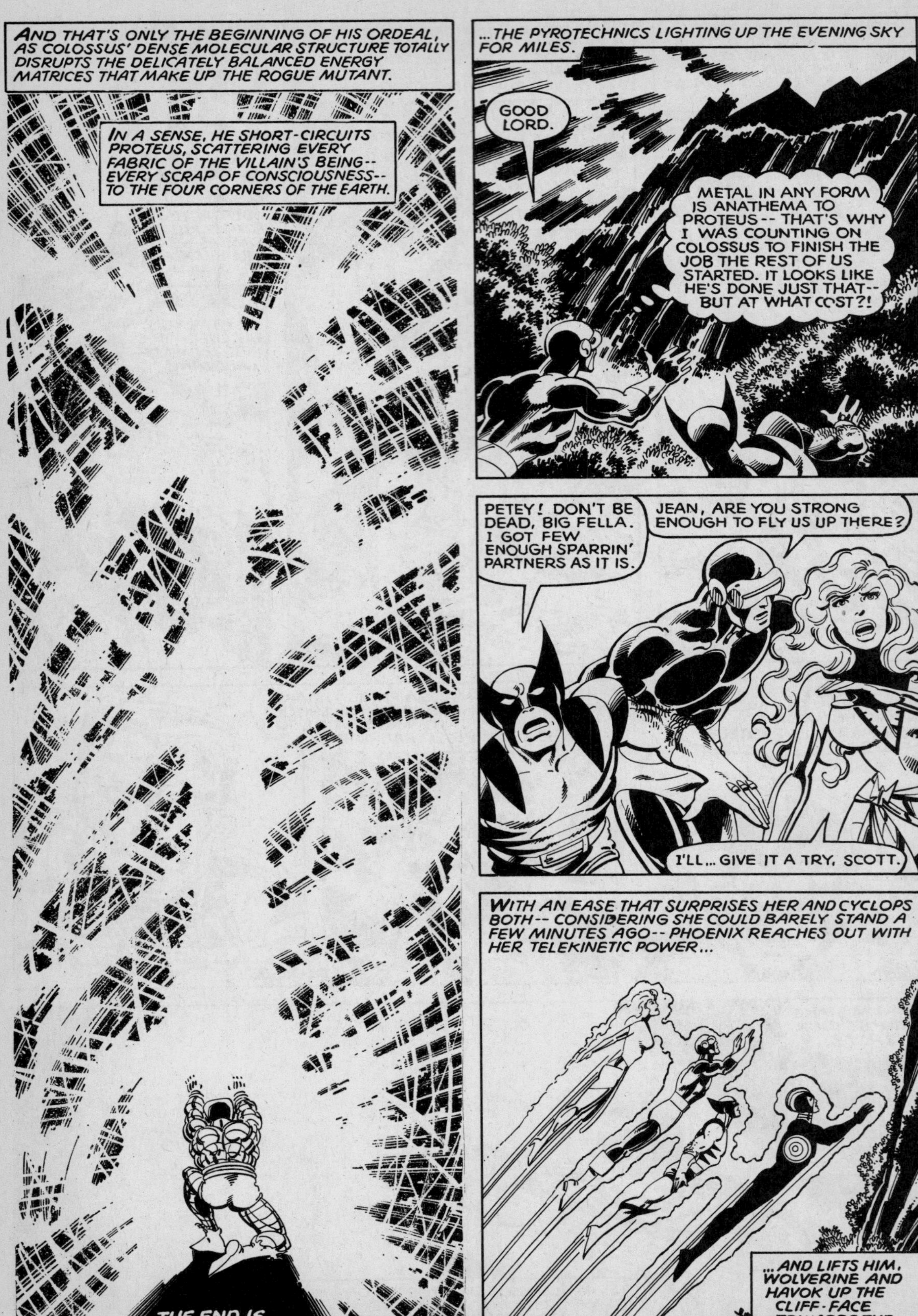
AND THAT'S ONLY THE BEGINNING OF HIS ORDEAL, AS COLOSSUS' DENSE MOLECULAR STRUCTURE TOTALLY DISRUPTS THE DELICATELY BALANCED ENERGY MATRICES THAT MAKE UP THE ROGUE MUTANT.
IN A SENSE, HE SHORT-CIRCUITS PROTEUS, SCATTERING EVERY FABRIC OF THE VILLAIN'S BEING-- EVERY SCRAP OF CONSCIOUSNESS-- TO THE FOUR CORNERS OF THE EARTH.
THE END IS INSTANTANEOUS...
...THE PYROTECHNICS LIGHTING UP THE EVENING SKY FOR MILES.
GOOD LORD.
METAL IN ANY FORM IS ANATHEMA TO PROTEUS -- THAT'S WHY I WAS COUNTING ON COLOSSUS TO FINISH THE JOB THE REST OF US STARTED. IT LOOKS LIKE HE'S DONE JUST THAT-- BUT AT WHAT COST?!
PETEY! DON'T BE DEAD, BIG FELLA. I GOT FEW ENOUGH SPARRIN' PARTNERS AS IT IS.
JEAN, ARE YOU STRONG ENOUGH TO FLY US UP THERE?
I'LL... GIVE IT A TRY, SCOTT.
WITH AN EASE THAT SURPRISES HER AND CYCLOPS BOTH-- CONSIDERING SHE COULD BARELY STAND A FEW MINUTES AGO-- PHOENIX REACHES OUT WITH HER TELEKINETIC POWER...
...AND LIFTS HIM, WOLVERINE AND HAVOK UP THE CLIFF-FACE TOWARDS THE CASTLE RAMPARTS.

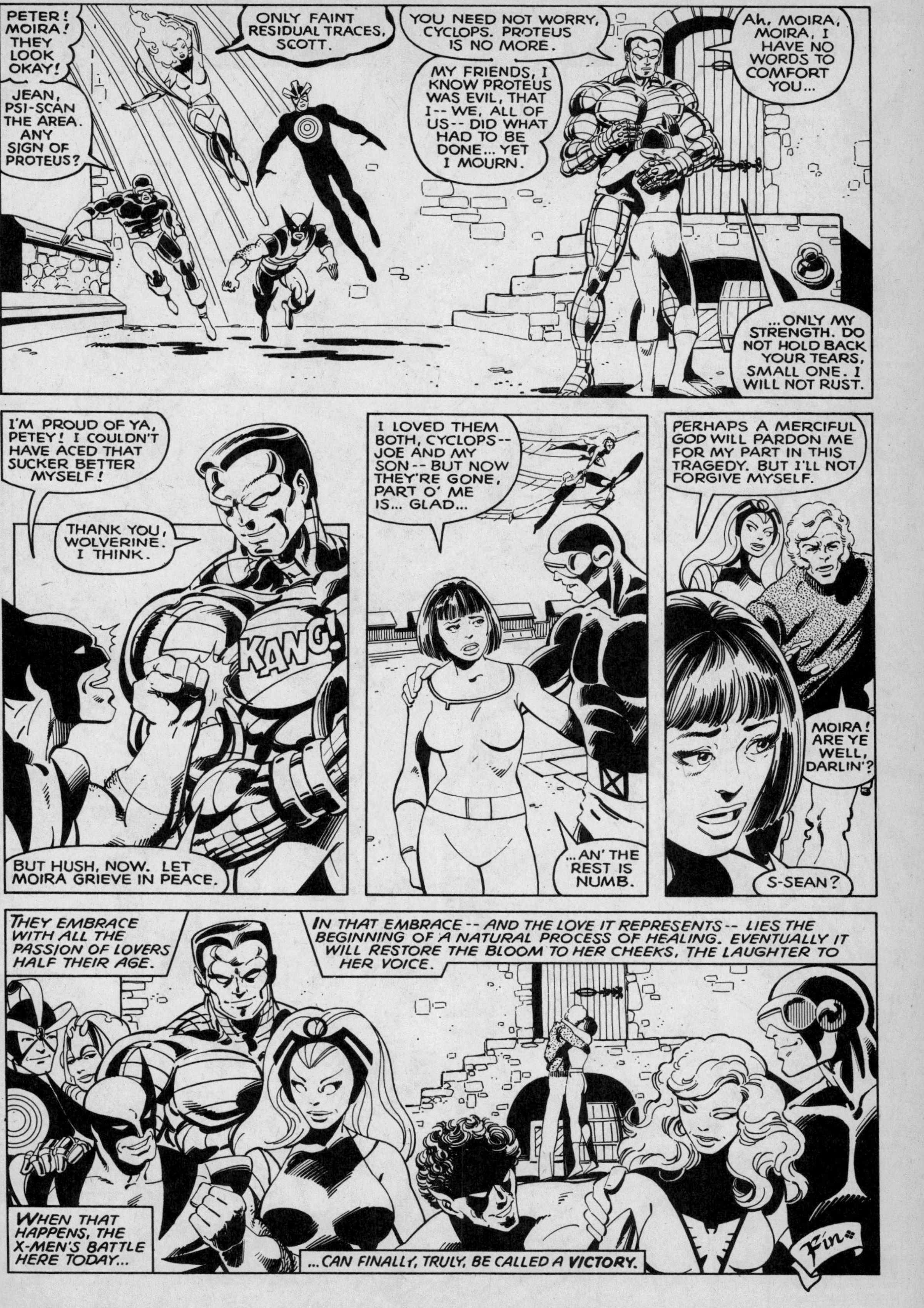
PETER! MOIRA! THEY LOOK OKAY!
JEAN, PSI-SCAN THE AREA. ANY SIGN OF PROTEUS?
ONLY FAINT RESIDUAL TRACES, SCOTT.
YOU NEED NOT WORRY, CYCLOPS. PROTEUS IS NO MORE.
MY FRIENDS, I KNOW PROTEUS WAS EVIL, THAT I-- WE, ALL OF US-- DID WHAT HAD TO BE DONE... YET I MOURN.
Ah, MOIRA, MOIRA, I HAVE NO WORDS TO COMFORT YOU...
...ONLY MY STRENGTH. DO NOT HOLD BACK YOUR TEARS, SMALL ONE. I WILL NOT RUST.
I'M PROUD OF YA, PETEY! I COULDN'T HAVE ACED THAT SUCKER BETTER MYSELF!
THANK YOU, WOLVERINE. I THINK.
KANG!
BUT HUSH, NOW. LET MOIRA GRIEVE IN PEACE.
I LOVED THEM BOTH, CYCLOPS-- JOE AND MY SON-- BUT NOW THEY'RE GONE, PART O' ME IS... GLAD...
...AN' THE REST IS NUMB.
PERHAPS A MERCIFUL GOD WILL PARDON ME FOR MY PART IN THIS TRAGEDY. BUT I'LL NOT FORGIVE MYSELF.
MOIRA! ARE YE WELL, DARLIN'?
S-SEAN?
THEY EMBRACE WITH ALL THE PASSION OF LOVERS HALF THEIR AGE.
IN THAT EMBRACE -- AND THE LOVE IT REPRESENTS -- LIES THE BEGINNING OF A NATURAL PROCESS OF HEALING. EVENTUALLY IT WILL RESTORE THE BLOOM TO HER CHEEKS, THE LAUGHTER TO HER VOICE.
WHEN THAT HAPPENS, THE X-MEN'S BATTLE HERE TODAY...
...CAN FINALLY, TRULY, BE CALLED A VICTORY.
Fin

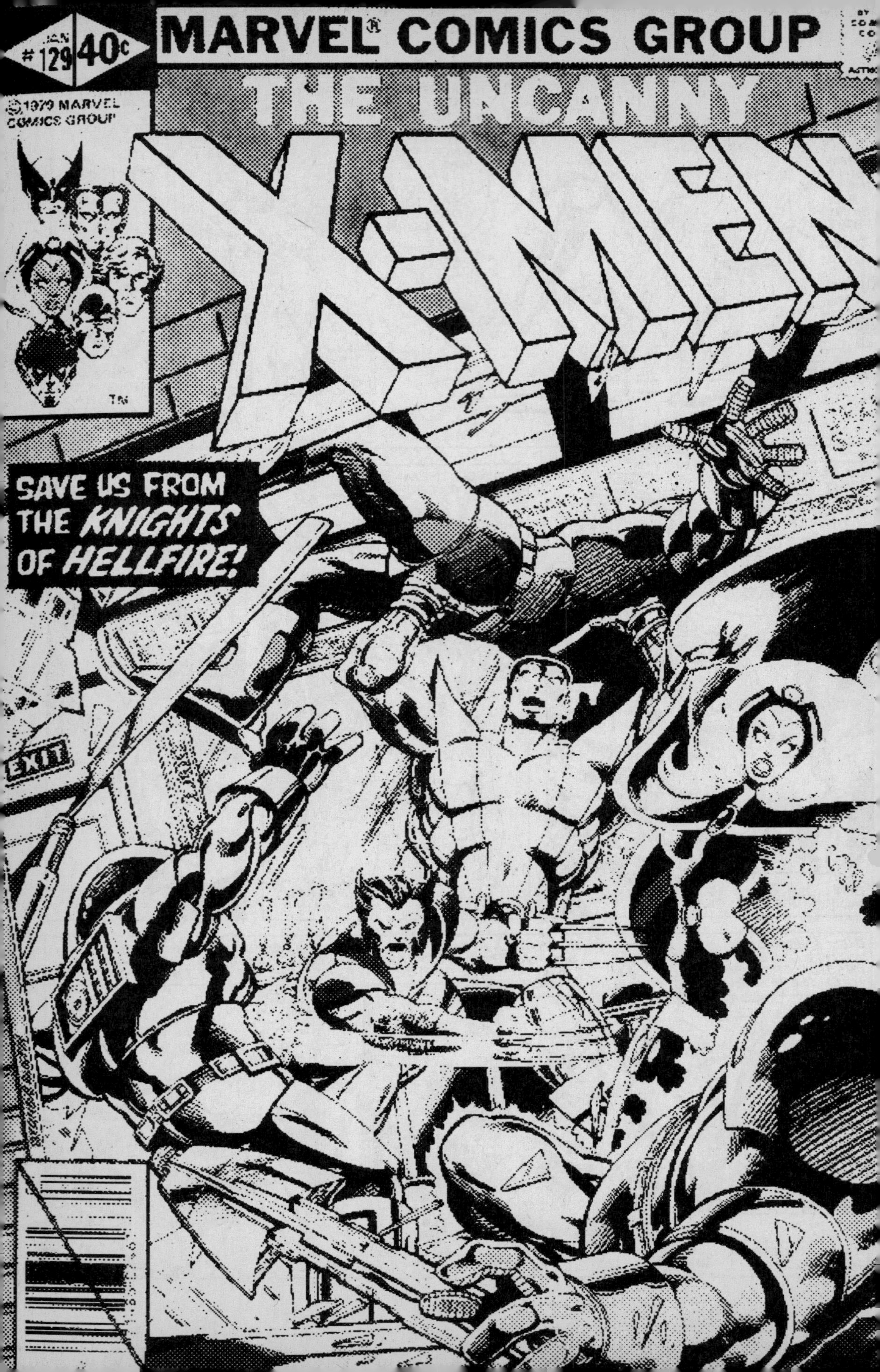

JAN # 129 40¢
MARVEL® COMICS GROUP
©1979 MARVEL COMICS GROUP
THE UNCANNY
X-MEN
TM
SAVE US FROM THE KNIGHTS OF HELLFIRE!
EXIT

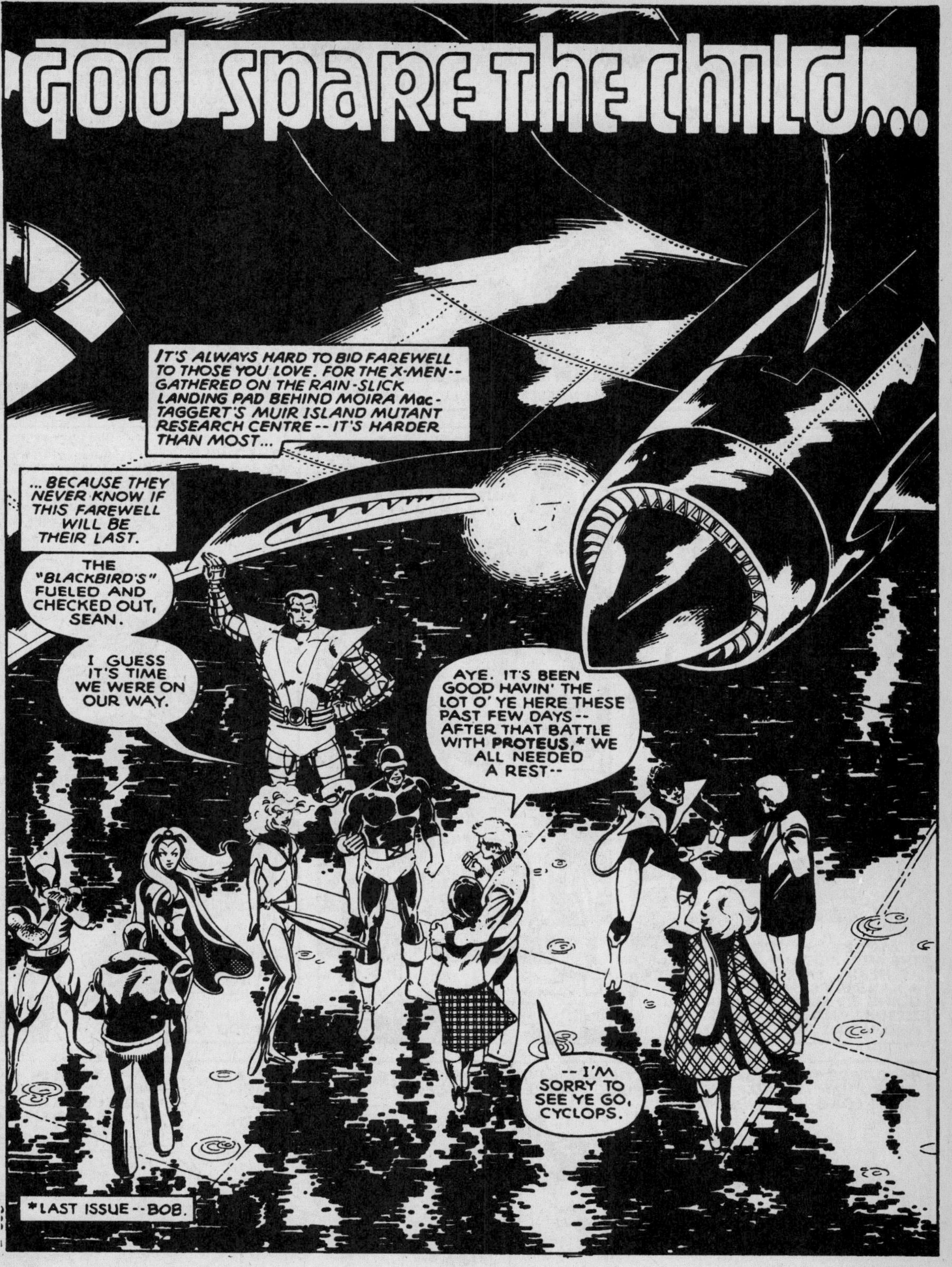

GOD SPARE THE CHILD...
IT'S ALWAYS HARD TO BID FAREWELL TO THOSE YOU LOVE. FOR THE X-MEN--GATHERED ON THE RAIN-SLICK LANDING PAD BEHIND MOIRA MacTAGGERT'S MUIR ISLAND MUTANT RESEARCH CENTRE--IT'S HARDER THAN MOST...
...BECAUSE THEY NEVER KNOW IF THIS FAREWELL WILL BE THEIR LAST.
THE "BLACKBIRD'S" FUELED AND CHECKED OUT, SEAN.
I GUESS IT'S TIME WE WERE ON OUR WAY.
AYE. IT'S BEEN GOOD HAVIN' THE LOT O' YE HERE THESE PAST FEW DAYS--AFTER THAT BATTLE WITH PROTEUS,* WE ALL NEEDED A REST--
--I'M SORRY TO SEE YE GO, CYCLOPS.
*LAST ISSUE--BOB.

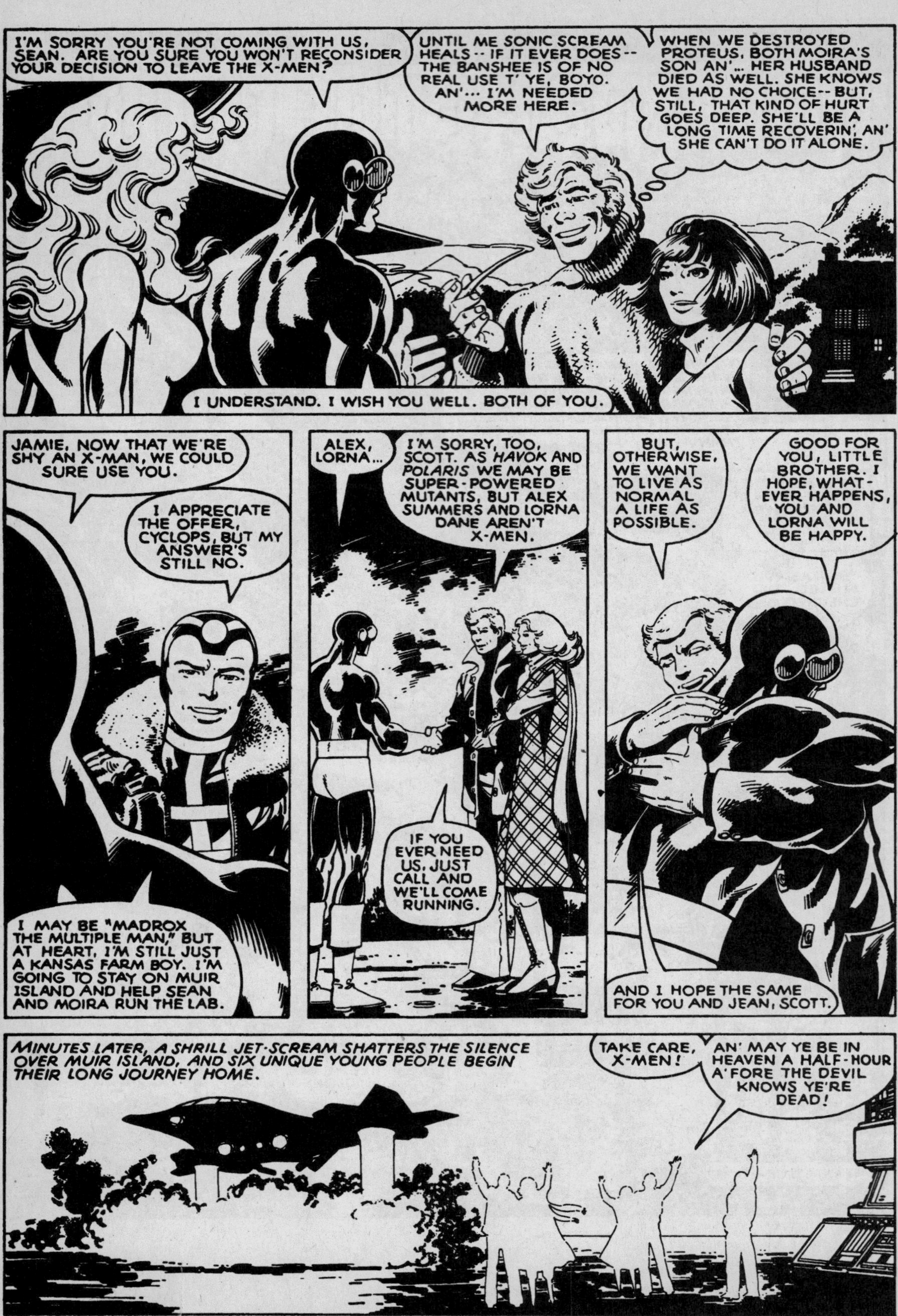
I'M SORRY YOU'RE NOT COMING WITH US, SEAN. ARE YOU SURE YOU WON'T RECONSIDER YOUR DECISION TO LEAVE THE X-MEN?
UNTIL ME SONIC SCREAM HEALS -- IF IT EVER DOES -- THE BANSHEE IS OF NO REAL USE T' YE, BOYO. AN'... I'M NEEDED MORE HERE.
WHEN WE DESTROYED PROTEUS, BOTH MOIRA'S SON AN'... HER HUSBAND DIED AS WELL. SHE KNOWS WE HAD NO CHOICE-- BUT, STILL, THAT KIND OF HURT GOES DEEP. SHE'LL BE A LONG TIME RECOVERIN', AN' SHE CAN'T DO IT ALONE.
I UNDERSTAND. I WISH YOU WELL. BOTH OF YOU.
JAMIE, NOW THAT WE'RE SHY AN X-MAN, WE COULD SURE USE YOU.
I APPRECIATE THE OFFER, CYCLOPS, BUT MY ANSWER'S STILL NO.
I MAY BE "MADROX THE MULTIPLE MAN," BUT AT HEART, I'M STILL JUST A KANSAS FARM BOY. I'M GOING TO STAY ON MUIR ISLAND AND HELP SEAN AND MOIRA RUN THE LAB.
ALEX, LORNA...
I'M SORRY, TOO, SCOTT. AS HAVOK AND POLARIS WE MAY BE SUPER-POWERED MUTANTS, BUT ALEX SUMMERS AND LORNA DANE AREN'T X-MEN.
IF YOU EVER NEED US, JUST CALL AND WE'LL COME RUNNING.
BUT, OTHERWISE, WE WANT TO LIVE AS NORMAL A LIFE AS POSSIBLE.
GOOD FOR YOU, LITTLE BROTHER. I HOPE, WHAT-EVER HAPPENS, YOU AND LORNA WILL BE HAPPY.
AND I HOPE THE SAME FOR YOU AND JEAN, SCOTT.
MINUTES LATER, A SHRILL JET-SCREAM SHATTERS THE SILENCE OVER MUIR ISLAND, AND SIX UNIQUE YOUNG PEOPLE BEGIN THEIR LONG JOURNEY HOME.
TAKE CARE, X-MEN!
AN' MAY YE BE IN HEAVEN A HALF-HOUR A'FORE THE DEVIL KNOWS YE'RE DEAD!

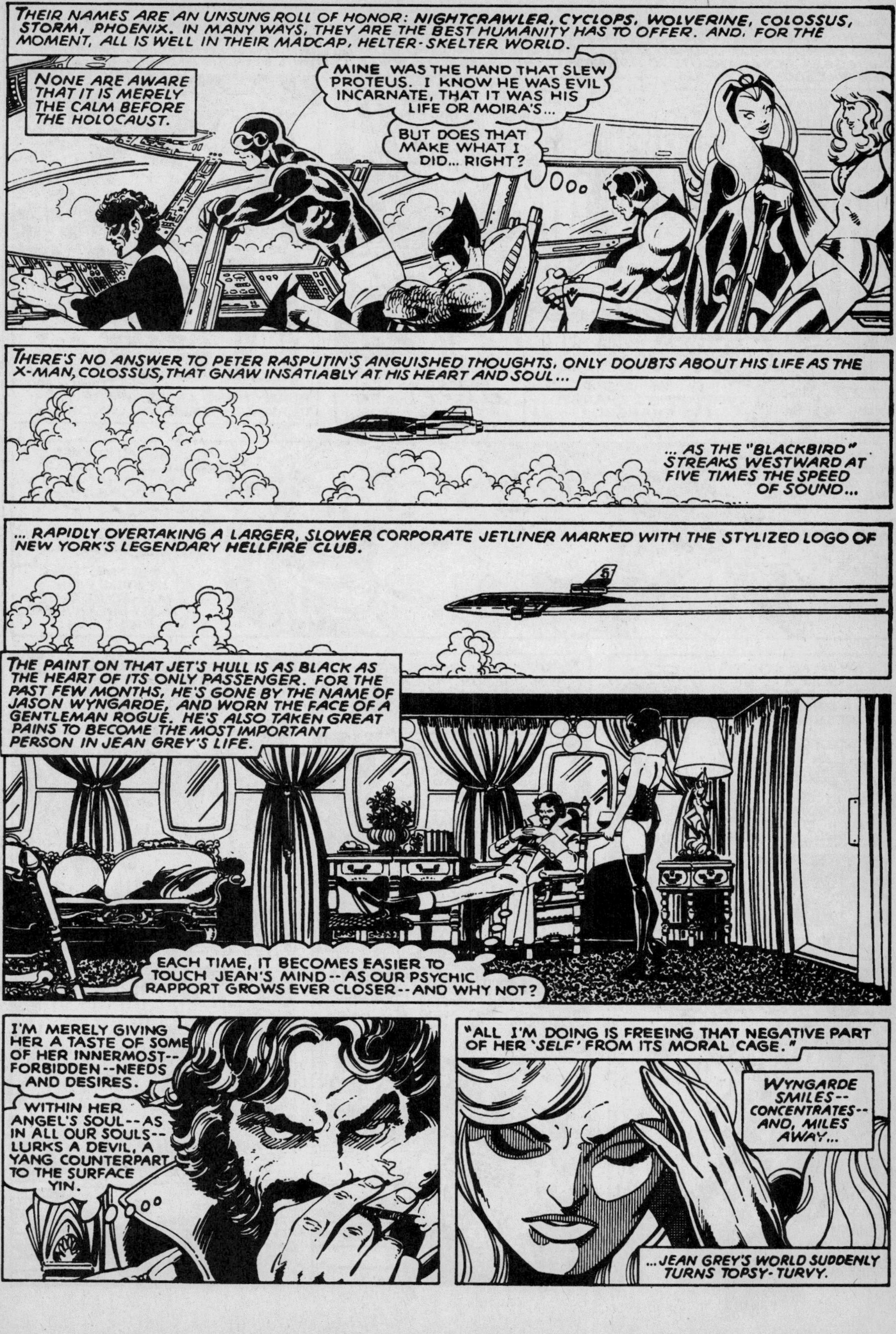
THEIR NAMES ARE AN UNSUNG ROLL OF HONOR: NIGHTCRAWLER, CYCLOPS, WOLVERINE, COLOSSUS, STORM, PHOENIX. IN MANY WAYS, THEY ARE THE BEST HUMANITY HAS TO OFFER. AND, FOR THE MOMENT, ALL IS WELL IN THEIR MADCAP, HELTER-SKELTER WORLD.
NONE ARE AWARE THAT IT IS MERELY THE CALM BEFORE THE HOLOCAUST.
MINE WAS THE HAND THAT SLEW PROTEUS. I KNOW HE WAS EVIL INCARNATE, THAT IT WAS HIS LIFE OR MOIRA'S...
BUT DOES THAT MAKE WHAT I DID... RIGHT?
THERE'S NO ANSWER TO PETER RASPUTIN'S ANGUISHED THOUGHTS, ONLY DOUBTS ABOUT HIS LIFE AS THE X-MAN, COLOSSUS, THAT GNAW INSATIABLY AT HIS HEART AND SOUL...
... AS THE "BLACKBIRD" STREAKS WESTWARD AT FIVE TIMES THE SPEED OF SOUND...
... RAPIDLY OVERTAKING A LARGER, SLOWER CORPORATE JETLINER MARKED WITH THE STYLIZED LOGO OF NEW YORK'S LEGENDARY HELLFIRE CLUB.
THE PAINT ON THAT JET'S HULL IS AS BLACK AS THE HEART OF ITS ONLY PASSENGER. FOR THE PAST FEW MONTHS, HE'S GONE BY THE NAME OF JASON WYNGARDE, AND WORN THE FACE OF A GENTLEMAN ROGUE. HE'S ALSO TAKEN GREAT PAINS TO BECOME THE MOST IMPORTANT PERSON IN JEAN GREY'S LIFE.
EACH TIME, IT BECOMES EASIER TO TOUCH JEAN'S MIND -- AS OUR PSYCHIC RAPPORT GROWS EVER CLOSER -- AND WHY NOT?
I'M MERELY GIVING HER A TASTE OF SOME OF HER INNERMOST -- FORBIDDEN -- NEEDS AND DESIRES.
WITHIN HER ANGEL'S SOUL -- AS IN ALL OUR SOULS -- LURKS A DEVIL, A YANG COUNTERPART TO THE SURFACE YIN.
"ALL I'M DOING IS FREEING THAT NEGATIVE PART OF HER 'SELF' FROM ITS MORAL CAGE."
WYNGARDE SMILES -- CONCENTRATES -- AND, MILES AWAY...
...JEAN GREY'S WORLD SUDDENLY TURNS TOPSY-TURVY.

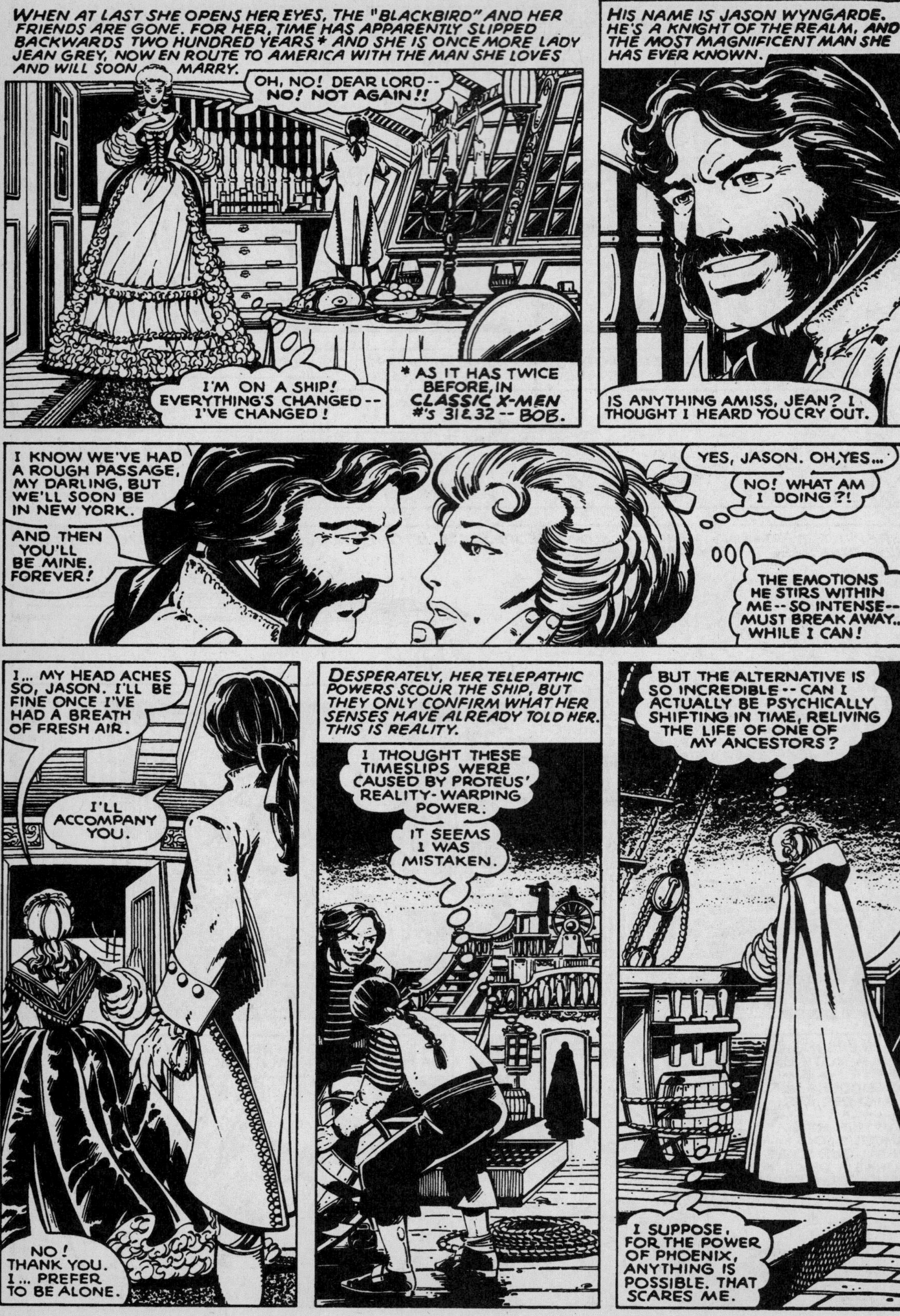

WHEN AT LAST SHE OPENS HER EYES, THE "BLACKBIRD" AND HER FRIENDS ARE GONE. FOR HER, TIME HAS APPARENTLY SLIPPED BACKWARDS TWO HUNDRED YEARS* AND SHE IS ONCE MORE LADY JEAN GREY, NOW EN ROUTE TO AMERICA WITH THE MAN SHE LOVES AND WILL SOON MARRY.
OH, NO! DEAR LORD-- NO! NOT AGAIN!!
I'M ON A SHIP! EVERYTHING'S CHANGED-- I'VE CHANGED!
* AS IT HAS TWICE BEFORE, IN CLASSIC X-MEN #'S 31 & 32 -- BOB.
HIS NAME IS JASON WYNGARDE. HE'S A KNIGHT OF THE REALM, AND THE MOST MAGNIFICENT MAN SHE HAS EVER KNOWN.
IS ANYTHING AMISS, JEAN? I THOUGHT I HEARD YOU CRY OUT.
I KNOW WE'VE HAD A ROUGH PASSAGE, MY DARLING, BUT WE'LL SOON BE IN NEW YORK.
AND THEN YOU'LL BE MINE, FOREVER!
YES, JASON. OH, YES...
NO! WHAT AM I DOING?!
THE EMOTIONS HE STIRS WITHIN ME -- SO INTENSE-- MUST BREAK AWAY... WHILE I CAN!
I... MY HEAD ACHES SO, JASON. I'LL BE FINE ONCE I'VE HAD A BREATH OF FRESH AIR.
I'LL ACCOMPANY YOU.
NO! THANK YOU. I... PREFER TO BE ALONE.
DESPERATELY, HER TELEPATHIC POWERS SCOUR THE SHIP, BUT THEY ONLY CONFIRM WHAT HER SENSES HAVE ALREADY TOLD HER. THIS IS REALITY.
I THOUGHT THESE TIMESLIPS WERE CAUSED BY PROTEUS' REALITY-WARPING POWER.
IT SEEMS I WAS MISTAKEN.
BUT THE ALTERNATIVE IS SO INCREDIBLE -- CAN I ACTUALLY BE PSYCHICALLY SHIFTING IN TIME, RELIVING THE LIFE OF ONE OF MY ANCESTORS?
I SUPPOSE, FOR THE POWER OF PHOENIX, ANYTHING IS POSSIBLE. THAT SCARES ME.

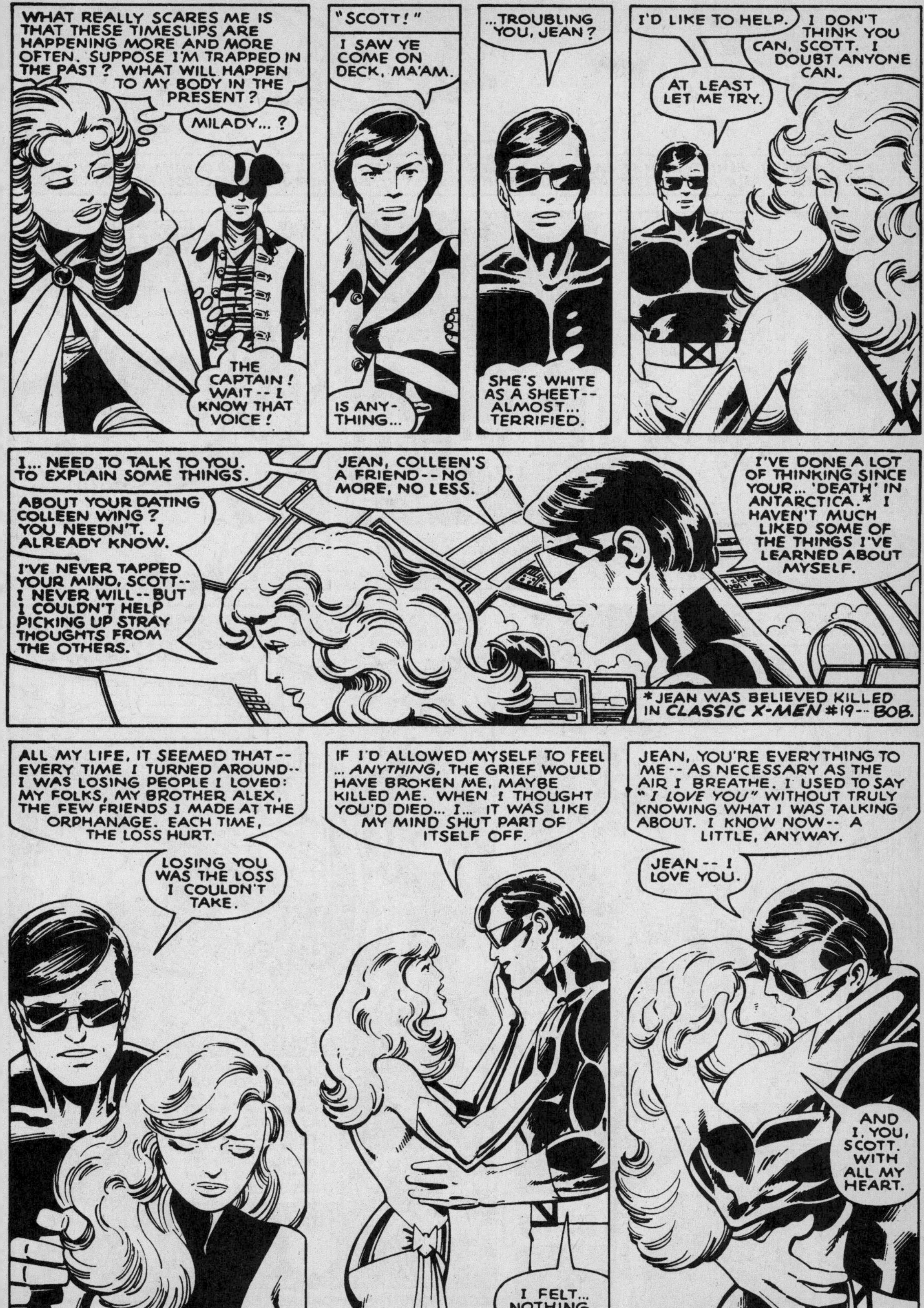
WHAT REALLY SCARES ME IS THAT THESE TIMESLIPS ARE HAPPENING MORE AND MORE OFTEN. SUPPOSE I'M TRAPPED IN THE PAST? WHAT WILL HAPPEN TO MY BODY IN THE PRESENT?
MILADY...?
THE CAPTAIN! WAIT-- I KNOW THAT VOICE!
"SCOTT!"
I SAW YE COME ON DECK, MA'AM.
IS ANY-THING...
...TROUBLING YOU, JEAN?
SHE'S WHITE AS A SHEET-- ALMOST... TERRIFIED.
I'D LIKE TO HELP.
I DON'T THINK YOU CAN, SCOTT. I DOUBT ANYONE CAN.
AT LEAST LET ME TRY.
I... NEED TO TALK TO YOU. TO EXPLAIN SOME THINGS.
ABOUT YOUR DATING COLLEEN WING? YOU NEEDN'T. I ALREADY KNOW.
I'VE NEVER TAPPED YOUR MIND, SCOTT-- I NEVER WILL--BUT I COULDN'T HELP PICKING UP STRAY THOUGHTS FROM THE OTHERS.
JEAN, COLLEEN'S A FRIEND--NO MORE, NO LESS.
I'VE DONE A LOT OF THINKING SINCE YOUR... 'DEATH' IN ANTARCTICA.* I HAVEN'T MUCH LIKED SOME OF THE THINGS I'VE LEARNED ABOUT MYSELF.
*JEAN WAS BELIEVED KILLED IN CLASSIC X-MEN #19-- BOB.
ALL MY LIFE, IT SEEMED THAT-- EVERY TIME I TURNED AROUND-- I WAS LOSING PEOPLE I LOVED: MY FOLKS, MY BROTHER ALEX, THE FEW FRIENDS I MADE AT THE ORPHANAGE. EACH TIME, THE LOSS HURT.
LOSING YOU WAS THE LOSS I COULDN'T TAKE.
IF I'D ALLOWED MYSELF TO FEEL ...ANYTHING, THE GRIEF WOULD HAVE BROKEN ME, MAYBE KILLED ME. WHEN I THOUGHT YOU'D DIED... I... IT WAS LIKE MY MIND SHUT PART OF ITSELF OFF.
I FELT... NOTHING.
JEAN, YOU'RE EVERYTHING TO ME--AS NECESSARY AS THE AIR I BREATHE. I USED TO SAY "I LOVE YOU" WITHOUT TRULY KNOWING WHAT I WAS TALKING ABOUT. I KNOW NOW-- A LITTLE, ANYWAY.
JEAN-- I LOVE YOU.
AND I, YOU, SCOTT. WITH ALL MY HEART.

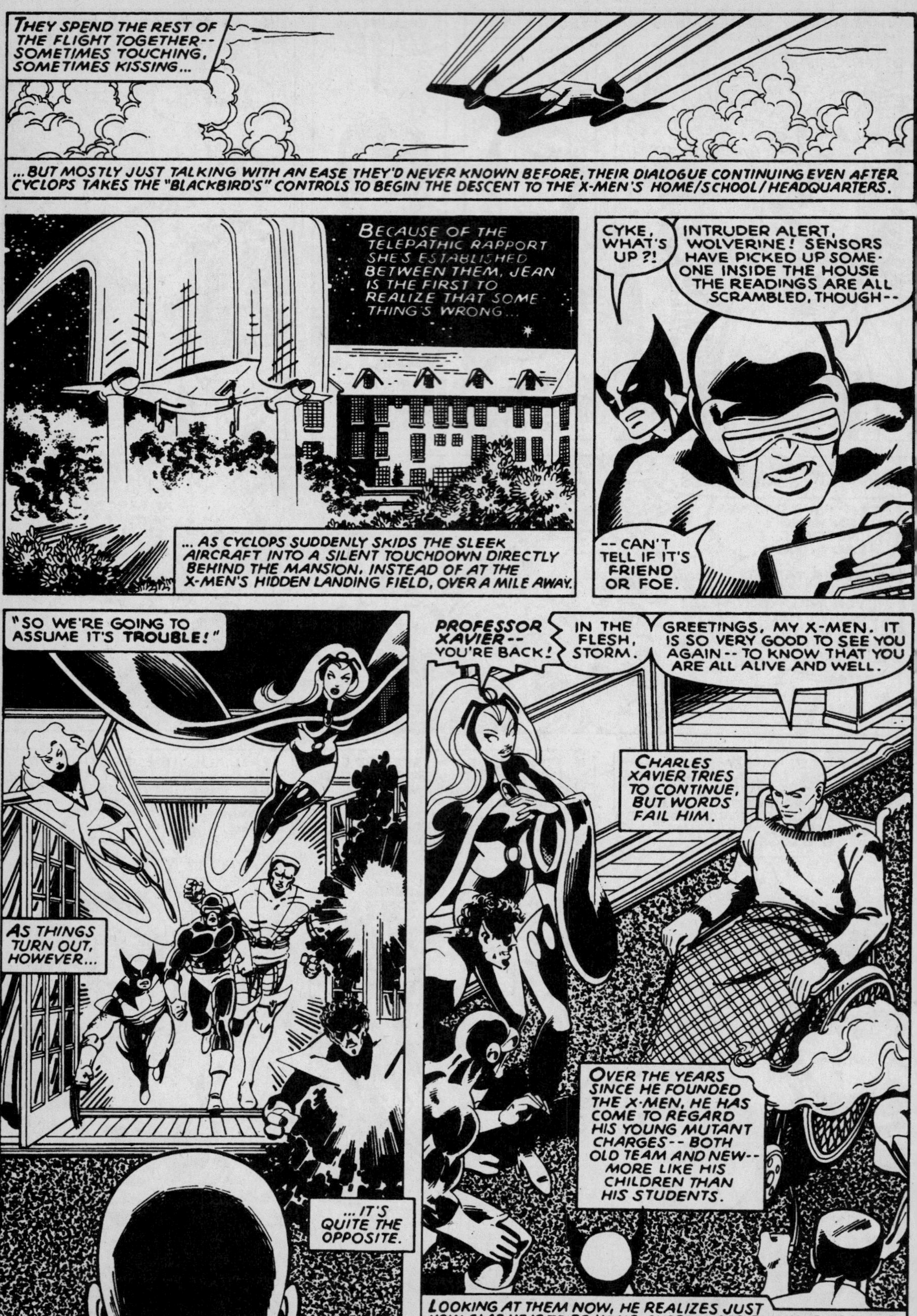
THEY SPEND THE REST OF THE FLIGHT TOGETHER-- SOMETIMES TOUCHING, SOMETIMES KISSING...
...BUT MOSTLY JUST TALKING WITH AN EASE THEY'D NEVER KNOWN BEFORE, THEIR DIALOGUE CONTINUING EVEN AFTER CYCLOPS TAKES THE "BLACKBIRD'S" CONTROLS TO BEGIN THE DESCENT TO THE X-MEN'S HOME/SCHOOL/HEADQUARTERS.
BECAUSE OF THE TELEPATHIC RAPPORT SHE'S ESTABLISHED BETWEEN THEM, JEAN IS THE FIRST TO REALIZE THAT SOMETHING'S WRONG...
...AS CYCLOPS SUDDENLY SKIDS THE SLEEK AIRCRAFT INTO A SILENT TOUCHDOWN DIRECTLY BEHIND THE MANSION, INSTEAD OF AT THE X-MEN'S HIDDEN LANDING FIELD, OVER A MILE AWAY.
CYKE, WHAT'S UP?!
INTRUDER ALERT, WOLVERINE! SENSORS HAVE PICKED UP SOMEONE INSIDE THE HOUSE THE READINGS ARE ALL SCRAMBLED, THOUGH--
--CAN'T TELL IF IT'S FRIEND OR FOE.
"SO WE'RE GOING TO ASSUME IT'S TROUBLE!"
AS THINGS TURN OUT, HOWEVER...
...IT'S QUITE THE OPPOSITE.
PROFESSOR XAVIER-- YOU'RE BACK!
IN THE FLESH, STORM.
GREETINGS, MY X-MEN. IT IS SO VERY GOOD TO SEE YOU AGAIN-- TO KNOW THAT YOU ARE ALL ALIVE AND WELL.
CHARLES XAVIER TRIES TO CONTINUE, BUT WORDS FAIL HIM.
OVER THE YEARS SINCE HE FOUNDED THE X-MEN, HE HAS COME TO REGARD HIS YOUNG MUTANT CHARGES-- BOTH OLD TEAM AND NEW-- MORE LIKE HIS CHILDREN THAN HIS STUDENTS.
LOOKING AT THEM NOW, HE REALIZES JUST HOW GLAD HE IS TO BE HOME, SURROUNDED BY THOSE HE LOVES.

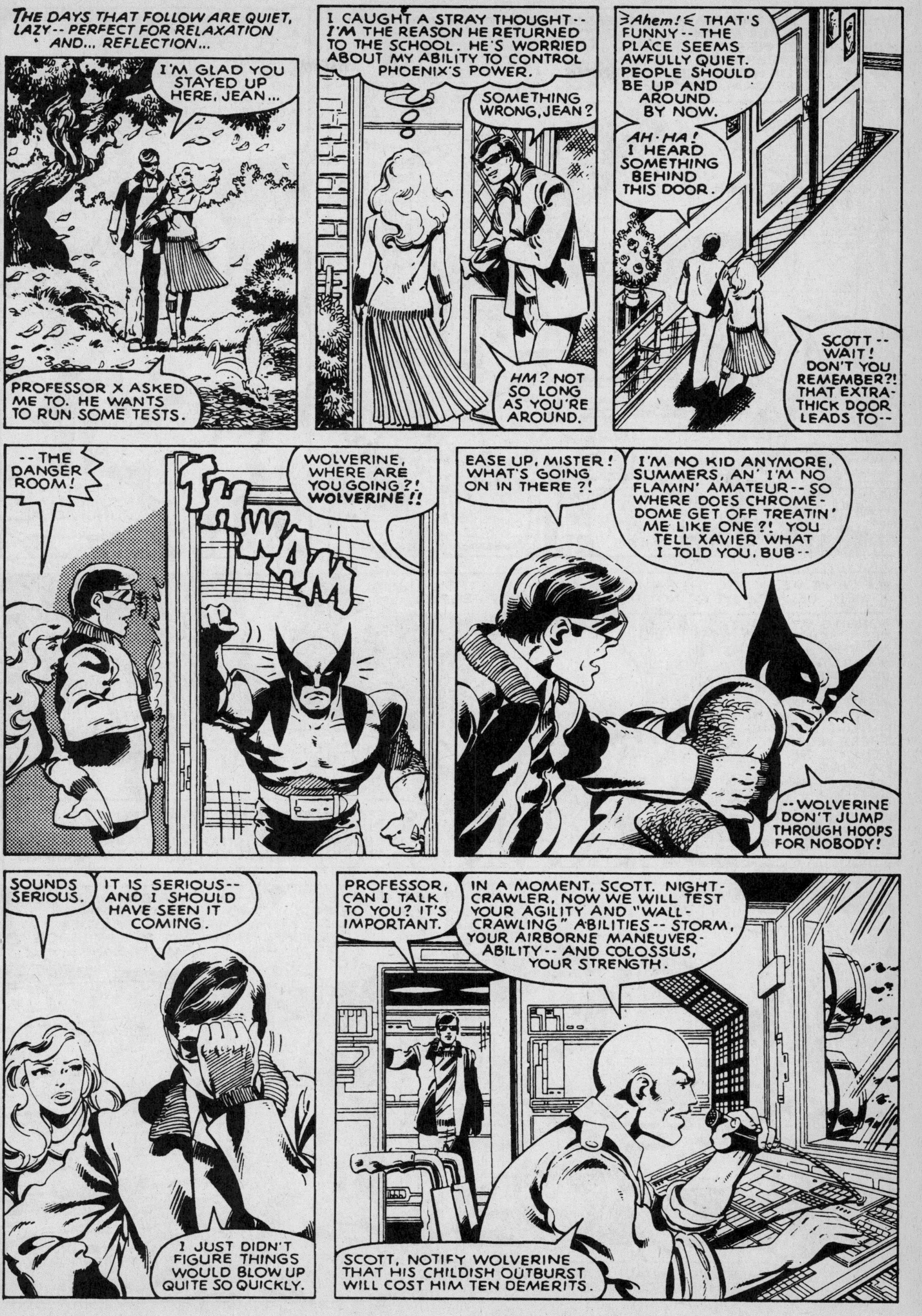

THE DAYS THAT FOLLOW ARE QUIET, LAZY -- PERFECT FOR RELAXATION AND... REFLECTION...
I'M GLAD YOU STAYED UP HERE, JEAN...
PROFESSOR X ASKED ME TO. HE WANTS TO RUN SOME TESTS.
I CAUGHT A STRAY THOUGHT -- I'M THE REASON HE RETURNED TO THE SCHOOL. HE'S WORRIED ABOUT MY ABILITY TO CONTROL PHOENIX'S POWER.
SOMETHING WRONG, JEAN?
HM? NOT SO LONG AS YOU'RE AROUND.
Ahem! THAT'S FUNNY -- THE PLACE SEEMS AWFULLY QUIET. PEOPLE SHOULD BE UP AND AROUND BY NOW.
AH-HA! I HEARD SOMETHING BEHIND THIS DOOR.
SCOTT -- WAIT! DON'T YOU REMEMBER?! THAT EXTRA-THICK DOOR LEADS TO --
-- THE DANGER ROOM!
THWAM
WOLVERINE, WHERE ARE YOU GOING?! WOLVERINE!!
EASE UP, MISTER! WHAT'S GOING ON IN THERE?!
I'M NO KID ANYMORE, SUMMERS, AN' I'M NO FLAMIN' AMATEUR -- SO WHERE DOES CHROME-DOME GET OFF TREATIN' ME LIKE ONE?! YOU TELL XAVIER WHAT I TOLD YOU, BUB --
-- WOLVERINE DON'T JUMP THROUGH HOOPS FOR NOBODY!
SOUNDS SERIOUS.
IT IS SERIOUS -- AND I SHOULD HAVE SEEN IT COMING.
I JUST DIDN'T FIGURE THINGS WOULD BLOW UP QUITE SO QUICKLY.
PROFESSOR, CAN I TALK TO YOU? IT'S IMPORTANT.
IN A MOMENT, SCOTT. NIGHTCRAWLER, NOW WE WILL TEST YOUR AGILITY AND "WALL-CRAWLING" ABILITIES -- STORM, YOUR AIRBORNE MANEUVERABILITY -- AND COLOSSUS, YOUR STRENGTH.
SCOTT, NOTIFY WOLVERINE THAT HIS CHILDISH OUTBURST WILL COST HIM TEN DEMERITS.

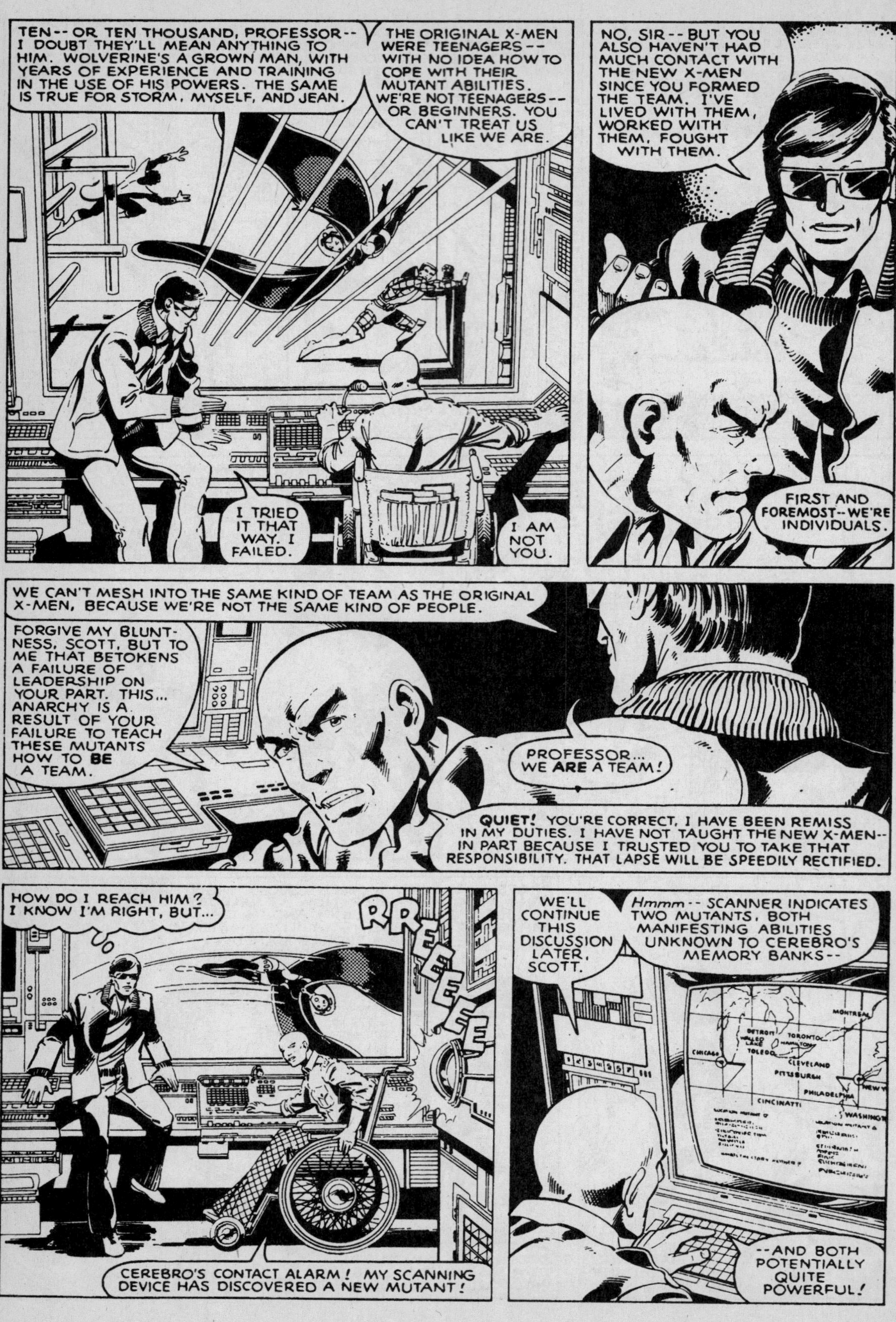

TEN-- OR TEN THOUSAND, PROFESSOR-- I DOUBT THEY'LL MEAN ANYTHING TO HIM. WOLVERINE'S A GROWN MAN, WITH YEARS OF EXPERIENCE AND TRAINING IN THE USE OF HIS POWERS. THE SAME IS TRUE FOR STORM, MYSELF, AND JEAN.
THE ORIGINAL X-MEN WERE TEENAGERS-- WITH NO IDEA HOW TO COPE WITH THEIR MUTANT ABILITIES. WE'RE NOT TEENAGERS-- OR BEGINNERS. YOU CAN'T TREAT US LIKE WE ARE.
I TRIED IT THAT WAY. I FAILED.
I AM NOT YOU.
NO, SIR-- BUT YOU ALSO HAVEN'T HAD MUCH CONTACT WITH THE NEW X-MEN SINCE YOU FORMED THE TEAM. I'VE LIVED WITH THEM, WORKED WITH THEM, FOUGHT WITH THEM.
FIRST AND FOREMOST--WE'RE INDIVIDUALS.
WE CAN'T MESH INTO THE SAME KIND OF TEAM AS THE ORIGINAL X-MEN, BECAUSE WE'RE NOT THE SAME KIND OF PEOPLE.
FORGIVE MY BLUNTNESS, SCOTT, BUT TO ME THAT BETOKENS A FAILURE OF LEADERSHIP ON YOUR PART. THIS... ANARCHY IS A RESULT OF YOUR FAILURE TO TEACH THESE MUTANTS HOW TO **BE** A TEAM.
PROFESSOR... WE **ARE** A TEAM!
QUIET! YOU'RE CORRECT, I HAVE BEEN REMISS IN MY DUTIES. I HAVE NOT TAUGHT THE NEW X-MEN-- IN PART BECAUSE I TRUSTED YOU TO TAKE THAT RESPONSIBILITY. THAT LAPSE WILL BE SPEEDILY RECTIFIED.
HOW DO I REACH HIM? I KNOW I'M RIGHT, BUT...
RREEEEE
CEREBRO'S CONTACT ALARM! MY SCANNING DEVICE HAS DISCOVERED A NEW MUTANT!
WE'LL CONTINUE THIS DISCUSSION LATER, SCOTT.
Hmmm-- SCANNER INDICATES TWO MUTANTS, BOTH MANIFESTING ABILITIES UNKNOWN TO CEREBRO'S MEMORY BANKS--
MONTREAL
DETROIT
TORONTO
CHICAGO
TOLEDO
CLEVELAND
PITTSBURGH
PHILADELPHIA
CINCINATTI
WASHINGTON
--AND BOTH POTENTIALLY QUITE POWERFUL!

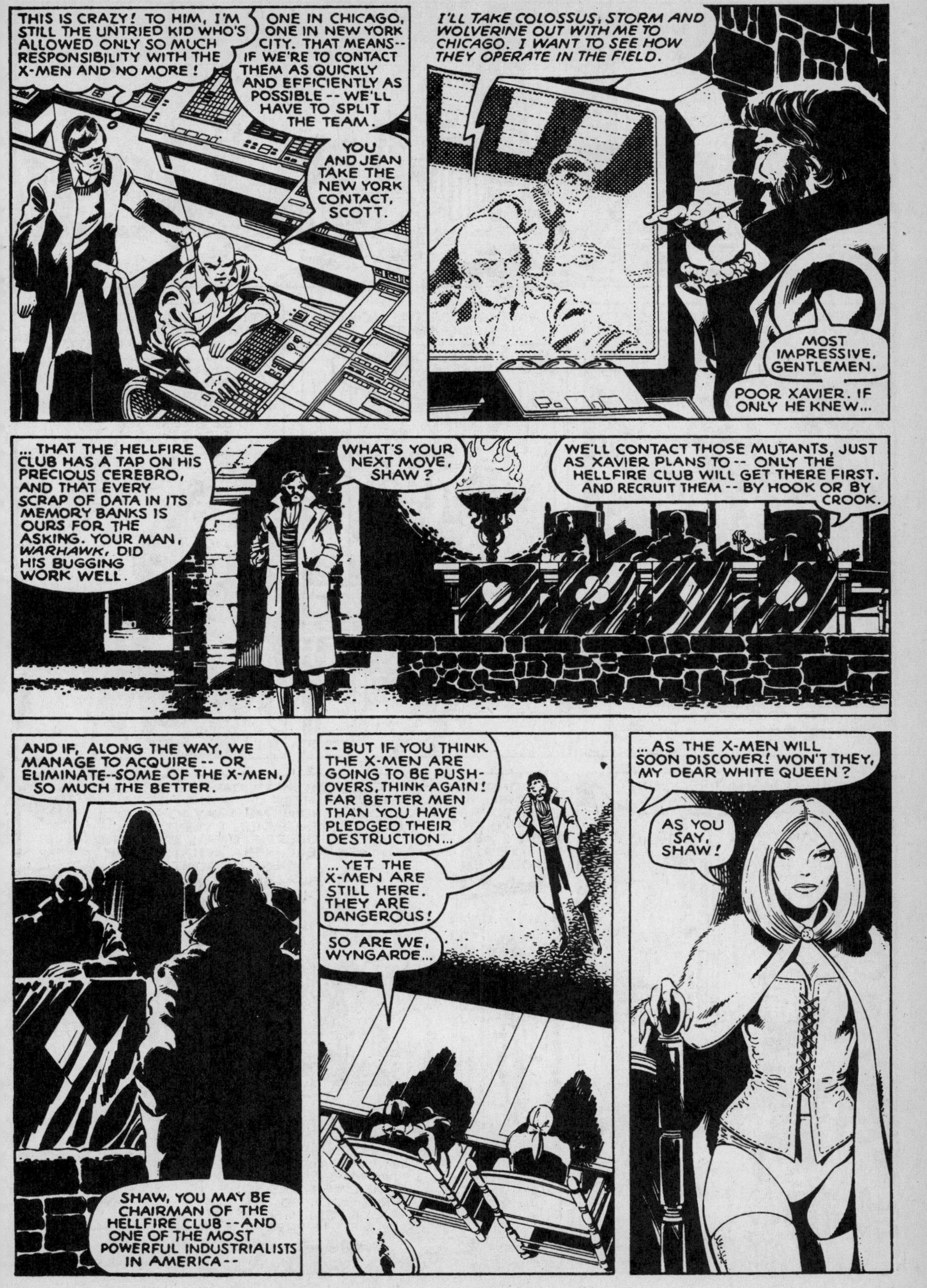
THIS IS CRAZY! TO HIM, I'M STILL THE UNTRIED KID WHO'S ALLOWED ONLY SO MUCH RESPONSIBILITY WITH THE X-MEN AND NO MORE!
ONE IN CHICAGO, ONE IN NEW YORK CITY. THAT MEANS-- IF WE'RE TO CONTACT THEM AS QUICKLY AND EFFICIENTLY AS POSSIBLE -- WE'LL HAVE TO SPLIT THE TEAM.
YOU AND JEAN TAKE THE NEW YORK CONTACT, SCOTT.
I'LL TAKE COLOSSUS, STORM AND WOLVERINE OUT WITH ME TO CHICAGO. I WANT TO SEE HOW THEY OPERATE IN THE FIELD.
MOST IMPRESSIVE, GENTLEMEN.
POOR XAVIER. IF ONLY HE KNEW...
... THAT THE HELLFIRE CLUB HAS A TAP ON HIS PRECIOUS CEREBRO, AND THAT EVERY SCRAP OF DATA IN ITS MEMORY BANKS IS OURS FOR THE ASKING. YOUR MAN, WARHAWK, DID HIS BUGGING WORK WELL.
WHAT'S YOUR NEXT MOVE, SHAW?
WE'LL CONTACT THOSE MUTANTS, JUST AS XAVIER PLANS TO -- ONLY THE HELLFIRE CLUB WILL GET THERE FIRST. AND RECRUIT THEM -- BY HOOK OR BY CROOK.
AND IF, ALONG THE WAY, WE MANAGE TO ACQUIRE -- OR ELIMINATE--SOME OF THE X-MEN, SO MUCH THE BETTER.
SHAW, YOU MAY BE CHAIRMAN OF THE HELLFIRE CLUB --AND ONE OF THE MOST POWERFUL INDUSTRIALISTS IN AMERICA--
-- BUT IF YOU THINK THE X-MEN ARE GOING TO BE PUSH-OVERS, THINK AGAIN! FAR BETTER MEN THAN YOU HAVE PLEDGED THEIR DESTRUCTION...
... YET THE X-MEN ARE STILL HERE. THEY ARE DANGEROUS!
SO ARE WE, WYNGARDE...
... AS THE X-MEN WILL SOON DISCOVER! WON'T THEY, MY DEAR WHITE QUEEN?
AS YOU SAY, SHAW!

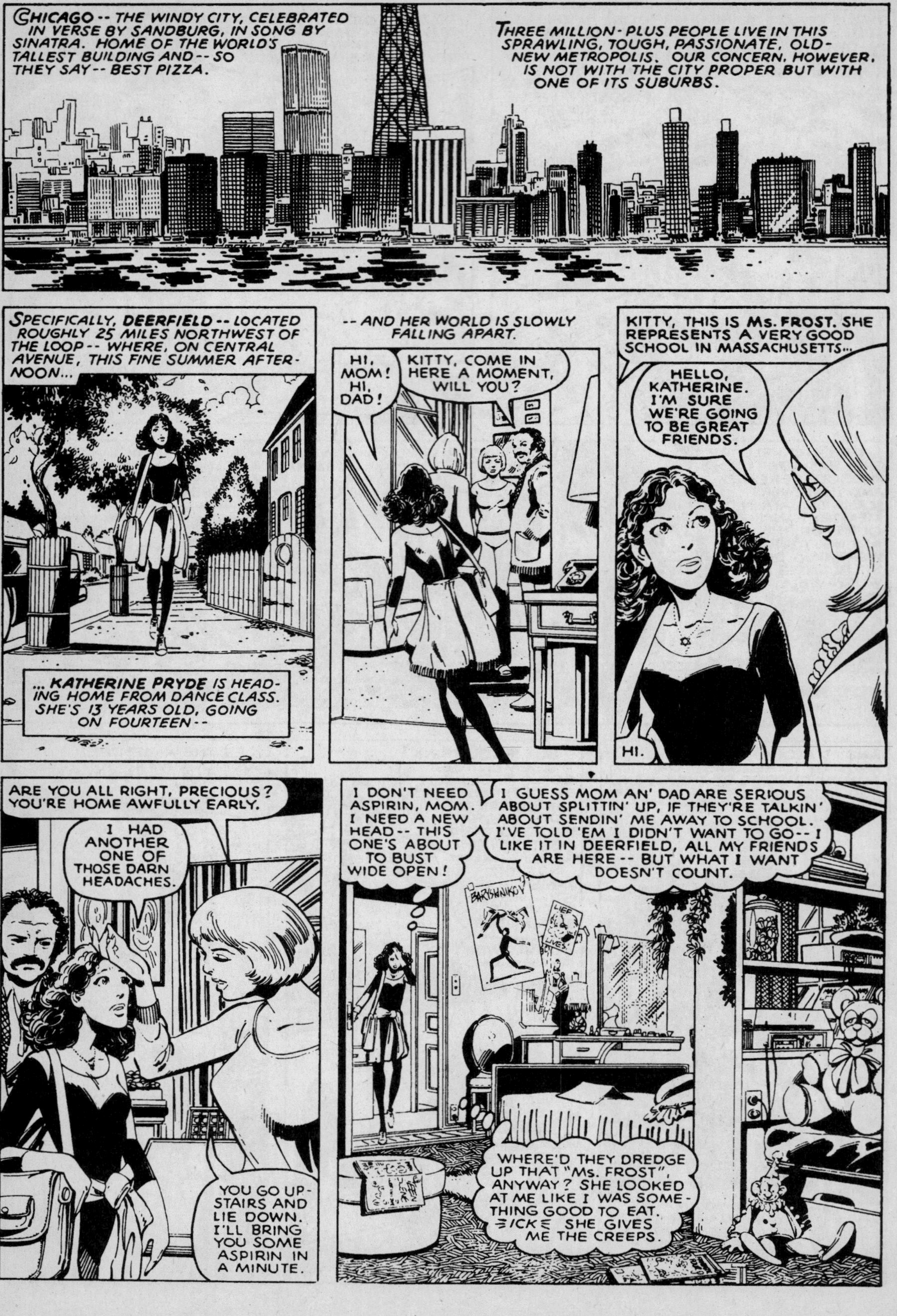
CHICAGO -- THE WINDY CITY, CELEBRATED IN VERSE BY SANDBURG, IN SONG BY SINATRA. HOME OF THE WORLD'S TALLEST BUILDING AND -- SO THEY SAY -- BEST PIZZA.
THREE MILLION-PLUS PEOPLE LIVE IN THIS SPRAWLING, TOUGH, PASSIONATE, OLD-NEW METROPOLIS. OUR CONCERN, HOWEVER, IS NOT WITH THE CITY PROPER BUT WITH ONE OF ITS SUBURBS.
SPECIFICALLY, DEERFIELD -- LOCATED ROUGHLY 25 MILES NORTHWEST OF THE LOOP -- WHERE, ON CENTRAL AVENUE, THIS FINE SUMMER AFTERNOON...
... KATHERINE PRYDE IS HEADING HOME FROM DANCE CLASS. SHE'S 13 YEARS OLD, GOING ON FOURTEEN --
-- AND HER WORLD IS SLOWLY FALLING APART.
HI, MOM! HI, DAD!
KITTY, COME IN HERE A MOMENT, WILL YOU?
KITTY, THIS IS Ms. FROST. SHE REPRESENTS A VERY GOOD SCHOOL IN MASSACHUSETTS...
HELLO, KATHERINE. I'M SURE WE'RE GOING TO BE GREAT FRIENDS.
HI.
ARE YOU ALL RIGHT, PRECIOUS? YOU'RE HOME AWFULLY EARLY.
I HAD ANOTHER ONE OF THOSE DARN HEADACHES.
YOU GO UPSTAIRS AND LIE DOWN. I'LL BRING YOU SOME ASPIRIN IN A MINUTE.
I DON'T NEED ASPIRIN, MOM. I NEED A NEW HEAD -- THIS ONE'S ABOUT TO BUST WIDE OPEN!
I GUESS MOM AN' DAD ARE SERIOUS ABOUT SPLITTIN' UP, IF THEY'RE TALKIN' ABOUT SENDIN' ME AWAY TO SCHOOL. I'VE TOLD 'EM I DIDN'T WANT TO GO -- I LIKE IT IN DEERFIELD, ALL MY FRIENDS ARE HERE -- BUT WHAT I WANT DOESN'T COUNT.
BARYSHNIKOV
WHERE'D THEY DREDGE UP THAT "Ms. FROST", ANYWAY? SHE LOOKED AT ME LIKE I WAS SOMETHING GOOD TO EAT. ≡ICK≡ SHE GIVES ME THE CREEPS.

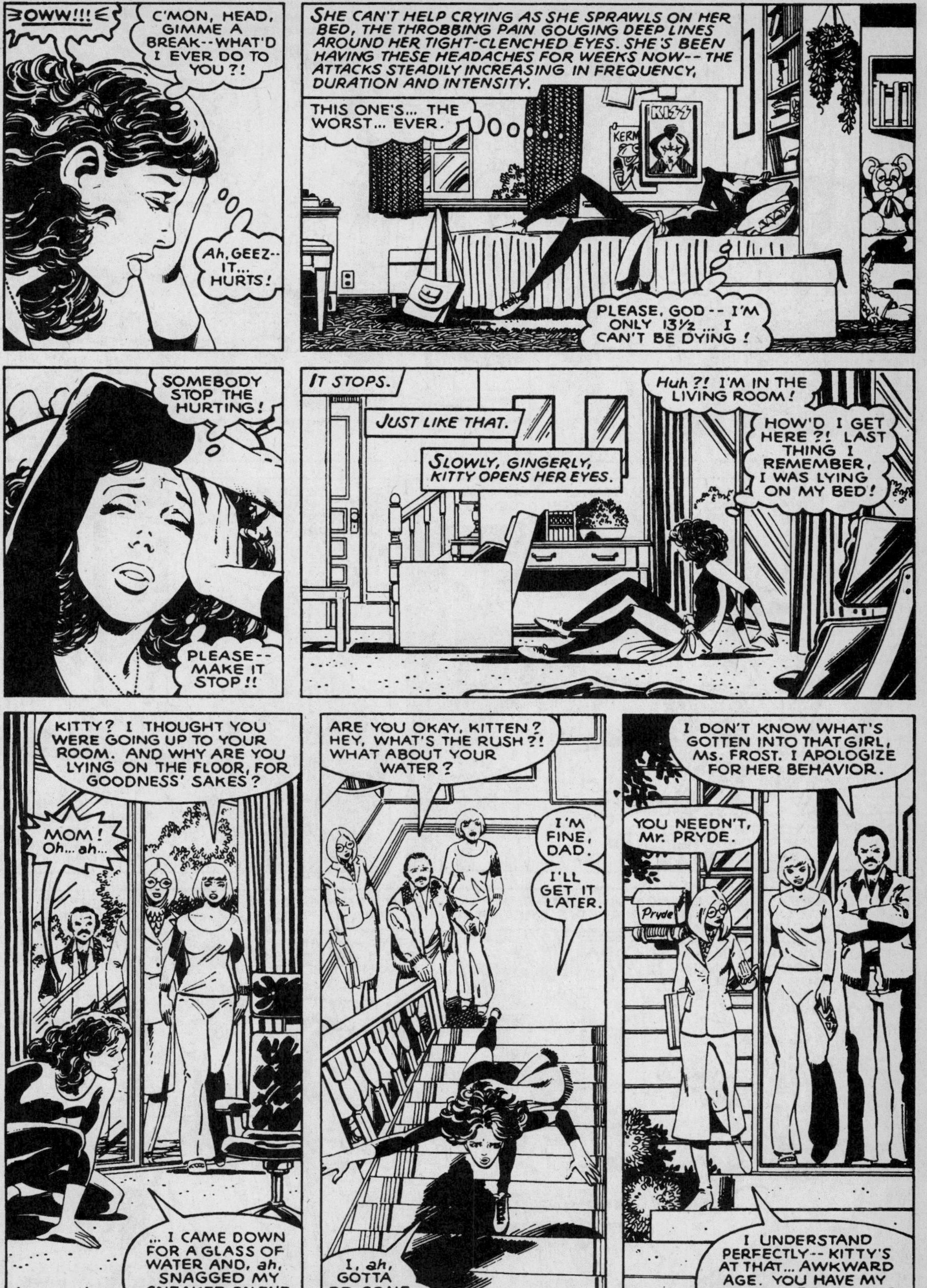
OWW!!!
C'MON, HEAD, GIMME A BREAK--WHAT'D I EVER DO TO YOU?!
Ah, GEEZ-- IT... HURTS!
SHE CAN'T HELP CRYING AS SHE SPRAWLS ON HER BED, THE THROBBING PAIN GOUGING DEEP LINES AROUND HER TIGHT-CLENCHED EYES. SHE'S BEEN HAVING THESE HEADACHES FOR WEEKS NOW-- THE ATTACKS STEADILY INCREASING IN FREQUENCY, DURATION AND INTENSITY.
THIS ONE'S... THE WORST... EVER.
KISS
PLEASE, GOD -- I'M ONLY 13½ ... I CAN'T BE DYING!
SOMEBODY STOP THE HURTING!
PLEASE-- MAKE IT STOP!!
IT STOPS.
JUST LIKE THAT.
SLOWLY, GINGERLY, KITTY OPENS HER EYES.
Huh?! I'M IN THE LIVING ROOM!
HOW'D I GET HERE?! LAST THING I REMEMBER, I WAS LYING ON MY BED!
KITTY? I THOUGHT YOU WERE GOING UP TO YOUR ROOM. AND WHY ARE YOU LYING ON THE FLOOR, FOR GOODNESS' SAKES?
MOM! Oh... ah...
... I CAME DOWN FOR A GLASS OF WATER AND, ah, SNAGGED MY SNEAKER ON THE CARPET. I FELL.
ARE YOU OKAY, KITTEN? HEY, WHAT'S THE RUSH?! WHAT ABOUT YOUR WATER?
I'M FINE, DAD.
I'LL GET IT LATER.
I, ah, GOTTA DO SOME HOMEWORK.
I DON'T KNOW WHAT'S GOTTEN INTO THAT GIRL, MS. FROST. I APOLOGIZE FOR HER BEHAVIOR.
YOU NEEDN'T, MR. PRYDE.
Pryde
I UNDERSTAND PERFECTLY-- KITTY'S AT THAT... AWKWARD AGE. YOU HAVE MY SCHOOL'S BROCHURES. I'LL BE IN TOUCH.

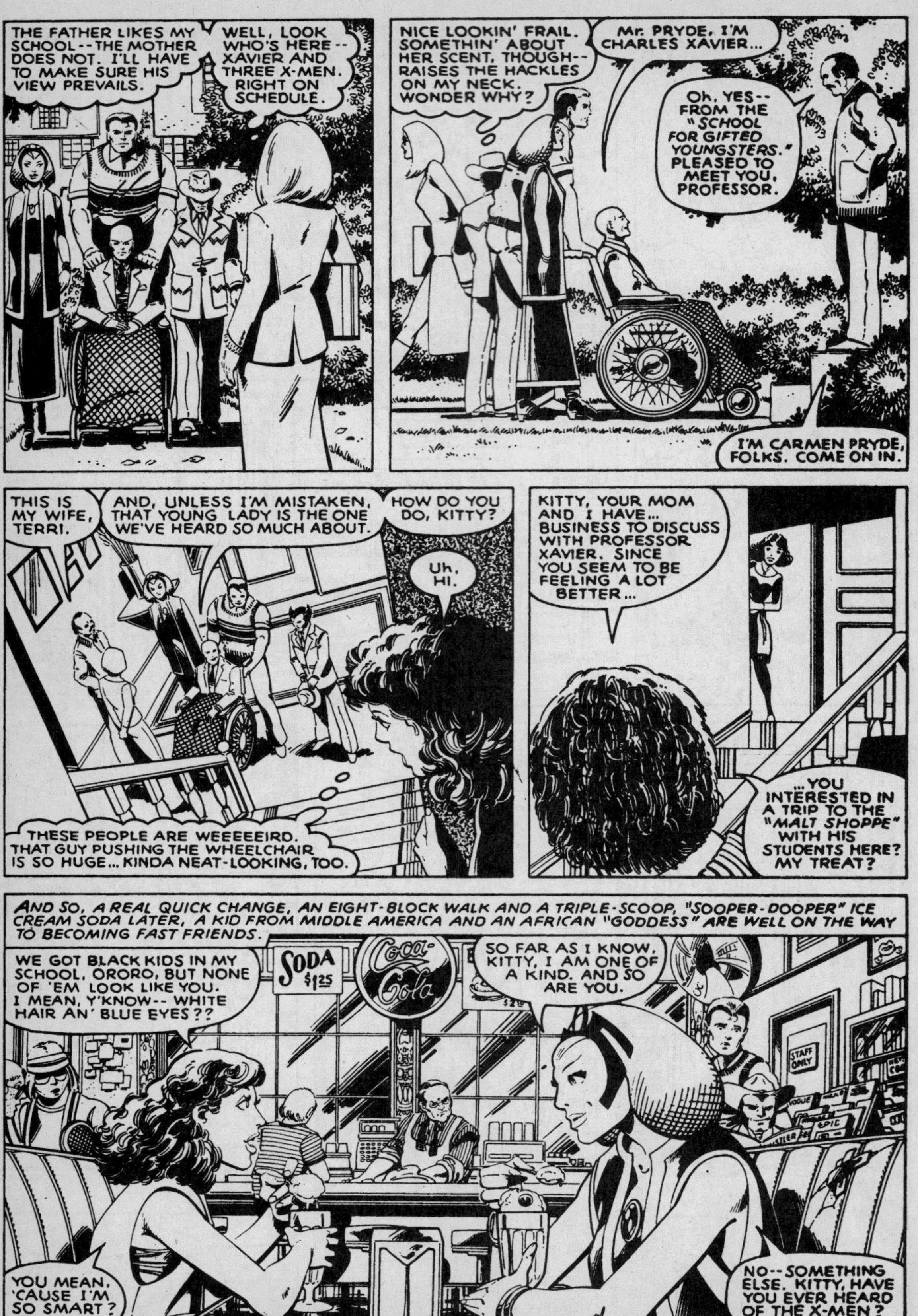

THE FATHER LIKES MY SCHOOL -- THE MOTHER DOES NOT. I'LL HAVE TO MAKE SURE HIS VIEW PREVAILS.
WELL, LOOK WHO'S HERE -- XAVIER AND THREE X-MEN. RIGHT ON SCHEDULE.
NICE LOOKIN' FRAIL. SOMETHIN' ABOUT HER SCENT, THOUGH-- RAISES THE HACKLES ON MY NECK. WONDER WHY?
Mr. PRYDE, I'M CHARLES XAVIER...
Oh, YES-- FROM THE "SCHOOL FOR GIFTED YOUNGSTERS." PLEASED TO MEET YOU, PROFESSOR.
I'M CARMEN PRYDE, FOLKS. COME ON IN.
THIS IS MY WIFE, TERRI.
AND, UNLESS I'M MISTAKEN, THAT YOUNG LADY IS THE ONE WE'VE HEARD SO MUCH ABOUT.
HOW DO YOU DO, KITTY?
Uh, HI.
THESE PEOPLE ARE WEEEEEIRD. THAT GUY PUSHING THE WHEELCHAIR IS SO HUGE... KINDA NEAT-LOOKING, TOO.
KITTY, YOUR MOM AND I HAVE... BUSINESS TO DISCUSS WITH PROFESSOR XAVIER. SINCE YOU SEEM TO BE FEELING A LOT BETTER...
...YOU INTERESTED IN A TRIP TO THE "MALT SHOPPE" WITH HIS STUDENTS HERE? MY TREAT?
AND SO, A REAL QUICK CHANGE, AN EIGHT-BLOCK WALK AND A TRIPLE-SCOOP, "SOOPER-DOOPER" ICE CREAM SODA LATER, A KID FROM MIDDLE AMERICA AND AN AFRICAN "GODDESS" ARE WELL ON THE WAY TO BECOMING FAST FRIENDS.
WE GOT BLACK KIDS IN MY SCHOOL, ORORO, BUT NONE OF 'EM LOOK LIKE YOU. I MEAN, Y'KNOW-- WHITE HAIR AN' BLUE EYES??
SODA $1.25
Coca-Cola
SO FAR AS I KNOW, KITTY, I AM ONE OF A KIND. AND SO ARE YOU.
STAFF ONLY
EPIC
YOU MEAN, 'CAUSE I'M SO SMART?
NO-- SOMETHING ELSE. KITTY, HAVE YOU EVER HEARD OF THE X-MEN?

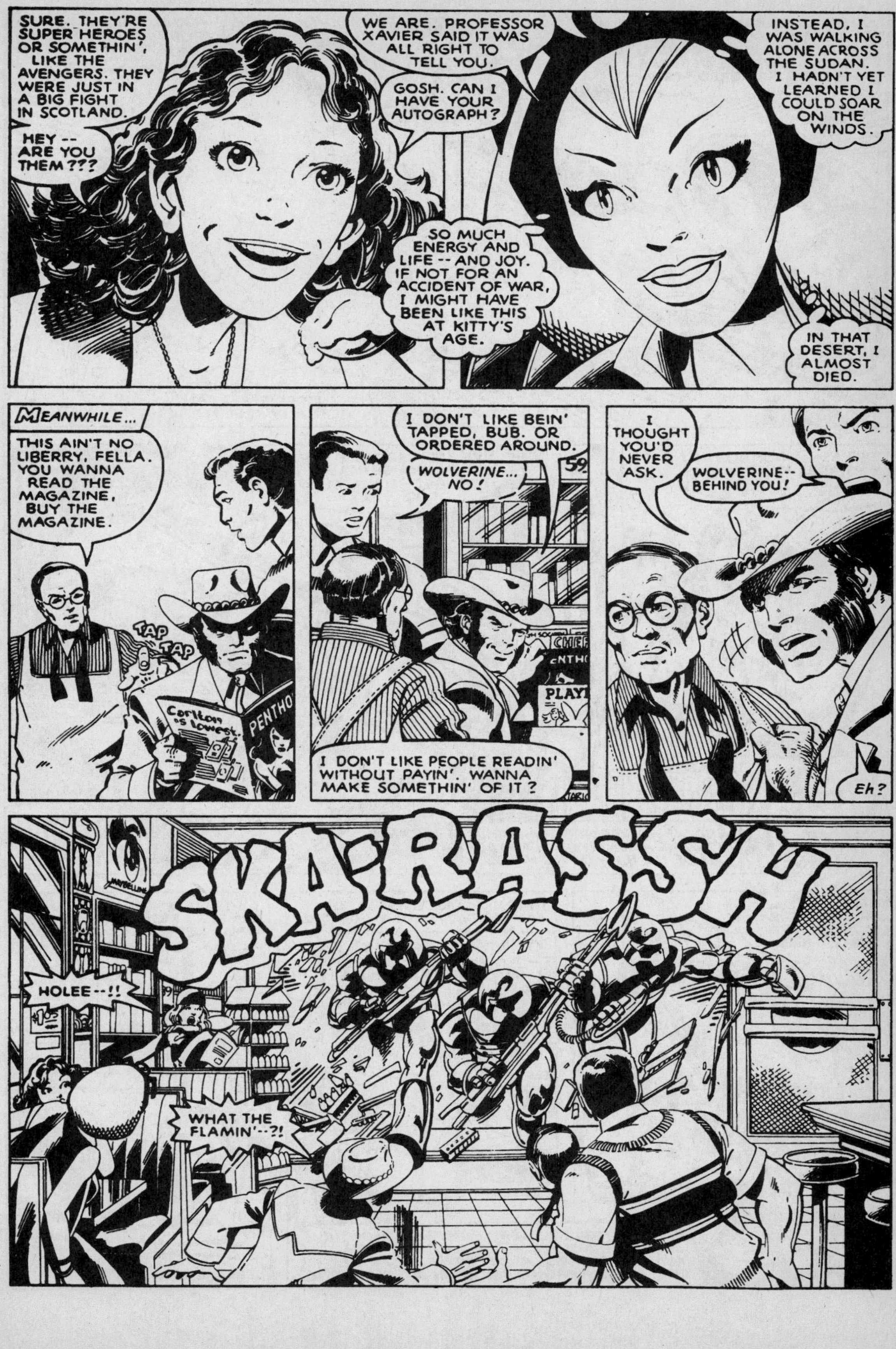

SURE. THEY'RE SUPER HEROES OR SOMETHIN', LIKE THE AVENGERS. THEY WERE JUST IN A BIG FIGHT IN SCOTLAND.
HEY -- ARE YOU THEM???
WE ARE. PROFESSOR XAVIER SAID IT WAS ALL RIGHT TO TELL YOU.
GOSH. CAN I HAVE YOUR AUTOGRAPH?
SO MUCH ENERGY AND LIFE -- AND JOY. IF NOT FOR AN ACCIDENT OF WAR, I MIGHT HAVE BEEN LIKE THIS AT KITTY'S AGE.
INSTEAD, I WAS WALKING ALONE ACROSS THE SUDAN. I HADN'T YET LEARNED I COULD SOAR ON THE WINDS.
IN THAT DESERT, I ALMOST DIED.
MEANWHILE...
THIS AIN'T NO LIBERRY, FELLA. YOU WANNA READ THE MAGAZINE, BUY THE MAGAZINE.
TAP TAP
I DON'T LIKE BEIN' TAPPED, BUB. OR ORDERED AROUND.
WOLVERINE... NO!
I DON'T LIKE PEOPLE READIN' WITHOUT PAYIN'. WANNA MAKE SOMETHIN' OF IT?
I THOUGHT YOU'D NEVER ASK.
WOLVERINE-- BEHIND YOU!
Eh?
SKA-RASSH
HOLEE--!!
WHAT THE FLAMIN'--?!

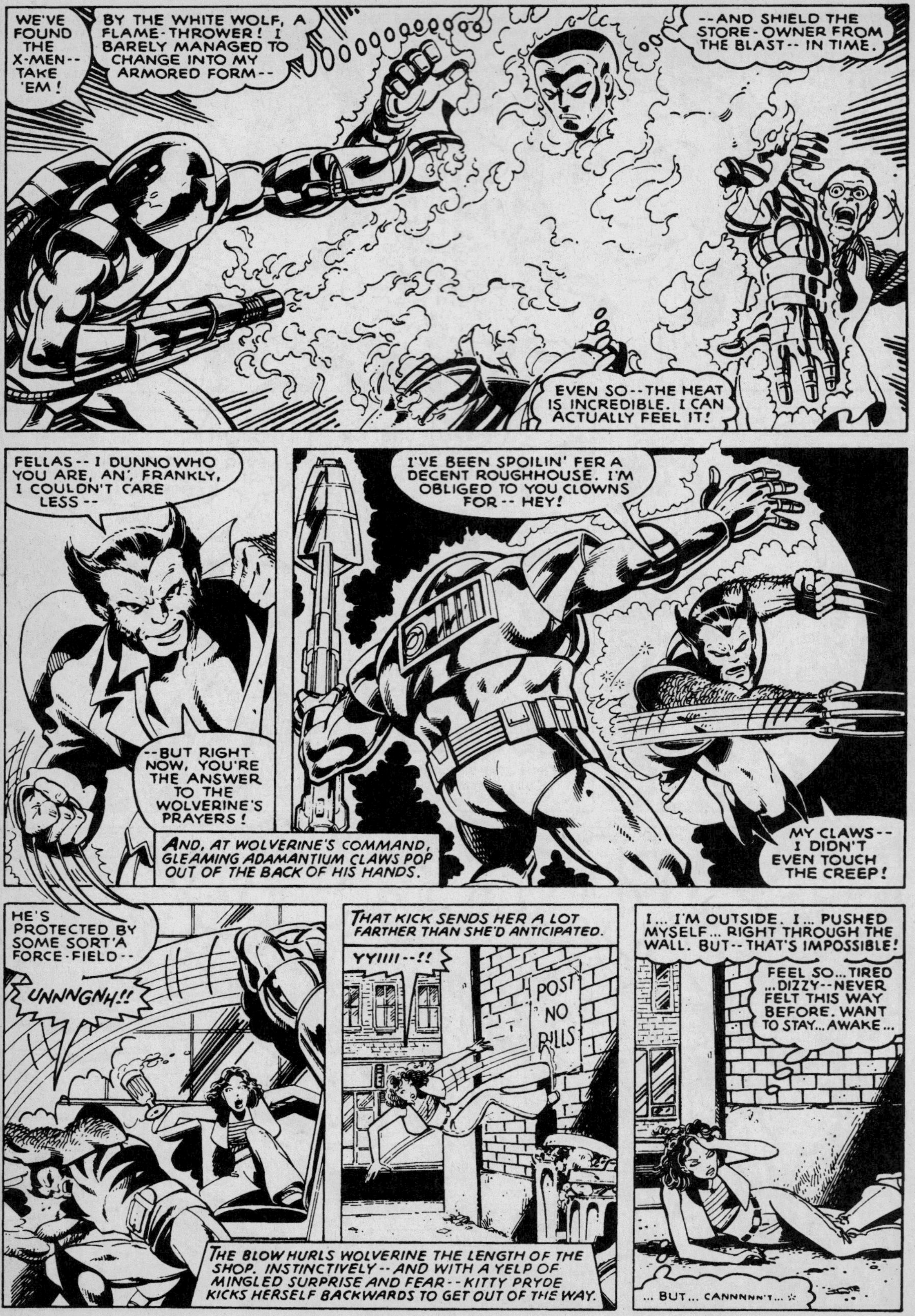

WE'VE FOUND THE X-MEN-- TAKE 'EM!
BY THE WHITE WOLF, A FLAME-THROWER! I BARELY MANAGED TO CHANGE INTO MY ARMORED FORM--
--AND SHIELD THE STORE-OWNER FROM THE BLAST-- IN TIME.
EVEN SO--THE HEAT IS INCREDIBLE. I CAN ACTUALLY FEEL IT!
FELLAS-- I DUNNO WHO YOU ARE, AN', FRANKLY, I COULDN'T CARE LESS--
--BUT RIGHT NOW, YOU'RE THE ANSWER TO THE WOLVERINE'S PRAYERS!
AND, AT WOLVERINE'S COMMAND, GLEAMING ADAMANTIUM CLAWS POP OUT OF THE BACK OF HIS HANDS.
I'VE BEEN SPOILIN' FER A DECENT ROUGHHOUSE. I'M OBLIGED TO YOU CLOWNS FOR-- HEY!
MY CLAWS-- I DIDN'T EVEN TOUCH THE CREEP!
HE'S PROTECTED BY SOME SORT'A FORCE-FIELD--
UNNNGNH!!
THE BLOW HURLS WOLVERINE THE LENGTH OF THE SHOP. INSTINCTIVELY-- AND WITH A YELP OF MINGLED SURPRISE AND FEAR--KITTY PRYDE KICKS HERSELF BACKWARDS TO GET OUT OF THE WAY.
THAT KICK SENDS HER A LOT FARTHER THAN SHE'D ANTICIPATED.
YYIIII--!!
POST NO BILLS
I... I'M OUTSIDE. I... PUSHED MYSELF... RIGHT THROUGH THE WALL. BUT--THAT'S IMPOSSIBLE!
FEEL SO... TIRED ...DIZZY--NEVER FELT THIS WAY BEFORE. WANT TO STAY... AWAKE...
... BUT... CANNNNN'T...

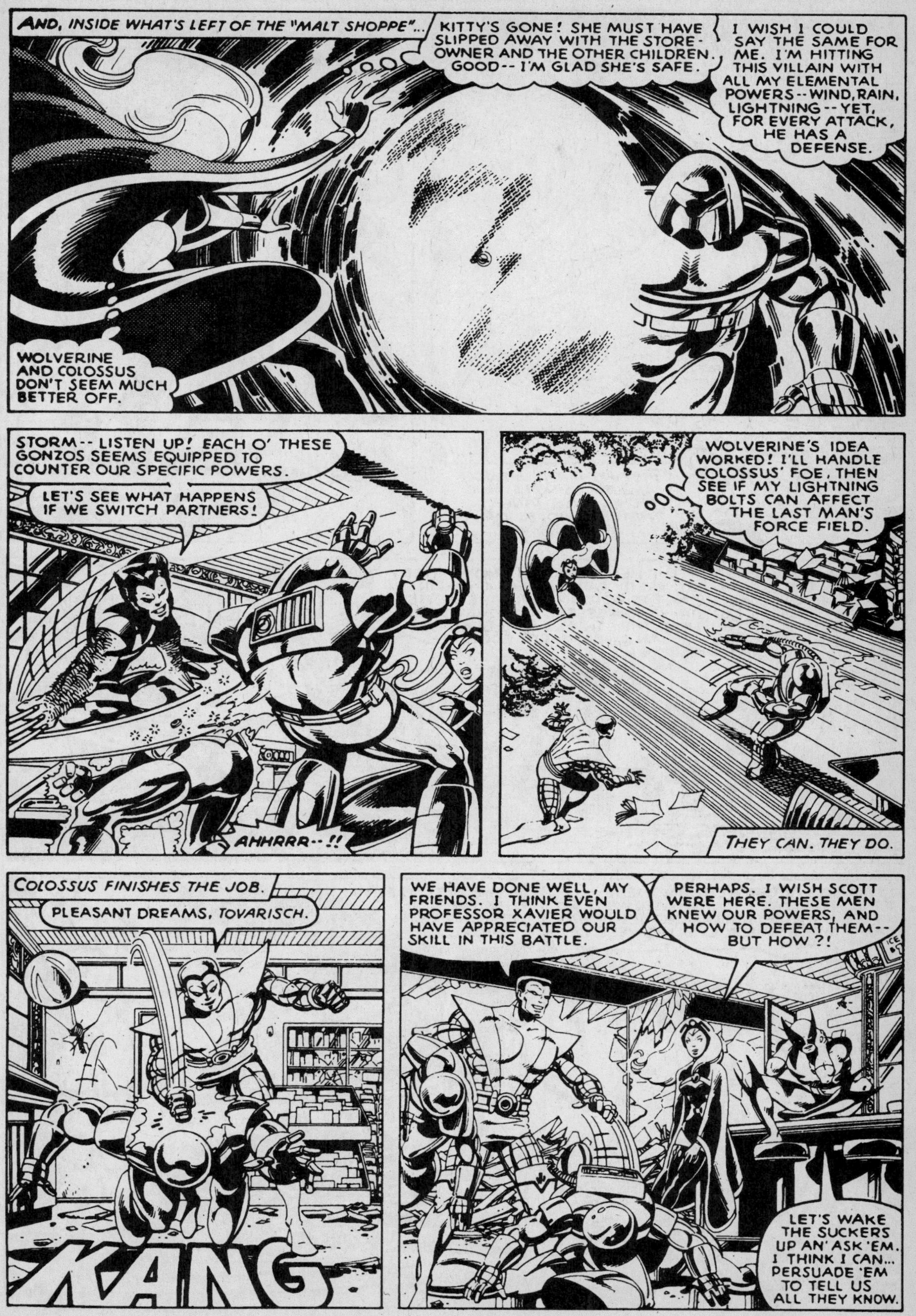
AND, INSIDE WHAT'S LEFT OF THE "MALT SHOPPE"...
KITTY'S GONE! SHE MUST HAVE SLIPPED AWAY WITH THE STORE-OWNER AND THE OTHER CHILDREN. GOOD-- I'M GLAD SHE'S SAFE.
I WISH I COULD SAY THE SAME FOR ME. I'M HITTING THIS VILLAIN WITH ALL MY ELEMENTAL POWERS--WIND, RAIN, LIGHTNING--YET, FOR EVERY ATTACK, HE HAS A DEFENSE.
WOLVERINE AND COLOSSUS DON'T SEEM MUCH BETTER OFF.
STORM-- LISTEN UP! EACH O' THESE GONZOS SEEMS EQUIPPED TO COUNTER OUR SPECIFIC POWERS.
LET'S SEE WHAT HAPPENS IF WE SWITCH PARTNERS!
AHHRRR--!!
WOLVERINE'S IDEA WORKED! I'LL HANDLE COLOSSUS' FOE, THEN SEE IF MY LIGHTNING BOLTS CAN AFFECT THE LAST MAN'S FORCE FIELD.
THEY CAN. THEY DO.
COLOSSUS FINISHES THE JOB.
PLEASANT DREAMS, TOVARISCH.
KANG
WE HAVE DONE WELL, MY FRIENDS. I THINK EVEN PROFESSOR XAVIER WOULD HAVE APPRECIATED OUR SKILL IN THIS BATTLE.
PERHAPS. I WISH SCOTT WERE HERE. THESE MEN KNEW OUR POWERS, AND HOW TO DEFEAT THEM-- BUT HOW?!
LET'S WAKE THE SUCKERS UP AN' ASK 'EM. I THINK I CAN... PERSUADE 'EM TO TELL US ALL THEY KNOW.

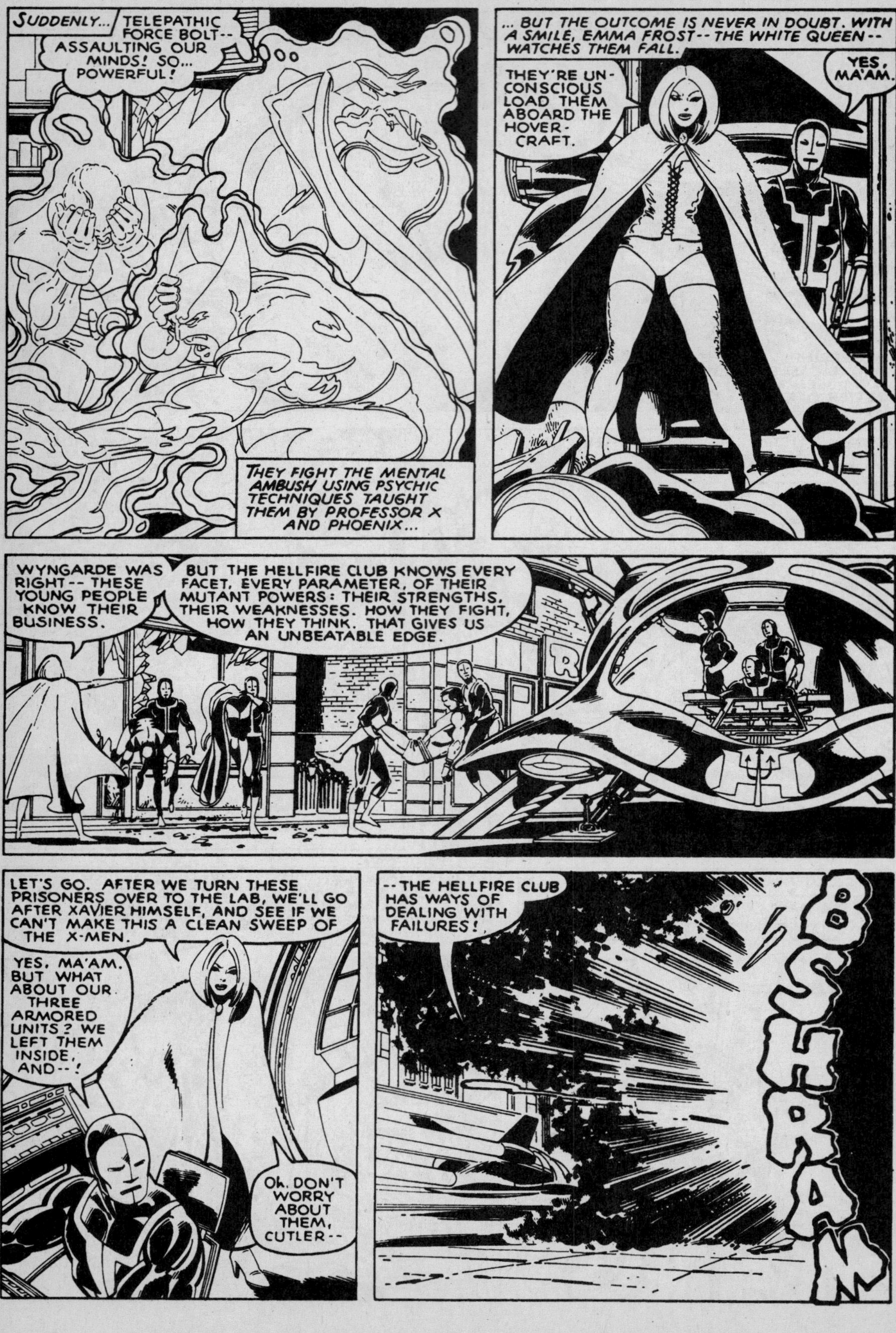
SUDDENLY...
TELEPATHIC FORCE BOLT-- ASSAULTING OUR MINDS! SO... POWERFUL!
THEY FIGHT THE MENTAL AMBUSH USING PSYCHIC TECHNIQUES TAUGHT THEM BY PROFESSOR X AND PHOENIX...
... BUT THE OUTCOME IS NEVER IN DOUBT. WITH A SMILE, EMMA FROST-- THE WHITE QUEEN-- WATCHES THEM FALL.
THEY'RE UNCONSCIOUS LOAD THEM ABOARD THE HOVER-CRAFT.
YES, MA'AM.
WYNGARDE WAS RIGHT-- THESE YOUNG PEOPLE KNOW THEIR BUSINESS.
BUT THE HELLFIRE CLUB KNOWS EVERY FACET, EVERY PARAMETER, OF THEIR MUTANT POWERS: THEIR STRENGTHS, THEIR WEAKNESSES. HOW THEY FIGHT, HOW THEY THINK. THAT GIVES US AN UNBEATABLE EDGE.
LET'S GO. AFTER WE TURN THESE PRISONERS OVER TO THE LAB, WE'LL GO AFTER XAVIER HIMSELF, AND SEE IF WE CAN'T MAKE THIS A CLEAN SWEEP OF THE X-MEN.
YES, MA'AM. BUT WHAT ABOUT OUR THREE ARMORED UNITS? WE LEFT THEM INSIDE, AND--!
Oh, DON'T WORRY ABOUT THEM, CUTLER--
--THE HELLFIRE CLUB HAS WAYS OF DEALING WITH FAILURES!
BSHRAM

THOSE MEN HAD POWER AND TRAINING SUFFICIENT TO DEFEAT THE X-MEN WITHOUT MY HELP. THEY BOTCHED THEIR JOB, AND NOW THE EXPLOSIVE CHARGES IN THEIR ARMOR HAVE REWARDED THEM FOR THEIR... "HANDY WORK".

DON'T ACT SO SHOCKED, CUTLER! WE PAY GOOD WAGES, WE EXPECT OUR MONEY'S WORTH.

STAYING ON BACK ROADS TO AVOID DETECTION, THE HOVERCRAFT MAKES ITS WAY SWIFTLY DOWN THE LAKE SHORE TOWARDS ITS BASE -- A MASSIVE INDUSTRIAL PARK ON THE OUTSKIRTS OF CHICAGO.

AND WITHIN THE CRAFT...

STRIP THEM -- SEARCH THEIR UNIFORMS AND THEIR PERSONS. CAREFULLY. REMOVE ANYTHING THAT MIGHT BE USED AS A WEAPON OR SIGNALLING DEVICE.

TAKE SPECIAL CARE WITH STORM. WE KNOW ABOUT THE LOCK-PICKS IN HER HEAD-DRESS -- MAKE SURE SHE HASN'T ANY OTHER SURPRISES. I'LL KEEP THEM TELEPATHICALLY SEDATED UNTIL WE REACH THE LAB.

WHAT ABOUT THE GIRL -- THE PRYDE KID?

SHE ESCAPED IN THE CONFUSION. THE X-MEN WERE ALWAYS OUR PRIMARY TARGET. NOW THAT WE HAVE THEM, SHE'LL KEEP.

WHEN WE WANT HER, WE KNOW WHERE TO FIND HER.

ACTUALLY, TO FIND KITTY, ALL THE WHITE QUEEN NEEDS TO DO IS TURN AROUND.

I DID IT! I CONCENTRATED-- AN' I'M WALKIN' RIGHT THROUGH THIS WALL FROM THE REAR COMPARTMENT!

I FEEL TINGLY ALL OVER -- BUT NOT AS TIRED AS THE LAST TIME. AN' MY HEADACHES ARE ALL GONE!

OH, NO! THAT CREEPY MISS FROST AND HER GOON SQUAD ARE HOLDING THE X-MEN PRISONERS. WHY... WHY DID I DECIDE TO SNOOP AROUND IN HERE?!

I... I GOTTA HELP 'EM, BUT HOW??? THESE GUYS HAVE GUNS-- AND SUPER-POWERS.

AN' I'M... ALL ALONE.

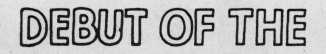

DEBUT OF THE Dazzler!

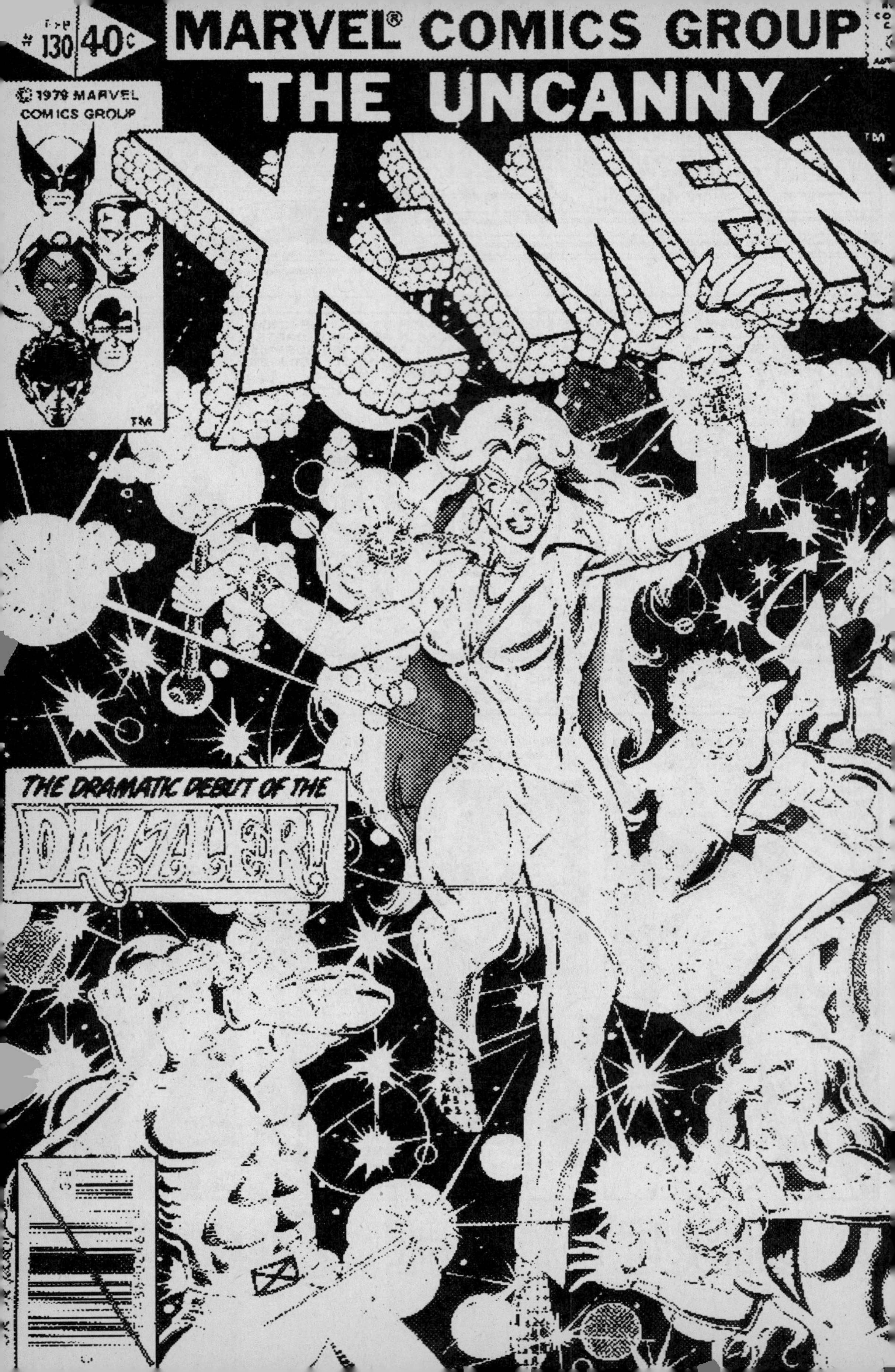

MARVEL® COMICS GROUP
130
40¢
THE UNCANNY
X-MEN
© 1979 MARVEL COMICS GROUP
THE DRAMATIC DEBUT OF THE
DAZZLER!

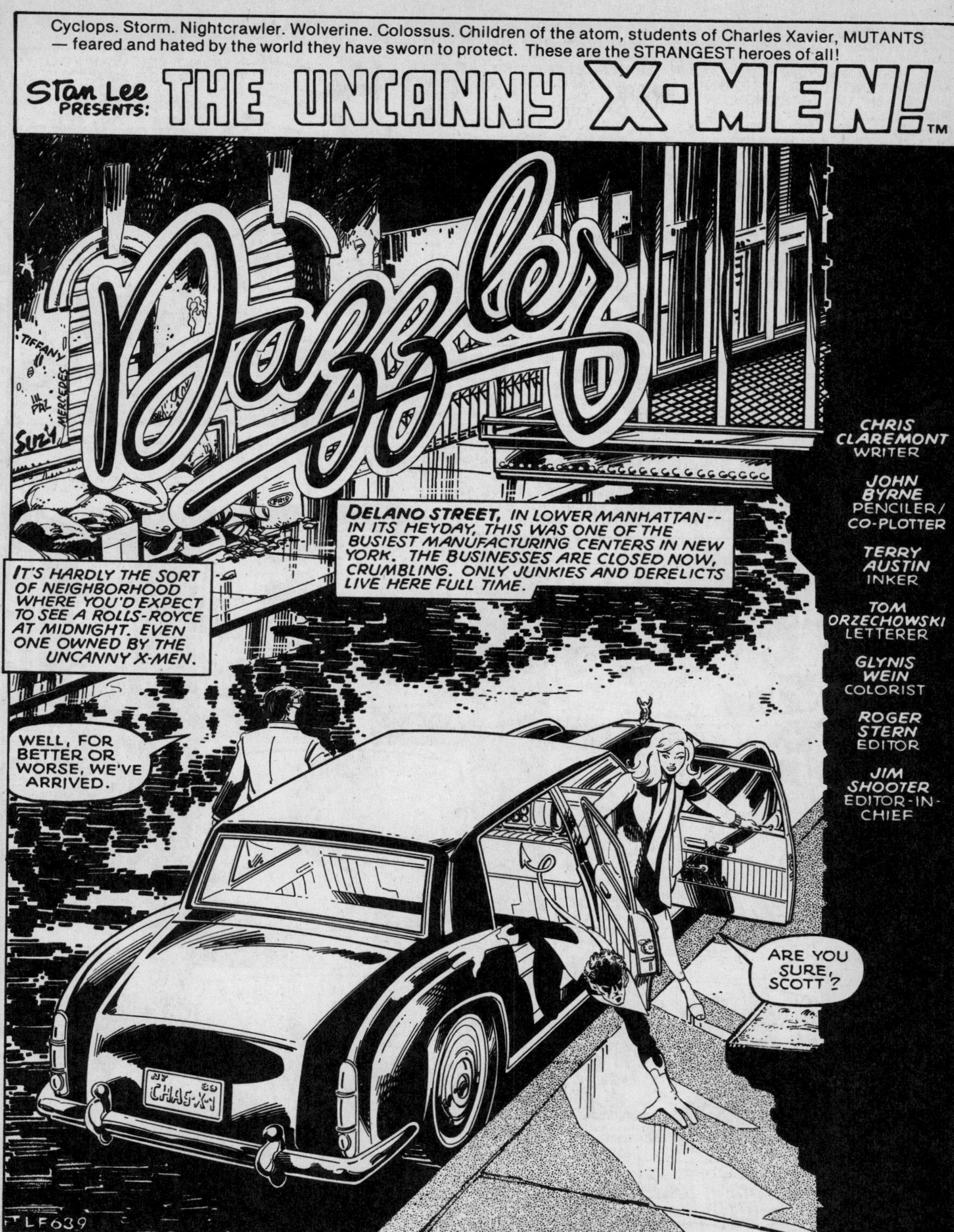
Cyclops. Storm. Nightcrawler. Wolverine. Colossus. Children of the atom, students of Charles Xavier, MUTANTS — feared and hated by the world they have sworn to protect. These are the STRANGEST heroes of all!
STAN LEE PRESENTS: THE UNCANNY X-MEN!™
Dazzler
DELANO STREET, IN LOWER MANHATTAN-- IN ITS HEYDAY, THIS WAS ONE OF THE BUSIEST MANUFACTURING CENTERS IN NEW YORK. THE BUSINESSES ARE CLOSED NOW, CRUMBLING. ONLY JUNKIES AND DERELICTS LIVE HERE FULL TIME.
IT'S HARDLY THE SORT OF NEIGHBORHOOD WHERE YOU'D EXPECT TO SEE A ROLLS-ROYCE AT MIDNIGHT. EVEN ONE OWNED BY THE UNCANNY X-MEN.
WELL, FOR BETTER OR WORSE, WE'VE ARRIVED.
ARE YOU SURE, SCOTT?
CHRIS CLAREMONT WRITER
JOHN BYRNE PENCILER/ CO-PLOTTER
TERRY AUSTIN INKER
TOM ORZECHOWSKI LETTERER
GLYNIS WEIN COLORIST
ROGER STERN EDITOR
JIM SHOOTER EDITOR-IN-CHIEF
CHAS-X-1
LF639

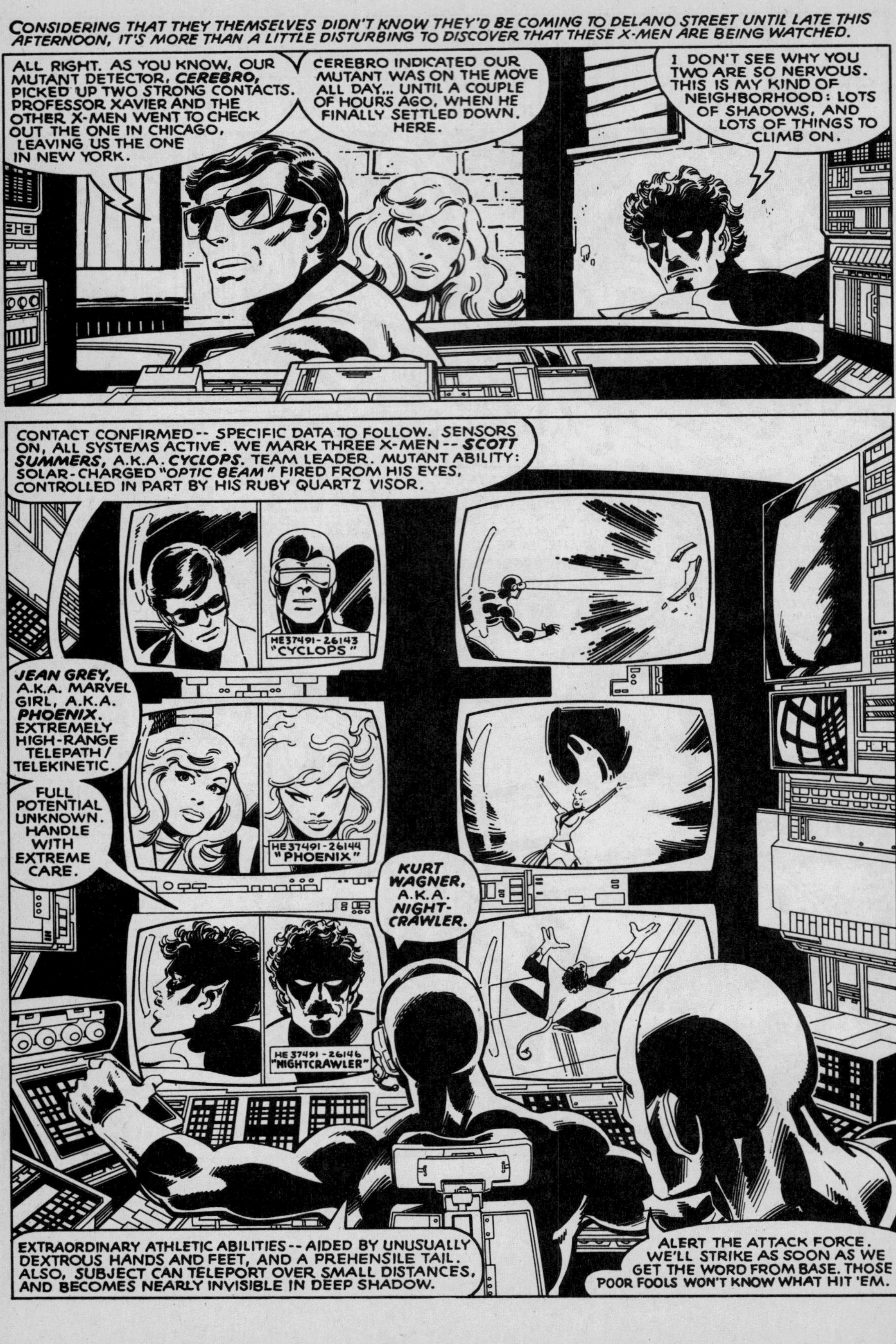
CONSIDERING THAT THEY THEMSELVES DIDN'T KNOW THEY'D BE COMING TO DELANO STREET UNTIL LATE THIS AFTERNOON, IT'S MORE THAN A LITTLE DISTURBING TO DISCOVER THAT THESE X-MEN ARE BEING WATCHED.
ALL RIGHT. AS YOU KNOW, OUR MUTANT DETECTOR, CEREBRO, PICKED UP TWO STRONG CONTACTS. PROFESSOR XAVIER AND THE OTHER X-MEN WENT TO CHECK OUT THE ONE IN CHICAGO, LEAVING US THE ONE IN NEW YORK.
CEREBRO INDICATED OUR MUTANT WAS ON THE MOVE ALL DAY... UNTIL A COUPLE OF HOURS AGO, WHEN HE FINALLY SETTLED DOWN. HERE.
I DON'T SEE WHY YOU TWO ARE SO NERVOUS. THIS IS MY KIND OF NEIGHBORHOOD: LOTS OF SHADOWS, AND LOTS OF THINGS TO CLIMB ON.
CONTACT CONFIRMED-- SPECIFIC DATA TO FOLLOW. SENSORS ON, ALL SYSTEMS ACTIVE. WE MARK THREE X-MEN-- SCOTT SUMMERS, A.K.A. CYCLOPS. TEAM LEADER. MUTANT ABILITY: SOLAR-CHARGED "OPTIC BEAM" FIRED FROM HIS EYES, CONTROLLED IN PART BY HIS RUBY QUARTZ VISOR.
HE37491-26143 "CYCLOPS"
JEAN GREY, A.K.A. MARVEL GIRL, A.K.A. PHOENIX. EXTREMELY HIGH-RANGE TELEPATH/TELEKINETIC.
FULL POTENTIAL UNKNOWN. HANDLE WITH EXTREME CARE.
HE37491-26144 "PHOENIX"
KURT WAGNER, A.K.A. NIGHT-CRAWLER.
HE37491-26146 "NIGHTCRAWLER"
EXTRAORDINARY ATHLETIC ABILITIES-- AIDED BY UNUSUALLY DEXTROUS HANDS AND FEET, AND A PREHENSILE TAIL. ALSO, SUBJECT CAN TELEPORT OVER SMALL DISTANCES, AND BECOMES NEARLY INVISIBLE IN DEEP SHADOW.
ALERT THE ATTACK FORCE. WE'LL STRIKE AS SOON AS WE GET THE WORD FROM BASE. THOSE POOR FOOLS WON'T KNOW WHAT HIT 'EM.

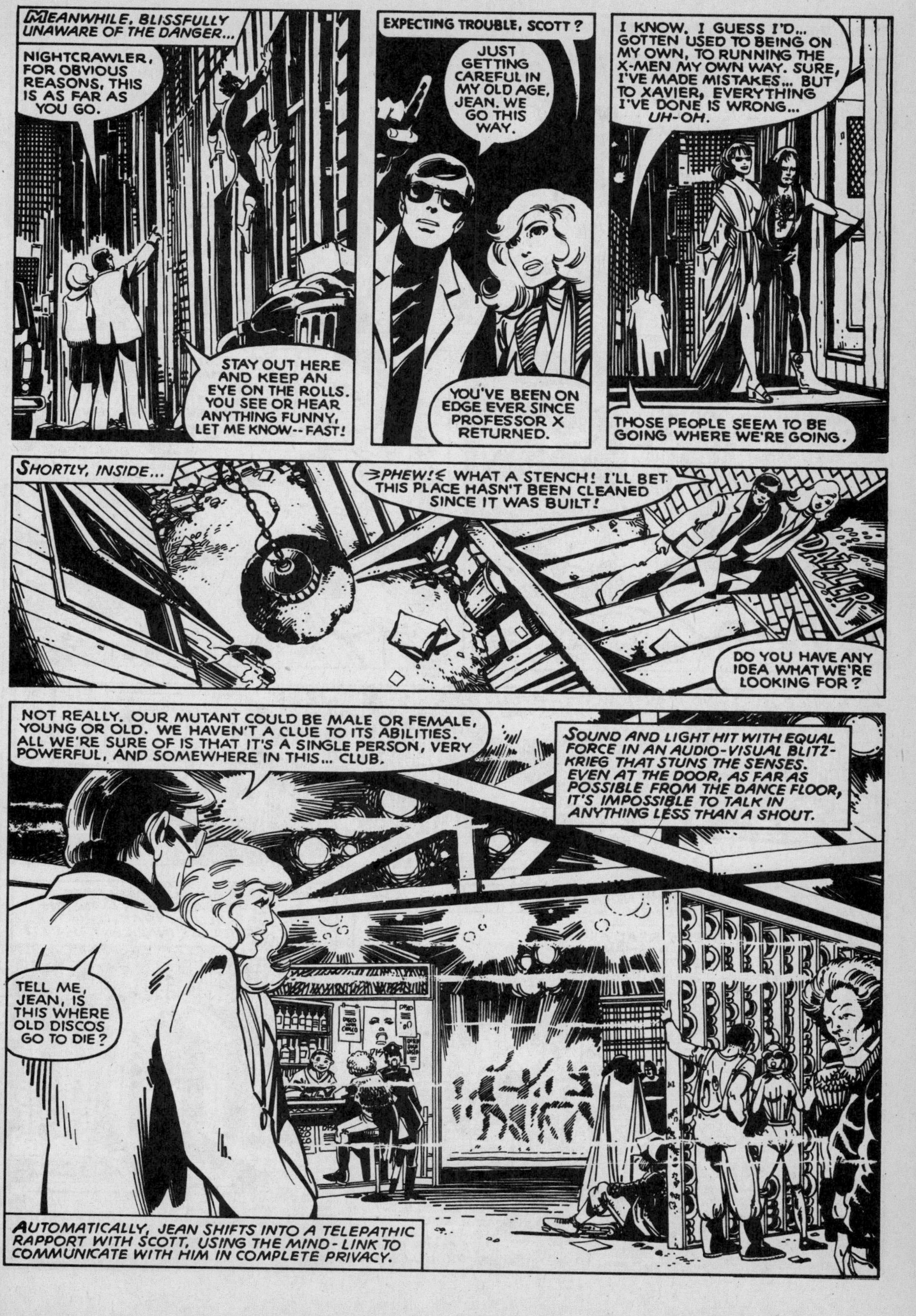
MEANWHILE, BLISSFULLY UNAWARE OF THE DANGER...
NIGHTCRAWLER, FOR OBVIOUS REASONS, THIS IS AS FAR AS YOU GO.
STAY OUT HERE AND KEEP AN EYE ON THE ROLLS. YOU SEE OR HEAR ANYTHING FUNNY, LET ME KNOW--FAST!
EXPECTING TROUBLE, SCOTT?
JUST GETTING CAREFUL IN MY OLD AGE, JEAN. WE GO THIS WAY.
YOU'VE BEEN ON EDGE EVER SINCE PROFESSOR X RETURNED.
I KNOW. I GUESS I'D... GOTTEN USED TO BEING ON MY OWN, TO RUNNING THE X-MEN MY OWN WAY. SURE, I'VE MADE MISTAKES... BUT TO XAVIER, EVERYTHING I'VE DONE IS WRONG... UH-OH.
THOSE PEOPLE SEEM TO BE GOING WHERE WE'RE GOING.
SHORTLY, INSIDE...
≯PHEW!≮ WHAT A STENCH! I'LL BET THIS PLACE HASN'T BEEN CLEANED SINCE IT WAS BUILT!
DAZZLER
DO YOU HAVE ANY IDEA WHAT WE'RE LOOKING FOR?
NOT REALLY. OUR MUTANT COULD BE MALE OR FEMALE, YOUNG OR OLD. WE HAVEN'T A CLUE TO ITS ABILITIES. ALL WE'RE SURE OF IS THAT IT'S A SINGLE PERSON, VERY POWERFUL, AND SOMEWHERE IN THIS... CLUB.
SOUND AND LIGHT HIT WITH EQUAL FORCE IN AN AUDIO-VISUAL BLITZ-KRIEG THAT STUNS THE SENSES. EVEN AT THE DOOR, AS FAR AS POSSIBLE FROM THE DANCE FLOOR, IT'S IMPOSSIBLE TO TALK IN ANYTHING LESS THAN A SHOUT.
TELL ME, JEAN, IS THIS WHERE OLD DISCOS GO TO DIE?
AUTOMATICALLY, JEAN SHIFTS INTO A TELEPATHIC RAPPORT WITH SCOTT, USING THE MIND-LINK TO COMMUNICATE WITH HIM IN COMPLETE PRIVACY.

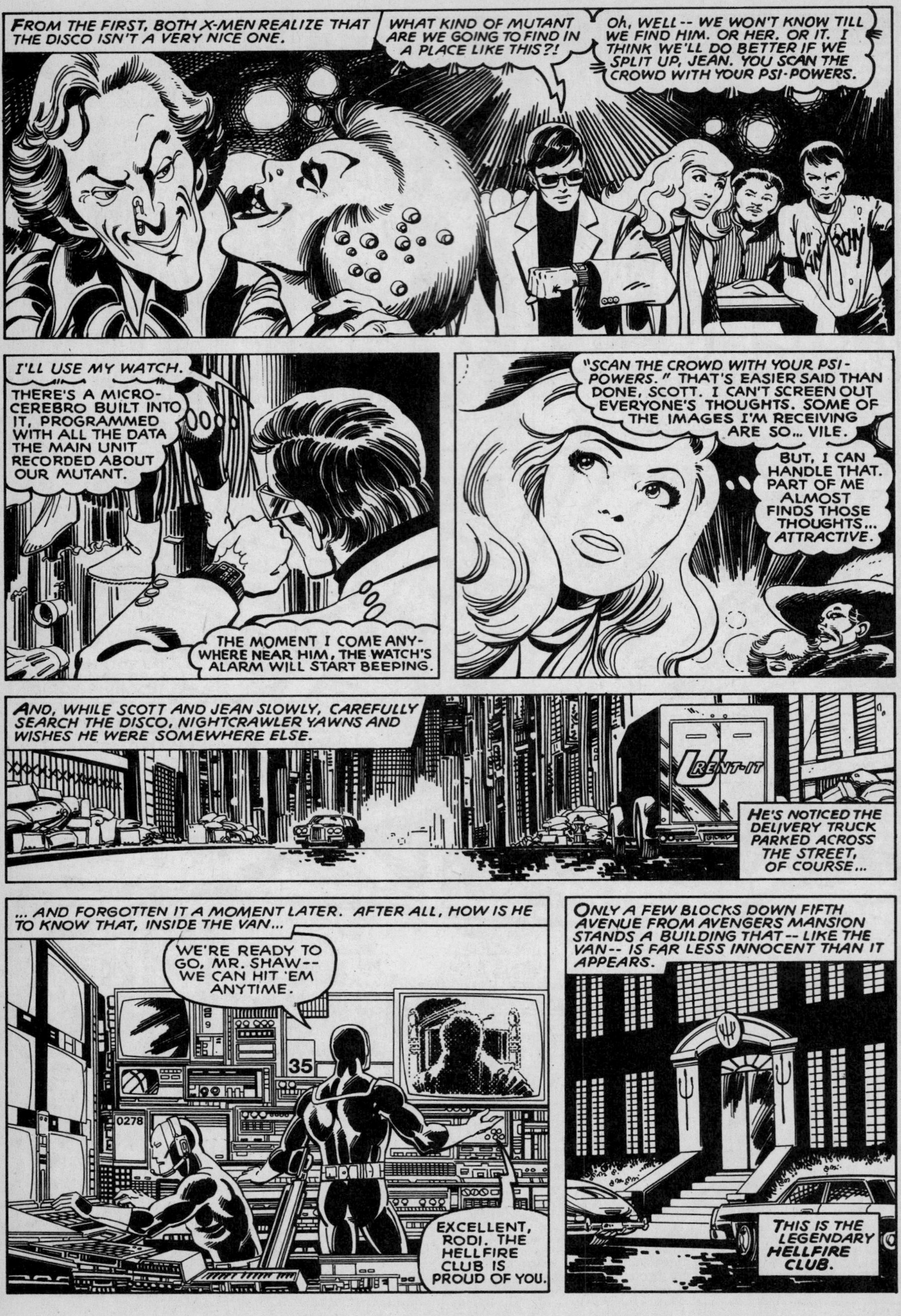

FROM THE FIRST, BOTH X-MEN REALIZE THAT THE DISCO ISN'T A VERY NICE ONE.
WHAT KIND OF MUTANT ARE WE GOING TO FIND IN A PLACE LIKE THIS?!
Oh, WELL -- WE WON'T KNOW TILL WE FIND HIM. OR HER. OR IT. I THINK WE'LL DO BETTER IF WE SPLIT UP, JEAN. YOU SCAN THE CROWD WITH YOUR PSI-POWERS.
I'LL USE MY WATCH.
THERE'S A MICRO-CEREBRO BUILT INTO IT, PROGRAMMED WITH ALL THE DATA THE MAIN UNIT RECORDED ABOUT OUR MUTANT.
THE MOMENT I COME ANYWHERE NEAR HIM, THE WATCH'S ALARM WILL START BEEPING.
"SCAN THE CROWD WITH YOUR PSI-POWERS." THAT'S EASIER SAID THAN DONE, SCOTT. I CAN'T SCREEN OUT EVERYONE'S THOUGHTS. SOME OF THE IMAGES I'M RECEIVING ARE SO... VILE.
BUT, I CAN HANDLE THAT. PART OF ME ALMOST FINDS THOSE THOUGHTS... ATTRACTIVE.
AND, WHILE SCOTT AND JEAN SLOWLY, CAREFULLY SEARCH THE DISCO, NIGHTCRAWLER YAWNS AND WISHES HE WERE SOMEWHERE ELSE.
RENT-IT
HE'S NOTICED THE DELIVERY TRUCK PARKED ACROSS THE STREET, OF COURSE...
... AND FORGOTTEN IT A MOMENT LATER. AFTER ALL, HOW IS HE TO KNOW THAT, INSIDE THE VAN...
WE'RE READY TO GO, MR. SHAW-- WE CAN HIT 'EM ANYTIME.
35
0278
EXCELLENT, RODI. THE HELLFIRE CLUB IS PROUD OF YOU.
ONLY A FEW BLOCKS DOWN FIFTH AVENUE FROM AVENGERS MANSION STANDS A BUILDING THAT -- LIKE THE VAN -- IS FAR LESS INNOCENT THAN IT APPEARS.
THIS IS THE LEGENDARY HELLFIRE CLUB.

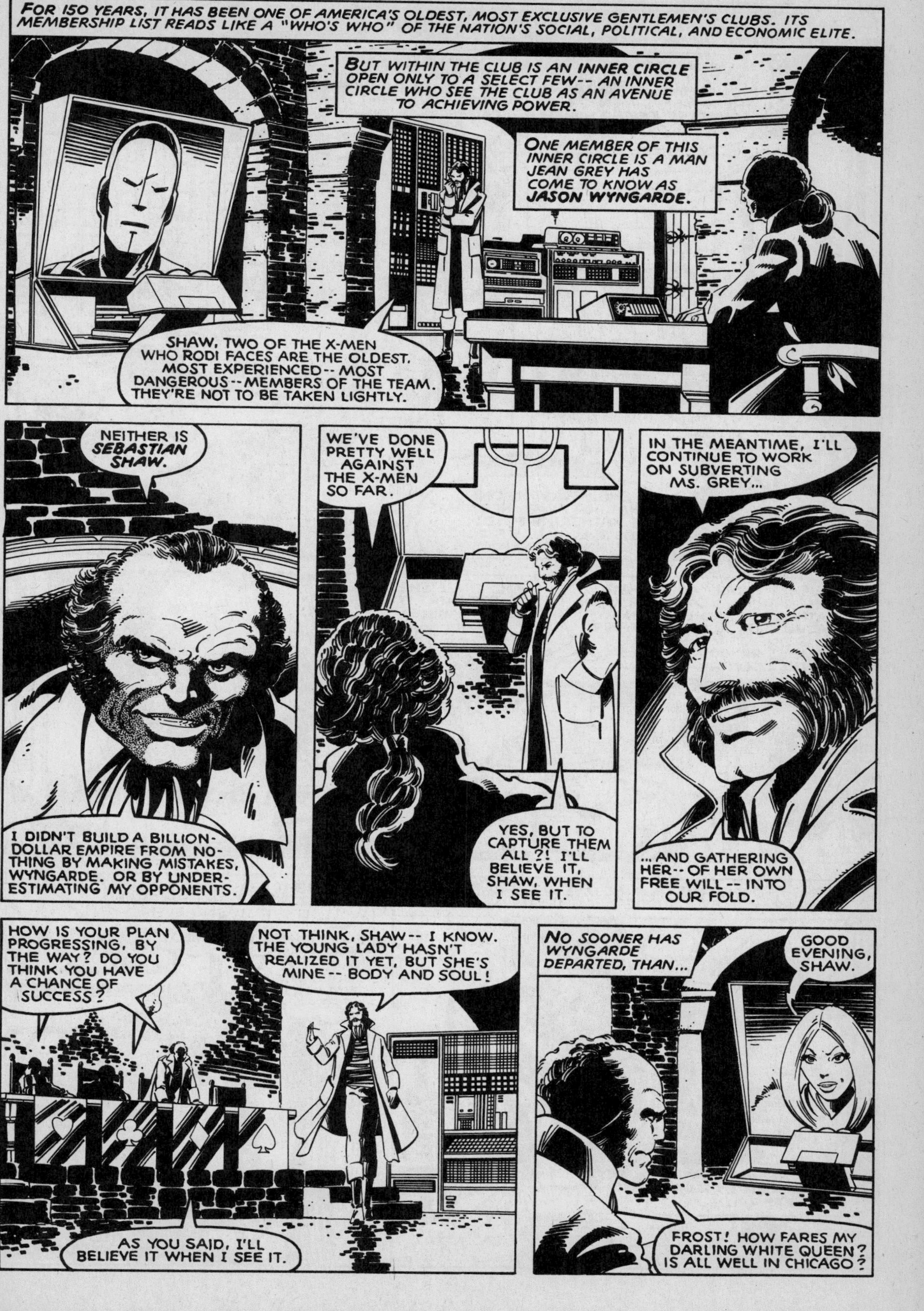
FOR 150 YEARS, IT HAS BEEN ONE OF AMERICA'S OLDEST, MOST EXCLUSIVE GENTLEMEN'S CLUBS. ITS MEMBERSHIP LIST READS LIKE A "WHO'S WHO" OF THE NATION'S SOCIAL, POLITICAL, AND ECONOMIC ELITE.
BUT WITHIN THE CLUB IS AN INNER CIRCLE OPEN ONLY TO A SELECT FEW-- AN INNER CIRCLE WHO SEE THE CLUB AS AN AVENUE TO ACHIEVING POWER.
ONE MEMBER OF THIS INNER CIRCLE IS A MAN JEAN GREY HAS COME TO KNOW AS JASON WYNGARDE.
SHAW, TWO OF THE X-MEN WHO RODI FACES ARE THE OLDEST, MOST EXPERIENCED-- MOST DANGEROUS--MEMBERS OF THE TEAM. THEY'RE NOT TO BE TAKEN LIGHTLY.
NEITHER IS SEBASTIAN SHAW.
I DIDN'T BUILD A BILLION-DOLLAR EMPIRE FROM NOTHING BY MAKING MISTAKES, WYNGARDE. OR BY UNDERESTIMATING MY OPPONENTS.
WE'VE DONE PRETTY WELL AGAINST THE X-MEN SO FAR.
YES, BUT TO CAPTURE THEM ALL ?! I'LL BELIEVE IT, SHAW, WHEN I SEE IT.
IN THE MEANTIME, I'LL CONTINUE TO WORK ON SUBVERTING MS. GREY...
...AND GATHERING HER-- OF HER OWN FREE WILL-- INTO OUR FOLD.
HOW IS YOUR PLAN PROGRESSING, BY THE WAY? DO YOU THINK YOU HAVE A CHANCE OF SUCCESS?
NOT THINK, SHAW-- I KNOW. THE YOUNG LADY HASN'T REALIZED IT YET, BUT SHE'S MINE-- BODY AND SOUL!
AS YOU SAID, I'LL BELIEVE IT WHEN I SEE IT.
NO SOONER HAS WYNGARDE DEPARTED, THAN...
GOOD EVENING, SHAW.
FROST! HOW FARES MY DARLING WHITE QUEEN? IS ALL WELL IN CHICAGO?

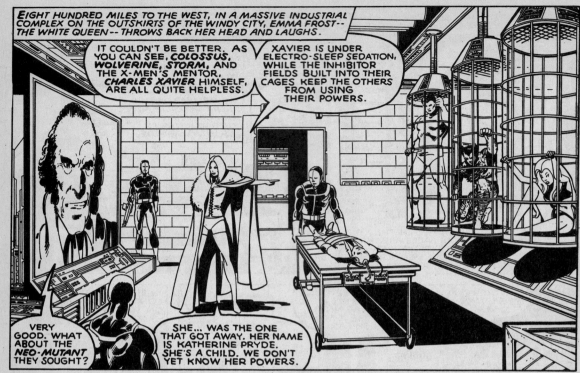

EIGHT HUNDRED MILES TO THE WEST, IN A MASSIVE INDUSTRIAL COMPLEX ON THE OUTSKIRTS OF THE WINDY CITY, EMMA FROST-- THE WHITE QUEEN -- THROWS BACK HER HEAD AND LAUGHS.

IT COULDN'T BE BETTER. AS YOU CAN SEE, *COLOSSUS*, *WOLVERINE*, *STORM*, AND THE X-MEN'S MENTOR, *CHARLES XAVIER* HIMSELF, ARE ALL QUITE HELPLESS.

XAVIER IS UNDER ELECTRO-SLEEP SEDATION, WHILE THE INHIBITOR FIELDS BUILT INTO THEIR CAGES KEEP THE OTHERS FROM USING THEIR POWERS.

VERY GOOD. WHAT ABOUT THE *NEO-MUTANT* THEY SOUGHT?

SHE... WAS THE ONE THAT GOT AWAY. HER NAME IS KATHERINE PRYDE. SHE'S A CHILD. WE DON'T YET KNOW HER POWERS.

WE NEEDN'T WORRY ABOUT HER, THOUGH. I THINK I CAN... PERSUADE HER FATHER TO ENROLL HER IN MY MASSACHUSETTS ACADEMY. AFTER ALL, IT IS ONE OF THE MOST PRESTIGIOUS PRIVATE SCHOOLS IN THE COUNTRY.

AND ONCE SHE'S THERE, SHE'S OURS FOR THE TAKING!

AS THE TWO VILLAINS TALK, NO ONE IN THE VAST HOLDING CHAMBER NOTICES A SUDDEN, SLIGHT STIR IN THE AIR...

...THAT HERALDS THE *UNORTHODOX* ENTRANCE OF KITTY PRYDE.

I DID IT AGAIN!

I THOUGHT REAL HARD-- AN' I WALKED RIGHT THROUGH THAT WALL, LIKE IT WASN'T EVEN THERE! IT GETS EASIER EACH TIME I DO IT, TOO!

OKAY, I'VE SNUCK MY WAY INTO HERE --

-- WHAT THE HECK DO I DO *NOW???*

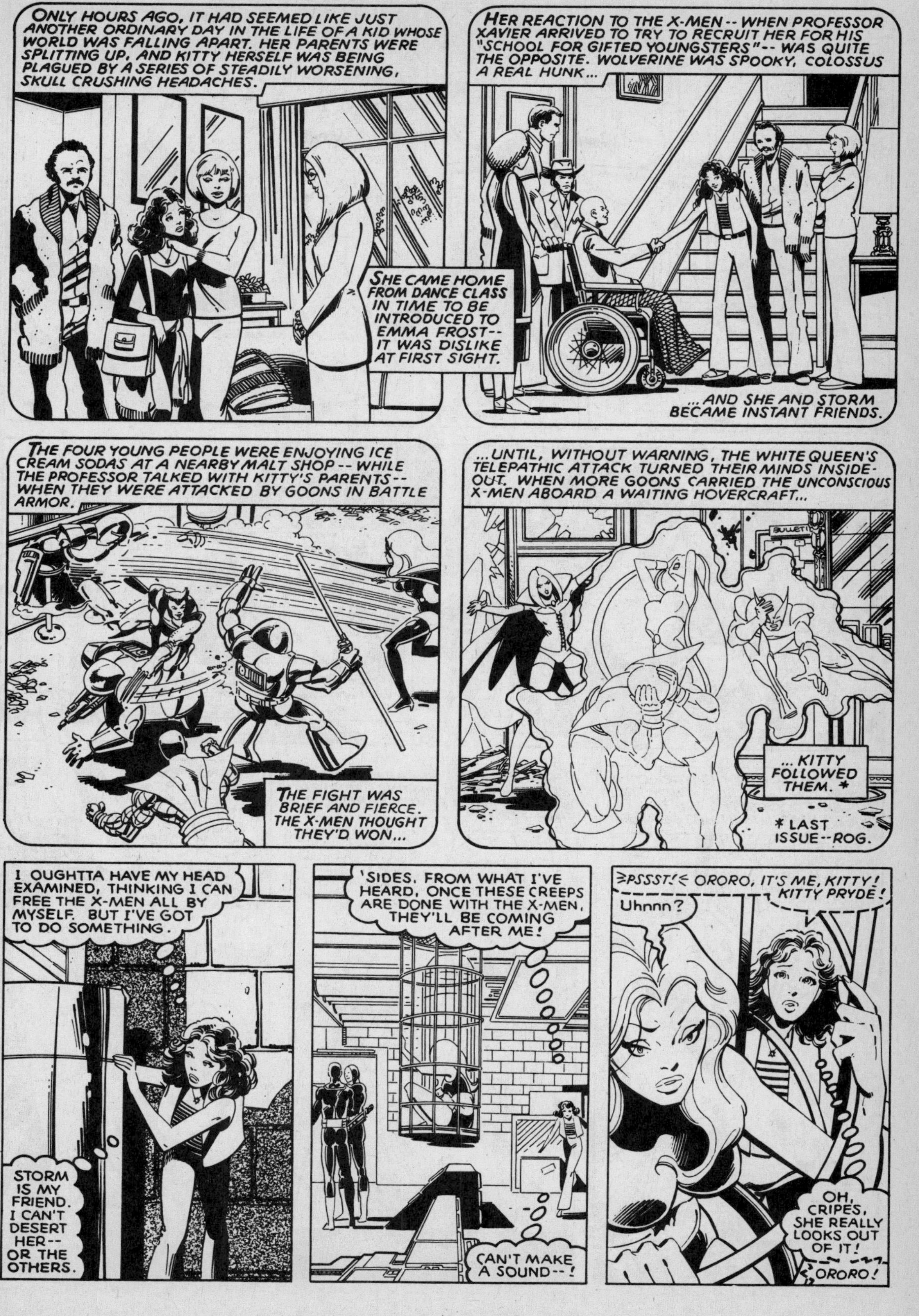
ONLY HOURS AGO, IT HAD SEEMED LIKE JUST ANOTHER ORDINARY DAY IN THE LIFE OF A KID WHOSE WORLD WAS FALLING APART. HER PARENTS WERE SPLITTING UP, AND KITTY HERSELF WAS BEING PLAGUED BY A SERIES OF STEADILY WORSENING, SKULL CRUSHING HEADACHES.
SHE CAME HOME FROM DANCE CLASS IN TIME TO BE INTRODUCED TO EMMA FROST-- IT WAS DISLIKE AT FIRST SIGHT.
HER REACTION TO THE X-MEN -- WHEN PROFESSOR XAVIER ARRIVED TO TRY TO RECRUIT HER FOR HIS "SCHOOL FOR GIFTED YOUNGSTERS" -- WAS QUITE THE OPPOSITE. WOLVERINE WAS SPOOKY, COLOSSUS A REAL HUNK...
...AND SHE AND STORM BECAME INSTANT FRIENDS.
THE FOUR YOUNG PEOPLE WERE ENJOYING ICE CREAM SODAS AT A NEARBY MALT SHOP -- WHILE THE PROFESSOR TALKED WITH KITTY'S PARENTS -- WHEN THEY WERE ATTACKED BY GOONS IN BATTLE ARMOR.
THE FIGHT WAS BRIEF AND FIERCE. THE X-MEN THOUGHT THEY'D WON...
...UNTIL, WITHOUT WARNING, THE WHITE QUEEN'S TELEPATHIC ATTACK TURNED THEIR MINDS INSIDE-OUT. WHEN MORE GOONS CARRIED THE UNCONSCIOUS X-MEN ABOARD A WAITING HOVERCRAFT...
... KITTY FOLLOWED THEM. *
* LAST ISSUE--ROG.
I OUGHTTA HAVE MY HEAD EXAMINED, THINKING I CAN FREE THE X-MEN ALL BY MYSELF. BUT I'VE GOT TO DO SOMETHING.
STORM IS MY FRIEND. I CAN'T DESERT HER-- OR THE OTHERS.
'SIDES, FROM WHAT I'VE HEARD, ONCE THESE CREEPS ARE DONE WITH THE X-MEN, THEY'LL BE COMING AFTER ME!
CAN'T MAKE A SOUND--!
PSSST! ORORO, IT'S ME, KITTY! KITTY PRYDE!
Uhnnn?
OH, CRIPES, SHE REALLY LOOKS OUT OF IT!
ORORO!

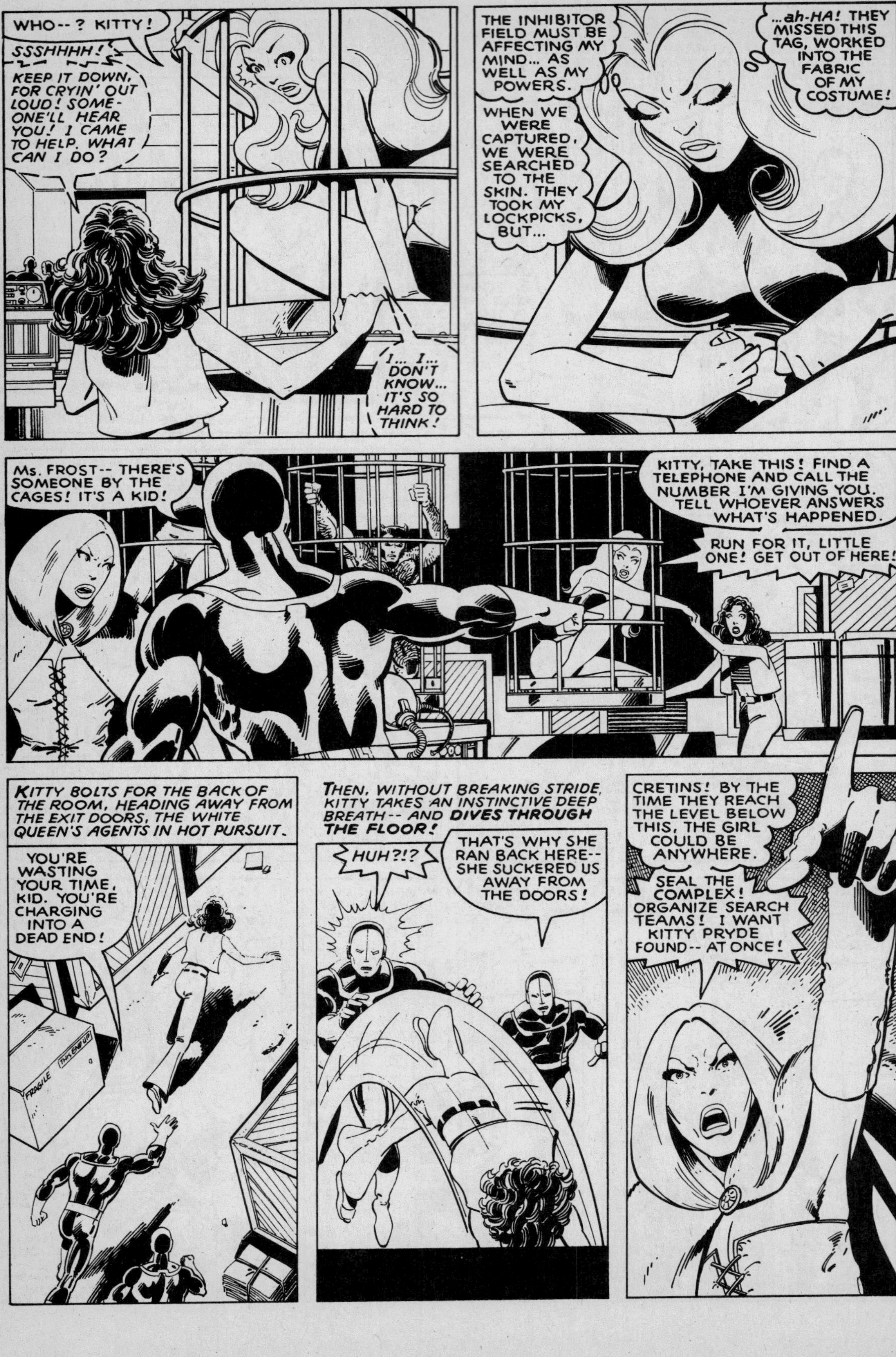
WHO--? KITTY!
SSSHHHH!
KEEP IT DOWN, FOR CRYIN' OUT LOUD! SOME-ONE'LL HEAR YOU! I CAME TO HELP. WHAT CAN I DO?
I... I... DON'T KNOW... IT'S SO HARD TO THINK!
THE INHIBITOR FIELD MUST BE AFFECTING MY MIND... AS WELL AS MY POWERS.
WHEN WE WERE CAPTURED, WE WERE SEARCHED TO THE SKIN. THEY TOOK MY LOCKPICKS, BUT...
...ah-HA! THEY MISSED THIS TAG, WORKED INTO THE FABRIC OF MY COSTUME!
Ms. FROST-- THERE'S SOMEONE BY THE CAGES! IT'S A KID!
KITTY, TAKE THIS! FIND A TELEPHONE AND CALL THE NUMBER I'M GIVING YOU. TELL WHOEVER ANSWERS WHAT'S HAPPENED.
RUN FOR IT, LITTLE ONE! GET OUT OF HERE!
KITTY BOLTS FOR THE BACK OF THE ROOM, HEADING AWAY FROM THE EXIT DOORS, THE WHITE QUEEN'S AGENTS IN HOT PURSUIT.
YOU'RE WASTING YOUR TIME, KID. YOU'RE CHARGING INTO A DEAD END!
FRAGILE
THEN, WITHOUT BREAKING STRIDE, KITTY TAKES AN INSTINCTIVE DEEP BREATH-- AND DIVES THROUGH THE FLOOR!
HUH?!?
THAT'S WHY SHE RAN BACK HERE-- SHE SUCKERED US AWAY FROM THE DOORS!
CRETINS! BY THE TIME THEY REACH THE LEVEL BELOW THIS, THE GIRL COULD BE ANYWHERE.
SEAL THE COMPLEX! ORGANIZE SEARCH TEAMS! I WANT KITTY PRYDE FOUND-- AT ONCE!

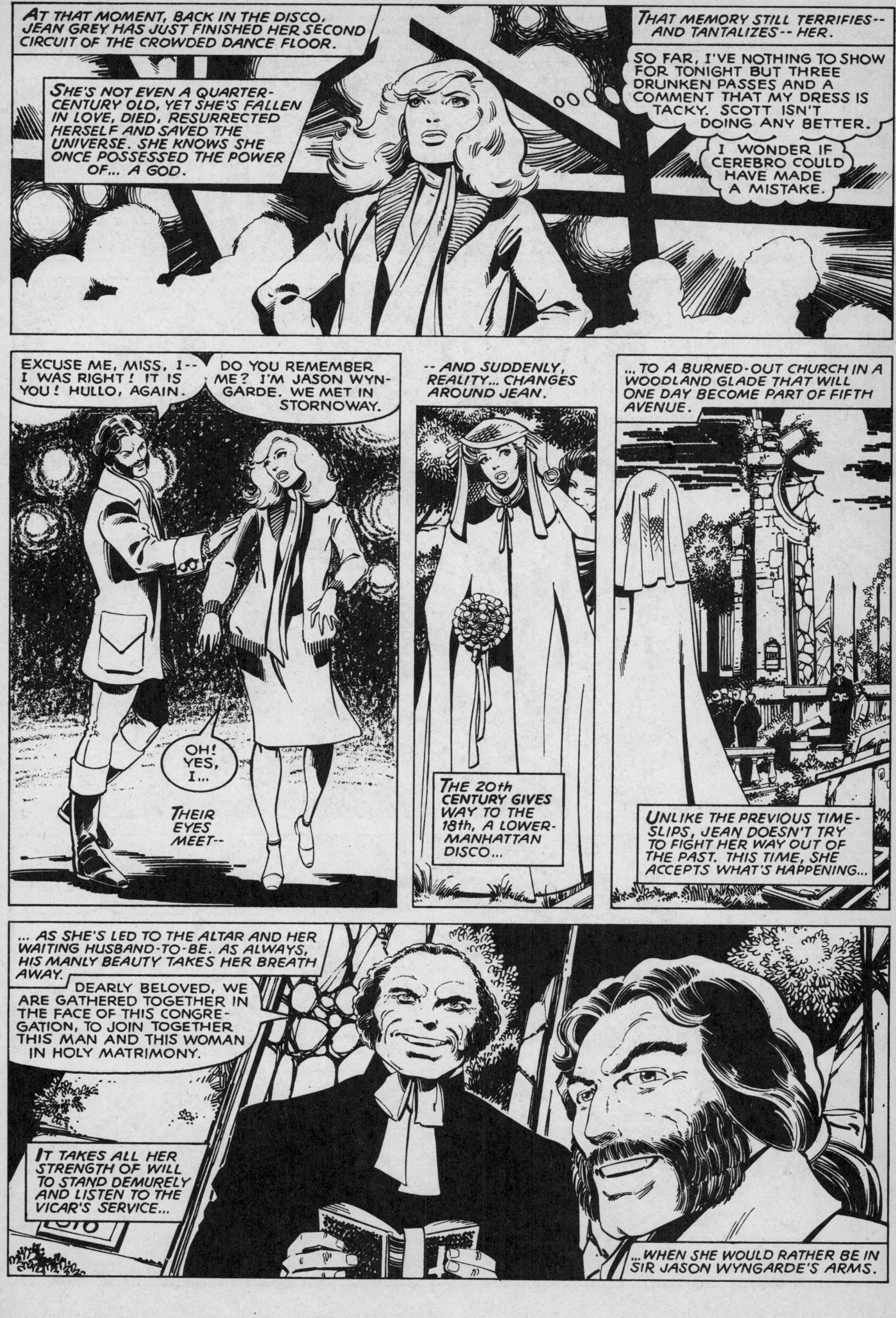

AT THAT MOMENT, BACK IN THE DISCO, JEAN GREY HAS JUST FINISHED HER SECOND CIRCUIT OF THE CROWDED DANCE FLOOR.
SHE'S NOT EVEN A QUARTER-CENTURY OLD, YET SHE'S FALLEN IN LOVE, DIED, RESURRECTED HERSELF AND SAVED THE UNIVERSE. SHE KNOWS SHE ONCE POSSESSED THE POWER OF... A GOD.
THAT MEMORY STILL TERRIFIES-- AND TANTALIZES-- HER.
SO FAR, I'VE NOTHING TO SHOW FOR TONIGHT BUT THREE DRUNKEN PASSES AND A COMMENT THAT MY DRESS IS TACKY. SCOTT ISN'T DOING ANY BETTER.
I WONDER IF CEREBRO COULD HAVE MADE A MISTAKE.
EXCUSE ME, MISS, I-- I WAS RIGHT! IT IS YOU! HULLO, AGAIN.
DO YOU REMEMBER ME? I'M JASON WYNGARDE. WE MET IN STORNOWAY.
OH! YES, I...
THEIR EYES MEET--
-- AND SUDDENLY, REALITY... CHANGES AROUND JEAN.
THE 20th CENTURY GIVES WAY TO THE 18th, A LOWER-MANHATTAN DISCO...
...TO A BURNED-OUT CHURCH IN A WOODLAND GLADE THAT WILL ONE DAY BECOME PART OF FIFTH AVENUE.
UNLIKE THE PREVIOUS TIME-SLIPS, JEAN DOESN'T TRY TO FIGHT HER WAY OUT OF THE PAST. THIS TIME, SHE ACCEPTS WHAT'S HAPPENING...
... AS SHE'S LED TO THE ALTAR AND HER WAITING HUSBAND-TO-BE. AS ALWAYS, HIS MANLY BEAUTY TAKES HER BREATH AWAY.
DEARLY BELOVED, WE ARE GATHERED TOGETHER IN THE FACE OF THIS CONGREGATION, TO JOIN TOGETHER THIS MAN AND THIS WOMAN IN HOLY MATRIMONY.
IT TAKES ALL HER STRENGTH OF WILL TO STAND DEMURELY AND LISTEN TO THE VICAR'S SERVICE...
...WHEN SHE WOULD RATHER BE IN SIR JASON WYNGARDE'S ARMS.

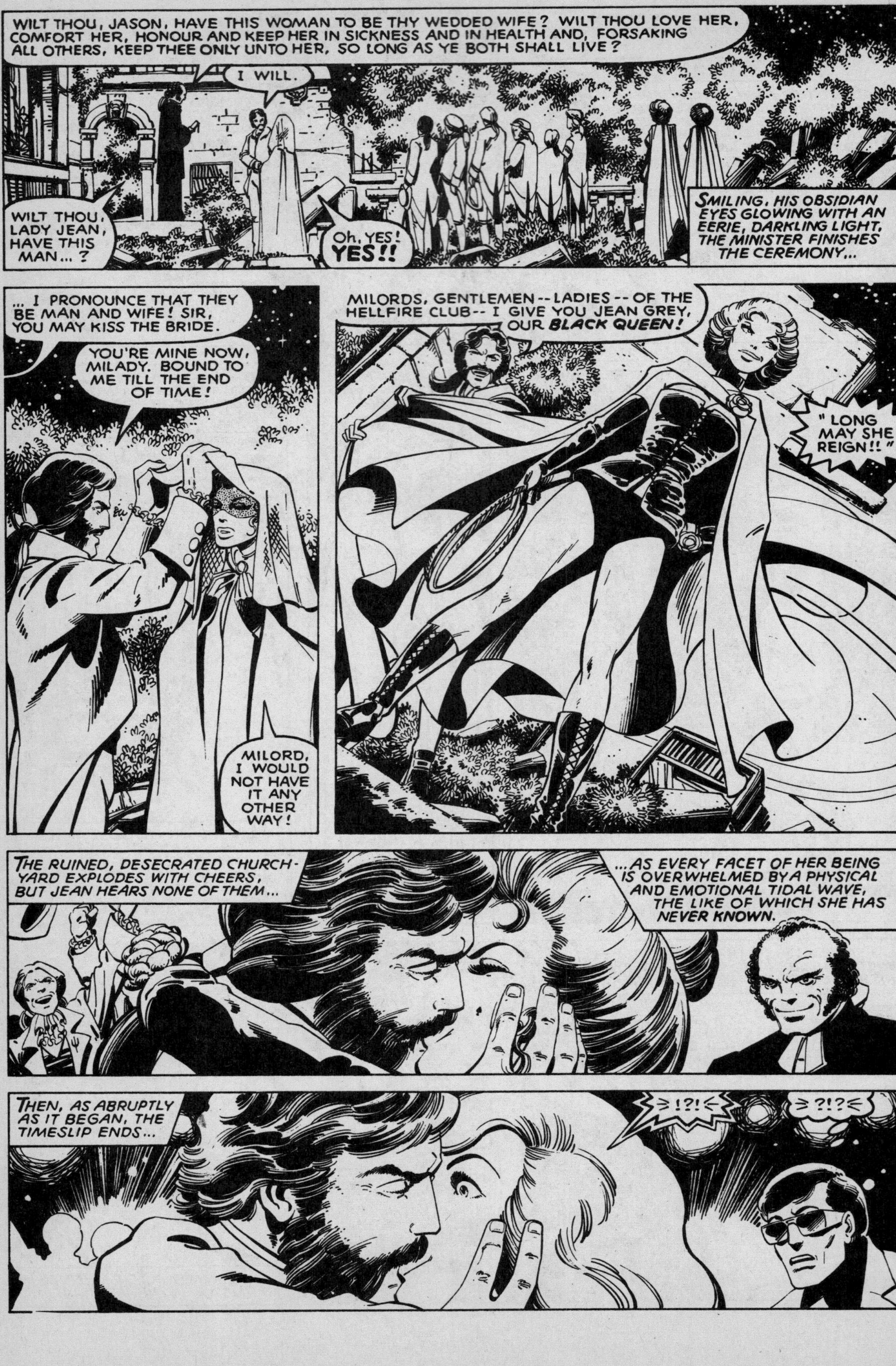
WILT THOU, JASON, HAVE THIS WOMAN TO BE THY WEDDED WIFE? WILT THOU LOVE HER, COMFORT HER, HONOUR AND KEEP HER IN SICKNESS AND IN HEALTH AND, FORSAKING ALL OTHERS, KEEP THEE ONLY UNTO HER, SO LONG AS YE BOTH SHALL LIVE?
I WILL.
WILT THOU, LADY JEAN, HAVE THIS MAN...?
Oh, YES! YES!!
SMILING, HIS OBSIDIAN EYES GLOWING WITH AN EERIE, DARKLING LIGHT, THE MINISTER FINISHES THE CEREMONY...
...I PRONOUNCE THAT THEY BE MAN AND WIFE! SIR, YOU MAY KISS THE BRIDE.
YOU'RE MINE NOW, MILADY. BOUND TO ME TILL THE END OF TIME!
MILORD, I WOULD NOT HAVE IT ANY OTHER WAY!
MILORDS, GENTLEMEN--LADIES--OF THE HELLFIRE CLUB--I GIVE YOU JEAN GREY, OUR BLACK QUEEN!
"LONG MAY SHE REIGN!!"
THE RUINED, DESECRATED CHURCH-YARD EXPLODES WITH CHEERS, BUT JEAN HEARS NONE OF THEM...
...AS EVERY FACET OF HER BEING IS OVERWHELMED BY A PHYSICAL AND EMOTIONAL TIDAL WAVE, THE LIKE OF WHICH SHE HAS NEVER KNOWN.
THEN, AS ABRUPTLY AS IT BEGAN, THE TIMESLIP ENDS...
!?!
?!?

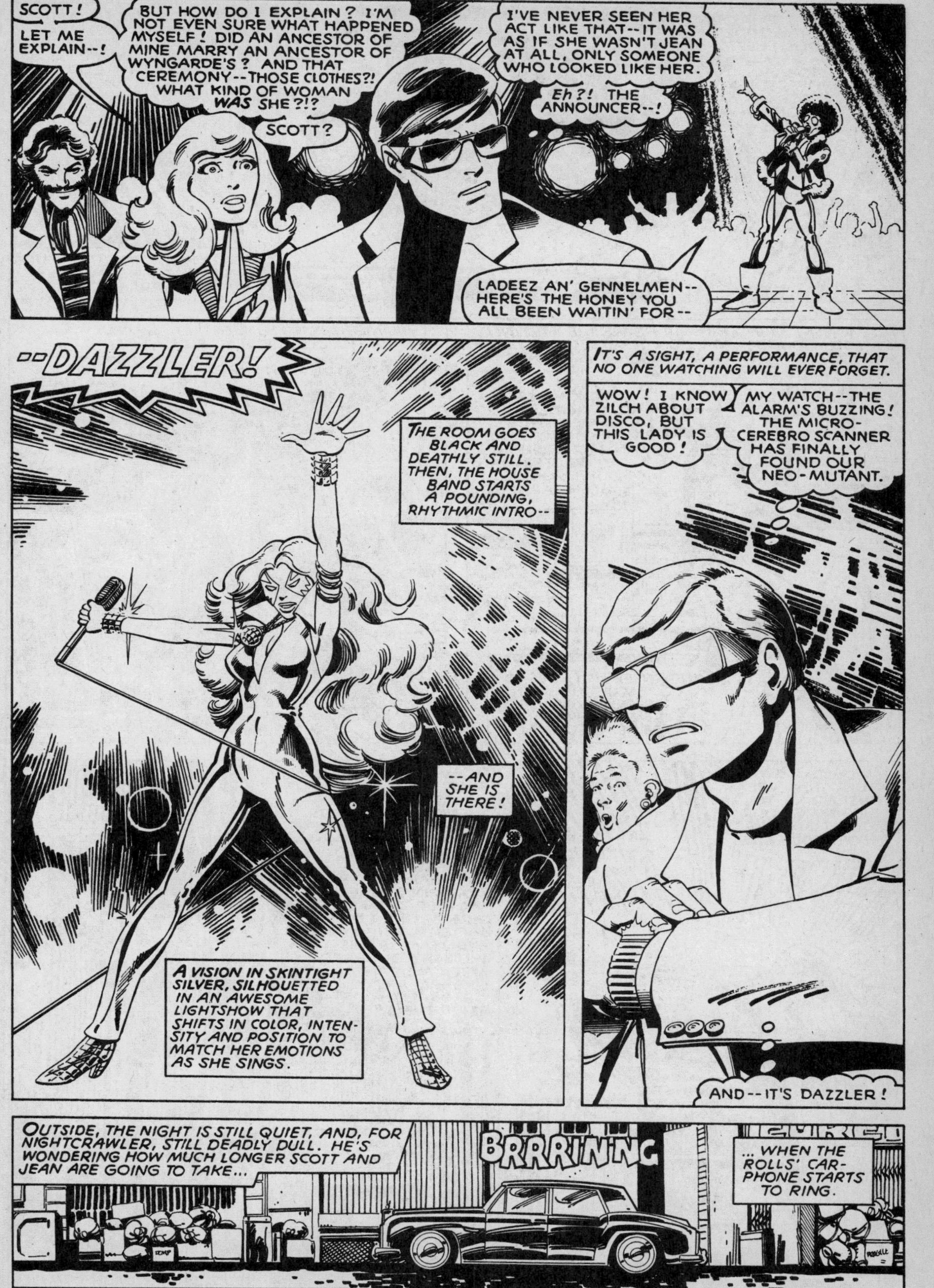
SCOTT!
LET ME EXPLAIN--!
BUT HOW DO I EXPLAIN? I'M NOT EVEN SURE WHAT HAPPENED MYSELF! DID AN ANCESTOR OF MINE MARRY AN ANCESTOR OF WYNGARDE'S? AND THAT CEREMONY--THOSE CLOTHES?! WHAT KIND OF WOMAN WAS SHE?!?
SCOTT?
I'VE NEVER SEEN HER ACT LIKE THAT--IT WAS AS IF SHE WASN'T JEAN AT ALL, ONLY SOMEONE WHO LOOKED LIKE HER.
Eh?! THE ANNOUNCER--!
LADEEZ AN' GENNELMEN--HERE'S THE HONEY YOU ALL BEEN WAITIN' FOR--
--DAZZLER!
THE ROOM GOES BLACK AND DEATHLY STILL. THEN, THE HOUSE BAND STARTS A POUNDING, RHYTHMIC INTRO--
--AND SHE IS THERE!
A VISION IN SKINTIGHT SILVER, SILHOUETTED IN AN AWESOME LIGHTSHOW THAT SHIFTS IN COLOR, INTENSITY AND POSITION TO MATCH HER EMOTIONS AS SHE SINGS.
IT'S A SIGHT, A PERFORMANCE, THAT NO ONE WATCHING WILL EVER FORGET.
WOW! I KNOW ZILCH ABOUT DISCO, BUT THIS LADY IS GOOD!
MY WATCH--THE ALARM'S BUZZING! THE MICRO-CEREBRO SCANNER HAS FINALLY FOUND OUR NEO-MUTANT.
AND--IT'S DAZZLER!
OUTSIDE, THE NIGHT IS STILL QUIET, AND, FOR NIGHTCRAWLER, STILL DEADLY DULL. HE'S WONDERING HOW MUCH LONGER SCOTT AND JEAN ARE GOING TO TAKE...
BRRRINNG
...WHEN THE ROLLS' CAR-PHONE STARTS TO RING.

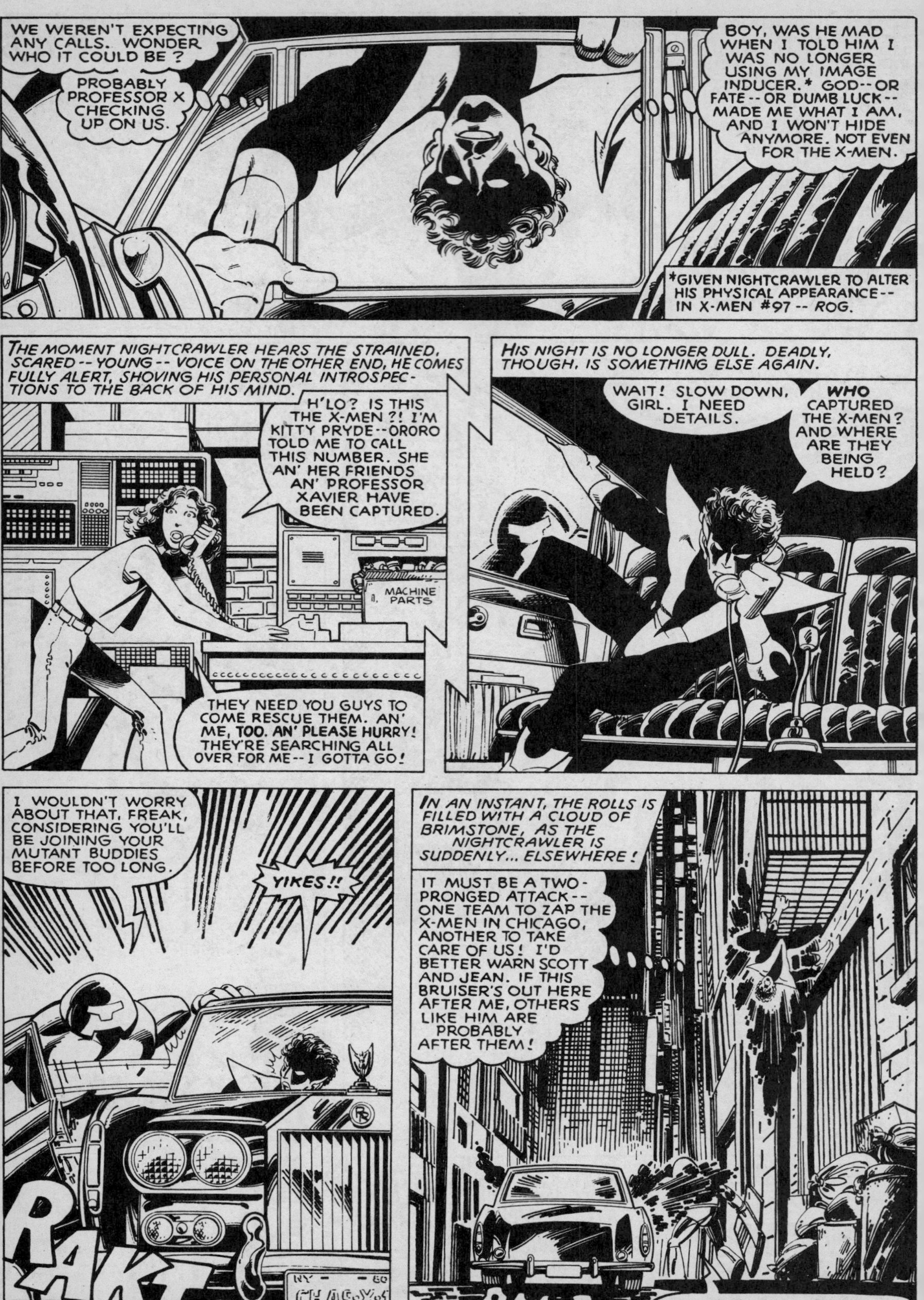
WE WEREN'T EXPECTING ANY CALLS. WONDER WHO IT COULD BE?
PROBABLY PROFESSOR X CHECKING UP ON US.
BOY, WAS HE MAD WHEN I TOLD HIM I WAS NO LONGER USING MY IMAGE INDUCER.* GOD--OR FATE--OR DUMB LUCK--MADE ME WHAT I AM, AND I WON'T HIDE ANYMORE. NOT EVEN FOR THE X-MEN.
*GIVEN NIGHTCRAWLER TO ALTER HIS PHYSICAL APPEARANCE--IN X-MEN #97 -- ROG.
THE MOMENT NIGHTCRAWLER HEARS THE STRAINED, SCARED--YOUNG--VOICE ON THE OTHER END, HE COMES FULLY ALERT, SHOVING HIS PERSONAL INTROSPECTIONS TO THE BACK OF HIS MIND.
H'LO? IS THIS THE X-MEN?! I'M KITTY PRYDE--ORORO TOLD ME TO CALL THIS NUMBER. SHE AN' HER FRIENDS AN' PROFESSOR XAVIER HAVE BEEN CAPTURED.
MACHINE PARTS
THEY NEED YOU GUYS TO COME RESCUE THEM. AN' ME, TOO. AN' PLEASE HURRY! THEY'RE SEARCHING ALL OVER FOR ME--I GOTTA GO!
HIS NIGHT IS NO LONGER DULL. DEADLY, THOUGH, IS SOMETHING ELSE AGAIN.
WAIT! SLOW DOWN, GIRL. I NEED DETAILS.
WHO CAPTURED THE X-MEN? AND WHERE ARE THEY BEING HELD?
I WOULDN'T WORRY ABOUT THAT, FREAK, CONSIDERING YOU'LL BE JOINING YOUR MUTANT BUDDIES BEFORE TOO LONG.
YIKES!!
RAKT
NY -- 80
CHAS-X-1
IN AN INSTANT, THE ROLLS IS FILLED WITH A CLOUD OF BRIMSTONE, AS THE NIGHTCRAWLER IS SUDDENLY... ELSEWHERE!
IT MUST BE A TWO-PRONGED ATTACK--ONE TEAM TO ZAP THE X-MEN IN CHICAGO, ANOTHER TO TAKE CARE OF US! I'D BETTER WARN SCOTT AND JEAN. IF THIS BRUISER'S OUT HERE AFTER ME, OTHERS LIKE HIM ARE PROBABLY AFTER THEM!
BAMF
TELEPORTING WON'T SAVE YOU THIS TIME, NIGHTCRAWLER!

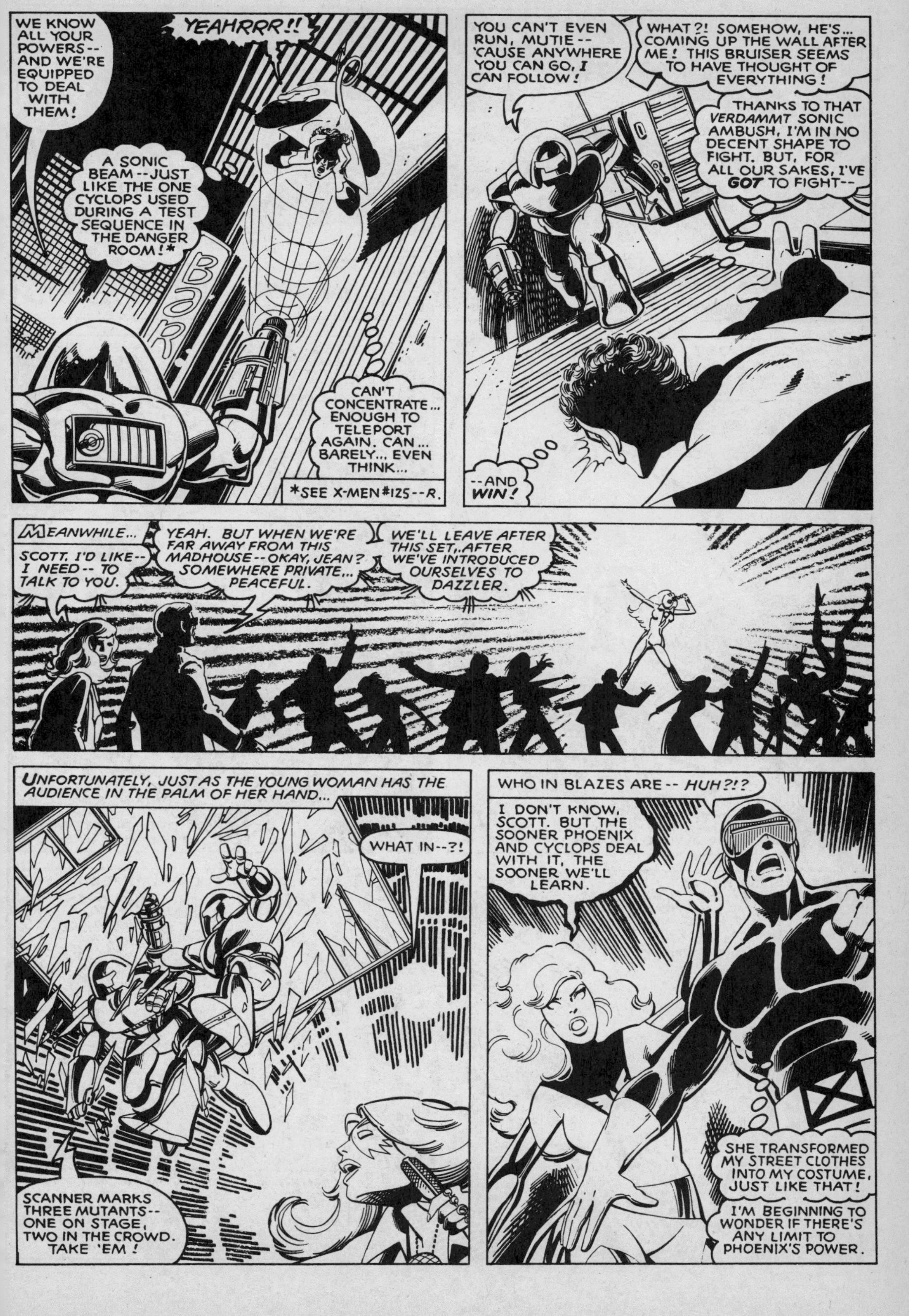
WE KNOW ALL YOUR POWERS-- AND WE'RE EQUIPPED TO DEAL WITH THEM!
YEAHRRR!!
A SONIC BEAM--JUST LIKE THE ONE CYCLOPS USED DURING A TEST SEQUENCE IN THE DANGER ROOM!*
BAR
CAN'T CONCENTRATE... ENOUGH TO TELEPORT AGAIN. CAN... BARELY... EVEN THINK...
*SEE X-MEN #125--R.
YOU CAN'T EVEN RUN, MUTIE-- 'CAUSE ANYWHERE YOU CAN GO, I CAN FOLLOW!
WHAT?! SOMEHOW, HE'S... COMING UP THE WALL AFTER ME! THIS BRUISER SEEMS TO HAVE THOUGHT OF EVERYTHING!
THANKS TO THAT VERDAMMT SONIC AMBUSH, I'M IN NO DECENT SHAPE TO FIGHT. BUT, FOR ALL OUR SAKES, I'VE GOT TO FIGHT--
--AND WIN!
MEANWHILE...
SCOTT, I'D LIKE-- I NEED-- TO TALK TO YOU.
YEAH. BUT WHEN WE'RE FAR AWAY FROM THIS MADHOUSE--OKAY, JEAN? SOMEWHERE PRIVATE... PEACEFUL.
WE'LL LEAVE AFTER THIS SET,,AFTER WE'VE INTRODUCED OURSELVES TO DAZZLER.
UNFORTUNATELY, JUST AS THE YOUNG WOMAN HAS THE AUDIENCE IN THE PALM OF HER HAND...
WHAT IN--?!
SCANNER MARKS THREE MUTANTS-- ONE ON STAGE, TWO IN THE CROWD. TAKE 'EM!
WHO IN BLAZES ARE-- HUH?!?
I DON'T KNOW, SCOTT. BUT THE SOONER PHOENIX AND CYCLOPS DEAL WITH IT, THE SOONER WE'LL LEARN.
SHE TRANSFORMED MY STREET CLOTHES INTO MY COSTUME, JUST LIKE THAT!
I'M BEGINNING TO WONDER IF THERE'S ANY LIMIT TO PHOENIX'S POWER.

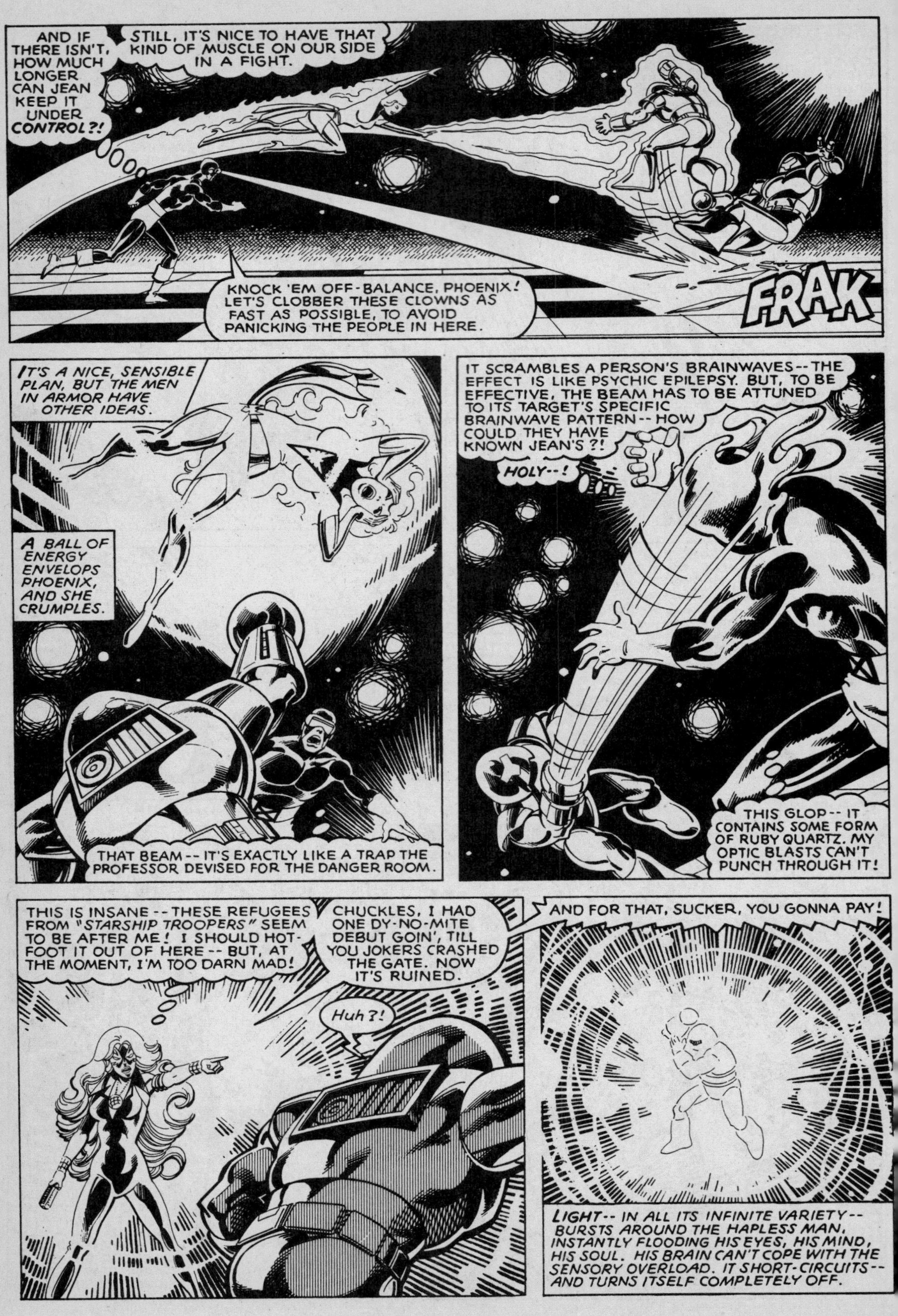
AND IF THERE ISN'T, HOW MUCH LONGER CAN JEAN KEEP IT UNDER CONTROL?!
STILL, IT'S NICE TO HAVE THAT KIND OF MUSCLE ON OUR SIDE IN A FIGHT.
KNOCK 'EM OFF-BALANCE, PHOENIX! LET'S CLOBBER THESE CLOWNS AS FAST AS POSSIBLE, TO AVOID PANICKING THE PEOPLE IN HERE.
FRAK
IT'S A NICE, SENSIBLE PLAN, BUT THE MEN IN ARMOR HAVE OTHER IDEAS.
A BALL OF ENERGY ENVELOPS PHOENIX, AND SHE CRUMPLES.
THAT BEAM -- IT'S EXACTLY LIKE A TRAP THE PROFESSOR DEVISED FOR THE DANGER ROOM.
IT SCRAMBLES A PERSON'S BRAINWAVES -- THE EFFECT IS LIKE PSYCHIC EPILEPSY. BUT, TO BE EFFECTIVE, THE BEAM HAS TO BE ATTUNED TO ITS TARGET'S SPECIFIC BRAINWAVE PATTERN -- HOW COULD THEY HAVE KNOWN JEAN'S?!
HOLY--!
THIS GLOP -- IT CONTAINS SOME FORM OF RUBY QUARTZ. MY OPTIC BLASTS CAN'T PUNCH THROUGH IT!
THIS IS INSANE -- THESE REFUGEES FROM "STARSHIP TROOPERS" SEEM TO BE AFTER ME! I SHOULD HOT-FOOT IT OUT OF HERE -- BUT, AT THE MOMENT, I'M TOO DARN MAD!
CHUCKLES, I HAD ONE DY-NO-MITE DEBUT GOIN', TILL YOU JOKERS CRASHED THE GATE. NOW IT'S RUINED.
Huh?!
AND FOR THAT, SUCKER, YOU GONNA PAY!
LIGHT -- IN ALL ITS INFINITE VARIETY -- BURSTS AROUND THE HAPLESS MAN, INSTANTLY FLOODING HIS EYES, HIS MIND, HIS SOUL. HIS BRAIN CAN'T COPE WITH THE SENSORY OVERLOAD. IT SHORT-CIRCUITS -- AND TURNS ITSELF COMPLETELY OFF.

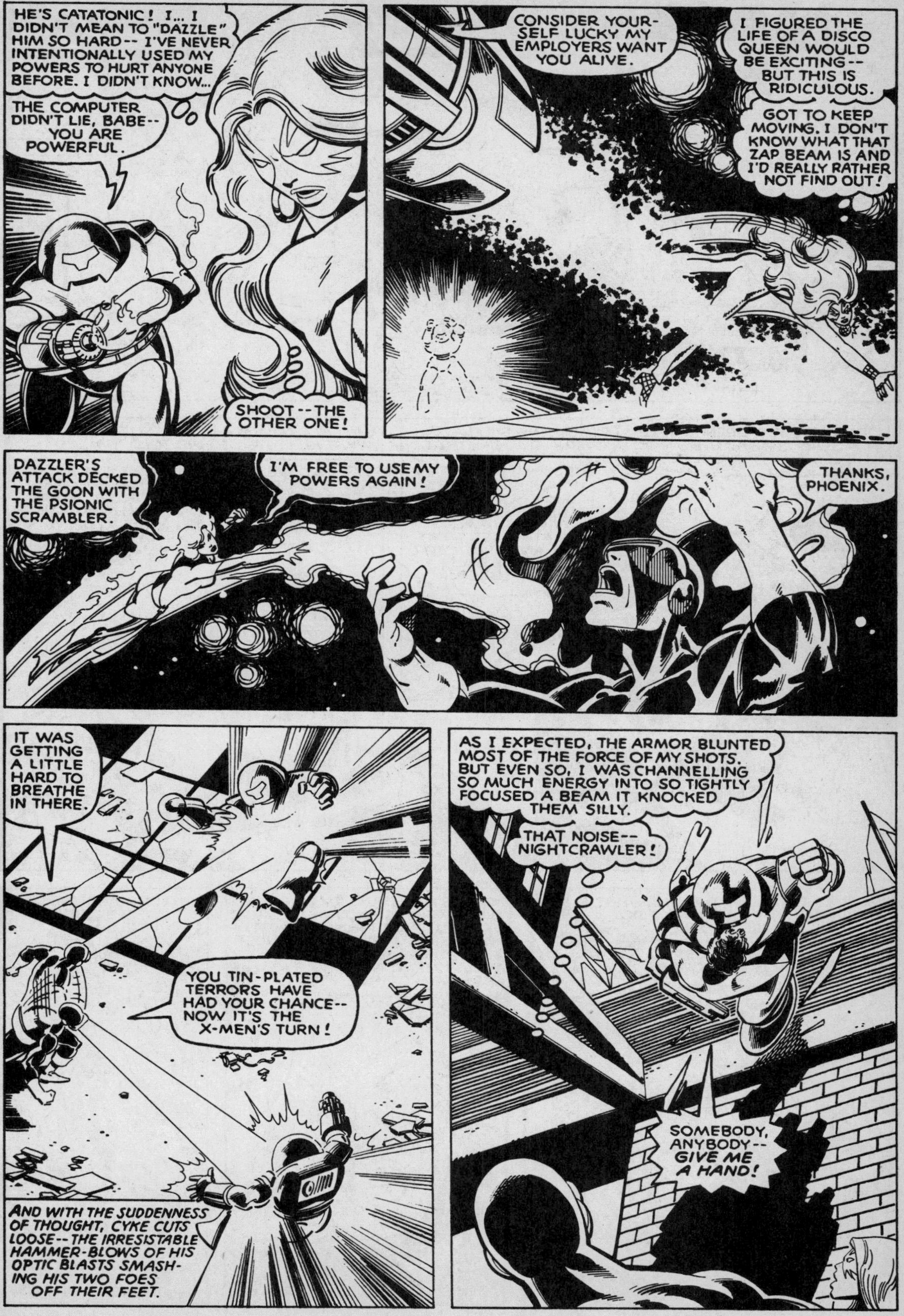
HE'S CATATONIC! I... I DIDN'T MEAN TO "DAZZLE" HIM SO HARD-- I'VE NEVER INTENTIONALLY USED MY POWERS TO HURT ANYONE BEFORE. I DIDN'T KNOW...
THE COMPUTER DIDN'T LIE, BABE-- YOU ARE POWERFUL.
SHOOT--THE OTHER ONE!
CONSIDER YOURSELF LUCKY MY EMPLOYERS WANT YOU ALIVE.
I FIGURED THE LIFE OF A DISCO QUEEN WOULD BE EXCITING-- BUT THIS IS RIDICULOUS.
GOT TO KEEP MOVING. I DON'T KNOW WHAT THAT ZAP BEAM IS AND I'D REALLY RATHER NOT FIND OUT!
DAZZLER'S ATTACK DECKED THE GOON WITH THE PSIONIC SCRAMBLER.
I'M FREE TO USE MY POWERS AGAIN!
THANKS, PHOENIX.
IT WAS GETTING A LITTLE HARD TO BREATHE IN THERE.
YOU TIN-PLATED TERRORS HAVE HAD YOUR CHANCE-- NOW IT'S THE X-MEN'S TURN!
AND WITH THE SUDDENNESS OF THOUGHT, CYKE CUTS LOOSE--THE IRRESISTABLE HAMMER-BLOWS OF HIS OPTIC BLASTS SMASHING HIS TWO FOES OFF THEIR FEET.
AS I EXPECTED, THE ARMOR BLUNTED MOST OF THE FORCE OF MY SHOTS. BUT EVEN SO, I WAS CHANNELLING SO MUCH ENERGY INTO SO TIGHTLY FOCUSED A BEAM IT KNOCKED THEM SILLY.
THAT NOISE-- NIGHTCRAWLER!
SOMEBODY, ANYBODY-- GIVE ME A HAND!

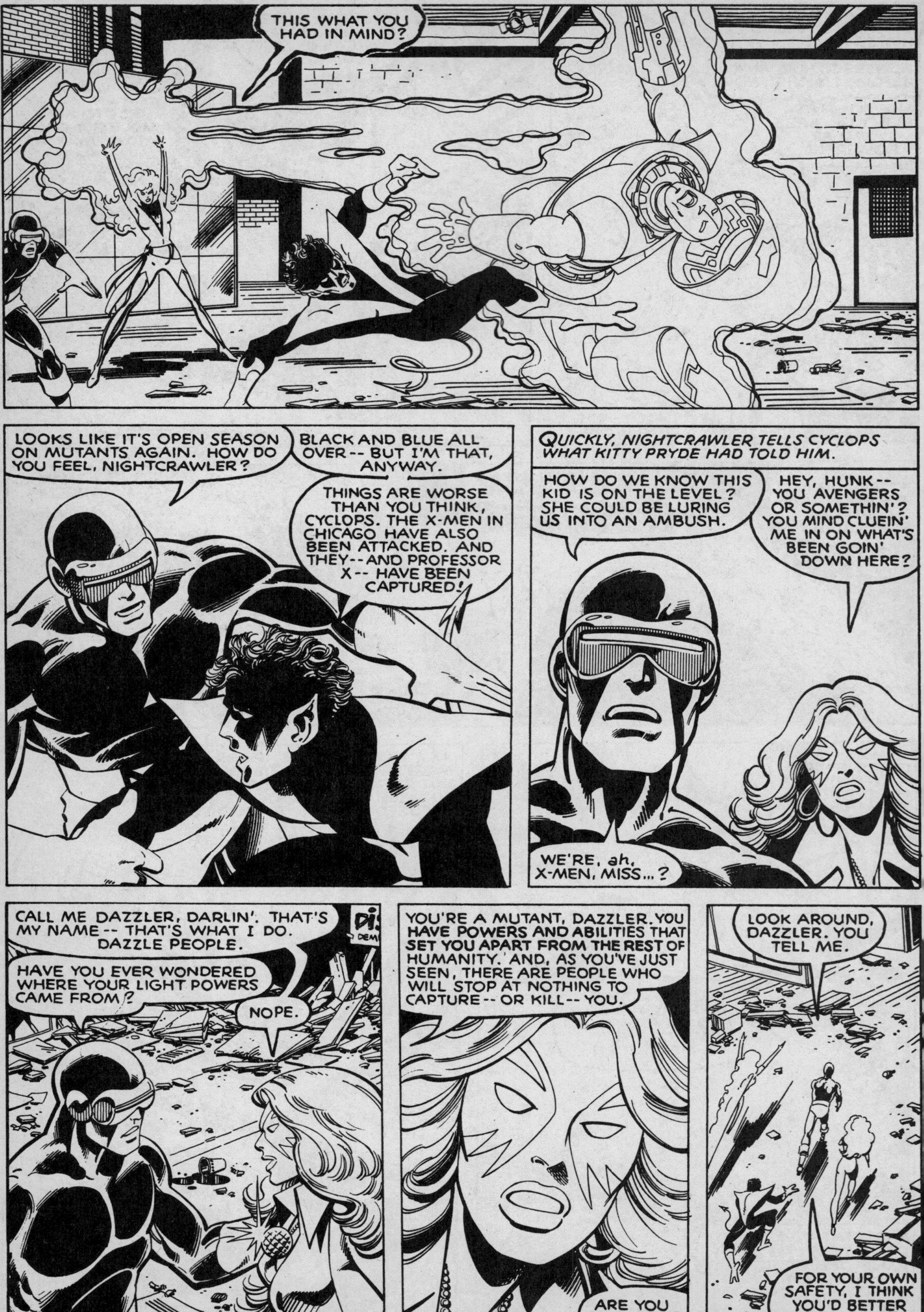
THIS WHAT YOU HAD IN MIND?
LOOKS LIKE IT'S OPEN SEASON ON MUTANTS AGAIN. HOW DO YOU FEEL, NIGHTCRAWLER?
BLACK AND BLUE ALL OVER -- BUT I'M THAT, ANYWAY.
THINGS ARE WORSE THAN YOU THINK, CYCLOPS. THE X-MEN IN CHICAGO HAVE ALSO BEEN ATTACKED. AND THEY -- AND PROFESSOR X -- HAVE BEEN CAPTURED!
QUICKLY, NIGHTCRAWLER TELLS CYCLOPS WHAT KITTY PRYDE HAD TOLD HIM.
HOW DO WE KNOW THIS KID IS ON THE LEVEL? SHE COULD BE LURING US INTO AN AMBUSH.
HEY, HUNK -- YOU AVENGERS OR SOMETHIN'? YOU MIND CLUEIN' ME IN ON WHAT'S BEEN GOIN' DOWN HERE?
WE'RE, ah, X-MEN, MISS...?
CALL ME DAZZLER, DARLIN'. THAT'S MY NAME -- THAT'S WHAT I DO. DAZZLE PEOPLE.
HAVE YOU EVER WONDERED WHERE YOUR LIGHT POWERS CAME FROM?
NOPE.
YOU'RE A MUTANT, DAZZLER. YOU HAVE POWERS AND ABILITIES THAT SET YOU APART FROM THE REST OF HUMANITY. AND, AS YOU'VE JUST SEEN, THERE ARE PEOPLE WHO WILL STOP AT NOTHING TO CAPTURE -- OR KILL -- YOU.
ARE YOU SERIOUS?
LOOK AROUND, DAZZLER. YOU TELL ME.
FOR YOUR OWN SAFETY, I THINK YOU'D BETTER COME WITH US.

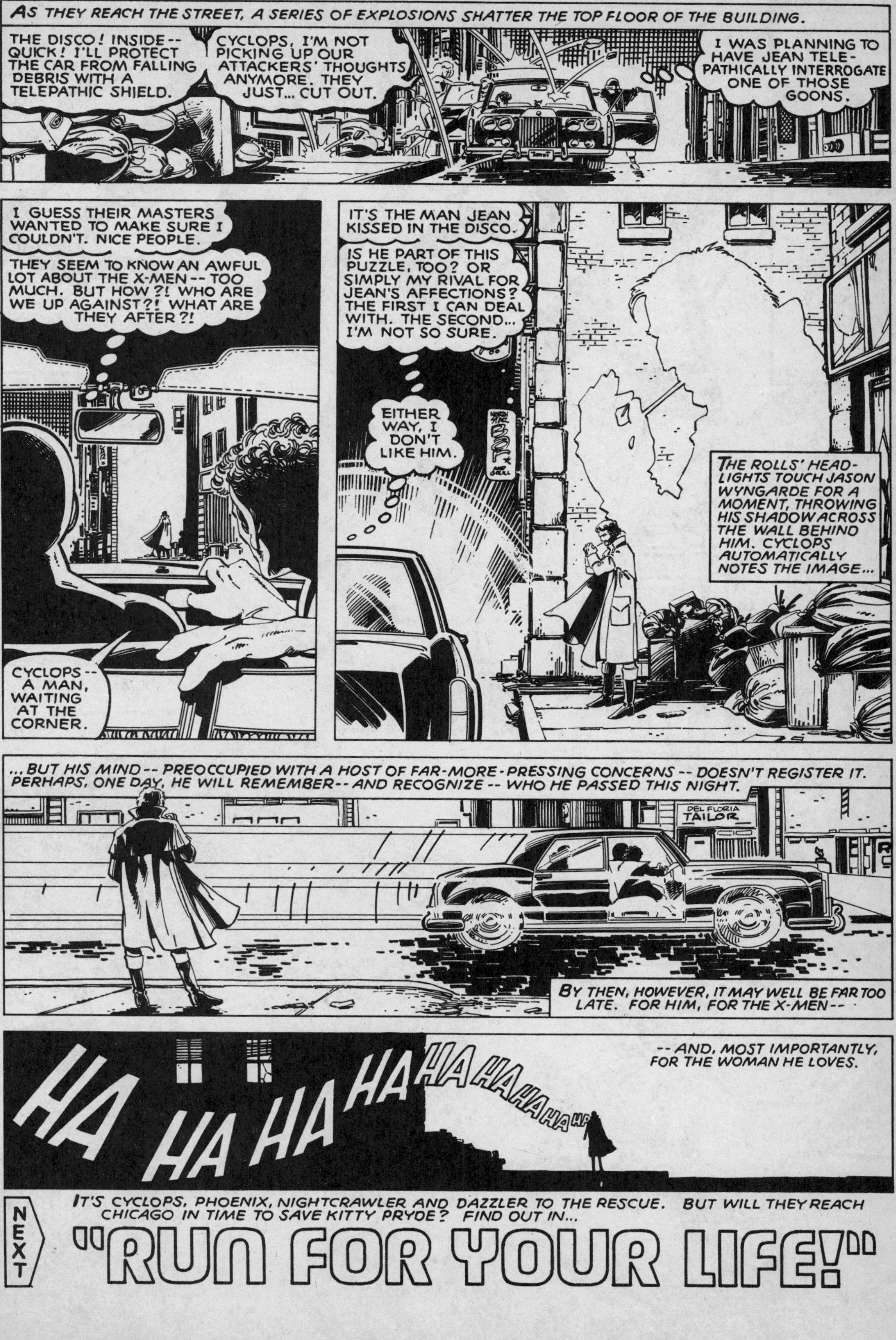
AS THEY REACH THE STREET, A SERIES OF EXPLOSIONS SHATTER THE TOP FLOOR OF THE BUILDING.
THE DISCO! INSIDE-- QUICK! I'LL PROTECT THE CAR FROM FALLING DEBRIS WITH A TELEPATHIC SHIELD.
CYCLOPS, I'M NOT PICKING UP OUR ATTACKERS' THOUGHTS ANYMORE. THEY JUST... CUT OUT.
I WAS PLANNING TO HAVE JEAN TELEPATHICALLY INTERROGATE ONE OF THOSE GOONS.
I GUESS THEIR MASTERS WANTED TO MAKE SURE I COULDN'T. NICE PEOPLE.
THEY SEEM TO KNOW AN AWFUL LOT ABOUT THE X-MEN -- TOO MUCH. BUT HOW?! WHO ARE WE UP AGAINST?! WHAT ARE THEY AFTER?!
CYCLOPS -- A MAN, WAITING AT THE CORNER.
IT'S THE MAN JEAN KISSED IN THE DISCO.
IS HE PART OF THIS PUZZLE, TOO? OR SIMPLY MY RIVAL FOR JEAN'S AFFECTIONS? THE FIRST I CAN DEAL WITH. THE SECOND... I'M NOT SO SURE.
EITHER WAY, I DON'T LIKE HIM.
THE ROLLS' HEADLIGHTS TOUCH JASON WYNGARDE FOR A MOMENT, THROWING HIS SHADOW ACROSS THE WALL BEHIND HIM. CYCLOPS AUTOMATICALLY NOTES THE IMAGE...
...BUT HIS MIND-- PREOCCUPIED WITH A HOST OF FAR-MORE-PRESSING CONCERNS -- DOESN'T REGISTER IT. PERHAPS, ONE DAY, HE WILL REMEMBER-- AND RECOGNIZE -- WHO HE PASSED THIS NIGHT.
DEL FLORIA TAILOR
BY THEN, HOWEVER, IT MAY WELL BE FAR TOO LATE. FOR HIM, FOR THE X-MEN--
-- AND, MOST IMPORTANTLY, FOR THE WOMAN HE LOVES.
HA HA HA HA HA HA HA HA HA HA HA
NEXT
IT'S CYCLOPS, PHOENIX, NIGHTCRAWLER AND DAZZLER TO THE RESCUE. BUT WILL THEY REACH CHICAGO IN TIME TO SAVE KITTY PRYDE? FIND OUT IN...
"RUN FOR YOUR LIFE!"

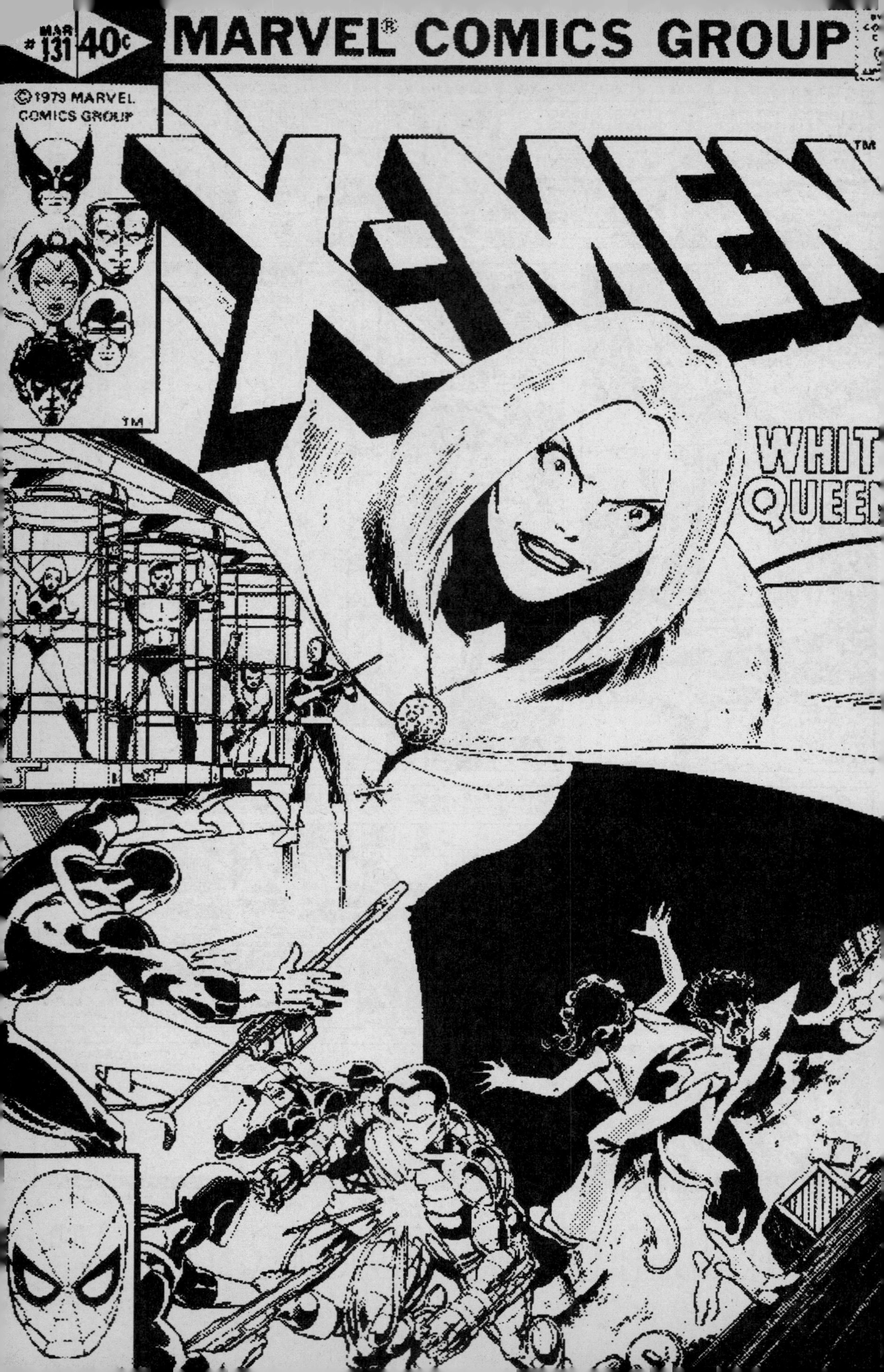

#131 MAR 40¢
MARVEL® COMICS GROUP
©1979 MARVEL COMICS GROUP
TM
X-MEN TM
WHIT
QUEE

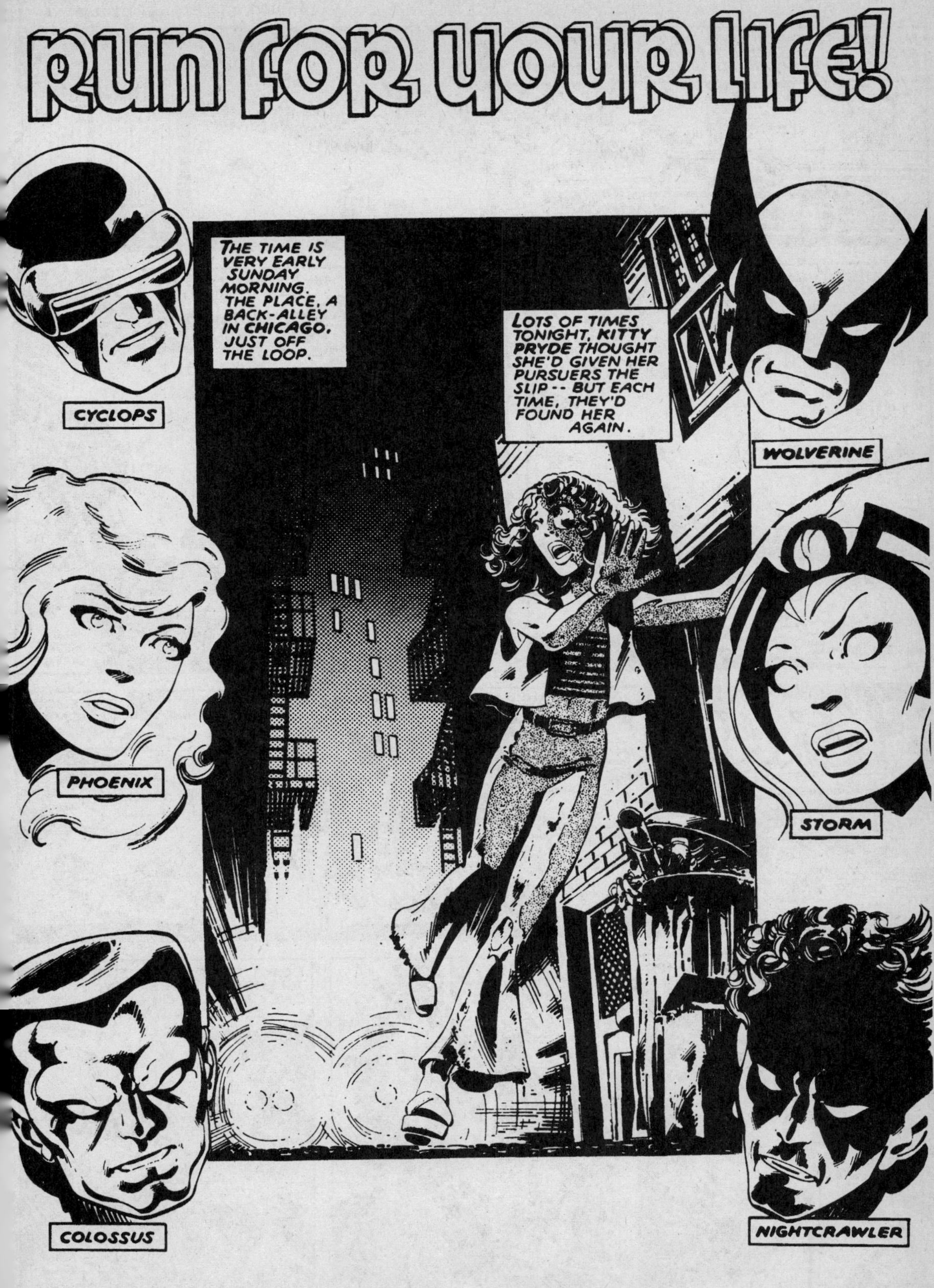
RUN FOR YOUR LIFE!
THE TIME IS VERY EARLY SUNDAY MORNING. THE PLACE, A BACK-ALLEY IN CHICAGO, JUST OFF THE LOOP.
LOTS OF TIMES TONIGHT, KITTY PRYDE THOUGHT SHE'D GIVEN HER PURSUERS THE SLIP -- BUT EACH TIME, THEY'D FOUND HER AGAIN.
CYCLOPS
WOLVERINE
PHOENIX
STORM
COLOSSUS
NIGHTCRAWLER

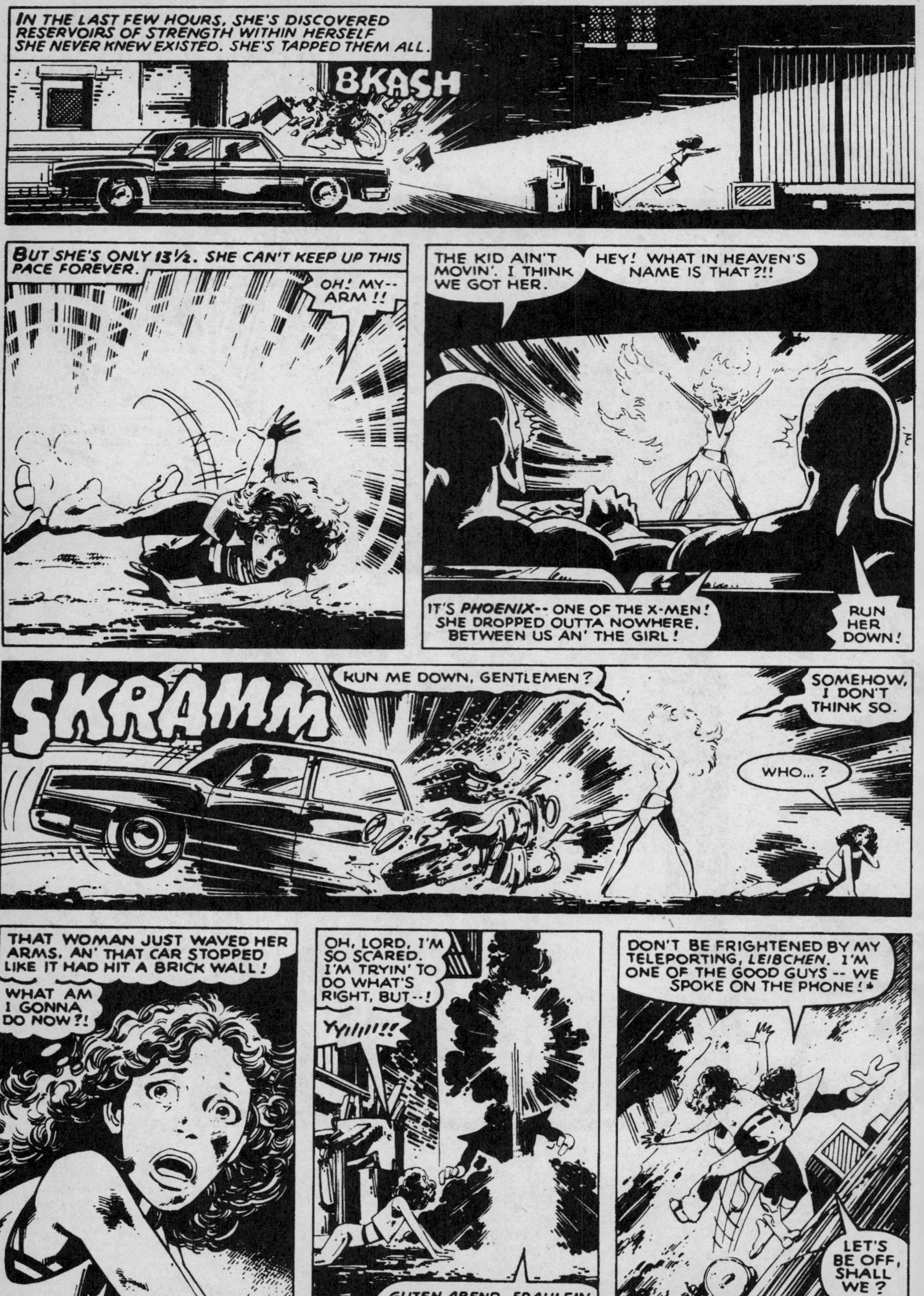
IN THE LAST FEW HOURS, SHE'S DISCOVERED RESERVOIRS OF STRENGTH WITHIN HERSELF SHE NEVER KNEW EXISTED. SHE'S TAPPED THEM ALL.
BKASH
BUT SHE'S ONLY 13½. SHE CAN'T KEEP UP THIS PACE FOREVER.
OH! MY-- ARM !!
THE KID AIN'T MOVIN'. I THINK WE GOT HER.
HEY! WHAT IN HEAVEN'S NAME IS THAT?!!
IT'S PHOENIX-- ONE OF THE X-MEN! SHE DROPPED OUTTA NOWHERE, BETWEEN US AN' THE GIRL!
RUN HER DOWN!
SKRAMM
RUN ME DOWN, GENTLEMEN?
SOMEHOW, I DON'T THINK SO.
WHO...?
THAT WOMAN JUST WAVED HER ARMS, AN' THAT CAR STOPPED LIKE IT HAD HIT A BRICK WALL!
WHAT AM I GONNA DO NOW?!
OH, LORD, I'M SO SCARED. I'M TRYIN' TO DO WHAT'S RIGHT, BUT--!
YYIIIII!!!
GUTEN ABEND, FRAULEIN PRYDE, I ASSUME?
DON'T BE FRIGHTENED BY MY TELEPORTING, LEIBCHEN. I'M ONE OF THE GOOD GUYS -- WE SPOKE ON THE PHONE!*
LET'S BE OFF, SHALL WE?
*LAST ISSUE--BOB.

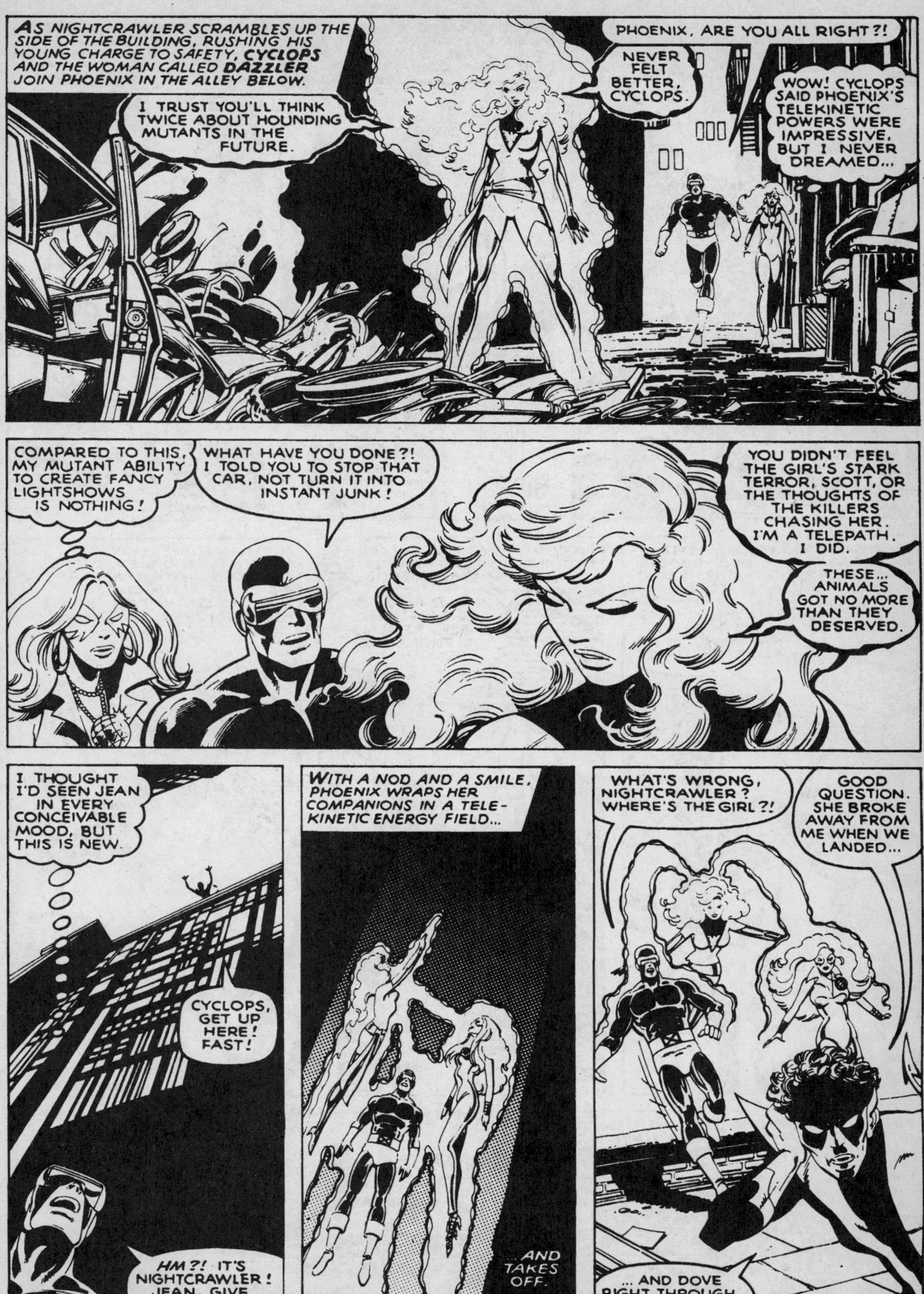
AS NIGHTCRAWLER SCRAMBLES UP THE SIDE OF THE BUILDING, RUSHING HIS YOUNG CHARGE TO SAFETY, CYCLOPS AND THE WOMAN CALLED DAZZLER JOIN PHOENIX IN THE ALLEY BELOW.
I TRUST YOU'LL THINK TWICE ABOUT HOUNDING MUTANTS IN THE FUTURE.
PHOENIX, ARE YOU ALL RIGHT?!
NEVER FELT BETTER, CYCLOPS.
WOW! CYCLOPS SAID PHOENIX'S TELEKINETIC POWERS WERE IMPRESSIVE, BUT I NEVER DREAMED...
COMPARED TO THIS, MY MUTANT ABILITY TO CREATE FANCY LIGHTSHOWS IS NOTHING!
WHAT HAVE YOU DONE?! I TOLD YOU TO STOP THAT CAR, NOT TURN IT INTO INSTANT JUNK!
YOU DIDN'T FEEL THE GIRL'S STARK TERROR, SCOTT, OR THE THOUGHTS OF THE KILLERS CHASING HER. I'M A TELEPATH. I DID.
THESE... ANIMALS GOT NO MORE THAN THEY DESERVED.
I THOUGHT I'D SEEN JEAN IN EVERY CONCEIVABLE MOOD, BUT THIS IS NEW.
CYCLOPS, GET UP HERE! FAST!
HM?! IT'S NIGHTCRAWLER! JEAN, GIVE US A LIFT!
WITH A NOD AND A SMILE, PHOENIX WRAPS HER COMPANIONS IN A TELEKINETIC ENERGY FIELD...
...AND TAKES OFF.
WHAT'S WRONG, NIGHTCRAWLER? WHERE'S THE GIRL?!
GOOD QUESTION. SHE BROKE AWAY FROM ME WHEN WE LANDED...
...AND DOVE RIGHT THROUGH THE ROOF!

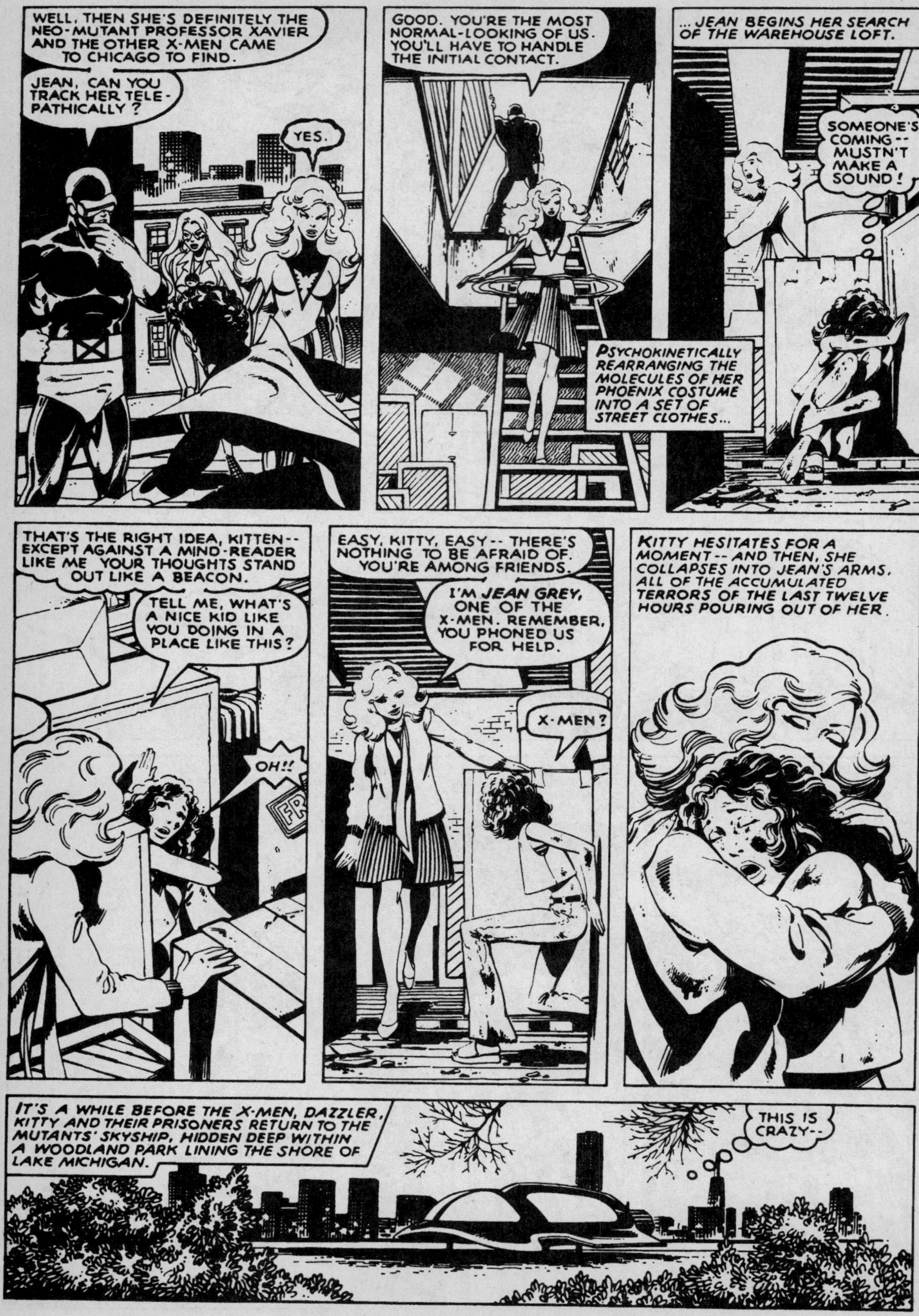

WELL, THEN SHE'S DEFINITELY THE NEO-MUTANT PROFESSOR XAVIER AND THE OTHER X-MEN CAME TO CHICAGO TO FIND.
JEAN, CAN YOU TRACK HER TELEPATHICALLY?
YES.
GOOD. YOU'RE THE MOST NORMAL-LOOKING OF US. YOU'LL HAVE TO HANDLE THE INITIAL CONTACT.
PSYCHOKINETICALLY REARRANGING THE MOLECULES OF HER PHOENIX COSTUME INTO A SET OF STREET CLOTHES...
...JEAN BEGINS HER SEARCH OF THE WAREHOUSE LOFT.
SOMEONE'S COMING -- MUSTN'T MAKE A SOUND!
THAT'S THE RIGHT IDEA, KITTEN -- EXCEPT AGAINST A MIND-READER LIKE ME YOUR THOUGHTS STAND OUT LIKE A BEACON.
TELL ME, WHAT'S A NICE KID LIKE YOU DOING IN A PLACE LIKE THIS?
OH!!
EASY, KITTY, EASY -- THERE'S NOTHING TO BE AFRAID OF. YOU'RE AMONG FRIENDS.
I'M JEAN GREY, ONE OF THE X-MEN. REMEMBER, YOU PHONED US FOR HELP.
X-MEN?
KITTY HESITATES FOR A MOMENT -- AND THEN, SHE COLLAPSES INTO JEAN'S ARMS, ALL OF THE ACCUMULATED TERRORS OF THE LAST TWELVE HOURS POURING OUT OF HER.
IT'S A WHILE BEFORE THE X-MEN, DAZZLER, KITTY AND THEIR PRISONERS RETURN TO THE MUTANTS' SKYSHIP, HIDDEN DEEP WITHIN A WOODLAND PARK LINING THE SHORE OF LAKE MICHIGAN.
THIS IS CRAZY--

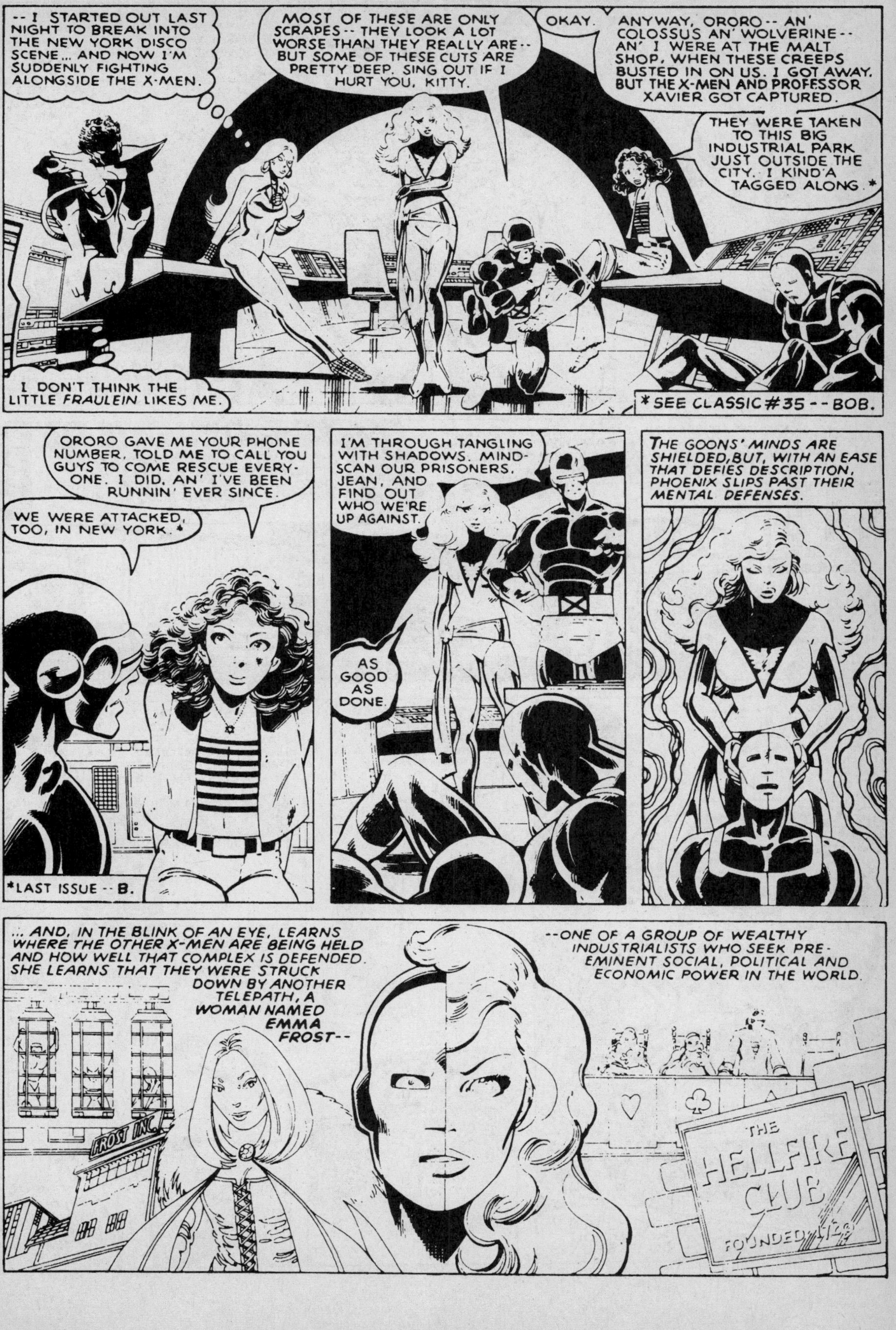
-- I STARTED OUT LAST NIGHT TO BREAK INTO THE NEW YORK DISCO SCENE... AND NOW I'M SUDDENLY FIGHTING ALONGSIDE THE X-MEN.
MOST OF THESE ARE ONLY SCRAPES -- THEY LOOK A LOT WORSE THAN THEY REALLY ARE -- BUT SOME OF THESE CUTS ARE PRETTY DEEP. SING OUT IF I HURT YOU, KITTY.
OKAY.
ANYWAY, ORORO -- AN' COLOSSUS AN' WOLVERINE -- AN' I WERE AT THE MALT SHOP, WHEN THESE CREEPS BUSTED IN ON US. I GOT AWAY, BUT THE X-MEN AND PROFESSOR XAVIER GOT CAPTURED.
THEY WERE TAKEN TO THIS BIG INDUSTRIAL PARK JUST OUTSIDE THE CITY. I KIND'A TAGGED ALONG.*
I DON'T THINK THE LITTLE FRAULEIN LIKES ME.
*SEE CLASSIC #35 -- BOB.
ORORO GAVE ME YOUR PHONE NUMBER, TOLD ME TO CALL YOU GUYS TO COME RESCUE EVERYONE. I DID, AN' I'VE BEEN RUNNIN' EVER SINCE.
WE WERE ATTACKED, TOO, IN NEW YORK.*
*LAST ISSUE -- B.
I'M THROUGH TANGLING WITH SHADOWS. MIND-SCAN OUR PRISONERS, JEAN, AND FIND OUT WHO WE'RE UP AGAINST.
AS GOOD AS DONE.
THE GOONS' MINDS ARE SHIELDED, BUT, WITH AN EASE THAT DEFIES DESCRIPTION, PHOENIX SLIPS PAST THEIR MENTAL DEFENSES.
... AND, IN THE BLINK OF AN EYE, LEARNS WHERE THE OTHER X-MEN ARE BEING HELD AND HOW WELL THAT COMPLEX IS DEFENDED. SHE LEARNS THAT THEY WERE STRUCK DOWN BY ANOTHER TELEPATH, A WOMAN NAMED EMMA FROST--
--ONE OF A GROUP OF WEALTHY INDUSTRIALISTS WHO SEEK PRE-EMINENT SOCIAL, POLITICAL AND ECONOMIC POWER IN THE WORLD.
FROST INC.
THE HELLFIRE CLUB
FOUNDED

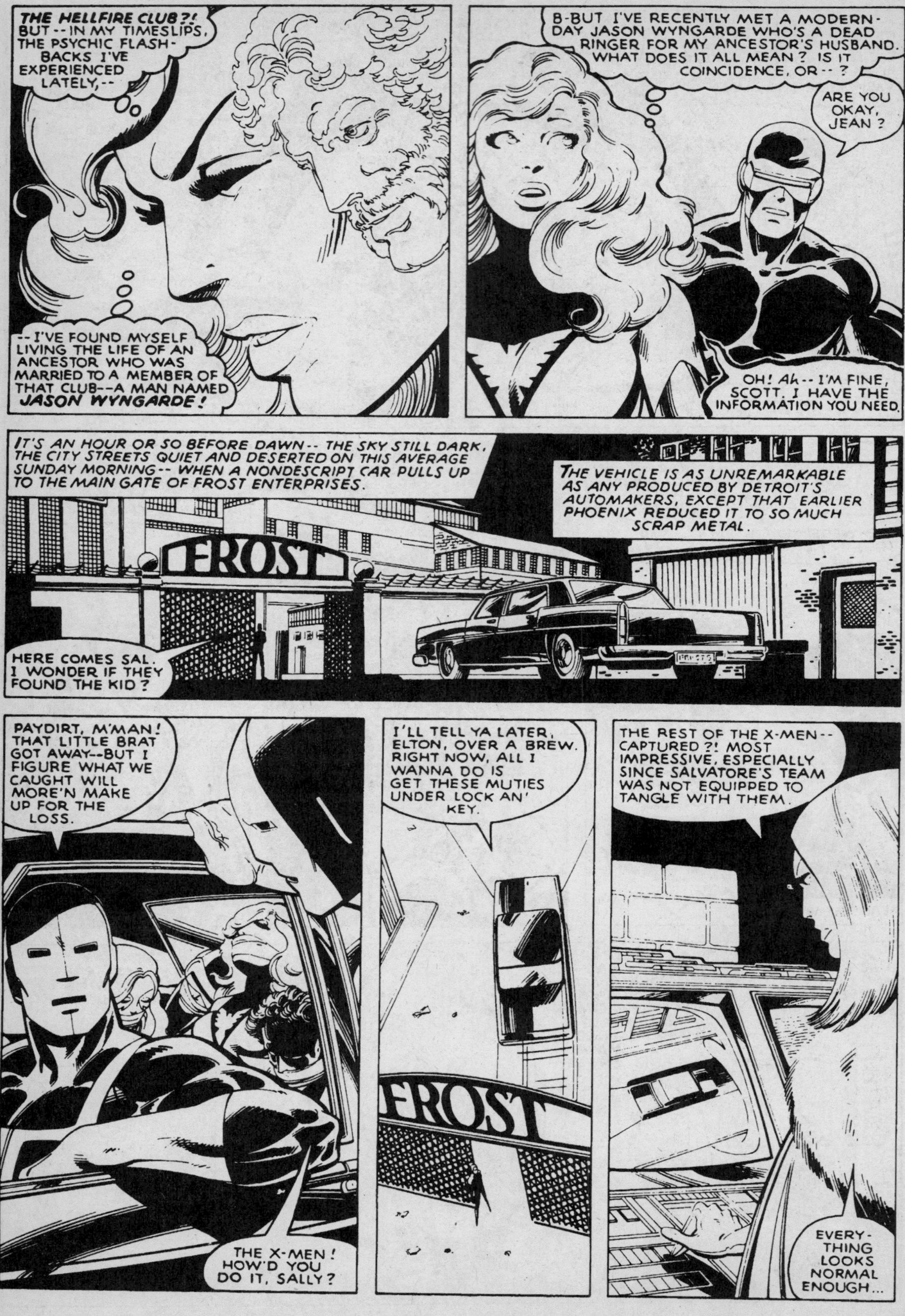
THE HELLFIRE CLUB?! BUT -- IN MY TIMESLIPS, THE PSYCHIC FLASH-BACKS I'VE EXPERIENCED LATELY, --
-- I'VE FOUND MYSELF LIVING THE LIFE OF AN ANCESTOR WHO WAS MARRIED TO A MEMBER OF THAT CLUB--A MAN NAMED JASON WYNGARDE!
B-BUT I'VE RECENTLY MET A MODERN-DAY JASON WYNGARDE WHO'S A DEAD RINGER FOR MY ANCESTOR'S HUSBAND. WHAT DOES IT ALL MEAN? IS IT COINCIDENCE, OR --?
ARE YOU OKAY, JEAN?
OH! Ah -- I'M FINE, SCOTT. I HAVE THE INFORMATION YOU NEED.
IT'S AN HOUR OR SO BEFORE DAWN -- THE SKY STILL DARK, THE CITY STREETS QUIET AND DESERTED ON THIS AVERAGE SUNDAY MORNING -- WHEN A NONDESCRIPT CAR PULLS UP TO THE MAIN GATE OF FROST ENTERPRISES.
FROST
THE VEHICLE IS AS UNREMARKABLE AS ANY PRODUCED BY DETROIT'S AUTOMAKERS, EXCEPT THAT EARLIER PHOENIX REDUCED IT TO SO MUCH SCRAP METAL.
HERE COMES SAL. I WONDER IF THEY FOUND THE KID?
PAYDIRT, M'MAN! THAT LITTLE BRAT GOT AWAY--BUT I FIGURE WHAT WE CAUGHT WILL MORE'N MAKE UP FOR THE LOSS.
THE X-MEN! HOW'D YOU DO IT, SALLY?
I'LL TELL YA LATER, ELTON, OVER A BREW. RIGHT NOW, ALL I WANNA DO IS GET THESE MUTIES UNDER LOCK AN' KEY.
FROST
THE REST OF THE X-MEN -- CAPTURED?! MOST IMPRESSIVE, ESPECIALLY SINCE SALVATORE'S TEAM WAS NOT EQUIPPED TO TANGLE WITH THEM.
EVERYTHING LOOKS NORMAL ENOUGH...

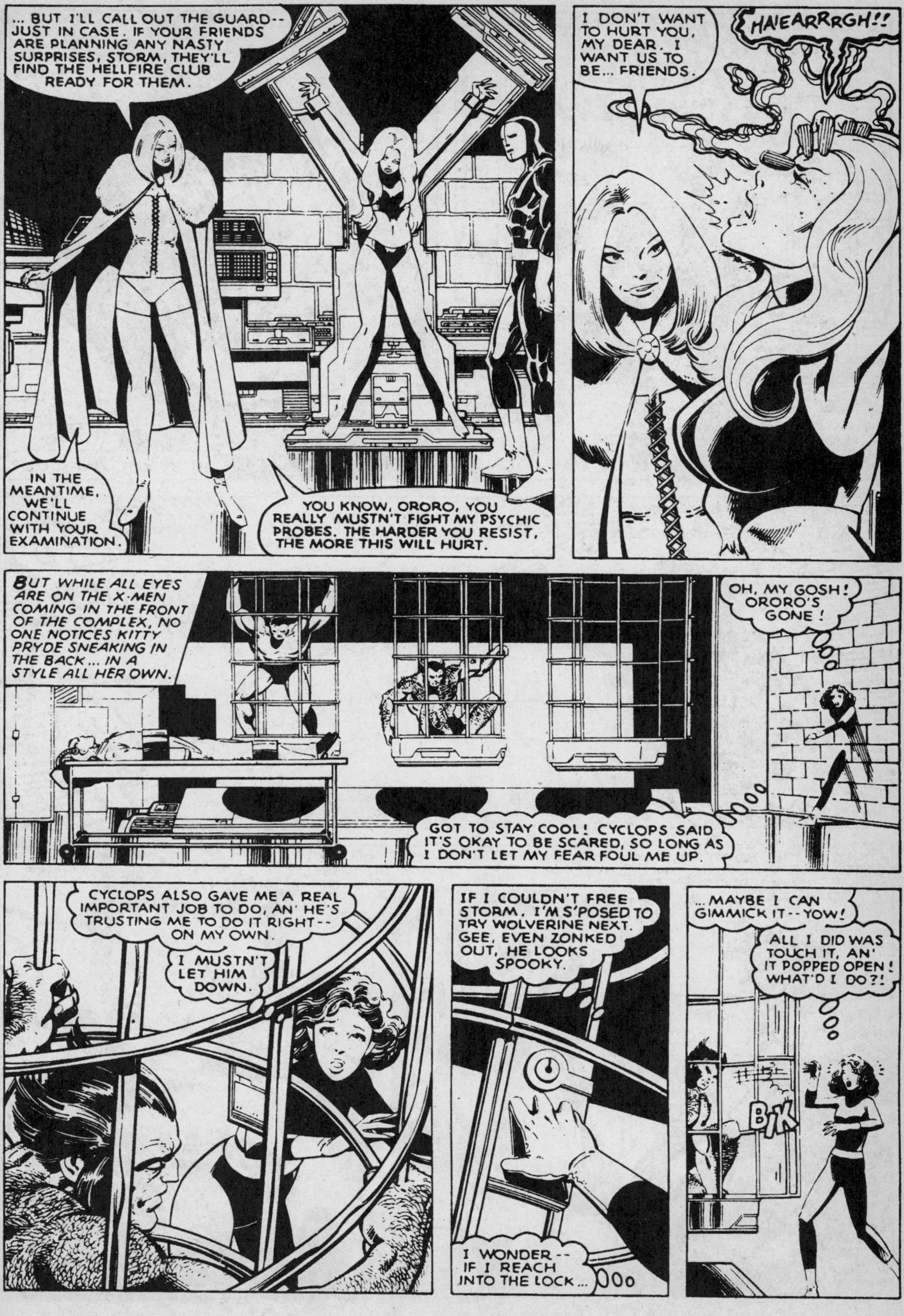
... BUT I'LL CALL OUT THE GUARD-- JUST IN CASE. IF YOUR FRIENDS ARE PLANNING ANY NASTY SURPRISES, STORM, THEY'LL FIND THE HELLFIRE CLUB READY FOR THEM.
IN THE MEANTIME, WE'LL CONTINUE WITH YOUR EXAMINATION.
YOU KNOW, ORORO, YOU REALLY MUSTN'T FIGHT MY PSYCHIC PROBES. THE HARDER YOU RESIST, THE MORE THIS WILL HURT.
I DON'T WANT TO HURT YOU, MY DEAR. I WANT US TO BE... FRIENDS.
CHAIEARRRGH!!
BUT WHILE ALL EYES ARE ON THE X-MEN COMING IN THE FRONT OF THE COMPLEX, NO ONE NOTICES KITTY PRYDE SNEAKING IN THE BACK... IN A STYLE ALL HER OWN.
OH, MY GOSH! ORORO'S GONE!
GOT TO STAY COOL! CYCLOPS SAID IT'S OKAY TO BE SCARED, SO LONG AS I DON'T LET MY FEAR FOUL ME UP.
CYCLOPS ALSO GAVE ME A REAL IMPORTANT JOB TO DO, AN' HE'S TRUSTING ME TO DO IT RIGHT-- ON MY OWN.
I MUSTN'T LET HIM DOWN.
IF I COULDN'T FREE STORM, I'M S'POSED TO TRY WOLVERINE NEXT. GEE, EVEN ZONKED OUT, HE LOOKS SPOOKY.
I WONDER-- IF I REACH INTO THE LOCK...
... MAYBE I CAN GIMMICK IT-- YOW!
BIK
ALL I DID WAS TOUCH IT, AN' IT POPPED OPEN! WHAT'D I DO?!

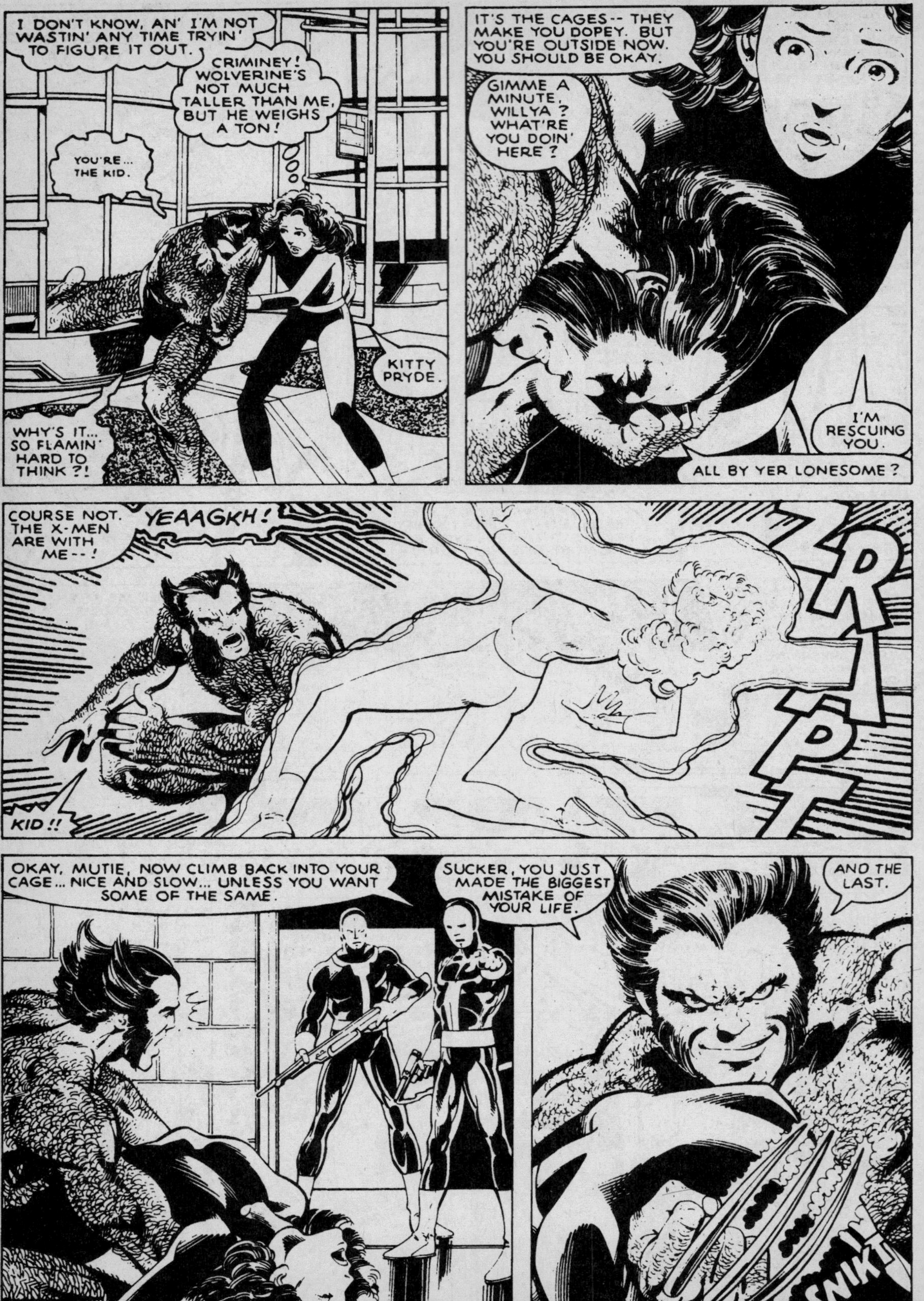
I DON'T KNOW, AN' I'M NOT WASTIN' ANY TIME TRYIN' TO FIGURE IT OUT.
CRIMINEY! WOLVERINE'S NOT MUCH TALLER THAN ME, BUT HE WEIGHS A TON!
YOU'RE... THE KID.
KITTY PRYDE.
WHY'S IT... SO FLAMIN' HARD TO THINK?!
IT'S THE CAGES-- THEY MAKE YOU DOPEY. BUT YOU'RE OUTSIDE NOW. YOU SHOULD BE OKAY.
GIMME A MINUTE, WILLYA? WHAT'RE YOU DOIN' HERE?
I'M RESCUING YOU.
ALL BY YER LONESOME?
COURSE NOT. THE X-MEN ARE WITH ME--!
YEAAGKH!
ZRAPT
KID!!
OKAY, MUTIE, NOW CLIMB BACK INTO YOUR CAGE... NICE AND SLOW... UNLESS YOU WANT SOME OF THE SAME.
SUCKER, YOU JUST MADE THE BIGGEST MISTAKE OF YOUR LIFE.
AND THE LAST.
SNIKT!

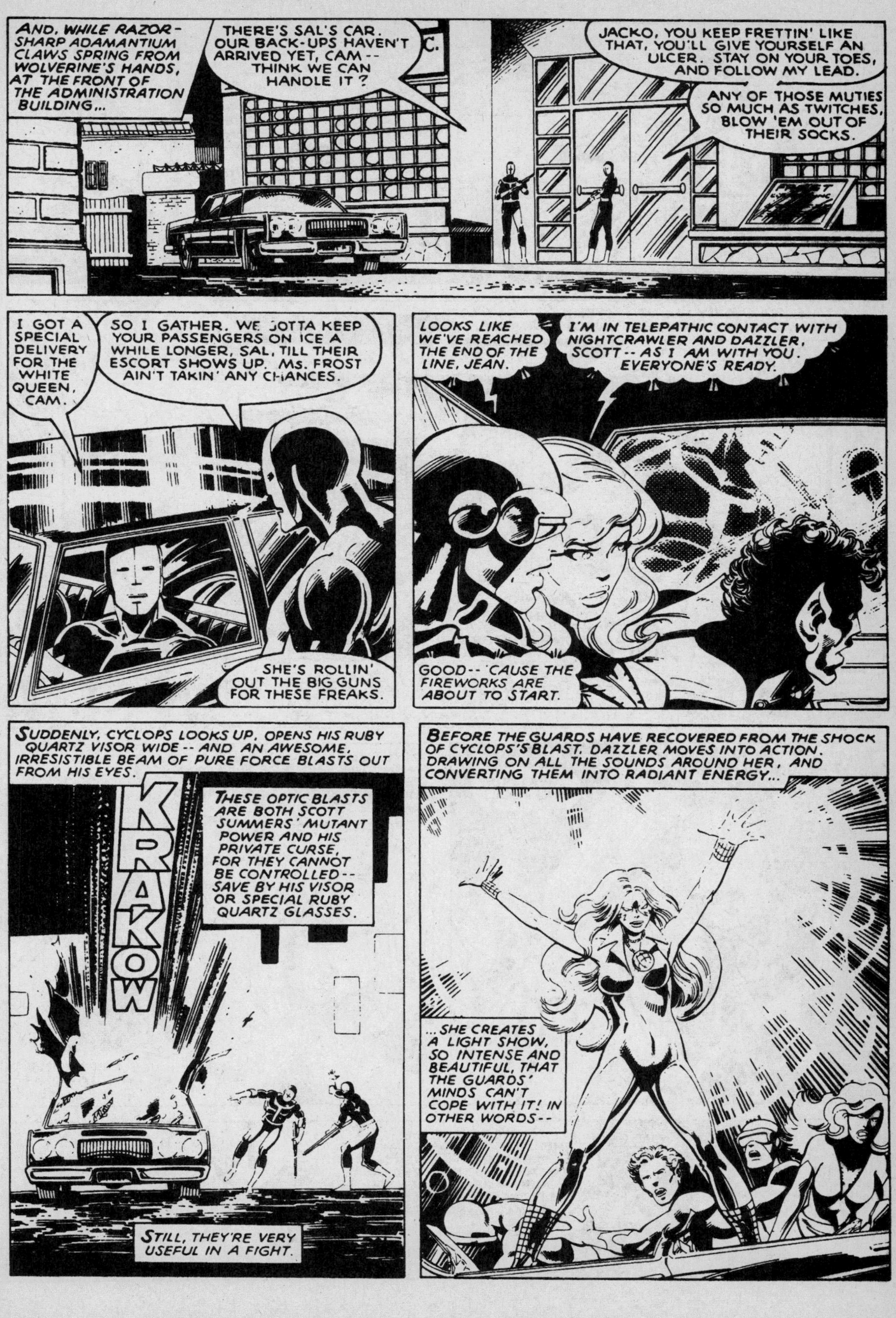

AND, WHILE RAZOR-SHARP ADAMANTIUM CLAWS SPRING FROM WOLVERINE'S HANDS, AT THE FRONT OF THE ADMINISTRATION BUILDING...
THERE'S SAL'S CAR. OUR BACK-UPS HAVEN'T ARRIVED YET, CAM -- THINK WE CAN HANDLE IT?
JACKO, YOU KEEP FRETTIN' LIKE THAT, YOU'LL GIVE YOURSELF AN ULCER. STAY ON YOUR TOES, AND FOLLOW MY LEAD.
ANY OF THOSE MUTIES SO MUCH AS TWITCHES, BLOW 'EM OUT OF THEIR SOCKS.
I GOT A SPECIAL DELIVERY FOR THE WHITE QUEEN, CAM.
SO I GATHER. WE GOTTA KEEP YOUR PASSENGERS ON ICE A WHILE LONGER, SAL, TILL THEIR ESCORT SHOWS UP. Ms. FROST AIN'T TAKIN' ANY CHANCES.
SHE'S ROLLIN' OUT THE BIG GUNS FOR THESE FREAKS.
LOOKS LIKE WE'VE REACHED THE END OF THE LINE, JEAN.
I'M IN TELEPATHIC CONTACT WITH NIGHTCRAWLER AND DAZZLER, SCOTT -- AS I AM WITH YOU. EVERYONE'S READY.
GOOD -- 'CAUSE THE FIREWORKS ARE ABOUT TO START.
SUDDENLY, CYCLOPS LOOKS UP, OPENS HIS RUBY QUARTZ VISOR WIDE -- AND AN AWESOME, IRRESISTIBLE BEAM OF PURE FORCE BLASTS OUT FROM HIS EYES.
KRAKOW
THESE OPTIC BLASTS ARE BOTH SCOTT SUMMERS' MUTANT POWER AND HIS PRIVATE CURSE, FOR THEY CANNOT BE CONTROLLED -- SAVE BY HIS VISOR OR SPECIAL RUBY QUARTZ GLASSES.
STILL, THEY'RE VERY USEFUL IN A FIGHT.
BEFORE THE GUARDS HAVE RECOVERED FROM THE SHOCK OF CYCLOPS'S BLAST, DAZZLER MOVES INTO ACTION, DRAWING ON ALL THE SOUNDS AROUND HER, AND CONVERTING THEM INTO RADIANT ENERGY...
...SHE CREATES A LIGHT SHOW, SO INTENSE AND BEAUTIFUL, THAT THE GUARDS' MINDS CAN'T COPE WITH IT! IN OTHER WORDS --

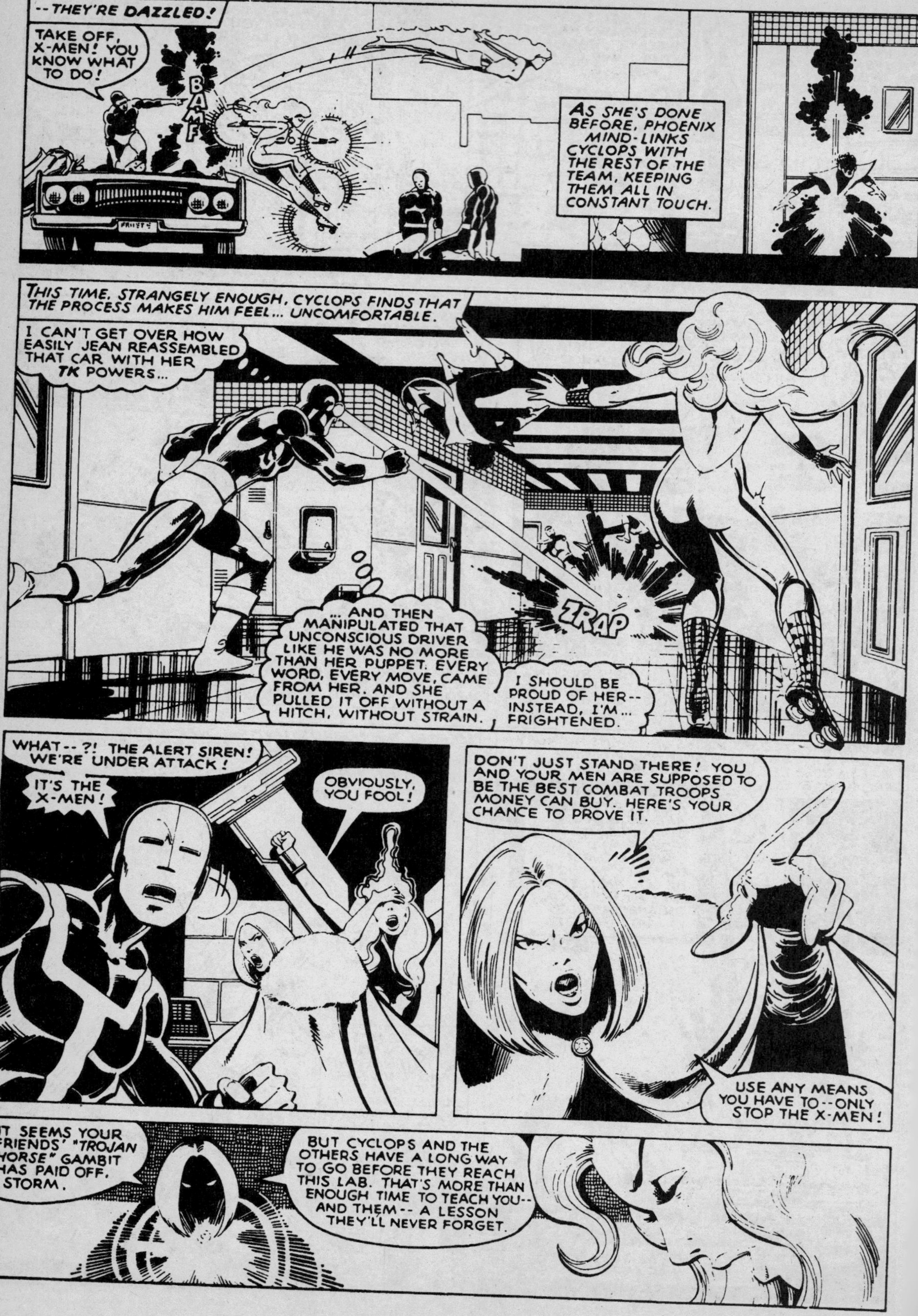
--THEY'RE DAZZLED!
TAKE OFF, X-MEN! YOU KNOW WHAT TO DO!
BAMF
AS SHE'S DONE BEFORE, PHOENIX MIND-LINKS CYCLOPS WITH THE REST OF THE TEAM, KEEPING THEM ALL IN CONSTANT TOUCH.
THIS TIME, STRANGELY ENOUGH, CYCLOPS FINDS THAT THE PROCESS MAKES HIM FEEL... UNCOMFORTABLE.
I CAN'T GET OVER HOW EASILY JEAN REASSEMBLED THAT CAR WITH HER TK POWERS...
ZRAP
... AND THEN MANIPULATED THAT UNCONSCIOUS DRIVER LIKE HE WAS NO MORE THAN HER PUPPET. EVERY WORD, EVERY MOVE, CAME FROM HER. AND SHE PULLED IT OFF WITHOUT A HITCH, WITHOUT STRAIN.
I SHOULD BE PROUD OF HER-- INSTEAD, I'M... FRIGHTENED.
WHAT--?! THE ALERT SIREN! WE'RE UNDER ATTACK!
IT'S THE X-MEN!
OBVIOUSLY, YOU FOOL!
DON'T JUST STAND THERE! YOU AND YOUR MEN ARE SUPPOSED TO BE THE BEST COMBAT TROOPS MONEY CAN BUY. HERE'S YOUR CHANCE TO PROVE IT.
USE ANY MEANS YOU HAVE TO--ONLY STOP THE X-MEN!
IT SEEMS YOUR FRIENDS' "TROJAN HORSE" GAMBIT HAS PAID OFF, STORM.
BUT CYCLOPS AND THE OTHERS HAVE A LONG WAY TO GO BEFORE THEY REACH THIS LAB. THAT'S MORE THAN ENOUGH TIME TO TEACH YOU-- AND THEM-- A LESSON THEY'LL NEVER FORGET.

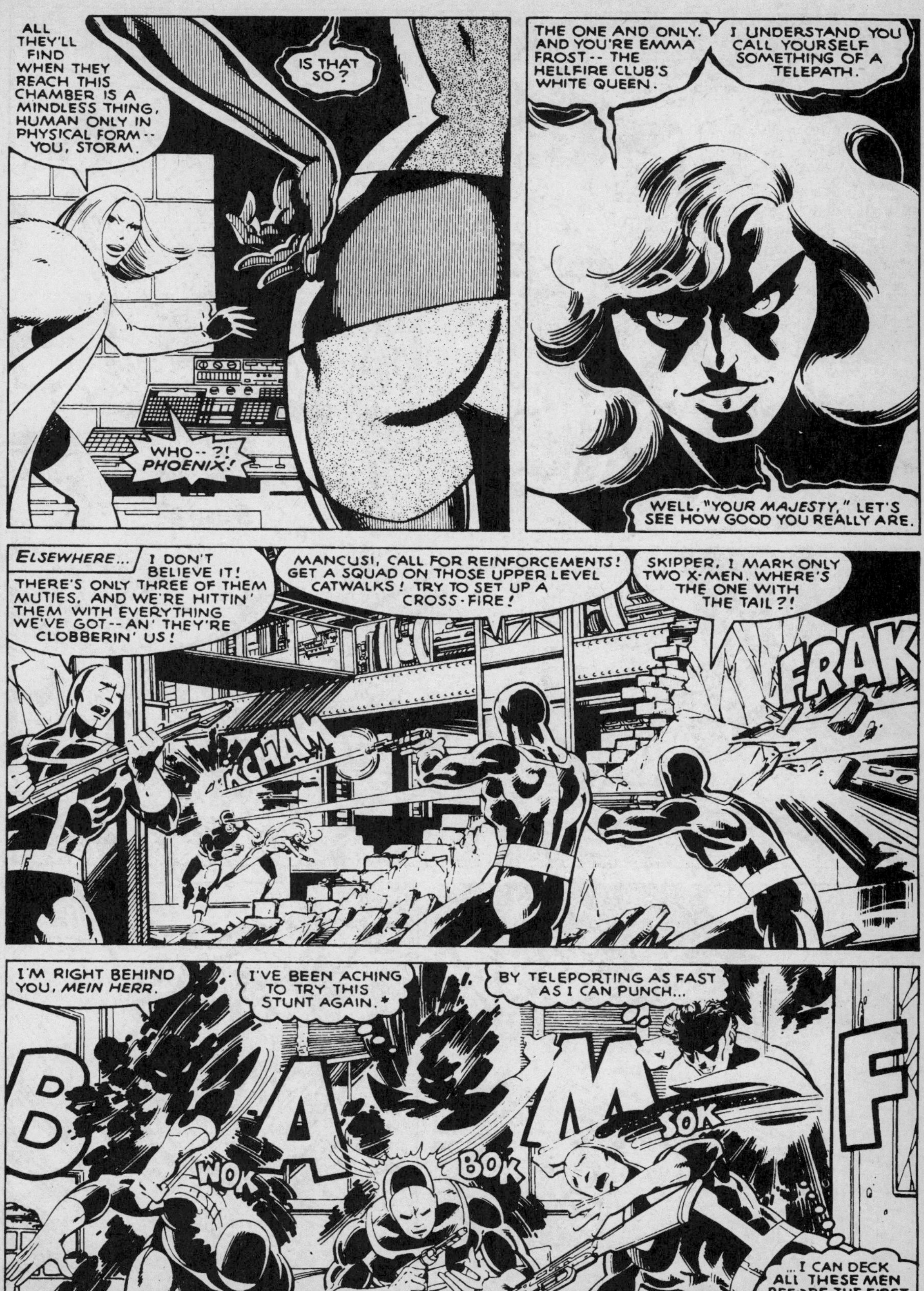
ALL THEY'LL FIND WHEN THEY REACH THIS CHAMBER IS A MINDLESS THING, HUMAN ONLY IN PHYSICAL FORM -- YOU, STORM.
IS THAT SO?
WHO--?! PHOENIX!
THE ONE AND ONLY. AND YOU'RE EMMA FROST -- THE HELLFIRE CLUB'S WHITE QUEEN.
I UNDERSTAND YOU CALL YOURSELF SOMETHING OF A TELEPATH.
WELL, "YOUR MAJESTY," LET'S SEE HOW GOOD YOU REALLY ARE.
ELSEWHERE...
I DON'T BELIEVE IT! THERE'S ONLY THREE OF THEM MUTIES, AND WE'RE HITTIN' THEM WITH EVERYTHING WE'VE GOT--AN' THEY'RE CLOBBERIN' US!
MANCUSI, CALL FOR REINFORCEMENTS! GET A SQUAD ON THOSE UPPER LEVEL CATWALKS! TRY TO SET UP A CROSS-FIRE!
SKIPPER, I MARK ONLY TWO X-MEN. WHERE'S THE ONE WITH THE TAIL?!
FRAK
KCHAM
I'M RIGHT BEHIND YOU, MEIN HERR.
I'VE BEEN ACHING TO TRY THIS STUNT AGAIN.*
BY TELEPORTING AS FAST AS I CAN PUNCH...
BAMF
WOK
BOK
SOK
...I CAN DECK ALL THESE MEN BEFORE THE FIRST ONE EVEN HITS THE GROUND!
*LAST USED IN CLASSIC #17--BOB.

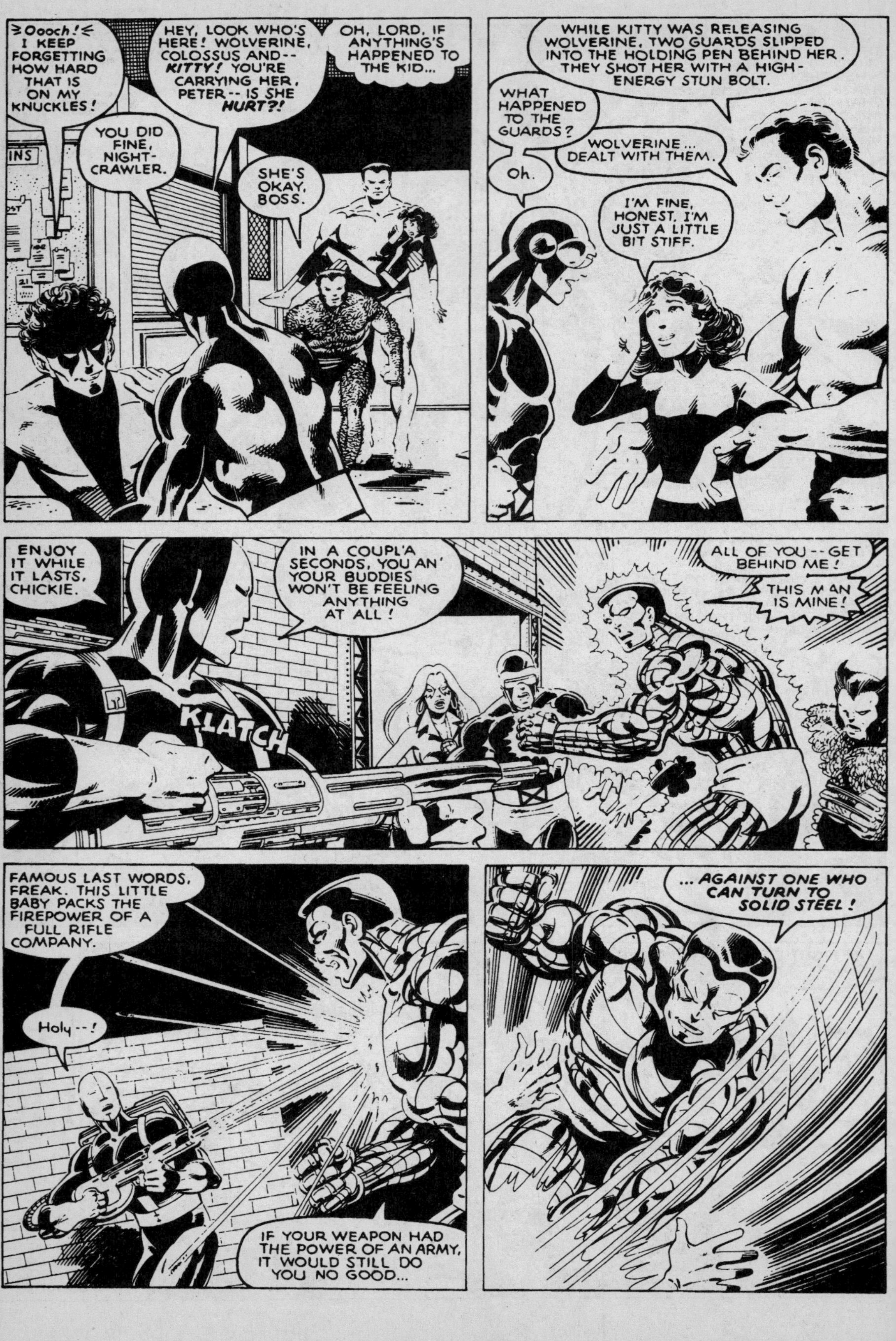
≥Oooch!≤ I KEEP FORGETTING HOW HARD THAT IS ON MY KNUCKLES!
HEY, LOOK WHO'S HERE! WOLVERINE, COLOSSUS AND-- KITTY! YOU'RE CARRYING HER, PETER-- IS SHE HURT?!
OH, LORD, IF ANYTHING'S HAPPENED TO THE KID...
YOU DID FINE, NIGHT-CRAWLER.
SHE'S OKAY, BOSS.
INS
WHAT HAPPENED TO THE GUARDS?
WHILE KITTY WAS RELEASING WOLVERINE, TWO GUARDS SLIPPED INTO THE HOLDING PEN BEHIND HER. THEY SHOT HER WITH A HIGH-ENERGY STUN BOLT.
WOLVERINE... DEALT WITH THEM.
Oh.
I'M FINE, HONEST. I'M JUST A LITTLE BIT STIFF.
ENJOY IT WHILE IT LASTS, CHICKIE.
IN A COUPL'A SECONDS, YOU AN' YOUR BUDDIES WON'T BE FEELING ANYTHING AT ALL!
KLATCH
ALL OF YOU-- GET BEHIND ME!
THIS MAN IS MINE!
FAMOUS LAST WORDS, FREAK. THIS LITTLE BABY PACKS THE FIREPOWER OF A FULL RIFLE COMPANY.
Holy--!
IF YOUR WEAPON HAD THE POWER OF AN ARMY, IT WOULD STILL DO YOU NO GOOD...
...AGAINST ONE WHO CAN TURN TO SOLID STEEL!

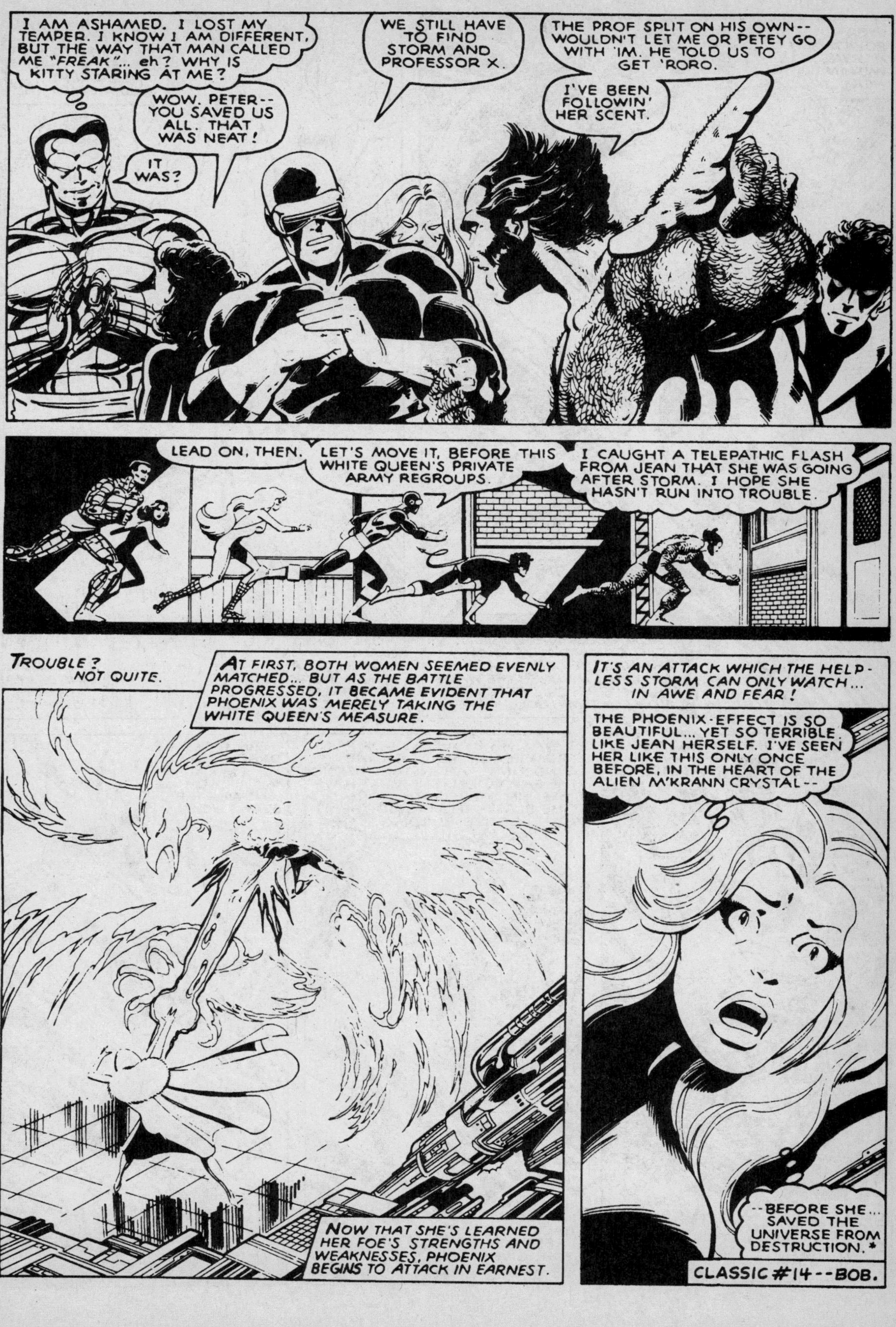
I AM ASHAMED. I LOST MY TEMPER. I KNOW I AM DIFFERENT, BUT THE WAY THAT MAN CALLED ME "FREAK"... eh? WHY IS KITTY STARING AT ME?
WOW. PETER-- YOU SAVED US ALL. THAT WAS NEAT!
IT WAS?
WE STILL HAVE TO FIND STORM AND PROFESSOR X.
THE PROF SPLIT ON HIS OWN-- WOULDN'T LET ME OR PETEY GO WITH 'IM. HE TOLD US TO GET 'RORO.
I'VE BEEN FOLLOWIN' HER SCENT.
LEAD ON, THEN.
LET'S MOVE IT, BEFORE THIS WHITE QUEEN'S PRIVATE ARMY REGROUPS.
I CAUGHT A TELEPATHIC FLASH FROM JEAN THAT SHE WAS GOING AFTER STORM. I HOPE SHE HASN'T RUN INTO TROUBLE.
TROUBLE? NOT QUITE.
AT FIRST, BOTH WOMEN SEEMED EVENLY MATCHED... BUT AS THE BATTLE PROGRESSED, IT BECAME EVIDENT THAT PHOENIX WAS MERELY TAKING THE WHITE QUEEN'S MEASURE.
NOW THAT SHE'S LEARNED HER FOE'S STRENGTHS AND WEAKNESSES, PHOENIX BEGINS TO ATTACK IN EARNEST.
IT'S AN ATTACK WHICH THE HELPLESS STORM CAN ONLY WATCH... IN AWE AND FEAR!
THE PHOENIX-EFFECT IS SO BEAUTIFUL... YET SO TERRIBLE. LIKE JEAN HERSELF. I'VE SEEN HER LIKE THIS ONLY ONCE BEFORE, IN THE HEART OF THE ALIEN M'KRANN CRYSTAL--
--BEFORE SHE... SAVED THE UNIVERSE FROM DESTRUCTION.*
CLASSIC #14--BOB.

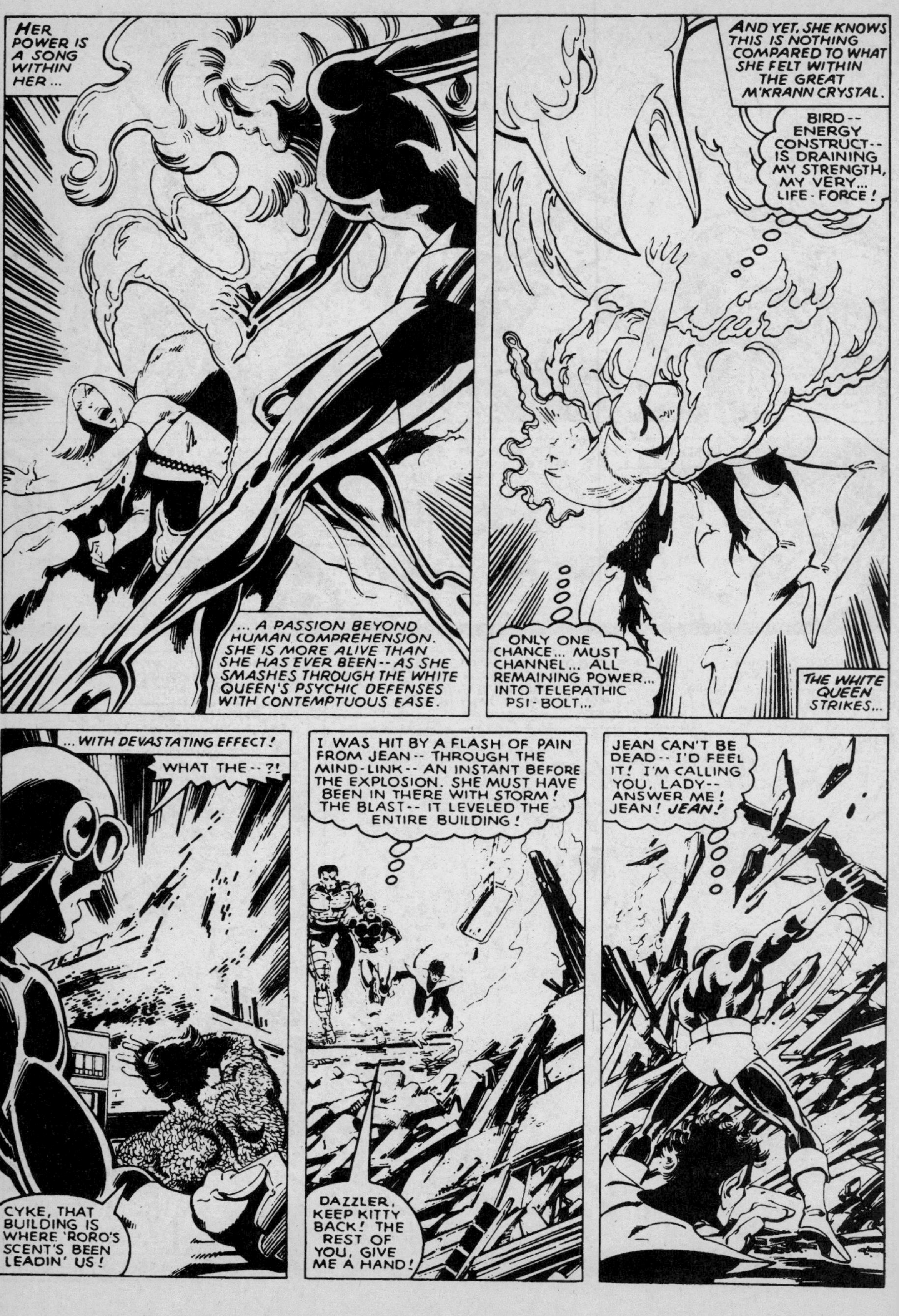
HER POWER IS A SONG WITHIN HER...
... A PASSION BEYOND HUMAN COMPREHENSION. SHE IS MORE ALIVE THAN SHE HAS EVER BEEN -- AS SHE SMASHES THROUGH THE WHITE QUEEN'S PSYCHIC DEFENSES WITH CONTEMPTUOUS EASE.
AND YET, SHE KNOWS THIS IS NOTHING COMPARED TO WHAT SHE FELT WITHIN THE GREAT M'KRANN CRYSTAL.
BIRD -- ENERGY CONSTRUCT -- IS DRAINING MY STRENGTH, MY VERY... LIFE-FORCE!
ONLY ONE CHANCE... MUST CHANNEL... ALL REMAINING POWER... INTO TELEPATHIC PSI-BOLT...
THE WHITE QUEEN STRIKES...
...WITH DEVASTATING EFFECT!
WHAT THE--?!
CYKE, THAT BUILDING IS WHERE 'RORO'S SCENT'S BEEN LEADIN' US!
I WAS HIT BY A FLASH OF PAIN FROM JEAN -- THROUGH THE MIND-LINK -- AN INSTANT BEFORE THE EXPLOSION. SHE MUST HAVE BEEN IN THERE WITH STORM! THE BLAST -- IT LEVELED THE ENTIRE BUILDING!
DAZZLER, KEEP KITTY BACK! THE REST OF YOU, GIVE ME A HAND!
JEAN CAN'T BE DEAD -- I'D FEEL IT! I'M CALLING YOU, LADY -- ANSWER ME! JEAN! JEAN!

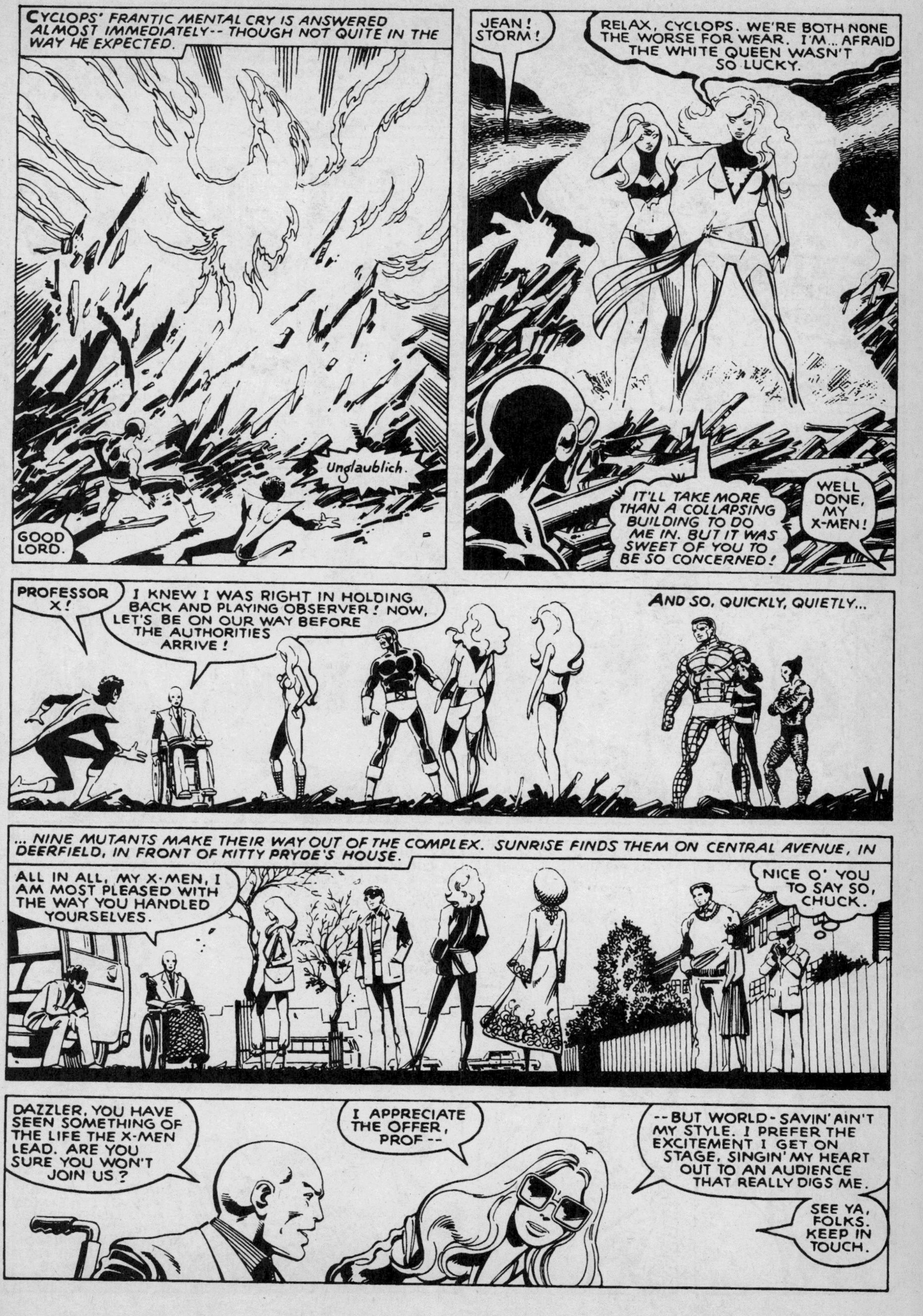
CYCLOPS' FRANTIC MENTAL CRY IS ANSWERED ALMOST IMMEDIATELY-- THOUGH NOT QUITE IN THE WAY HE EXPECTED.
Unglaublich.
GOOD LORD.
JEAN! STORM!
RELAX, CYCLOPS. WE'RE BOTH NONE THE WORSE FOR WEAR. I'M... AFRAID THE WHITE QUEEN WASN'T SO LUCKY.
IT'LL TAKE MORE THAN A COLLAPSING BUILDING TO DO ME IN. BUT IT WAS SWEET OF YOU TO BE SO CONCERNED!
WELL DONE, MY X-MEN!
PROFESSOR X!
I KNEW I WAS RIGHT IN HOLDING BACK AND PLAYING OBSERVER! NOW, LET'S BE ON OUR WAY BEFORE THE AUTHORITIES ARRIVE!
AND SO, QUICKLY, QUIETLY...
... NINE MUTANTS MAKE THEIR WAY OUT OF THE COMPLEX. SUNRISE FINDS THEM ON CENTRAL AVENUE, IN DEERFIELD, IN FRONT OF KITTY PRYDE'S HOUSE.
ALL IN ALL, MY X-MEN, I AM MOST PLEASED WITH THE WAY YOU HANDLED YOURSELVES.
NICE O' YOU TO SAY SO, CHUCK.
DAZZLER, YOU HAVE SEEN SOMETHING OF THE LIFE THE X-MEN LEAD. ARE YOU SURE YOU WON'T JOIN US?
I APPRECIATE THE OFFER, PROF--
--BUT WORLD-SAVIN' AIN'T MY STYLE. I PREFER THE EXCITEMENT I GET ON STAGE, SINGIN' MY HEART OUT TO AN AUDIENCE THAT REALLY DIGS ME.
SEE YA, FOLKS. KEEP IN TOUCH.

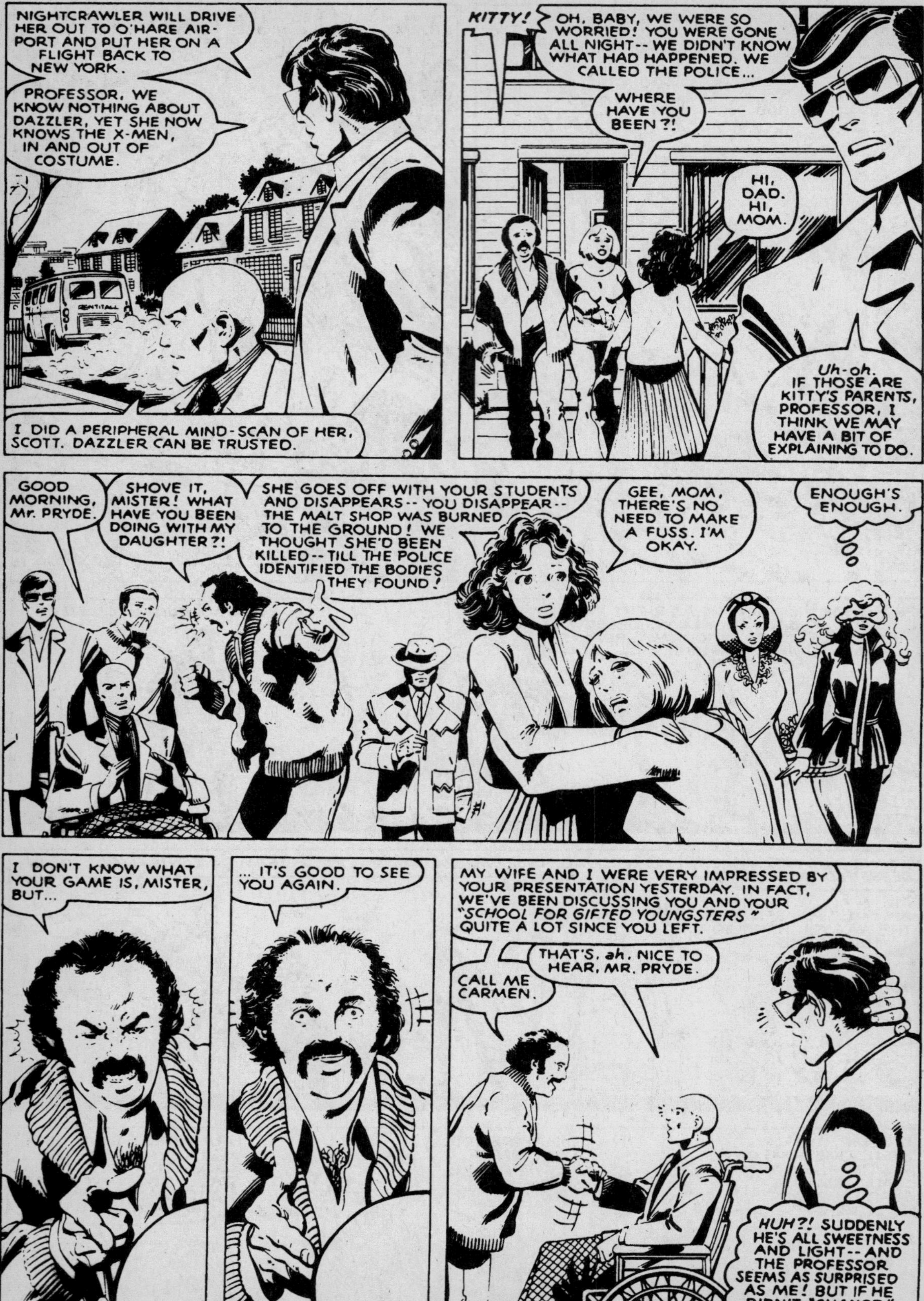
NIGHTCRAWLER WILL DRIVE HER OUT TO O'HARE AIRPORT AND PUT HER ON A FLIGHT BACK TO NEW YORK.
PROFESSOR, WE KNOW NOTHING ABOUT DAZZLER, YET SHE NOW KNOWS THE X-MEN, IN AND OUT OF COSTUME.
I DID A PERIPHERAL MIND-SCAN OF HER, SCOTT. DAZZLER CAN BE TRUSTED.
KITTY!
OH, BABY, WE WERE SO WORRIED! YOU WERE GONE ALL NIGHT-- WE DIDN'T KNOW WHAT HAD HAPPENED. WE CALLED THE POLICE...
WHERE HAVE YOU BEEN?!
HI, DAD. HI, MOM.
Uh-oh. IF THOSE ARE KITTY'S PARENTS, PROFESSOR, I THINK WE MAY HAVE A BIT OF EXPLAINING TO DO.
GOOD MORNING, Mr. PRYDE.
SHOVE IT, MISTER! WHAT HAVE YOU BEEN DOING WITH MY DAUGHTER?!
SHE GOES OFF WITH YOUR STUDENTS AND DISAPPEARS-- YOU DISAPPEAR-- THE MALT SHOP WAS BURNED TO THE GROUND! WE THOUGHT SHE'D BEEN KILLED-- TILL THE POLICE IDENTIFIED THE BODIES THEY FOUND!
GEE, MOM, THERE'S NO NEED TO MAKE A FUSS. I'M OKAY.
ENOUGH'S ENOUGH.
I DON'T KNOW WHAT YOUR GAME IS, MISTER, BUT...
... IT'S GOOD TO SEE YOU AGAIN.
MY WIFE AND I WERE VERY IMPRESSED BY YOUR PRESENTATION YESTERDAY. IN FACT, WE'VE BEEN DISCUSSING YOU AND YOUR "SCHOOL FOR GIFTED YOUNGSTERS" QUITE A LOT SINCE YOU LEFT.
CALL ME CARMEN.
THAT'S, ah, NICE TO HEAR, MR. PRYDE.
HUH?! SUDDENLY HE'S ALL SWEETNESS AND LIGHT-- AND THE PROFESSOR SEEMS AS SURPRISED AS ME! BUT IF HE DIDN'T "CHANGE" PRYDE'S MIND, WHO--?

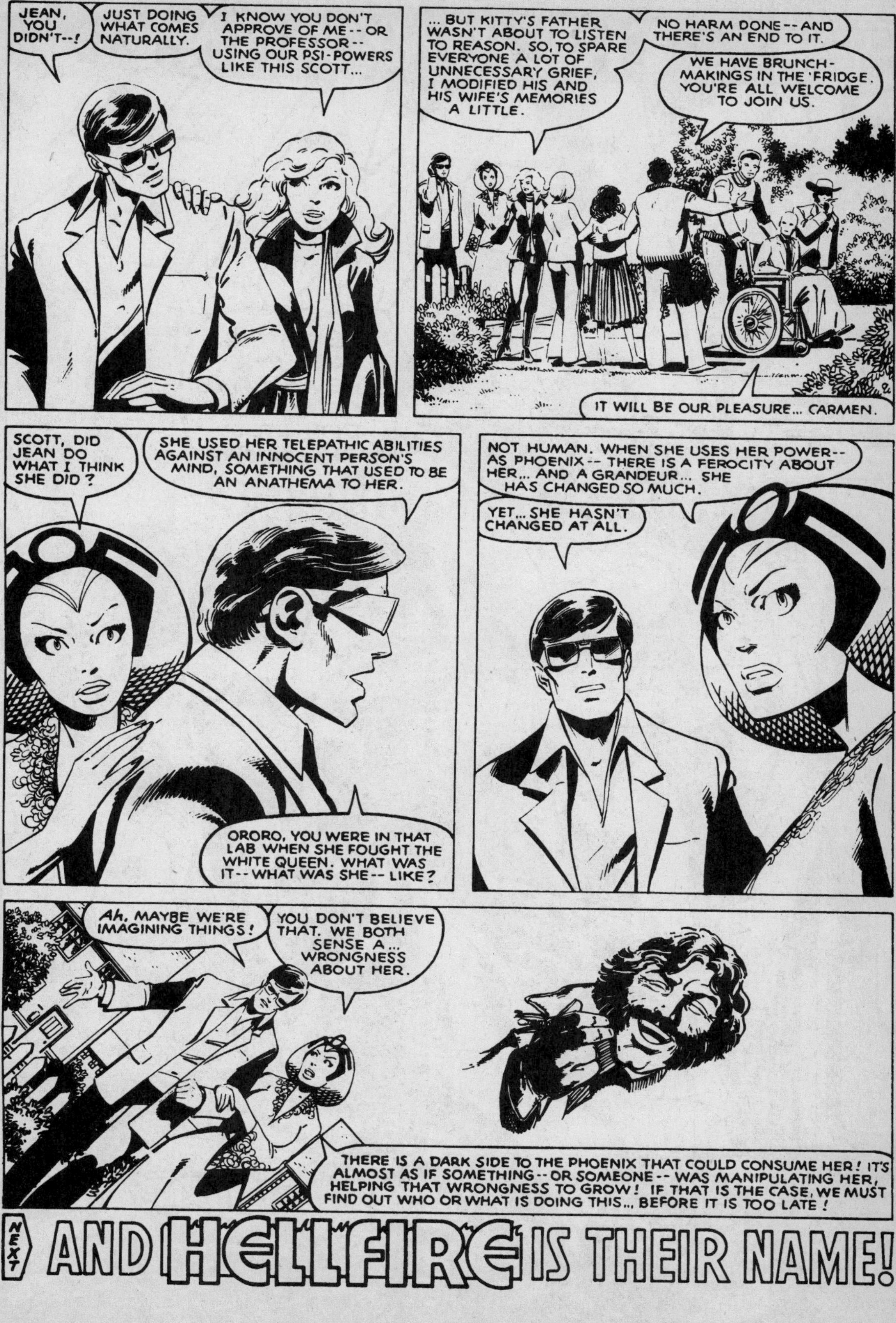
JEAN, YOU DIDN'T--!
JUST DOING WHAT COMES NATURALLY.
I KNOW YOU DON'T APPROVE OF ME -- OR THE PROFESSOR -- USING OUR PSI-POWERS LIKE THIS SCOTT...
... BUT KITTY'S FATHER WASN'T ABOUT TO LISTEN TO REASON. SO, TO SPARE EVERYONE A LOT OF UNNECESSARY GRIEF, I MODIFIED HIS AND HIS WIFE'S MEMORIES A LITTLE.
NO HARM DONE -- AND THERE'S AN END TO IT.
WE HAVE BRUNCH-MAKINGS IN THE 'FRIDGE. YOU'RE ALL WELCOME TO JOIN US.
IT WILL BE OUR PLEASURE... CARMEN.
SCOTT, DID JEAN DO WHAT I THINK SHE DID?
SHE USED HER TELEPATHIC ABILITIES AGAINST AN INNOCENT PERSON'S MIND, SOMETHING THAT USED TO BE AN ANATHEMA TO HER.
ORORO, YOU WERE IN THAT LAB WHEN SHE FOUGHT THE WHITE QUEEN. WHAT WAS IT -- WHAT WAS SHE -- LIKE?
NOT HUMAN. WHEN SHE USES HER POWER -- AS PHOENIX -- THERE IS A FEROCITY ABOUT HER... AND A GRANDEUR... SHE HAS CHANGED SO MUCH.
YET... SHE HASN'T CHANGED AT ALL.
Ah, MAYBE WE'RE IMAGINING THINGS!
YOU DON'T BELIEVE THAT. WE BOTH SENSE A... WRONGNESS ABOUT HER.
THERE IS A DARK SIDE TO THE PHOENIX THAT COULD CONSUME HER! IT'S ALMOST AS IF SOMETHING -- OR SOMEONE -- WAS MANIPULATING HER, HELPING THAT WRONGNESS TO GROW! IF THAT IS THE CASE, WE MUST FIND OUT WHO OR WHAT IS DOING THIS... BEFORE IT IS TOO LATE!
NEXT
AND HELLFIRE IS THEIR NAME!

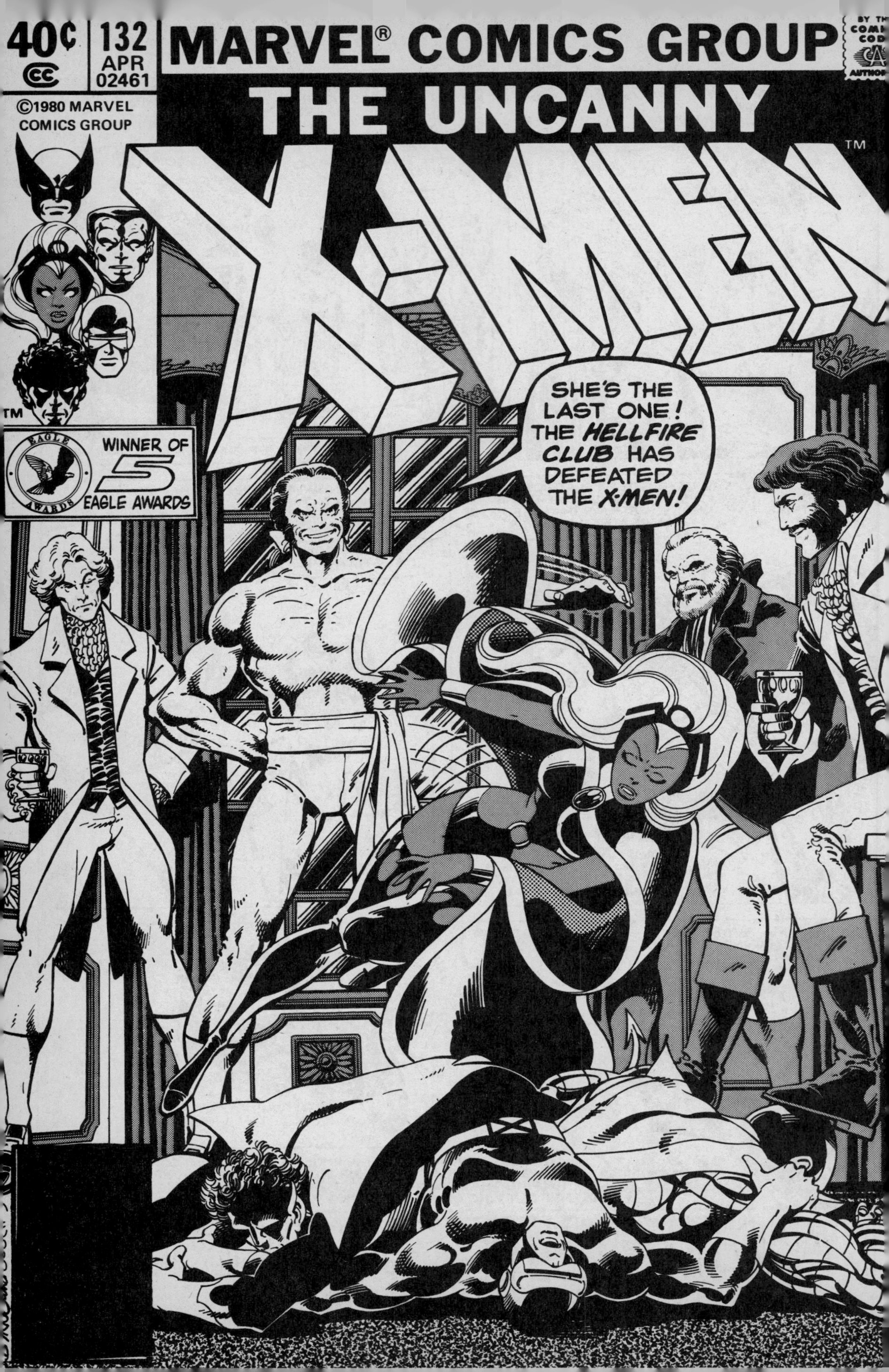

40¢
132
APR
02461
MARVEL® COMICS GROUP
©1980 MARVEL COMICS GROUP
THE UNCANNY
X-MEN™
WINNER OF 5 EAGLE AWARDS
SHE'S THE LAST ONE! THE HELLFIRE CLUB HAS DEFEATED THE X-MEN!

Cyclops. Storm. Nightcrawler. Wolverine. Colossus. Children of the atom, students of Charles Xavier, MUTANTS — feared and hated by the world they have sworn to protect. These are the STRANGEST heroes of all!

STAN LEE PRESENTS: THE UNCANNY X-MEN! ™

CHRIS CLAREMONT · JOHN BYRNE | TERRY AUSTIN | TOM ORZECHOWSKI, letterer | JIM SALICRUP | JIM SHOOTER
WRITER / CO-PLOTTERS / PENCILER | INKER | GLYNIS WEIN, colorist | EDITOR | Ed.-IN-CHIEF

AND Hellfire IS THEIR name!

IN NEW MEXICO, ALONG THE CONTINENTAL DIVIDE -- LITERALLY MILES FROM ANYWHERE-- STANDS A VERY SPECIAL HOUSE, OWNED BY A VERY SPECIAL YOUNG MAN.

SCOTTY! LONG TIME, NO SEE, OL' BUDDY!

WELCOME TO ANGEL'S AERIE, X-MEN. MY HOME AWAY FROM HOME.

HE WAS CHRISTENED WARREN WORTHINGTON III, HEIR APPARENT TO ONE OF AMERICA'S LARGER PRIVATE FORTUNES.

IN LATER YEARS, HE BECAME SOMEWHAT BETTER KNOWN AS THE HIGH-FLYING ANGEL, ONE OF THE FOUNDING MEMBERS OF THE UNCANNY X-MEN.

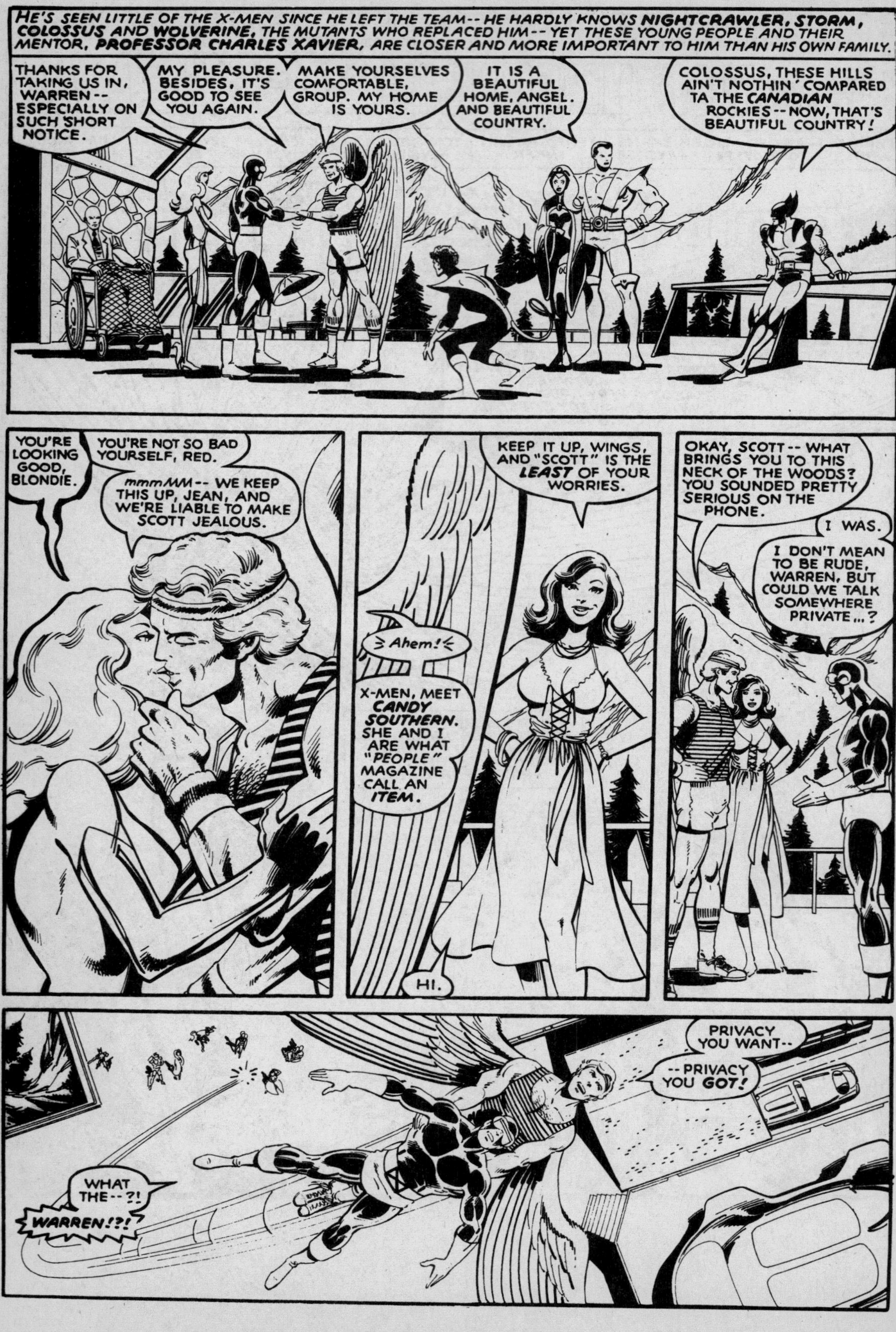
HE'S SEEN LITTLE OF THE X-MEN SINCE HE LEFT THE TEAM-- HE HARDLY KNOWS NIGHTCRAWLER, STORM, COLOSSUS AND WOLVERINE, THE MUTANTS WHO REPLACED HIM-- YET THESE YOUNG PEOPLE AND THEIR MENTOR, PROFESSOR CHARLES XAVIER, ARE CLOSER AND MORE IMPORTANT TO HIM THAN HIS OWN FAMILY.
THANKS FOR TAKING US IN, WARREN-- ESPECIALLY ON SUCH SHORT NOTICE.
MY PLEASURE. BESIDES, IT'S GOOD TO SEE YOU AGAIN.
MAKE YOURSELVES COMFORTABLE, GROUP. MY HOME IS YOURS.
IT IS A BEAUTIFUL HOME, ANGEL. AND BEAUTIFUL COUNTRY.
COLOSSUS, THESE HILLS AIN'T NOTHIN' COMPARED TA THE CANADIAN ROCKIES-- NOW, THAT'S BEAUTIFUL COUNTRY!
YOU'RE LOOKING GOOD, BLONDIE.
YOU'RE NOT SO BAD YOURSELF, RED.
mmmMM-- WE KEEP THIS UP, JEAN, AND WE'RE LIABLE TO MAKE SCOTT JEALOUS.
KEEP IT UP, WINGS, AND "SCOTT" IS THE LEAST OF YOUR WORRIES.
Ahem!
X-MEN, MEET CANDY SOUTHERN. SHE AND I ARE WHAT "PEOPLE" MAGAZINE CALL AN ITEM.
HI.
OKAY, SCOTT-- WHAT BRINGS YOU TO THIS NECK OF THE WOODS? YOU SOUNDED PRETTY SERIOUS ON THE PHONE.
I WAS.
I DON'T MEAN TO BE RUDE, WARREN, BUT COULD WE TALK SOMEWHERE PRIVATE...?
PRIVACY YOU WANT--
--PRIVACY YOU GOT!
WHAT THE--?!
WARREN!?!

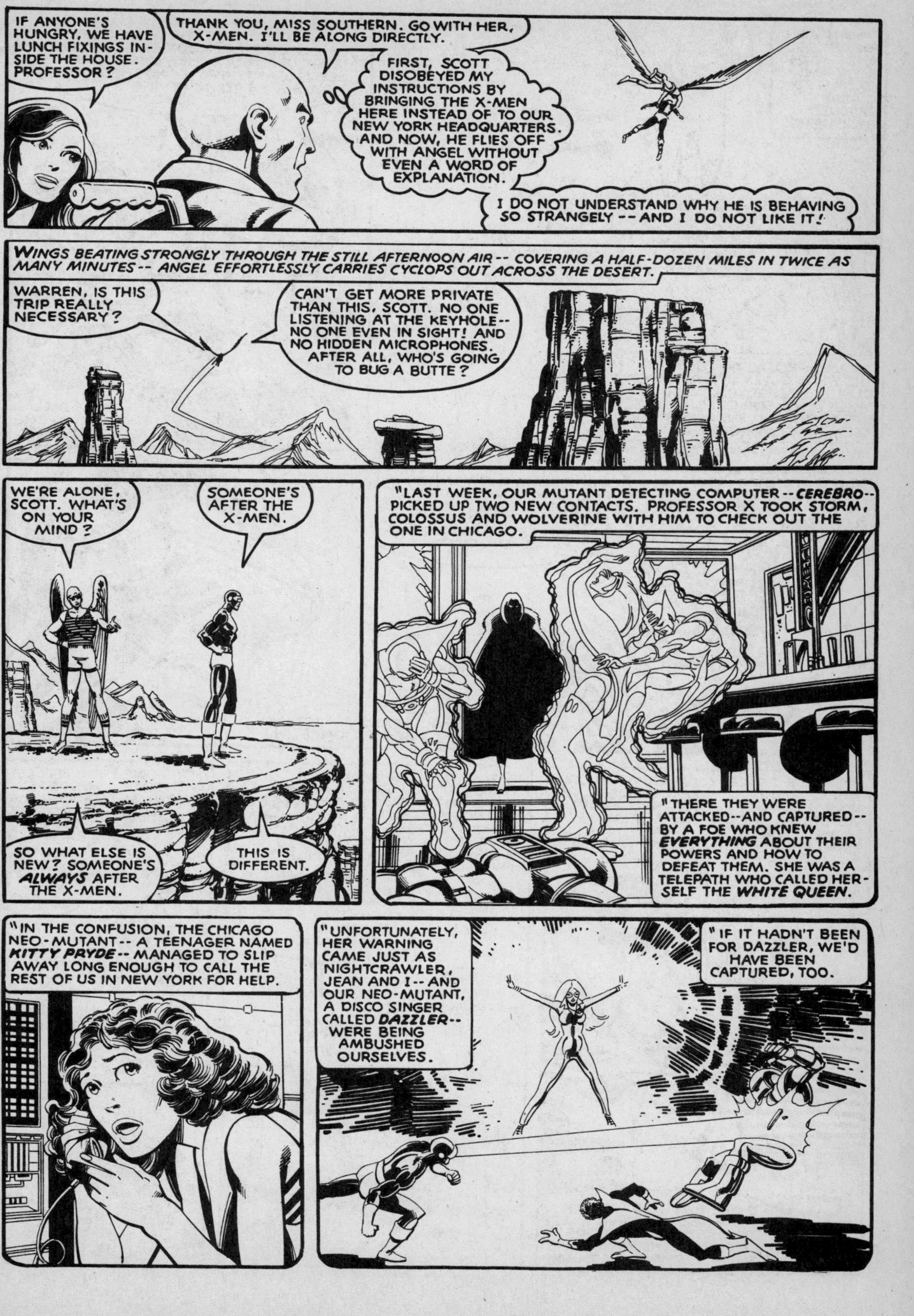
IF ANYONE'S HUNGRY, WE HAVE LUNCH FIXINGS INSIDE THE HOUSE. PROFESSOR?
THANK YOU, MISS SOUTHERN. GO WITH HER, X-MEN. I'LL BE ALONG DIRECTLY.
FIRST, SCOTT DISOBEYED MY INSTRUCTIONS BY BRINGING THE X-MEN HERE INSTEAD OF TO OUR NEW YORK HEADQUARTERS. AND NOW, HE FLIES OFF WITH ANGEL WITHOUT EVEN A WORD OF EXPLANATION.
I DO NOT UNDERSTAND WHY HE IS BEHAVING SO STRANGELY -- AND I DO NOT LIKE IT!
WINGS BEATING STRONGLY THROUGH THE STILL AFTERNOON AIR -- COVERING A HALF-DOZEN MILES IN TWICE AS MANY MINUTES -- ANGEL EFFORTLESSLY CARRIES CYCLOPS OUT ACROSS THE DESERT.
WARREN, IS THIS TRIP REALLY NECESSARY?
CAN'T GET MORE PRIVATE THAN THIS, SCOTT. NO ONE LISTENING AT THE KEYHOLE -- NO ONE EVEN IN SIGHT! AND NO HIDDEN MICROPHONES. AFTER ALL, WHO'S GOING TO BUG A BUTTE?
WE'RE ALONE, SCOTT. WHAT'S ON YOUR MIND?
SOMEONE'S AFTER THE X-MEN.
SO WHAT ELSE IS NEW? SOMEONE'S ALWAYS AFTER THE X-MEN.
THIS IS DIFFERENT.
"LAST WEEK, OUR MUTANT DETECTING COMPUTER -- CEREBRO -- PICKED UP TWO NEW CONTACTS. PROFESSOR X TOOK STORM, COLOSSUS AND WOLVERINE WITH HIM TO CHECK OUT THE ONE IN CHICAGO.
"THERE THEY WERE ATTACKED -- AND CAPTURED -- BY A FOE WHO KNEW EVERYTHING ABOUT THEIR POWERS AND HOW TO DEFEAT THEM. SHE WAS A TELEPATH WHO CALLED HERSELF THE WHITE QUEEN.
"IN THE CONFUSION, THE CHICAGO NEO-MUTANT -- A TEENAGER NAMED KITTY PRYDE -- MANAGED TO SLIP AWAY LONG ENOUGH TO CALL THE REST OF US IN NEW YORK FOR HELP.
"UNFORTUNATELY, HER WARNING CAME JUST AS NIGHTCRAWLER, JEAN AND I -- AND OUR NEO-MUTANT, A DISCO SINGER CALLED DAZZLER -- WERE BEING AMBUSHED OURSELVES.
"IF IT HADN'T BEEN FOR DAZZLER, WE'D HAVE BEEN CAPTURED, TOO.

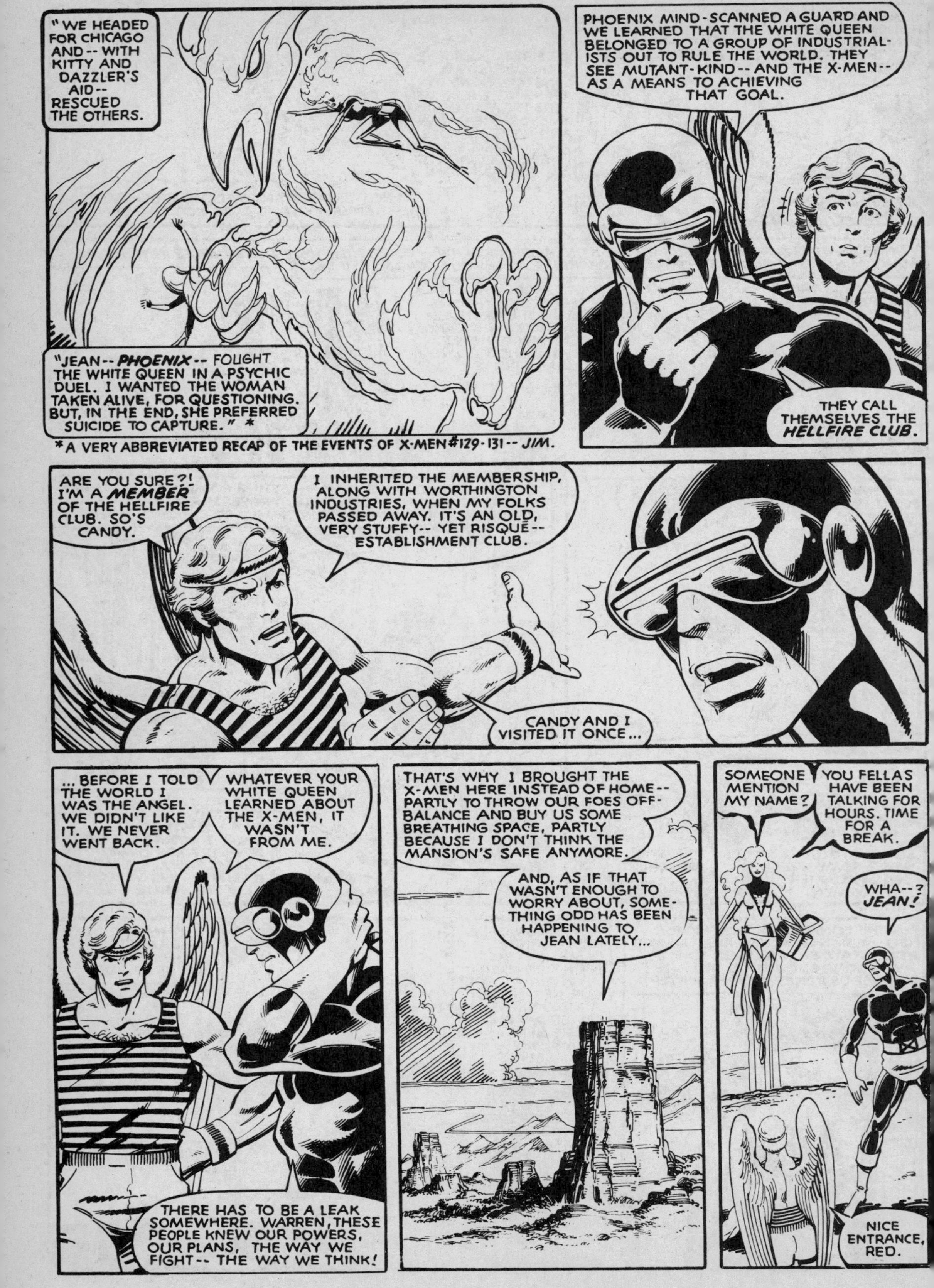
"WE HEADED FOR CHICAGO AND -- WITH KITTY AND DAZZLER'S AID -- RESCUED THE OTHERS.
"JEAN -- PHOENIX -- FOUGHT THE WHITE QUEEN IN A PSYCHIC DUEL. I WANTED THE WOMAN TAKEN ALIVE, FOR QUESTIONING. BUT, IN THE END, SHE PREFERRED SUICIDE TO CAPTURE." *
* A VERY ABBREVIATED RECAP OF THE EVENTS OF X-MEN #129-131 -- JIM.
PHOENIX MIND-SCANNED A GUARD AND WE LEARNED THAT THE WHITE QUEEN BELONGED TO A GROUP OF INDUSTRIALISTS OUT TO RULE THE WORLD. THEY SEE MUTANT-KIND -- AND THE X-MEN -- AS A MEANS TO ACHIEVING THAT GOAL.
THEY CALL THEMSELVES THE HELLFIRE CLUB.
ARE YOU SURE?! I'M A MEMBER OF THE HELLFIRE CLUB. SO'S CANDY.
I INHERITED THE MEMBERSHIP, ALONG WITH WORTHINGTON INDUSTRIES, WHEN MY FOLKS PASSED AWAY. IT'S AN OLD, VERY STUFFY -- YET RISQUÉ -- ESTABLISHMENT CLUB.
CANDY AND I VISITED IT ONCE...
... BEFORE I TOLD THE WORLD I WAS THE ANGEL. WE DIDN'T LIKE IT. WE NEVER WENT BACK.
WHATEVER YOUR WHITE QUEEN LEARNED ABOUT THE X-MEN, IT WASN'T FROM ME.
THERE HAS TO BE A LEAK SOMEWHERE. WARREN, THESE PEOPLE KNEW OUR POWERS, OUR PLANS, THE WAY WE FIGHT -- THE WAY WE THINK!
THAT'S WHY I BROUGHT THE X-MEN HERE INSTEAD OF HOME -- PARTLY TO THROW OUR FOES OFF-BALANCE AND BUY US SOME BREATHING SPACE, PARTLY BECAUSE I DON'T THINK THE MANSION'S SAFE ANYMORE.
AND, AS IF THAT WASN'T ENOUGH TO WORRY ABOUT, SOMETHING ODD HAS BEEN HAPPENING TO JEAN LATELY...
SOMEONE MENTION MY NAME?
YOU FELLAS HAVE BEEN TALKING FOR HOURS. TIME FOR A BREAK.
WHA--? JEAN!
NICE ENTRANCE, RED.

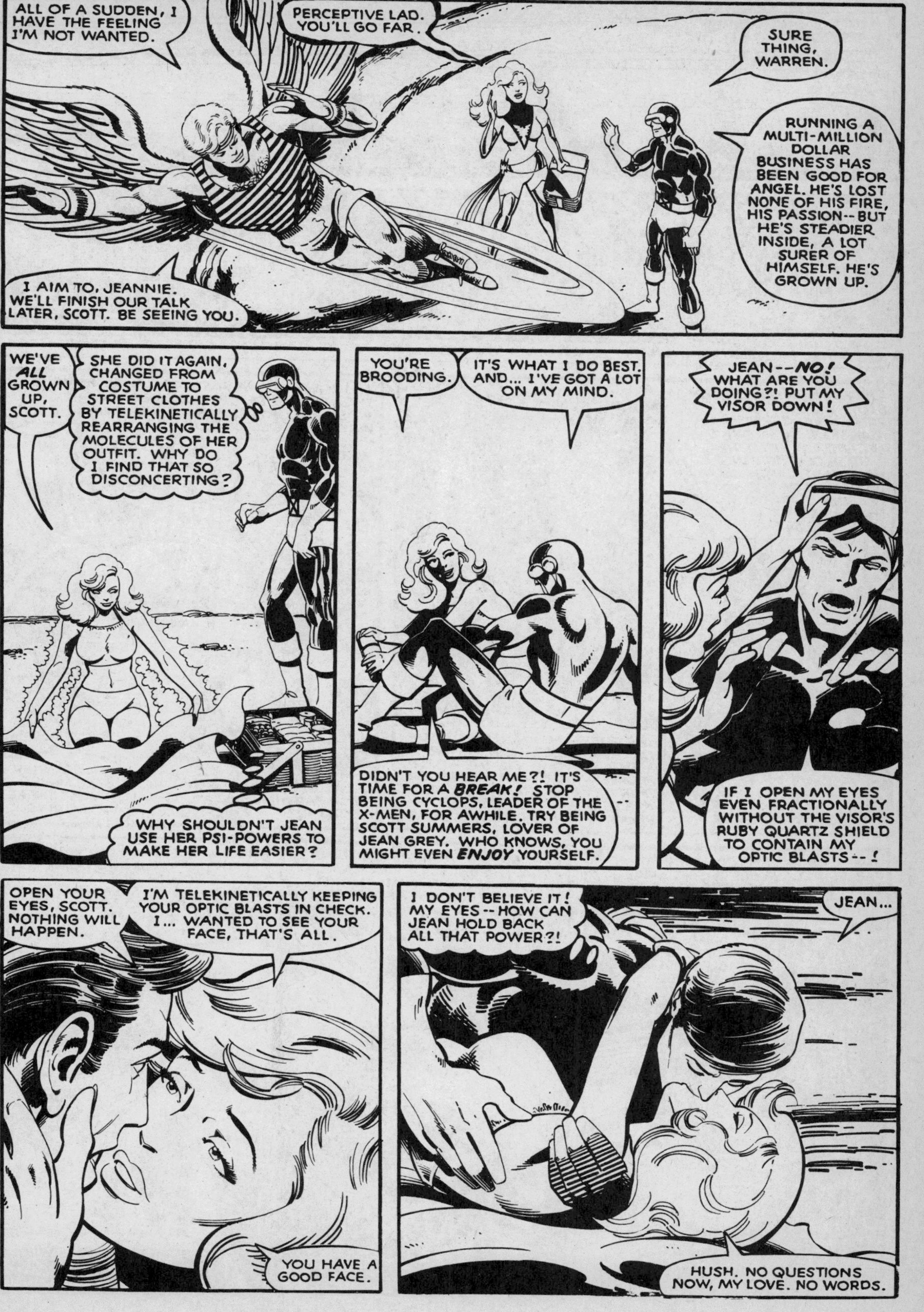
ALL OF A SUDDEN, I HAVE THE FEELING I'M NOT WANTED.
PERCEPTIVE LAD. YOU'LL GO FAR.
I AIM TO, JEANNIE. WE'LL FINISH OUR TALK LATER, SCOTT. BE SEEING YOU.
SURE THING, WARREN.
RUNNING A MULTI-MILLION DOLLAR BUSINESS HAS BEEN GOOD FOR ANGEL. HE'S LOST NONE OF HIS FIRE, HIS PASSION-- BUT HE'S STEADIER INSIDE, A LOT SURER OF HIMSELF. HE'S GROWN UP.
WE'VE ALL GROWN UP, SCOTT.
SHE DID IT AGAIN, CHANGED FROM COSTUME TO STREET CLOTHES BY TELEKINETICALLY REARRANGING THE MOLECULES OF HER OUTFIT. WHY DO I FIND THAT SO DISCONCERTING?
WHY SHOULDN'T JEAN USE HER PSI-POWERS TO MAKE HER LIFE EASIER?
YOU'RE BROODING.
IT'S WHAT I DO BEST. AND... I'VE GOT A LOT ON MY MIND.
DIDN'T YOU HEAR ME?! IT'S TIME FOR A BREAK! STOP BEING CYCLOPS, LEADER OF THE X-MEN, FOR AWHILE. TRY BEING SCOTT SUMMERS, LOVER OF JEAN GREY. WHO KNOWS, YOU MIGHT EVEN ENJOY YOURSELF.
JEAN--NO! WHAT ARE YOU DOING?! PUT MY VISOR DOWN!
IF I OPEN MY EYES EVEN FRACTIONALLY WITHOUT THE VISOR'S RUBY QUARTZ SHIELD TO CONTAIN MY OPTIC BLASTS--!
OPEN YOUR EYES, SCOTT. NOTHING WILL HAPPEN.
I'M TELEKINETICALLY KEEPING YOUR OPTIC BLASTS IN CHECK. I... WANTED TO SEE YOUR FACE, THAT'S ALL.
YOU HAVE A GOOD FACE.
I DON'T BELIEVE IT! MY EYES--HOW CAN JEAN HOLD BACK ALL THAT POWER?!
JEAN...
HUSH. NO QUESTIONS NOW, MY LOVE. NO WORDS.

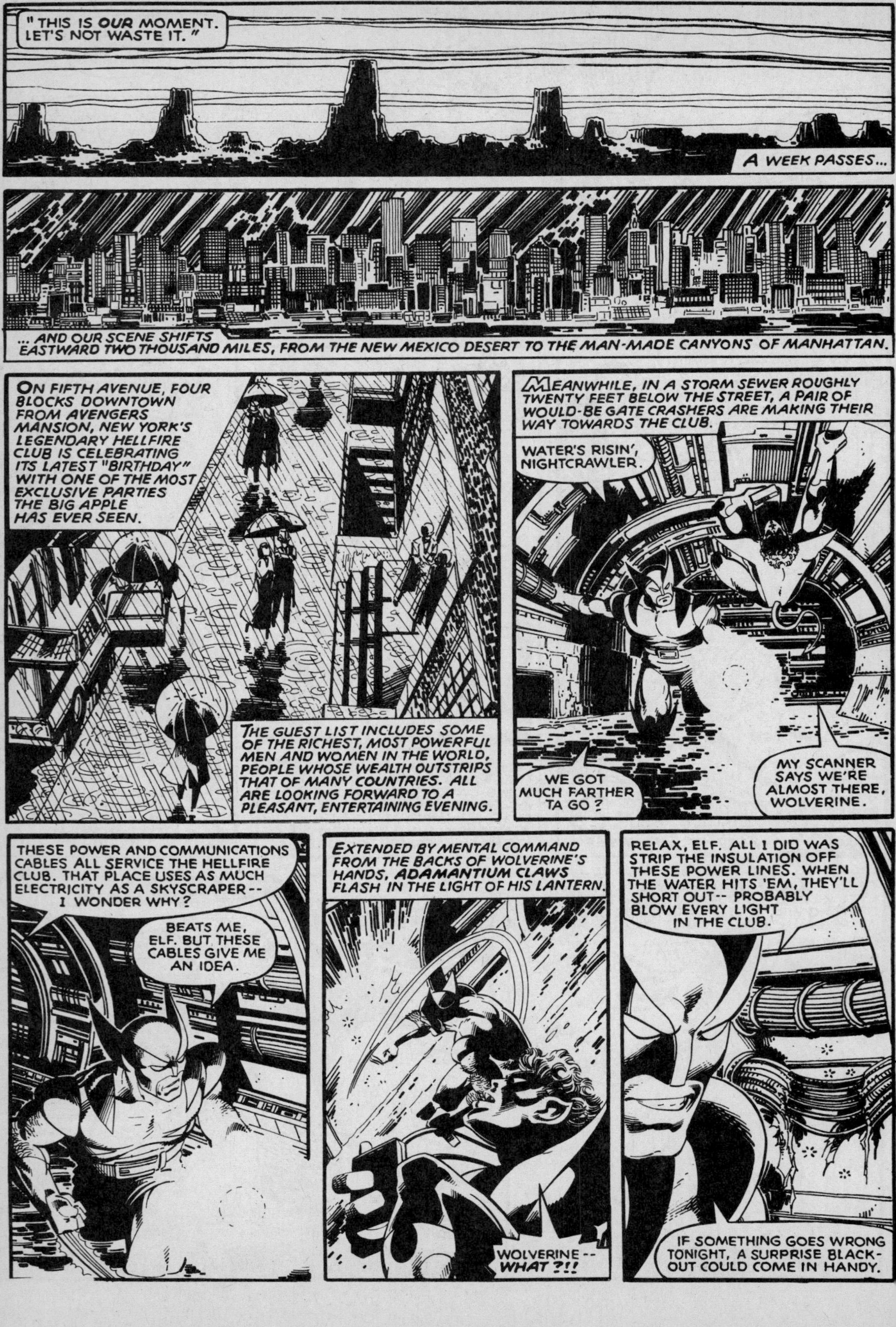
"THIS IS OUR MOMENT. LET'S NOT WASTE IT."
A WEEK PASSES...
...AND OUR SCENE SHIFTS EASTWARD TWO THOUSAND MILES, FROM THE NEW MEXICO DESERT TO THE MAN-MADE CANYONS OF MANHATTAN.
ON FIFTH AVENUE, FOUR BLOCKS DOWNTOWN FROM AVENGERS MANSION, NEW YORK'S LEGENDARY HELLFIRE CLUB IS CELEBRATING ITS LATEST "BIRTHDAY" WITH ONE OF THE MOST EXCLUSIVE PARTIES THE BIG APPLE HAS EVER SEEN.
THE GUEST LIST INCLUDES SOME OF THE RICHEST, MOST POWERFUL MEN AND WOMEN IN THE WORLD, PEOPLE WHOSE WEALTH OUTSTRIPS THAT OF MANY COUNTRIES. ALL ARE LOOKING FORWARD TO A PLEASANT, ENTERTAINING EVENING.
MEANWHILE, IN A STORM SEWER ROUGHLY TWENTY FEET BELOW THE STREET, A PAIR OF WOULD-BE GATE CRASHERS ARE MAKING THEIR WAY TOWARDS THE CLUB.
WATER'S RISIN', NIGHTCRAWLER.
WE GOT MUCH FARTHER TA GO?
MY SCANNER SAYS WE'RE ALMOST THERE, WOLVERINE.
THESE POWER AND COMMUNICATIONS CABLES ALL SERVICE THE HELLFIRE CLUB. THAT PLACE USES AS MUCH ELECTRICITY AS A SKYSCRAPER -- I WONDER WHY?
BEATS ME, ELF. BUT THESE CABLES GIVE ME AN IDEA.
EXTENDED BY MENTAL COMMAND FROM THE BACKS OF WOLVERINE'S HANDS, ADAMANTIUM CLAWS FLASH IN THE LIGHT OF HIS LANTERN.
WOLVERINE -- WHAT?!!
RELAX, ELF. ALL I DID WAS STRIP THE INSULATION OFF THESE POWER LINES. WHEN THE WATER HITS 'EM, THEY'LL SHORT OUT-- PROBABLY BLOW EVERY LIGHT IN THE CLUB.
IF SOMETHING GOES WRONG TONIGHT, A SURPRISE BLACK-OUT COULD COME IN HANDY.

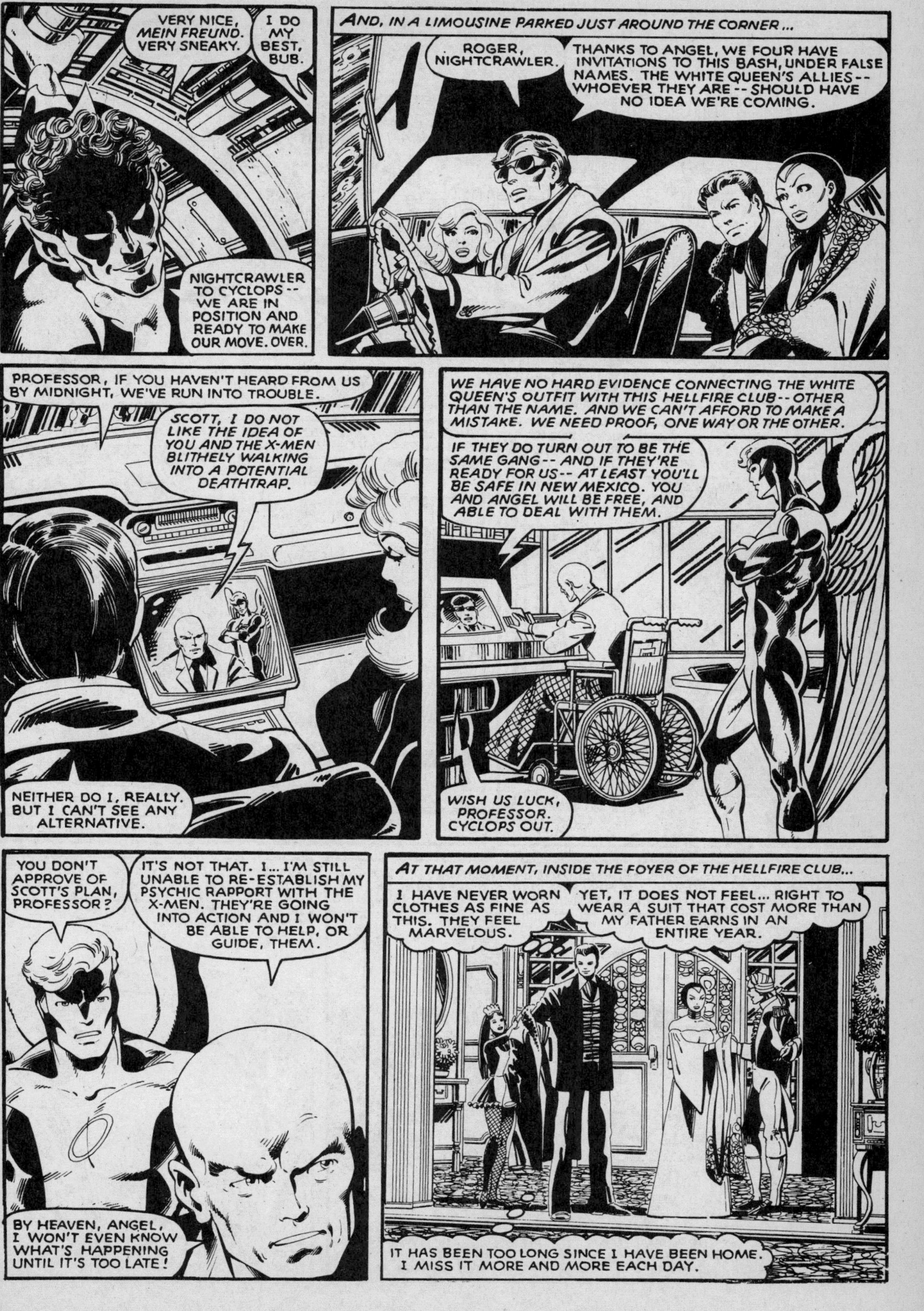

VERY NICE, MEIN FREUND. VERY SNEAKY.
I DO MY BEST, BUB.
NIGHTCRAWLER TO CYCLOPS -- WE ARE IN POSITION AND READY TO MAKE OUR MOVE. OVER.
AND, IN A LIMOUSINE PARKED JUST AROUND THE CORNER...
ROGER, NIGHTCRAWLER.
THANKS TO ANGEL, WE FOUR HAVE INVITATIONS TO THIS BASH, UNDER FALSE NAMES. THE WHITE QUEEN'S ALLIES -- WHOEVER THEY ARE -- SHOULD HAVE NO IDEA WE'RE COMING.
PROFESSOR, IF YOU HAVEN'T HEARD FROM US BY MIDNIGHT, WE'VE RUN INTO TROUBLE.
SCOTT, I DO NOT LIKE THE IDEA OF YOU AND THE X-MEN BLITHELY WALKING INTO A POTENTIAL DEATHTRAP.
NEITHER DO I, REALLY. BUT I CAN'T SEE ANY ALTERNATIVE.
WE HAVE NO HARD EVIDENCE CONNECTING THE WHITE QUEEN'S OUTFIT WITH THIS HELLFIRE CLUB -- OTHER THAN THE NAME. AND WE CAN'T AFFORD TO MAKE A MISTAKE. WE NEED PROOF, ONE WAY OR THE OTHER.
IF THEY DO TURN OUT TO BE THE SAME GANG -- AND IF THEY'RE READY FOR US -- AT LEAST YOU'LL BE SAFE IN NEW MEXICO. YOU AND ANGEL WILL BE FREE, AND ABLE TO DEAL WITH THEM.
WISH US LUCK, PROFESSOR. CYCLOPS OUT.
YOU DON'T APPROVE OF SCOTT'S PLAN, PROFESSOR?
IT'S NOT THAT. I... I'M STILL UNABLE TO RE-ESTABLISH MY PSYCHIC RAPPORT WITH THE X-MEN. THEY'RE GOING INTO ACTION AND I WON'T BE ABLE TO HELP, OR GUIDE, THEM.
BY HEAVEN, ANGEL, I WON'T EVEN KNOW WHAT'S HAPPENING UNTIL IT'S TOO LATE!
AT THAT MOMENT, INSIDE THE FOYER OF THE HELLFIRE CLUB...
I HAVE NEVER WORN CLOTHES AS FINE AS THIS. THEY FEEL MARVELOUS.
YET, IT DOES NOT FEEL... RIGHT TO WEAR A SUIT THAT COST MORE THAN MY FATHER EARNS IN AN ENTIRE YEAR.
IT HAS BEEN TOO LONG SINCE I HAVE BEEN HOME. I MISS IT MORE AND MORE EACH DAY.

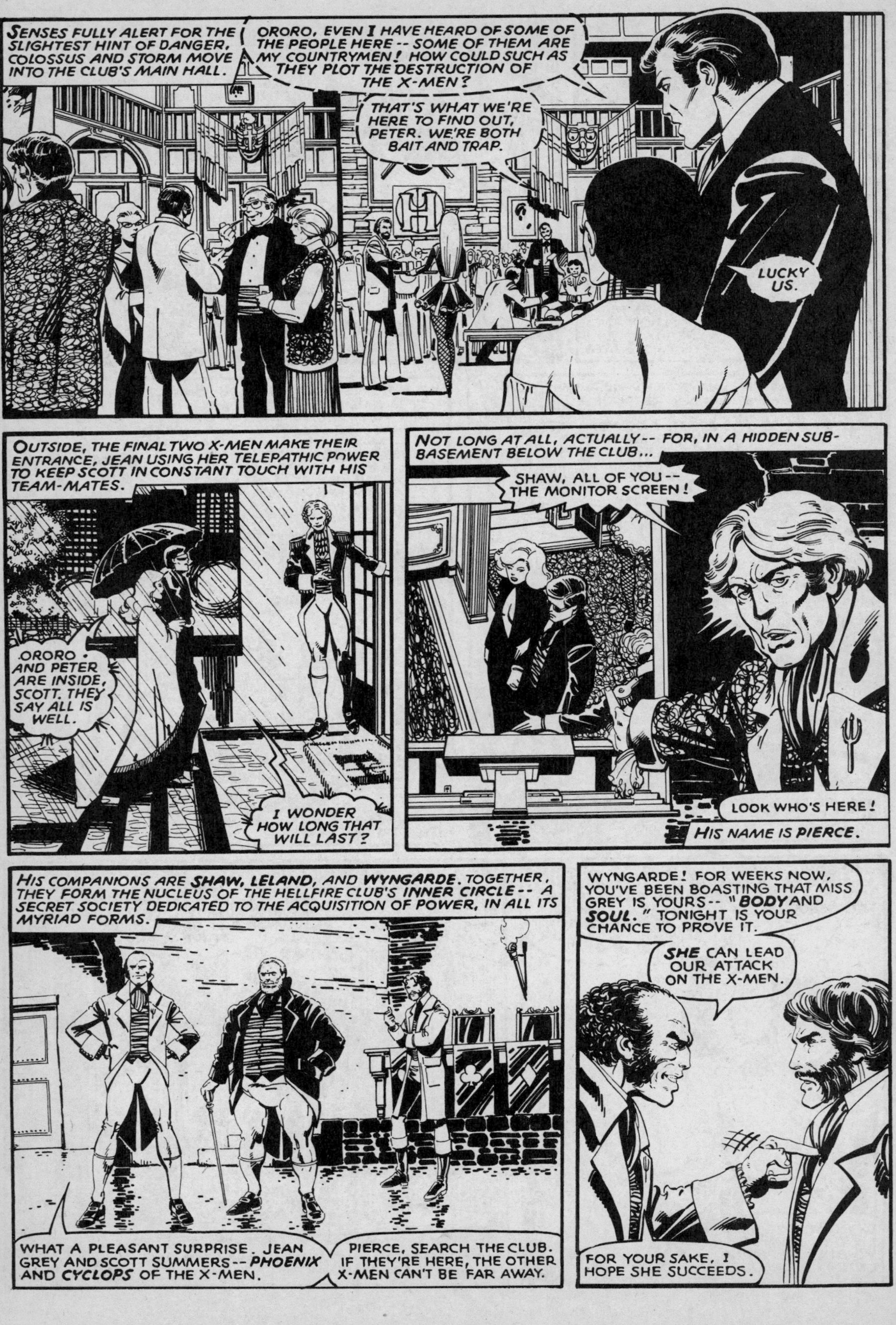
SENSES FULLY ALERT FOR THE SLIGHTEST HINT OF DANGER, COLOSSUS AND STORM MOVE INTO THE CLUB'S MAIN HALL.
ORORO, EVEN I HAVE HEARD OF SOME OF THE PEOPLE HERE -- SOME OF THEM ARE MY COUNTRYMEN! HOW COULD SUCH AS THEY PLOT THE DESTRUCTION OF THE X-MEN?
THAT'S WHAT WE'RE HERE TO FIND OUT, PETER. WE'RE BOTH BAIT AND TRAP.
LUCKY US.
OUTSIDE, THE FINAL TWO X-MEN MAKE THEIR ENTRANCE, JEAN USING HER TELEPATHIC POWER TO KEEP SCOTT IN CONSTANT TOUCH WITH HIS TEAM-MATES.
ORORO AND PETER ARE INSIDE, SCOTT. THEY SAY ALL IS WELL.
I WONDER HOW LONG THAT WILL LAST?
NOT LONG AT ALL, ACTUALLY -- FOR, IN A HIDDEN SUB-BASEMENT BELOW THE CLUB...
SHAW, ALL OF YOU -- THE MONITOR SCREEN!
LOOK WHO'S HERE!
HIS NAME IS PIERCE.
HIS COMPANIONS ARE SHAW, LELAND, AND WYNGARDE. TOGETHER, THEY FORM THE NUCLEUS OF THE HELLFIRE CLUB'S INNER CIRCLE -- A SECRET SOCIETY DEDICATED TO THE ACQUISITION OF POWER, IN ALL ITS MYRIAD FORMS.
WHAT A PLEASANT SURPRISE. JEAN GREY AND SCOTT SUMMERS -- PHOENIX AND CYCLOPS OF THE X-MEN.
PIERCE, SEARCH THE CLUB. IF THEY'RE HERE, THE OTHER X-MEN CAN'T BE FAR AWAY.
WYNGARDE! FOR WEEKS NOW, YOU'VE BEEN BOASTING THAT MISS GREY IS YOURS -- "BODY AND SOUL." TONIGHT IS YOUR CHANCE TO PROVE IT.
SHE CAN LEAD OUR ATTACK ON THE X-MEN.
FOR YOUR SAKE, I HOPE SHE SUCCEEDS.

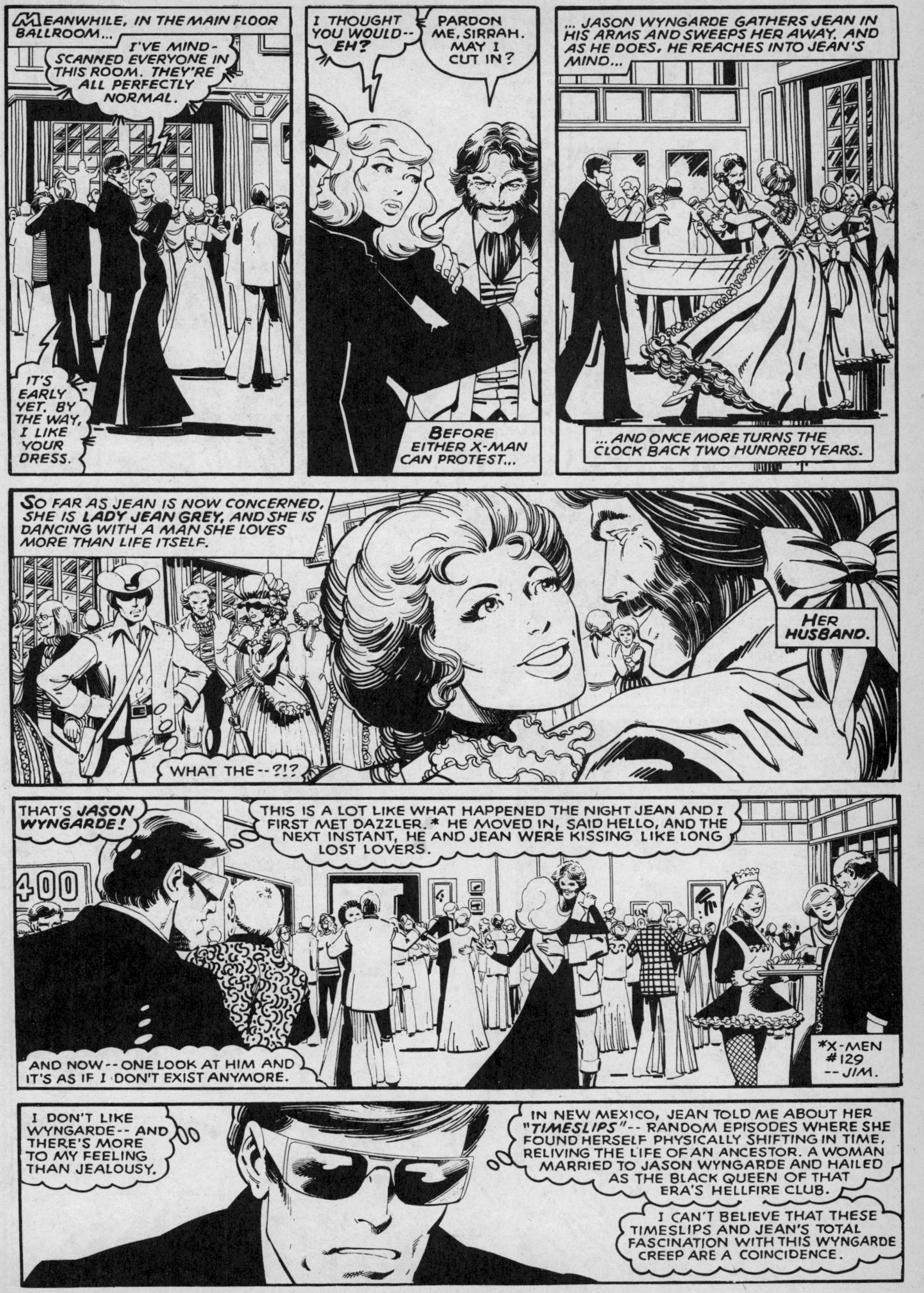
MEANWHILE, IN THE MAIN FLOOR BALLROOM...
I'VE MIND-SCANNED EVERYONE IN THIS ROOM. THEY'RE ALL PERFECTLY NORMAL.
IT'S EARLY YET. BY THE WAY, I LIKE YOUR DRESS.
I THOUGHT YOU WOULD-- EH?
PARDON ME, SIRRAH. MAY I CUT IN?
BEFORE EITHER X-MAN CAN PROTEST...
... JASON WYNGARDE GATHERS JEAN IN HIS ARMS AND SWEEPS HER AWAY. AND AS HE DOES, HE REACHES INTO JEAN'S MIND...
... AND ONCE MORE TURNS THE CLOCK BACK TWO HUNDRED YEARS.
SO FAR AS JEAN IS NOW CONCERNED, SHE IS LADY JEAN GREY, AND SHE IS DANCING WITH A MAN SHE LOVES MORE THAN LIFE ITSELF.
HER HUSBAND.
WHAT THE--?!?
THAT'S JASON WYNGARDE!
THIS IS A LOT LIKE WHAT HAPPENED THE NIGHT JEAN AND I FIRST MET DAZZLER.* HE MOVED IN, SAID HELLO, AND THE NEXT INSTANT, HE AND JEAN WERE KISSING LIKE LONG LOST LOVERS.
400
AND NOW-- ONE LOOK AT HIM AND IT'S AS IF I DON'T EXIST ANYMORE.
*X-MEN #129 --JIM.
I DON'T LIKE WYNGARDE-- AND THERE'S MORE TO MY FEELING THAN JEALOUSY.
IN NEW MEXICO, JEAN TOLD ME ABOUT HER "TIMESLIPS"-- RANDOM EPISODES WHERE SHE FOUND HERSELF PHYSICALLY SHIFTING IN TIME, RELIVING THE LIFE OF AN ANCESTOR. A WOMAN MARRIED TO JASON WYNGARDE AND HAILED AS THE BLACK QUEEN OF THAT ERA'S HELLFIRE CLUB.
I CAN'T BELIEVE THAT THESE TIMESLIPS AND JEAN'S TOTAL FASCINATION WITH THIS WYNGARDE CREEP ARE A COINCIDENCE.

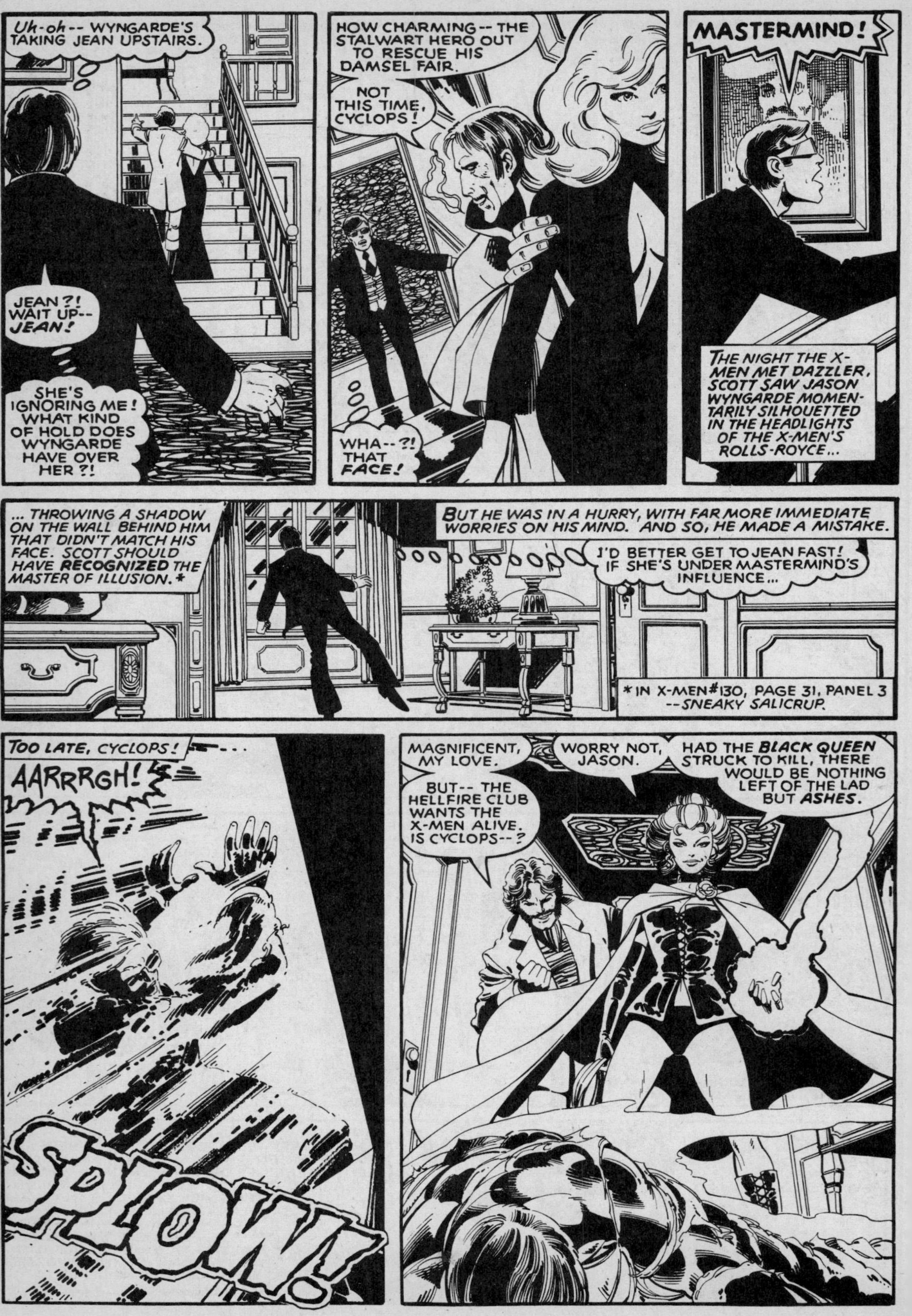
Uh-oh -- WYNGARDE'S TAKING JEAN UPSTAIRS.
JEAN?! WAIT UP-- JEAN!
SHE'S IGNORING ME! WHAT KIND OF HOLD DOES WYNGARDE HAVE OVER HER?!
HOW CHARMING -- THE STALWART HERO OUT TO RESCUE HIS DAMSEL FAIR.
NOT THIS TIME, CYCLOPS!
WHA--?! THAT FACE!
MASTERMIND!
THE NIGHT THE X-MEN MET DAZZLER, SCOTT SAW JASON WYNGARDE MOMENTARILY SILHOUETTED IN THE HEADLIGHTS OF THE X-MEN'S ROLLS-ROYCE...
... THROWING A SHADOW ON THE WALL BEHIND HIM THAT DIDN'T MATCH HIS FACE. SCOTT SHOULD HAVE RECOGNIZED THE MASTER OF ILLUSION.*
BUT HE WAS IN A HURRY, WITH FAR MORE IMMEDIATE WORRIES ON HIS MIND. AND SO, HE MADE A MISTAKE.
I'D BETTER GET TO JEAN FAST! IF SHE'S UNDER MASTERMIND'S INFLUENCE...
*IN X-MEN #130, PAGE 31, PANEL 3 --SNEAKY SALICRUP.
TOO LATE, CYCLOPS!
AARRRGH!
SPLOW!
MAGNIFICENT, MY LOVE.
BUT-- THE HELLFIRE CLUB WANTS THE X-MEN ALIVE. IS CYCLOPS--?
WORRY NOT, JASON.
HAD THE BLACK QUEEN STRUCK TO KILL, THERE WOULD BE NOTHING LEFT OF THE LAD BUT ASHES.

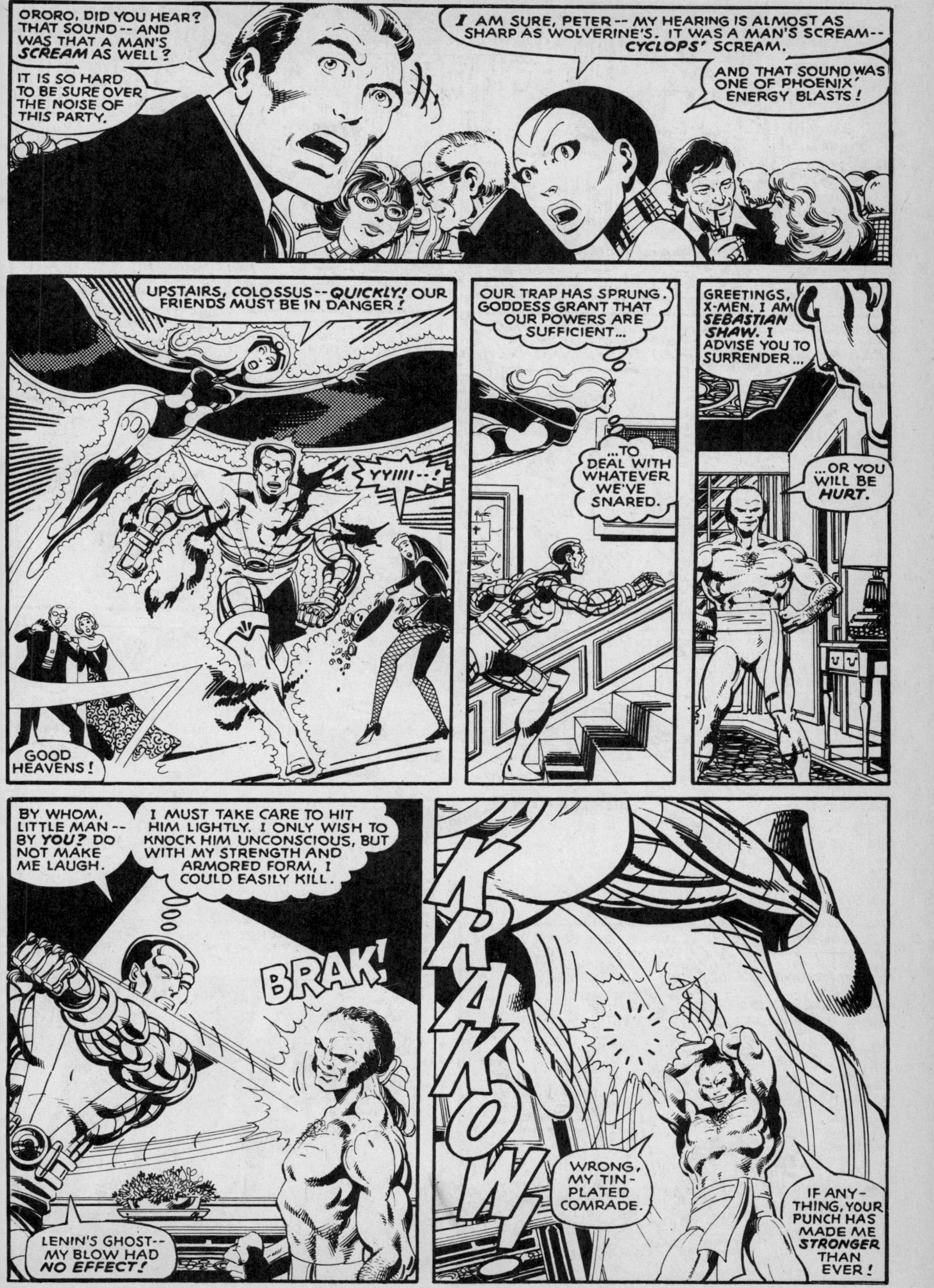
ORORO, DID YOU HEAR? THAT SOUND -- AND WAS THAT A MAN'S SCREAM AS WELL?
IT IS SO HARD TO BE SURE OVER THE NOISE OF THIS PARTY.
I AM SURE, PETER -- MY HEARING IS ALMOST AS SHARP AS WOLVERINE'S. IT WAS A MAN'S SCREAM -- CYCLOPS' SCREAM.
AND THAT SOUND WAS ONE OF PHOENIX' ENERGY BLASTS!
UPSTAIRS, COLOSSUS -- QUICKLY! OUR FRIENDS MUST BE IN DANGER!
YYIIII --!
GOOD HEAVENS!
OUR TRAP HAS SPRUNG. GODDESS GRANT THAT OUR POWERS ARE SUFFICIENT...
...TO DEAL WITH WHATEVER WE'VE SNARED.
GREETINGS, X-MEN. I AM SEBASTIAN SHAW. I ADVISE YOU TO SURRENDER...
...OR YOU WILL BE HURT.
BY WHOM, LITTLE MAN -- BY YOU? DO NOT MAKE ME LAUGH.
I MUST TAKE CARE TO HIT HIM LIGHTLY. I ONLY WISH TO KNOCK HIM UNCONSCIOUS, BUT WITH MY STRENGTH AND ARMORED FORM, I COULD EASILY KILL.
BRAK!
LENIN'S GHOST -- MY BLOW HAD NO EFFECT!
KRAKOW!
WRONG, MY TIN-PLATED COMRADE.
IF ANYTHING, YOUR PUNCH HAS MADE ME STRONGER THAN EVER!

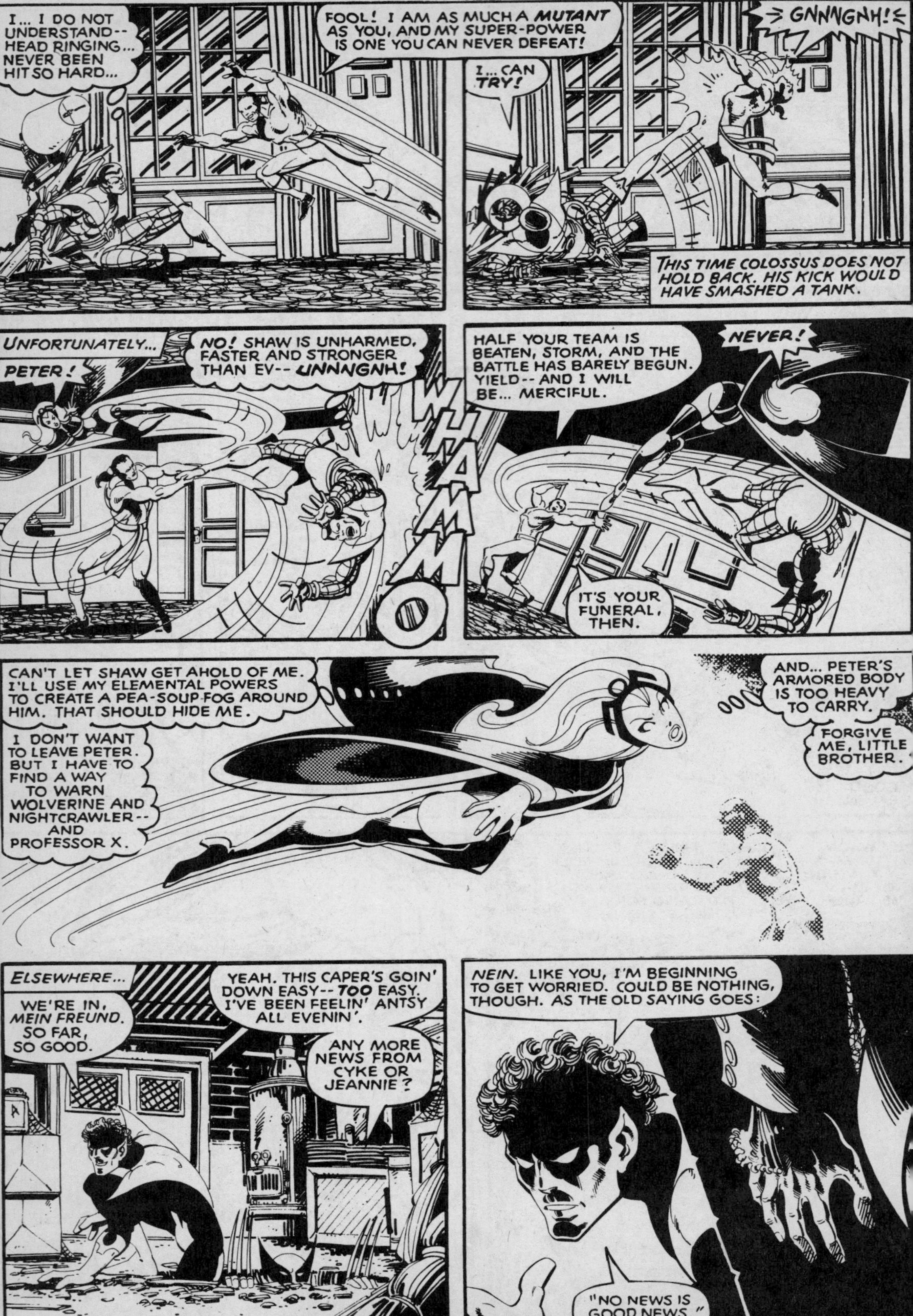

I... I DO NOT UNDERSTAND-- HEAD RINGING... NEVER BEEN HIT SO HARD...
FOOL! I AM AS MUCH A MUTANT AS YOU, AND MY SUPER-POWER IS ONE YOU CAN NEVER DEFEAT!
I... CAN TRY!
GNNNGNH!
THIS TIME COLOSSUS DOES NOT HOLD BACK. HIS KICK WOULD HAVE SMASHED A TANK.
UNFORTUNATELY...
PETER!
NO! SHAW IS UNHARMED, FASTER AND STRONGER THAN EV-- UNNNGNH!
WHAMMO
HALF YOUR TEAM IS BEATEN, STORM, AND THE BATTLE HAS BARELY BEGUN. YIELD-- AND I WILL BE... MERCIFUL.
NEVER!
IT'S YOUR FUNERAL, THEN.
CAN'T LET SHAW GET AHOLD OF ME. I'LL USE MY ELEMENTAL POWERS TO CREATE A PEA-SOUP FOG AROUND HIM. THAT SHOULD HIDE ME.
I DON'T WANT TO LEAVE PETER. BUT I HAVE TO FIND A WAY TO WARN WOLVERINE AND NIGHTCRAWLER-- AND PROFESSOR X.
AND... PETER'S ARMORED BODY IS TOO HEAVY TO CARRY.
FORGIVE ME, LITTLE BROTHER.
ELSEWHERE...
WE'RE IN, MEIN FREUND. SO FAR, SO GOOD.
YEAH. THIS CAPER'S GOIN' DOWN EASY-- TOO EASY. I'VE BEEN FEELIN' ANTSY ALL EVENIN'.
ANY MORE NEWS FROM CYKE OR JEANNIE?
NEIN. LIKE YOU, I'M BEGINNING TO GET WORRIED. COULD BE NOTHING, THOUGH. AS THE OLD SAYING GOES:
"NO NEWS IS GOOD NEWS."

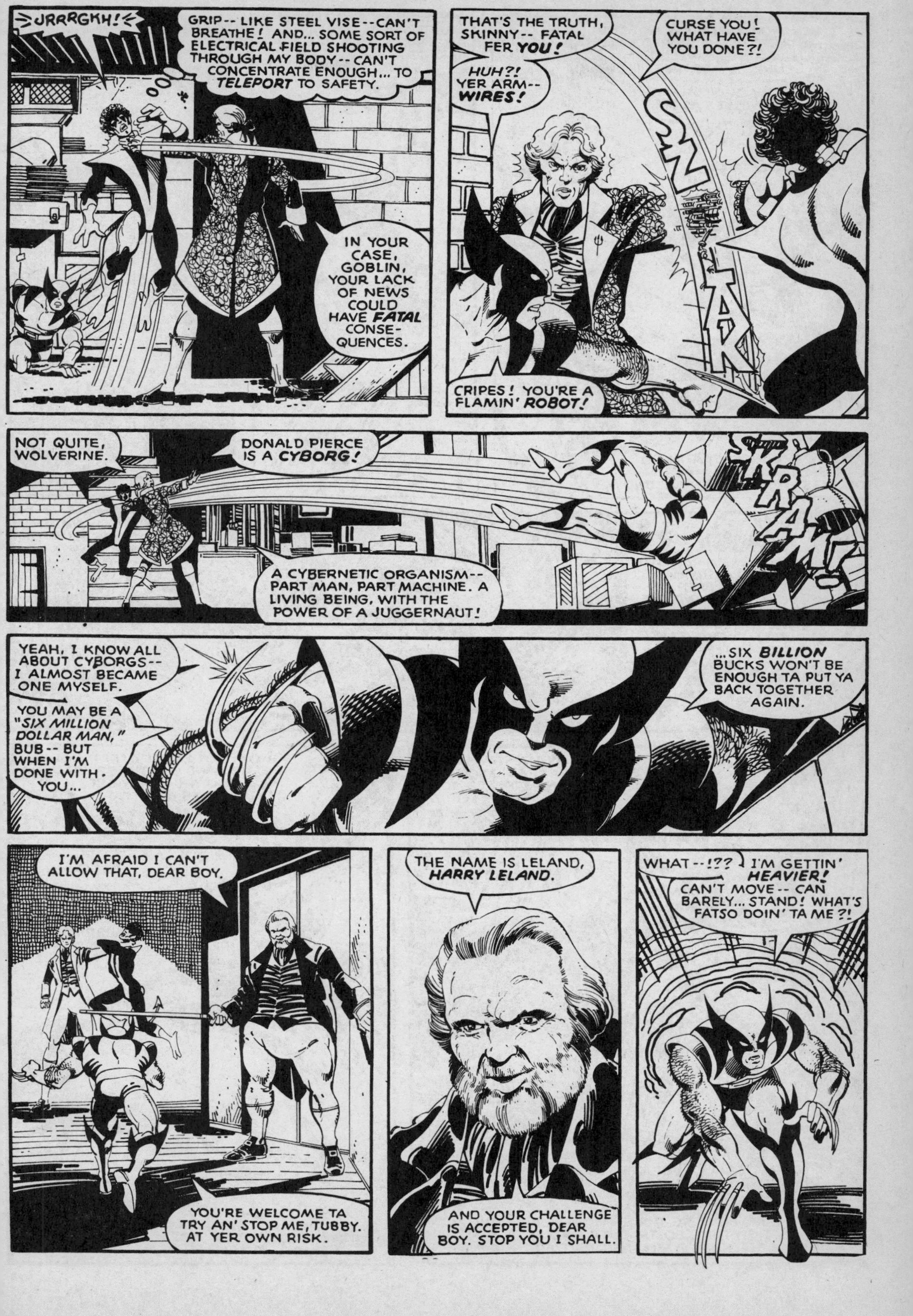
JRRRGKH!
GRIP-- LIKE STEEL VISE--CAN'T BREATHE! AND... SOME SORT OF ELECTRICAL FIELD SHOOTING THROUGH MY BODY--CAN'T CONCENTRATE ENOUGH... TO TELEPORT TO SAFETY.
IN YOUR CASE, GOBLIN, YOUR LACK OF NEWS COULD HAVE FATAL CONSE-QUENCES.
THAT'S THE TRUTH, SKINNY-- FATAL FER YOU!
HUH?! YER ARM-- WIRES!
CURSE YOU! WHAT HAVE YOU DONE?!
SNIKT
CRIPES! YOU'RE A FLAMIN' ROBOT!
NOT QUITE, WOLVERINE.
DONALD PIERCE IS A CYBORG!
SKRAM!
A CYBERNETIC ORGANISM-- PART MAN, PART MACHINE. A LIVING BEING, WITH THE POWER OF A JUGGERNAUT!
YEAH, I KNOW ALL ABOUT CYBORGS-- I ALMOST BECAME ONE MYSELF.
YOU MAY BE A "SIX MILLION DOLLAR MAN," BUB-- BUT WHEN I'M DONE WITH YOU...
...SIX BILLION BUCKS WON'T BE ENOUGH TA PUT YA BACK TOGETHER AGAIN.
I'M AFRAID I CAN'T ALLOW THAT, DEAR BOY.
YOU'RE WELCOME TA TRY AN' STOP ME, TUBBY. AT YER OWN RISK.
THE NAME IS LELAND, HARRY LELAND.
AND YOUR CHALLENGE IS ACCEPTED, DEAR BOY. STOP YOU I SHALL.
WHAT--!?? I'M GETTIN' HEAVIER!
CAN'T MOVE-- CAN BARELY... STAND! WHAT'S FATSO DOIN' TA ME?!

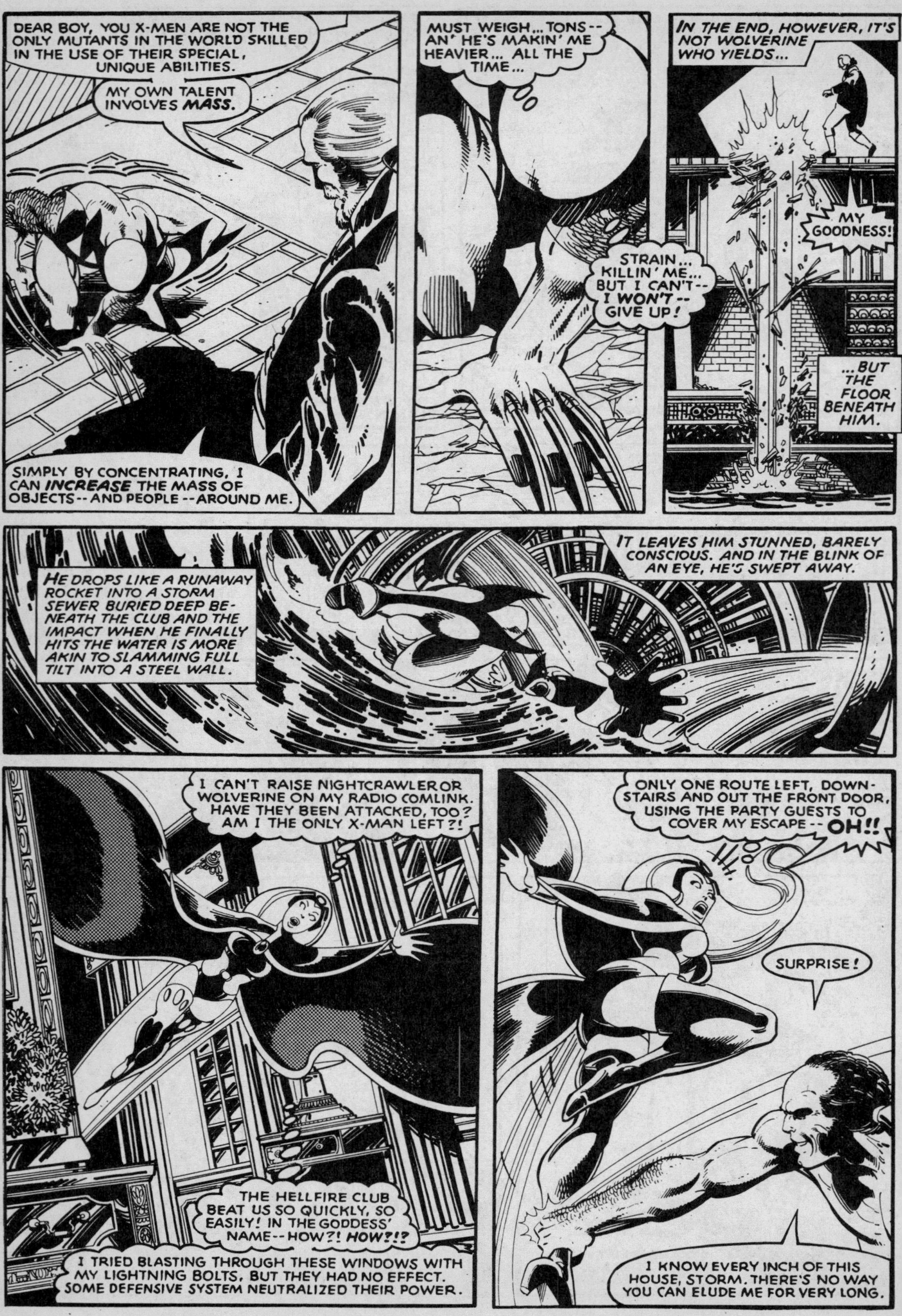
DEAR BOY, YOU X-MEN ARE NOT THE ONLY MUTANTS IN THE WORLD SKILLED IN THE USE OF THEIR SPECIAL, UNIQUE ABILITIES.
MY OWN TALENT INVOLVES MASS.
SIMPLY BY CONCENTRATING, I CAN INCREASE THE MASS OF OBJECTS -- AND PEOPLE -- AROUND ME.
MUST WEIGH... TONS -- AN' HE'S MAKIN' ME HEAVIER... ALL THE TIME...
STRAIN... KILLIN' ME... BUT I CAN'T -- I WON'T -- GIVE UP!
IN THE END, HOWEVER, IT'S NOT WOLVERINE WHO YIELDS...
MY GOODNESS!
...BUT THE FLOOR BENEATH HIM.
HE DROPS LIKE A RUNAWAY ROCKET INTO A STORM SEWER BURIED DEEP BENEATH THE CLUB AND THE IMPACT WHEN HE FINALLY HITS THE WATER IS MORE AKIN TO SLAMMING FULL TILT INTO A STEEL WALL.
IT LEAVES HIM STUNNED, BARELY CONSCIOUS. AND IN THE BLINK OF AN EYE, HE'S SWEPT AWAY.
I CAN'T RAISE NIGHTCRAWLER OR WOLVERINE ON MY RADIO COMLINK. HAVE THEY BEEN ATTACKED, TOO? AM I THE ONLY X-MAN LEFT?!
THE HELLFIRE CLUB BEAT US SO QUICKLY, SO EASILY! IN THE GODDESS' NAME -- HOW?! HOW?!?
I TRIED BLASTING THROUGH THESE WINDOWS WITH MY LIGHTNING BOLTS, BUT THEY HAD NO EFFECT. SOME DEFENSIVE SYSTEM NEUTRALIZED THEIR POWER.
ONLY ONE ROUTE LEFT, DOWNSTAIRS AND OUT THE FRONT DOOR, USING THE PARTY GUESTS TO COVER MY ESCAPE -- OH!!
SURPRISE!
I KNOW EVERY INCH OF THIS HOUSE, STORM. THERE'S NO WAY YOU CAN ELUDE ME FOR VERY LONG.

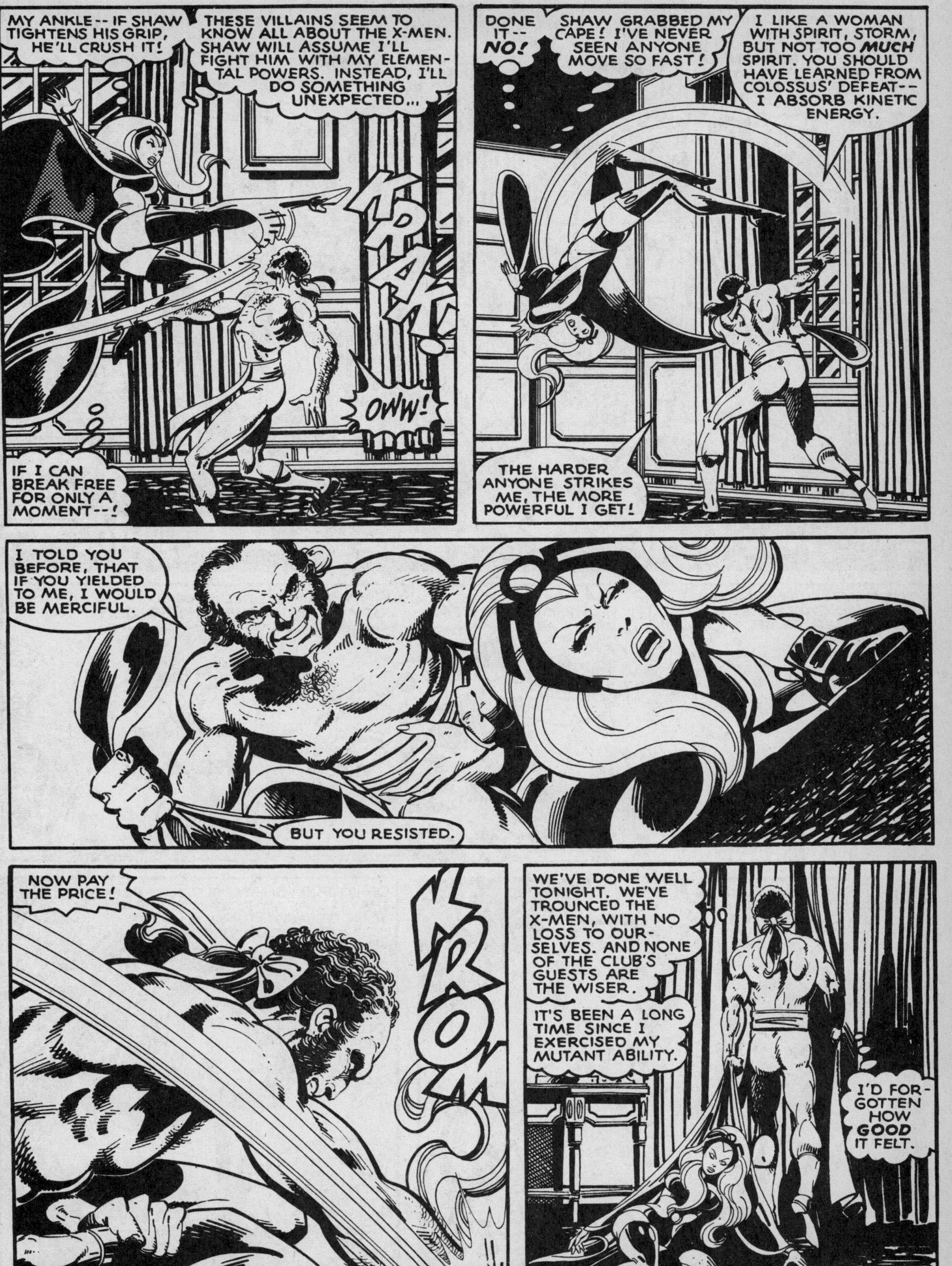

MY ANKLE -- IF SHAW TIGHTENS HIS GRIP, HE'LL CRUSH IT!
THESE VILLAINS SEEM TO KNOW ALL ABOUT THE X-MEN. SHAW WILL ASSUME I'LL FIGHT HIM WITH MY ELEMENTAL POWERS. INSTEAD, I'LL DO SOMETHING UNEXPECTED...
KRAK!
OWW!
IF I CAN BREAK FREE FOR ONLY A MOMENT --!
DONE IT -- NO!
SHAW GRABBED MY CAPE! I'VE NEVER SEEN ANYONE MOVE SO FAST!
I LIKE A WOMAN WITH SPIRIT, STORM, BUT NOT TOO MUCH SPIRIT. YOU SHOULD HAVE LEARNED FROM COLOSSUS' DEFEAT -- I ABSORB KINETIC ENERGY.
THE HARDER ANYONE STRIKES ME, THE MORE POWERFUL I GET!
I TOLD YOU BEFORE, THAT IF YOU YIELDED TO ME, I WOULD BE MERCIFUL.
BUT YOU RESISTED.
NOW PAY THE PRICE!
KROOM
WE'VE DONE WELL TONIGHT. WE'VE TROUNCED THE X-MEN, WITH NO LOSS TO OURSELVES. AND NONE OF THE CLUB'S GUESTS ARE THE WISER.
IT'S BEEN A LONG TIME SINCE I EXERCISED MY MUTANT ABILITY.
I'D FORGOTTEN HOW GOOD IT FELT.

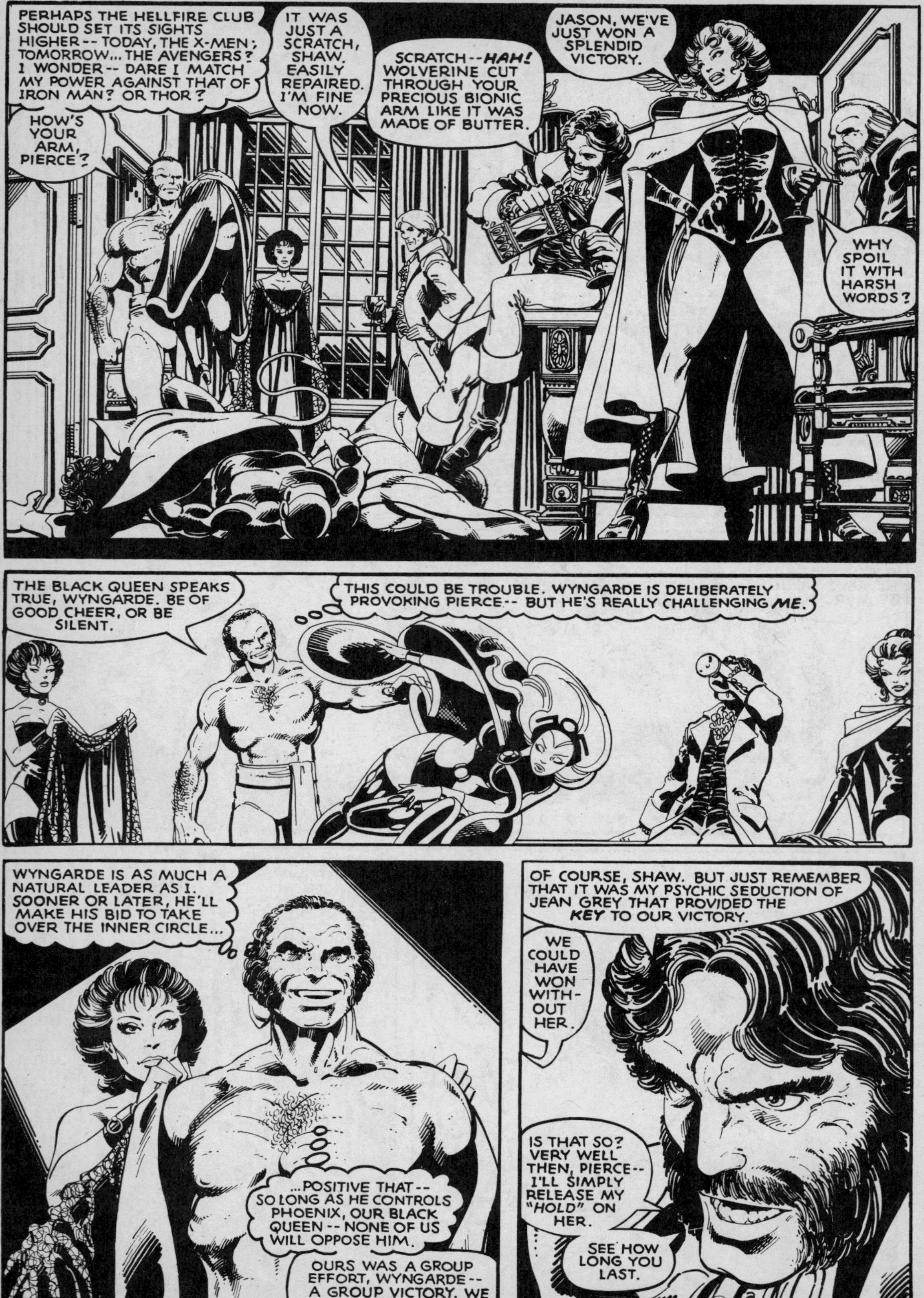
PERHAPS THE HELLFIRE CLUB SHOULD SET ITS SIGHTS HIGHER -- TODAY, THE X-MEN; TOMORROW... THE AVENGERS? I WONDER -- DARE I MATCH MY POWER AGAINST THAT OF IRON MAN? OR THOR?
HOW'S YOUR ARM, PIERCE?
IT WAS JUST A SCRATCH, SHAW. EASILY REPAIRED. I'M FINE NOW.
SCRATCH -- HAH! WOLVERINE CUT THROUGH YOUR PRECIOUS BIONIC ARM LIKE IT WAS MADE OF BUTTER.
JASON, WE'VE JUST WON A SPLENDID VICTORY.
WHY SPOIL IT WITH HARSH WORDS?
THE BLACK QUEEN SPEAKS TRUE, WYNGARDE. BE OF GOOD CHEER, OR BE SILENT.
THIS COULD BE TROUBLE. WYNGARDE IS DELIBERATELY PROVOKING PIERCE -- BUT HE'S REALLY CHALLENGING ME.
WYNGARDE IS AS MUCH A NATURAL LEADER AS I. SOONER OR LATER, HE'LL MAKE HIS BID TO TAKE OVER THE INNER CIRCLE...
...POSITIVE THAT -- SO LONG AS HE CONTROLS PHOENIX, OUR BLACK QUEEN -- NONE OF US WILL OPPOSE HIM.
OURS WAS A GROUP EFFORT, WYNGARDE -- A GROUP VICTORY. WE ALL DID OUR PART.
OF COURSE, SHAW. BUT JUST REMEMBER THAT IT WAS MY PSYCHIC SEDUCTION OF JEAN GREY THAT PROVIDED THE KEY TO OUR VICTORY.
WE COULD HAVE WON WITH-OUT HER.
IS THAT SO? VERY WELL THEN, PIERCE -- I'LL SIMPLY RELEASE MY "HOLD" ON HER.
SEE HOW LONG YOU LAST.

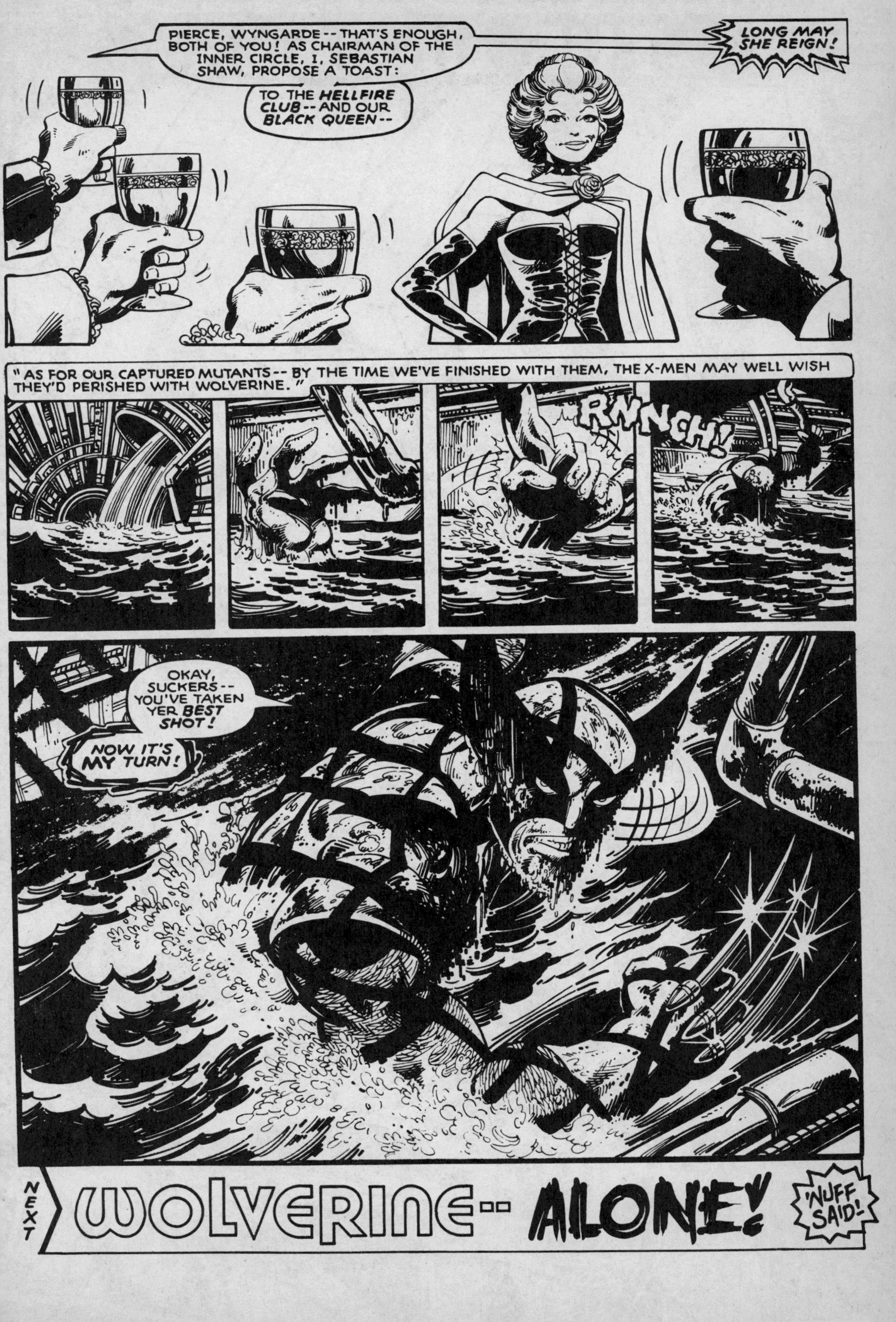

PIERCE, WYNGARDE -- THAT'S ENOUGH, BOTH OF YOU! AS CHAIRMAN OF THE INNER CIRCLE, I, SEBASTIAN SHAW, PROPOSE A TOAST:
TO THE HELLFIRE CLUB -- AND OUR BLACK QUEEN --
LONG MAY SHE REIGN!
"AS FOR OUR CAPTURED MUTANTS -- BY THE TIME WE'VE FINISHED WITH THEM, THE X-MEN MAY WELL WISH THEY'D PERISHED WITH WOLVERINE."
RNNCH!
OKAY, SUCKERS -- YOU'VE TAKEN YER BEST SHOT!
NOW IT'S MY TURN!
NEXT
WOLVERINE -- ALONE!
'NUFF SAID!

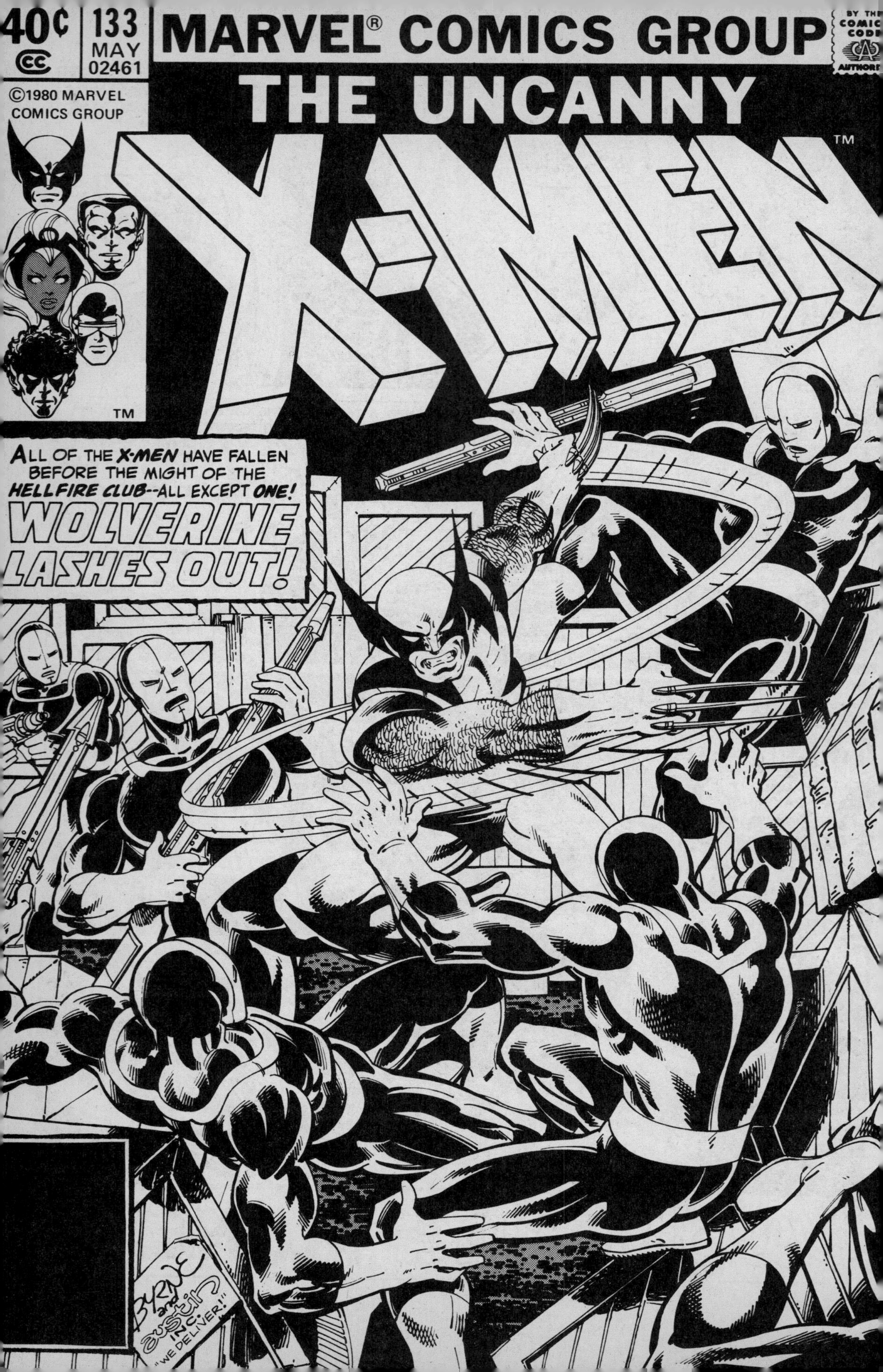

40¢
CC
133
MAY
02461
MARVEL® COMICS GROUP
©1980 MARVEL
COMICS GROUP
THE UNCANNY
X-MEN™
TM
ALL OF THE X-MEN HAVE FALLEN BEFORE THE MIGHT OF THE HELLFIRE CLUB--ALL EXCEPT ONE!
WOLVERINE LASHES OUT!
BYRNE and austin INC. "WE DELIVER!"

Cyclops. Storm. Nightcrawler. Wolverine. Colossus. Children of the atom, students of Charles Xavier, MUTANTS — feared and hated by the world they have sworn to protect. These are the STRANGEST heroes of all!

Stan Lee PRESENTS: THE UNCANNY X-MEN!™

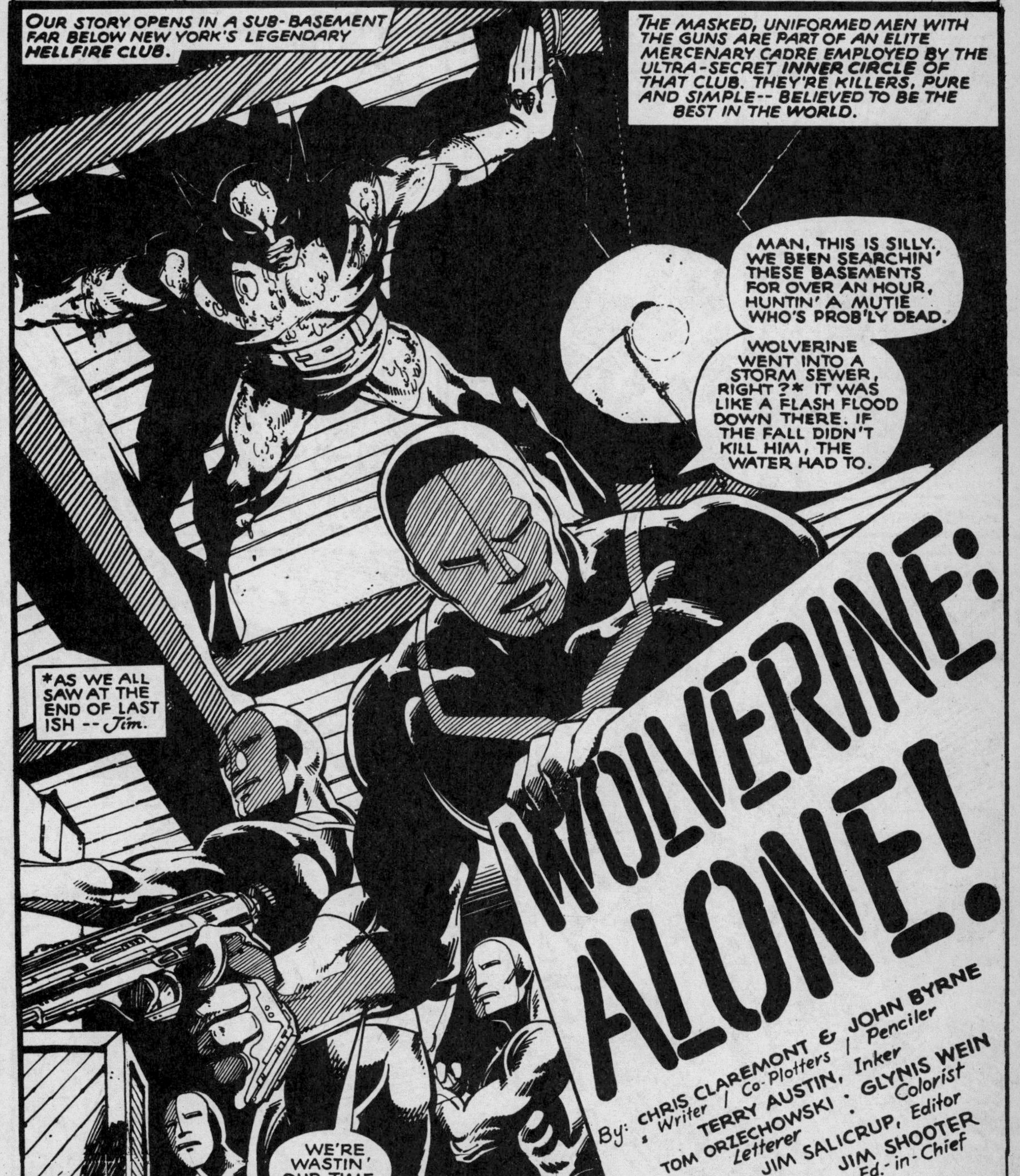

OUR STORY OPENS IN A SUB-BASEMENT FAR BELOW NEW YORK'S LEGENDARY HELLFIRE CLUB.
THE MASKED, UNIFORMED MEN WITH THE GUNS ARE PART OF AN ELITE MERCENARY CADRE EMPLOYED BY THE ULTRA-SECRET INNER CIRCLE OF THAT CLUB. THEY'RE KILLERS, PURE AND SIMPLE-- BELIEVED TO BE THE BEST IN THE WORLD.
MAN, THIS IS SILLY. WE BEEN SEARCHIN' THESE BASEMENTS FOR OVER AN HOUR, HUNTIN' A MUTIE WHO'S PROB'LY DEAD.
WOLVERINE WENT INTO A STORM SEWER, RIGHT?* IT WAS LIKE A FLASH FLOOD DOWN THERE. IF THE FALL DIDN'T KILL HIM, THE WATER HAD TO.
*AS WE ALL SAW AT THE END OF LAST ISH -- Jim.
WE'RE WASTIN' OUR TIME.
WOLVERINE: ALONE!
By: CHRIS CLAREMONT & JOHN BYRNE
Writer / Co-Plotters / Penciler
TERRY AUSTIN, Inker
TOM ORZECHOWSKI · GLYNIS WEIN
Letterer · Colorist
JIM SALICRUP, Editor
JIM SHOOTER
Ed.-in-Chief

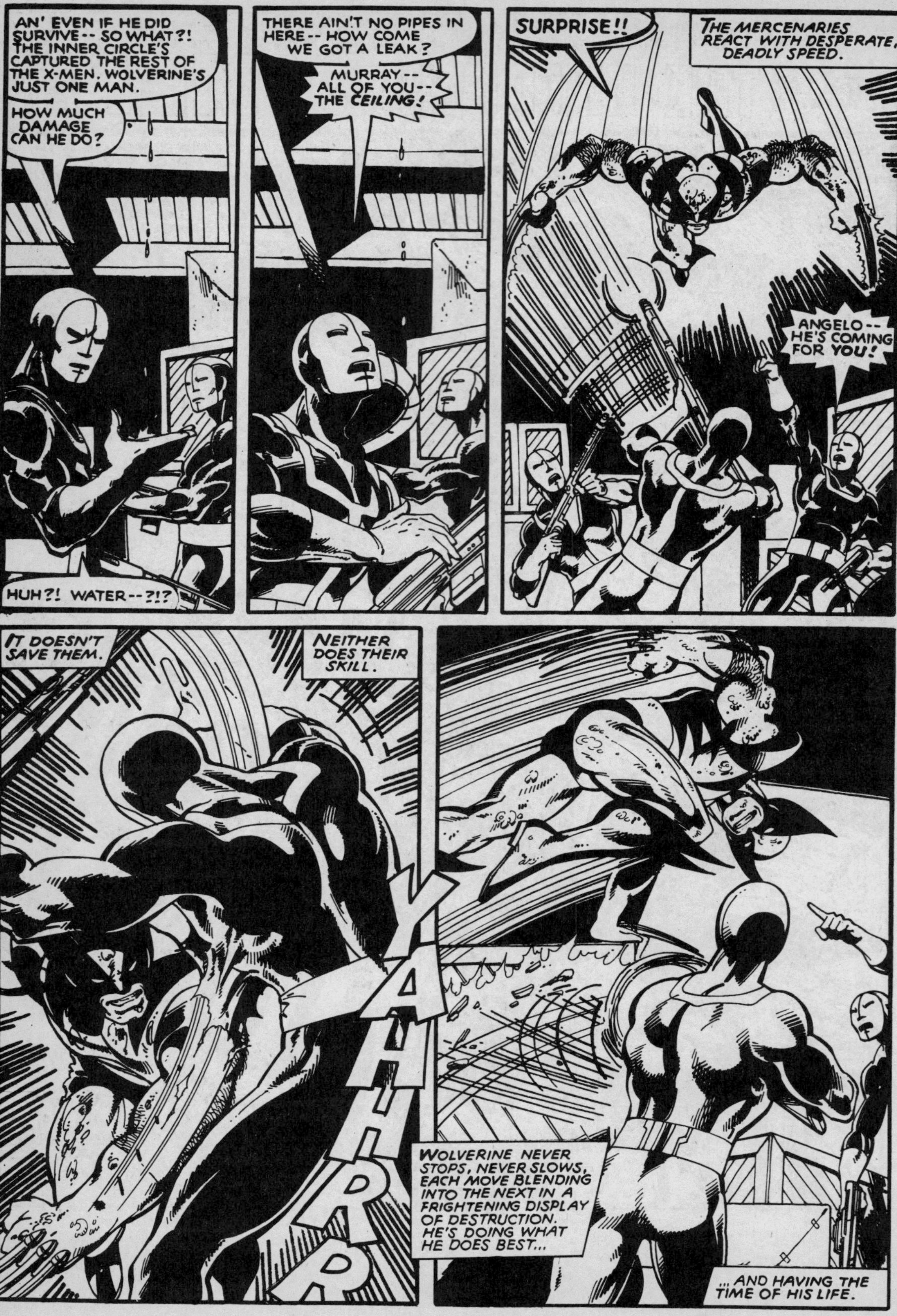
AN' EVEN IF HE DID SURVIVE-- SO WHAT?! THE INNER CIRCLE'S CAPTURED THE REST OF THE X-MEN. WOLVERINE'S JUST ONE MAN.
HOW MUCH DAMAGE CAN HE DO?
HUH?! WATER--?!?
THERE AIN'T NO PIPES IN HERE-- HOW COME WE GOT A LEAK?
MURRAY-- ALL OF YOU-- THE CEILING!
SURPRISE!!
THE MERCENARIES REACT WITH DESPERATE, DEADLY SPEED.
ANGELO-- HE'S COMING FOR YOU!
IT DOESN'T SAVE THEM.
NEITHER DOES THEIR SKILL.
YAAHHRR
WOLVERINE NEVER STOPS, NEVER SLOWS, EACH MOVE BLENDING INTO THE NEXT IN A FRIGHTENING DISPLAY OF DESTRUCTION. HE'S DOING WHAT HE DOES BEST...
...AND HAVING THE TIME OF HIS LIFE.

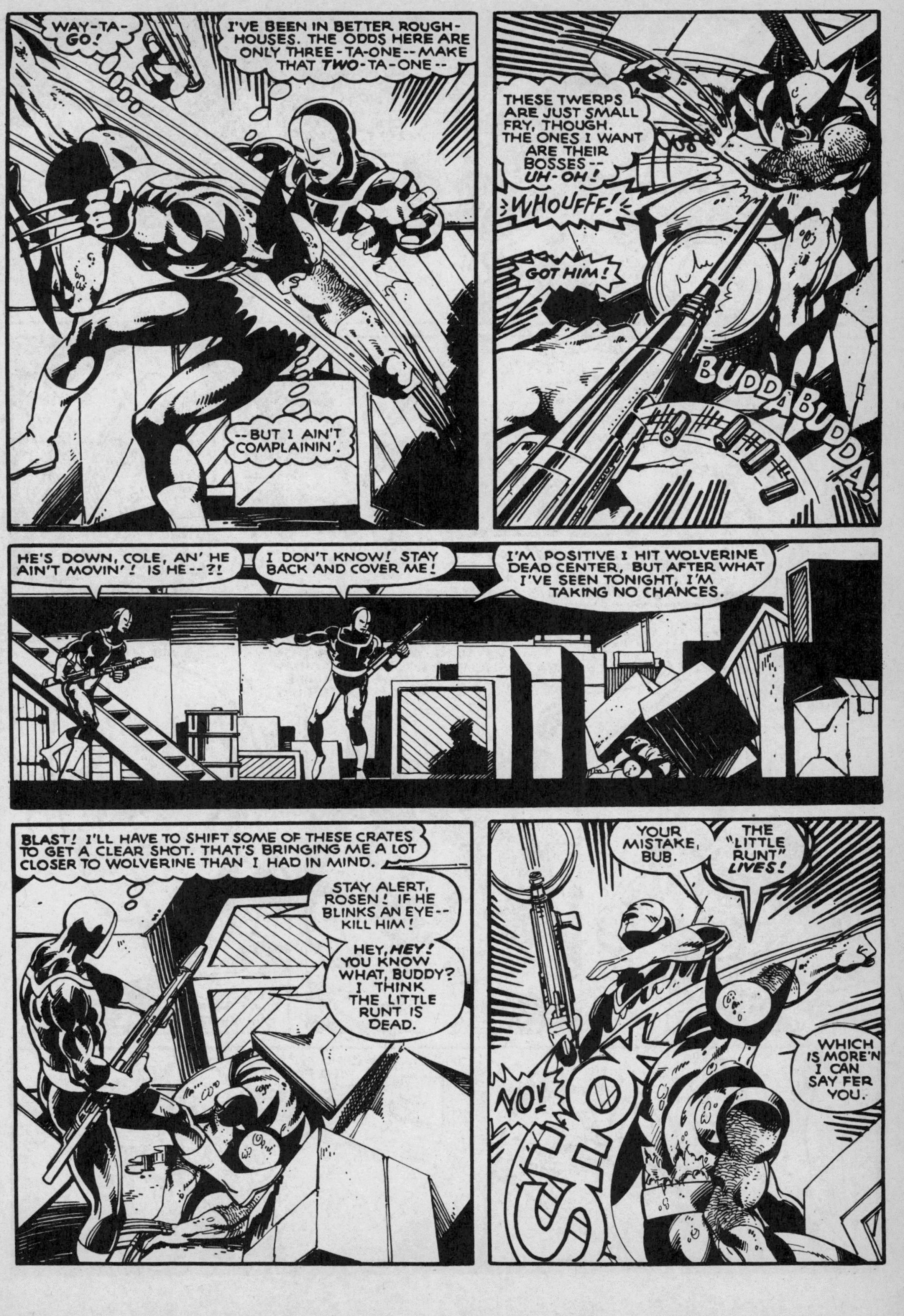
WAY-TA-GO!
I'VE BEEN IN BETTER ROUGH-HOUSES. THE ODDS HERE ARE ONLY THREE-TA-ONE--MAKE THAT TWO-TA-ONE--
--BUT I AIN'T COMPLAININ'.
THESE TWERPS ARE JUST SMALL FRY, THOUGH. THE ONES I WANT ARE THEIR BOSSES--UH-OH!
WHOUFFF!
GOT HIM!
BUDDABUDDA!
HE'S DOWN, COLE, AN' HE AIN'T MOVIN'! IS HE--?!
I DON'T KNOW! STAY BACK AND COVER ME!
I'M POSITIVE I HIT WOLVERINE DEAD CENTER, BUT AFTER WHAT I'VE SEEN TONIGHT, I'M TAKING NO CHANCES.
BLAST! I'LL HAVE TO SHIFT SOME OF THESE CRATES TO GET A CLEAR SHOT. THAT'S BRINGING ME A LOT CLOSER TO WOLVERINE THAN I HAD IN MIND.
STAY ALERT, ROSEN! IF HE BLINKS AN EYE--KILL HIM!
HEY, HEY! YOU KNOW WHAT, BUDDY? I THINK THE LITTLE RUNT IS DEAD.
YOUR MISTAKE, BUB.
THE "LITTLE RUNT" LIVES!
NO!
SHOK
WHICH IS MORE'N I CAN SAY FER YOU.

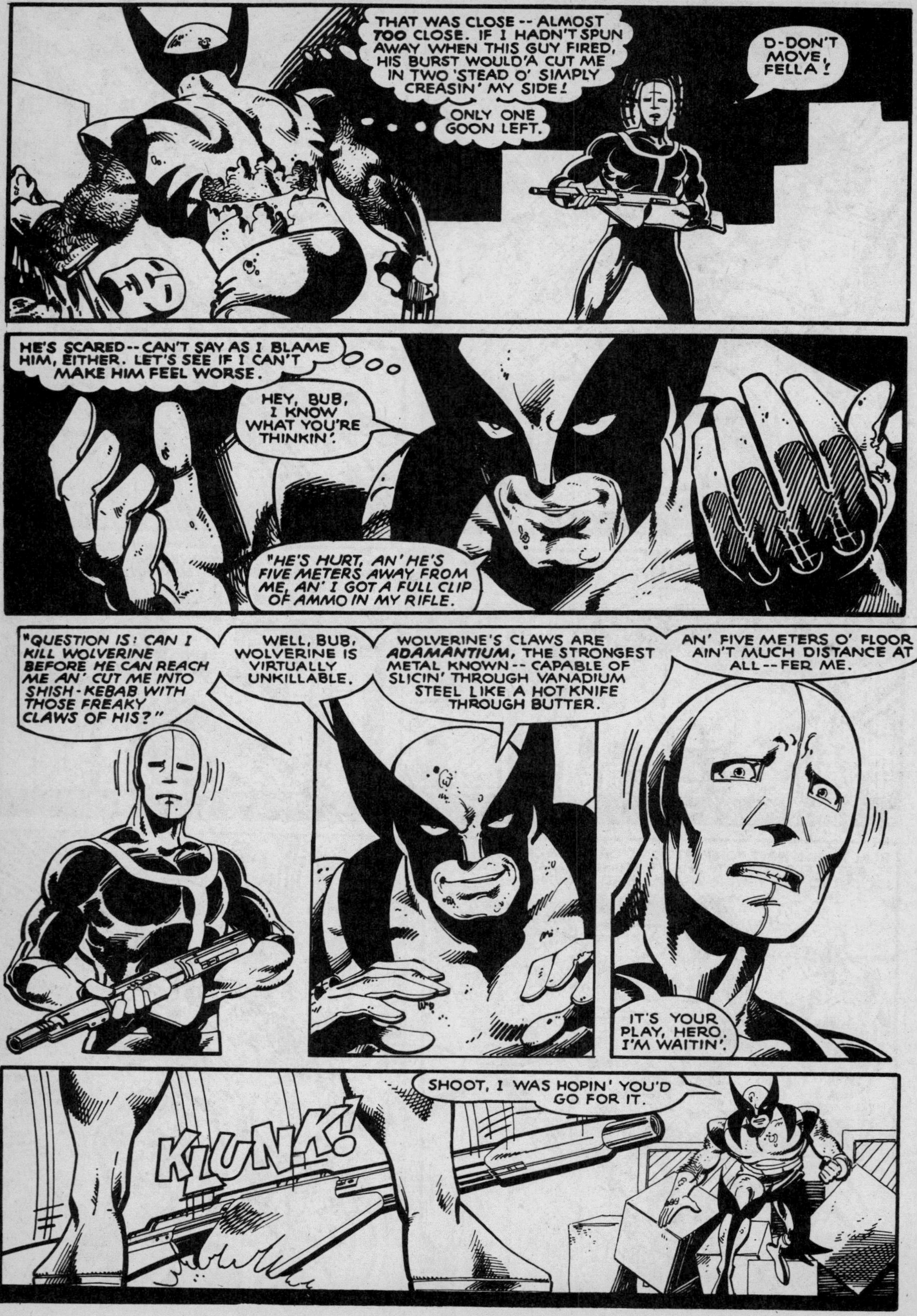
THAT WAS CLOSE -- ALMOST TOO CLOSE. IF I HADN'T SPUN AWAY WHEN THIS GUY FIRED, HIS BURST WOULD'A CUT ME IN TWO 'STEAD O' SIMPLY CREASIN' MY SIDE!
ONLY ONE GOON LEFT.
D-DON'T MOVE, FELLA!
HE'S SCARED--CAN'T SAY AS I BLAME HIM, EITHER. LET'S SEE IF I CAN'T MAKE HIM FEEL WORSE.
HEY, BUB, I KNOW WHAT YOU'RE THINKIN'.
"HE'S HURT, AN' HE'S FIVE METERS AWAY FROM ME, AN' I GOT A FULL CLIP OF AMMO IN MY RIFLE.
"QUESTION IS: CAN I KILL WOLVERINE BEFORE HE CAN REACH ME AN' CUT ME INTO SHISH-KEBAB WITH THOSE FREAKY CLAWS OF HIS?"
WELL, BUB, WOLVERINE IS VIRTUALLY UNKILLABLE.
WOLVERINE'S CLAWS ARE ADAMANTIUM, THE STRONGEST METAL KNOWN-- CAPABLE OF SLICIN' THROUGH VANADIUM STEEL LIKE A HOT KNIFE THROUGH BUTTER.
AN' FIVE METERS O' FLOOR AIN'T MUCH DISTANCE AT ALL--FER ME.
IT'S YOUR PLAY, HERO. I'M WAITIN'.
KLUNK!
SHOOT, I WAS HOPIN' YOU'D GO FOR IT.

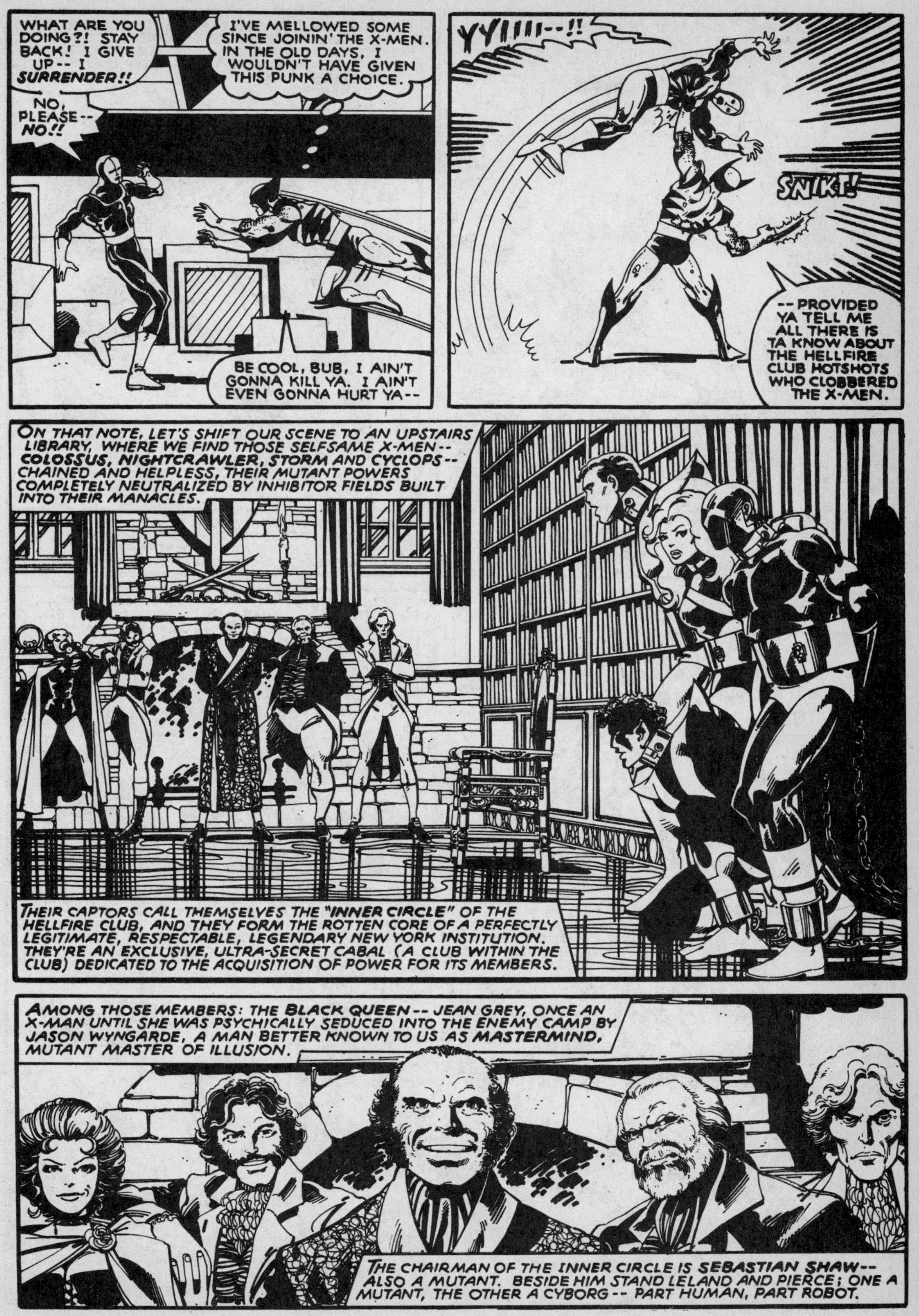

WHAT ARE YOU DOING?! STAY BACK! I GIVE UP -- I SURRENDER!!
I'VE MELLOWED SOME SINCE JOININ' THE X-MEN. IN THE OLD DAYS, I WOULDN'T HAVE GIVEN THIS PUNK A CHOICE.
NO, PLEASE -- NO!!
BE COOL, BUB, I AIN'T GONNA KILL YA. I AIN'T EVEN GONNA HURT YA --
YYIIIII--!!
SNIKT!
-- PROVIDED YA TELL ME ALL THERE IS TA KNOW ABOUT THE HELLFIRE CLUB HOTSHOTS WHO CLOBBERED THE X-MEN.
ON THAT NOTE, LET'S SHIFT OUR SCENE TO AN UPSTAIRS LIBRARY, WHERE WE FIND THOSE SELFSAME X-MEN -- COLOSSUS, NIGHTCRAWLER, STORM AND CYCLOPS -- CHAINED AND HELPLESS, THEIR MUTANT POWERS COMPLETELY NEUTRALIZED BY INHIBITOR FIELDS BUILT INTO THEIR MANACLES.
THEIR CAPTORS CALL THEMSELVES THE "INNER CIRCLE" OF THE HELLFIRE CLUB, AND THEY FORM THE ROTTEN CORE OF A PERFECTLY LEGITIMATE, RESPECTABLE, LEGENDARY NEW YORK INSTITUTION. THEY'RE AN EXCLUSIVE, ULTRA-SECRET CABAL (A CLUB WITHIN THE CLUB) DEDICATED TO THE ACQUISITION OF POWER FOR ITS MEMBERS.
AMONG THOSE MEMBERS: THE BLACK QUEEN -- JEAN GREY, ONCE AN X-MAN UNTIL SHE WAS PSYCHICALLY SEDUCED INTO THE ENEMY CAMP BY JASON WYNGARDE, A MAN BETTER KNOWN TO US AS MASTERMIND, MUTANT MASTER OF ILLUSION.
THE CHAIRMAN OF THE INNER CIRCLE IS SEBASTIAN SHAW -- ALSO A MUTANT. BESIDE HIM STAND LELAND AND PIERCE; ONE A MUTANT, THE OTHER A CYBORG -- PART HUMAN, PART ROBOT.

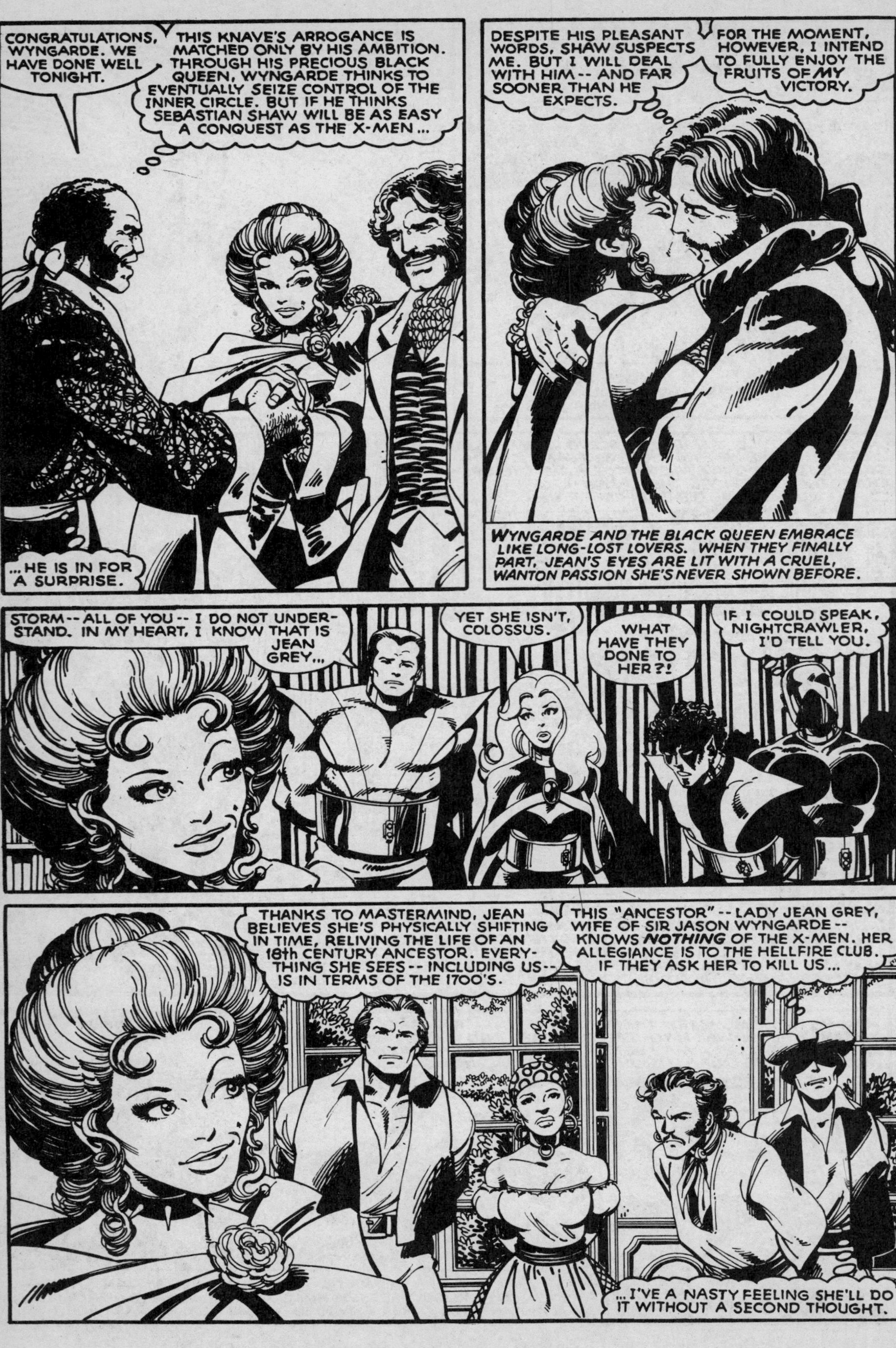
CONGRATULATIONS, WYNGARDE. WE HAVE DONE WELL TONIGHT.
THIS KNAVE'S ARROGANCE IS MATCHED ONLY BY HIS AMBITION. THROUGH HIS PRECIOUS BLACK QUEEN, WYNGARDE THINKS TO EVENTUALLY SEIZE CONTROL OF THE INNER CIRCLE. BUT IF HE THINKS SEBASTIAN SHAW WILL BE AS EASY A CONQUEST AS THE X-MEN...
...HE IS IN FOR A SURPRISE.
DESPITE HIS PLEASANT WORDS, SHAW SUSPECTS ME. BUT I WILL DEAL WITH HIM -- AND FAR SOONER THAN HE EXPECTS.
FOR THE MOMENT, HOWEVER, I INTEND TO FULLY ENJOY THE FRUITS OF MY VICTORY.
WYNGARDE AND THE BLACK QUEEN EMBRACE LIKE LONG-LOST LOVERS. WHEN THEY FINALLY PART, JEAN'S EYES ARE LIT WITH A CRUEL, WANTON PASSION SHE'S NEVER SHOWN BEFORE.
STORM -- ALL OF YOU -- I DO NOT UNDERSTAND. IN MY HEART, I KNOW THAT IS JEAN GREY...
YET SHE ISN'T, COLOSSUS.
WHAT HAVE THEY DONE TO HER?!
IF I COULD SPEAK, NIGHTCRAWLER, I'D TELL YOU.
THANKS TO MASTERMIND, JEAN BELIEVES SHE'S PHYSICALLY SHIFTING IN TIME, RELIVING THE LIFE OF AN 18th CENTURY ANCESTOR. EVERYTHING SHE SEES -- INCLUDING US -- IS IN TERMS OF THE 1700'S.
THIS "ANCESTOR" -- LADY JEAN GREY, WIFE OF SIR JASON WYNGARDE -- KNOWS NOTHING OF THE X-MEN. HER ALLEGIANCE IS TO THE HELLFIRE CLUB. IF THEY ASK HER TO KILL US...
...I'VE A NASTY FEELING SHE'LL DO IT WITHOUT A SECOND THOUGHT.

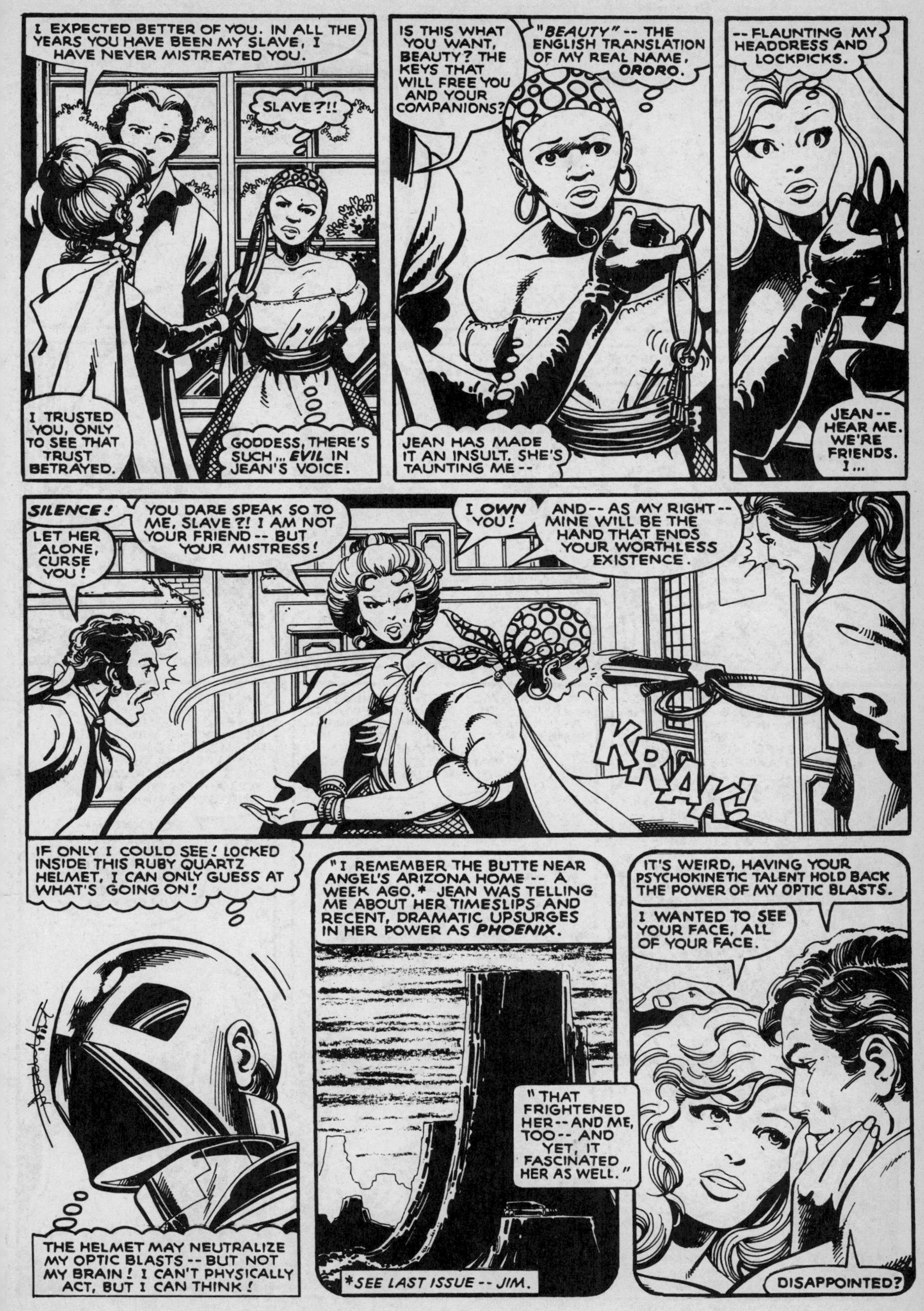
I EXPECTED BETTER OF YOU. IN ALL THE YEARS YOU HAVE BEEN MY SLAVE, I HAVE NEVER MISTREATED YOU.
SLAVE?!!
I TRUSTED YOU, ONLY TO SEE THAT TRUST BETRAYED.
GODDESS, THERE'S SUCH... EVIL IN JEAN'S VOICE.
IS THIS WHAT YOU WANT, BEAUTY? THE KEYS THAT WILL FREE YOU AND YOUR COMPANIONS?
"BEAUTY" -- THE ENGLISH TRANSLATION OF MY REAL NAME, ORORO.
JEAN HAS MADE IT AN INSULT. SHE'S TAUNTING ME --
-- FLAUNTING MY HEADDRESS AND LOCKPICKS.
JEAN -- HEAR ME. WE'RE FRIENDS. I...
SILENCE!
LET HER ALONE, CURSE YOU!
YOU DARE SPEAK SO TO ME, SLAVE?! I AM NOT YOUR FRIEND -- BUT YOUR MISTRESS!
I OWN YOU!
AND -- AS MY RIGHT -- MINE WILL BE THE HAND THAT ENDS YOUR WORTHLESS EXISTENCE.
KRAK!
IF ONLY I COULD SEE! LOCKED INSIDE THIS RUBY QUARTZ HELMET, I CAN ONLY GUESS AT WHAT'S GOING ON!
THE HELMET MAY NEUTRALIZE MY OPTIC BLASTS -- BUT NOT MY BRAIN! I CAN'T PHYSICALLY ACT, BUT I CAN THINK!
"I REMEMBER THE BUTTE NEAR ANGEL'S ARIZONA HOME -- A WEEK AGO.* JEAN WAS TELLING ME ABOUT HER TIMESLIPS AND RECENT, DRAMATIC UPSURGES IN HER POWER AS PHOENIX.
"THAT FRIGHTENED HER -- AND ME, TOO -- AND YET, IT FASCINATED HER AS WELL."
*SEE LAST ISSUE -- JIM.
IT'S WEIRD, HAVING YOUR PSYCHOKINETIC TALENT HOLD BACK THE POWER OF MY OPTIC BLASTS.
I WANTED TO SEE YOUR FACE, ALL OF YOUR FACE.
DISAPPOINTED?

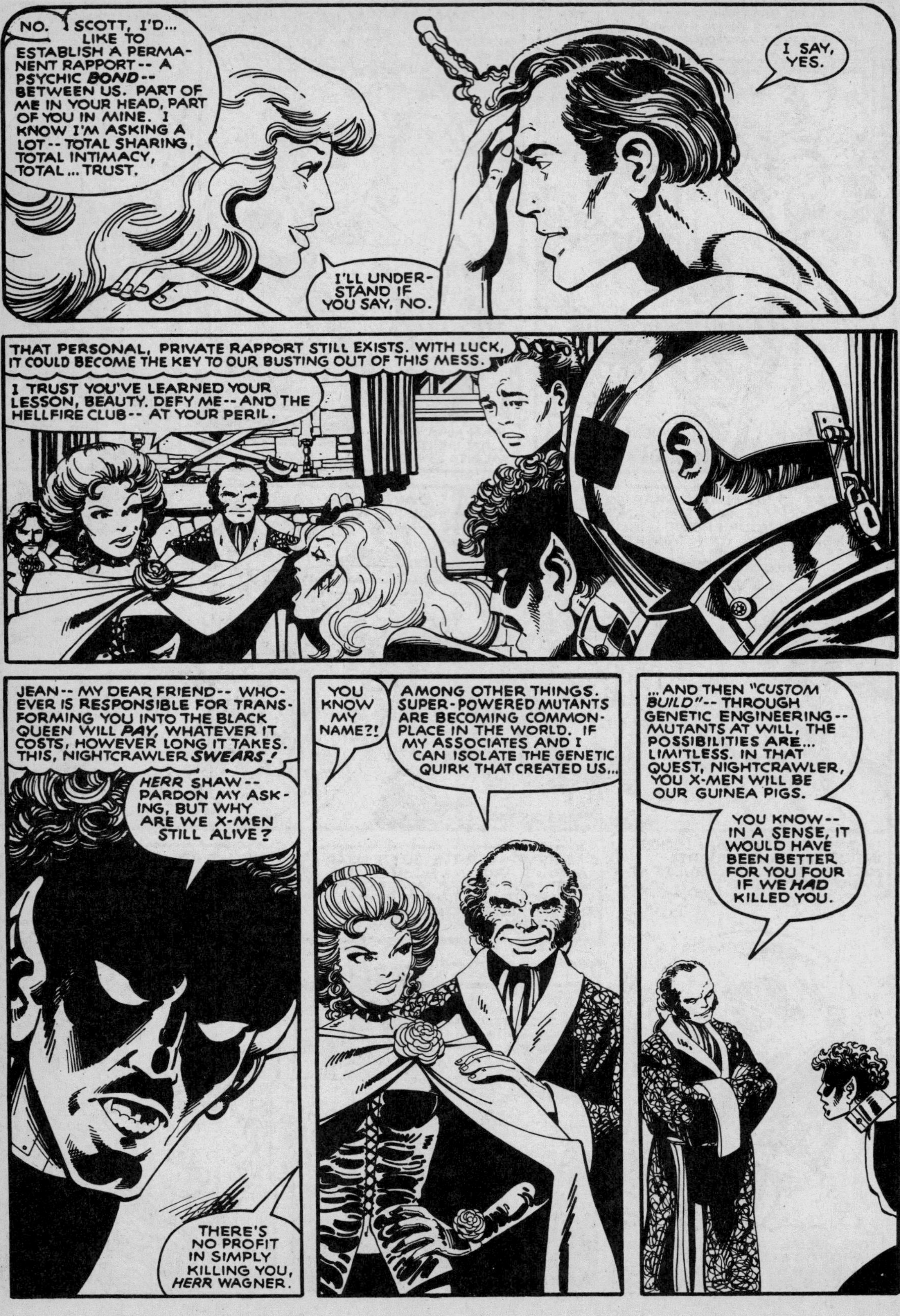
NO.
SCOTT, I'D... LIKE TO ESTABLISH A PERMANENT RAPPORT -- A PSYCHIC BOND -- BETWEEN US. PART OF ME IN YOUR HEAD, PART OF YOU IN MINE. I KNOW I'M ASKING A LOT -- TOTAL SHARING, TOTAL INTIMACY, TOTAL ... TRUST.
I'LL UNDERSTAND IF YOU SAY, NO.
I SAY, YES.
THAT PERSONAL, PRIVATE RAPPORT STILL EXISTS. WITH LUCK, IT COULD BECOME THE KEY TO OUR BUSTING OUT OF THIS MESS.
I TRUST YOU'VE LEARNED YOUR LESSON, BEAUTY. DEFY ME -- AND THE HELLFIRE CLUB -- AT YOUR PERIL.
JEAN -- MY DEAR FRIEND -- WHOEVER IS RESPONSIBLE FOR TRANSFORMING YOU INTO THE BLACK QUEEN WILL PAY, WHATEVER IT COSTS, HOWEVER LONG IT TAKES. THIS, NIGHTCRAWLER SWEARS!
HERR SHAW -- PARDON MY ASKING, BUT WHY ARE WE X-MEN STILL ALIVE?
THERE'S NO PROFIT IN SIMPLY KILLING YOU, HERR WAGNER.
YOU KNOW MY NAME?!
AMONG OTHER THINGS. SUPER-POWERED MUTANTS ARE BECOMING COMMONPLACE IN THE WORLD. IF MY ASSOCIATES AND I CAN ISOLATE THE GENETIC QUIRK THAT CREATED US...
...AND THEN "CUSTOM BUILD" -- THROUGH GENETIC ENGINEERING -- MUTANTS AT WILL, THE POSSIBILITIES ARE... LIMITLESS. IN THAT QUEST, NIGHTCRAWLER, YOU X-MEN WILL BE OUR GUINEA PIGS.
YOU KNOW -- IN A SENSE, IT WOULD HAVE BEEN BETTER FOR YOU FOUR IF WE HAD KILLED YOU.

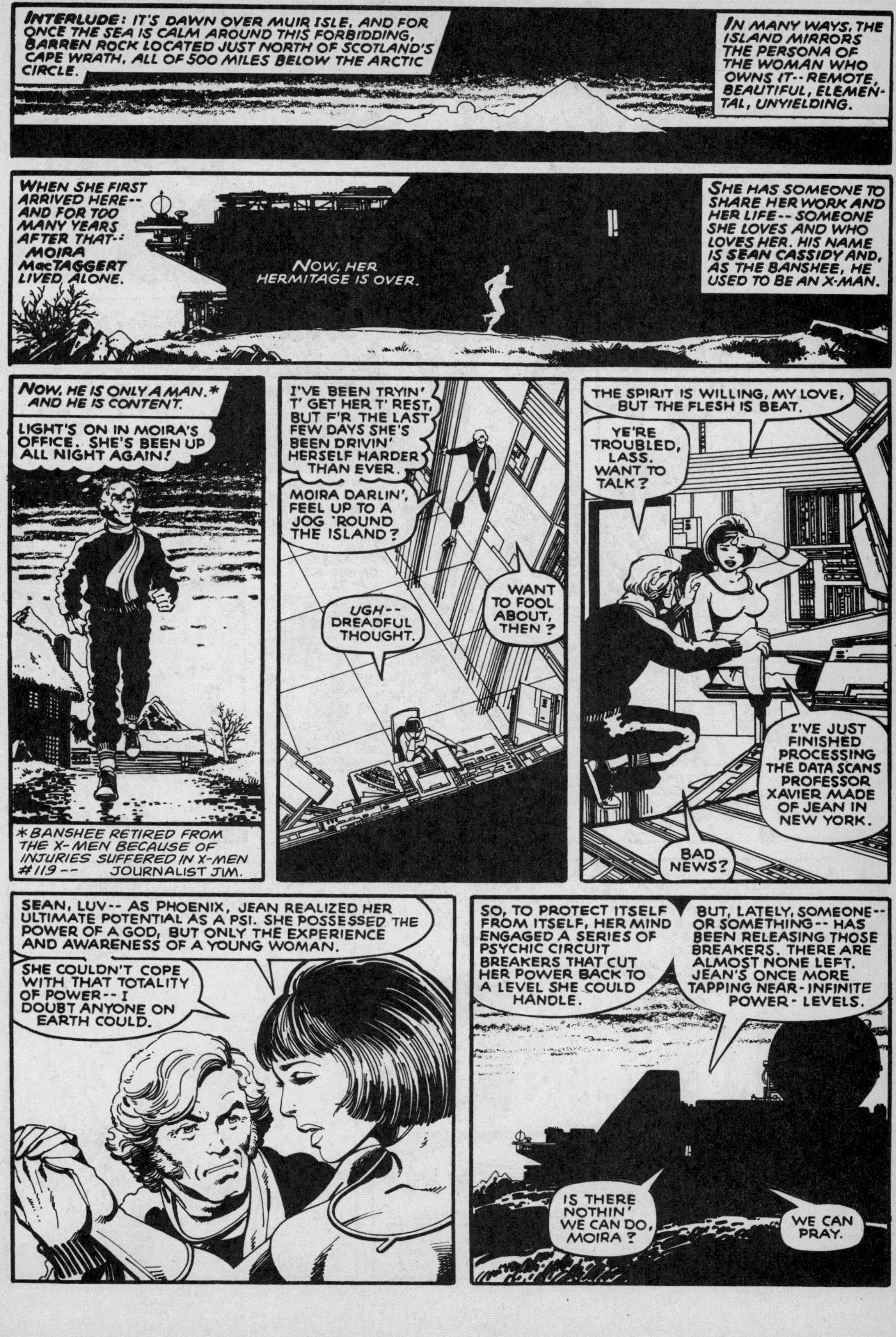
INTERLUDE: IT'S DAWN OVER MUIR ISLE, AND FOR ONCE THE SEA IS CALM AROUND THIS FORBIDDING, BARREN ROCK LOCATED JUST NORTH OF SCOTLAND'S CAPE WRATH, ALL OF 500 MILES BELOW THE ARCTIC CIRCLE.
IN MANY WAYS, THE ISLAND MIRRORS THE PERSONA OF THE WOMAN WHO OWNS IT-- REMOTE, BEAUTIFUL, ELEMENTAL, UNYIELDING.
WHEN SHE FIRST ARRIVED HERE-- AND FOR TOO MANY YEARS AFTER THAT-: MOIRA MacTAGGERT LIVED ALONE.
NOW, HER HERMITAGE IS OVER.
SHE HAS SOMEONE TO SHARE HER WORK AND HER LIFE-- SOMEONE SHE LOVES AND WHO LOVES HER. HIS NAME IS SEAN CASSIDY AND, AS THE BANSHEE, HE USED TO BE AN X-MAN.
NOW, HE IS ONLY A MAN.* AND HE IS CONTENT.
LIGHT'S ON IN MOIRA'S OFFICE. SHE'S BEEN UP ALL NIGHT AGAIN!
*BANSHEE RETIRED FROM THE X-MEN BECAUSE OF INJURIES SUFFERED IN X-MEN #119 -- JOURNALIST JIM.
I'VE BEEN TRYIN' T' GET HER T' REST, BUT F'R THE LAST FEW DAYS SHE'S BEEN DRIVIN' HERSELF HARDER THAN EVER.
MOIRA DARLIN', FEEL UP TO A JOG 'ROUND THE ISLAND?
UGH-- DREADFUL THOUGHT.
WANT TO FOOL ABOUT, THEN?
THE SPIRIT IS WILLING, MY LOVE, BUT THE FLESH IS BEAT.
YE'RE TROUBLED, LASS. WANT TO TALK?
I'VE JUST FINISHED PROCESSING THE DATA SCANS PROFESSOR XAVIER MADE OF JEAN IN NEW YORK.
BAD NEWS?
SEAN, LUV-- AS PHOENIX, JEAN REALIZED HER ULTIMATE POTENTIAL AS A PSI. SHE POSSESSED THE POWER OF A GOD, BUT ONLY THE EXPERIENCE AND AWARENESS OF A YOUNG WOMAN.
SHE COULDN'T COPE WITH THAT TOTALITY OF POWER-- I DOUBT ANYONE ON EARTH COULD.
SO, TO PROTECT ITSELF FROM ITSELF, HER MIND ENGAGED A SERIES OF PSYCHIC CIRCUIT BREAKERS THAT CUT HER POWER BACK TO A LEVEL SHE COULD HANDLE.
BUT, LATELY, SOMEONE-- OR SOMETHING-- HAS BEEN RELEASING THOSE BREAKERS. THERE ARE ALMOST NONE LEFT. JEAN'S ONCE MORE TAPPING NEAR-INFINITE POWER-LEVELS.
IS THERE NOTHIN' WE CAN DO, MOIRA?
WE CAN PRAY.

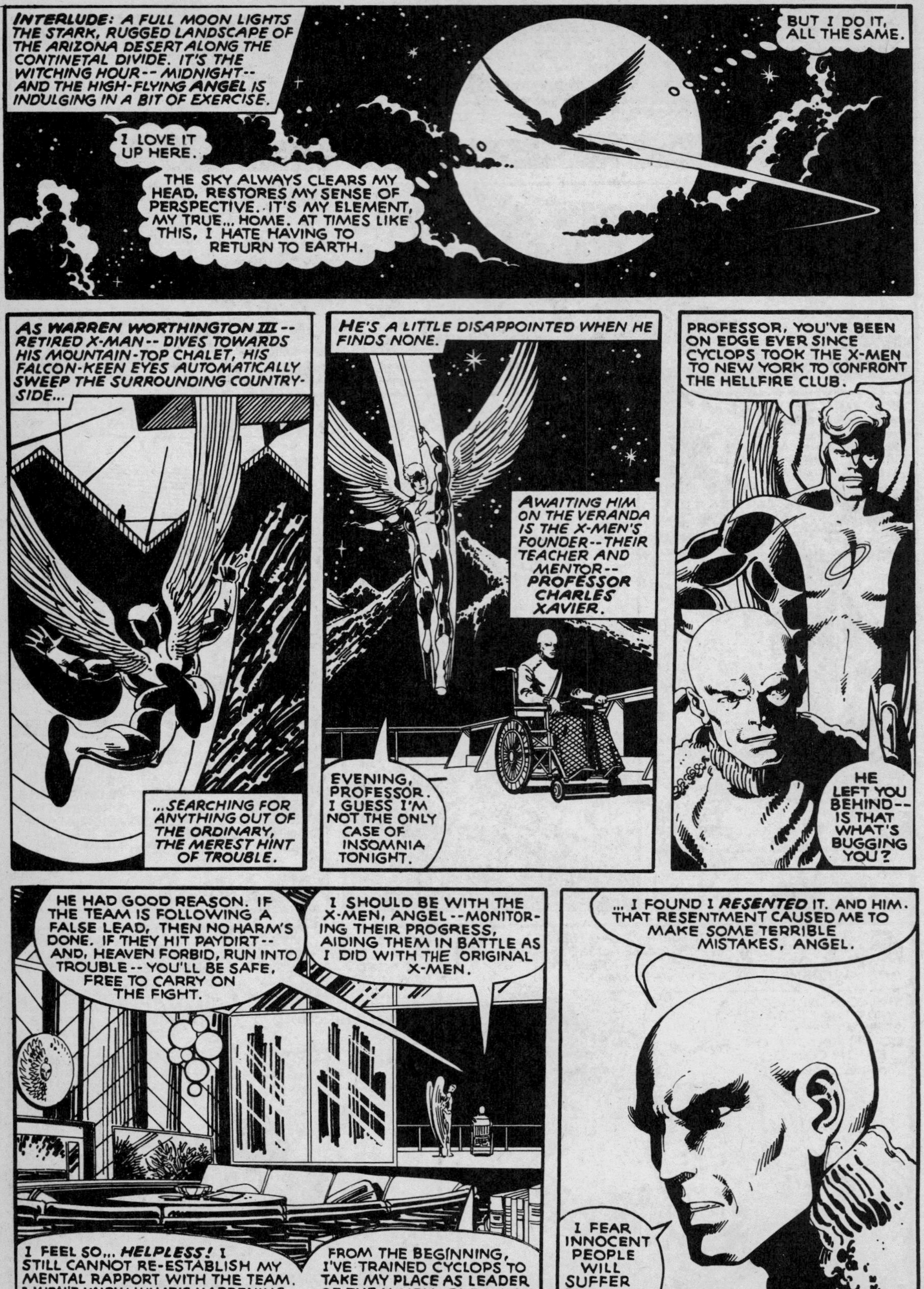

INTERLUDE: A FULL MOON LIGHTS THE STARK, RUGGED LANDSCAPE OF THE ARIZONA DESERT ALONG THE CONTINETAL DIVIDE. IT'S THE WITCHING HOUR-- MIDNIGHT-- AND THE HIGH-FLYING ANGEL IS INDULGING IN A BIT OF EXERCISE.
I LOVE IT UP HERE.
THE SKY ALWAYS CLEARS MY HEAD, RESTORES MY SENSE OF PERSPECTIVE. IT'S MY ELEMENT, MY TRUE... HOME. AT TIMES LIKE THIS, I HATE HAVING TO RETURN TO EARTH.
BUT I DO IT, ALL THE SAME.
AS WARREN WORTHINGTON III -- RETIRED X-MAN -- DIVES TOWARDS HIS MOUNTAIN-TOP CHALET, HIS FALCON-KEEN EYES AUTOMATICALLY SWEEP THE SURROUNDING COUNTRY-SIDE...
...SEARCHING FOR ANYTHING OUT OF THE ORDINARY, THE MEREST HINT OF TROUBLE.
HE'S A LITTLE DISAPPOINTED WHEN HE FINDS NONE.
AWAITING HIM ON THE VERANDA IS THE X-MEN'S FOUNDER-- THEIR TEACHER AND MENTOR-- PROFESSOR CHARLES XAVIER.
EVENING, PROFESSOR. I GUESS I'M NOT THE ONLY CASE OF INSOMNIA TONIGHT.
PROFESSOR, YOU'VE BEEN ON EDGE EVER SINCE CYCLOPS TOOK THE X-MEN TO NEW YORK TO CONFRONT THE HELLFIRE CLUB.
HE LEFT YOU BEHIND-- IS THAT WHAT'S BUGGING YOU?
HE HAD GOOD REASON. IF THE TEAM IS FOLLOWING A FALSE LEAD, THEN NO HARM'S DONE. IF THEY HIT PAYDIRT-- AND, HEAVEN FORBID, RUN INTO TROUBLE -- YOU'LL BE SAFE, FREE TO CARRY ON THE FIGHT.
I SHOULD BE WITH THE X-MEN, ANGEL -- MONITORING THEIR PROGRESS, AIDING THEM IN BATTLE AS I DID WITH THE ORIGINAL X-MEN.
I FEEL SO... HELPLESS! I STILL CANNOT RE-ESTABLISH MY MENTAL RAPPORT WITH THE TEAM. I WON'T KNOW WHAT'S HAPPENING TO THEM UNTIL IT'S TOO LATE!
FROM THE BEGINNING, I'VE TRAINED CYCLOPS TO TAKE MY PLACE AS LEADER OF THE X-MEN. BUT WHEN THAT DAY FINALLY CAME...
... I FOUND I RESENTED IT. AND HIM. THAT RESENTMENT CAUSED ME TO MAKE SOME TERRIBLE MISTAKES, ANGEL.
I FEAR INNOCENT PEOPLE WILL SUFFER BECAUSE OF THEM.

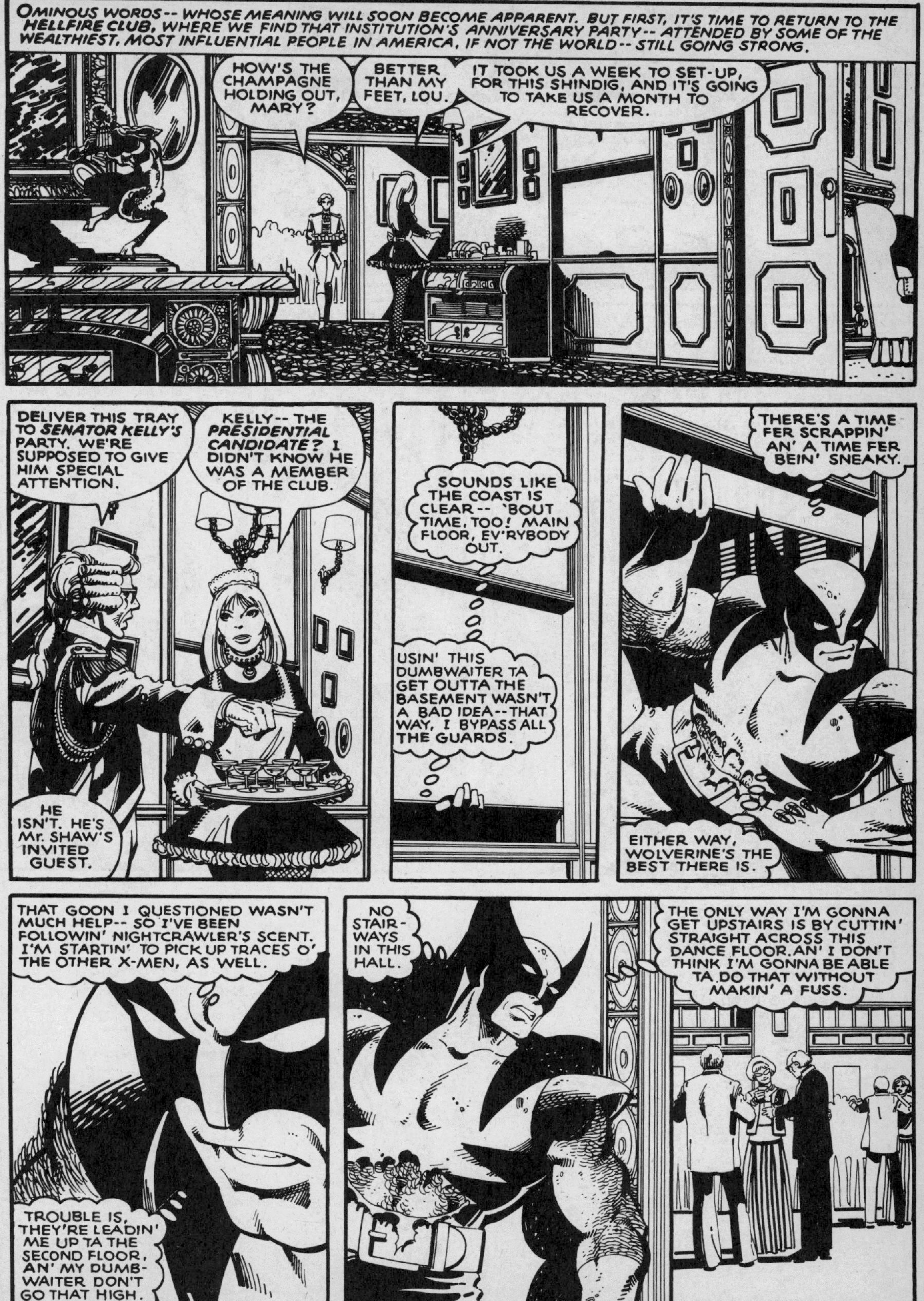
OMINOUS WORDS -- WHOSE MEANING WILL SOON BECOME APPARENT. BUT FIRST, IT'S TIME TO RETURN TO THE HELLFIRE CLUB, WHERE WE FIND THAT INSTITUTION'S ANNIVERSARY PARTY -- ATTENDED BY SOME OF THE WEALTHIEST, MOST INFLUENTIAL PEOPLE IN AMERICA, IF NOT THE WORLD -- STILL GOING STRONG.
HOW'S THE CHAMPAGNE HOLDING OUT, MARY?
BETTER THAN MY FEET, LOU.
IT TOOK US A WEEK TO SET-UP, FOR THIS SHINDIG, AND IT'S GOING TO TAKE US A MONTH TO RECOVER.
DELIVER THIS TRAY TO SENATOR KELLY'S PARTY. WE'RE SUPPOSED TO GIVE HIM SPECIAL ATTENTION.
KELLY -- THE PRESIDENTIAL CANDIDATE? I DIDN'T KNOW HE WAS A MEMBER OF THE CLUB.
HE ISN'T. HE'S Mr. SHAW'S INVITED GUEST.
SOUNDS LIKE THE COAST IS CLEAR -- 'BOUT TIME, TOO! MAIN FLOOR, EV'RYBODY OUT.
USIN' THIS DUMBWAITER TA GET OUTTA THE BASEMENT WASN'T A BAD IDEA -- THAT WAY, I BYPASS ALL THE GUARDS.
THERE'S A TIME FER SCRAPPIN' AN' A TIME FER BEIN' SNEAKY.
EITHER WAY, WOLVERINE'S THE BEST THERE IS.
THAT GOON I QUESTIONED WASN'T MUCH HELP -- SO I'VE BEEN FOLLOWIN' NIGHTCRAWLER'S SCENT. I'M STARTIN' TO PICK UP TRACES O' THE OTHER X-MEN, AS WELL.
TROUBLE IS, THEY'RE LEADIN' ME UP TA THE SECOND FLOOR, AN' MY DUMB-WAITER DON'T GO THAT HIGH.
NO STAIR-WAYS IN THIS HALL.
THE ONLY WAY I'M GONNA GET UPSTAIRS IS BY CUTTIN' STRAIGHT ACROSS THIS DANCE FLOOR. AN' I DON'T THINK I'M GONNA BE ABLE TA DO THAT WITHOUT MAKIN' A FUSS.

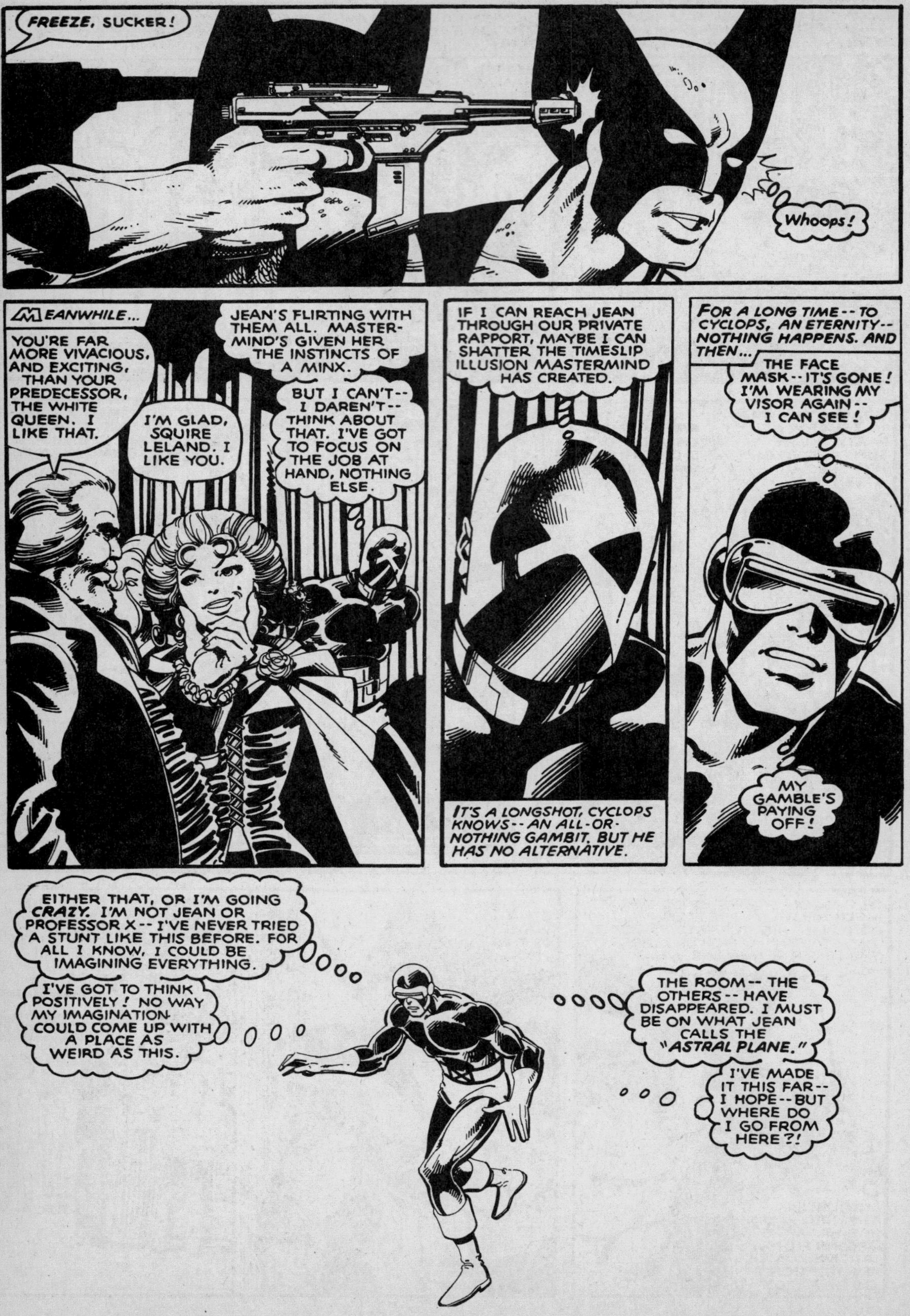
FREEZE, SUCKER!
Whoops!
MEANWHILE...
YOU'RE FAR MORE VIVACIOUS, AND EXCITING, THAN YOUR PREDECESSOR, THE WHITE QUEEN. I LIKE THAT.
I'M GLAD, SQUIRE LELAND. I LIKE YOU.
JEAN'S FLIRTING WITH THEM ALL. MASTER-MIND'S GIVEN HER THE INSTINCTS OF A MINX.
BUT I CAN'T-- I DAREN'T-- THINK ABOUT THAT. I'VE GOT TO FOCUS ON THE JOB AT HAND, NOTHING ELSE.
IF I CAN REACH JEAN THROUGH OUR PRIVATE RAPPORT, MAYBE I CAN SHATTER THE TIMESLIP ILLUSION MASTERMIND HAS CREATED.
IT'S A LONGSHOT, CYCLOPS KNOWS-- AN ALL-OR-NOTHING GAMBIT. BUT HE HAS NO ALTERNATIVE.
FOR A LONG TIME-- TO CYCLOPS, AN ETERNITY-- NOTHING HAPPENS. AND THEN...
THE FACE MASK-- IT'S GONE! I'M WEARING MY VISOR AGAIN-- I CAN SEE!
MY GAMBLE'S PAYING OFF!
EITHER THAT, OR I'M GOING CRAZY. I'M NOT JEAN OR PROFESSOR X-- I'VE NEVER TRIED A STUNT LIKE THIS BEFORE. FOR ALL I KNOW, I COULD BE IMAGINING EVERYTHING.
I'VE GOT TO THINK POSITIVELY! NO WAY MY IMAGINATION COULD COME UP WITH A PLACE AS WEIRD AS THIS.
THE ROOM-- THE OTHERS-- HAVE DISAPPEARED. I MUST BE ON WHAT JEAN CALLS THE "ASTRAL PLANE."
I'VE MADE IT THIS FAR-- I HOPE-- BUT WHERE DO I GO FROM HERE?!

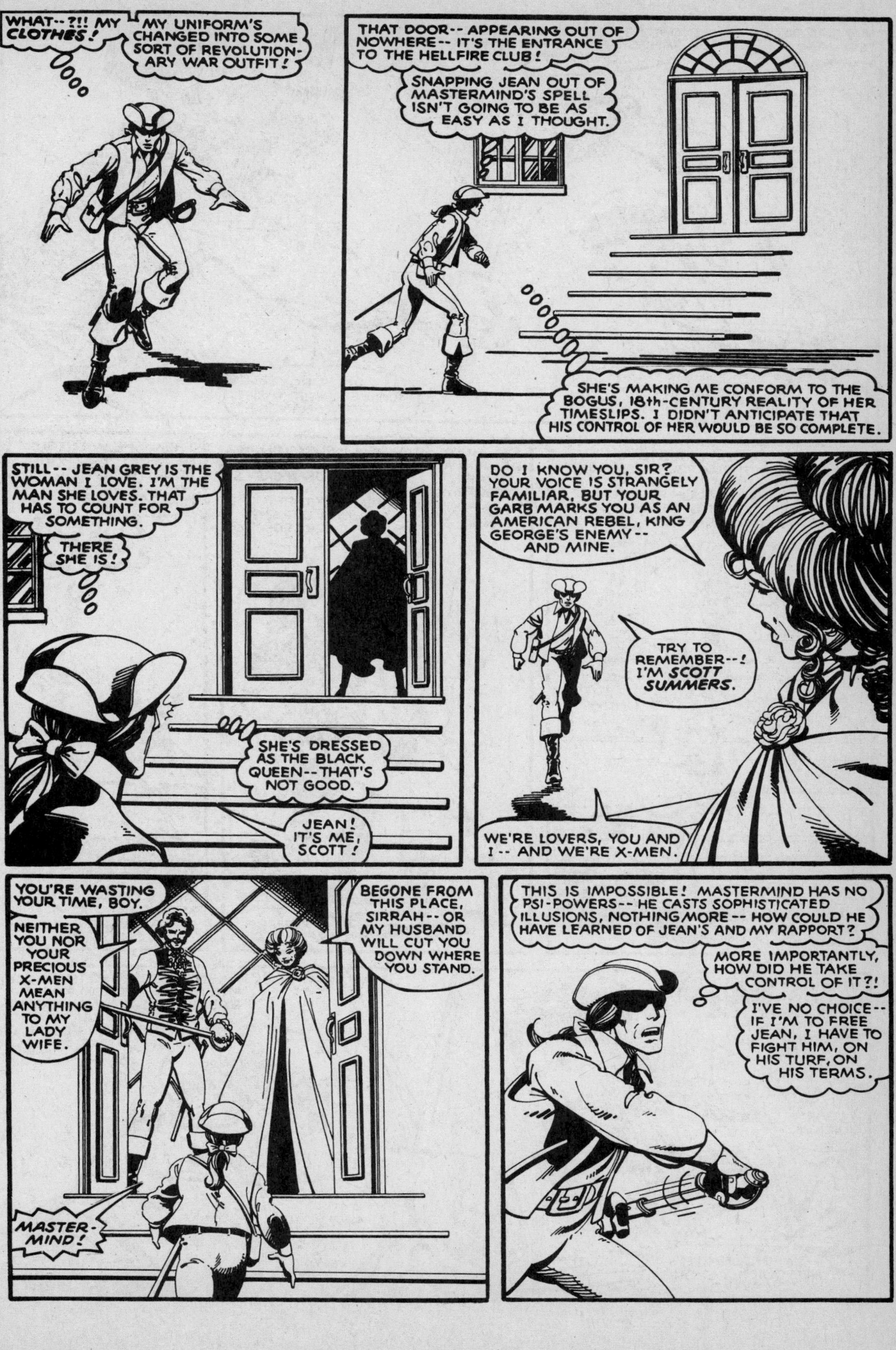
WHAT--?!! MY CLOTHES!
MY UNIFORM'S CHANGED INTO SOME SORT OF REVOLUTIONARY WAR OUTFIT!
THAT DOOR-- APPEARING OUT OF NOWHERE-- IT'S THE ENTRANCE TO THE HELLFIRE CLUB!
SNAPPING JEAN OUT OF MASTERMIND'S SPELL ISN'T GOING TO BE AS EASY AS I THOUGHT.
SHE'S MAKING ME CONFORM TO THE BOGUS, 18th-CENTURY REALITY OF HER TIMESLIPS. I DIDN'T ANTICIPATE THAT HIS CONTROL OF HER WOULD BE SO COMPLETE.
STILL-- JEAN GREY IS THE WOMAN I LOVE. I'M THE MAN SHE LOVES. THAT HAS TO COUNT FOR SOMETHING.
THERE SHE IS!
SHE'S DRESSED AS THE BLACK QUEEN--THAT'S NOT GOOD.
JEAN! IT'S ME, SCOTT!
DO I KNOW YOU, SIR? YOUR VOICE IS STRANGELY FAMILIAR, BUT YOUR GARB MARKS YOU AS AN AMERICAN REBEL, KING GEORGE'S ENEMY-- AND MINE.
TRY TO REMEMBER--! I'M SCOTT SUMMERS.
WE'RE LOVERS, YOU AND I-- AND WE'RE X-MEN.
YOU'RE WASTING YOUR TIME, BOY.
NEITHER YOU NOR YOUR PRECIOUS X-MEN MEAN ANYTHING TO MY LADY WIFE.
BEGONE FROM THIS PLACE, SIRRAH-- OR MY HUSBAND WILL CUT YOU DOWN WHERE YOU STAND.
MASTERMIND!
THIS IS IMPOSSIBLE! MASTERMIND HAS NO PSI-POWERS-- HE CASTS SOPHISTICATED ILLUSIONS, NOTHING MORE-- HOW COULD HE HAVE LEARNED OF JEAN'S AND MY RAPPORT?
MORE IMPORTANTLY, HOW DID HE TAKE CONTROL OF IT?!
I'VE NO CHOICE-- IF I'M TO FREE JEAN, I HAVE TO FIGHT HIM, ON HIS TURF, ON HIS TERMS.

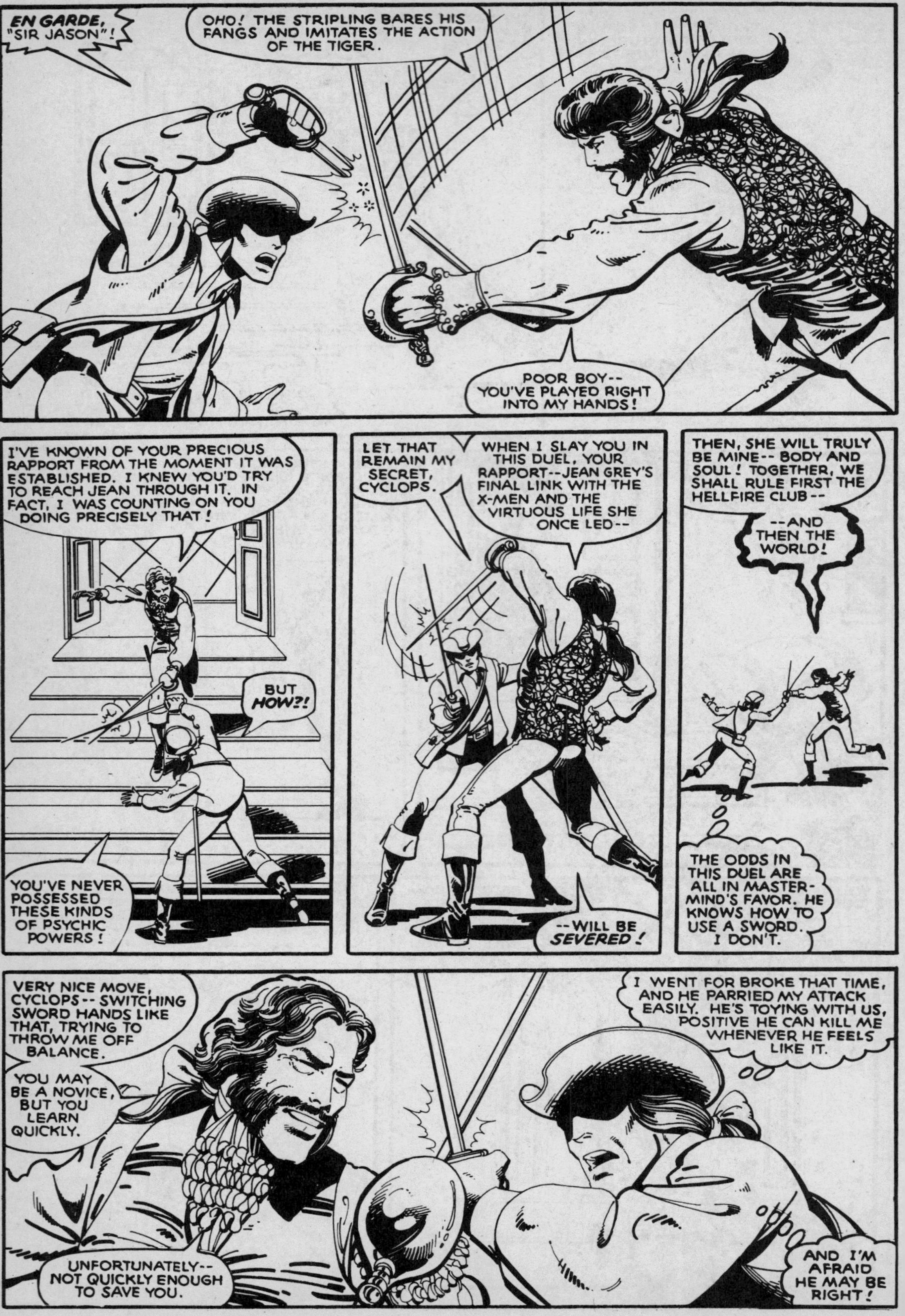

EN GARDE, "SIR JASON"!
OHO! THE STRIPLING BARES HIS FANGS AND IMITATES THE ACTION OF THE TIGER.
POOR BOY-- YOU'VE PLAYED RIGHT INTO MY HANDS!
I'VE KNOWN OF YOUR PRECIOUS RAPPORT FROM THE MOMENT IT WAS ESTABLISHED. I KNEW YOU'D TRY TO REACH JEAN THROUGH IT. IN FACT, I WAS COUNTING ON YOU DOING PRECISELY THAT!
BUT HOW?!
YOU'VE NEVER POSSESSED THESE KINDS OF PSYCHIC POWERS!
LET THAT REMAIN MY SECRET, CYCLOPS.
WHEN I SLAY YOU IN THIS DUEL, YOUR RAPPORT--JEAN GREY'S FINAL LINK WITH THE X-MEN AND THE VIRTUOUS LIFE SHE ONCE LED--
--WILL BE SEVERED!
THEN, SHE WILL TRULY BE MINE-- BODY AND SOUL! TOGETHER, WE SHALL RULE FIRST THE HELLFIRE CLUB--
--AND THEN THE WORLD!
THE ODDS IN THIS DUEL ARE ALL IN MASTER-MIND'S FAVOR. HE KNOWS HOW TO USE A SWORD. I DON'T.
VERY NICE MOVE, CYCLOPS-- SWITCHING SWORD HANDS LIKE THAT, TRYING TO THROW ME OFF BALANCE.
YOU MAY BE A NOVICE, BUT YOU LEARN QUICKLY.
UNFORTUNATELY-- NOT QUICKLY ENOUGH TO SAVE YOU.
I WENT FOR BROKE THAT TIME, AND HE PARRIED MY ATTACK EASILY. HE'S TOYING WITH US, POSITIVE HE CAN KILL ME WHENEVER HE FEELS LIKE IT.
AND I'M AFRAID HE MAY BE RIGHT!

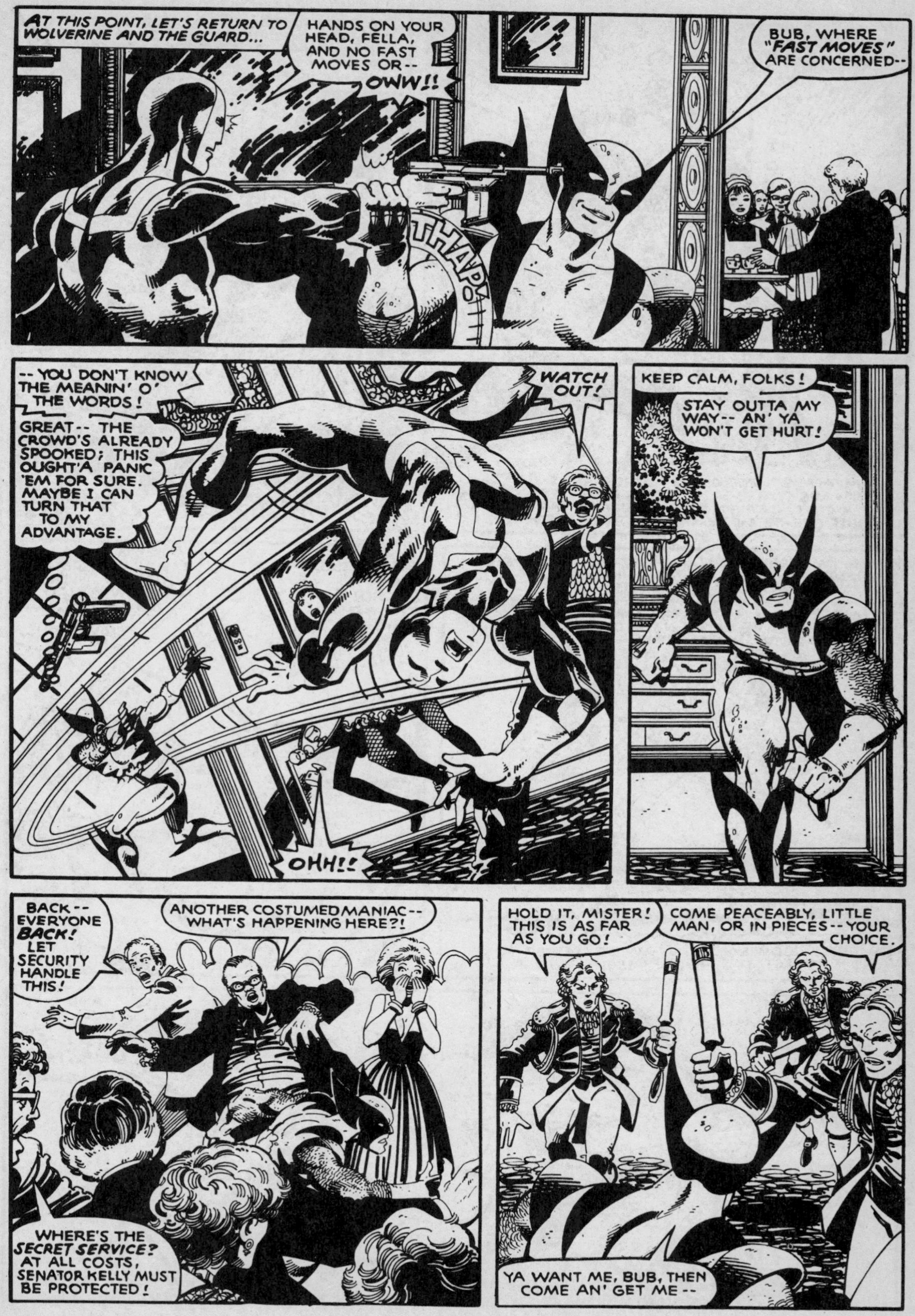
AT THIS POINT, LET'S RETURN TO WOLVERINE AND THE GUARD...
HANDS ON YOUR HEAD, FELLA, AND NO FAST MOVES OR--
OWW!!
THAP
BUB, WHERE "FAST MOVES" ARE CONCERNED--
--YOU DON'T KNOW THE MEANIN' O' THE WORDS!
GREAT-- THE CROWD'S ALREADY SPOOKED; THIS OUGHT'A PANIC 'EM FOR SURE. MAYBE I CAN TURN THAT TO MY ADVANTAGE.
WATCH OUT!
OHH!!
KEEP CALM, FOLKS!
STAY OUTTA MY WAY-- AN' YA WON'T GET HURT!
BACK-- EVERYONE BACK! LET SECURITY HANDLE THIS!
ANOTHER COSTUMED MANIAC-- WHAT'S HAPPENING HERE?!
WHERE'S THE SECRET SERVICE? AT ALL COSTS, SENATOR KELLY MUST BE PROTECTED!
HOLD IT, MISTER! THIS IS AS FAR AS YOU GO!
COME PEACEABLY, LITTLE MAN, OR IN PIECES-- YOUR CHOICE.
YA WANT ME, BUB, THEN COME AN' GET ME--

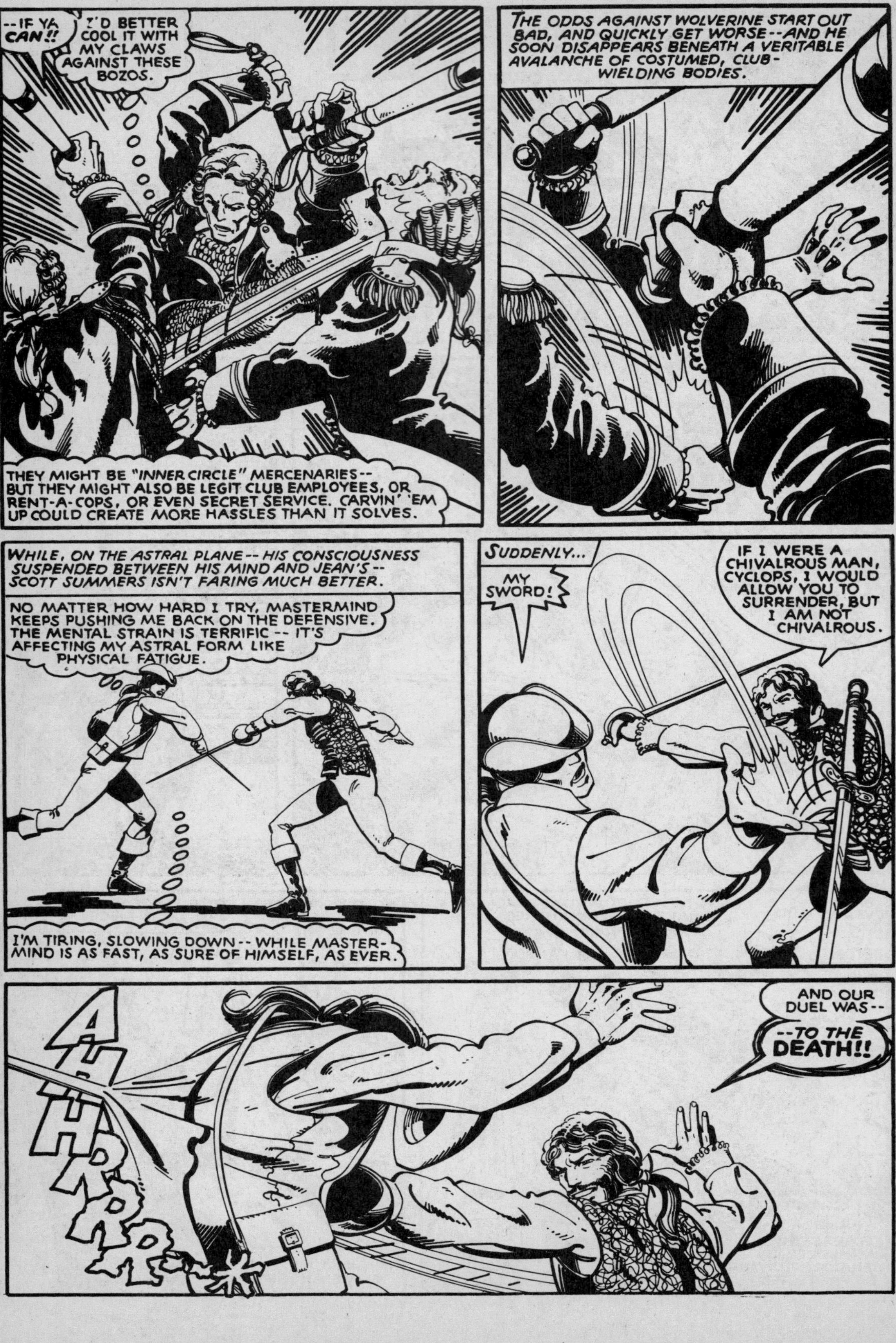
--IF YA CAN!!
I'D BETTER COOL IT WITH MY CLAWS AGAINST THESE BOZOS.
THEY MIGHT BE "INNER CIRCLE" MERCENARIES-- BUT THEY MIGHT ALSO BE LEGIT CLUB EMPLOYEES, OR RENT-A-COPS, OR EVEN SECRET SERVICE. CARVIN' 'EM UP COULD CREATE MORE HASSLES THAN IT SOLVES.
THE ODDS AGAINST WOLVERINE START OUT BAD, AND QUICKLY GET WORSE--AND HE SOON DISAPPEARS BENEATH A VERITABLE AVALANCHE OF COSTUMED, CLUB-WIELDING BODIES.
WHILE, ON THE ASTRAL PLANE--HIS CONSCIOUSNESS SUSPENDED BETWEEN HIS MIND AND JEAN'S--SCOTT SUMMERS ISN'T FARING MUCH BETTER.
NO MATTER HOW HARD I TRY, MASTERMIND KEEPS PUSHING ME BACK ON THE DEFENSIVE. THE MENTAL STRAIN IS TERRIFIC -- IT'S AFFECTING MY ASTRAL FORM LIKE PHYSICAL FATIGUE.
I'M TIRING, SLOWING DOWN--WHILE MASTER-MIND IS AS FAST, AS SURE OF HIMSELF, AS EVER.
SUDDENLY...
MY SWORD!
IF I WERE A CHIVALROUS MAN, CYCLOPS, I WOULD ALLOW YOU TO SURRENDER, BUT I AM NOT CHIVALROUS.
AHHRRR
AND OUR DUEL WAS--
--TO THE DEATH!!

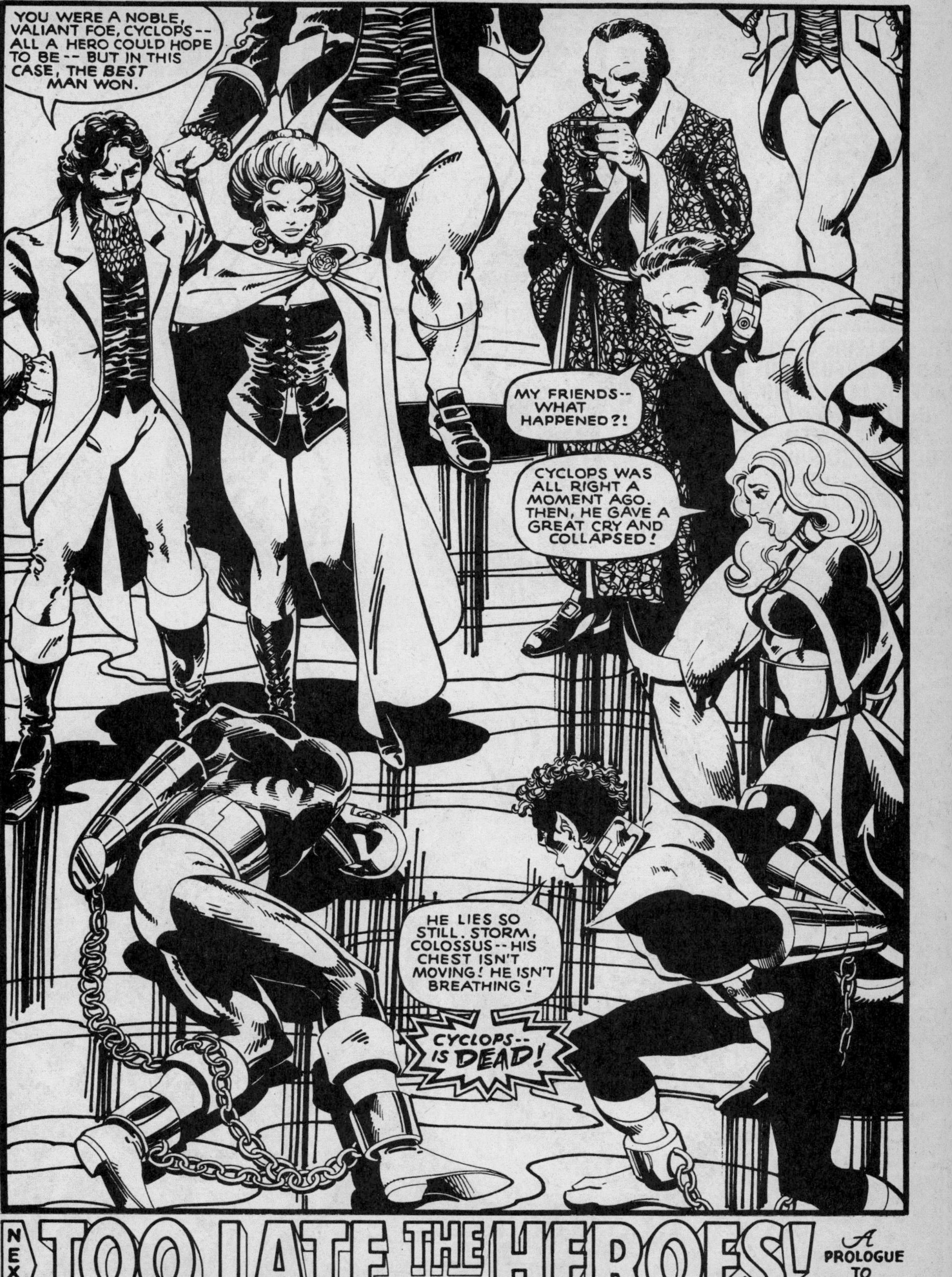
YOU WERE A NOBLE, VALIANT FOE, CYCLOPS -- ALL A HERO COULD HOPE TO BE -- BUT IN THIS CASE, THE *BEST* MAN WON.
MY FRIENDS -- WHAT HAPPENED?!
CYCLOPS WAS ALL RIGHT A MOMENT AGO. THEN, HE GAVE A GREAT CRY AND COLLAPSED!
HE LIES SO STILL. STORM, COLOSSUS -- HIS CHEST ISN'T MOVING! HE ISN'T BREATHING!
CYCLOPS -- IS *DEAD*!

NEXT: TOO LATE, THE HEROES! *A* PROLOGUE TO *DISASTER!*

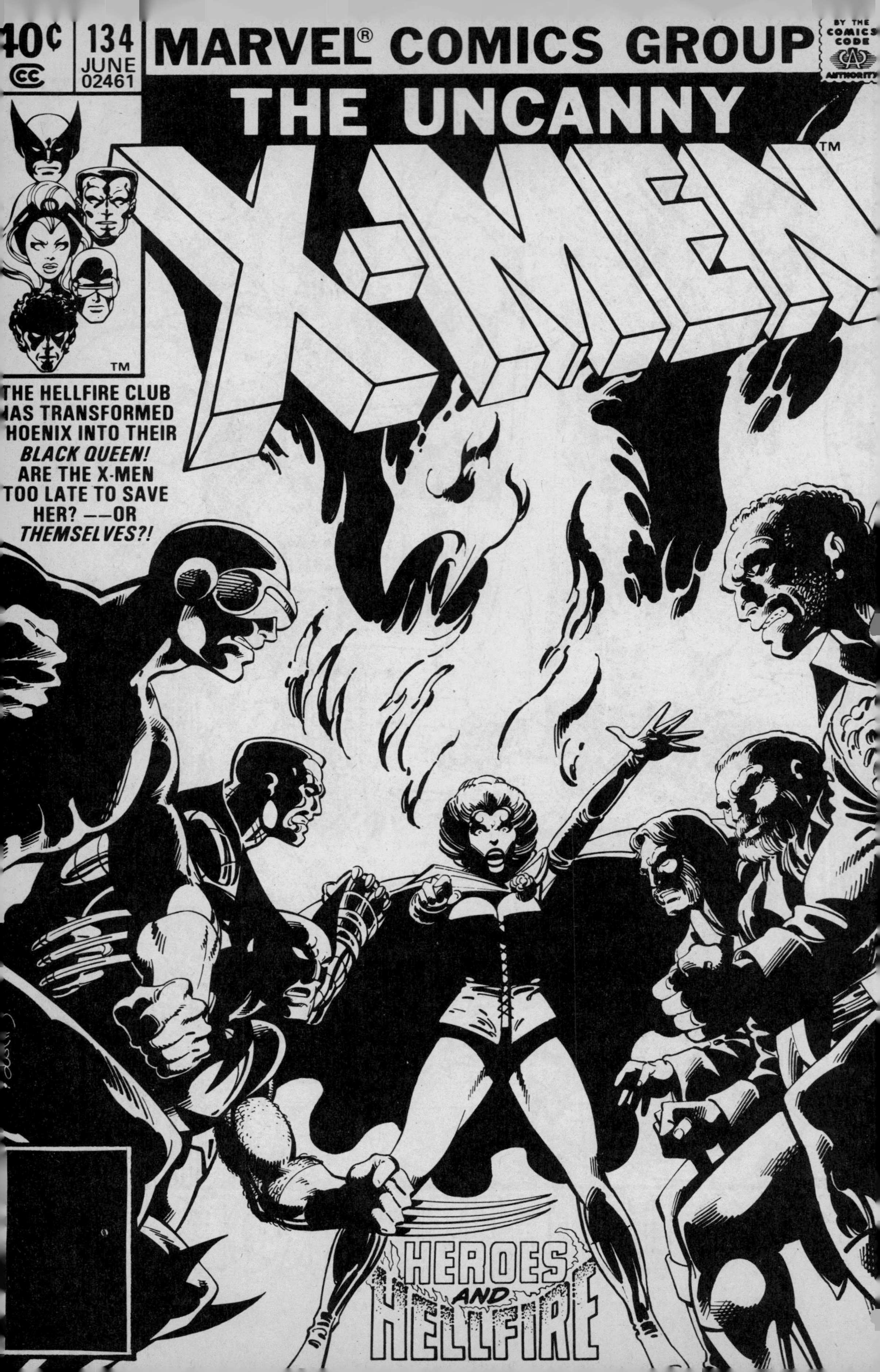
40¢
134
JUNE
02461
CC
MARVEL® COMICS GROUP
APPROVED BY THE COMICS CODE AUTHORITY
THE UNCANNY
X-MEN™
TM
THE HELLFIRE CLUB HAS TRANSFORMED PHOENIX INTO THEIR BLACK QUEEN! ARE THE X-MEN TOO LATE TO SAVE HER? ——OR THEMSELVES?!
HEROES AND HELLFIRE

Cyclops. Storm. Nightcrawler. Wolverine. Colossus. Children of the atom, students of Charles Xavier, MUTANTS — feared and hated by the world they have sworn to protect. These are the STRANGEST heroes of all!

Stan Lee PRESENTS: **THE UNCANNY X-MEN!** TM

A TALE OF TRIUMPH AND TERROR CRAFTED BY

CHRIS CLAREMONT & JOHN BYRNE WRITER / CO-PLOTTERS / PENCILER | TERRY AUSTIN INKER | TOM ORZECHOWSKI, letterer BOB SHAREN, colorist | JIM SALICRUP EDITOR | JIM SHOOTER Ed.-IN-CHIEF

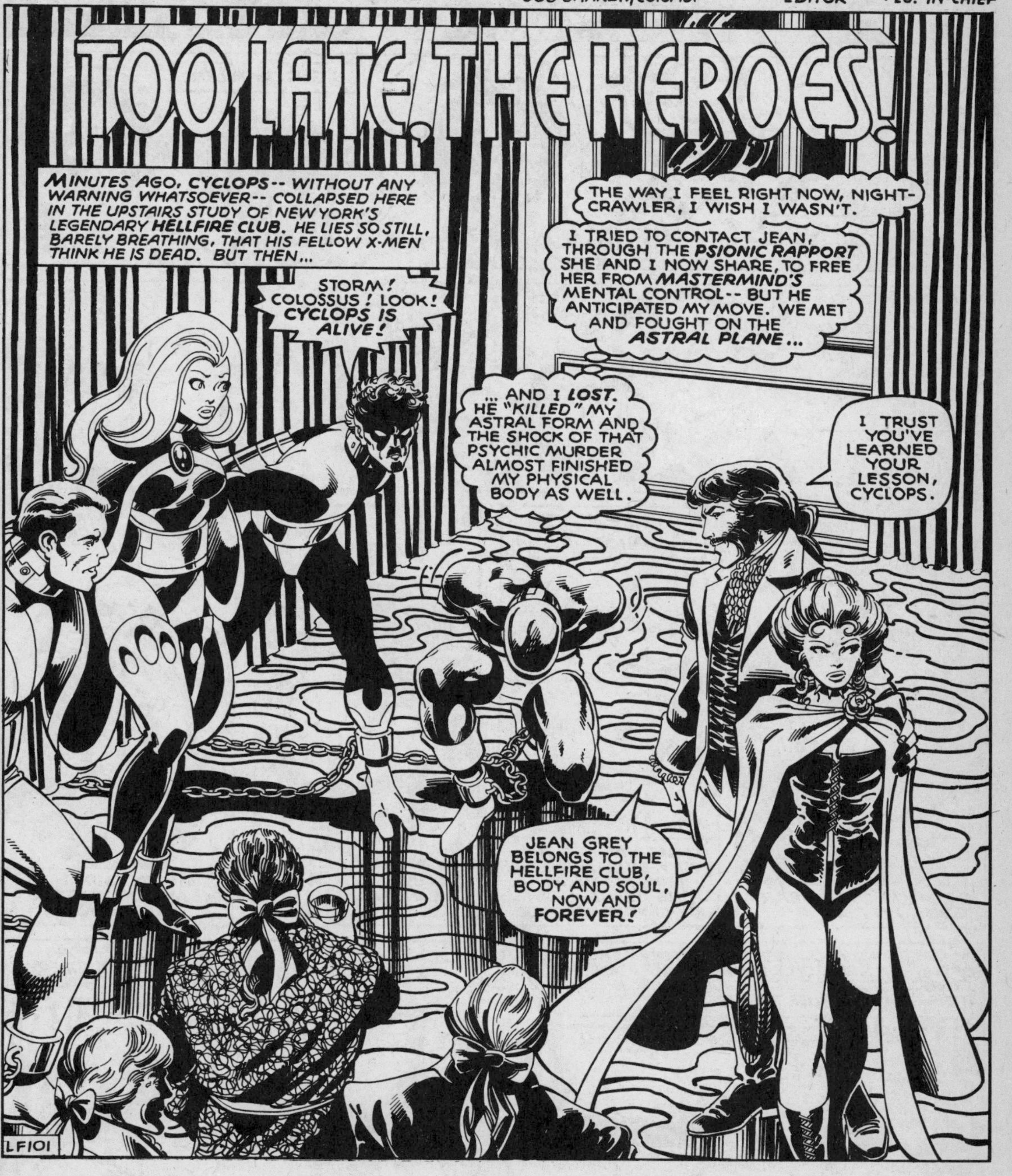
TOO LATE, THE HEROES!
MINUTES AGO, CYCLOPS-- WITHOUT ANY WARNING WHATSOEVER-- COLLAPSED HERE IN THE UPSTAIRS STUDY OF NEW YORK'S LEGENDARY HELLFIRE CLUB. HE LIES SO STILL, BARELY BREATHING, THAT HIS FELLOW X-MEN THINK HE IS DEAD. BUT THEN...
STORM! COLOSSUS! LOOK! CYCLOPS IS ALIVE!
THE WAY I FEEL RIGHT NOW, NIGHT-CRAWLER, I WISH I WASN'T.
I TRIED TO CONTACT JEAN, THROUGH THE PSIONIC RAPPORT SHE AND I NOW SHARE, TO FREE HER FROM MASTERMIND'S MENTAL CONTROL-- BUT HE ANTICIPATED MY MOVE. WE MET AND FOUGHT ON THE ASTRAL PLANE...
... AND I LOST. HE "KILLED" MY ASTRAL FORM AND THE SHOCK OF THAT PSYCHIC MURDER ALMOST FINISHED MY PHYSICAL BODY AS WELL.
I TRUST YOU'VE LEARNED YOUR LESSON, CYCLOPS.
JEAN GREY BELONGS TO THE HELLFIRE CLUB, BODY AND SOUL, NOW AND FOREVER!
LF101

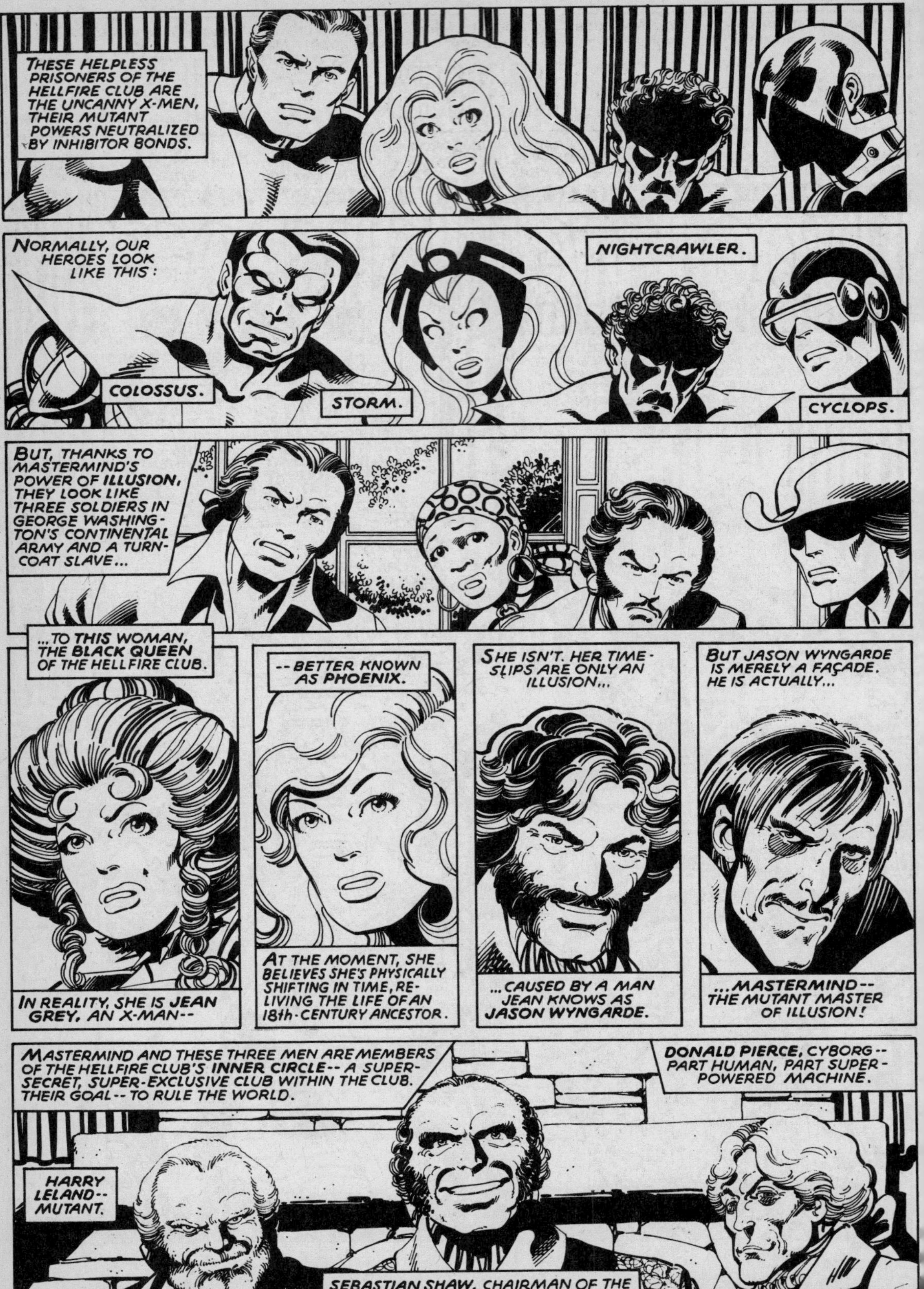
THESE HELPLESS PRISONERS OF THE HELLFIRE CLUB ARE THE UNCANNY X-MEN, THEIR MUTANT POWERS NEUTRALIZED BY INHIBITOR BONDS.
NORMALLY, OUR HEROES LOOK LIKE THIS:
COLOSSUS.
STORM.
NIGHTCRAWLER.
CYCLOPS.
BUT, THANKS TO MASTERMIND'S POWER OF ILLUSION, THEY LOOK LIKE THREE SOLDIERS IN GEORGE WASHINGTON'S CONTINENTAL ARMY AND A TURNCOAT SLAVE...
...TO THIS WOMAN, THE BLACK QUEEN OF THE HELLFIRE CLUB.
IN REALITY, SHE IS JEAN GREY, AN X-MAN--
--BETTER KNOWN AS PHOENIX.
AT THE MOMENT, SHE BELIEVES SHE'S PHYSICALLY SHIFTING IN TIME, RELIVING THE LIFE OF AN 18th-CENTURY ANCESTOR.
SHE ISN'T. HER TIME-SLIPS ARE ONLY AN ILLUSION...
...CAUSED BY A MAN JEAN KNOWS AS JASON WYNGARDE.
BUT JASON WYNGARDE IS MERELY A FAÇADE. HE IS ACTUALLY...
...MASTERMIND-- THE MUTANT MASTER OF ILLUSION!
MASTERMIND AND THESE THREE MEN ARE MEMBERS OF THE HELLFIRE CLUB'S INNER CIRCLE-- A SUPER-SECRET, SUPER-EXCLUSIVE CLUB WITHIN THE CLUB. THEIR GOAL-- TO RULE THE WORLD.
DONALD PIERCE, CYBORG-- PART HUMAN, PART SUPER-POWERED MACHINE.
HARRY LELAND-- MUTANT.
SEBASTIAN SHAW, CHAIRMAN OF THE INNER CIRCLE-- ALSO A MUTANT.

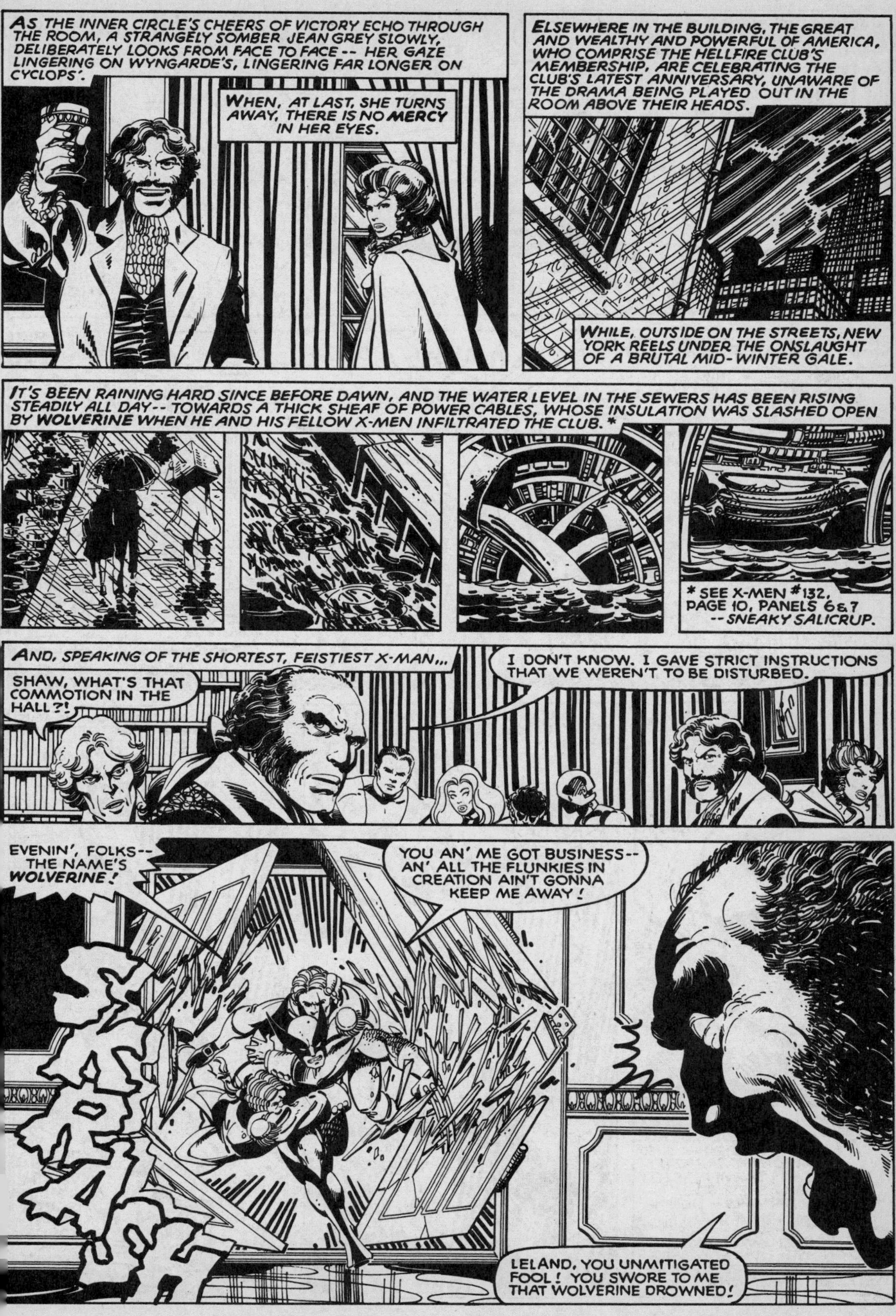
AS THE INNER CIRCLE'S CHEERS OF VICTORY ECHO THROUGH THE ROOM, A STRANGELY SOMBER JEAN GREY SLOWLY, DELIBERATELY LOOKS FROM FACE TO FACE -- HER GAZE LINGERING ON WYNGARDE'S, LINGERING FAR LONGER ON CYCLOPS'.
WHEN, AT LAST, SHE TURNS AWAY, THERE IS NO MERCY IN HER EYES.
ELSEWHERE IN THE BUILDING, THE GREAT AND WEALTHY AND POWERFUL OF AMERICA, WHO COMPRISE THE HELLFIRE CLUB'S MEMBERSHIP, ARE CELEBRATING THE CLUB'S LATEST ANNIVERSARY, UNAWARE OF THE DRAMA BEING PLAYED OUT IN THE ROOM ABOVE THEIR HEADS.
WHILE, OUTSIDE ON THE STREETS, NEW YORK REELS UNDER THE ONSLAUGHT OF A BRUTAL MID-WINTER GALE.
IT'S BEEN RAINING HARD SINCE BEFORE DAWN, AND THE WATER LEVEL IN THE SEWERS HAS BEEN RISING STEADILY ALL DAY-- TOWARDS A THICK SHEAF OF POWER CABLES, WHOSE INSULATION WAS SLASHED OPEN BY WOLVERINE WHEN HE AND HIS FELLOW X-MEN INFILTRATED THE CLUB. *
* SEE X-MEN #132, PAGE 10, PANELS 6&7 -- SNEAKY SALICRUP.
AND, SPEAKING OF THE SHORTEST, FEISTIEST X-MAN...
SHAW, WHAT'S THAT COMMOTION IN THE HALL?!
I DON'T KNOW. I GAVE STRICT INSTRUCTIONS THAT WE WEREN'T TO BE DISTURBED.
EVENIN', FOLKS-- THE NAME'S WOLVERINE!
YOU AN' ME GOT BUSINESS-- AN' ALL THE FLUNKIES IN CREATION AIN'T GONNA KEEP ME AWAY!
SKRASH
LELAND, YOU UNMITIGATED FOOL! YOU SWORE TO ME THAT WOLVERINE DROWNED!

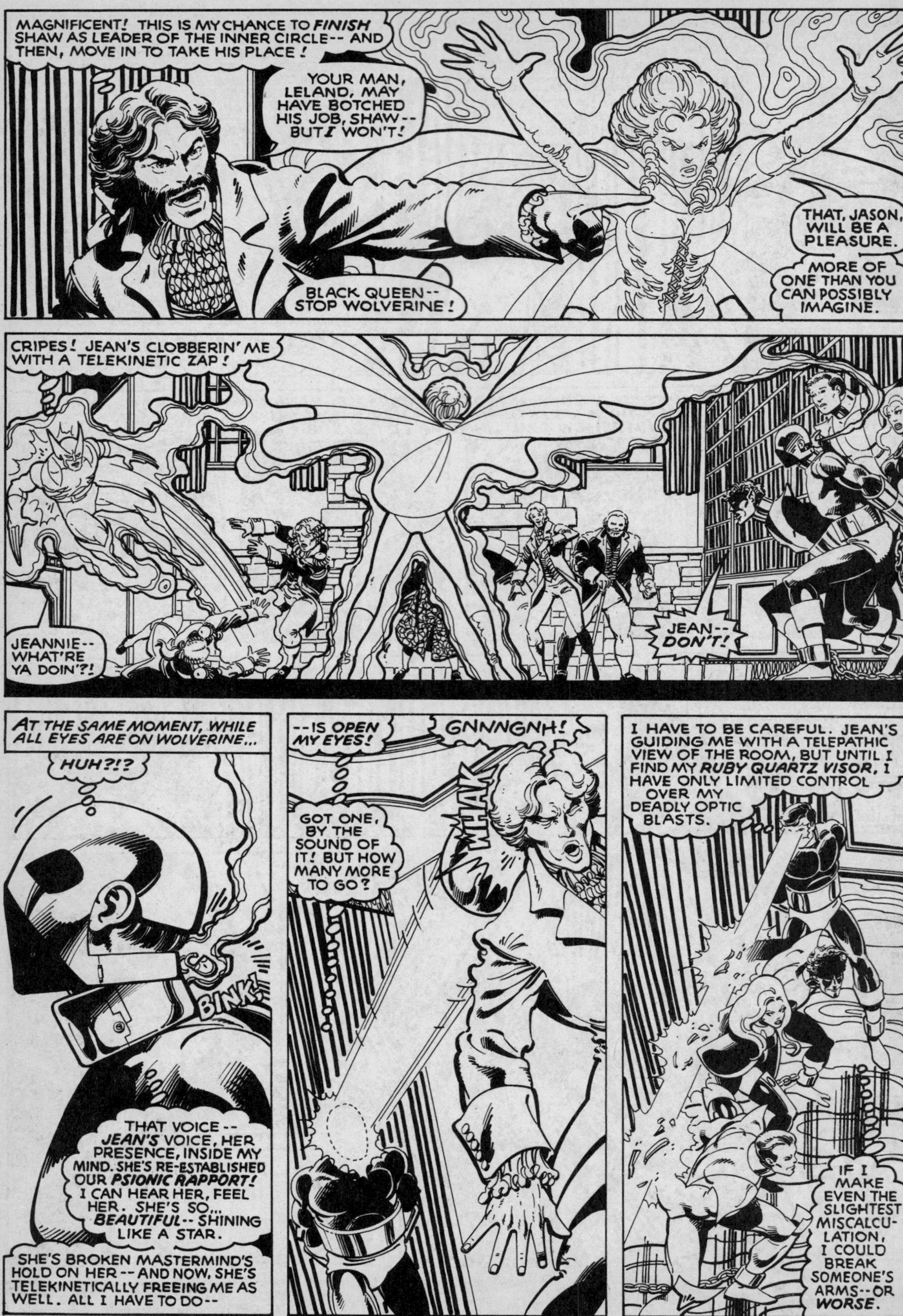
MAGNIFICENT! THIS IS MY CHANCE TO FINISH SHAW AS LEADER OF THE INNER CIRCLE-- AND THEN, MOVE IN TO TAKE HIS PLACE!
YOUR MAN, LELAND, MAY HAVE BOTCHED HIS JOB, SHAW-- BUT I WON'T!
BLACK QUEEN-- STOP WOLVERINE!
THAT, JASON, WILL BE A PLEASURE.
MORE OF ONE THAN YOU CAN POSSIBLY IMAGINE.
CRIPES! JEAN'S CLOBBERIN' ME WITH A TELEKINETIC ZAP!
JEANNIE-- WHAT'RE YA DOIN'?!
JEAN-- DON'T!
AT THE SAME MOMENT, WHILE ALL EYES ARE ON WOLVERINE...
HUH?!?
BINK!
THAT VOICE -- JEAN'S VOICE, HER PRESENCE, INSIDE MY MIND. SHE'S RE-ESTABLISHED OUR PSIONIC RAPPORT! I CAN HEAR HER, FEEL HER. SHE'S SO... BEAUTIFUL-- SHINING LIKE A STAR.
SHE'S BROKEN MASTERMIND'S HOLD ON HER -- AND NOW, SHE'S TELEKINETICALLY FREEING ME AS WELL. ALL I HAVE TO DO--
--IS OPEN MY EYES!
GNNNGNH!
WHAK
GOT ONE, BY THE SOUND OF IT! BUT HOW MANY MORE TO GO?
I HAVE TO BE CAREFUL. JEAN'S GUIDING ME WITH A TELEPATHIC VIEW OF THE ROOM, BUT UNTIL I FIND MY RUBY QUARTZ VISOR, I HAVE ONLY LIMITED CONTROL OVER MY DEADLY OPTIC BLASTS.
IF I MAKE EVEN THE SLIGHTEST MISCALCULATION, I COULD BREAK SOMEONE'S ARMS--OR WORSE.

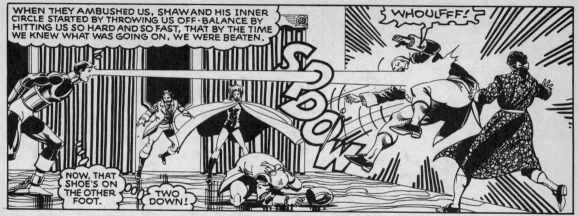

WHEN THEY AMBUSHED US, SHAW AND HIS INNER CIRCLE STARTED BY THROWING US OFF-BALANCE BY HITTING US SO HARD AND SO FAST, THAT BY THE TIME WE KNEW WHAT WAS GOING ON, WE WERE BEATEN.

WHOULFFF!

NOW, THAT SHOE'S ON THE OTHER FOOT.

TWO DOWN!

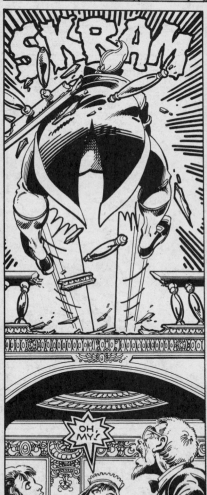

SKRAM

OH MY!

GO, WOLVERINE!

JEANNIE! YOU'RE WORKIN' ON THE SIDE O' THE ANGELS AFTER ALL! NICE -- SNEAKY -- MOVES, LADY. YOU'RE A WOMAN AFTER MY OWN HEART.

I KNOW. I WISH I WASN'T.

NEVER SAY DIE, eh, CYCLOPS? WE BEAT YOU X-MEN ONCE. WE CAN DO SO AGAIN.

YOUR VAUNTED OPTIC BLASTS MEAN NOTHING TO A MAN CAPABLE OF ABSORBING ALL FORMS OF KINETIC ENERGY. THE HARDER YOU HIT ME -- WITH ANYTHING -- THE STRONGER I GET!

HEY, LELAND! LAST TIME WE TUSSLED, YOU NEARLY TRASHED ME. *

YOU OWE ME A REMATCH, BUB, AN' I'M HERE TA COLLECT. WITH INTEREST!

*X-MEN #132--SCORE-KEEPER SALICRUP.

WHO SAID I WAS GOING TO HIT YOU, SHAW?

WHAT--?! THE FLOOR!!

HAPPY LANDINGS!

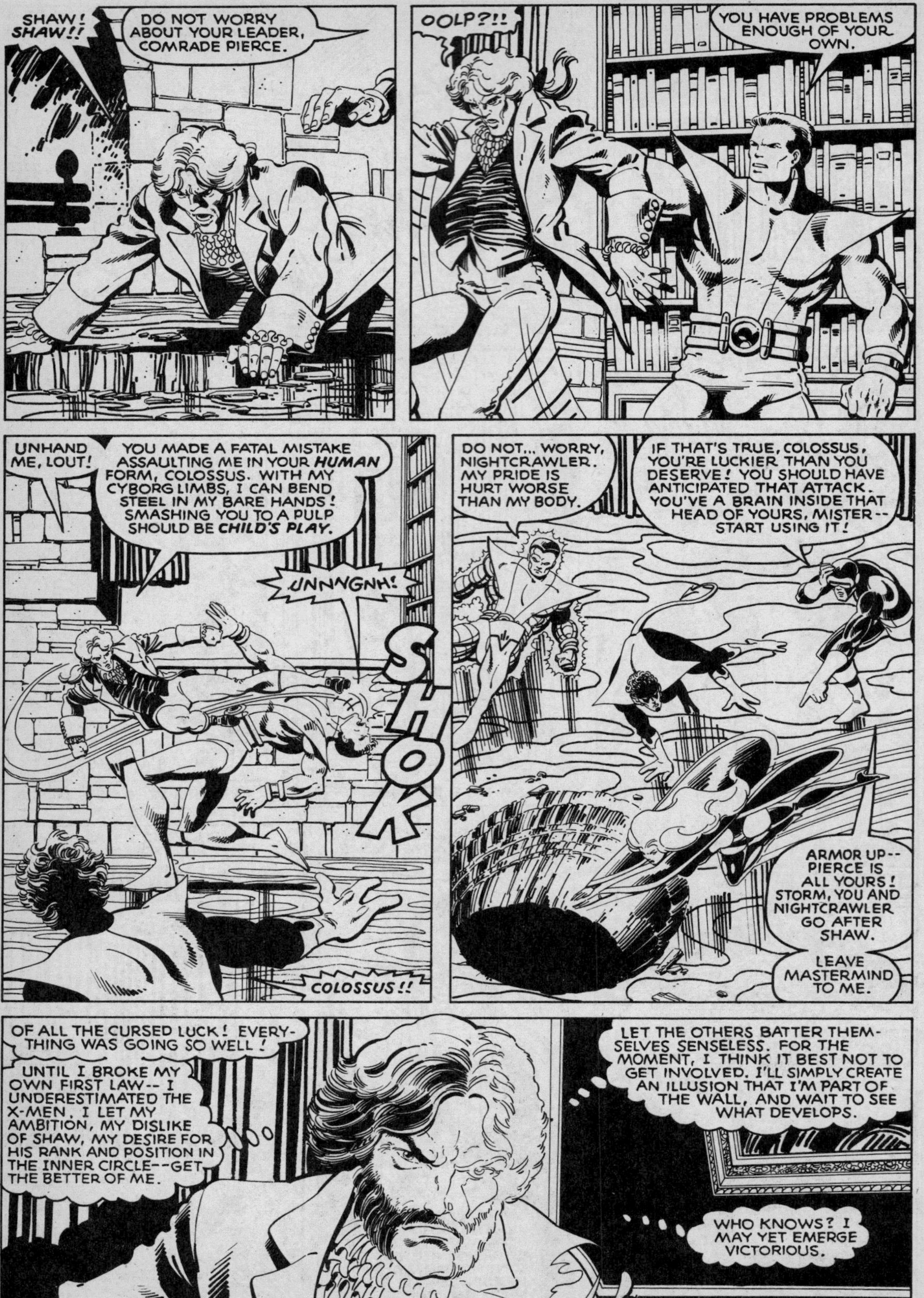
SHAW! SHAW!!
DO NOT WORRY ABOUT YOUR LEADER, COMRADE PIERCE.
OOLP?!!
YOU HAVE PROBLEMS ENOUGH OF YOUR OWN.
UNHAND ME, LOUT!
YOU MADE A FATAL MISTAKE ASSAULTING ME IN YOUR HUMAN FORM, COLOSSUS. WITH MY CYBORG LIMBS, I CAN BEND STEEL IN MY BARE HANDS! SMASHING YOU TO A PULP SHOULD BE CHILD'S PLAY.
UNNNGNH!
SHOK
COLOSSUS!!
DO NOT... WORRY, NIGHTCRAWLER. MY PRIDE IS HURT WORSE THAN MY BODY.
IF THAT'S TRUE, COLOSSUS, YOU'RE LUCKIER THAN YOU DESERVE! YOU SHOULD HAVE ANTICIPATED THAT ATTACK. YOU'VE A BRAIN INSIDE THAT HEAD OF YOURS, MISTER-- START USING IT!
ARMOR UP-- PIERCE IS ALL YOURS! STORM, YOU AND NIGHTCRAWLER GO AFTER SHAW.
LEAVE MASTERMIND TO ME.
OF ALL THE CURSED LUCK! EVERYTHING WAS GOING SO WELL!
UNTIL I BROKE MY OWN FIRST LAW-- I UNDERESTIMATED THE X-MEN. I LET MY AMBITION, MY DISLIKE OF SHAW, MY DESIRE FOR HIS RANK AND POSITION IN THE INNER CIRCLE--GET THE BETTER OF ME.
LET THE OTHERS BATTER THEMSELVES SENSELESS. FOR THE MOMENT, I THINK IT BEST NOT TO GET INVOLVED. I'LL SIMPLY CREATE AN ILLUSION THAT I'M PART OF THE WALL, AND WAIT TO SEE WHAT DEVELOPS.
WHO KNOWS? I MAY YET EMERGE VICTORIOUS.

HEADS UP, TUBBY! AN' SAY YER PRAYERS!

IT'S A MANIAC!

CALL THE POLICE-- HURRY!

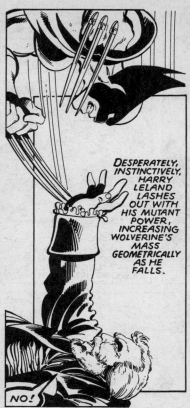

DESPERATELY, INSTINCTIVELY, HARRY LELAND LASHES OUT WITH HIS MUTANT POWER, INCREASING WOLVERINE'S MASS GEOMETRICALLY AS HE FALLS.

NO!

TOO LATE, LELAND REALIZES THAT THAT'S THE LAST THING HE SHOULD HAVE DONE.

NO!!

AT THAT MOMENT, IN ONE OF THE MANY SECRET PASSAGES THAT HONEYCOMB THIS VENERABLE MANHATTAN TOWNHOUSE...

CYCLOPS IS A BORN LEADER, AS GOOD AS I EXPECTED. HE FOUND ONE OPENING, ONE FLAW IN OUR DEFENSES, AND IN A MATTER OF SECONDS HE HAD US ON THE ROPES. I LIKE THAT.

BUT HE HAD HELP-- AND I'VE AN UNCOMFORTABLE FEELING I KNOW FROM WHAT SOURCE. WYNGARDE'S PUPPET, I FEAR, HAS CUT HER STRINGS.

IF THAT'S TRUE, I PITY THE PUPPET MASTER.

WHAT-- NIGHTCRAWLER, TELEPORTING ON TOP OF ME!!

BOO! STORM SAYS I SHOULDN'T HIT YOU, HERR SHAW. THAT'S FINE WITH ME.

ANYONE CAN PUNCH. NIGHTCRAWLER IS GOING TO CLOBBER YOU IN STYLE.

FOR ALL SHAW'S MUTANT STRENGTH, HE'S STILL ONLY HUMAN. HE'S VULNERABLE TO TEMPERATURE SHIFTS. SO, IF I USE MY ELEMENTAL POWERS TO SURROUND HIM WITH A FIELD OF EXTREME COLD-- A MICRO-BLIZZARD-- I SHOULD BE ABLE TO FREEZE THE FIGHT OUT OF HIM.

WITH A SLIGHT ASSIST FROM STORM, MY FRIEND.

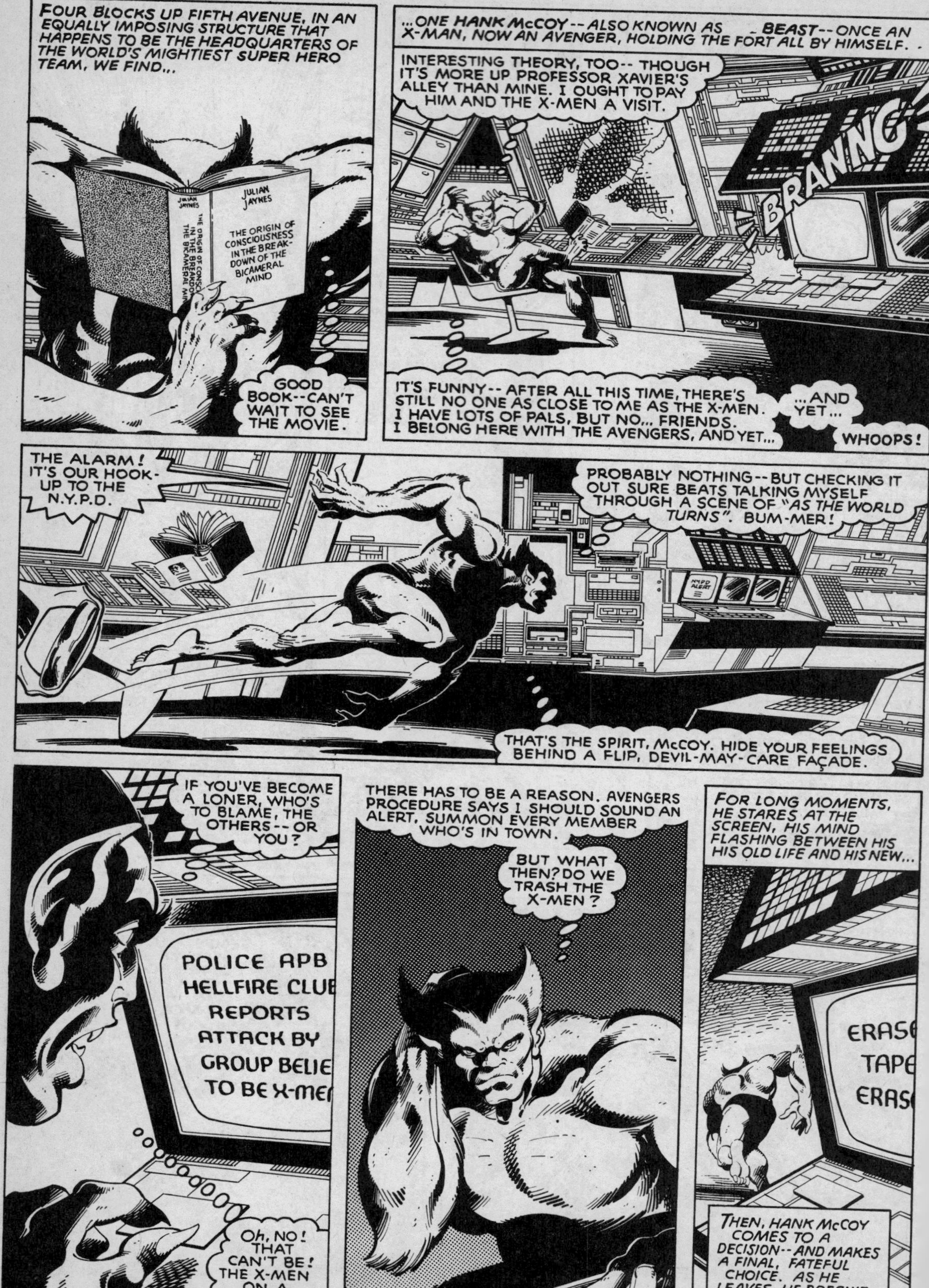
FOUR BLOCKS UP FIFTH AVENUE, IN AN EQUALLY IMPOSING STRUCTURE THAT HAPPENS TO BE THE HEADQUARTERS OF THE WORLD'S MIGHTIEST SUPER HERO TEAM, WE FIND...
JULIAN JAYNES
THE ORIGIN OF CONSCIOUSNESS IN THE BREAK-DOWN OF THE BICAMERAL MIND
GOOD BOOK--CAN'T WAIT TO SEE THE MOVIE.
...ONE HANK McCOY -- ALSO KNOWN AS BEAST -- ONCE AN X-MAN, NOW AN AVENGER, HOLDING THE FORT ALL BY HIMSELF.
INTERESTING THEORY, TOO-- THOUGH IT'S MORE UP PROFESSOR XAVIER'S ALLEY THAN MINE. I OUGHT TO PAY HIM AND THE X-MEN A VISIT.
BRANNG!
IT'S FUNNY-- AFTER ALL THIS TIME, THERE'S STILL NO ONE AS CLOSE TO ME AS THE X-MEN. I HAVE LOTS OF PALS, BUT NO... FRIENDS. I BELONG HERE WITH THE AVENGERS, AND YET...
...AND YET...
WHOOPS!
THE ALARM! IT'S OUR HOOK-UP TO THE N.Y.P.D.
PROBABLY NOTHING--BUT CHECKING IT OUT SURE BEATS TALKING MYSELF THROUGH A SCENE OF "AS THE WORLD TURNS". BUM-MER!
NYPD ALERT
THAT'S THE SPIRIT, McCOY. HIDE YOUR FEELINGS BEHIND A FLIP, DEVIL-MAY-CARE FAÇADE.
IF YOU'VE BECOME A LONER, WHO'S TO BLAME, THE OTHERS--OR YOU?
POLICE APB HELLFIRE CLUB REPORTS ATTACK BY GROUP BELIE TO BE X-MEN
OH, NO! THAT CAN'T BE! THE X-MEN ON A RAMPAGE?!
THERE HAS TO BE A REASON. AVENGERS PROCEDURE SAYS I SHOULD SOUND AN ALERT, SUMMON EVERY MEMBER WHO'S IN TOWN.
BUT WHAT THEN? DO WE TRASH THE X-MEN?
FOR LONG MOMENTS, HE STARES AT THE SCREEN, HIS MIND FLASHING BETWEEN HIS HIS OLD LIFE AND HIS NEW...
ERAS TAPE ERAS
THEN, HANK McCOY COMES TO A DECISION--AND MAKES A FINAL, FATEFUL CHOICE. AS HE LEAVES, HE DOESN'T LOOK BACK.

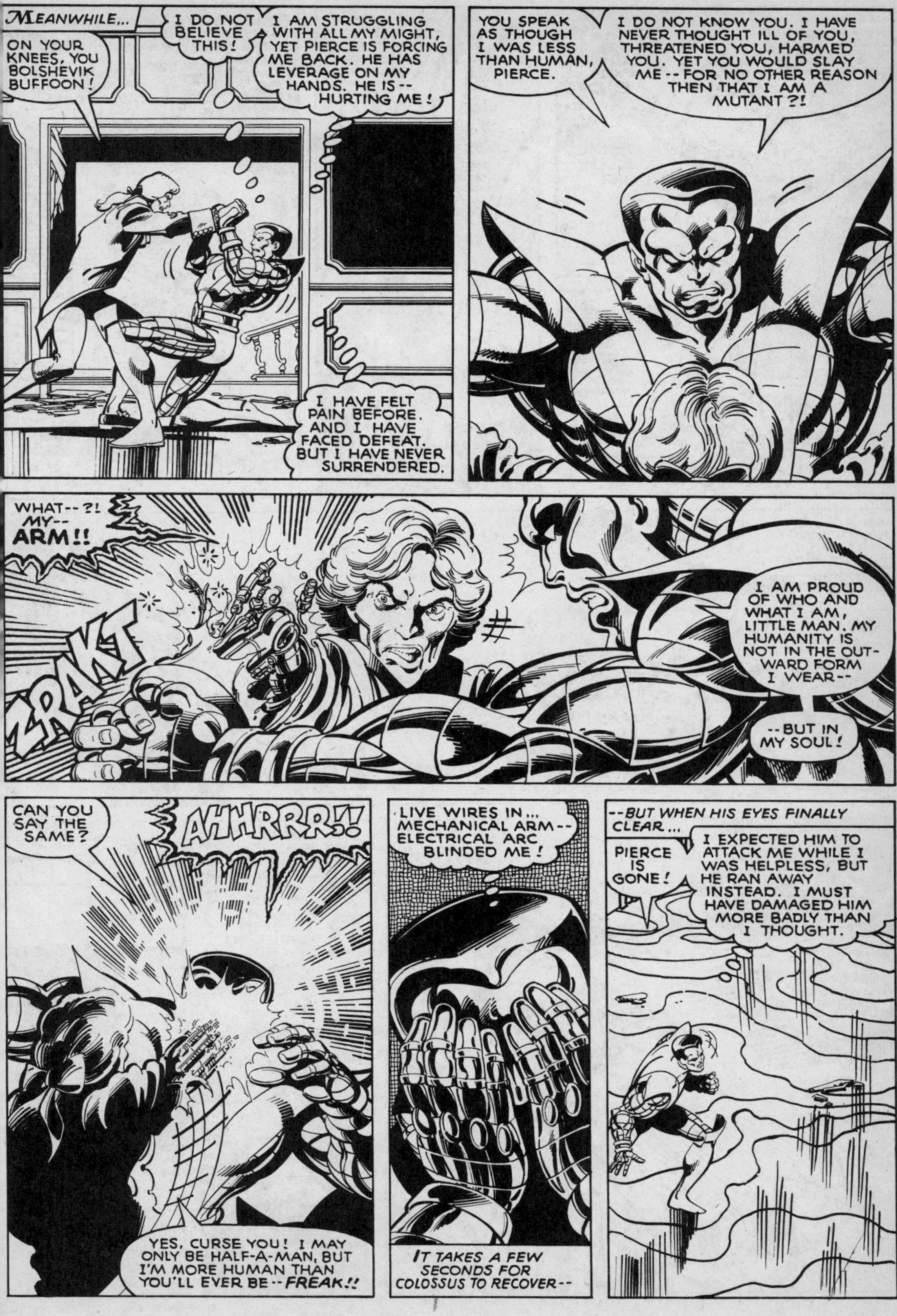
MEANWHILE...
ON YOUR KNEES, YOU BOLSHEVIK BUFFOON!
I DO NOT BELIEVE THIS!
I AM STRUGGLING WITH ALL MY MIGHT, YET PIERCE IS FORCING ME BACK. HE HAS LEVERAGE ON MY HANDS. HE IS -- HURTING ME!
I HAVE FELT PAIN BEFORE. AND I HAVE FACED DEFEAT. BUT I HAVE NEVER SURRENDERED.
YOU SPEAK AS THOUGH I WAS LESS THAN HUMAN, PIERCE.
I DO NOT KNOW YOU. I HAVE NEVER THOUGHT ILL OF YOU, THREATENED YOU, HARMED YOU. YET YOU WOULD SLAY ME -- FOR NO OTHER REASON THEN THAT I AM A MUTANT?!
WHAT--?! MY-- ARM!!
ZRAKT
I AM PROUD OF WHO AND WHAT I AM, LITTLE MAN. MY HUMANITY IS NOT IN THE OUTWARD FORM I WEAR--
--BUT IN MY SOUL!
CAN YOU SAY THE SAME?
AHHRRR!!
YES, CURSE YOU! I MAY ONLY BE HALF-A-MAN, BUT I'M MORE HUMAN THAN YOU'LL EVER BE -- FREAK!!
LIVE WIRES IN ... MECHANICAL ARM -- ELECTRICAL ARC BLINDED ME!
IT TAKES A FEW SECONDS FOR COLOSSUS TO RECOVER--
--BUT WHEN HIS EYES FINALLY CLEAR...
PIERCE IS GONE!
I EXPECTED HIM TO ATTACK ME WHILE I WAS HELPLESS, BUT HE RAN AWAY INSTEAD. I MUST HAVE DAMAGED HIM MORE BADLY THAN I THOUGHT.

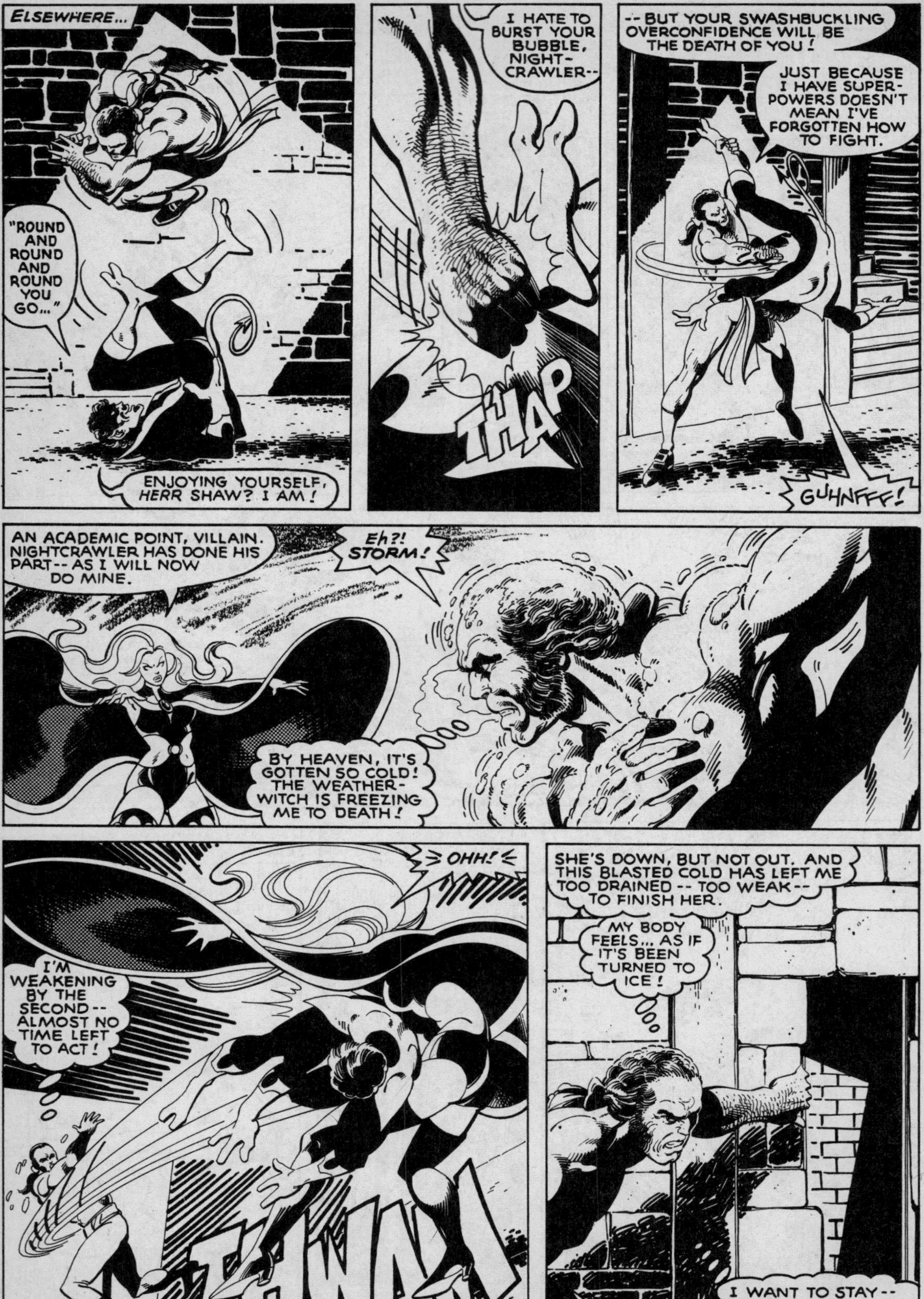
ELSEWHERE...
"ROUND AND ROUND AND ROUND YOU GO..."
ENJOYING YOURSELF, HERR SHAW? I AM!
I HATE TO BURST YOUR BUBBLE, NIGHT-CRAWLER--
THAP
--BUT YOUR SWASHBUCKLING OVERCONFIDENCE WILL BE THE DEATH OF YOU!
JUST BECAUSE I HAVE SUPER-POWERS DOESN'T MEAN I'VE FORGOTTEN HOW TO FIGHT.
GUHNFFF!
AN ACADEMIC POINT, VILLAIN. NIGHTCRAWLER HAS DONE HIS PART-- AS I WILL NOW DO MINE.
Eh?! STORM!
BY HEAVEN, IT'S GOTTEN SO COLD! THE WEATHER-WITCH IS FREEZING ME TO DEATH!
OHH!
I'M WEAKENING BY THE SECOND-- ALMOST NO TIME LEFT TO ACT!
THWAM
SHE'S DOWN, BUT NOT OUT. AND THIS BLASTED COLD HAS LEFT ME TOO DRAINED -- TOO WEAK-- TO FINISH HER.
MY BODY FEELS... AS IF IT'S BEEN TURNED TO ICE!
I WANT TO STAY-- TO FIGHT-- BUT I DARE NOT.

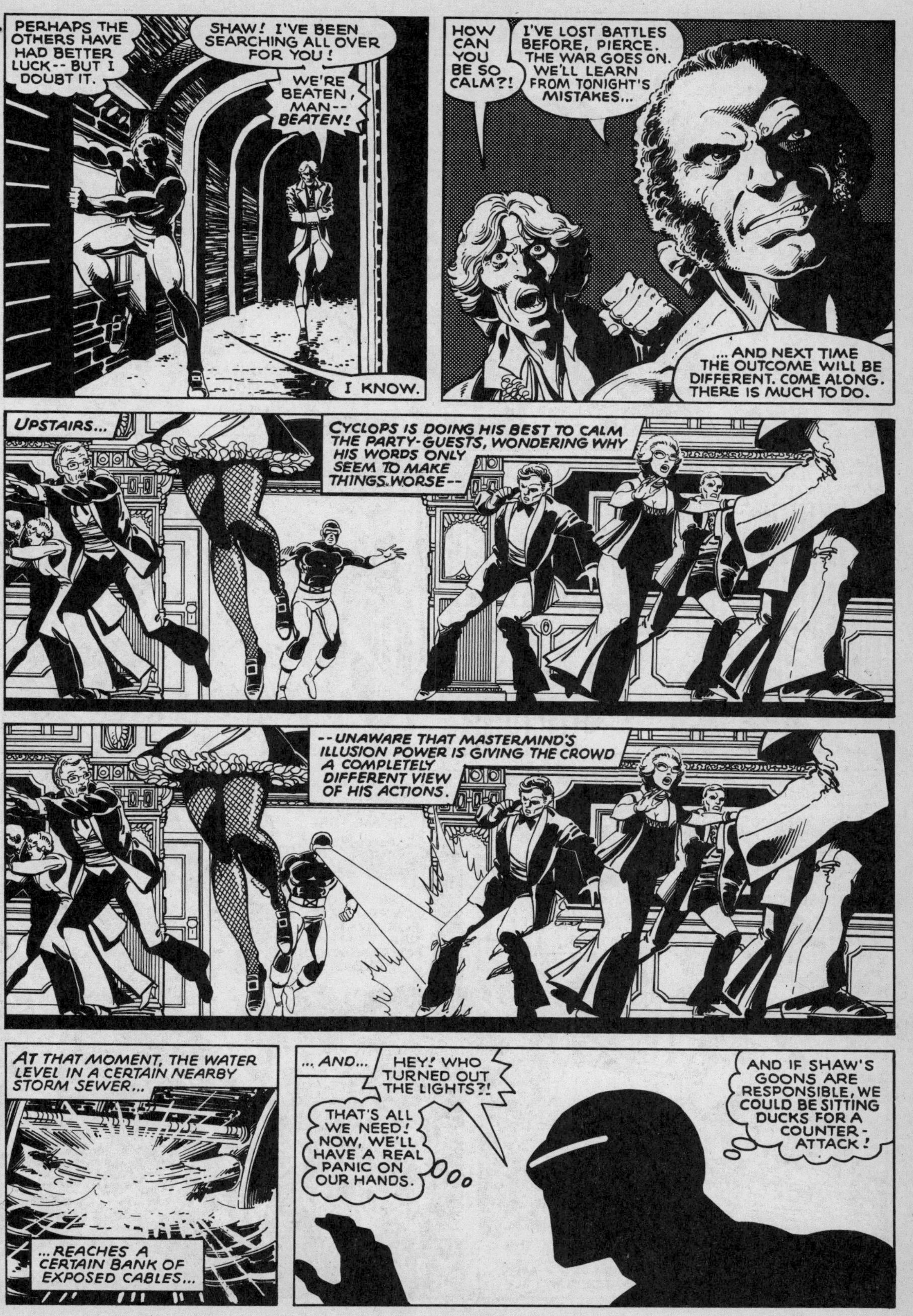
PERHAPS THE OTHERS HAVE HAD BETTER LUCK-- BUT I DOUBT IT.
SHAW! I'VE BEEN SEARCHING ALL OVER FOR YOU!
WE'RE BEATEN, MAN-- BEATEN!
I KNOW.
HOW CAN YOU BE SO CALM?!
I'VE LOST BATTLES BEFORE, PIERCE. THE WAR GOES ON. WE'LL LEARN FROM TONIGHT'S MISTAKES...
... AND NEXT TIME THE OUTCOME WILL BE DIFFERENT. COME ALONG. THERE IS MUCH TO DO.
UPSTAIRS...
CYCLOPS IS DOING HIS BEST TO CALM THE PARTY-GUESTS, WONDERING WHY HIS WORDS ONLY SEEM TO MAKE THINGS WORSE--
--UNAWARE THAT MASTERMIND'S ILLUSION POWER IS GIVING THE CROWD A COMPLETELY DIFFERENT VIEW OF HIS ACTIONS.
AT THAT MOMENT, THE WATER LEVEL IN A CERTAIN NEARBY STORM SEWER...
...REACHES A CERTAIN BANK OF EXPOSED CABLES...
... AND...
HEY! WHO TURNED OUT THE LIGHTS?!
THAT'S ALL WE NEED! NOW, WE'LL HAVE A REAL PANIC ON OUR HANDS.
AND IF SHAW'S GOONS ARE RESPONSIBLE, WE COULD BE SITTING DUCKS FOR A COUNTER-ATTACK!

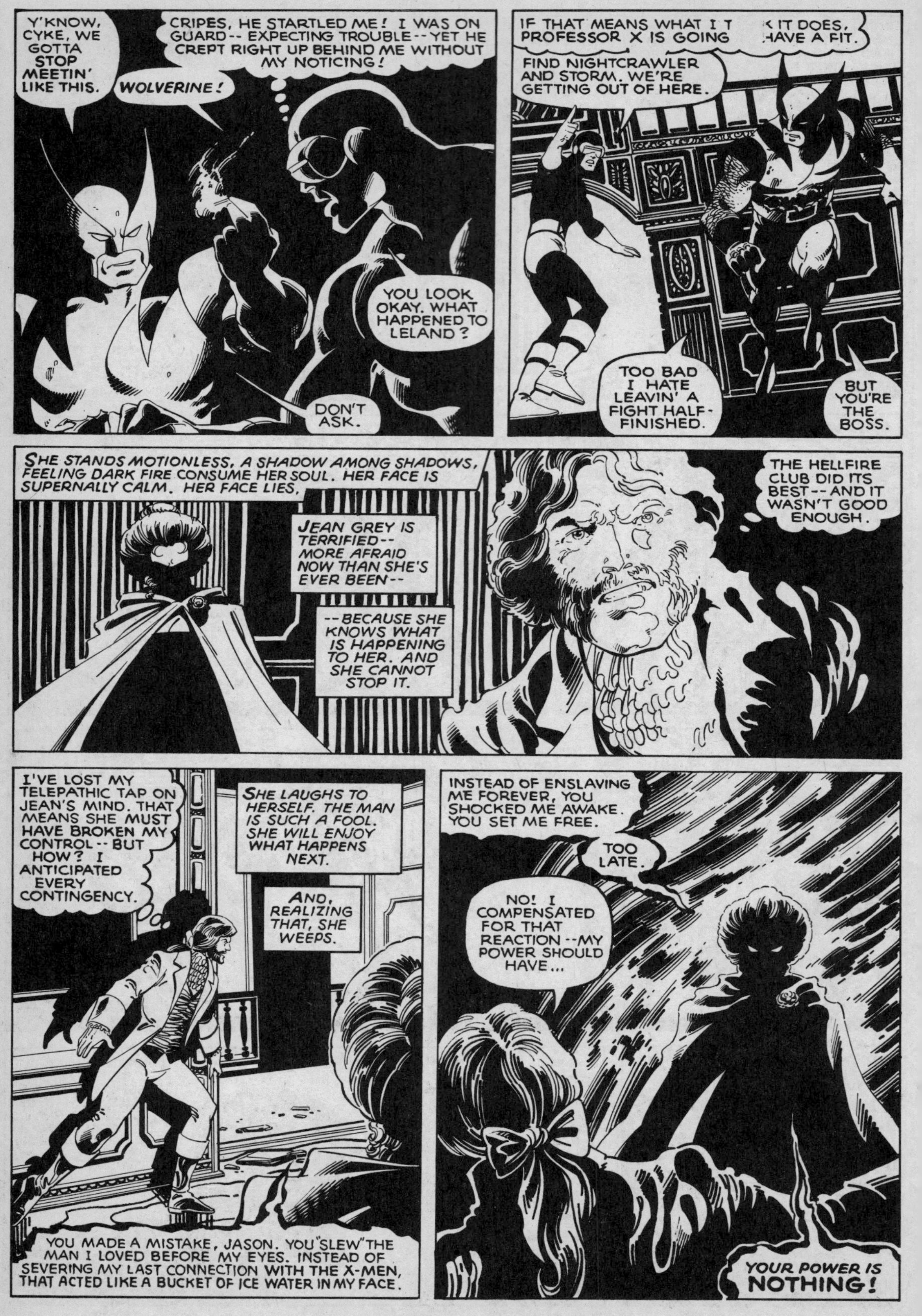
Y'KNOW, CYKE, WE GOTTA STOP MEETIN' LIKE THIS.
WOLVERINE!
CRIPES, HE STARTLED ME! I WAS ON GUARD -- EXPECTING TROUBLE -- YET HE CREPT RIGHT UP BEHIND ME WITHOUT MY NOTICING!
YOU LOOK OKAY. WHAT HAPPENED TO LELAND?
DON'T ASK.
IF THAT MEANS WHAT I T K IT DOES, PROFESSOR X IS GOING HAVE A FIT.
FIND NIGHTCRAWLER AND STORM. WE'RE GETTING OUT OF HERE.
TOO BAD I HATE LEAVIN' A FIGHT HALF-FINISHED.
BUT YOU'RE THE BOSS.
SHE STANDS MOTIONLESS, A SHADOW AMONG SHADOWS, FEELING DARK FIRE CONSUME HER SOUL. HER FACE IS SUPERNALLY CALM. HER FACE LIES.
JEAN GREY IS TERRIFIED-- MORE AFRAID NOW THAN SHE'S EVER BEEN--
--BECAUSE SHE KNOWS WHAT IS HAPPENING TO HER. AND SHE CANNOT STOP IT.
THE HELLFIRE CLUB DID ITS BEST -- AND IT WASN'T GOOD ENOUGH.
I'VE LOST MY TELEPATHIC TAP ON JEAN'S MIND. THAT MEANS SHE MUST HAVE BROKEN MY CONTROL -- BUT HOW? I ANTICIPATED EVERY CONTINGENCY.
SHE LAUGHS TO HERSELF. THE MAN IS SUCH A FOOL. SHE WILL ENJOY WHAT HAPPENS NEXT.
AND, REALIZING THAT, SHE WEEPS.
YOU MADE A MISTAKE, JASON. YOU "SLEW" THE MAN I LOVED BEFORE MY EYES. INSTEAD OF SEVERING MY LAST CONNECTION WITH THE X-MEN, THAT ACTED LIKE A BUCKET OF ICE WATER IN MY FACE.
INSTEAD OF ENSLAVING ME FOREVER, YOU SHOCKED ME AWAKE. YOU SET ME FREE.
TOO LATE.
NO! I COMPENSATED FOR THAT REACTION -- MY POWER SHOULD HAVE...
YOUR POWER IS NOTHING!

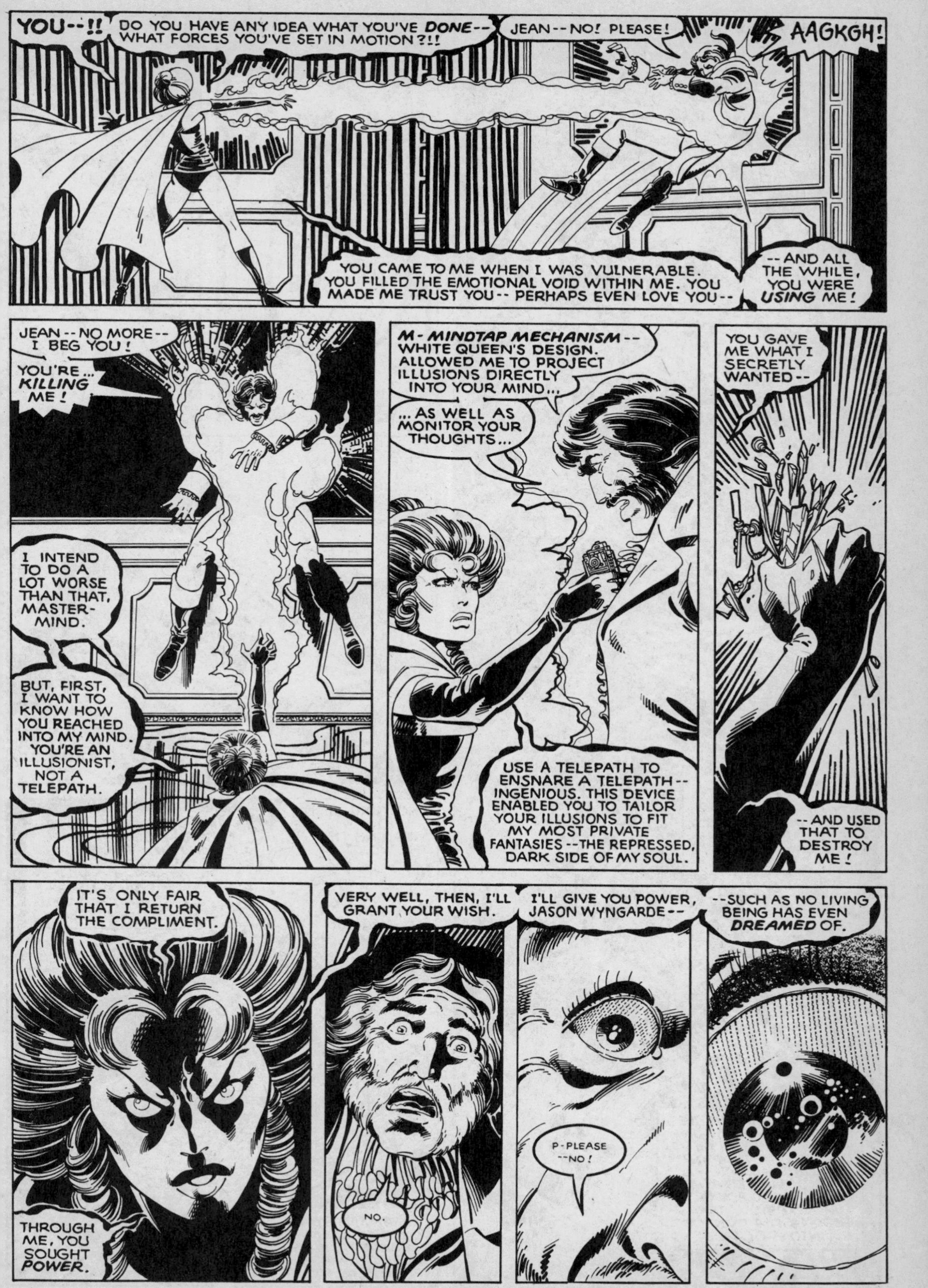
YOU--!! DO YOU HAVE ANY IDEA WHAT YOU'VE DONE-- WHAT FORCES YOU'VE SET IN MOTION?!!
JEAN--NO! PLEASE!
AAGKGH!
YOU CAME TO ME WHEN I WAS VULNERABLE. YOU FILLED THE EMOTIONAL VOID WITHIN ME. YOU MADE ME TRUST YOU-- PERHAPS EVEN LOVE YOU--
--AND ALL THE WHILE, YOU WERE USING ME!
JEAN--NO MORE-- I BEG YOU!
YOU'RE... KILLING ME!
I INTEND TO DO A LOT WORSE THAN THAT, MASTERMIND.
BUT, FIRST, I WANT TO KNOW HOW YOU REACHED INTO MY MIND. YOU'RE AN ILLUSIONIST, NOT A TELEPATH.
M-MINDTAP MECHANISM-- WHITE QUEEN'S DESIGN. ALLOWED ME TO PROJECT ILLUSIONS DIRECTLY INTO YOUR MIND...
...AS WELL AS MONITOR YOUR THOUGHTS...
USE A TELEPATH TO ENSNARE A TELEPATH-- INGENIOUS. THIS DEVICE ENABLED YOU TO TAILOR YOUR ILLUSIONS TO FIT MY MOST PRIVATE FANTASIES--THE REPRESSED, DARK SIDE OF MY SOUL.
YOU GAVE ME WHAT I SECRETLY WANTED--
--AND USED THAT TO DESTROY ME!
IT'S ONLY FAIR THAT I RETURN THE COMPLIMENT.
THROUGH ME, YOU SOUGHT POWER.
VERY WELL, THEN, I'LL GRANT YOUR WISH.
NO.
I'LL GIVE YOU POWER, JASON WYNGARDE--
P-PLEASE --NO!
--SUCH AS NO LIVING BEING HAS EVEN DREAMED OF.

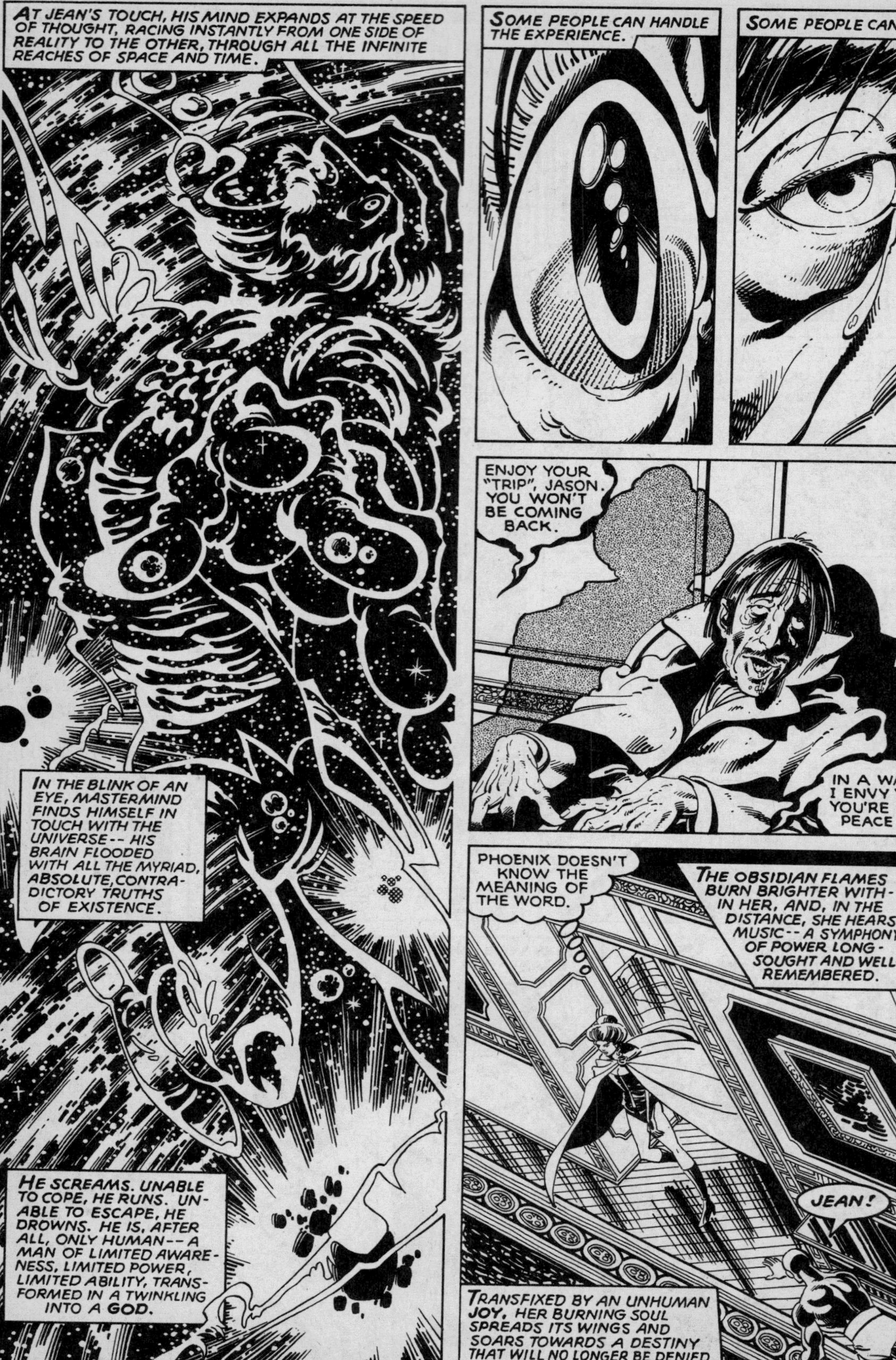
AT JEAN'S TOUCH, HIS MIND EXPANDS AT THE SPEED OF THOUGHT, RACING INSTANTLY FROM ONE SIDE OF REALITY TO THE OTHER, THROUGH ALL THE INFINITE REACHES OF SPACE AND TIME.
IN THE BLINK OF AN EYE, MASTERMIND FINDS HIMSELF IN TOUCH WITH THE UNIVERSE-- HIS BRAIN FLOODED WITH ALL THE MYRIAD, ABSOLUTE, CONTRA-DICTORY TRUTHS OF EXISTENCE.
HE SCREAMS. UNABLE TO COPE, HE RUNS. UN-ABLE TO ESCAPE, HE DROWNS. HE IS, AFTER ALL, ONLY HUMAN-- A MAN OF LIMITED AWARE-NESS, LIMITED POWER, LIMITED ABILITY, TRANS-FORMED IN A TWINKLING INTO A GOD.
SOME PEOPLE CAN HANDLE THE EXPERIENCE.
SOME PEOPLE CAN'T.
ENJOY YOUR "TRIP", JASON. YOU WON'T BE COMING BACK.
IN A WAY, I ENVY YOU. YOU'RE AT PEACE.
PHOENIX DOESN'T KNOW THE MEANING OF THE WORD.
THE OBSIDIAN FLAMES BURN BRIGHTER WITH-IN HER, AND, IN THE DISTANCE, SHE HEARS MUSIC-- A SYMPHONY OF POWER LONG-SOUGHT AND WELL-REMEMBERED.
JEAN!
TRANSFIXED BY AN UNHUMAN JOY, HER BURNING SOUL SPREADS ITS WINGS AND SOARS TOWARDS A DESTINY THAT WILL NO LONGER BE DENIED.

Panel 1 (left):
I'VE BEEN SEARCHING ALL OVER FOR YOU. ARE YOU ALL RIGHT?

SCOTT-- I... I...

SOMETHING'S WRONG! SHE'S DAMPING DOWN THE PSYCHIC RAPPORT WE SHARE-- HIDING FROM ME!

MASTERMIND WAS UP HERE-- IS HE--?!!

Panel 2 (right):
STILL CONTROLLING ME? NO. I... TOOK CARE OF HIM.

WHAT'S THE MATTER? JEAN, TALK TO ME-- LET ME HELP!

YOU CAN'T HELP, MY LOVE. NO ONE CAN.

JEAN-- WAIT!

Panel 3:
ALL PRESENT, CYKE-- WHAT NOW?

WE RUN FOR IT, SHORT-STUFF!

I'M RECEIVING MULTIPLE MENTAL IMPRESSIONS-- THE POLICE ARE CLOSING IN ON THIS BUILDING, AND THEY MEAN TO ARREST THE X-MEN.

IF THEY CAPTURE US, YOU CAN BET SHAW AND THE HELLFIRE CLUB WILL MAKE ANY CRIMINAL CHARGES STICK. SO, LET'S SCOOT!

Panel 4:
THIS MOMENT IS YOURS, X-MEN. ENJOY IT WHILE YOU CAN.

BECAUSE, BEFORE I'M FINISHED, YOU'LL BE KNOWN THROUGHOUT THE LAND-- THROUGHOUT THE WORLD--

--AS PUBLIC ENEMY NUMBER ONE!

Panel 5:
WHY WON'T JEAN LET ME REACH HER-- ON ANY LEVEL? WHAT IS SHE SO AFRAID OF?!

NOTHING MUCH I CAN DO ABOUT IT NOW-- AT LEAST, UNTIL WE'RE SAFELY ON OUR WAY. ONCE WE'RE AIRBORNE, THOUGH, AND THE PRESSURE'S OFF, THEN MAYBE SHE'LL TALK TO ME.

CYCLOPS TOUCHES A CONTROL STUD ON HIS WRISTWATCH...

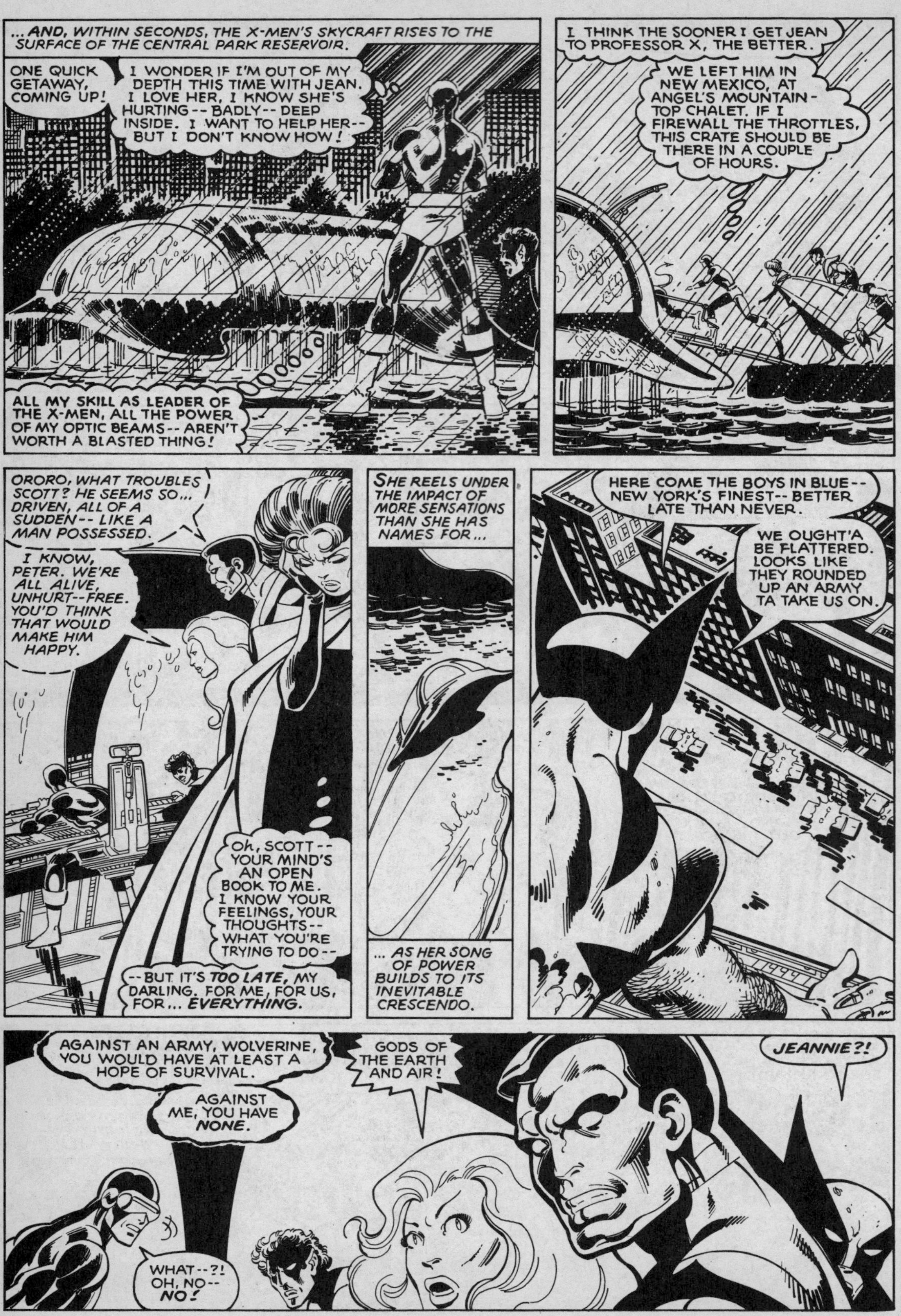
...AND, WITHIN SECONDS, THE X-MEN'S SKYCRAFT RISES TO THE SURFACE OF THE CENTRAL PARK RESERVOIR.
ONE QUICK GETAWAY, COMING UP!
I WONDER IF I'M OUT OF MY DEPTH THIS TIME WITH JEAN. I LOVE HER, I KNOW SHE'S HURTING -- BADLY -- DEEP INSIDE. I WANT TO HELP HER -- BUT I DON'T KNOW HOW!
ALL MY SKILL AS LEADER OF THE X-MEN, ALL THE POWER OF MY OPTIC BEAMS -- AREN'T WORTH A BLASTED THING!
I THINK THE SOONER I GET JEAN TO PROFESSOR X, THE BETTER.
WE LEFT HIM IN NEW MEXICO, AT ANGEL'S MOUNTAIN-TOP CHALET. IF I FIREWALL THE THROTTLES, THIS CRATE SHOULD BE THERE IN A COUPLE OF HOURS.
ORORO, WHAT TROUBLES SCOTT? HE SEEMS SO... DRIVEN, ALL OF A SUDDEN -- LIKE A MAN POSSESSED.
I KNOW, PETER. WE'RE ALL ALIVE, UNHURT--FREE. YOU'D THINK THAT WOULD MAKE HIM HAPPY.
Oh, SCOTT -- YOUR MIND'S AN OPEN BOOK TO ME. I KNOW YOUR FEELINGS, YOUR THOUGHTS -- WHAT YOU'RE TRYING TO DO --
-- BUT IT'S TOO LATE, MY DARLING. FOR ME, FOR US, FOR... EVERYTHING.
SHE REELS UNDER THE IMPACT OF MORE SENSATIONS THAN SHE HAS NAMES FOR...
... AS HER SONG OF POWER BUILDS TO ITS INEVITABLE CRESCENDO.
HERE COME THE BOYS IN BLUE -- NEW YORK'S FINEST -- BETTER LATE THAN NEVER.
WE OUGHT'A BE FLATTERED. LOOKS LIKE THEY ROUNDED UP AN ARMY TA TAKE US ON.
AGAINST AN ARMY, WOLVERINE, YOU WOULD HAVE AT LEAST A HOPE OF SURVIVAL.
AGAINST ME, YOU HAVE NONE.
GODS OF THE EARTH AND AIR!
JEANNIE?!
WHAT--?! OH, NO-- NO!

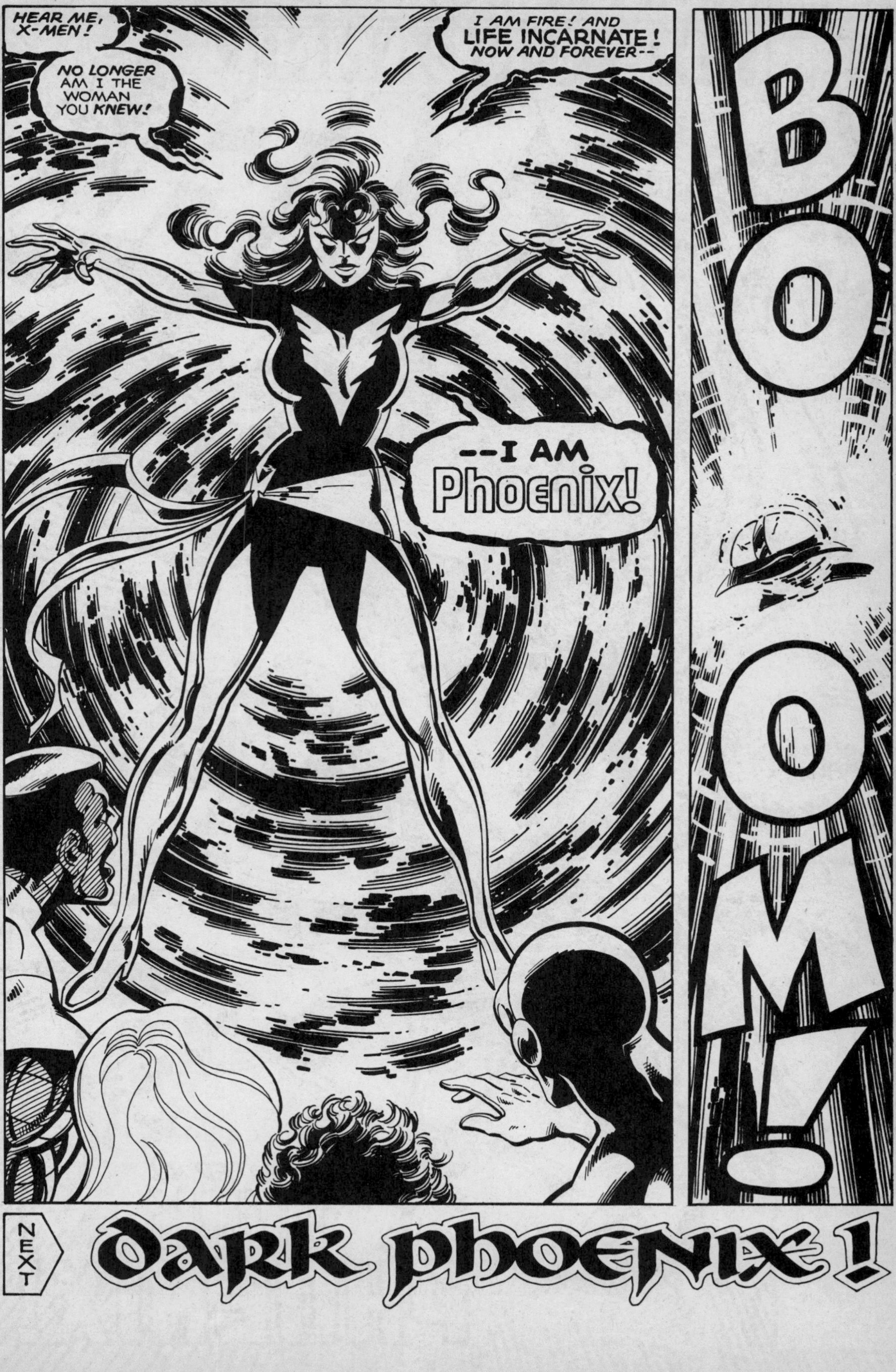
HEAR ME, X-MEN!
NO LONGER AM I THE WOMAN YOU KNEW!
I AM FIRE! AND LIFE INCARNATE! NOW AND FOREVER--
--I AM Phoenix!
BOOM!
NEXT
Dark Phoenix!

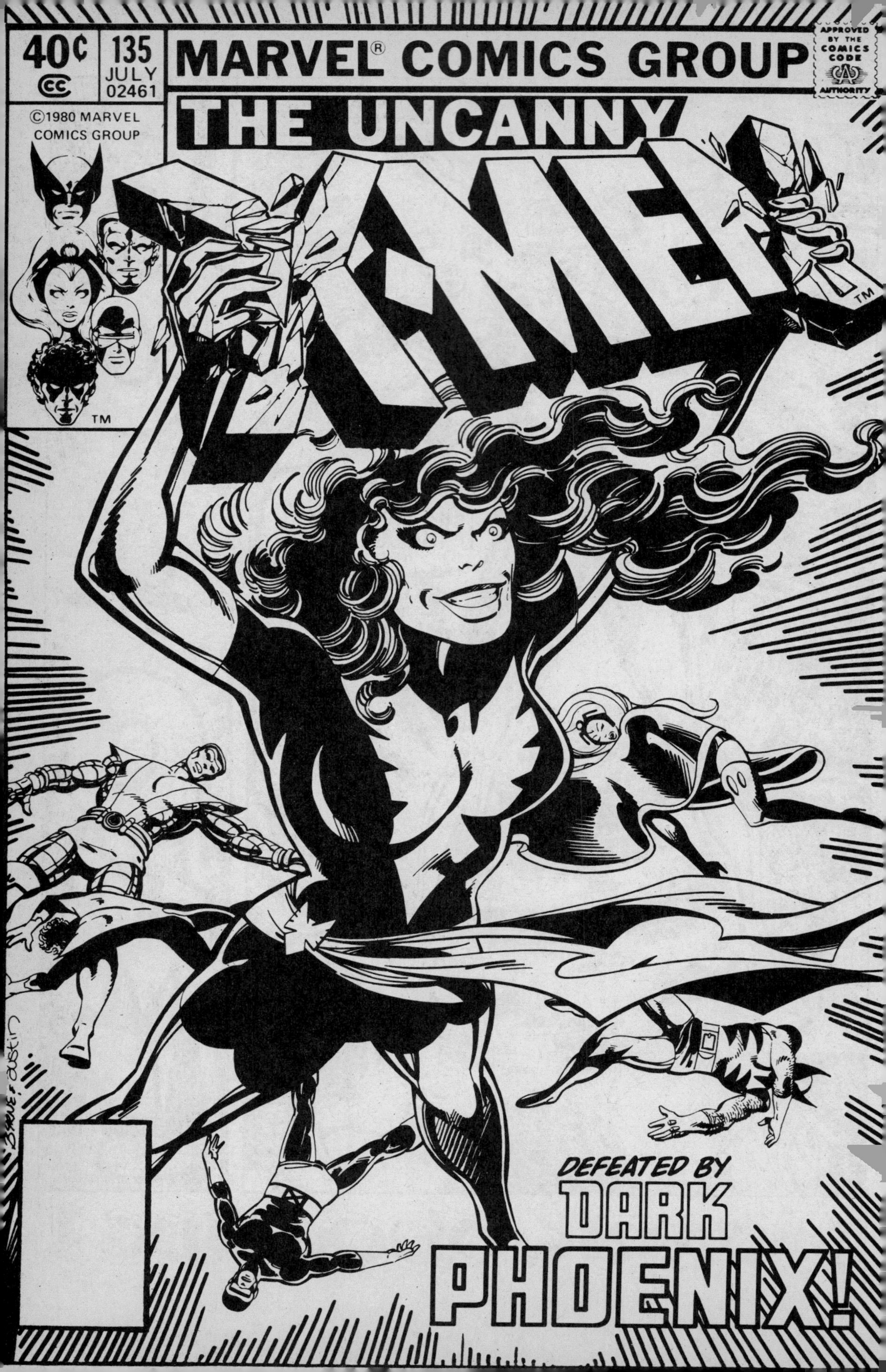

40¢
CC
135
JULY
02461
MARVEL® COMICS GROUP
APPROVED BY THE COMICS CODE AUTHORITY
©1980 MARVEL COMICS GROUP
THE UNCANNY
X-MEN
TM
DEFEATED BY
DARK
PHOENIX!
BYRNE & AUSTIN

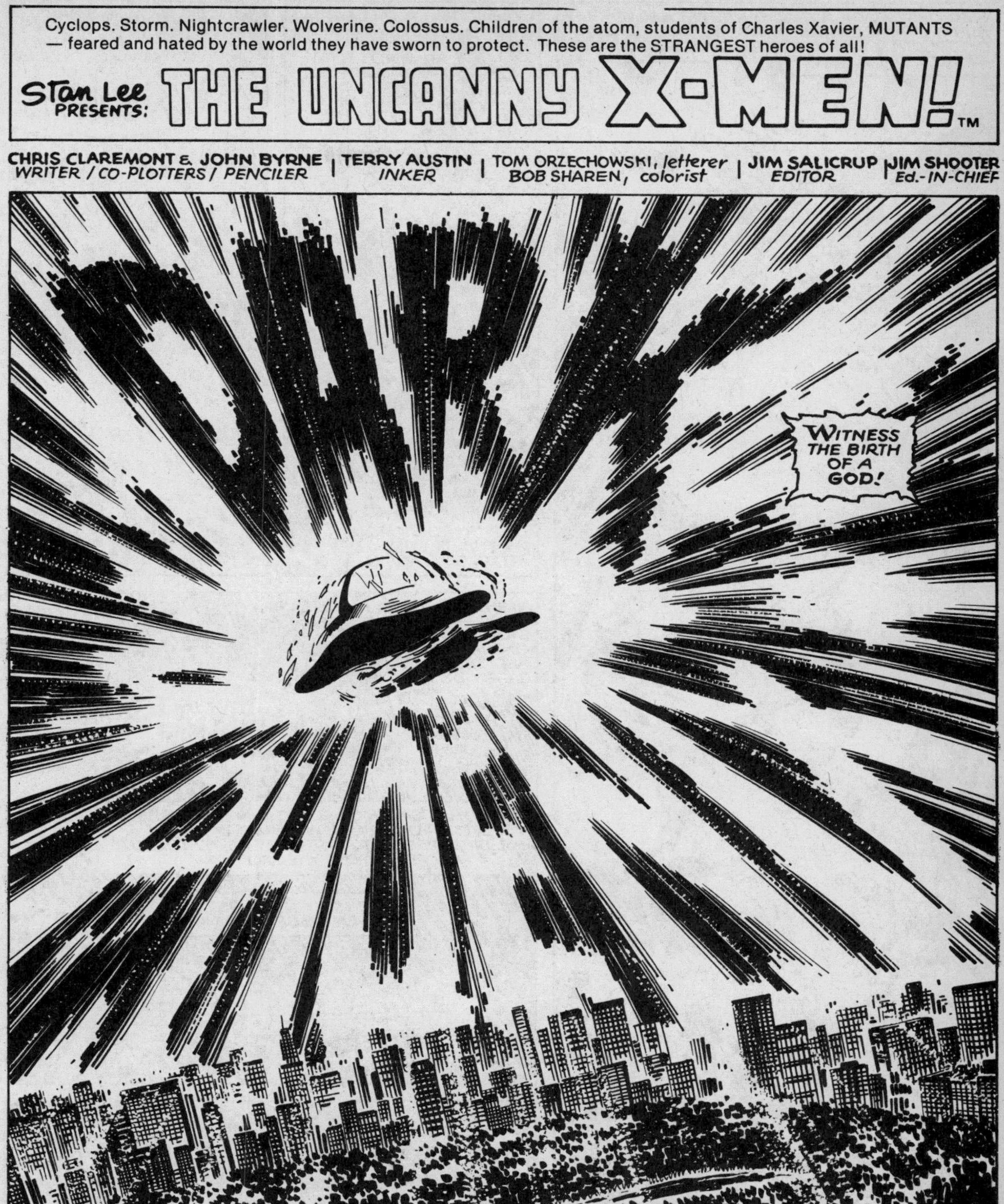

Cyclops. Storm. Nightcrawler. Wolverine. Colossus. Children of the atom, students of Charles Xavier, MUTANTS — feared and hated by the world they have sworn to protect. These are the STRANGEST heroes of all!
Stan Lee PRESENTS: THE UNCANNY X-MEN!™
CHRIS CLAREMONT & JOHN BYRNE WRITER / CO-PLOTTERS / PENCILER | TERRY AUSTIN INKER | TOM ORZECHOWSKI, letterer BOB SHAREN, colorist | JIM SALICRUP EDITOR | JIM SHOOTER Ed.-IN-CHIEF
WITNESS THE BIRTH OF A GOD!
HER NAME IS JEAN GREY. A YOUNG WOMAN OF EXTRAORDINARY BEAUTY, STRENGTH, COURAGE, PASSION. A SUPER-POWERED MUTANT TELEPATH/ TELEKINETIC. A CHARTER MEMBER OF THE UNCANNY X-MEN.
NONE OF THAT HAS CHANGED. AND YET-- EVERYTHING HAS CHANGED.

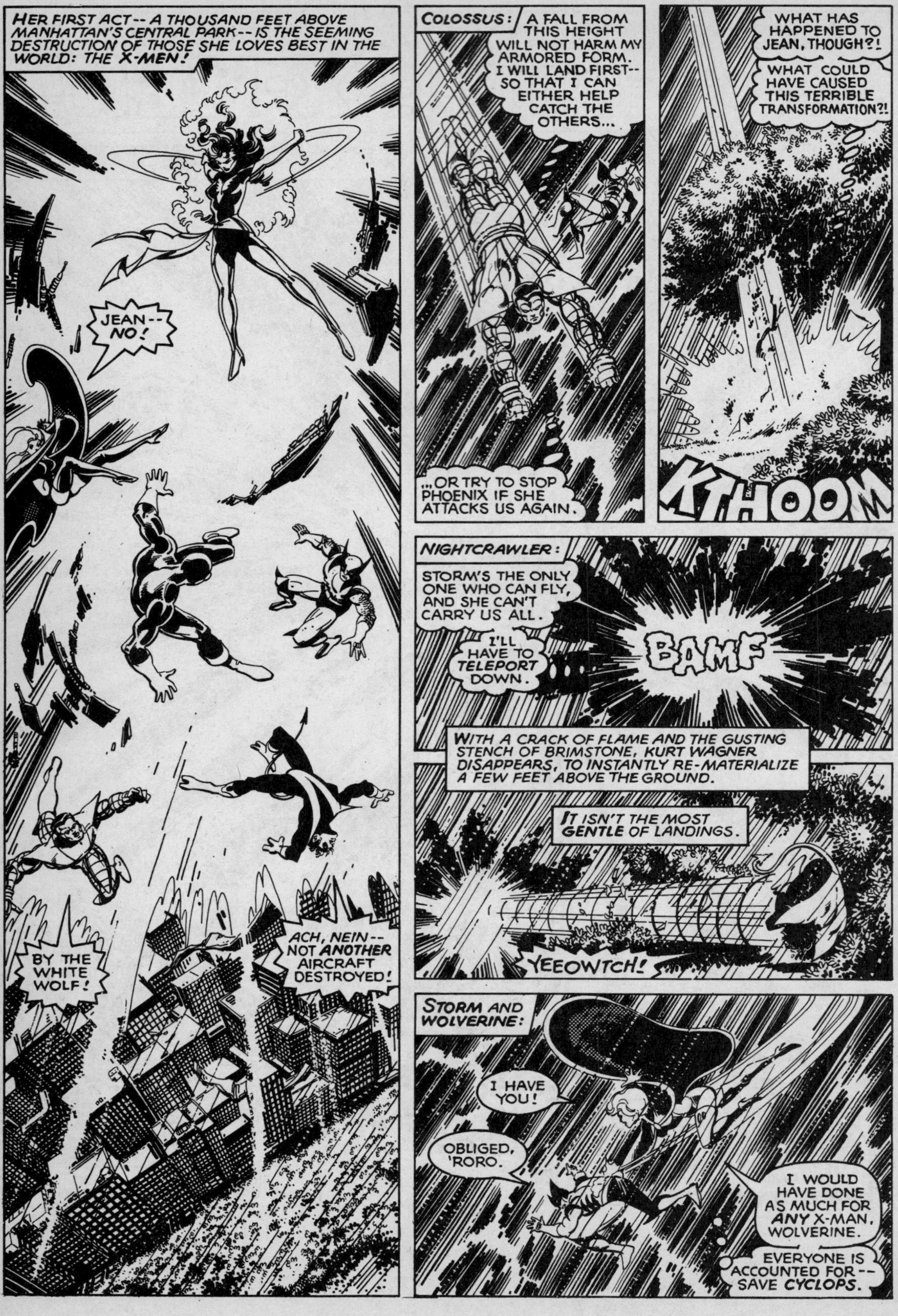
HER FIRST ACT -- A THOUSAND FEET ABOVE MANHATTAN'S CENTRAL PARK -- IS THE SEEMING DESTRUCTION OF THOSE SHE LOVES BEST IN THE WORLD: THE X-MEN!
JEAN -- NO!
BY THE WHITE WOLF!
ACH, NEIN -- NOT ANOTHER AIRCRAFT DESTROYED!
COLOSSUS:
A FALL FROM THIS HEIGHT WILL NOT HARM MY ARMORED FORM. I WILL LAND FIRST -- SO THAT I CAN EITHER HELP CATCH THE OTHERS...
...OR TRY TO STOP PHOENIX IF SHE ATTACKS US AGAIN.
WHAT HAS HAPPENED TO JEAN, THOUGH?!
WHAT COULD HAVE CAUSED THIS TERRIBLE TRANSFORMATION?!
KTHOOM
NIGHTCRAWLER:
STORM'S THE ONLY ONE WHO CAN FLY, AND SHE CAN'T CARRY US ALL.
I'LL HAVE TO TELEPORT DOWN.
BAMF
WITH A CRACK OF FLAME AND THE GUSTING STENCH OF BRIMSTONE, KURT WAGNER DISAPPEARS, TO INSTANTLY RE-MATERIALIZE A FEW FEET ABOVE THE GROUND.
IT ISN'T THE MOST GENTLE OF LANDINGS.
YEEOWTCH!
STORM AND WOLVERINE:
I HAVE YOU!
OBLIGED, 'RORO.
I WOULD HAVE DONE AS MUCH FOR ANY X-MAN, WOLVERINE.
EVERYONE IS ACCOUNTED FOR -- SAVE CYCLOPS.

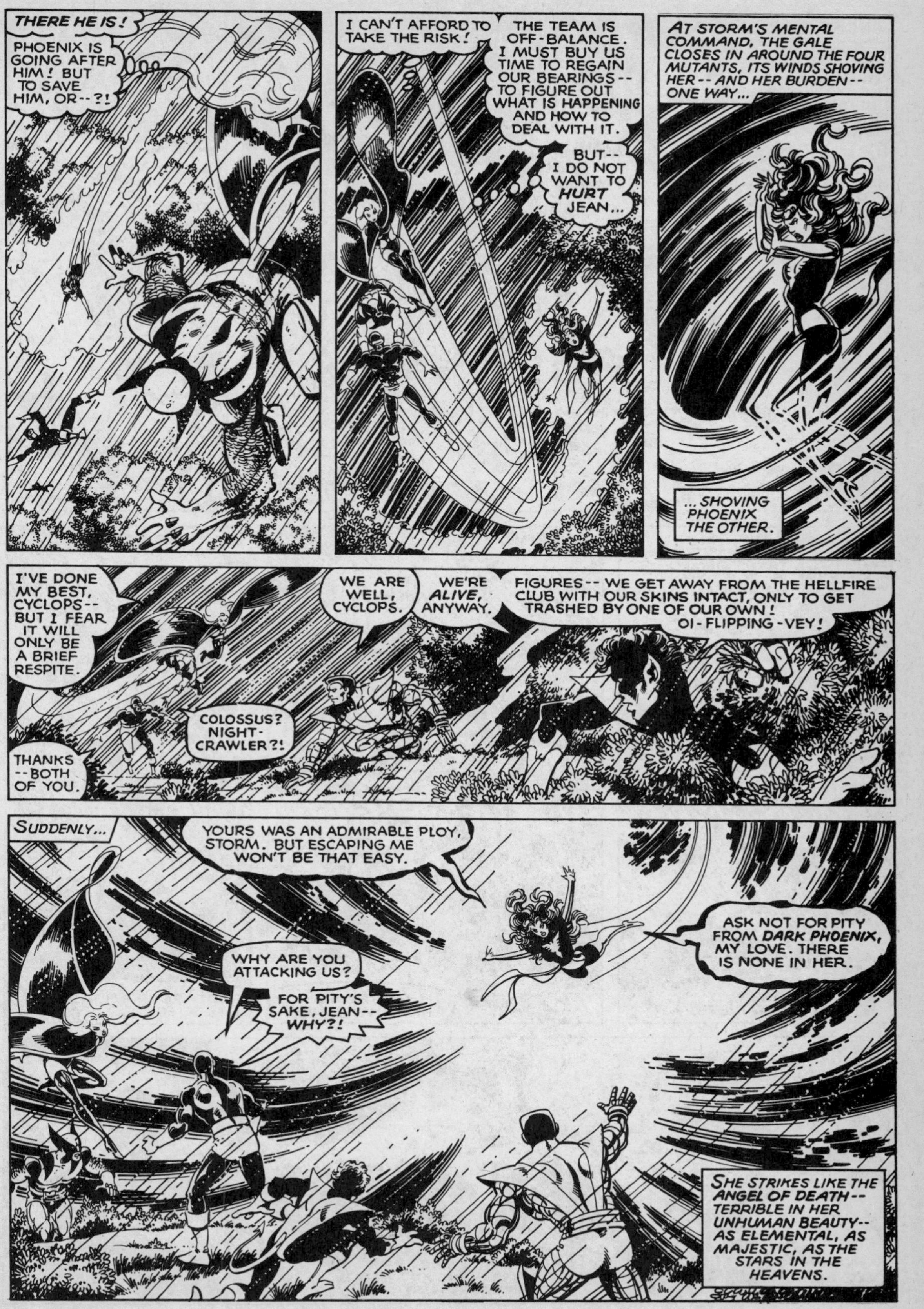
THERE HE IS!
PHOENIX IS GOING AFTER HIM! BUT TO SAVE HIM, OR--?!
I CAN'T AFFORD TO TAKE THE RISK!
THE TEAM IS OFF-BALANCE. I MUST BUY US TIME TO REGAIN OUR BEARINGS -- TO FIGURE OUT WHAT IS HAPPENING AND HOW TO DEAL WITH IT.
BUT-- I DO NOT WANT TO HURT JEAN...
AT STORM'S MENTAL COMMAND, THE GALE CLOSES IN AROUND THE FOUR MUTANTS, ITS WINDS SHOVING HER -- AND HER BURDEN -- ONE WAY...
...SHOVING PHOENIX THE OTHER.
I'VE DONE MY BEST, CYCLOPS -- BUT I FEAR IT WILL ONLY BE A BRIEF RESPITE.
WE ARE WELL, CYCLOPS.
WE'RE ALIVE, ANYWAY.
FIGURES -- WE GET AWAY FROM THE HELLFIRE CLUB WITH OUR SKINS INTACT, ONLY TO GET TRASHED BY ONE OF OUR OWN!
OI-FLIPPING-VEY!
COLOSSUS? NIGHT-CRAWLER?!
THANKS --BOTH OF YOU.
SUDDENLY...
YOURS WAS AN ADMIRABLE PLOY, STORM. BUT ESCAPING ME WON'T BE THAT EASY.
WHY ARE YOU ATTACKING US?
FOR PITY'S SAKE, JEAN-- WHY?!
ASK NOT FOR PITY FROM DARK PHOENIX, MY LOVE. THERE IS NONE IN HER.
SHE STRIKES LIKE THE ANGEL OF DEATH -- TERRIBLE IN HER UNHUMAN BEAUTY -- AS ELEMENTAL, AS MAJESTIC, AS THE STARS IN THE HEAVENS.

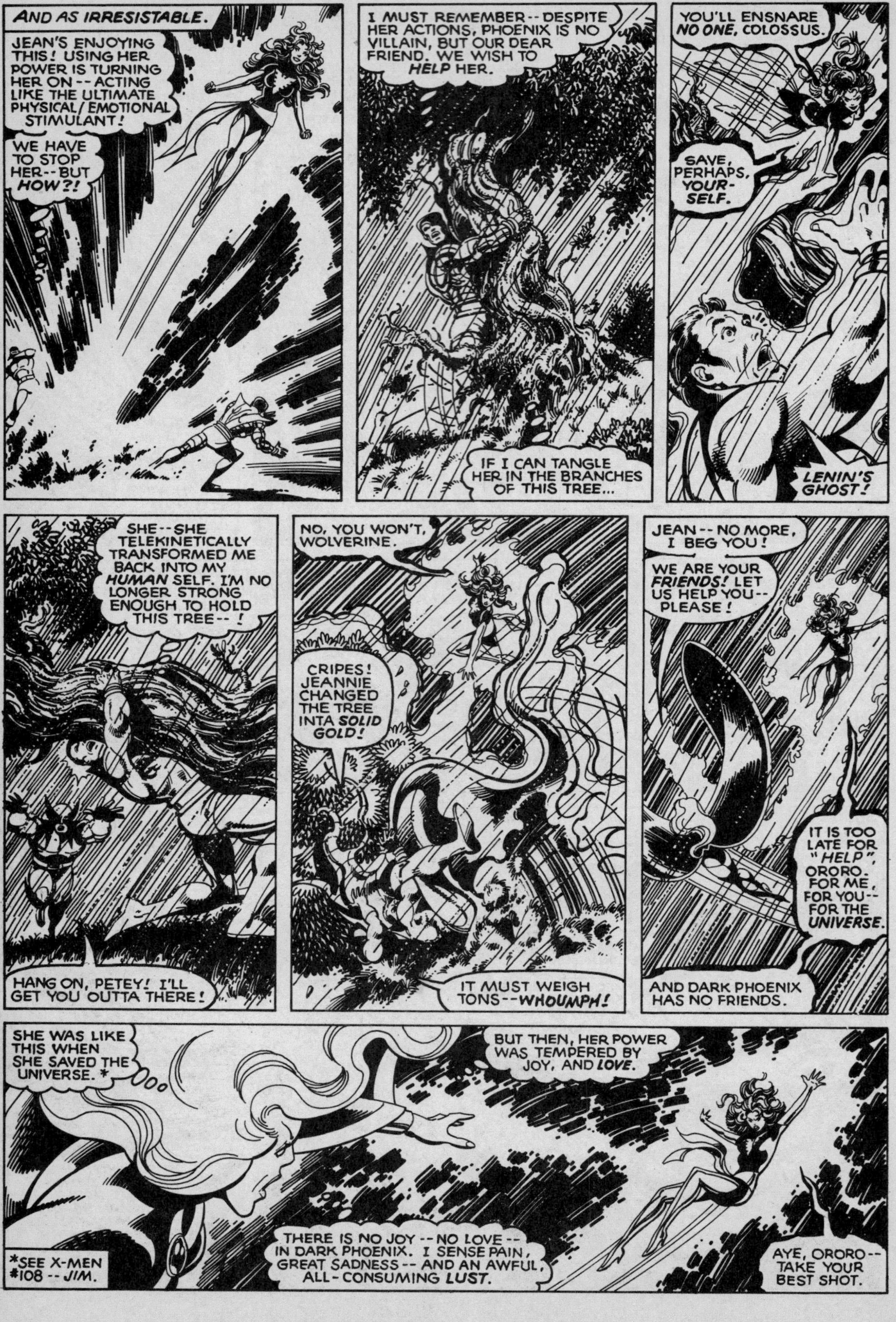
AND AS IRRESISTABLE.
JEAN'S ENJOYING THIS! USING HER POWER IS TURNING HER ON -- ACTING LIKE THE ULTIMATE PHYSICAL/EMOTIONAL STIMULANT!
WE HAVE TO STOP HER-- BUT HOW?!
I MUST REMEMBER -- DESPITE HER ACTIONS, PHOENIX IS NO VILLAIN, BUT OUR DEAR FRIEND. WE WISH TO HELP HER.
IF I CAN TANGLE HER IN THE BRANCHES OF THIS TREE...
YOU'LL ENSNARE NO ONE, COLOSSUS.
SAVE, PERHAPS, YOURSELF.
LENIN'S GHOST!
SHE--SHE TELEKINETICALLY TRANSFORMED ME BACK INTO MY HUMAN SELF. I'M NO LONGER STRONG ENOUGH TO HOLD THIS TREE-- !
HANG ON, PETEY! I'LL GET YOU OUTTA THERE!
NO, YOU WON'T, WOLVERINE.
CRIPES! JEANNIE CHANGED THE TREE INTA SOLID GOLD!
IT MUST WEIGH TONS--WHOUMPH!
JEAN -- NO MORE, I BEG YOU!
WE ARE YOUR FRIENDS! LET US HELP YOU-- PLEASE!
IT IS TOO LATE FOR "HELP", ORORO. FOR ME, FOR YOU-- FOR THE UNIVERSE.
AND DARK PHOENIX HAS NO FRIENDS.
SHE WAS LIKE THIS WHEN SHE SAVED THE UNIVERSE.*
BUT THEN, HER POWER WAS TEMPERED BY JOY, AND LOVE.
THERE IS NO JOY -- NO LOVE -- IN DARK PHOENIX. I SENSE PAIN, GREAT SADNESS -- AND AN AWFUL, ALL-CONSUMING LUST.
AYE, ORORO -- TAKE YOUR BEST SHOT.
*SEE X-MEN #108 -- JIM.

I'D RATHER END THIS QUICKLY.

AARRGH!

FOR ALL YOUR SKILL--AND POWER-- ORORO, YOU HAVEN'T A PRAYER AGAINST ME. I CAN PICK YOUR MIND CLEAN IN THE BLINK OF AN EYE--KNOW YOUR PLANS THE MOMENT YOU THINK OF THEM.

"AND *MY* POWER... DEFIES COMPREHENSION."

STORM! IMAGES -- HITTING ME THROUGH THE PSYCHIC *RAPPORT* I SHARE WITH JEAN-- BLACK FLAMES CONSUMING HER SOUL! MYSTICAL ALLUSIONS -- I DON'T UNDERSTAND--LOST... DROWNING... ALONE ...

CYCLOPS, WE'RE THE ONLY ONES LEFT! WHAT CAN WE DO?!

NOT A THING, NIGHTCRAWLER.

SHE HITS THEM A HUNDRED DIFFERENT WAYS AT ONCE--

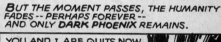

-- AND THE LAST TWO X-MEN DROP IN THEIR TRACKS.

I DIDN'T WANT THIS, MY DEAR ONES -- AND YET, IT WAS SOME- THING I *HAD* TO DO.

BY STRIKING *YOU* DOWN, I CUT MYSELF FREE OF THE LAST TIES BINDING ME TO THE PERSON I WAS, THE LIFE I LED.

FOR A MOMENT, THE GODDESS- MASQUE SLIPS -- AND JEAN GREY'S FACE SHATTERS WITH A GRIEF THAT TRANSCENDS THOUGHT.

BUT THE MOMENT PASSES, THE HUMANITY FADES -- PERHAPS FOREVER -- AND ONLY DARK PHOENIX REMAINS.

YOU AND I ARE QUITS NOW, X-MEN. OUR PATHS WILL CROSS NO MORE.

MY DESTINY LIES IN THE *STARS!*

SHE REACHES FOR THE SKY-- SUMMONING THE LIGHTNING-- LAUGHING AS THE AWESOME BOLTS OF ENERGY CARESS HER BODY LIKE A LOVER.

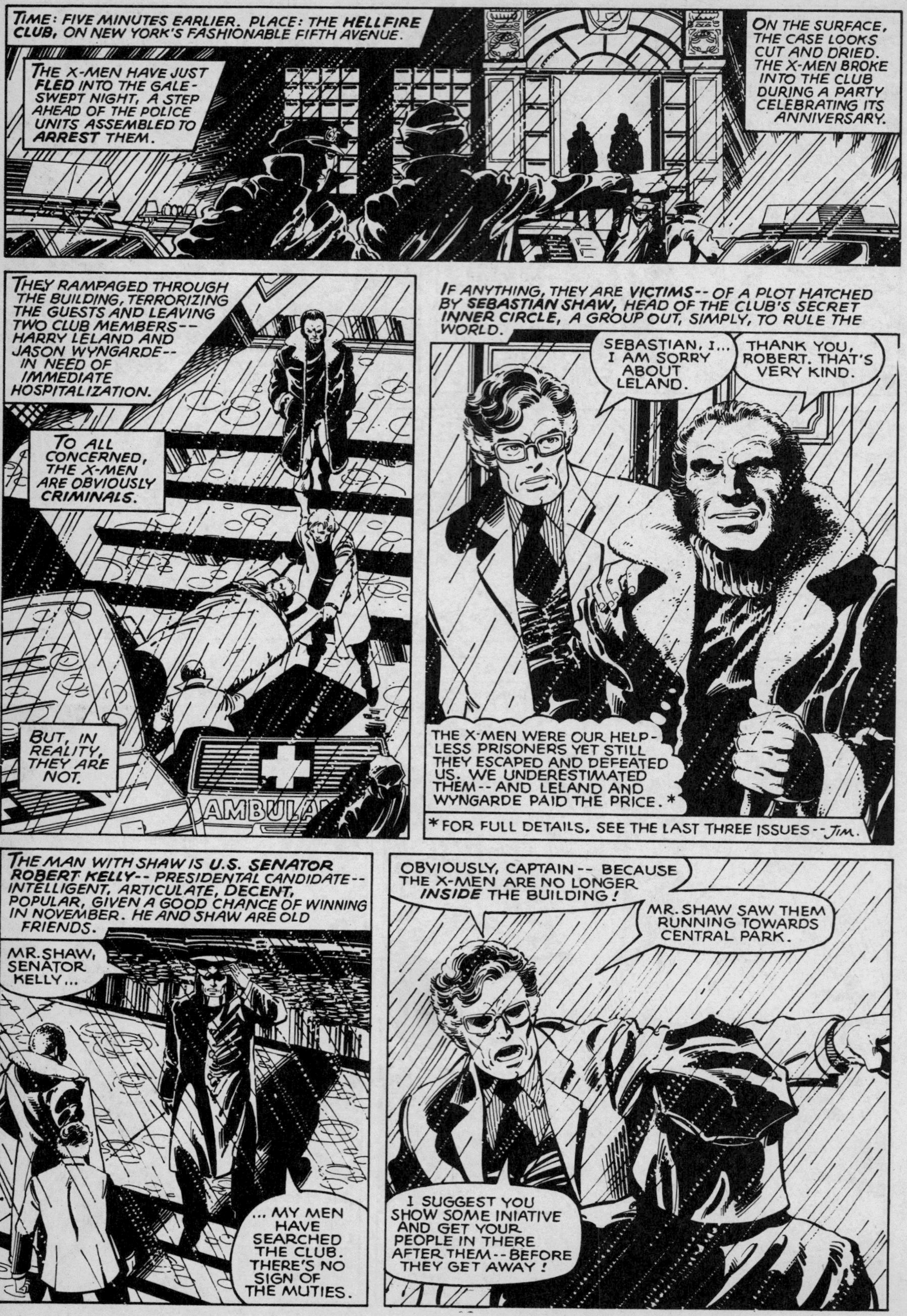
TIME: FIVE MINUTES EARLIER. PLACE: THE HELLFIRE CLUB, ON NEW YORK'S FASHIONABLE FIFTH AVENUE.
THE X-MEN HAVE JUST FLED INTO THE GALE-SWEPT NIGHT, A STEP AHEAD OF THE POLICE UNITS ASSEMBLED TO ARREST THEM.
ON THE SURFACE, THE CASE LOOKS CUT AND DRIED. THE X-MEN BROKE INTO THE CLUB DURING A PARTY CELEBRATING ITS ANNIVERSARY.
THEY RAMPAGED THROUGH THE BUILDING, TERRORIZING THE GUESTS AND LEAVING TWO CLUB MEMBERS-- HARRY LELAND AND JASON WYNGARDE-- IN NEED OF IMMEDIATE HOSPITALIZATION.
TO ALL CONCERNED, THE X-MEN ARE OBVIOUSLY CRIMINALS.
BUT, IN REALITY, THEY ARE NOT.
AMBULA
IF ANYTHING, THEY ARE VICTIMS-- OF A PLOT HATCHED BY SEBASTIAN SHAW, HEAD OF THE CLUB'S SECRET INNER CIRCLE, A GROUP OUT, SIMPLY, TO RULE THE WORLD.
SEBASTIAN, I... I AM SORRY ABOUT LELAND.
THANK YOU, ROBERT. THAT'S VERY KIND.
THE X-MEN WERE OUR HELPLESS PRISONERS YET STILL THEY ESCAPED AND DEFEATED US. WE UNDERESTIMATED THEM-- AND LELAND AND WYNGARDE PAID THE PRICE.*
*FOR FULL DETAILS, SEE THE LAST THREE ISSUES--JIM.
THE MAN WITH SHAW IS U.S. SENATOR ROBERT KELLY-- PRESIDENTAL CANDIDATE-- INTELLIGENT, ARTICULATE, DECENT, POPULAR, GIVEN A GOOD CHANCE OF WINNING IN NOVEMBER. HE AND SHAW ARE OLD FRIENDS.
MR. SHAW, SENATOR KELLY...
...MY MEN HAVE SEARCHED THE CLUB. THERE'S NO SIGN OF THE MUTIES.
OBVIOUSLY, CAPTAIN-- BECAUSE THE X-MEN ARE NO LONGER INSIDE THE BUILDING!
MR. SHAW SAW THEM RUNNING TOWARDS CENTRAL PARK.
I SUGGEST YOU SHOW SOME INIATIVE AND GET YOUR PEOPLE IN THERE AFTER THEM--BEFORE THEY GET AWAY!

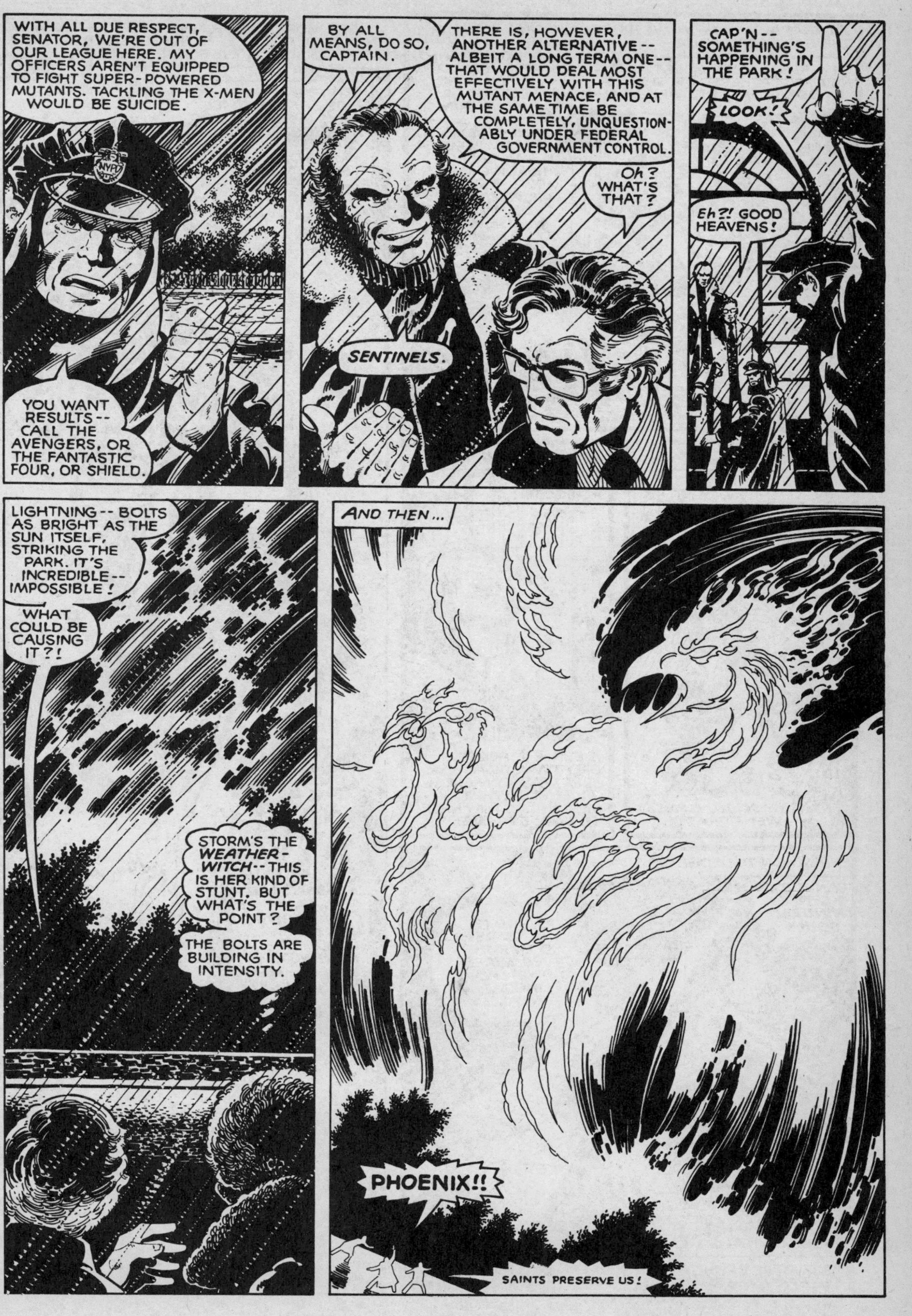

WITH ALL DUE RESPECT, SENATOR, WE'RE OUT OF OUR LEAGUE HERE. MY OFFICERS AREN'T EQUIPPED TO FIGHT SUPER-POWERED MUTANTS. TACKLING THE X-MEN WOULD BE SUICIDE.
YOU WANT RESULTS -- CALL THE AVENGERS, OR THE FANTASTIC FOUR, OR SHIELD.
BY ALL MEANS, DO SO, CAPTAIN.
THERE IS, HOWEVER, ANOTHER ALTERNATIVE -- ALBEIT A LONG TERM ONE -- THAT WOULD DEAL MOST EFFECTIVELY WITH THIS MUTANT MENACE, AND AT THE SAME TIME BE COMPLETELY, UNQUESTIONABLY UNDER FEDERAL GOVERNMENT CONTROL.
Oh? WHAT'S THAT?
SENTINELS.
CAP'N -- SOMETHING'S HAPPENING IN THE PARK!
LOOK!
Eh?! GOOD HEAVENS!
LIGHTNING -- BOLTS AS BRIGHT AS THE SUN ITSELF, STRIKING THE PARK. IT'S INCREDIBLE -- IMPOSSIBLE!
WHAT COULD BE CAUSING IT?!
STORM'S THE WEATHER-WITCH -- THIS IS HER KIND OF STUNT. BUT WHAT'S THE POINT?
THE BOLTS ARE BUILDING IN INTENSITY.
AND THEN...
PHOENIX!!
SAINTS PRESERVE US!

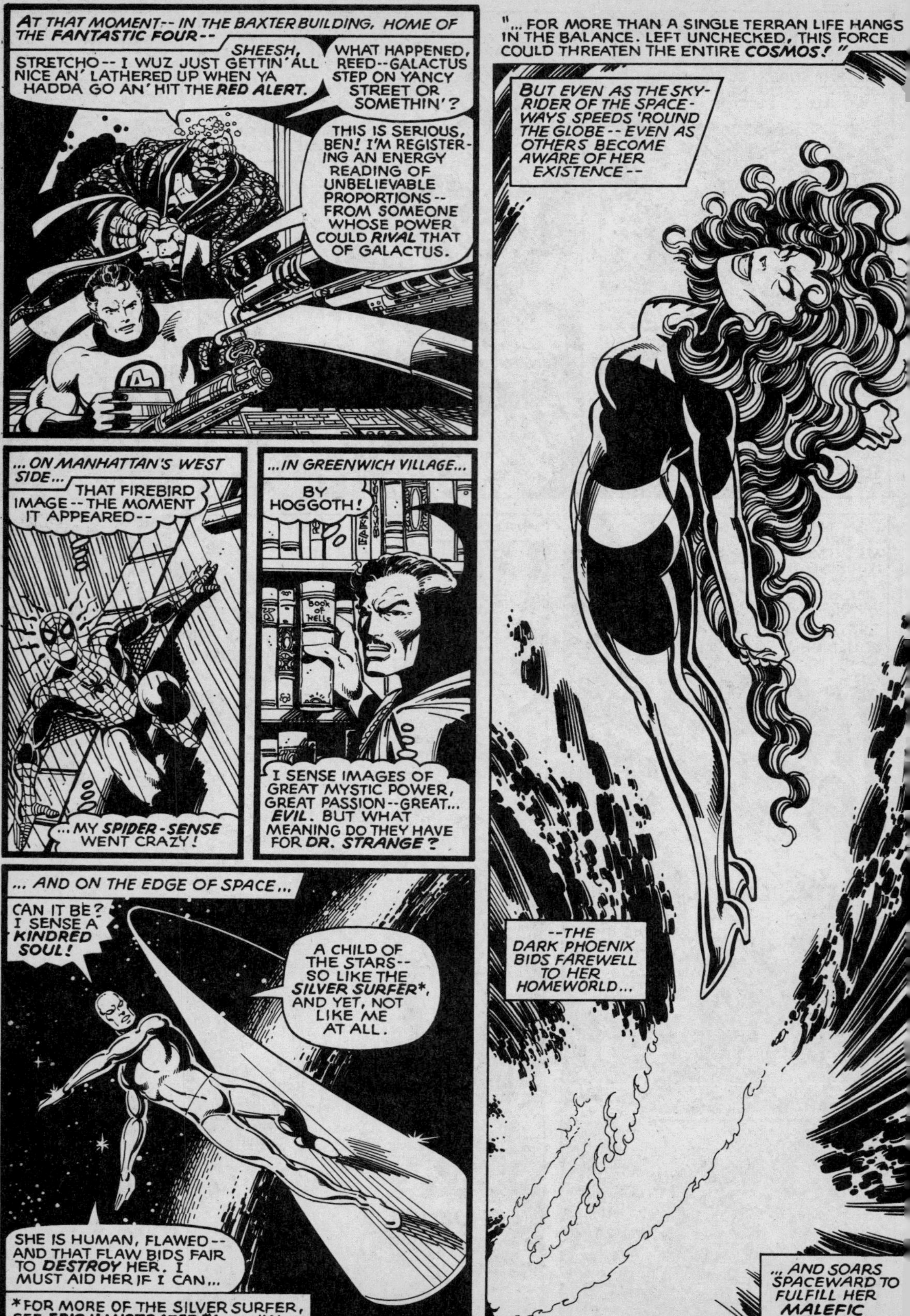
AT THAT MOMENT-- IN THE BAXTER BUILDING, HOME OF THE FANTASTIC FOUR--
SHEESH, STRETCHO-- I WUZ JUST GETTIN' ALL NICE AN' LATHERED UP WHEN YA HADDA GO AN' HIT THE RED ALERT.
WHAT HAPPENED, REED--GALACTUS STEP ON YANCY STREET OR SOMETHIN'?
THIS IS SERIOUS, BEN! I'M REGISTERING AN ENERGY READING OF UNBELIEVABLE PROPORTIONS-- FROM SOMEONE WHOSE POWER COULD RIVAL THAT OF GALACTUS.
...ON MANHATTAN'S WEST SIDE...
THAT FIREBIRD IMAGE--THE MOMENT IT APPEARED--
...MY SPIDER-SENSE WENT CRAZY!
...IN GREENWICH VILLAGE...
BY HOGGOTH!
BOOK OF HELLS
I SENSE IMAGES OF GREAT MYSTIC POWER, GREAT PASSION--GREAT... EVIL. BUT WHAT MEANING DO THEY HAVE FOR DR. STRANGE?
... AND ON THE EDGE OF SPACE...
CAN IT BE? I SENSE A KINDRED SOUL!
A CHILD OF THE STARS-- SO LIKE THE SILVER SURFER*, AND YET, NOT LIKE ME AT ALL.
SHE IS HUMAN, FLAWED-- AND THAT FLAW BIDS FAIR TO DESTROY HER. I MUST AID HER IF I CAN...
*FOR MORE OF THE SILVER SURFER, SEE EPIC ILLUSTRATED #1 -- JIM.
"... FOR MORE THAN A SINGLE TERRAN LIFE HANGS IN THE BALANCE. LEFT UNCHECKED, THIS FORCE COULD THREATEN THE ENTIRE COSMOS!"
BUT EVEN AS THE SKY-RIDER OF THE SPACEWAYS SPEEDS 'ROUND THE GLOBE -- EVEN AS OTHERS BECOME AWARE OF HER EXISTENCE--
--THE DARK PHOENIX BIDS FAREWELL TO HER HOMEWORLD...
...AND SOARS SPACEWARD TO FULFILL HER MALEFIC DESTINY.

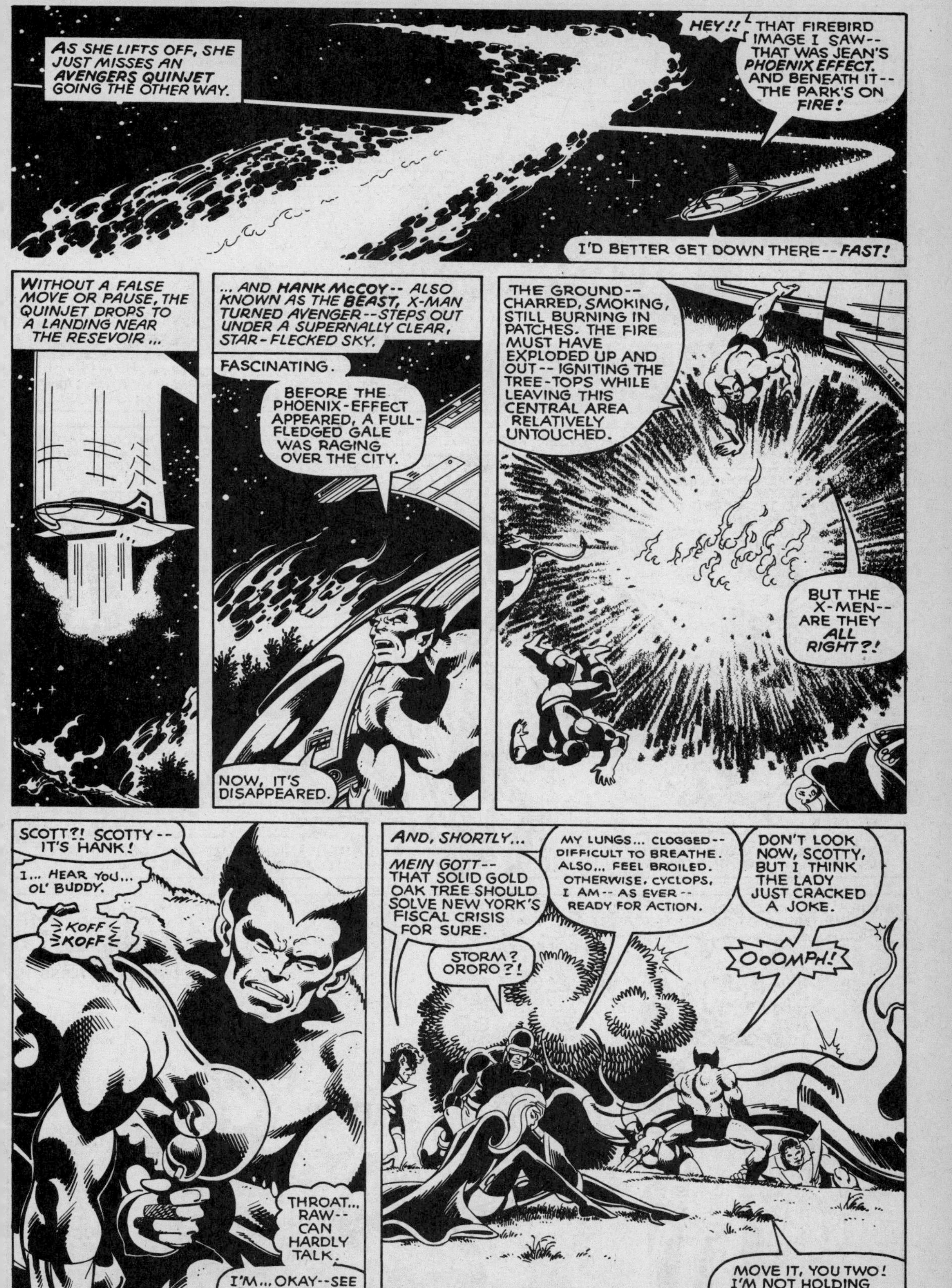
AS SHE LIFTS OFF, SHE JUST MISSES AN AVENGERS QUINJET GOING THE OTHER WAY.
HEY!! THAT FIREBIRD IMAGE I SAW-- THAT WAS JEAN'S PHOENIX EFFECT. AND BENEATH IT-- THE PARK'S ON FIRE!
I'D BETTER GET DOWN THERE--FAST!
WITHOUT A FALSE MOVE OR PAUSE, THE QUINJET DROPS TO A LANDING NEAR THE RESEVOIR...
...AND HANK McCOY-- ALSO KNOWN AS THE BEAST, X-MAN TURNED AVENGER--STEPS OUT UNDER A SUPERNALLY CLEAR, STAR-FLECKED SKY.
FASCINATING.
BEFORE THE PHOENIX-EFFECT APPEARED, A FULL-FLEDGED GALE WAS RAGING OVER THE CITY.
NOW, IT'S DISAPPEARED.
THE GROUND-- CHARRED, SMOKING, STILL BURNING IN PATCHES. THE FIRE MUST HAVE EXPLODED UP AND OUT--IGNITING THE TREE-TOPS WHILE LEAVING THIS CENTRAL AREA RELATIVELY UNTOUCHED.
BUT THE X-MEN-- ARE THEY ALL RIGHT?!
SCOTT?! SCOTTY-- IT'S HANK!
I... HEAR YOU... OL' BUDDY.
KOFF KOFF
THROAT... RAW-- CAN HARDLY TALK.
I'M...OKAY--SEE TO OTHERS.
AND, SHORTLY...
MEIN GOTT-- THAT SOLID GOLD OAK TREE SHOULD SOLVE NEW YORK'S FISCAL CRISIS FOR SURE.
STORM? ORORO?!
MY LUNGS... CLOGGED-- DIFFICULT TO BREATHE. ALSO... FEEL BROILED. OTHERWISE, CYCLOPS, I AM-- AS EVER-- READY FOR ACTION.
DON'T LOOK NOW, SCOTTY, BUT I THINK THE LADY JUST CRACKED A JOKE.
OOOMPH!
MOVE IT, YOU TWO! I'M NOT HOLDING THIS ALL NIGHT!

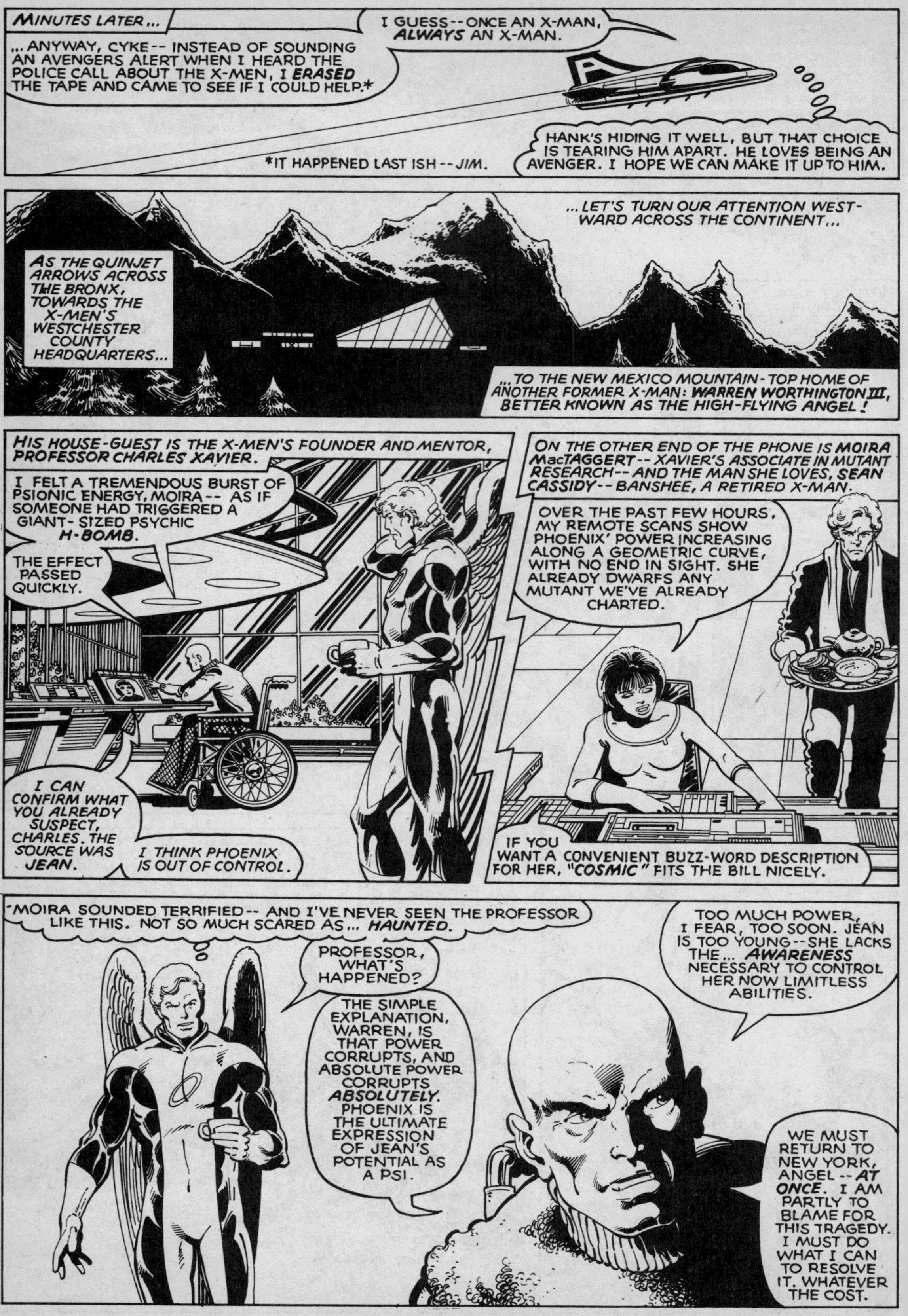

MINUTES LATER...
...ANYWAY, CYKE -- INSTEAD OF SOUNDING AN AVENGERS ALERT WHEN I HEARD THE POLICE CALL ABOUT THE X-MEN, I ERASED THE TAPE AND CAME TO SEE IF I COULD HELP.*
I GUESS -- ONCE AN X-MAN, ALWAYS AN X-MAN.
*IT HAPPENED LAST ISH -- JIM.
HANK'S HIDING IT WELL, BUT THAT CHOICE IS TEARING HIM APART. HE LOVES BEING AN AVENGER. I HOPE WE CAN MAKE IT UP TO HIM.
AS THE QUINJET ARROWS ACROSS THE BRONX, TOWARDS THE X-MEN'S WESTCHESTER COUNTY HEADQUARTERS...
...LET'S TURN OUR ATTENTION WESTWARD ACROSS THE CONTINENT...
...TO THE NEW MEXICO MOUNTAIN-TOP HOME OF ANOTHER FORMER X-MAN: WARREN WORTHINGTON III, BETTER KNOWN AS THE HIGH-FLYING ANGEL!
HIS HOUSE-GUEST IS THE X-MEN'S FOUNDER AND MENTOR, PROFESSOR CHARLES XAVIER.
I FELT A TREMENDOUS BURST OF PSIONIC ENERGY, MOIRA -- AS IF SOMEONE HAD TRIGGERED A GIANT-SIZED PSYCHIC H-BOMB.
THE EFFECT PASSED QUICKLY.
I CAN CONFIRM WHAT YOU ALREADY SUSPECT, CHARLES. THE SOURCE WAS JEAN.
I THINK PHOENIX IS OUT OF CONTROL.
ON THE OTHER END OF THE PHONE IS MOIRA MacTAGGERT -- XAVIER'S ASSOCIATE IN MUTANT RESEARCH -- AND THE MAN SHE LOVES, SEAN CASSIDY -- BANSHEE, A RETIRED X-MAN.
OVER THE PAST FEW HOURS, MY REMOTE SCANS SHOW PHOENIX' POWER INCREASING ALONG A GEOMETRIC CURVE, WITH NO END IN SIGHT. SHE ALREADY DWARFS ANY MUTANT WE'VE ALREADY CHARTED.
IF YOU WANT A CONVENIENT BUZZ-WORD DESCRIPTION FOR HER, "COSMIC" FITS THE BILL NICELY.
MOIRA SOUNDED TERRIFIED -- AND I'VE NEVER SEEN THE PROFESSOR LIKE THIS. NOT SO MUCH SCARED AS... HAUNTED.
PROFESSOR, WHAT'S HAPPENED?
THE SIMPLE EXPLANATION, WARREN, IS THAT POWER CORRUPTS, AND ABSOLUTE POWER CORRUPTS ABSOLUTELY. PHOENIX IS THE ULTIMATE EXPRESSION OF JEAN'S POTENTIAL AS A PSI.
TOO MUCH POWER, I FEAR, TOO SOON. JEAN IS TOO YOUNG -- SHE LACKS THE... AWARENESS NECESSARY TO CONTROL HER NOW LIMITLESS ABILITIES.
WE MUST RETURN TO NEW YORK, ANGEL -- AT ONCE. I AM PARTLY TO BLAME FOR THIS TRAGEDY. I MUST DO WHAT I CAN TO RESOLVE IT. WHATEVER THE COST.

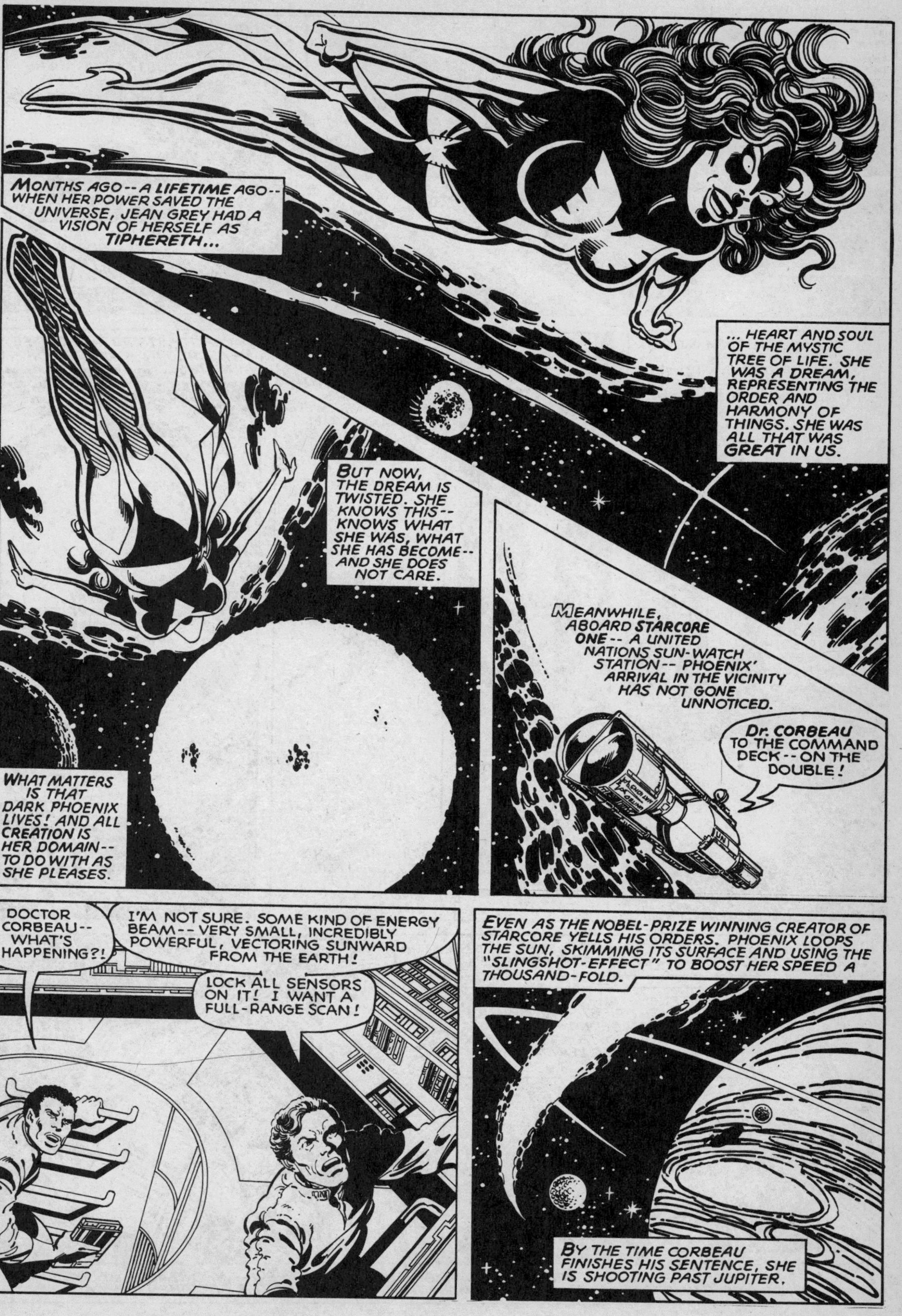
MONTHS AGO--A LIFETIME AGO--WHEN HER POWER SAVED THE UNIVERSE, JEAN GREY HAD A VISION OF HERSELF AS TIPHERETH...
...HEART AND SOUL OF THE MYSTIC TREE OF LIFE. SHE WAS A DREAM, REPRESENTING THE ORDER AND HARMONY OF THINGS. SHE WAS ALL THAT WAS GREAT IN US.
BUT NOW, THE DREAM IS TWISTED. SHE KNOWS THIS--KNOWS WHAT SHE WAS, WHAT SHE HAS BECOME--AND SHE DOES NOT CARE.
WHAT MATTERS IS THAT DARK PHOENIX LIVES! AND ALL CREATION IS HER DOMAIN--TO DO WITH AS SHE PLEASES.
MEANWHILE, ABOARD STARCORE ONE--A UNITED NATIONS SUN-WATCH STATION--PHOENIX' ARRIVAL IN THE VICINITY HAS NOT GONE UNNOTICED.
Dr. CORBEAU TO THE COMMAND DECK--ON THE DOUBLE!
DOCTOR CORBEAU--WHAT'S HAPPENING?!
I'M NOT SURE. SOME KIND OF ENERGY BEAM--VERY SMALL, INCREDIBLY POWERFUL, VECTORING SUNWARD FROM THE EARTH!
LOCK ALL SENSORS ON IT! I WANT A FULL-RANGE SCAN!
EVEN AS THE NOBEL-PRIZE WINNING CREATOR OF STARCORE YELLS HIS ORDERS, PHOENIX LOOPS THE SUN, SKIMMING ITS SURFACE AND USING THE "SLINGSHOT-EFFECT" TO BOOST HER SPEED A THOUSAND-FOLD.
BY THE TIME CORBEAU FINISHES HIS SENTENCE, SHE IS SHOOTING PAST JUPITER.

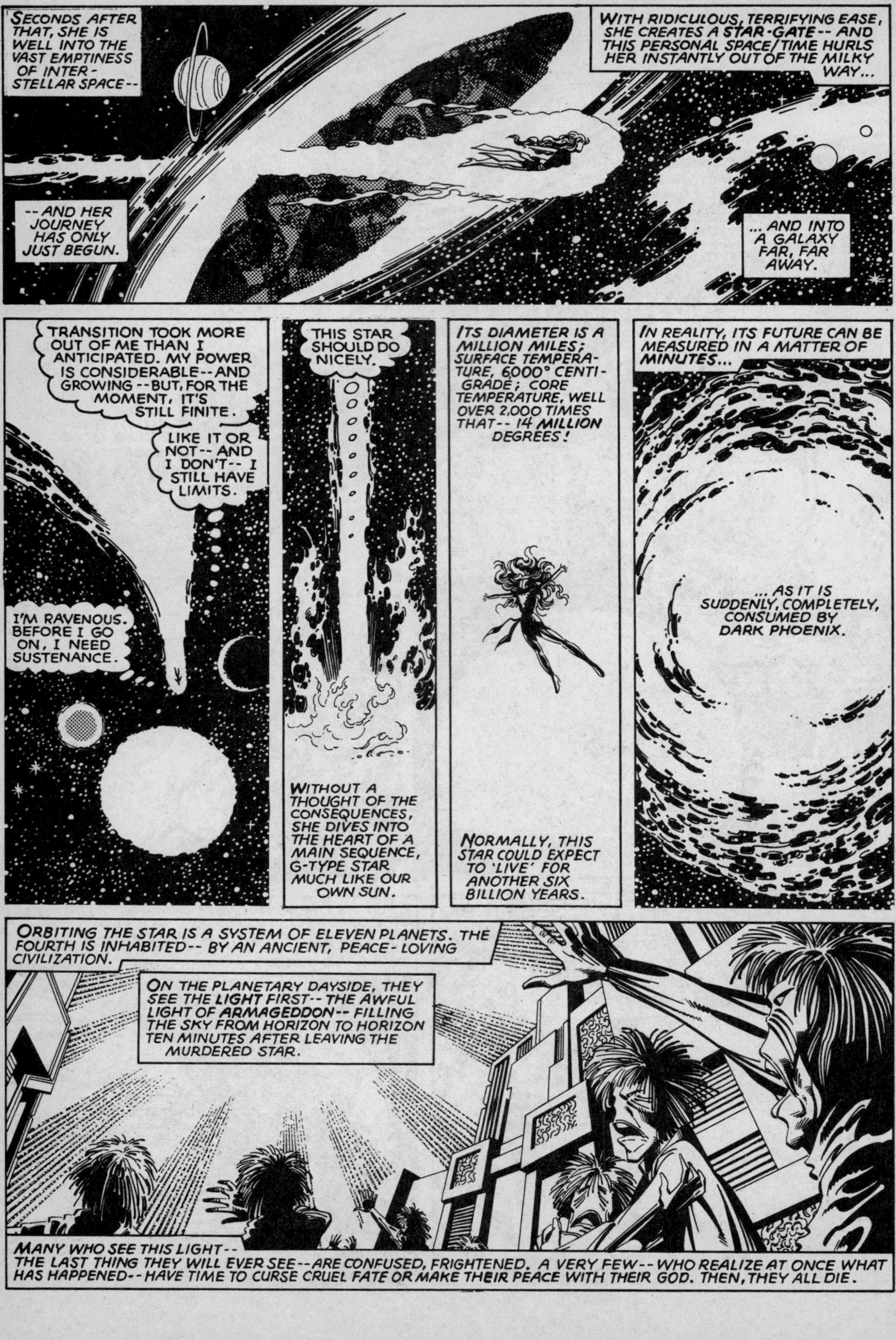
SECONDS AFTER THAT, SHE IS WELL INTO THE VAST EMPTINESS OF INTER-STELLAR SPACE--
--AND HER JOURNEY HAS ONLY JUST BEGUN.
WITH RIDICULOUS, TERRIFYING EASE, SHE CREATES A STAR-GATE-- AND THIS PERSONAL SPACE/TIME HURLS HER INSTANTLY OUT OF THE MILKY WAY...
...AND INTO A GALAXY FAR, FAR AWAY.
TRANSITION TOOK MORE OUT OF ME THAN I ANTICIPATED. MY POWER IS CONSIDERABLE--AND GROWING--BUT, FOR THE MOMENT, IT'S STILL FINITE.
LIKE IT OR NOT-- AND I DON'T-- I STILL HAVE LIMITS.
I'M RAVENOUS. BEFORE I GO ON, I NEED SUSTENANCE.
THIS STAR SHOULD DO NICELY.
WITHOUT A THOUGHT OF THE CONSEQUENCES, SHE DIVES INTO THE HEART OF A MAIN SEQUENCE, G-TYPE STAR MUCH LIKE OUR OWN SUN.
ITS DIAMETER IS A MILLION MILES; SURFACE TEMPERATURE, 6000° CENTIGRADE; CORE TEMPERATURE, WELL OVER 2,000 TIMES THAT-- 14 MILLION DEGREES!
NORMALLY, THIS STAR COULD EXPECT TO 'LIVE' FOR ANOTHER SIX BILLION YEARS.
IN REALITY, ITS FUTURE CAN BE MEASURED IN A MATTER OF MINUTES...
...AS IT IS SUDDENLY, COMPLETELY, CONSUMED BY DARK PHOENIX.
ORBITING THE STAR IS A SYSTEM OF ELEVEN PLANETS. THE FOURTH IS INHABITED-- BY AN ANCIENT, PEACE-LOVING CIVILIZATION.
ON THE PLANETARY DAYSIDE, THEY SEE THE LIGHT FIRST-- THE AWFUL LIGHT OF ARMAGEDDON-- FILLING THE SKY FROM HORIZON TO HORIZON TEN MINUTES AFTER LEAVING THE MURDERED STAR.
MANY WHO SEE THIS LIGHT-- THE LAST THING THEY WILL EVER SEE--ARE CONFUSED, FRIGHTENED. A VERY FEW--WHO REALIZE AT ONCE WHAT HAS HAPPENED--HAVE TIME TO CURSE CRUEL FATE OR MAKE THEIR PEACE WITH THEIR GOD. THEN, THEY ALL DIE.

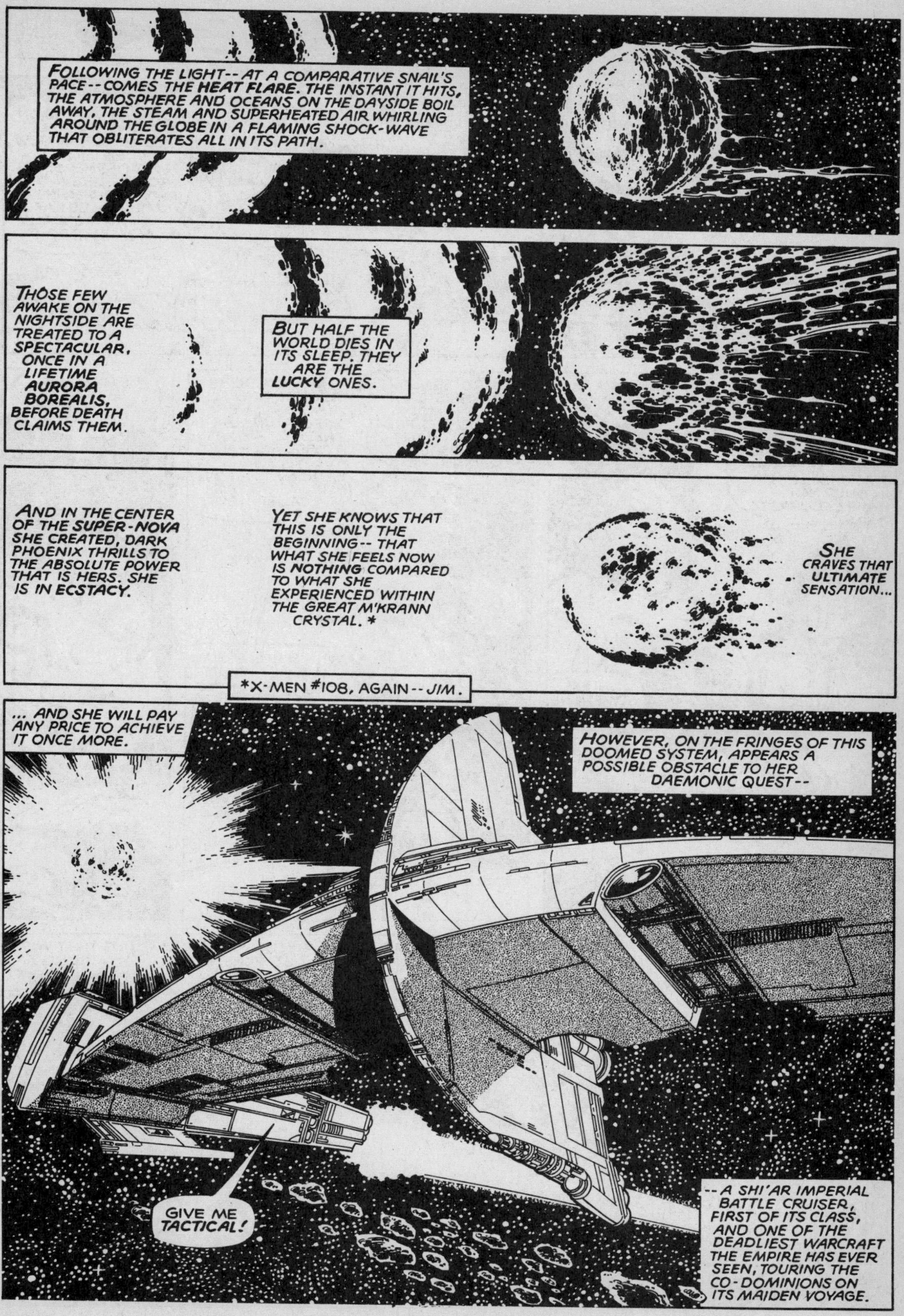
FOLLOWING THE LIGHT-- AT A COMPARATIVE SNAIL'S PACE-- COMES THE HEAT FLARE. THE INSTANT IT HITS, THE ATMOSPHERE AND OCEANS ON THE DAYSIDE BOIL AWAY, THE STEAM AND SUPERHEATED AIR WHIRLING AROUND THE GLOBE IN A FLAMING SHOCK-WAVE THAT OBLITERATES ALL IN ITS PATH.
THOSE FEW AWAKE ON THE NIGHTSIDE ARE TREATED TO A SPECTACULAR, ONCE IN A LIFETIME AURORA BOREALIS, BEFORE DEATH CLAIMS THEM.
BUT HALF THE WORLD DIES IN ITS SLEEP. THEY ARE THE LUCKY ONES.
AND IN THE CENTER OF THE SUPER-NOVA SHE CREATED, DARK PHOENIX THRILLS TO THE ABSOLUTE POWER THAT IS HERS. SHE IS IN ECSTACY.
YET SHE KNOWS THAT THIS IS ONLY THE BEGINNING-- THAT WHAT SHE FEELS NOW IS NOTHING COMPARED TO WHAT SHE EXPERIENCED WITHIN THE GREAT M'KRANN CRYSTAL. *
SHE CRAVES THAT ULTIMATE SENSATION...
*X-MEN #108, AGAIN-- JIM.
... AND SHE WILL PAY ANY PRICE TO ACHIEVE IT ONCE MORE.
HOWEVER, ON THE FRINGES OF THIS DOOMED SYSTEM, APPEARS A POSSIBLE OBSTACLE TO HER DAEMONIC QUEST--
GIVE ME TACTICAL!
-- A SHI'AR IMPERIAL BATTLE CRUISER, FIRST OF ITS CLASS, AND ONE OF THE DEADLIEST WARCRAFT THE EMPIRE HAS EVER SEEN, TOURING THE CO-DOMINIONS ON ITS MAIDEN VOYAGE.

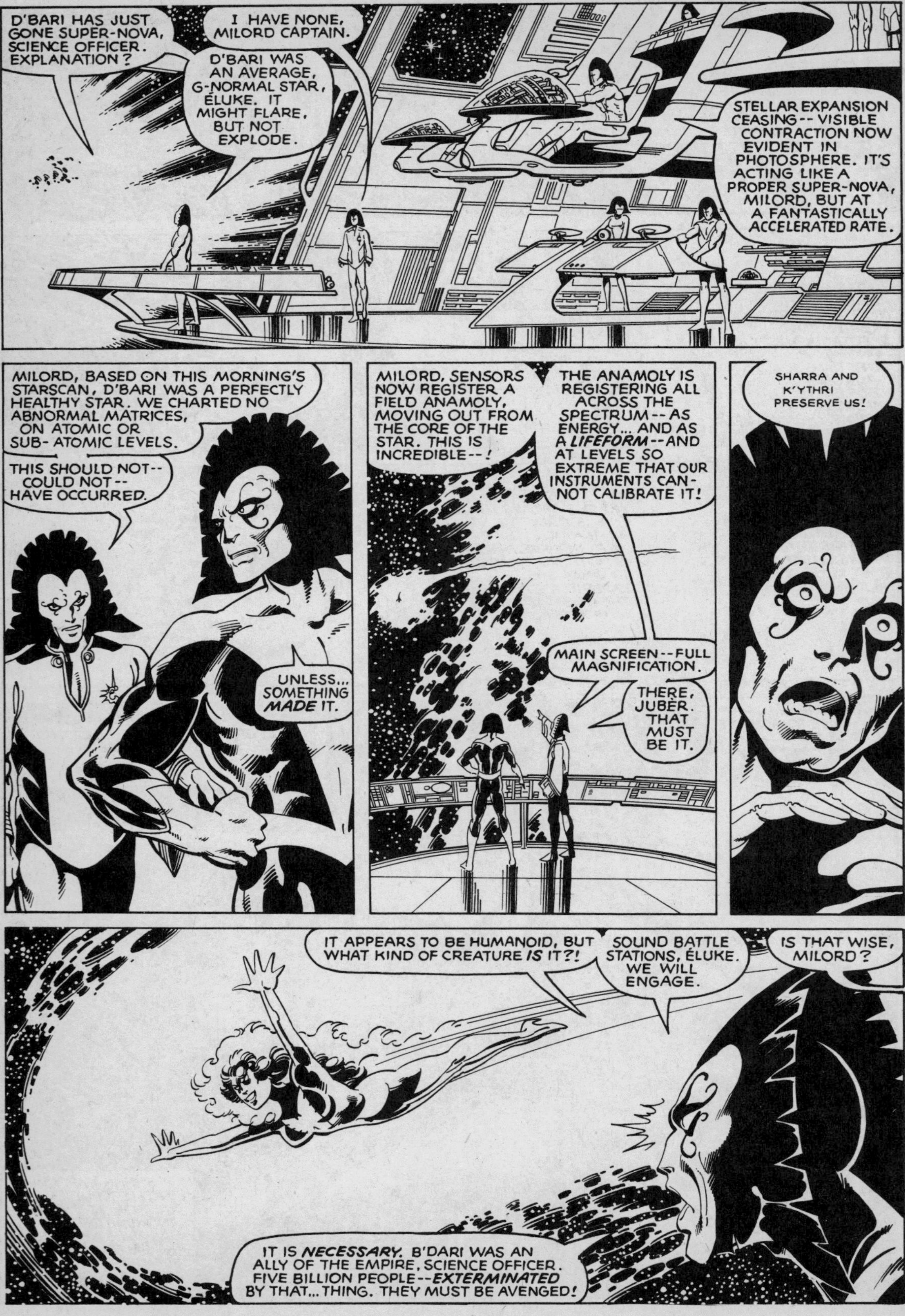

D'BARI HAS JUST GONE SUPER-NOVA, SCIENCE OFFICER. EXPLANATION?
I HAVE NONE, MILORD CAPTAIN.
D'BARI WAS AN AVERAGE, G-NORMAL STAR, ÉLUKE. IT MIGHT FLARE, BUT NOT EXPLODE.
STELLAR EXPANSION CEASING-- VISIBLE CONTRACTION NOW EVIDENT IN PHOTOSPHERE. IT'S ACTING LIKE A PROPER SUPER-NOVA, MILORD, BUT AT A FANTASTICALLY ACCELERATED RATE.
MILORD, BASED ON THIS MORNING'S STARSCAN, D'BARI WAS A PERFECTLY HEALTHY STAR. WE CHARTED NO ABNORMAL MATRICES, ON ATOMIC OR SUB-ATOMIC LEVELS.
THIS SHOULD NOT-- COULD NOT-- HAVE OCCURRED.
UNLESS... SOMETHING *MADE* IT.
MILORD, SENSORS NOW REGISTER A FIELD ANAMOLY, MOVING OUT FROM THE CORE OF THE STAR. THIS IS INCREDIBLE--!
THE ANAMOLY IS REGISTERING ALL ACROSS THE SPECTRUM-- AS ENERGY... AND AS A *LIFEFORM*-- AND AT LEVELS SO EXTREME THAT OUR INSTRUMENTS CANNOT CALIBRATE IT!
MAIN SCREEN-- FULL MAGNIFICATION.
THERE, JUBER. THAT MUST BE IT.
SHARRA AND K'YTHRI PRESERVE US!
IT APPEARS TO BE HUMANOID, BUT WHAT KIND OF CREATURE *IS* IT?!
SOUND BATTLE STATIONS, ÉLUKE. WE WILL ENGAGE.
IS THAT WISE, MILORD?
IT IS *NECESSARY.* B'DARI WAS AN ALLY OF THE EMPIRE, SCIENCE OFFICER. FIVE BILLION PEOPLE-- *EXTERMINATED* BY THAT... THING. THEY MUST BE AVENGED!

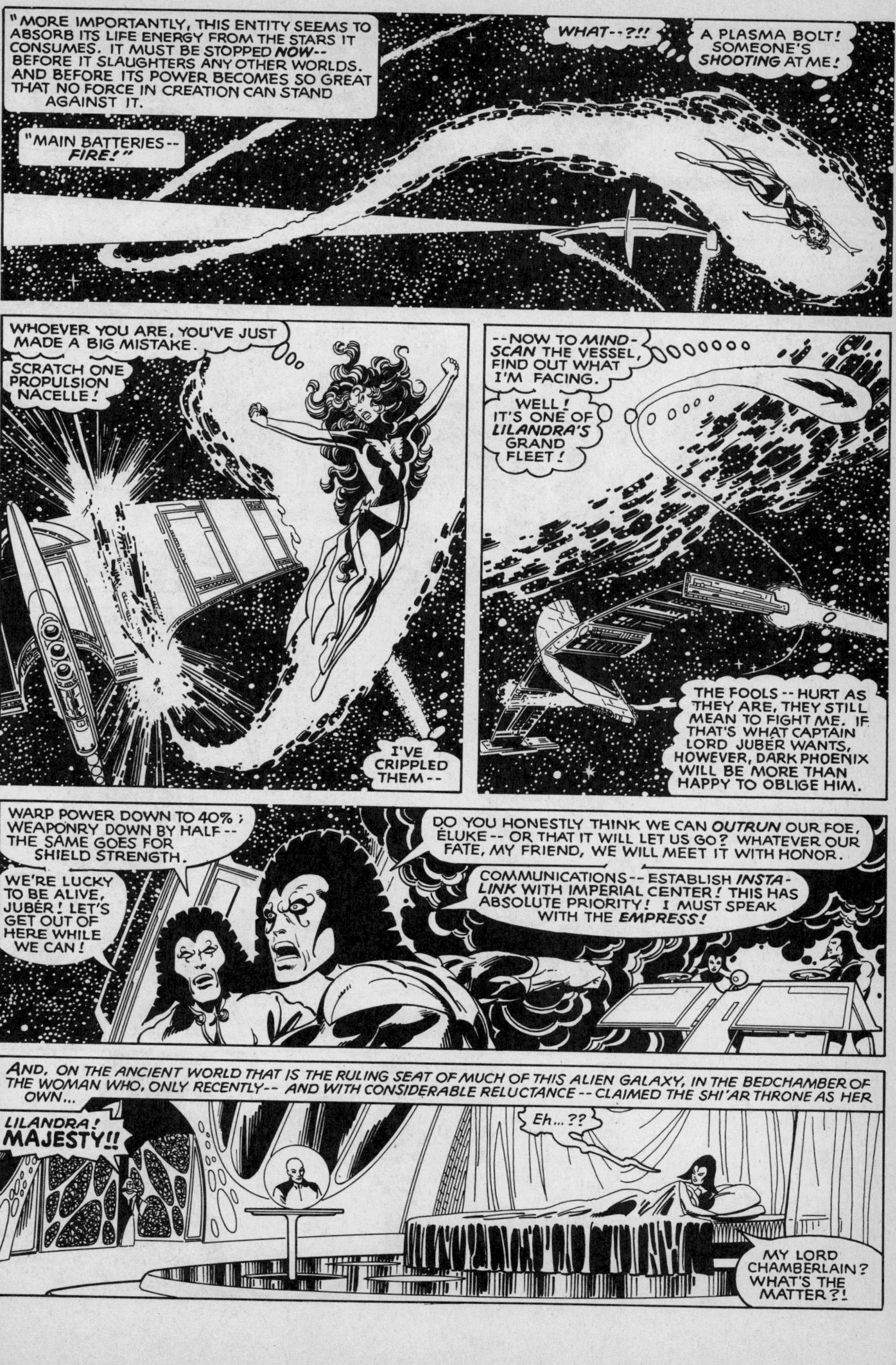
"MORE IMPORTANTLY, THIS ENTITY SEEMS TO ABSORB ITS LIFE ENERGY FROM THE STARS IT CONSUMES. IT MUST BE STOPPED NOW-- BEFORE IT SLAUGHTERS ANY OTHER WORLDS. AND BEFORE ITS POWER BECOMES SO GREAT THAT NO FORCE IN CREATION CAN STAND AGAINST IT.
"MAIN BATTERIES-- FIRE!"
WHAT--?!!
A PLASMA BOLT! SOMEONE'S SHOOTING AT ME!
WHOEVER YOU ARE, YOU'VE JUST MADE A BIG MISTAKE.
SCRATCH ONE PROPULSION NACELLE!
I'VE CRIPPLED THEM--
--NOW TO MIND-SCAN THE VESSEL, FIND OUT WHAT I'M FACING.
WELL! IT'S ONE OF LILANDRA'S GRAND FLEET!
THE FOOLS -- HURT AS THEY ARE, THEY STILL MEAN TO FIGHT ME. IF THAT'S WHAT CAPTAIN LORD JUBER WANTS, HOWEVER, DARK PHOENIX WILL BE MORE THAN HAPPY TO OBLIGE HIM.
WARP POWER DOWN TO 40%; WEAPONRY DOWN BY HALF-- THE SAME GOES FOR SHIELD STRENGTH.
WE'RE LUCKY TO BE ALIVE, JUBÉR! LET'S GET OUT OF HERE WHILE WE CAN!
DO YOU HONESTLY THINK WE CAN OUTRUN OUR FOE, ÉLUKE -- OR THAT IT WILL LET US GO? WHATEVER OUR FATE, MY FRIEND, WE WILL MEET IT WITH HONOR.
COMMUNICATIONS-- ESTABLISH INSTA-LINK WITH IMPERIAL CENTER! THIS HAS ABSOLUTE PRIORITY! I MUST SPEAK WITH THE EMPRESS!
AND, ON THE ANCIENT WORLD THAT IS THE RULING SEAT OF MUCH OF THIS ALIEN GALAXY, IN THE BEDCHAMBER OF THE WOMAN WHO, ONLY RECENTLY-- AND WITH CONSIDERABLE RELUCTANCE --CLAIMED THE SHI'AR THRONE AS HER OWN...
LILANDRA! MAJESTY!!
Eh...??
MY LORD CHAMBERLAIN? WHAT'S THE MATTER?!

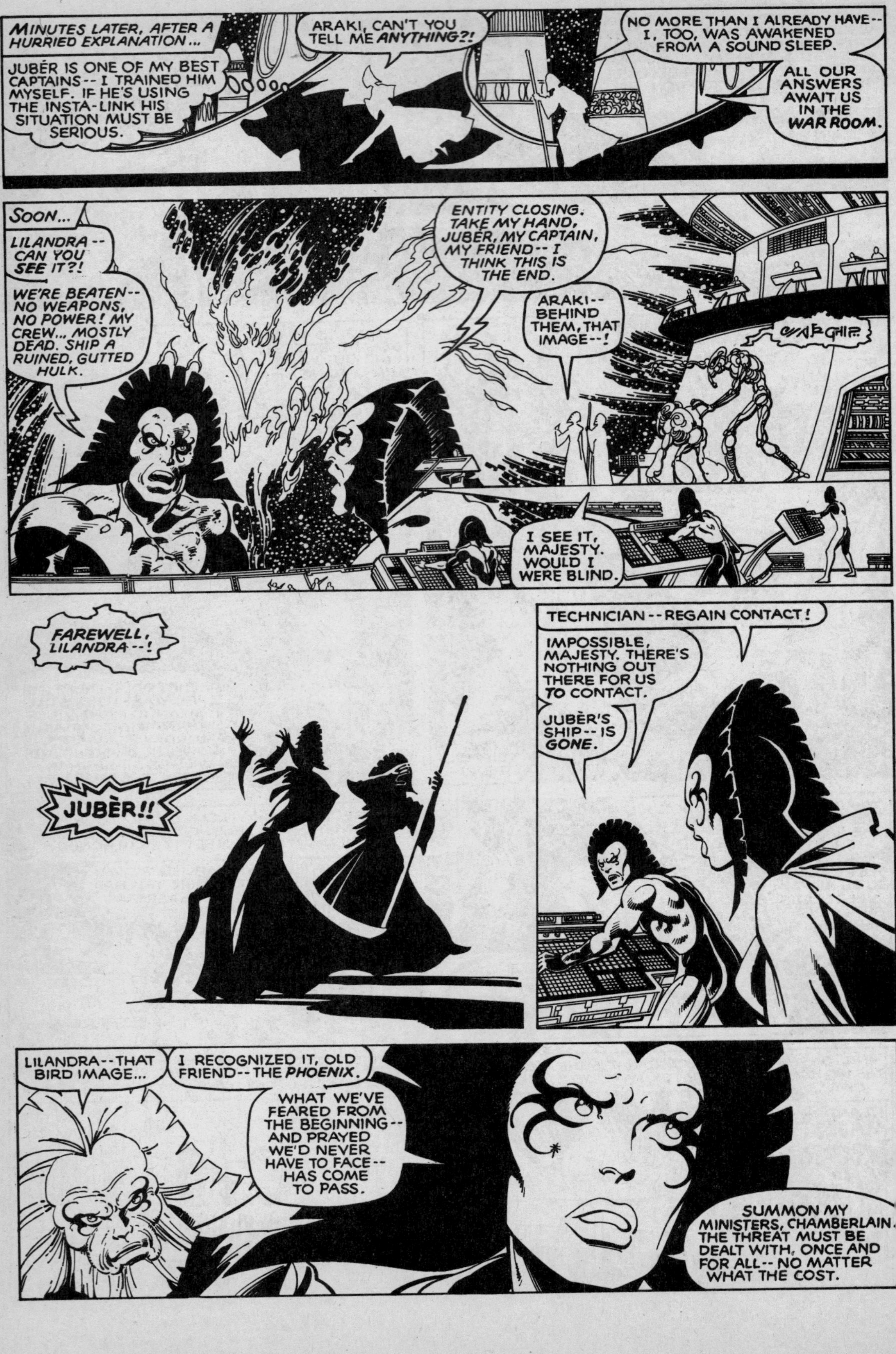
MINUTES LATER, AFTER A HURRIED EXPLANATION...
JUBÈR IS ONE OF MY BEST CAPTAINS-- I TRAINED HIM MYSELF. IF HE'S USING THE INSTA-LINK HIS SITUATION MUST BE SERIOUS.
ARAKI, CAN'T YOU TELL ME ANYTHING?!
NO MORE THAN I ALREADY HAVE-- I, TOO, WAS AWAKENED FROM A SOUND SLEEP.
ALL OUR ANSWERS AWAIT US IN THE WAR ROOM.
SOON...
LILANDRA-- CAN YOU SEE IT?!
WE'RE BEATEN-- NO WEAPONS, NO POWER! MY CREW... MOSTLY DEAD. SHIP A RUINED, GUTTED HULK.
ENTITY CLOSING. TAKE MY HAND, JUBER, MY CAPTAIN, MY FRIEND-- I THINK THIS IS THE END.
ARAKI-- BEHIND THEM, THAT IMAGE--!
I SEE IT, MAJESTY. WOULD I WERE BLIND.
FAREWELL, LILANDRA--!
JUBÈR!!
TECHNICIAN--REGAIN CONTACT!
IMPOSSIBLE, MAJESTY. THERE'S NOTHING OUT THERE FOR US TO CONTACT.
JUBÈR'S SHIP-- IS GONE.
LILANDRA--THAT BIRD IMAGE...
I RECOGNIZED IT, OLD FRIEND--THE PHOENIX.
WHAT WE'VE FEARED FROM THE BEGINNING-- AND PRAYED WE'D NEVER HAVE TO FACE-- HAS COME TO PASS.
SUMMON MY MINISTERS, CHAMBERLAIN. THE THREAT MUST BE DEALT WITH, ONCE AND FOR ALL-- NO MATTER WHAT THE COST.

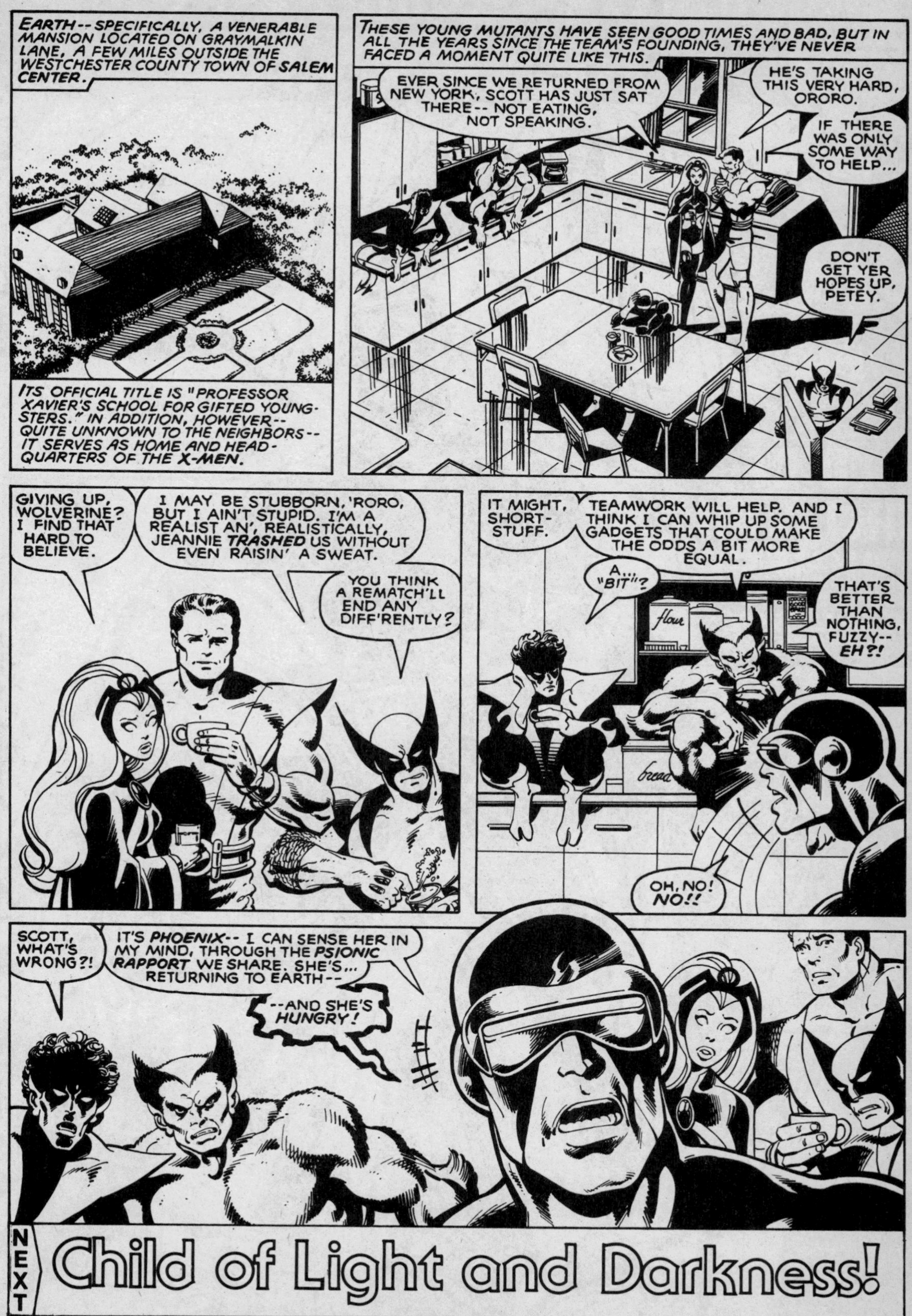
EARTH -- SPECIFICALLY, A VENERABLE MANSION LOCATED ON GRAYMALKIN LANE, A FEW MILES OUTSIDE THE WESTCHESTER COUNTY TOWN OF SALEM CENTER.
ITS OFFICIAL TITLE IS "PROFESSOR XAVIER'S SCHOOL FOR GIFTED YOUNGSTERS." IN ADDITION, HOWEVER -- QUITE UNKNOWN TO THE NEIGHBORS -- IT SERVES AS HOME AND HEADQUARTERS OF THE X-MEN.
THESE YOUNG MUTANTS HAVE SEEN GOOD TIMES AND BAD, BUT IN ALL THE YEARS SINCE THE TEAM'S FOUNDING, THEY'VE NEVER FACED A MOMENT QUITE LIKE THIS.
EVER SINCE WE RETURNED FROM NEW YORK, SCOTT HAS JUST SAT THERE -- NOT EATING, NOT SPEAKING.
HE'S TAKING THIS VERY HARD, ORORO.
IF THERE WAS ONLY SOME WAY TO HELP...
DON'T GET YER HOPES UP, PETEY.
GIVING UP, WOLVERINE? I FIND THAT HARD TO BELIEVE.
I MAY BE STUBBORN, 'RORO, BUT I AIN'T STUPID. I'M A REALIST AN', REALISTICALLY, JEANNIE TRASHED US WITHOUT EVEN RAISIN' A SWEAT.
YOU THINK A REMATCH'LL END ANY DIFF'RENTLY?
IT MIGHT, SHORT-STUFF.
TEAMWORK WILL HELP. AND I THINK I CAN WHIP UP SOME GADGETS THAT COULD MAKE THE ODDS A BIT MORE EQUAL.
A... "BIT"?
THAT'S BETTER THAN NOTHING, FUZZY-- EH?!
flour
bread
OH, NO! NO!!
SCOTT, WHAT'S WRONG?!
IT'S PHOENIX-- I CAN SENSE HER IN MY MIND, THROUGH THE PSIONIC RAPPORT WE SHARE. SHE'S... RETURNING TO EARTH--
--AND SHE'S HUNGRY!
NEXT
Child of Light and Darkness!

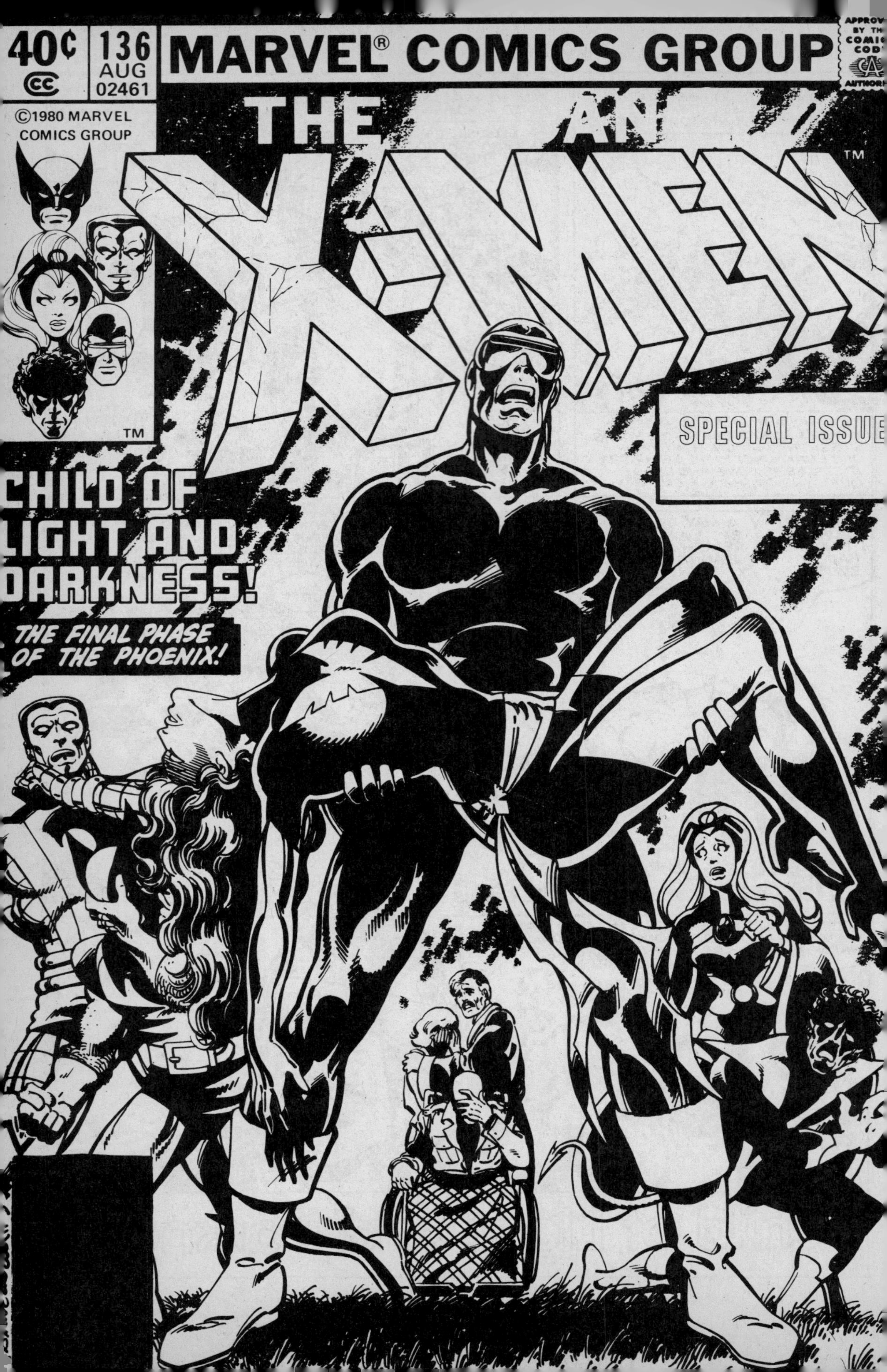

40¢
136
AUG
02461
MARVEL® COMICS GROUP
©1980 MARVEL COMICS GROUP
THE X-MEN
TM
SPECIAL ISSUE
CHILD OF LIGHT AND DARKNESS!
THE FINAL PHASE OF THE PHOENIX!

Cyclops. Storm. Nightcrawler. Wolverine. Colossus. Children of the atom, students of Charles Xavier, MUTANTS — feared and hated by the world they have sworn to protect. These are the STRANGEST heroes of all!

STan Lee PRESENTS: THE UNCANNY X-MEN! ™

child of light and darkness!

CHRIS CLAREMONT · JOHN BYRNE | TERRY AUSTIN | TOM ORZECHOWSKI, *letterer* | JIM SALICRUP | JIM SHOOTER
WRITER · CO-PLOTTERS · PENCILER | INKER | GLYNIS WEIN, *colorist* | EDITOR | EDITOR-IN-CHIEF

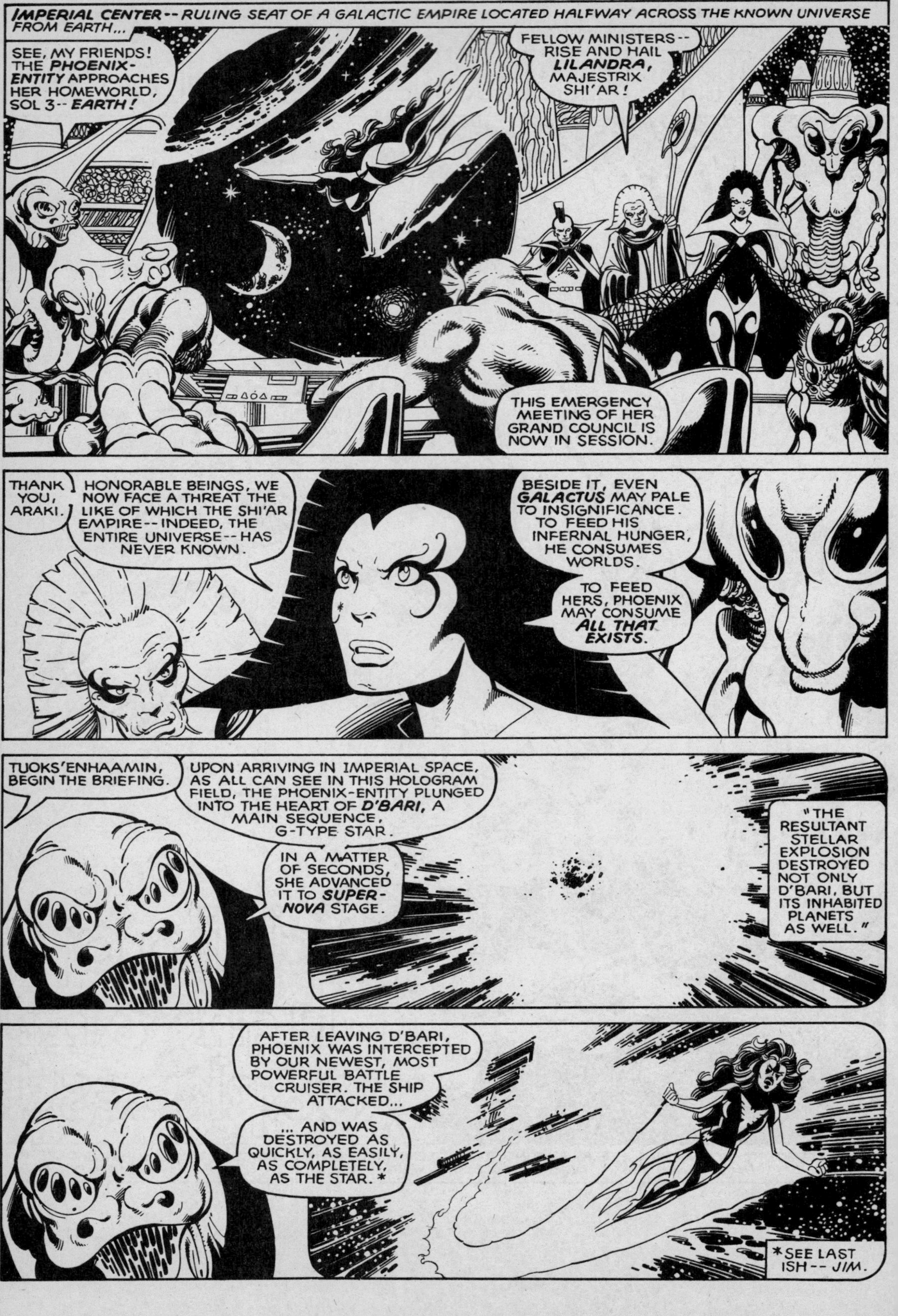
IMPERIAL CENTER -- RULING SEAT OF A GALACTIC EMPIRE LOCATED HALFWAY ACROSS THE KNOWN UNIVERSE FROM EARTH...
SEE, MY FRIENDS! THE PHOENIX-ENTITY APPROACHES HER HOMEWORLD, SOL 3 -- EARTH!
FELLOW MINISTERS -- RISE AND HAIL LILANDRA, MAJESTRIX SHI'AR!
THIS EMERGENCY MEETING OF HER GRAND COUNCIL IS NOW IN SESSION.
THANK YOU, ARAKI.
HONORABLE BEINGS, WE NOW FACE A THREAT THE LIKE OF WHICH THE SHI'AR EMPIRE -- INDEED, THE ENTIRE UNIVERSE -- HAS NEVER KNOWN.
BESIDE IT, EVEN GALACTUS MAY PALE TO INSIGNIFICANCE. TO FEED HIS INFERNAL HUNGER, HE CONSUMES WORLDS.
TO FEED HERS, PHOENIX MAY CONSUME ALL THAT EXISTS.
TUOKS'ENHAAMIN, BEGIN THE BRIEFING.
UPON ARRIVING IN IMPERIAL SPACE, AS ALL CAN SEE IN THIS HOLOGRAM FIELD, THE PHOENIX-ENTITY PLUNGED INTO THE HEART OF D'BARI, A MAIN SEQUENCE, G-TYPE STAR.
IN A MATTER OF SECONDS, SHE ADVANCED IT TO SUPER-NOVA STAGE.
"THE RESULTANT STELLAR EXPLOSION DESTROYED NOT ONLY D'BARI, BUT ITS INHABITED PLANETS AS WELL."
AFTER LEAVING D'BARI, PHOENIX WAS INTERCEPTED BY OUR NEWEST, MOST POWERFUL BATTLE CRUISER. THE SHIP ATTACKED...
... AND WAS DESTROYED AS QUICKLY, AS EASILY, AS COMPLETELY, AS THE STAR. *
*SEE LAST ISH -- JIM.

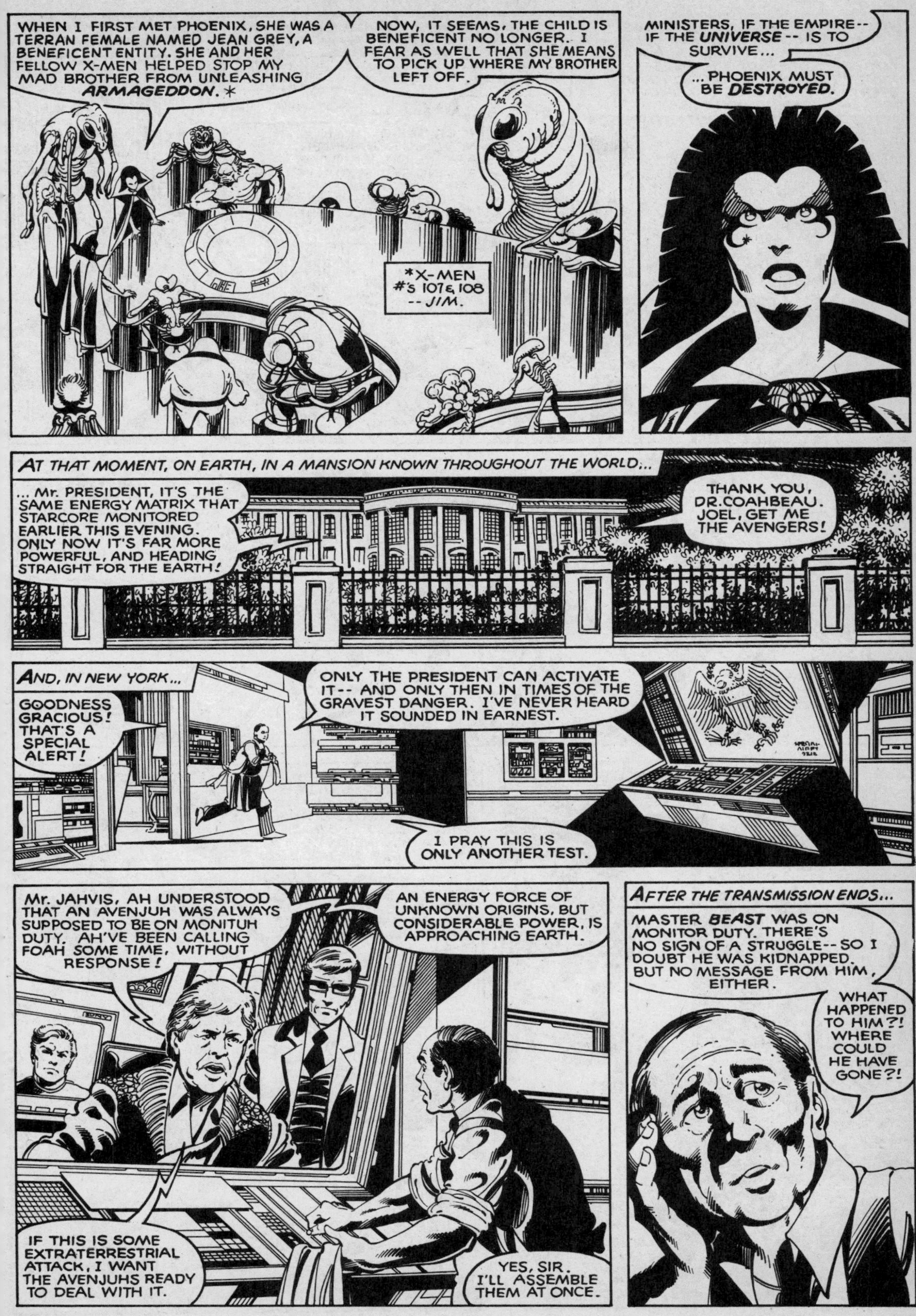

WHEN I FIRST MET PHOENIX, SHE WAS A TERRAN FEMALE NAMED JEAN GREY, A BENEFICENT ENTITY. SHE AND HER FELLOW X-MEN HELPED STOP MY MAD BROTHER FROM UNLEASHING ARMAGEDDON.*
NOW, IT SEEMS, THE CHILD IS BENEFICENT NO LONGER. I FEAR AS WELL THAT SHE MEANS TO PICK UP WHERE MY BROTHER LEFT OFF.
*X-MEN #'S 107 & 108 --JIM.
MINISTERS, IF THE EMPIRE-- IF THE UNIVERSE -- IS TO SURVIVE...
...PHOENIX MUST BE DESTROYED.
AT THAT MOMENT, ON EARTH, IN A MANSION KNOWN THROUGHOUT THE WORLD...
...Mr. PRESIDENT, IT'S THE SAME ENERGY MATRIX THAT STARCORE MONITORED EARLIER THIS EVENING. ONLY NOW IT'S FAR MORE POWERFUL, AND HEADING STRAIGHT FOR THE EARTH!
THANK YOU, DR. COAHBEAU. JOEL, GET ME THE AVENGERS!
AND, IN NEW YORK...
GOODNESS GRACIOUS! THAT'S A SPECIAL ALERT!
ONLY THE PRESIDENT CAN ACTIVATE IT-- AND ONLY THEN IN TIMES OF THE GRAVEST DANGER. I'VE NEVER HEARD IT SOUNDED IN EARNEST.
I PRAY THIS IS ONLY ANOTHER TEST.
Mr. JAHVIS, AH UNDERSTOOD THAT AN AVENJUH WAS ALWAYS SUPPOSED TO BE ON MONITUH DUTY. AH'VE BEEN CALLING FOAH SOME TIME, WITHOUT RESPONSE!
AN ENERGY FORCE OF UNKNOWN ORIGINS, BUT CONSIDERABLE POWER, IS APPROACHING EARTH.
IF THIS IS SOME EXTRATERRESTRIAL ATTACK, I WANT THE AVENJUHS READY TO DEAL WITH IT.
YES, SIR. I'LL ASSEMBLE THEM AT ONCE.
AFTER THE TRANSMISSION ENDS...
MASTER BEAST WAS ON MONITOR DUTY. THERE'S NO SIGN OF A STRUGGLE-- SO I DOUBT HE WAS KIDNAPPED. BUT NO MESSAGE FROM HIM, EITHER.
WHAT HAPPENED TO HIM?! WHERE COULD HE HAVE GONE?!

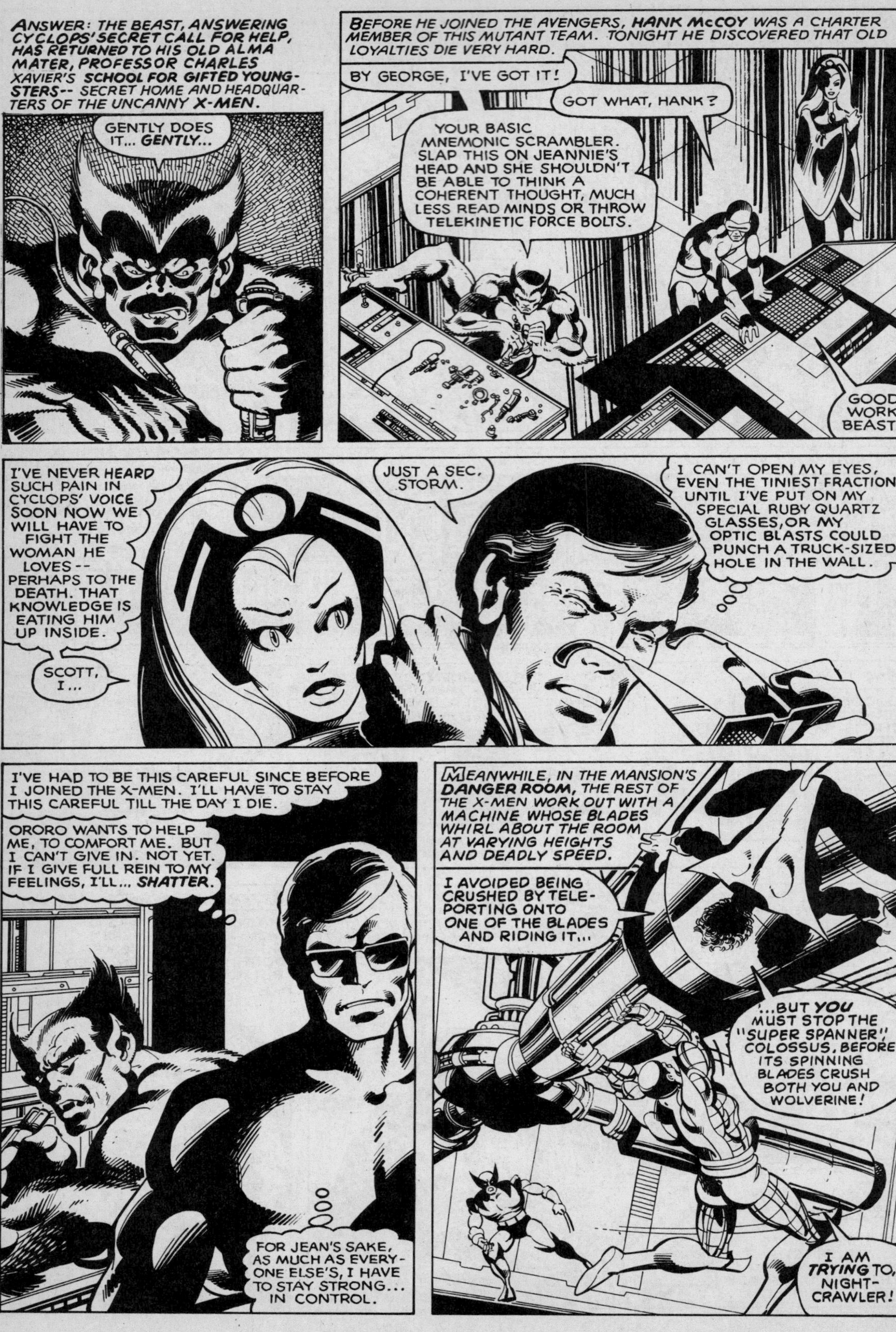
ANSWER: THE BEAST, ANSWERING CYCLOPS' SECRET CALL FOR HELP, HAS RETURNED TO HIS OLD ALMA MATER, PROFESSOR CHARLES XAVIER'S SCHOOL FOR GIFTED YOUNGSTERS-- SECRET HOME AND HEADQUARTERS OF THE UNCANNY X-MEN.
GENTLY DOES IT... GENTLY...
BEFORE HE JOINED THE AVENGERS, HANK McCOY WAS A CHARTER MEMBER OF THIS MUTANT TEAM. TONIGHT HE DISCOVERED THAT OLD LOYALTIES DIE VERY HARD.
BY GEORGE, I'VE GOT IT!
GOT WHAT, HANK?
YOUR BASIC MNEMONIC SCRAMBLER. SLAP THIS ON JEANNIE'S HEAD AND SHE SHOULDN'T BE ABLE TO THINK A COHERENT THOUGHT, MUCH LESS READ MINDS OR THROW TELEKINETIC FORCE BOLTS.
GOOD WORK, BEAST.
I'VE NEVER HEARD SUCH PAIN IN CYCLOPS' VOICE SOON NOW WE WILL HAVE TO FIGHT THE WOMAN HE LOVES -- PERHAPS TO THE DEATH. THAT KNOWLEDGE IS EATING HIM UP INSIDE.
SCOTT, I...
JUST A SEC, STORM.
I CAN'T OPEN MY EYES, EVEN THE TINIEST FRACTION, UNTIL I'VE PUT ON MY SPECIAL RUBY QUARTZ GLASSES, OR MY OPTIC BLASTS COULD PUNCH A TRUCK-SIZED HOLE IN THE WALL.
I'VE HAD TO BE THIS CAREFUL SINCE BEFORE I JOINED THE X-MEN. I'LL HAVE TO STAY THIS CAREFUL TILL THE DAY I DIE.
ORORO WANTS TO HELP ME, TO COMFORT ME. BUT I CAN'T GIVE IN. NOT YET. IF I GIVE FULL REIN TO MY FEELINGS, I'LL... SHATTER.
FOR JEAN'S SAKE, AS MUCH AS EVERY-ONE ELSE'S, I HAVE TO STAY STRONG... IN CONTROL.
MEANWHILE, IN THE MANSION'S DANGER ROOM, THE REST OF THE X-MEN WORK OUT WITH A MACHINE WHOSE BLADES WHIRL ABOUT THE ROOM AT VARYING HEIGHTS AND DEADLY SPEED.
I AVOIDED BEING CRUSHED BY TELE-PORTING ONTO ONE OF THE BLADES AND RIDING IT...
...BUT YOU MUST STOP THE "SUPER SPANNER" COLOSSUS, BEFORE ITS SPINNING BLADES CRUSH BOTH YOU AND WOLVERINE!
I AM TRYING TO, NIGHT-CRAWLER!

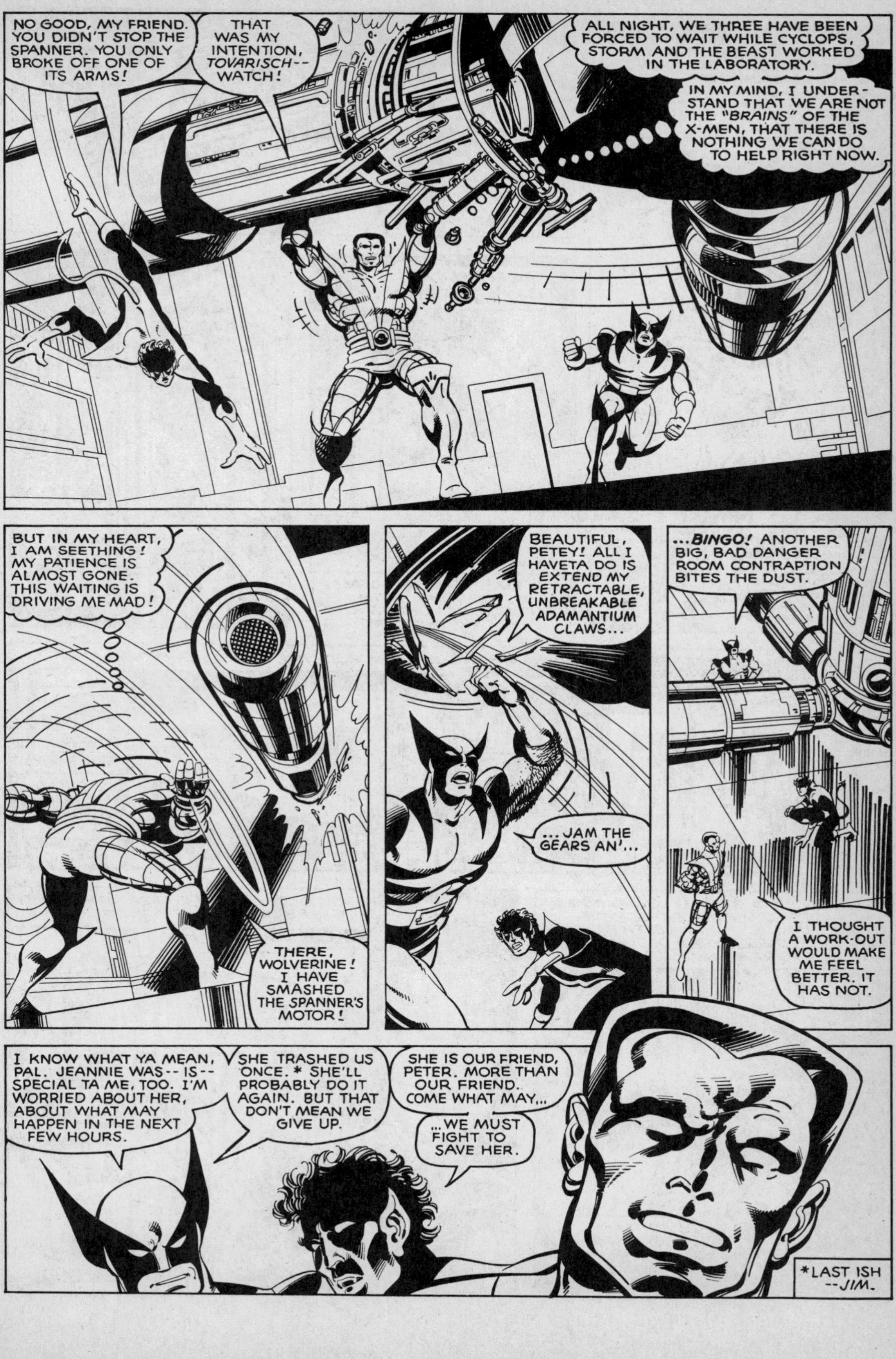
NO GOOD, MY FRIEND. YOU DIDN'T STOP THE SPANNER. YOU ONLY BROKE OFF ONE OF ITS ARMS!
THAT WAS MY INTENTION, *TOVARISCH*-- WATCH!
ALL NIGHT, WE THREE HAVE BEEN FORCED TO WAIT WHILE CYCLOPS, STORM AND THE BEAST WORKED IN THE LABORATORY.
IN MY MIND, I UNDERSTAND THAT WE ARE NOT THE "*BRAINS*" OF THE X-MEN, THAT THERE IS NOTHING WE CAN DO TO HELP RIGHT NOW.
BUT IN MY HEART, I AM SEETHING! MY PATIENCE IS ALMOST GONE. THIS WAITING IS DRIVING ME MAD!
THERE, WOLVERINE! I HAVE SMASHED THE *SPANNER'S* MOTOR!
BEAUTIFUL, PETEY! ALL I HAVETA DO IS EXTEND MY RETRACTABLE, UNBREAKABLE ADAMANTIUM CLAWS...
...JAM THE GEARS AN'...
...*BINGO!* ANOTHER BIG, BAD DANGER ROOM CONTRAPTION BITES THE DUST.
I THOUGHT A WORK-OUT WOULD MAKE ME FEEL BETTER. IT HAS NOT.
I KNOW WHAT YA MEAN, PAL. JEANNIE WAS-- IS-- SPECIAL TA ME, TOO. I'M WORRIED ABOUT HER, ABOUT WHAT MAY HAPPEN IN THE NEXT FEW HOURS.
SHE TRASHED US ONCE.* SHE'LL PROBABLY DO IT AGAIN. BUT THAT DON'T MEAN WE GIVE UP.
SHE IS OUR FRIEND, PETER. MORE THAN OUR FRIEND. COME WHAT MAY...
...WE MUST FIGHT TO SAVE HER.
*LAST ISH --JIM.

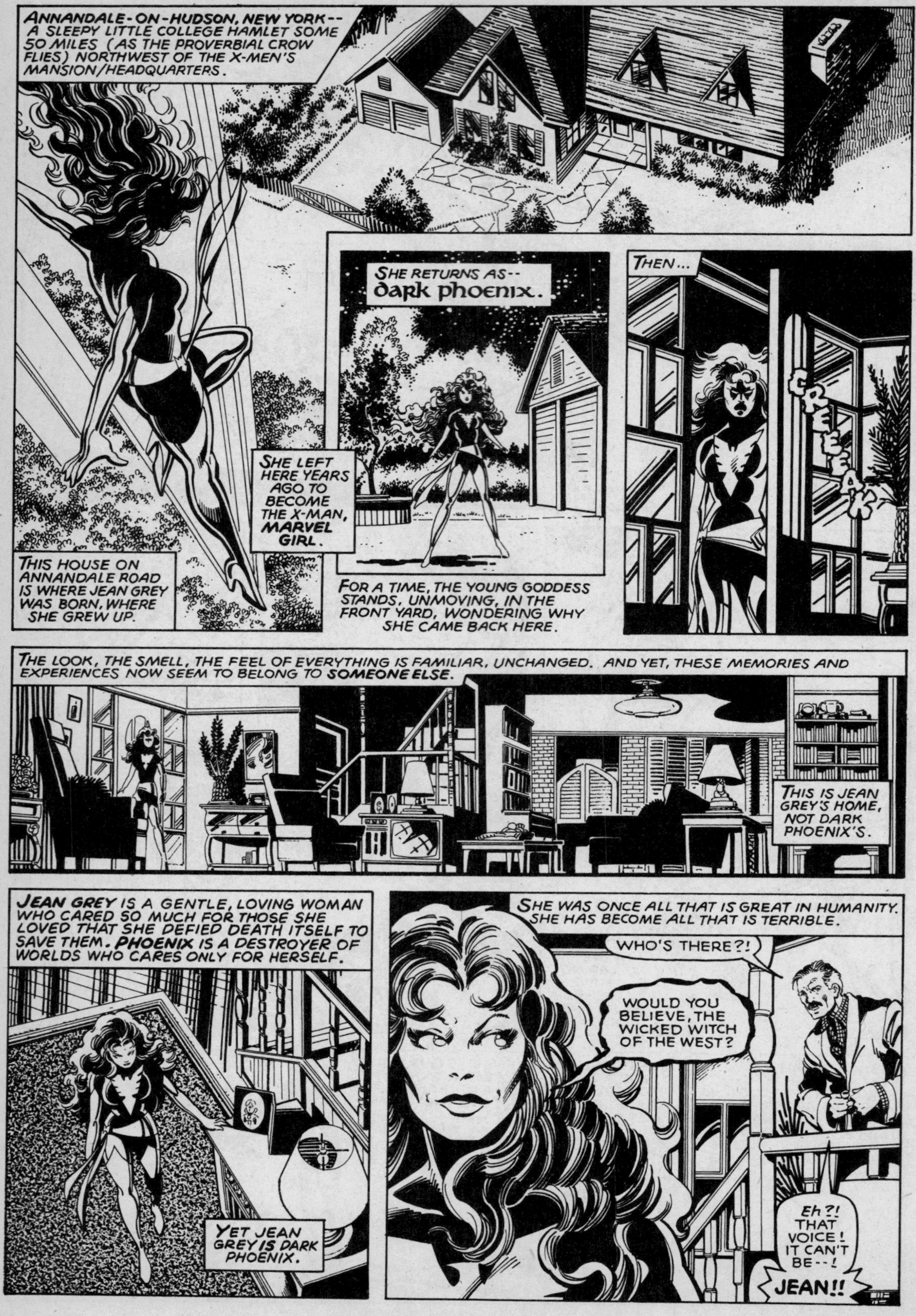
ANNANDALE-ON-HUDSON, NEW YORK-- A SLEEPY LITTLE COLLEGE HAMLET SOME 50 MILES (AS THE PROVERBIAL CROW FLIES) NORTHWEST OF THE X-MEN'S MANSION/HEADQUARTERS.
THIS HOUSE ON ANNANDALE ROAD IS WHERE JEAN GREY WAS BORN, WHERE SHE GREW UP.
SHE LEFT HERE YEARS AGO TO BECOME THE X-MAN, MARVEL GIRL.
SHE RETURNS AS-- dark phoenix.
FOR A TIME, THE YOUNG GODDESS STANDS, UNMOVING, IN THE FRONT YARD, WONDERING WHY SHE CAME BACK HERE.
THEN...
CREEEAK
THE LOOK, THE SMELL, THE FEEL OF EVERYTHING IS FAMILIAR, UNCHANGED. AND YET, THESE MEMORIES AND EXPERIENCES NOW SEEM TO BELONG TO SOMEONE ELSE.
THIS IS JEAN GREY'S HOME, NOT DARK PHOENIX'S.
JEAN GREY IS A GENTLE, LOVING WOMAN WHO CARED SO MUCH FOR THOSE SHE LOVED THAT SHE DEFIED DEATH ITSELF TO SAVE THEM. PHOENIX IS A DESTROYER OF WORLDS WHO CARES ONLY FOR HERSELF.
YET JEAN GREY IS DARK PHOENIX.
SHE WAS ONCE ALL THAT IS GREAT IN HUMANITY. SHE HAS BECOME ALL THAT IS TERRIBLE.
WHO'S THERE?!
WOULD YOU BELIEVE, THE WICKED WITCH OF THE WEST?
Eh?! THAT VOICE! IT CAN'T BE--!
JEAN!!

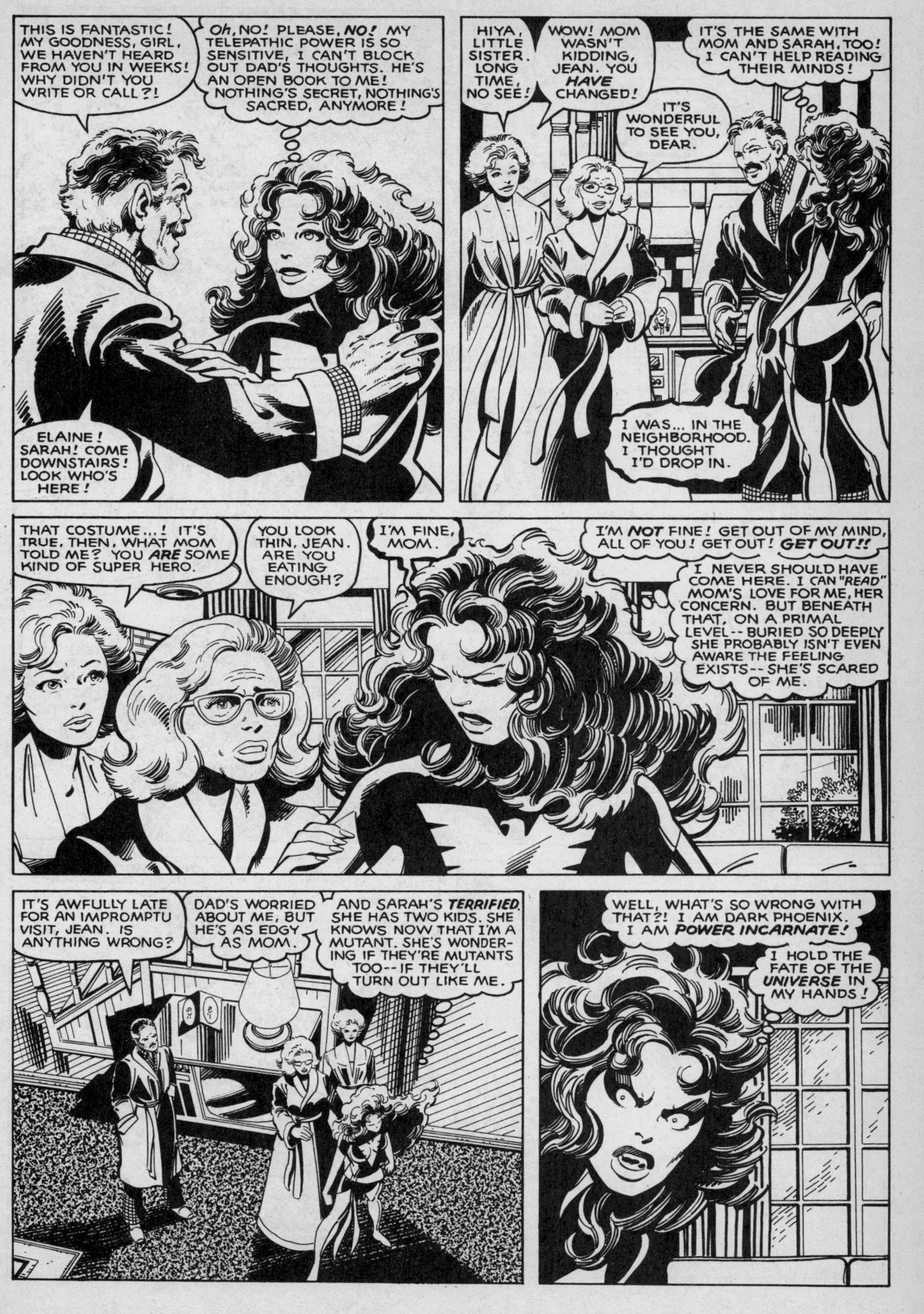
THIS IS FANTASTIC! MY GOODNESS, GIRL, WE HAVEN'T HEARD FROM YOU IN WEEKS! WHY DIDN'T YOU WRITE OR CALL?!
Oh, NO! PLEASE, NO! MY TELEPATHIC POWER IS SO SENSITIVE, I CAN'T BLOCK OUT DAD'S THOUGHTS. HE'S AN OPEN BOOK TO ME! NOTHING'S SECRET, NOTHING'S SACRED, ANYMORE!
ELAINE! SARAH! COME DOWNSTAIRS! LOOK WHO'S HERE!
HIYA, LITTLE SISTER. LONG TIME, NO SEE!
WOW! MOM WASN'T KIDDING, JEAN. YOU HAVE CHANGED!
IT'S THE SAME WITH MOM AND SARAH, TOO! I CAN'T HELP READING THEIR MINDS!
IT'S WONDERFUL TO SEE YOU, DEAR.
I WAS... IN THE NEIGHBORHOOD. I THOUGHT I'D DROP IN.
THAT COSTUME...! IT'S TRUE, THEN, WHAT MOM TOLD ME? YOU ARE SOME KIND OF SUPER HERO.
YOU LOOK THIN, JEAN. ARE YOU EATING ENOUGH?
I'M FINE, MOM.
I'M NOT FINE! GET OUT OF MY MIND, ALL OF YOU! GET OUT! GET OUT!!
I NEVER SHOULD HAVE COME HERE. I CAN "READ" MOM'S LOVE FOR ME, HER CONCERN. BUT BENEATH THAT, ON A PRIMAL LEVEL -- BURIED SO DEEPLY SHE PROBABLY ISN'T EVEN AWARE THE FEELING EXISTS -- SHE'S SCARED OF ME.
IT'S AWFULLY LATE FOR AN IMPROMPTU VISIT, JEAN. IS ANYTHING WRONG?
DAD'S WORRIED ABOUT ME, BUT HE'S AS EDGY AS MOM.
AND SARAH'S TERRIFIED. SHE HAS TWO KIDS. SHE KNOWS NOW THAT I'M A MUTANT. SHE'S WONDERING IF THEY'RE MUTANTS TOO -- IF THEY'LL TURN OUT LIKE ME.
WELL, WHAT'S SO WRONG WITH THAT?! I AM DARK PHOENIX. I AM POWER INCARNATE!
I HOLD THE FATE OF THE UNIVERSE IN MY HANDS!
7

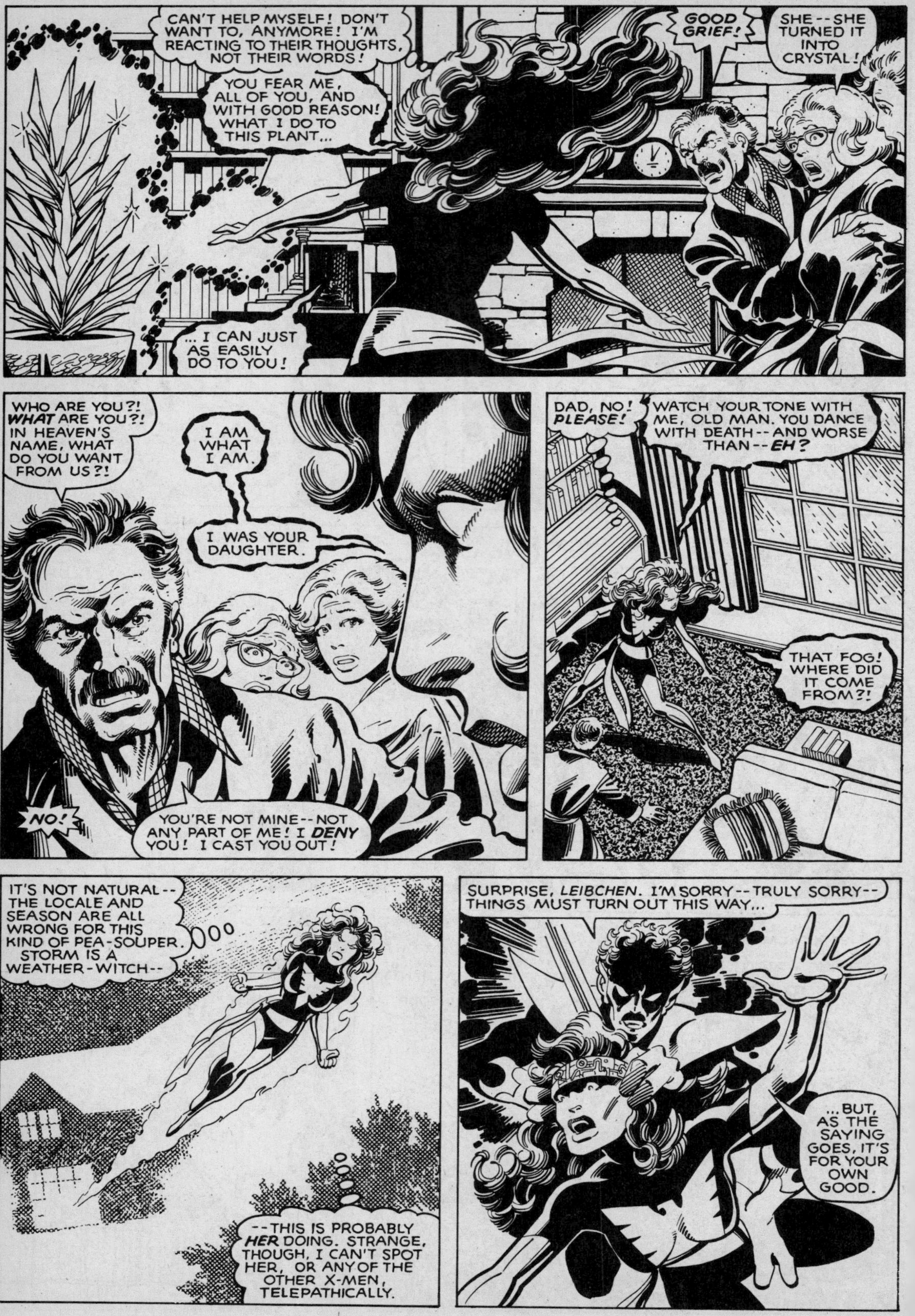
CAN'T HELP MYSELF! DON'T WANT TO, ANYMORE! I'M REACTING TO THEIR THOUGHTS, NOT THEIR WORDS!
YOU FEAR ME, ALL OF YOU, AND WITH GOOD REASON! WHAT I DO TO THIS PLANT...
...I CAN JUST AS EASILY DO TO YOU!
GOOD GRIEF!
SHE--SHE TURNED IT INTO CRYSTAL!
WHO ARE YOU?! WHAT ARE YOU?! IN HEAVEN'S NAME, WHAT DO YOU WANT FROM US?!
I AM WHAT I AM.
I WAS YOUR DAUGHTER.
NO!
YOU'RE NOT MINE--NOT ANY PART OF ME! I DENY YOU! I CAST YOU OUT!
DAD, NO! PLEASE!
WATCH YOUR TONE WITH ME, OLD MAN. YOU DANCE WITH DEATH--AND WORSE THAN--EH?
THAT FOG! WHERE DID IT COME FROM?!
IT'S NOT NATURAL-- THE LOCALE AND SEASON ARE ALL WRONG FOR THIS KIND OF PEA-SOUPER. STORM IS A WEATHER-WITCH--
--THIS IS PROBABLY HER DOING. STRANGE, THOUGH, I CAN'T SPOT HER, OR ANY OF THE OTHER X-MEN, TELEPATHICALLY.
SURPRISE, LEIBCHEN. I'M SORRY--TRULY SORRY-- THINGS MUST TURN OUT THIS WAY...
...BUT, AS THE SAYING GOES, IT'S FOR YOUR OWN GOOD.

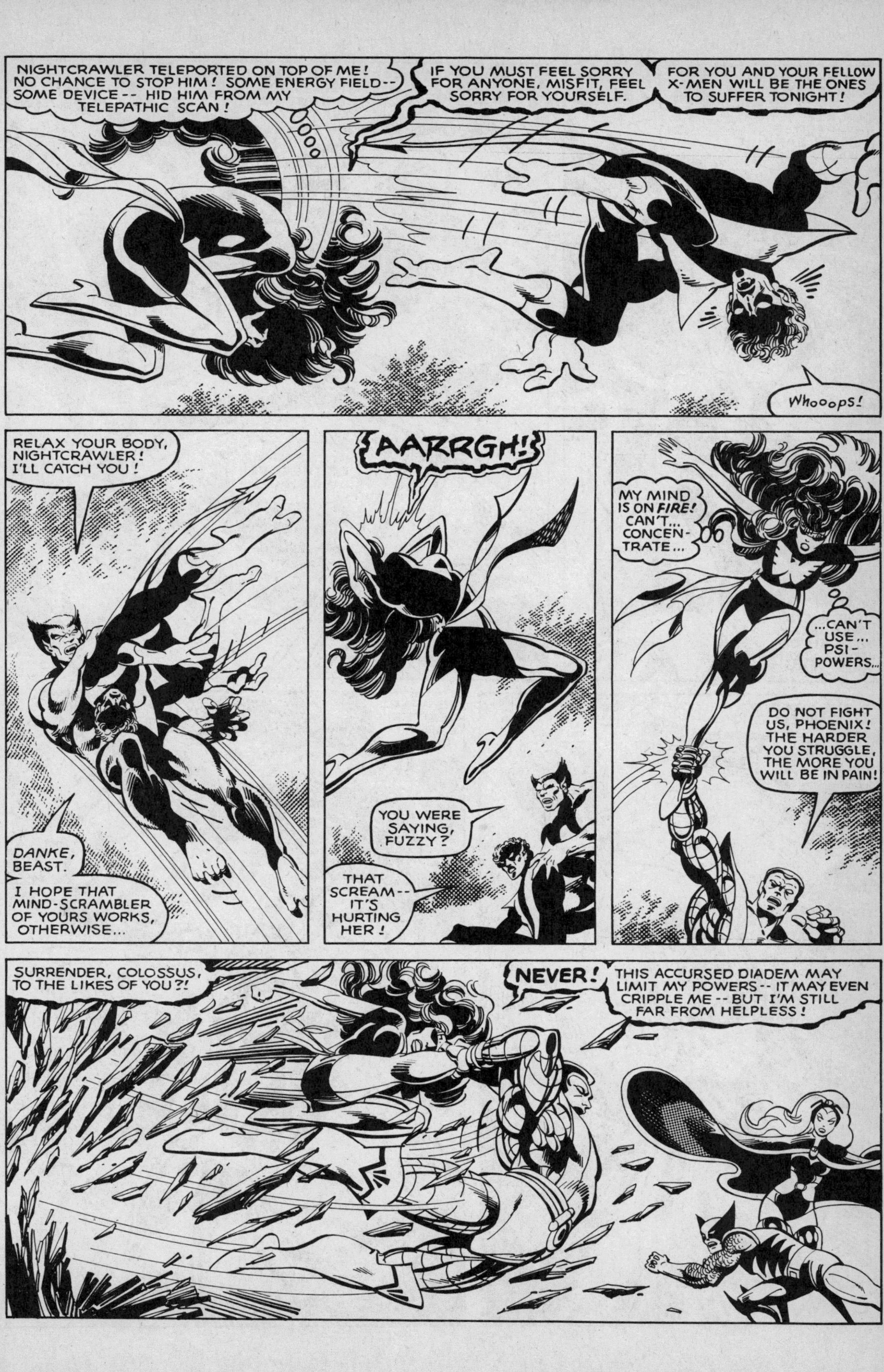

NIGHTCRAWLER TELEPORTED ON TOP OF ME! NO CHANCE TO STOP HIM! SOME ENERGY FIELD-- SOME DEVICE -- HID HIM FROM MY TELEPATHIC SCAN!
IF YOU MUST FEEL SORRY FOR ANYONE, MISFIT, FEEL SORRY FOR YOURSELF.
FOR YOU AND YOUR FELLOW X-MEN WILL BE THE ONES TO SUFFER TONIGHT!
Whoooops!
RELAX YOUR BODY, NIGHTCRAWLER! I'LL CATCH YOU!
DANKE, BEAST.
I HOPE THAT MIND-SCRAMBLER OF YOURS WORKS, OTHERWISE...
AARRGH!
YOU WERE SAYING, FUZZY?
THAT SCREAM-- IT'S HURTING HER!
MY MIND IS ON FIRE! CAN'T... CONCEN-TRATE...
...CAN'T USE... PSI-POWERS...
DO NOT FIGHT US, PHOENIX! THE HARDER YOU STRUGGLE, THE MORE YOU WILL BE IN PAIN!
SURRENDER, COLOSSUS, TO THE LIKES OF YOU?!
NEVER!
THIS ACCURSED DIADEM MAY LIMIT MY POWERS -- IT MAY EVEN CRIPPLE ME -- BUT I'M STILL FAR FROM HELPLESS!

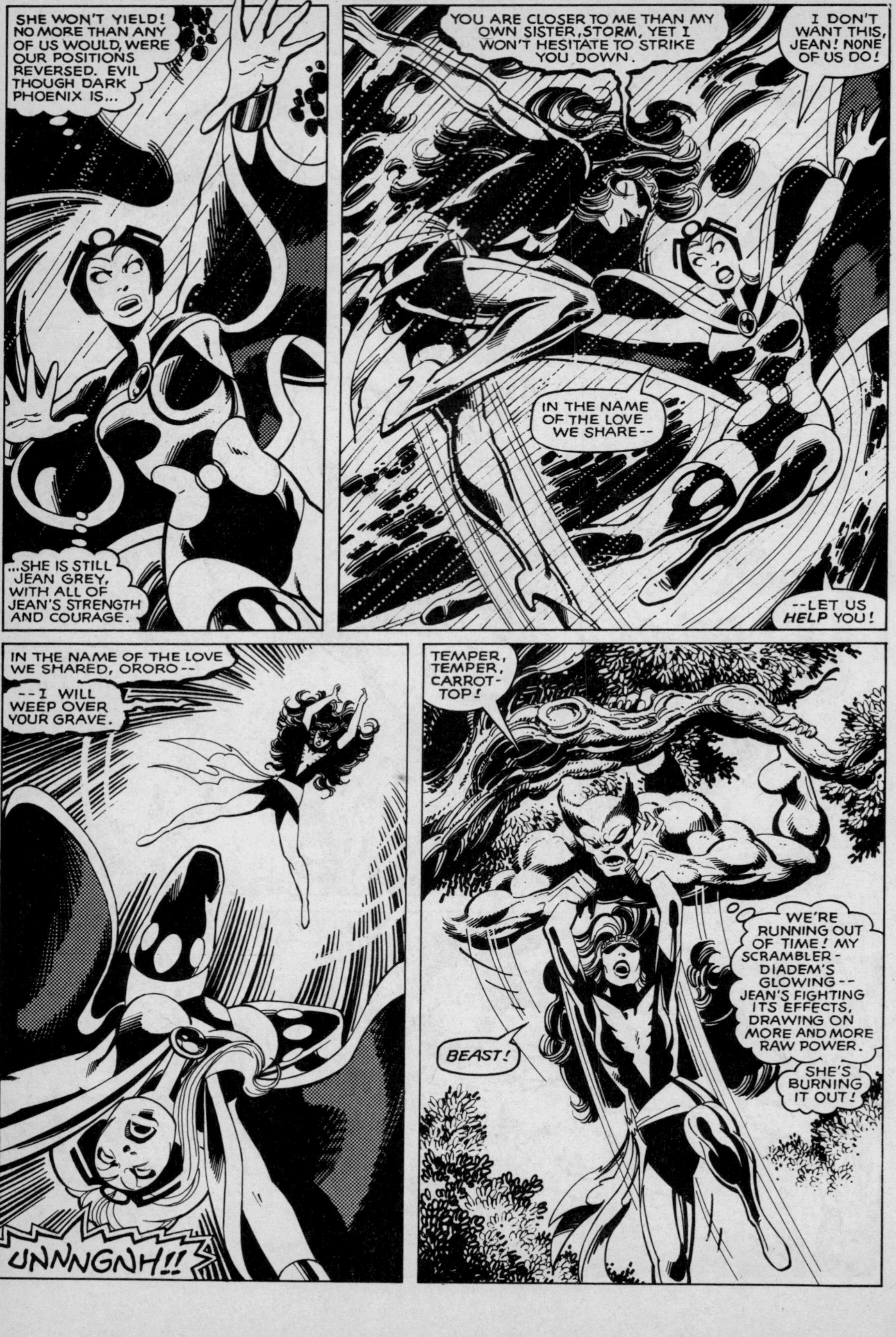
SHE WON'T YIELD! NO MORE THAN ANY OF US WOULD, WERE OUR POSITIONS REVERSED. EVIL THOUGH DARK PHOENIX IS...
...SHE IS STILL JEAN GREY, WITH ALL OF JEAN'S STRENGTH AND COURAGE.
YOU ARE CLOSER TO ME THAN MY OWN SISTER, STORM, YET I WON'T HESITATE TO STRIKE YOU DOWN.
I DON'T WANT THIS, JEAN! NONE OF US DO!
IN THE NAME OF THE LOVE WE SHARE--
--LET US HELP YOU!
IN THE NAME OF THE LOVE WE SHARED, ORORO--
--I WILL WEEP OVER YOUR GRAVE.
UNNNGNH!!
TEMPER, TEMPER, CARROT-TOP!
WE'RE RUNNING OUT OF TIME! MY SCRAMBLER-DIADEM'S GLOWING--JEAN'S FIGHTING ITS EFFECTS, DRAWING ON MORE AND MORE RAW POWER.
SHE'S BURNING IT OUT!
BEAST!

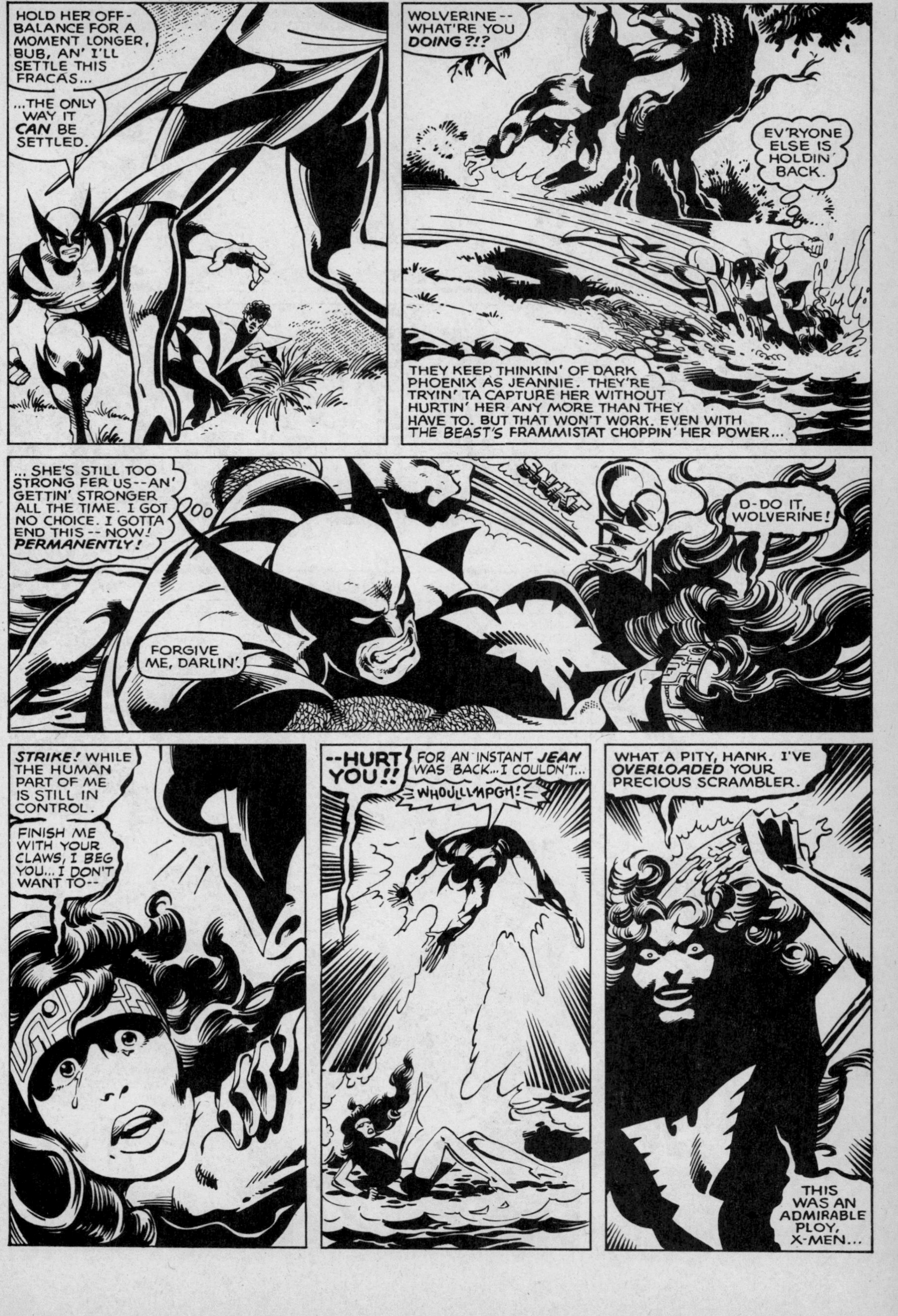
HOLD HER OFF-BALANCE FOR A MOMENT LONGER, BUB, AN' I'LL SETTLE THIS FRACAS...
...THE ONLY WAY IT CAN BE SETTLED.
WOLVERINE -- WHAT'RE YOU DOING?!?
EV'RYONE ELSE IS HOLDIN' BACK.
THEY KEEP THINKIN' OF DARK PHOENIX AS JEANNIE. THEY'RE TRYIN' TA CAPTURE HER WITHOUT HURTIN' HER ANY MORE THAN THEY HAVE TO. BUT THAT WON'T WORK. EVEN WITH THE BEAST'S FRAMMISTAT CHOPPIN' HER POWER...
... SHE'S STILL TOO STRONG FER US--AN' GETTIN' STRONGER ALL THE TIME. I GOT NO CHOICE. I GOTTA END THIS -- NOW! PERMANENTLY!
SNIKT
D-DO IT, WOLVERINE!
FORGIVE ME, DARLIN'.
STRIKE! WHILE THE HUMAN PART OF ME IS STILL IN CONTROL.
FINISH ME WITH YOUR CLAWS, I BEG YOU... I DON'T WANT TO--
--HURT YOU!!
FOR AN INSTANT JEAN WAS BACK... I COULDN'T...
WHOULLLMPGH!
WHAT A PITY, HANK. I'VE OVERLOADED YOUR PRECIOUS SCRAMBLER.
THIS WAS AN ADMIRABLE PLOY, X-MEN...

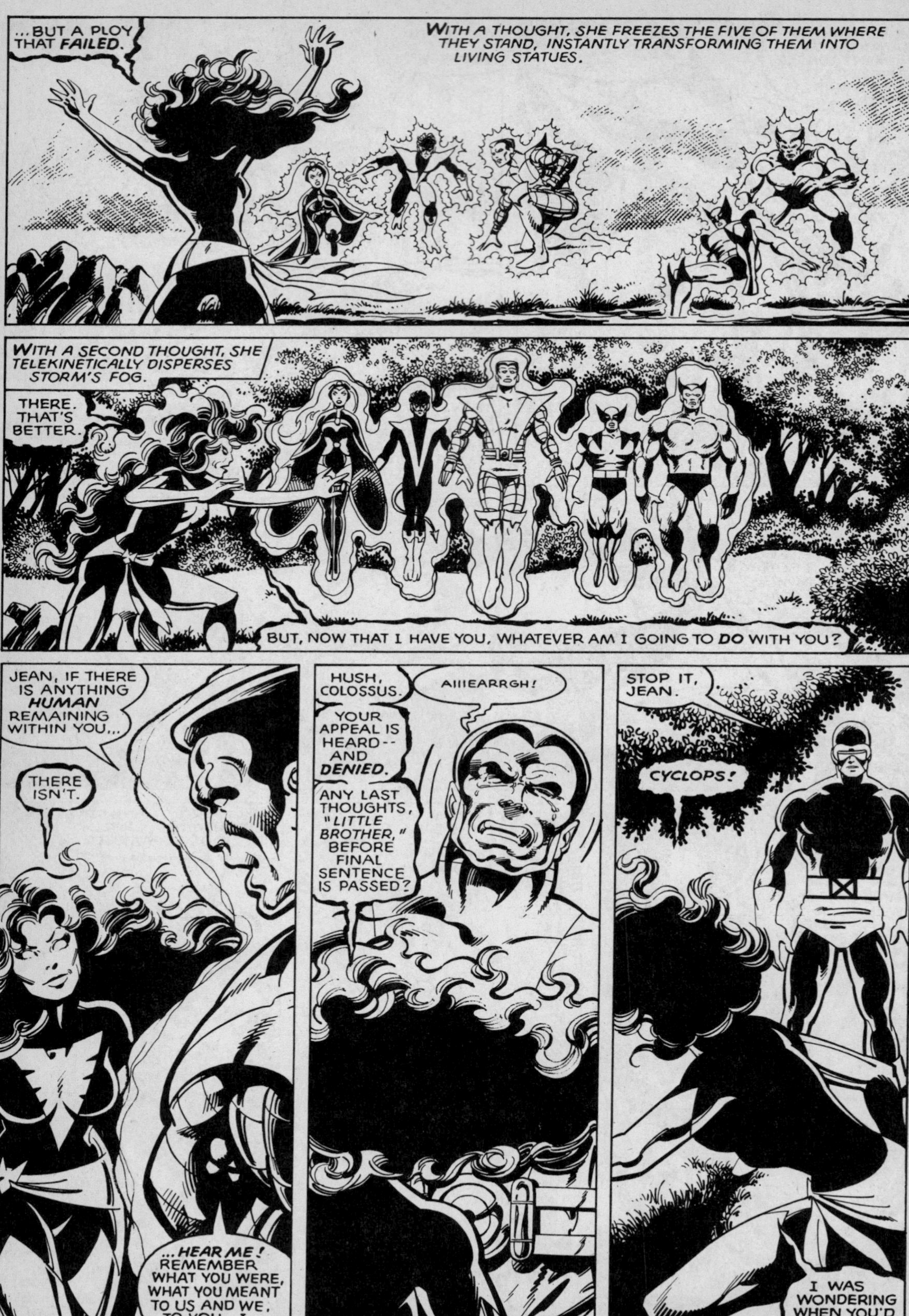
...BUT A PLOY THAT FAILED.
WITH A THOUGHT, SHE FREEZES THE FIVE OF THEM WHERE THEY STAND, INSTANTLY TRANSFORMING THEM INTO LIVING STATUES.
WITH A SECOND THOUGHT, SHE TELEKINETICALLY DISPERSES STORM'S FOG.
THERE. THAT'S BETTER.
BUT, NOW THAT I HAVE YOU, WHATEVER AM I GOING TO DO WITH YOU?
JEAN, IF THERE IS ANYTHING HUMAN REMAINING WITHIN YOU...
THERE ISN'T.
...HEAR ME! REMEMBER WHAT YOU WERE, WHAT YOU MEANT TO US AND WE, TO YOU. I...
HUSH, COLOSSUS.
AIIIEARRGH!
YOUR APPEAL IS HEARD-- AND DENIED.
ANY LAST THOUGHTS, "LITTLE BROTHER," BEFORE FINAL SENTENCE IS PASSED?
STOP IT, JEAN.
CYCLOPS!
I WAS WONDERING WHEN YOU'D TURN UP.

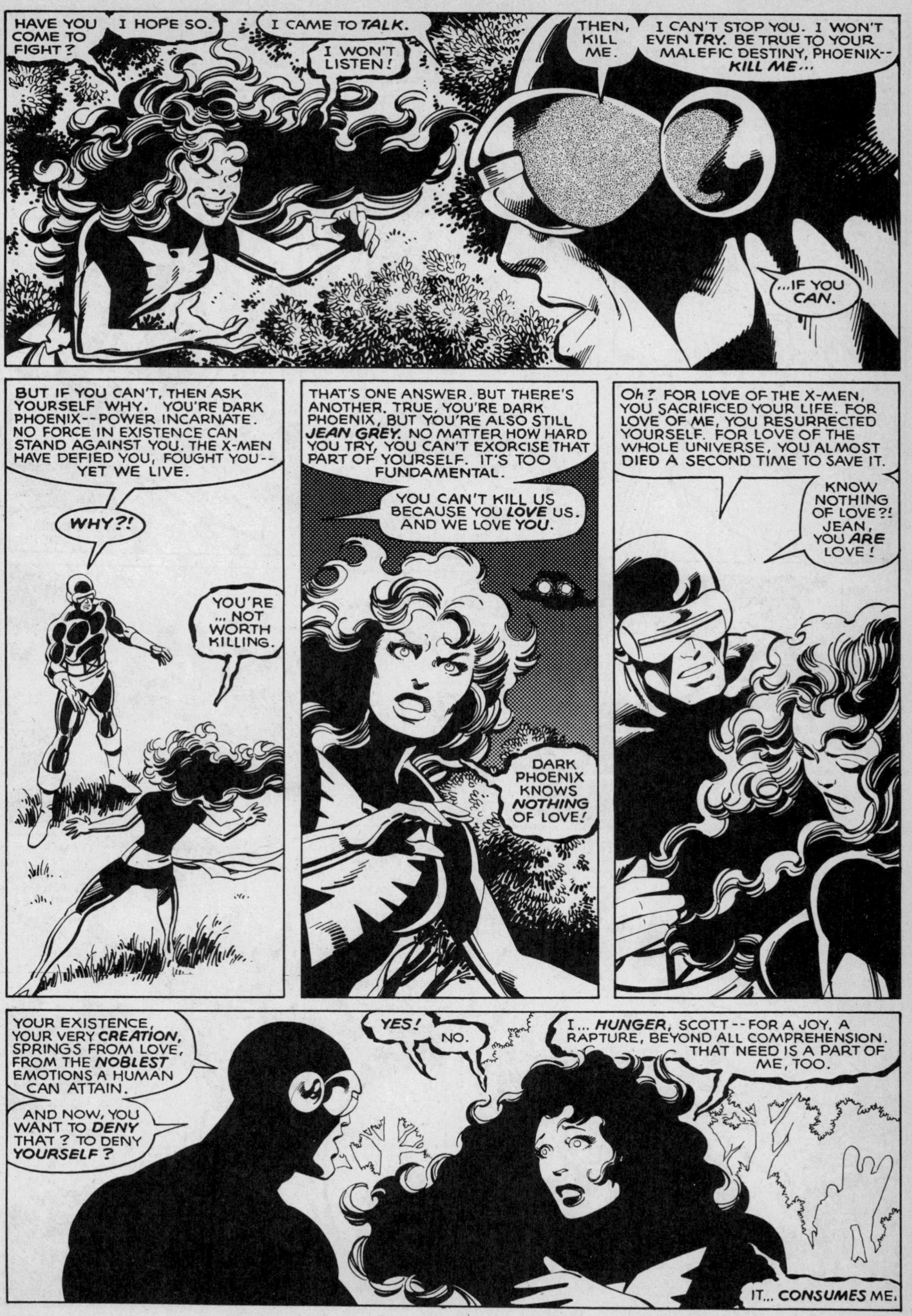
HAVE YOU COME TO FIGHT?
I HOPE SO.
I CAME TO TALK.
I WON'T LISTEN!
THEN, KILL ME.
I CAN'T STOP YOU. I WON'T EVEN TRY. BE TRUE TO YOUR MALEFIC DESTINY, PHOENIX-- KILL ME...
...IF YOU CAN.
BUT IF YOU CAN'T, THEN ASK YOURSELF WHY. YOU'RE DARK PHOENIX--POWER INCARNATE. NO FORCE IN EXISTENCE CAN STAND AGAINST YOU. THE X-MEN HAVE DEFIED YOU, FOUGHT YOU-- YET WE LIVE.
WHY?!
YOU'RE ... NOT WORTH KILLING.
THAT'S ONE ANSWER. BUT THERE'S ANOTHER. TRUE, YOU'RE DARK PHOENIX, BUT YOU'RE ALSO STILL JEAN GREY. NO MATTER HOW HARD YOU TRY, YOU CAN'T EXORCISE THAT PART OF YOURSELF. IT'S TOO FUNDAMENTAL.
YOU CAN'T KILL US BECAUSE YOU LOVE US. AND WE LOVE YOU.
DARK PHOENIX KNOWS NOTHING OF LOVE!
Oh? FOR LOVE OF THE X-MEN, YOU SACRIFICED YOUR LIFE. FOR LOVE OF ME, YOU RESURRECTED YOURSELF. FOR LOVE OF THE WHOLE UNIVERSE, YOU ALMOST DIED A SECOND TIME TO SAVE IT.
KNOW NOTHING OF LOVE?! JEAN, YOU ARE LOVE!
YOUR EXISTENCE, YOUR VERY CREATION, SPRINGS FROM LOVE, FROM THE NOBLEST EMOTIONS A HUMAN CAN ATTAIN.
AND NOW, YOU WANT TO DENY THAT? TO DENY YOURSELF?
YES!
NO.
I... HUNGER, SCOTT--FOR A JOY, A RAPTURE, BEYOND ALL COMPREHENSION. THAT NEED IS A PART OF ME, TOO.
IT... CONSUMES ME.

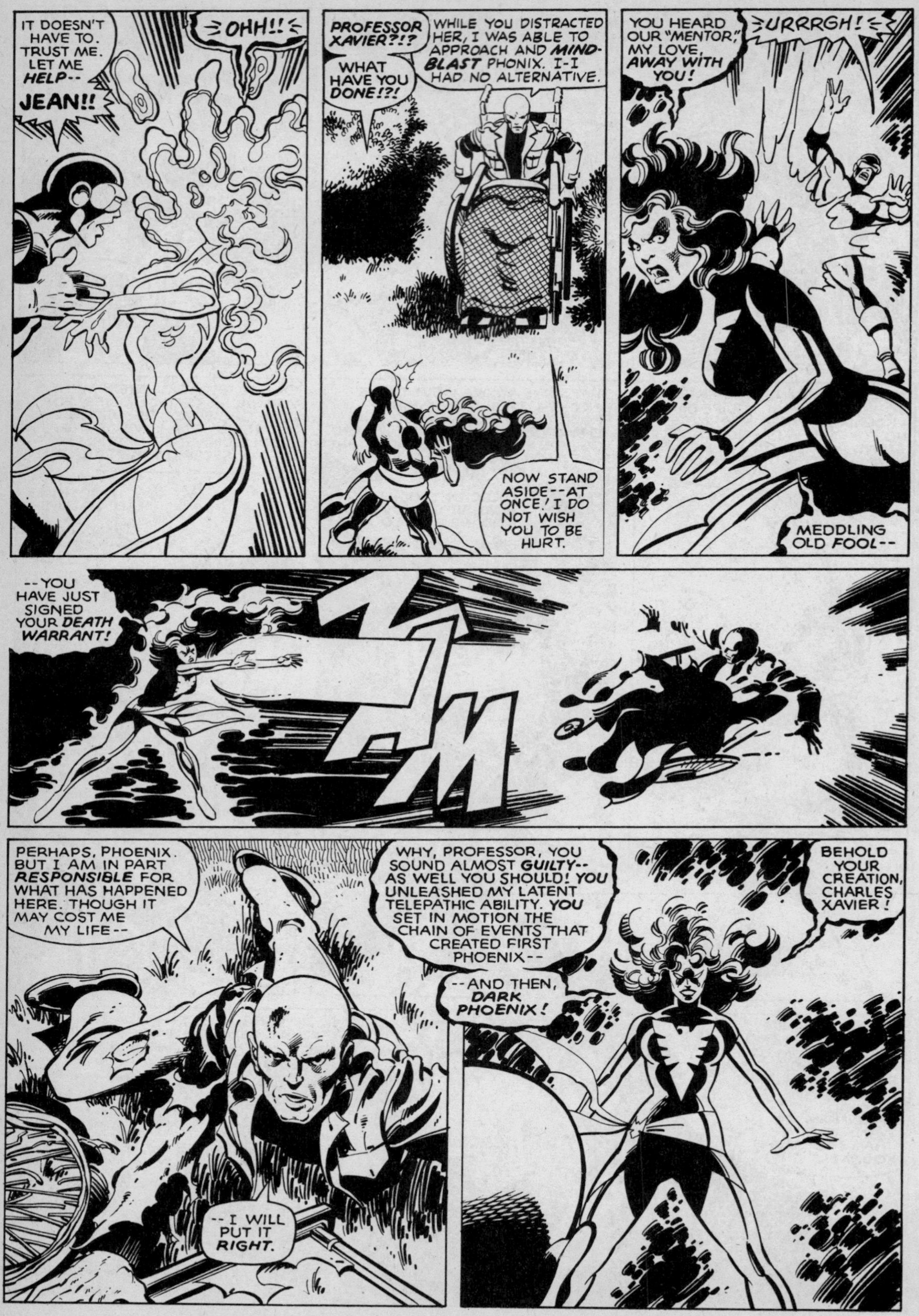
IT DOESN'T HAVE TO. TRUST ME. LET ME HELP--
JEAN!!
OHH!!
PROFESSOR XAVIER?!?
WHAT HAVE YOU DONE!?!
WHILE YOU DISTRACTED HER, I WAS ABLE TO APPROACH AND MIND-BLAST PHONIX. I-I HAD NO ALTERNATIVE.
NOW STAND ASIDE--AT ONCE! I DO NOT WISH YOU TO BE HURT.
YOU HEARD OUR "MENTOR," MY LOVE. AWAY WITH YOU!
URRRGH!
MEDDLING OLD FOOL--
--YOU HAVE JUST SIGNED YOUR DEATH WARRANT!
ZZM
PERHAPS, PHOENIX. BUT I AM IN PART RESPONSIBLE FOR WHAT HAS HAPPENED HERE. THOUGH IT MAY COST ME MY LIFE--
--I WILL PUT IT RIGHT.
WHY, PROFESSOR, YOU SOUND ALMOST GUILTY--AS WELL YOU SHOULD! YOU UNLEASHED MY LATENT TELEPATHIC ABILITY. YOU SET IN MOTION THE CHAIN OF EVENTS THAT CREATED FIRST PHOENIX--
--AND THEN, DARK PHOENIX!
BEHOLD YOUR CREATION, CHARLES XAVIER!

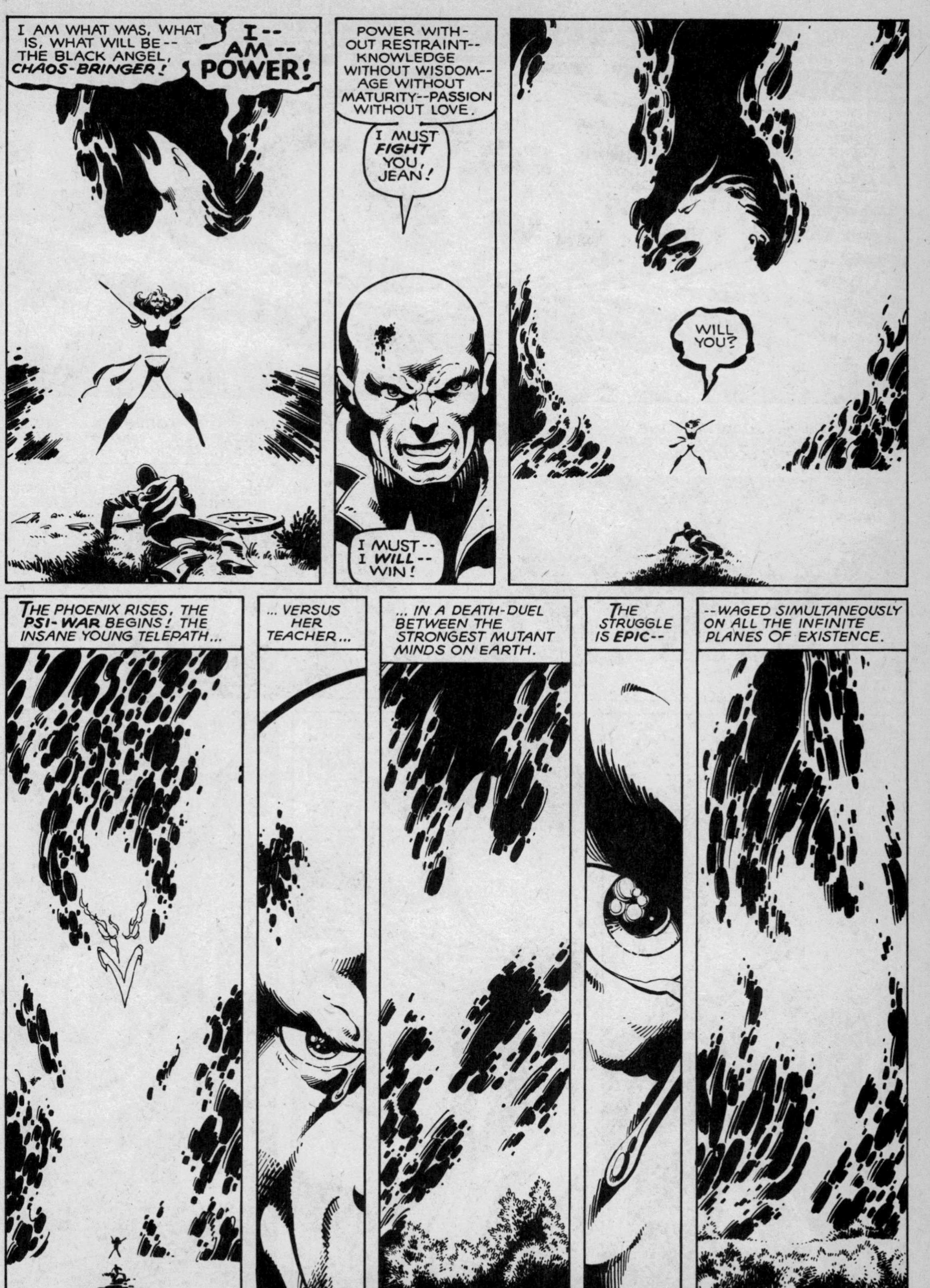
I AM WHAT WAS, WHAT IS, WHAT WILL BE-- THE BLACK ANGEL, CHAOS-BRINGER!
I-- AM-- POWER!
POWER WITHOUT RESTRAINT-- KNOWLEDGE WITHOUT WISDOM-- AGE WITHOUT MATURITY--PASSION WITHOUT LOVE.
I MUST FIGHT YOU, JEAN!
I MUST-- I WILL-- WIN!
WILL YOU?
THE PHOENIX RISES. THE PSI-WAR BEGINS! THE INSANE YOUNG TELEPATH...
... VERSUS HER TEACHER...
... IN A DEATH-DUEL BETWEEN THE STRONGEST MUTANT MINDS ON EARTH.
THE STRUGGLE IS EPIC--
--WAGED SIMULTANEOUSLY ON ALL THE INFINITE PLANES OF EXISTENCE.

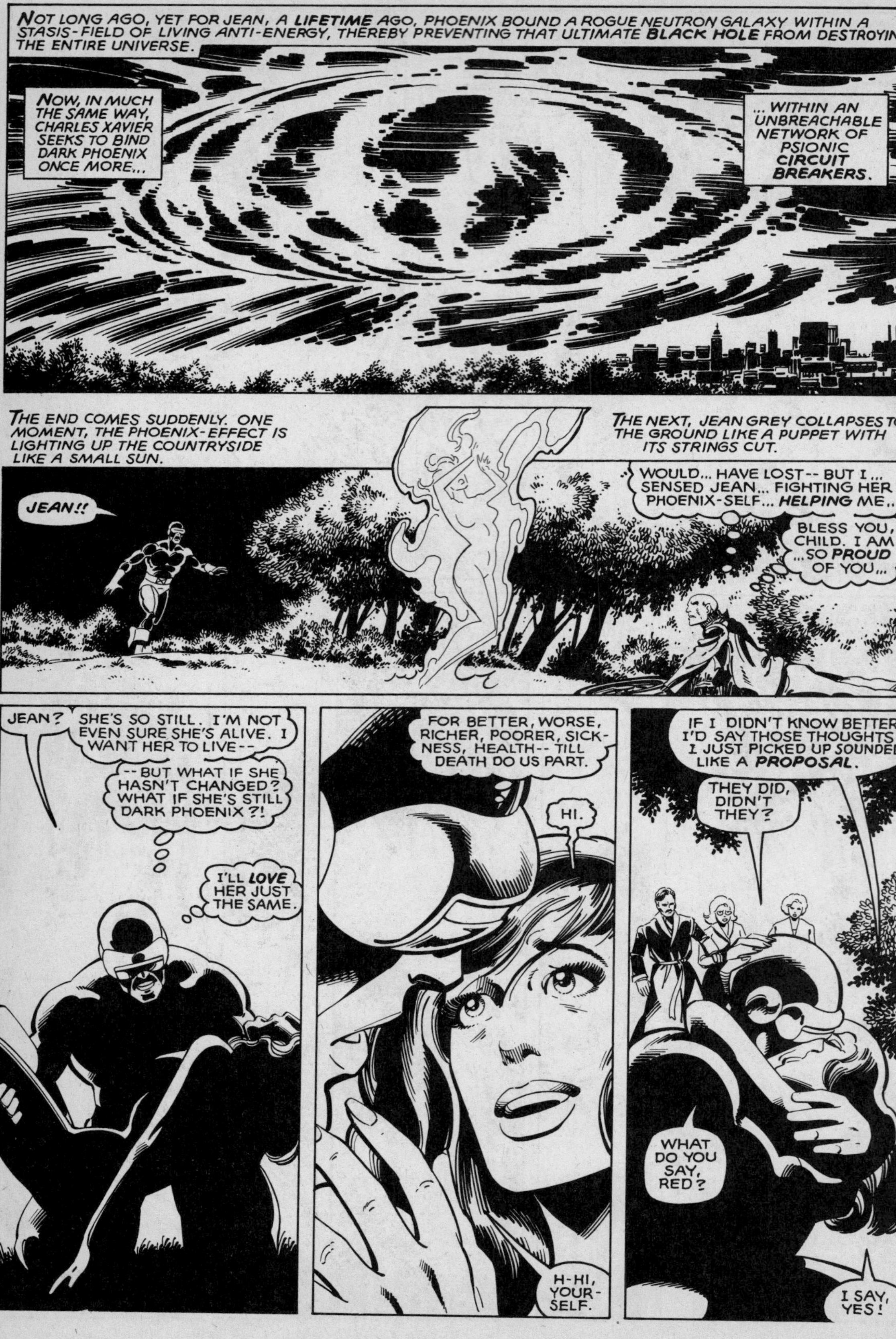
NOT LONG AGO, YET FOR JEAN, A LIFETIME AGO, PHOENIX BOUND A ROGUE NEUTRON GALAXY WITHIN A STASIS-FIELD OF LIVING ANTI-ENERGY, THEREBY PREVENTING THAT ULTIMATE BLACK HOLE FROM DESTROYING THE ENTIRE UNIVERSE.
NOW, IN MUCH THE SAME WAY, CHARLES XAVIER SEEKS TO BIND DARK PHOENIX ONCE MORE...
...WITHIN AN UNBREACHABLE NETWORK OF PSIONIC CIRCUIT BREAKERS.
THE END COMES SUDDENLY. ONE MOMENT, THE PHOENIX-EFFECT IS LIGHTING UP THE COUNTRYSIDE LIKE A SMALL SUN.
THE NEXT, JEAN GREY COLLAPSES TO THE GROUND LIKE A PUPPET WITH ITS STRINGS CUT.
JEAN!!
...WOULD... HAVE LOST-- BUT I... SENSED JEAN... FIGHTING HER PHOENIX-SELF... HELPING ME...
BLESS YOU, CHILD. I AM ...SO PROUD OF YOU...
JEAN?
SHE'S SO STILL. I'M NOT EVEN SURE SHE'S ALIVE. I WANT HER TO LIVE--
--BUT WHAT IF SHE HASN'T CHANGED? WHAT IF SHE'S STILL DARK PHOENIX?!
I'LL LOVE HER JUST THE SAME.
FOR BETTER, WORSE, RICHER, POORER, SICKNESS, HEALTH-- TILL DEATH DO US PART.
HI.
H-HI, YOURSELF.
IF I DIDN'T KNOW BETTER, I'D SAY THOSE THOUGHTS I JUST PICKED UP SOUNDED LIKE A PROPOSAL.
THEY DID, DIDN'T THEY?
WHAT DO YOU SAY, RED?
I SAY, YES!

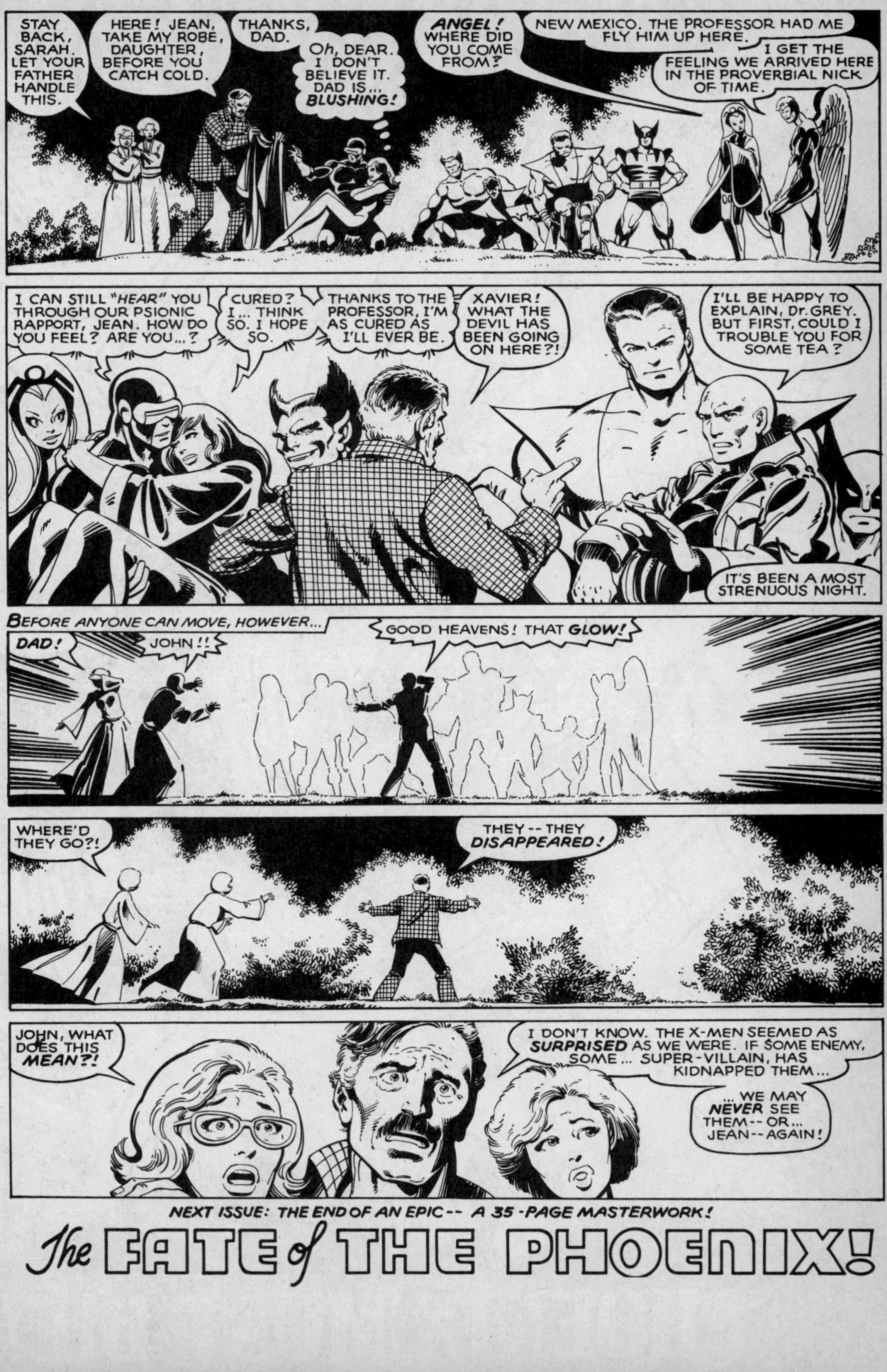
STAY BACK, SARAH. LET YOUR FATHER HANDLE THIS.
HERE! JEAN, TAKE MY ROBE, DAUGHTER, BEFORE YOU CATCH COLD.
THANKS, DAD.
Oh, DEAR. I DON'T BELIEVE IT. DAD IS... BLUSHING!
ANGEL! WHERE DID YOU COME FROM?
NEW MEXICO. THE PROFESSOR HAD ME FLY HIM UP HERE.
I GET THE FEELING WE ARRIVED HERE IN THE PROVERBIAL NICK OF TIME.
I CAN STILL "HEAR" YOU THROUGH OUR PSIONIC RAPPORT, JEAN. HOW DO YOU FEEL? ARE YOU...?
CURED? I... THINK SO. I HOPE SO.
THANKS TO THE PROFESSOR, I'M AS CURED AS I'LL EVER BE.
XAVIER! WHAT THE DEVIL HAS BEEN GOING ON HERE?!
I'LL BE HAPPY TO EXPLAIN, Dr. GREY. BUT FIRST, COULD I TROUBLE YOU FOR SOME TEA?
IT'S BEEN A MOST STRENUOUS NIGHT.
BEFORE ANYONE CAN MOVE, HOWEVER...
DAD!
JOHN!!
GOOD HEAVENS! THAT GLOW!
WHERE'D THEY GO?!
THEY -- THEY DISAPPEARED!
JOHN, WHAT DOES THIS MEAN?!
I DON'T KNOW. THE X-MEN SEEMED AS SURPRISED AS WE WERE. IF SOME ENEMY, SOME... SUPER-VILLAIN, HAS KIDNAPPED THEM...
... WE MAY NEVER SEE THEM -- OR... JEAN -- AGAIN!
NEXT ISSUE: THE END OF AN EPIC -- A 35-PAGE MASTERWORK!
The FATE of THE PHOENIX!

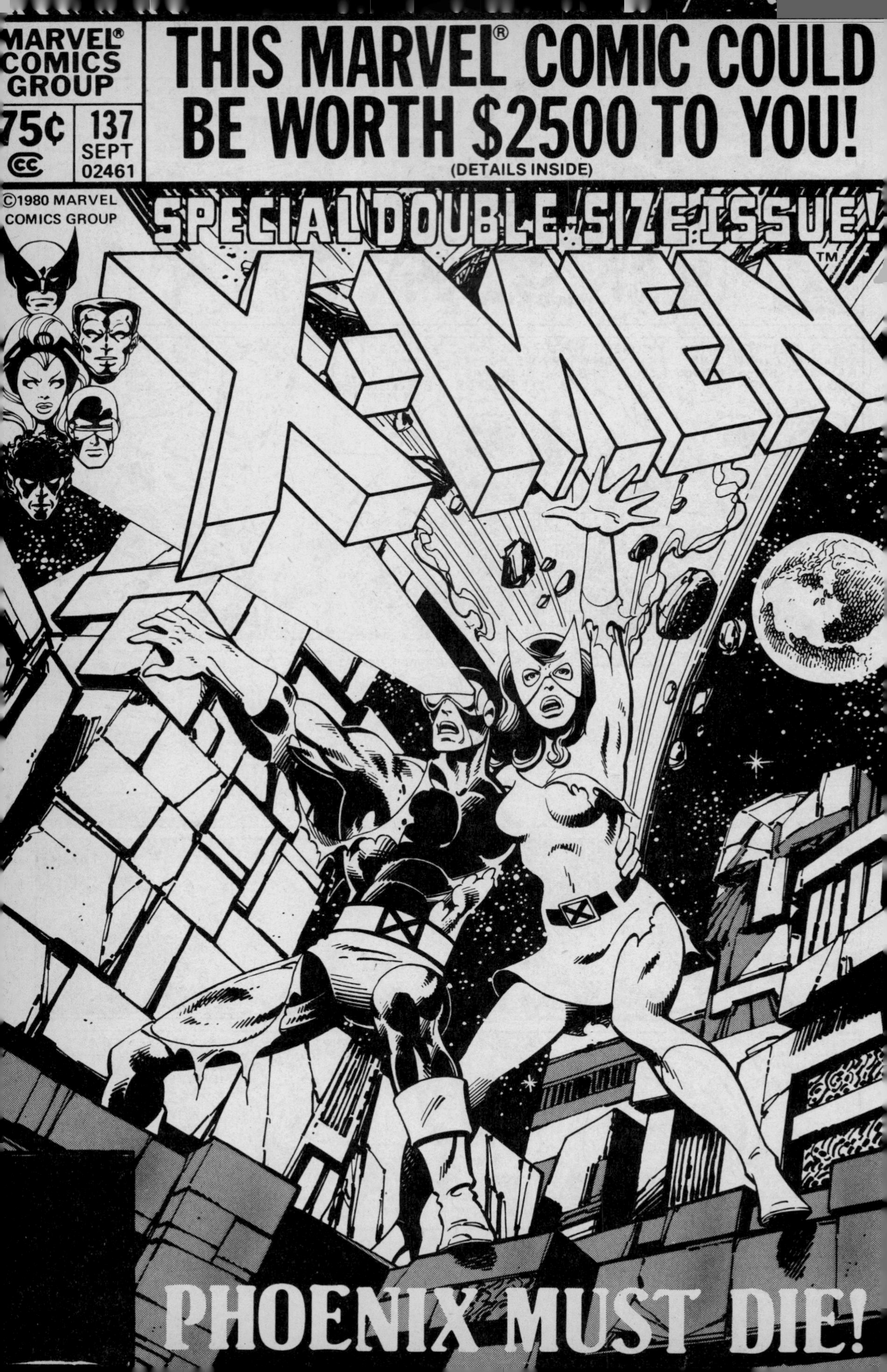
MARVEL® COMICS GROUP
75¢
CC
137
SEPT
02461
THIS MARVEL® COMIC COULD BE WORTH $2500 TO YOU!
(DETAILS INSIDE)
©1980 MARVEL COMICS GROUP
SPECIAL DOUBLE-SIZE ISSUE!
X-MEN™
PHOENIX MUST DIE!

Seventeen years ago, this month, *Stan Lee* and *Jack Kirby* chronicled the first adventure of one of the strangest super hero teams ever created — and a ***legend*** was born! Today, *Chris Claremont*, *John Byrne* and *Terry Austin* proudly celebrate that anniversary and ***reaffirm*** that legend!

Stan Lee PRESENTS: THE UNCANNY X-MEN!™

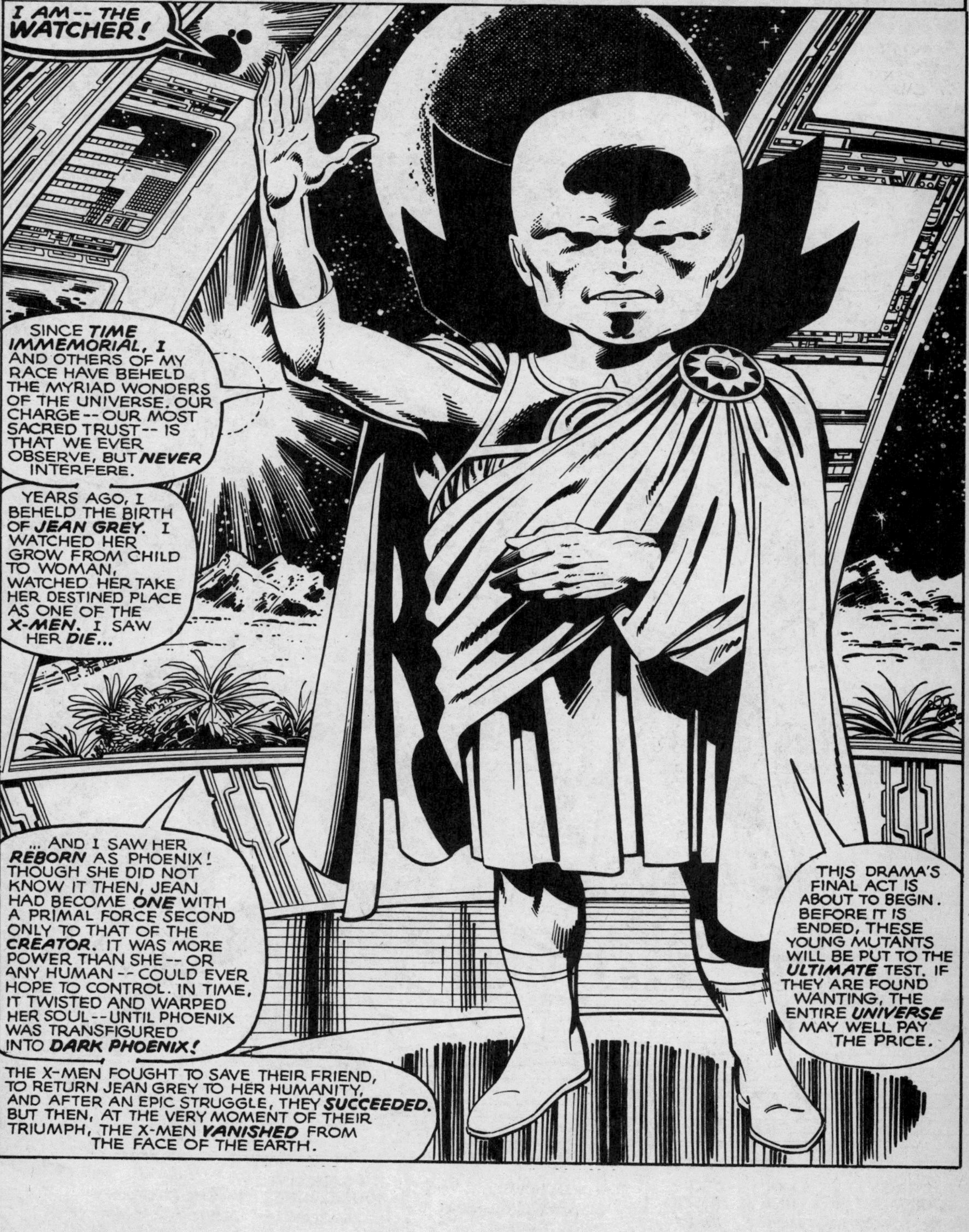

I AM -- THE WATCHER!
SINCE TIME IMMEMORIAL, I AND OTHERS OF MY RACE HAVE BEHELD THE MYRIAD WONDERS OF THE UNIVERSE. OUR CHARGE -- OUR MOST SACRED TRUST -- IS THAT WE EVER OBSERVE, BUT NEVER INTERFERE.
YEARS AGO, I BEHELD THE BIRTH OF JEAN GREY. I WATCHED HER GROW FROM CHILD TO WOMAN, WATCHED HER TAKE HER DESTINED PLACE AS ONE OF THE X-MEN. I SAW HER DIE...
... AND I SAW HER REBORN AS PHOENIX! THOUGH SHE DID NOT KNOW IT THEN, JEAN HAD BECOME ONE WITH A PRIMAL FORCE SECOND ONLY TO THAT OF THE CREATOR. IT WAS MORE POWER THAN SHE -- OR ANY HUMAN -- COULD EVER HOPE TO CONTROL. IN TIME, IT TWISTED AND WARPED HER SOUL -- UNTIL PHOENIX WAS TRANSFIGURED INTO DARK PHOENIX!
THIS DRAMA'S FINAL ACT IS ABOUT TO BEGIN. BEFORE IT IS ENDED, THESE YOUNG MUTANTS WILL BE PUT TO THE ULTIMATE TEST. IF THEY ARE FOUND WANTING, THE ENTIRE UNIVERSE MAY WELL PAY THE PRICE.
THE X-MEN FOUGHT TO SAVE THEIR FRIEND, TO RETURN JEAN GREY TO HER HUMANITY, AND AFTER AN EPIC STRUGGLE, THEY SUCCEEDED. BUT THEN, AT THE VERY MOMENT OF THEIR TRIUMPH, THE X-MEN VANISHED FROM THE FACE OF THE EARTH.

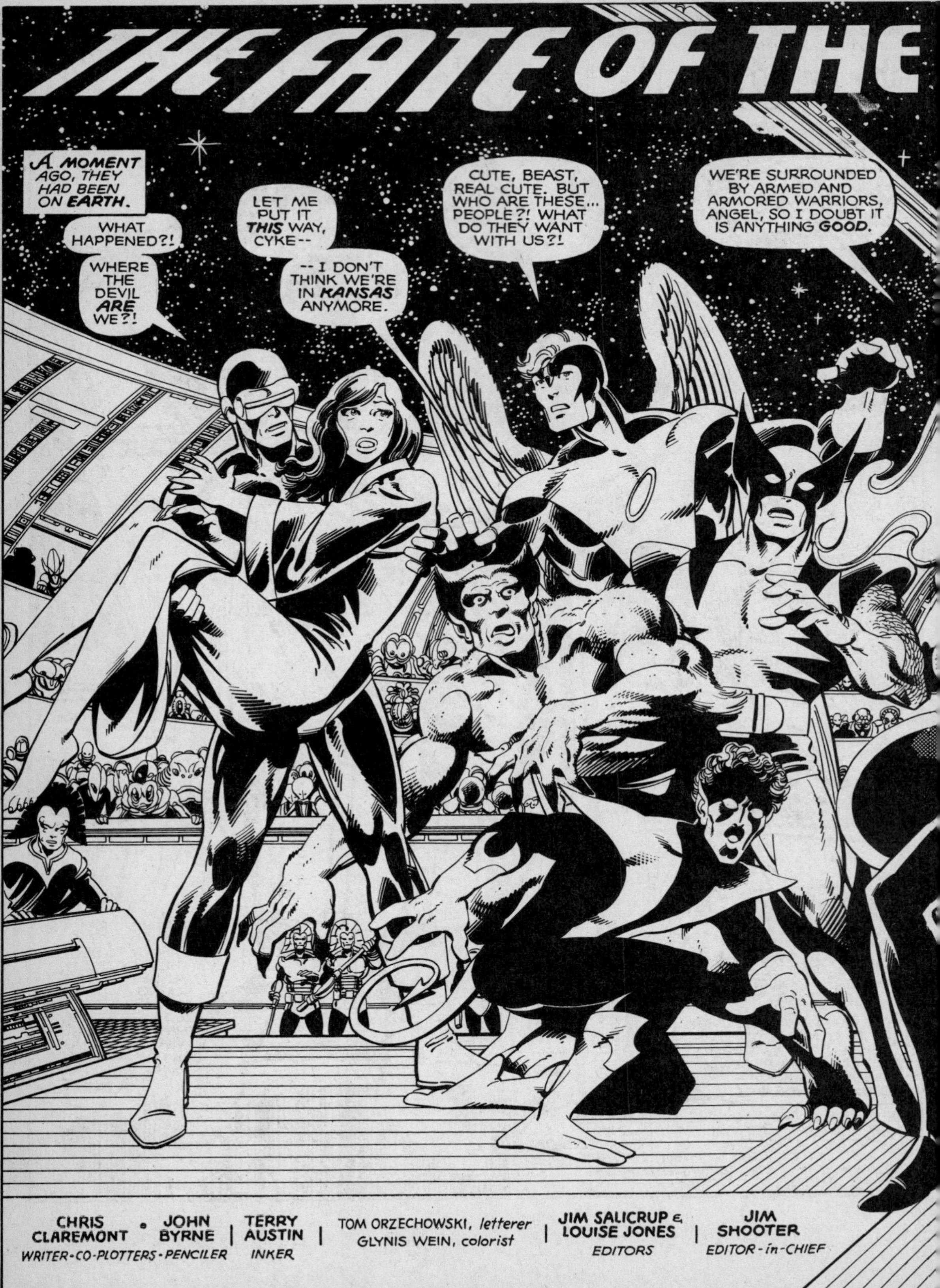
THE FATE OF THE
A MOMENT AGO, THEY HAD BEEN ON EARTH.
WHAT HAPPENED?!
WHERE THE DEVIL ARE WE?!
LET ME PUT IT THIS WAY, CYKE--
-- I DON'T THINK WE'RE IN KANSAS ANYMORE.
CUTE, BEAST, REAL CUTE. BUT WHO ARE THESE... PEOPLE?! WHAT DO THEY WANT WITH US?!
WE'RE SURROUNDED BY ARMED AND ARMORED WARRIORS, ANGEL, SO I DOUBT IT IS ANYTHING GOOD.
CHRIS CLAREMONT • JOHN BYRNE
WRITER-CO-PLOTTERS-PENCILER
TERRY AUSTIN
INKER
TOM ORZECHOWSKI, letterer
GLYNIS WEIN, colorist
JIM SALICRUP & LOUISE JONES
EDITORS
JIM SHOOTER
EDITOR-in-CHIEF

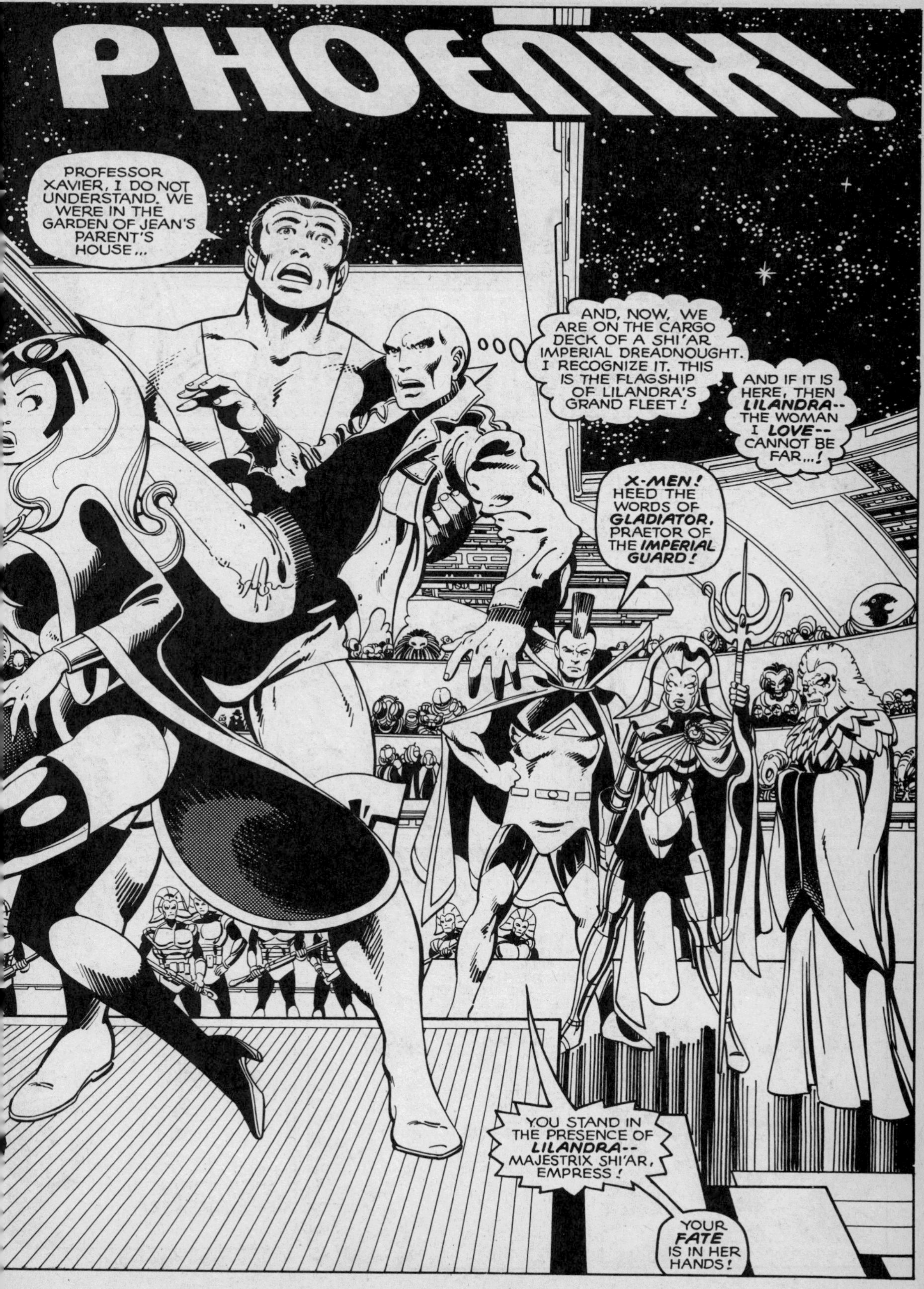
PHOENIX!
PROFESSOR XAVIER, I DO NOT UNDERSTAND. WE WERE IN THE GARDEN OF JEAN'S PARENT'S HOUSE...
AND, NOW, WE ARE ON THE CARGO DECK OF A SHI'AR IMPERIAL DREADNOUGHT. I RECOGNIZE IT. THIS IS THE FLAGSHIP OF LILANDRA'S GRAND FLEET!
AND IF IT IS HERE, THEN LILANDRA-- THE WOMAN I LOVE-- CANNOT BE FAR...!
X-MEN! HEED THE WORDS OF GLADIATOR, PRAETOR OF THE IMPERIAL GUARD!
YOU STAND IN THE PRESENCE OF LILANDRA-- MAJESTRIX SHI'AR, EMPRESS!
YOUR FATE IS IN HER HANDS!

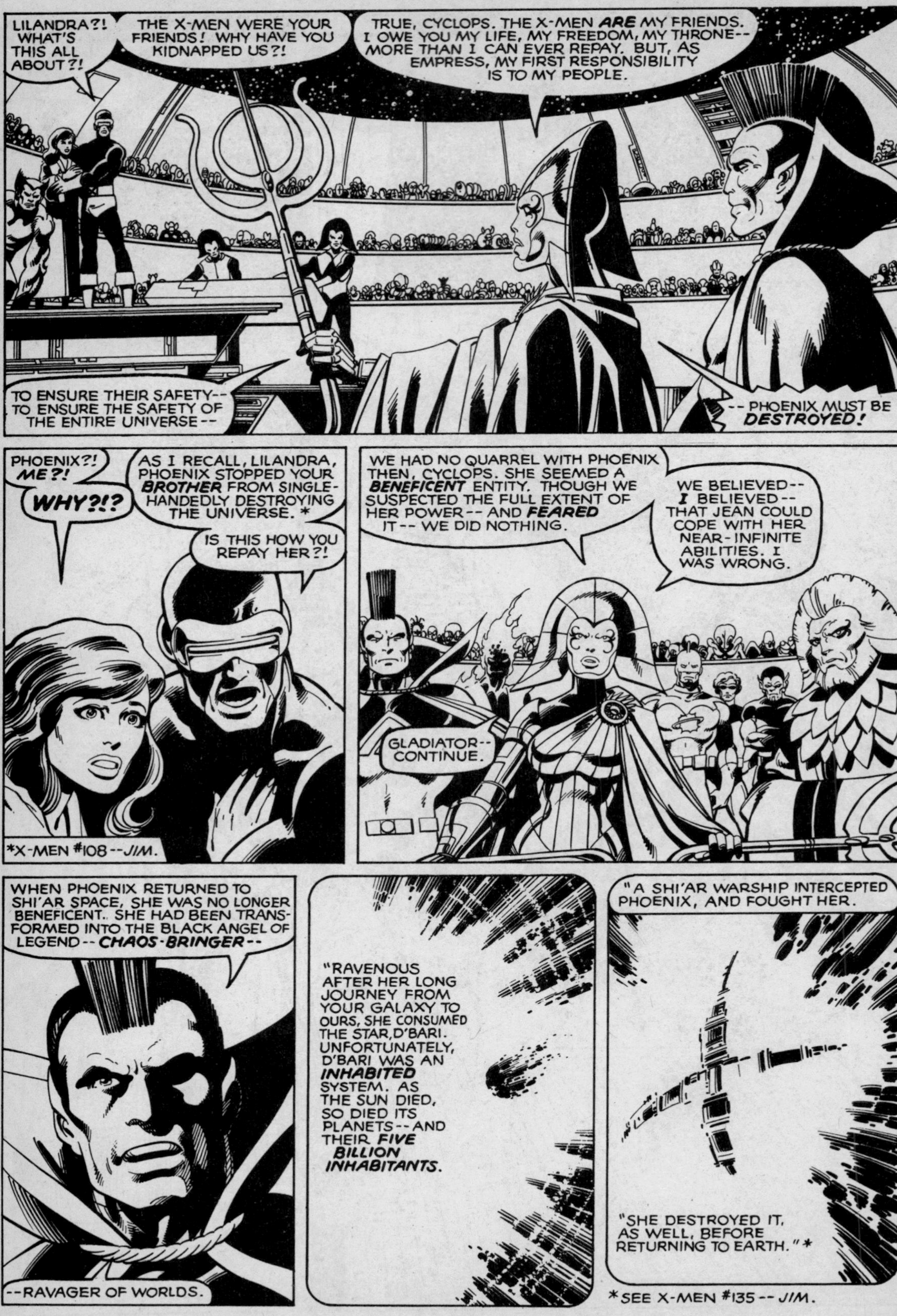

LILANDRA?! WHAT'S THIS ALL ABOUT?!
THE X-MEN WERE YOUR FRIENDS! WHY HAVE YOU KIDNAPPED US?!
TRUE, CYCLOPS. THE X-MEN ARE MY FRIENDS. I OWE YOU MY LIFE, MY FREEDOM, MY THRONE-- MORE THAN I CAN EVER REPAY. BUT, AS EMPRESS, MY FIRST RESPONSIBILITY IS TO MY PEOPLE.
TO ENSURE THEIR SAFETY-- TO ENSURE THE SAFETY OF THE ENTIRE UNIVERSE--
--PHOENIX MUST BE DESTROYED!
PHOENIX?! ME?!
WHY?!?
AS I RECALL, LILANDRA, PHOENIX STOPPED YOUR BROTHER FROM SINGLE-HANDEDLY DESTROYING THE UNIVERSE. *
IS THIS HOW YOU REPAY HER?!
*X-MEN #108--JIM.
WE HAD NO QUARREL WITH PHOENIX THEN, CYCLOPS. SHE SEEMED A BENEFICENT ENTITY. THOUGH WE SUSPECTED THE FULL EXTENT OF HER POWER-- AND FEARED IT-- WE DID NOTHING.
WE BELIEVED-- I BELIEVED-- THAT JEAN COULD COPE WITH HER NEAR-INFINITE ABILITIES. I WAS WRONG.
GLADIATOR-- CONTINUE.
WHEN PHOENIX RETURNED TO SHI'AR SPACE, SHE WAS NO LONGER BENEFICENT.. SHE HAD BEEN TRANSFORMED INTO THE BLACK ANGEL OF LEGEND-- CHAOS-BRINGER--
--RAVAGER OF WORLDS.
"RAVENOUS AFTER HER LONG JOURNEY FROM YOUR GALAXY TO OURS, SHE CONSUMED THE STAR, D'BARI. UNFORTUNATELY, D'BARI WAS AN INHABITED SYSTEM. AS THE SUN DIED, SO DIED ITS PLANETS-- AND THEIR FIVE BILLION INHABITANTS.
"A SHI'AR WARSHIP INTERCEPTED PHOENIX, AND FOUGHT HER.
"SHE DESTROYED IT, AS WELL, BEFORE RETURNING TO EARTH." *
*SEE X-MEN #135 -- JIM.

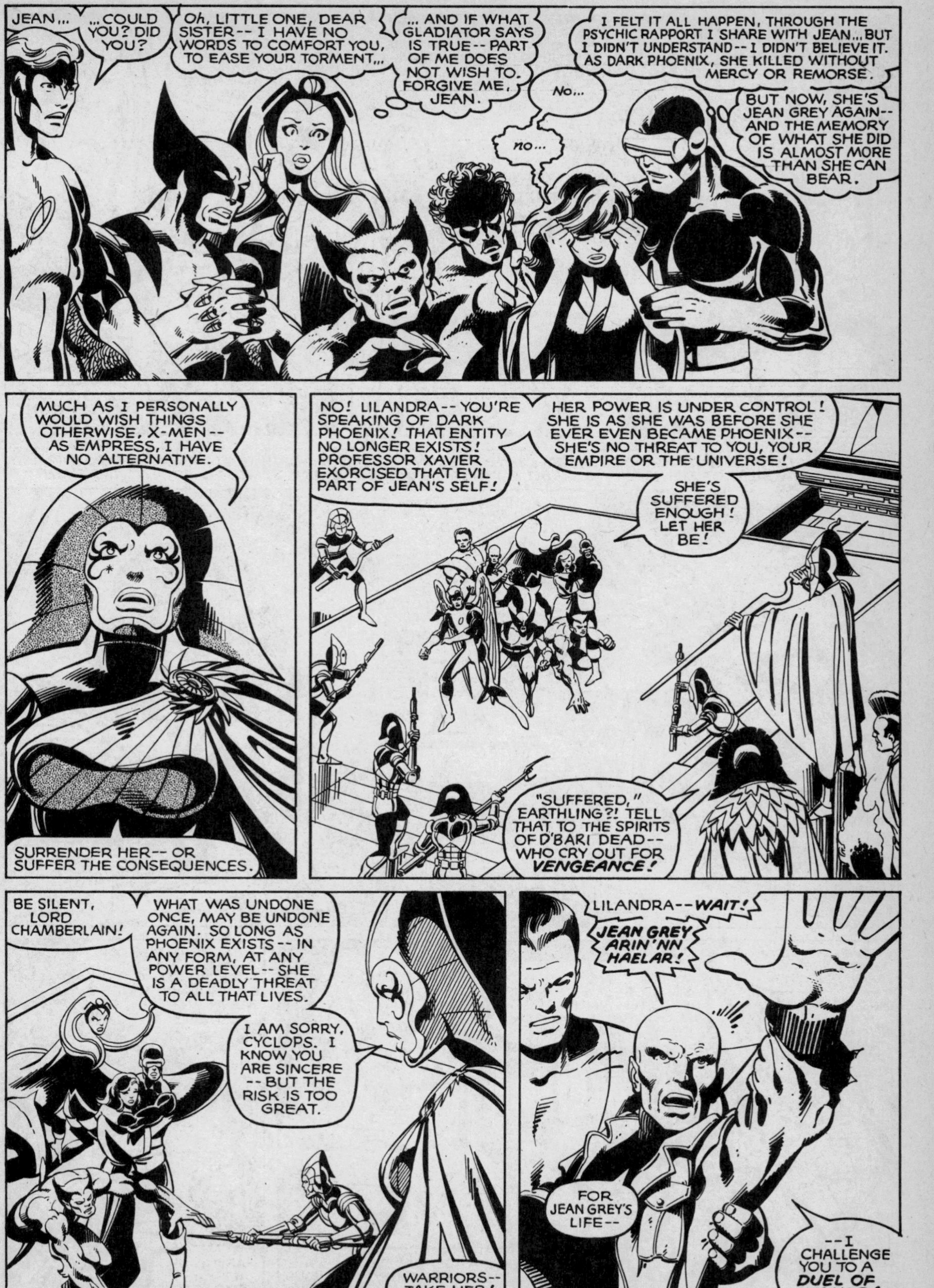

JEAN...
...COULD YOU? DID YOU?
Oh, LITTLE ONE, DEAR SISTER-- I HAVE NO WORDS TO COMFORT YOU, TO EASE YOUR TORMENT...
... AND IF WHAT GLADIATOR SAYS IS TRUE-- PART OF ME DOES NOT WISH TO. FORGIVE ME, JEAN.
No...
no...
I FELT IT ALL HAPPEN, THROUGH THE PSYCHIC RAPPORT I SHARE WITH JEAN... BUT I DIDN'T UNDERSTAND-- I DIDN'T BELIEVE IT. AS DARK PHOENIX, SHE KILLED WITHOUT MERCY OR REMORSE.
BUT NOW, SHE'S JEAN GREY AGAIN-- AND THE MEMORY OF WHAT SHE DID IS ALMOST MORE THAN SHE CAN BEAR.
MUCH AS I PERSONALLY WOULD WISH THINGS OTHERWISE, X-MEN-- AS EMPRESS, I HAVE NO ALTERNATIVE.
SURRENDER HER-- OR SUFFER THE CONSEQUENCES.
NO! LILANDRA-- YOU'RE SPEAKING OF DARK PHOENIX! THAT ENTITY NO LONGER EXISTS! PROFESSOR XAVIER EXORCISED THAT EVIL PART OF JEAN'S SELF!
HER POWER IS UNDER CONTROL! SHE IS AS SHE WAS BEFORE SHE EVER EVEN BECAME PHOENIX-- SHE'S NO THREAT TO YOU, YOUR EMPIRE OR THE UNIVERSE!
SHE'S SUFFERED ENOUGH! LET HER BE!
"SUFFERED," EARTHLING?! TELL THAT TO THE SPIRITS OF D'BARI DEAD-- WHO CRY OUT FOR VENGEANCE!
BE SILENT, LORD CHAMBERLAIN!
WHAT WAS UNDONE ONCE, MAY BE UNDONE AGAIN. SO LONG AS PHOENIX EXISTS-- IN ANY FORM, AT ANY POWER LEVEL-- SHE IS A DEADLY THREAT TO ALL THAT LIVES.
I AM SORRY, CYCLOPS. I KNOW YOU ARE SINCERE-- BUT THE RISK IS TOO GREAT.
WARRIORS-- TAKE HER!
LILANDRA-- WAIT!
JEAN GREY ARIN'NN HAELAR!
FOR JEAN GREY'S LIFE--
--I CHALLENGE YOU TO A DUEL OF HONOR!

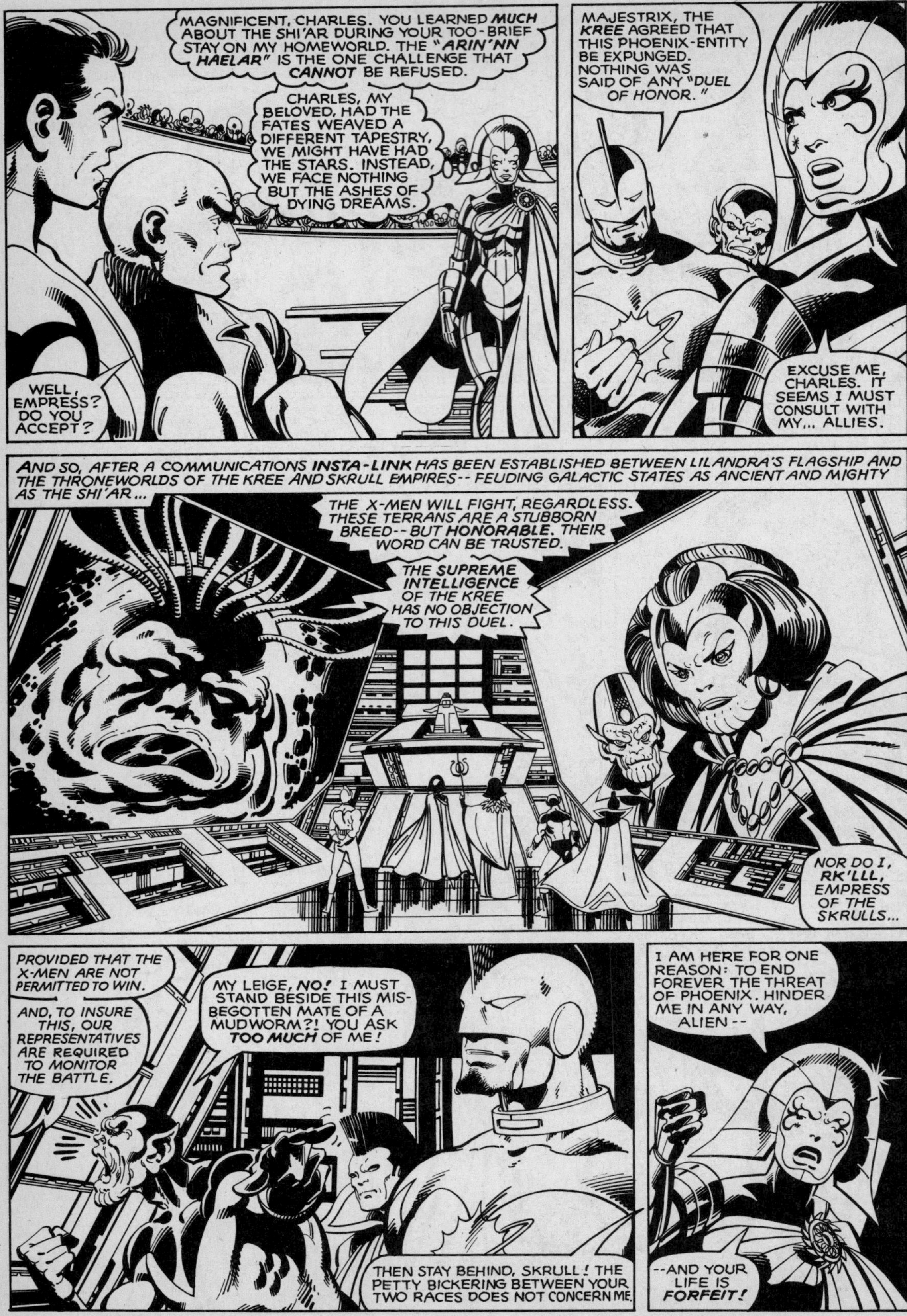
MAGNIFICENT, CHARLES. YOU LEARNED MUCH ABOUT THE SHI'AR DURING YOUR TOO-BRIEF STAY ON MY HOMEWORLD. THE "ARIN'NN HAELAR" IS THE ONE CHALLENGE THAT CANNOT BE REFUSED.
CHARLES, MY BELOVED, HAD THE FATES WEAVED A DIFFERENT TAPESTRY, WE MIGHT HAVE HAD THE STARS. INSTEAD, WE FACE NOTHING BUT THE ASHES OF DYING DREAMS.
WELL, EMPRESS? DO YOU ACCEPT?
MAJESTRIX, THE KREE AGREED THAT THIS PHOENIX-ENTITY BE EXPUNGED. NOTHING WAS SAID OF ANY "DUEL OF HONOR."
EXCUSE ME, CHARLES. IT SEEMS I MUST CONSULT WITH MY... ALLIES.
AND SO, AFTER A COMMUNICATIONS INSTA-LINK HAS BEEN ESTABLISHED BETWEEN LILANDRA'S FLAGSHIP AND THE THRONEWORLDS OF THE KREE AND SKRULL EMPIRES-- FEUDING GALACTIC STATES AS ANCIENT AND MIGHTY AS THE SHI'AR...
THE X-MEN WILL FIGHT, REGARDLESS. THESE TERRANS ARE A STUBBORN BREED-- BUT HONORABLE. THEIR WORD CAN BE TRUSTED.
THE SUPREME INTELLIGENCE OF THE KREE HAS NO OBJECTION TO THIS DUEL.
NOR DO I, RK'LLL, EMPRESS OF THE SKRULLS...
PROVIDED THAT THE X-MEN ARE NOT PERMITTED TO WIN.
AND, TO INSURE THIS, OUR REPRESENTATIVES ARE REQUIRED TO MONITOR THE BATTLE.
MY LEIGE, NO! I MUST STAND BESIDE THIS MIS-BEGOTTEN MATE OF A MUDWORM?! YOU ASK TOO MUCH OF ME!
THEN STAY BEHIND, SKRULL! THE PETTY BICKERING BETWEEN YOUR TWO RACES DOES NOT CONCERN ME.
I AM HERE FOR ONE REASON: TO END FOREVER THE THREAT OF PHOENIX. HINDER ME IN ANY WAY, ALIEN --
--AND YOUR LIFE IS FORFEIT!

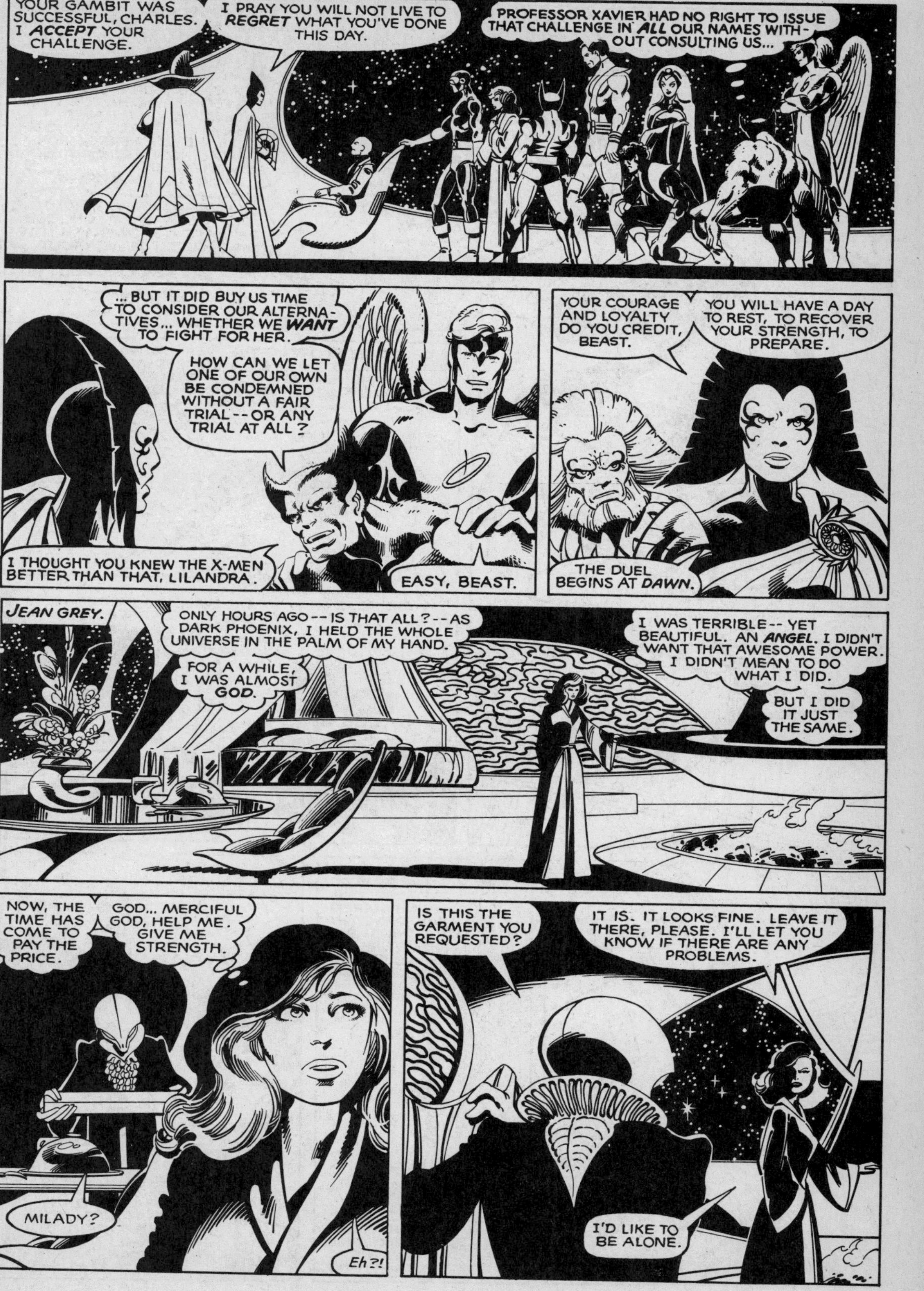
YOUR GAMBIT WAS SUCCESSFUL, CHARLES. I ACCEPT YOUR CHALLENGE.
I PRAY YOU WILL NOT LIVE TO REGRET WHAT YOU'VE DONE THIS DAY.
PROFESSOR XAVIER HAD NO RIGHT TO ISSUE THAT CHALLENGE IN ALL OUR NAMES WITHOUT CONSULTING US...
...BUT IT DID BUY US TIME TO CONSIDER OUR ALTERNATIVES... WHETHER WE WANT TO FIGHT FOR HER.
HOW CAN WE LET ONE OF OUR OWN BE CONDEMNED WITHOUT A FAIR TRIAL--OR ANY TRIAL AT ALL?
I THOUGHT YOU KNEW THE X-MEN BETTER THAN THAT, LILANDRA.
EASY, BEAST.
YOUR COURAGE AND LOYALTY DO YOU CREDIT, BEAST.
YOU WILL HAVE A DAY TO REST, TO RECOVER YOUR STRENGTH, TO PREPARE.
THE DUEL BEGINS AT DAWN.
JEAN GREY.
ONLY HOURS AGO--IS THAT ALL?--AS DARK PHOENIX, I HELD THE WHOLE UNIVERSE IN THE PALM OF MY HAND.
FOR A WHILE, I WAS ALMOST GOD.
I WAS TERRIBLE-- YET BEAUTIFUL. AN ANGEL. I DIDN'T WANT THAT AWESOME POWER. I DIDN'T MEAN TO DO WHAT I DID.
BUT I DID IT JUST THE SAME.
NOW, THE TIME HAS COME TO PAY THE PRICE.
GOD... MERCIFUL GOD, HELP ME. GIVE ME STRENGTH.
MILADY?
Eh?!
IS THIS THE GARMENT YOU REQUESTED?
IT IS. IT LOOKS FINE. LEAVE IT THERE, PLEASE. I'LL LET YOU KNOW IF THERE ARE ANY PROBLEMS.
I'D LIKE TO BE ALONE.

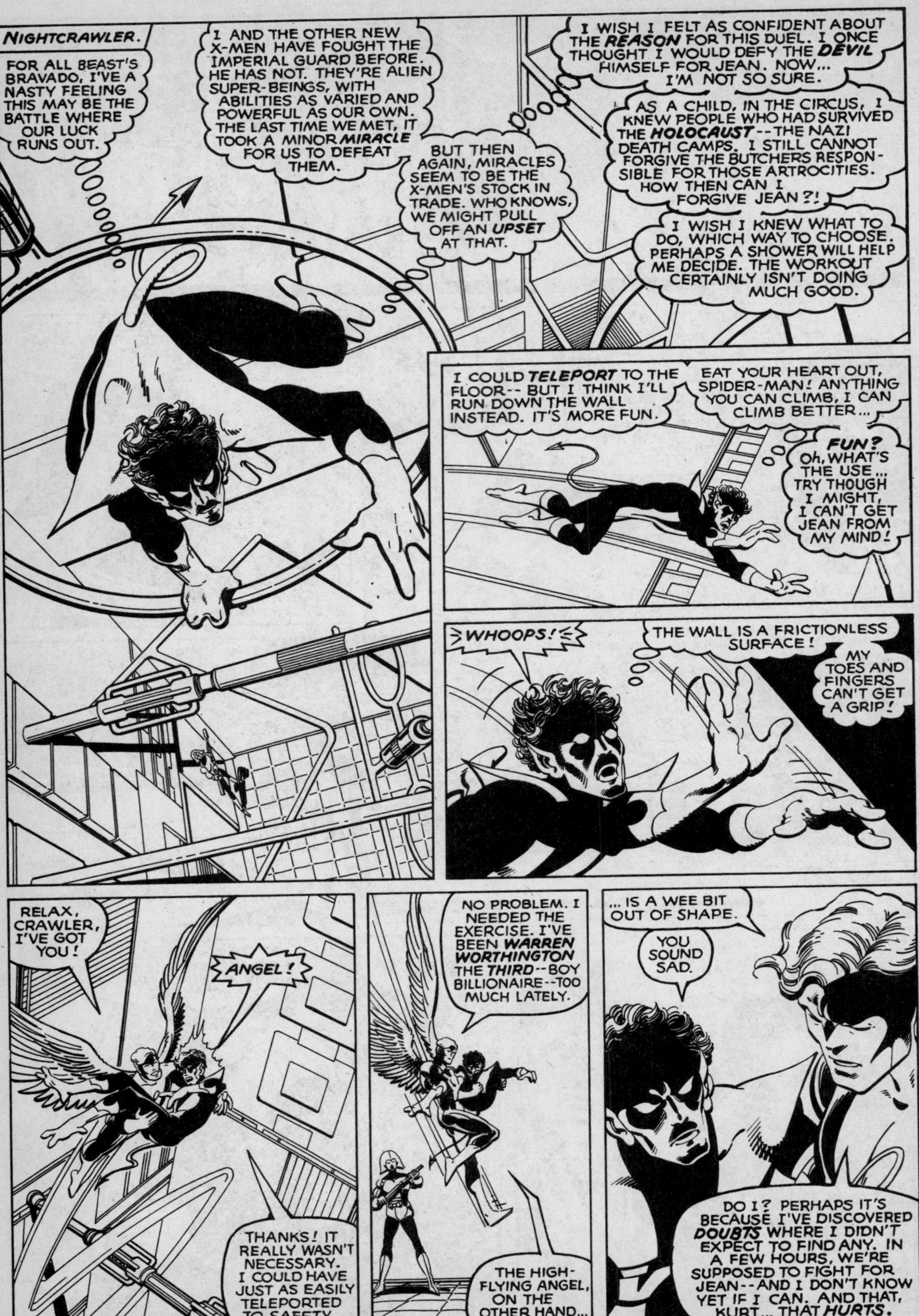
NIGHTCRAWLER.
FOR ALL BEAST'S BRAVADO, I'VE A NASTY FEELING THIS MAY BE THE BATTLE WHERE OUR LUCK RUNS OUT.
I AND THE OTHER NEW X-MEN HAVE FOUGHT THE IMPERIAL GUARD BEFORE. HE HAS NOT. THEY'RE ALIEN SUPER-BEINGS, WITH ABILITIES AS VARIED AND POWERFUL AS OUR OWN. THE LAST TIME WE MET, IT TOOK A MINOR MIRACLE FOR US TO DEFEAT THEM.
BUT THEN AGAIN, MIRACLES SEEM TO BE THE X-MEN'S STOCK IN TRADE. WHO KNOWS, WE MIGHT PULL OFF AN UPSET AT THAT.
I WISH I FELT AS CONFIDENT ABOUT THE REASON FOR THIS DUEL. I ONCE THOUGHT I WOULD DEFY THE DEVIL HIMSELF FOR JEAN. NOW... I'M NOT SO SURE.
AS A CHILD, IN THE CIRCUS, I KNEW PEOPLE WHO HAD SURVIVED THE HOLOCAUST -- THE NAZI DEATH CAMPS. I STILL CANNOT FORGIVE THE BUTCHERS RESPONSIBLE FOR THOSE ARTROCITIES. HOW THEN CAN I FORGIVE JEAN ?!
I WISH I KNEW WHAT TO DO, WHICH WAY TO CHOOSE. PERHAPS A SHOWER WILL HELP ME DECIDE. THE WORKOUT CERTAINLY ISN'T DOING MUCH GOOD.
I COULD TELEPORT TO THE FLOOR-- BUT I THINK I'LL RUN DOWN THE WALL INSTEAD. IT'S MORE FUN.
EAT YOUR HEART OUT, SPIDER-MAN! ANYTHING YOU CAN CLIMB, I CAN CLIMB BETTER...
FUN? Oh, WHAT'S THE USE... TRY THOUGH I MIGHT, I CAN'T GET JEAN FROM MY MIND!
WHOOPS!
THE WALL IS A FRICTIONLESS SURFACE!
MY TOES AND FINGERS CAN'T GET A GRIP!
RELAX, CRAWLER, I'VE GOT YOU!
ANGEL!
THANKS! IT REALLY WASN'T NECESSARY. I COULD HAVE JUST AS EASILY TELEPORTED TO SAFETY.
NO PROBLEM. I NEEDED THE EXERCISE. I'VE BEEN WARREN WORTHINGTON THE THIRD--BOY BILLIONAIRE--TOO MUCH LATELY.
THE HIGH-FLYING ANGEL, ON THE OTHER HAND...
... IS A WEE BIT OUT OF SHAPE.
YOU SOUND SAD.
DO I? PERHAPS IT'S BECAUSE I'VE DISCOVERED DOUBTS WHERE I DIDN'T EXPECT TO FIND ANY. IN A FEW HOURS, WE'RE SUPPOSED TO FIGHT FOR JEAN--AND I DON'T KNOW YET IF I CAN. AND THAT, KURT... THAT HURTS.

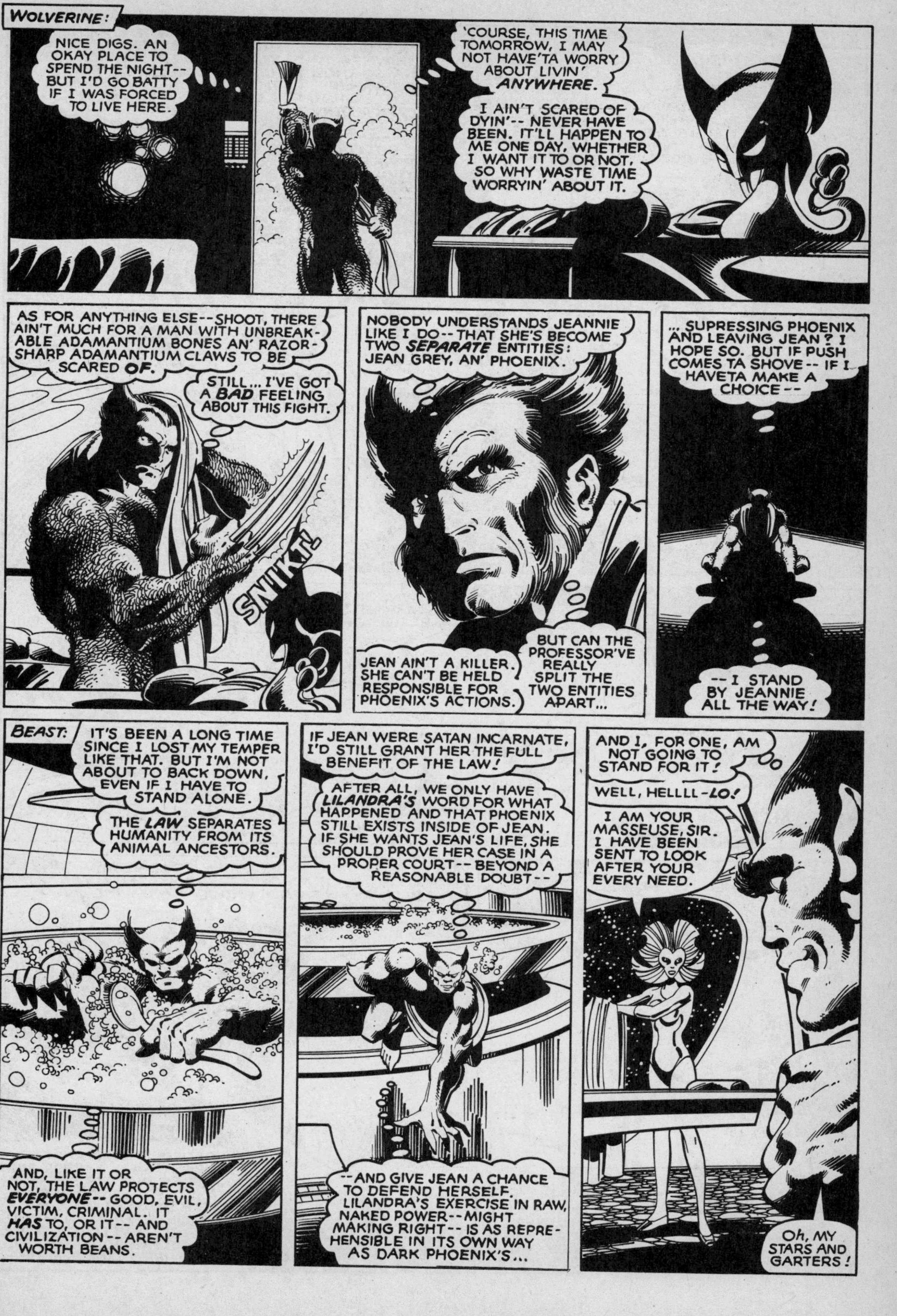
WOLVERINE:
NICE DIGS. AN OKAY PLACE TO SPEND THE NIGHT-- BUT I'D GO BATTY IF I WAS FORCED TO LIVE HERE.
'COURSE, THIS TIME TOMORROW, I MAY NOT HAVE'TA WORRY ABOUT LIVIN' ANYWHERE.
I AIN'T SCARED OF DYIN'-- NEVER HAVE BEEN. IT'LL HAPPEN TO ME ONE DAY, WHETHER I WANT IT TO OR NOT, SO WHY WASTE TIME WORRYIN' ABOUT IT.
AS FOR ANYTHING ELSE--SHOOT, THERE AIN'T MUCH FOR A MAN WITH UNBREAKABLE ADAMANTIUM BONES AN' RAZOR-SHARP ADAMANTIUM CLAWS TO BE SCARED OF.
STILL... I'VE GOT A BAD FEELING ABOUT THIS FIGHT.
SNIKT!
NOBODY UNDERSTANDS JEANNIE LIKE I DO--THAT SHE'S BECOME TWO SEPARATE ENTITIES: JEAN GREY, AN' PHOENIX.
JEAN AIN'T A KILLER. SHE CAN'T BE HELD RESPONSIBLE FOR PHOENIX'S ACTIONS.
BUT CAN THE PROFESSOR'VE REALLY SPLIT THE TWO ENTITIES APART...
... SUPRESSING PHOENIX AND LEAVING JEAN? I HOPE SO. BUT IF PUSH COMES TA SHOVE-- IF I HAVETA MAKE A CHOICE--
-- I STAND BY JEANNIE ALL THE WAY!
BEAST:
IT'S BEEN A LONG TIME SINCE I LOST MY TEMPER LIKE THAT. BUT I'M NOT ABOUT TO BACK DOWN, EVEN IF I HAVE TO STAND ALONE.
THE LAW SEPARATES HUMANITY FROM ITS ANIMAL ANCESTORS.
AND, LIKE IT OR NOT, THE LAW PROTECTS EVERYONE-- GOOD, EVIL, VICTIM, CRIMINAL. IT HAS TO, OR IT-- AND CIVILIZATION-- AREN'T WORTH BEANS.
IF JEAN WERE SATAN INCARNATE, I'D STILL GRANT HER THE FULL BENEFIT OF THE LAW!
AFTER ALL, WE ONLY HAVE LILANDRA'S WORD FOR WHAT HAPPENED AND THAT PHOENIX STILL EXISTS INSIDE OF JEAN. IF SHE WANTS JEAN'S LIFE, SHE SHOULD PROVE HER CASE IN A PROPER COURT-- BEYOND A REASONABLE DOUBT--
--AND GIVE JEAN A CHANCE TO DEFEND HERSELF. LILANDRA'S EXERCISE IN RAW, NAKED POWER--MIGHT MAKING RIGHT-- IS AS REPREHENSIBLE IN ITS OWN WAY AS DARK PHOENIX'S...
AND I, FOR ONE, AM NOT GOING TO STAND FOR IT!
WELL, HELLLL-LO!
I AM YOUR MASSEUSE, SIR. I HAVE BEEN SENT TO LOOK AFTER YOUR EVERY NEED.
Oh, MY STARS AND GARTERS!

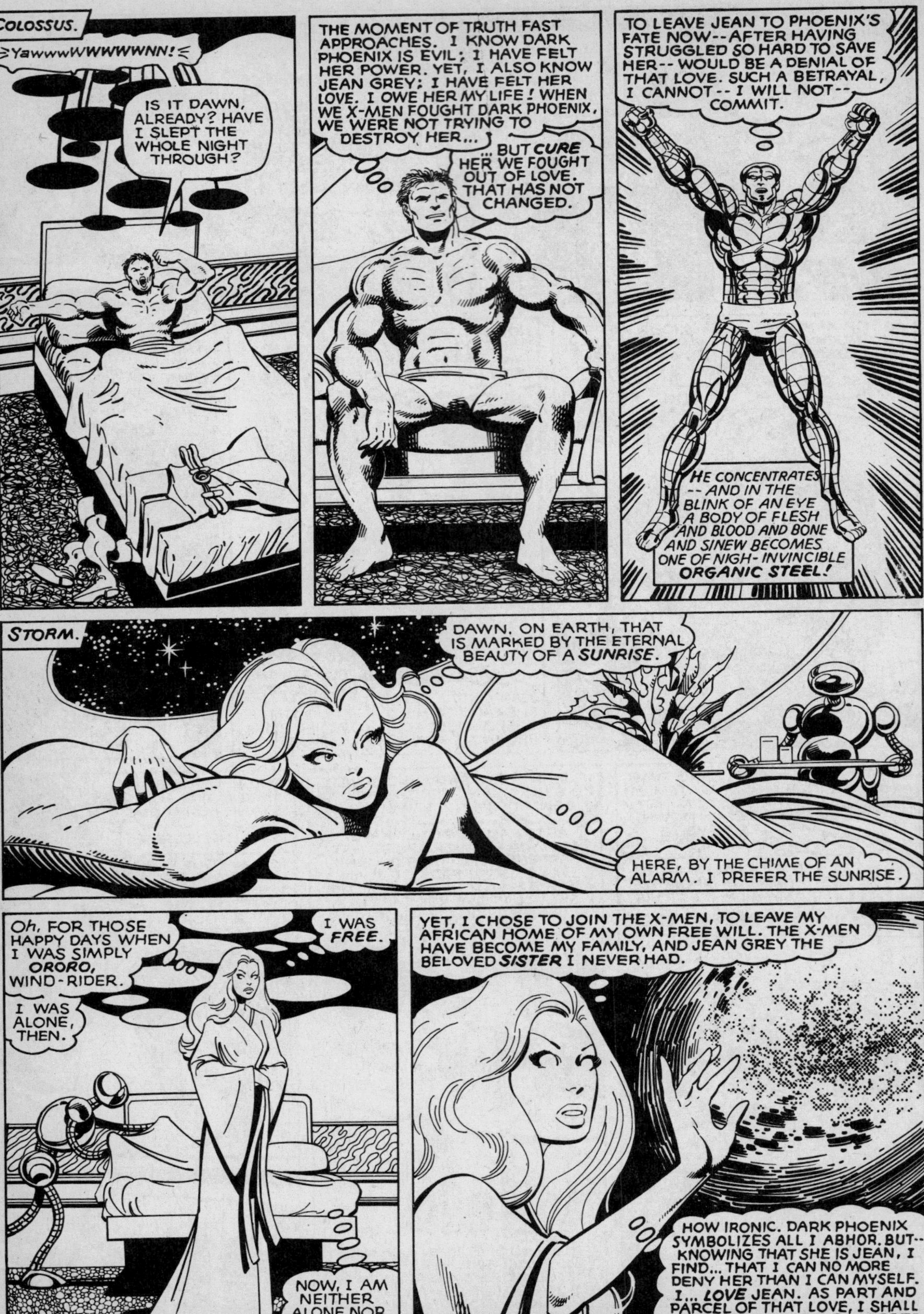
COLOSSUS.
YawwwWWWWWNN!
IS IT DAWN, ALREADY? HAVE I SLEPT THE WHOLE NIGHT THROUGH?
THE MOMENT OF TRUTH FAST APPROACHES. I KNOW DARK PHOENIX IS EVIL; I HAVE FELT HER POWER. YET, I ALSO KNOW JEAN GREY; I HAVE FELT HER LOVE. I OWE HER MY LIFE! WHEN WE X-MEN FOUGHT DARK PHOENIX, WE WERE NOT TRYING TO DESTROY HER...
... BUT CURE HER WE FOUGHT OUT OF LOVE. THAT HAS NOT CHANGED.
TO LEAVE JEAN TO PHOENIX'S FATE NOW--AFTER HAVING STRUGGLED SO HARD TO SAVE HER-- WOULD BE A DENIAL OF THAT LOVE. SUCH A BETRAYAL, I CANNOT -- I WILL NOT -- COMMIT.
HE CONCENTRATES -- AND IN THE BLINK OF AN EYE A BODY OF FLESH AND BLOOD AND BONE AND SINEW BECOMES ONE OF NIGH-INVINCIBLE ORGANIC STEEL!
STORM.
DAWN, ON EARTH, THAT IS MARKED BY THE ETERNAL BEAUTY OF A SUNRISE.
HERE, BY THE CHIME OF AN ALARM. I PREFER THE SUNRISE.
Oh, FOR THOSE HAPPY DAYS WHEN I WAS SIMPLY ORORO, WIND-RIDER.
I WAS FREE.
I WAS ALONE, THEN.
NOW, I AM NEITHER ALONE NOR FREE. AND RARELY HAPPY.
YET, I CHOSE TO JOIN THE X-MEN, TO LEAVE MY AFRICAN HOME OF MY OWN FREE WILL. THE X-MEN HAVE BECOME MY FAMILY, AND JEAN GREY THE BELOVED SISTER I NEVER HAD.
HOW IRONIC. DARK PHOENIX SYMBOLIZES ALL I ABHOR. BUT-- KNOWING THAT SHE IS JEAN, I FIND... THAT I CAN NO MORE DENY HER THAN I CAN MYSELF. I... LOVE JEAN. AS PART AND PARCEL OF THAT LOVE, I SHALL USE MY ELEMENTAL POWERS TO DEFEND HER TO THE DEATH.

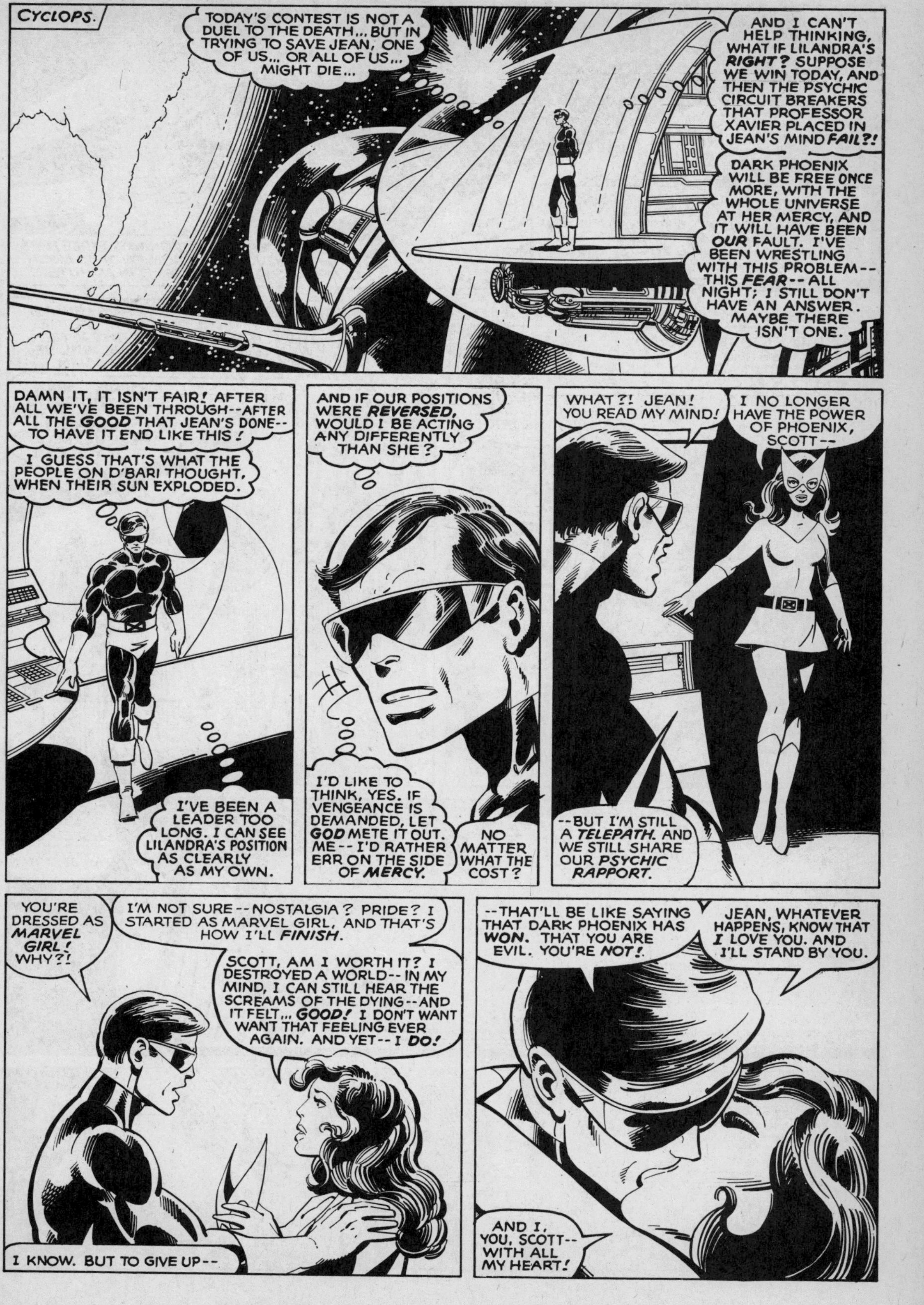

CYCLOPS.
TODAY'S CONTEST IS NOT A DUEL TO THE DEATH... BUT IN TRYING TO SAVE JEAN, ONE OF US... OR ALL OF US... MIGHT DIE...
AND I CAN'T HELP THINKING, WHAT IF LILANDRA'S RIGHT? SUPPOSE WE WIN TODAY, AND THEN THE PSYCHIC CIRCUIT BREAKERS THAT PROFESSOR XAVIER PLACED IN JEAN'S MIND FAIL?!
DARK PHOENIX WILL BE FREE ONCE MORE, WITH THE WHOLE UNIVERSE AT HER MERCY, AND IT WILL HAVE BEEN OUR FAULT. I'VE BEEN WRESTLING WITH THIS PROBLEM-- THIS FEAR-- ALL NIGHT; I STILL DON'T HAVE AN ANSWER. MAYBE THERE ISN'T ONE.
DAMN IT, IT ISN'T FAIR! AFTER ALL WE'VE BEEN THROUGH--AFTER ALL THE GOOD THAT JEAN'S DONE-- TO HAVE IT END LIKE THIS!
I GUESS THAT'S WHAT THE PEOPLE ON D'BARI THOUGHT, WHEN THEIR SUN EXPLODED.
I'VE BEEN A LEADER TOO LONG. I CAN SEE LILANDRA'S POSITION AS CLEARLY AS MY OWN.
AND IF OUR POSITIONS WERE REVERSED, WOULD I BE ACTING ANY DIFFERENTLY THAN SHE?
I'D LIKE TO THINK, YES. IF VENGEANCE IS DEMANDED, LET GOD METE IT OUT. ME-- I'D RATHER ERR ON THE SIDE OF MERCY.
NO MATTER WHAT THE COST?
WHAT?! JEAN! YOU READ MY MIND!
I NO LONGER HAVE THE POWER OF PHOENIX, SCOTT--
--BUT I'M STILL A TELEPATH. AND WE STILL SHARE OUR PSYCHIC RAPPORT.
YOU'RE DRESSED AS MARVEL GIRL! WHY?!
I'M NOT SURE--NOSTALGIA? PRIDE? I STARTED AS MARVEL GIRL, AND THAT'S HOW I'LL FINISH.
SCOTT, AM I WORTH IT? I DESTROYED A WORLD-- IN MY MIND, I CAN STILL HEAR THE SCREAMS OF THE DYING--AND IT FELT... GOOD! I DON'T WANT WANT THAT FEELING EVER AGAIN. AND YET-- I DO!
I KNOW. BUT TO GIVE UP--
--THAT'LL BE LIKE SAYING THAT DARK PHOENIX HAS WON. THAT YOU ARE EVIL. YOU'RE NOT!.
JEAN, WHATEVER HAPPENS, KNOW THAT I LOVE YOU. AND I'LL STAND BY YOU.
AND I, YOU, SCOTT-- WITH ALL MY HEART!

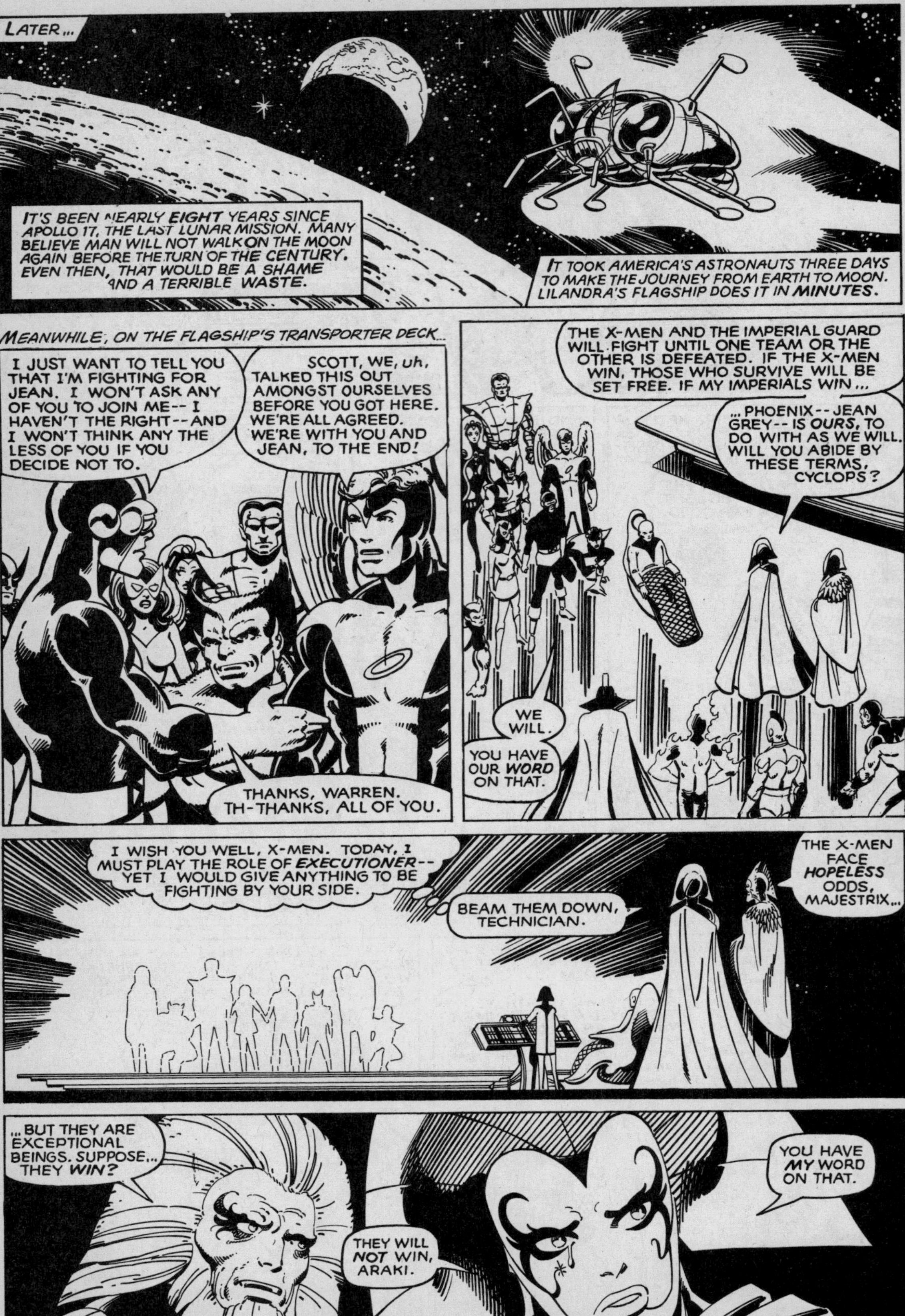
LATER...
IT'S BEEN NEARLY EIGHT YEARS SINCE APOLLO 17, THE LAST LUNAR MISSION. MANY BELIEVE MAN WILL NOT WALK ON THE MOON AGAIN BEFORE THE TURN OF THE CENTURY. EVEN THEN, THAT WOULD BE A SHAME AND A TERRIBLE WASTE.
IT TOOK AMERICA'S ASTRONAUTS THREE DAYS TO MAKE THE JOURNEY FROM EARTH TO MOON. LILANDRA'S FLAGSHIP DOES IT IN MINUTES.
MEANWHILE, ON THE FLAGSHIP'S TRANSPORTER DECK...
I JUST WANT TO TELL YOU THAT I'M FIGHTING FOR JEAN. I WON'T ASK ANY OF YOU TO JOIN ME-- I HAVEN'T THE RIGHT-- AND I WON'T THINK ANY THE LESS OF YOU IF YOU DECIDE NOT TO.
SCOTT, WE, uh, TALKED THIS OUT AMONGST OURSELVES BEFORE YOU GOT HERE. WE'RE ALL AGREED. WE'RE WITH YOU AND JEAN, TO THE END!
THANKS, WARREN. TH-THANKS, ALL OF YOU.
THE X-MEN AND THE IMPERIAL GUARD WILL FIGHT UNTIL ONE TEAM OR THE OTHER IS DEFEATED. IF THE X-MEN WIN, THOSE WHO SURVIVE WILL BE SET FREE. IF MY IMPERIALS WIN...
... PHOENIX-- JEAN GREY-- IS OURS, TO DO WITH AS WE WILL. WILL YOU ABIDE BY THESE TERMS, CYCLOPS?
WE WILL.
YOU HAVE OUR WORD ON THAT.
I WISH YOU WELL, X-MEN. TODAY, I MUST PLAY THE ROLE OF EXECUTIONER-- YET I WOULD GIVE ANYTHING TO BE FIGHTING BY YOUR SIDE.
BEAM THEM DOWN, TECHNICIAN.
THE X-MEN FACE HOPELESS ODDS, MAJESTRIX...
... BUT THEY ARE EXCEPTIONAL BEINGS. SUPPOSE... THEY WIN?
THEY WILL NOT WIN, ARAKI.
YOU HAVE MY WORD ON THAT.

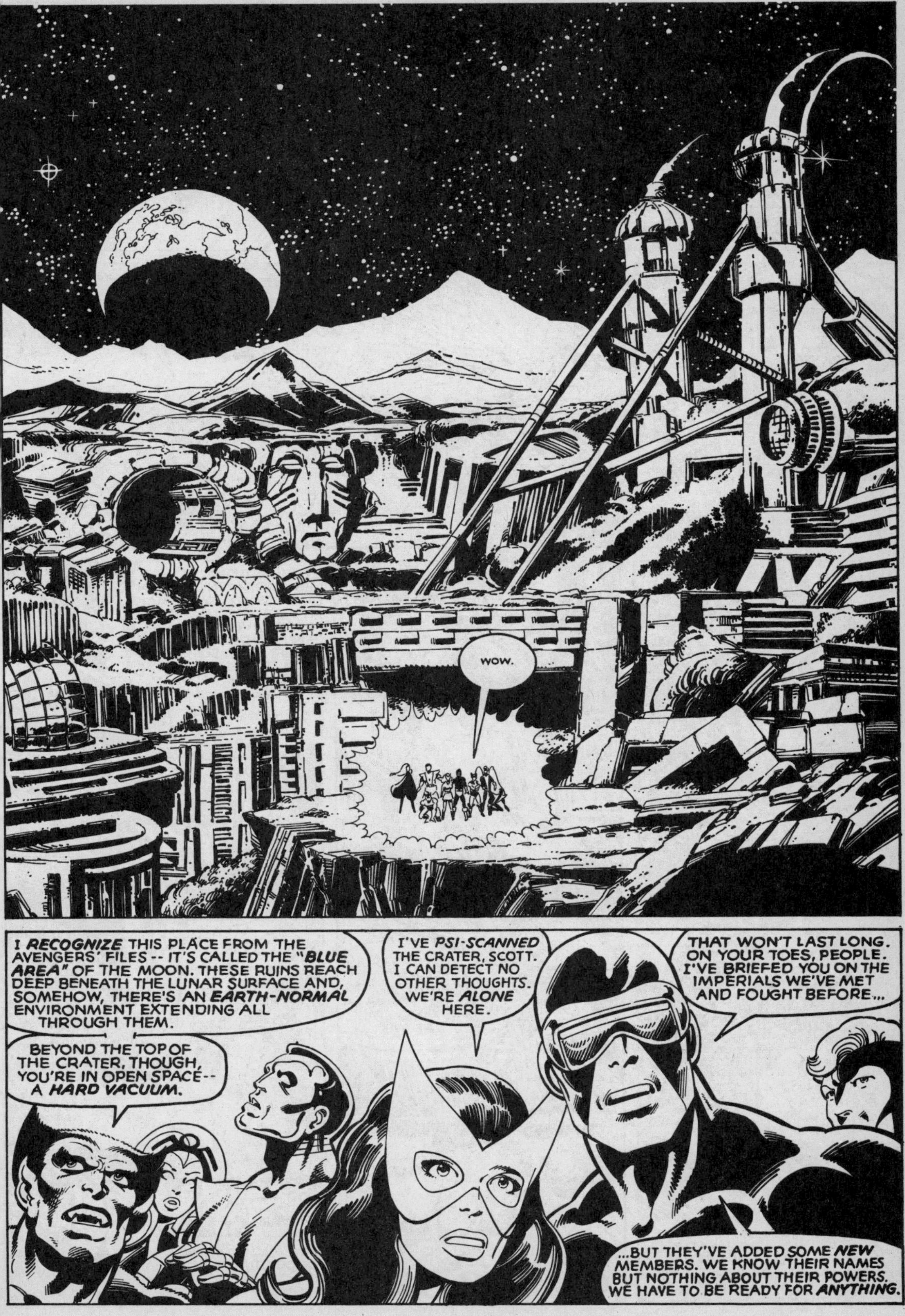

WOW.
I RECOGNIZE THIS PLACE FROM THE AVENGERS' FILES -- IT'S CALLED THE "BLUE AREA" OF THE MOON. THESE RUINS REACH DEEP BENEATH THE LUNAR SURFACE AND, SOMEHOW, THERE'S AN EARTH-NORMAL ENVIRONMENT EXTENDING ALL THROUGH THEM.
BEYOND THE TOP OF THE CRATER, THOUGH, YOU'RE IN OPEN SPACE -- A HARD VACUUM.
I'VE PSI-SCANNED THE CRATER, SCOTT. I CAN DETECT NO OTHER THOUGHTS. WE'RE ALONE HERE.
THAT WON'T LAST LONG. ON YOUR TOES, PEOPLE. I'VE BRIEFED YOU ON THE IMPERIALS WE'VE MET AND FOUGHT BEFORE...
...BUT THEY'VE ADDED SOME NEW MEMBERS. WE KNOW THEIR NAMES BUT NOTHING ABOUT THEIR POWERS. WE HAVE TO BE READY FOR ANYTHING.

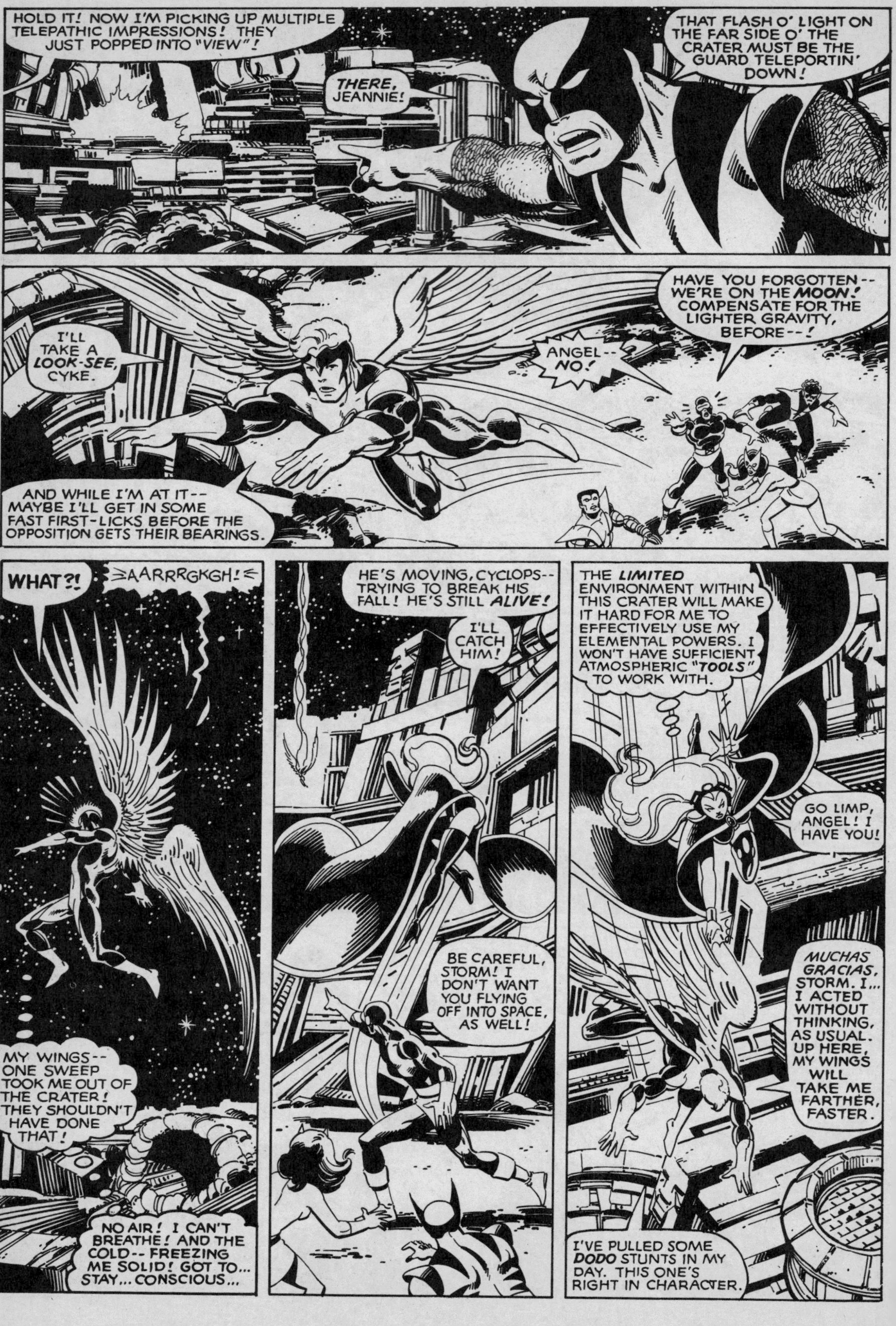
HOLD IT! NOW I'M PICKING UP MULTIPLE TELEPATHIC IMPRESSIONS! THEY JUST POPPED INTO "VIEW"!
THERE, JEANNIE!
THAT FLASH O' LIGHT ON THE FAR SIDE O' THE CRATER MUST BE THE GUARD TELEPORTIN' DOWN!
I'LL TAKE A LOOK-SEE, CYKE.
AND WHILE I'M AT IT-- MAYBE I'LL GET IN SOME FAST FIRST-LICKS BEFORE THE OPPOSITION GETS THEIR BEARINGS.
ANGEL-- NO!
HAVE YOU FORGOTTEN-- WE'RE ON THE MOON! COMPENSATE FOR THE LIGHTER GRAVITY, BEFORE--!
WHAT?!
AARRRGKGH!
MY WINGS-- ONE SWEEP TOOK ME OUT OF THE CRATER! THEY SHOULDN'T HAVE DONE THAT!
NO AIR! I CAN'T BREATHE! AND THE COLD-- FREEZING ME SOLID! GOT TO... STAY... CONSCIOUS...
HE'S MOVING, CYCLOPS-- TRYING TO BREAK HIS FALL! HE'S STILL ALIVE!
I'LL CATCH HIM!
BE CAREFUL, STORM! I DON'T WANT YOU FLYING OFF INTO SPACE, AS WELL!
THE LIMITED ENVIRONMENT WITHIN THIS CRATER WILL MAKE IT HARD FOR ME TO EFFECTIVELY USE MY ELEMENTAL POWERS. I WON'T HAVE SUFFICIENT ATMOSPHERIC "TOOLS" TO WORK WITH.
GO LIMP, ANGEL! I HAVE YOU!
MUCHAS GRACIAS, STORM. I... I ACTED WITHOUT THINKING, AS USUAL. UP HERE, MY WINGS WILL TAKE ME FARTHER, FASTER.
I'VE PULLED SOME DODO STUNTS IN MY DAY. THIS ONE'S RIGHT IN CHARACTER.

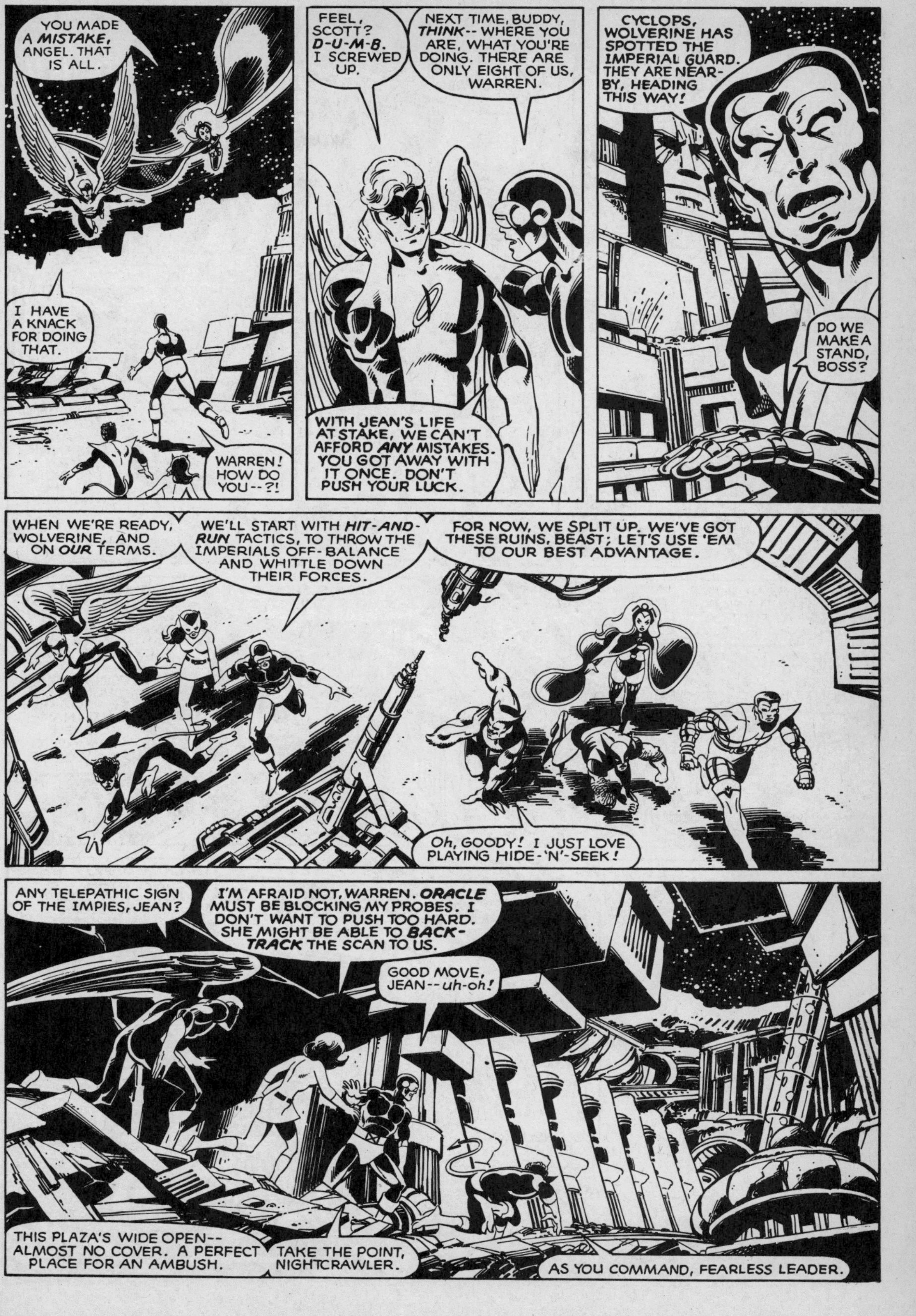

YOU MADE A MISTAKE, ANGEL. THAT IS ALL.
I HAVE A KNACK FOR DOING THAT.
WARREN! HOW DO YOU--?!
FEEL, SCOTT? D-U-M-B. I SCREWED UP.
NEXT TIME, BUDDY, THINK-- WHERE YOU ARE, WHAT YOU'RE DOING. THERE ARE ONLY EIGHT OF US, WARREN.
WITH JEAN'S LIFE AT STAKE, WE CAN'T AFFORD ANY MISTAKES. YOU GOT AWAY WITH IT ONCE. DON'T PUSH YOUR LUCK.
CYCLOPS, WOLVERINE HAS SPOTTED THE IMPERIAL GUARD. THEY ARE NEARBY, HEADING THIS WAY!
DO WE MAKE A STAND, BOSS?
WHEN WE'RE READY, WOLVERINE, AND ON OUR TERMS.
WE'LL START WITH HIT-AND-RUN TACTICS, TO THROW THE IMPERIALS OFF-BALANCE AND WHITTLE DOWN THEIR FORCES.
FOR NOW, WE SPLIT UP. WE'VE GOT THESE RUINS, BEAST; LET'S USE 'EM TO OUR BEST ADVANTAGE.
Oh, GOODY! I JUST LOVE PLAYING HIDE-'N'-SEEK!
ANY TELEPATHIC SIGN OF THE IMPIES, JEAN?
I'M AFRAID NOT, WARREN. ORACLE MUST BE BLOCKING MY PROBES. I DON'T WANT TO PUSH TOO HARD. SHE MIGHT BE ABLE TO BACK-TRACK THE SCAN TO US.
GOOD MOVE, JEAN--uh-oh!
THIS PLAZA'S WIDE OPEN-- ALMOST NO COVER. A PERFECT PLACE FOR AN AMBUSH.
TAKE THE POINT, NIGHTCRAWLER.
AS YOU COMMAND, FEARLESS LEADER.

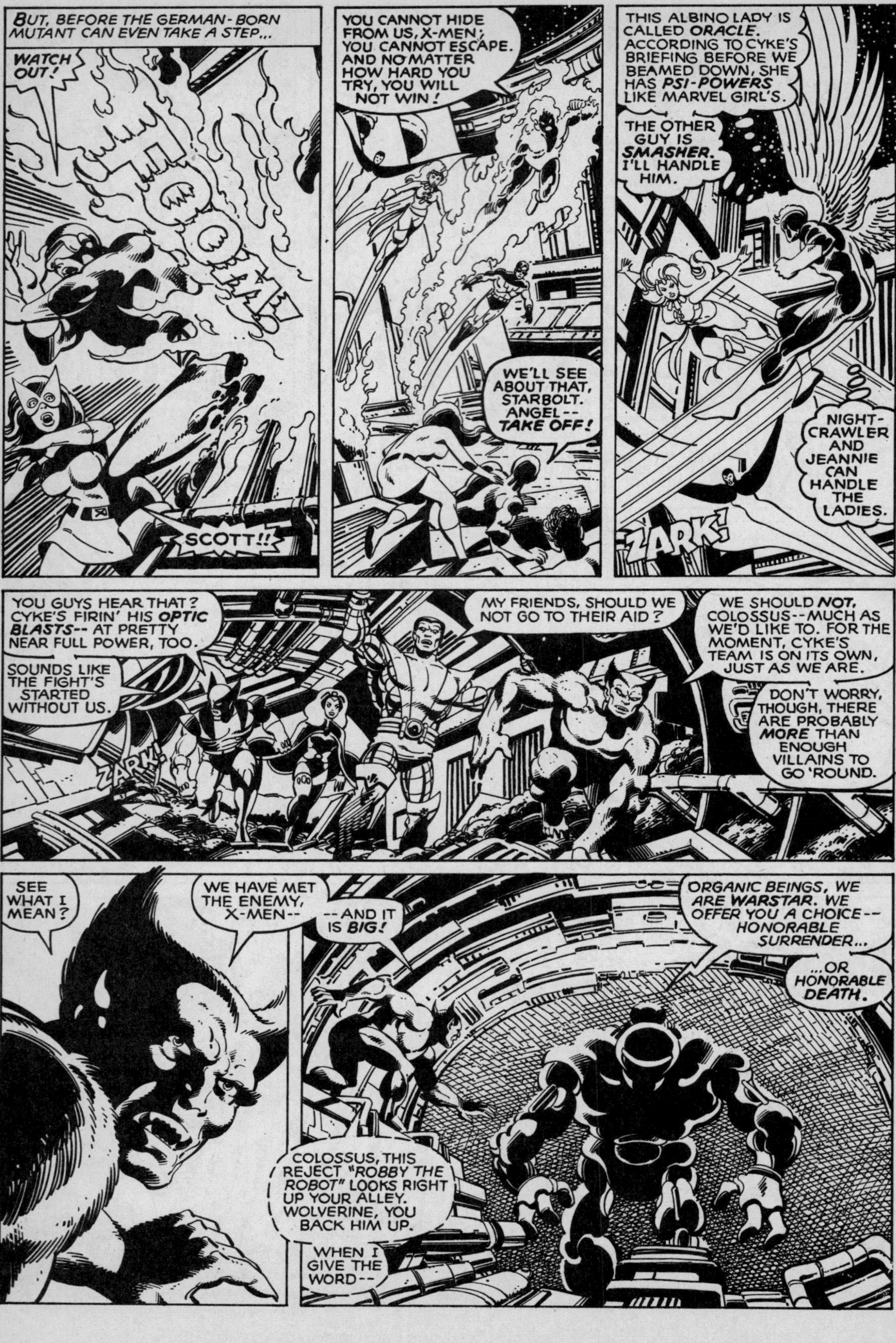
BUT, BEFORE THE GERMAN-BORN MUTANT CAN EVEN TAKE A STEP...
WATCH OUT!
BOOM
SCOTT!!
YOU CANNOT HIDE FROM US, X-MEN; YOU CANNOT ESCAPE. AND NO MATTER HOW HARD YOU TRY, YOU WILL NOT WIN!
WE'LL SEE ABOUT THAT, STARBOLT. ANGEL-- TAKE OFF!
THIS ALBINO LADY IS CALLED ORACLE. ACCORDING TO CYKE'S BRIEFING BEFORE WE BEAMED DOWN, SHE HAS PSI-POWERS LIKE MARVEL GIRL'S.
THE OTHER GUY IS SMASHER. I'LL HANDLE HIM.
NIGHT-CRAWLER AND JEANNIE CAN HANDLE THE LADIES.
ZARK!
YOU GUYS HEAR THAT? CYKE'S FIRIN' HIS OPTIC BLASTS-- AT PRETTY NEAR FULL POWER, TOO.
SOUNDS LIKE THE FIGHT'S STARTED WITHOUT US.
ZARK
MY FRIENDS, SHOULD WE NOT GO TO THEIR AID?
WE SHOULD NOT, COLOSSUS--MUCH AS WE'D LIKE TO. FOR THE MOMENT, CYKE'S TEAM IS ON ITS OWN, JUST AS WE ARE.
DON'T WORRY, THOUGH, THERE ARE PROBABLY MORE THAN ENOUGH VILLAINS TO GO 'ROUND.
SEE WHAT I MEAN?
WE HAVE MET THE ENEMY, X-MEN--
--AND IT IS BIG!
ORGANIC BEINGS, WE ARE WARSTAR. WE OFFER YOU A CHOICE-- HONORABLE SURRENDER...
...OR HONORABLE DEATH.
COLOSSUS, THIS REJECT "ROBBY THE ROBOT" LOOKS RIGHT UP YOUR ALLEY. WOLVERINE, YOU BACK HIM UP.
WHEN I GIVE THE WORD--

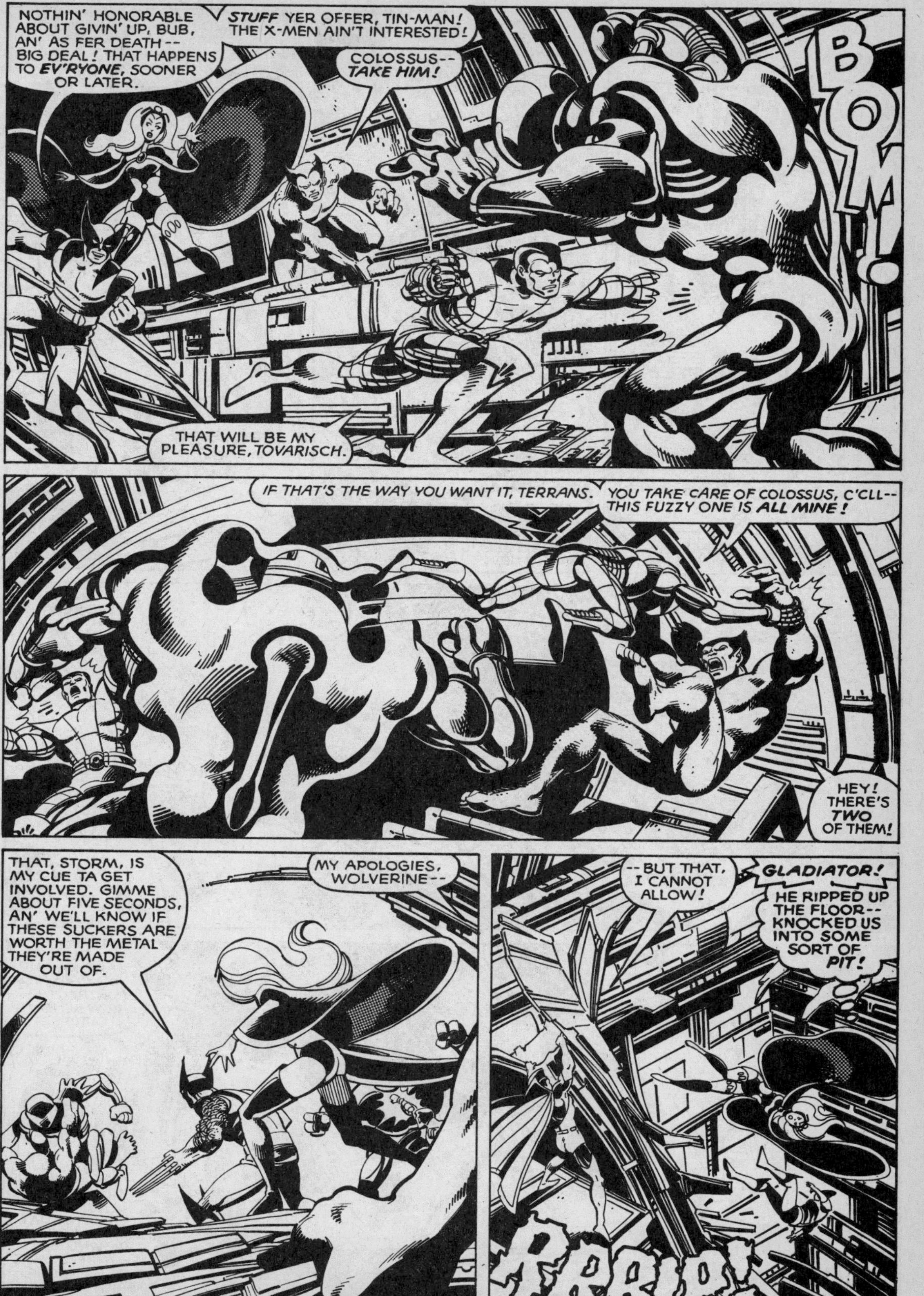
NOTHIN' HONORABLE ABOUT GIVIN' UP, BUB, AN' AS FER DEATH -- BIG DEAL! THAT HAPPENS TO EV'RYONE, SOONER OR LATER.
STUFF YER OFFER, TIN-MAN! THE X-MEN AIN'T INTERESTED!
COLOSSUS-- TAKE HIM!
BOOM!
THAT WILL BE MY PLEASURE, TOVARISCH.
IF THAT'S THE WAY YOU WANT IT, TERRANS.
YOU TAKE CARE OF COLOSSUS, C'CLL-- THIS FUZZY ONE IS ALL MINE!
HEY! THERE'S TWO OF THEM!
THAT, STORM, IS MY CUE TA GET INVOLVED. GIMME ABOUT FIVE SECONDS, AN' WE'LL KNOW IF THESE SUCKERS ARE WORTH THE METAL THEY'RE MADE OUT OF.
MY APOLOGIES, WOLVERINE--
--BUT THAT, I CANNOT ALLOW!
GLADIATOR!
HE RIPPED UP THE FLOOR-- KNOCKED US INTO SOME SORT OF PIT!
RRRIP!

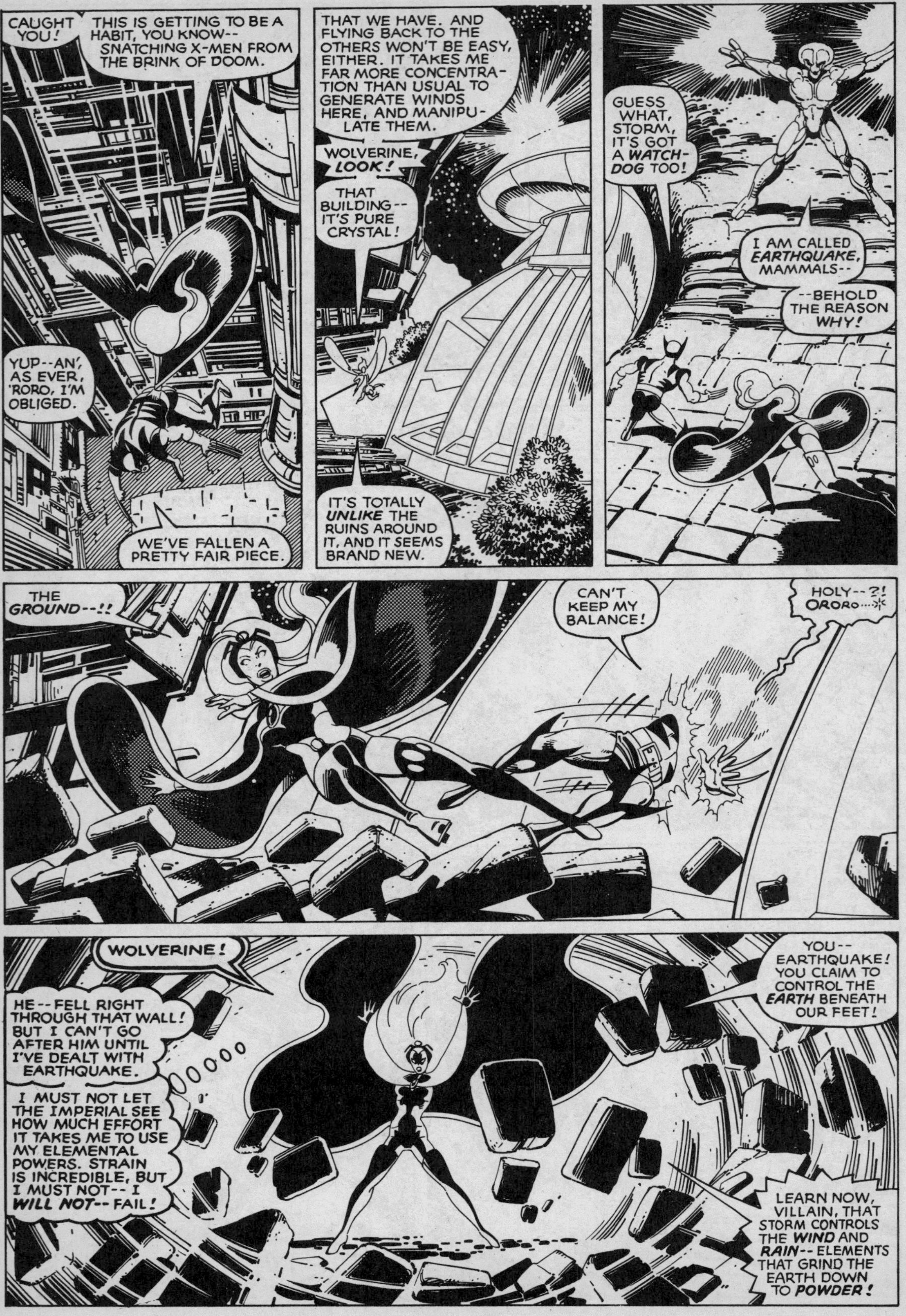
CAUGHT YOU!
THIS IS GETTING TO BE A HABIT, YOU KNOW-- SNATCHING X-MEN FROM THE BRINK OF DOOM.
YUP--AN', AS EVER, 'RORO, I'M OBLIGED.
WE'VE FALLEN A PRETTY FAIR PIECE.
THAT WE HAVE. AND FLYING BACK TO THE OTHERS WON'T BE EASY, EITHER. IT TAKES ME FAR MORE CONCENTRATION THAN USUAL TO GENERATE WINDS HERE, AND MANIPULATE THEM.
WOLVERINE, LOOK!
THAT BUILDING-- IT'S PURE CRYSTAL!
IT'S TOTALLY UNLIKE THE RUINS AROUND IT, AND IT SEEMS BRAND NEW.
GUESS WHAT, STORM, IT'S GOT A WATCH-DOG TOO!
I AM CALLED EARTHQUAKE, MAMMALS--
--BEHOLD THE REASON WHY!
THE GROUND--!!
CAN'T KEEP MY BALANCE!
HOLY--?! ORORO...!
WOLVERINE!
HE--FELL RIGHT THROUGH THAT WALL! BUT I CAN'T GO AFTER HIM UNTIL I'VE DEALT WITH EARTHQUAKE.
I MUST NOT LET THE IMPERIAL SEE HOW MUCH EFFORT IT TAKES ME TO USE MY ELEMENTAL POWERS. STRAIN IS INCREDIBLE, BUT I MUST NOT-- I WILL NOT-- FAIL!
YOU-- EARTHQUAKE! YOU CLAIM TO CONTROL THE EARTH BENEATH OUR FEET!
LEARN NOW, VILLAIN, THAT STORM CONTROLS THE WIND AND RAIN-- ELEMENTS THAT GRIND THE EARTH DOWN TO POWDER!

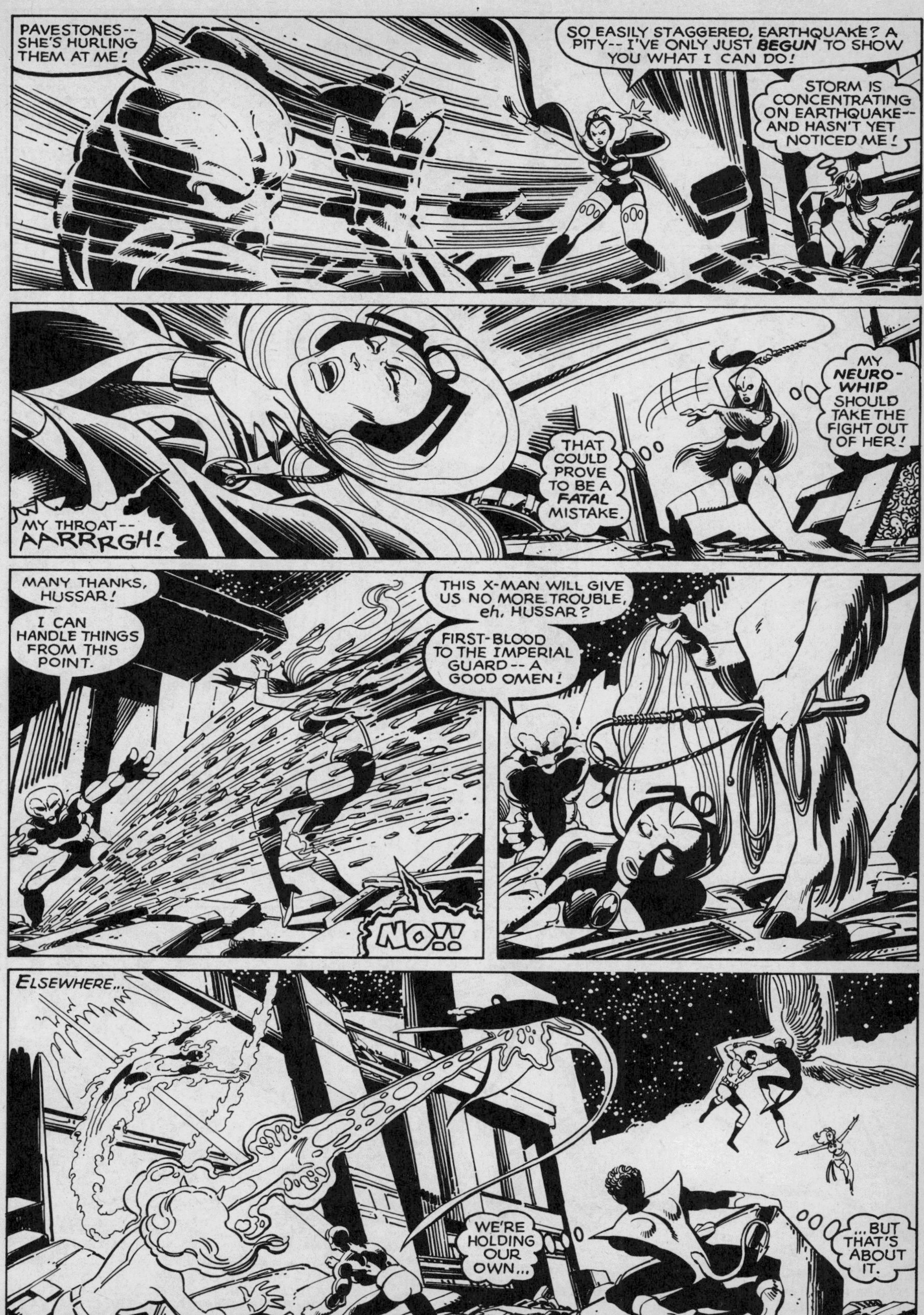
PAVESTONES-- SHE'S HURLING THEM AT ME!
SO EASILY STAGGERED, EARTHQUAKE? A PITY-- I'VE ONLY JUST BEGUN TO SHOW YOU WHAT I CAN DO!
STORM IS CONCENTRATING ON EARTHQUAKE-- AND HASN'T YET NOTICED ME!
MY NEURO-WHIP SHOULD TAKE THE FIGHT OUT OF HER!
THAT COULD PROVE TO BE A FATAL MISTAKE.
MY THROAT-- AARRRGH!
MANY THANKS, HUSSAR!
I CAN HANDLE THINGS FROM THIS POINT.
NO!!
THIS X-MAN WILL GIVE US NO MORE TROUBLE, eh, HUSSAR?
FIRST-BLOOD TO THE IMPERIAL GUARD-- A GOOD OMEN!
ELSEWHERE...
WE'RE HOLDING OUR OWN...
...BUT THAT'S ABOUT IT.

OUR POWERS AND TACTICAL SKILLS ARE PRETTY EVENLY MATCHED -- EXCEPT THAT *ALL* OF OUR FOES CAN FLY.

CYCLOPS AND JEAN CAN STRIKE AT LONG-RANGE, AND ANGEL CAN FIGHT THEM IN THEIR ELEMENT.

BUT I'M JUST A GLORIFIED *ACROBAT.* ALL THE MANEUVERS I'VE LEARNED TO COUNTER AN AIRBORNE ATTACK, WERE WORKED OUT WITH *STORM.* ANGEL DOESN'T KNOW THEM, AND THERE'S NO TIME TO TEACH -- *WHAT?!*

ANGEL! *LOOK OUT!* ORACLE'S MOVING IN BEHIND YOU!

M-MY MIND -- EVERY...THING... SUDDENLY GONE ...*BLOOEY!*

TOO LATE, NIGHTCRAWLER! I'VE *STUNNED* HIM!

AND WHILE THIS ANGEL-BEING IS HELPLESS...

...*SMASHER* WILL FINISH HIM OFF...

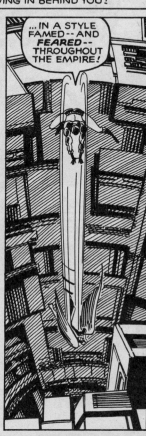

...IN A STYLE FAMED -- AND *FEARED* -- THROUGHOUT THE EMPIRE!

MEIN GOTT -- ANGEL'S TRAVELLING LIKE A *ROCKET!*

I CAN'T SEE BOTTOM -- THIS MUST BE A DEEP PIT. I HOPE IT'S A *STRAIGHT* ONE AS WELL.

I'VE GOT TO 'PORT AHEAD OF ANGEL, THEN TRY TO BREAK HIS FALL!

IT'LL BE RISKY. IF I *MATERIALIZE* IN OR AROUND A PHYSICAL OBJECT, I'LL GET MYSELF A QUICK AND VERY MESSY DEATH. BUT I'M ANGEL'S *ONLY* HOPE; I HAVE TO AT LEAST *TRY!*

THERE'S A FLASH OF FLAME, A GUSTING STENCH OF BRIMSTONE, A "BAMF" OF IMPLODING AIR -- AS NIGHTCRAWLER DISAPPEARS -- AND THEN, THERE IS ONLY SILENCE.

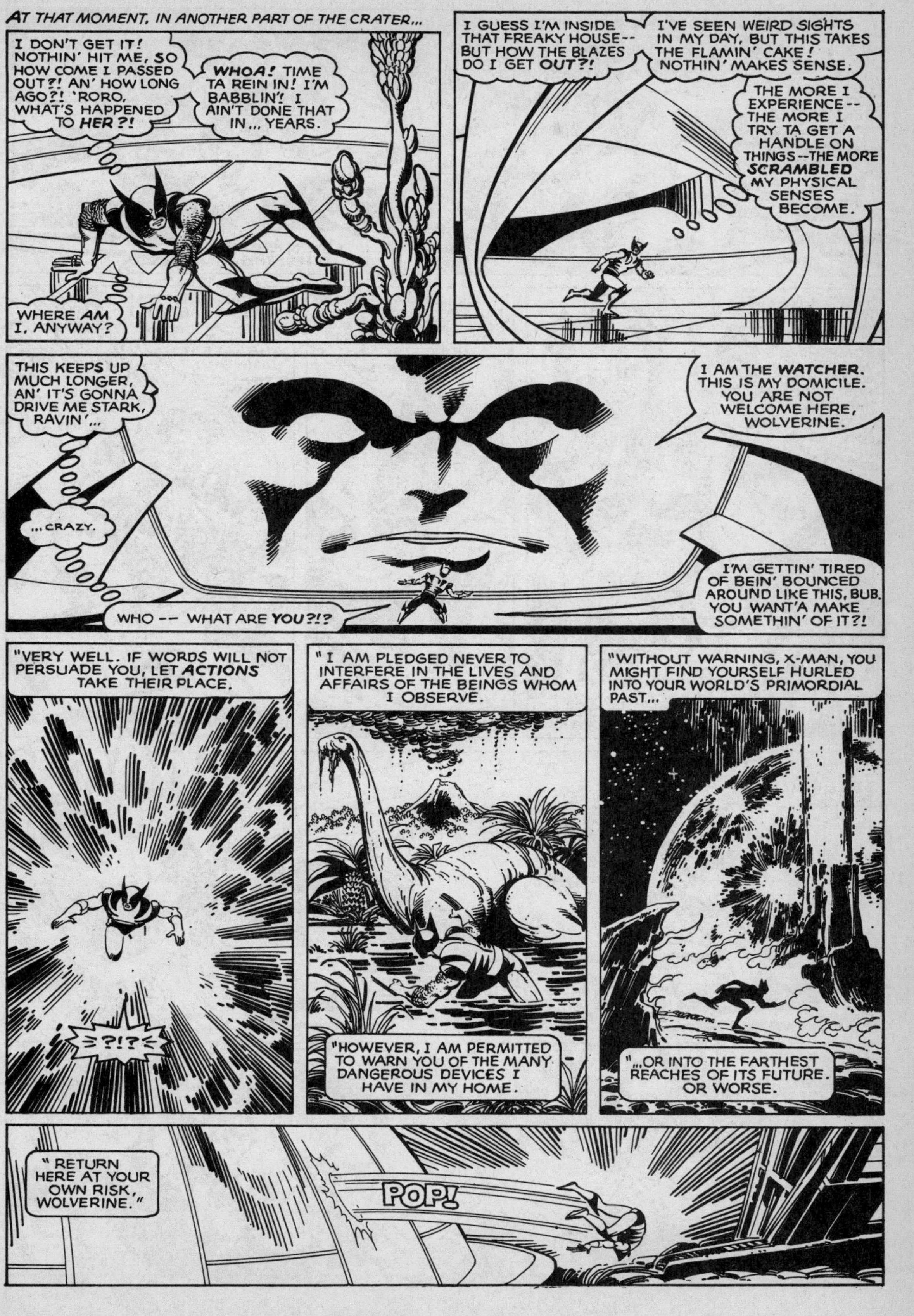
AT THAT MOMENT, IN ANOTHER PART OF THE CRATER...
I DON'T GET IT! NOTHIN' HIT ME, SO HOW COME I PASSED OUT?! AN' HOW LONG AGO?! 'RORO, WHAT'S HAPPENED TO HER?!
WHOA! TIME TA REIN IN! I'M BABBLIN'! I AIN'T DONE THAT IN... YEARS.
WHERE AM I, ANYWAY?
I GUESS I'M INSIDE THAT FREAKY HOUSE-- BUT HOW THE BLAZES DO I GET OUT?!
I'VE SEEN WEIRD SIGHTS IN MY DAY, BUT THIS TAKES THE FLAMIN' CAKE! NOTHIN' MAKES SENSE.
THE MORE I EXPERIENCE -- THE MORE I TRY TA GET A HANDLE ON THINGS --THE MORE SCRAMBLED MY PHYSICAL SENSES BECOME.
THIS KEEPS UP MUCH LONGER, AN' IT'S GONNA DRIVE ME STARK, RAVIN'...
...CRAZY.
WHO -- WHAT ARE YOU?!?
I AM THE WATCHER. THIS IS MY DOMICILE. YOU ARE NOT WELCOME HERE, WOLVERINE.
I'M GETTIN' TIRED OF BEIN' BOUNCED AROUND LIKE THIS, BUB. YOU WANT'A MAKE SOMETHIN' OF IT?!
"VERY WELL. IF WORDS WILL NOT PERSUADE YOU, LET ACTIONS TAKE THEIR PLACE.
?!?
"I AM PLEDGED NEVER TO INTERFERE IN THE LIVES AND AFFAIRS OF THE BEINGS WHOM I OBSERVE.
"HOWEVER, I AM PERMITTED TO WARN YOU OF THE MANY DANGEROUS DEVICES I HAVE IN MY HOME.
"WITHOUT WARNING, X-MAN, YOU MIGHT FIND YOURSELF HURLED INTO YOUR WORLD'S PRIMORDIAL PAST...
"...OR INTO THE FARTHEST REACHES OF ITS FUTURE. OR WORSE.
"RETURN HERE AT YOUR OWN RISK, WOLVERINE."
POP!

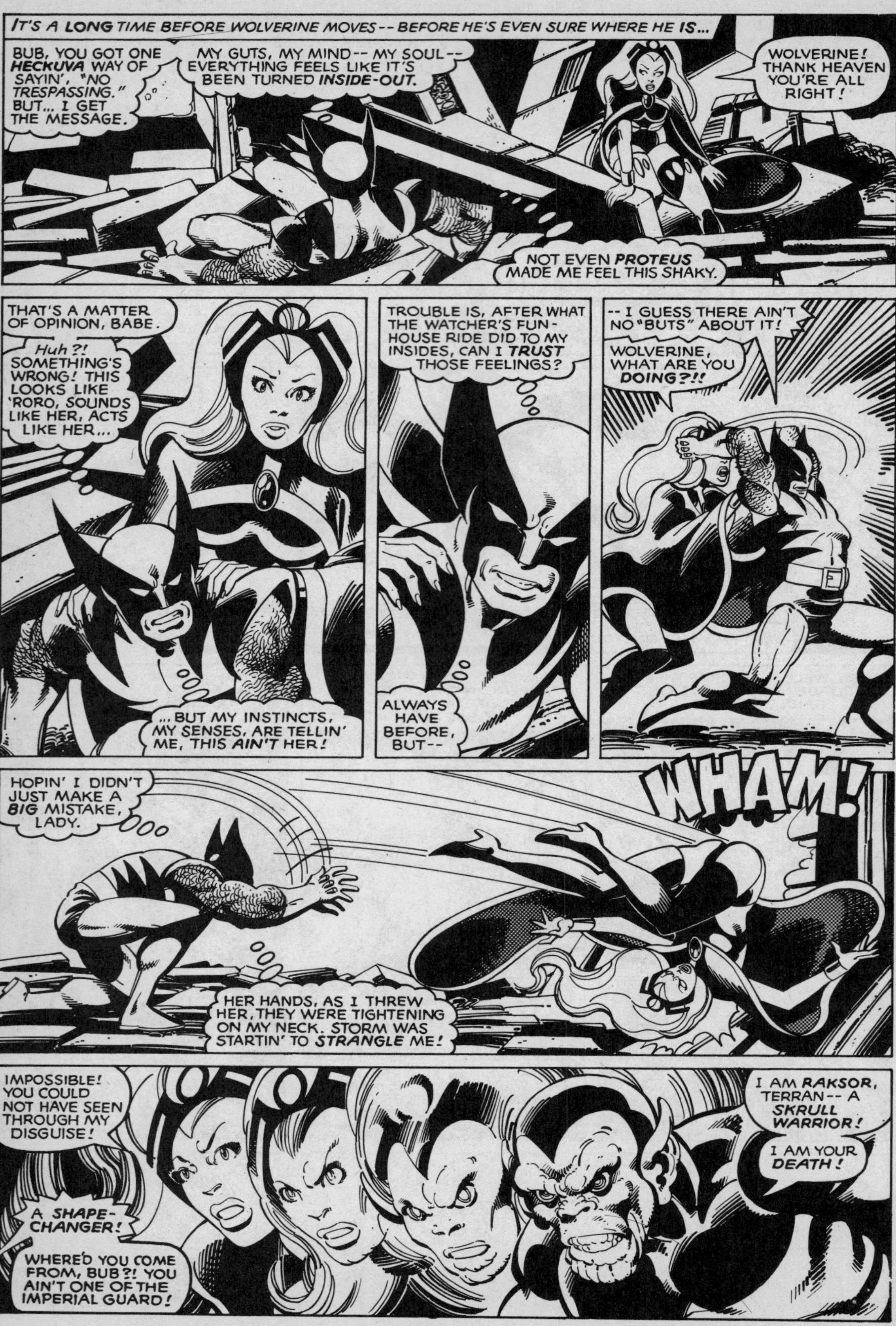

IT'S A LONG TIME BEFORE WOLVERINE MOVES -- BEFORE HE'S EVEN SURE WHERE HE IS...
BUB, YOU GOT ONE HECKUVA WAY OF SAYIN', "NO TRESPASSING." BUT... I GET THE MESSAGE.
MY GUTS, MY MIND -- MY SOUL -- EVERYTHING FEELS LIKE IT'S BEEN TURNED INSIDE-OUT.
WOLVERINE! THANK HEAVEN YOU'RE ALL RIGHT!
NOT EVEN PROTEUS MADE ME FEEL THIS SHAKY.
THAT'S A MATTER OF OPINION, BABE.
Huh?! SOMETHING'S WRONG! THIS LOOKS LIKE 'RORO, SOUNDS LIKE HER, ACTS LIKE HER...
...BUT MY INSTINCTS, MY SENSES, ARE TELLIN' ME, THIS AIN'T HER!
TROUBLE IS, AFTER WHAT THE WATCHER'S FUN-HOUSE RIDE DID TO MY INSIDES, CAN I TRUST THOSE FEELINGS?
ALWAYS HAVE BEFORE, BUT--
-- I GUESS THERE AIN'T NO "BUTS" ABOUT IT!
WOLVERINE, WHAT ARE YOU DOING?!!
HOPIN' I DIDN'T JUST MAKE A BIG MISTAKE, LADY.
WHAM!
HER HANDS, AS I THREW HER, THEY WERE TIGHTENING ON MY NECK. STORM WAS STARTIN' TO STRANGLE ME!
IMPOSSIBLE! YOU COULD NOT HAVE SEEN THROUGH MY DISGUISE!
A SHAPE-CHANGER!
WHERE'D YOU COME FROM, BUB?! YOU AIN'T ONE OF THE IMPERIAL GUARD!
I AM RAKSOR, TERRAN -- A SKRULL WARRIOR!
I AM YOUR DEATH!

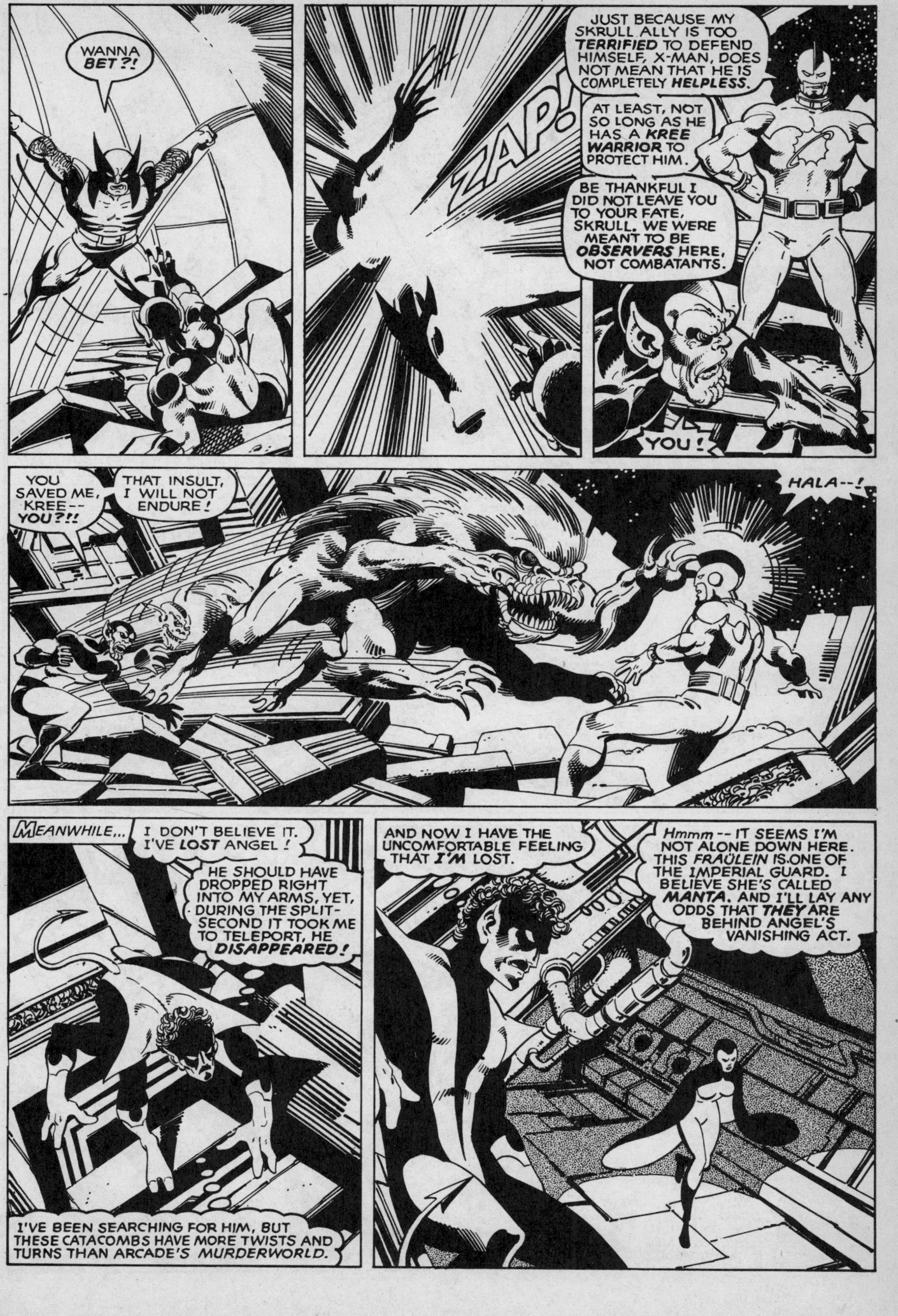

WANNA BET?!
ZAP!
JUST BECAUSE MY SKRULL ALLY IS TOO TERRIFIED TO DEFEND HIMSELF, X-MAN, DOES NOT MEAN THAT HE IS COMPLETELY HELPLESS.
AT LEAST, NOT SO LONG AS HE HAS A KREE WARRIOR TO PROTECT HIM.
BE THANKFUL I DID NOT LEAVE YOU TO YOUR FATE, SKRULL. WE WERE MEANT TO BE OBSERVERS HERE, NOT COMBATANTS.
YOU!
YOU SAVED ME, KREE-- YOU?!!
THAT INSULT, I WILL NOT ENDURE!
HALA--!
MEANWHILE...
I DON'T BELIEVE IT. I'VE LOST ANGEL!
HE SHOULD HAVE DROPPED RIGHT INTO MY ARMS, YET, DURING THE SPLIT-SECOND IT TOOK ME TO TELEPORT, HE DISAPPEARED!
I'VE BEEN SEARCHING FOR HIM, BUT THESE CATACOMBS HAVE MORE TWISTS AND TURNS THAN ARCADE'S MURDERWORLD.
AND NOW I HAVE THE UNCOMFORTABLE FEELING THAT I'M LOST.
Hmmm -- IT SEEMS I'M NOT ALONE DOWN HERE. THIS FRÄULEIN IS ONE OF THE IMPERIAL GUARD. I BELIEVE SHE'S CALLED MANTA. AND I'LL LAY ANY ODDS THAT THEY ARE BEHIND ANGEL'S VANISHING ACT.

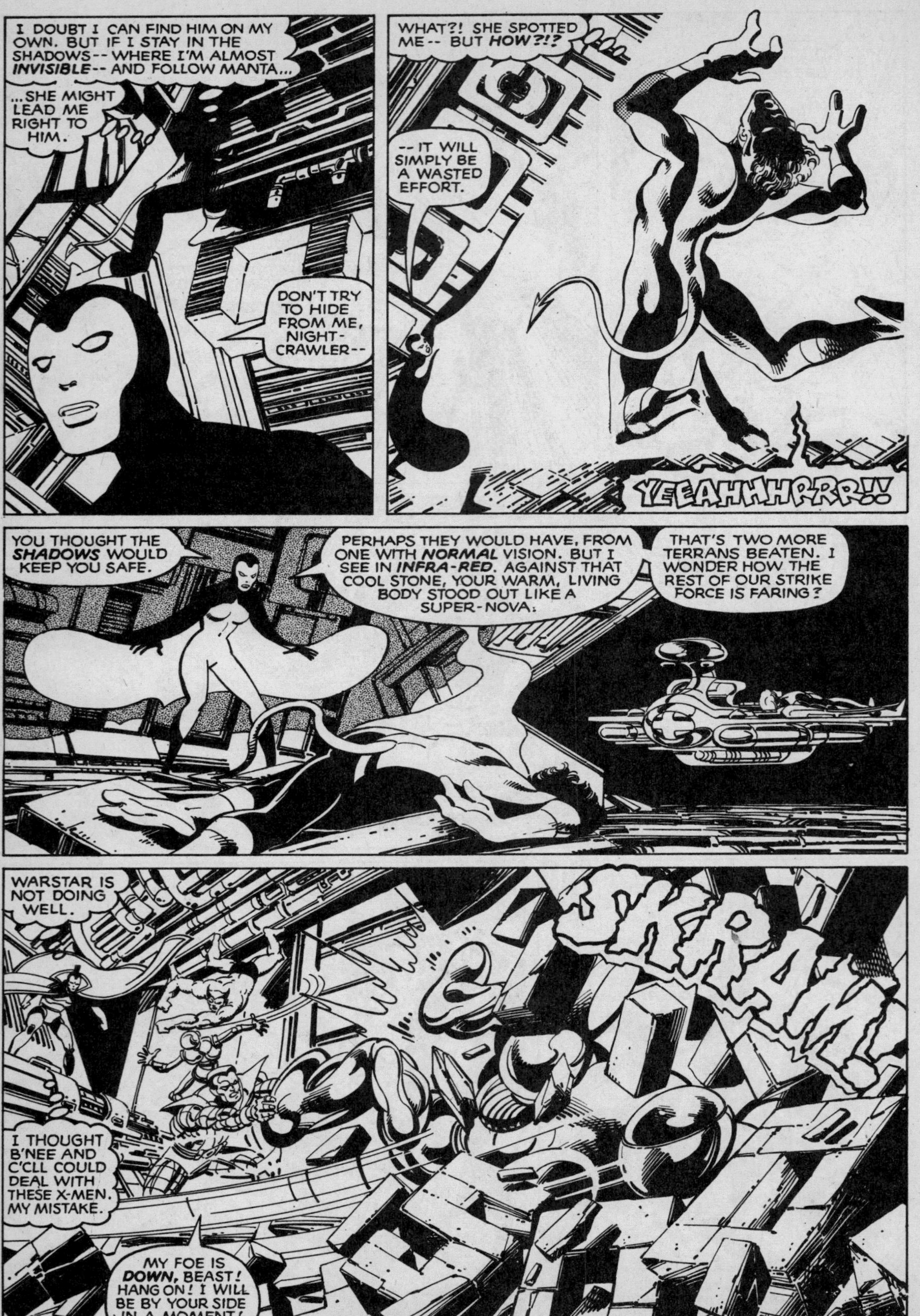
I DOUBT I CAN FIND HIM ON MY OWN. BUT IF I STAY IN THE SHADOWS-- WHERE I'M ALMOST INVISIBLE-- AND FOLLOW MANTA...
...SHE MIGHT LEAD ME RIGHT TO HIM.
DON'T TRY TO HIDE FROM ME, NIGHT-CRAWLER--
WHAT?! SHE SPOTTED ME-- BUT HOW?!?
--IT WILL SIMPLY BE A WASTED EFFORT.
YEEAHHHRRR!!
YOU THOUGHT THE SHADOWS WOULD KEEP YOU SAFE.
PERHAPS THEY WOULD HAVE, FROM ONE WITH NORMAL VISION. BUT I SEE IN INFRA-RED. AGAINST THAT COOL STONE, YOUR WARM, LIVING BODY STOOD OUT LIKE A SUPER-NOVA.
THAT'S TWO MORE TERRANS BEATEN. I WONDER HOW THE REST OF OUR STRIKE FORCE IS FARING?
WARSTAR IS NOT DOING WELL.
SKRAM!
I THOUGHT B'NEE AND C'LL COULD DEAL WITH THESE X-MEN. MY MISTAKE.
MY FOE IS DOWN, BEAST! HANG ON! I WILL BE BY YOUR SIDE IN A MOMENT!

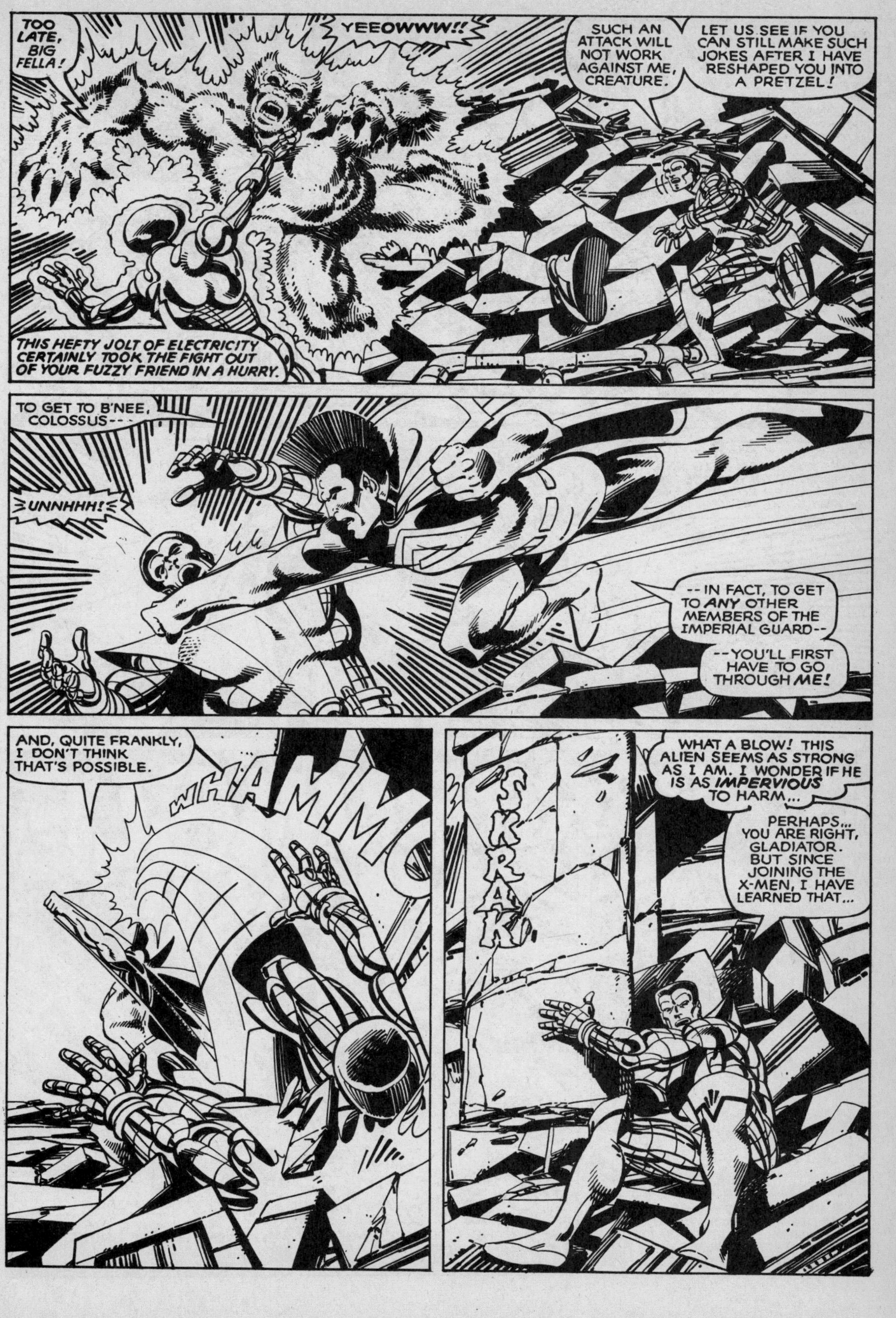
TOO LATE, BIG FELLA!
YEEOWWW!!
SUCH AN ATTACK WILL NOT WORK AGAINST ME, CREATURE.
LET US SEE IF YOU CAN STILL MAKE SUCH JOKES AFTER I HAVE RESHAPED YOU INTO A PRETZEL!
THIS HEFTY JOLT OF ELECTRICITY CERTAINLY TOOK THE FIGHT OUT OF YOUR FUZZY FRIEND IN A HURRY.
TO GET TO B'NEE, COLOSSUS---
UNNHHH!
-- IN FACT, TO GET TO ANY OTHER MEMBERS OF THE IMPERIAL GUARD--
--YOU'LL FIRST HAVE TO GO THROUGH ME!
AND, QUITE FRANKLY, I DON'T THINK THAT'S POSSIBLE.
WHAMMM
WHAT A BLOW! THIS ALIEN SEEMS AS STRONG AS I AM. I WONDER IF HE IS AS IMPERVIOUS TO HARM...
SKRAK
PERHAPS... YOU ARE RIGHT, GLADIATOR. BUT SINCE JOINING THE X-MEN, I HAVE LEARNED THAT...

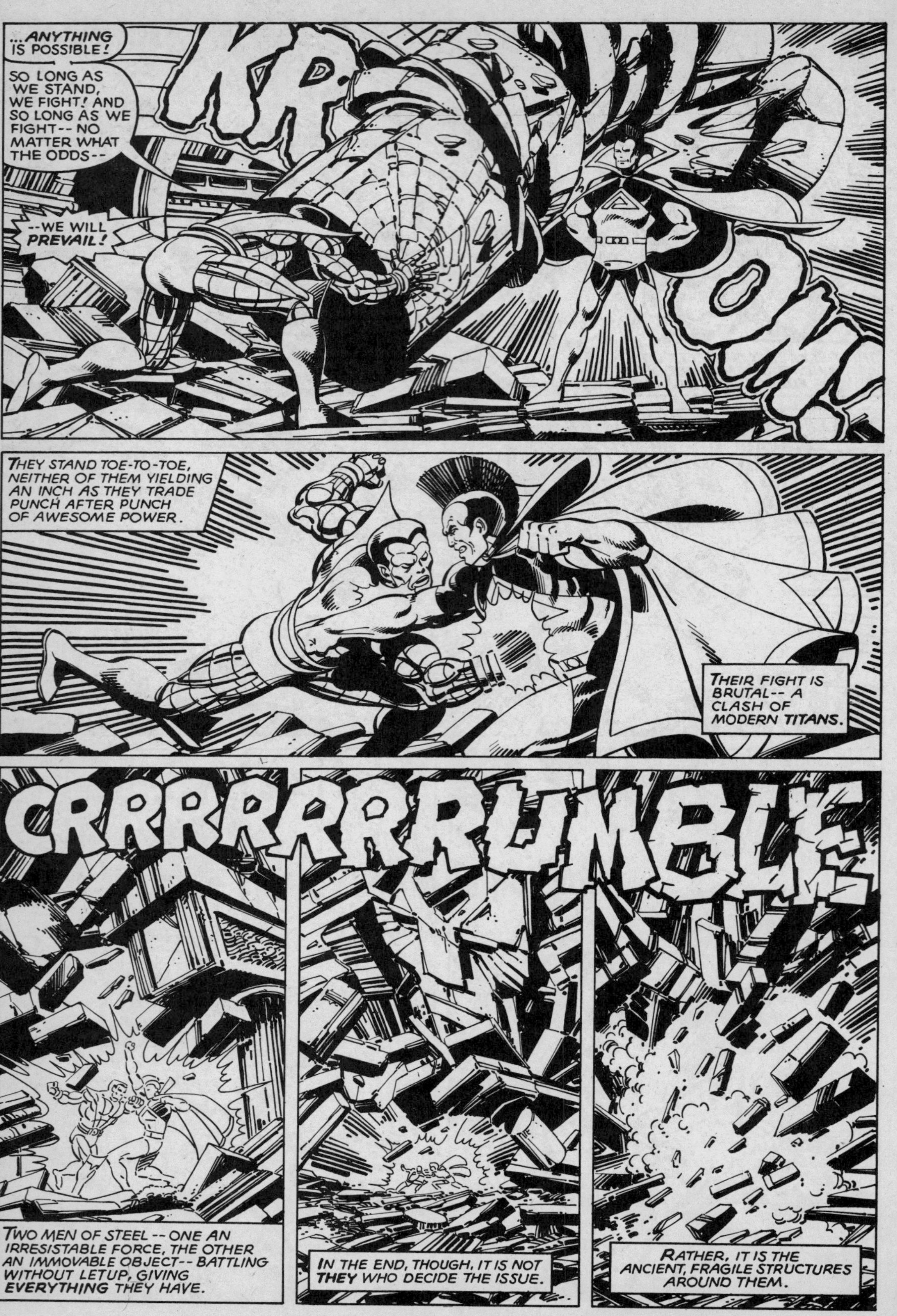
...ANYTHING IS POSSIBLE!
SO LONG AS WE STAND, WE FIGHT! AND SO LONG AS WE FIGHT-- NO MATTER WHAT THE ODDS--
--WE WILL PREVAIL!
KRA-BOOM!
THEY STAND TOE-TO-TOE, NEITHER OF THEM YIELDING AN INCH AS THEY TRADE PUNCH AFTER PUNCH OF AWESOME POWER.
THEIR FIGHT IS BRUTAL-- A CLASH OF MODERN TITANS.
CRRRRRRRUMBLE!
TWO MEN OF STEEL -- ONE AN IRRESISTABLE FORCE, THE OTHER AN IMMOVABLE OBJECT-- BATTLING WITHOUT LETUP, GIVING EVERYTHING THEY HAVE.
IN THE END, THOUGH, IT IS NOT THEY WHO DECIDE THE ISSUE.
RATHER, IT IS THE ANCIENT, FRAGILE STRUCTURES AROUND THEM.

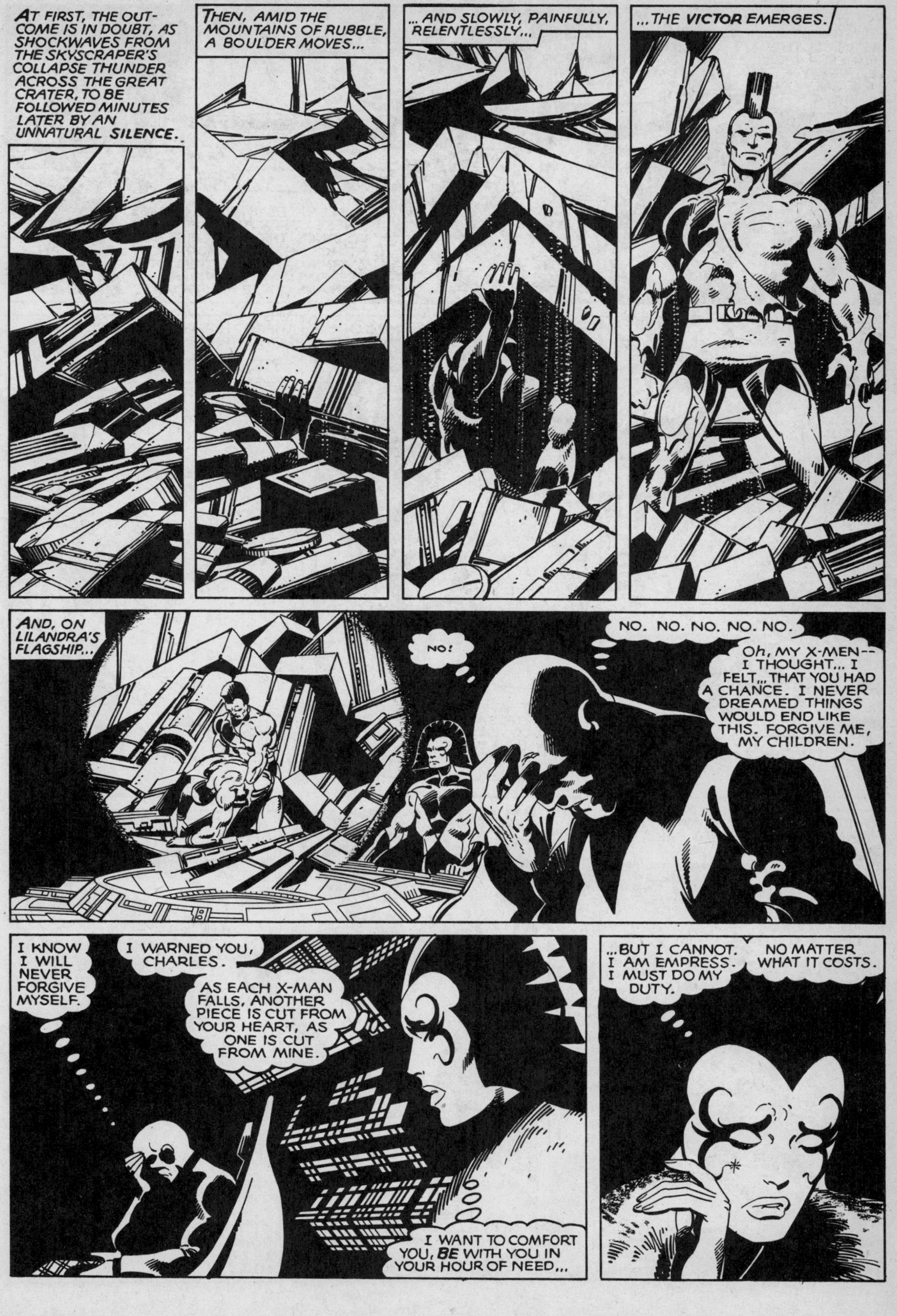
AT FIRST, THE OUTCOME IS IN DOUBT, AS SHOCKWAVES FROM THE SKYSCRAPER'S COLLAPSE THUNDER ACROSS THE GREAT CRATER, TO BE FOLLOWED MINUTES LATER BY AN UNNATURAL SILENCE.
THEN, AMID THE MOUNTAINS OF RUBBLE, A BOULDER MOVES...
...AND SLOWLY, PAINFULLY, RELENTLESSLY...
...THE VICTOR EMERGES.
AND, ON LILANDRA'S FLAGSHIP...
NO!
NO. NO. NO. NO. NO.
Oh, MY X-MEN-- I THOUGHT... I FELT... THAT YOU HAD A CHANCE. I NEVER DREAMED THINGS WOULD END LIKE THIS. FORGIVE ME, MY CHILDREN.
I KNOW I WILL NEVER FORGIVE MYSELF.
I WARNED YOU, CHARLES.
AS EACH X-MAN FALLS, ANOTHER PIECE IS CUT FROM YOUR HEART, AS ONE IS CUT FROM MINE.
I WANT TO COMFORT YOU, BE WITH YOU IN YOUR HOUR OF NEED...
...BUT I CANNOT. I AM EMPRESS. I MUST DO MY DUTY.
NO MATTER WHAT IT COSTS.

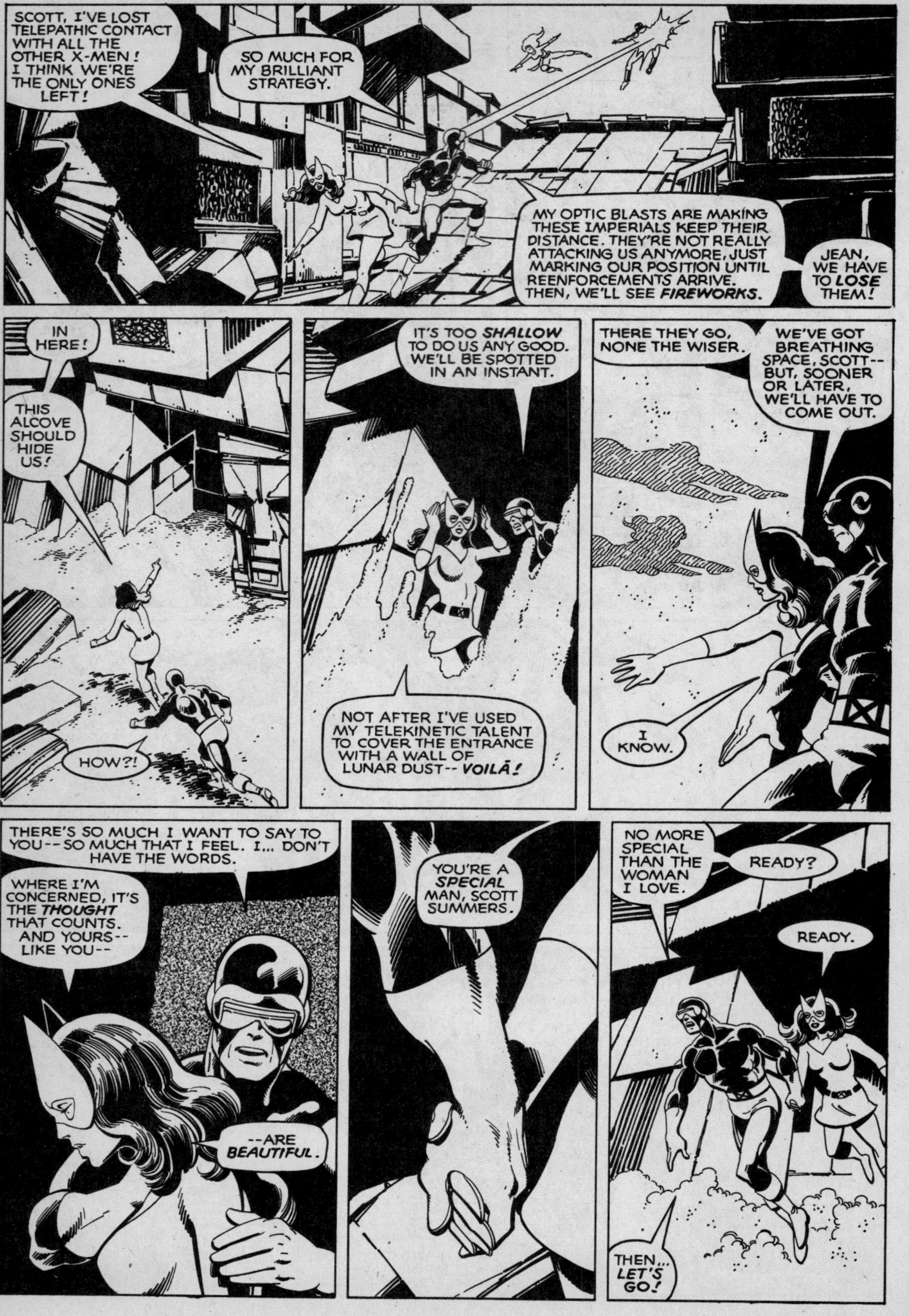
SCOTT, I'VE LOST TELEPATHIC CONTACT WITH ALL THE OTHER X-MEN! I THINK WE'RE THE ONLY ONES LEFT!
SO MUCH FOR MY BRILLIANT STRATEGY.
MY OPTIC BLASTS ARE MAKING THESE IMPERIALS KEEP THEIR DISTANCE. THEY'RE NOT REALLY ATTACKING US ANYMORE, JUST MARKING OUR POSITION UNTIL REENFORCEMENTS ARRIVE. THEN, WE'LL SEE FIREWORKS.
JEAN, WE HAVE TO LOSE THEM!
IN HERE!
THIS ALCOVE SHOULD HIDE US!
HOW?!
IT'S TOO SHALLOW TO DO US ANY GOOD. WE'LL BE SPOTTED IN AN INSTANT.
NOT AFTER I'VE USED MY TELEKINETIC TALENT TO COVER THE ENTRANCE WITH A WALL OF LUNAR DUST-- VOILÀ!
THERE THEY GO, NONE THE WISER.
WE'VE GOT BREATHING SPACE, SCOTT-- BUT, SOONER OR LATER, WE'LL HAVE TO COME OUT.
I KNOW.
THERE'S SO MUCH I WANT TO SAY TO YOU-- SO MUCH THAT I FEEL. I... DON'T HAVE THE WORDS.
WHERE I'M CONCERNED, IT'S THE THOUGHT THAT COUNTS. AND YOURS-- LIKE YOU--
--ARE BEAUTIFUL.
YOU'RE A SPECIAL MAN, SCOTT SUMMERS.
NO MORE SPECIAL THAN THE WOMAN I LOVE.
READY?
READY.
THEN... LET'S GO!

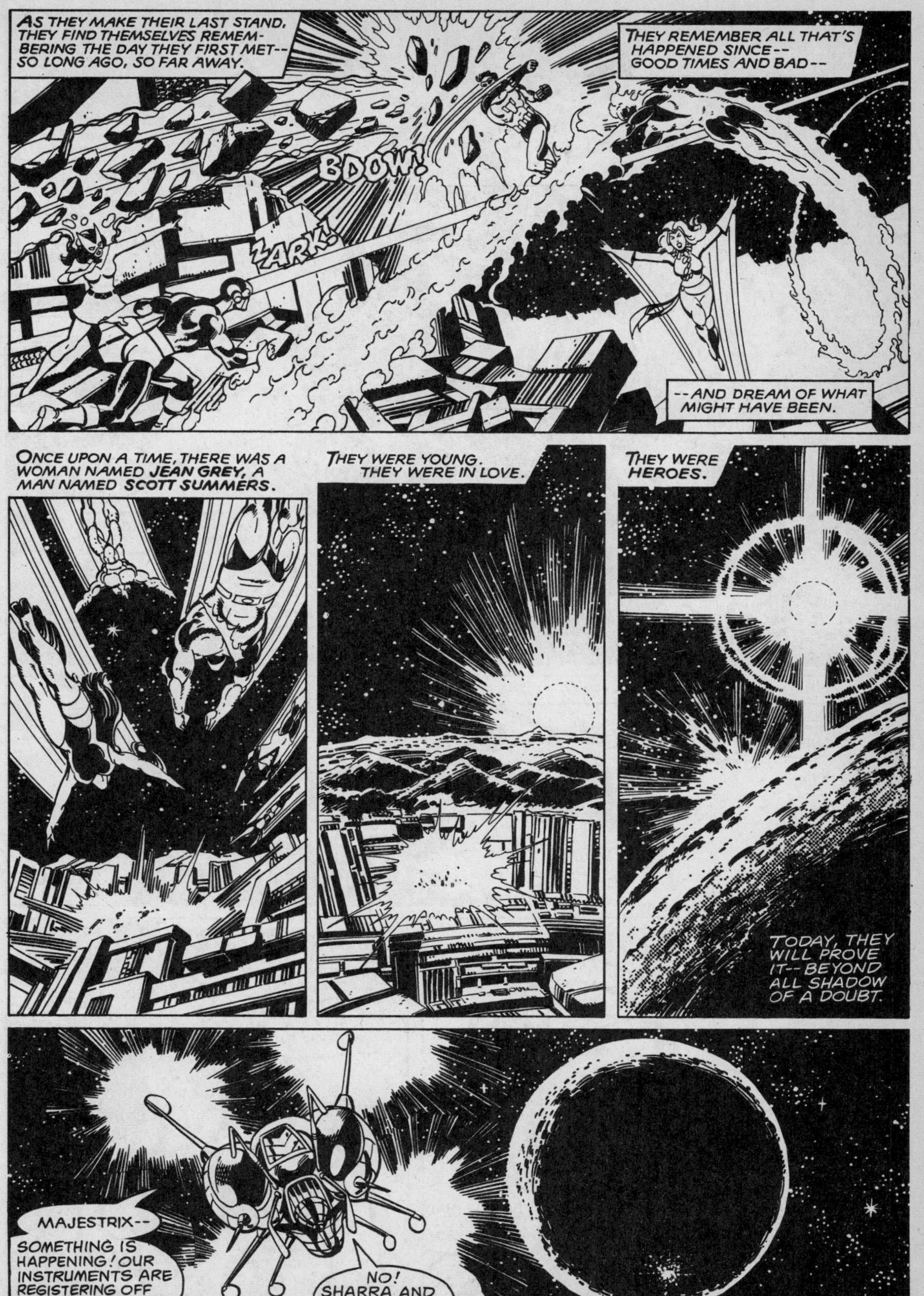

AS THEY MAKE THEIR LAST STAND, THEY FIND THEMSELVES REMEMBERING THE DAY THEY FIRST MET-- SO LONG AGO, SO FAR AWAY.
THEY REMEMBER ALL THAT'S HAPPENED SINCE-- GOOD TIMES AND BAD--
BDOW!
ZARK!
--AND DREAM OF WHAT MIGHT HAVE BEEN.
ONCE UPON A TIME, THERE WAS A WOMAN NAMED JEAN GREY, A MAN NAMED SCOTT SUMMERS.
THEY WERE YOUNG. THEY WERE IN LOVE.
THEY WERE HEROES.
TODAY, THEY WILL PROVE IT--BEYOND ALL SHADOW OF A DOUBT.
MAJESTRIX--
SOMETHING IS HAPPENING! OUR INSTRUMENTS ARE REGISTERING OFF THEIR SCALES!
NO! SHARRA AND K'YTHRI--NO!!

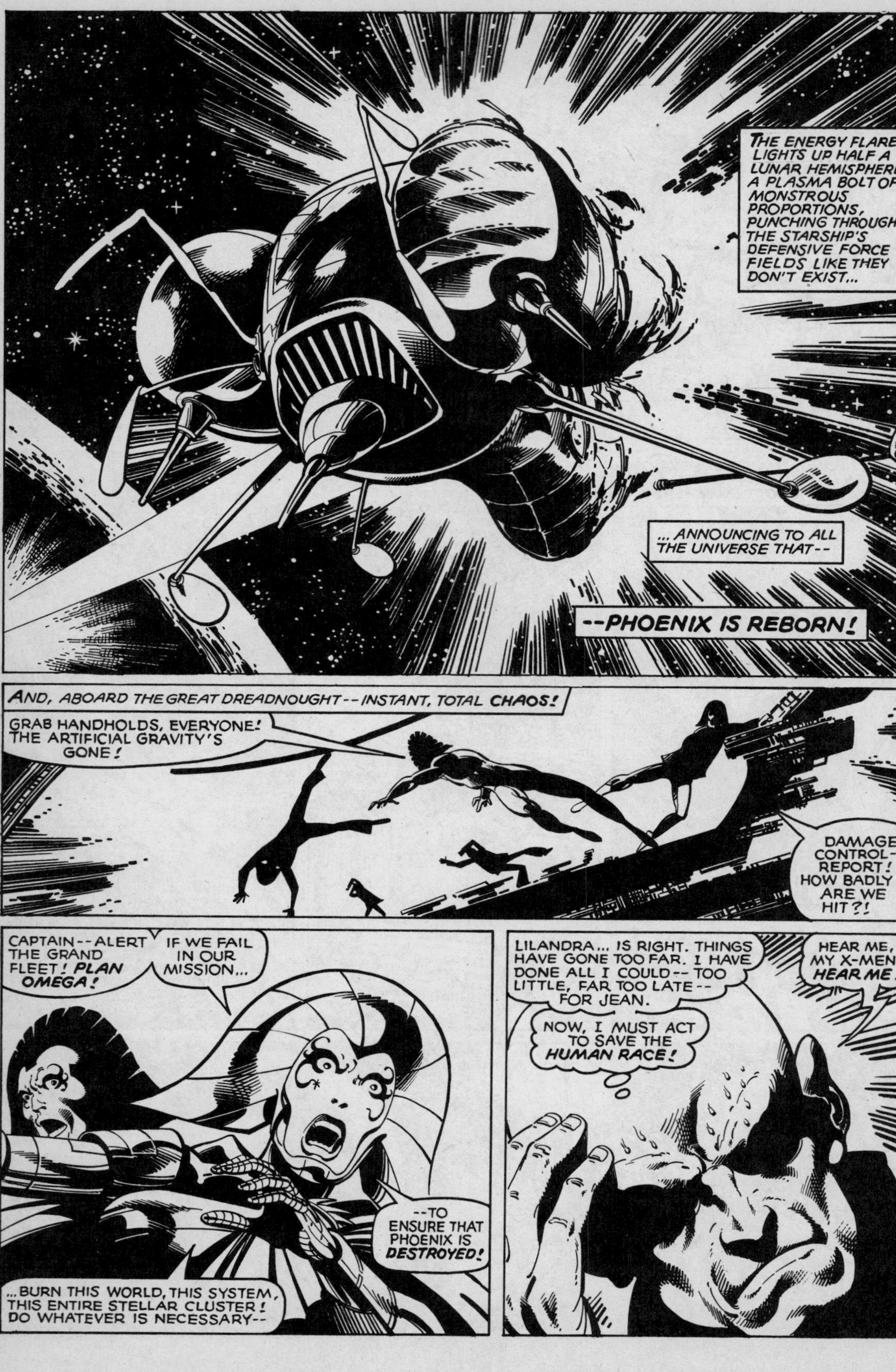
THE ENERGY FLARE LIGHTS UP HALF A LUNAR HEMISPHERE, A PLASMA BOLT OF MONSTROUS PROPORTIONS, PUNCHING THROUGH THE STARSHIP'S DEFENSIVE FORCE FIELDS LIKE THEY DON'T EXIST...
...ANNOUNCING TO ALL THE UNIVERSE THAT--
--PHOENIX IS REBORN!
AND, ABOARD THE GREAT DREADNOUGHT--INSTANT, TOTAL CHAOS!
GRAB HANDHOLDS, EVERYONE! THE ARTIFICIAL GRAVITY'S GONE!
DAMAGE CONTROL--REPORT! HOW BADLY ARE WE HIT?!
CAPTAIN--ALERT THE GRAND FLEET! PLAN OMEGA!
IF WE FAIL IN OUR MISSION...
...BURN THIS WORLD, THIS SYSTEM, THIS ENTIRE STELLAR CLUSTER! DO WHATEVER IS NECESSARY--
--TO ENSURE THAT PHOENIX IS DESTROYED!
LILANDRA... IS RIGHT. THINGS HAVE GONE TOO FAR. I HAVE DONE ALL I COULD--TOO LITTLE, FAR TOO LATE--FOR JEAN.
NOW, I MUST ACT TO SAVE THE HUMAN RACE!
HEAR ME, MY X-MEN! HEAR ME!

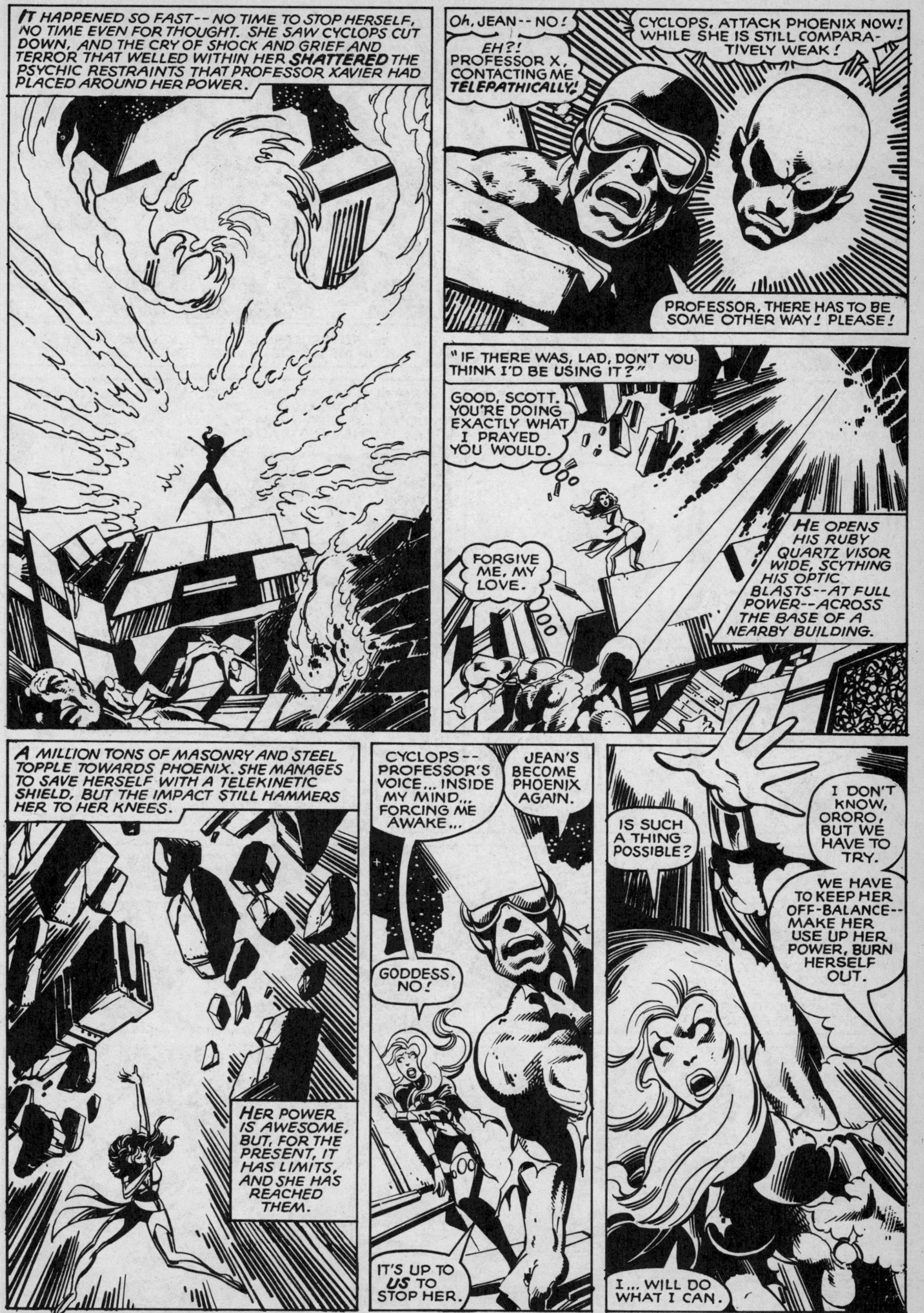
IT HAPPENED SO FAST-- NO TIME TO STOP HERSELF, NO TIME EVEN FOR THOUGHT. SHE SAW CYCLOPS CUT DOWN, AND THE CRY OF SHOCK AND GRIEF AND TERROR THAT WELLED WITHIN HER SHATTERED THE PSYCHIC RESTRAINTS THAT PROFESSOR XAVIER HAD PLACED AROUND HER POWER.
Oh, JEAN-- NO!
EH?! PROFESSOR X, CONTACTING ME TELEPATHICALLY!
CYCLOPS, ATTACK PHOENIX NOW! WHILE SHE IS STILL COMPARATIVELY WEAK!
PROFESSOR, THERE HAS TO BE SOME OTHER WAY! PLEASE!
"IF THERE WAS, LAD, DON'T YOU THINK I'D BE USING IT?"
GOOD, SCOTT. YOU'RE DOING EXACTLY WHAT I PRAYED YOU WOULD.
FORGIVE ME, MY LOVE.
HE OPENS HIS RUBY QUARTZ VISOR WIDE, SCYTHING HIS OPTIC BLASTS--AT FULL POWER--ACROSS THE BASE OF A NEARBY BUILDING.
A MILLION TONS OF MASONRY AND STEEL TOPPLE TOWARDS PHOENIX. SHE MANAGES TO SAVE HERSELF WITH A TELEKINETIC SHIELD, BUT THE IMPACT STILL HAMMERS HER TO HER KNEES.
HER POWER IS AWESOME, BUT, FOR THE PRESENT, IT HAS LIMITS, AND SHE HAS REACHED THEM.
CYCLOPS-- PROFESSOR'S VOICE... INSIDE MY MIND... FORCING ME AWAKE...
JEAN'S BECOME PHOENIX AGAIN.
GODDESS, NO!
IT'S UP TO US TO STOP HER.
IS SUCH A THING POSSIBLE?
I DON'T KNOW, ORORO, BUT WE HAVE TO TRY.
WE HAVE TO KEEP HER OFF-BALANCE-- MAKE HER USE UP HER POWER, BURN HERSELF OUT.
I... WILL DO WHAT I CAN.

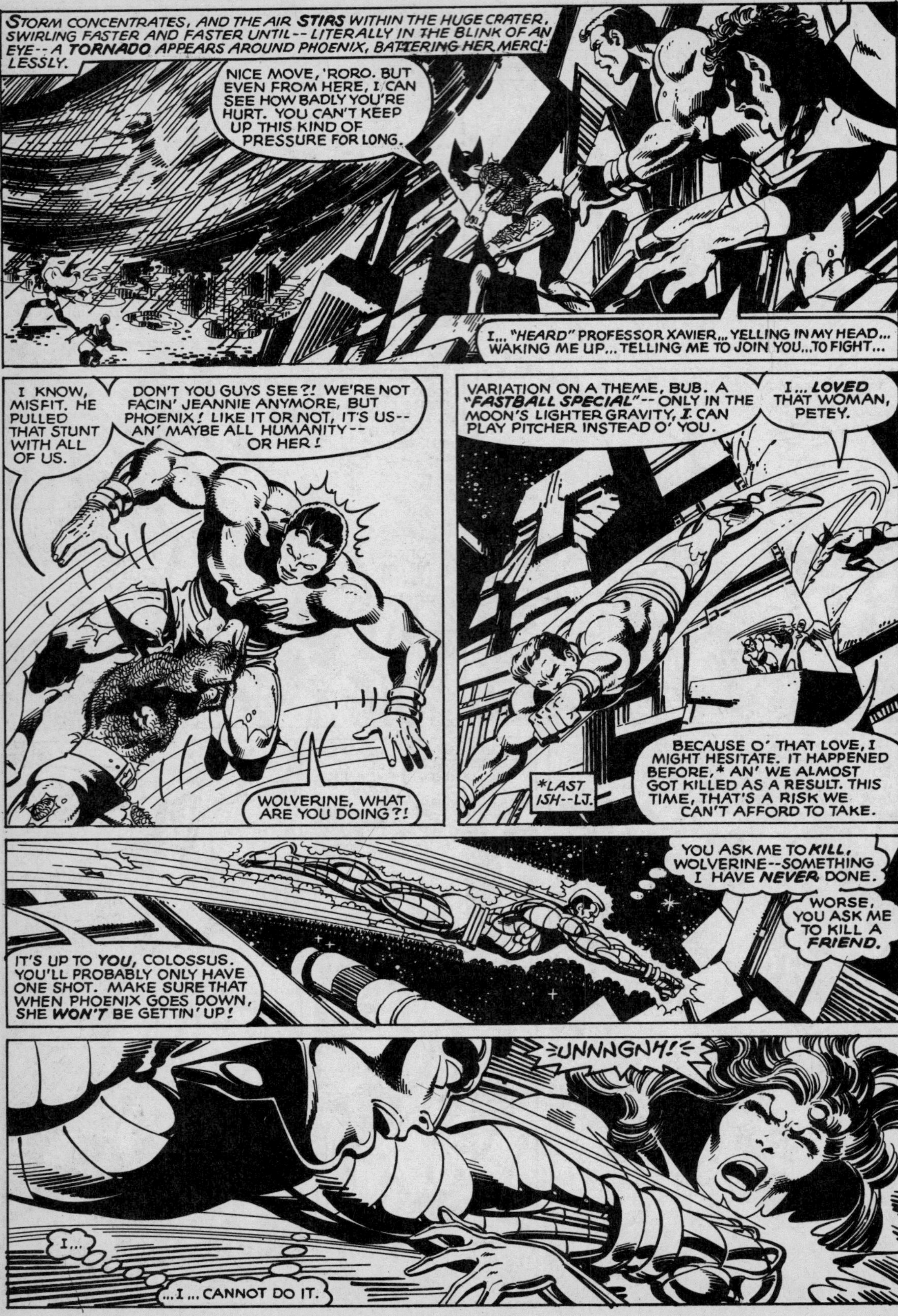
STORM CONCENTRATES, AND THE AIR STIRS WITHIN THE HUGE CRATER, SWIRLING FASTER AND FASTER UNTIL-- LITERALLY IN THE BLINK OF AN EYE-- A TORNADO APPEARS AROUND PHOENIX, BATTERING HER MERCILESSLY.
NICE MOVE, 'RORO. BUT EVEN FROM HERE, I CAN SEE HOW BADLY YOU'RE HURT. YOU CAN'T KEEP UP THIS KIND OF PRESSURE FOR LONG.
I... "HEARD" PROFESSOR XAVIER... YELLING IN MY HEAD... WAKING ME UP... TELLING ME TO JOIN YOU... TO FIGHT...
I KNOW, MISFIT. HE PULLED THAT STUNT WITH ALL OF US.
DON'T YOU GUYS SEE?! WE'RE NOT FACIN' JEANNIE ANYMORE, BUT PHOENIX! LIKE IT OR NOT, IT'S US-- AN' MAYBE ALL HUMANITY-- OR HER!
WOLVERINE, WHAT ARE YOU DOING?!
VARIATION ON A THEME, BUB. A "FASTBALL SPECIAL"-- ONLY IN THE MOON'S LIGHTER GRAVITY, I CAN PLAY PITCHER INSTEAD O' YOU.
I... LOVED THAT WOMAN, PETEY.
BECAUSE O' THAT LOVE, I MIGHT HESITATE. IT HAPPENED BEFORE,* AN' WE ALMOST GOT KILLED AS A RESULT. THIS TIME, THAT'S A RISK WE CAN'T AFFORD TO TAKE.
*LAST ISH--LJ.
IT'S UP TO YOU, COLOSSUS. YOU'LL PROBABLY ONLY HAVE ONE SHOT. MAKE SURE THAT WHEN PHOENIX GOES DOWN, SHE WON'T BE GETTIN' UP!
YOU ASK ME TO KILL, WOLVERINE--SOMETHING I HAVE NEVER DONE.
WORSE, YOU ASK ME TO KILL A FRIEND.
UNNNGNH!
I...
...I... CANNOT DO IT.

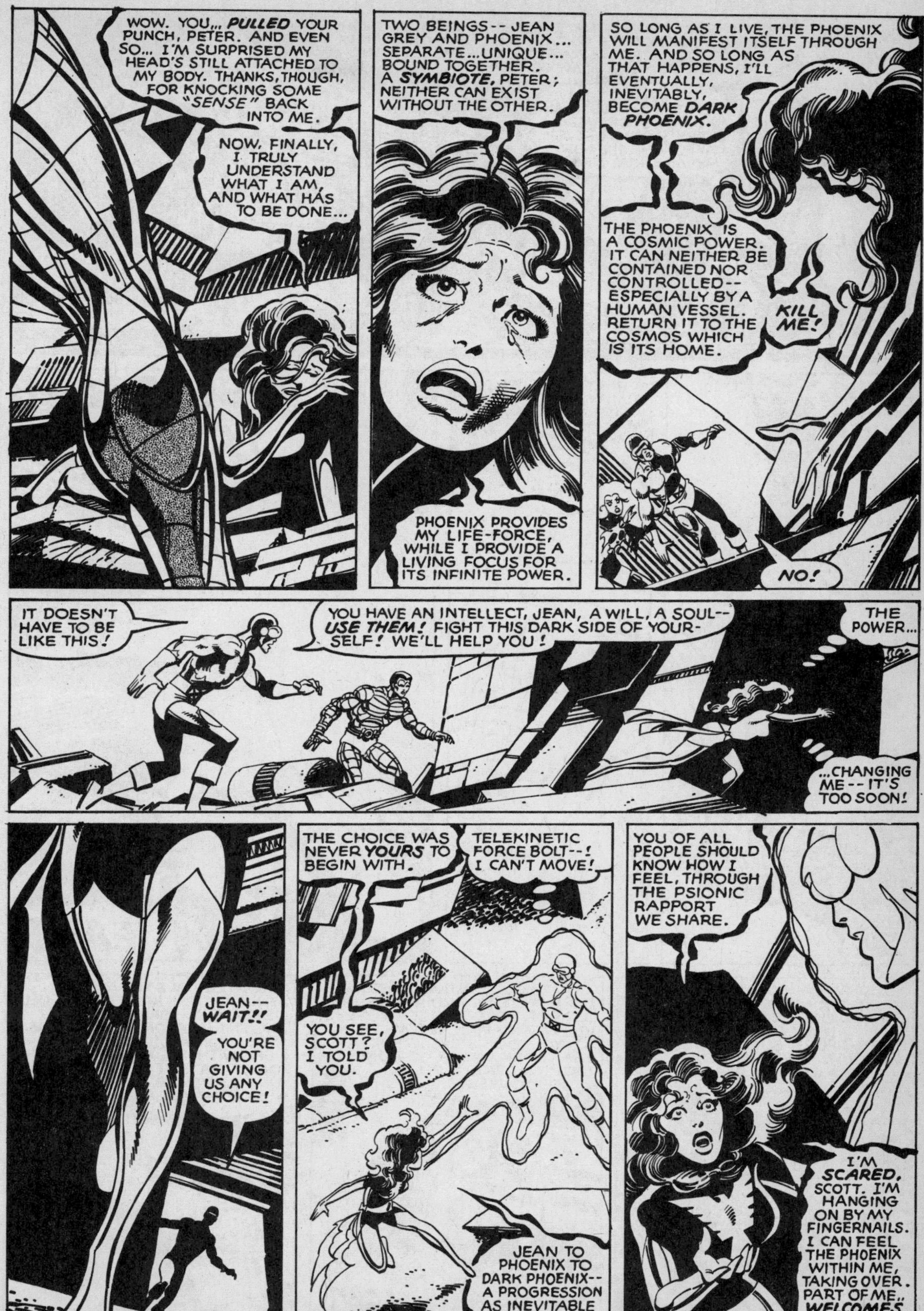
WOW. YOU... PULLED YOUR PUNCH, PETER. AND EVEN SO... I'M SURPRISED MY HEAD'S STILL ATTACHED TO MY BODY. THANKS, THOUGH, FOR KNOCKING SOME "SENSE" BACK INTO ME.
NOW, FINALLY, I TRULY UNDERSTAND WHAT I AM, AND WHAT HAS TO BE DONE...
TWO BEINGS -- JEAN GREY AND PHOENIX... SEPARATE... UNIQUE... BOUND TOGETHER. A SYMBIOTE, PETER; NEITHER CAN EXIST WITHOUT THE OTHER.
PHOENIX PROVIDES MY LIFE-FORCE, WHILE I PROVIDE A LIVING FOCUS FOR ITS INFINITE POWER.
SO LONG AS I LIVE, THE PHOENIX WILL MANIFEST ITSELF THROUGH ME. AND SO LONG AS THAT HAPPENS, I'LL EVENTUALLY, INEVITABLY, BECOME DARK PHOENIX.
THE PHOENIX IS A COSMIC POWER. IT CAN NEITHER BE CONTAINED NOR CONTROLLED -- ESPECIALLY BY A HUMAN VESSEL. RETURN IT TO THE COSMOS WHICH IS ITS HOME.
KILL ME!
NO!
IT DOESN'T HAVE TO BE LIKE THIS!
YOU HAVE AN INTELLECT, JEAN, A WILL, A SOUL -- USE THEM! FIGHT THIS DARK SIDE OF YOURSELF! WE'LL HELP YOU!
THE POWER...
...CHANGING ME -- IT'S TOO SOON!
JEAN -- WAIT!!
YOU'RE NOT GIVING US ANY CHOICE!
THE CHOICE WAS NEVER YOURS TO BEGIN WITH.
TELEKINETIC FORCE BOLT --! I CAN'T MOVE!
YOU SEE, SCOTT? I TOLD YOU.
JEAN TO PHOENIX TO DARK PHOENIX -- A PROGRESSION AS INEVITABLE AS DEATH.
YOU OF ALL PEOPLE SHOULD KNOW HOW I FEEL, THROUGH THE PSIONIC RAPPORT WE SHARE.
I'M SCARED, SCOTT. I'M HANGING ON BY MY FINGERNAILS. I CAN FEEL THE PHOENIX WITHIN ME, TAKING OVER. PART OF ME.. WELCOMES IT.

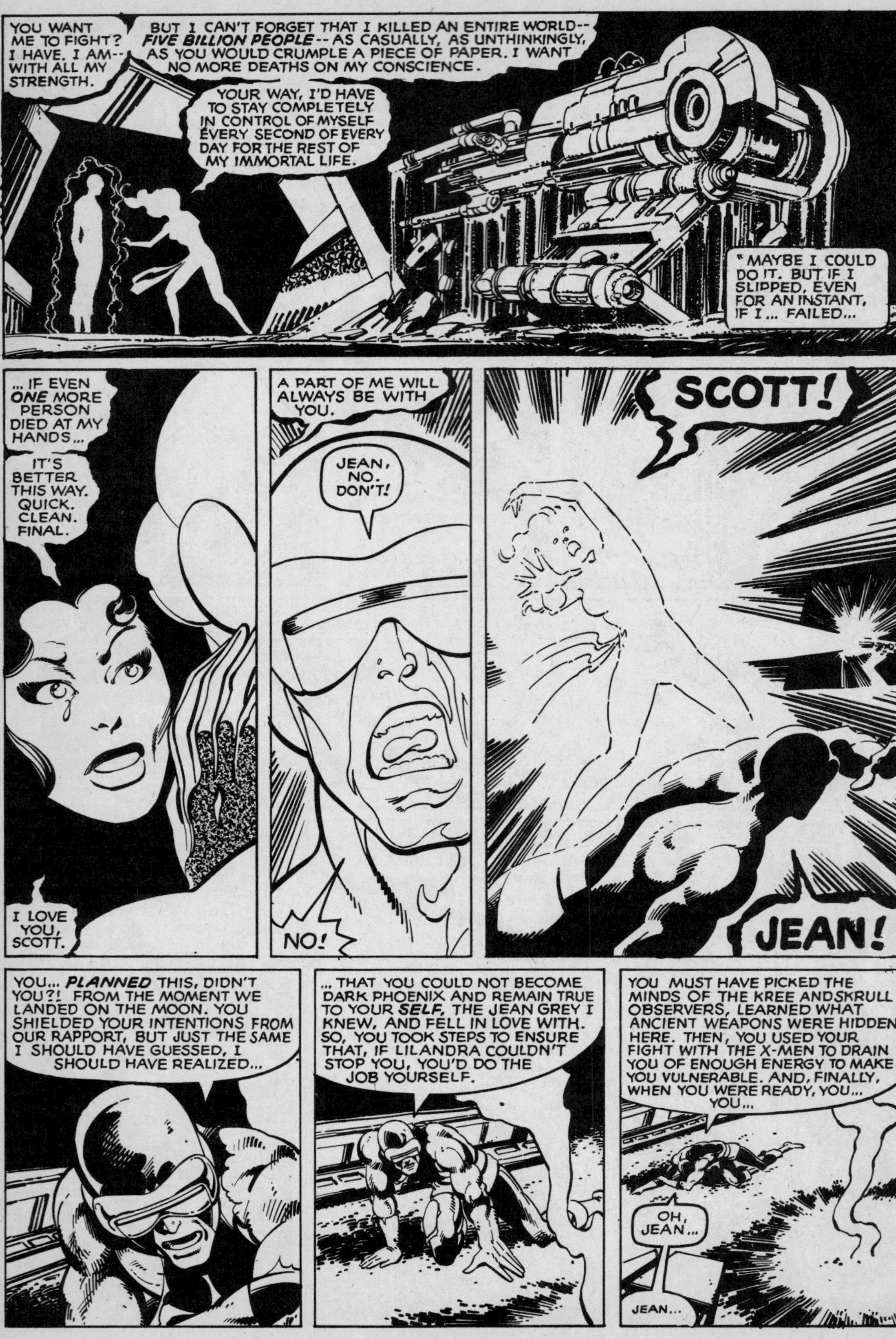
YOU WANT ME TO FIGHT? I HAVE. I AM-- WITH ALL MY STRENGTH.
BUT I CAN'T FORGET THAT I KILLED AN ENTIRE WORLD-- FIVE BILLION PEOPLE -- AS CASUALLY, AS UNTHINKINGLY, AS YOU WOULD CRUMPLE A PIECE OF PAPER. I WANT NO MORE DEATHS ON MY CONSCIENCE.
YOUR WAY, I'D HAVE TO STAY COMPLETELY IN CONTROL OF MYSELF EVERY SECOND OF EVERY DAY FOR THE REST OF MY IMMORTAL LIFE.
"MAYBE I COULD DO IT. BUT IF I SLIPPED, EVEN FOR AN INSTANT, IF I... FAILED...
... IF EVEN ONE MORE PERSON DIED AT MY HANDS...
IT'S BETTER THIS WAY. QUICK. CLEAN. FINAL.
I LOVE YOU, SCOTT.
A PART OF ME WILL ALWAYS BE WITH YOU.
JEAN, NO. DON'T!
NO!
SCOTT!
JEAN!
YOU... PLANNED THIS, DIDN'T YOU?! FROM THE MOMENT WE LANDED ON THE MOON. YOU SHIELDED YOUR INTENTIONS FROM OUR RAPPORT, BUT JUST THE SAME I SHOULD HAVE GUESSED, I SHOULD HAVE REALIZED...
... THAT YOU COULD NOT BECOME DARK PHOENIX AND REMAIN TRUE TO YOUR SELF, THE JEAN GREY I KNEW, AND FELL IN LOVE WITH. SO, YOU TOOK STEPS TO ENSURE THAT, IF LILANDRA COULDN'T STOP YOU, YOU'D DO THE JOB YOURSELF.
YOU MUST HAVE PICKED THE MINDS OF THE KREE AND SKRULL OBSERVERS, LEARNED WHAT ANCIENT WEAPONS WERE HIDDEN HERE. THEN, YOU USED YOUR FIGHT WITH THE X-MEN TO DRAIN YOU OF ENOUGH ENERGY TO MAKE YOU VULNERABLE. AND, FINALLY, WHEN YOU WERE READY, YOU... YOU...
OH, JEAN...
JEAN...

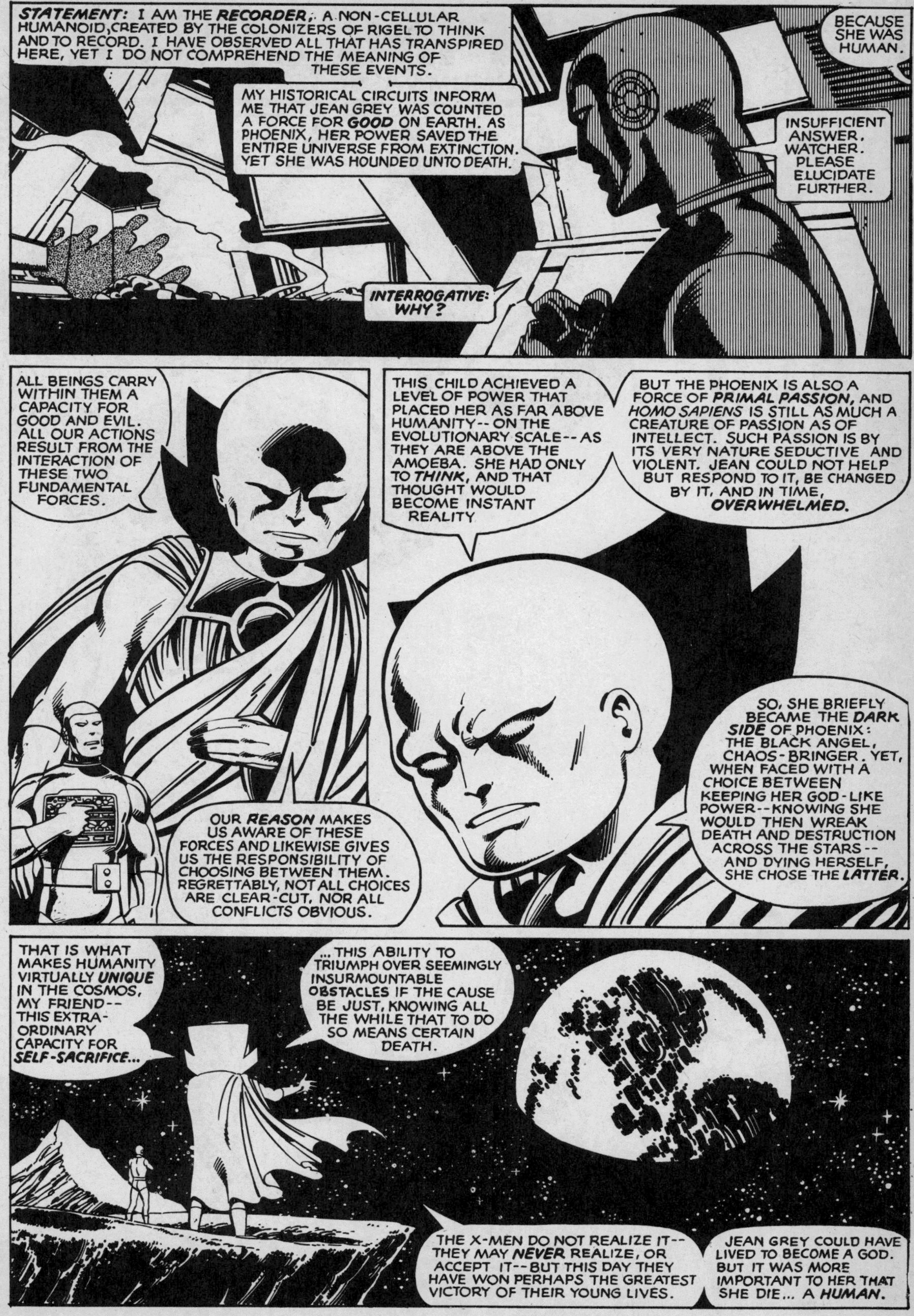
STATEMENT: I AM THE RECORDER, A NON-CELLULAR HUMANOID, CREATED BY THE COLONIZERS OF RIGEL TO THINK AND TO RECORD. I HAVE OBSERVED ALL THAT HAS TRANSPIRED HERE, YET I DO NOT COMPREHEND THE MEANING OF THESE EVENTS.
MY HISTORICAL CIRCUITS INFORM ME THAT JEAN GREY WAS COUNTED A FORCE FOR GOOD ON EARTH. AS PHOENIX, HER POWER SAVED THE ENTIRE UNIVERSE FROM EXTINCTION. YET SHE WAS HOUNDED UNTO DEATH.
INTERROGATIVE: WHY?
BECAUSE SHE WAS HUMAN.
INSUFFICIENT ANSWER, WATCHER. PLEASE ELUCIDATE FURTHER.
ALL BEINGS CARRY WITHIN THEM A CAPACITY FOR GOOD AND EVIL. ALL OUR ACTIONS RESULT FROM THE INTERACTION OF THESE TWO FUNDAMENTAL FORCES.
OUR REASON MAKES US AWARE OF THESE FORCES AND LIKEWISE GIVES US THE RESPONSIBILITY OF CHOOSING BETWEEN THEM. REGRETTABLY, NOT ALL CHOICES ARE CLEAR-CUT, NOR ALL CONFLICTS OBVIOUS.
THIS CHILD ACHIEVED A LEVEL OF POWER THAT PLACED HER AS FAR ABOVE HUMANITY-- ON THE EVOLUTIONARY SCALE-- AS THEY ARE ABOVE THE AMOEBA. SHE HAD ONLY TO THINK, AND THAT THOUGHT WOULD BECOME INSTANT REALITY.
BUT THE PHOENIX IS ALSO A FORCE OF PRIMAL PASSION, AND HOMO SAPIENS IS STILL AS MUCH A CREATURE OF PASSION AS OF INTELLECT. SUCH PASSION IS BY ITS VERY NATURE SEDUCTIVE AND VIOLENT. JEAN COULD NOT HELP BUT RESPOND TO IT, BE CHANGED BY IT, AND IN TIME, OVERWHELMED.
SO, SHE BRIEFLY BECAME THE DARK SIDE OF PHOENIX: THE BLACK ANGEL, CHAOS-BRINGER. YET, WHEN FACED WITH A CHOICE BETWEEN KEEPING HER GOD-LIKE POWER--KNOWING SHE WOULD THEN WREAK DEATH AND DESTRUCTION ACROSS THE STARS-- AND DYING HERSELF, SHE CHOSE THE LATTER.
THAT IS WHAT MAKES HUMANITY VIRTUALLY UNIQUE IN THE COSMOS, MY FRIEND-- THIS EXTRA-ORDINARY CAPACITY FOR SELF-SACRIFICE...
... THIS ABILITY TO TRIUMPH OVER SEEMINGLY INSURMOUNTABLE OBSTACLES IF THE CAUSE BE JUST, KNOWING ALL THE WHILE THAT TO DO SO MEANS CERTAIN DEATH.
THE X-MEN DO NOT REALIZE IT-- THEY MAY NEVER REALIZE, OR ACCEPT IT-- BUT THIS DAY THEY HAVE WON PERHAPS THE GREATEST VICTORY OF THEIR YOUNG LIVES.
JEAN GREY COULD HAVE LIVED TO BECOME A GOD. BUT IT WAS MORE IMPORTANT TO HER THAT SHE DIE... A HUMAN.

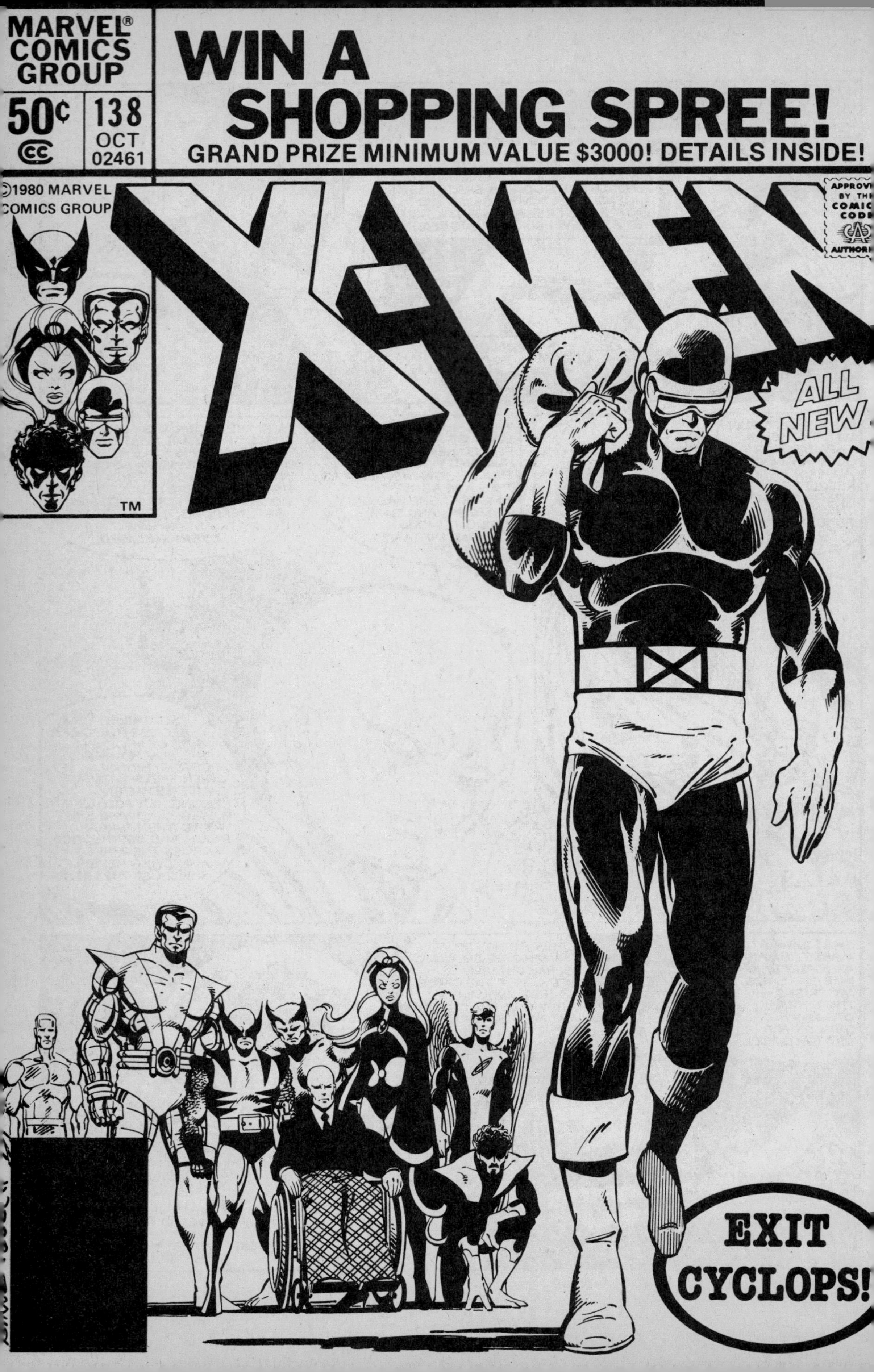
MARVEL® COMICS GROUP
50¢
138
OCT
02461
WIN A SHOPPING SPREE!
GRAND PRIZE MINIMUM VALUE $3000! DETAILS INSIDE!
©1980 MARVEL COMICS GROUP
X-MEN
TM
ALL NEW
EXIT CYCLOPS!

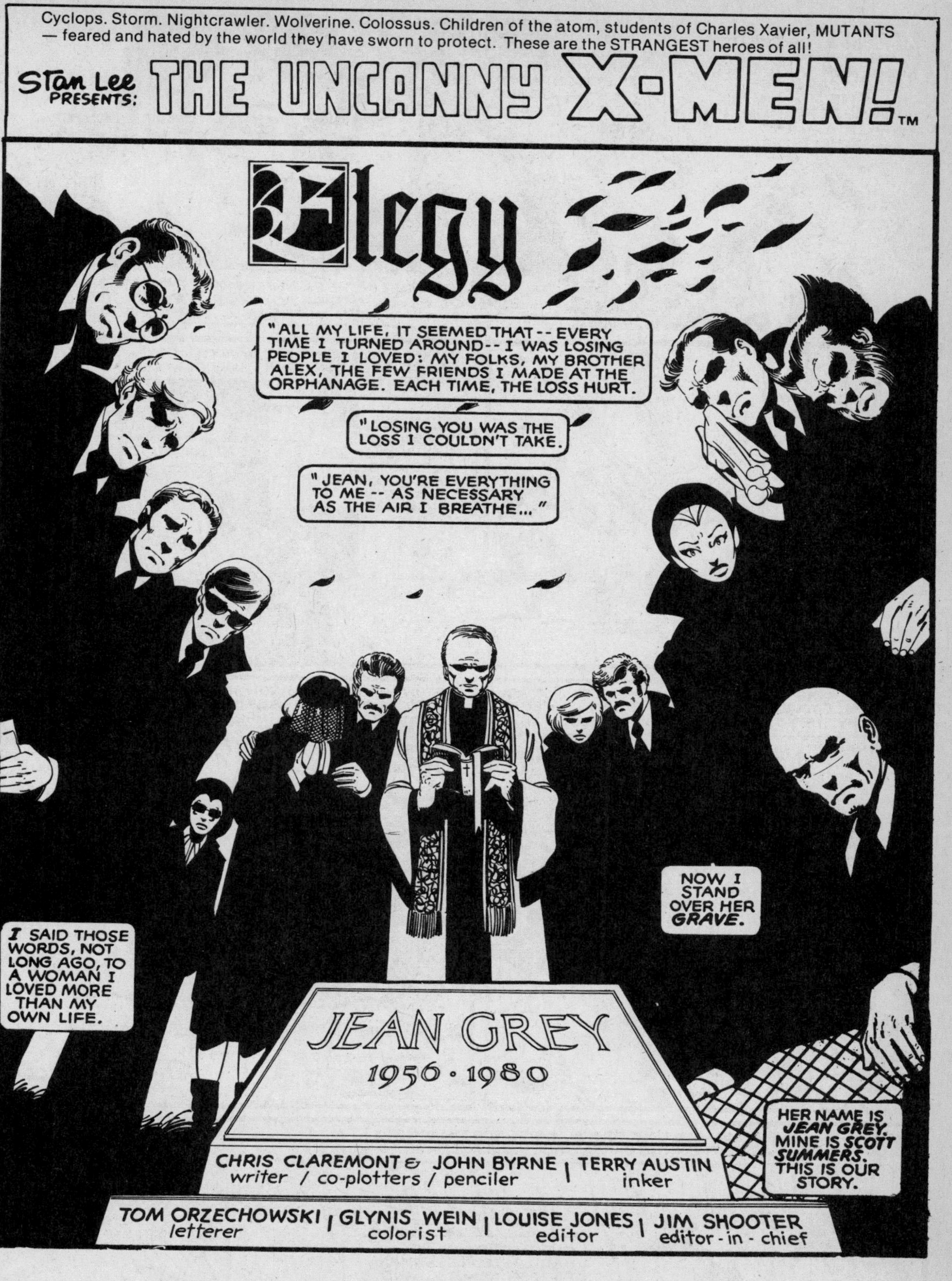
Cyclops. Storm. Nightcrawler. Wolverine. Colossus. Children of the atom, students of Charles Xavier, MUTANTS — feared and hated by the world they have sworn to protect. These are the STRANGEST heroes of all!
Stan Lee PRESENTS: THE UNCANNY X-MEN!™
Elegy
"ALL MY LIFE, IT SEEMED THAT -- EVERY TIME I TURNED AROUND -- I WAS LOSING PEOPLE I LOVED: MY FOLKS, MY BROTHER ALEX, THE FEW FRIENDS I MADE AT THE ORPHANAGE. EACH TIME, THE LOSS HURT.
"LOSING YOU WAS THE LOSS I COULDN'T TAKE.
"JEAN, YOU'RE EVERYTHING TO ME -- AS NECESSARY AS THE AIR I BREATHE..."
I SAID THOSE WORDS, NOT LONG AGO, TO A WOMAN I LOVED MORE THAN MY OWN LIFE.
NOW I STAND OVER HER GRAVE.
HER NAME IS JEAN GREY. MINE IS SCOTT SUMMERS. THIS IS OUR STORY.
JEAN GREY
1956 · 1980
CHRIS CLAREMONT & JOHN BYRNE writer / co-plotters / penciler | TERRY AUSTIN inker
TOM ORZECHOWSKI letterer | GLYNIS WEIN colorist | LOUISE JONES editor | JIM SHOOTER editor-in-chief

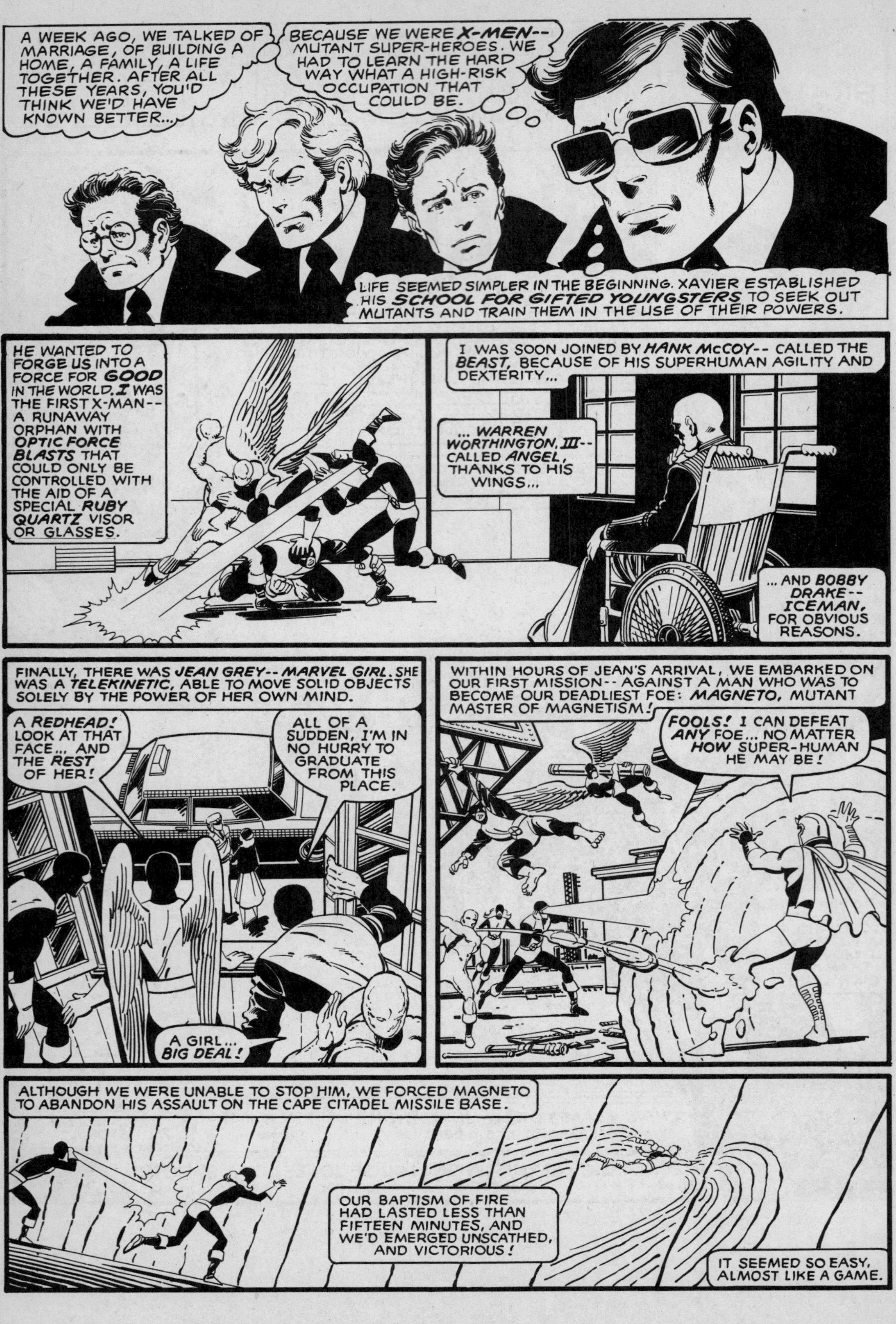
A WEEK AGO, WE TALKED OF MARRIAGE, OF BUILDING A HOME, A FAMILY, A LIFE TOGETHER. AFTER ALL THESE YEARS, YOU'D THINK WE'D HAVE KNOWN BETTER...
BECAUSE WE WERE X-MEN-- MUTANT SUPER-HEROES. WE HAD TO LEARN THE HARD WAY WHAT A HIGH-RISK OCCUPATION THAT COULD BE.
LIFE SEEMED SIMPLER IN THE BEGINNING. XAVIER ESTABLISHED HIS SCHOOL FOR GIFTED YOUNGSTERS TO SEEK OUT MUTANTS AND TRAIN THEM IN THE USE OF THEIR POWERS.
HE WANTED TO FORGE US INTO A FORCE FOR GOOD IN THE WORLD. I WAS THE FIRST X-MAN-- A RUNAWAY ORPHAN WITH OPTIC FORCE BLASTS THAT COULD ONLY BE CONTROLLED WITH THE AID OF A SPECIAL RUBY QUARTZ VISOR OR GLASSES.
I WAS SOON JOINED BY HANK McCOY-- CALLED THE BEAST, BECAUSE OF HIS SUPERHUMAN AGILITY AND DEXTERITY...
... WARREN WORTHINGTON, III-- CALLED ANGEL, THANKS TO HIS WINGS...
... AND BOBBY DRAKE-- ICEMAN, FOR OBVIOUS REASONS.
FINALLY, THERE WAS JEAN GREY-- MARVEL GIRL. SHE WAS A TELEKINETIC, ABLE TO MOVE SOLID OBJECTS SOLELY BY THE POWER OF HER OWN MIND.
A REDHEAD! LOOK AT THAT FACE... AND THE REST OF HER!
ALL OF A SUDDEN, I'M IN NO HURRY TO GRADUATE FROM THIS PLACE.
A GIRL... BIG DEAL!
WITHIN HOURS OF JEAN'S ARRIVAL, WE EMBARKED ON OUR FIRST MISSION-- AGAINST A MAN WHO WAS TO BECOME OUR DEADLIEST FOE: MAGNETO, MUTANT MASTER OF MAGNETISM!
FOOLS! I CAN DEFEAT ANY FOE... NO MATTER HOW SUPER-HUMAN HE MAY BE!
ALTHOUGH WE WERE UNABLE TO STOP HIM, WE FORCED MAGNETO TO ABANDON HIS ASSAULT ON THE CAPE CITADEL MISSILE BASE.
OUR BAPTISM OF FIRE HAD LASTED LESS THAN FIFTEEN MINUTES, AND WE'D EMERGED UNSCATHED, AND VICTORIOUS!
IT SEEMED SO EASY, ALMOST LIKE A GAME.

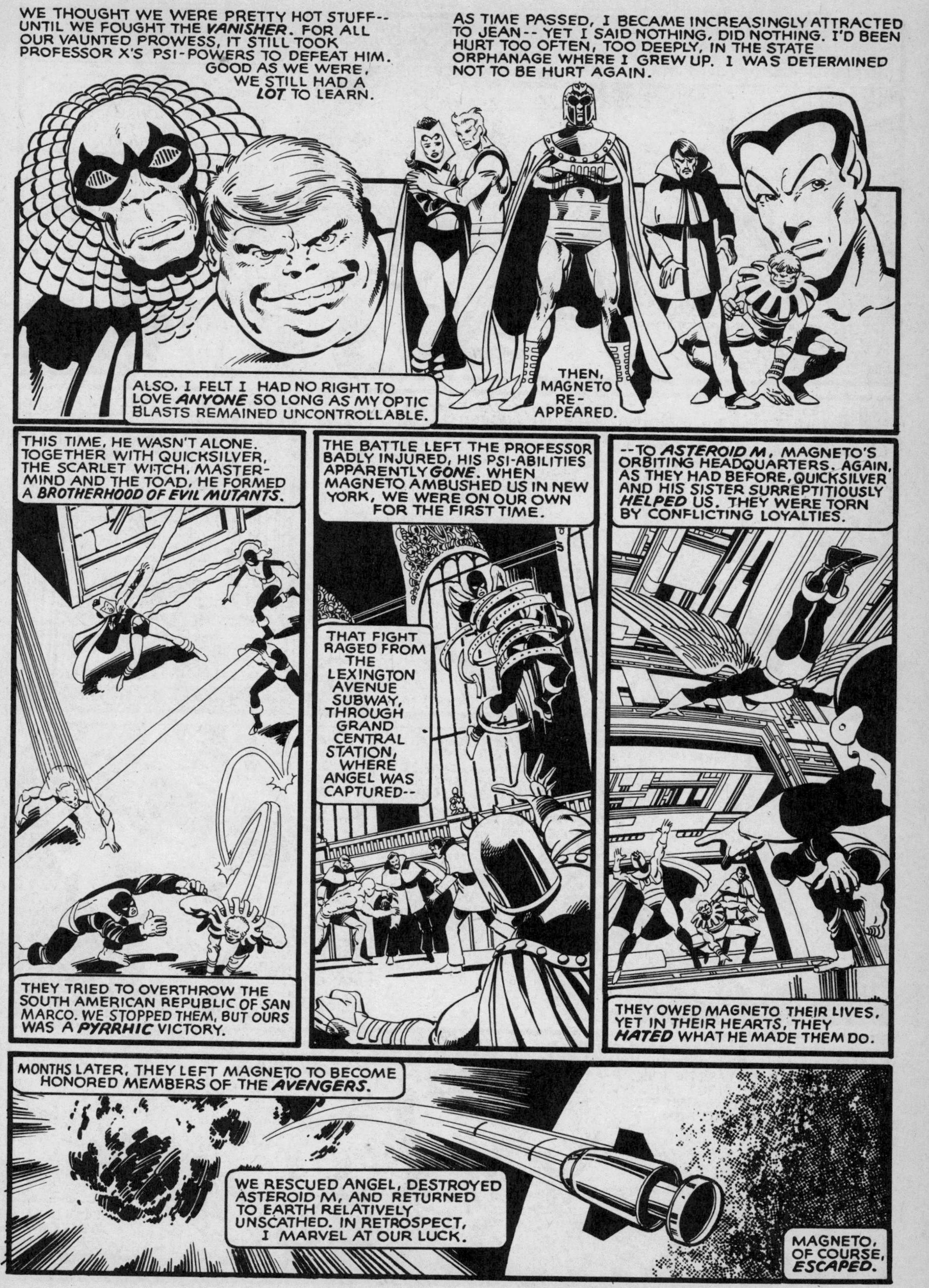
WE THOUGHT WE WERE PRETTY HOT STUFF--UNTIL WE FOUGHT THE VANISHER. FOR ALL OUR VAUNTED PROWESS, IT STILL TOOK PROFESSOR X'S PSI-POWERS TO DEFEAT HIM. GOOD AS WE WERE, WE STILL HAD A LOT TO LEARN.
AS TIME PASSED, I BECAME INCREASINGLY ATTRACTED TO JEAN-- YET I SAID NOTHING, DID NOTHING. I'D BEEN HURT TOO OFTEN, TOO DEEPLY, IN THE STATE ORPHANAGE WHERE I GREW UP. I WAS DETERMINED NOT TO BE HURT AGAIN.
ALSO, I FELT I HAD NO RIGHT TO LOVE ANYONE SO LONG AS MY OPTIC BLASTS REMAINED UNCONTROLLABLE.
THEN, MAGNETO RE-APPEARED.
THIS TIME, HE WASN'T ALONE. TOGETHER WITH QUICKSILVER, THE SCARLET WITCH, MASTERMIND AND THE TOAD, HE FORMED A BROTHERHOOD OF EVIL MUTANTS.
THEY TRIED TO OVERTHROW THE SOUTH AMERICAN REPUBLIC OF SAN MARCO. WE STOPPED THEM, BUT OURS WAS A PYRRHIC VICTORY.
THE BATTLE LEFT THE PROFESSOR BADLY INJURED, HIS PSI-ABILITIES APPARENTLY GONE. WHEN MAGNETO AMBUSHED US IN NEW YORK, WE WERE ON OUR OWN FOR THE FIRST TIME.
THAT FIGHT RAGED FROM THE LEXINGTON AVENUE SUBWAY, THROUGH GRAND CENTRAL STATION, WHERE ANGEL WAS CAPTURED--
--TO ASTEROID M, MAGNETO'S ORBITING HEADQUARTERS. AGAIN, AS THEY HAD BEFORE, QUICKSILVER AND HIS SISTER SURREPTITIOUSLY HELPED US. THEY WERE TORN BY CONFLICTING LOYALTIES.
THEY OWED MAGNETO THEIR LIVES, YET IN THEIR HEARTS, THEY HATED WHAT HE MADE THEM DO.
MONTHS LATER, THEY LEFT MAGNETO TO BECOME HONORED MEMBERS OF THE AVENGERS.
WE RESCUED ANGEL, DESTROYED ASTEROID M, AND RETURNED TO EARTH RELATIVELY UNSCATHED. IN RETROSPECT, I MARVEL AT OUR LUCK.
MAGNETO, OF COURSE, ESCAPED.

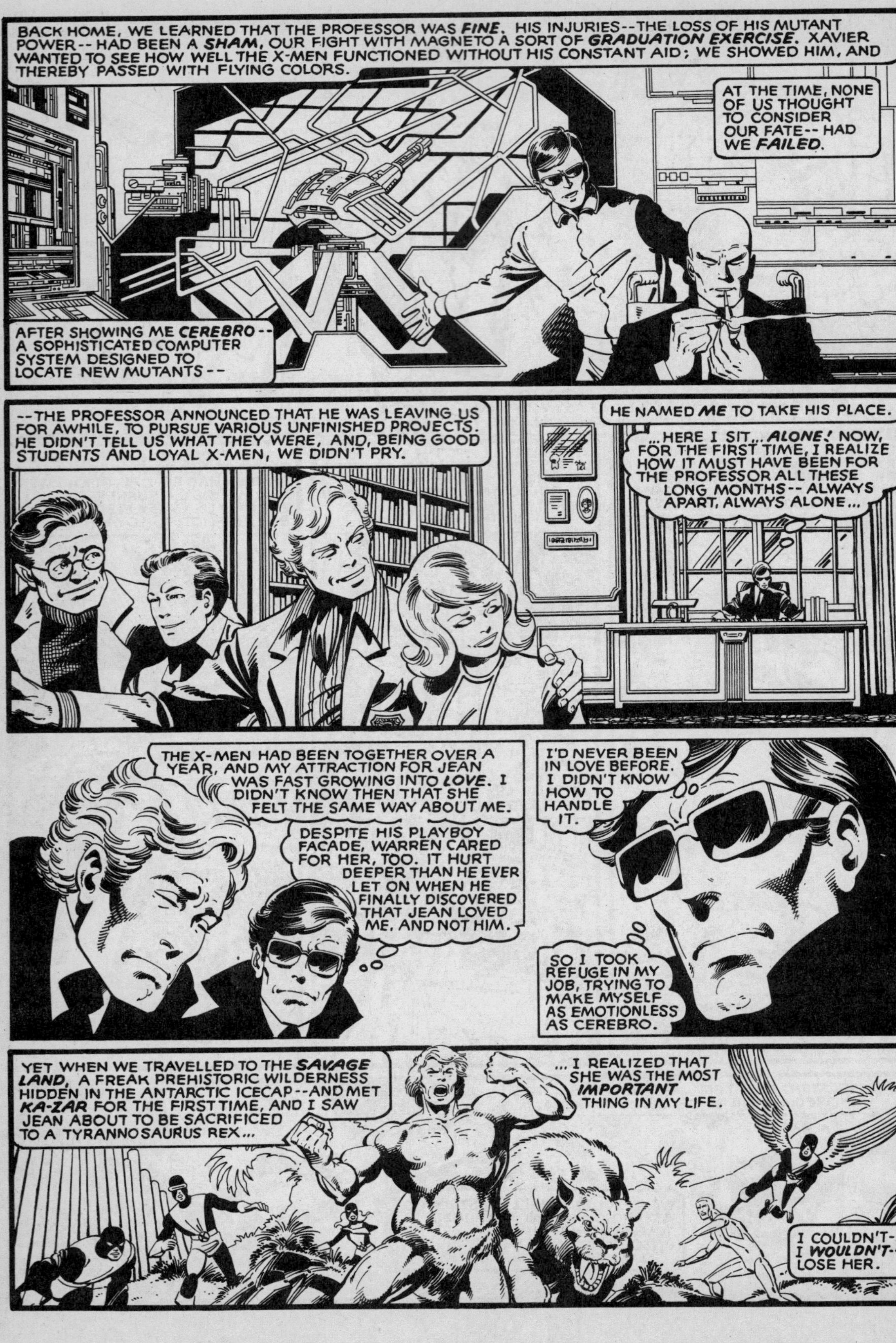
BACK HOME, WE LEARNED THAT THE PROFESSOR WAS FINE. HIS INJURIES--THE LOSS OF HIS MUTANT POWER--HAD BEEN A SHAM, OUR FIGHT WITH MAGNETO A SORT OF GRADUATION EXERCISE. XAVIER WANTED TO SEE HOW WELL THE X-MEN FUNCTIONED WITHOUT HIS CONSTANT AID; WE SHOWED HIM, AND THEREBY PASSED WITH FLYING COLORS.
AT THE TIME, NONE OF US THOUGHT TO CONSIDER OUR FATE--HAD WE FAILED.
AFTER SHOWING ME CEREBRO--A SOPHISTICATED COMPUTER SYSTEM DESIGNED TO LOCATE NEW MUTANTS--
--THE PROFESSOR ANNOUNCED THAT HE WAS LEAVING US FOR AWHILE, TO PURSUE VARIOUS UNFINISHED PROJECTS. HE DIDN'T TELL US WHAT THEY WERE, AND, BEING GOOD STUDENTS AND LOYAL X-MEN, WE DIDN'T PRY.
HE NAMED ME TO TAKE HIS PLACE.
...HERE I SIT... ALONE! NOW, FOR THE FIRST TIME, I REALIZE HOW IT MUST HAVE BEEN FOR THE PROFESSOR ALL THESE LONG MONTHS--ALWAYS APART, ALWAYS ALONE...
THE X-MEN HAD BEEN TOGETHER OVER A YEAR, AND MY ATTRACTION FOR JEAN WAS FAST GROWING INTO LOVE. I DIDN'T KNOW THEN THAT SHE FELT THE SAME WAY ABOUT ME.
DESPITE HIS PLAYBOY FACADE, WARREN CARED FOR HER, TOO. IT HURT DEEPER THAN HE EVER LET ON WHEN HE FINALLY DISCOVERED THAT JEAN LOVED ME, AND NOT HIM.
I'D NEVER BEEN IN LOVE BEFORE. I DIDN'T KNOW HOW TO HANDLE IT.
SO I TOOK REFUGE IN MY JOB, TRYING TO MAKE MYSELF AS EMOTIONLESS AS CEREBRO.
YET WHEN WE TRAVELLED TO THE SAVAGE LAND, A FREAK PREHISTORIC WILDERNESS HIDDEN IN THE ANTARCTIC ICECAP--AND MET KA-ZAR FOR THE FIRST TIME, AND I SAW JEAN ABOUT TO BE SACRIFICED TO A TYRANNOSAURUS REX...
...I REALIZED THAT SHE WAS THE MOST IMPORTANT THING IN MY LIFE.
I COULDN'T--I WOULDN'T--LOSE HER.

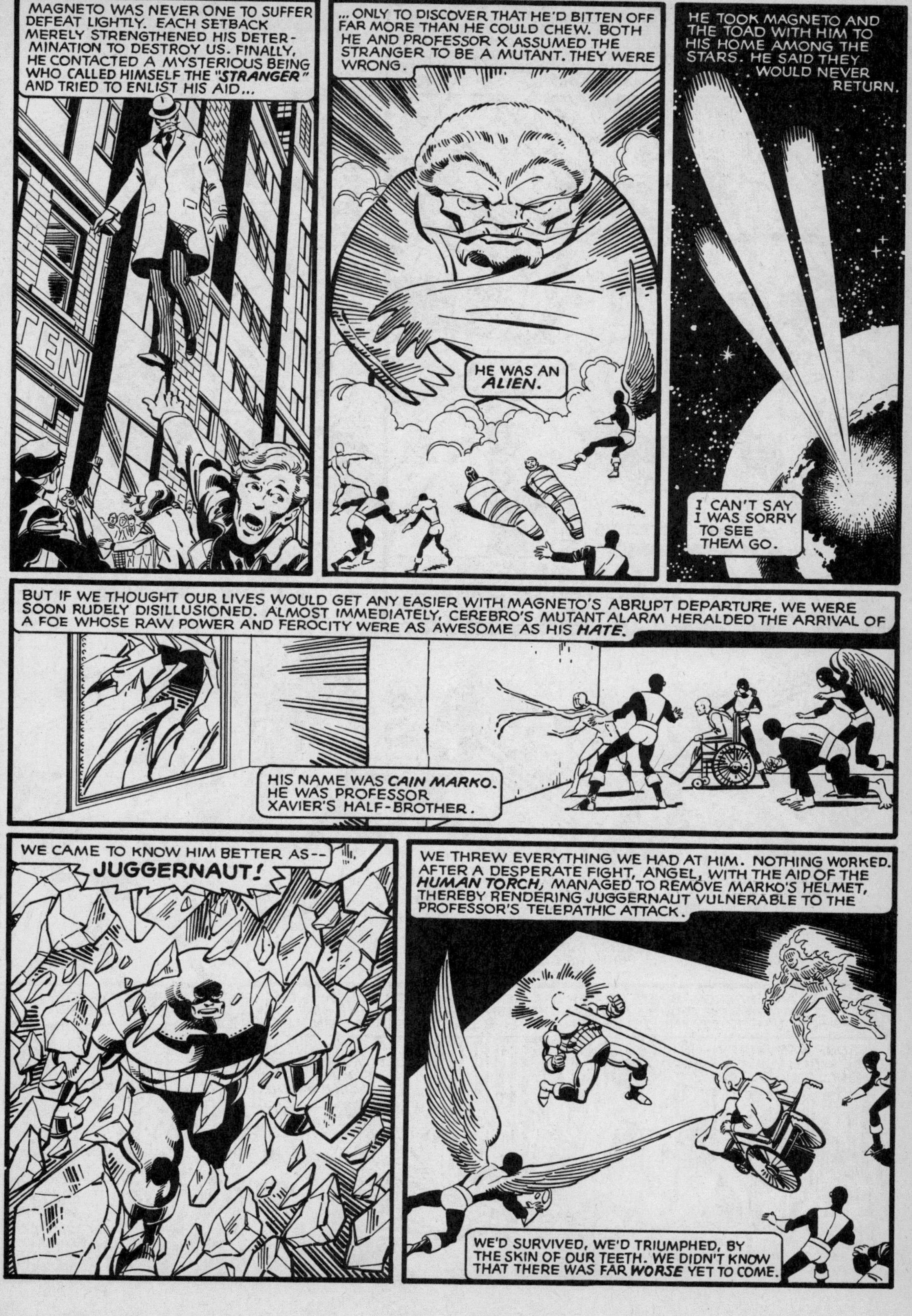
MAGNETO WAS NEVER ONE TO SUFFER DEFEAT LIGHTLY. EACH SETBACK MERELY STRENGTHENED HIS DETERMINATION TO DESTROY US. FINALLY, HE CONTACTED A MYSTERIOUS BEING WHO CALLED HIMSELF THE "STRANGER" AND TRIED TO ENLIST HIS AID...
TEN
...ONLY TO DISCOVER THAT HE'D BITTEN OFF FAR MORE THAN HE COULD CHEW. BOTH HE AND PROFESSOR X ASSUMED THE STRANGER TO BE A MUTANT. THEY WERE WRONG.
HE WAS AN ALIEN.
HE TOOK MAGNETO AND THE TOAD WITH HIM TO HIS HOME AMONG THE STARS. HE SAID THEY WOULD NEVER RETURN.
I CAN'T SAY I WAS SORRY TO SEE THEM GO.
BUT IF WE THOUGHT OUR LIVES WOULD GET ANY EASIER WITH MAGNETO'S ABRUPT DEPARTURE, WE WERE SOON RUDELY DISILLUSIONED. ALMOST IMMEDIATELY, CEREBRO'S MUTANT ALARM HERALDED THE ARRIVAL OF A FOE WHOSE RAW POWER AND FEROCITY WERE AS AWESOME AS HIS HATE.
HIS NAME WAS CAIN MARKO. HE WAS PROFESSOR XAVIER'S HALF-BROTHER.
WE CAME TO KNOW HIM BETTER AS-- JUGGERNAUT!
WE THREW EVERYTHING WE HAD AT HIM. NOTHING WORKED. AFTER A DESPERATE FIGHT, ANGEL, WITH THE AID OF THE HUMAN TORCH, MANAGED TO REMOVE MARKO'S HELMET, THEREBY RENDERING JUGGERNAUT VULNERABLE TO THE PROFESSOR'S TELEPATHIC ATTACK.
WE'D SURVIVED. WE'D TRIUMPHED, BY THE SKIN OF OUR TEETH. WE DIDN'T KNOW THAT THERE WAS FAR WORSE YET TO COME.

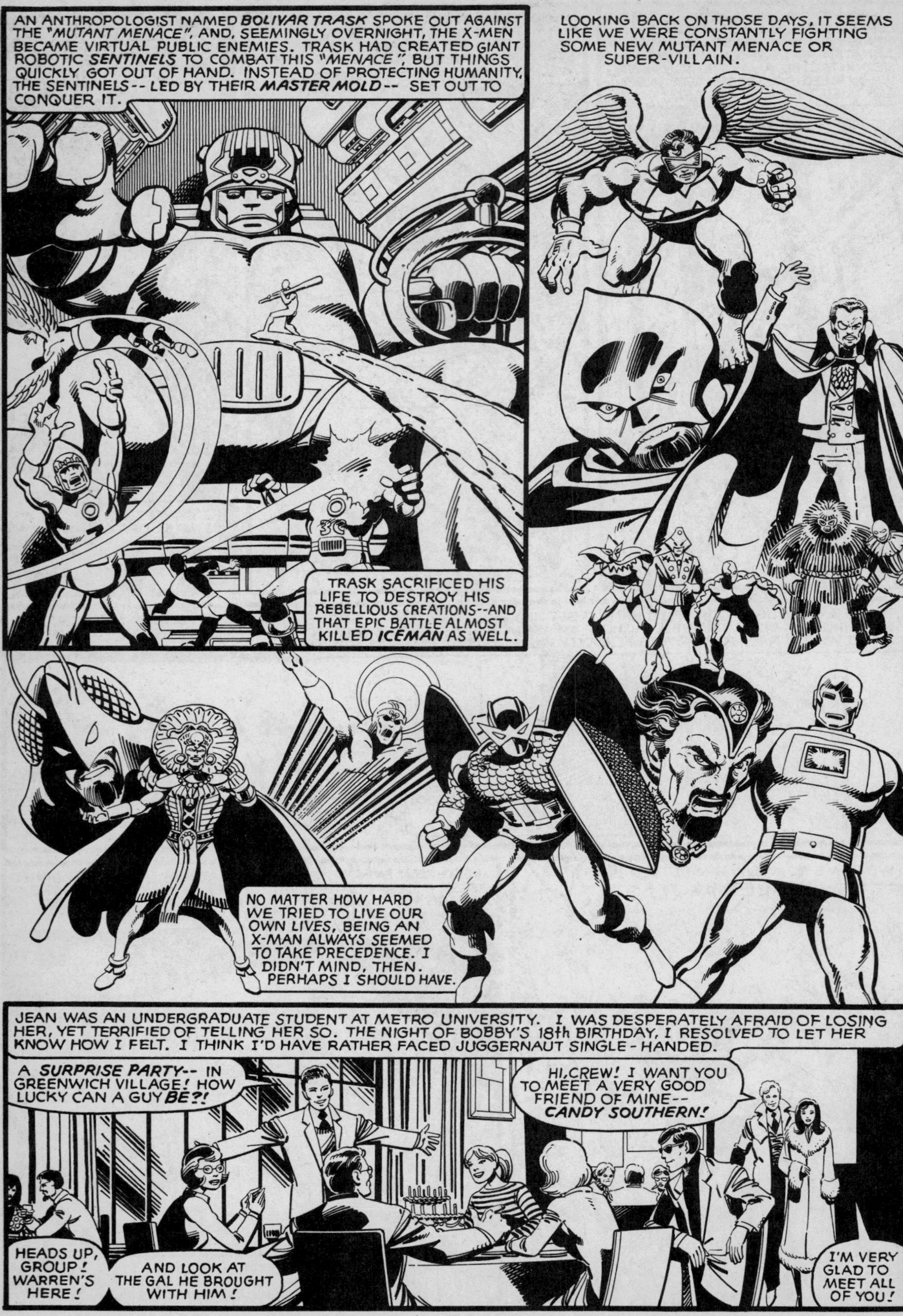
AN ANTHROPOLOGIST NAMED BOLIVAR TRASK SPOKE OUT AGAINST THE "MUTANT MENACE", AND, SEEMINGLY OVERNIGHT, THE X-MEN BECAME VIRTUAL PUBLIC ENEMIES. TRASK HAD CREATED GIANT ROBOTIC SENTINELS TO COMBAT THIS "MENACE", BUT THINGS QUICKLY GOT OUT OF HAND. INSTEAD OF PROTECTING HUMANITY, THE SENTINELS-- LED BY THEIR MASTER MOLD-- SET OUT TO CONQUER IT.
TRASK SACRIFICED HIS LIFE TO DESTROY HIS REBELLIOUS CREATIONS--AND THAT EPIC BATTLE ALMOST KILLED ICEMAN AS WELL.
LOOKING BACK ON THOSE DAYS, IT SEEMS LIKE WE WERE CONSTANTLY FIGHTING SOME NEW MUTANT MENACE OR SUPER-VILLAIN.
NO MATTER HOW HARD WE TRIED TO LIVE OUR OWN LIVES, BEING AN X-MAN ALWAYS SEEMED TO TAKE PRECEDENCE. I DIDN'T MIND, THEN. PERHAPS I SHOULD HAVE.
JEAN WAS AN UNDERGRADUATE STUDENT AT METRO UNIVERSITY. I WAS DESPERATELY AFRAID OF LOSING HER, YET TERRIFIED OF TELLING HER SO. THE NIGHT OF BOBBY'S 18th BIRTHDAY, I RESOLVED TO LET HER KNOW HOW I FELT. I THINK I'D HAVE RATHER FACED JUGGERNAUT SINGLE-HANDED.
A SURPRISE PARTY-- IN GREENWICH VILLAGE! HOW LUCKY CAN A GUY BE?!
HEADS UP, GROUP! WARREN'S HERE!
AND LOOK AT THE GAL HE BROUGHT WITH HIM!
HI, CREW! I WANT YOU TO MEET A VERY GOOD FRIEND OF MINE-- CANDY SOUTHERN!
I'M VERY GLAD TO MEET ALL OF YOU!

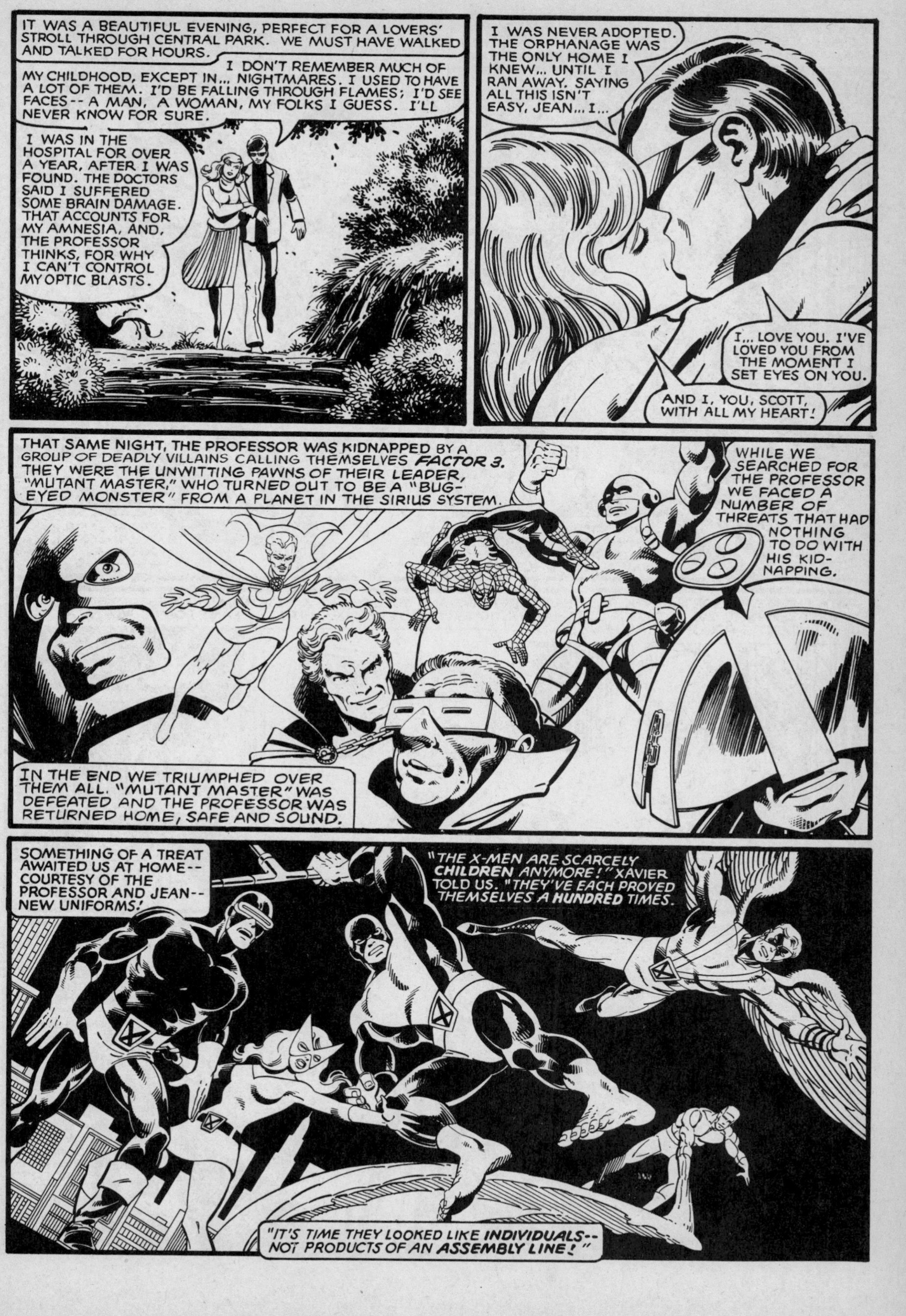
IT WAS A BEAUTIFUL EVENING, PERFECT FOR A LOVERS' STROLL THROUGH CENTRAL PARK. WE MUST HAVE WALKED AND TALKED FOR HOURS.
I DON'T REMEMBER MUCH OF MY CHILDHOOD, EXCEPT IN... NIGHTMARES. I USED TO HAVE A LOT OF THEM. I'D BE FALLING THROUGH FLAMES; I'D SEE FACES -- A MAN, A WOMAN, MY FOLKS I GUESS. I'LL NEVER KNOW FOR SURE.
I WAS IN THE HOSPITAL FOR OVER A YEAR, AFTER I WAS FOUND. THE DOCTORS SAID I SUFFERED SOME BRAIN DAMAGE. THAT ACCOUNTS FOR MY AMNESIA, AND, THE PROFESSOR THINKS, FOR WHY I CAN'T CONTROL MY OPTIC BLASTS.
I WAS NEVER ADOPTED. THE ORPHANAGE WAS THE ONLY HOME I KNEW... UNTIL I RAN AWAY. SAYING ALL THIS ISN'T EASY, JEAN... I...
I... LOVE YOU. I'VE LOVED YOU FROM THE MOMENT I SET EYES ON YOU.
AND I, YOU, SCOTT, WITH ALL MY HEART!
THAT SAME NIGHT, THE PROFESSOR WAS KIDNAPPED BY A GROUP OF DEADLY VILLAINS CALLING THEMSELVES FACTOR 3. THEY WERE THE UNWITTING PAWNS OF THEIR LEADER, "MUTANT MASTER," WHO TURNED OUT TO BE A "BUG-EYED MONSTER" FROM A PLANET IN THE SIRIUS SYSTEM.
WHILE WE SEARCHED FOR THE PROFESSOR WE FACED A NUMBER OF THREATS THAT HAD NOTHING TO DO WITH HIS KID-NAPPING.
IN THE END WE TRIUMPHED OVER THEM ALL. "MUTANT MASTER" WAS DEFEATED AND THE PROFESSOR WAS RETURNED HOME, SAFE AND SOUND.
SOMETHING OF A TREAT AWAITED US AT HOME-- COURTESY OF THE PROFESSOR AND JEAN-- NEW UNIFORMS!
"THE X-MEN ARE SCARCELY CHILDREN ANYMORE!" XAVIER TOLD US. "THEY'VE EACH PROVED THEMSELVES A HUNDRED TIMES.
"IT'S TIME THEY LOOKED LIKE INDIVIDUALS-- NOT PRODUCTS OF AN ASSEMBLY LINE!"

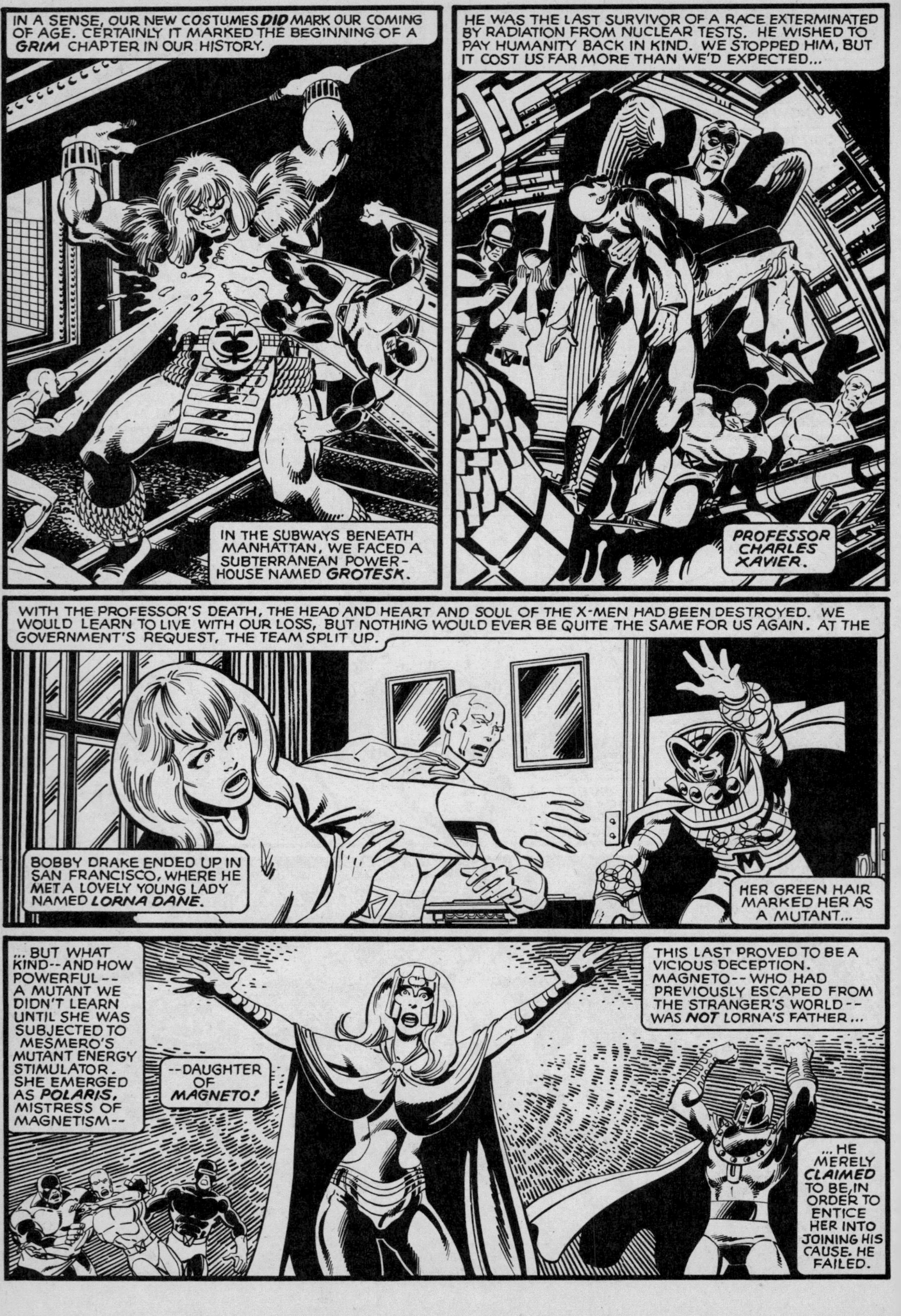
IN A SENSE, OUR NEW COSTUMES DID MARK OUR COMING OF AGE. CERTAINLY IT MARKED THE BEGINNING OF A GRIM CHAPTER IN OUR HISTORY.
IN THE SUBWAYS BENEATH MANHATTAN, WE FACED A SUBTERRANEAN POWER-HOUSE NAMED GROTESK.
HE WAS THE LAST SURVIVOR OF A RACE EXTERMINATED BY RADIATION FROM NUCLEAR TESTS. HE WISHED TO PAY HUMANITY BACK IN KIND. WE STOPPED HIM, BUT IT COST US FAR MORE THAN WE'D EXPECTED...
PROFESSOR CHARLES XAVIER.
WITH THE PROFESSOR'S DEATH, THE HEAD AND HEART AND SOUL OF THE X-MEN HAD BEEN DESTROYED. WE WOULD LEARN TO LIVE WITH OUR LOSS, BUT NOTHING WOULD EVER BE QUITE THE SAME FOR US AGAIN. AT THE GOVERNMENT'S REQUEST, THE TEAM SPLIT UP.
BOBBY DRAKE ENDED UP IN SAN FRANCISCO, WHERE HE MET A LOVELY YOUNG LADY NAMED LORNA DANE.
HER GREEN HAIR MARKED HER AS A MUTANT...
... BUT WHAT KIND--AND HOW POWERFUL-- A MUTANT WE DIDN'T LEARN UNTIL SHE WAS SUBJECTED TO MESMERO'S MUTANT ENERGY STIMULATOR. SHE EMERGED AS POLARIS, MISTRESS OF MAGNETISM--
--DAUGHTER OF MAGNETO!
THIS LAST PROVED TO BE A VICIOUS DECEPTION. MAGNETO--WHO HAD PREVIOUSLY ESCAPED FROM THE STRANGER'S WORLD-- WAS NOT LORNA'S FATHER...
...HE MERELY CLAIMED TO BE, IN ORDER TO ENTICE HER INTO JOINING HIS CAUSE. HE FAILED.

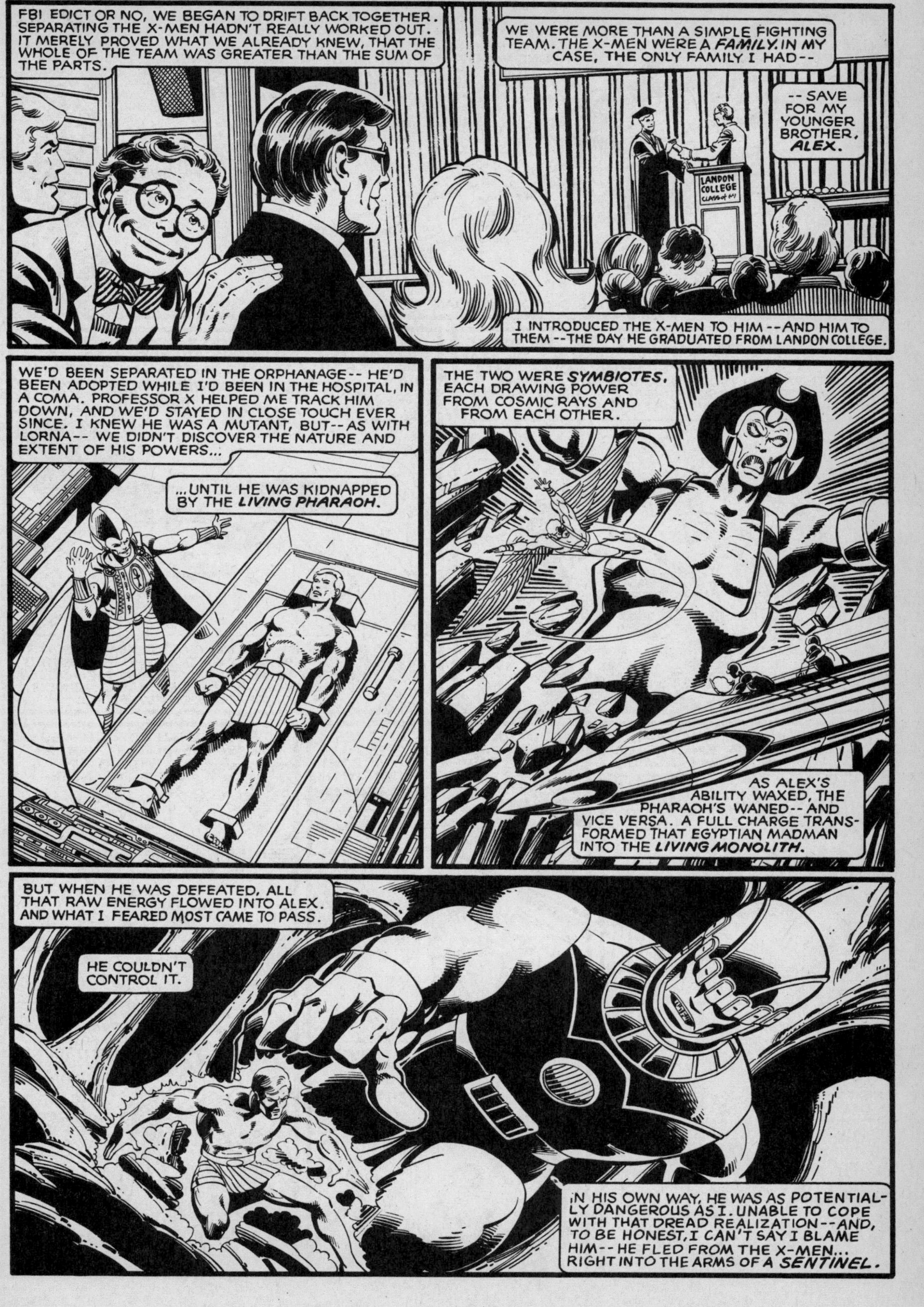
FBI EDICT OR NO, WE BEGAN TO DRIFT BACK TOGETHER. SEPARATING THE X-MEN HADN'T REALLY WORKED OUT. IT MERELY PROVED WHAT WE ALREADY KNEW, THAT THE WHOLE OF THE TEAM WAS GREATER THAN THE SUM OF THE PARTS.
WE WERE MORE THAN A SIMPLE FIGHTING TEAM. THE X-MEN WERE A FAMILY. IN MY CASE, THE ONLY FAMILY I HAD--
-- SAVE FOR MY YOUNGER BROTHER, ALEX.
LANDON COLLEGE
I INTRODUCED THE X-MEN TO HIM --AND HIM TO THEM --THE DAY HE GRADUATED FROM LANDON COLLEGE.
WE'D BEEN SEPARATED IN THE ORPHANAGE-- HE'D BEEN ADOPTED WHILE I'D BEEN IN THE HOSPITAL, IN A COMA. PROFESSOR X HELPED ME TRACK HIM DOWN, AND WE'D STAYED IN CLOSE TOUCH EVER SINCE. I KNEW HE WAS A MUTANT, BUT-- AS WITH LORNA-- WE DIDN'T DISCOVER THE NATURE AND EXTENT OF HIS POWERS...
...UNTIL HE WAS KIDNAPPED BY THE LIVING PHARAOH.
THE TWO WERE SYMBIOTES, EACH DRAWING POWER FROM COSMIC RAYS AND FROM EACH OTHER.
AS ALEX'S ABILITY WAXED, THE PHARAOH'S WANED-- AND VICE VERSA. A FULL CHARGE TRANSFORMED THAT EGYPTIAN MADMAN INTO THE LIVING MONOLITH.
BUT WHEN HE WAS DEFEATED, ALL THAT RAW ENERGY FLOWED INTO ALEX. AND WHAT I FEARED MOST CAME TO PASS.
HE COULDN'T CONTROL IT.
IN HIS OWN WAY, HE WAS AS POTENTIALLY DANGEROUS AS I. UNABLE TO COPE WITH THAT DREAD REALIZATION--AND, TO BE HONEST, I CAN'T SAY I BLAME HIM-- HE FLED FROM THE X-MEN... RIGHT INTO THE ARMS OF A SENTINEL.

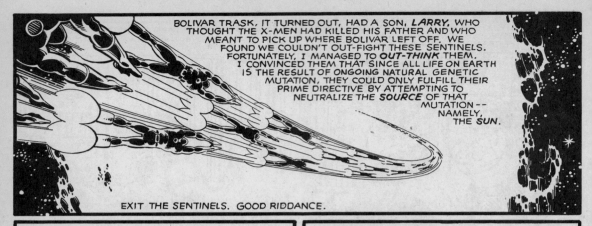

BOLIVAR TRASK, IT TURNED OUT, HAD A SON, *LARRY,* WHO THOUGHT THE X-MEN HAD KILLED HIS FATHER AND WHO MEANT TO PICK UP WHERE BOLIVAR LEFT OFF. WE FOUND WE COULDN'T OUT-FIGHT THESE SENTINELS. FORTUNATELY, I MANAGED TO *OUT-THINK* THEM. I CONVINCED THEM THAT SINCE ALL LIFE ON EARTH IS THE RESULT OF ONGOING NATURAL GENETIC MUTATION, THEY COULD ONLY FULFILL THEIR PRIME DIRECTIVE BY ATTEMPTING TO NEUTRALIZE THE *SOURCE* OF THAT MUTATION -- NAMELY, THE *SUN.*

EXIT THE *SENTINELS.* GOOD RIDDANCE.

BUT WE'D SUFFERED A CASUALTY... ALEX. WE RUSHED HIM TO A COLLEAGUE OF THE PROFESSOR'S, *DR. KARL LYKOS...* NOT ONE OF OUR BRIGHTER MOVES. LYKOS, UNFORTUNATELY, WAS A NON-MUTANT VARIENT WHO EXISTED BY ABSORBING THE LIFE FORCE FROM OTHER BEINGS. DOING THAT TO ALEX,...

...TRANSFORMED LYKOS INTO *SAURON* -- A HUMANOID PTERODACTYL WITH HYPNOTIC/ILLUSION POWERS THAT PUT BOTH MESMERO AND MASTERMIND TO SHAME.

LYKOS WAS A DRIVEN, TORMENTED SOUL, BUT BASICALLY A GOOD MAN. HE WANTED ONLY TO BE WORTHY OF *TANYA ANDERSSEN,* THE WOMAN HE LOVED. SAURON, THOUGH, WAS A CREATURE OF *PURE EVIL.*

WE FOUGHT HIM IN NEW YORK, AND FOLLOWED HIM WHEN HE FLED TO HIS HOME IN *TIERRA DEL FUEGO.*

KARL!!

THERE, RATHER THAN SURVIVE BY KILLING TANYA, LYKOS TOOK HIS OWN LIFE.

OUR UNSUCCESSFUL QUEST TO RECOVER LYKOS' BODY LED TO KA-ZAR'S SAVAGE LAND, AND YET ANOTHER CONFRONTATION WITH MAGNETO.

HE FOUGHT HARD, AS USUAL. HE LOST.

NO SOONER HAD WE RETURNED HOME THAN WE FACED YET ANOTHER MUTANT THREAT, A JAPANESE YOUTH: *SHIRO YASHIDA-- SUNFIRE!*

HE WASN'T EVIL, MERELY MISGUIDED-- BUT IT TOOK THE VIOLENT DEATH OF HIS FATHER TO SHOW HIM THE ERROR OF HIS WAYS.

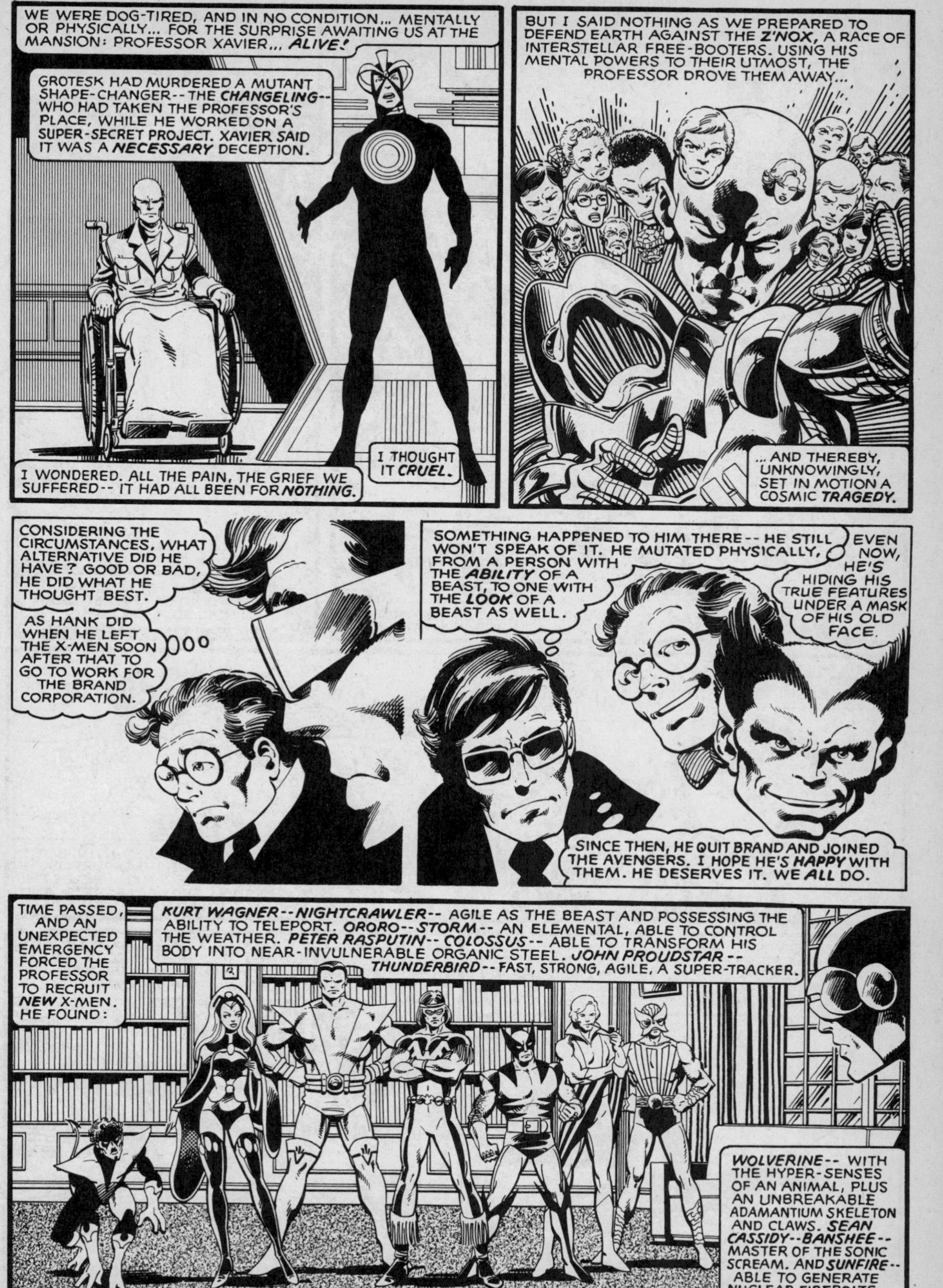
WE WERE DOG-TIRED, AND IN NO CONDITION... MENTALLY OR PHYSICALLY... FOR THE SURPRISE AWAITING US AT THE MANSION: PROFESSOR XAVIER... ALIVE!
GROTESK HAD MURDERED A MUTANT SHAPE-CHANGER--THE CHANGELING--WHO HAD TAKEN THE PROFESSOR'S PLACE, WHILE HE WORKED ON A SUPER-SECRET PROJECT. XAVIER SAID IT WAS A NECESSARY DECEPTION.
I WONDERED. ALL THE PAIN, THE GRIEF WE SUFFERED--IT HAD ALL BEEN FOR NOTHING.
I THOUGHT IT CRUEL.
BUT I SAID NOTHING AS WE PREPARED TO DEFEND EARTH AGAINST THE Z'NOX, A RACE OF INTERSTELLAR FREE-BOOTERS. USING HIS MENTAL POWERS TO THEIR UTMOST, THE PROFESSOR DROVE THEM AWAY...
...AND THEREBY, UNKNOWINGLY, SET IN MOTION A COSMIC TRAGEDY.
CONSIDERING THE CIRCUMSTANCES, WHAT ALTERNATIVE DID HE HAVE? GOOD OR BAD, HE DID WHAT HE THOUGHT BEST.
AS HANK DID WHEN HE LEFT THE X-MEN SOON AFTER THAT TO GO TO WORK FOR THE BRAND CORPORATION.
SOMETHING HAPPENED TO HIM THERE--HE STILL WON'T SPEAK OF IT. HE MUTATED PHYSICALLY, FROM A PERSON WITH THE ABILITY OF A BEAST, TO ONE WITH THE LOOK OF A BEAST AS WELL.
EVEN NOW, HE'S HIDING HIS TRUE FEATURES UNDER A MASK OF HIS OLD FACE.
SINCE THEN, HE QUIT BRAND AND JOINED THE AVENGERS. I HOPE HE'S HAPPY WITH THEM. HE DESERVES IT. WE ALL DO.
TIME PASSED, AND AN UNEXPECTED EMERGENCY FORCED THE PROFESSOR TO RECRUIT NEW X-MEN. HE FOUND:
KURT WAGNER--NIGHTCRAWLER--AGILE AS THE BEAST AND POSSESSING THE ABILITY TO TELEPORT. ORORO--STORM--AN ELEMENTAL, ABLE TO CONTROL THE WEATHER. PETER RASPUTIN--COLOSSUS--ABLE TO TRANSFORM HIS BODY INTO NEAR-INVULNERABLE ORGANIC STEEL. JOHN PROUDSTAR--THUNDERBIRD--FAST, STRONG, AGILE, A SUPER-TRACKER.
WOLVERINE--WITH THE HYPER-SENSES OF AN ANIMAL, PLUS AN UNBREAKABLE ADAMANTIUM SKELETON AND CLAWS. SEAN CASSIDY--BANSHEE--MASTER OF THE SONIC SCREAM. AND SUNFIRE--ABLE TO GENERATE NUCLEAR FIREBOLTS.

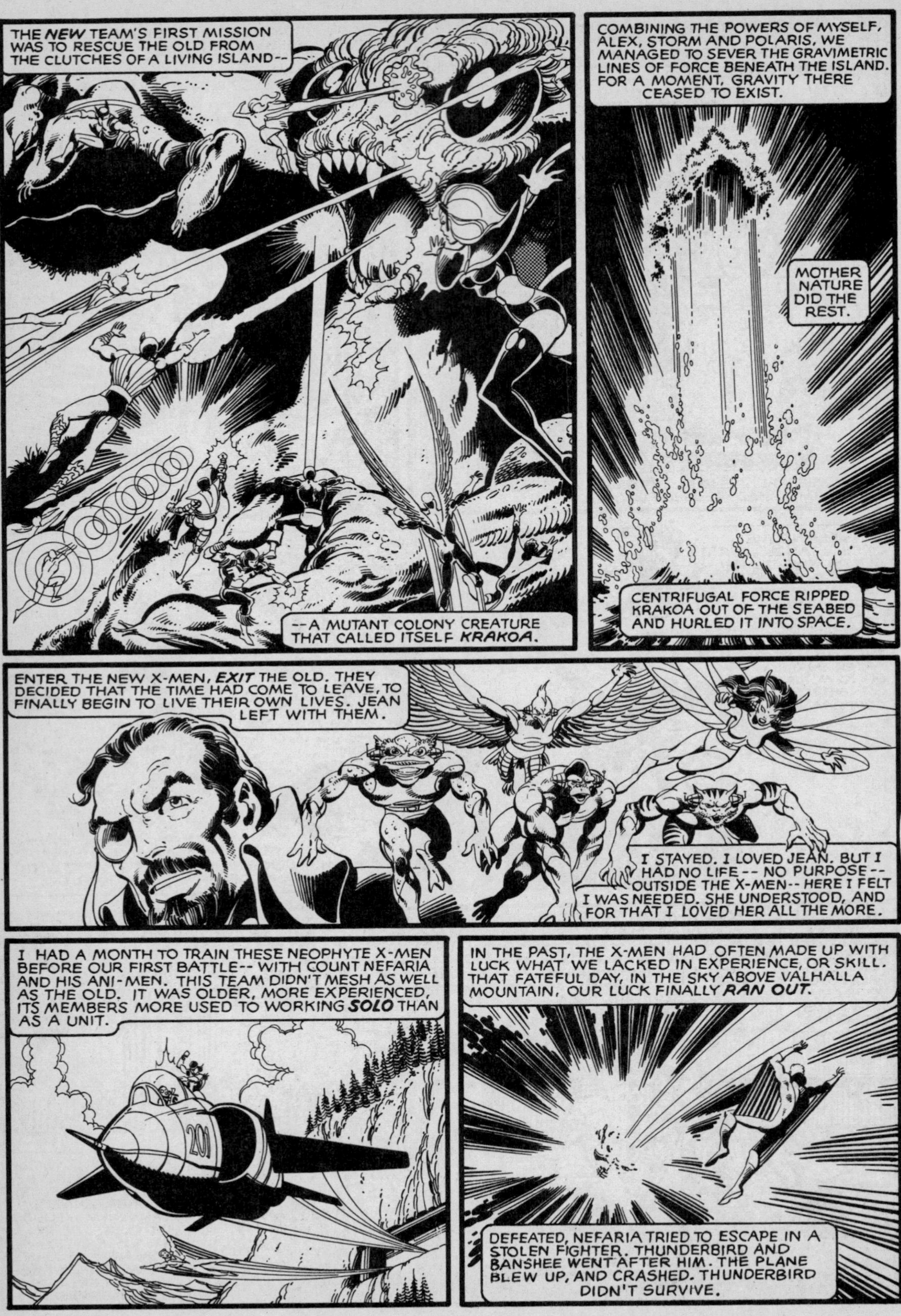
THE *NEW* TEAM'S FIRST MISSION WAS TO RESCUE THE OLD FROM THE CLUTCHES OF A LIVING ISLAND--
--A MUTANT COLONY CREATURE THAT CALLED ITSELF *KRAKOA*.
COMBINING THE POWERS OF MYSELF, ALEX, STORM AND POLARIS, WE MANAGED TO SEVER THE GRAVIMETRIC LINES OF FORCE BENEATH THE ISLAND. FOR A MOMENT, GRAVITY THERE CEASED TO EXIST.
MOTHER NATURE DID THE REST.
CENTRIFUGAL FORCE RIPPED KRAKOA OUT OF THE SEABED AND HURLED IT INTO SPACE.
ENTER THE NEW X-MEN, *EXIT* THE OLD. THEY DECIDED THAT THE TIME HAD COME TO LEAVE, TO FINALLY BEGIN TO LIVE THEIR OWN LIVES. JEAN LEFT WITH THEM.
I STAYED. I LOVED JEAN. BUT I HAD NO LIFE -- NO PURPOSE -- OUTSIDE THE X-MEN-- HERE I FELT I WAS NEEDED. SHE UNDERSTOOD, AND FOR THAT I LOVED HER ALL THE MORE.
I HAD A MONTH TO TRAIN THESE NEOPHYTE X-MEN BEFORE OUR FIRST BATTLE-- WITH COUNT NEFARIA AND HIS ANI-MEN. THIS TEAM DIDN'T MESH AS WELL AS THE OLD. IT WAS OLDER, MORE EXPERIENCED, ITS MEMBERS MORE USED TO WORKING *SOLO* THAN AS A UNIT.
201
IN THE PAST, THE X-MEN HAD OFTEN MADE UP WITH LUCK WHAT WE LACKED IN EXPERIENCE, OR SKILL. THAT FATEFUL DAY, IN THE SKY ABOVE VALHALLA MOUNTAIN, OUR LUCK FINALLY *RAN OUT*.
DEFEATED, NEFARIA TRIED TO ESCAPE IN A STOLEN FIGHTER. THUNDERBIRD AND BANSHEE WENT AFTER HIM. THE PLANE BLEW UP, AND CRASHED. THUNDERBIRD DIDN'T SURVIVE.

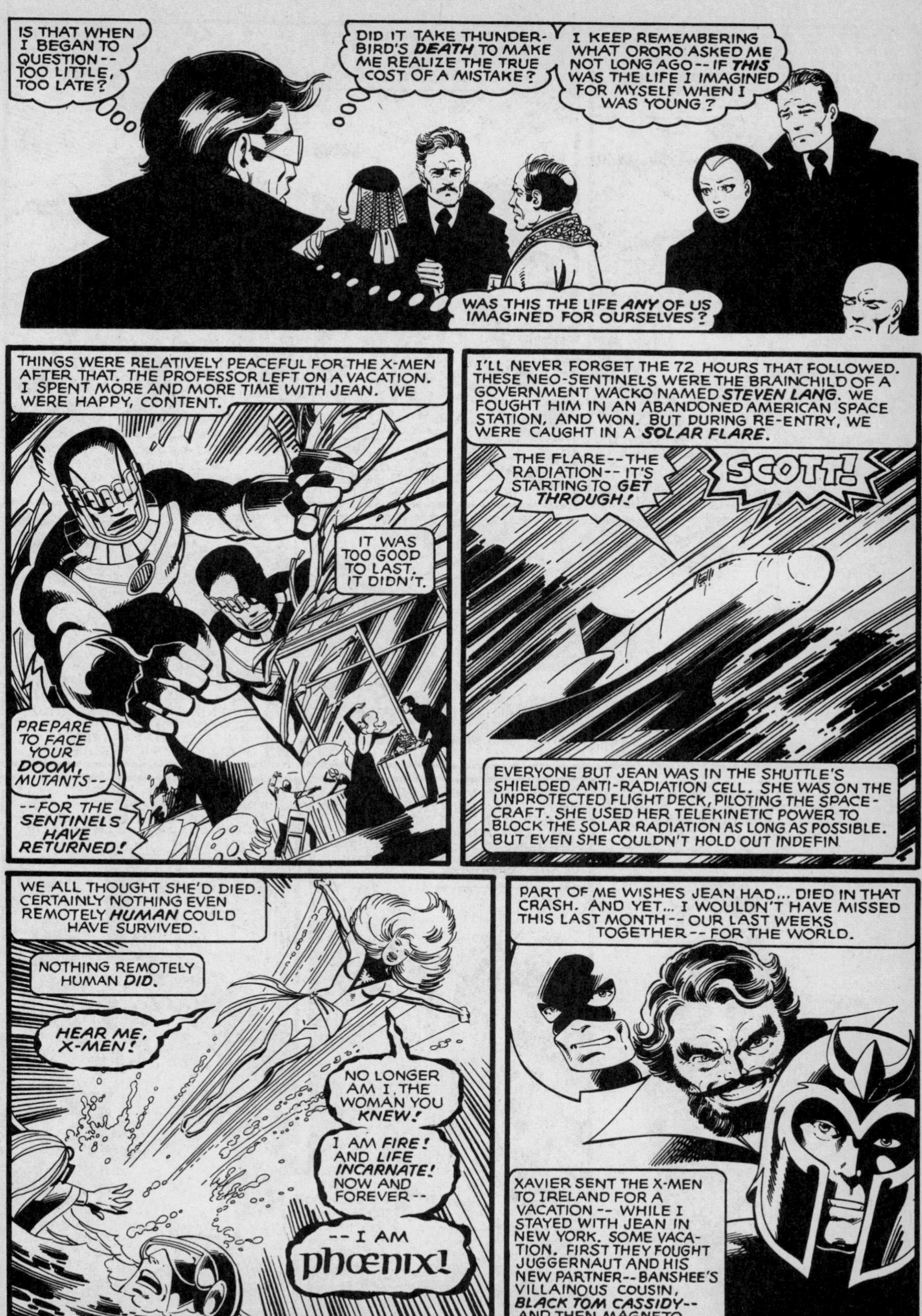
IS THAT WHEN I BEGAN TO QUESTION-- TOO LITTLE, TOO LATE?
DID IT TAKE THUNDERBIRD'S DEATH TO MAKE ME REALIZE THE TRUE COST OF A MISTAKE?
I KEEP REMEMBERING WHAT ORORO ASKED ME NOT LONG AGO-- IF THIS WAS THE LIFE I IMAGINED FOR MYSELF WHEN I WAS YOUNG?
WAS THIS THE LIFE ANY OF US IMAGINED FOR OURSELVES?
THINGS WERE RELATIVELY PEACEFUL FOR THE X-MEN AFTER THAT. THE PROFESSOR LEFT ON A VACATION. I SPENT MORE AND MORE TIME WITH JEAN. WE WERE HAPPY, CONTENT.
IT WAS TOO GOOD TO LAST. IT DIDN'T.
PREPARE TO FACE YOUR DOOM, MUTANTS--
--FOR THE SENTINELS HAVE RETURNED!
I'LL NEVER FORGET THE 72 HOURS THAT FOLLOWED. THESE NEO-SENTINELS WERE THE BRAINCHILD OF A GOVERNMENT WACKO NAMED STEVEN LANG. WE FOUGHT HIM IN AN ABANDONED AMERICAN SPACE STATION, AND WON. BUT DURING RE-ENTRY, WE WERE CAUGHT IN A SOLAR FLARE.
THE FLARE--THE RADIATION-- IT'S STARTING TO GET THROUGH!
SCOTT!
EVERYONE BUT JEAN WAS IN THE SHUTTLE'S SHIELDED ANTI-RADIATION CELL. SHE WAS ON THE UNPROTECTED FLIGHT DECK, PILOTING THE SPACE-CRAFT. SHE USED HER TELEKINETIC POWER TO BLOCK THE SOLAR RADIATION AS LONG AS POSSIBLE. BUT EVEN SHE COULDN'T HOLD OUT INDEFIN
WE ALL THOUGHT SHE'D DIED. CERTAINLY NOTHING EVEN REMOTELY HUMAN COULD HAVE SURVIVED.
NOTHING REMOTELY HUMAN DID.
HEAR ME, X-MEN!
NO LONGER AM I THE WOMAN YOU KNEW!
I AM FIRE! AND LIFE INCARNATE! NOW AND FOREVER--
--I AM PHOENIX!
PART OF ME WISHES JEAN HAD... DIED IN THAT CRASH. AND YET... I WOULDN'T HAVE MISSED THIS LAST MONTH-- OUR LAST WEEKS TOGETHER-- FOR THE WORLD.
XAVIER SENT THE X-MEN TO IRELAND FOR A VACATION -- WHILE I STAYED WITH JEAN IN NEW YORK. SOME VACATION. FIRST THEY FOUGHT JUGGERNAUT AND HIS NEW PARTNER--BANSHEE'S VILLAINOUS COUSIN, BLACK TOM CASSIDY-- AND THEN MAGNETO.

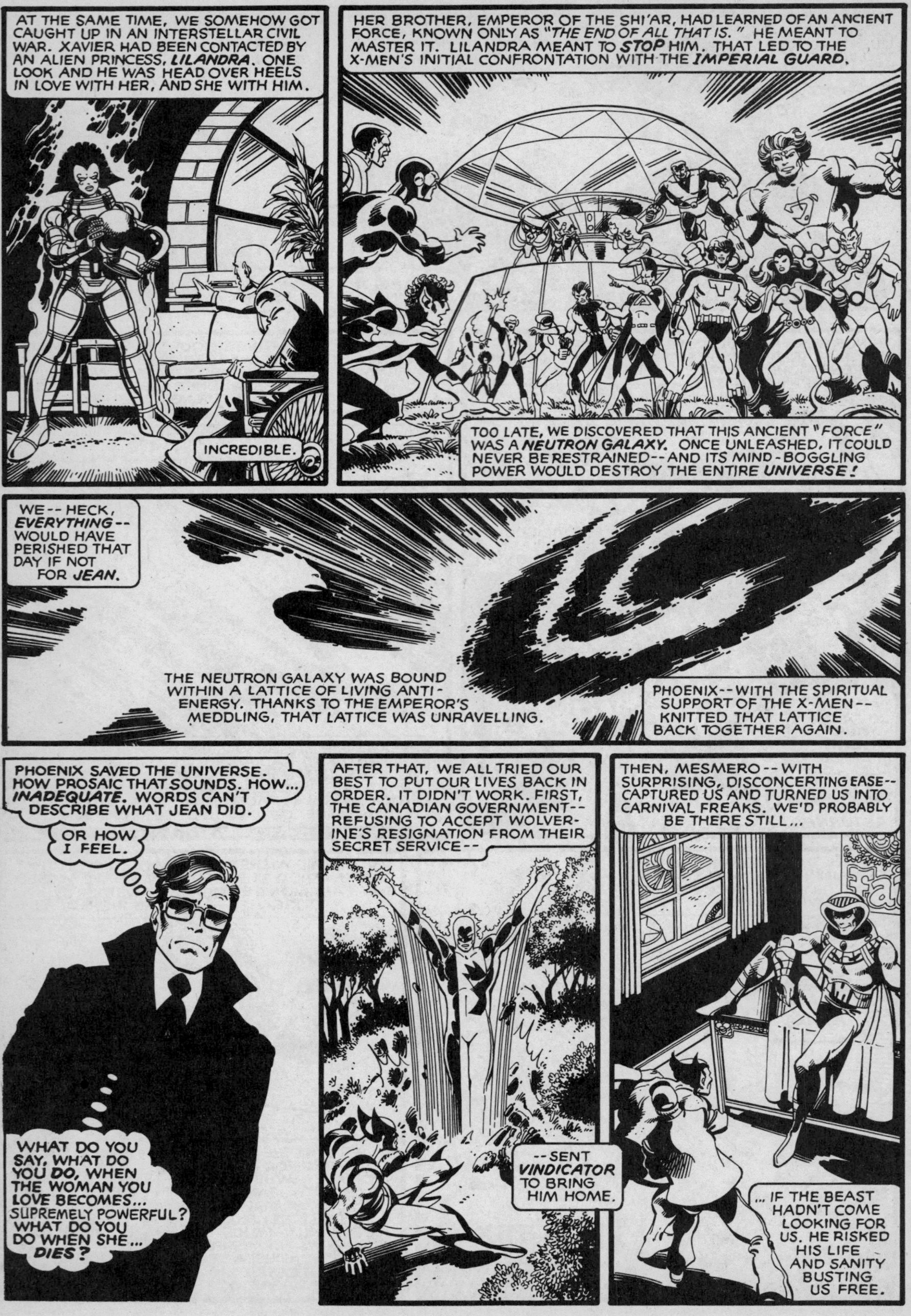

AT THE SAME TIME, WE SOMEHOW GOT CAUGHT UP IN AN INTERSTELLAR CIVIL WAR. XAVIER HAD BEEN CONTACTED BY AN ALIEN PRINCESS, LILANDRA. ONE LOOK AND HE WAS HEAD OVER HEELS IN LOVE WITH HER, AND SHE WITH HIM.
INCREDIBLE.
HER BROTHER, EMPEROR OF THE SHI'AR, HAD LEARNED OF AN ANCIENT FORCE, KNOWN ONLY AS "THE END OF ALL THAT IS." HE MEANT TO MASTER IT. LILANDRA MEANT TO STOP HIM. THAT LED TO THE X-MEN'S INITIAL CONFRONTATION WITH THE IMPERIAL GUARD.
TOO LATE, WE DISCOVERED THAT THIS ANCIENT "FORCE" WAS A NEUTRON GALAXY. ONCE UNLEASHED, IT COULD NEVER BE RESTRAINED--AND ITS MIND-BOGGLING POWER WOULD DESTROY THE ENTIRE UNIVERSE!
WE--HECK, EVERYTHING--WOULD HAVE PERISHED THAT DAY IF NOT FOR JEAN.
THE NEUTRON GALAXY WAS BOUND WITHIN A LATTICE OF LIVING ANTI-ENERGY. THANKS TO THE EMPEROR'S MEDDLING, THAT LATTICE WAS UNRAVELLING.
PHOENIX--WITH THE SPIRITUAL SUPPORT OF THE X-MEN--KNITTED THAT LATTICE BACK TOGETHER AGAIN.
PHOENIX SAVED THE UNIVERSE. HOW PROSAIC THAT SOUNDS. HOW... INADEQUATE. WORDS CAN'T DESCRIBE WHAT JEAN DID.
OR HOW I FEEL.
WHAT DO YOU SAY, WHAT DO YOU DO, WHEN THE WOMAN YOU LOVE BECOMES... SUPREMELY POWERFUL? WHAT DO YOU DO WHEN SHE... DIES?
AFTER THAT, WE ALL TRIED OUR BEST TO PUT OUR LIVES BACK IN ORDER. IT DIDN'T WORK. FIRST, THE CANADIAN GOVERNMENT--REFUSING TO ACCEPT WOLVERINE'S RESIGNATION FROM THEIR SECRET SERVICE--
--SENT VINDICATOR TO BRING HIM HOME.
THEN, MESMERO--WITH SURPRISING, DISCONCERTING EASE--CAPTURED US AND TURNED US INTO CARNIVAL FREAKS. WE'D PROBABLY BE THERE STILL...
...IF THE BEAST HADN'T COME LOOKING FOR US. HE RISKED HIS LIFE AND SANITY BUSTING US FREE.

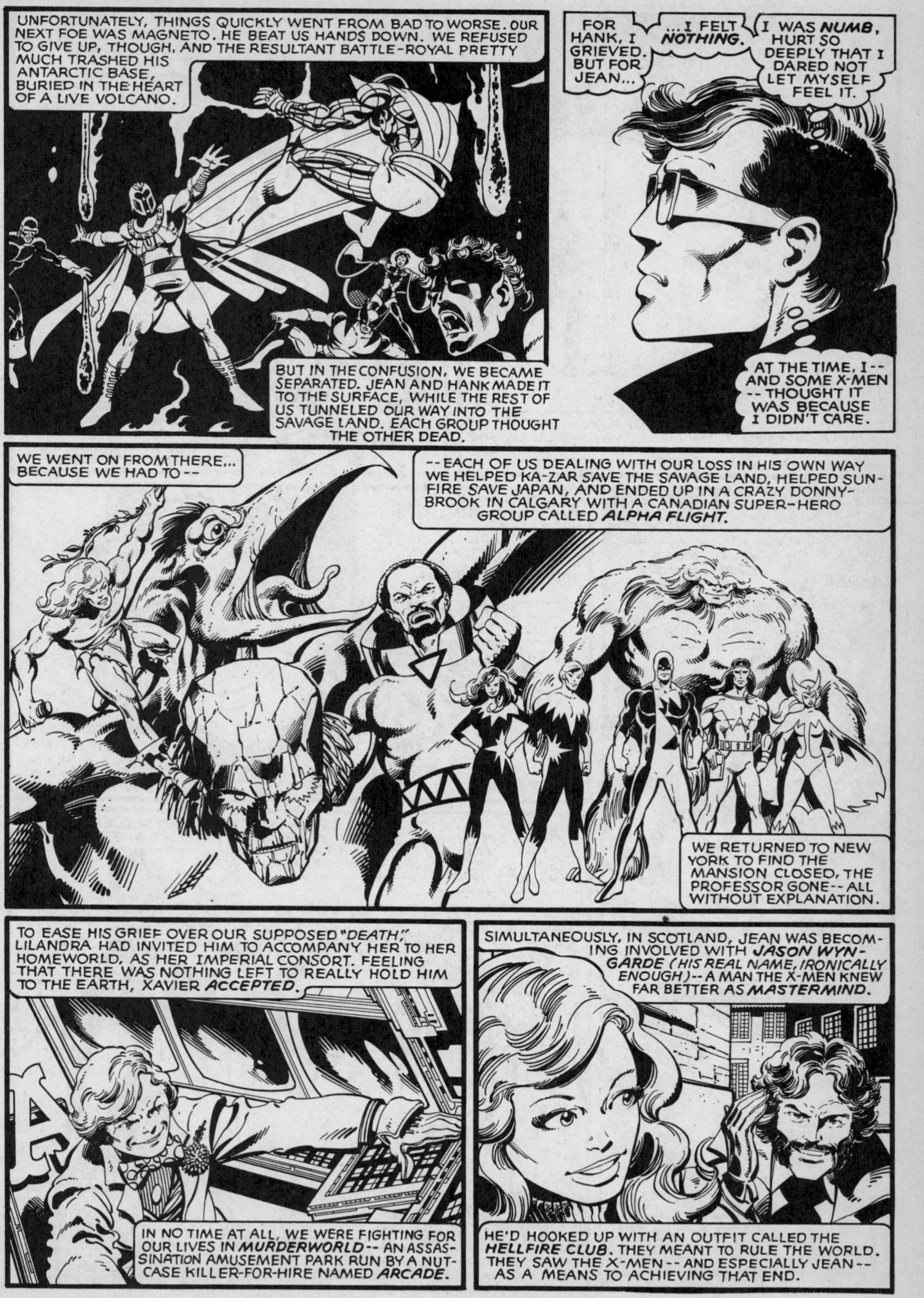
UNFORTUNATELY, THINGS QUICKLY WENT FROM BAD TO WORSE. OUR NEXT FOE WAS MAGNETO. HE BEAT US HANDS DOWN. WE REFUSED TO GIVE UP, THOUGH. AND THE RESULTANT BATTLE-ROYAL PRETTY MUCH TRASHED HIS ANTARCTIC BASE, BURIED IN THE HEART OF A LIVE VOLCANO.
BUT IN THE CONFUSION, WE BECAME SEPARATED. JEAN AND HANK MADE IT TO THE SURFACE, WHILE THE REST OF US TUNNELED OUR WAY INTO THE SAVAGE LAND. EACH GROUP THOUGHT THE OTHER DEAD.
FOR HANK, I GRIEVED. BUT FOR JEAN...
...I FELT NOTHING.
I WAS NUMB, HURT SO DEEPLY THAT I DARED NOT LET MYSELF FEEL IT.
AT THE TIME, I -- AND SOME X-MEN -- THOUGHT IT WAS BECAUSE I DIDN'T CARE.
WE WENT ON FROM THERE... BECAUSE WE HAD TO --
-- EACH OF US DEALING WITH OUR LOSS IN HIS OWN WAY WE HELPED KA-ZAR SAVE THE SAVAGE LAND, HELPED SUNFIRE SAVE JAPAN, AND ENDED UP IN A CRAZY DONNYBROOK IN CALGARY WITH A CANADIAN SUPER-HERO GROUP CALLED ALPHA FLIGHT.
WE RETURNED TO NEW YORK TO FIND THE MANSION CLOSED, THE PROFESSOR GONE -- ALL WITHOUT EXPLANATION.
TO EASE HIS GRIEF OVER OUR SUPPOSED "DEATH," LILANDRA HAD INVITED HIM TO ACCOMPANY HER TO HER HOMEWORLD, AS HER IMPERIAL CONSORT. FEELING THAT THERE WAS NOTHING LEFT TO REALLY HOLD HIM TO THE EARTH, XAVIER ACCEPTED.
IN NO TIME AT ALL, WE WERE FIGHTING FOR OUR LIVES IN MURDERWORLD -- AN ASSASSINATION AMUSEMENT PARK RUN BY A NUT-CASE KILLER-FOR-HIRE NAMED ARCADE.
SIMULTANEOUSLY, IN SCOTLAND, JEAN WAS BECOMING INVOLVED WITH JASON WYNGARDE (HIS REAL NAME, IRONICALLY ENOUGH) -- A MAN THE X-MEN KNEW FAR BETTER AS MASTERMIND.
HE'D HOOKED UP WITH AN OUTFIT CALLED THE HELLFIRE CLUB. THEY MEANT TO RULE THE WORLD. THEY SAW THE X-MEN -- AND ESPECIALLY JEAN -- AS A MEANS TO ACHIEVING THAT END.

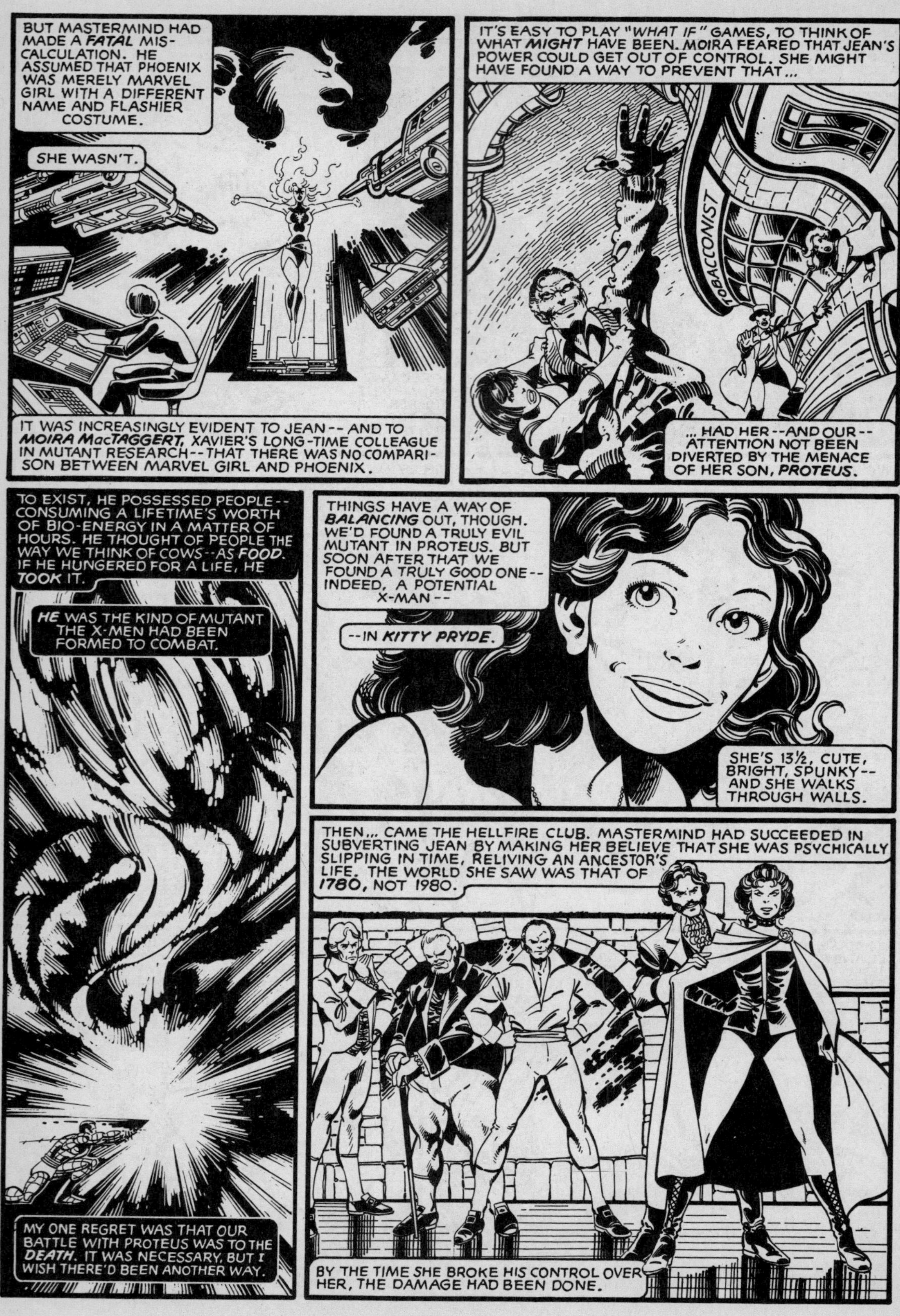

BUT MASTERMIND HAD MADE A **FATAL** MIS-CALCULATION. HE ASSUMED THAT PHOENIX WAS MERELY MARVEL GIRL WITH A DIFFERENT NAME AND FLASHIER COSTUME.
SHE WASN'T.
IT WAS INCREASINGLY EVIDENT TO JEAN-- AND TO **MOIRA MacTAGGERT,** XAVIER'S LONG-TIME COLLEAGUE IN MUTANT RESEARCH--THAT THERE WAS NO COMPARI-SON BETWEEN MARVEL GIRL AND PHOENIX.
IT'S EASY TO PLAY "*WHAT IF*" GAMES, TO THINK OF WHAT **MIGHT** HAVE BEEN. MOIRA FEARED THAT JEAN'S POWER COULD GET OUT OF CONTROL. SHE MIGHT HAVE FOUND A WAY TO PREVENT THAT...
TOBACCONIST
...HAD HER--AND OUR-- ATTENTION NOT BEEN DIVERTED BY THE MENACE OF HER SON, **PROTEUS.**
TO EXIST, HE POSSESSED PEOPLE-- CONSUMING A LIFETIME'S WORTH OF BIO-ENERGY IN A MATTER OF HOURS. HE THOUGHT OF PEOPLE THE WAY WE THINK OF COWS--AS **FOOD.** IF HE HUNGERED FOR A LIFE, HE **TOOK** IT.
HE WAS THE KIND OF MUTANT THE X-MEN HAD BEEN FORMED TO COMBAT.
MY ONE REGRET WAS THAT OUR BATTLE WITH PROTEUS WAS TO THE **DEATH.** IT WAS NECESSARY, BUT I WISH THERE'D BEEN ANOTHER WAY.
THINGS HAVE A WAY OF **BALANCING** OUT, THOUGH. WE'D FOUND A TRULY EVIL MUTANT IN PROTEUS. BUT SOON AFTER THAT WE FOUND A TRULY GOOD ONE-- INDEED, A POTENTIAL X-MAN--
--IN **KITTY PRYDE.**
SHE'S 13½, CUTE, BRIGHT, SPUNKY-- AND SHE WALKS THROUGH WALLS.
THEN... CAME THE HELLFIRE CLUB. MASTERMIND HAD SUCCEEDED IN SUBVERTING JEAN BY MAKING HER BELIEVE THAT SHE WAS PSYCHICALLY SLIPPING IN TIME, RELIVING AN ANCESTOR'S LIFE. THE WORLD SHE SAW WAS THAT OF **1780,** NOT 1980.
BY THE TIME SHE BROKE HIS CONTROL OVER HER, THE DAMAGE HAD BEEN DONE.

NO LONGER WAS SHE PHOENIX, CHILD OF LIGHT AND LAUGHTER. SHE WAS *DARK PHOENIX*, THE BLACK ANGEL, CHAOS-BRINGER.

RAVAGER OF WORLDS.

AT HER HANDS, AN ENTIRE STAR SYSTEM-- FIVE BILLION PEOPLE -- DIED. SHE WAS DRIVEN BY NEEDS, DESIRES, PASSIONS THAT NONE OF US CAN COMPREHEND-- AFTER ALL, WE'RE ONLY HUMAN. PHOENIX WAS A STEP BEYOND.

BUT... SHE WAS STILL THE WOMAN I LOVED. I HAD TO TRY TO SAVE HER. I TRIED TO TALK HER DOWN. I WAS REACHING HER WHEN PROFESSOR X STEPPED IN. I USED REASON...HE USED *FORCE*. WHO'S TO SAY WHICH OF US HAD THE *BETTER* WAY?

HE AND PHOENIX FACED OFF IN A *PSI-WAR*. HE WON. JEAN WAS "*CURED*," THE POWER OF THE PHOENIX ONCE MORE UNDER CONTROL. I ASKED HER TO MARRY ME. SHE SAID, YES. HAPPY ENDING.

NOT SO.

ENTER LILANDRA, DETERMINED TO ELIMINATE PHOENIX AS A THREAT ONCE AND FOR ALL.

WHEN HER IMPERIAL GUARD FAILED JEAN FINISHED THE JOB HERSELF.

SCOTT!

JEAN!

THIS... IS PAIN BEYOND PAIN. I NEVER KNEW A BODY COULD HURT SO MUCH AND STILL FUNCTION.

I'M NOT SURE I WANT TO CALL THIS "*LIVING*."

HOW ARE YOU BEARING UP, SCOTT? I KNOW HOW MUCH YOU LOVED JEAN, AND SHE YOU. I KNOW HOW HARD ALL THIS MUST BE...

DON'T WORRY ABOUT ME, SIR. I'LL BE FINE. BUT HOW ARE *YOU*? AND *MRS. GREY*?

SURVIVING.

PROFESSOR GREY, I SPEAK FOR ALL SHI'AR WHEN I SAY HOW... SORRY WE ARE AT YOUR DAUGHTER'S DEATH. YOUR GRIEF IS OURS.

THANK YOU, YOUR..., MAJESTY. THAT'S VERY KIND.

SO LONG AS I RULE, SO LONG AS SHI'AR ENDURES, JEAN GREY'S NAME AND MEMORY WILL BE

SHE GAVE HER LIFE, THAT THE *UNIVERSE* MIGHT LIVE.

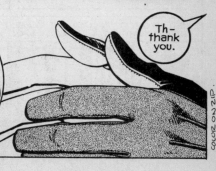

PLEASE ACCEPT THIS GIFT. IT IS A HOLEMPATHIC MATRIX CRYSTAL. TOUCH IT, AND YOU WILL NOT ONLY SEE A 3-DIMENSIONAL IMAGE OF JEAN, BUT FEEL THE ESSENCE OF HER PERSONALITY AS WELL. THIS WAY, A PART OF HER WILL BE WITH YOU, ALWAYS.

Th-thank you.

COLOR 012 ZIP

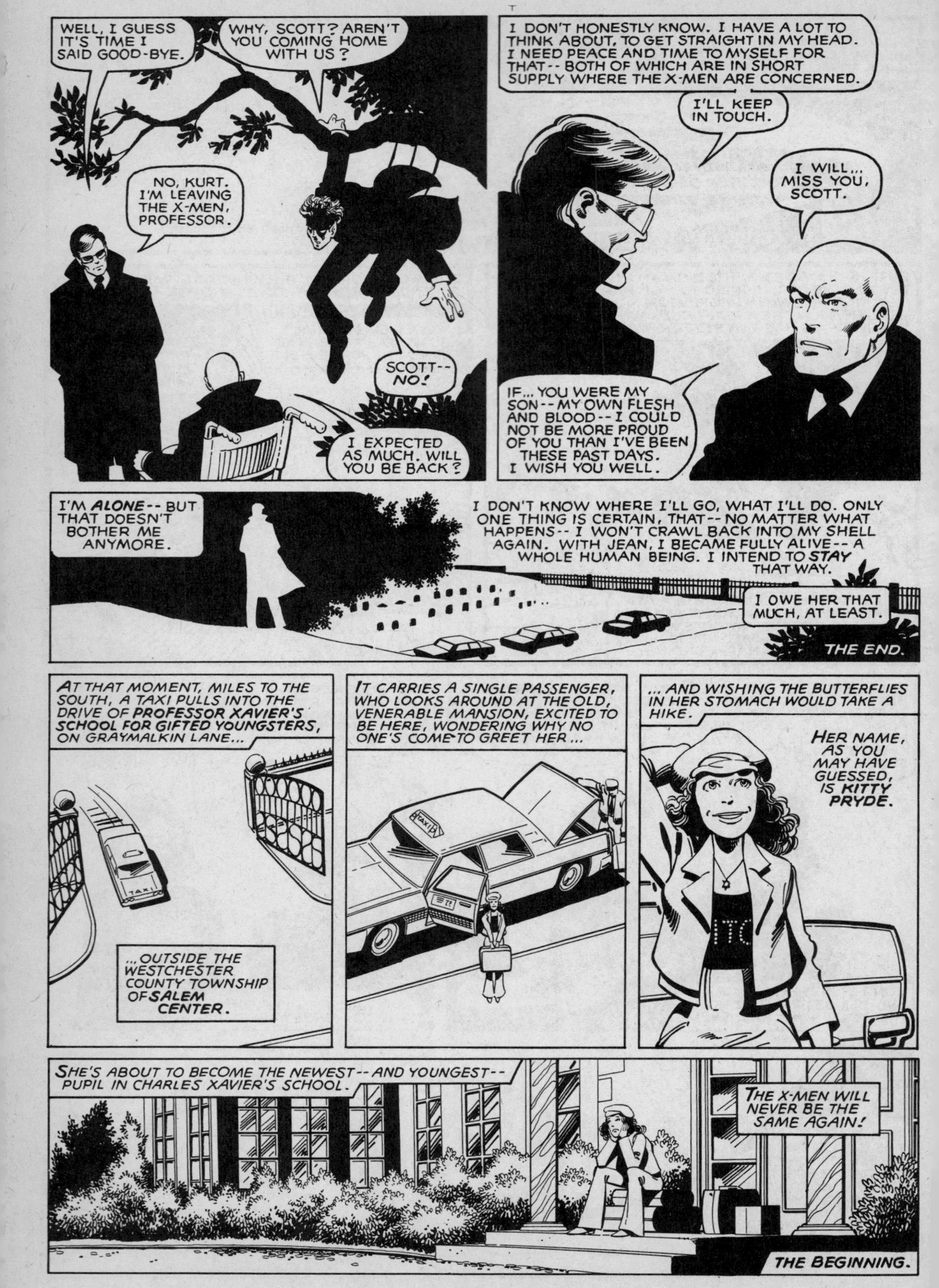
WELL, I GUESS IT'S TIME I SAID GOOD-BYE.
WHY, SCOTT? AREN'T YOU COMING HOME WITH US?
NO, KURT. I'M LEAVING THE X-MEN, PROFESSOR.
SCOTT-- NO!
I EXPECTED AS MUCH. WILL YOU BE BACK?
I DON'T HONESTLY KNOW. I HAVE A LOT TO THINK ABOUT, TO GET STRAIGHT IN MY HEAD. I NEED PEACE AND TIME TO MYSELF FOR THAT-- BOTH OF WHICH ARE IN SHORT SUPPLY WHERE THE X-MEN ARE CONCERNED.
I'LL KEEP IN TOUCH.
I WILL... MISS YOU, SCOTT.
IF... YOU WERE MY SON-- MY OWN FLESH AND BLOOD-- I COULD NOT BE MORE PROUD OF YOU THAN I'VE BEEN THESE PAST DAYS. I WISH YOU WELL.
I'M ALONE-- BUT THAT DOESN'T BOTHER ME ANYMORE.
I DON'T KNOW WHERE I'LL GO, WHAT I'LL DO. ONLY ONE THING IS CERTAIN, THAT-- NO MATTER WHAT HAPPENS-- I WON'T CRAWL BACK INTO MY SHELL AGAIN. WITH JEAN, I BECAME FULLY ALIVE-- A WHOLE HUMAN BEING. I INTEND TO STAY THAT WAY.
I OWE HER THAT MUCH, AT LEAST.
THE END.
AT THAT MOMENT, MILES TO THE SOUTH, A TAXI PULLS INTO THE DRIVE OF PROFESSOR XAVIER'S SCHOOL FOR GIFTED YOUNGSTERS, ON GRAYMALKIN LANE...
TAXI
...OUTSIDE THE WESTCHESTER COUNTY TOWNSHIP OF SALEM CENTER.
IT CARRIES A SINGLE PASSENGER, WHO LOOKS AROUND AT THE OLD, VENERABLE MANSION, EXCITED TO BE HERE, WONDERING WHY NO ONE'S COME TO GREET HER...
...AND WISHING THE BUTTERFLIES IN HER STOMACH WOULD TAKE A HIKE.
HER NAME, AS YOU MAY HAVE GUESSED, IS KITTY PRYDE.
SHE'S ABOUT TO BECOME THE NEWEST-- AND YOUNGEST-- PUPIL IN CHARLES XAVIER'S SCHOOL.
THE X-MEN WILL NEVER BE THE SAME AGAIN!
THE BEGINNING.

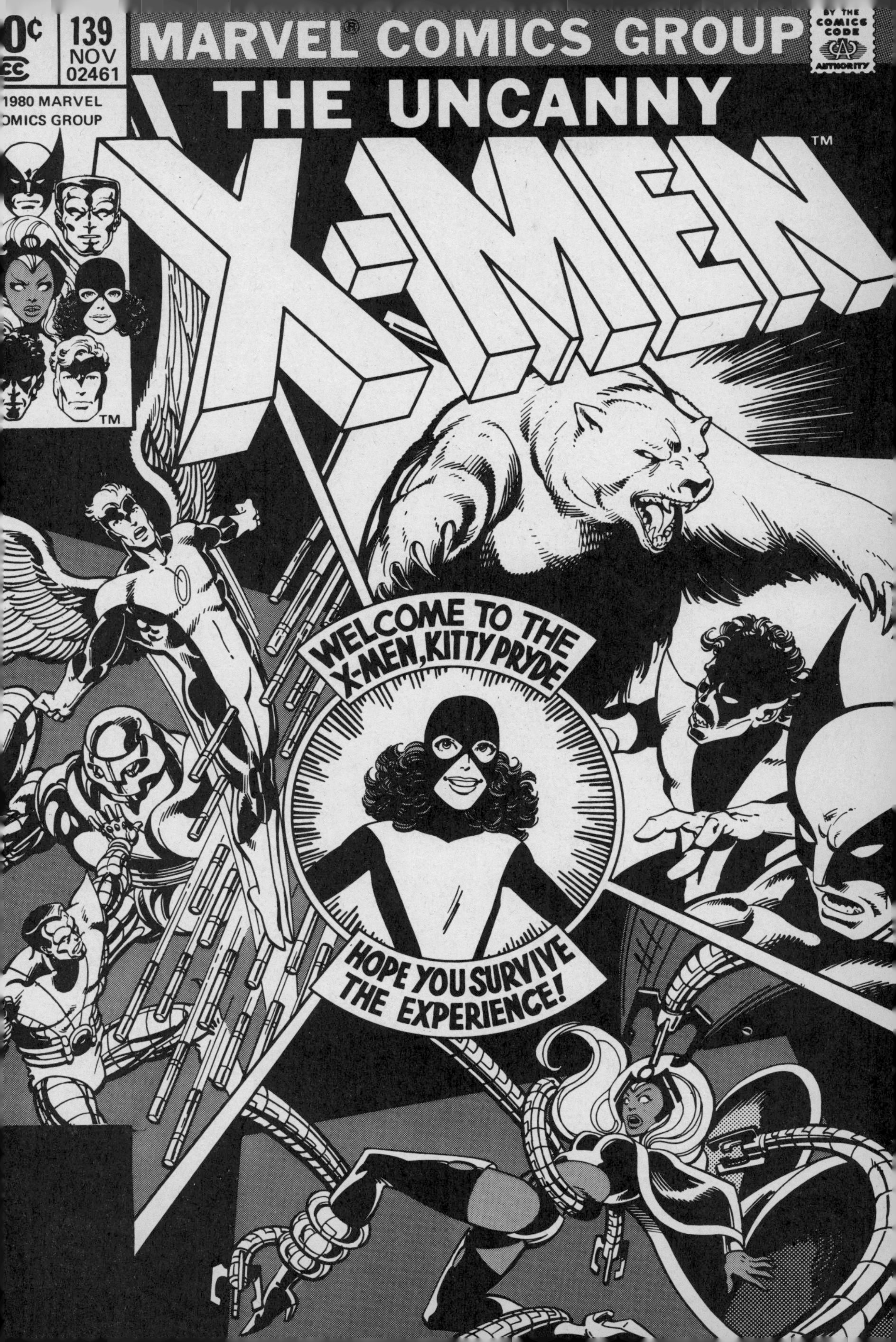

0¢
139
NOV
02461
CC
1980 MARVEL
OMICS GROUP
MARVEL® COMICS GROUP
BY THE COMICS CODE AUTHORITY
THE UNCANNY
X-MEN™
TM
WELCOME TO THE X-MEN, KITTY PRYDE
HOPE YOU SURVIVE THE EXPERIENCE!

Cyclops. Storm. Nightcrawler. Wolverine. Colossus. Children of the atom, students of Charles Xavier, MUTANTS — feared and hated by the world they have sworn to protect. These are the STRANGEST heroes of all!

Stan Lee PRESENTS: THE UNCANNY X-MEN!™

CHRIS CLAREMONT WRITER | JOHN BYRNE PLOT-PENCILS | TERRY AUSTIN INKER | TOM ORZECHOWSKI, letterer GLYNIS WEIN, colorist | LOUISE JONES EDITOR | JIM SHOOTER Ed. in CHIEF

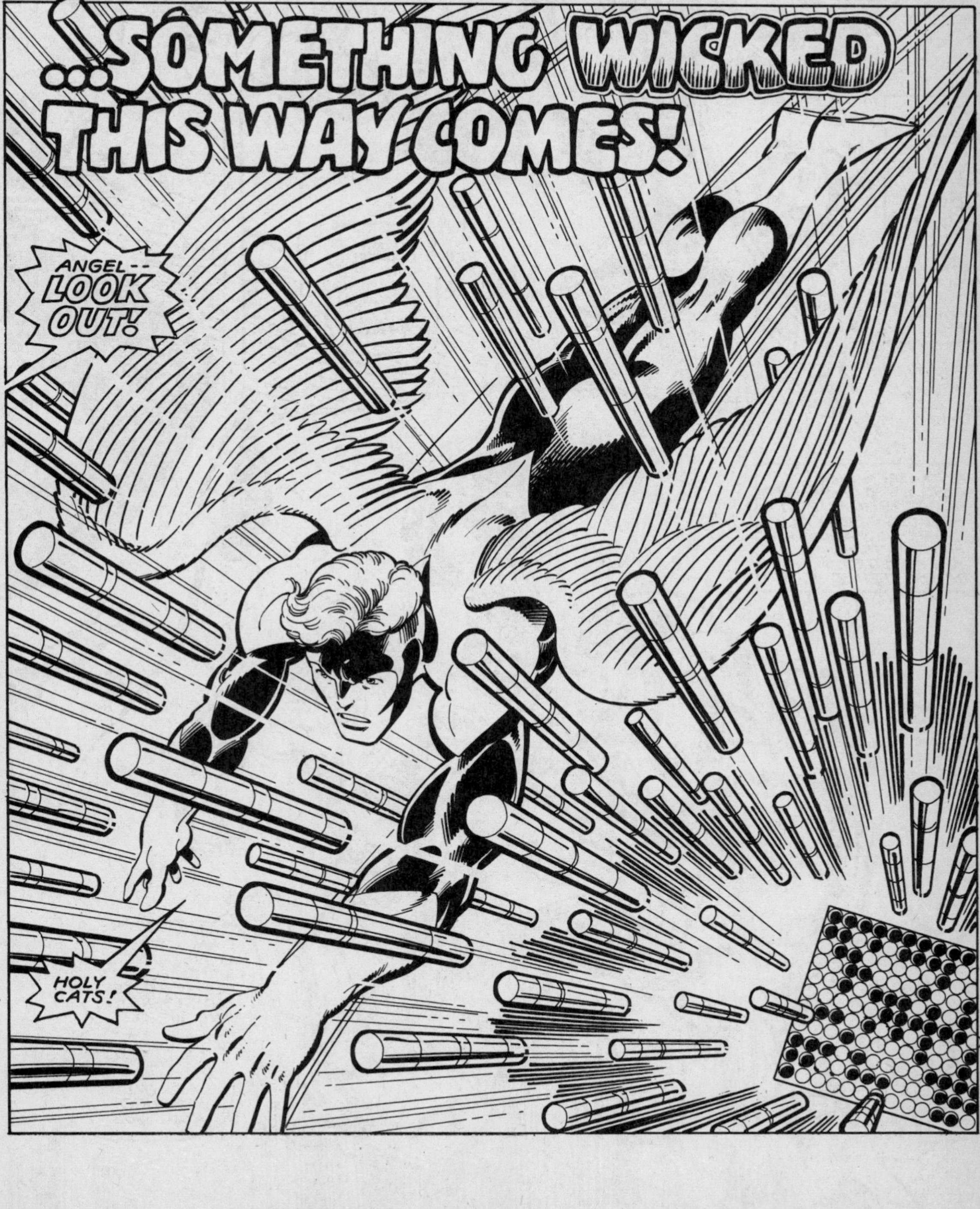
...SOMETHING WICKED THIS WAY COMES!
ANGEL-- LOOK OUT!
HOLY CATS!

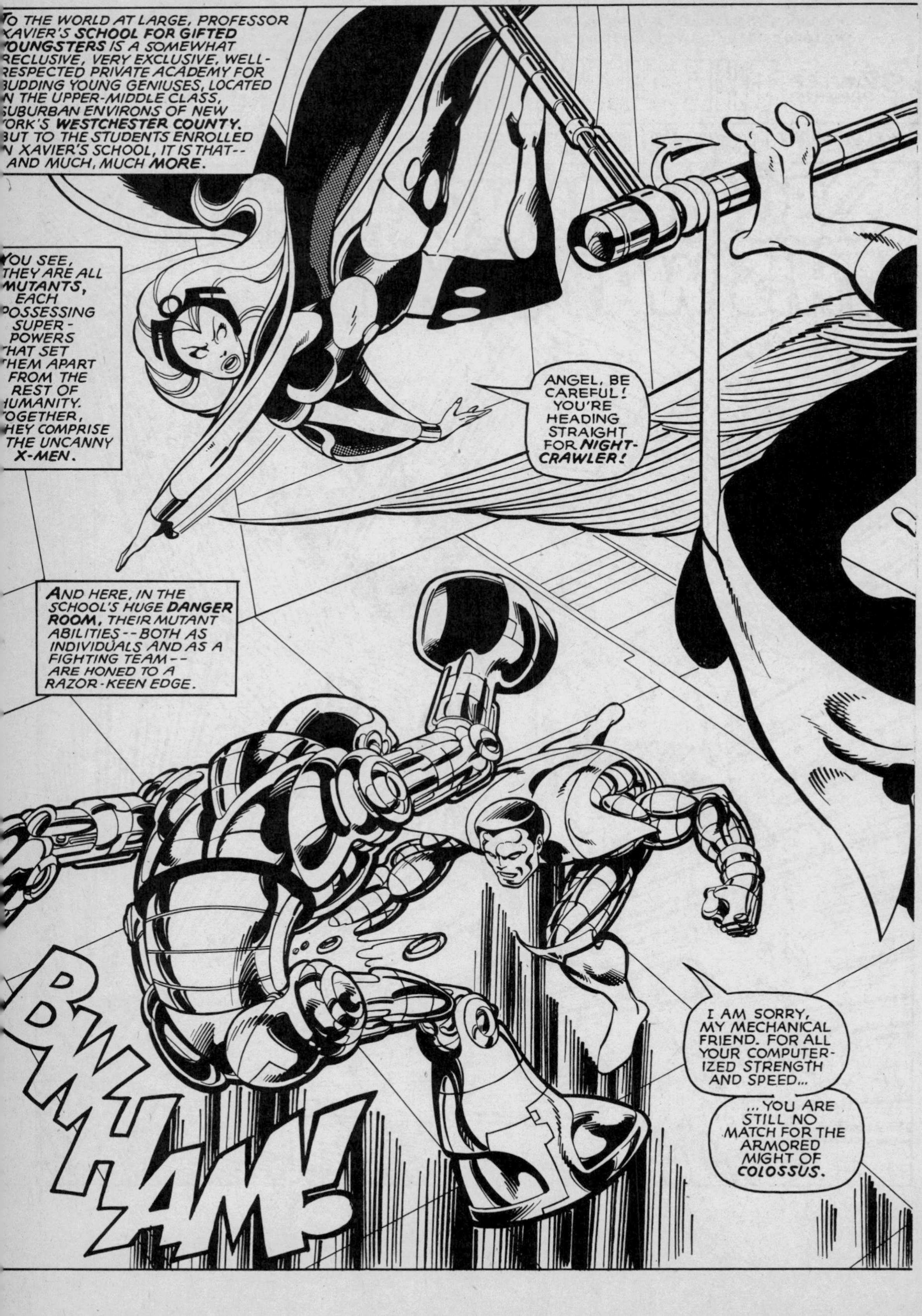
TO THE WORLD AT LARGE, PROFESSOR XAVIER'S SCHOOL FOR GIFTED YOUNGSTERS IS A SOMEWHAT RECLUSIVE, VERY EXCLUSIVE, WELL-RESPECTED PRIVATE ACADEMY FOR BUDDING YOUNG GENIUSES, LOCATED IN THE UPPER-MIDDLE CLASS, SUBURBAN ENVIRONS OF NEW YORK'S WESTCHESTER COUNTY. BUT TO THE STUDENTS ENROLLED IN XAVIER'S SCHOOL, IT IS THAT--AND MUCH, MUCH MORE.
YOU SEE, THEY ARE ALL MUTANTS, EACH POSSESSING SUPER-POWERS THAT SET THEM APART FROM THE REST OF HUMANITY. TOGETHER, THEY COMPRISE THE UNCANNY X-MEN.
ANGEL, BE CAREFUL! YOU'RE HEADING STRAIGHT FOR NIGHT-CRAWLER!
AND HERE, IN THE SCHOOL'S HUGE DANGER ROOM, THEIR MUTANT ABILITIES--BOTH AS INDIVIDUALS AND AS A FIGHTING TEAM--ARE HONED TO A RAZOR-KEEN EDGE.
BWHAM!
I AM SORRY, MY MECHANICAL FRIEND. FOR ALL YOUR COMPUTER-IZED STRENGTH AND SPEED...
...YOU ARE STILL NO MATCH FOR THE ARMORED MIGHT OF COLOSSUS.

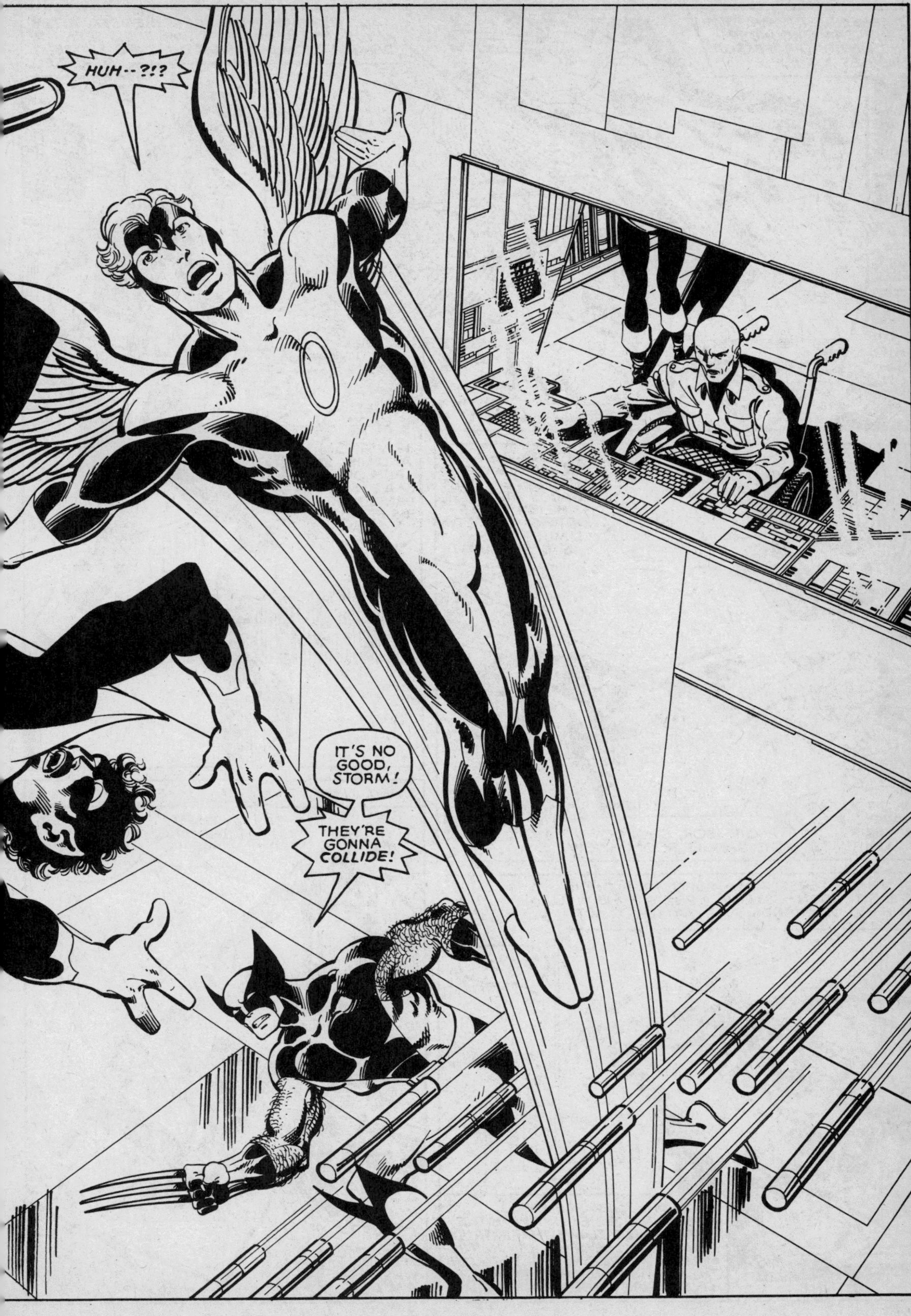
HUH--?!?
IT'S NO GOOD, STORM!
THEY'RE GONNA COLLIDE!

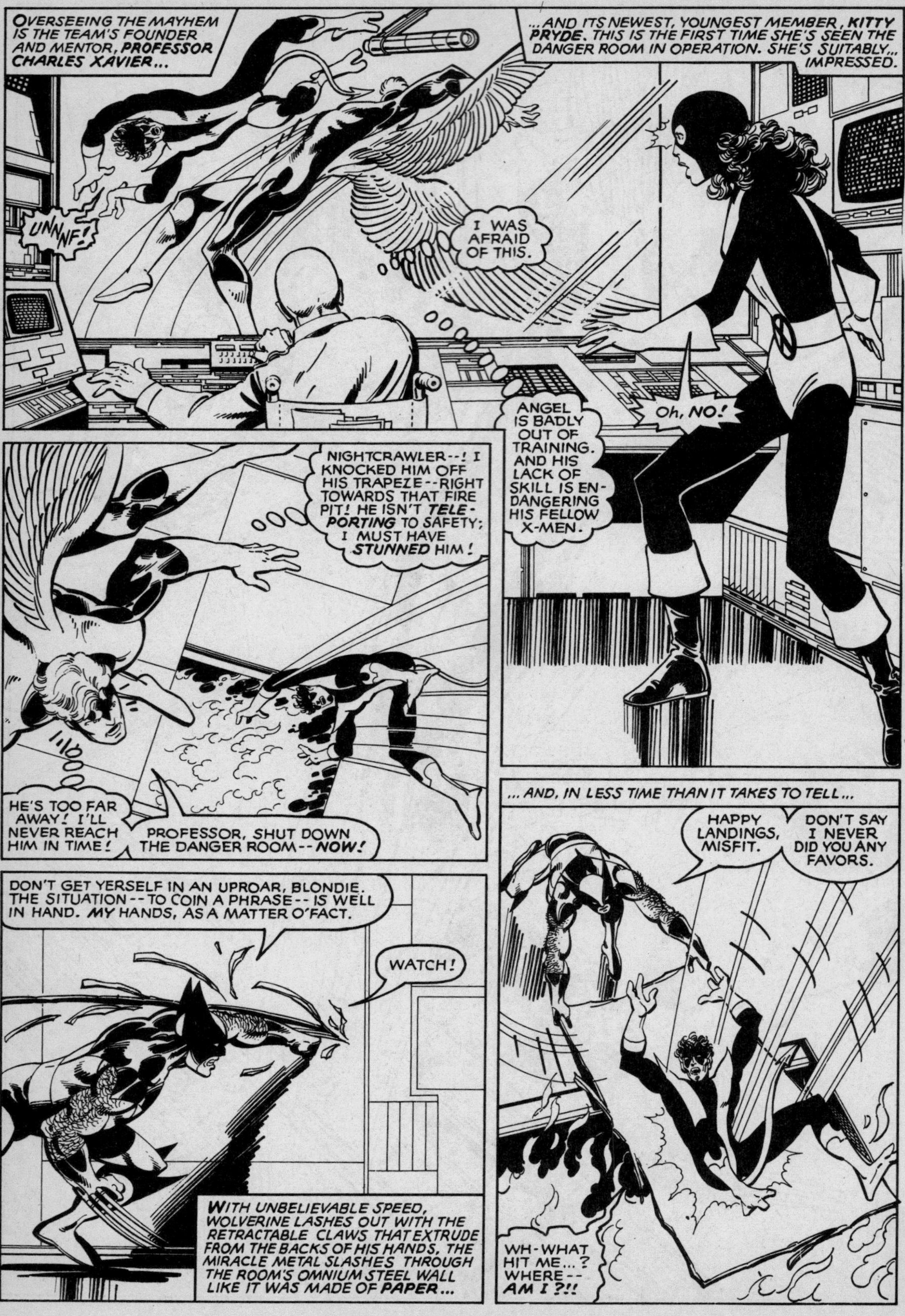
OVERSEEING THE MAYHEM IS THE TEAM'S FOUNDER AND MENTOR, PROFESSOR CHARLES XAVIER...
...AND ITS NEWEST, YOUNGEST MEMBER, KITTY PRYDE. THIS IS THE FIRST TIME SHE'S SEEN THE DANGER ROOM IN OPERATION. SHE'S SUITABLY... IMPRESSED.
UNNNF!
I WAS AFRAID OF THIS.
ANGEL IS BADLY OUT OF TRAINING. AND HIS LACK OF SKILL IS ENDANGERING HIS FELLOW X-MEN.
Oh, NO!
NIGHTCRAWLER--! I KNOCKED HIM OFF HIS TRAPEZE--RIGHT TOWARDS THAT FIRE PIT! HE ISN'T TELE-PORTING TO SAFETY; I MUST HAVE STUNNED HIM!
HE'S TOO FAR AWAY! I'LL NEVER REACH HIM IN TIME!
PROFESSOR, SHUT DOWN THE DANGER ROOM--NOW!
...AND, IN LESS TIME THAN IT TAKES TO TELL...
HAPPY LANDINGS, MISFIT.
DON'T SAY I NEVER DID YOU ANY FAVORS.
DON'T GET YERSELF IN AN UPROAR, BLONDIE. THE SITUATION--TO COIN A PHRASE--IS WELL IN HAND. MY HANDS, AS A MATTER O'FACT.
WATCH!
WITH UNBELIEVABLE SPEED, WOLVERINE LASHES OUT WITH THE RETRACTABLE CLAWS THAT EXTRUDE FROM THE BACKS OF HIS HANDS, THE MIRACLE METAL SLASHES THROUGH THE ROOM'S OMNIUM STEEL WALL LIKE IT WAS MADE OF PAPER...
WH-WHAT HIT ME...? WHERE--AM I?!!

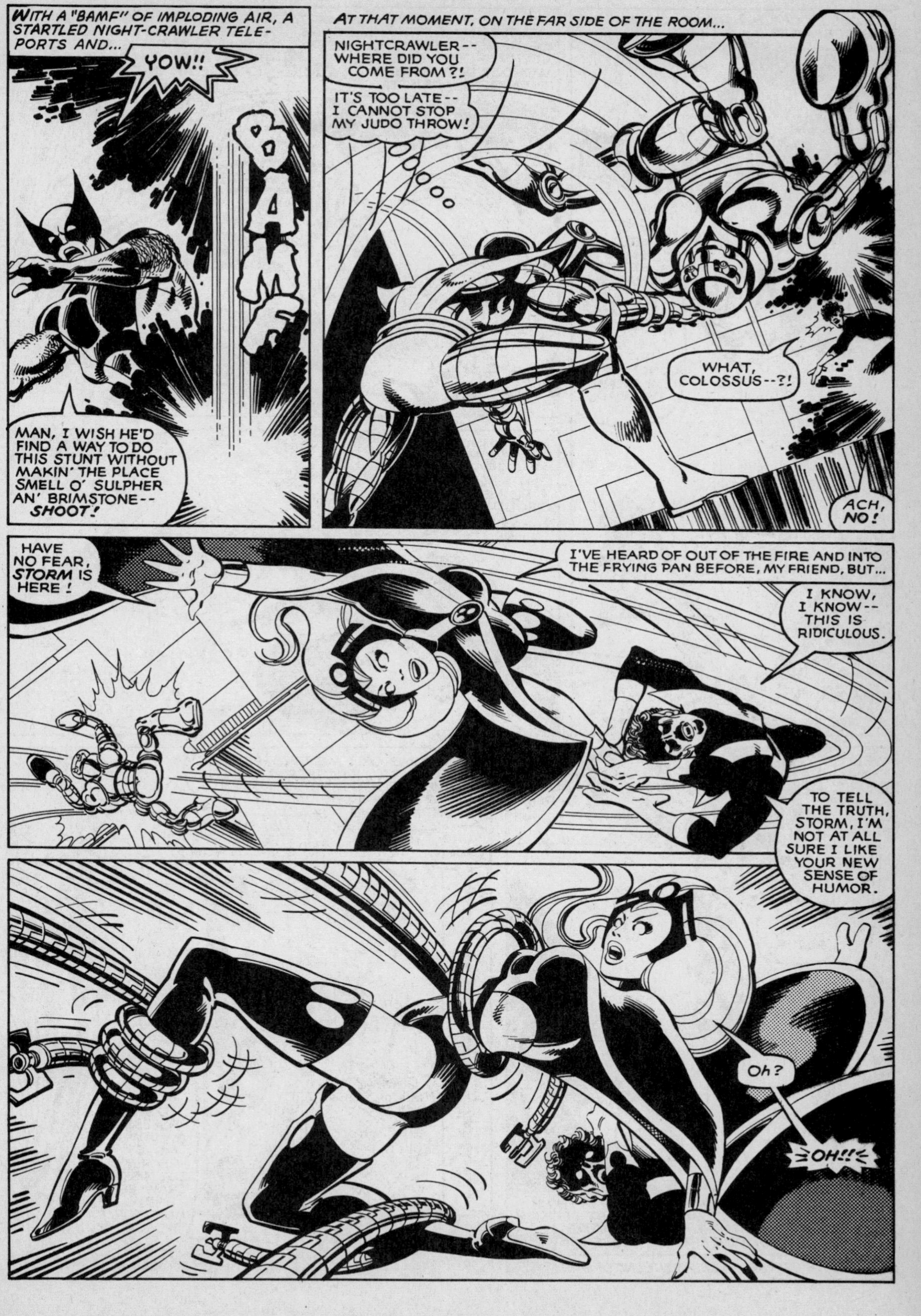
WITH A "BAMF" OF IMPLODING AIR, A STARTLED NIGHT-CRAWLER TELE-PORTS AND...
YOW!!
BAMF
MAN, I WISH HE'D FIND A WAY TO DO THIS STUNT WITHOUT MAKIN' THE PLACE SMELL O' SULPHER AN' BRIMSTONE-- SHOOT!
AT THAT MOMENT, ON THE FAR SIDE OF THE ROOM...
NIGHTCRAWLER-- WHERE DID YOU COME FROM?!
IT'S TOO LATE-- I CANNOT STOP MY JUDO THROW!
WHAT, COLOSSUS--?!
ACH, NO!
HAVE NO FEAR, STORM IS HERE!
I'VE HEARD OF OUT OF THE FIRE AND INTO THE FRYING PAN BEFORE, MY FRIEND, BUT...
I KNOW, I KNOW-- THIS IS RIDICULOUS.
TO TELL THE TRUTH, STORM, I'M NOT AT ALL SURE I LIKE YOUR NEW SENSE OF HUMOR.
Oh?
OH!!

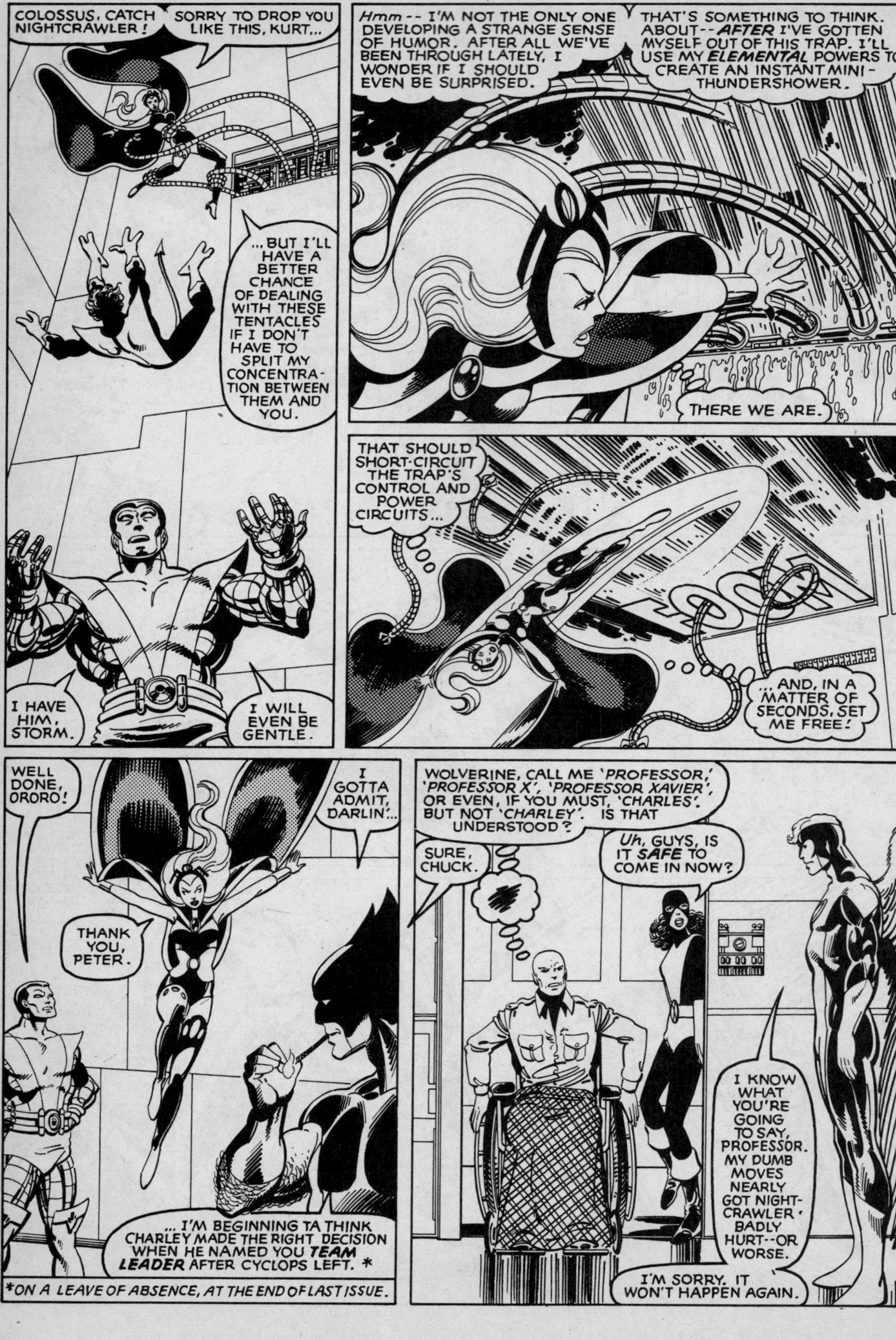

COLOSSUS, CATCH NIGHTCRAWLER!
SORRY TO DROP YOU LIKE THIS, KURT...
...BUT I'LL HAVE A BETTER CHANCE OF DEALING WITH THESE TENTACLES IF I DON'T HAVE TO SPLIT MY CONCENTRATION BETWEEN THEM AND YOU.
I HAVE HIM, STORM.
I WILL EVEN BE GENTLE.
Hmm -- I'M NOT THE ONLY ONE DEVELOPING A STRANGE SENSE OF HUMOR. AFTER ALL WE'VE BEEN THROUGH LATELY, I WONDER IF I SHOULD EVEN BE SURPRISED.
THAT'S SOMETHING TO THINK. ABOUT-- ***AFTER*** I'VE GOTTEN MYSELF OUT OF THIS TRAP. I'LL USE MY ***ELEMENTAL*** POWERS TO CREATE AN INSTANT MINI-THUNDERSHOWER.
THERE WE ARE.
THAT SHOULD SHORT-CIRCUIT THE TRAP'S CONTROL AND POWER CIRCUITS...
...AND, IN A MATTER OF SECONDS, SET ME FREE!
WELL DONE, ORORO!
THANK YOU, PETER.
I GOTTA ADMIT, DARLIN'...
...I'M BEGINNING TA THINK CHARLEY MADE THE RIGHT DECISION WHEN HE NAMED YOU ***TEAM LEADER*** AFTER CYCLOPS LEFT. *
*ON A LEAVE OF ABSENCE, AT THE END OF LAST ISSUE.
WOLVERINE, CALL ME '*PROFESSOR*,' '*PROFESSOR X*', '*PROFESSOR XAVIER*', OR EVEN, IF YOU MUST, '*CHARLES*'. BUT NOT '*CHARLEY*'. IS THAT UNDERSTOOD?
SURE, CHUCK.
Uh, GUYS, IS IT ***SAFE*** TO COME IN NOW?
I KNOW WHAT YOU'RE GOING TO SAY, PROFESSOR. MY DUMB MOVES NEARLY GOT NIGHT-CRAWLER BADLY HURT--OR WORSE.
I'M SORRY. IT WON'T HAPPEN AGAIN.

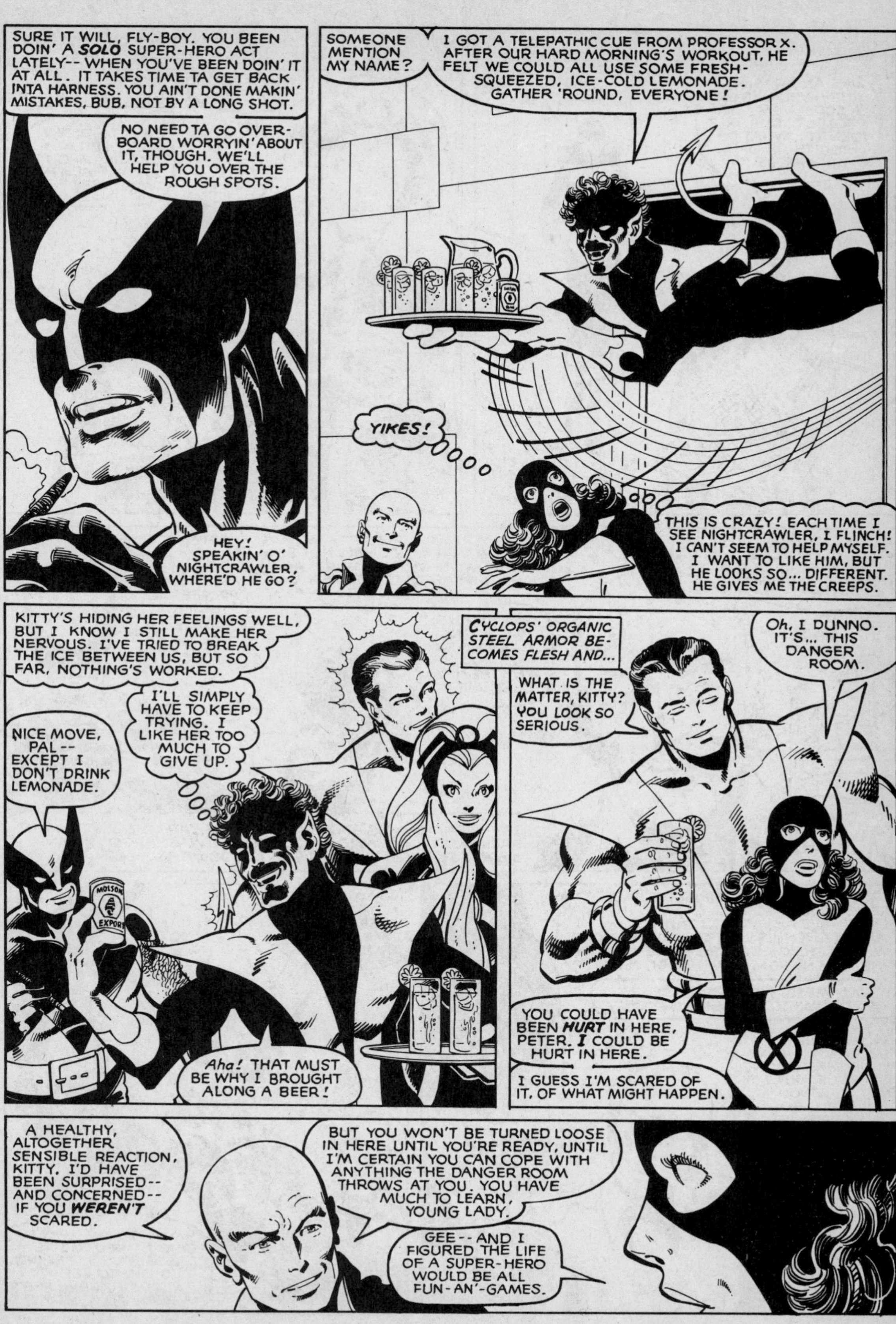
SURE IT WILL, FLY-BOY. YOU BEEN DOIN' A SOLO SUPER-HERO ACT LATELY-- WHEN YOU'VE BEEN DOIN' IT AT ALL. IT TAKES TIME TA GET BACK INTA HARNESS. YOU AIN'T DONE MAKIN' MISTAKES, BUB, NOT BY A LONG SHOT.
NO NEED TA GO OVERBOARD WORRYIN' ABOUT IT, THOUGH. WE'LL HELP YOU OVER THE ROUGH SPOTS.
HEY! SPEAKIN' O' NIGHTCRAWLER, WHERE'D HE GO?
SOMEONE MENTION MY NAME?
I GOT A TELEPATHIC CUE FROM PROFESSOR X. AFTER OUR HARD MORNING'S WORKOUT, HE FELT WE COULD ALL USE SOME FRESH-SQUEEZED, ICE-COLD LEMONADE. GATHER 'ROUND, EVERYONE!
YIKES!
THIS IS CRAZY! EACH TIME I SEE NIGHTCRAWLER, I FLINCH! I CAN'T SEEM TO HELP MYSELF. I WANT TO LIKE HIM, BUT HE LOOKS SO... DIFFERENT. HE GIVES ME THE CREEPS.
KITTY'S HIDING HER FEELINGS WELL, BUT I KNOW I STILL MAKE HER NERVOUS. I'VE TRIED TO BREAK THE ICE BETWEEN US, BUT SO FAR, NOTHING'S WORKED.
I'LL SIMPLY HAVE TO KEEP TRYING. I LIKE HER TOO MUCH TO GIVE UP.
NICE MOVE, PAL-- EXCEPT I DON'T DRINK LEMONADE.
MOLSON EXPORT
Aha! THAT MUST BE WHY I BROUGHT ALONG A BEER!
CYCLOPS' ORGANIC STEEL ARMOR BECOMES FLESH AND...
WHAT IS THE MATTER, KITTY? YOU LOOK SO SERIOUS.
Oh, I DUNNO. IT'S... THIS DANGER ROOM.
YOU COULD HAVE BEEN HURT IN HERE, PETER. I COULD BE HURT IN HERE.
I GUESS I'M SCARED OF IT, OF WHAT MIGHT HAPPEN.
A HEALTHY, ALTOGETHER SENSIBLE REACTION, KITTY. I'D HAVE BEEN SURPRISED-- AND CONCERNED-- IF YOU WEREN'T SCARED.
BUT YOU WON'T BE TURNED LOOSE IN HERE UNTIL YOU'RE READY, UNTIL I'M CERTAIN YOU CAN COPE WITH ANYTHING THE DANGER ROOM THROWS AT YOU. YOU HAVE MUCH TO LEARN, YOUNG LADY.
GEE-- AND I FIGURED THE LIFE OF A SUPER-HERO WOULD BE ALL FUN-AN'-GAMES.

IF ONLY IT WERE.

AS AN X-MAN, KITTY, YOU'LL NEED A *CODE-NAME*, TO PROTECT YOUR TRUE IDENTITY. WHAT DO YOU THINK OF *"ARIEL"*?

YUCK. NO OFFENSE, PROFESSOR, BUT DO I HAVE TO TAKE IT?

I MEAN, IT'S ...OKAY, BUT IT DOESN'T REALLY SEND ME.

WELL NOW, LITTLE ONE, WE CERTAINLY WOULDN'T WANT TO GIVE YOU A NAME YOU DON'T LIKE. LET'S SEE...

WHAT ABOUT *"SPRITE"*?

YEAH... YEAH!

BUT I BETTER NOT HEAR ANY CRACKS ABOUT PEOPLE PULLIN' MY *"TAB!"*

OUCH! X-MEN, I PROPOSE A TOAST-- TO OUR NEWEST MEMBER: *"SPRITE!"*

I HOPE YOU WILL BE HAPPY WITH US, KITTY. I PRAY YOU WILL NOT BE HURT, AS WE HAVE BEEN HURT. AND YET, I FEAR THAT, SOONER OR LATER, YOU *WILL*.

WOLVERINE, I'VE BEEN MEANING TO ASK YOU: *WHY* THE NEW COSTUME?

WHY *NOT*?

PROFESSOR, GOT A MINUTE?

I'VE BEEN THINKING ABOUT MY HASSLES WITH THE GOVERNMENT BACK HOME IN *CANADA*. YOU KNOW I WAS PART O' THEIR *SECRET SERVICE* 'TIL I RESIGNED TO JOIN THE X-MEN.

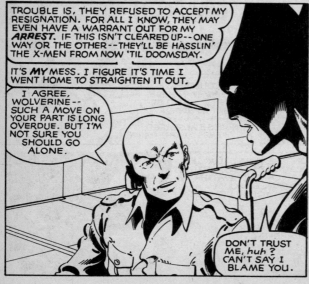

TROUBLE IS, THEY REFUSED TO ACCEPT MY RESIGNATION. FOR ALL I KNOW, THEY MAY EVEN HAVE A WARRANT OUT FOR MY *ARREST*. IF THIS ISN'T CLEARED UP-- ONE WAY OR THE OTHER--THEY'LL BE HASSLIN' THE X-MEN FROM NOW 'TIL DOOMSDAY.

IT'S *MY* MESS. I FIGURE IT'S TIME I WENT HOME TO STRAIGHTEN IT OUT.

I AGREE, WOLVERINE-- SUCH A MOVE ON YOUR PART IS LONG OVERDUE. BUT I'M NOT SURE YOU SHOULD GO ALONE.

DON'T TRUST ME, huh? CAN'T SAY I BLAME YOU.

WANT'A PLAY *"CHAPERONE,"* MISFIT? KEEP ME OUT OF TROUBLE?

WHY NOT?

MY MOTHER ALWAYS SAID I LIKED TO LIVE DANGEROUSLY. BESIDES, I'D LIKE TO SEE *AURORA* AGAIN; SHE'S A REAL *"FOXY LADY."*

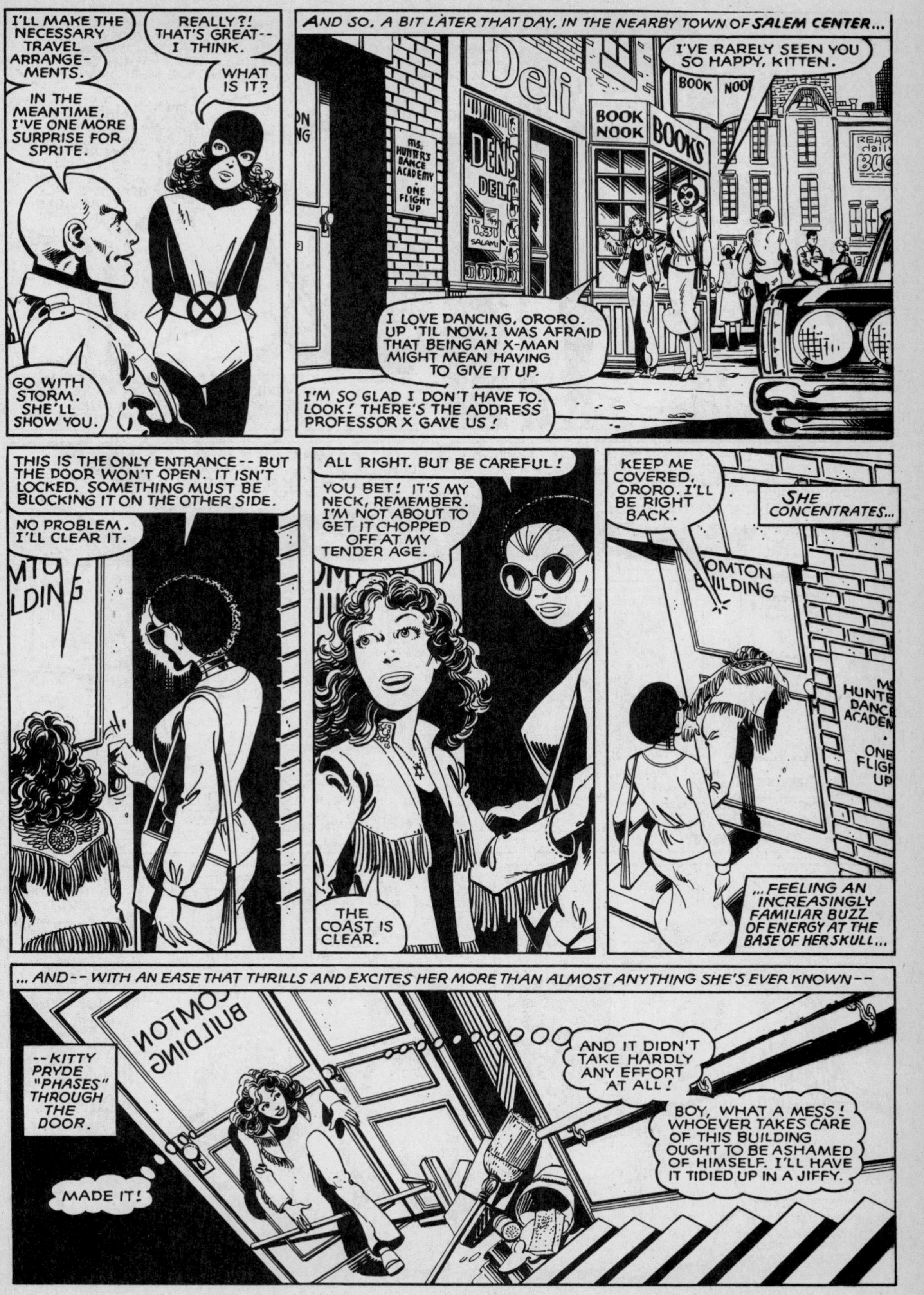

I'LL MAKE THE NECESSARY TRAVEL ARRANGE-MENTS.
IN THE MEANTIME, I'VE ONE MORE SURPRISE FOR SPRITE.
REALLY?! THAT'S GREAT-- I THINK.
WHAT IS IT?
GO WITH STORM. SHE'LL SHOW YOU.
AND SO, A BIT LATER THAT DAY, IN THE NEARBY TOWN OF SALEM CENTER...
Deli
DEN'S DELI
MS. HUNTER'S DANCE ACADEMY ONE FLIGHT UP
SALAMI
BOOK NOOK
BOOKS
I'VE RARELY SEEN YOU SO HAPPY, KITTEN.
I LOVE DANCING, ORORO. UP 'TIL NOW, I WAS AFRAID THAT BEING AN X-MAN MIGHT MEAN HAVING TO GIVE IT UP.
I'M SO GLAD I DON'T HAVE TO. LOOK! THERE'S THE ADDRESS PROFESSOR X GAVE US!
THIS IS THE ONLY ENTRANCE-- BUT THE DOOR WON'T OPEN. IT ISN'T LOCKED. SOMETHING MUST BE BLOCKING IT ON THE OTHER SIDE.
NO PROBLEM. I'LL CLEAR IT.
ALL RIGHT. BUT BE CAREFUL!
YOU BET! IT'S MY NECK, REMEMBER. I'M NOT ABOUT TO GET IT CHOPPED OFF AT MY TENDER AGE.
THE COAST IS CLEAR.
KEEP ME COVERED, ORORO. I'LL BE RIGHT BACK.
SHE CONCENTRATES...
COMTON BUILDING
...FEELING AN INCREASINGLY FAMILIAR BUZZ OF ENERGY AT THE BASE OF HER SKULL...
... AND-- WITH AN EASE THAT THRILLS AND EXCITES HER MORE THAN ALMOST ANYTHING SHE'S EVER KNOWN--
--KITTY PRYDE "PHASES" THROUGH THE DOOR.
MADE IT!
AND IT DIDN'T TAKE HARDLY ANY EFFORT AT ALL!
BOY, WHAT A MESS! WHOEVER TAKES CARE OF THIS BUILDING OUGHT TO BE ASHAMED OF HIMSELF. I'LL HAVE IT TIDIED UP IN A JIFFY.

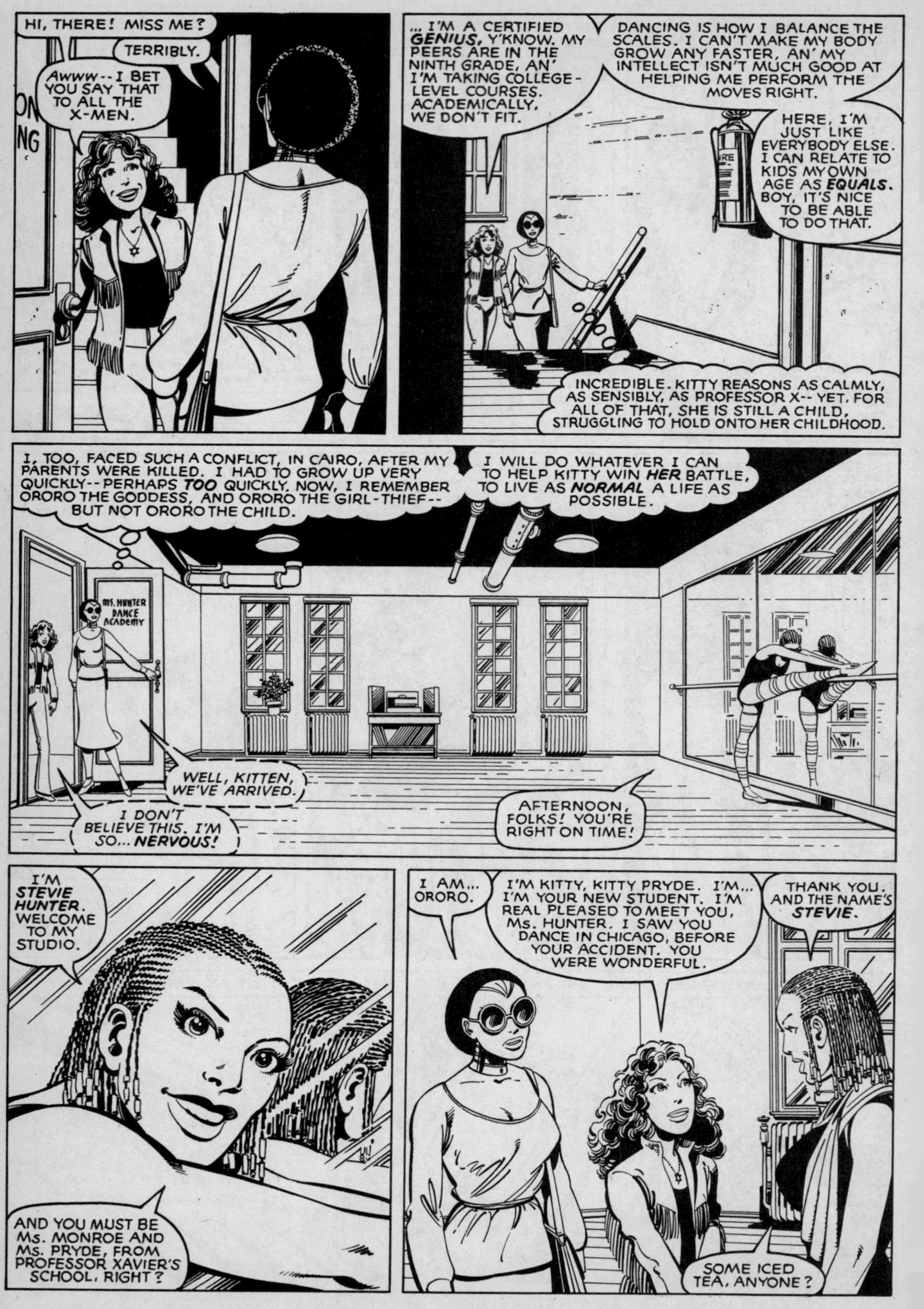
HI, THERE! MISS ME?
TERRIBLY.
Awww-- I BET YOU SAY THAT TO ALL THE X-MEN.
... I'M A CERTIFIED GENIUS, Y'KNOW. MY PEERS ARE IN THE NINTH GRADE, AN' I'M TAKING COLLEGE-LEVEL COURSES. ACADEMICALLY, WE DON'T FIT.
DANCING IS HOW I BALANCE THE SCALES. I CAN'T MAKE MY BODY GROW ANY FASTER, AN' MY INTELLECT ISN'T MUCH GOOD AT HELPING ME PERFORM THE MOVES RIGHT.
HERE, I'M JUST LIKE EVERYBODY ELSE. I CAN RELATE TO KIDS MY OWN AGE AS EQUALS. BOY, IT'S NICE TO BE ABLE TO DO THAT.
INCREDIBLE. KITTY REASONS AS CALMLY, AS SENSIBLY, AS PROFESSOR X-- YET, FOR ALL OF THAT, SHE IS STILL A CHILD, STRUGGLING TO HOLD ONTO HER CHILDHOOD.
I, TOO, FACED SUCH A CONFLICT, IN CAIRO, AFTER MY PARENTS WERE KILLED. I HAD TO GROW UP VERY QUICKLY-- PERHAPS TOO QUICKLY. NOW, I REMEMBER ORORO THE GODDESS, AND ORORO THE GIRL-THIEF-- BUT NOT ORORO THE CHILD.
I WILL DO WHATEVER I CAN TO HELP KITTY WIN HER BATTLE, TO LIVE AS NORMAL A LIFE AS POSSIBLE.
MS. HUNTER DANCE ACADEMY
WELL, KITTEN, WE'VE ARRIVED.
I DON'T BELIEVE THIS. I'M SO... NERVOUS!
AFTERNOON, FOLKS! YOU'RE RIGHT ON TIME!
I'M STEVIE HUNTER. WELCOME TO MY STUDIO.
AND YOU MUST BE Ms. MONROE AND Ms. PRYDE, FROM PROFESSOR XAVIER'S SCHOOL, RIGHT?
I AM... ORORO.
I'M KITTY, KITTY PRYDE. I'M... I'M YOUR NEW STUDENT. I'M REAL PLEASED TO MEET YOU, Ms. HUNTER. I SAW YOU DANCE IN CHICAGO, BEFORE YOUR ACCIDENT. YOU WERE WONDERFUL.
THANK YOU. AND THE NAME'S STEVIE.
SOME ICED TEA, ANYONE?

WITH THAT, AN EFFERVESCENT, ENTHUSIASTIC KITTY, AND SURPRISINGLY, A SLIGHTLY WARY STORM, GET TO KNOW KITTY'S NEW DANCE TEACHER OVER A POT OF ICED HERBAL TEA...

THIS IS LAURIER DRIVE, A PLEASANT, WHITE-COLLAR NEIGHBORHOOD. MOST OF THESE MODEST, SEMI-DETACHED HOUSES ARE OWNED BY PROFESSIONAL PEOPLE -- TEACHERS, DOCTORS, LAWYERS, GOVERNMENT WORKERS, ALL JUST GETTING STARTED IN THEIR VARIOUS FIELDS...

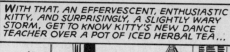

...AS WE SHIFT OUR SCENE AHEAD A DAY, AND SOME THREE HUNDRED MILES TO THE NORTHWEST, FROM THE SUBURBS OF NEW YORK CITY TO THOSE OF OTTAWA, CAPITAL OF CANADA.

... AMONG THEM -- IN NUMBER 138A -- A BRILLIANT, MAVERICK RESEARCH PHYSICIST NAMED JAMES MacDONALD HUDSON...

... AND HIS WIFE, HEATHER, AN EXECUTIVE SECRETARY FOR YUKON OIL, ONE OF THE COUNTRY'S BIGGEST ENERGY CONGLOMERATES.

IT WAS NICE OF MR. BERESFORD TO GIVE ME THE DAY OFF. BUT AFTER ALL THE HOURS I PUT IN HELPING HIM PREPARE FOR THIS MONTH'S BOARD MEETING...

... I DESERVE IT.

THAT OVERTIME MONEY WILL COME IN HANDY -- AND WITH JAMIE AWAY ON GOVERNMENT BUSINESS, MY EXTRA WORK DIDN'T CAUSE ANY HASSLES AT HOME.

HOME-- UGH!

ALL I'VE DONE THIS PAST WEEK WAS TOUCH BASE LONG ENOUGH TO GRAB SOME SLEEP...

...SHOWER, AND CHANGE MY CLOTHES. THE PLACE IS PROBABLY AN UNHOLY MESS.

FIGURES-- NOTHING BUT BILLS.

HOW CAN SO LITTLE COST SO MUCH?

BETWEEN US, JAMIE AND I MAKE A RESPECTABLE SALARY -- YET WE STILL HAVE TO STRAIN TO MAKE ENDS MEET. WE WANT CHILDREN, BUT HOW ARE WE GOING TO AFFORD THEM?

WHAT THE--?! OUR FRONT DOOR'S OPEN!

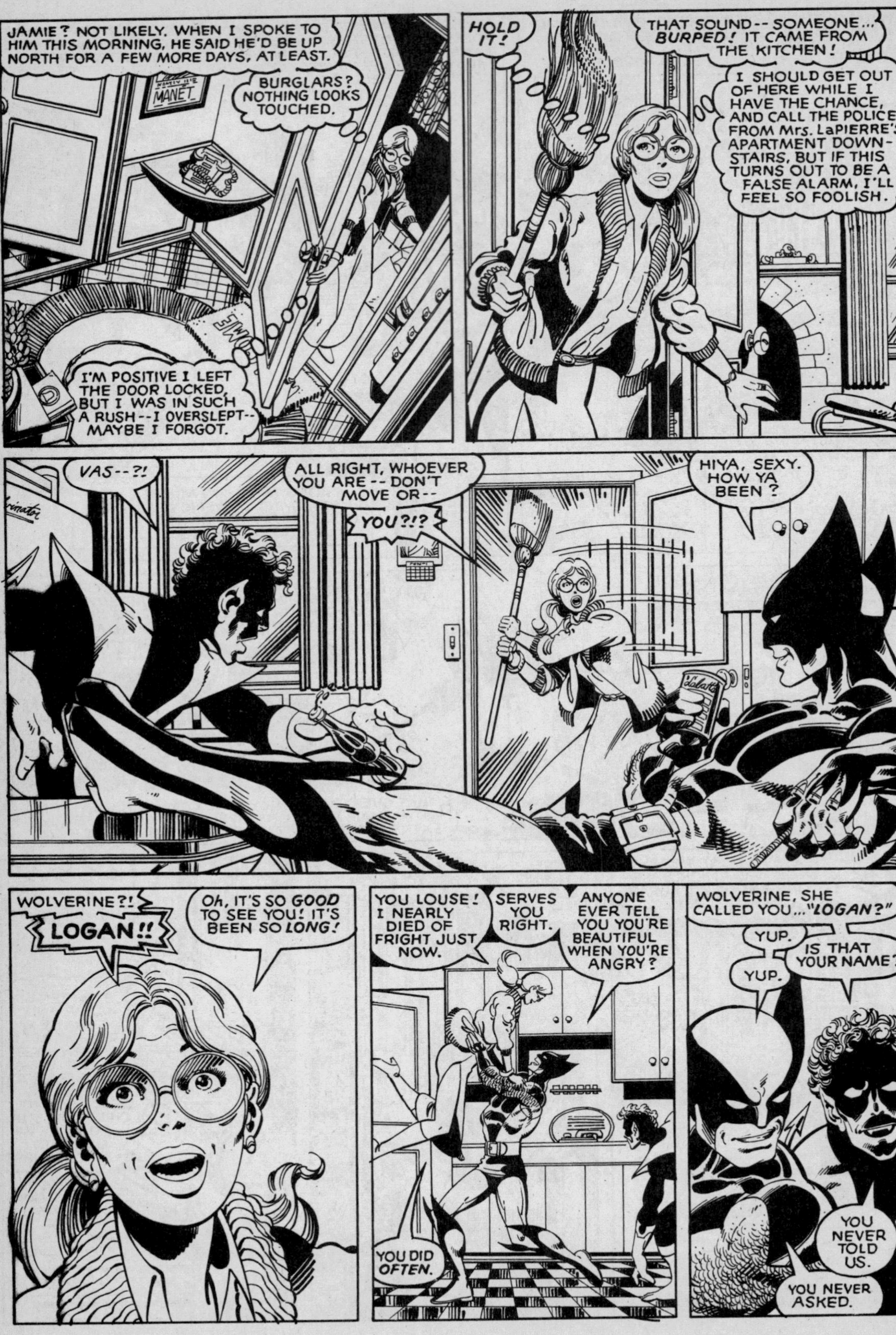
JAMIE? NOT LIKELY. WHEN I SPOKE TO HIM THIS MORNING, HE SAID HE'D BE UP NORTH FOR A FEW MORE DAYS, AT LEAST.
BURGLARS? NOTHING LOOKS TOUCHED.
MANET
I'M POSITIVE I LEFT THE DOOR LOCKED, BUT I WAS IN SUCH A RUSH--I OVERSLEPT--MAYBE I FORGOT.
HOLD IT!
THAT SOUND--SOMEONE... BURPED! IT CAME FROM THE KITCHEN!
I SHOULD GET OUT OF HERE WHILE I HAVE THE CHANCE, AND CALL THE POLICE FROM Mrs. LaPIERRE'S APARTMENT DOWN-STAIRS, BUT IF THIS TURNS OUT TO BE A FALSE ALARM, I'LL FEEL SO FOOLISH.
VAS--?!
ALL RIGHT, WHOEVER YOU ARE--DON'T MOVE OR--
YOU?!?
HIYA, SEXY. HOW YA BEEN?
WOLVERINE?!
LOGAN!!
Oh, IT'S SO GOOD TO SEE YOU! IT'S BEEN SO LONG!
YOU LOUSE! I NEARLY DIED OF FRIGHT JUST NOW.
SERVES YOU RIGHT.
ANYONE EVER TELL YOU YOU'RE BEAUTIFUL WHEN YOU'RE ANGRY?
YOU DID OFTEN.
WOLVERINE, SHE CALLED YOU... "LOGAN?"
YUP.
IS THAT YOUR NAME?
YUP.
YOU NEVER TOLD US.
YOU NEVER ASKED.

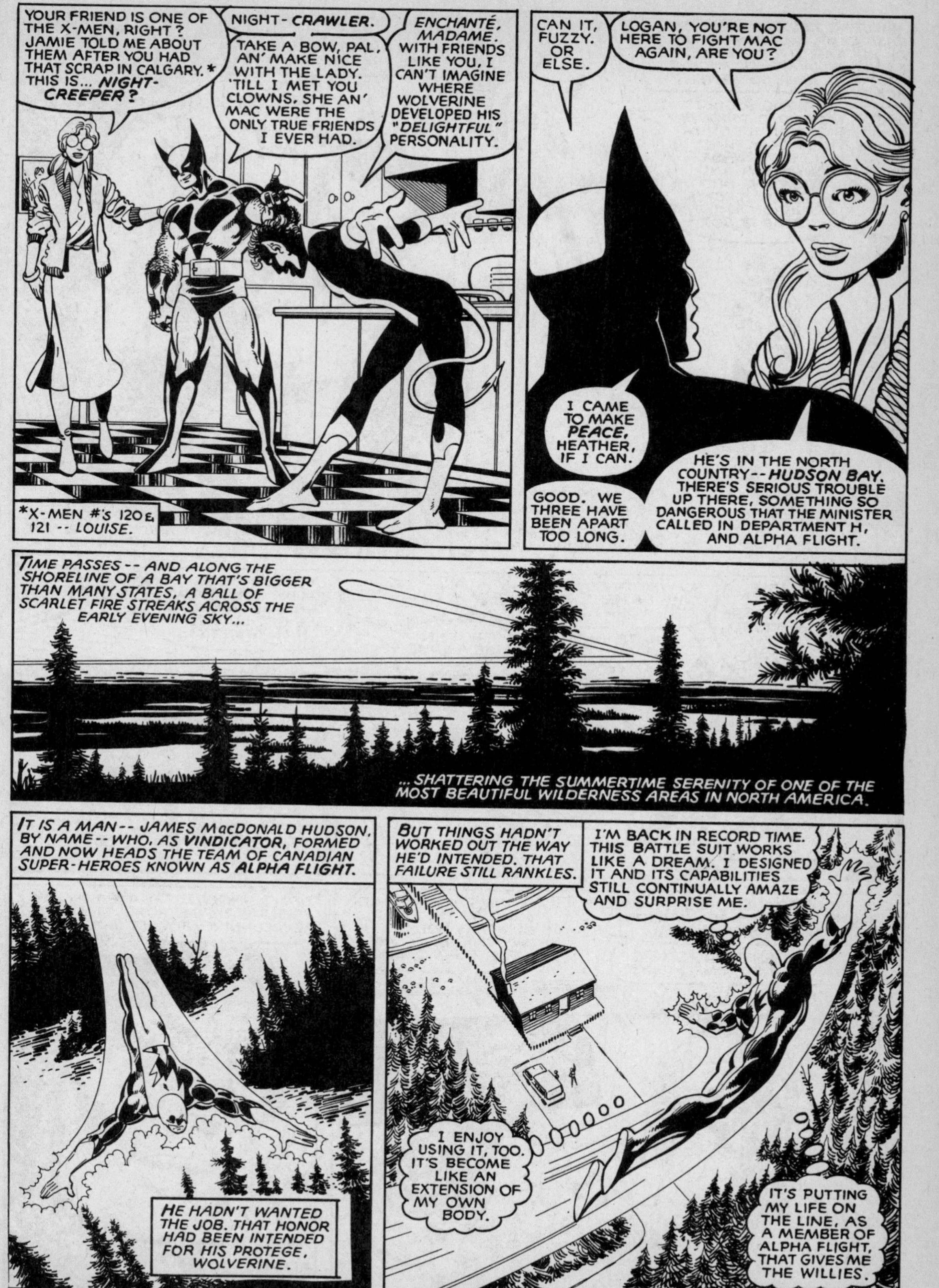
YOUR FRIEND IS ONE OF THE X-MEN, RIGHT? JAMIE TOLD ME ABOUT THEM AFTER YOU HAD THAT SCRAP IN CALGARY.* THIS IS... NIGHT-CREEPER?
NIGHT-CRAWLER.
TAKE A BOW, PAL, AN' MAKE NICE WITH THE LADY. 'TILL I MET YOU CLOWNS, SHE AN' MAC WERE THE ONLY TRUE FRIENDS I EVER HAD.
ENCHANTÉ, MADAME. WITH FRIENDS LIKE YOU, I CAN'T IMAGINE WHERE WOLVERINE DEVELOPED HIS "DELIGHTFUL" PERSONALITY.
*X-MEN #'s 120 & 121 -- LOUISE.
CAN IT, FUZZY. OR ELSE.
LOGAN, YOU'RE NOT HERE TO FIGHT MAC AGAIN, ARE YOU?
I CAME TO MAKE PEACE, HEATHER, IF I CAN.
GOOD. WE THREE HAVE BEEN APART TOO LONG.
HE'S IN THE NORTH COUNTRY--HUDSON BAY. THERE'S SERIOUS TROUBLE UP THERE, SOMETHING SO DANGEROUS THAT THE MINISTER CALLED IN DEPARTMENT H, AND ALPHA FLIGHT.
TIME PASSES-- AND ALONG THE SHORELINE OF A BAY THAT'S BIGGER THAN MANY STATES, A BALL OF SCARLET FIRE STREAKS ACROSS THE EARLY EVENING SKY...
...SHATTERING THE SUMMERTIME SERENITY OF ONE OF THE MOST BEAUTIFUL WILDERNESS AREAS IN NORTH AMERICA.
IT IS A MAN-- JAMES MacDONALD HUDSON, BY NAME-- WHO, AS VINDICATOR, FORMED AND NOW HEADS THE TEAM OF CANADIAN SUPER-HEROES KNOWN AS ALPHA FLIGHT.
HE HADN'T WANTED THE JOB. THAT HONOR HAD BEEN INTENDED FOR HIS PROTEGE, WOLVERINE.
BUT THINGS HADN'T WORKED OUT THE WAY HE'D INTENDED. THAT FAILURE STILL RANKLES.
I'M BACK IN RECORD TIME. THIS BATTLE SUIT WORKS LIKE A DREAM. I DESIGNED IT AND ITS CAPABILITIES STILL CONTINUALLY AMAZE AND SURPRISE ME.
I ENJOY USING IT, TOO. IT'S BECOME LIKE AN EXTENSION OF MY OWN BODY.
IT'S PUTTING MY LIFE ON THE LINE, AS A MEMBER OF ALPHA FLIGHT, THAT GIVES ME THE WILLIES.

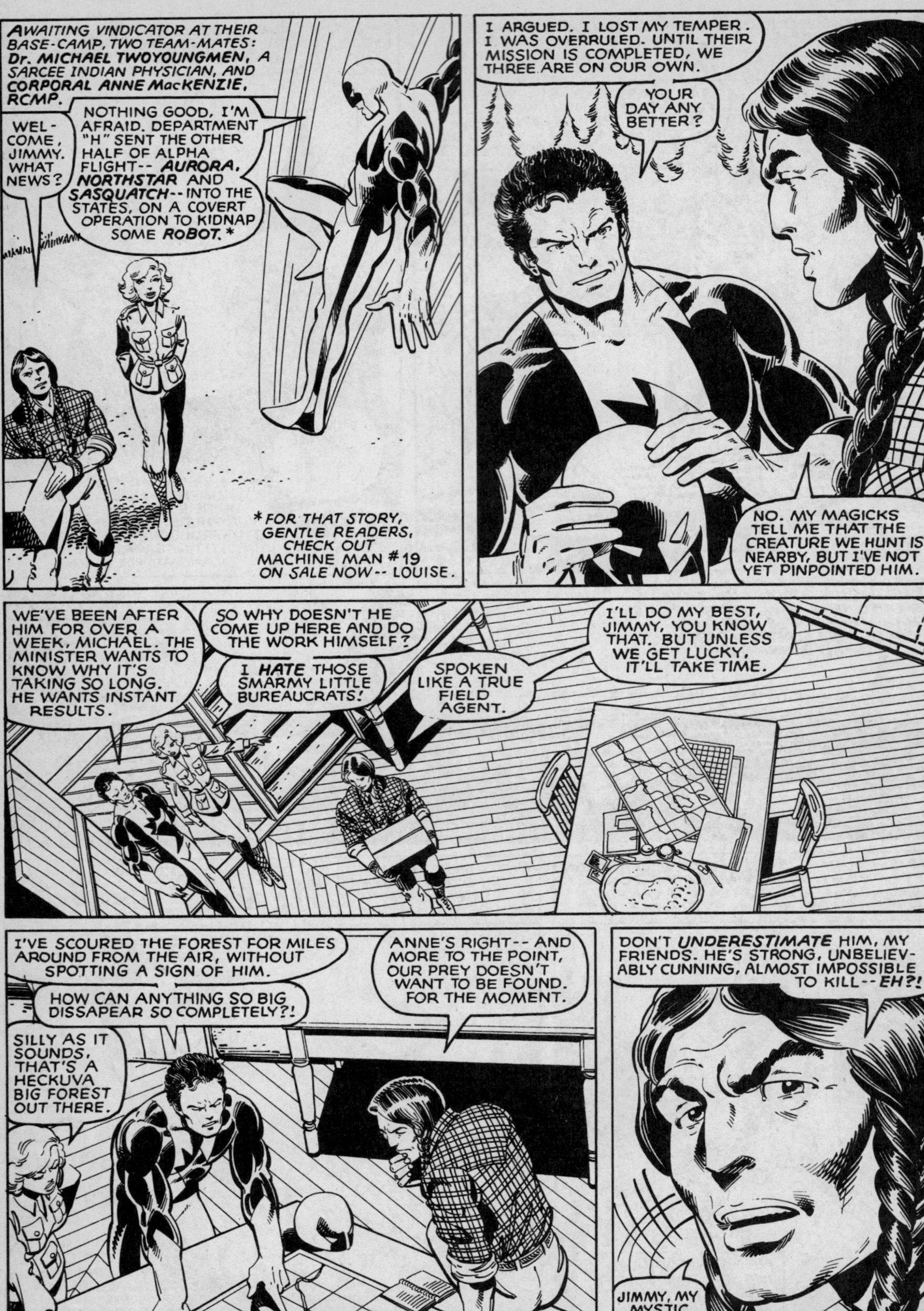

AWAITING VINDICATOR AT THEIR BASE-CAMP, TWO TEAM-MATES: Dr. MICHAEL TWOYOUNGMEN, A SARCEE INDIAN PHYSICIAN, AND CORPORAL ANNE MacKENZIE, RCMP.
WEL-COME, JIMMY. WHAT NEWS?
NOTHING GOOD, I'M AFRAID. DEPARTMENT "H" SENT THE OTHER HALF OF ALPHA FLIGHT-- AURORA, NORTHSTAR AND SASQUATCH-- INTO THE STATES, ON A COVERT OPERATION TO KIDNAP SOME ROBOT.*
*FOR THAT STORY, GENTLE READERS, CHECK OUT MACHINE MAN #19 ON SALE NOW-- LOUISE.
I ARGUED. I LOST MY TEMPER. I WAS OVERRULED. UNTIL THEIR MISSION IS COMPLETED, WE THREE ARE ON OUR OWN.
YOUR DAY ANY BETTER?
NO. MY MAGICKS TELL ME THAT THE CREATURE WE HUNT IS NEARBY, BUT I'VE NOT YET PINPOINTED HIM.
WE'VE BEEN AFTER HIM FOR OVER A WEEK, MICHAEL. THE MINISTER WANTS TO KNOW WHY IT'S TAKING SO LONG. HE WANTS INSTANT RESULTS.
SO WHY DOESN'T HE COME UP HERE AND DO THE WORK HIMSELF?
I HATE THOSE SMARMY LITTLE BUREAUCRATS!
SPOKEN LIKE A TRUE FIELD AGENT.
I'LL DO MY BEST, JIMMY, YOU KNOW THAT. BUT UNLESS WE GET LUCKY, IT'LL TAKE TIME.
I'VE SCOURED THE FOREST FOR MILES AROUND FROM THE AIR, WITHOUT SPOTTING A SIGN OF HIM.
HOW CAN ANYTHING SO BIG DISSAPEAR SO COMPLETELY?!
SILLY AS IT SOUNDS, THAT'S A HECKUVA BIG FOREST OUT THERE.
ANNE'S RIGHT-- AND MORE TO THE POINT, OUR PREY DOESN'T WANT TO BE FOUND. FOR THE MOMENT.
DON'T UNDERESTIMATE HIM, MY FRIENDS. HE'S STRONG, UNBELIEV-ABLY CUNNING, ALMOST IMPOSSIBLE TO KILL-- EH?!
JIMMY, MY MYSTIC ALARMS-- INTRUDERS!

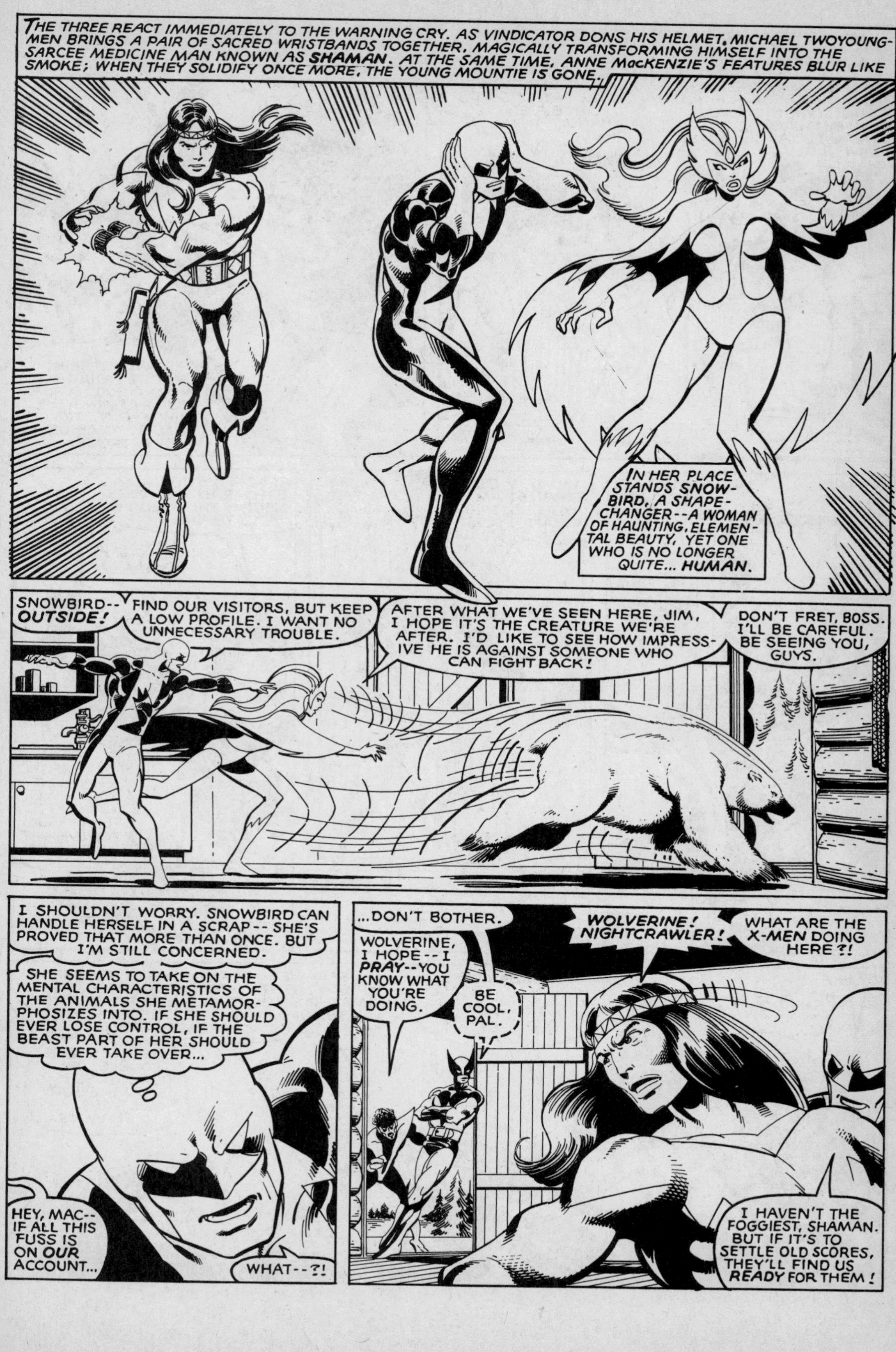
THE THREE REACT IMMEDIATELY TO THE WARNING CRY. AS VINDICATOR DONS HIS HELMET, MICHAEL TWOYOUNG-MEN BRINGS A PAIR OF SACRED WRISTBANDS TOGETHER, MAGICALLY TRANSFORMING HIMSELF INTO THE SARCEE MEDICINE MAN KNOWN AS SHAMAN. AT THE SAME TIME, ANNE MacKENZIE'S FEATURES BLUR LIKE SMOKE; WHEN THEY SOLIDIFY ONCE MORE, THE YOUNG MOUNTIE IS GONE.
IN HER PLACE STANDS SNOWBIRD, A SHAPE-CHANGER--A WOMAN OF HAUNTING, ELEMENTAL BEAUTY, YET ONE WHO IS NO LONGER QUITE... HUMAN.
SNOWBIRD--OUTSIDE!
FIND OUR VISITORS, BUT KEEP A LOW PROFILE. I WANT NO UNNECESSARY TROUBLE.
AFTER WHAT WE'VE SEEN HERE, JIM, I HOPE IT'S THE CREATURE WE'RE AFTER. I'D LIKE TO SEE HOW IMPRESSIVE HE IS AGAINST SOMEONE WHO CAN FIGHT BACK!
DON'T FRET, BOSS. I'LL BE CAREFUL. BE SEEING YOU, GUYS.
I SHOULDN'T WORRY. SNOWBIRD CAN HANDLE HERSELF IN A SCRAP-- SHE'S PROVED THAT MORE THAN ONCE. BUT I'M STILL CONCERNED.
SHE SEEMS TO TAKE ON THE MENTAL CHARACTERISTICS OF THE ANIMALS SHE METAMORPHOSIZES INTO. IF SHE SHOULD EVER LOSE CONTROL, IF THE BEAST PART OF HER SHOULD EVER TAKE OVER...
HEY, MAC-- IF ALL THIS FUSS IS ON OUR ACCOUNT...
WHAT--?!
...DON'T BOTHER.
WOLVERINE, I HOPE--I PRAY--YOU KNOW WHAT YOU'RE DOING.
BE COOL, PAL.
WOLVERINE! NIGHTCRAWLER!
WHAT ARE THE X-MEN DOING HERE?!
I HAVEN'T THE FOGGIEST, SHAMAN. BUT IF IT'S TO SETTLE OLD SCORES, THEY'LL FIND US READY FOR THEM!

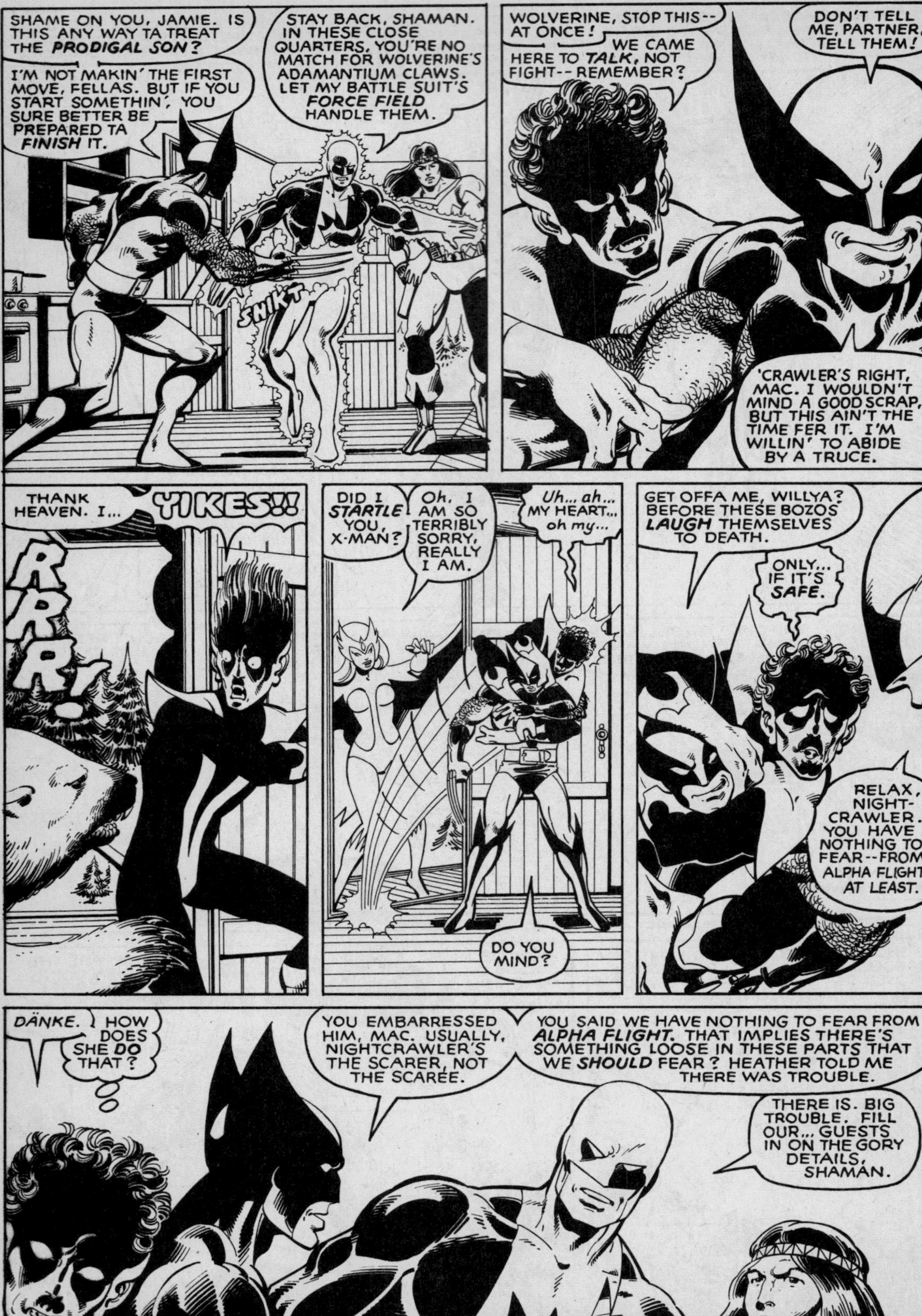
SHAME ON YOU, JAMIE. IS THIS ANY WAY TA TREAT THE PRODIGAL SON?
I'M NOT MAKIN' THE FIRST MOVE, FELLAS. BUT IF YOU START SOMETHIN', YOU SURE BETTER BE PREPARED TA FINISH IT.
STAY BACK, SHAMAN. IN THESE CLOSE QUARTERS, YOU'RE NO MATCH FOR WOLVERINE'S ADAMANTIUM CLAWS. LET MY BATTLE SUIT'S FORCE FIELD HANDLE THEM.
SNIKT
WOLVERINE, STOP THIS-- AT ONCE!
WE CAME HERE TO TALK, NOT FIGHT-- REMEMBER?
DON'T TELL ME, PARTNER, TELL THEM!
'CRAWLER'S RIGHT, MAC. I WOULDN'T MIND A GOOD SCRAP, BUT THIS AIN'T THE TIME FER IT. I'M WILLIN' TO ABIDE BY A TRUCE.
THANK HEAVEN. I...
YIKES!!
RRRR!
DID I STARTLE YOU, X-MAN?
Oh, I AM SO TERRIBLY SORRY, REALLY I AM.
Uh... ah... MY HEART... oh my...
DO YOU MIND?
GET OFFA ME, WILLYA? BEFORE THESE BOZOS LAUGH THEMSELVES TO DEATH.
ONLY... IF IT'S SAFE.
RELAX, NIGHT-CRAWLER. YOU HAVE NOTHING TO FEAR--FROM ALPHA FLIGHT, AT LEAST.
DÄNKE.
HOW DOES SHE DO THAT?
YOU EMBARRESSED HIM, MAC. USUALLY, NIGHTCRAWLER'S THE SCARER, NOT THE SCAREE.
YOU SAID WE HAVE NOTHING TO FEAR FROM ALPHA FLIGHT. THAT IMPLIES THERE'S SOMETHING LOOSE IN THESE PARTS THAT WE SHOULD FEAR? HEATHER TOLD ME THERE WAS TROUBLE.
THERE IS. BIG TROUBLE. FILL OUR... GUESTS IN ON THE GORY DETAILS, SHAMAN.

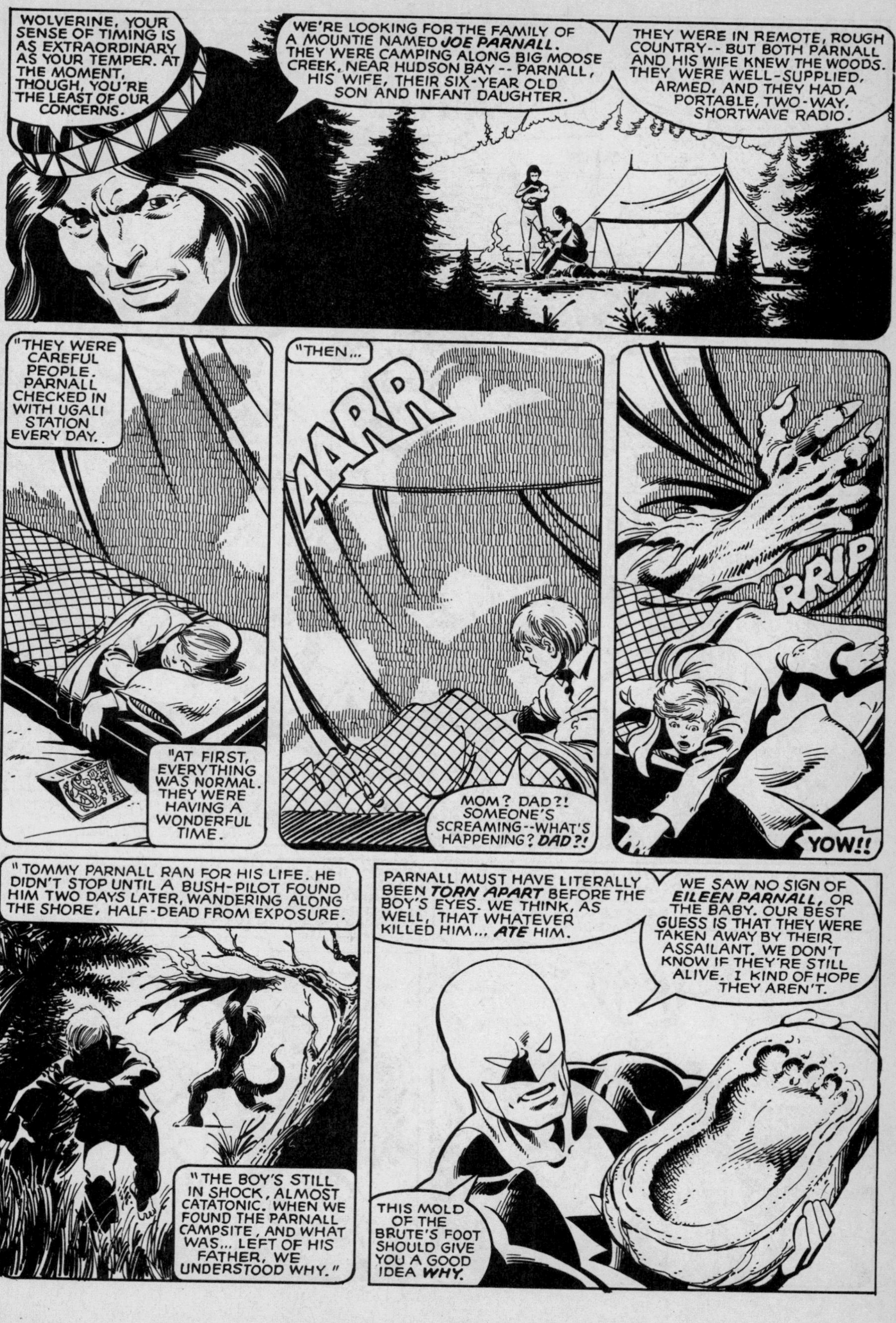
WOLVERINE, YOUR SENSE OF TIMING IS AS EXTRAORDINARY AS YOUR TEMPER. AT THE MOMENT, THOUGH, YOU'RE THE LEAST OF OUR CONCERNS.
WE'RE LOOKING FOR THE FAMILY OF A MOUNTIE NAMED JOE PARNALL. THEY WERE CAMPING ALONG BIG MOOSE CREEK, NEAR HUDSON BAY -- PARNALL, HIS WIFE, THEIR SIX-YEAR OLD SON AND INFANT DAUGHTER.
THEY WERE IN REMOTE, ROUGH COUNTRY-- BUT BOTH PARNALL AND HIS WIFE KNEW THE WOODS. THEY WERE WELL-SUPPLIED, ARMED, AND THEY HAD A PORTABLE, TWO-WAY, SHORTWAVE RADIO.
"THEY WERE CAREFUL PEOPLE. PARNALL CHECKED IN WITH UGALI STATION EVERY DAY..
"AT FIRST, EVERYTHING WAS NORMAL. THEY WERE HAVING A WONDERFUL TIME.
"THEN...
AARR
MOM? DAD?! SOMEONE'S SCREAMING--WHAT'S HAPPENING? DAD?!
RRIP
YOW!!
"TOMMY PARNALL RAN FOR HIS LIFE. HE DIDN'T STOP UNTIL A BUSH-PILOT FOUND HIM TWO DAYS LATER, WANDERING ALONG THE SHORE, HALF-DEAD FROM EXPOSURE.
"THE BOY'S STILL IN SHOCK, ALMOST CATATONIC. WHEN WE FOUND THE PARNALL CAMPSITE, AND WHAT WAS... LEFT OF HIS FATHER, WE UNDERSTOOD WHY."
PARNALL MUST HAVE LITERALLY BEEN TORN APART BEFORE THE BOY'S EYES. WE THINK, AS WELL, THAT WHATEVER KILLED HIM... ATE HIM.
WE SAW NO SIGN OF EILEEN PARNALL, OR THE BABY. OUR BEST GUESS IS THAT THEY WERE TAKEN AWAY BY THEIR ASSAILANT. WE DON'T KNOW IF THEY'RE STILL ALIVE. I KIND OF HOPE THEY AREN'T.
THIS MOLD OF THE BRUTE'S FOOT SHOULD GIVE YOU A GOOD IDEA WHY.

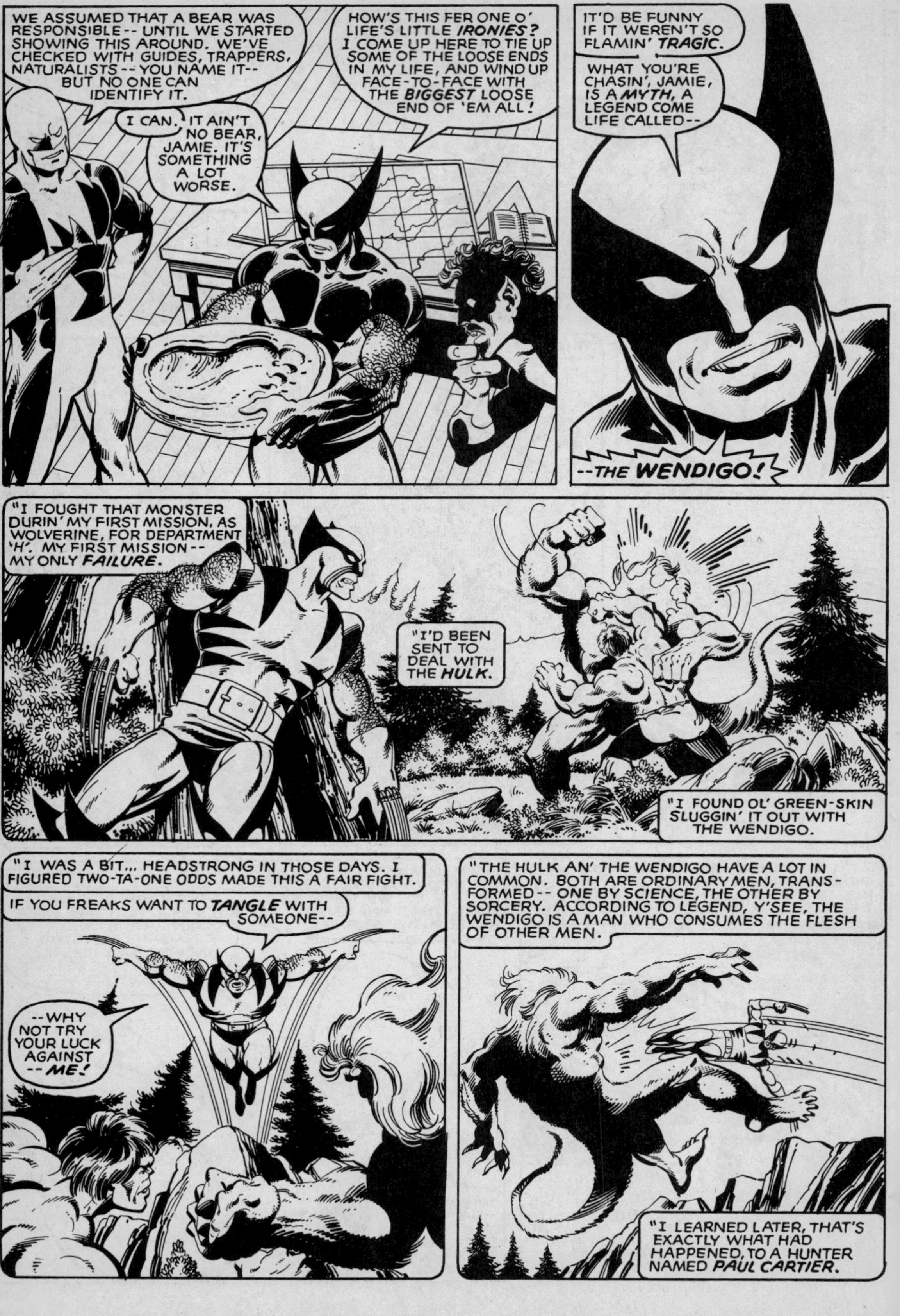
WE ASSUMED THAT A BEAR WAS RESPONSIBLE -- UNTIL WE STARTED SHOWING THIS AROUND. WE'VE CHECKED WITH GUIDES, TRAPPERS, NATURALISTS -- YOU NAME IT -- BUT NO ONE CAN IDENTIFY IT.
I CAN.
IT AIN'T NO BEAR, JAMIE. IT'S SOMETHING A LOT WORSE.
HOW'S THIS FER ONE O' LIFE'S LITTLE IRONIES? I COME UP HERE TO TIE UP SOME OF THE LOOSE ENDS IN MY LIFE, AND WIND UP FACE-TO-FACE WITH THE BIGGEST LOOSE END OF 'EM ALL!
IT'D BE FUNNY IF IT WEREN'T SO FLAMIN' TRAGIC.
WHAT YOU'RE CHASIN', JAMIE, IS A MYTH, A LEGEND COME LIFE CALLED--
--THE WENDIGO!
"I FOUGHT THAT MONSTER DURIN' MY FIRST MISSION, AS WOLVERINE, FOR DEPARTMENT 'H'. MY FIRST MISSION -- MY ONLY FAILURE.
"I'D BEEN SENT TO DEAL WITH THE HULK.
"I FOUND OL' GREEN-SKIN SLUGGIN' IT OUT WITH THE WENDIGO.
"I WAS A BIT... HEADSTRONG IN THOSE DAYS. I FIGURED TWO-TA-ONE ODDS MADE THIS A FAIR FIGHT.
IF YOU FREAKS WANT TO TANGLE WITH SOMEONE--
--WHY NOT TRY YOUR LUCK AGAINST --ME!
"THE HULK AN' THE WENDIGO HAVE A LOT IN COMMON. BOTH ARE ORDINARY MEN, TRANSFORMED -- ONE BY SCIENCE, THE OTHER BY SORCERY. ACCORDING TO LEGEND, Y'SEE, THE WENDIGO IS A MAN WHO CONSUMES THE FLESH OF OTHER MEN.
"I LEARNED LATER, THAT'S EXACTLY WHAT HAD HAPPENED, TO A HUNTER NAMED PAUL CARTIER.

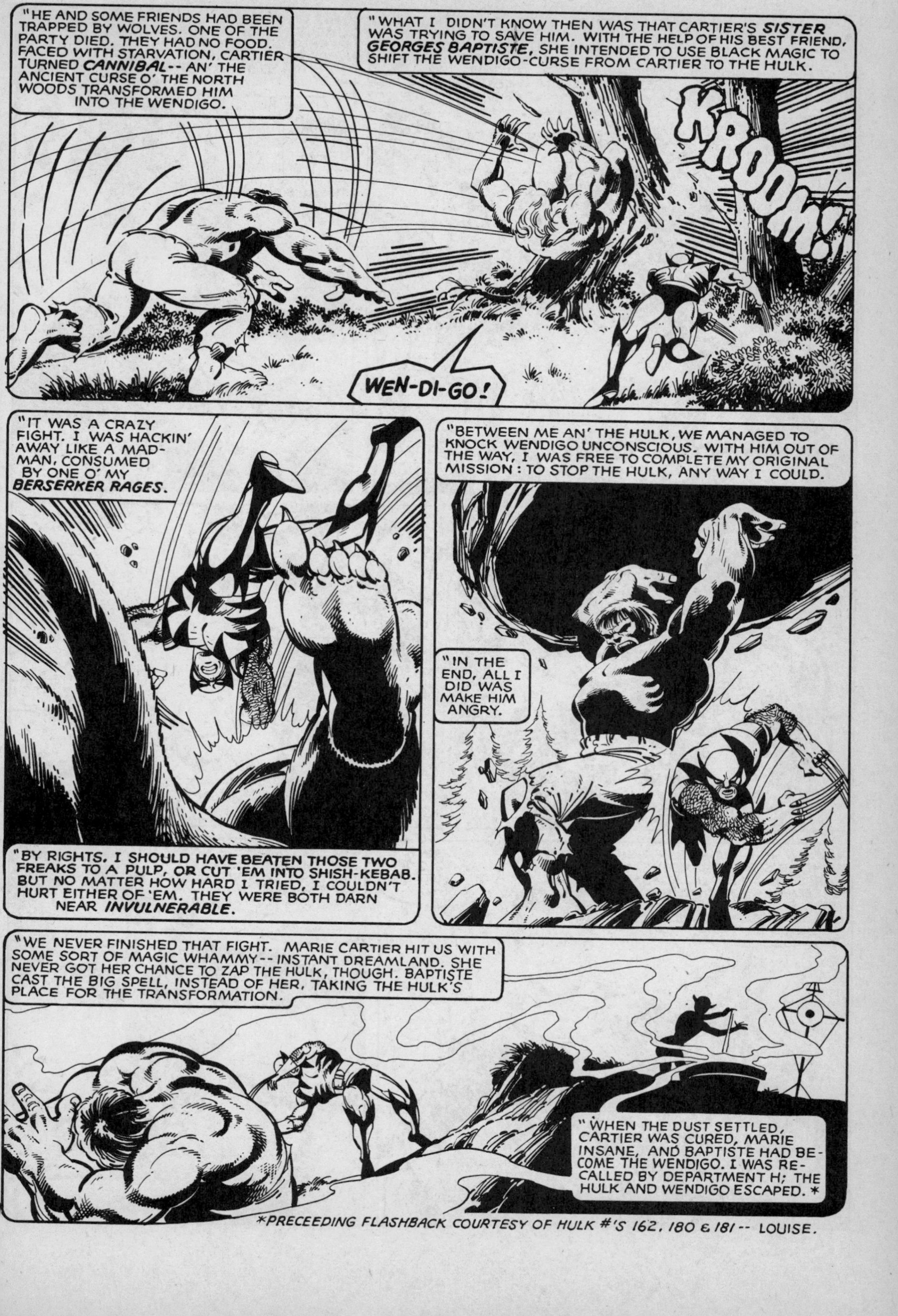
"HE AND SOME FRIENDS HAD BEEN TRAPPED BY WOLVES. ONE OF THE PARTY DIED. THEY HAD NO FOOD. FACED WITH STARVATION, CARTIER TURNED CANNIBAL-- AN' THE ANCIENT CURSE O' THE NORTH WOODS TRANSFORMED HIM INTO THE WENDIGO.
"WHAT I DIDN'T KNOW THEN WAS THAT CARTIER'S SISTER WAS TRYING TO SAVE HIM. WITH THE HELP OF HIS BEST FRIEND, GEORGES BAPTISTE, SHE INTENDED TO USE BLACK MAGIC TO SHIFT THE WENDIGO-CURSE FROM CARTIER TO THE HULK.
KROOM!
WEN-DI-GO!
"IT WAS A CRAZY FIGHT. I WAS HACKIN' AWAY LIKE A MAD-MAN, CONSUMED BY ONE O' MY BERSERKER RAGES.
"BY RIGHTS, I SHOULD HAVE BEATEN THOSE TWO FREAKS TO A PULP, OR CUT 'EM INTO SHISH-KEBAB. BUT NO MATTER HOW HARD I TRIED, I COULDN'T HURT EITHER OF 'EM. THEY WERE BOTH DARN NEAR INVULNERABLE.
"BETWEEN ME AN' THE HULK, WE MANAGED TO KNOCK WENDIGO UNCONSCIOUS. WITH HIM OUT OF THE WAY, I WAS FREE TO COMPLETE MY ORIGINAL MISSION : TO STOP THE HULK, ANY WAY I COULD.
"IN THE END, ALL I DID WAS MAKE HIM ANGRY.
"WE NEVER FINISHED THAT FIGHT. MARIE CARTIER HIT US WITH SOME SORT OF MAGIC WHAMMY-- INSTANT DREAMLAND. SHE NEVER GOT HER CHANCE TO ZAP THE HULK, THOUGH. BAPTISTE CAST THE BIG SPELL, INSTEAD OF HER, TAKING THE HULK'S PLACE FOR THE TRANSFORMATION.
"WHEN THE DUST SETTLED, CARTIER WAS CURED, MARIE INSANE, AND BAPTISTE HAD BE-COME THE WENDIGO. I WAS RE-CALLED BY DEPARTMENT H; THE HULK AND WENDIGO ESCAPED. *
*PRECEEDING FLASHBACK COURTESY OF HULK #'S 162, 180 & 181 -- LOUISE.

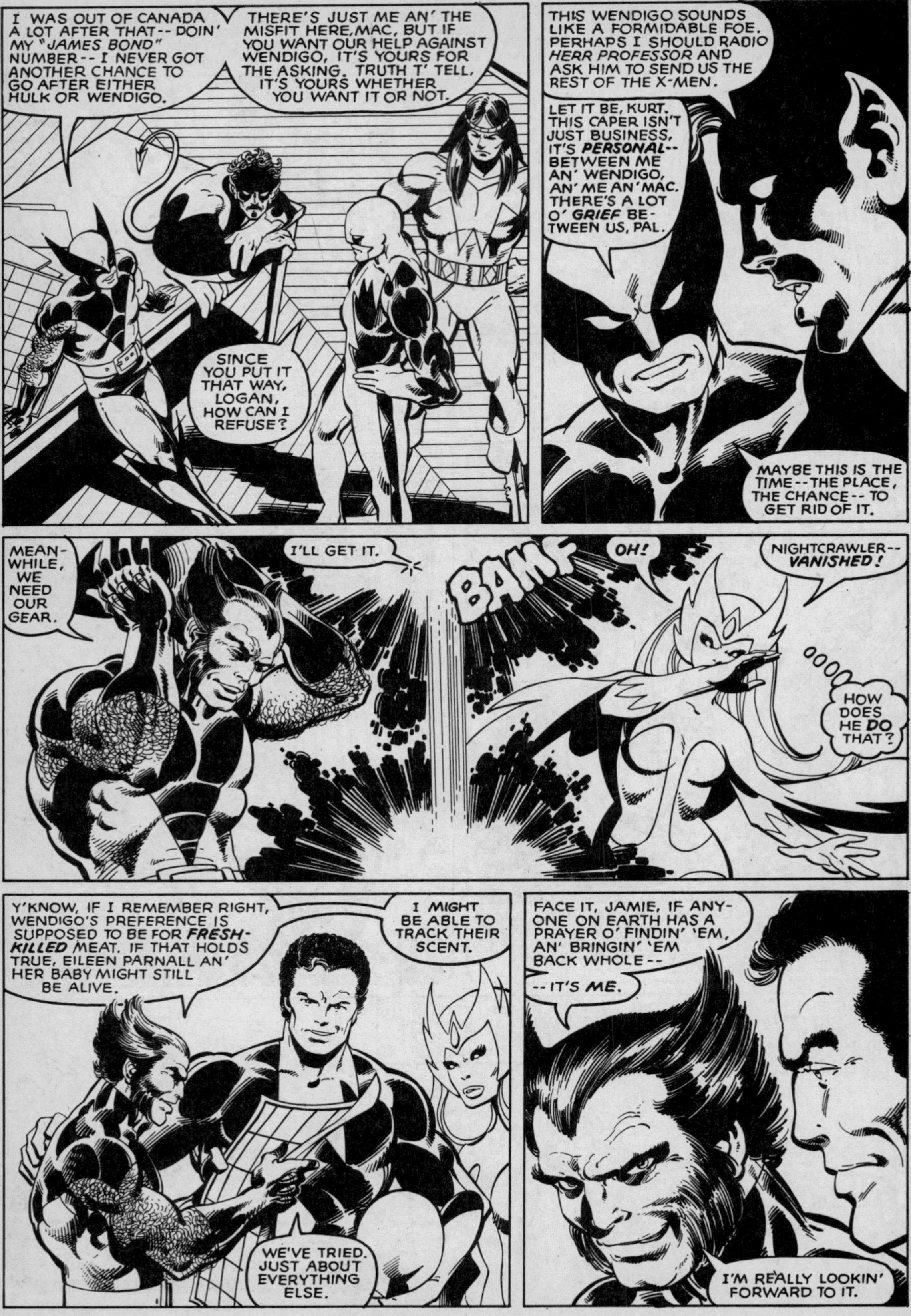

I WAS OUT OF CANADA A LOT AFTER THAT-- DOIN' MY "JAMES BOND" NUMBER-- I NEVER GOT ANOTHER CHANCE TO GO AFTER EITHER HULK OR WENDIGO.
THERE'S JUST ME AN' THE MISFIT HERE, MAC, BUT IF YOU WANT OUR HELP AGAINST WENDIGO, IT'S YOURS FOR THE ASKING. TRUTH T' TELL, IT'S YOURS WHETHER YOU WANT IT OR NOT.
SINCE YOU PUT IT THAT WAY, LOGAN, HOW CAN I REFUSE?
THIS WENDIGO SOUNDS LIKE A FORMIDABLE FOE. PERHAPS I SHOULD RADIO HERR PROFESSOR AND ASK HIM TO SEND US THE REST OF THE X-MEN.
LET IT BE, KURT. THIS CAPER ISN'T JUST BUSINESS, IT'S PERSONAL-- BETWEEN ME AN' WENDIGO, AN' ME AN' MAC. THERE'S A LOT O' GRIEF BE-TWEEN US, PAL.
MAYBE THIS IS THE TIME-- THE PLACE, THE CHANCE-- TO GET RID OF IT.
MEAN-WHILE, WE NEED OUR GEAR.
I'LL GET IT.
BAMF
OH!
NIGHTCRAWLER-- VANISHED!
HOW DOES HE DO THAT?
Y'KNOW, IF I REMEMBER RIGHT, WENDIGO'S PREFERENCE IS SUPPOSED TO BE FOR FRESH-KILLED MEAT. IF THAT HOLDS TRUE, EILEEN PARNALL AN' HER BABY MIGHT STILL BE ALIVE.
I MIGHT BE ABLE TO TRACK THEIR SCENT.
WE'VE TRIED. JUST ABOUT EVERYTHING ELSE.
FACE IT, JAMIE, IF ANY-ONE ON EARTH HAS A PRAYER O' FINDIN' 'EM, AN' BRINGIN' 'EM BACK WHOLE--
-- IT'S ME.
I'M REALLY LOOKIN' FORWARD TO IT.

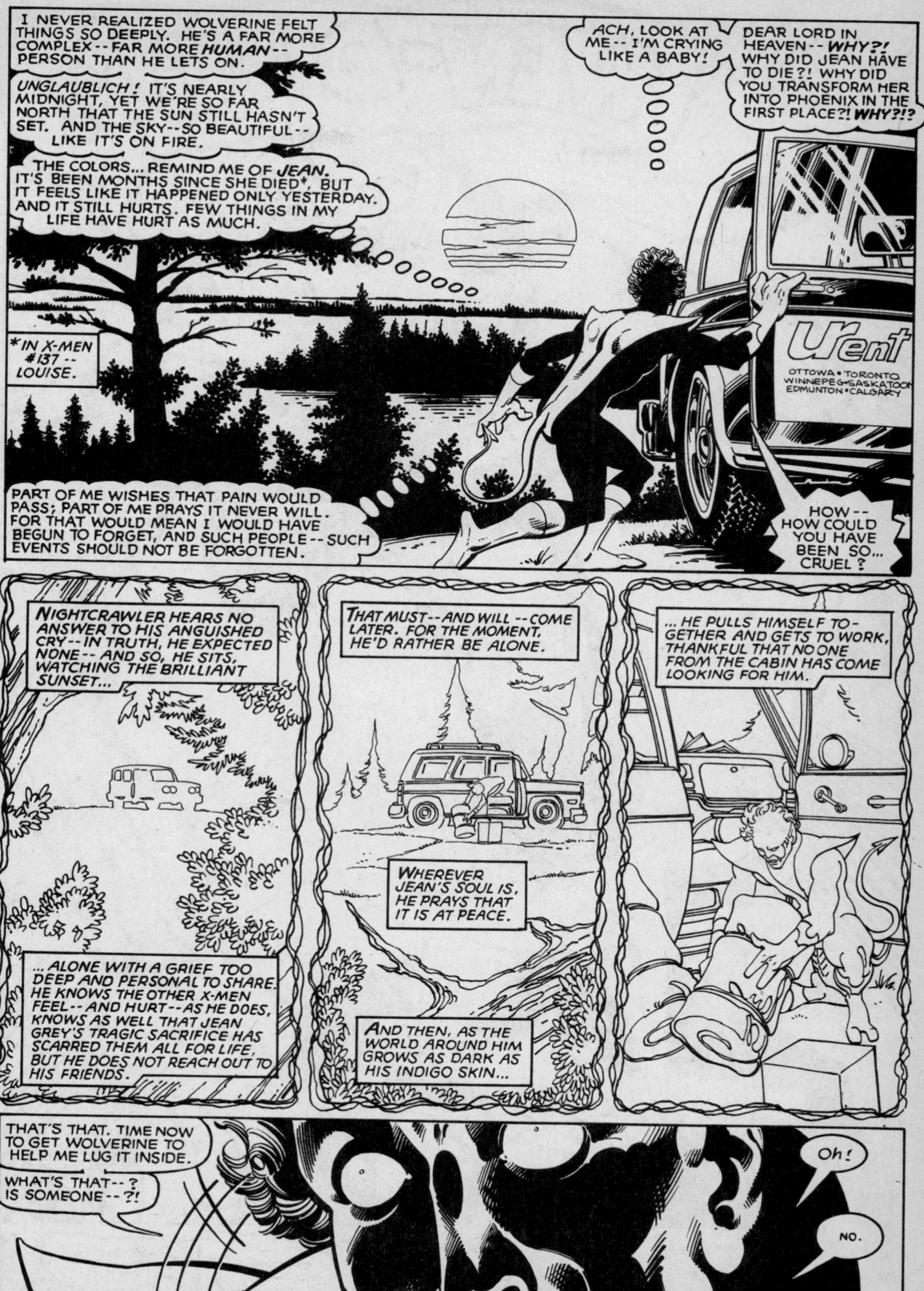
I NEVER REALIZED WOLVERINE FELT THINGS SO DEEPLY. HE'S A FAR MORE COMPLEX -- FAR MORE HUMAN -- PERSON THAN HE LETS ON.
UNGLAUBLICH! IT'S NEARLY MIDNIGHT, YET WE'RE SO FAR NORTH THAT THE SUN STILL HASN'T SET. AND THE SKY -- SO BEAUTIFUL -- LIKE IT'S ON FIRE.
THE COLORS... REMIND ME OF JEAN. IT'S BEEN MONTHS SINCE SHE DIED*, BUT IT FEELS LIKE IT HAPPENED ONLY YESTERDAY. AND IT STILL HURTS. FEW THINGS IN MY LIFE HAVE HURT AS MUCH.
*IN X-MEN #137 -- LOUISE.
PART OF ME WISHES THAT PAIN WOULD PASS; PART OF ME PRAYS IT NEVER WILL. FOR THAT WOULD MEAN I WOULD HAVE BEGUN TO FORGET, AND SUCH PEOPLE -- SUCH EVENTS SHOULD NOT BE FORGOTTEN.
ACH, LOOK AT ME -- I'M CRYING LIKE A BABY!
DEAR LORD IN HEAVEN -- WHY?! WHY DID JEAN HAVE TO DIE?! WHY DID YOU TRANSFORM HER INTO PHOENIX IN THE FIRST PLACE?! WHY?!?
Urent
OTTOWA • TORONTO
WINNEPEG • SASKATOON
EDMUNTON • CALGARY
HOW -- HOW COULD YOU HAVE BEEN SO... CRUEL?
NIGHTCRAWLER HEARS NO ANSWER TO HIS ANGUISHED CRY -- IN TRUTH, HE EXPECTED NONE -- AND SO, HE SITS, WATCHING THE BRILLIANT SUNSET...
...ALONE WITH A GRIEF TOO DEEP AND PERSONAL TO SHARE. HE KNOWS THE OTHER X-MEN FEEL -- AND HURT -- AS HE DOES, KNOWS AS WELL THAT JEAN GREY'S TRAGIC SACRIFICE HAS SCARRED THEM ALL FOR LIFE, BUT HE DOES NOT REACH OUT TO HIS FRIENDS.
THAT MUST -- AND WILL -- COME LATER. FOR THE MOMENT, HE'D RATHER BE ALONE.
WHEREVER JEAN'S SOUL IS, HE PRAYS THAT IT IS AT PEACE.
AND THEN, AS THE WORLD AROUND HIM GROWS AS DARK AS HIS INDIGO SKIN...
...HE PULLS HIMSELF TOGETHER AND GETS TO WORK, THANKFUL THAT NO ONE FROM THE CABIN HAS COME LOOKING FOR HIM.
THAT'S THAT. TIME NOW TO GET WOLVERINE TO HELP ME LUG IT INSIDE.
WHAT'S THAT --? IS SOMEONE --?!
Oh!
NO.

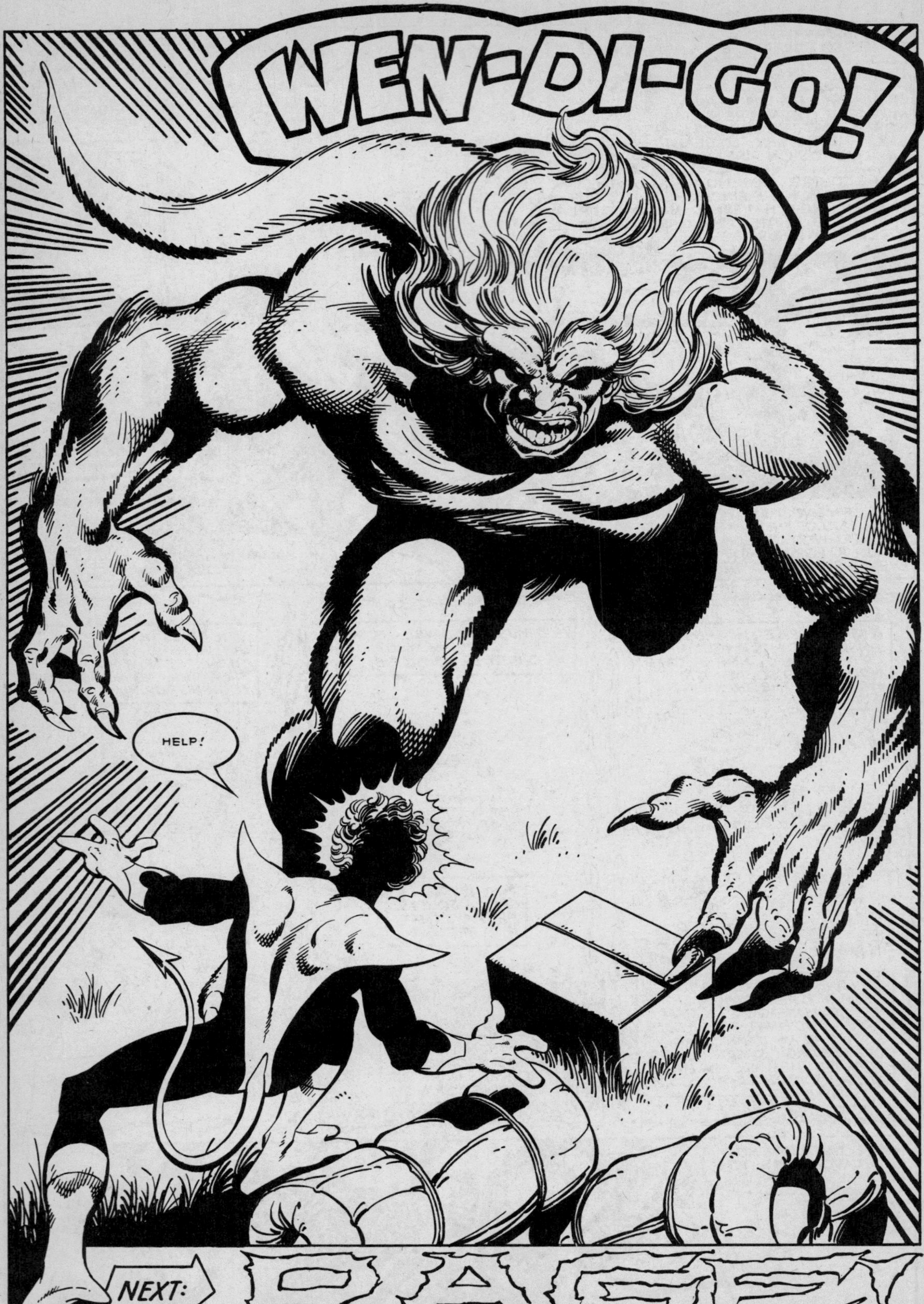

WEN-DI-GO!
HELP!
NEXT: RAGE!

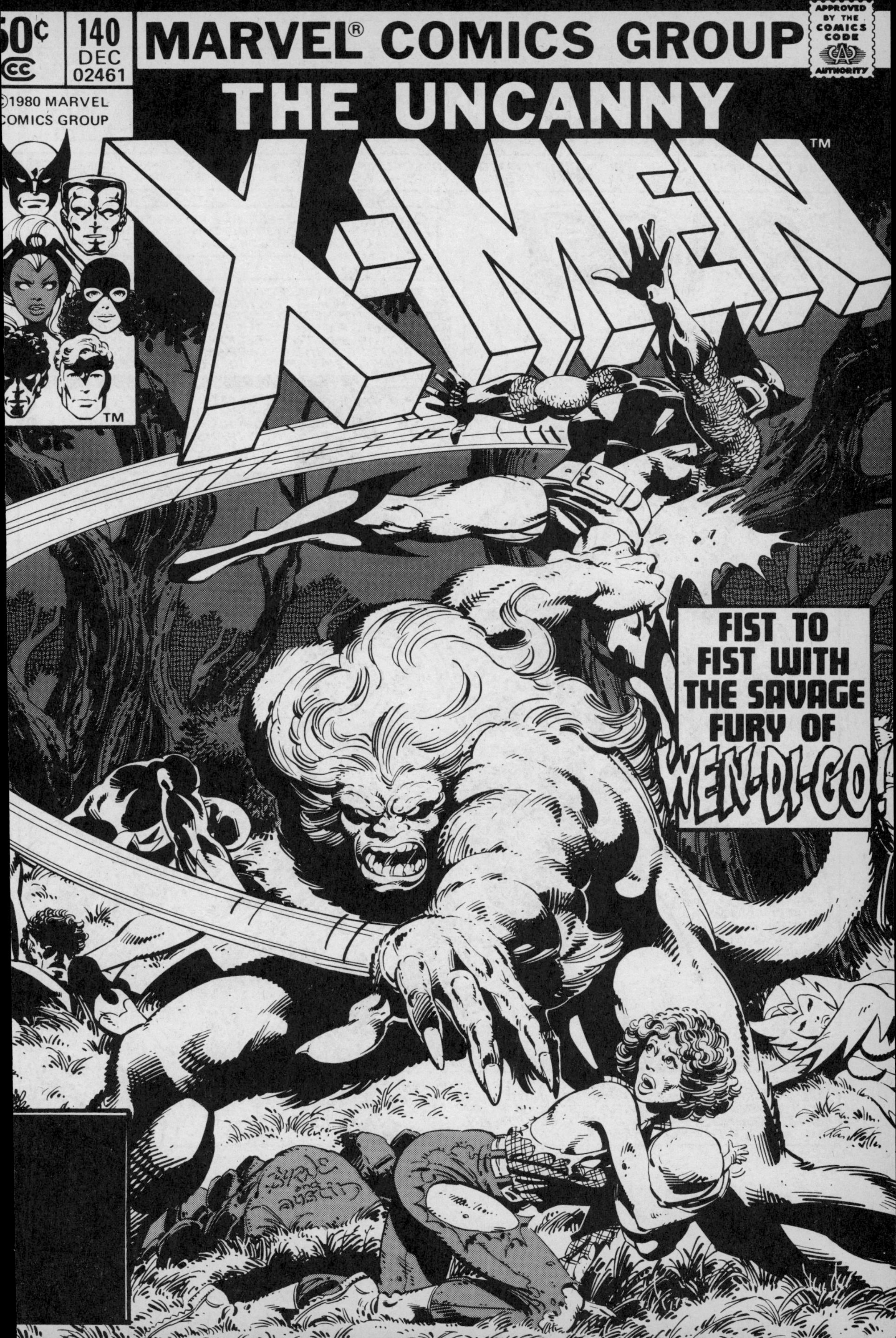

50¢
CC
140
DEC
02461
MARVEL® COMICS GROUP
APPROVED BY THE COMICS CODE AUTHORITY
©1980 MARVEL COMICS GROUP
THE UNCANNY
X-MEN™
TM
FIST TO FIST WITH THE SAVAGE FURY OF
WEN-DI-GO!

Cyclops. Storm. Nightcrawler. Wolverine. Colossus. Children of the atom, students of Charles Xavier, MUTANTS — feared and hated by the world they have sworn to protect. These are the STRANGEST heroes of all!

Stan Lee PRESENTS: THE UNCANNY X-MEN!™

CHRIS CLAREMONT WRITER | JOHN BYRNE PLOT-PENCILS | TERRY AUSTIN INKER | TOM ORZECHOWSKI, letterer GLYNIS WEIN, colorist | LOUISE JONES EDITOR | JIM SHOOTER Ed. IN CHIEF

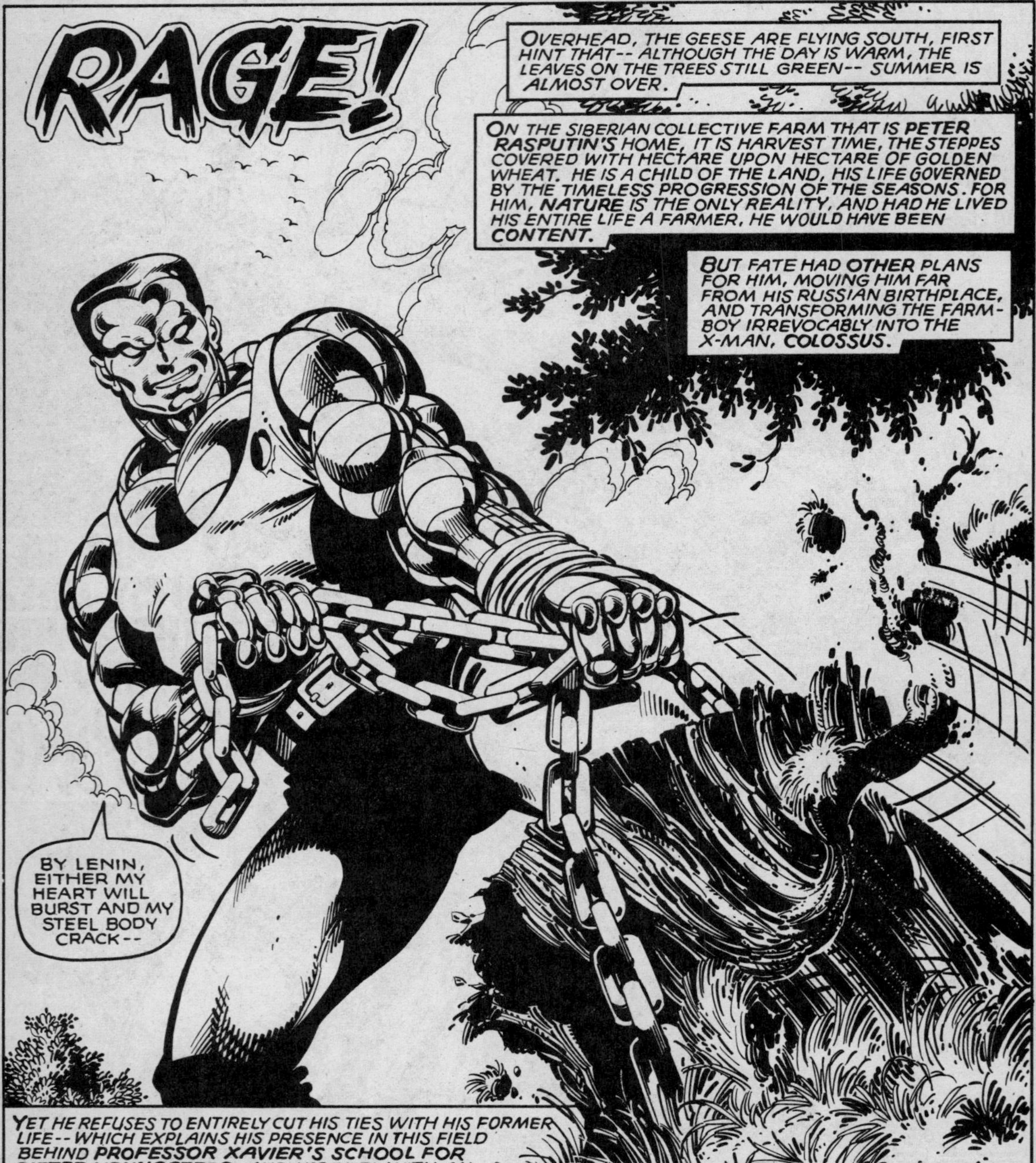
RAGE!
OVERHEAD, THE GEESE ARE FLYING SOUTH, FIRST HINT THAT-- ALTHOUGH THE DAY IS WARM, THE LEAVES ON THE TREES STILL GREEN-- SUMMER IS ALMOST OVER.
ON THE SIBERIAN COLLECTIVE FARM THAT IS PETER RASPUTIN'S HOME, IT IS HARVEST TIME, THE STEPPES COVERED WITH HECTARE UPON HECTARE OF GOLDEN WHEAT. HE IS A CHILD OF THE LAND, HIS LIFE GOVERNED BY THE TIMELESS PROGRESSION OF THE SEASONS. FOR HIM, NATURE IS THE ONLY REALITY, AND HAD HE LIVED HIS ENTIRE LIFE A FARMER, HE WOULD HAVE BEEN CONTENT.
BUT FATE HAD OTHER PLANS FOR HIM, MOVING HIM FAR FROM HIS RUSSIAN BIRTHPLACE, AND TRANSFORMING THE FARM-BOY IRREVOCABLY INTO THE X-MAN, COLOSSUS.
BY LENIN, EITHER MY HEART WILL BURST AND MY STEEL BODY CRACK--
YET HE REFUSES TO ENTIRELY CUT HIS TIES WITH HIS FORMER LIFE-- WHICH EXPLAINS HIS PRESENCE IN THIS FIELD BEHIND PROFESSOR XAVIER'S SCHOOL FOR GIFTED YOUNGSTERS, AND HIS DUEL WITH AN OLD, WITHERED TREE STUMP.
LF 256

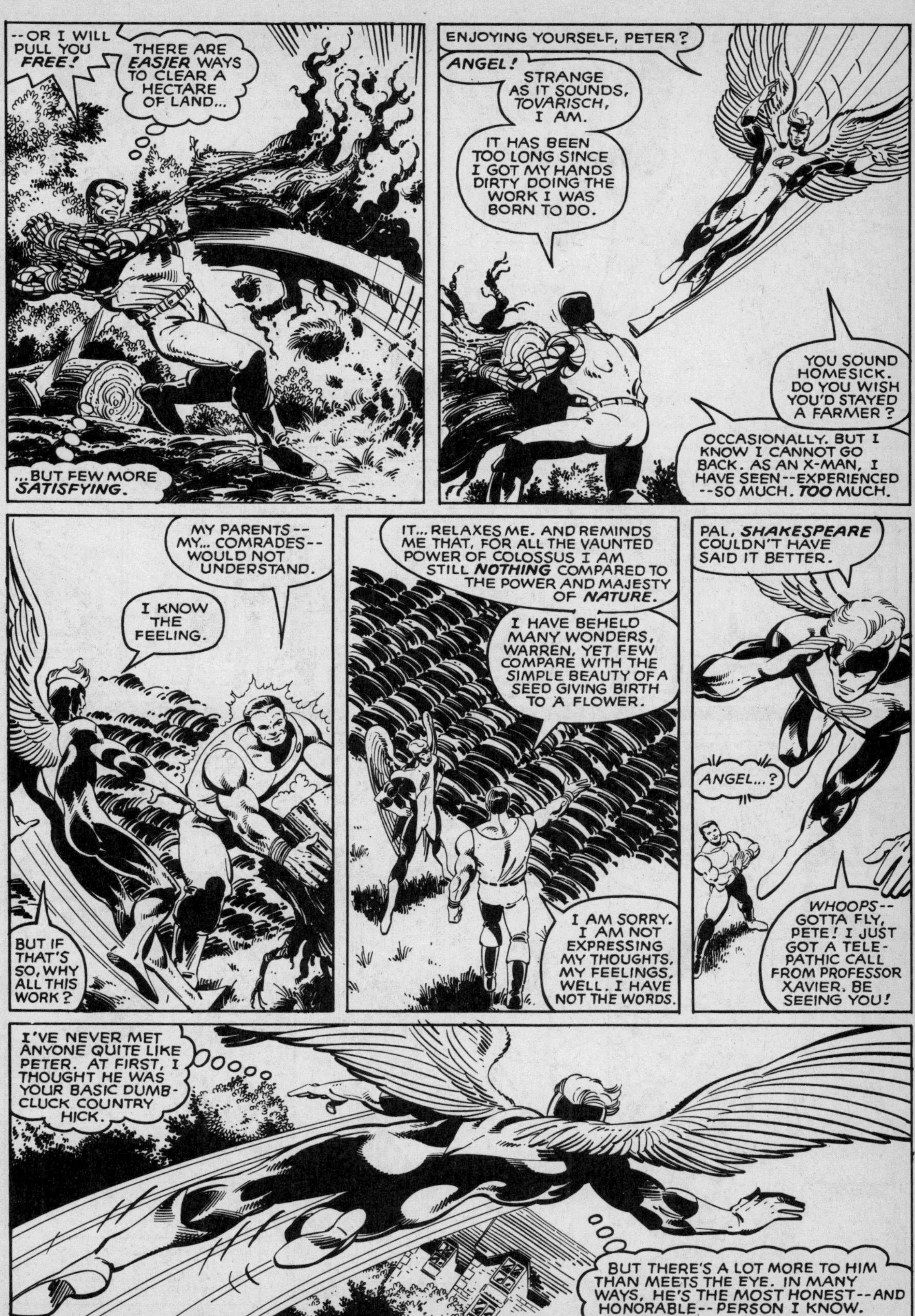
--OR I WILL PULL YOU FREE!
THERE ARE EASIER WAYS TO CLEAR A HECTARE OF LAND...
...BUT FEW MORE SATISFYING.
ENJOYING YOURSELF, PETER?
ANGEL!
STRANGE AS IT SOUNDS, TOVARISCH, I AM.
IT HAS BEEN TOO LONG SINCE I GOT MY HANDS DIRTY DOING THE WORK I WAS BORN TO DO.
YOU SOUND HOMESICK. DO YOU WISH YOU'D STAYED A FARMER?
OCCASIONALLY. BUT I KNOW I CANNOT GO BACK. AS AN X-MAN, I HAVE SEEN--EXPERIENCED--SO MUCH. TOO MUCH.
MY PARENTS--MY... COMRADES--WOULD NOT UNDERSTAND.
I KNOW THE FEELING.
BUT IF THAT'S SO, WHY ALL THIS WORK?
IT... RELAXES ME. AND REMINDS ME THAT, FOR ALL THE VAUNTED POWER OF COLOSSUS I AM STILL NOTHING COMPARED TO THE POWER AND MAJESTY OF NATURE.
I HAVE BEHELD MANY WONDERS, WARREN, YET FEW COMPARE WITH THE SIMPLE BEAUTY OF A SEED GIVING BIRTH TO A FLOWER.
I AM SORRY. I AM NOT EXPRESSING MY THOUGHTS, MY FEELINGS, WELL. I HAVE NOT THE WORDS.
PAL, SHAKESPEARE COULDN'T HAVE SAID IT BETTER.
ANGEL...?
WHOOPS--GOTTA FLY, PETE! I JUST GOT A TELE-PATHIC CALL FROM PROFESSOR XAVIER. BE SEEING YOU!
I'VE NEVER MET ANYONE QUITE LIKE PETER. AT FIRST, I THOUGHT HE WAS YOUR BASIC DUMB-CLUCK COUNTRY HICK.
BUT THERE'S A LOT MORE TO HIM THAN MEETS THE EYE. IN MANY WAYS, HE'S THE MOST HONEST--AND HONORABLE--PERSON I KNOW.

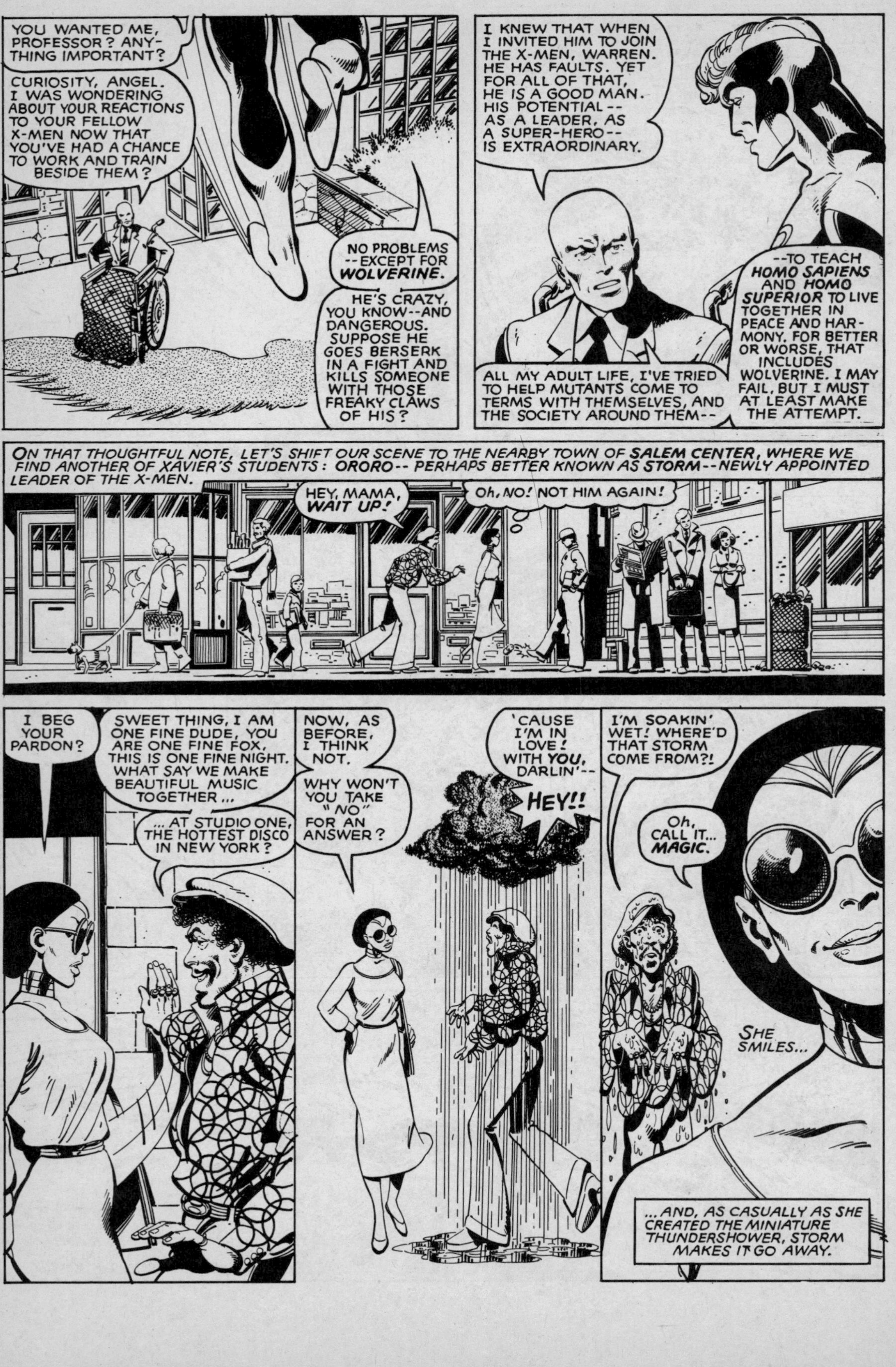
YOU WANTED ME, PROFESSOR? ANYTHING IMPORTANT?
CURIOSITY, ANGEL. I WAS WONDERING ABOUT YOUR REACTIONS TO YOUR FELLOW X-MEN NOW THAT YOU'VE HAD A CHANCE TO WORK AND TRAIN BESIDE THEM?
NO PROBLEMS --EXCEPT FOR WOLVERINE.
HE'S CRAZY, YOU KNOW--AND DANGEROUS. SUPPOSE HE GOES BERSERK IN A FIGHT AND KILLS SOMEONE WITH THOSE FREAKY CLAWS OF HIS?
I KNEW THAT WHEN I INVITED HIM TO JOIN THE X-MEN, WARREN. HE HAS FAULTS. YET FOR ALL OF THAT, HE IS A GOOD MAN. HIS POTENTIAL -- AS A LEADER, AS A SUPER-HERO -- IS EXTRAORDINARY.
ALL MY ADULT LIFE, I'VE TRIED TO HELP MUTANTS COME TO TERMS WITH THEMSELVES, AND THE SOCIETY AROUND THEM--
--TO TEACH HOMO SAPIENS AND HOMO SUPERIOR TO LIVE TOGETHER IN PEACE AND HARMONY. FOR BETTER OR WORSE, THAT INCLUDES WOLVERINE. I MAY FAIL, BUT I MUST AT LEAST MAKE THE ATTEMPT.
ON THAT THOUGHTFUL NOTE, LET'S SHIFT OUR SCENE TO THE NEARBY TOWN OF SALEM CENTER, WHERE WE FIND ANOTHER OF XAVIER'S STUDENTS: ORORO-- PERHAPS BETTER KNOWN AS STORM--NEWLY APPOINTED LEADER OF THE X-MEN.
HEY, MAMA, WAIT UP!
Oh, NO! NOT HIM AGAIN!
I BEG YOUR PARDON?
SWEET THING, I AM ONE FINE DUDE, YOU ARE ONE FINE FOX, THIS IS ONE FINE NIGHT. WHAT SAY WE MAKE BEAUTIFUL MUSIC TOGETHER...
...AT STUDIO ONE, THE HOTTEST DISCO IN NEW YORK?
NOW, AS BEFORE, I THINK NOT.
WHY WON'T YOU TAKE "NO" FOR AN ANSWER?
'CAUSE I'M IN LOVE! WITH YOU, DARLIN'--
HEY!!
I'M SOAKIN' WET! WHERE'D THAT STORM COME FROM?!
Oh, CALL IT... MAGIC.
SHE SMILES...
...AND, AS CASUALLY AS SHE CREATED THE MINIATURE THUNDERSHOWER, STORM MAKES IT GO AWAY.

Panel 1: A FEW MINUTES LATER, A FEW BLOCKS FURTHER ON...

THERE'S *KITTY*, AND HER NEW DANCE TEACHER, *STEVIE HUNTER*. THEY SEEM TO BE GETTING ALONG FAMOUSLY.

THAT SHOULDN'T BOTHER ME, BUT IT DOES. I'VE BEEN ON EDGE SINCE THE MOMENT WE MET. I KEEP TELLING MYSELF SUCH FEELINGS ARE ABSURD.

Panel 2: STEVIE IS ONE OF THE NICEST WOMEN *I'VE* EVER MET -- YET THE FEELINGS... REMAIN.

HIYA, 'RORO. BOY, YOU SHOULD HAVE STUCK AROUND TO WATCH THE CLASS. IT WAS *GREAT!*

OUR KITTEN HAS REAL TALENT, ORORO -- ONCE WE SMOOTH DOWN HER CONSIDERABLE ROUGH EDGES.

"OUR" KITTEN?

Panel 3: CAN I INTEREST YOU BOTH IN A BITE TO EAT? AFTER A DAY TEACHING BUDDING BARYSHNIKOV'S AND MAKAROVA'S, I'M FAMISHED.

THANK YOU, STEVIE, BUT NO, WE MUST BE GETTING BACK TO THE SCHOOL.

SORRY, STEVIE. DUTY CALLS! SEEYA!

SOME OTHER TIME, PER-HAPS.

FOR *SURE!*

Panel 4: *KITTY!*

WHAT DO YOU THINK YOU'RE DOING, FLAUNTING YOUR POWER LIKE THAT?! SUPPOSE SOMEONE SEES YOU?!

I CHECKED BEFORE I DID IT, ORORO. NOBODY'S AROUND.

Panel 5: I'M SORRY. IT'S JUST THAT... USING MY POWER -- WALKING THROUGH SOLID OBJECTS -- IS *FUN!*

I KNOW, LITTLE ONE. BUT PLEASE BE MORE CAREFUL.

Panel 6:

OKAY. ORORO, ARE YOU FEELING ALL RIGHT? YOU'RE ON AN AWFULLY SHORT FUSE ALL OF A SUDDEN. IS IT ME, OR ...?

GODDESS, THE CHILD IS PERCEPTIVE!

N-NO, KITTEN. IT'S NOT YOU.

I'M, *ah,* CONCERNED FOR WOLVERINE AND NIGHTCRAWLER. WE'VE HEARD NOTHING FROM THEM SINCE THEY LEFT FOR CANADA THIS MORNING. I HOPE THEY HAVEN'T RUN INTO TROUBLE.

To FIND OUT...

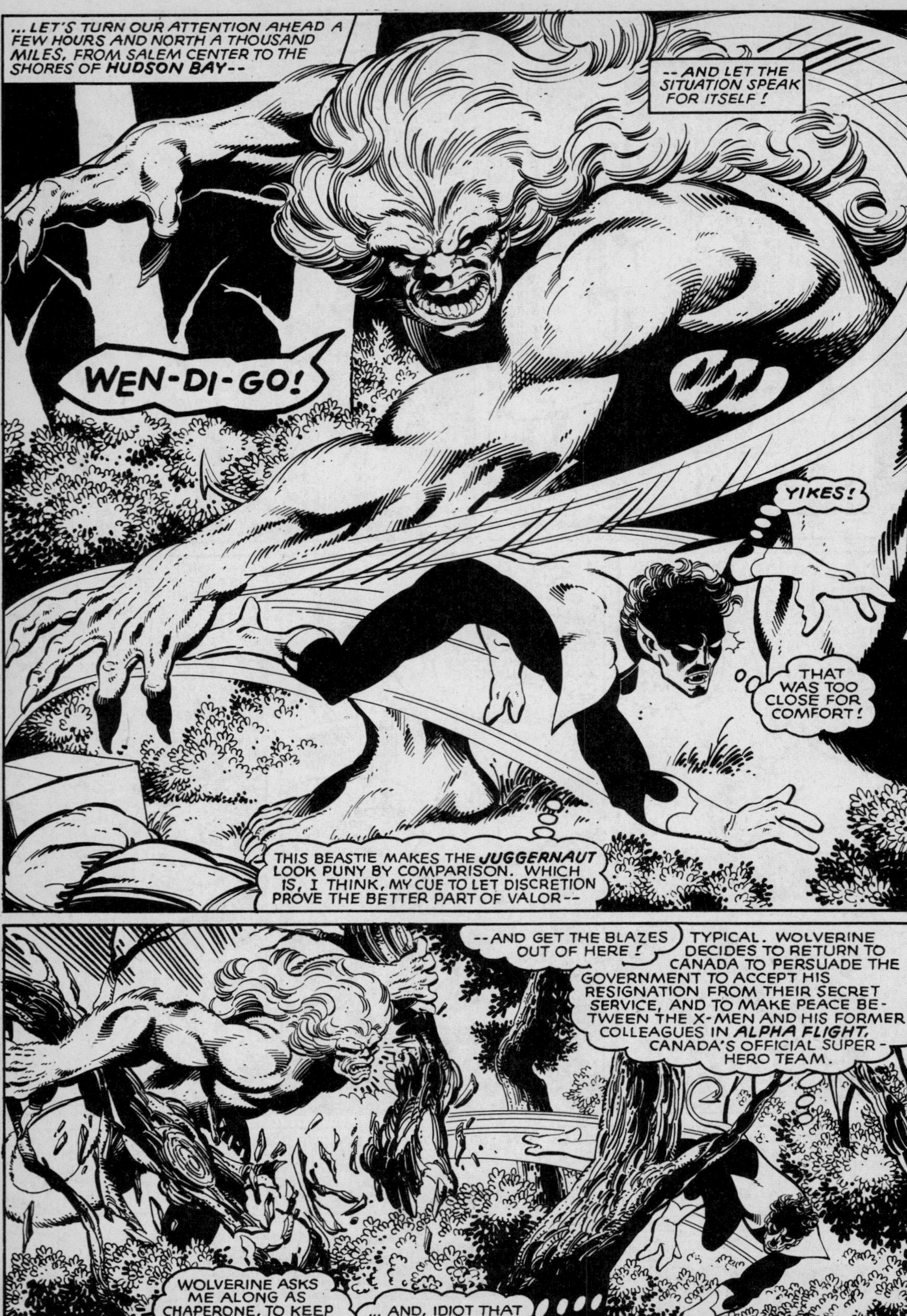
...LET'S TURN OUR ATTENTION AHEAD A FEW HOURS AND NORTH A THOUSAND MILES, FROM SALEM CENTER TO THE SHORES OF HUDSON BAY--
--AND LET THE SITUATION SPEAK FOR ITSELF!
WEN-DI-GO!
YIKES!
THAT WAS TOO CLOSE FOR COMFORT!
THIS BEASTIE MAKES THE JUGGERNAUT LOOK PUNY BY COMPARISON. WHICH IS, I THINK, MY CUE TO LET DISCRETION PROVE THE BETTER PART OF VALOR--
--AND GET THE BLAZES OUT OF HERE!
TYPICAL. WOLVERINE DECIDES TO RETURN TO CANADA TO PERSUADE THE GOVERNMENT TO ACCEPT HIS RESIGNATION FROM THEIR SECRET SERVICE, AND TO MAKE PEACE BETWEEN THE X-MEN AND HIS FORMER COLLEAGUES IN ALPHA FLIGHT, CANADA'S OFFICIAL SUPER-HERO TEAM.
WOLVERINE ASKS ME ALONG AS CHAPERONE, TO KEEP HIM OUT OF TROUBLE...
...AND, IDIOT THAT I AM, I ACCEPT.

SO, OF COURSE, WITH ALL EYES ON WOLVERINE, THE PROVERBIAL ROOF FALLS IN ON *ME!*

I'M NOT STAYING AHEAD OF THE MONSTER ON THE GROUND.

IT'S TOO RISKY TO TELE-PORT UNLESS I ABSOLUTELY HAVE TO. PERHAPS *I'LL* HAVE BETTER LUCK IN THE TREETOPS. HE LOOKS TOO BULKY TO CLIMB AFTER ME.

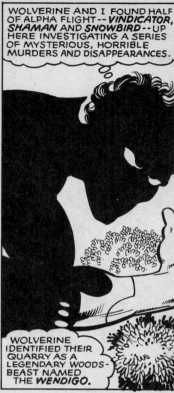

WOLVERINE AND I FOUND HALF OF ALPHA FLIGHT -- *VINDICATOR, SHAMAN* AND *SNOWBIRD* -- UP HERE INVESTIGATING A SERIES OF MYSTERIOUS, HORRIBLE MURDERS AND DISAPPEARANCES.

WOLVERINE IDENTIFIED THEIR QUARRY AS A LEGENDARY WOODS-BEAST NAMED THE *WENDIGO.*

FROM THIS HULK'S BATTLE CRY, *HE* MUST BE IT!

MY *TREE* -- OH, NO!

SHAK!

WEN-DI-GO!

AARRRGH!

GRIP LIKE A VISE -- CRUSHING ME! CLAWS... CUTTING INTO ME!

WENDIGO... TOO STRONG. I CAN'T... BREAK FREE.

ONLY HOPE... FOCUS CONCEN-TRATION... IGNORE PAIN... BUT IT'S SO *HARD!* I HURT... SO MUCH! BUT -- I *MUST!*

A PSYCHIC SWITCH CLOSES IN NIGHTCRAWLER'S MIND -- AND WITH THE TRADITIONAL CRACK OF FLAME AND GUSTING STENCH OF BRIMSTONE...

BAMF

... HE TELEPORTS OUT OF WENDIGO'S GRASP.

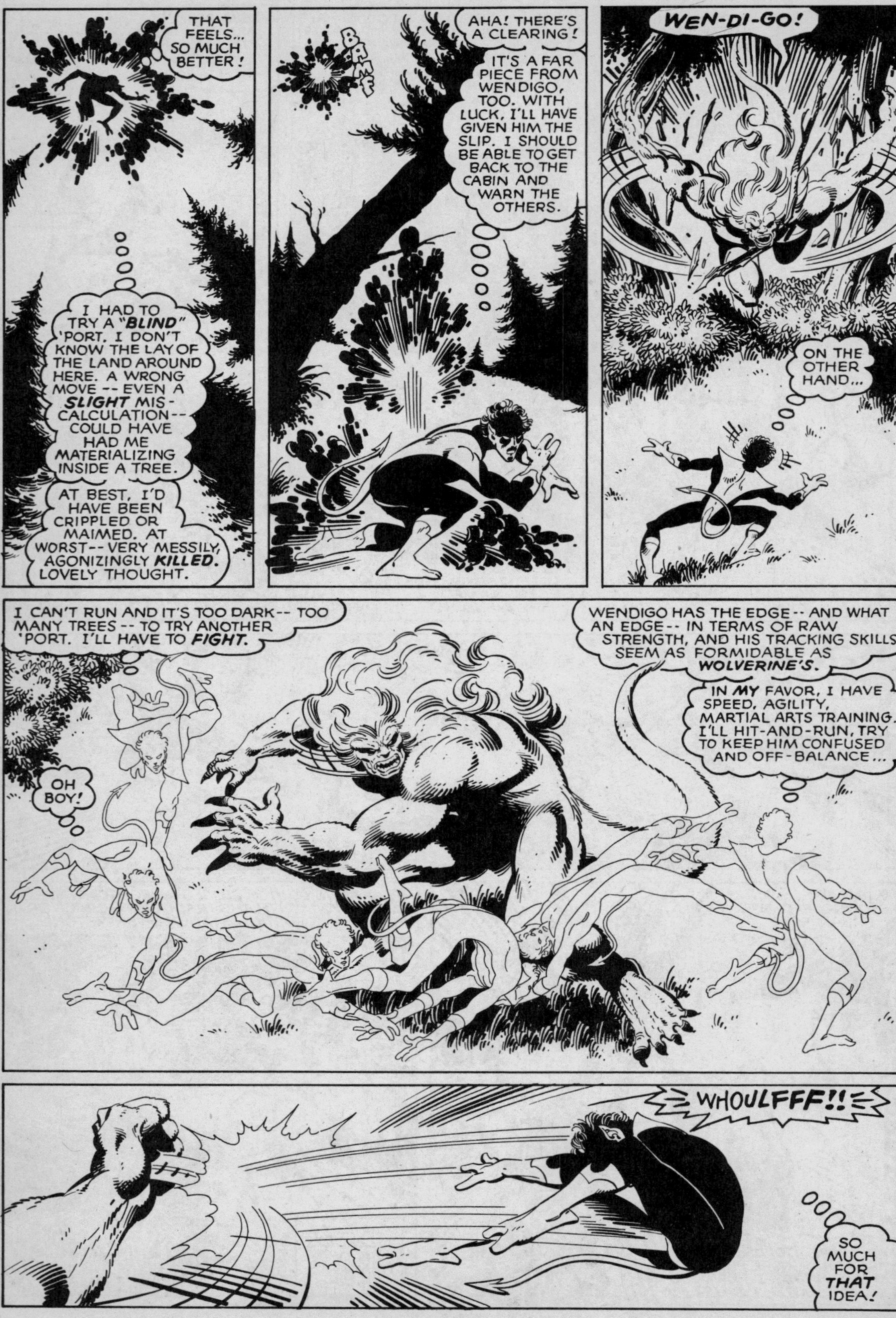

THAT FEELS... SO MUCH BETTER!
I HAD TO TRY A "BLIND" 'PORT. I DON'T KNOW THE LAY OF THE LAND AROUND HERE. A WRONG MOVE -- EVEN A SLIGHT MIS-CALCULATION-- COULD HAVE HAD ME MATERIALIZING INSIDE A TREE.
AT BEST, I'D HAVE BEEN CRIPPLED OR MAIMED. AT WORST-- VERY MESSILY, AGONIZINGLY KILLED. LOVELY THOUGHT.
BAMF
AHA! THERE'S A CLEARING!
IT'S A FAR PIECE FROM WENDIGO, TOO. WITH LUCK, I'LL HAVE GIVEN HIM THE SLIP. I SHOULD BE ABLE TO GET BACK TO THE CABIN AND WARN THE OTHERS.
WEN-DI-GO!
ON THE OTHER HAND...
I CAN'T RUN AND IT'S TOO DARK-- TOO MANY TREES -- TO TRY ANOTHER 'PORT. I'LL HAVE TO FIGHT.
OH BOY!
WENDIGO HAS THE EDGE -- AND WHAT AN EDGE -- IN TERMS OF RAW STRENGTH, AND HIS TRACKING SKILLS SEEM AS FORMIDABLE AS WOLVERINE'S.
IN MY FAVOR, I HAVE SPEED, AGILITY, MARTIAL ARTS TRAINING. I'LL HIT-AND-RUN, TRY TO KEEP HIM CONFUSED AND OFF-BALANCE...
WHOULFFF!!
SO MUCH FOR THAT IDEA!

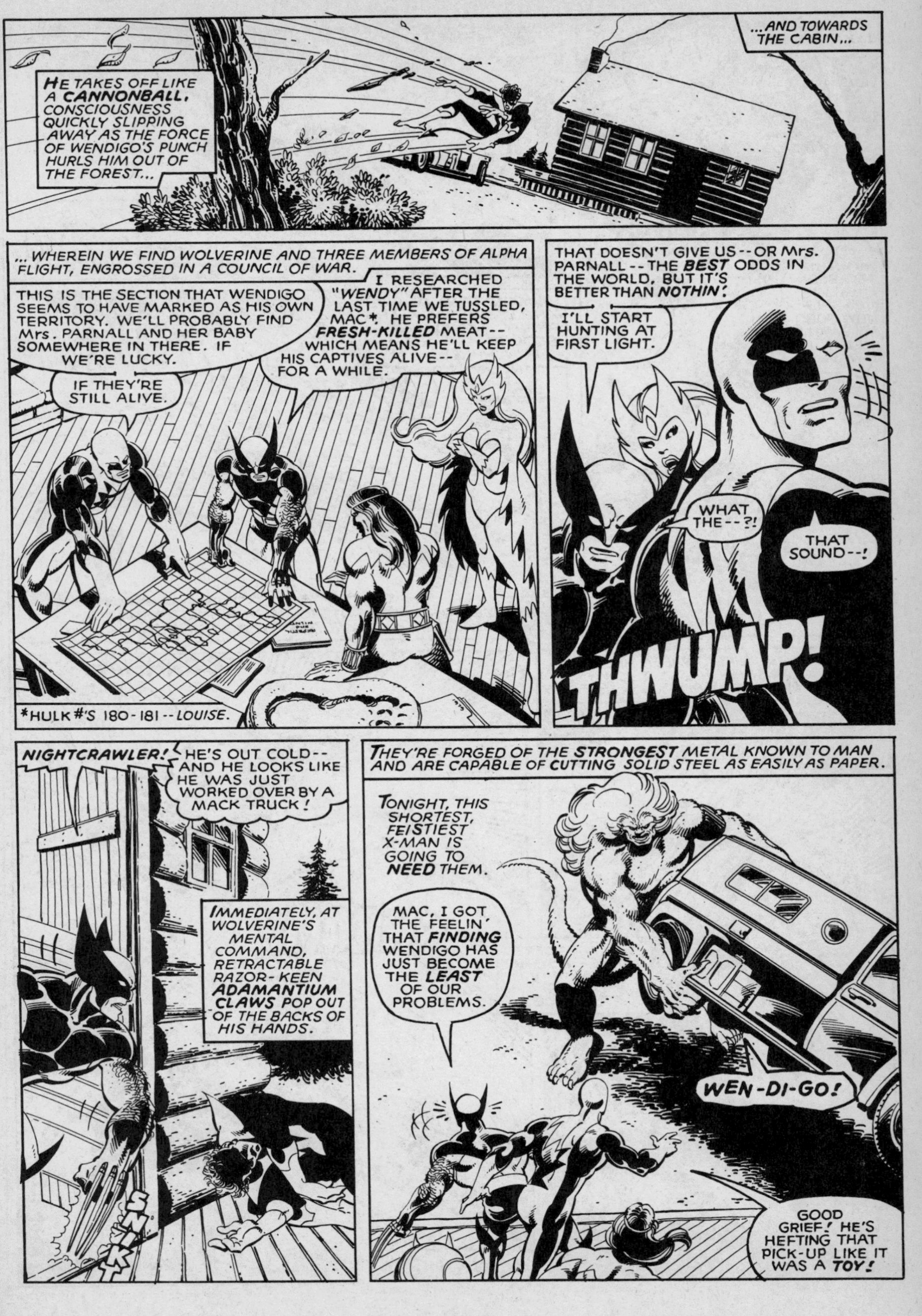

HE TAKES OFF LIKE A CANNONBALL, CONSCIOUSNESS QUICKLY SLIPPING AWAY AS THE FORCE OF WENDIGO'S PUNCH HURLS HIM OUT OF THE FOREST...
...AND TOWARDS THE CABIN...
...WHEREIN WE FIND WOLVERINE AND THREE MEMBERS OF ALPHA FLIGHT, ENGROSSED IN A COUNCIL OF WAR.
THIS IS THE SECTION THAT WENDIGO SEEMS TO HAVE MARKED AS HIS OWN TERRITORY. WE'LL PROBABLY FIND Mrs. PARNALL AND HER BABY SOMEWHERE IN THERE. IF WE'RE LUCKY.
IF THEY'RE STILL ALIVE.
I RESEARCHED "WENDY" AFTER THE LAST TIME WE TUSSLED, MAC*. HE PREFERS FRESH-KILLED MEAT--WHICH MEANS HE'LL KEEP HIS CAPTIVES ALIVE--FOR A WHILE.
*HULK #'S 180-181 --LOUISE.
THAT DOESN'T GIVE US--OR Mrs. PARNALL--THE BEST ODDS IN THE WORLD, BUT IT'S BETTER THAN NOTHIN'.
I'LL START HUNTING AT FIRST LIGHT.
WHAT THE--?!
THAT SOUND--!
THWUMP!
NIGHTCRAWLER!
HE'S OUT COLD--AND HE LOOKS LIKE HE WAS JUST WORKED OVER BY A MACK TRUCK!
IMMEDIATELY, AT WOLVERINE'S MENTAL COMMAND, RETRACTABLE RAZOR-KEEN ADAMANTIUM CLAWS POP OUT OF THE BACKS OF HIS HANDS.
SNIKT
THEY'RE FORGED OF THE STRONGEST METAL KNOWN TO MAN AND ARE CAPABLE OF CUTTING SOLID STEEL AS EASILY AS PAPER.
TONIGHT, THIS SHORTEST, FEISTIEST X-MAN IS GOING TO NEED THEM.
MAC, I GOT THE FEELIN' THAT FINDING WENDIGO HAS JUST BECOME THE LEAST OF OUR PROBLEMS.
WEN-DI-GO!
GOOD GRIEF! HE'S HEFTING THAT PICK-UP LIKE IT WAS A TOY!

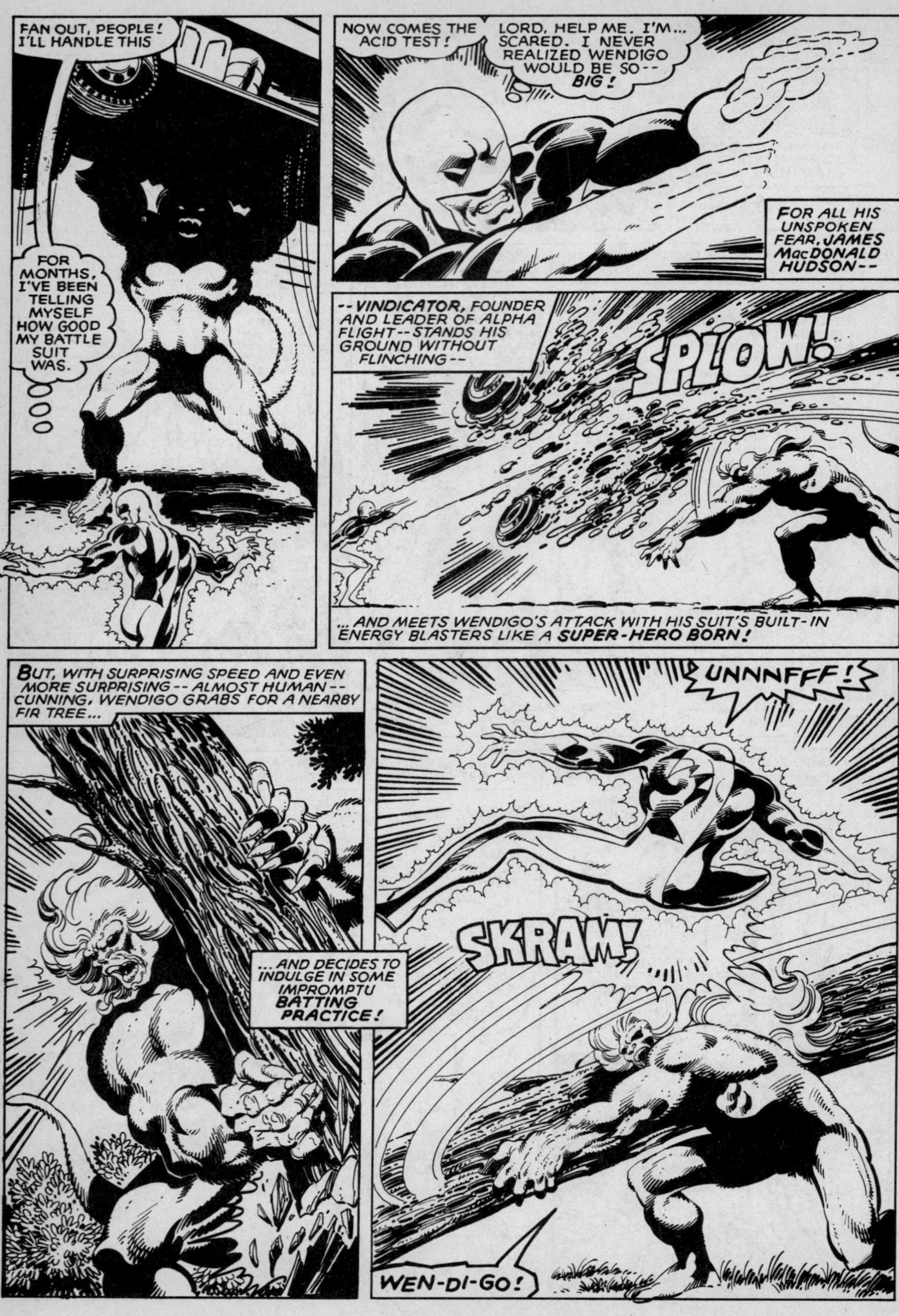
FAN OUT, PEOPLE! I'LL HANDLE THIS
FOR MONTHS, I'VE BEEN TELLING MYSELF HOW GOOD MY BATTLE SUIT WAS.
NOW COMES THE ACID TEST!
LORD, HELP ME. I'M... SCARED. I NEVER REALIZED WENDIGO WOULD BE SO-- BIG!
FOR ALL HIS UNSPOKEN FEAR, JAMES MacDONALD HUDSON--
--VINDICATOR, FOUNDER AND LEADER OF ALPHA FLIGHT--STANDS HIS GROUND WITHOUT FLINCHING--
SPLOW!
...AND MEETS WENDIGO'S ATTACK WITH HIS SUIT'S BUILT-IN ENERGY BLASTERS LIKE A SUPER-HERO BORN!
BUT, WITH SURPRISING SPEED AND EVEN MORE SURPRISING--ALMOST HUMAN--CUNNING, WENDIGO GRABS FOR A NEARBY FIR TREE...
...AND DECIDES TO INDULGE IN SOME IMPROMPTU BATTING PRACTICE!
UNNNFFF!
SKRAM!
WEN-DI-GO!

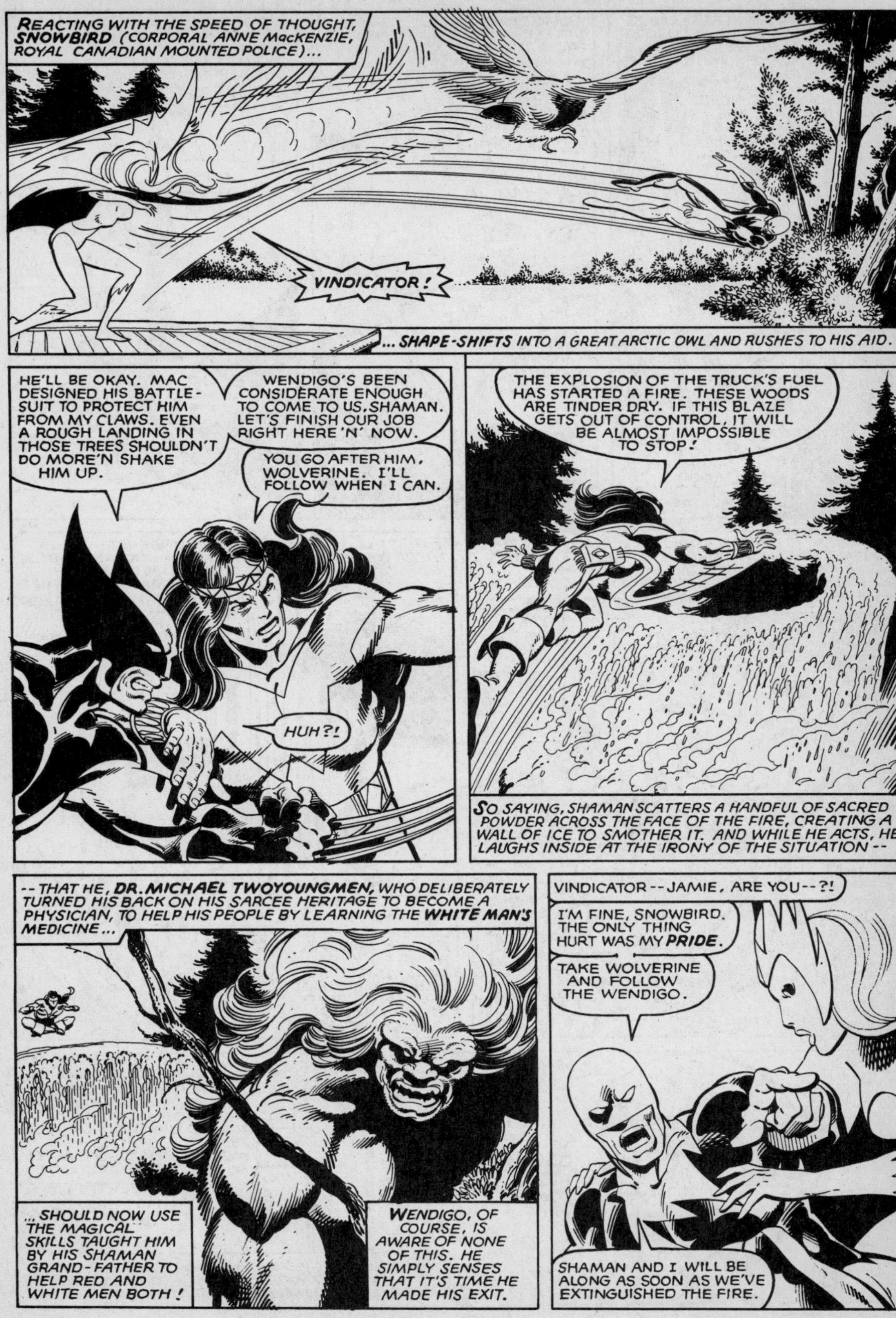
REACTING WITH THE SPEED OF THOUGHT, SNOWBIRD (CORPORAL ANNE MacKENZIE, ROYAL CANADIAN MOUNTED POLICE)...
VINDICATOR!
...SHAPE-SHIFTS INTO A GREAT ARCTIC OWL AND RUSHES TO HIS AID.
HE'LL BE OKAY. MAC DESIGNED HIS BATTLE-SUIT TO PROTECT HIM FROM MY CLAWS. EVEN A ROUGH LANDING IN THOSE TREES SHOULDN'T DO MORE'N SHAKE HIM UP.
WENDIGO'S BEEN CONSIDERATE ENOUGH TO COME TO US, SHAMAN. LET'S FINISH OUR JOB RIGHT HERE 'N' NOW.
YOU GO AFTER HIM, WOLVERINE. I'LL FOLLOW WHEN I CAN.
HUH?!
THE EXPLOSION OF THE TRUCK'S FUEL HAS STARTED A FIRE. THESE WOODS ARE TINDER DRY. IF THIS BLAZE GETS OUT OF CONTROL, IT WILL BE ALMOST IMPOSSIBLE TO STOP!
SO SAYING, SHAMAN SCATTERS A HANDFUL OF SACRED POWDER ACROSS THE FACE OF THE FIRE, CREATING A WALL OF ICE TO SMOTHER IT. AND WHILE HE ACTS, HE LAUGHS INSIDE AT THE IRONY OF THE SITUATION --
-- THAT HE, DR. MICHAEL TWOYOUNGMEN, WHO DELIBERATELY TURNED HIS BACK ON HIS SARCEE HERITAGE TO BECOME A PHYSICIAN, TO HELP HIS PEOPLE BY LEARNING THE WHITE MAN'S MEDICINE...
...SHOULD NOW USE THE MAGICAL SKILLS TAUGHT HIM BY HIS SHAMAN GRAND-FATHER TO HELP RED AND WHITE MEN BOTH!
WENDIGO, OF COURSE, IS AWARE OF NONE OF THIS. HE SIMPLY SENSES THAT IT'S TIME HE MADE HIS EXIT.
VINDICATOR -- JAMIE, ARE YOU--?!
I'M FINE, SNOWBIRD. THE ONLY THING HURT WAS MY PRIDE.
TAKE WOLVERINE AND FOLLOW THE WENDIGO.
SHAMAN AND I WILL BE ALONG AS SOON AS WE'VE EXTINGUISHED THE FIRE.

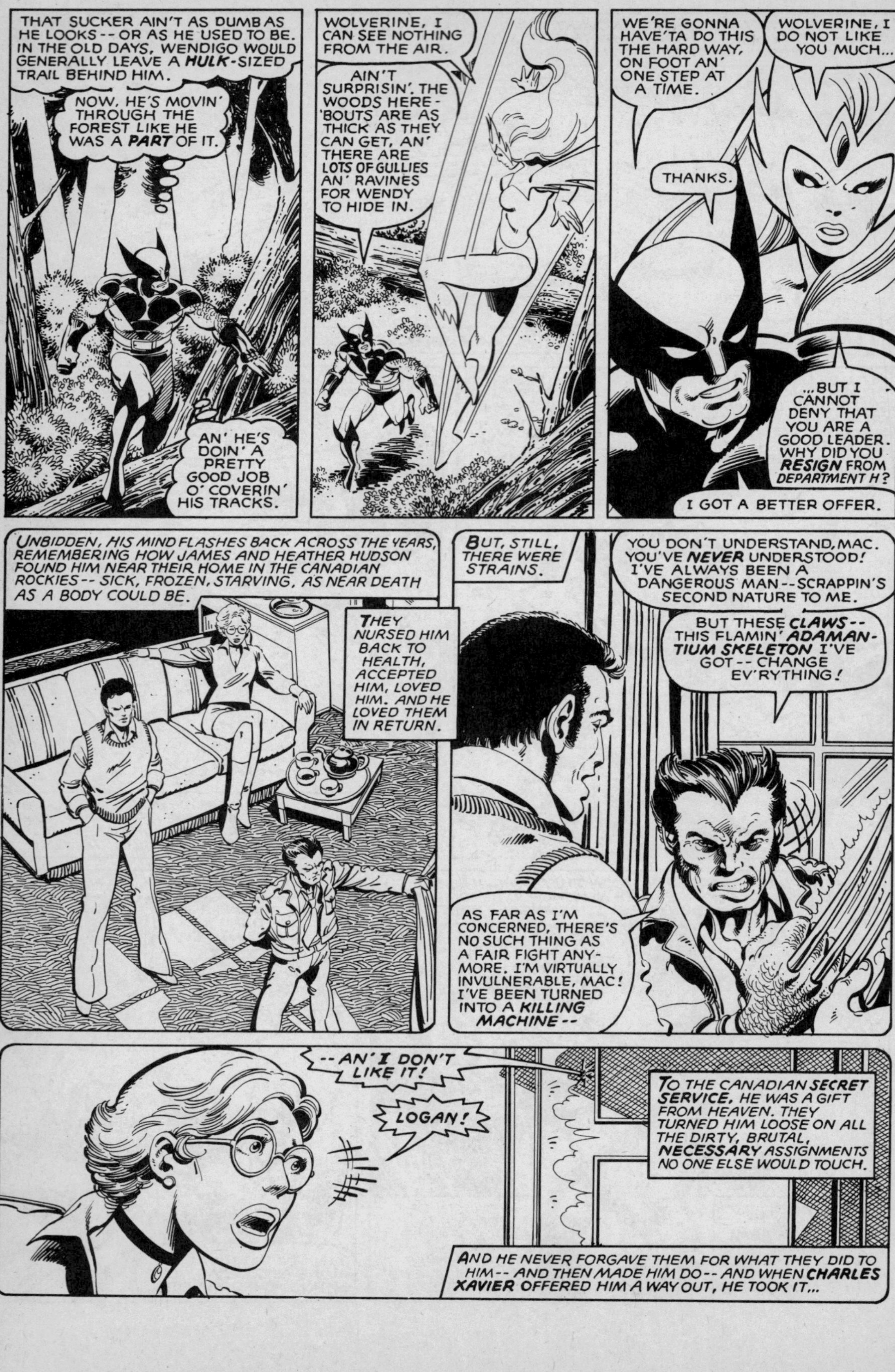

THAT SUCKER AIN'T AS DUMB AS HE LOOKS -- OR AS HE USED TO BE. IN THE OLD DAYS, WENDIGO WOULD GENERALLY LEAVE A HULK-SIZED TRAIL BEHIND HIM.
NOW, HE'S MOVIN' THROUGH THE FOREST LIKE HE WAS A PART OF IT.
AN' HE'S DOIN' A PRETTY GOOD JOB O' COVERIN' HIS TRACKS.
WOLVERINE, I CAN SEE NOTHING FROM THE AIR.
AIN'T SURPRISIN'. THE WOODS HERE-'BOUTS ARE AS THICK AS THEY CAN GET, AN' THERE ARE LOTS OF GULLIES AN' RAVINES FOR WENDY TO HIDE IN.
WE'RE GONNA HAVE'TA DO THIS THE HARD WAY, ON FOOT AN' ONE STEP AT A TIME.
WOLVERINE, I DO NOT LIKE YOU MUCH...
THANKS.
...BUT I CANNOT DENY THAT YOU ARE A GOOD LEADER. WHY DID YOU RESIGN FROM DEPARTMENT H?
I GOT A BETTER OFFER.
UNBIDDEN, HIS MIND FLASHES BACK ACROSS THE YEARS, REMEMBERING HOW JAMES AND HEATHER HUDSON FOUND HIM NEAR THEIR HOME IN THE CANADIAN ROCKIES -- SICK, FROZEN, STARVING, AS NEAR DEATH AS A BODY COULD BE.
THEY NURSED HIM BACK TO HEALTH, ACCEPTED HIM, LOVED HIM. AND HE LOVED THEM IN RETURN.
BUT, STILL, THERE WERE STRAINS.
YOU DON'T UNDERSTAND, MAC. YOU'VE NEVER UNDERSTOOD! I'VE ALWAYS BEEN A DANGEROUS MAN -- SCRAPPIN'S SECOND NATURE TO ME.
BUT THESE CLAWS -- THIS FLAMIN' ADAMANTIUM SKELETON I'VE GOT -- CHANGE EV'RYTHING!
AS FAR AS I'M CONCERNED, THERE'S NO SUCH THING AS A FAIR FIGHT ANY-MORE. I'M VIRTUALLY INVULNERABLE, MAC! I'VE BEEN TURNED INTO A KILLING MACHINE --
-- AN' I DON'T LIKE IT!
LOGAN!
TO THE CANADIAN SECRET SERVICE, HE WAS A GIFT FROM HEAVEN. THEY TURNED HIM LOOSE ON ALL THE DIRTY, BRUTAL, NECESSARY ASSIGNMENTS NO ONE ELSE WOULD TOUCH.
AND HE NEVER FORGAVE THEM FOR WHAT THEY DID TO HIM -- AND THEN MADE HIM DO -- AND WHEN CHARLES XAVIER OFFERED HIM A WAY OUT, HE TOOK IT...

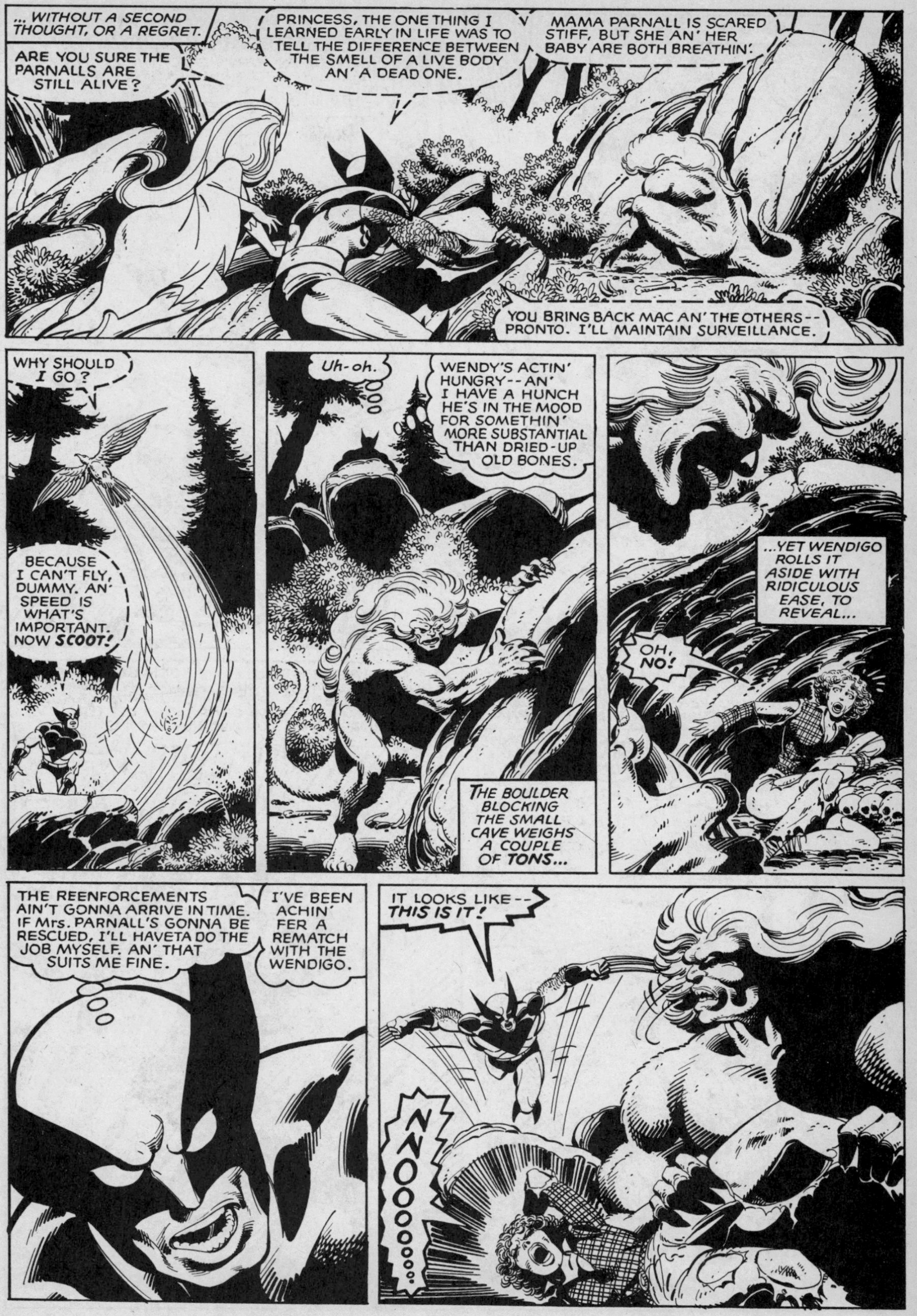
...WITHOUT A SECOND THOUGHT, OR A REGRET.
ARE YOU SURE THE PARNALLS ARE STILL ALIVE?
PRINCESS, THE ONE THING I LEARNED EARLY IN LIFE WAS TO TELL THE DIFFERENCE BETWEEN THE SMELL OF A LIVE BODY AN' A DEAD ONE.
MAMA PARNALL IS SCARED STIFF, BUT SHE AN' HER BABY ARE BOTH BREATHIN'.
YOU BRING BACK MAC AN' THE OTHERS-- PRONTO. I'LL MAINTAIN SURVEILLANCE.
WHY SHOULD I GO?
BECAUSE I CAN'T FLY, DUMMY. AN' SPEED IS WHAT'S IMPORTANT. NOW SCOOT!
Uh-oh.
WENDY'S ACTIN' HUNGRY-- AN' I HAVE A HUNCH HE'S IN THE MOOD FOR SOMETHIN' MORE SUBSTANTIAL THAN DRIED-UP OLD BONES.
THE BOULDER BLOCKING THE SMALL CAVE WEIGHS A COUPLE OF TONS...
...YET WENDIGO ROLLS IT ASIDE WITH RIDICULOUS EASE, TO REVEAL...
OH, NO!
THE REENFORCEMENTS AIN'T GONNA ARRIVE IN TIME. IF Mrs. PARNALL'S GONNA BE RESCUED, I'LL HAVETA DO THE JOB MYSELF. AN' THAT SUITS ME FINE.
I'VE BEEN ACHIN' FER A REMATCH WITH THE WENDIGO.
IT LOOKS LIKE-- THIS IS IT!
NNOOOOOooo

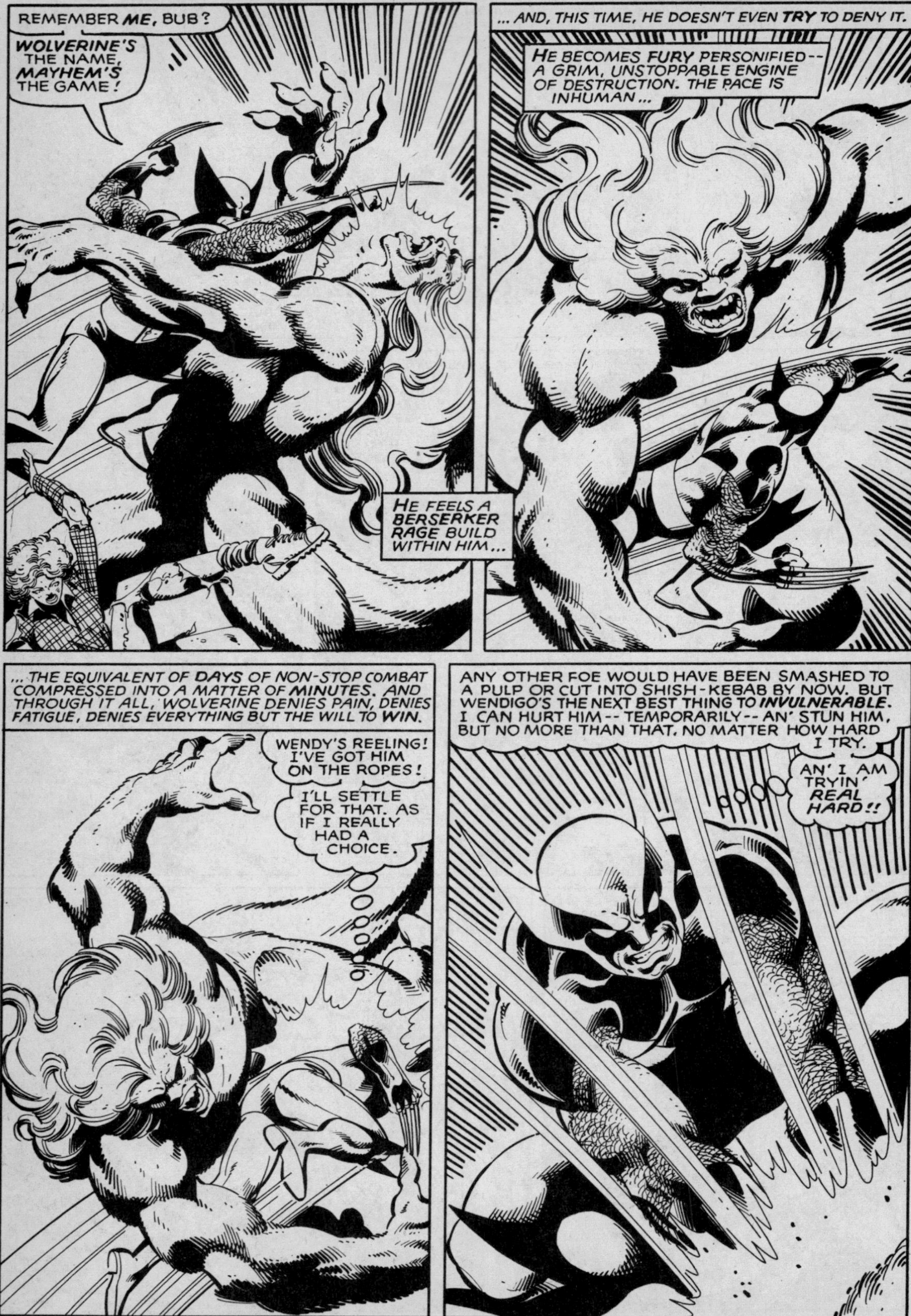

REMEMBER ME, BUB?
WOLVERINE'S THE NAME, MAYHEM'S THE GAME!
HE FEELS A BERSERKER RAGE BUILD WITHIN HIM...
... AND, THIS TIME, HE DOESN'T EVEN TRY TO DENY IT.
HE BECOMES FURY PERSONIFIED -- A GRIM, UNSTOPPABLE ENGINE OF DESTRUCTION. THE PACE IS INHUMAN...
... THE EQUIVALENT OF DAYS OF NON-STOP COMBAT COMPRESSED INTO A MATTER OF MINUTES. AND THROUGH IT ALL, WOLVERINE DENIES PAIN, DENIES FATIGUE, DENIES EVERYTHING BUT THE WILL TO WIN.
WENDY'S REELING! I'VE GOT HIM ON THE ROPES!
I'LL SETTLE FOR THAT. AS IF I REALLY HAD A CHOICE.
ANY OTHER FOE WOULD HAVE BEEN SMASHED TO A PULP OR CUT INTO SHISH-KEBAB BY NOW. BUT WENDIGO'S THE NEXT BEST THING TO INVULNERABLE. I CAN HURT HIM -- TEMPORARILY -- AN' STUN HIM, BUT NO MORE THAN THAT. NO MATTER HOW HARD I TRY.
AN' I AM TRYIN' REAL HARD!!

whooo...

HE'S DOWN... AN' OUT. FINALLY. MY ADRENALIN SURGE -- MY PATENTED "BERSERKER RAGE" -- IS FADIN' FAST. BEEN... A LONG TIME SINCE I FELT THIS... POOPED.

CAN'T FOLD, THOUGH -- NOT 'TIL I GET THE LADY AN' HER KID OUT O' HARM'S WAY.

M-Mrs. PARNALL...? NAME'S WOLVERINE. BE COOL, MA'AM, I'M ONE O' THE GOOD GUYS.

CAN YOU TRAVEL? THE SOONER WE'RE AWAY FROM HERE, THE BETTER. I CAN'T GUARANTEE HOW LONG SHAGGY'LL STAY IN SLUMBER-LAND.

I... CAN WALK.

THAT'S A START. WE'LL PICK UP SPEED AS WE GO ALONG, AS YOU GET YOUR STRENGTH BACK.

M-MY HUSBAND, JOE -- I HEARD HIM SCREAM. I... SAW--! IT WAS... HORRIBLE. AND... AND MY BOY, TOMMY...?

TOMMY'S FINE. HE'S IN THE HOSPITAL.

THANK GOD.

THAT'S ONLY PART O' THE TRUTH. BUT HOW DO I TELL HER THAT THE BOY'S IN CATATONIC SHOCK -- ALMOST A KIND OF LIVING DEATH?!

HUH?! THAT SHADOW--!

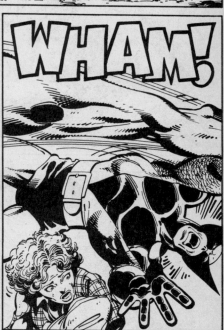

WHAM!

WEN-DI-GO!

OF ALL... THE DUMB... MISTAKES. I... DROPPED MY GUARD...

WENDY... HAS EDGE. ALL I CAN DO... IS RIDE THINGS OUT...

... AN' HOPE FOR... THE BEST...

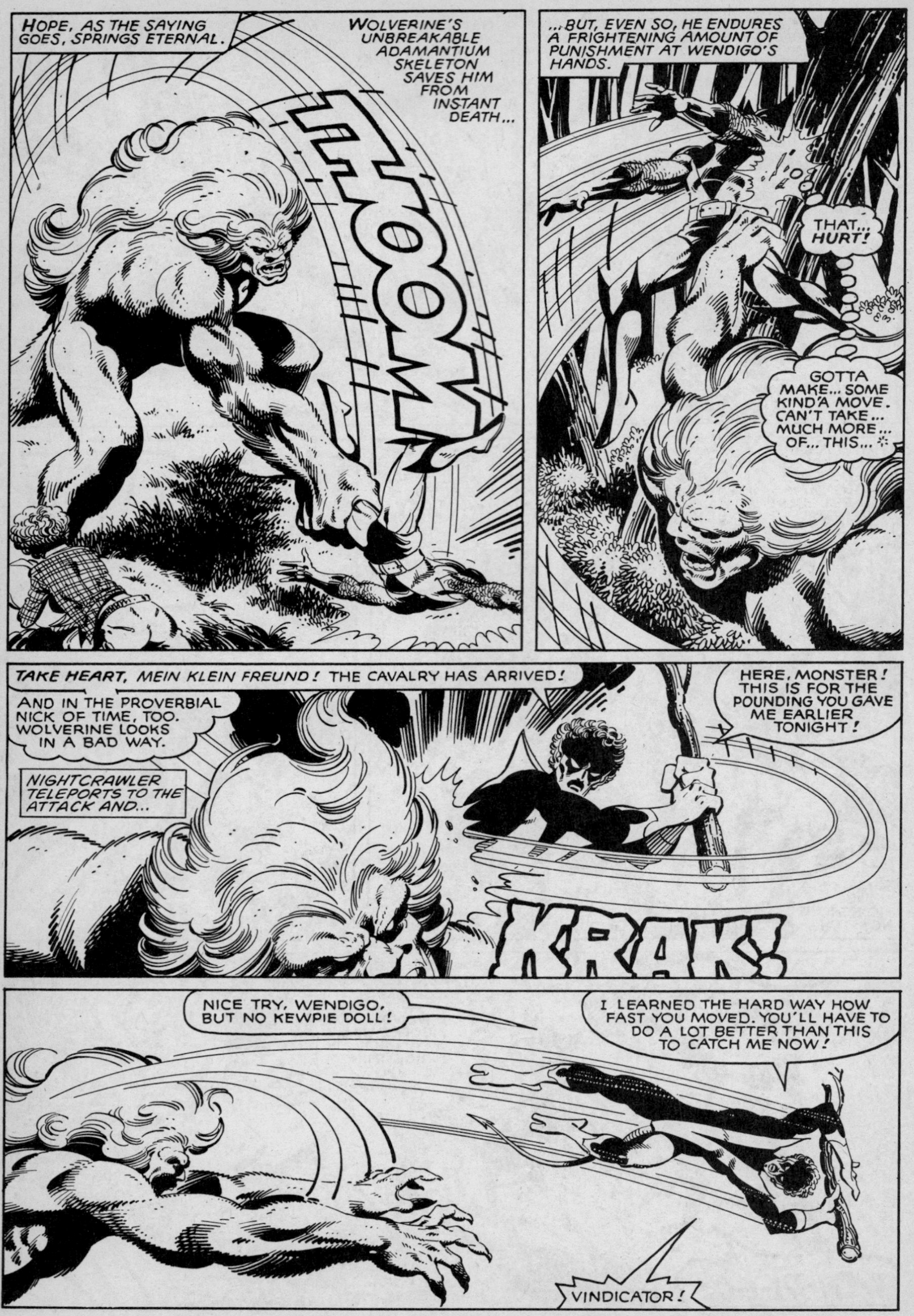
HOPE, AS THE SAYING GOES, SPRINGS ETERNAL.
WOLVERINE'S UNBREAKABLE ADAMANTIUM SKELETON SAVES HIM FROM INSTANT DEATH...
THOOOM
...BUT, EVEN SO, HE ENDURES A FRIGHTENING AMOUNT OF PUNISHMENT AT WENDIGO'S HANDS.
THAT... HURT!
GOTTA MAKE... SOME KIND'A MOVE. CAN'T TAKE... MUCH MORE... OF... THIS...
TAKE HEART, MEIN KLEIN FREUND! THE CAVALRY HAS ARRIVED!
AND IN THE PROVERBIAL NICK OF TIME, TOO. WOLVERINE LOOKS IN A BAD WAY.
NIGHTCRAWLER TELEPORTS TO THE ATTACK AND...
HERE, MONSTER! THIS IS FOR THE POUNDING YOU GAVE ME EARLIER TONIGHT!
KRAK!
NICE TRY, WENDIGO, BUT NO KEWPIE DOLL!
I LEARNED THE HARD WAY HOW FAST YOU MOVED. YOU'LL HAVE TO DO A LOT BETTER THAN THIS TO CATCH ME NOW!
VINDICATOR!

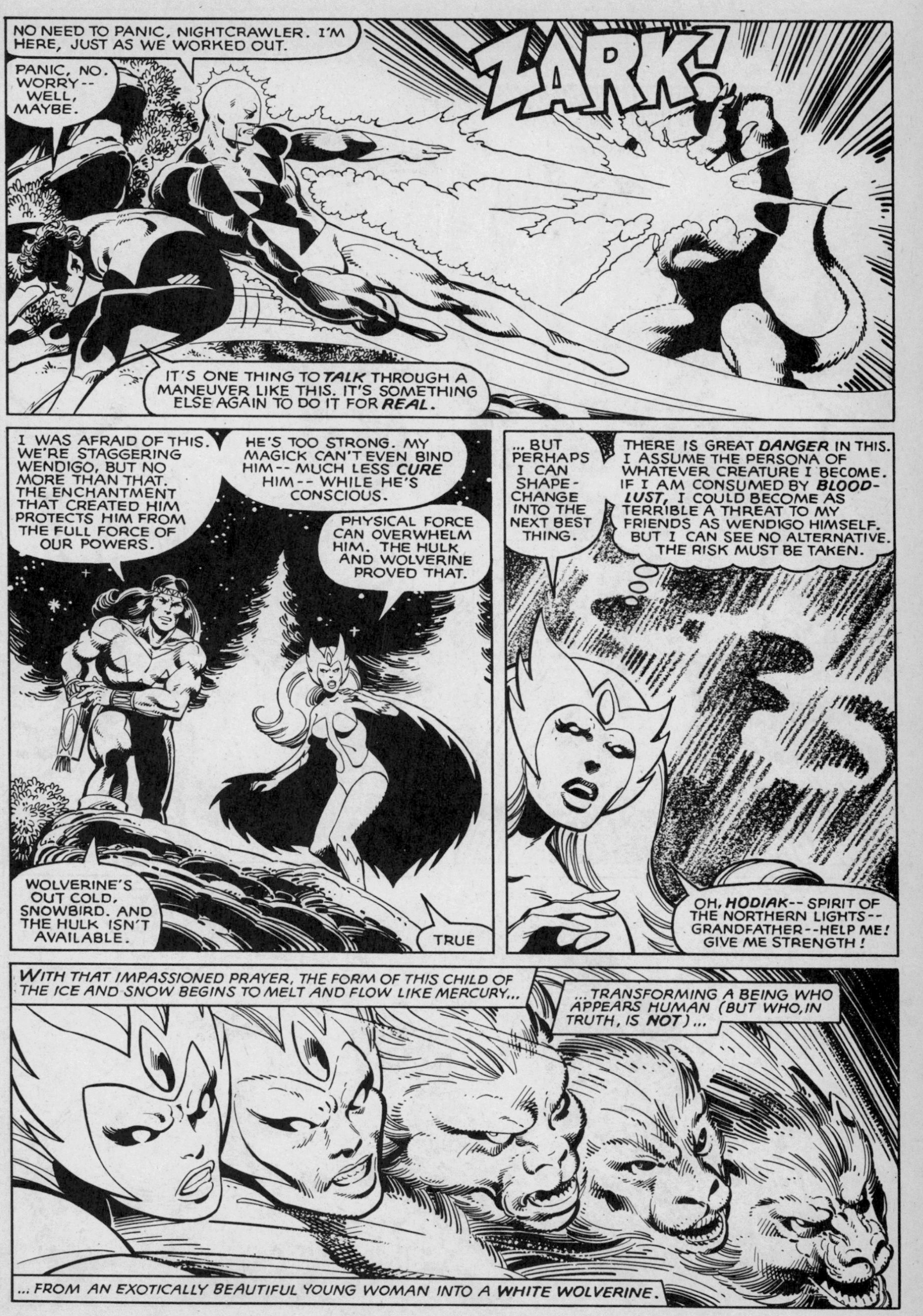
NO NEED TO PANIC, NIGHTCRAWLER. I'M HERE, JUST AS WE WORKED OUT.
PANIC, NO. WORRY-- WELL, MAYBE.
ZARK!
IT'S ONE THING TO TALK THROUGH A MANEUVER LIKE THIS. IT'S SOMETHING ELSE AGAIN TO DO IT FOR REAL.
I WAS AFRAID OF THIS. WE'RE STAGGERING WENDIGO, BUT NO MORE THAN THAT. THE ENCHANTMENT THAT CREATED HIM PROTECTS HIM FROM THE FULL FORCE OF OUR POWERS.
HE'S TOO STRONG. MY MAGICK CAN'T EVEN BIND HIM-- MUCH LESS CURE HIM-- WHILE HE'S CONSCIOUS.
PHYSICAL FORCE CAN OVERWHELM HIM. THE HULK AND WOLVERINE PROVED THAT.
WOLVERINE'S OUT COLD, SNOWBIRD. AND THE HULK ISN'T AVAILABLE.
TRUE
... BUT PERHAPS I CAN SHAPE-CHANGE INTO THE NEXT BEST THING.
THERE IS GREAT DANGER IN THIS. I ASSUME THE PERSONA OF WHATEVER CREATURE I BECOME. IF I AM CONSUMED BY BLOOD-LUST, I COULD BECOME AS TERRIBLE A THREAT TO MY FRIENDS AS WENDIGO HIMSELF. BUT I CAN SEE NO ALTERNATIVE. THE RISK MUST BE TAKEN.
OH, HODIAK-- SPIRIT OF THE NORTHERN LIGHTS-- GRANDFATHER--HELP ME! GIVE ME STRENGTH!
WITH THAT IMPASSIONED PRAYER, THE FORM OF THIS CHILD OF THE ICE AND SNOW BEGINS TO MELT AND FLOW LIKE MERCURY...
...TRANSFORMING A BEING WHO APPEARS HUMAN (BUT WHO, IN TRUTH, IS NOT)...
... FROM AN EXOTICALLY BEAUTIFUL YOUNG WOMAN INTO A WHITE WOLVERINE.

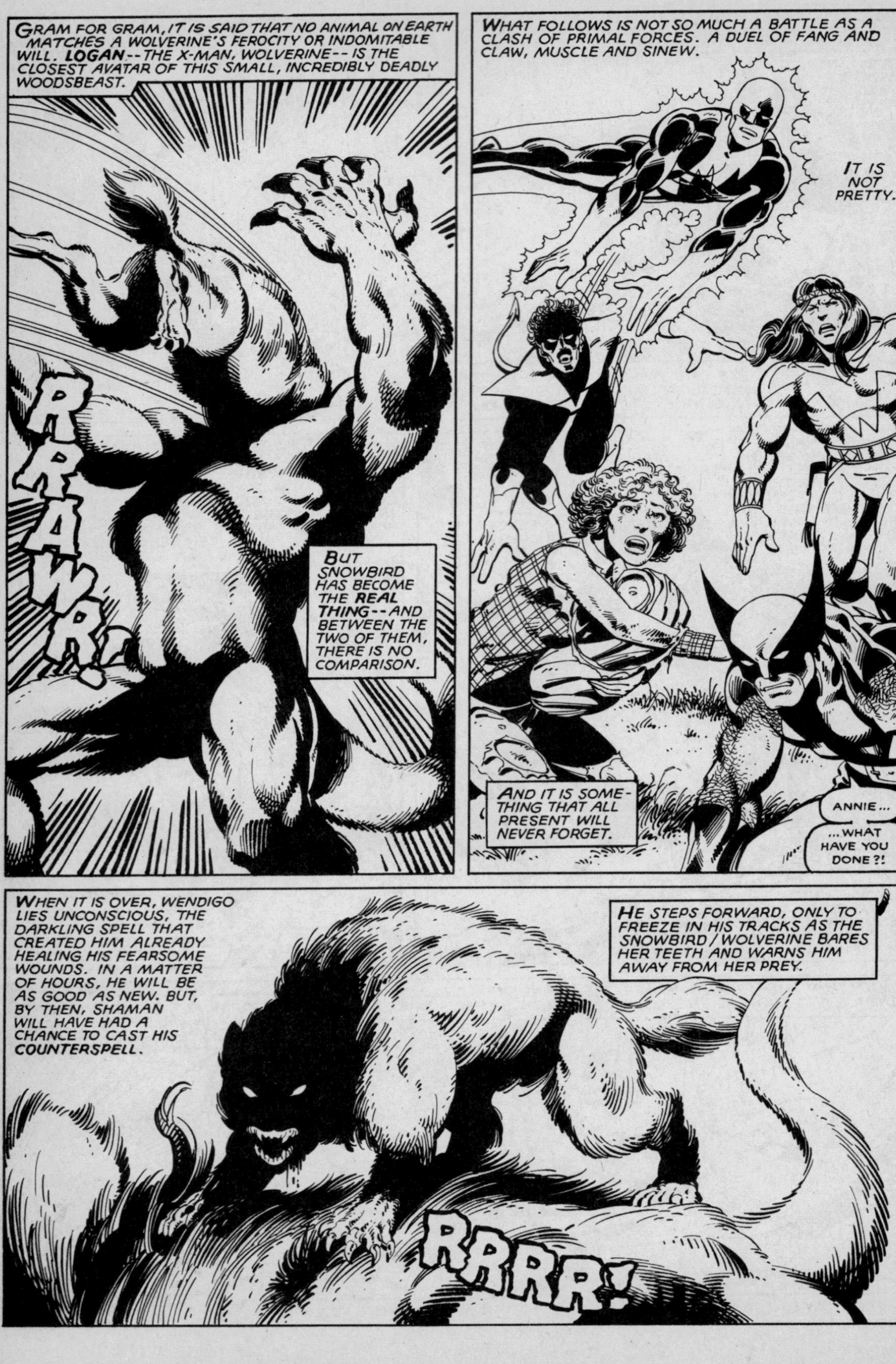
GRAM FOR GRAM, IT IS SAID THAT NO ANIMAL ON EARTH MATCHES A WOLVERINE'S FEROCITY OR INDOMITABLE WILL. LOGAN--THE X-MAN, WOLVERINE--IS THE CLOSEST AVATAR OF THIS SMALL, INCREDIBLY DEADLY WOODSBEAST.
RRAWR!
BUT SNOWBIRD HAS BECOME THE REAL THING--AND BETWEEN THE TWO OF THEM, THERE IS NO COMPARISON.
WHAT FOLLOWS IS NOT SO MUCH A BATTLE AS A CLASH OF PRIMAL FORCES. A DUEL OF FANG AND CLAW, MUSCLE AND SINEW.
IT IS NOT PRETTY.
AND IT IS SOMETHING THAT ALL PRESENT WILL NEVER FORGET.
ANNIE...
...WHAT HAVE YOU DONE?!
WHEN IT IS OVER, WENDIGO LIES UNCONSCIOUS, THE DARKLING SPELL THAT CREATED HIM ALREADY HEALING HIS FEARSOME WOUNDS. IN A MATTER OF HOURS, HE WILL BE AS GOOD AS NEW. BUT, BY THEN, SHAMAN WILL HAVE HAD A CHANCE TO CAST HIS COUNTERSPELL.
HE STEPS FORWARD, ONLY TO FREEZE IN HIS TRACKS AS THE SNOWBIRD/WOLVERINE BARES HER TEETH AND WARNS HIM AWAY FROM HER PREY.
RRRRR!

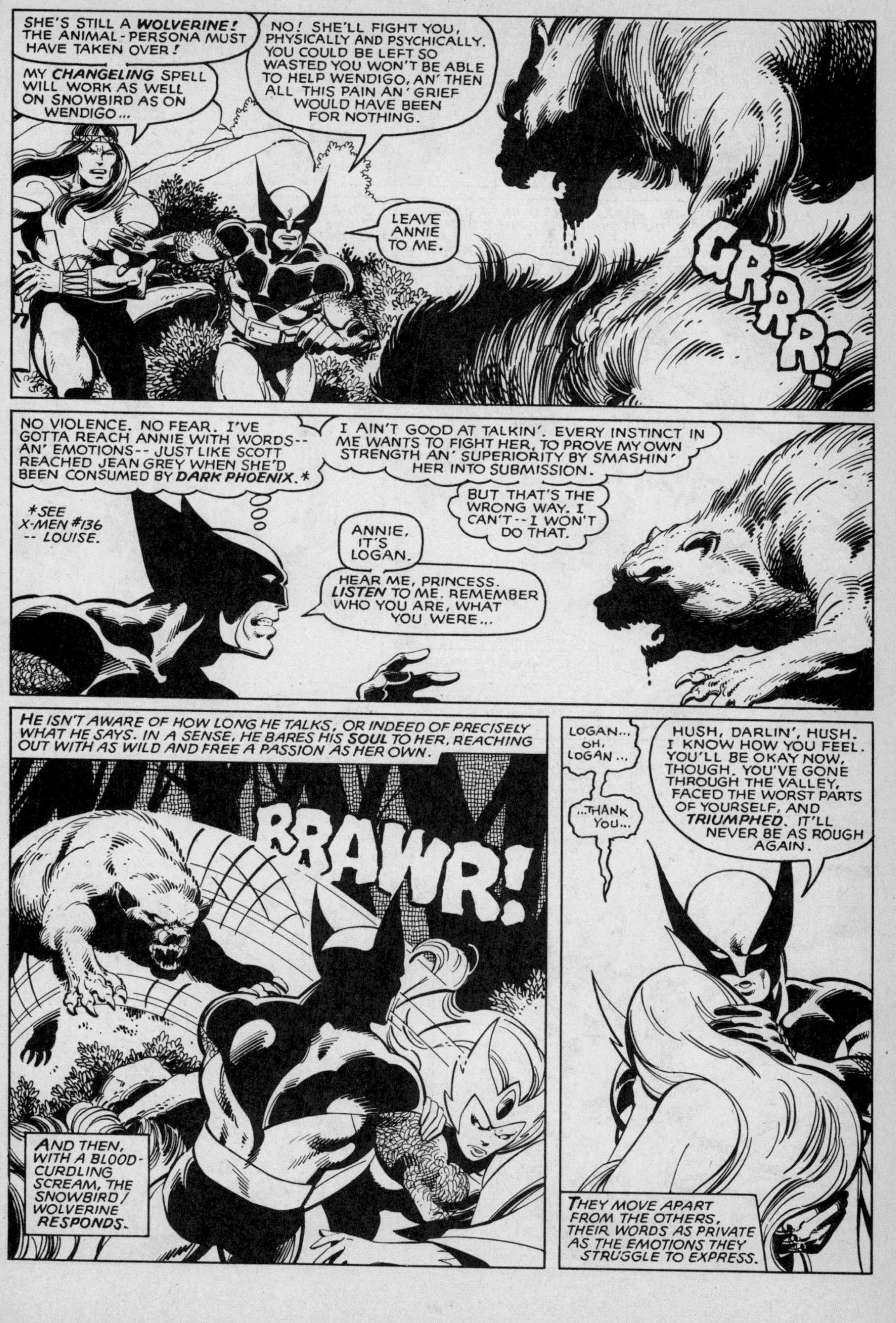
SHE'S STILL A WOLVERINE! THE ANIMAL-PERSONA MUST HAVE TAKEN OVER!
MY CHANGELING SPELL WILL WORK AS WELL ON SNOWBIRD AS ON WENDIGO...
NO! SHE'LL FIGHT YOU, PHYSICALLY AND PSYCHICALLY. YOU COULD BE LEFT SO WASTED YOU WON'T BE ABLE TO HELP WENDIGO, AN' THEN ALL THIS PAIN AN' GRIEF WOULD HAVE BEEN FOR NOTHING.
LEAVE ANNIE TO ME.
GRRR!
NO VIOLENCE. NO FEAR. I'VE GOTTA REACH ANNIE WITH WORDS-- AN' EMOTIONS-- JUST LIKE SCOTT REACHED JEAN GREY WHEN SHE'D BEEN CONSUMED BY DARK PHOENIX.*
I AIN'T GOOD AT TALKIN'. EVERY INSTINCT IN ME WANTS TO FIGHT HER, TO PROVE MY OWN STRENGTH AN' SUPERIORITY BY SMASHIN' HER INTO SUBMISSION.
*SEE X-MEN #136 -- LOUISE.
BUT THAT'S THE WRONG WAY. I CAN'T -- I WON'T DO THAT.
ANNIE, IT'S LOGAN.
HEAR ME, PRINCESS. LISTEN TO ME. REMEMBER WHO YOU ARE, WHAT YOU WERE...
HE ISN'T AWARE OF HOW LONG HE TALKS, OR INDEED OF PRECISELY WHAT HE SAYS. IN A SENSE, HE BARES HIS SOUL TO HER, REACHING OUT WITH AS WILD AND FREE A PASSION AS HER OWN.
BRAWR!
AND THEN, WITH A BLOOD-CURDLING SCREAM, THE SNOWBIRD/ WOLVERINE RESPONDS.
LOGAN... OH, LOGAN...
...THANK YOU...
HUSH, DARLIN', HUSH. I KNOW HOW YOU FEEL. YOU'LL BE OKAY NOW, THOUGH. YOU'VE GONE THROUGH THE VALLEY, FACED THE WORST PARTS OF YOURSELF, AND TRIUMPHED. IT'LL NEVER BE AS ROUGH AGAIN.
THEY MOVE APART FROM THE OTHERS, THEIR WORDS AS PRIVATE AS THE EMOTIONS THEY STRUGGLE TO EXPRESS.

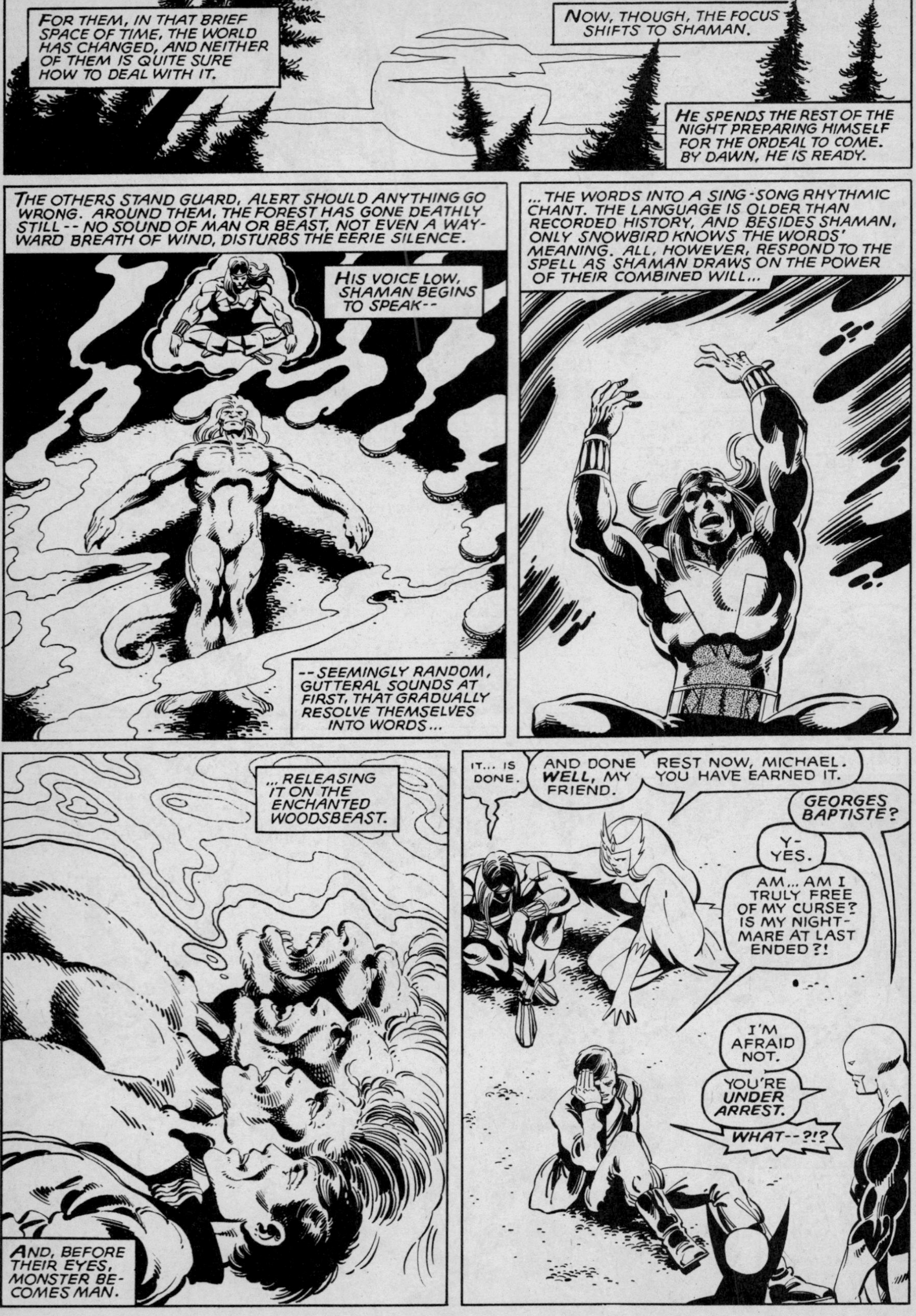
FOR THEM, IN THAT BRIEF SPACE OF TIME, THE WORLD HAS CHANGED, AND NEITHER OF THEM IS QUITE SURE HOW TO DEAL WITH IT.
NOW, THOUGH, THE FOCUS SHIFTS TO SHAMAN.
HE SPENDS THE REST OF THE NIGHT PREPARING HIMSELF FOR THE ORDEAL TO COME. BY DAWN, HE IS READY.
THE OTHERS STAND GUARD, ALERT SHOULD ANYTHING GO WRONG. AROUND THEM, THE FOREST HAS GONE DEATHLY STILL -- NO SOUND OF MAN OR BEAST, NOT EVEN A WAYWARD BREATH OF WIND, DISTURBS THE EERIE SILENCE.
HIS VOICE LOW, SHAMAN BEGINS TO SPEAK--
--SEEMINGLY RANDOM, GUTTERAL SOUNDS AT FIRST, THAT GRADUALLY RESOLVE THEMSELVES INTO WORDS...
...THE WORDS INTO A SING-SONG RHYTHMIC CHANT. THE LANGUAGE IS OLDER THAN RECORDED HISTORY, AND BESIDES SHAMAN, ONLY SNOWBIRD KNOWS THE WORDS' MEANING. ALL, HOWEVER, RESPOND TO THE SPELL AS SHAMAN DRAWS ON THE POWER OF THEIR COMBINED WILL...
...RELEASING IT ON THE ENCHANTED WOODSBEAST.
AND, BEFORE THEIR EYES, MONSTER BECOMES MAN.
IT... IS DONE.
AND DONE WELL, MY FRIEND.
REST NOW, MICHAEL. YOU HAVE EARNED IT.
GEORGES BAPTISTE?
Y-YES.
AM... AM I TRULY FREE OF MY CURSE? IS MY NIGHTMARE AT LAST ENDED?!
I'M AFRAID NOT.
YOU'RE UNDER ARREST.
WHAT--?!?

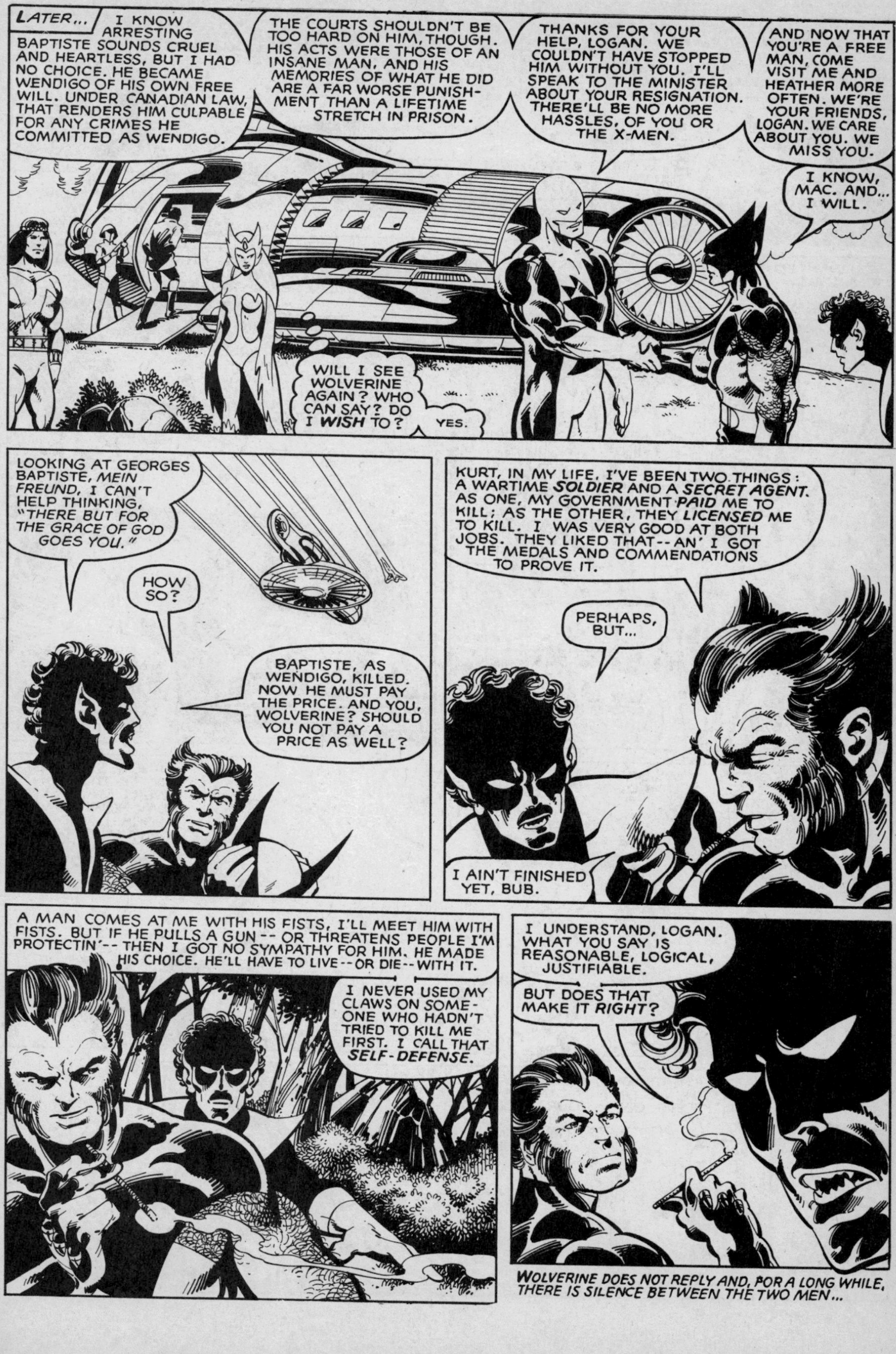
LATER...
I KNOW ARRESTING BAPTISTE SOUNDS CRUEL AND HEARTLESS, BUT I HAD NO CHOICE. HE BECAME WENDIGO OF HIS OWN FREE WILL. UNDER CANADIAN LAW, THAT RENDERS HIM CULPABLE FOR ANY CRIMES HE COMMITTED AS WENDIGO.
THE COURTS SHOULDN'T BE TOO HARD ON HIM, THOUGH. HIS ACTS WERE THOSE OF AN INSANE MAN, AND HIS MEMORIES OF WHAT HE DID ARE A FAR WORSE PUNISHMENT THAN A LIFETIME STRETCH IN PRISON.
THANKS FOR YOUR HELP, LOGAN. WE COULDN'T HAVE STOPPED HIM WITHOUT YOU. I'LL SPEAK TO THE MINISTER ABOUT YOUR RESIGNATION. THERE'LL BE NO MORE HASSLES, OF YOU OR THE X-MEN.
AND NOW THAT YOU'RE A FREE MAN, COME VISIT ME AND HEATHER MORE OFTEN. WE'RE YOUR FRIENDS, LOGAN. WE CARE ABOUT YOU. WE MISS YOU.
I KNOW, MAC. AND... I WILL.
WILL I SEE WOLVERINE AGAIN? WHO CAN SAY? DO I WISH TO?
YES.
LOOKING AT GEORGES BAPTISTE, MEIN FREUND, I CAN'T HELP THINKING, "THERE BUT FOR THE GRACE OF GOD GOES YOU."
HOW SO?
BAPTISTE, AS WENDIGO, KILLED. NOW HE MUST PAY THE PRICE. AND YOU, WOLVERINE? SHOULD YOU NOT PAY A PRICE AS WELL?
KURT, IN MY LIFE, I'VE BEEN TWO THINGS: A WARTIME SOLDIER AND A SECRET AGENT. AS ONE, MY GOVERNMENT PAID ME TO KILL; AS THE OTHER, THEY LICENSED ME TO KILL. I WAS VERY GOOD AT BOTH JOBS. THEY LIKED THAT-- AN' I GOT THE MEDALS AND COMMENDATIONS TO PROVE IT.
PERHAPS, BUT...
I AIN'T FINISHED YET, BUB.
A MAN COMES AT ME WITH HIS FISTS, I'LL MEET HIM WITH FISTS. BUT IF HE PULLS A GUN -- OR THREATENS PEOPLE I'M PROTECTIN'-- THEN I GOT NO SYMPATHY FOR HIM. HE MADE HIS CHOICE. HE'LL HAVE TO LIVE--OR DIE--WITH IT.
I NEVER USED MY CLAWS ON SOMEONE WHO HADN'T TRIED TO KILL ME FIRST. I CALL THAT SELF-DEFENSE.
I UNDERSTAND, LOGAN. WHAT YOU SAY IS REASONABLE, LOGICAL, JUSTIFIABLE.
BUT DOES THAT MAKE IT RIGHT?
WOLVERINE DOES NOT REPLY AND, FOR A LONG WHILE, THERE IS SILENCE BETWEEN THE TWO MEN...

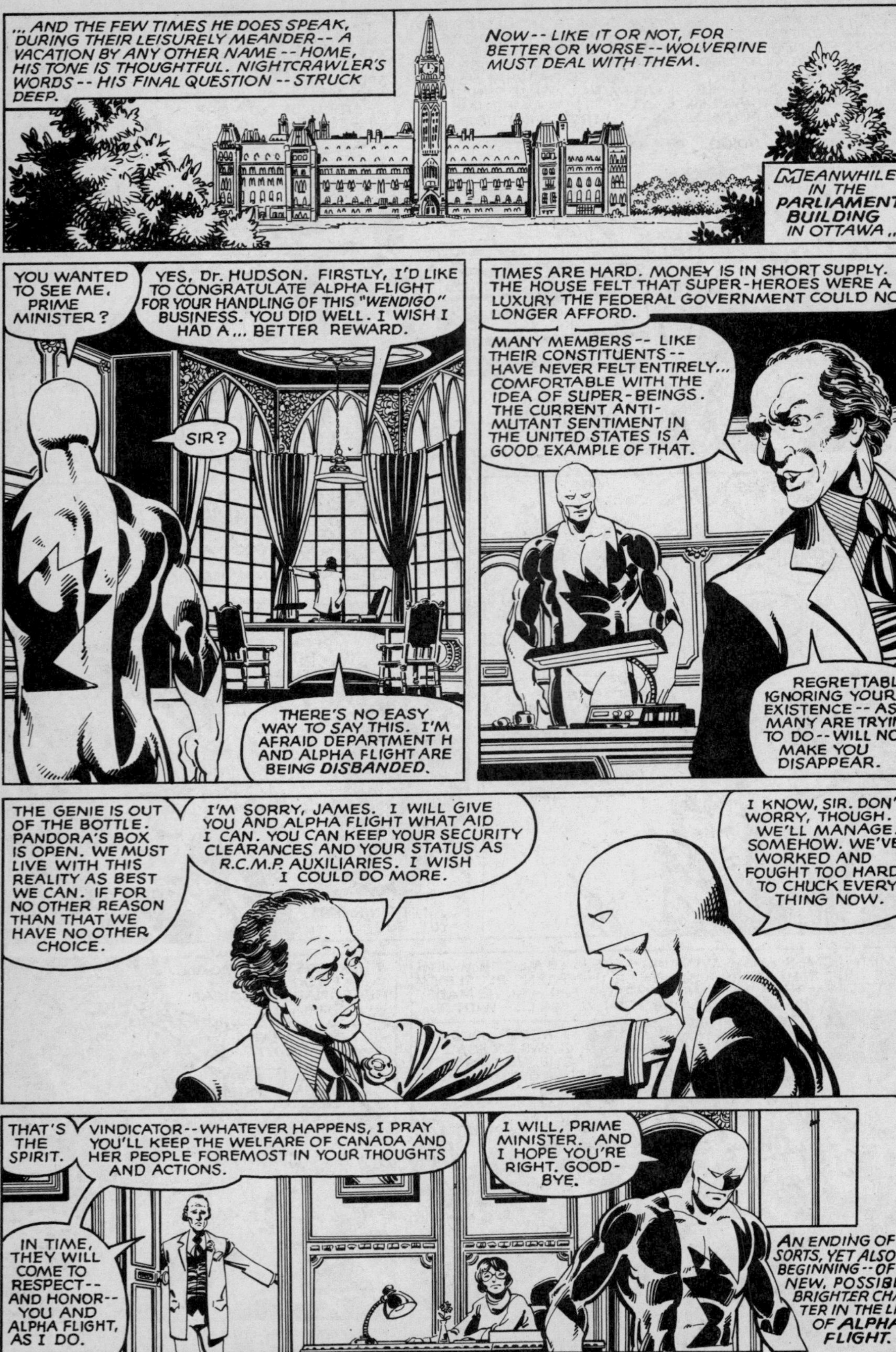
...AND THE FEW TIMES HE DOES SPEAK, DURING THEIR LEISURELY MEANDER -- A VACATION BY ANY OTHER NAME -- HOME, HIS TONE IS THOUGHTFUL. NIGHTCRAWLER'S WORDS -- HIS FINAL QUESTION -- STRUCK DEEP.
NOW -- LIKE IT OR NOT, FOR BETTER OR WORSE -- WOLVERINE MUST DEAL WITH THEM.
MEANWHILE, IN THE PARLIAMENT BUILDING IN OTTAWA...
YOU WANTED TO SEE ME, PRIME MINISTER?
YES, Dr. HUDSON. FIRSTLY, I'D LIKE TO CONGRATULATE ALPHA FLIGHT FOR YOUR HANDLING OF THIS "WENDIGO" BUSINESS. YOU DID WELL. I WISH I HAD A... BETTER REWARD.
SIR?
THERE'S NO EASY WAY TO SAY THIS. I'M AFRAID DEPARTMENT H AND ALPHA FLIGHT ARE BEING DISBANDED.
TIMES ARE HARD. MONEY IS IN SHORT SUPPLY. THE HOUSE FELT THAT SUPER-HEROES WERE A LUXURY THE FEDERAL GOVERNMENT COULD NO LONGER AFFORD.
MANY MEMBERS -- LIKE THEIR CONSTITUENTS -- HAVE NEVER FELT ENTIRELY... COMFORTABLE WITH THE IDEA OF SUPER-BEINGS. THE CURRENT ANTI-MUTANT SENTIMENT IN THE UNITED STATES IS A GOOD EXAMPLE OF THAT.
REGRETTABLY, IGNORING YOUR EXISTENCE -- AS MANY ARE TRYING TO DO -- WILL NOT MAKE YOU DISAPPEAR.
THE GENIE IS OUT OF THE BOTTLE. PANDORA'S BOX IS OPEN. WE MUST LIVE WITH THIS REALITY AS BEST WE CAN. IF FOR NO OTHER REASON THAN THAT WE HAVE NO OTHER CHOICE.
I'M SORRY, JAMES. I WILL GIVE YOU AND ALPHA FLIGHT WHAT AID I CAN. YOU CAN KEEP YOUR SECURITY CLEARANCES AND YOUR STATUS AS R.C.M.P. AUXILIARIES. I WISH I COULD DO MORE.
I KNOW, SIR. DON'T WORRY, THOUGH. WE'LL MANAGE. SOMEHOW. WE'VE WORKED AND FOUGHT TOO HARD TO CHUCK EVERYTHING NOW.
THAT'S THE SPIRIT.
VINDICATOR -- WHATEVER HAPPENS, I PRAY YOU'LL KEEP THE WELFARE OF CANADA AND HER PEOPLE FOREMOST IN YOUR THOUGHTS AND ACTIONS.
IN TIME, THEY WILL COME TO RESPECT -- AND HONOR -- YOU AND ALPHA FLIGHT, AS I DO.
I WILL, PRIME MINISTER. AND I HOPE YOU'RE RIGHT. GOOD-BYE.
AN ENDING OF SORTS, YET ALSO A BEGINNING -- OF A NEW, POSSIBLY BRIGHTER CHAPTER IN THE LIFE OF ALPHA FLIGHT.

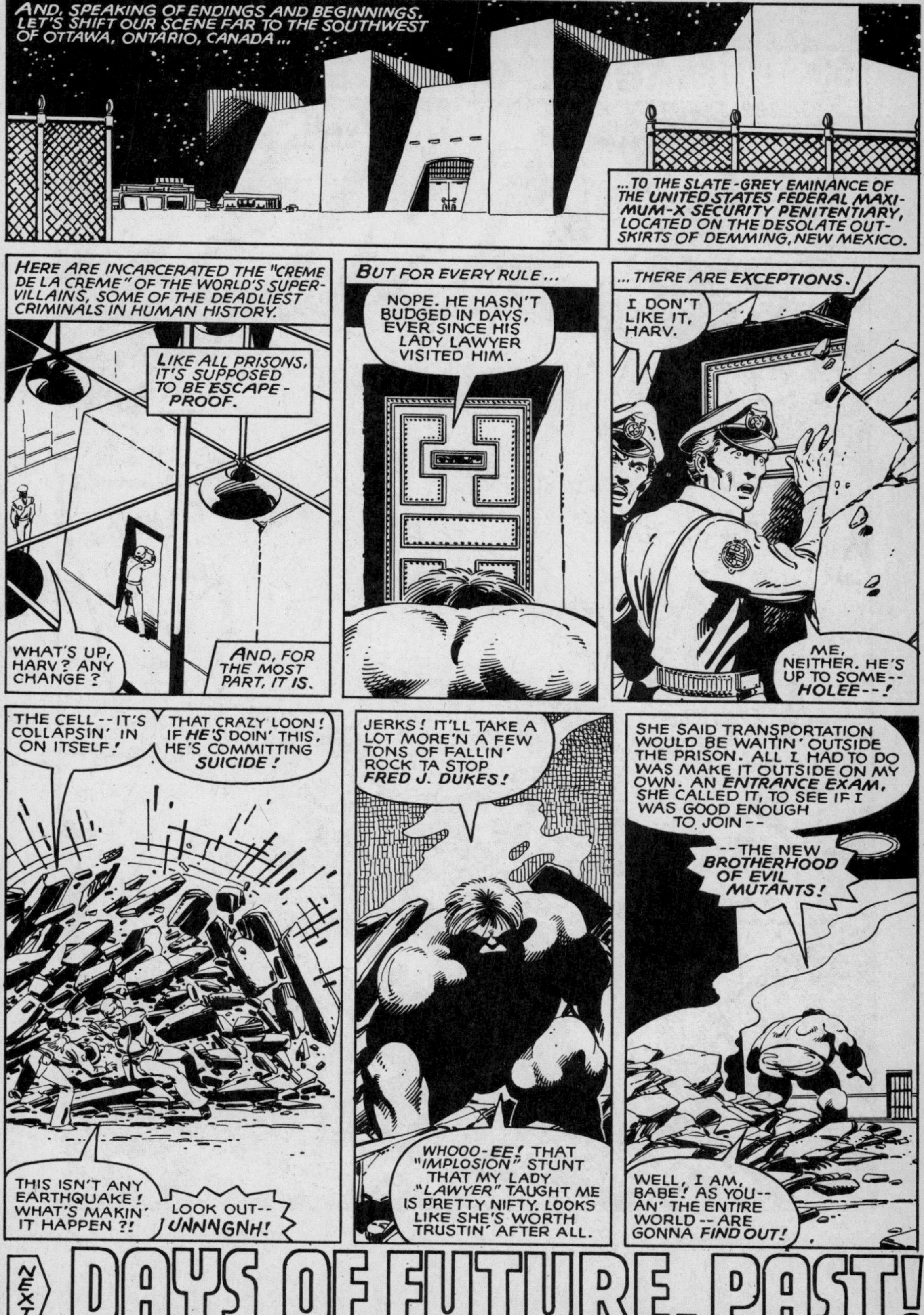
AND, SPEAKING OF ENDINGS AND BEGINNINGS, LET'S SHIFT OUR SCENE FAR TO THE SOUTHWEST OF OTTAWA, ONTARIO, CANADA...
...TO THE SLATE-GREY EMINANCE OF THE UNITED STATES FEDERAL MAXIMUM-X SECURITY PENITENTIARY, LOCATED ON THE DESOLATE OUTSKIRTS OF DEMMING, NEW MEXICO.
HERE ARE INCARCERATED THE "CREME DE LA CREME" OF THE WORLD'S SUPER-VILLAINS, SOME OF THE DEADLIEST CRIMINALS IN HUMAN HISTORY.
LIKE ALL PRISONS, IT'S SUPPOSED TO BE ESCAPE-PROOF.
WHAT'S UP, HARV? ANY CHANGE?
AND, FOR THE MOST PART, IT IS.
BUT FOR EVERY RULE...
NOPE. HE HASN'T BUDGED IN DAYS, EVER SINCE HIS LADY LAWYER VISITED HIM.
...THERE ARE EXCEPTIONS.
I DON'T LIKE IT, HARV.
ME, NEITHER. HE'S UP TO SOME-- HOLEE--!
THE CELL--IT'S COLLAPSIN' IN ON ITSELF!
THAT CRAZY LOON! IF HE'S DOIN' THIS, HE'S COMMITTING SUICIDE!
THIS ISN'T ANY EARTHQUAKE! WHAT'S MAKIN' IT HAPPEN ?!
LOOK OUT-- UNNNGNH!
JERKS! IT'LL TAKE A LOT MORE'N A FEW TONS OF FALLIN' ROCK TA STOP FRED J. DUKES!
WHOOO-EE! THAT "IMPLOSION" STUNT THAT MY LADY "LAWYER" TAUGHT ME IS PRETTY NIFTY. LOOKS LIKE SHE'S WORTH TRUSTIN' AFTER ALL.
SHE SAID TRANSPORTATION WOULD BE WAITIN' OUTSIDE THE PRISON. ALL I HAD TO DO WAS MAKE IT OUTSIDE ON MY OWN. AN ENTRANCE EXAM, SHE CALLED IT, TO SEE IF I WAS GOOD ENOUGH TO JOIN--
--THE NEW BROTHERHOOD OF EVIL MUTANTS!
WELL, I AM, BABE! AS YOU-- AN' THE ENTIRE WORLD--ARE GONNA FIND OUT!

NEXT DAYS OF FUTURE, PAST!

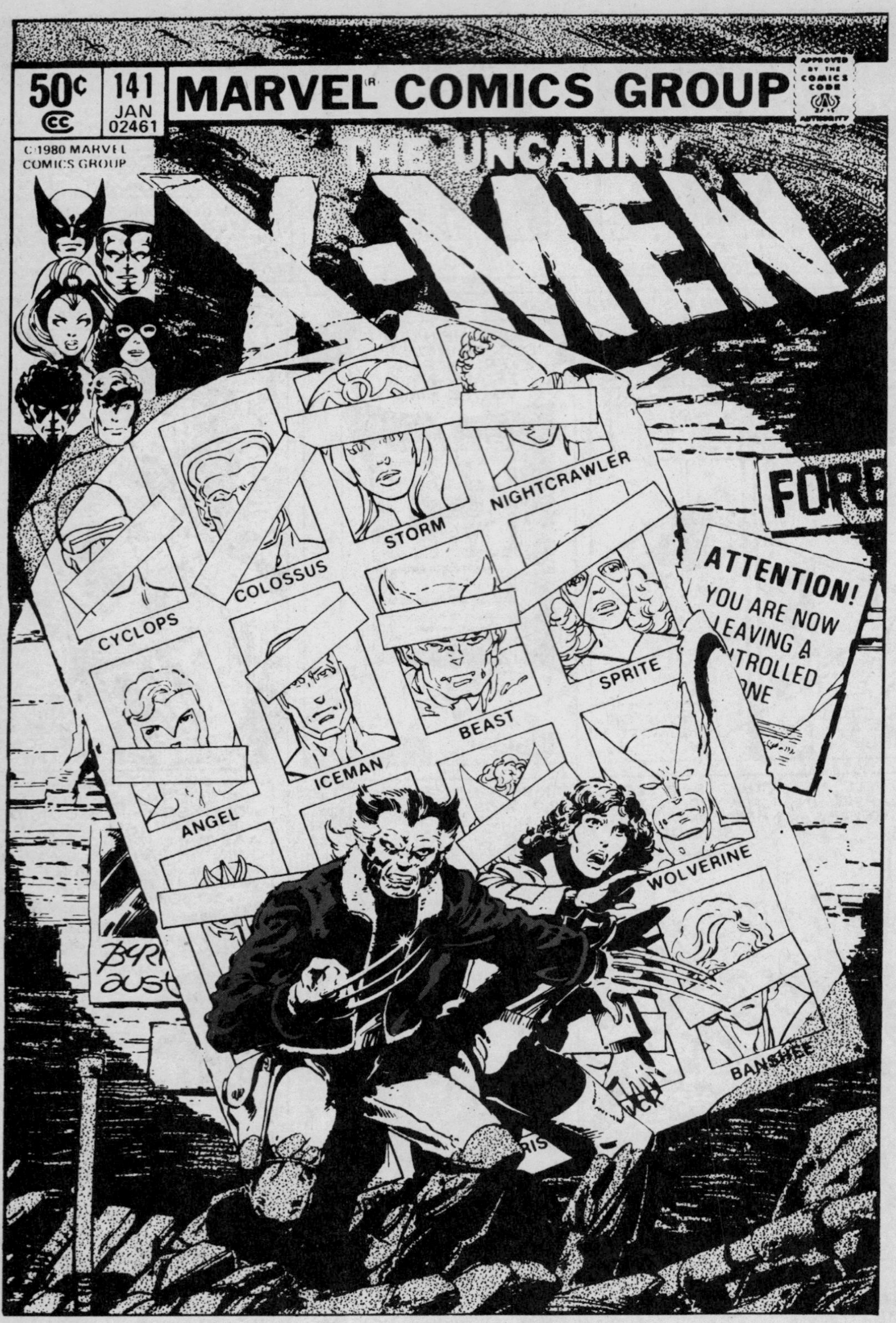
50¢
141
JAN
02461
MARVEL COMICS GROUP
APPROVED BY THE COMICS CODE AUTHORITY
©1980 MARVEL COMICS GROUP
THE UNCANNY
X-MEN
CYCLOPS
COLOSSUS
STORM
NIGHTCRAWLER
SPRITE
BEAST
ICEMAN
ANGEL
WOLVERINE
BANSHEE
ATTENTION!
YOU ARE NOW
LEAVING A

STAN LEE PRESENTS: **THE UNCANNY X-MEN!**

CHRIS CLAREMONT · JOHN BYRNE | TERRY AUSTIN | TOM ORZECHOWSKI, letterer | LOUISE JONES | JIM SHOOTER
WRITER · CO-PLOTTERS · ARTIST | INKER | GLYNIS WEIN, colorist | EDITOR | Ed.-IN-CHIEF

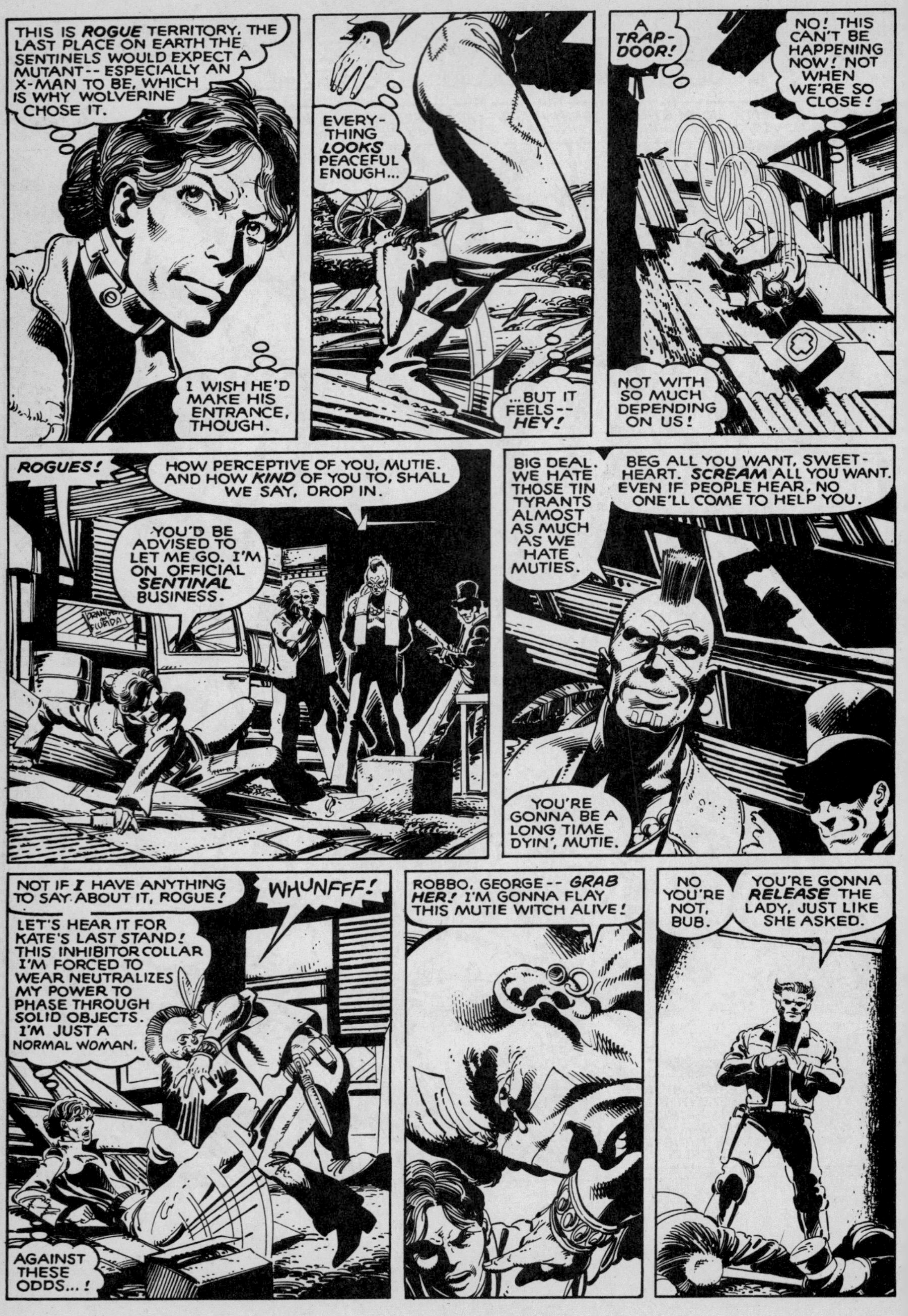
THIS IS ROGUE TERRITORY, THE LAST PLACE ON EARTH THE SENTINELS WOULD EXPECT A MUTANT-- ESPECIALLY AN X-MAN TO BE, WHICH IS WHY WOLVERINE CHOSE IT.
I WISH HE'D MAKE HIS ENTRANCE, THOUGH.
EVERY-THING LOOKS PEACEFUL ENOUGH...
...BUT IT FEELS-- HEY!
A TRAP-DOOR!
NO! THIS CAN'T BE HAPPENING NOW! NOT WHEN WE'RE SO CLOSE!
NOT WITH SO MUCH DEPENDING ON US!
ROGUES!
HOW PERCEPTIVE OF YOU, MUTIE. AND HOW KIND OF YOU TO, SHALL WE SAY, DROP IN.
YOU'D BE ADVISED TO LET ME GO. I'M ON OFFICIAL SENTINAL BUSINESS.
BIG DEAL. WE HATE THOSE TIN TYRANTS ALMOST AS MUCH AS WE HATE MUTIES.
BEG ALL YOU WANT, SWEET-HEART. SCREAM ALL YOU WANT. EVEN IF PEOPLE HEAR, NO ONE'LL COME TO HELP YOU.
YOU'RE GONNA BE A LONG TIME DYIN', MUTIE.
NOT IF I HAVE ANYTHING TO SAY ABOUT IT, ROGUE!
LET'S HEAR IT FOR KATE'S LAST STAND! THIS INHIBITOR COLLAR I'M FORCED TO WEAR NEUTRALIZES MY POWER TO PHASE THROUGH SOLID OBJECTS. I'M JUST A NORMAL WOMAN.
WHUNFFF!
AGAINST THESE ODDS...!
ROBBO, GEORGE-- GRAB HER! I'M GONNA FLAY THIS MUTIE WITCH ALIVE!
NO YOU'RE NOT, BUB.
YOU'RE GONNA RELEASE THE LADY, JUST LIKE SHE ASKED.

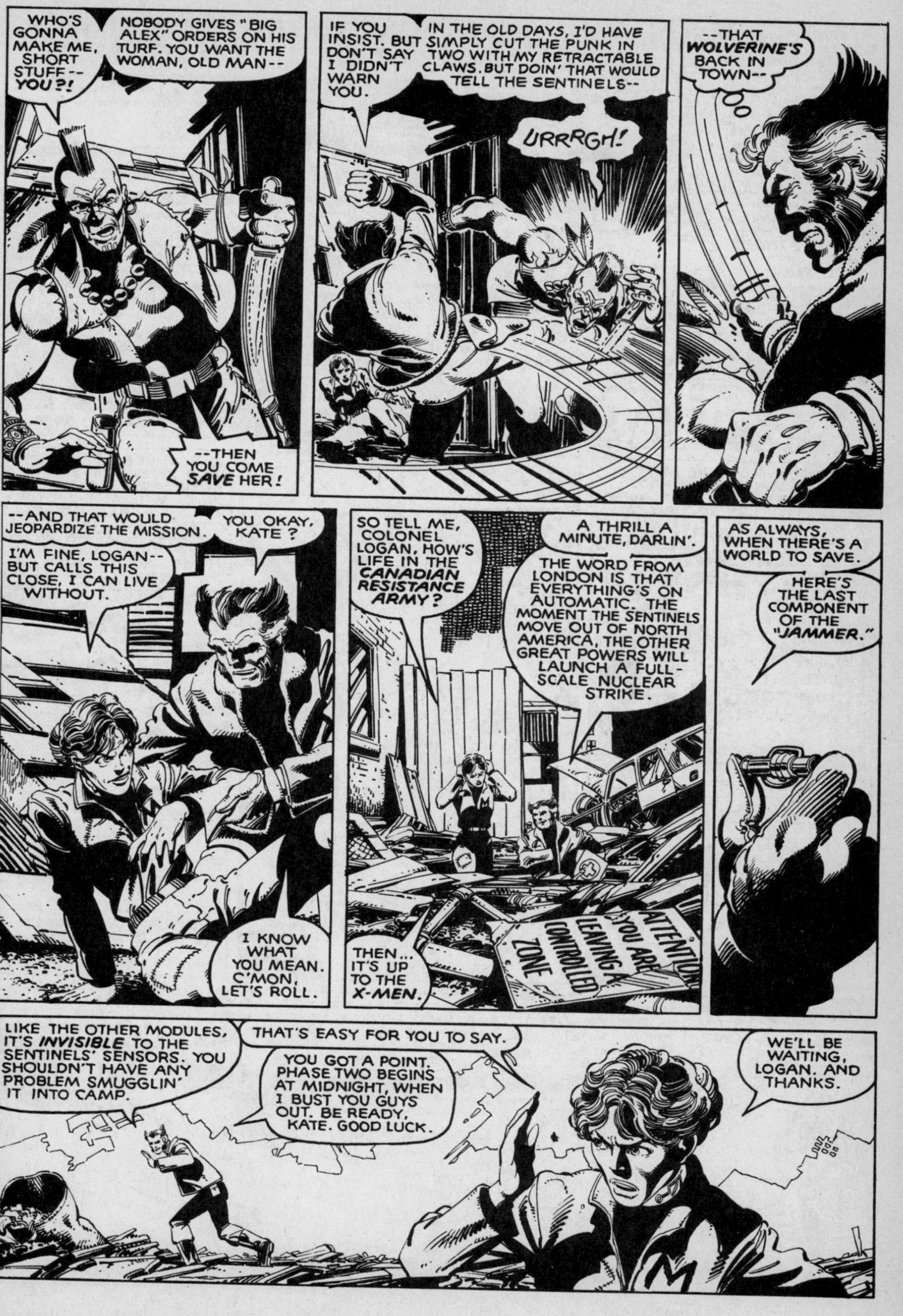
WHO'S GONNA MAKE ME, SHORT STUFF-- YOU?!
NOBODY GIVES "BIG ALEX" ORDERS ON HIS TURF. YOU WANT THE WOMAN, OLD MAN--
--THEN YOU COME SAVE HER!
IF YOU INSIST. BUT DON'T SAY I DIDN'T WARN YOU.
IN THE OLD DAYS, I'D HAVE SIMPLY CUT THE PUNK IN TWO WITH MY RETRACTABLE CLAWS. BUT DOIN' THAT WOULD TELL THE SENTINELS--
URRRGH!
--THAT WOLVERINE'S BACK IN TOWN--
--AND THAT WOULD JEOPARDIZE THE MISSION.
YOU OKAY, KATE?
I'M FINE, LOGAN-- BUT CALLS THIS CLOSE, I CAN LIVE WITHOUT.
I KNOW WHAT YOU MEAN. C'MON, LET'S ROLL.
SO TELL ME, COLONEL LOGAN, HOW'S LIFE IN THE CANADIAN RESISTANCE ARMY?
A THRILL A MINUTE, DARLIN'.
THE WORD FROM LONDON IS THAT EVERYTHING'S ON AUTOMATIC. THE MOMENT THE SENTINELS MOVE OUT OF NORTH AMERICA, THE OTHER GREAT POWERS WILL LAUNCH A FULL-SCALE NUCLEAR STRIKE.
THEN... IT'S UP TO THE X-MEN.
ATTENTIO YOU ARE LEAVING A CONTROLLED ZONE
AS ALWAYS, WHEN THERE'S A WORLD TO SAVE.
HERE'S THE LAST COMPONENT OF THE "JAMMER."
LIKE THE OTHER MODULES, IT'S INVISIBLE TO THE SENTINELS' SENSORS. YOU SHOULDN'T HAVE ANY PROBLEM SMUGGLIN' IT INTO CAMP.
THAT'S EASY FOR YOU TO SAY.
YOU GOT A POINT. PHASE TWO BEGINS AT MIDNIGHT, WHEN I BUST YOU GUYS OUT. BE READY, KATE. GOOD LUCK.
WE'LL BE WAITING, LOGAN. AND THANKS.

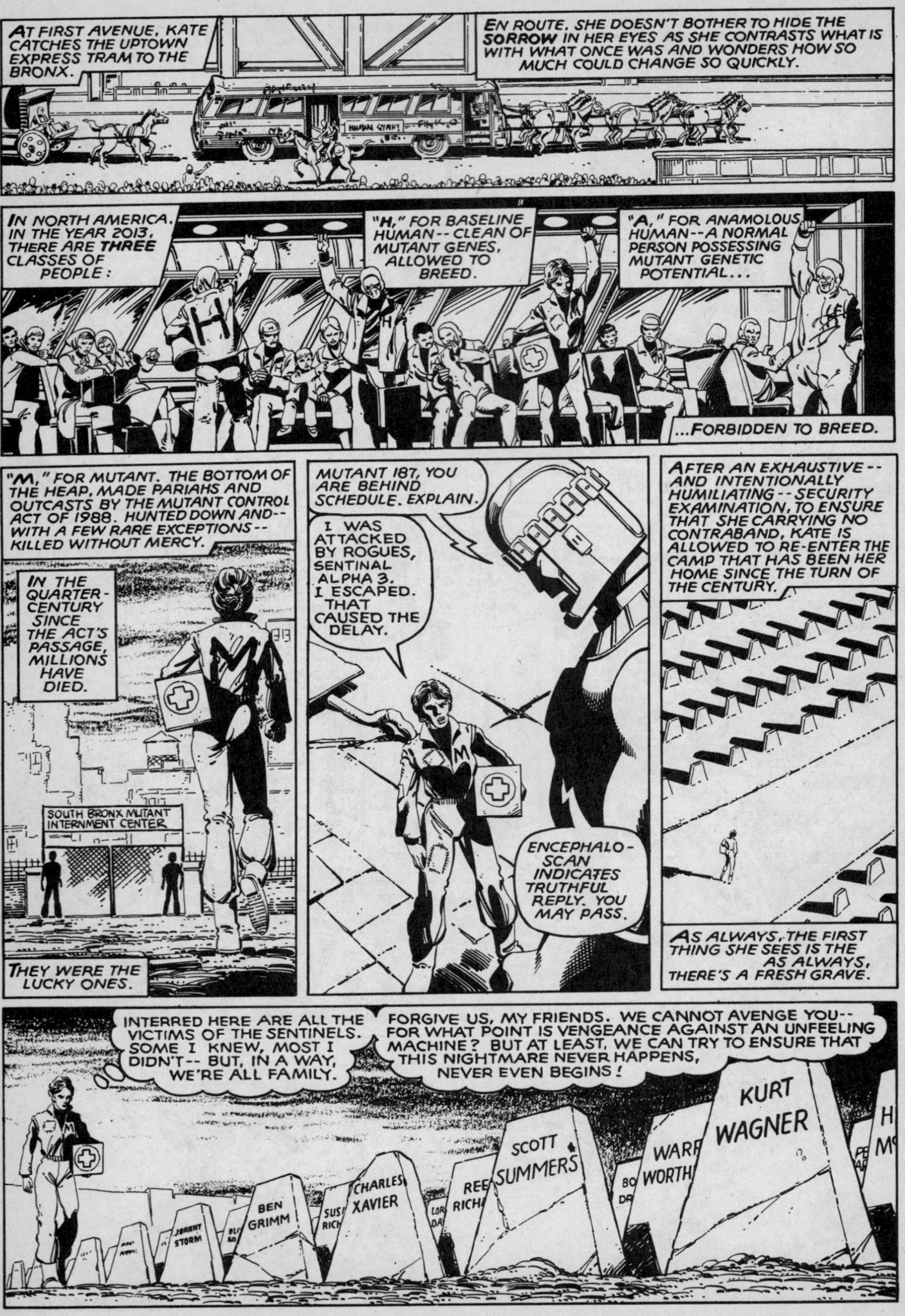

AT FIRST AVENUE, KATE CATCHES THE UPTOWN EXPRESS TRAM TO THE BRONX.
EN ROUTE, SHE DOESN'T BOTHER TO HIDE THE SORROW IN HER EYES AS SHE CONTRASTS WHAT IS WITH WHAT ONCE WAS AND WONDERS HOW SO MUCH COULD CHANGE SO QUICKLY.
IN NORTH AMERICA, IN THE YEAR 2013, THERE ARE THREE CLASSES OF PEOPLE:
"H," FOR BASELINE HUMAN--CLEAN OF MUTANT GENES, ALLOWED TO BREED.
"A," FOR ANAMOLOUS HUMAN--A NORMAL PERSON POSSESSING MUTANT GENETIC POTENTIAL...
...FORBIDDEN TO BREED.
"M," FOR MUTANT. THE BOTTOM OF THE HEAP, MADE PARIAHS AND OUTCASTS BY THE MUTANT CONTROL ACT OF 1988. HUNTED DOWN AND--WITH A FEW RARE EXCEPTIONS--KILLED WITHOUT MERCY.
IN THE QUARTER-CENTURY SINCE THE ACT'S PASSAGE, MILLIONS HAVE DIED.
SOUTH BRONX MUTANT INTERNMENT CENTER
THEY WERE THE LUCKY ONES.
MUTANT 187, YOU ARE BEHIND SCHEDULE. EXPLAIN.
I WAS ATTACKED BY ROGUES, SENTINAL ALPHA 3. I ESCAPED. THAT CAUSED THE DELAY.
ENCEPHALO-SCAN INDICATES TRUTHFUL REPLY. YOU MAY PASS.
AFTER AN EXHAUSTIVE--AND INTENTIONALLY HUMILIATING--SECURITY EXAMINATION, TO ENSURE THAT SHE CARRYING NO CONTRABAND, KATE IS ALLOWED TO RE-ENTER THE CAMP THAT HAS BEEN HER HOME SINCE THE TURN OF THE CENTURY.
AS ALWAYS, THE FIRST THING SHE SEES IS THE AS ALWAYS, THERE'S A FRESH GRAVE.
INTERRED HERE ARE ALL THE VICTIMS OF THE SENTINELS. SOME I KNEW, MOST I DIDN'T--BUT, IN A WAY, WE'RE ALL FAMILY.
FORGIVE US, MY FRIENDS. WE CANNOT AVENGE YOU--FOR WHAT POINT IS VENGEANCE AGAINST AN UNFEELING MACHINE? BUT AT LEAST, WE CAN TRY TO ENSURE THAT THIS NIGHTMARE NEVER HAPPENS, NEVER EVEN BEGINS!
KURT WAGNER
SCOTT SUMMERS
CHARLES XAVIER
BEN GRIMM
JOHNNY STORM

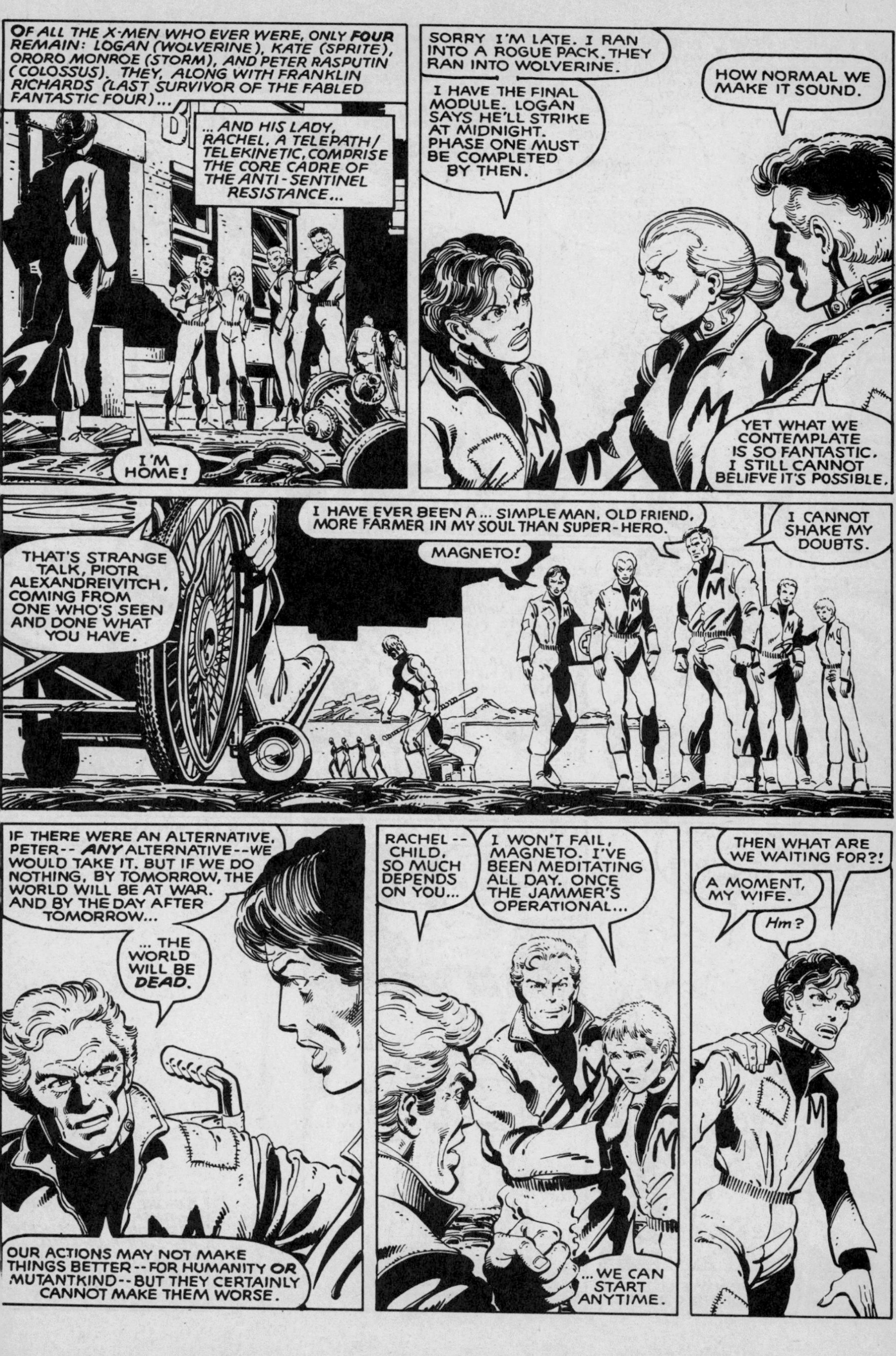

OF ALL THE X-MEN WHO EVER WERE, ONLY FOUR REMAIN: LOGAN (WOLVERINE), KATE (SPRITE), ORORO MONROE (STORM), AND PETER RASPUTIN (COLOSSUS). THEY, ALONG WITH FRANKLIN RICHARDS (LAST SURVIVOR OF THE FABLED FANTASTIC FOUR)...
... AND HIS LADY, RACHEL, A TELEPATH/TELEKINETIC, COMPRISE THE CORE CADRE OF THE ANTI-SENTINEL RESISTANCE...
I'M HOME!
SORRY I'M LATE. I RAN INTO A ROGUE PACK. THEY RAN INTO WOLVERINE.
I HAVE THE FINAL MODULE. LOGAN SAYS HE'LL STRIKE AT MIDNIGHT. PHASE ONE MUST BE COMPLETED BY THEN.
HOW NORMAL WE MAKE IT SOUND.
YET WHAT WE CONTEMPLATE IS SO FANTASTIC. I STILL CANNOT BELIEVE IT'S POSSIBLE.
THAT'S STRANGE TALK, PIOTR ALEXANDREIVITCH, COMING FROM ONE WHO'S SEEN AND DONE WHAT YOU HAVE.
I HAVE EVER BEEN A... SIMPLE MAN, OLD FRIEND, MORE FARMER IN MY SOUL THAN SUPER-HERO.
MAGNETO!
I CANNOT SHAKE MY DOUBTS.
IF THERE WERE AN ALTERNATIVE, PETER-- ANY ALTERNATIVE--WE WOULD TAKE IT. BUT IF WE DO NOTHING, BY TOMORROW, THE WORLD WILL BE AT WAR. AND BY THE DAY AFTER TOMORROW...
... THE WORLD WILL BE DEAD.
OUR ACTIONS MAY NOT MAKE THINGS BETTER--FOR HUMANITY OR MUTANTKIND--BUT THEY CERTAINLY CANNOT MAKE THEM WORSE.
RACHEL-- CHILD, SO MUCH DEPENDS ON YOU...
I WON'T FAIL, MAGNETO. I'VE BEEN MEDITATING ALL DAY. ONCE THE JAMMER'S OPERATIONAL...
...WE CAN START ANYTIME.
THEN WHAT ARE WE WAITING FOR?!
A MOMENT, MY WIFE.
Hm?

AS I SAID, I HAVE DOUBTS. CAN OUR MAD, DESPERATE PLAN WORK? MORE IMPORTANTLY, *SHOULD* IT? WE ARE TOYING WITH THE BASIC FABRIC OF REALITY.

AND IF WE SUCCEED, WHAT WILL HAPPEN TO US, TO OUR LOVE? IT MIGHT CEASE TO EXIST, ALONG WITH THE SENTINELS.

THAT'S A RISK WE HAVE TO TAKE. WHAT DOES THE LOVE OF TWO PEOPLE MATTER AGAINST THE LIVES OF BILLIONS?

I AM SELFISH. IT MATTERS TO ME.

PETER, IF OUR LOVE WAS MEANT TO BE, IT *WILL* BE. ONLY THIS TIME IN A WORLD WHERE OUR CHILDREN CAN GROW UP *FREE* AND *UNAFRAID!*

THE SENTINELS KILLED MY FRIENDS AND THEY KILLED MY...MY BABIES.

IF CHANGING THE PAST HOLDS OUT EVEN THE SLIGHTEST HOPE OF SAVING THEM, I'LL DO IT. WHATEVER THE COST.

I LOVE YOU, KATE.

AND I, YOU, PETER...

...FROM THE MOMENT WE FIRST MET.

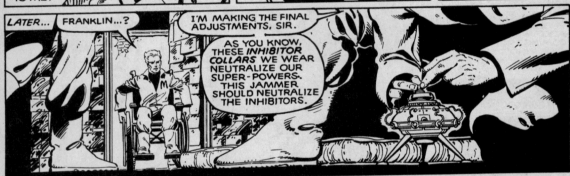

LATER... FRANKLIN...?

I'M MAKING THE FINAL ADJUSTMENTS, SIR.

AS YOU KNOW, THESE *INHIBITOR COLLARS* WE WEAR NEUTRALIZE OUR SUPER-POWERS. THIS JAMMER SHOULD NEUTRALIZE THE INHIBITORS.

INSIDE THIS ROOM, WE'LL BE AS STRONG AS WE EVER WERE, FOR AS LONG AS THE UNIT'S POWER CELLS FUNCTION.

BY THEN, WE'LL BE FREE OF THE COLLARS.

LAY BACK AND RELAX, KATE.

THIS IS CRAZY. I'VE GOT BUTTERFLIES IN MY STOMACH.

HUSH!

SORRY.

BREATHE WITH ME.

"LET YOUR MIND BECOME *ONE* WITH MINE, AND OUR MINDS ONE WITH *ALL*."

BEFORE SHE KNOWS IT, KATHERINE PRYDE-RASPUTIN IS ENTRANCED, HER SOUL FLUNG OUT ACROSS THE ABYSS OF ETERNITY. WHAT HAPPENS NEXT IS ANYBODY'S GUESS.

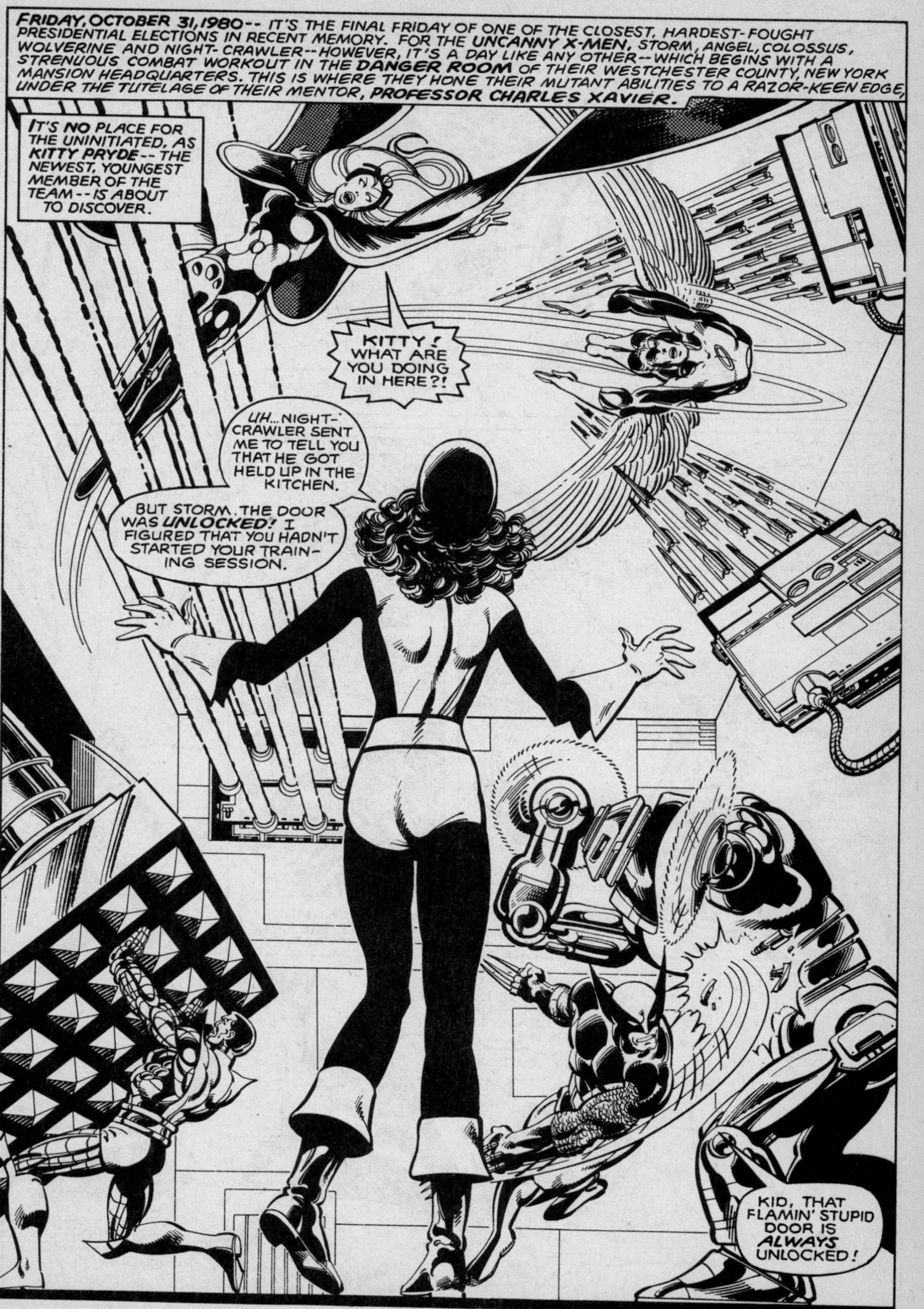
FRIDAY, OCTOBER 31, 1980-- IT'S THE FINAL FRIDAY OF ONE OF THE CLOSEST, HARDEST-FOUGHT PRESIDENTIAL ELECTIONS IN RECENT MEMORY. FOR THE UNCANNY X-MEN, STORM, ANGEL, COLOSSUS, WOLVERINE AND NIGHT-CRAWLER--HOWEVER, IT'S A DAY LIKE ANY OTHER--WHICH BEGINS WITH A STRENUOUS COMBAT WORKOUT IN THE DANGER ROOM OF THEIR WESTCHESTER COUNTY, NEW YORK MANSION HEADQUARTERS. THIS IS WHERE THEY HONE THEIR MUTANT ABILITIES TO A RAZOR-KEEN EDGE, UNDER THE TUTELAGE OF THEIR MENTOR, PROFESSOR CHARLES XAVIER.
IT'S NO PLACE FOR THE UNINITIATED, AS KITTY PRYDE -- THE NEWEST, YOUNGEST MEMBER OF THE TEAM -- IS ABOUT TO DISCOVER.
KITTY! WHAT ARE YOU DOING IN HERE?!
UH... NIGHT-CRAWLER SENT ME TO TELL YOU THAT HE GOT HELD UP IN THE KITCHEN.
BUT STORM, THE DOOR WAS UNLOCKED! I FIGURED THAT YOU HADN'T STARTED YOUR TRAINING SESSION.
KID, THAT FLAMIN' STUPID DOOR IS ALWAYS UNLOCKED!

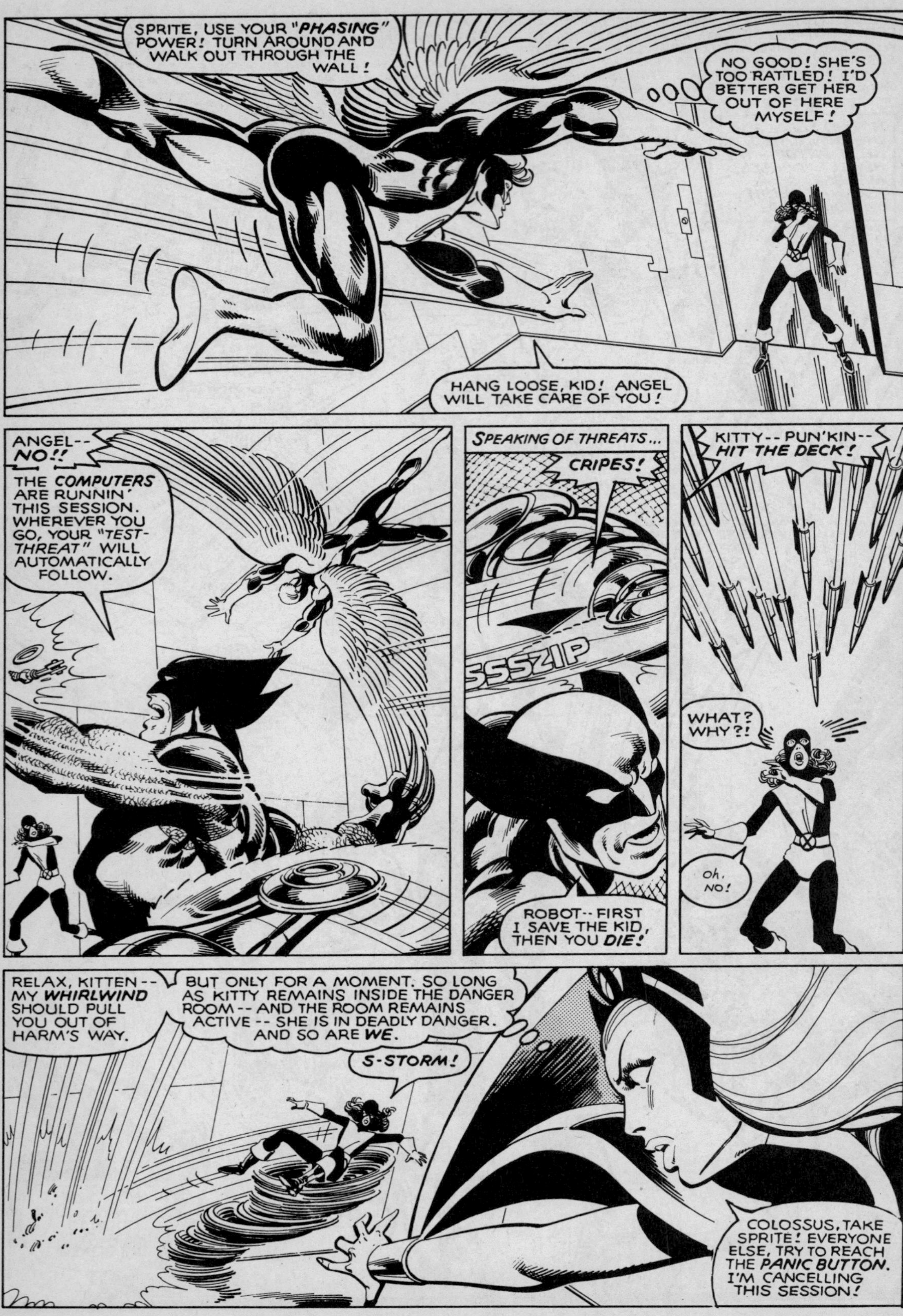

SPRITE, USE YOUR "PHASING" POWER! TURN AROUND AND WALK OUT THROUGH THE WALL!
NO GOOD! SHE'S TOO RATTLED! I'D BETTER GET HER OUT OF HERE MYSELF!
HANG LOOSE, KID! ANGEL WILL TAKE CARE OF YOU!
ANGEL-- NO!!
THE COMPUTERS ARE RUNNIN' THIS SESSION. WHEREVER YOU GO, YOUR "TEST-THREAT" WILL AUTOMATICALLY FOLLOW.
SPEAKING OF THREATS...
CRIPES!
SSSZIP
ROBOT-- FIRST I SAVE THE KID, THEN YOU DIE!
KITTY-- PUN'KIN-- HIT THE DECK!
WHAT? WHY?!
Oh, NO!
RELAX, KITTEN-- MY WHIRLWIND SHOULD PULL YOU OUT OF HARM'S WAY.
BUT ONLY FOR A MOMENT. SO LONG AS KITTY REMAINS INSIDE THE DANGER ROOM -- AND THE ROOM REMAINS ACTIVE -- SHE IS IN DEADLY DANGER. AND SO ARE WE.
S-STORM!
COLOSSUS, TAKE SPRITE! EVERYONE ELSE, TRY TO REACH THE PANIC BUTTON. I'M CANCELLING THIS SESSION!

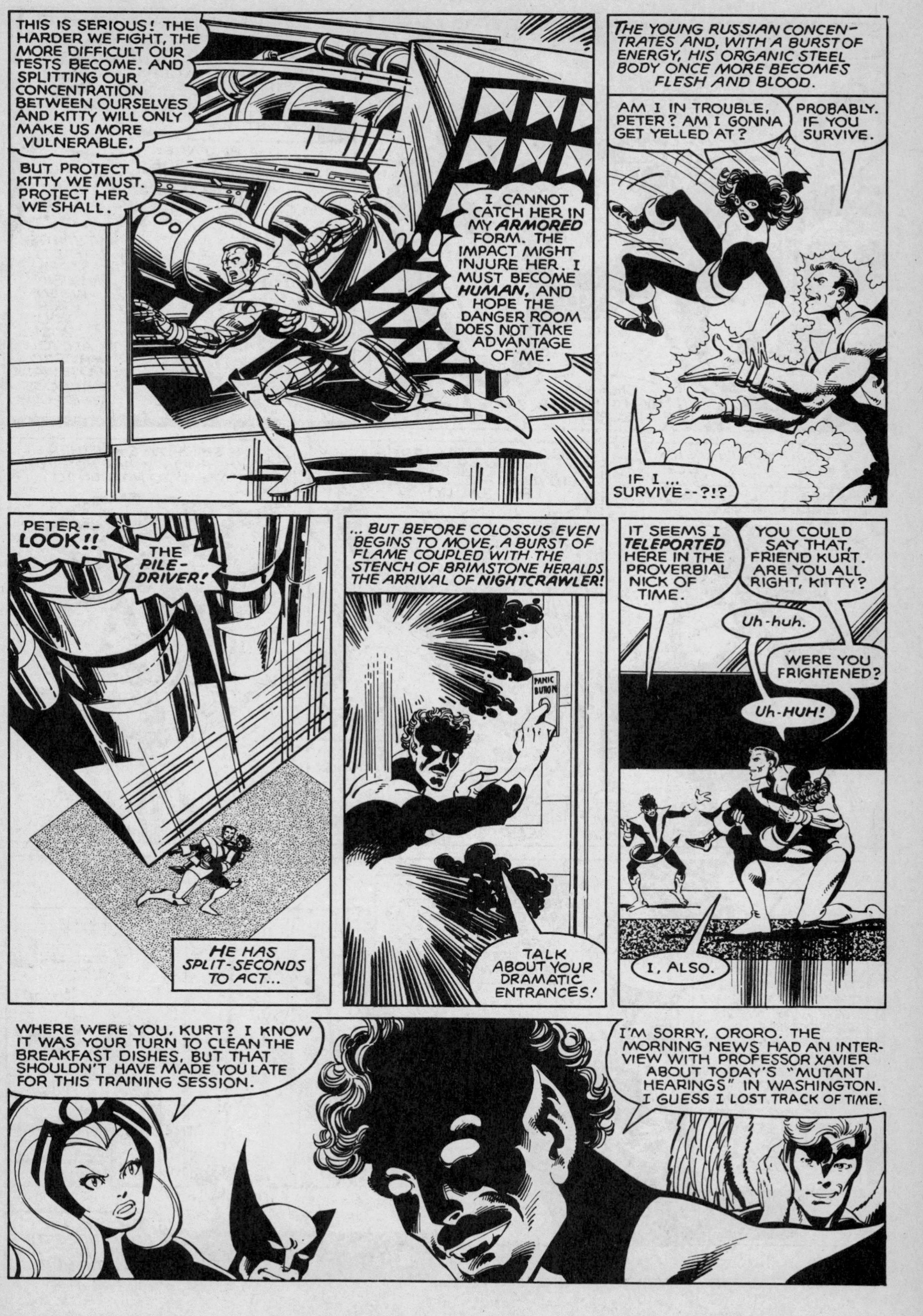

THIS IS SERIOUS! THE HARDER WE FIGHT, THE MORE DIFFICULT OUR TESTS BECOME. AND SPLITTING OUR CONCENTRATION BETWEEN OURSELVES AND KITTY WILL ONLY MAKE US MORE VULNERABLE.
BUT PROTECT KITTY WE MUST. PROTECT HER WE SHALL.
I CANNOT CATCH HER IN MY ARMORED FORM. THE IMPACT MIGHT INJURE HER. I MUST BECOME HUMAN, AND HOPE THE DANGER ROOM DOES NOT TAKE ADVANTAGE OF ME.
THE YOUNG RUSSIAN CONCENTRATES AND, WITH A BURST OF ENERGY, HIS ORGANIC STEEL BODY ONCE MORE BECOMES FLESH AND BLOOD.
AM I IN TROUBLE, PETER? AM I GONNA GET YELLED AT?
PROBABLY. IF YOU SURVIVE.
IF I ... SURVIVE--?!?
PETER-- LOOK!!
THE PILE-DRIVER!
HE HAS SPLIT-SECONDS TO ACT...
... BUT BEFORE COLOSSUS EVEN BEGINS TO MOVE, A BURST OF FLAME COUPLED WITH THE STENCH OF BRIMSTONE HERALDS THE ARRIVAL OF NIGHTCRAWLER!
PANIC BUTTON
TALK ABOUT YOUR DRAMATIC ENTRANCES!
IT SEEMS I TELEPORTED HERE IN THE PROVERBIAL NICK OF TIME.
YOU COULD SAY THAT, FRIEND KURT. ARE YOU ALL RIGHT, KITTY?
Uh-huh.
WERE YOU FRIGHTENED?
Uh-HUH!
I, ALSO.
WHERE WERE YOU, KURT? I KNOW IT WAS YOUR TURN TO CLEAN THE BREAKFAST DISHES, BUT THAT SHOULDN'T HAVE MADE YOU LATE FOR THIS TRAINING SESSION.
I'M SORRY, ORORO. THE MORNING NEWS HAD AN INTERVIEW WITH PROFESSOR XAVIER ABOUT TODAY'S "MUTANT HEARINGS" IN WASHINGTON. I GUESS I LOST TRACK OF TIME.

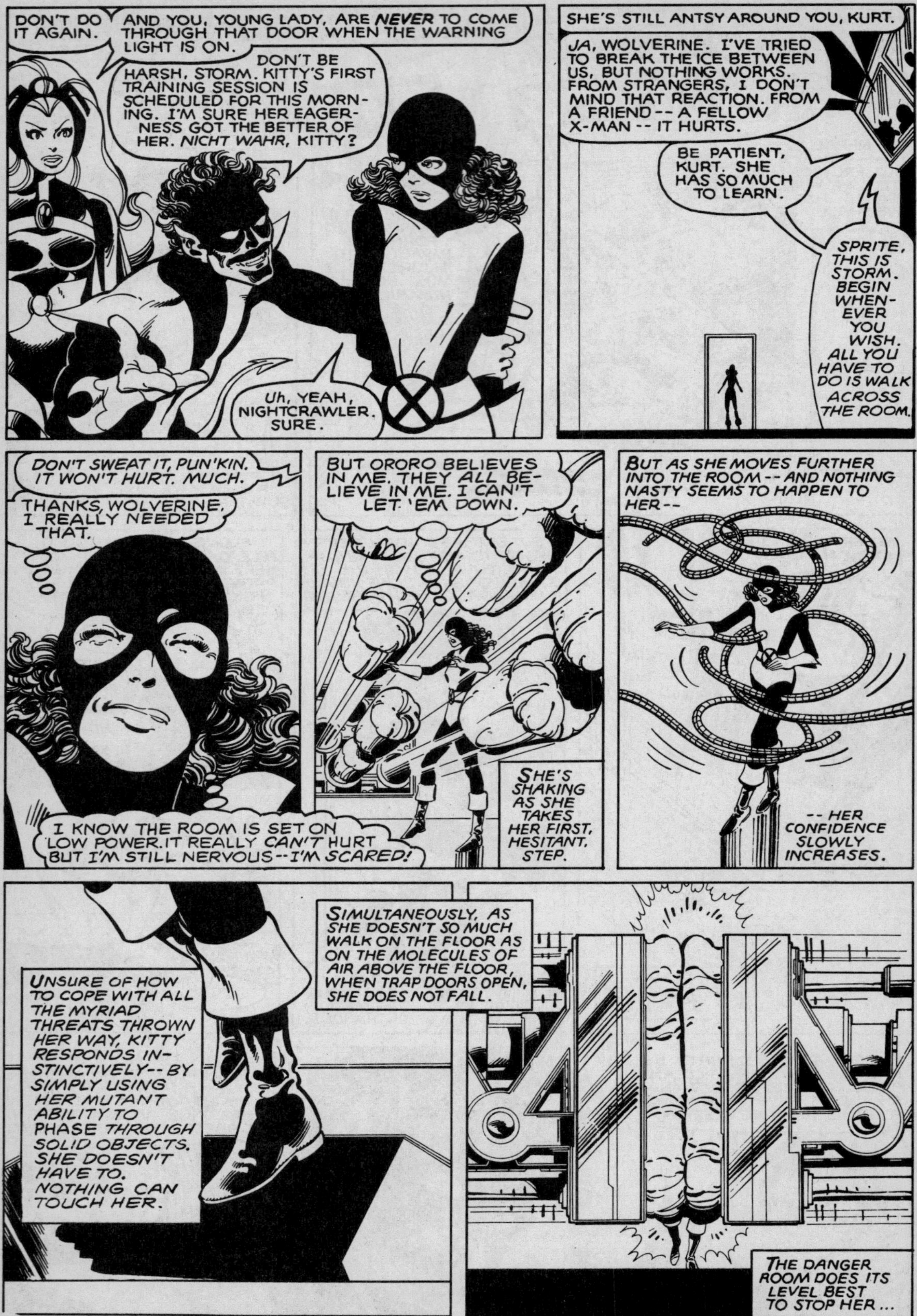
DON'T DO IT AGAIN.
AND YOU, YOUNG LADY, ARE NEVER TO COME THROUGH THAT DOOR WHEN THE WARNING LIGHT IS ON.
DON'T BE HARSH, STORM. KITTY'S FIRST TRAINING SESSION IS SCHEDULED FOR THIS MORNING. I'M SURE HER EAGERNESS GOT THE BETTER OF HER. NICHT WAHR, KITTY?
Uh, YEAH, NIGHTCRAWLER. SURE.
SHE'S STILL ANTSY AROUND YOU, KURT.
JA, WOLVERINE. I'VE TRIED TO BREAK THE ICE BETWEEN US, BUT NOTHING WORKS. FROM STRANGERS, I DON'T MIND THAT REACTION. FROM A FRIEND -- A FELLOW X-MAN -- IT HURTS.
BE PATIENT, KURT. SHE HAS SO MUCH TO LEARN.
SPRITE, THIS IS STORM. BEGIN WHENEVER YOU WISH. ALL YOU HAVE TO DO IS WALK ACROSS THE ROOM.
DON'T SWEAT IT, PUN'KIN. IT WON'T HURT. MUCH.
THANKS, WOLVERINE. I REALLY NEEDED THAT.
I KNOW THE ROOM IS SET ON LOW POWER. IT REALLY CAN'T HURT BUT I'M STILL NERVOUS -- I'M SCARED!
BUT ORORO BELIEVES IN ME. THEY ALL BELIEVE IN ME. I CAN'T LET 'EM DOWN.
SHE'S SHAKING AS SHE TAKES HER FIRST, HESITANT, STEP.
BUT AS SHE MOVES FURTHER INTO THE ROOM -- AND NOTHING NASTY SEEMS TO HAPPEN TO HER --
-- HER CONFIDENCE SLOWLY INCREASES.
UNSURE OF HOW TO COPE WITH ALL THE MYRIAD THREATS THROWN HER WAY, KITTY RESPONDS INSTINCTIVELY -- BY SIMPLY USING HER MUTANT ABILITY TO PHASE THROUGH SOLID OBJECTS. SHE DOESN'T HAVE TO. NOTHING CAN TOUCH HER.
SIMULTANEOUSLY, AS SHE DOESN'T SO MUCH WALK ON THE FLOOR AS ON THE MOLECULES OF AIR ABOVE THE FLOOR, WHEN TRAP DOORS OPEN, SHE DOES NOT FALL.
THE DANGER ROOM DOES ITS LEVEL BEST TO STOP HER ...

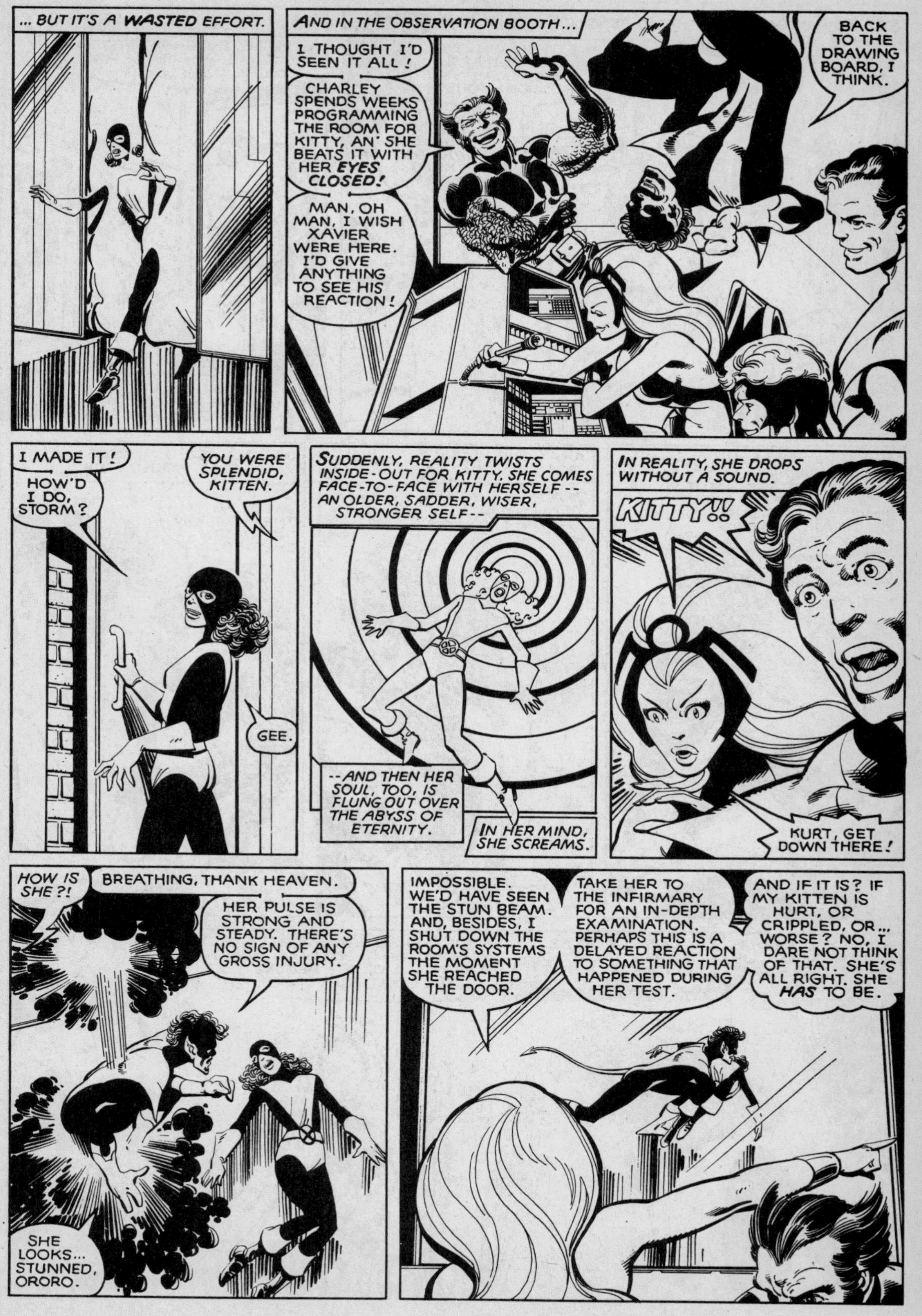
... BUT IT'S A WASTED EFFORT.
AND IN THE OBSERVATION BOOTH...
I THOUGHT I'D SEEN IT ALL!
CHARLEY SPENDS WEEKS PROGRAMMING THE ROOM FOR KITTY, AN' SHE BEATS IT WITH HER EYES CLOSED!
MAN, OH MAN, I WISH XAVIER WERE HERE. I'D GIVE ANYTHING TO SEE HIS REACTION!
BACK TO THE DRAWING BOARD, I THINK.
I MADE IT!
HOW'D I DO, STORM?
YOU WERE SPLENDID, KITTEN.
GEE.
SUDDENLY, REALITY TWISTS INSIDE-OUT FOR KITTY. SHE COMES FACE-TO-FACE WITH HERSELF -- AN OLDER, SADDER, WISER, STRONGER SELF--
--AND THEN HER SOUL, TOO, IS FLUNG OUT OVER THE ABYSS OF ETERNITY.
IN HER MIND, SHE SCREAMS.
IN REALITY, SHE DROPS WITHOUT A SOUND.
KITTY!!
KURT, GET DOWN THERE!
HOW IS SHE?!
BREATHING, THANK HEAVEN.
HER PULSE IS STRONG AND STEADY. THERE'S NO SIGN OF ANY GROSS INJURY.
SHE LOOKS... STUNNED, ORORO.
IMPOSSIBLE. WE'D HAVE SEEN THE STUN BEAM. AND, BESIDES, I SHUT DOWN THE ROOM'S SYSTEMS THE MOMENT SHE REACHED THE DOOR.
TAKE HER TO THE INFIRMARY FOR AN IN-DEPTH EXAMINATION. PERHAPS THIS IS A DELAYED REACTION TO SOMETHING THAT HAPPENED DURING HER TEST.
AND IF IT IS? IF MY KITTEN IS HURT, OR CRIPPLED, OR... WORSE? NO, I DARE NOT THINK OF THAT. SHE'S ALL RIGHT. SHE HAS TO BE.

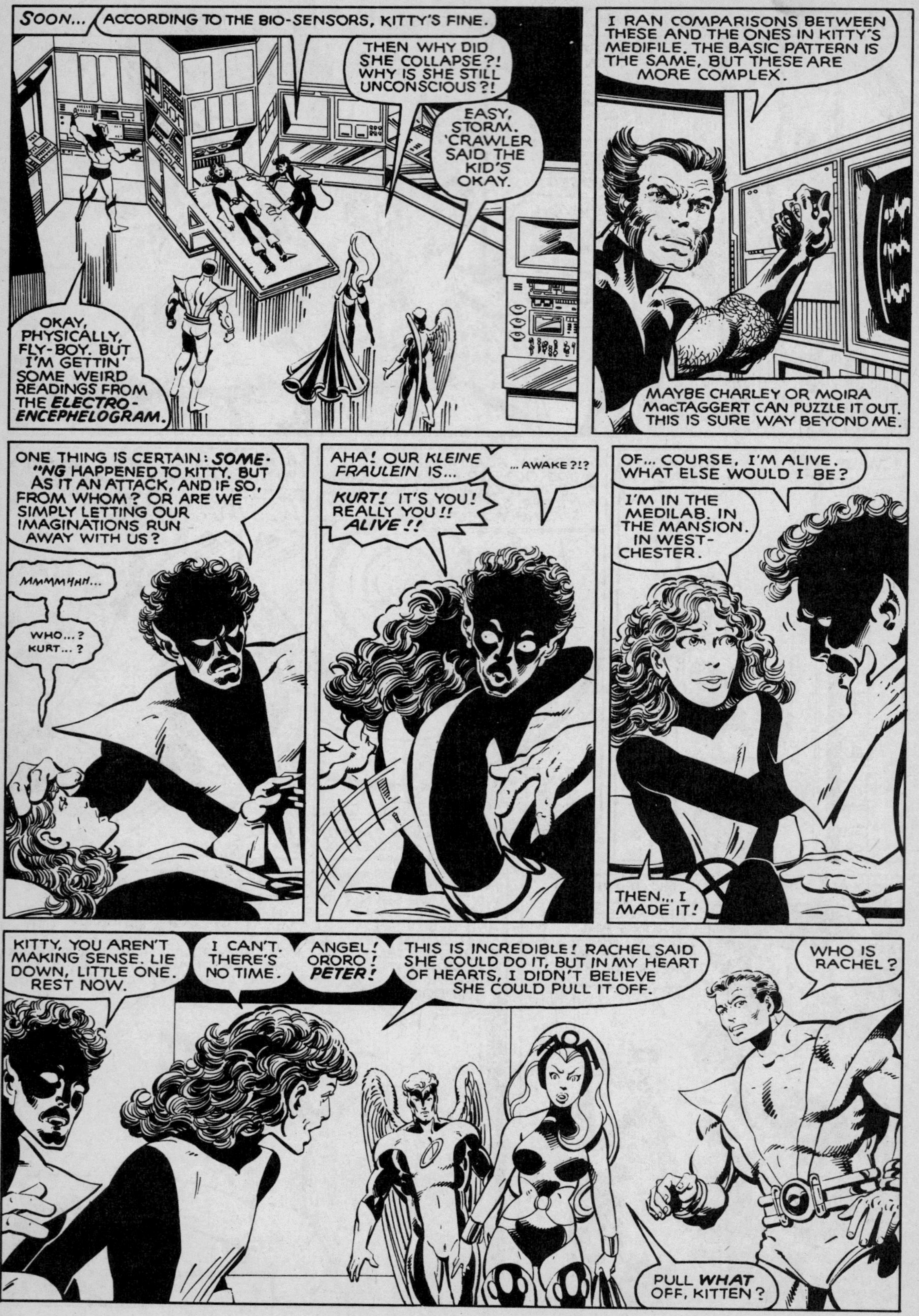
SOON...
ACCORDING TO THE BIO-SENSORS, KITTY'S FINE.
THEN WHY DID SHE COLLAPSE?! WHY IS SHE STILL UNCONSCIOUS?!
EASY, STORM. 'CRAWLER SAID THE KID'S OKAY.
OKAY, PHYSICALLY, FLY-BOY. BUT I'M GETTIN' SOME WEIRD READINGS FROM THE ELECTRO-ENCEPHELOGRAM.
I RAN COMPARISONS BETWEEN THESE AND THE ONES IN KITTY'S MEDIFILE. THE BASIC PATTERN IS THE SAME, BUT THESE ARE MORE COMPLEX.
MAYBE CHARLEY OR MOIRA MacTAGGERT CAN PUZZLE IT OUT. THIS IS SURE WAY BEYOND ME.
ONE THING IS CERTAIN: SOME- 'NG HAPPENED TO KITTY, BUT AS IT AN ATTACK, AND IF SO, FROM WHOM? OR ARE WE SIMPLY LETTING OUR IMAGINATIONS RUN AWAY WITH US?
MMMMHHH...
WHO...? KURT...?
AHA! OUR KLEINE FRAULEIN IS...
...AWAKE?!?
KURT! IT'S YOU! REALLY YOU!! ALIVE!!
OF... COURSE, I'M ALIVE. WHAT ELSE WOULD I BE?
I'M IN THE MEDILAB. IN THE MANSION. IN WEST-CHESTER.
THEN... I MADE IT!
KITTY, YOU AREN'T MAKING SENSE. LIE DOWN, LITTLE ONE. REST NOW.
I CAN'T. THERE'S NO TIME.
ANGEL! ORORO! PETER!
THIS IS INCREDIBLE! RACHEL SAID SHE COULD DO IT, BUT IN MY HEART OF HEARTS, I DIDN'T BELIEVE SHE COULD PULL IT OFF.
WHO IS RACHEL?
PULL WHAT OFF, KITTEN?

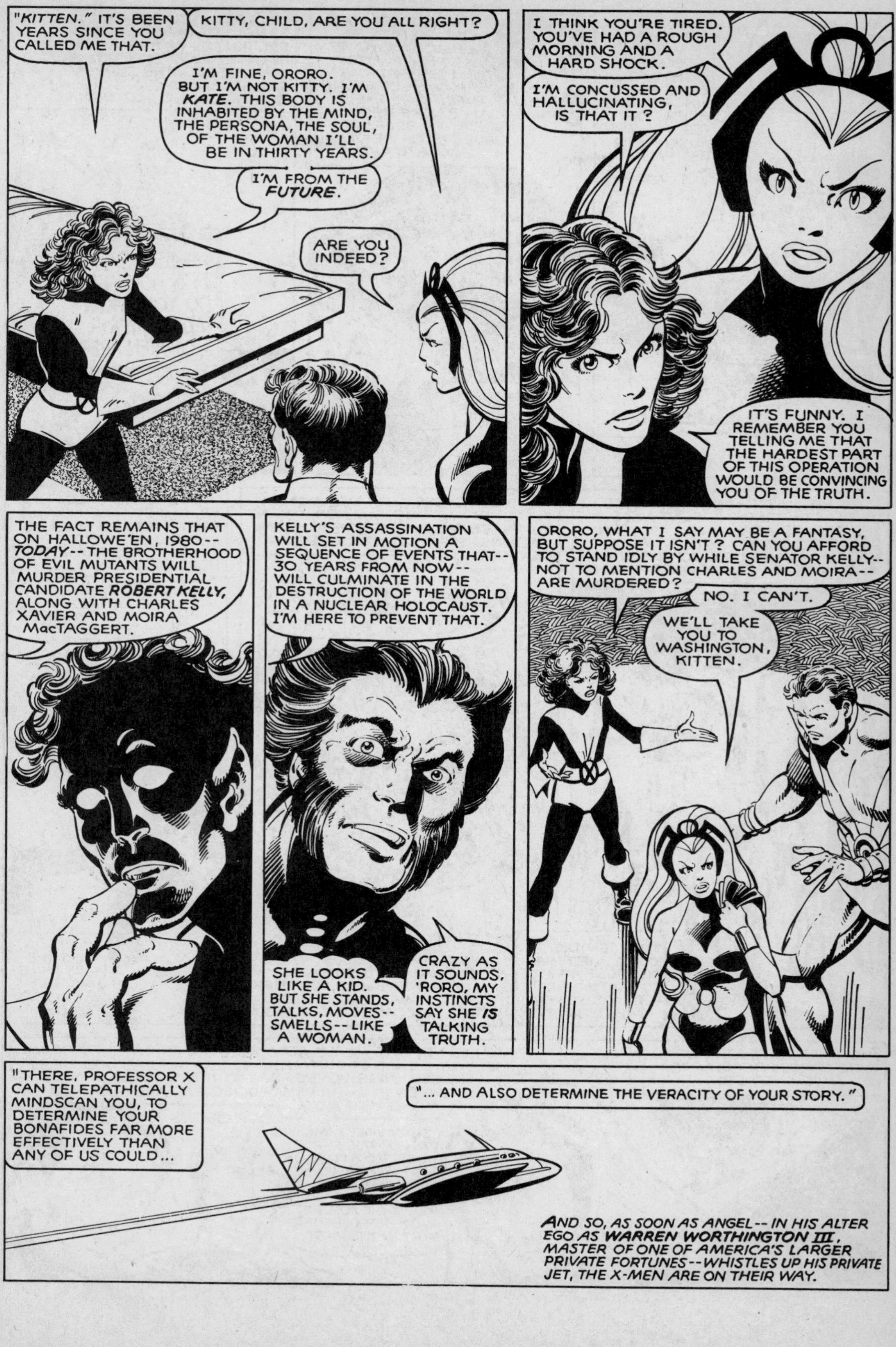
"KITTEN." IT'S BEEN YEARS SINCE YOU CALLED ME THAT.
KITTY, CHILD, ARE YOU ALL RIGHT?
I'M FINE, ORORO. BUT I'M NOT KITTY. I'M KATE. THIS BODY IS INHABITED BY THE MIND, THE PERSONA, THE SOUL, OF THE WOMAN I'LL BE IN THIRTY YEARS.
I'M FROM THE FUTURE.
ARE YOU INDEED?
I THINK YOU'RE TIRED. YOU'VE HAD A ROUGH MORNING AND A HARD SHOCK.
I'M CONCUSSED AND HALLUCINATING, IS THAT IT?
IT'S FUNNY. I REMEMBER YOU TELLING ME THAT THE HARDEST PART OF THIS OPERATION WOULD BE CONVINCING YOU OF THE TRUTH.
THE FACT REMAINS THAT ON HALLOWE'EN, 1980-- TODAY-- THE BROTHERHOOD OF EVIL MUTANTS WILL MURDER PRESIDENTIAL CANDIDATE ROBERT KELLY, ALONG WITH CHARLES XAVIER AND MOIRA MacTAGGERT.
KELLY'S ASSASSINATION WILL SET IN MOTION A SEQUENCE OF EVENTS THAT-- 30 YEARS FROM NOW-- WILL CULMINATE IN THE DESTRUCTION OF THE WORLD IN A NUCLEAR HOLOCAUST. I'M HERE TO PREVENT THAT.
SHE LOOKS LIKE A KID. BUT SHE STANDS, TALKS, MOVES-- SMELLS-- LIKE A WOMAN.
CRAZY AS IT SOUNDS, 'RORO, MY INSTINCTS SAY SHE IS TALKING TRUTH.
ORORO, WHAT I SAY MAY BE A FANTASY, BUT SUPPOSE IT ISN'T? CAN YOU AFFORD TO STAND IDLY BY WHILE SENATOR KELLY-- NOT TO MENTION CHARLES AND MOIRA-- ARE MURDERED?
NO. I CAN'T.
WE'LL TAKE YOU TO WASHINGTON, KITTEN.
"THERE, PROFESSOR X CAN TELEPATHICALLY MINDSCAN YOU, TO DETERMINE YOUR BONAFIDES FAR MORE EFFECTIVELY THAN ANY OF US COULD...
"... AND ALSO DETERMINE THE VERACITY OF YOUR STORY."
AND SO, AS SOON AS ANGEL-- IN HIS ALTER EGO AS WARREN WORTHINGTON III, MASTER OF ONE OF AMERICA'S LARGER PRIVATE FORTUNES-- WHISTLES UP HIS PRIVATE JET, THE X-MEN ARE ON THEIR WAY.

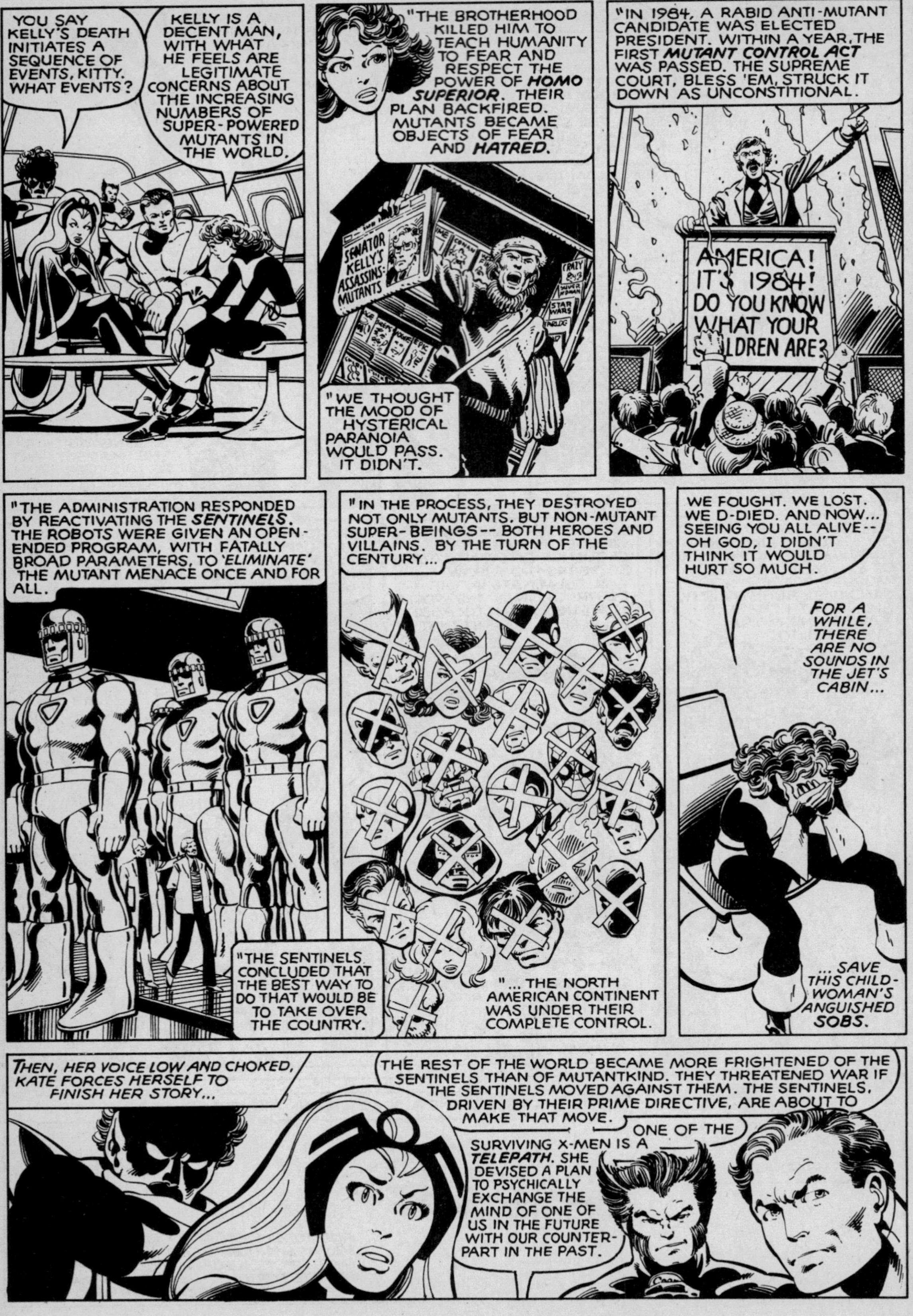
YOU SAY KELLY'S DEATH INITIATES A SEQUENCE OF EVENTS, KITTY. WHAT EVENTS?
KELLY IS A DECENT MAN, WITH WHAT HE FEELS ARE LEGITIMATE CONCERNS ABOUT THE INCREASING NUMBERS OF SUPER-POWERED MUTANTS IN THE WORLD.
"THE BROTHERHOOD KILLED HIM TO TEACH HUMANITY TO FEAR AND RESPECT THE POWER OF HOMO SUPERIOR. THEIR PLAN BACKFIRED. MUTANTS BECAME OBJECTS OF FEAR AND HATRED.
SENATOR KELLY'S ASSASSINS: MUTANTS
STAR WARS
"WE THOUGHT THE MOOD OF HYSTERICAL PARANOIA WOULD PASS. IT DIDN'T.
"IN 1984, A RABID ANTI-MUTANT CANDIDATE WAS ELECTED PRESIDENT. WITHIN A YEAR, THE FIRST MUTANT CONTROL ACT WAS PASSED. THE SUPREME COURT, BLESS 'EM, STRUCK IT DOWN AS UNCONSTITIONAL.
AMERICA! IT'S 1984! DO YOU KNOW WHAT YOUR ...LDREN ARE?
"THE ADMINISTRATION RESPONDED BY REACTIVATING THE SENTINELS. THE ROBOTS WERE GIVEN AN OPEN-ENDED PROGRAM, WITH FATALLY BROAD PARAMETERS, TO 'ELIMINATE' THE MUTANT MENACE ONCE AND FOR ALL.
"THE SENTINELS CONCLUDED THAT THE BEST WAY TO DO THAT WOULD BE TO TAKE OVER THE COUNTRY.
"IN THE PROCESS, THEY DESTROYED NOT ONLY MUTANTS. BUT NON-MUTANT SUPER-BEINGS-- BOTH HEROES AND VILLAINS. BY THE TURN OF THE CENTURY...
"... THE NORTH AMERICAN CONTINENT WAS UNDER THEIR COMPLETE CONTROL.
WE FOUGHT. WE LOST. WE D-DIED. AND NOW... SEEING YOU ALL ALIVE-- OH GOD, I DIDN'T THINK IT WOULD HURT SO MUCH.
FOR A WHILE, THERE ARE NO SOUNDS IN THE JET'S CABIN...
... SAVE THIS CHILD-WOMAN'S ANGUISHED SOBS.
THEN, HER VOICE LOW AND CHOKED, KATE FORCES HERSELF TO FINISH HER STORY...
THE REST OF THE WORLD BECAME MORE FRIGHTENED OF THE SENTINELS THAN OF MUTANTKIND. THEY THREATENED WAR IF THE SENTINELS MOVED AGAINST THEM. THE SENTINELS, DRIVEN BY THEIR PRIME DIRECTIVE, ARE ABOUT TO MAKE THAT MOVE.
ONE OF THE SURVIVING X-MEN IS A TELEPATH. SHE DEVISED A PLAN TO PSYCHICALLY EXCHANGE THE MIND OF ONE OF US IN THE FUTURE WITH OUR COUNTER-PART IN THE PAST.

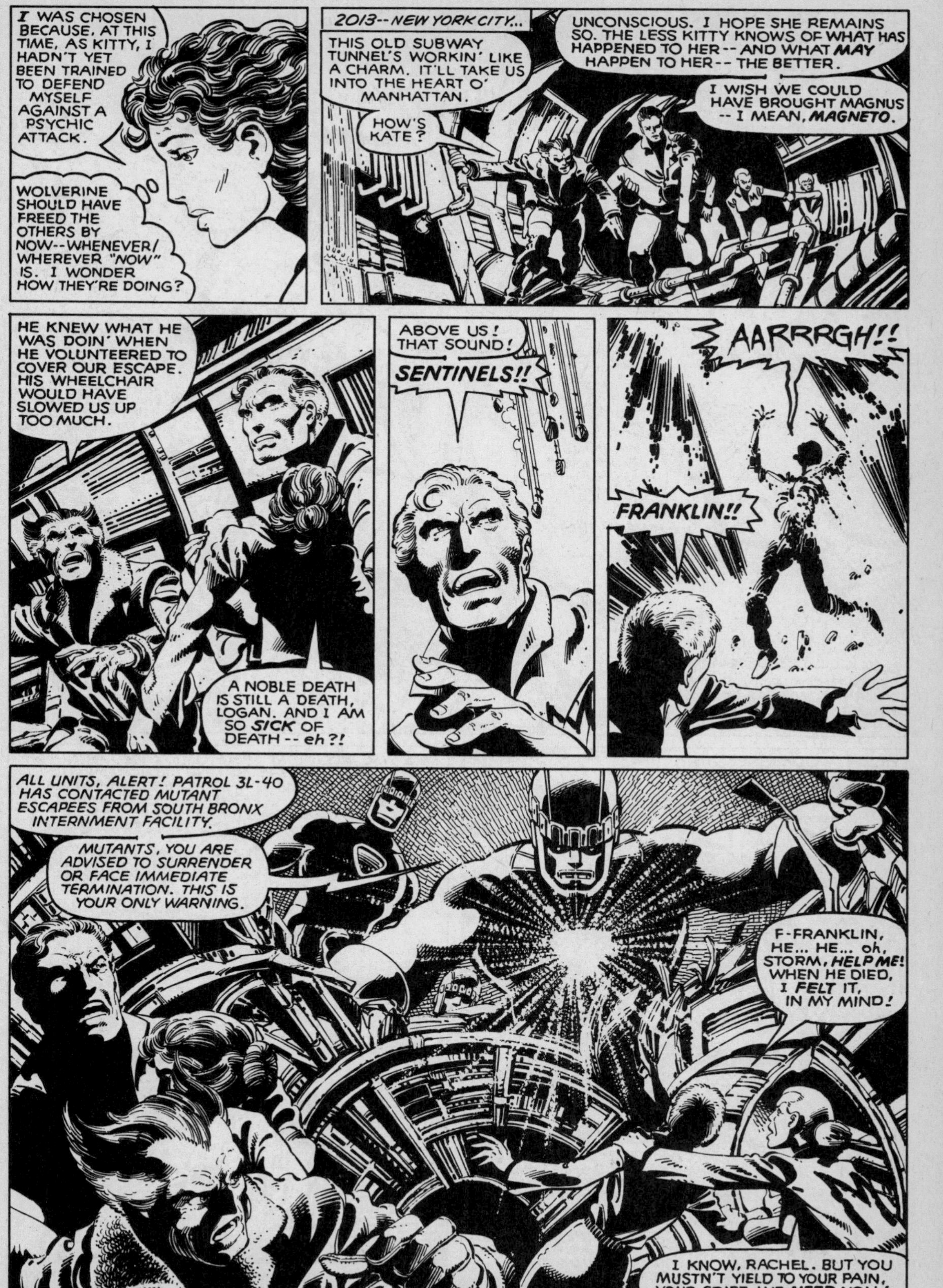
I WAS CHOSEN BECAUSE, AT THIS TIME, AS KITTY, I HADN'T YET BEEN TRAINED TO DEFEND MYSELF AGAINST A PSYCHIC ATTACK.
WOLVERINE SHOULD HAVE FREED THE OTHERS BY NOW--WHENEVER/ WHEREVER "NOW" IS. I WONDER HOW THEY'RE DOING?
2013--NEW YORK CITY...
THIS OLD SUBWAY TUNNEL'S WORKIN' LIKE A CHARM. IT'LL TAKE US INTO THE HEART O' MANHATTAN.
HOW'S KATE?
UNCONSCIOUS. I HOPE SHE REMAINS SO. THE LESS KITTY KNOWS OF WHAT HAS HAPPENED TO HER-- AND WHAT MAY HAPPEN TO HER-- THE BETTER.
I WISH WE COULD HAVE BROUGHT MAGNUS -- I MEAN, MAGNETO.
HE KNEW WHAT HE WAS DOIN' WHEN HE VOLUNTEERED TO COVER OUR ESCAPE. HIS WHEELCHAIR WOULD HAVE SLOWED US UP TOO MUCH.
A NOBLE DEATH IS STILL A DEATH, LOGAN. AND I AM SO SICK OF DEATH -- eh?!
ABOVE US! THAT SOUND!
SENTINELS!!
AARRRGH!!
FRANKLIN!!
ALL UNITS, ALERT! PATROL 3L-40 HAS CONTACTED MUTANT ESCAPEES FROM SOUTH BRONX INTERNMENT FACILITY.
MUTANTS, YOU ARE ADVISED TO SURRENDER OR FACE IMMEDIATE TERMINATION. THIS IS YOUR ONLY WARNING.
F-FRANKLIN, HE... HE... oh, STORM, HELP ME! WHEN HE DIED, I FELT IT, IN MY MIND!
I KNOW, RACHEL. BUT YOU MUSTN'T YIELD TO YOUR PAIN, YOUR GRIEF. WE NEED YOU!

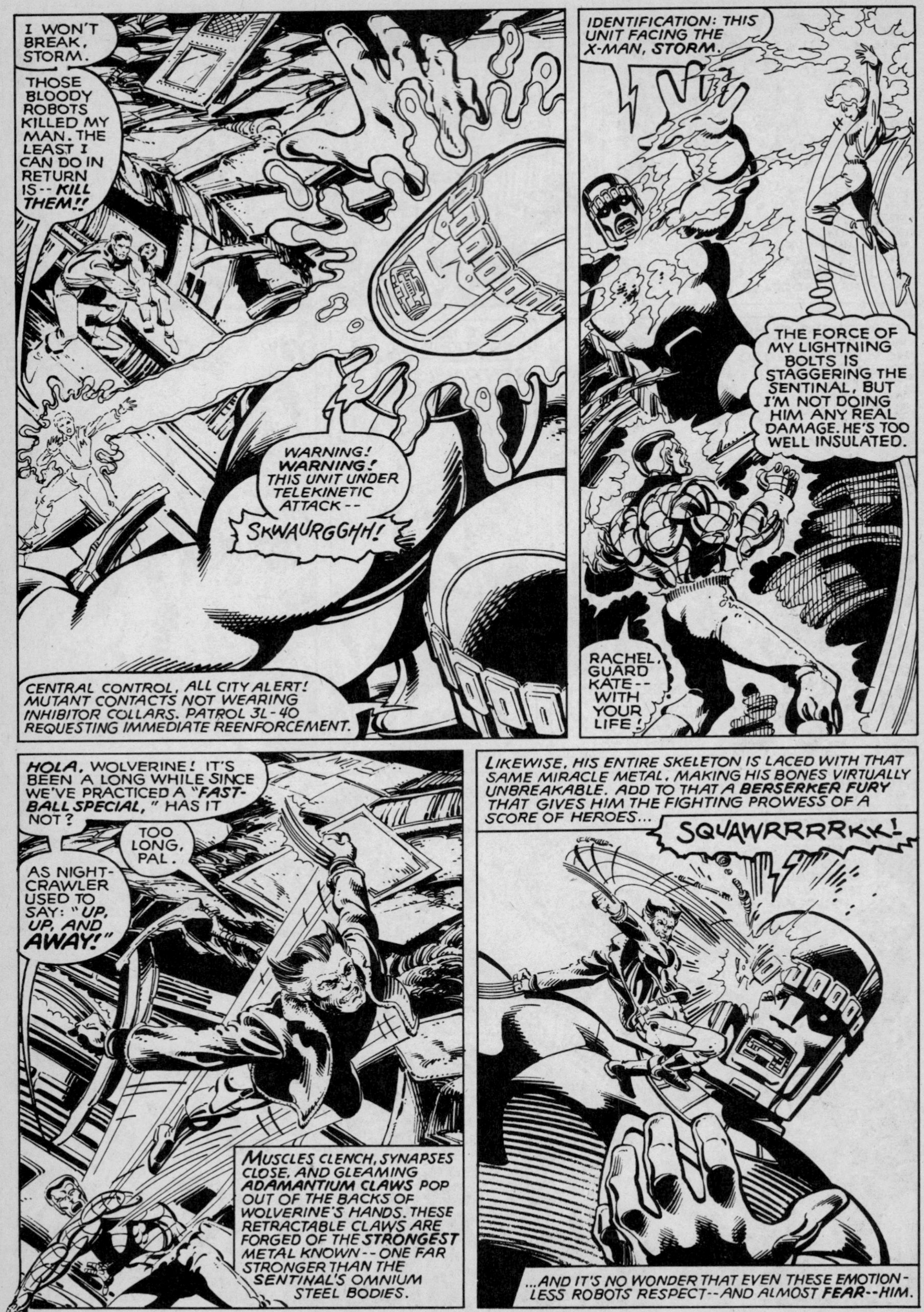

I WON'T BREAK, STORM.
THOSE BLOODY ROBOTS KILLED MY MAN. THE LEAST I CAN DO IN RETURN IS-- KILL THEM!!
WARNING! WARNING! THIS UNIT UNDER TELEKINETIC ATTACK--
SKWAURGGHH!
CENTRAL CONTROL, ALL CITY ALERT! MUTANT CONTACTS NOT WEARING INHIBITOR COLLARS. PATROL 3L-40 REQUESTING IMMEDIATE REENFORCEMENT.
IDENTIFICATION: THIS UNIT FACING THE X-MAN, STORM.
THE FORCE OF MY LIGHTNING BOLTS IS STAGGERING THE SENTINAL, BUT I'M NOT DOING HIM ANY REAL DAMAGE. HE'S TOO WELL INSULATED.
RACHEL, GUARD KATE-- WITH YOUR LIFE!
HOLA, WOLVERINE! IT'S BEEN A LONG WHILE SINCE WE'VE PRACTICED A "FAST-BALL SPECIAL," HAS IT NOT?
TOO LONG, PAL.
AS NIGHT-CRAWLER USED TO SAY: "UP, UP, AND AWAY!"
MUSCLES CLENCH, SYNAPSES CLOSE, AND GLEAMING ADAMANTIUM CLAWS POP OUT OF THE BACKS OF WOLVERINE'S HANDS. THESE RETRACTABLE CLAWS ARE FORGED OF THE STRONGEST METAL KNOWN--ONE FAR STRONGER THAN THE SENTINAL'S OMNIUM STEEL BODIES.
LIKEWISE, HIS ENTIRE SKELETON IS LACED WITH THAT SAME MIRACLE METAL, MAKING HIS BONES VIRTUALLY UNBREAKABLE. ADD TO THAT A BERSERKER FURY THAT GIVES HIM THE FIGHTING PROWESS OF A SCORE OF HEROES...
SQUAWRRRRKK!
...AND IT'S NO WONDER THAT EVEN THESE EMOTION-LESS ROBOTS RESPECT--AND ALMOST FEAR--HIM.

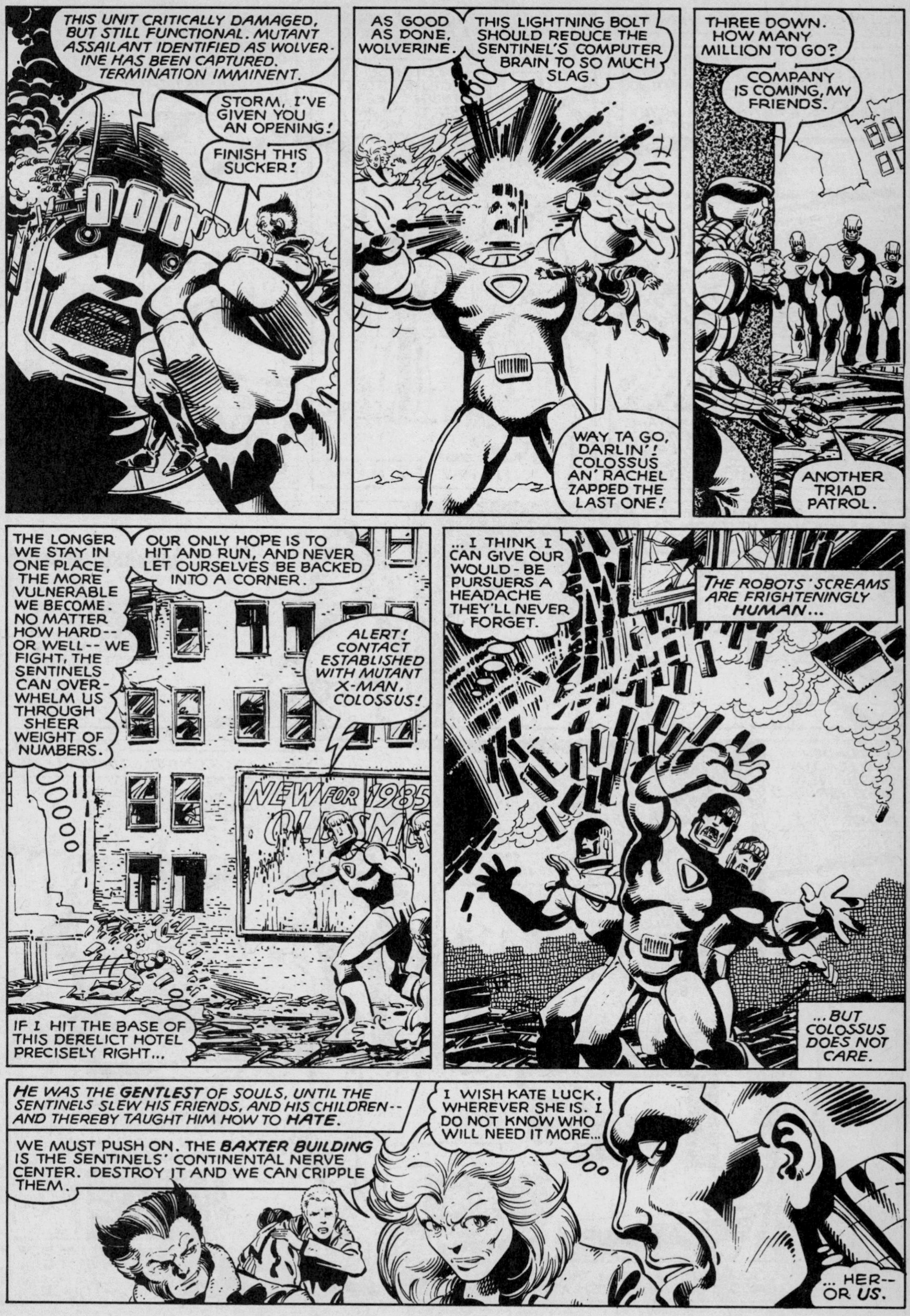
THIS UNIT CRITICALLY DAMAGED, BUT STILL FUNCTIONAL. MUTANT ASSAILANT IDENTIFIED AS WOLVERINE HAS BEEN CAPTURED. TERMINATION IMMINENT.
STORM, I'VE GIVEN YOU AN OPENING!
FINISH THIS SUCKER!
AS GOOD AS DONE, WOLVERINE.
THIS LIGHTNING BOLT SHOULD REDUCE THE SENTINEL'S COMPUTER BRAIN TO SO MUCH SLAG.
WAY TA GO, DARLIN'! COLOSSUS AN' RACHEL ZAPPED THE LAST ONE!
THREE DOWN. HOW MANY MILLION TO GO?
COMPANY IS COMING, MY FRIENDS.
ANOTHER TRIAD PATROL.
THE LONGER WE STAY IN ONE PLACE, THE MORE VULNERABLE WE BECOME. NO MATTER HOW HARD-- OR WELL-- WE FIGHT, THE SENTINELS CAN OVERWHELM US THROUGH SHEER WEIGHT OF NUMBERS.
OUR ONLY HOPE IS TO HIT AND RUN, AND NEVER LET OURSELVES BE BACKED INTO A CORNER.
ALERT! CONTACT ESTABLISHED WITH MUTANT X-MAN, COLOSSUS!
NEW FOR 1985
IF I HIT THE BASE OF THIS DERELICT HOTEL PRECISELY RIGHT...
...I THINK I CAN GIVE OUR WOULD-BE PURSUERS A HEADACHE THEY'LL NEVER FORGET.
THE ROBOTS' SCREAMS ARE FRIGHTENINGLY HUMAN...
...BUT COLOSSUS DOES NOT CARE.
HE WAS THE GENTLEST OF SOULS, UNTIL THE SENTINELS SLEW HIS FRIENDS, AND HIS CHILDREN-- AND THEREBY TAUGHT HIM HOW TO HATE.
WE MUST PUSH ON. THE BAXTER BUILDING IS THE SENTINELS' CONTINENTAL NERVE CENTER. DESTROY IT AND WE CAN CRIPPLE THEM.
I WISH KATE LUCK, WHEREVER SHE IS. I DO NOT KNOW WHO WILL NEED IT MORE...
...HER-- OR US.

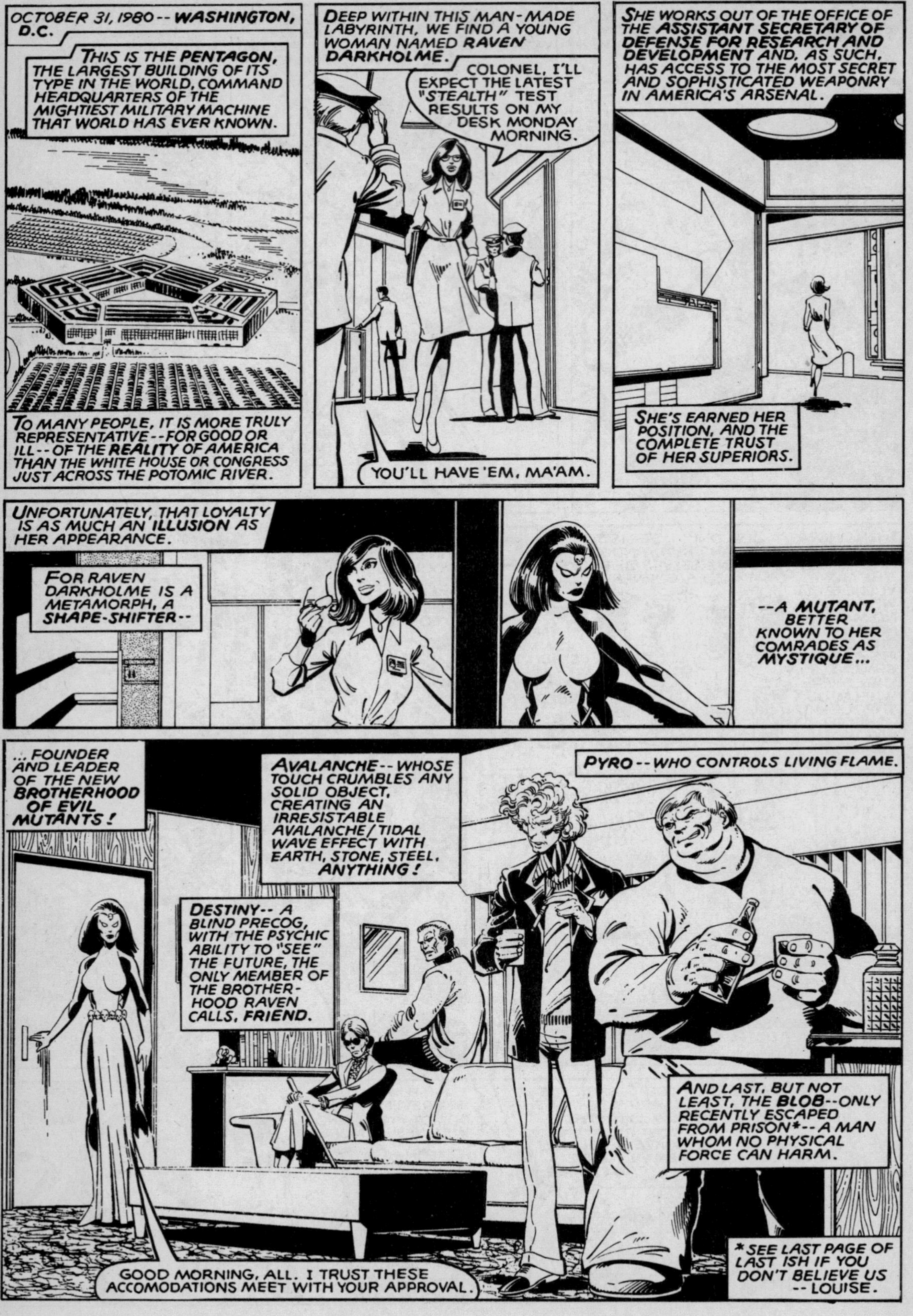
OCTOBER 31, 1980 -- WASHINGTON, D.C.
THIS IS THE PENTAGON, THE LARGEST BUILDING OF ITS TYPE IN THE WORLD, COMMAND HEADQUARTERS OF THE MIGHTIEST MILITARY MACHINE THAT WORLD HAS EVER KNOWN.
TO MANY PEOPLE, IT IS MORE TRULY REPRESENTATIVE -- FOR GOOD OR ILL -- OF THE REALITY OF AMERICA THAN THE WHITE HOUSE OR CONGRESS JUST ACROSS THE POTOMIC RIVER.
DEEP WITHIN THIS MAN-MADE LABYRINTH, WE FIND A YOUNG WOMAN NAMED RAVEN DARKHOLME.
COLONEL, I'LL EXPECT THE LATEST "STEALTH" TEST RESULTS ON MY DESK MONDAY MORNING.
YOU'LL HAVE 'EM, MA'AM.
SHE WORKS OUT OF THE OFFICE OF THE ASSISTANT SECRETARY OF DEFENSE FOR RESEARCH AND DEVELOPMENT AND, AS SUCH, HAS ACCESS TO THE MOST SECRET AND SOPHISTICATED WEAPONRY IN AMERICA'S ARSENAL.
SHE'S EARNED HER POSITION, AND THE COMPLETE TRUST OF HER SUPERIORS.
UNFORTUNATELY, THAT LOYALTY IS AS MUCH AN ILLUSION AS HER APPEARANCE.
FOR RAVEN DARKHOLME IS A METAMORPH, A SHAPE-SHIFTER--
--A MUTANT, BETTER KNOWN TO HER COMRADES AS MYSTIQUE...
...FOUNDER AND LEADER OF THE NEW BROTHERHOOD OF EVIL MUTANTS!
AVALANCHE -- WHOSE TOUCH CRUMBLES ANY SOLID OBJECT, CREATING AN IRRESISTABLE AVALANCHE/TIDAL WAVE EFFECT WITH EARTH, STONE, STEEL, ANYTHING!
PYRO -- WHO CONTROLS LIVING FLAME.
DESTINY -- A BLIND PRECOG, WITH THE PSYCHIC ABILITY TO "SEE" THE FUTURE, THE ONLY MEMBER OF THE BROTHERHOOD RAVEN CALLS, FRIEND.
AND LAST, BUT NOT LEAST, THE BLOB -- ONLY RECENTLY ESCAPED FROM PRISON* -- A MAN WHOM NO PHYSICAL FORCE CAN HARM.
GOOD MORNING, ALL. I TRUST THESE ACCOMODATIONS MEET WITH YOUR APPROVAL.
*SEE LAST PAGE OF LAST ISH IF YOU DON'T BELIEVE US -- LOUISE.

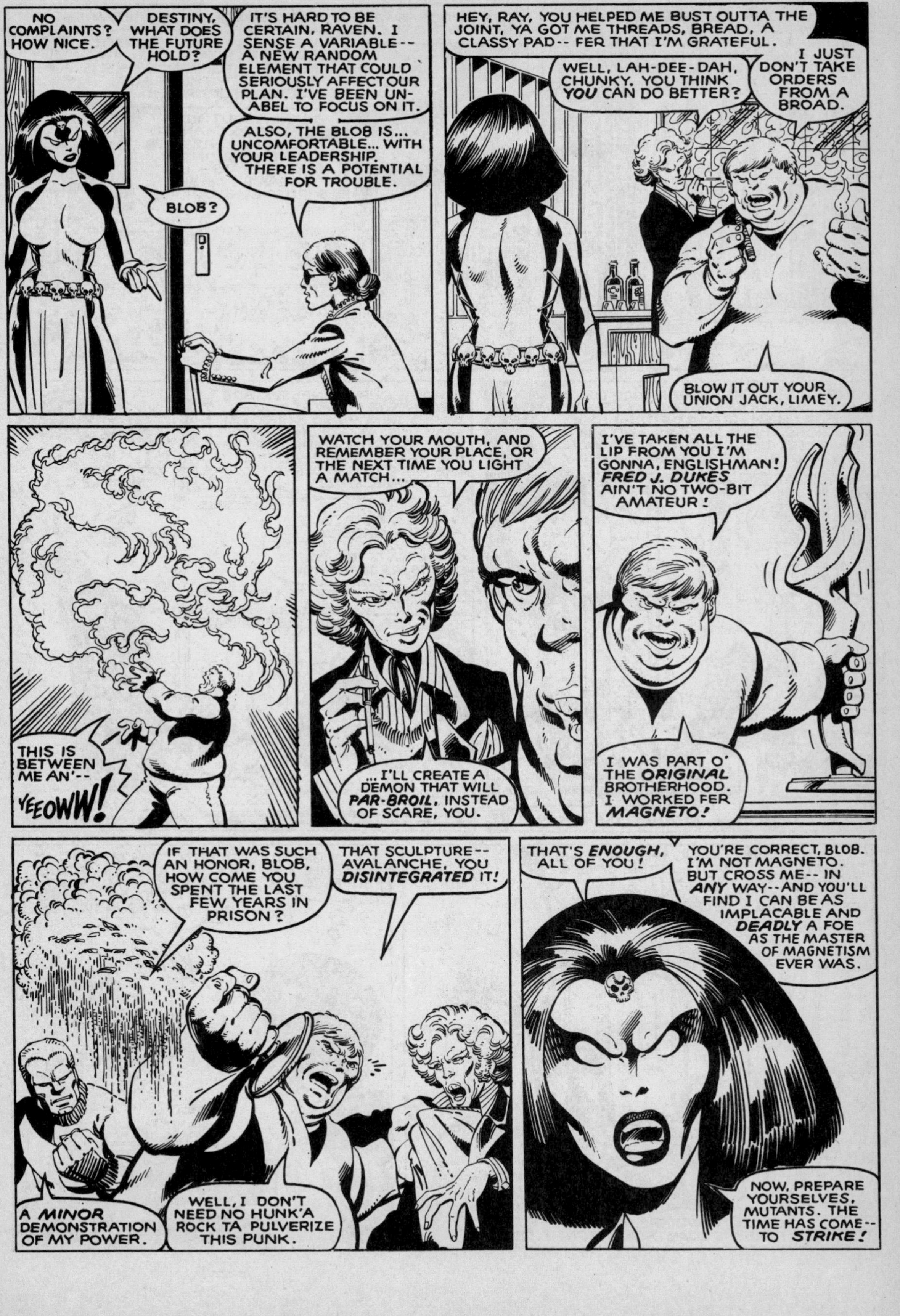
NO COMPLAINTS? HOW NICE.
DESTINY, WHAT DOES THE FUTURE HOLD?
IT'S HARD TO BE CERTAIN, RAVEN. I SENSE A VARIABLE-- A NEW RANDOM ELEMENT THAT COULD SERIOUSLY AFFECT OUR PLAN. I'VE BEEN UNABEL TO FOCUS ON IT.
ALSO, THE BLOB IS... UNCOMFORTABLE... WITH YOUR LEADERSHIP. THERE IS A POTENTIAL FOR TROUBLE.
BLOB?
HEY, RAY, YOU HELPED ME BUST OUTTA THE JOINT, YA GOT ME THREADS, BREAD, A CLASSY PAD-- FER THAT I'M GRATEFUL.
I JUST DON'T TAKE ORDERS FROM A BROAD.
WELL, LAH-DEE-DAH, CHUNKY. YOU THINK YOU CAN DO BETTER?
BLOW IT OUT YOUR UNION JACK, LIMEY.
THIS IS BETWEEN ME AN'--
YEEOWW!
WATCH YOUR MOUTH, AND REMEMBER YOUR PLACE, OR THE NEXT TIME YOU LIGHT A MATCH...
...I'LL CREATE A DEMON THAT WILL PAR-BROIL, INSTEAD OF SCARE, YOU.
I'VE TAKEN ALL THE LIP FROM YOU I'M GONNA, ENGLISHMAN! FRED J. DUKES AIN'T NO TWO-BIT AMATEUR!
I WAS PART O' THE ORIGINAL BROTHERHOOD. I WORKED FER MAGNETO!
IF THAT WAS SUCH AN HONOR, BLOB, HOW COME YOU SPENT THE LAST FEW YEARS IN PRISON?
THAT SCULPTURE-- AVALANCHE, YOU DISINTEGRATED IT!
A MINOR DEMONSTRATION OF MY POWER.
WELL, I DON'T NEED NO HUNK'A ROCK TA PULVERIZE THIS PUNK.
THAT'S ENOUGH, ALL OF YOU!
YOU'RE CORRECT, BLOB. I'M NOT MAGNETO. BUT CROSS ME-- IN ANY WAY--AND YOU'LL FIND I CAN BE AS IMPLACABLE AND DEADLY A FOE AS THE MASTER OF MAGNETISM EVER WAS.
NOW, PREPARE YOURSELVES, MUTANTS. THE TIME HAS COME-- TO STRIKE!

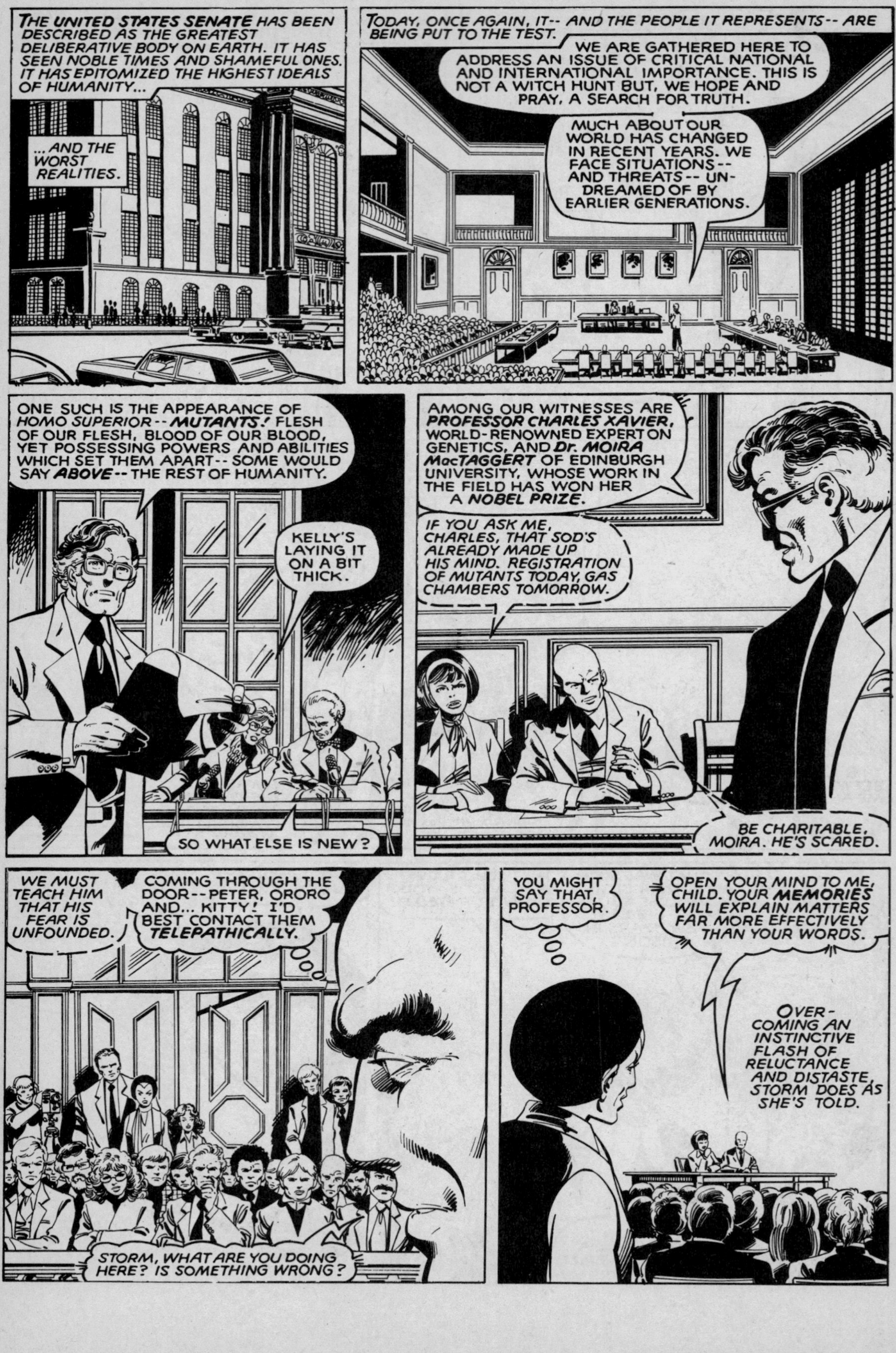

THE UNITED STATES SENATE HAS BEEN DESCRIBED AS THE GREATEST DELIBERATIVE BODY ON EARTH. IT HAS SEEN NOBLE TIMES AND SHAMEFUL ONES. IT HAS EPITOMIZED THE HIGHEST IDEALS OF HUMANITY...
...AND THE WORST REALITIES.
TODAY, ONCE AGAIN, IT-- AND THE PEOPLE IT REPRESENTS-- ARE BEING PUT TO THE TEST.
WE ARE GATHERED HERE TO ADDRESS AN ISSUE OF CRITICAL NATIONAL AND INTERNATIONAL IMPORTANCE. THIS IS NOT A WITCH HUNT BUT, WE HOPE AND PRAY, A SEARCH FOR TRUTH.
MUCH ABOUT OUR WORLD HAS CHANGED IN RECENT YEARS. WE FACE SITUATIONS-- AND THREATS-- UNDREAMED OF BY EARLIER GENERATIONS.
ONE SUCH IS THE APPEARANCE OF HOMO SUPERIOR-- MUTANTS! FLESH OF OUR FLESH, BLOOD OF OUR BLOOD, YET POSSESSING POWERS AND ABILITIES WHICH SET THEM APART-- SOME WOULD SAY ABOVE-- THE REST OF HUMANITY.
KELLY'S LAYING IT ON A BIT THICK.
SO WHAT ELSE IS NEW?
AMONG OUR WITNESSES ARE PROFESSOR CHARLES XAVIER, WORLD-RENOWNED EXPERT ON GENETICS, AND Dr. MOIRA MacTAGGERT OF EDINBURGH UNIVERSITY, WHOSE WORK IN THE FIELD HAS WON HER A NOBEL PRIZE.
IF YOU ASK ME, CHARLES, THAT SOD'S ALREADY MADE UP HIS MIND. REGISTRATION OF MUTANTS TODAY, GAS CHAMBERS TOMORROW.
BE CHARITABLE, MOIRA. HE'S SCARED.
WE MUST TEACH HIM THAT HIS FEAR IS UNFOUNDED.
COMING THROUGH THE DOOR-- PETER, ORORO AND... KITTY! I'D BEST CONTACT THEM TELEPATHICALLY.
STORM, WHAT ARE YOU DOING HERE? IS SOMETHING WRONG?
YOU MIGHT SAY THAT, PROFESSOR.
OPEN YOUR MIND TO ME, CHILD. YOUR MEMORIES WILL EXPLAIN MATTERS FAR MORE EFFECTIVELY THAN YOUR WORDS.
OVERCOMING AN INSTINCTIVE FLASH OF RELUCTANCE AND DISTASTE, STORM DOES AS SHE'S TOLD.

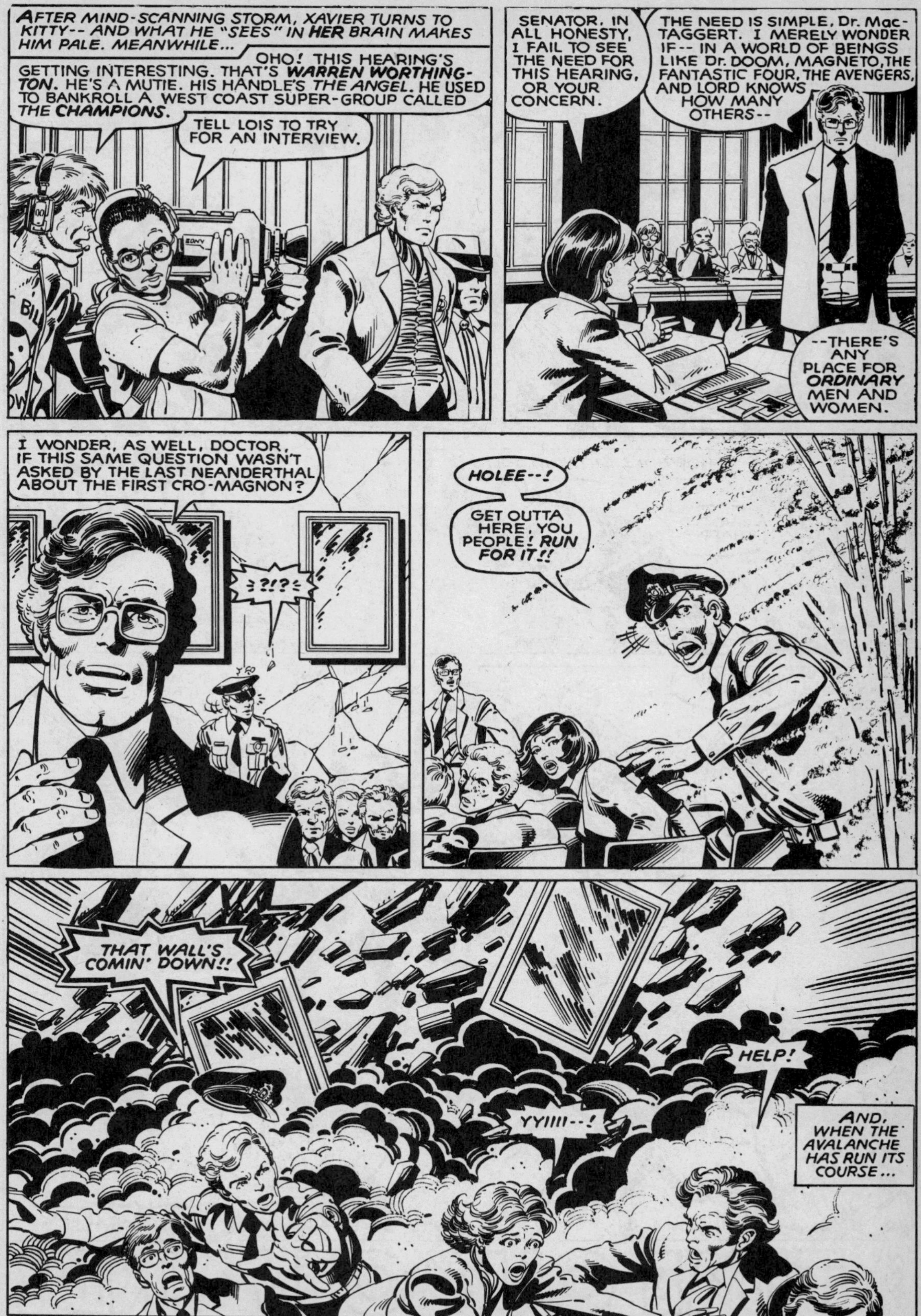

AFTER MIND-SCANNING STORM, XAVIER TURNS TO KITTY-- AND WHAT HE "SEES" IN HER BRAIN MAKES HIM PALE. MEANWHILE...
OHO! THIS HEARING'S GETTING INTERESTING. THAT'S WARREN WORTHINGTON. HE'S A MUTIE. HIS HANDLE'S THE ANGEL. HE USED TO BANKROLL A WEST COAST SUPER-GROUP CALLED THE CHAMPIONS.
TELL LOIS TO TRY FOR AN INTERVIEW.
SENATOR. IN ALL HONESTY, I FAIL TO SEE THE NEED FOR THIS HEARING, OR YOUR CONCERN.
THE NEED IS SIMPLE, Dr. MacTAGGERT. I MERELY WONDER IF-- IN A WORLD OF BEINGS LIKE Dr. DOOM, MAGNETO, THE FANTASTIC FOUR, THE AVENGERS, AND LORD KNOWS HOW MANY OTHERS--
--THERE'S ANY PLACE FOR ORDINARY MEN AND WOMEN.
I WONDER, AS WELL, DOCTOR, IF THIS SAME QUESTION WASN'T ASKED BY THE LAST NEANDERTHAL ABOUT THE FIRST CRO-MAGNON?
?!?
HOLEE--!
GET OUTTA HERE, YOU PEOPLE! RUN FOR IT!!
THAT WALL'S COMIN' DOWN!!
HELP!
YYIIII--!
AND, WHEN THE AVALANCHE HAS RUN ITS COURSE...

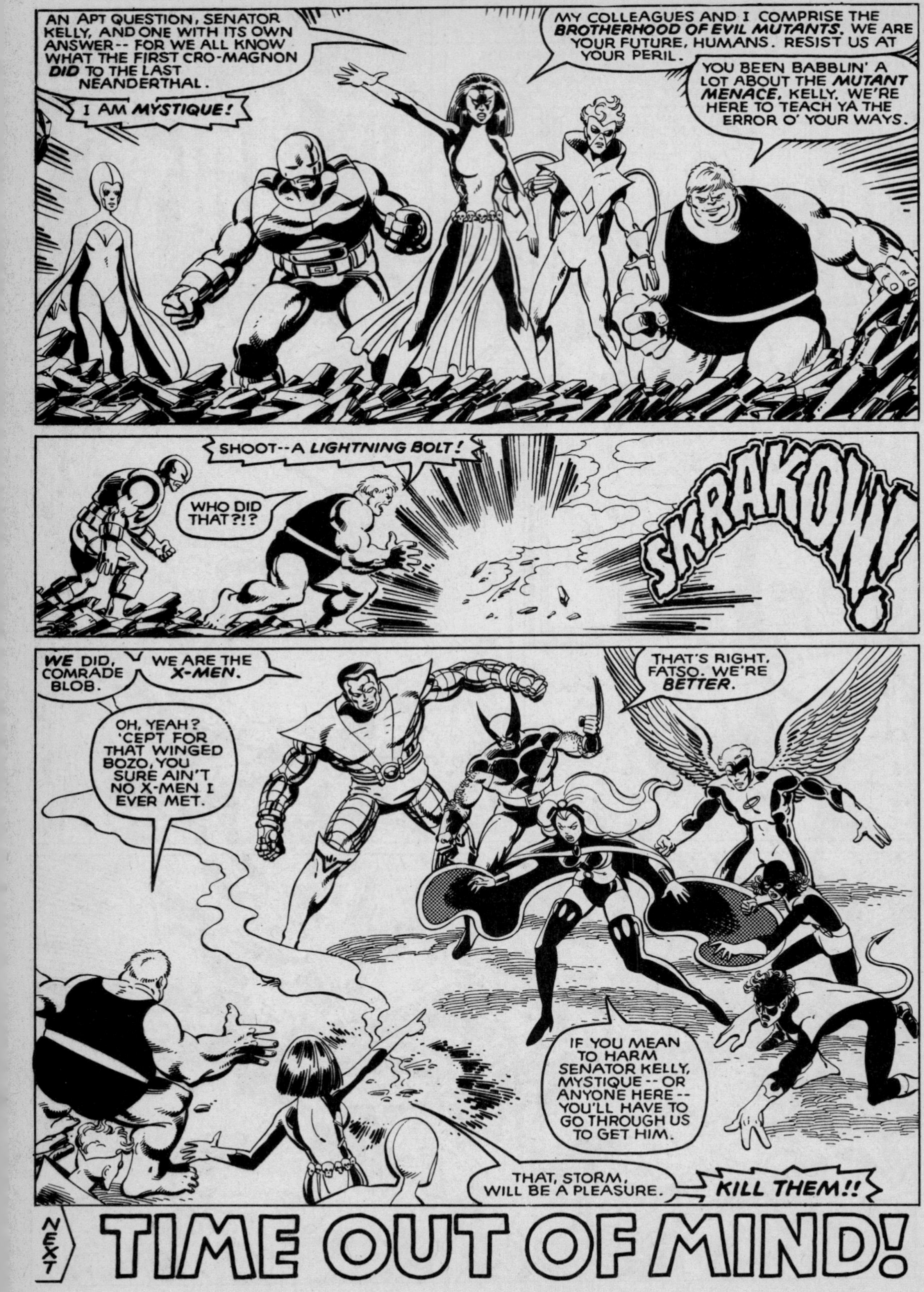
AN APT QUESTION, SENATOR KELLY, AND ONE WITH ITS OWN ANSWER-- FOR WE ALL KNOW WHAT THE FIRST CRO-MAGNON DID TO THE LAST NEANDERTHAL.
I AM MYSTIQUE!
MY COLLEAGUES AND I COMPRISE THE BROTHERHOOD OF EVIL MUTANTS. WE ARE YOUR FUTURE, HUMANS. RESIST US AT YOUR PERIL.
YOU BEEN BABBLIN' A LOT ABOUT THE MUTANT MENACE, KELLY. WE'RE HERE TO TEACH YA THE ERROR O' YOUR WAYS.
SHOOT--A LIGHTNING BOLT!
WHO DID THAT?!?
SKRAKOW!
WE DID, COMRADE BLOB.
WE ARE THE X-MEN.
THAT'S RIGHT, FATSO. WE'RE BETTER.
OH, YEAH? 'CEPT FOR THAT WINGED BOZO, YOU SURE AIN'T NO X-MEN I EVER MET.
IF YOU MEAN TO HARM SENATOR KELLY, MYSTIQUE -- OR ANYONE HERE -- YOU'LL HAVE TO GO THROUGH US TO GET HIM.
THAT, STORM, WILL BE A PLEASURE.
KILL THEM!!

NEXT TIME OUT OF MIND!

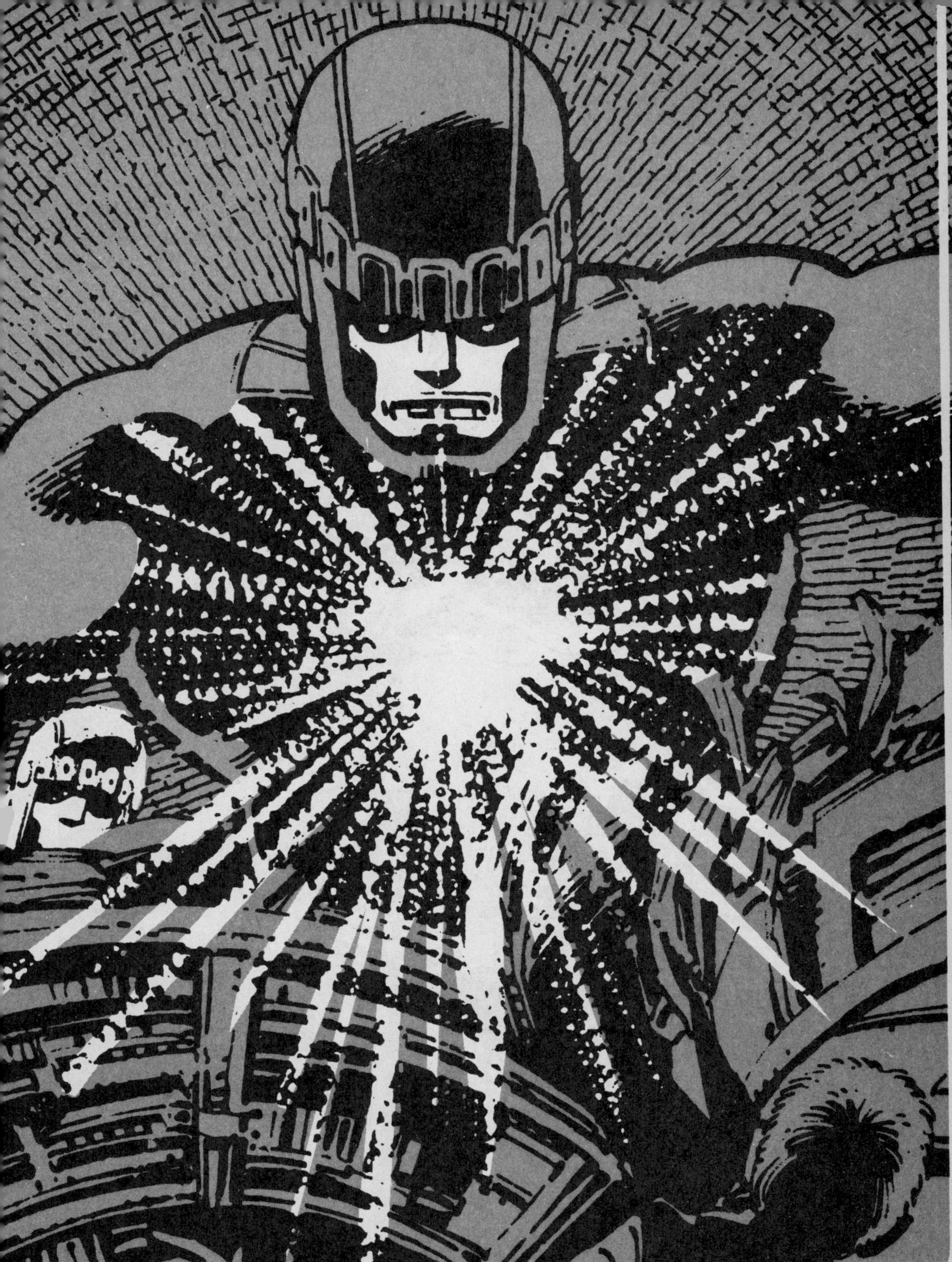

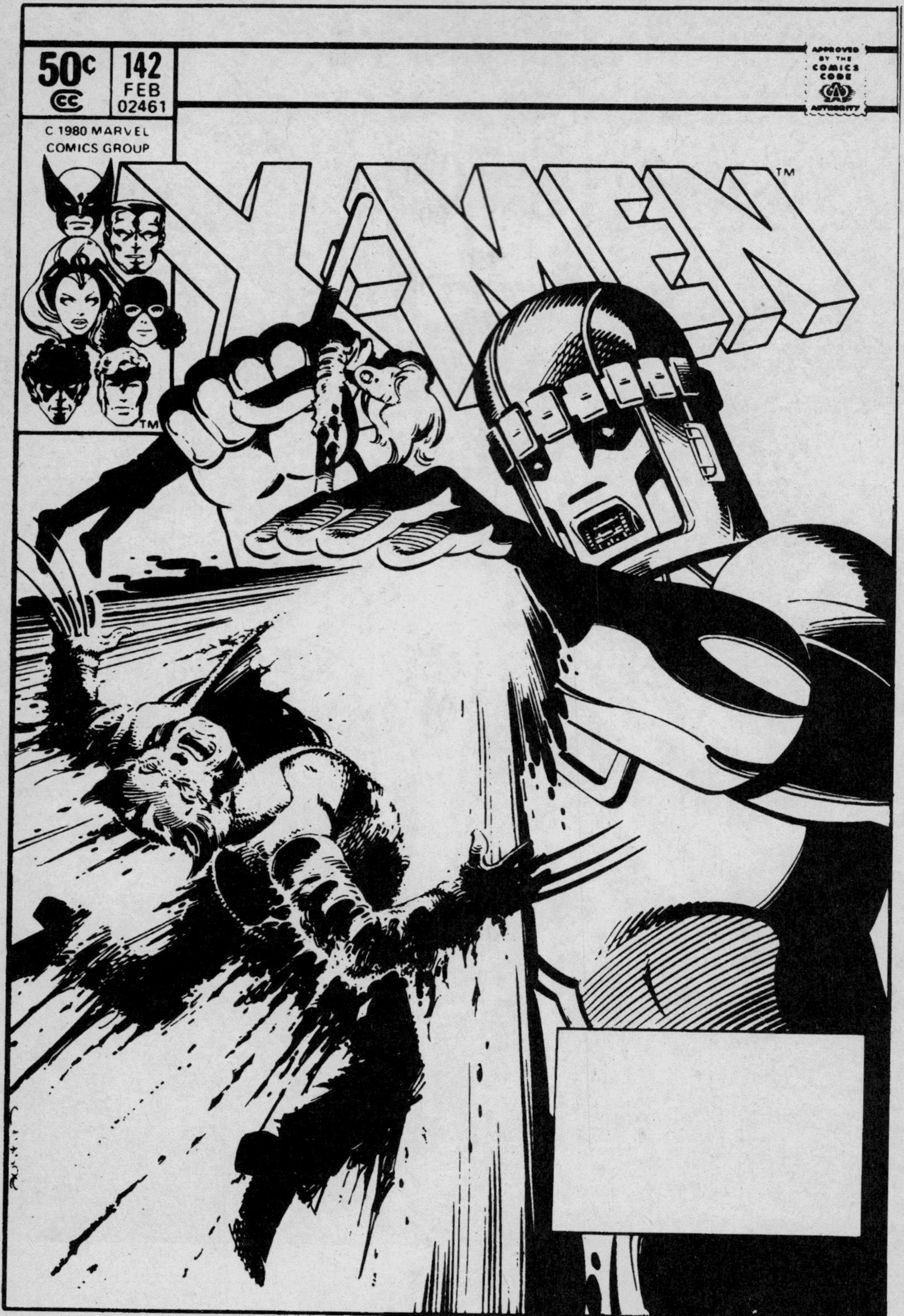
50¢
CC
142
FEB
02461
C 1980 MARVEL
COMICS GROUP
X-MEN
TM
APPROVED
BY THE
COMICS
CODE
AUTHORITY

STAN LEE presents: **THE UNCANNY X-MEN!**

CHRIS CLAREMONT • JOHN BYRNE | TERRY AUSTIN | GLYNIS WEIN, colorist | LOUISE JONES | JIM SHOOTER
WRITER / CO-PLOTTERS / PENCILER | INKER | TOM ORZECHOWSKI, letterer | EDITOR | Ed.-IN-CHIEF

THIS IS A TALE OF TWO WORLDS -- AND OF THE *CHILD/WOMAN* WHO SOUGHT TO SAVE THEM.

MIND OUT OF TIME!

1980-- THE UNCANNY X-MEN (WOLVERINE, COLOSSUS, STORM, ANGEL, SPRITE & NIGHTCRAWLER) FACE OFF AGAINST THE NEWLY-RECONSTITUTED *BROTHERHOOD OF EVIL MUTANTS* IN A HEARING ROOM OF THE UNITED STATES SENATE.

2013-- THE REMNANTS OF THAT SELF-SAME TEAM OF MUTANT SUPER-HEROES FIGHT FOR THEIR LIVES AGAINST THE NIGH-IRRESISTIBLE MIGHT OF THE *SENTINELS*...

...IN A LAST-DITCH ATTEMPT TO SAVE THEIR WORLD FROM IMMINENT *NUCLEAR* ARMAGEDDON.

AND LINKING THESE TWO WORLDS, THESE TWO DESPERATE BATTLES, IS *KATHERINE PRYDE.* IN HER HANDS LIES THE FATE OF MUTANTKIND, OF HUMANITY, OF THE EARTH ITSELF. FAILURE IS UNTHINKABLE, YET SUCCESS MAY WELL BE IMPOSSIBLE -- FOR SHE SEEKS TO *CHANGE HISTORY.*

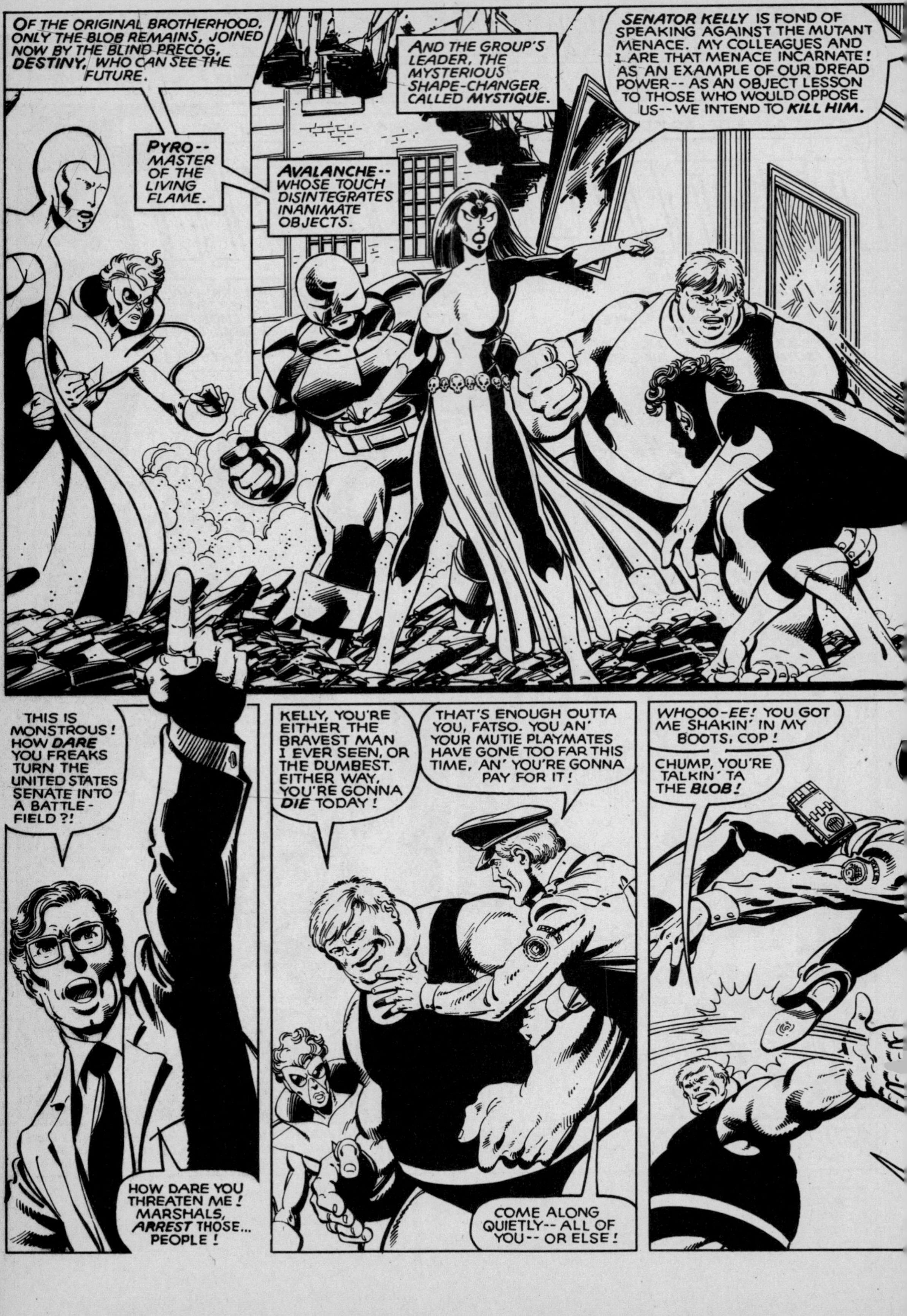

OF THE ORIGINAL BROTHERHOOD, ONLY THE BLOB REMAINS, JOINED NOW BY THE BLIND PRECOG, DESTINY, WHO CAN SEE THE FUTURE.
PYRO-- MASTER OF THE LIVING FLAME.
AVALANCHE-- WHOSE TOUCH DISINTEGRATES INANIMATE OBJECTS.
AND THE GROUP'S LEADER, THE MYSTERIOUS SHAPE-CHANGER CALLED MYSTIQUE.
SENATOR KELLY IS FOND OF SPEAKING AGAINST THE MUTANT MENACE. MY COLLEAGUES AND I ARE THAT MENACE INCARNATE! AS AN EXAMPLE OF OUR DREAD POWER-- AS AN OBJECT LESSON TO THOSE WHO WOULD OPPOSE US-- WE INTEND TO KILL HIM.
THIS IS MONSTROUS! HOW DARE YOU FREAKS TURN THE UNITED STATES SENATE INTO A BATTLE-FIELD?!
HOW DARE YOU THREATEN ME! MARSHALS, ARREST THOSE... PEOPLE!
KELLY, YOU'RE EITHER THE BRAVEST MAN I EVER SEEN, OR THE DUMBEST. EITHER WAY, YOU'RE GONNA DIE TODAY!
THAT'S ENOUGH OUTTA YOU, FATSO. YOU AN' YOUR MUTIE PLAYMATES HAVE GONE TOO FAR THIS TIME, AN' YOU'RE GONNA PAY FOR IT!
COME ALONG QUIETLY-- ALL OF YOU-- OR ELSE!
WHOOO-EE! YOU GOT ME SHAKIN' IN MY BOOTS, COP!
CHUMP, YOU'RE TALKIN' TA THE BLOB!

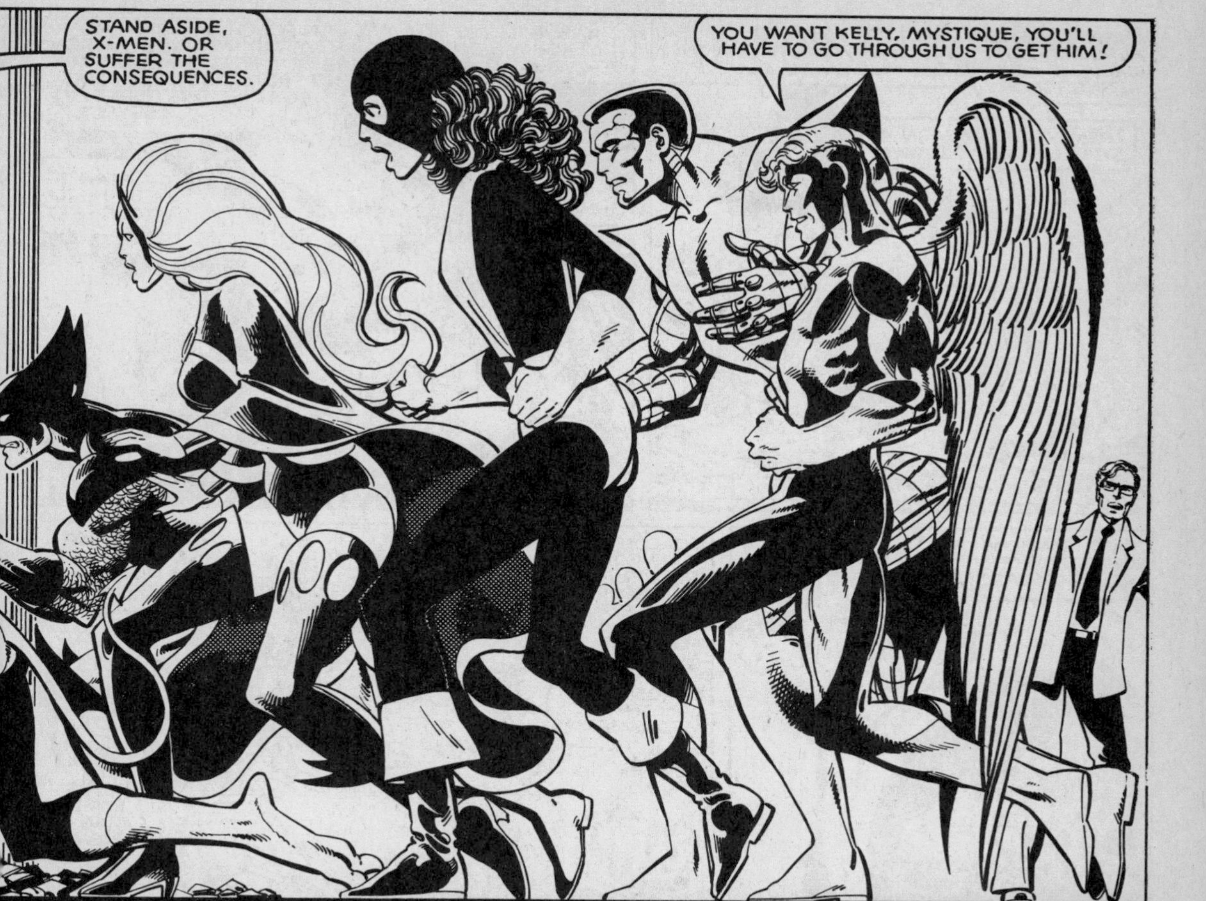
STAND ASIDE, X-MEN. OR SUFFER THE CONSEQUENCES.
YOU WANT KELLY, MYSTIQUE, YOU'LL HAVE TO GO THROUGH US TO GET HIM!

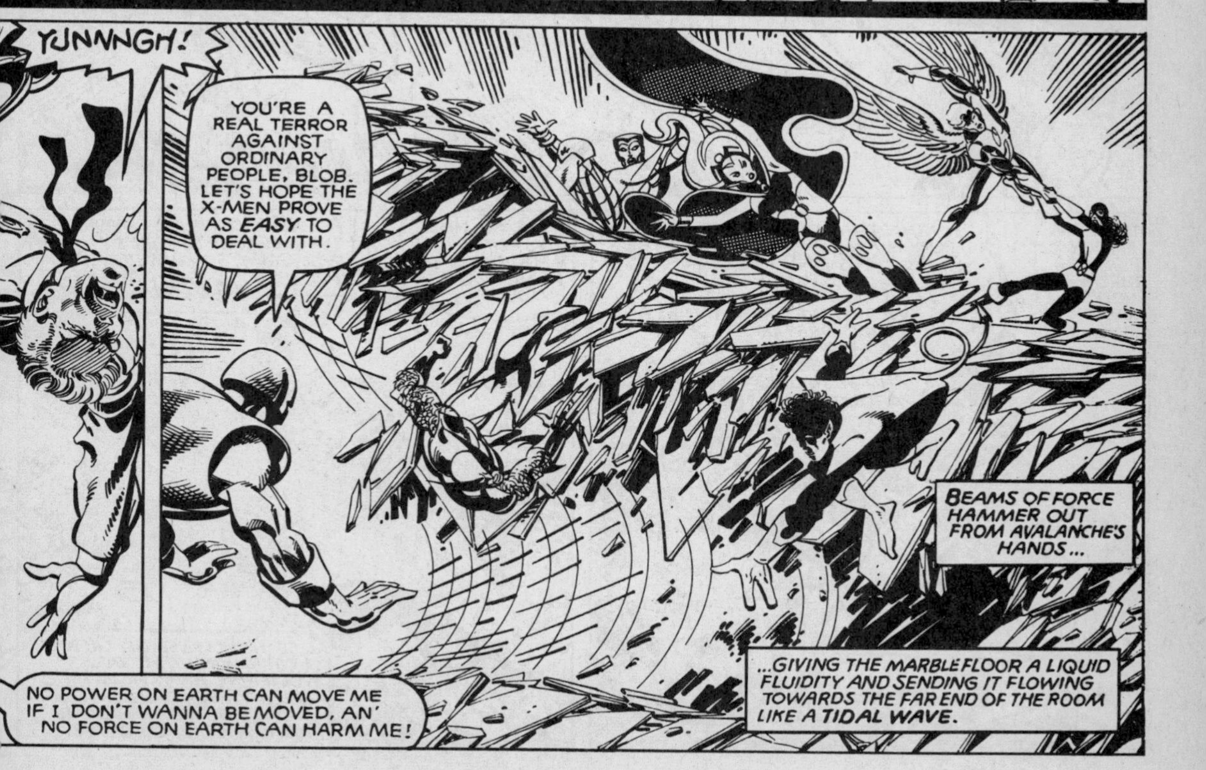
YUNNNGH!
YOU'RE A REAL TERROR AGAINST ORDINARY PEOPLE, BLOB. LET'S HOPE THE X-MEN PROVE AS EASY TO DEAL WITH.
NO POWER ON EARTH CAN MOVE ME IF I DON'T WANNA BE MOVED, AN' NO FORCE ON EARTH CAN HARM ME!
BEAMS OF FORCE HAMMER OUT FROM AVALANCHE'S HANDS...
...GIVING THE MARBLE FLOOR A LIQUID FLUIDITY AND SENDING IT FLOWING TOWARDS THE FAR END OF THE ROOM LIKE A TIDAL WAVE.

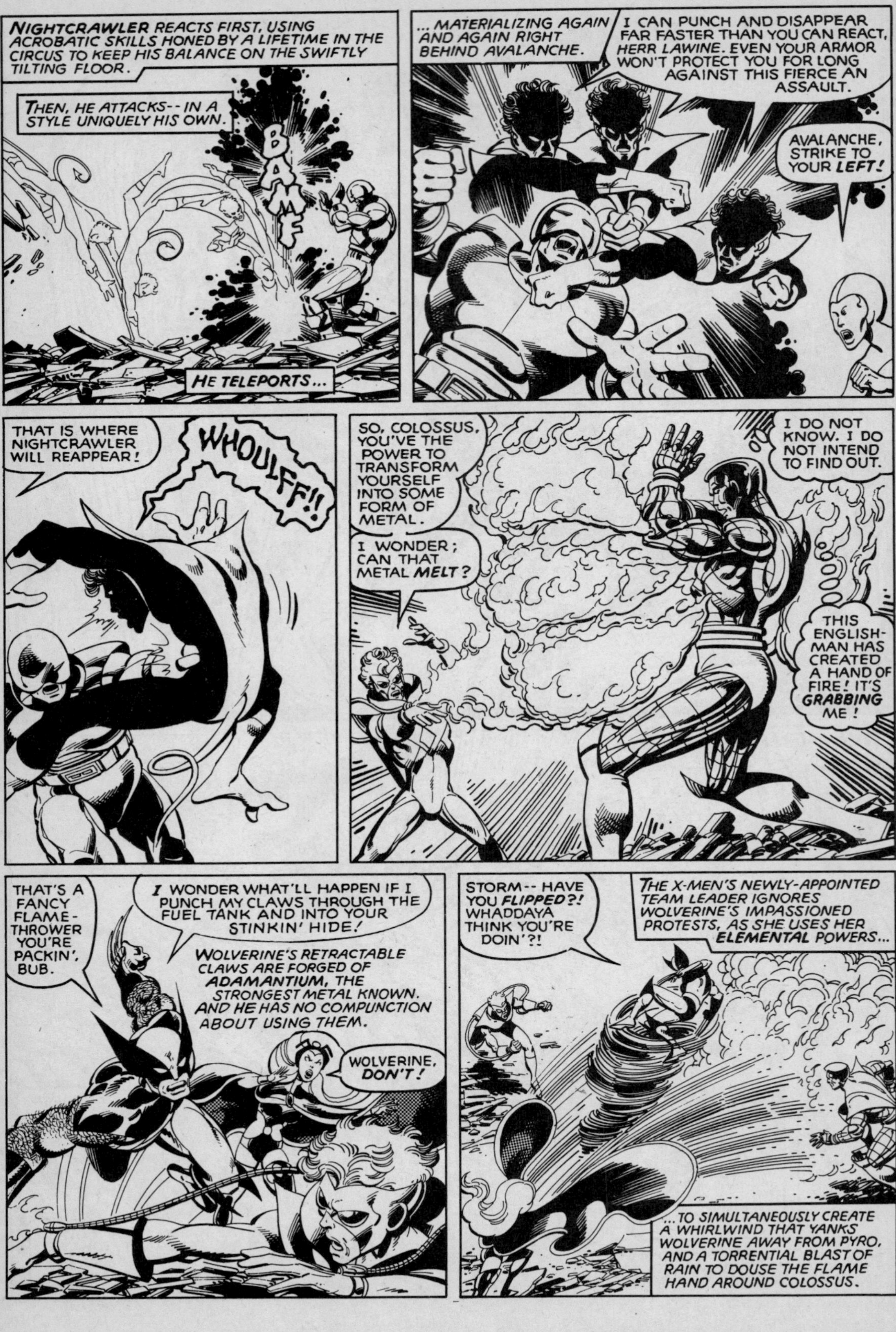
NIGHTCRAWLER REACTS FIRST, USING ACROBATIC SKILLS HONED BY A LIFETIME IN THE CIRCUS TO KEEP HIS BALANCE ON THE SWIFTLY TILTING FLOOR.
THEN, HE ATTACKS-- IN A STYLE UNIQUELY HIS OWN.
BAMF
HE TELEPORTS...
...MATERIALIZING AGAIN AND AGAIN RIGHT BEHIND AVALANCHE.
I CAN PUNCH AND DISAPPEAR FAR FASTER THAN YOU CAN REACT, HERR LAWINE. EVEN YOUR ARMOR WON'T PROTECT YOU FOR LONG AGAINST THIS FIERCE AN ASSAULT.
AVALANCHE, STRIKE TO YOUR LEFT!
THAT IS WHERE NIGHTCRAWLER WILL REAPPEAR!
WHOULFFF!!
SO, COLOSSUS, YOU'VE THE POWER TO TRANSFORM YOURSELF INTO SOME FORM OF METAL.
I WONDER; CAN THAT METAL MELT?
I DO NOT KNOW. I DO NOT INTEND TO FIND OUT.
THIS ENGLISH-MAN HAS CREATED A HAND OF FIRE! IT'S GRABBING ME!
THAT'S A FANCY FLAME-THROWER YOU'RE PACKIN', BUB.
I WONDER WHAT'LL HAPPEN IF I PUNCH MY CLAWS THROUGH THE FUEL TANK AND INTO YOUR STINKIN' HIDE!
WOLVERINE'S RETRACTABLE CLAWS ARE FORGED OF ADAMANTIUM, THE STRONGEST METAL KNOWN. AND HE HAS NO COMPUNCTION ABOUT USING THEM.
WOLVERINE, DON'T!
STORM-- HAVE YOU FLIPPED?! WHADDAYA THINK YOU'RE DOIN'?!
THE X-MEN'S NEWLY-APPOINTED TEAM LEADER IGNORES WOLVERINE'S IMPASSIONED PROTESTS, AS SHE USES HER ELEMENTAL POWERS...
...TO SIMULTANEOUSLY CREATE A WHIRLWIND THAT YANKS WOLVERINE AWAY FROM PYRO, AND A TORRENTIAL BLAST OF RAIN TO DOUSE THE FLAME HAND AROUND COLOSSUS.

Panel 1: NICE MOVE, STORM. WITH THE COUNTRY'S GROWING ANTI-MUTANT SENTIMENT, THE LAST THING WE NEED IS WOLVIE CARVING SOMEONE UP-- EVEN IF IT IS A VILLAIN.

ANGEL, FIND SENATOR KELLY! HE MUST BE PROTECTED AT ANY COST!

Panel 2: NEARBY, SCRAMBLING FOR THEIR LIVES, ARE THE X-MEN'S FOUNDER AND MENTOR, *PROFESSOR CHARLES XAVIER*, AND HIS COLLEAGUE IN MUTANT RESEARCH-- ALSO, HIS ONE-TIME LOVE-- *MOIRA MacTAGGERT*.

CHARLES, WHAT THE DEVIL IS HAPPENING?!

IT'S ALMOST TOO FANTASTIC TO BELIEVE. SOMEHOW, THE MIND AND PERSONA OF THE *ADULT* KATE PRYDE-- FROM 30 YEARS IN THE FUTURE-- HAS PSYCHICALLY EXCHANGED PLACES WITH THAT OF HER TEEN-AGED SELF.

THE BODY OF *SPRITE* IS INHABITED BY THE CONSCIOUSNESS OF THE WOMAN SHE WILL ONE DAY BECOME.

Panel 3: THAT'S DAFT!

MOIRA, I TELEPATHICALLY SCANNED HER MIND. IT IS THE *TRUTH*.

PROFESSOR XAVIER, LET'S GET YOU AND Dr. MacTAGGERT OUT OF HERE!

Panel 4: THAT'S THE FIRST SENSIBLE SUGGESTION I'VE HEARD ALL MORNING!

CHARLES, IF YOU'RE RIGHT-- IF TIME TRAVEL IS POSSIBLE, IF AS A RESULT HISTORY IS... MUTABLE-- WE'LL HAVE TO REDEFINE OUR CONCEPT OF REALITY ITSELF.

WE'LL NEVER BE COMPLETELY SURE WHAT... IS... FROM ONE MOMENT TO THE NEXT. THAT'S... *FRIGHTENING!*

PERHAPS.

YOU'LL BE SAFE HERE.

600

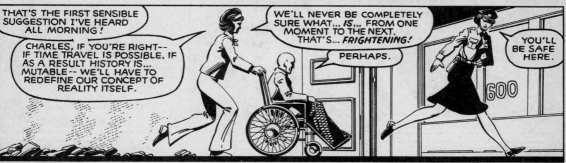

Panel 5: THANK GOODNESS.

WAIT! MOIRA, I SENSE SOME SORT OF ENERGY FIELD AROUND THIS WOMAN. SHE IS *NOT* WHAT SHE SEEMS--

AARGKGH!

YOU SPOTTED THE ELECTRONIC *DAMPER* FIELD WHICH KEPT YOU FROM READING MY MIND, XAVIER...

Panel 6: ...UNTIL IT WAS *TOO LATE* TO DO YOU ANY GOOD.

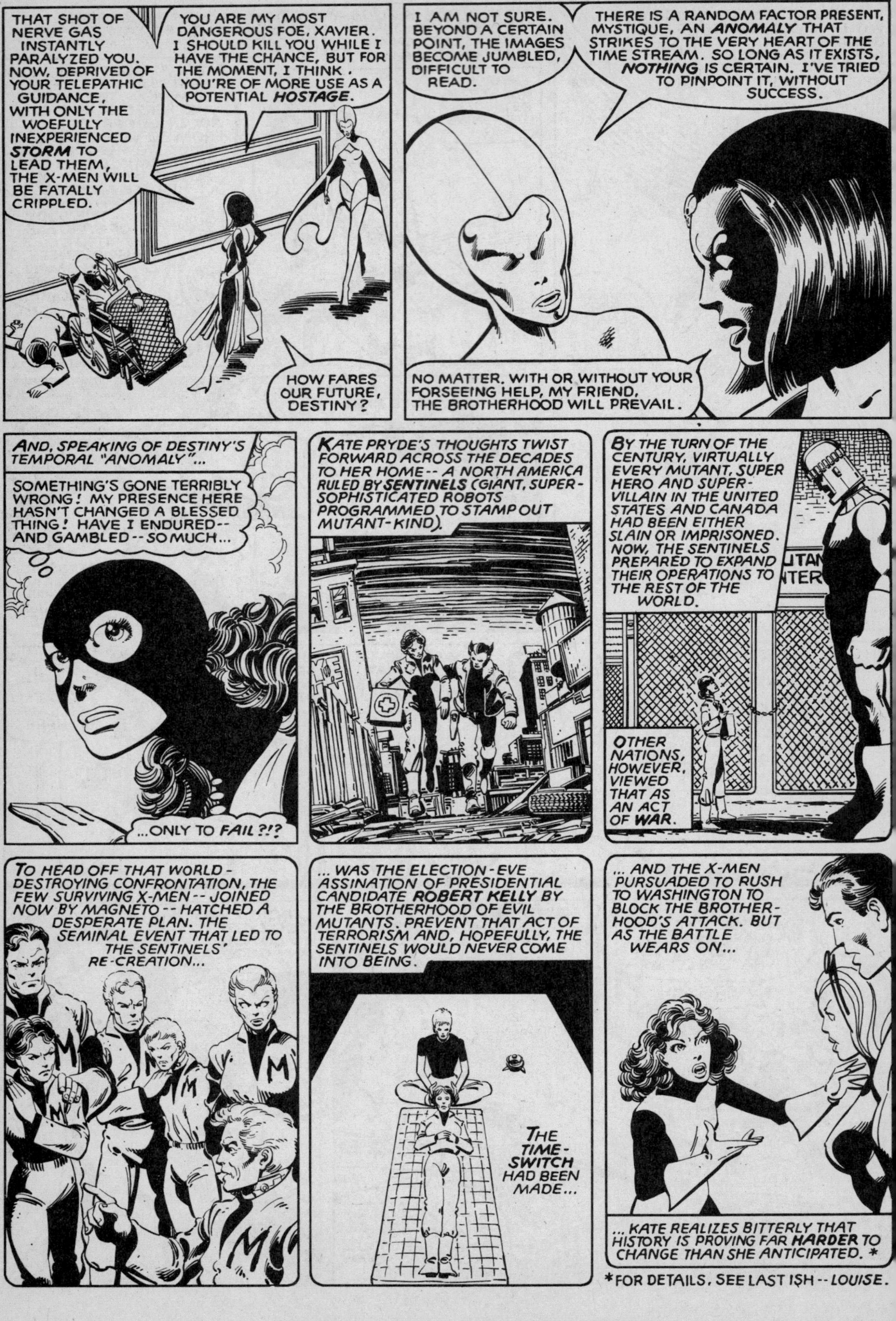
THAT SHOT OF NERVE GAS INSTANTLY PARALYZED YOU. NOW, DEPRIVED OF YOUR TELEPATHIC GUIDANCE, WITH ONLY THE WOEFULLY INEXPERIENCED STORM TO LEAD THEM, THE X-MEN WILL BE FATALLY CRIPPLED.
YOU ARE MY MOST DANGEROUS FOE, XAVIER. I SHOULD KILL YOU WHILE I HAVE THE CHANCE, BUT FOR THE MOMENT, I THINK. YOU'RE OF MORE USE AS A POTENTIAL HOSTAGE.
HOW FARES OUR FUTURE, DESTINY?
I AM NOT SURE. BEYOND A CERTAIN POINT, THE IMAGES BECOME JUMBLED, DIFFICULT TO READ.
THERE IS A RANDOM FACTOR PRESENT, MYSTIQUE, AN ANOMALY THAT STRIKES TO THE VERY HEART OF THE TIME STREAM. SO LONG AS IT EXISTS, NOTHING IS CERTAIN. I'VE TRIED TO PINPOINT IT, WITHOUT SUCCESS.
NO MATTER. WITH OR WITHOUT YOUR FORSEEING HELP, MY FRIEND, THE BROTHERHOOD WILL PREVAIL.
AND, SPEAKING OF DESTINY'S TEMPORAL "ANOMALY"...
SOMETHING'S GONE TERRIBLY WRONG! MY PRESENCE HERE HASN'T CHANGED A BLESSED THING! HAVE I ENDURED-- AND GAMBLED -- SO MUCH...
...ONLY TO FAIL?!?
KATE PRYDE'S THOUGHTS TWIST FORWARD ACROSS THE DECADES TO HER HOME -- A NORTH AMERICA RULED BY SENTINELS (GIANT, SUPER-SOPHISTICATED ROBOTS PROGRAMMED TO STAMP OUT MUTANT-KIND).
BY THE TURN OF THE CENTURY, VIRTUALLY EVERY MUTANT, SUPER HERO AND SUPER-VILLAIN IN THE UNITED STATES AND CANADA HAD BEEN EITHER SLAIN OR IMPRISONED. NOW, THE SENTINELS PREPARED TO EXPAND THEIR OPERATIONS TO THE REST OF THE WORLD.
OTHER NATIONS, HOWEVER, VIEWED THAT AS AN ACT OF WAR.
TO HEAD OFF THAT WORLD-DESTROYING CONFRONTATION, THE FEW SURVIVING X-MEN -- JOINED NOW BY MAGNETO -- HATCHED A DESPERATE PLAN. THE SEMINAL EVENT THAT LED TO THE SENTINELS' RE-CREATION...
... WAS THE ELECTION-EVE ASSINATION OF PRESIDENTIAL CANDIDATE ROBERT KELLY BY THE BROTHERHOOD OF EVIL MUTANTS. PREVENT THAT ACT OF TERRORISM AND, HOPEFULLY, THE SENTINELS WOULD NEVER COME INTO BEING.
THE TIME-SWITCH HAD BEEN MADE...
... AND THE X-MEN PURSUADED TO RUSH TO WASHINGTON TO BLOCK THE BROTHER-HOOD'S ATTACK. BUT AS THE BATTLE WEARS ON...
... KATE REALIZES BITTERLY THAT HISTORY IS PROVING FAR HARDER TO CHANGE THAN SHE ANTICIPATED. *
*FOR DETAILS, SEE LAST IŞH -- LOUISE.

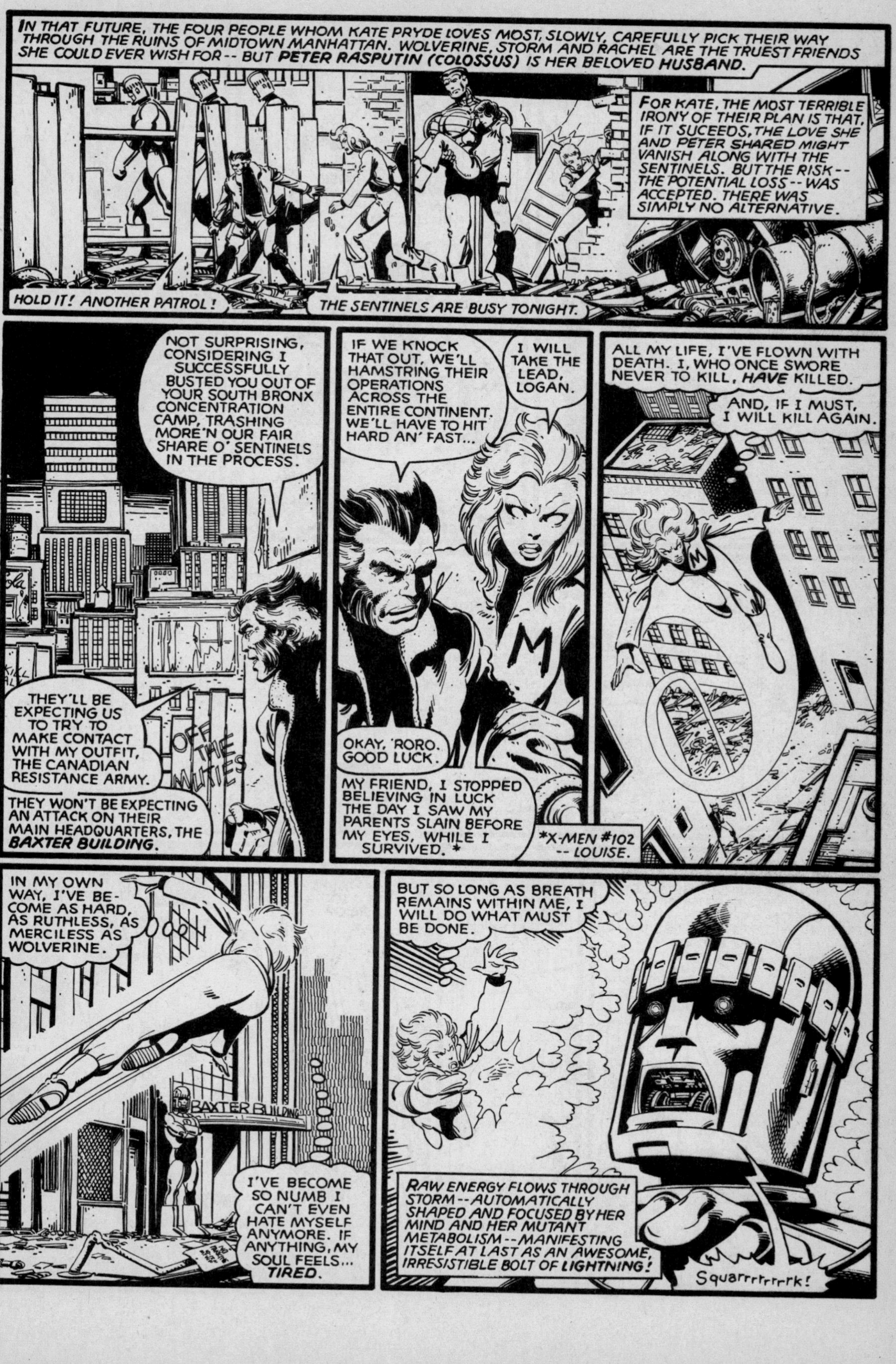

IN THAT FUTURE, THE FOUR PEOPLE WHOM KATE PRYDE LOVES MOST, SLOWLY, CAREFULLY PICK THEIR WAY THROUGH THE RUINS OF MIDTOWN MANHATTAN. WOLVERINE, STORM AND RACHEL ARE THE TRUEST FRIENDS SHE COULD EVER WISH FOR -- BUT PETER RASPUTIN (COLOSSUS) IS HER BELOVED HUSBAND.
FOR KATE, THE MOST TERRIBLE IRONY OF THEIR PLAN IS THAT, IF IT SUCEEDS, THE LOVE SHE AND PETER SHARED MIGHT VANISH ALONG WITH THE SENTINELS. BUT THE RISK -- THE POTENTIAL LOSS -- WAS ACCEPTED. THERE WAS SIMPLY NO ALTERNATIVE.
HOLD IT! ANOTHER PATROL!
THE SENTINELS ARE BUSY TONIGHT.
NOT SURPRISING, CONSIDERING I SUCCESSFULLY BUSTED YOU OUT OF YOUR SOUTH BRONX CONCENTRATION CAMP, TRASHING MORE'N OUR FAIR SHARE O' SENTINELS IN THE PROCESS.
THEY'LL BE EXPECTING US TO TRY TO MAKE CONTACT WITH MY OUTFIT, THE CANADIAN RESISTANCE ARMY.
THEY WON'T BE EXPECTING AN ATTACK ON THEIR MAIN HEADQUARTERS, THE BAXTER BUILDING.
OFF THE MUTIES
IF WE KNOCK THAT OUT, WE'LL HAMSTRING THEIR OPERATIONS ACROSS THE ENTIRE CONTINENT. WE'LL HAVE TO HIT HARD AN' FAST...
I WILL TAKE THE LEAD, LOGAN.
OKAY, 'RORO. GOOD LUCK.
MY FRIEND, I STOPPED BELIEVING IN LUCK THE DAY I SAW MY PARENTS SLAIN BEFORE MY EYES, WHILE I SURVIVED. *
*X-MEN #102 -- LOUISE.
ALL MY LIFE, I'VE FLOWN WITH DEATH. I, WHO ONCE SWORE NEVER TO KILL, HAVE KILLED.
AND, IF I MUST, I WILL KILL AGAIN.
IN MY OWN WAY, I'VE BECOME AS HARD, AS RUTHLESS, AS MERCILESS AS WOLVERINE.
BAXTER BUILDING
I'VE BECOME SO NUMB I CAN'T EVEN HATE MYSELF ANYMORE. IF ANYTHING, MY SOUL FEELS... TIRED.
BUT SO LONG AS BREATH REMAINS WITHIN ME, I WILL DO WHAT MUST BE DONE.
RAW ENERGY FLOWS THROUGH STORM -- AUTOMATICALLY SHAPED AND FOCUSED BY HER MIND AND HER MUTANT METABOLISM -- MANIFESTING ITSELF AT LAST AS AN AWESOME, IRRESISTIBLE BOLT OF LIGHTNING!
Squarrrrrrrrk!

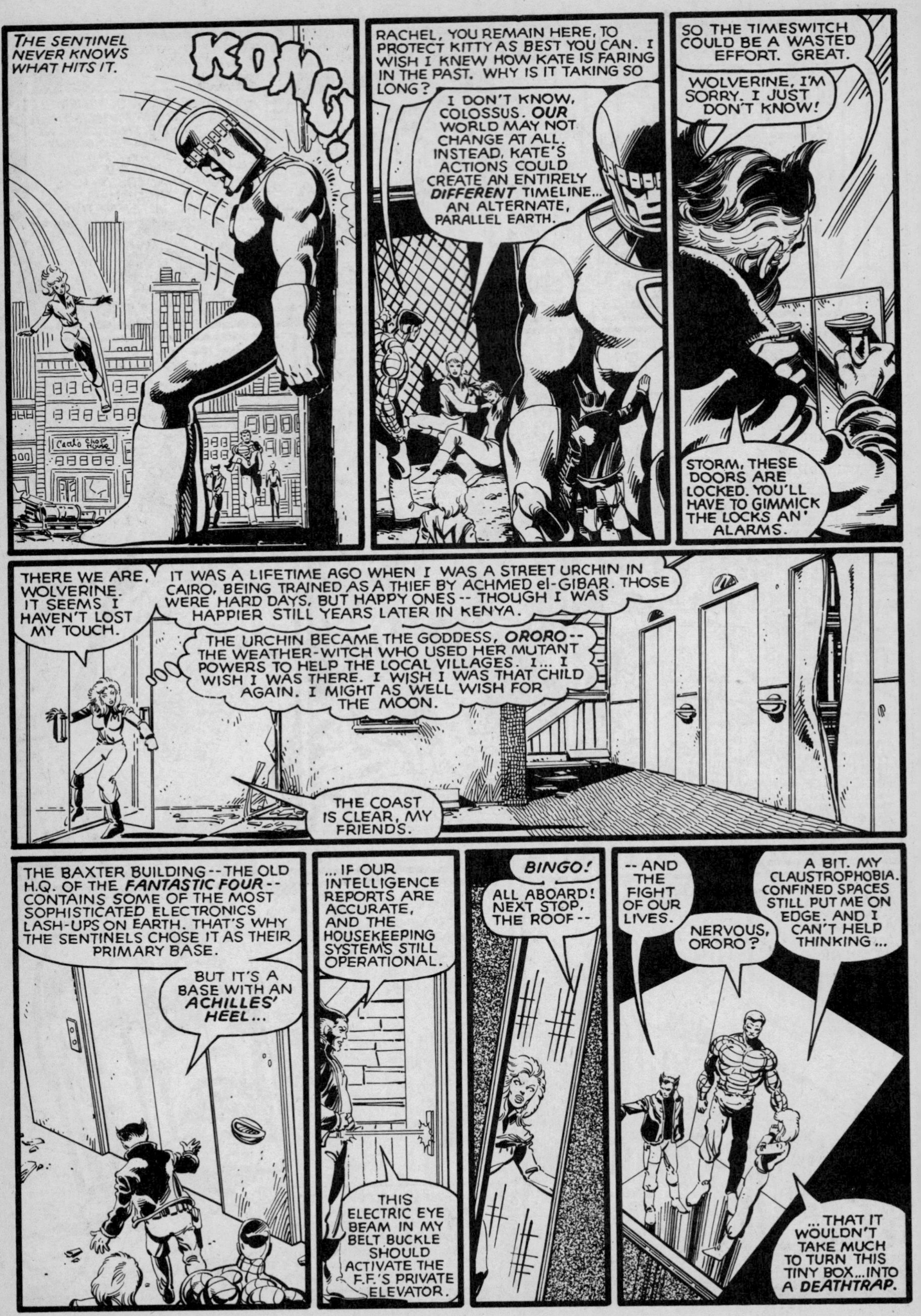
THE SENTINEL NEVER KNOWS WHAT HITS IT.
KONG!
RACHEL, YOU REMAIN HERE, TO PROTECT KITTY AS BEST YOU CAN. I WISH I KNEW HOW KATE IS FARING IN THE PAST. WHY IS IT TAKING SO LONG?
I DON'T KNOW, COLOSSUS. OUR WORLD MAY NOT CHANGE AT ALL. INSTEAD, KATE'S ACTIONS COULD CREATE AN ENTIRELY DIFFERENT TIMELINE... AN ALTERNATE, PARALLEL EARTH.
SO THE TIMESWITCH COULD BE A WASTED EFFORT. GREAT.
WOLVERINE, I'M SORRY. I JUST DON'T KNOW!
STORM, THESE DOORS ARE LOCKED. YOU'LL HAVE TO GIMMICK THE LOCKS AN' ALARMS.
THERE WE ARE, WOLVERINE. IT SEEMS I HAVEN'T LOST MY TOUCH.
IT WAS A LIFETIME AGO WHEN I WAS A STREET URCHIN IN CAIRO, BEING TRAINED AS A THIEF BY ACHMED el-GIBAR. THOSE WERE HARD DAYS, BUT HAPPY ONES -- THOUGH I WAS HAPPIER STILL YEARS LATER IN KENYA.
THE URCHIN BECAME THE GODDESS, ORORO -- THE WEATHER-WITCH WHO USED HER MUTANT POWERS TO HELP THE LOCAL VILLAGES. I... I WISH I WAS THERE. I WISH I WAS THAT CHILD AGAIN. I MIGHT AS WELL WISH FOR THE MOON.
THE COAST IS CLEAR, MY FRIENDS.
THE BAXTER BUILDING -- THE OLD H.Q. OF THE FANTASTIC FOUR -- CONTAINS SOME OF THE MOST SOPHISTICATED ELECTRONICS LASH-UPS ON EARTH. THAT'S WHY THE SENTINELS CHOSE IT AS THEIR PRIMARY BASE.
BUT IT'S A BASE WITH AN ACHILLES' HEEL...
...IF OUR INTELLIGENCE REPORTS ARE ACCURATE, AND THE HOUSEKEEPING SYSTEM'S STILL OPERATIONAL.
THIS ELECTRIC EYE BEAM IN MY BELT BUCKLE SHOULD ACTIVATE THE F.F.'S PRIVATE ELEVATOR.
BINGO!
ALL ABOARD! NEXT STOP, THE ROOF --
-- AND THE FIGHT OF OUR LIVES.
NERVOUS, ORORO?
A BIT. MY CLAUSTROPHOBIA. CONFINED SPACES STILL PUT ME ON EDGE. AND I CAN'T HELP THINKING...
...THAT IT WOULDN'T TAKE MUCH TO TURN THIS TINY BOX... INTO A DEATHTRAP.

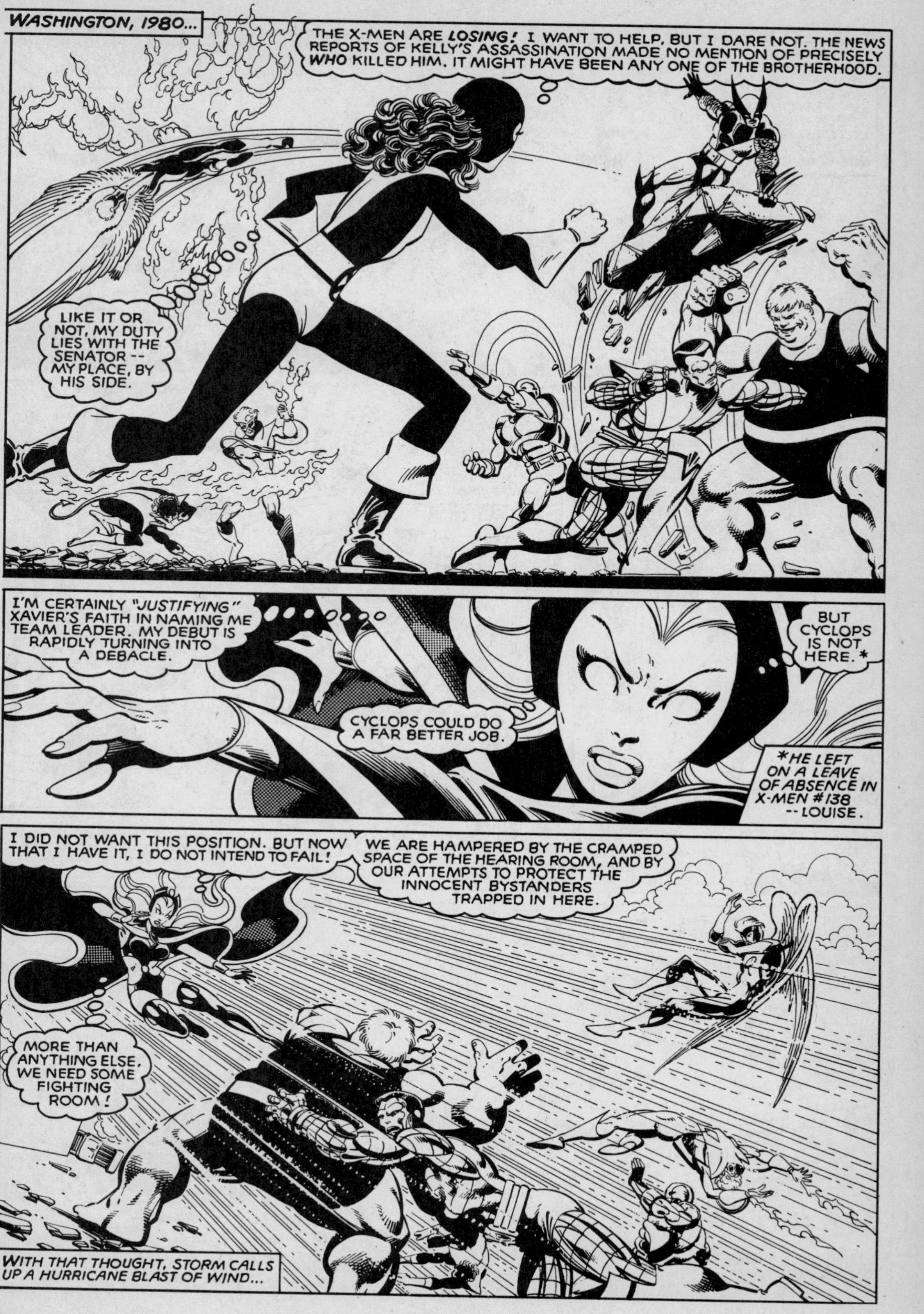
WASHINGTON, 1980...
THE X-MEN ARE LOSING! I WANT TO HELP, BUT I DARE NOT. THE NEWS REPORTS OF KELLY'S ASSASSINATION MADE NO MENTION OF PRECISELY WHO KILLED HIM. IT MIGHT HAVE BEEN ANY ONE OF THE BROTHERHOOD.
LIKE IT OR NOT, MY DUTY LIES WITH THE SENATOR -- MY PLACE, BY HIS SIDE.
I'M CERTAINLY "JUSTIFYING" XAVIER'S FAITH IN NAMING ME TEAM LEADER. MY DEBUT IS RAPIDLY TURNING INTO A DEBACLE.
CYCLOPS COULD DO A FAR BETTER JOB.
BUT CYCLOPS IS NOT HERE.*
*HE LEFT ON A LEAVE OF ABSENCE IN X-MEN #138 -- LOUISE.
I DID NOT WANT THIS POSITION. BUT NOW THAT I HAVE IT, I DO NOT INTEND TO FAIL!
WE ARE HAMPERED BY THE CRAMPED SPACE OF THE HEARING ROOM, AND BY OUR ATTEMPTS TO PROTECT THE INNOCENT BYSTANDERS TRAPPED IN HERE.
MORE THAN ANYTHING ELSE, WE NEED SOME FIGHTING ROOM!
WITH THAT THOUGHT, STORM CALLS UP A HURRICANE BLAST OF WIND...

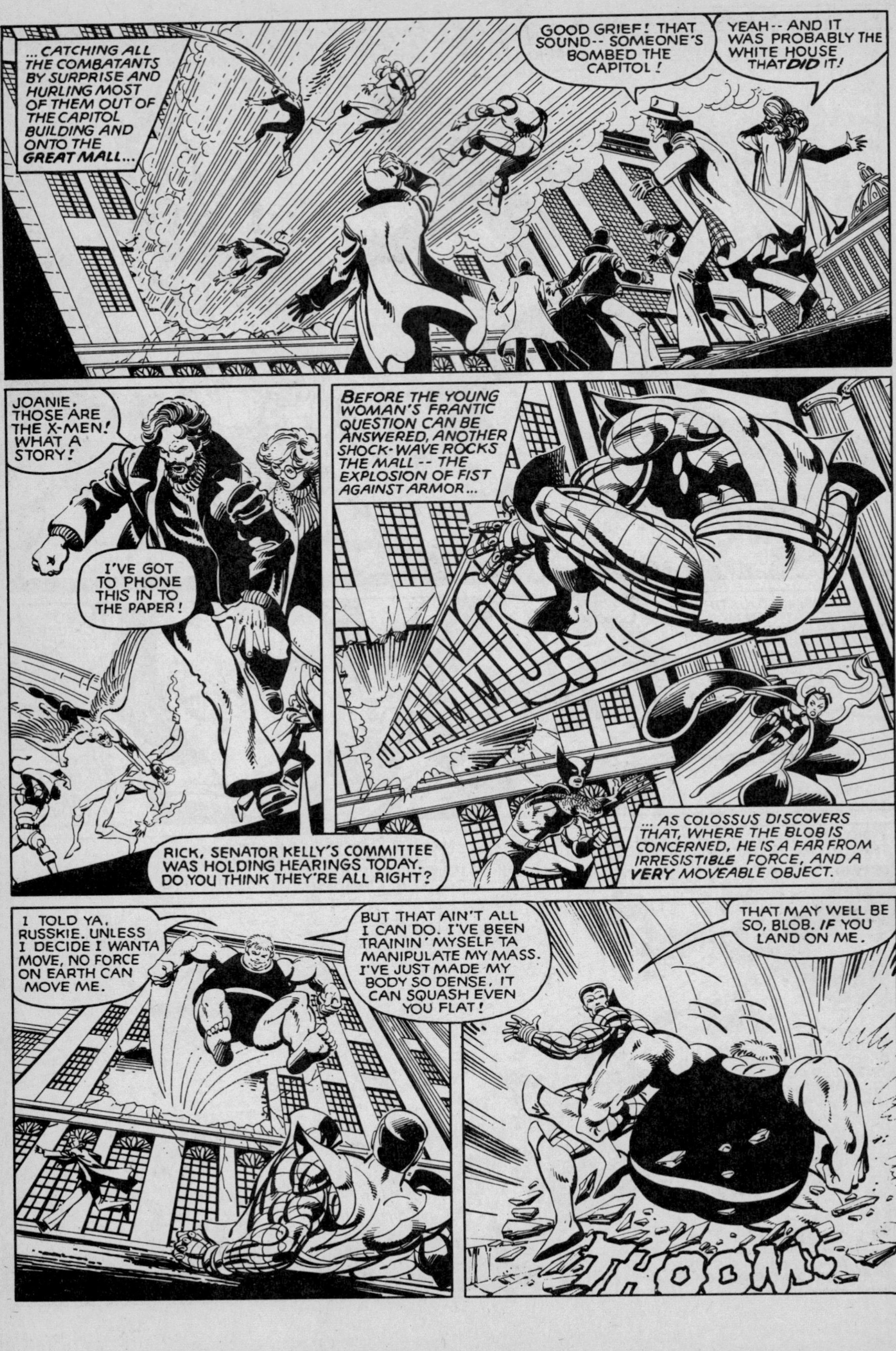

...CATCHING ALL THE COMBATANTS BY SURPRISE AND HURLING MOST OF THEM OUT OF THE CAPITOL BUILDING AND ONTO THE GREAT MALL...
GOOD GRIEF! THAT SOUND-- SOMEONE'S BOMBED THE CAPITOL!
YEAH-- AND IT WAS PROBABLY THE WHITE HOUSE THAT DID IT!
JOANIE, THOSE ARE THE X-MEN! WHAT A STORY!
I'VE GOT TO PHONE THIS IN TO THE PAPER!
RICK, SENATOR KELLY'S COMMITTEE WAS HOLDING HEARINGS TODAY. DO YOU THINK THEY'RE ALL RIGHT?
BEFORE THE YOUNG WOMAN'S FRANTIC QUESTION CAN BE ANSWERED, ANOTHER SHOCK-WAVE ROCKS THE MALL -- THE EXPLOSION OF FIST AGAINST ARMOR...
WHAMM!
...AS COLOSSUS DISCOVERS THAT, WHERE THE BLOB IS CONCERNED, HE IS A FAR FROM IRRESISTIBLE FORCE, AND A VERY MOVEABLE OBJECT.
I TOLD YA, RUSSKIE. UNLESS I DECIDE I WANTA MOVE, NO FORCE ON EARTH CAN MOVE ME.
BUT THAT AIN'T ALL I CAN DO. I'VE BEEN TRAININ' MYSELF TA MANIPULATE MY MASS. I'VE JUST MADE MY BODY SO DENSE, IT CAN SQUASH EVEN YOU FLAT!
THAT MAY WELL BE SO, BLOB. IF YOU LAND ON ME.
THOOM!

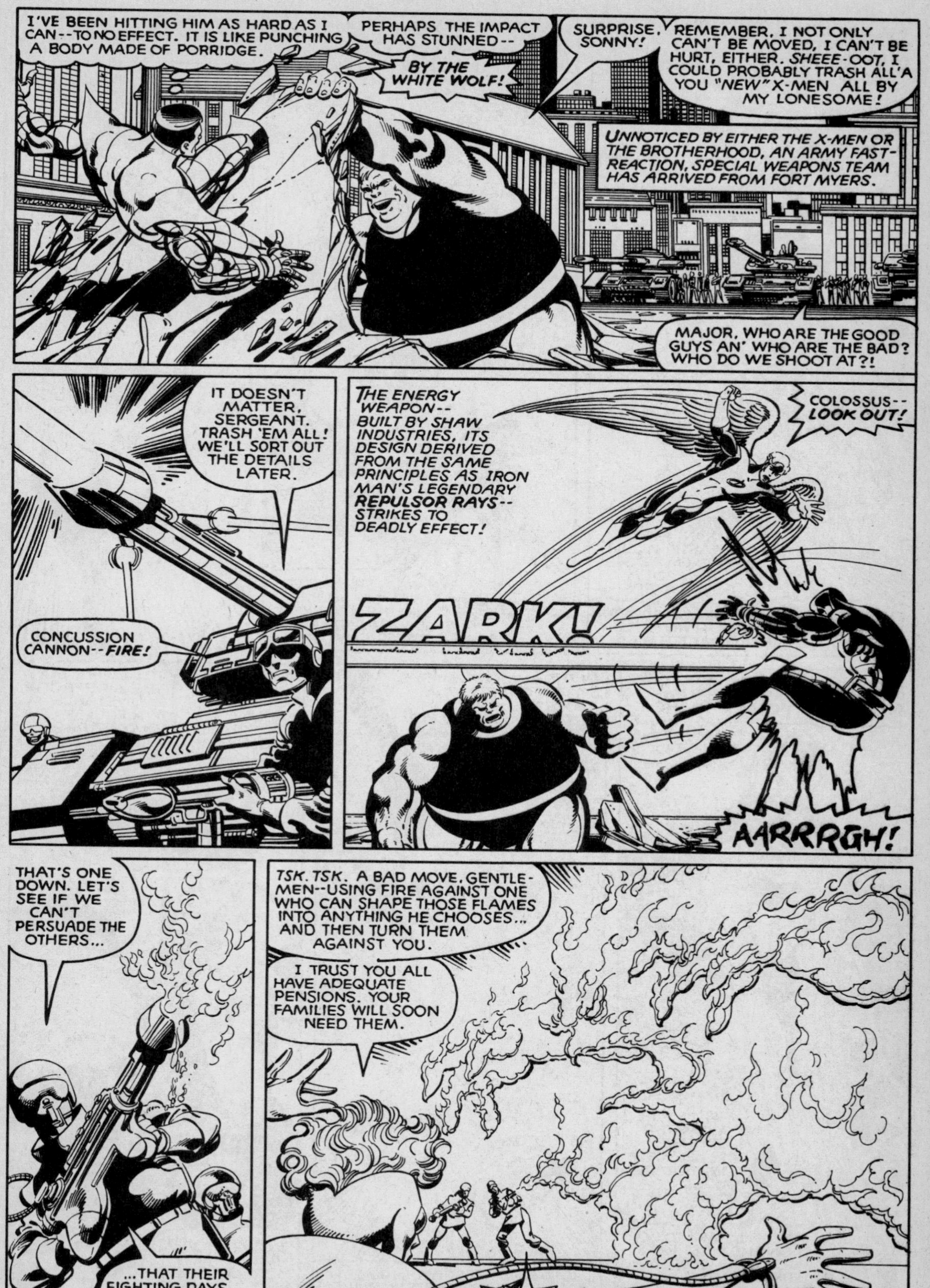

I'VE BEEN HITTING HIM AS HARD AS I CAN--TO NO EFFECT. IT IS LIKE PUNCHING A BODY MADE OF PORRIDGE.
PERHAPS THE IMPACT HAS STUNNED--
BY THE WHITE WOLF!
SURPRISE, SONNY!
REMEMBER, I NOT ONLY CAN'T BE MOVED, I CAN'T BE HURT, EITHER. SHEEE-OOT, I COULD PROBABLY TRASH ALL'A YOU "NEW" X-MEN ALL BY MY LONESOME!
UNNOTICED BY EITHER THE X-MEN OR THE BROTHERHOOD, AN ARMY FAST-REACTION, SPECIAL WEAPONS TEAM HAS ARRIVED FROM FORT MYERS.
MAJOR, WHO ARE THE GOOD GUYS AN' WHO ARE THE BAD? WHO DO WE SHOOT AT?!
IT DOESN'T MATTER, SERGEANT. TRASH 'EM ALL! WE'LL SORT OUT THE DETAILS LATER.
CONCUSSION CANNON--FIRE!
THE ENERGY WEAPON--BUILT BY SHAW INDUSTRIES, ITS DESIGN DERIVED FROM THE SAME PRINCIPLES AS IRON MAN'S LEGENDARY REPULSOR RAYS--STRIKES TO DEADLY EFFECT!
COLOSSUS--LOOK OUT!
ZARK!
AARRRGH!
THAT'S ONE DOWN. LET'S SEE IF WE CAN'T PERSUADE THE OTHERS...
...THAT THEIR FIGHTING DAYS ARE OVER.
TSK. TSK. A BAD MOVE, GENTLEMEN--USING FIRE AGAINST ONE WHO CAN SHAPE THOSE FLAMES INTO ANYTHING HE CHOOSES... AND THEN TURN THEM AGAINST YOU.
I TRUST YOU ALL HAVE ADEQUATE PENSIONS. YOUR FAMILIES WILL SOON NEED THEM.
S-SARGE--!!

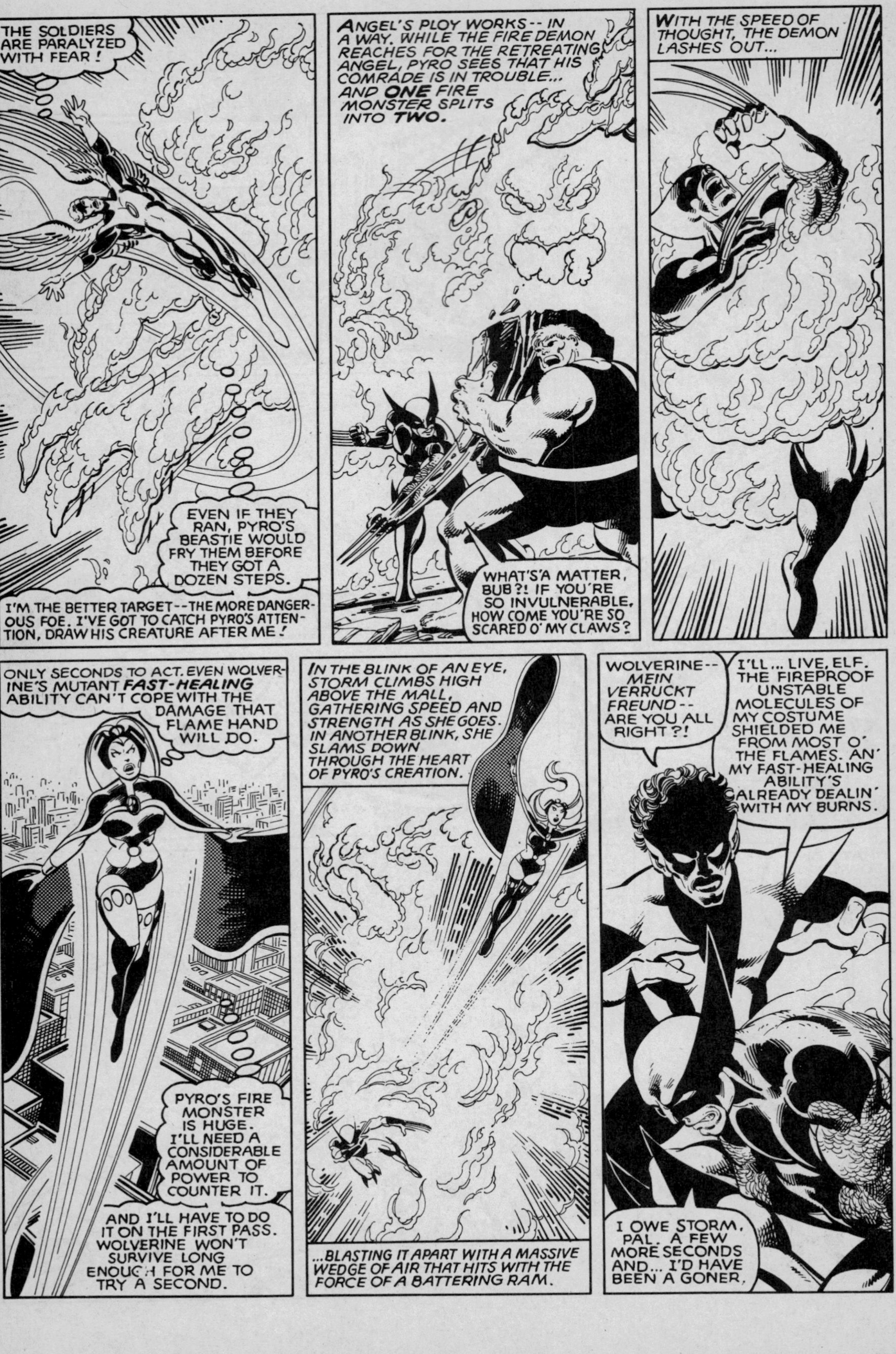
THE SOLDIERS ARE PARALYZED WITH FEAR!
EVEN IF THEY RAN, PYRO'S BEASTIE WOULD FRY THEM BEFORE THEY GOT A DOZEN STEPS.
I'M THE BETTER TARGET--THE MORE DANGEROUS FOE. I'VE GOT TO CATCH PYRO'S ATTENTION, DRAW HIS CREATURE AFTER ME!
ANGEL'S PLOY WORKS--IN A WAY. WHILE THE FIRE DEMON REACHES FOR THE RETREATING ANGEL, PYRO SEES THAT HIS COMRADE IS IN TROUBLE... AND ONE FIRE MONSTER SPLITS INTO TWO.
WHAT'S'A MATTER, BUB?! IF YOU'RE SO INVULNERABLE, HOW COME YOU'RE SO SCARED O' MY CLAWS?
WITH THE SPEED OF THOUGHT, THE DEMON LASHES OUT...
ONLY SECONDS TO ACT. EVEN WOLVERINE'S MUTANT FAST-HEALING ABILITY CAN'T COPE WITH THE DAMAGE THAT FLAME HAND WILL DO.
PYRO'S FIRE MONSTER IS HUGE. I'LL NEED A CONSIDERABLE AMOUNT OF POWER TO COUNTER IT.
AND I'LL HAVE TO DO IT ON THE FIRST PASS. WOLVERINE WON'T SURVIVE LONG ENOUGH FOR ME TO TRY A SECOND.
IN THE BLINK OF AN EYE, STORM CLIMBS HIGH ABOVE THE MALL, GATHERING SPEED AND STRENGTH AS SHE GOES. IN ANOTHER BLINK, SHE SLAMS DOWN THROUGH THE HEART OF PYRO'S CREATION.
...BLASTING IT APART WITH A MASSIVE WEDGE OF AIR THAT HITS WITH THE FORCE OF A BATTERING RAM.
WOLVERINE--MEIN VERRUCKT FREUND--ARE YOU ALL RIGHT?!
I'LL... LIVE, ELF. THE FIREPROOF UNSTABLE MOLECULES OF MY COSTUME SHIELDED ME FROM MOST O' THE FLAMES. AN' MY FAST-HEALING ABILITY'S ALREADY DEALIN' WITH MY BURNS.
I OWE STORM, PAL. A FEW MORE SECONDS AND... I'D HAVE BEEN A GONER.

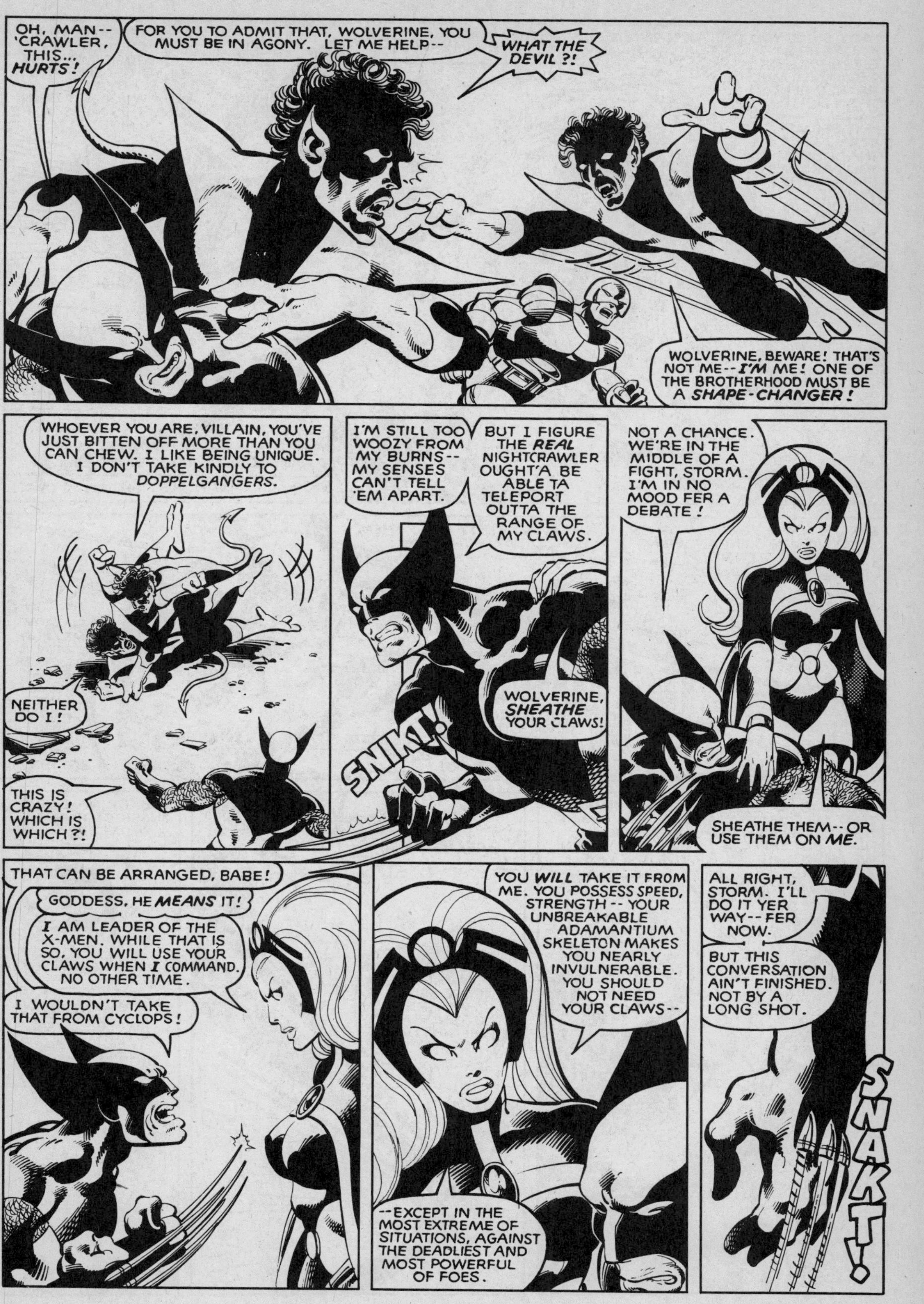

OH, MAN-- 'CRAWLER, THIS... HURTS!
FOR YOU TO ADMIT THAT, WOLVERINE, YOU MUST BE IN AGONY. LET ME HELP--
WHAT THE DEVIL?!
WOLVERINE, BEWARE! THAT'S NOT ME-- I'M ME! ONE OF THE BROTHERHOOD MUST BE A SHAPE-CHANGER!
WHOEVER YOU ARE, VILLAIN, YOU'VE JUST BITTEN OFF MORE THAN YOU CAN CHEW. I LIKE BEING UNIQUE. I DON'T TAKE KINDLY TO DOPPELGANGERS.
NEITHER DO I!
THIS IS CRAZY! WHICH IS WHICH?!
I'M STILL TOO WOOZY FROM MY BURNS-- MY SENSES CAN'T TELL 'EM APART.
BUT I FIGURE THE REAL NIGHTCRAWLER OUGHT'A BE ABLE TA TELEPORT OUTTA THE RANGE OF MY CLAWS.
WOLVERINE, SHEATHE YOUR CLAWS!
SNIKT!
NOT A CHANCE. WE'RE IN THE MIDDLE OF A FIGHT, STORM. I'M IN NO MOOD FER A DEBATE!
SHEATHE THEM-- OR USE THEM ON ME.
THAT CAN BE ARRANGED, BABE!
GODDESS, HE MEANS IT!
I AM LEADER OF THE X-MEN. WHILE THAT IS SO, YOU WILL USE YOUR CLAWS WHEN I COMMAND. NO OTHER TIME.
I WOULDN'T TAKE THAT FROM CYCLOPS!
YOU WILL TAKE IT FROM ME. YOU POSSESS SPEED, STRENGTH -- YOUR UNBREAKABLE ADAMANTIUM SKELETON MAKES YOU NEARLY INVULNERABLE. YOU SHOULD NOT NEED YOUR CLAWS--
--EXCEPT IN THE MOST EXTREME OF SITUATIONS, AGAINST THE DEADLIEST AND MOST POWERFUL OF FOES.
ALL RIGHT, STORM. I'LL DO IT YER WAY-- FER NOW.
BUT THIS CONVERSATION AIN'T FINISHED. NOT BY A LONG SHOT.
SNAKT!

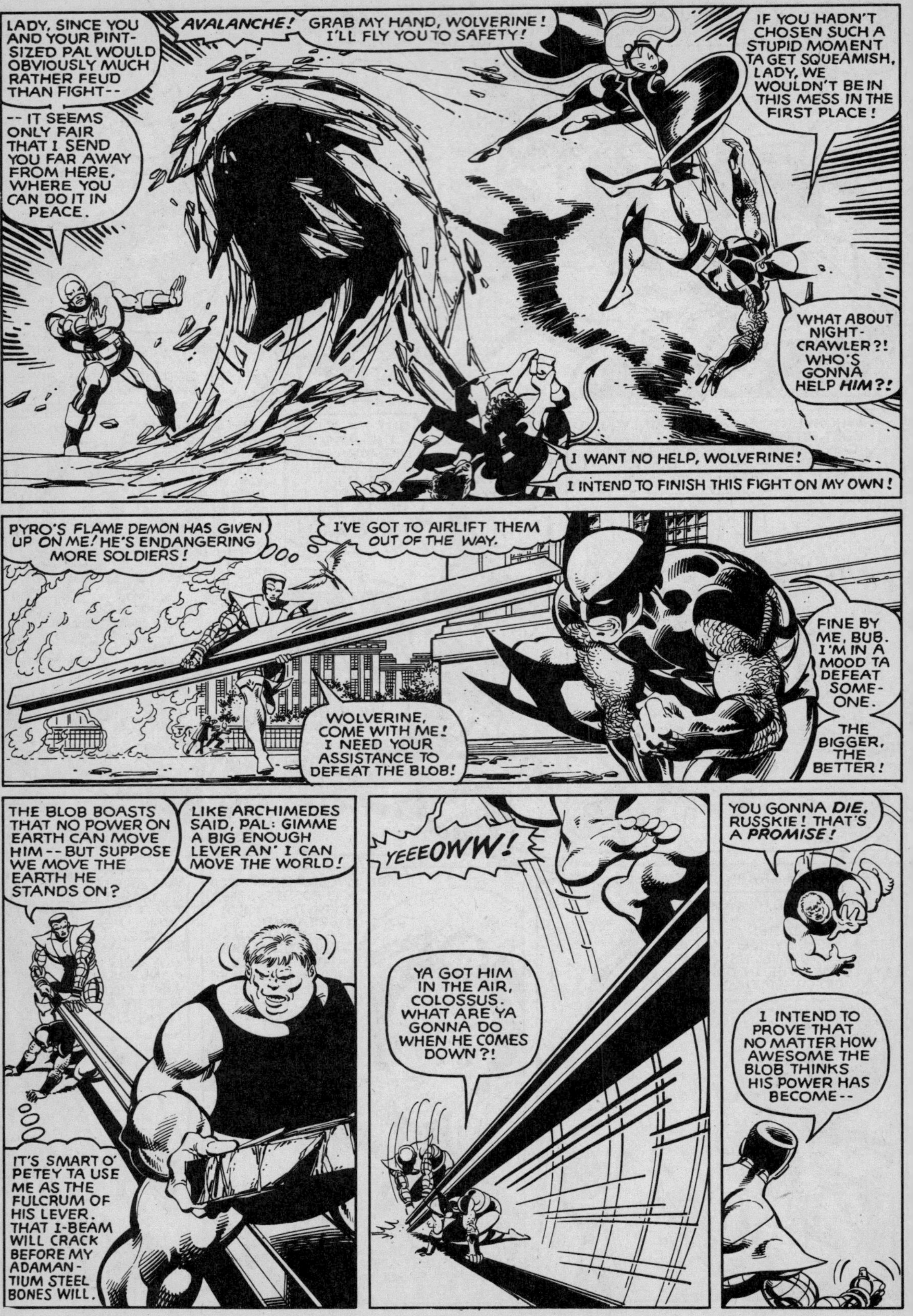
LADY, SINCE YOU AND YOUR PINT-SIZED PAL WOULD OBVIOUSLY MUCH RATHER FEUD THAN FIGHT--
-- IT SEEMS ONLY FAIR THAT I SEND YOU FAR AWAY FROM HERE, WHERE YOU CAN DO IT IN PEACE.
AVALANCHE!
GRAB MY HAND, WOLVERINE! I'LL FLY YOU TO SAFETY!
IF YOU HADN'T CHOSEN SUCH A STUPID MOMENT TA GET SQUEAMISH, LADY, WE WOULDN'T BE IN THIS MESS IN THE FIRST PLACE!
WHAT ABOUT NIGHT-CRAWLER?! WHO'S GONNA HELP HIM?!
I WANT NO HELP, WOLVERINE!
I INTEND TO FINISH THIS FIGHT ON MY OWN!
PYRO'S FLAME DEMON HAS GIVEN UP ON ME! HE'S ENDANGERING MORE SOLDIERS!
I'VE GOT TO AIRLIFT THEM OUT OF THE WAY.
WOLVERINE, COME WITH ME! I NEED YOUR ASSISTANCE TO DEFEAT THE BLOB!
FINE BY ME, BUB. I'M IN A MOOD TA DEFEAT SOME-ONE.
THE BIGGER, THE BETTER!
THE BLOB BOASTS THAT NO POWER ON EARTH CAN MOVE HIM -- BUT SUPPOSE WE MOVE THE EARTH HE STANDS ON?
LIKE ARCHIMEDES SAID, PAL: GIMME A BIG ENOUGH LEVER AN' I CAN MOVE THE WORLD!
IT'S SMART O' PETEY TA USE ME AS THE FULCRUM OF HIS LEVER. THAT I-BEAM WILL CRACK BEFORE MY ADAMAN-TIUM STEEL BONES WILL.
YEEEOWW!
YA GOT HIM IN THE AIR, COLOSSUS. WHAT ARE YA GONNA DO WHEN HE COMES DOWN?!
YOU GONNA DIE, RUSSKIE! THAT'S A PROMISE!
I INTEND TO PROVE THAT NO MATTER HOW AWESOME THE BLOB THINKS HIS POWER HAS BECOME--

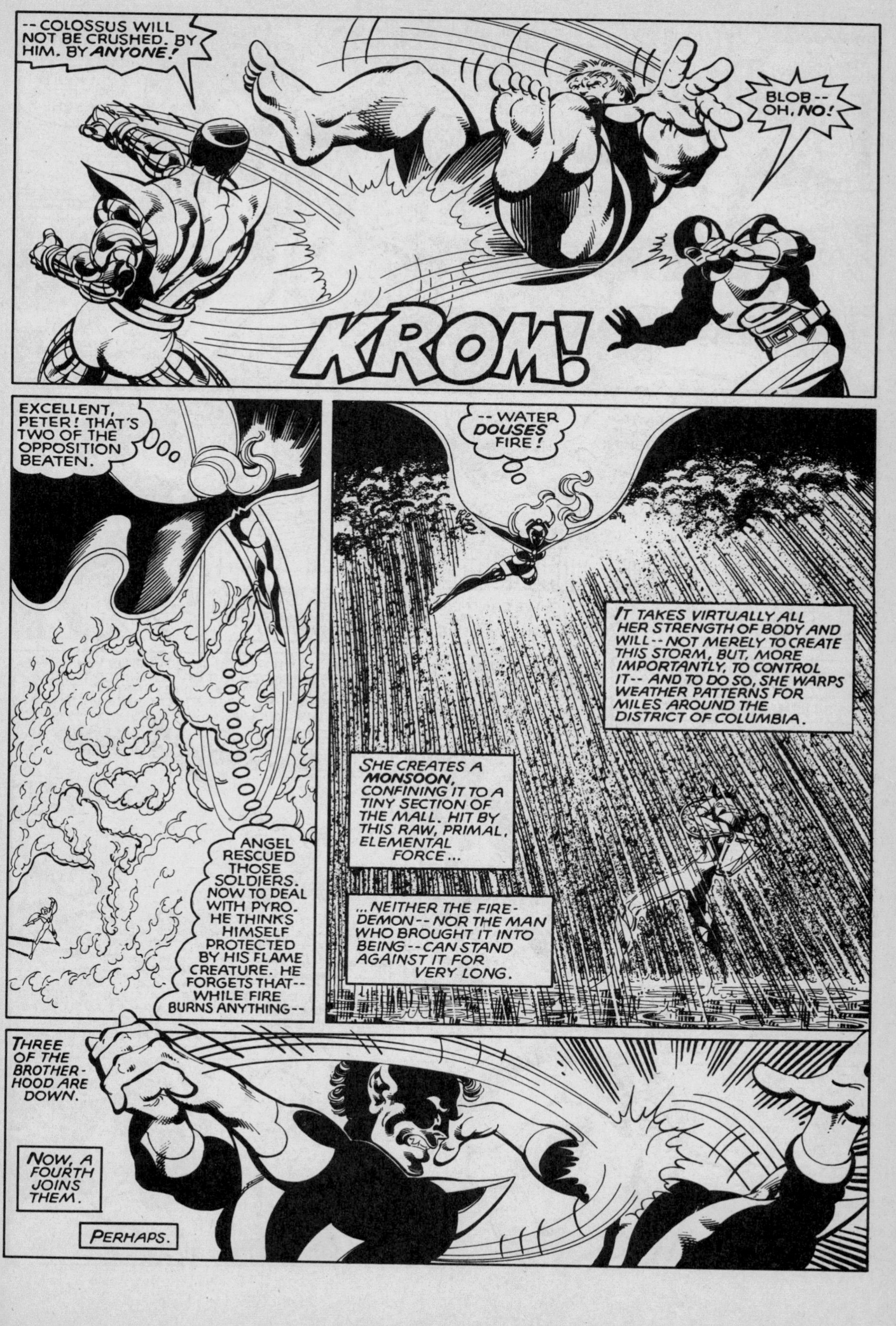

-- COLOSSUS WILL NOT BE CRUSHED. BY HIM. BY ANYONE!
BLOB -- OH, NO!
KROM!
EXCELLENT, PETER! THAT'S TWO OF THE OPPOSITION BEATEN.
ANGEL RESCUED THOSE SOLDIERS. NOW TO DEAL WITH PYRO. HE THINKS HIMSELF PROTECTED BY HIS FLAME CREATURE. HE FORGETS THAT -- WHILE FIRE BURNS ANYTHING --
-- WATER DOUSES FIRE!
IT TAKES VIRTUALLY ALL HER STRENGTH OF BODY AND WILL -- NOT MERELY TO CREATE THIS STORM, BUT, MORE IMPORTANTLY, TO CONTROL IT -- AND TO DO SO, SHE WARPS WEATHER PATTERNS FOR MILES AROUND THE DISTRICT OF COLUMBIA.
SHE CREATES A MONSOON, CONFINING IT TO A TINY SECTION OF THE MALL. HIT BY THIS RAW, PRIMAL, ELEMENTAL FORCE...
...NEITHER THE FIRE-DEMON -- NOR THE MAN WHO BROUGHT IT INTO BEING -- CAN STAND AGAINST IT FOR VERY LONG.
THREE OF THE BROTHERHOOD ARE DOWN.
NOW, A FOURTH JOINS THEM.
PERHAPS.

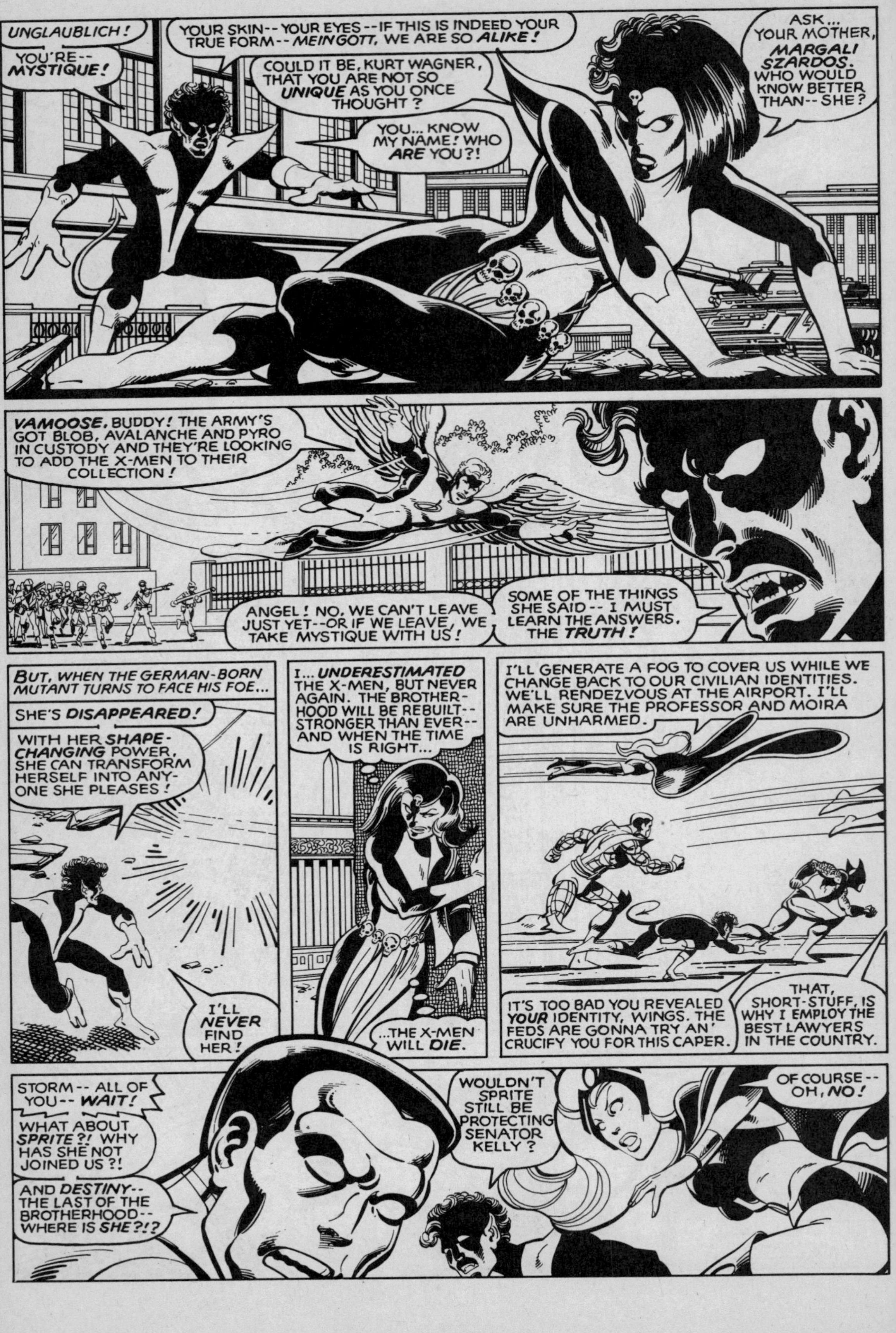
UNGLAUBLICH!
YOU'RE-- MYSTIQUE!
YOUR SKIN-- YOUR EYES--IF THIS IS INDEED YOUR TRUE FORM-- MEIN GOTT, WE ARE SO ALIKE!
COULD IT BE, KURT WAGNER, THAT YOU ARE NOT SO UNIQUE AS YOU ONCE THOUGHT?
YOU... KNOW MY NAME! WHO ARE YOU?!
ASK... YOUR MOTHER, MARGALI SZARDOS. WHO WOULD KNOW BETTER THAN-- SHE?
VAMOOSE, BUDDY! THE ARMY'S GOT BLOB, AVALANCHE AND PYRO IN CUSTODY AND THEY'RE LOOKING TO ADD THE X-MEN TO THEIR COLLECTION!
ANGEL! NO, WE CAN'T LEAVE JUST YET--OR IF WE LEAVE, WE TAKE MYSTIQUE WITH US!
SOME OF THE THINGS SHE SAID -- I MUST LEARN THE ANSWERS. THE TRUTH!
BUT, WHEN THE GERMAN-BORN MUTANT TURNS TO FACE HIS FOE...
SHE'S DISAPPEARED!
WITH HER SHAPE-CHANGING POWER, SHE CAN TRANSFORM HERSELF INTO ANYONE SHE PLEASES!
I'LL NEVER FIND HER!
I... UNDERESTIMATED THE X-MEN, BUT NEVER AGAIN. THE BROTHERHOOD WILL BE REBUILT--STRONGER THAN EVER--AND WHEN THE TIME IS RIGHT...
...THE X-MEN WILL DIE.
I'LL GENERATE A FOG TO COVER US WHILE WE CHANGE BACK TO OUR CIVILIAN IDENTITIES. WE'LL RENDEZVOUS AT THE AIRPORT. I'LL MAKE SURE THE PROFESSOR AND MOIRA ARE UNHARMED.
IT'S TOO BAD YOU REVEALED YOUR IDENTITY, WINGS. THE FEDS ARE GONNA TRY AN' CRUCIFY YOU FOR THIS CAPER.
THAT, SHORT-STUFF, IS WHY I EMPLOY THE BEST LAWYERS IN THE COUNTRY.
STORM -- ALL OF YOU-- WAIT!
WHAT ABOUT SPRITE?! WHY HAS SHE NOT JOINED US?!
AND DESTINY-- THE LAST OF THE BROTHERHOOD-- WHERE IS SHE?!?
WOULDN'T SPRITE STILL BE PROTECTING SENATOR KELLY?
OF COURSE-- OH, NO!

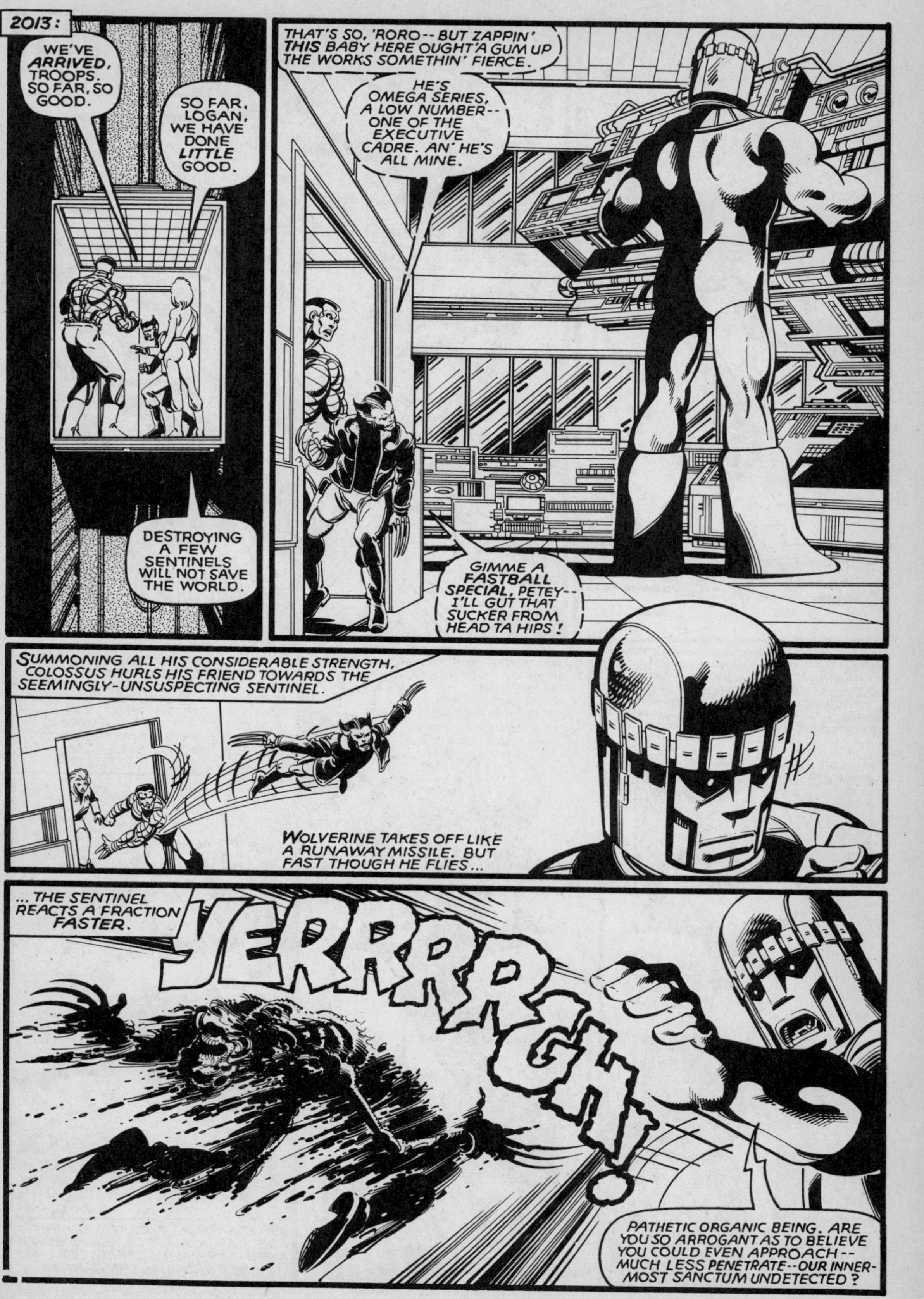
2013:
WE'VE ARRIVED, TROOPS. SO FAR, SO GOOD.
SO FAR, LOGAN, WE HAVE DONE LITTLE GOOD.
DESTROYING A FEW SENTINELS WILL NOT SAVE THE WORLD.
THAT'S SO, 'RORO -- BUT ZAPPIN' THIS BABY HERE OUGHT'A GUM UP THE WORKS SOMETHIN' FIERCE.
HE'S OMEGA SERIES, A LOW NUMBER -- ONE OF THE EXECUTIVE CADRE. AN' HE'S ALL MINE.
GIMME A FASTBALL SPECIAL, PETEY -- I'LL GUT THAT SUCKER FROM HEAD TA HIPS!
SUMMONING ALL HIS CONSIDERABLE STRENGTH, COLOSSUS HURLS HIS FRIEND TOWARDS THE SEEMINGLY-UNSUSPECTING SENTINEL.
WOLVERINE TAKES OFF LIKE A RUNAWAY MISSILE. BUT FAST THOUGH HE FLIES...
... THE SENTINEL REACTS A FRACTION FASTER.
YERRRRGH!
PATHETIC ORGANIC BEING. ARE YOU SO ARROGANT AS TO BELIEVE YOU COULD EVEN APPROACH -- MUCH LESS PENETRATE -- OUR INNER-MOST SANCTUM UNDETECTED?

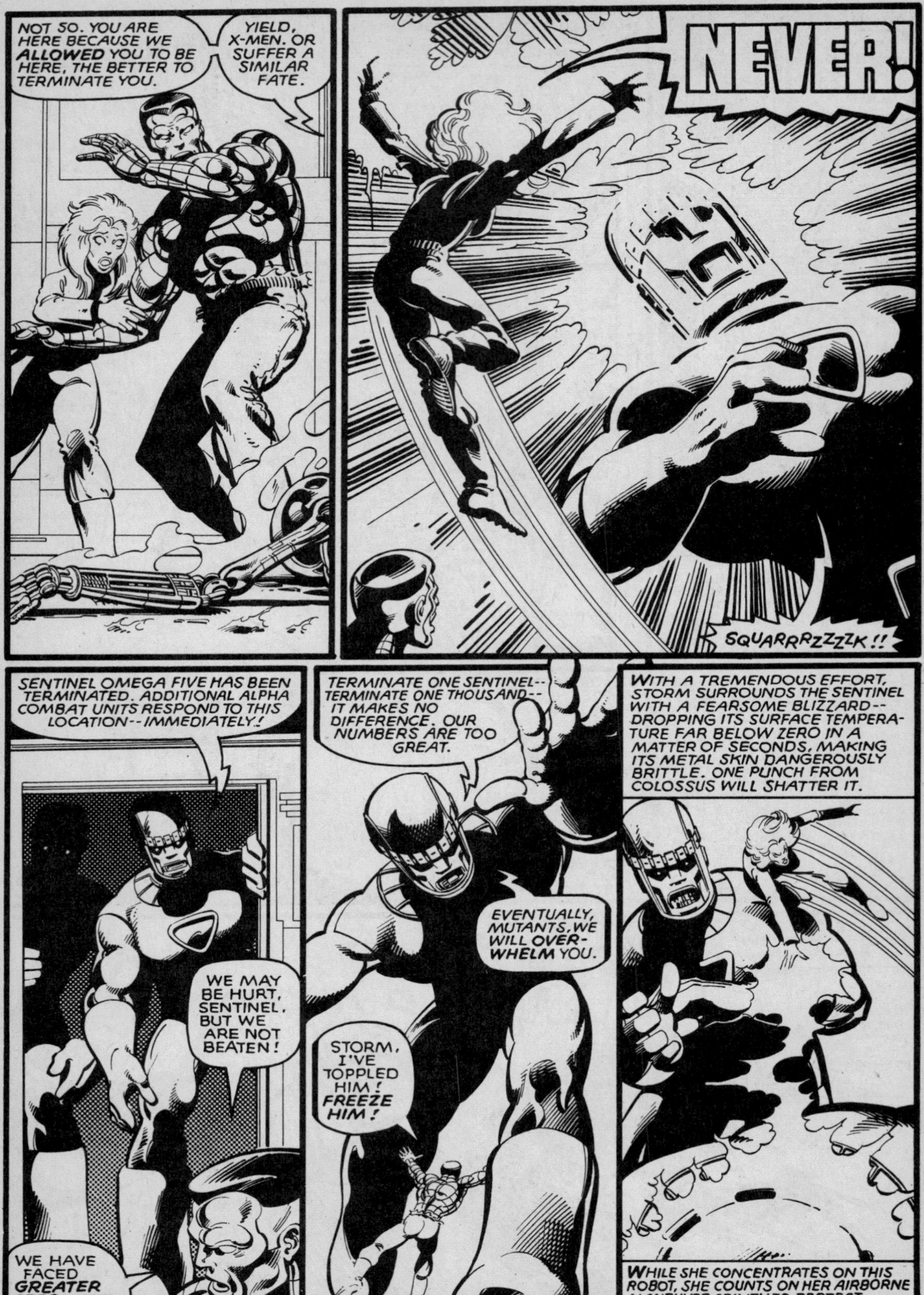
NOT SO. YOU ARE HERE BECAUSE WE ALLOWED YOU TO BE HERE, THE BETTER TO TERMINATE YOU.
YIELD, X-MEN. OR SUFFER A SIMILAR FATE.
NEVER!
SQUARRRZZZZK!!
SENTINEL OMEGA FIVE HAS BEEN TERMINATED. ADDITIONAL ALPHA COMBAT UNITS RESPOND TO THIS LOCATION--IMMEDIATELY!
WE MAY BE HURT, SENTINEL, BUT WE ARE NOT BEATEN!
WE HAVE FACED GREATER ODDS--AND TRIUMPHED!
TERMINATE ONE SENTINEL--TERMINATE ONE THOUSAND--IT MAKES NO DIFFERENCE. OUR NUMBERS ARE TOO GREAT.
EVENTUALLY, MUTANTS, WE WILL OVERWHELM YOU.
STORM, I'VE TOPPLED HIM! FREEZE HIM!
WITH A TREMENDOUS EFFORT, STORM SURROUNDS THE SENTINEL WITH A FEARSOME BLIZZARD--DROPPING ITS SURFACE TEMPERATURE FAR BELOW ZERO IN A MATTER OF SECONDS, MAKING ITS METAL SKIN DANGEROUSLY BRITTLE. ONE PUNCH FROM COLOSSUS WILL SHATTER IT.
WHILE SHE CONCENTRATES ON THIS ROBOT, SHE COUNTS ON HER AIRBORNE MANEUVERABILITY TO PROTECT HER FROM ITS COMPANION.

THIS TIME, SHE HOPES IN VAIN.

PETER!!

ORORO!!

PETER RASPUTIN WAS EVER A *GENTLE* MAN, A MAN OF PEACE, A MAN WHO-- LIKE THE WOMAN HE HOLDS IN HIS ARMS-- THOUGHT *LIFE* THE MOST PRECIOUS OF GIFTS, AND *LOVE* THE MOST PRECIOUS CELEBRATION OF THAT GIFT.

ORORO WAS A *SISTER* TO HIM, THE BEST FRIEND HE EVER HAD. AND HE FINDS THAT HER DEATH IS... *UNENDURABLE.*

BOOM!

HIS HANDS RED WITH HER BLOOD, HE *SCREAMS.* AND, MOMENTS LATER, WHEN HE FEELS HIMSELF GRIPPED BY A MURDEROUS BERSERKER FURY TO RIVAL WOLVERINE'S, HE *WELCOMES* IT.

ON THE STREET FAR BELOW, TEARS STREAM DOWN RACHEL'S FACE-- BUT SHE MAKES NO MOVE TO WIPE THEM AWAY.

INSTEAD SHE HOLDS THE UNCONSCIOUS BODY OF *KATHERINE PRYDE-RASPUTIN*-- WITHIN WHICH RESIDES THE MIND AND SOUL OF KITTY PRYDE--TIGHTER TO HER BREAST.

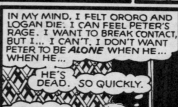

IN MY MIND, I FELT ORORO AND LOGAN DIE. I CAN FEEL PETER'S RAGE. I WANT TO BREAK CONTACT, BUT I... I CAN'T. I DON'T WANT PETER TO BE *ALONE* WHEN HE... WHEN HE...

HE'S DEAD. SO QUICKLY.

FUNNY. I'VE EXPERIENCED DEATH SO OFTEN IN THE MINDS OF OTHERS, YET I'M TERRIFIED OF DYING MYSELF.

IF KATE'S BODY DIES HERE, WILL HER MIND BE TRAPPED IN THE PAST? IF SO, I WISH HER A... *HAPPIER* LIFE THAN THE ONE SHE LIVED.

WE DID ALL WE COULD, MY DARLING KATE.

NOW, IT'S UP TO *YOU.*

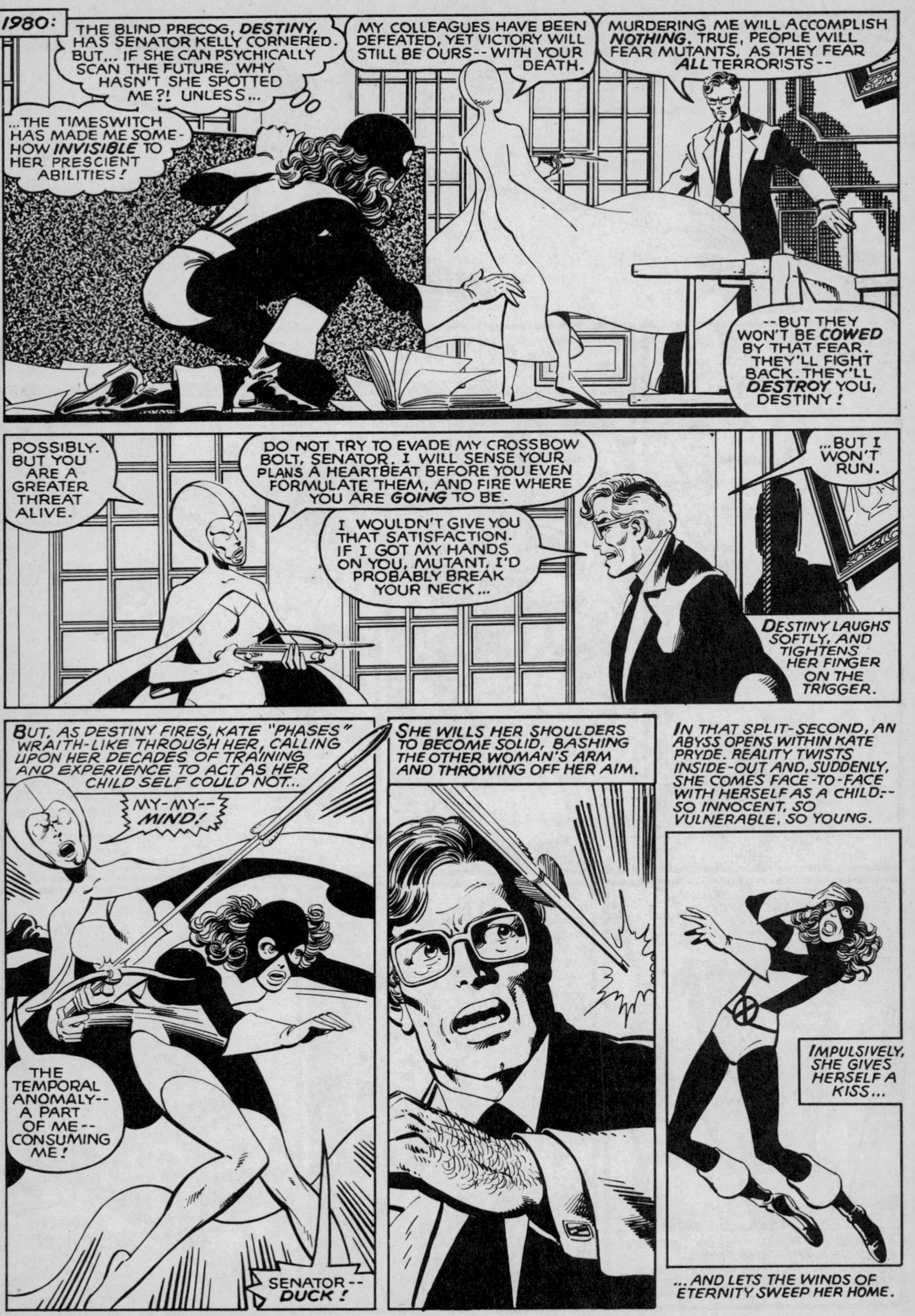

1980:
THE BLIND PRECOG, DESTINY, HAS SENATOR KELLY CORNERED. BUT... IF SHE CAN PSYCHICALLY SCAN THE FUTURE, WHY HASN'T SHE SPOTTED ME?! UNLESS...
...THE TIMESWITCH HAS MADE ME SOMEHOW INVISIBLE TO HER PRESCIENT ABILITIES!
MY COLLEAGUES HAVE BEEN DEFEATED, YET VICTORY WILL STILL BE OURS-- WITH YOUR DEATH.
MURDERING ME WILL ACCOMPLISH NOTHING. TRUE, PEOPLE WILL FEAR MUTANTS, AS THEY FEAR ALL TERRORISTS--
--BUT THEY WON'T BE COWED BY THAT FEAR. THEY'LL FIGHT BACK. THEY'LL DESTROY YOU, DESTINY!
POSSIBLY. BUT YOU ARE A GREATER THREAT ALIVE.
DO NOT TRY TO EVADE MY CROSSBOW BOLT, SENATOR. I WILL SENSE YOUR PLANS A HEARTBEAT BEFORE YOU EVEN FORMULATE THEM, AND FIRE WHERE YOU ARE GOING TO BE.
I WOULDN'T GIVE YOU THAT SATISFACTION. IF I GOT MY HANDS ON YOU, MUTANT, I'D PROBABLY BREAK YOUR NECK...
...BUT I WON'T RUN.
DESTINY LAUGHS SOFTLY, AND TIGHTENS HER FINGER ON THE TRIGGER.
BUT, AS DESTINY FIRES, KATE "PHASES" WRAITH-LIKE THROUGH HER, CALLING UPON HER DECADES OF TRAINING AND EXPERIENCE TO ACT AS HER CHILD SELF COULD NOT...
MY-MY-- MIND!
THE TEMPORAL ANOMALY-- A PART OF ME-- CONSUMING ME!
SENATOR-- DUCK!
SHE WILLS HER SHOULDERS TO BECOME SOLID, BASHING THE OTHER WOMAN'S ARM AND THROWING OFF HER AIM.
IN THAT SPLIT-SECOND, AN ABYSS OPENS WITHIN KATE PRYDE. REALITY TWISTS INSIDE-OUT AND, SUDDENLY, SHE COMES FACE-TO-FACE WITH HERSELF AS A CHILD:-- SO INNOCENT, SO VULNERABLE, SO YOUNG.
IMPULSIVELY, SHE GIVES HERSELF A KISS...
...AND LETS THE WINDS OF ETERNITY SWEEP HER HOME.

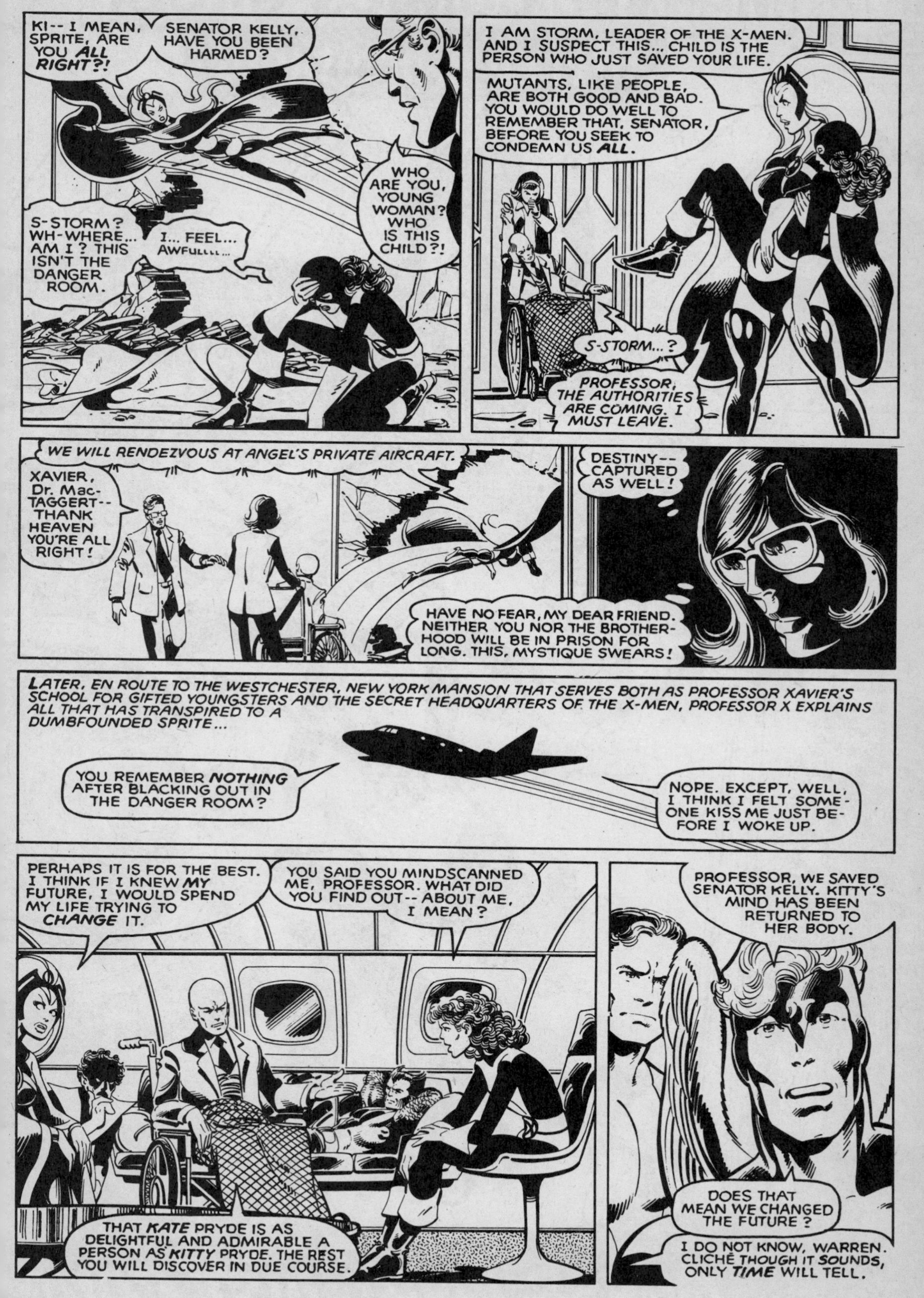
KI-- I MEAN, SPRITE, ARE YOU ALL RIGHT?!
SENATOR KELLY, HAVE YOU BEEN HARMED?
WHO ARE YOU, YOUNG WOMAN? WHO IS THIS CHILD?!
S-STORM? WH-WHERE... AM I? THIS ISN'T THE DANGER ROOM.
I... FEEL... AWFULLLL...
I AM STORM, LEADER OF THE X-MEN. AND I SUSPECT THIS... CHILD IS THE PERSON WHO JUST SAVED YOUR LIFE.
MUTANTS, LIKE PEOPLE, ARE BOTH GOOD AND BAD. YOU WOULD DO WELL TO REMEMBER THAT, SENATOR, BEFORE YOU SEEK TO CONDEMN US ALL.
S-STORM...?
PROFESSOR, THE AUTHORITIES ARE COMING. I MUST LEAVE.
WE WILL RENDEZVOUS AT ANGEL'S PRIVATE AIRCRAFT.
XAVIER, Dr. MacTAGGERT-- THANK HEAVEN YOU'RE ALL RIGHT!
DESTINY-- CAPTURED AS WELL!
HAVE NO FEAR, MY DEAR FRIEND. NEITHER YOU NOR THE BROTHERHOOD WILL BE IN PRISON FOR LONG. THIS, MYSTIQUE SWEARS!
LATER, EN ROUTE TO THE WESTCHESTER, NEW YORK MANSION THAT SERVES BOTH AS PROFESSOR XAVIER'S SCHOOL FOR GIFTED YOUNGSTERS AND THE SECRET HEADQUARTERS OF THE X-MEN, PROFESSOR X EXPLAINS ALL THAT HAS TRANSPIRED TO A DUMBFOUNDED SPRITE...
YOU REMEMBER NOTHING AFTER BLACKING OUT IN THE DANGER ROOM?
NOPE. EXCEPT, WELL, I THINK I FELT SOMEONE KISS ME JUST BEFORE I WOKE UP.
PERHAPS IT IS FOR THE BEST. I THINK IF I KNEW MY FUTURE, I WOULD SPEND MY LIFE TRYING TO CHANGE IT.
YOU SAID YOU MINDSCANNED ME, PROFESSOR. WHAT DID YOU FIND OUT-- ABOUT ME, I MEAN?
THAT KATE PRYDE IS AS DELIGHTFUL AND ADMIRABLE A PERSON AS KITTY PRYDE. THE REST YOU WILL DISCOVER IN DUE COURSE.
PROFESSOR, WE SAVED SENATOR KELLY. KITTY'S MIND HAS BEEN RETURNED TO HER BODY.
DOES THAT MEAN WE CHANGED THE FUTURE?
I DO NOT KNOW, WARREN. CLICHÉ THOUGH IT SOUNDS, ONLY TIME WILL TELL.

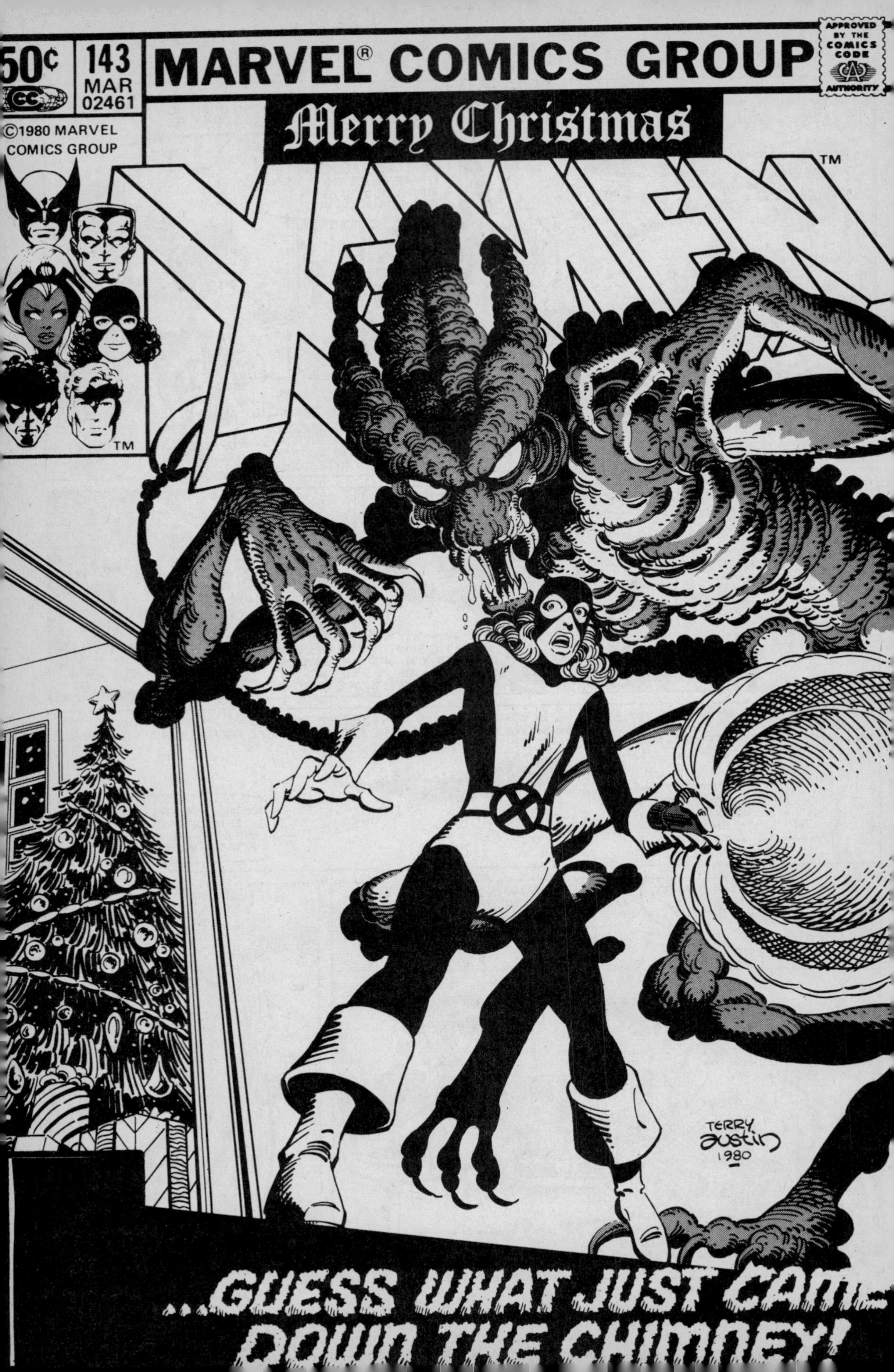

50¢
143
MAR
02461
MARVEL® COMICS GROUP
APPROVED BY THE COMICS CODE AUTHORITY
©1980 MARVEL COMICS GROUP
Merry Christmas
X-MEN™
TM
TERRY AUSTIN 1980
...GUESS WHAT JUST CAM-
DOWN THE CHIMNEY!

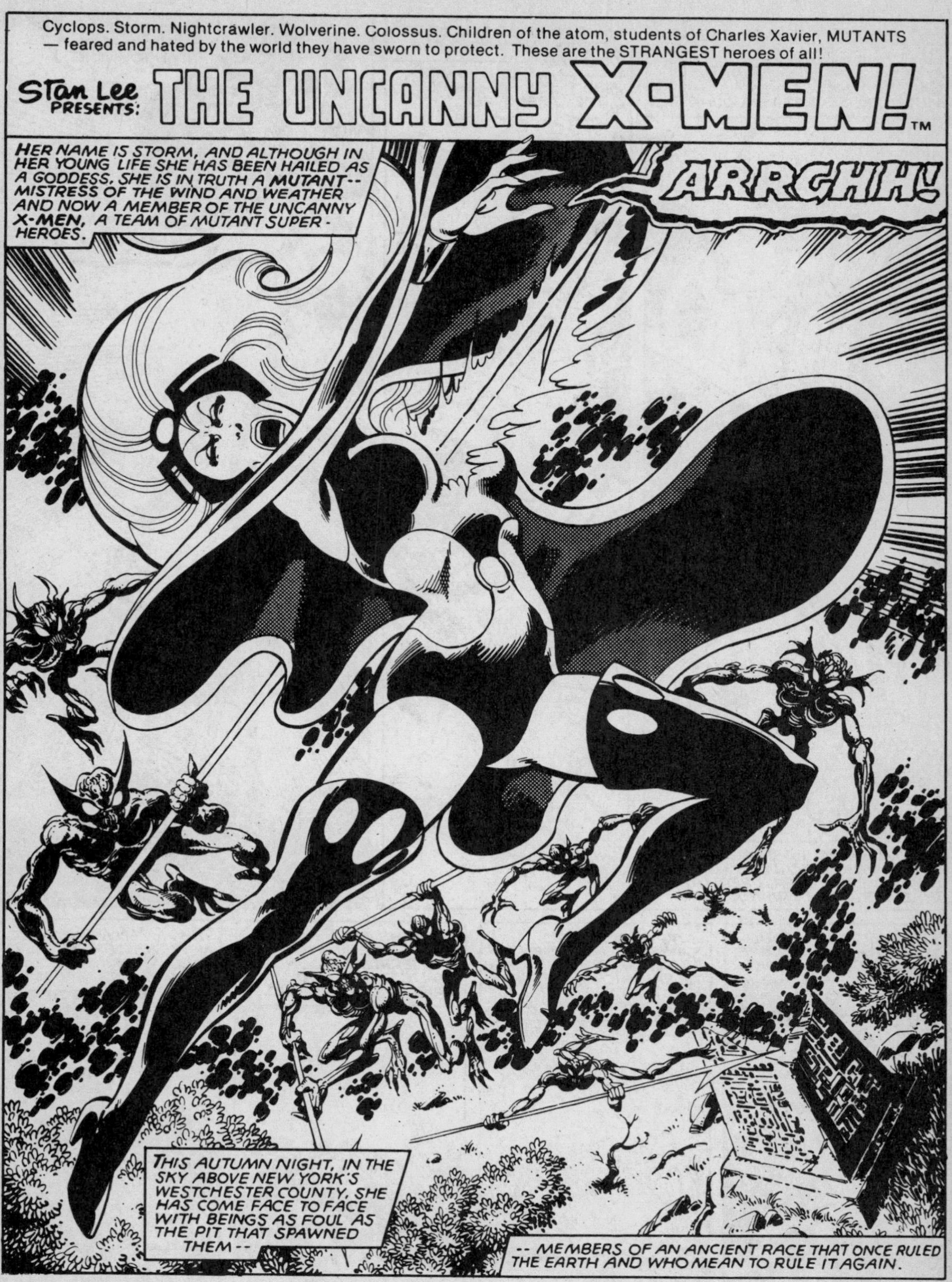
Cyclops. Storm. Nightcrawler. Wolverine. Colossus. Children of the atom, students of Charles Xavier, MUTANTS — feared and hated by the world they have sworn to protect. These are the STRANGEST heroes of all!
Stan Lee PRESENTS: THE UNCANNY X-MEN!™
HER NAME IS STORM, AND ALTHOUGH IN HER YOUNG LIFE SHE HAS BEEN HAILED AS A GODDESS, SHE IS IN TRUTH A MUTANT-- MISTRESS OF THE WIND AND WEATHER AND NOW A MEMBER OF THE UNCANNY X-MEN, A TEAM OF MUTANT SUPER-HEROES.
ARRGHH!
THIS AUTUMN NIGHT, IN THE SKY ABOVE NEW YORK'S WESTCHESTER COUNTY, SHE HAS COME FACE TO FACE WITH BEINGS AS FOUL AS THE PIT THAT SPAWNED THEM --
-- MEMBERS OF AN ANCIENT RACE THAT ONCE RULED THE EARTH AND WHO MEAN TO RULE IT AGAIN.

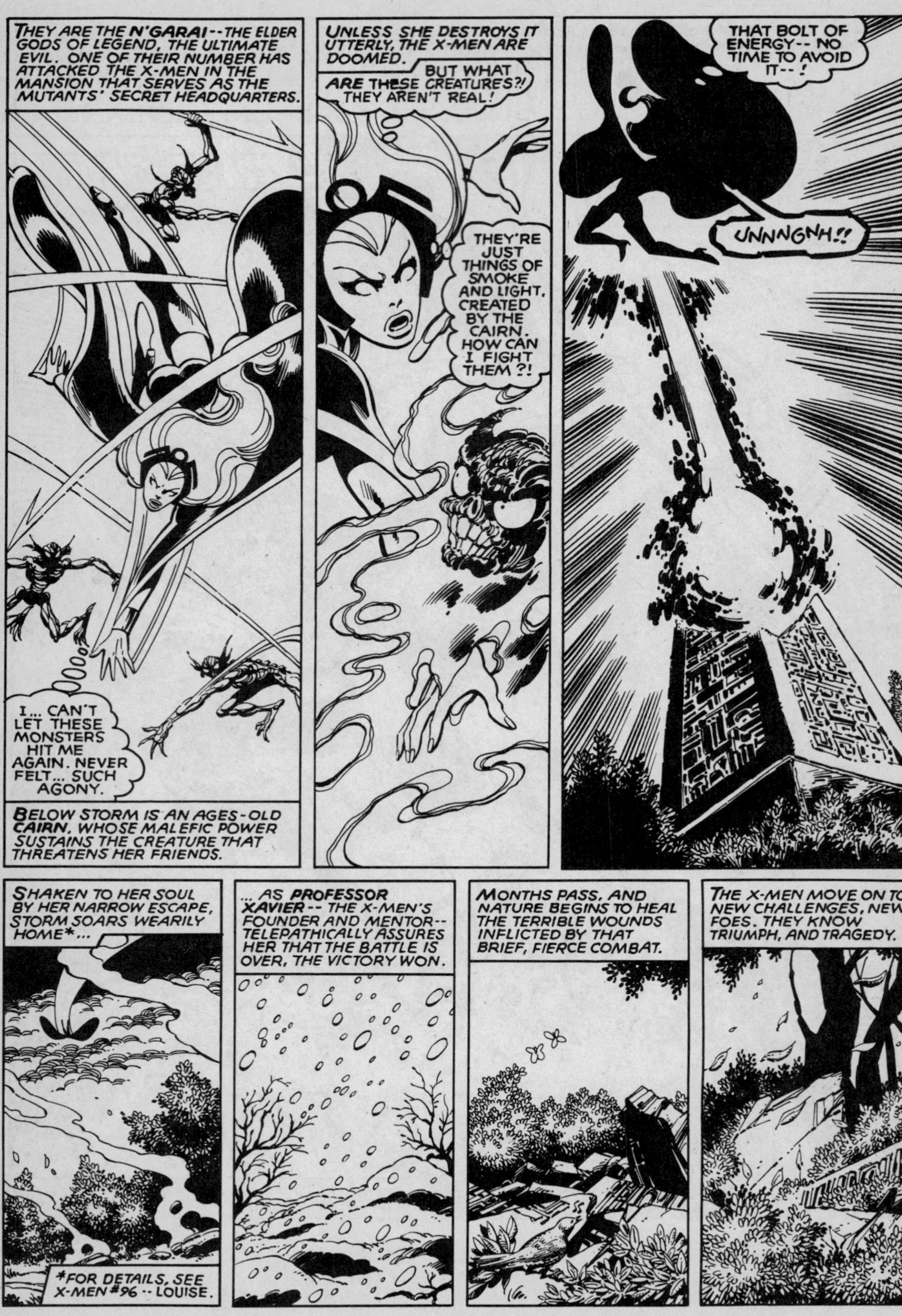
THEY ARE THE N'GARAI--THE ELDER GODS OF LEGEND, THE ULTIMATE EVIL. ONE OF THEIR NUMBER HAS ATTACKED THE X-MEN IN THE MANSION THAT SERVES AS THE MUTANTS' SECRET HEADQUARTERS.
I... CAN'T LET THESE MONSTERS HIT ME AGAIN. NEVER FELT... SUCH AGONY.
BELOW STORM IS AN AGES-OLD CAIRN, WHOSE MALEFIC POWER SUSTAINS THE CREATURE THAT THREATENS HER FRIENDS.
UNLESS SHE DESTROYS IT UTTERLY, THE X-MEN ARE DOOMED.
BUT WHAT ARE THESE CREATURES?! THEY AREN'T REAL!
THEY'RE JUST THINGS OF SMOKE AND LIGHT, CREATED BY THE CAIRN. HOW CAN I FIGHT THEM?!
THAT BOLT OF ENERGY-- NO TIME TO AVOID IT--!
UNNNGNH!!
SHAKEN TO HER SOUL BY HER NARROW ESCAPE, STORM SOARS WEARILY HOME*...
*FOR DETAILS, SEE X-MEN #96 -- LOUISE.
...AS PROFESSOR XAVIER -- THE X-MEN'S FOUNDER AND MENTOR-- TELEPATHICALLY ASSURES HER THAT THE BATTLE IS OVER, THE VICTORY WON.
MONTHS PASS, AND NATURE BEGINS TO HEAL THE TERRIBLE WOUNDS INFLICTED BY THAT BRIEF, FIERCE COMBAT.
THE X-MEN MOVE ON TO NEW CHALLENGES, NEW FOES. THEY KNOW TRIUMPH, AND TRAGEDY.

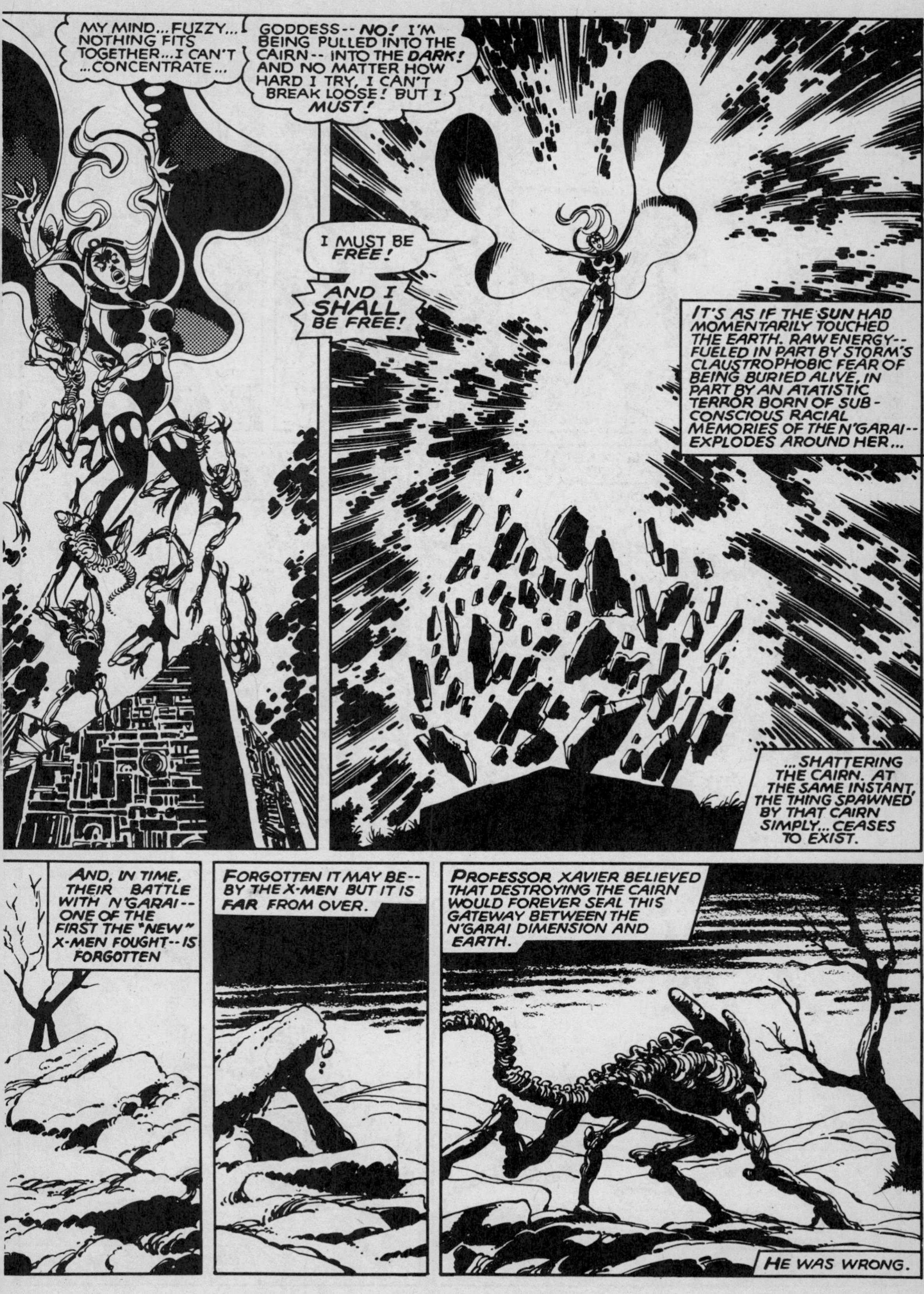
MY MIND... FUZZY... NOTHING FITS TOGETHER... I CAN'T ...CONCENTRATE...
GODDESS-- NO! I'M BEING PULLED INTO THE CAIRN-- INTO THE DARK! AND NO MATTER HOW HARD I TRY, I CAN'T BREAK LOOSE! BUT I MUST!
I MUST BE FREE!
AND I SHALL BE FREE!
IT'S AS IF THE SUN HAD MOMENTARILY TOUCHED THE EARTH. RAW ENERGY-- FUELED IN PART BY STORM'S CLAUSTROPHOBIC FEAR OF BEING BURIED ALIVE, IN PART BY AN ATATISTIC TERROR BORN OF SUB-CONSCIOUS RACIAL MEMORIES OF THE N'GARAI-- EXPLODES AROUND HER...
...SHATTERING THE CAIRN. AT THE SAME INSTANT, THE THING SPAWNED BY THAT CAIRN SIMPLY... CEASES TO EXIST.
AND, IN TIME, THEIR BATTLE WITH N'GARAI-- ONE OF THE FIRST THE "NEW" X-MEN FOUGHT-- IS FORGOTTEN
FORGOTTEN IT MAY BE-- BY THE X-MEN BUT IT IS FAR FROM OVER.
PROFESSOR XAVIER BELIEVED THAT DESTROYING THE CAIRN WOULD FOREVER SEAL THIS GATEWAY BETWEEN THE N'GARAI DIMENSION AND EARTH.
HE WAS WRONG.

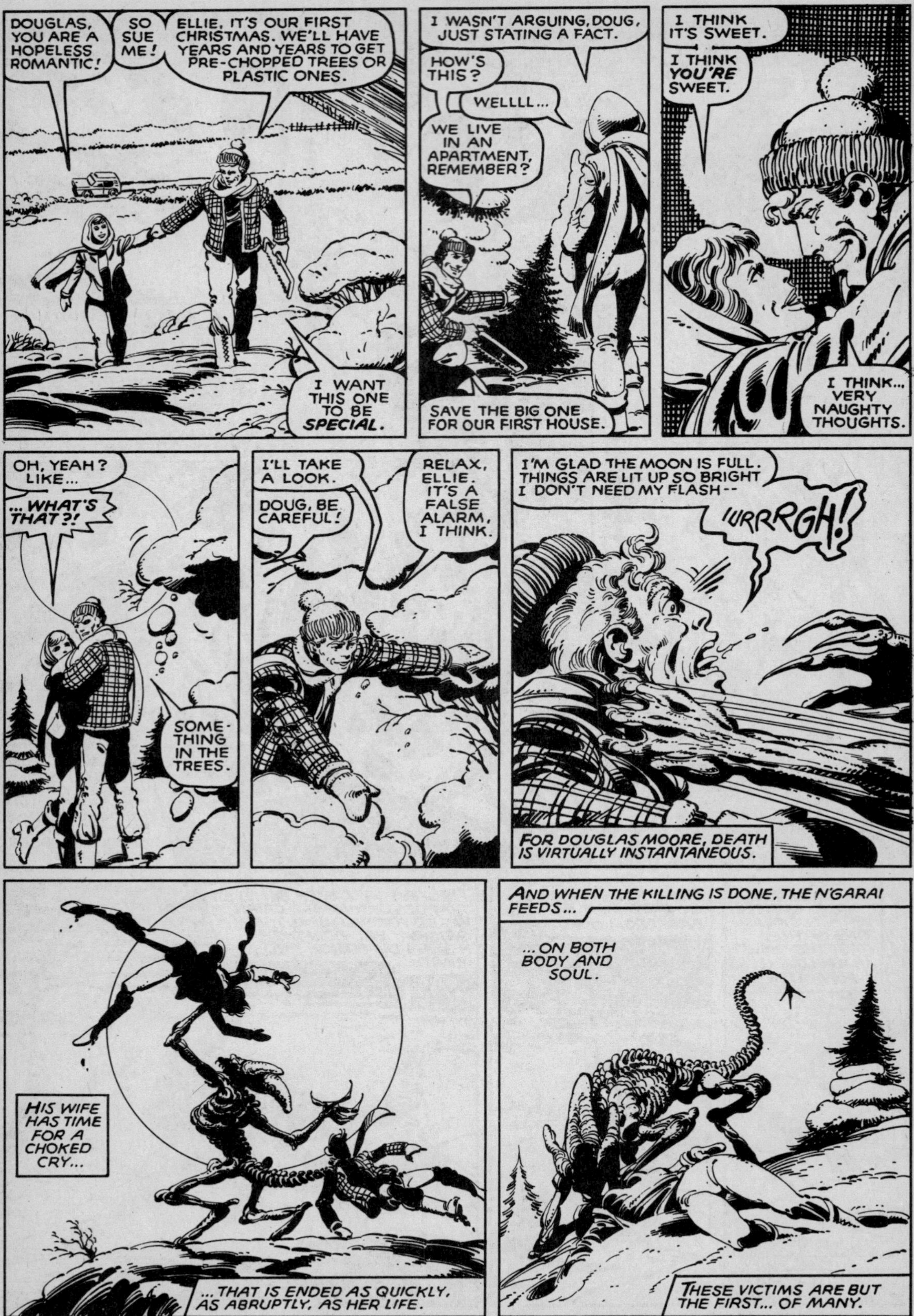

DOUGLAS, YOU ARE A HOPELESS ROMANTIC!
SO SUE ME!
ELLIE, IT'S OUR FIRST CHRISTMAS. WE'LL HAVE YEARS AND YEARS TO GET PRE-CHOPPED TREES OR PLASTIC ONES.
I WANT THIS ONE TO BE SPECIAL.
I WASN'T ARGUING, DOUG, JUST STATING A FACT.
HOW'S THIS?
WELLLL...
WE LIVE IN AN APARTMENT, REMEMBER?
SAVE THE BIG ONE FOR OUR FIRST HOUSE.
I THINK IT'S SWEET.
I THINK YOU'RE SWEET.
I THINK... VERY NAUGHTY THOUGHTS.
OH, YEAH? LIKE...
...WHAT'S THAT?!
SOMETHING IN THE TREES.
I'LL TAKE A LOOK.
DOUG, BE CAREFUL!
RELAX, ELLIE. IT'S A FALSE ALARM, I THINK.
I'M GLAD THE MOON IS FULL. THINGS ARE LIT UP SO BRIGHT I DON'T NEED MY FLASH--
IURRRGH!
FOR DOUGLAS MOORE, DEATH IS VIRTUALLY INSTANTANEOUS.
HIS WIFE HAS TIME FOR A CHOKED CRY...
...THAT IS ENDED AS QUICKLY, AS ABRUPTLY, AS HER LIFE.
AND WHEN THE KILLING IS DONE, THE N'GARAI FEEDS...
...ON BOTH BODY AND SOUL.
THESE VICTIMS ARE BUT THE FIRST... OF MANY.

'TWAS THE NIGHT BEFORE CHRISTMAS, AND ALL THROUGH THE HOUSE, THE X-MEN ARE STIRRING.

IT'S BEEN A QUIET MONTH SINCE THEIR BATTLE IN WASHINGTON, D.C., WITH THE NEW BROTHERHOOD OF EVIL MUTANTS* -- AND THEY'VE SPENT THE TIME CATCHING THEIR BREATH, HONING OLD SKILLS, LEARNING NEW ONES.

NO DAY, NO OPPORTUNITY, IS WASTED. WHICH IS WHY, EVEN ON CHRISTMAS EVE, KITTY PRYDE -- THE NEWEST AND YOUNGEST MEMBER OF THE TEAM -- MUST SPEND AN HOUR UNDER PROFESSOR XAVIER'S INSTRUCTION (IN ADDITION TO HER SCHOOLWORK) LEARNING ALL THERE IS TO KNOW ABOUT THE X-MEN, THEIR ABILITIES, THEIR EQUIPMENT.

ONCE MORE, KITTY. "BLACKBIRD" IGNITION PROCEDURE, FROM THE BEGINNING.

Sigh.

MASTER SWITCH, ON. BRAKES, LOCKED. THROTTLES TO...

PROFESSOR, THE CAR IS READY. IT'S, ah, GETTING LATE.

*LAST ISH -- L.

CHRIS CLAREMONT · JOHN BYRNE | TERRY AUSTIN | TOM ORZECHOWSKI, letterer | LOUISE JONES | JIM SHOOTER
WRITER / CO-PLOTTERS / PENCILER | INKER | GLYNIS WEIN, colorist | EDITOR | Ed.-in-CHIEF

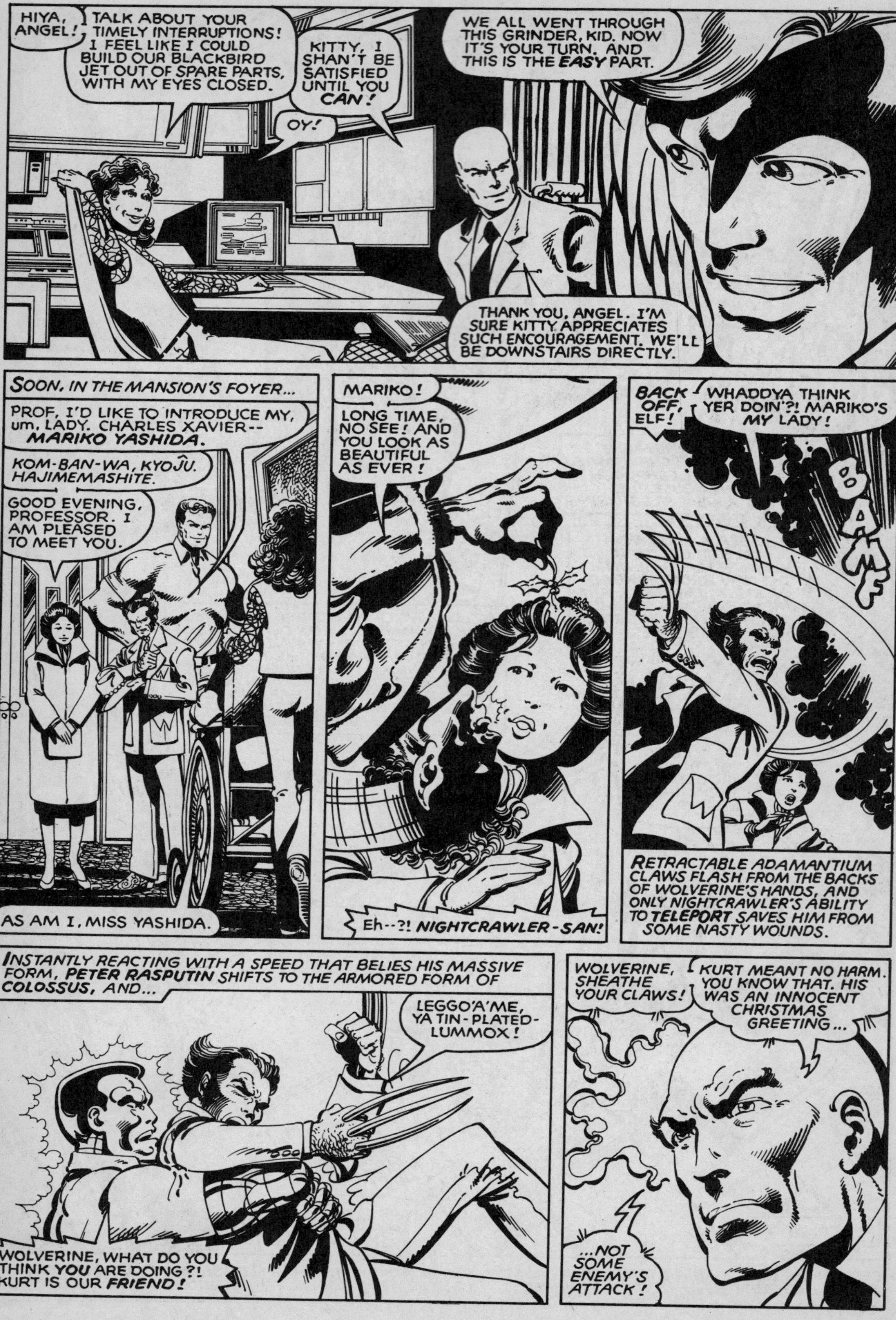
HIYA, ANGEL!
TALK ABOUT YOUR TIMELY INTERRUPTIONS! I FEEL LIKE I COULD BUILD OUR BLACKBIRD JET OUT OF SPARE PARTS, WITH MY EYES CLOSED.
KITTY, I SHAN'T BE SATISFIED UNTIL YOU CAN!
OY!
WE ALL WENT THROUGH THIS GRINDER, KID. NOW IT'S YOUR TURN. AND THIS IS THE EASY PART.
THANK YOU, ANGEL. I'M SURE KITTY APPRECIATES SUCH ENCOURAGEMENT. WE'LL BE DOWNSTAIRS DIRECTLY.
SOON, IN THE MANSION'S FOYER...
PROF, I'D LIKE TO INTRODUCE MY, um, LADY. CHARLES XAVIER-- MARIKO YASHIDA.
KOM-BAN-WA, KYOJU. HAJIMEMASHITE.
GOOD EVENING, PROFESSOR. I AM PLEASED TO MEET YOU.
AS AM I, MISS YASHIDA.
MARIKO!
LONG TIME, NO SEE! AND YOU LOOK AS BEAUTIFUL AS EVER!
Eh--?! NIGHTCRAWLER-SAN!
BACK OFF, ELF!
WHADDYA THINK YER DOIN'?! MARIKO'S MY LADY!
BAMF
RETRACTABLE ADAMANTIUM CLAWS FLASH FROM THE BACKS OF WOLVERINE'S HANDS, AND ONLY NIGHTCRAWLER'S ABILITY TO TELEPORT SAVES HIM FROM SOME NASTY WOUNDS.
INSTANTLY REACTING WITH A SPEED THAT BELIES HIS MASSIVE FORM, PETER RASPUTIN SHIFTS TO THE ARMORED FORM OF COLOSSUS, AND...
LEGGO'A'ME, YA TIN-PLATED-LUMMOX!
WOLVERINE, WHAT DO YOU THINK YOU ARE DOING?! KURT IS OUR FRIEND!
WOLVERINE, SHEATHE YOUR CLAWS!
KURT MEANT NO HARM. YOU KNOW THAT. HIS WAS AN INNOCENT CHRISTMAS GREETING...
...NOT SOME ENEMY'S ATTACK!

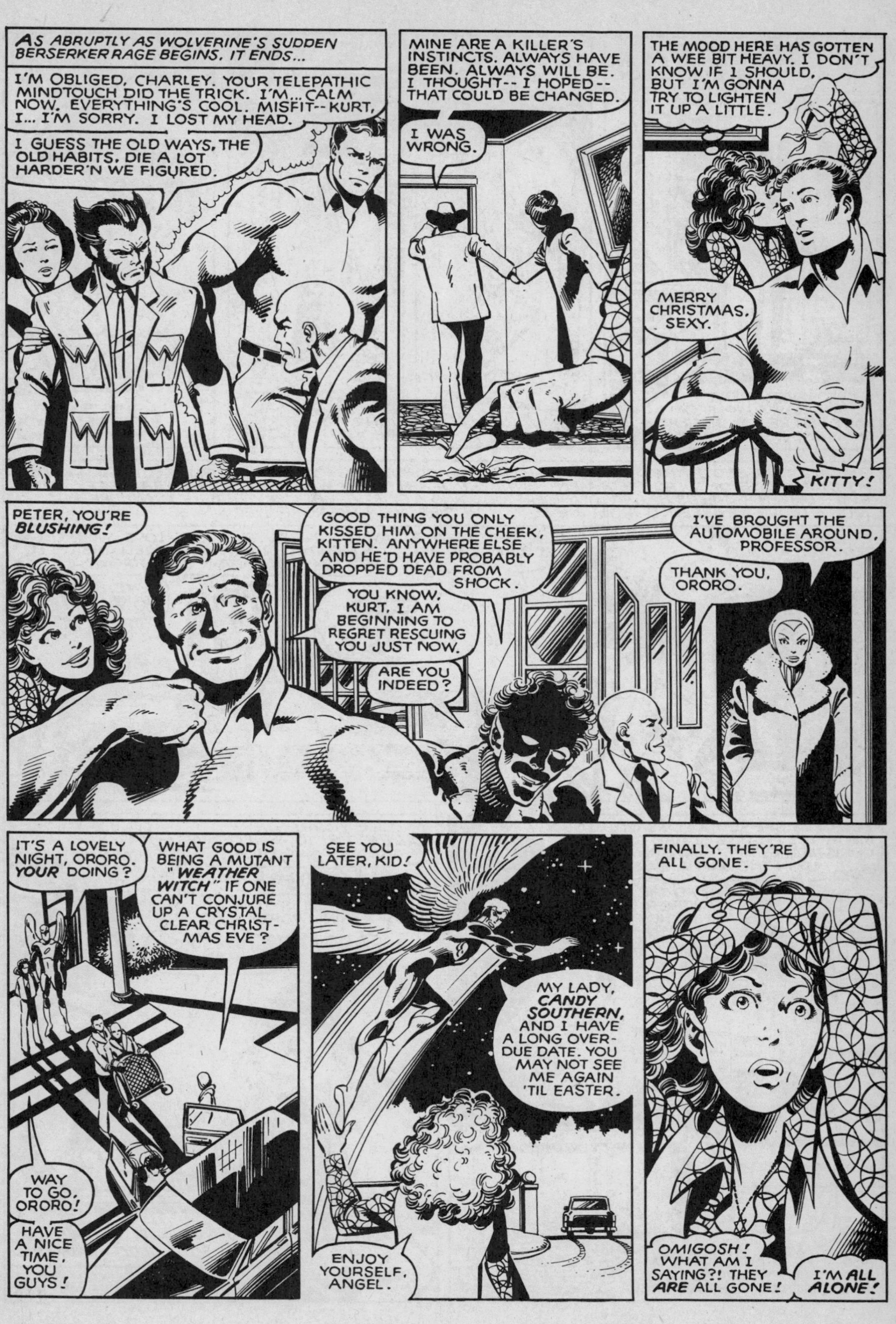
AS ABRUPTLY AS WOLVERINE'S SUDDEN BERSERKER RAGE BEGINS, IT ENDS...
I'M OBLIGED, CHARLEY. YOUR TELEPATHIC MINDTOUCH DID THE TRICK. I'M... CALM NOW. EVERYTHING'S COOL. MISFIT-- KURT, I... I'M SORRY. I LOST MY HEAD.
I GUESS THE OLD WAYS, THE OLD HABITS, DIE A LOT HARDER'N WE FIGURED.
MINE ARE A KILLER'S INSTINCTS. ALWAYS HAVE BEEN. ALWAYS WILL BE. I THOUGHT-- I HOPED-- THAT COULD BE CHANGED.
I WAS WRONG.
THE MOOD HERE HAS GOTTEN A WEE BIT HEAVY. I DON'T KNOW IF I SHOULD, BUT I'M GONNA TRY TO LIGHTEN IT UP A LITTLE.
MERRY CHRISTMAS, SEXY.
KITTY!
PETER, YOU'RE BLUSHING!
GOOD THING YOU ONLY KISSED HIM ON THE CHEEK, KITTEN. ANYWHERE ELSE AND HE'D HAVE PROBABLY DROPPED DEAD FROM SHOCK.
YOU KNOW, KURT, I AM BEGINNING TO REGRET RESCUING YOU JUST NOW.
ARE YOU INDEED?
I'VE BROUGHT THE AUTOMOBILE AROUND, PROFESSOR.
THANK YOU, ORORO.
IT'S A LOVELY NIGHT, ORORO. YOUR DOING?
WHAT GOOD IS BEING A MUTANT "WEATHER WITCH" IF ONE CAN'T CONJURE UP A CRYSTAL CLEAR CHRISTMAS EVE?
WAY TO GO, ORORO!
HAVE A NICE TIME, YOU GUYS!
SEE YOU LATER, KID!
MY LADY, CANDY SOUTHERN, AND I HAVE A LONG OVERDUE DATE. YOU MAY NOT SEE ME AGAIN 'TIL EASTER.
ENJOY YOURSELF, ANGEL.
FINALLY. THEY'RE ALL GONE.
OMIGOSH! WHAT AM I SAYING?! THEY ARE ALL GONE!
I'M ALL ALONE!

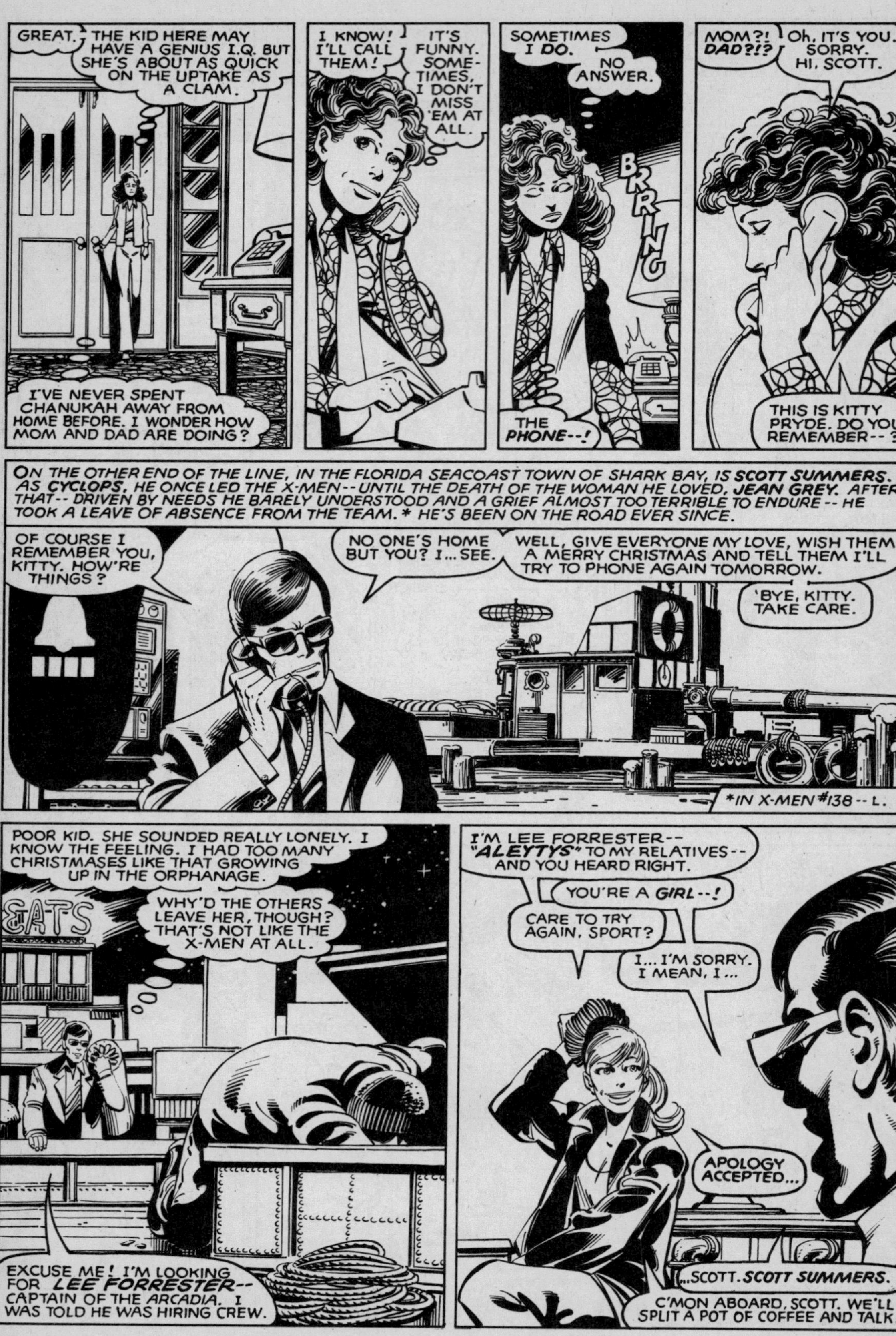
GREAT. THE KID HERE MAY HAVE A GENIUS I.Q. BUT SHE'S ABOUT AS QUICK ON THE UPTAKE AS A CLAM.
I'VE NEVER SPENT CHANUKAH AWAY FROM HOME BEFORE. I WONDER HOW MOM AND DAD ARE DOING?
I KNOW! I'LL CALL THEM!
IT'S FUNNY. SOMETIMES, I DON'T MISS 'EM AT ALL.
SOMETIMES I DO.
NO ANSWER.
BRRING
THE PHONE--!
MOM?! DAD?!?
Oh, IT'S YOU. SORRY. HI, SCOTT.
THIS IS KITTY PRYDE. DO YOU REMEMBER--?
ON THE OTHER END OF THE LINE, IN THE FLORIDA SEACOAST TOWN OF SHARK BAY, IS SCOTT SUMMERS. AS CYCLOPS, HE ONCE LED THE X-MEN--UNTIL THE DEATH OF THE WOMAN HE LOVED, JEAN GREY. AFTER THAT--DRIVEN BY NEEDS HE BARELY UNDERSTOOD AND A GRIEF ALMOST TOO TERRIBLE TO ENDURE--HE TOOK A LEAVE OF ABSENCE FROM THE TEAM.* HE'S BEEN ON THE ROAD EVER SINCE.
OF COURSE I REMEMBER YOU, KITTY. HOW'RE THINGS?
NO ONE'S HOME BUT YOU? I...SEE.
WELL, GIVE EVERYONE MY LOVE, WISH THEM A MERRY CHRISTMAS AND TELL THEM I'LL TRY TO PHONE AGAIN TOMORROW.
'BYE, KITTY. TAKE CARE.
*IN X-MEN #138--L.
POOR KID. SHE SOUNDED REALLY LONELY. I KNOW THE FEELING. I HAD TOO MANY CHRISTMASES LIKE THAT GROWING UP IN THE ORPHANAGE.
WHY'D THE OTHERS LEAVE HER, THOUGH? THAT'S NOT LIKE THE X-MEN AT ALL.
EATS
EXCUSE ME! I'M LOOKING FOR LEE FORRESTER--CAPTAIN OF THE ARCADIA. I WAS TOLD HE WAS HIRING CREW.
I'M LEE FORRESTER--"ALEYTYS" TO MY RELATIVES--AND YOU HEARD RIGHT.
YOU'RE A GIRL--!
CARE TO TRY AGAIN, SPORT?
I...I'M SORRY. I MEAN, I...
APOLOGY ACCEPTED...
...SCOTT. SCOTT SUMMERS.
C'MON ABOARD, SCOTT. WE'LL SPLIT A POT OF COFFEE AND TALK.

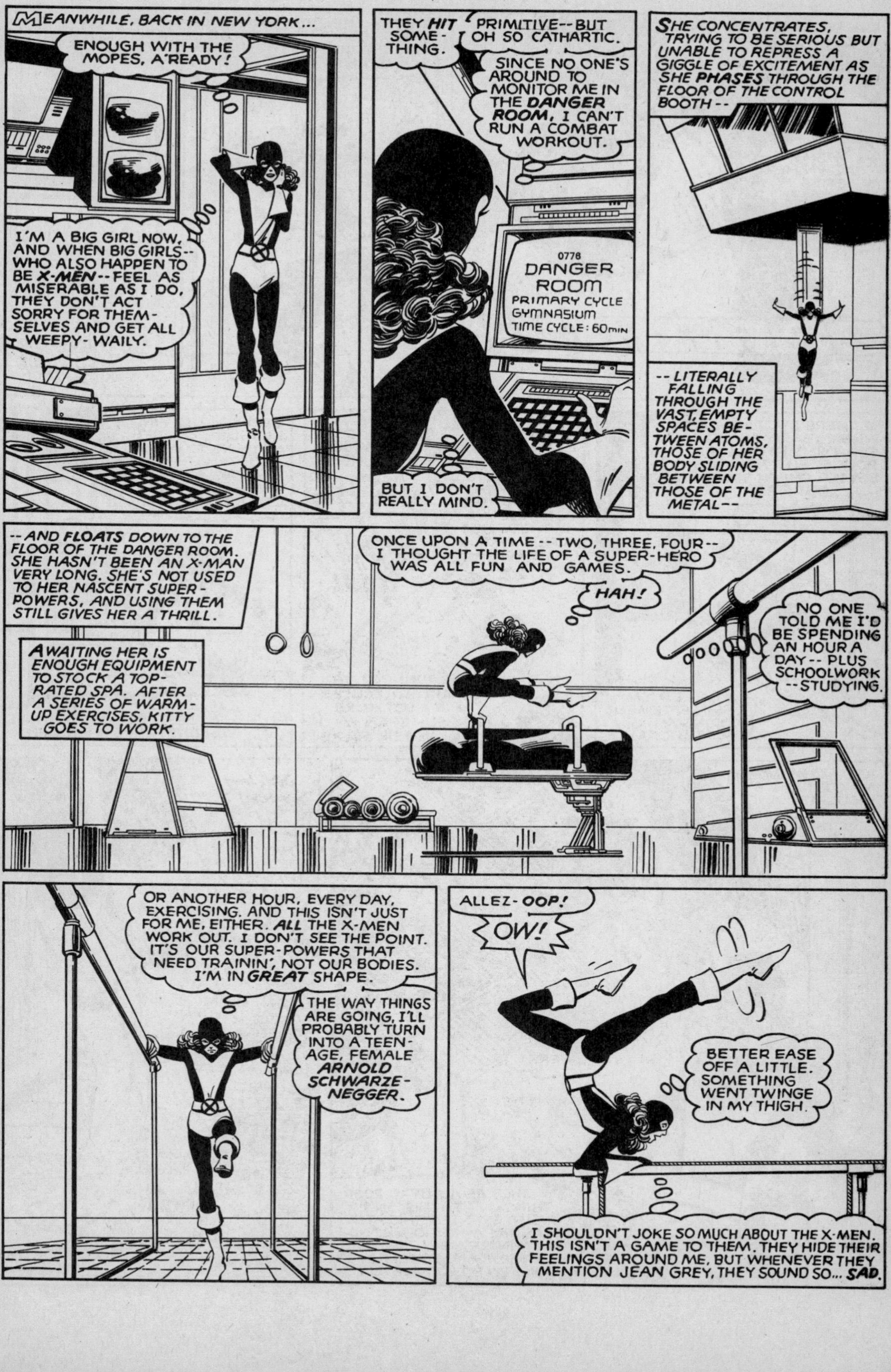
MEANWHILE, BACK IN NEW YORK...
ENOUGH WITH THE MOPES, A'READY!
I'M A BIG GIRL NOW, AND WHEN BIG GIRLS--WHO ALSO HAPPEN TO BE X-MEN--FEEL AS MISERABLE AS I DO, THEY DON'T ACT SORRY FOR THEMSELVES AND GET ALL WEEPY-WAILY.
THEY HIT SOMETHING.
PRIMITIVE--BUT OH SO CATHARTIC.
SINCE NO ONE'S AROUND TO MONITOR ME IN THE DANGER ROOM, I CAN'T RUN A COMBAT WORKOUT.
0778
DANGER ROOM
PRIMARY CYCLE
GYMNASIUM
TIME CYCLE: 60MIN
BUT I DON'T REALLY MIND.
SHE CONCENTRATES, TRYING TO BE SERIOUS BUT UNABLE TO REPRESS A GIGGLE OF EXCITEMENT AS SHE PHASES THROUGH THE FLOOR OF THE CONTROL BOOTH--
--LITERALLY FALLING THROUGH THE VAST, EMPTY SPACES BETWEEN ATOMS, THOSE OF HER BODY SLIDING BETWEEN THOSE OF THE METAL--
--AND FLOATS DOWN TO THE FLOOR OF THE DANGER ROOM. SHE HASN'T BEEN AN X-MAN VERY LONG. SHE'S NOT USED TO HER NASCENT SUPER-POWERS, AND USING THEM STILL GIVES HER A THRILL.
AWAITING HER IS ENOUGH EQUIPMENT TO STOCK A TOP-RATED SPA. AFTER A SERIES OF WARM-UP EXERCISES, KITTY GOES TO WORK.
ONCE UPON A TIME--TWO, THREE, FOUR--I THOUGHT THE LIFE OF A SUPER-HERO WAS ALL FUN AND GAMES.
HAH!
NO ONE TOLD ME I'D BE SPENDING AN HOUR A DAY--PLUS SCHOOLWORK--STUDYING.
OR ANOTHER HOUR, EVERY DAY, EXERCISING. AND THIS ISN'T JUST FOR ME, EITHER. ALL THE X-MEN WORK OUT. I DON'T SEE THE POINT. IT'S OUR SUPER-POWERS THAT NEED TRAININ', NOT OUR BODIES. I'M IN GREAT SHAPE.
THE WAY THINGS ARE GOING, I'LL PROBABLY TURN INTO A TEENAGE, FEMALE ARNOLD SCHWARZENEGGER.
ALLEZ-OOP!
OW!
BETTER EASE OFF A LITTLE. SOMETHING WENT TWINGE IN MY THIGH.
I SHOULDN'T JOKE SO MUCH ABOUT THE X-MEN. THIS ISN'T A GAME TO THEM. THEY HIDE THEIR FEELINGS AROUND ME, BUT WHENEVER THEY MENTION JEAN GREY, THEY SOUND SO... SAD.

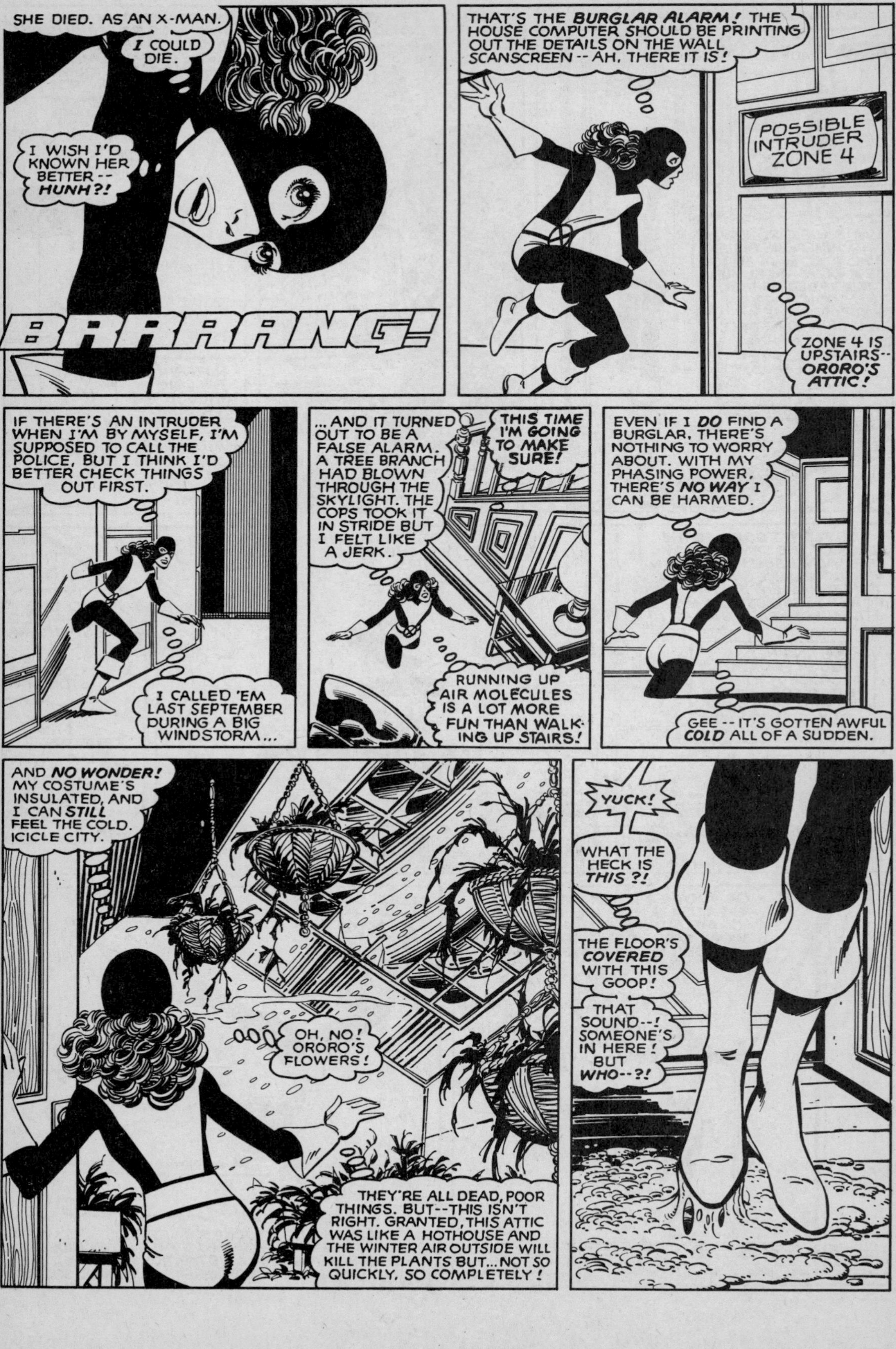
SHE DIED. AS AN X-MAN.
I COULD DIE.
I WISH I'D KNOWN HER BETTER -- HUNH?!
BRRRANG!
THAT'S THE BURGLAR ALARM! THE HOUSE COMPUTER SHOULD BE PRINTING OUT THE DETAILS ON THE WALL SCANSCREEN -- AH, THERE IT IS!
POSSIBLE INTRUDER ZONE 4
ZONE 4 IS UPSTAIRS-- ORORO'S ATTIC!
IF THERE'S AN INTRUDER WHEN I'M BY MYSELF, I'M SUPPOSED TO CALL THE POLICE, BUT I THINK I'D BETTER CHECK THINGS OUT FIRST.
I CALLED 'EM LAST SEPTEMBER DURING A BIG WINDSTORM...
...AND IT TURNED OUT TO BE A FALSE ALARM. A TREE BRANCH HAD BLOWN THROUGH THE SKYLIGHT. THE COPS TOOK IT IN STRIDE BUT I FELT LIKE A JERK.
THIS TIME I'M GOING TO MAKE SURE!
RUNNING UP AIR MOLECULES IS A LOT MORE FUN THAN WALKING UP STAIRS!
EVEN IF I DO FIND A BURGLAR, THERE'S NOTHING TO WORRY ABOUT. WITH MY PHASING POWER, THERE'S NO WAY I CAN BE HARMED.
GEE -- IT'S GOTTEN AWFUL COLD ALL OF A SUDDEN.
AND NO WONDER! MY COSTUME'S INSULATED, AND I CAN STILL FEEL THE COLD. ICICLE CITY.
OH, NO! ORORO'S FLOWERS!
THEY'RE ALL DEAD, POOR THINGS. BUT--THIS ISN'T RIGHT. GRANTED, THIS ATTIC WAS LIKE A HOTHOUSE AND THE WINTER AIR OUTSIDE WILL KILL THE PLANTS BUT... NOT SO QUICKLY, SO COMPLETELY!
YUCK!
WHAT THE HECK IS THIS?!
THE FLOOR'S COVERED WITH THIS GOOP!
THAT SOUND--! SOMEONE'S IN HERE! BUT WHO--?!

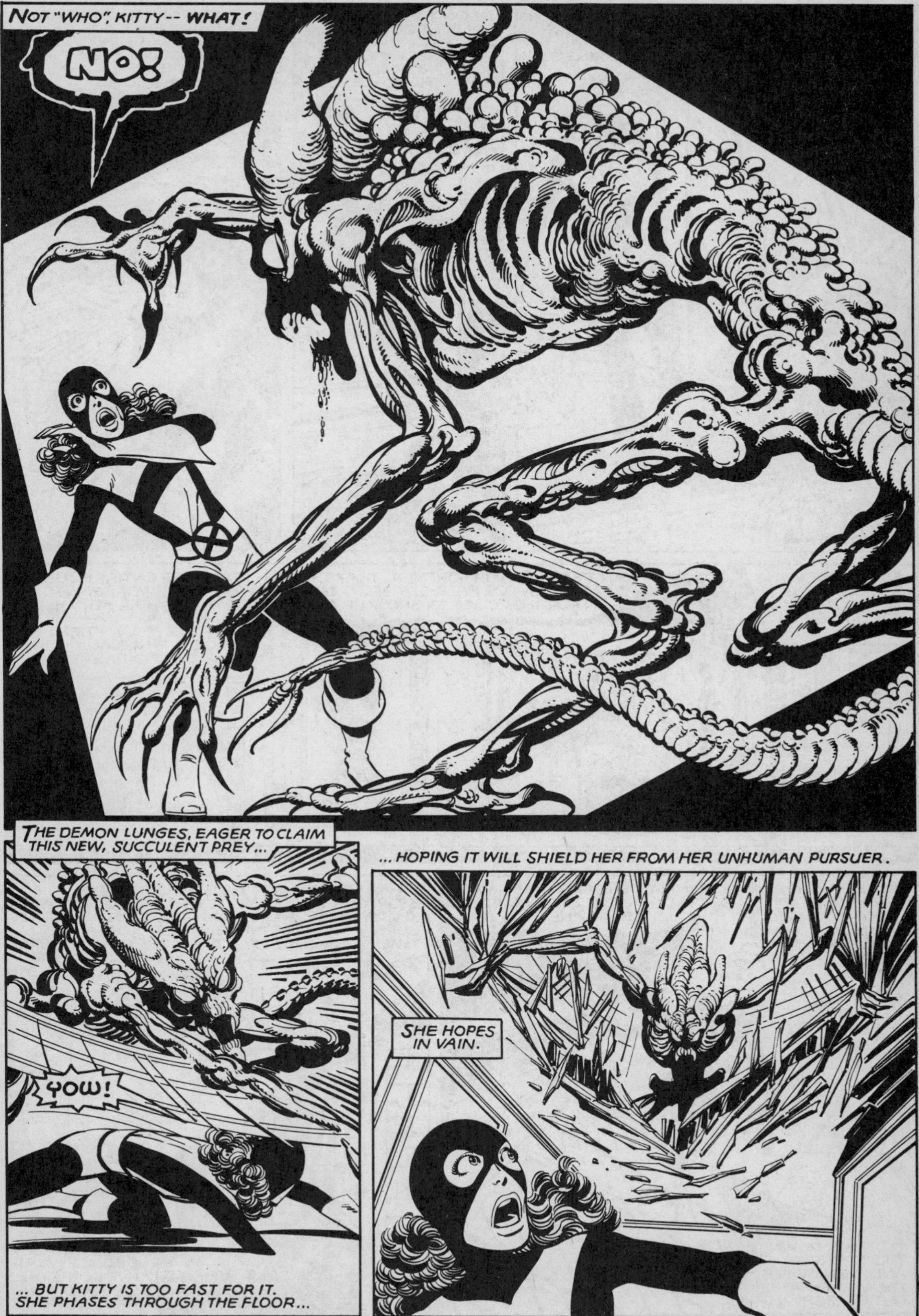
NOT "WHO", KITTY -- WHAT!
NO!
THE DEMON LUNGES, EAGER TO CLAIM THIS NEW, SUCCULENT PREY...
YOW!
... BUT KITTY IS TOO FAST FOR IT. SHE PHASES THROUGH THE FLOOR...
... HOPING IT WILL SHIELD HER FROM HER UNHUMAN PURSUER.
SHE HOPES IN VAIN.

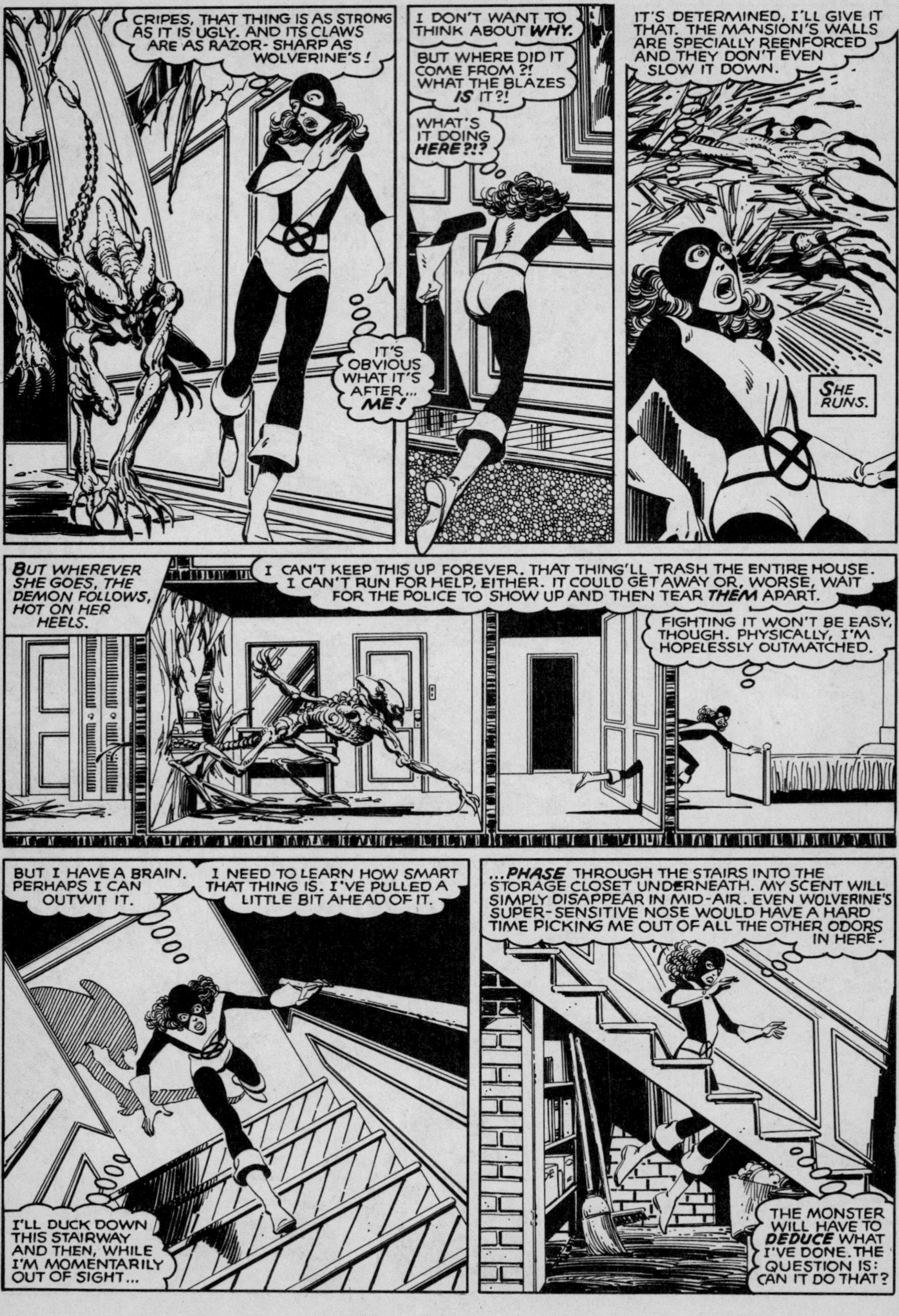

CRIPES, THAT THING IS AS STRONG AS IT IS UGLY. AND ITS CLAWS ARE AS RAZOR-SHARP AS WOLVERINE'S!
IT'S OBVIOUS WHAT IT'S AFTER... ME!
I DON'T WANT TO THINK ABOUT WHY.
BUT WHERE DID IT COME FROM?! WHAT THE BLAZES IS IT?!
WHAT'S IT DOING HERE?!?
IT'S DETERMINED, I'LL GIVE IT THAT. THE MANSION'S WALLS ARE SPECIALLY REENFORCED AND THEY DON'T EVEN SLOW IT DOWN.
SHE RUNS.
BUT WHEREVER SHE GOES, THE DEMON FOLLOWS, HOT ON HER HEELS.
I CAN'T KEEP THIS UP FOREVER. THAT THING'LL TRASH THE ENTIRE HOUSE. I CAN'T RUN FOR HELP, EITHER. IT COULD GET AWAY OR, WORSE, WAIT FOR THE POLICE TO SHOW UP AND THEN TEAR THEM APART.
FIGHTING IT WON'T BE EASY, THOUGH. PHYSICALLY, I'M HOPELESSLY OUTMATCHED.
BUT I HAVE A BRAIN. PERHAPS I CAN OUTWIT IT.
I NEED TO LEARN HOW SMART THAT THING IS. I'VE PULLED A LITTLE BIT AHEAD OF IT.
I'LL DUCK DOWN THIS STAIRWAY AND THEN, WHILE I'M MOMENTARILY OUT OF SIGHT...
...PHASE THROUGH THE STAIRS INTO THE STORAGE CLOSET UNDERNEATH. MY SCENT WILL SIMPLY DISAPPEAR IN MID-AIR. EVEN WOLVERINE'S SUPER-SENSITIVE NOSE WOULD HAVE A HARD TIME PICKING ME OUT OF ALL THE OTHER ODORS IN HERE.
THE MONSTER WILL HAVE TO DEDUCE WHAT I'VE DONE. THE QUESTION IS: CAN IT DO THAT?

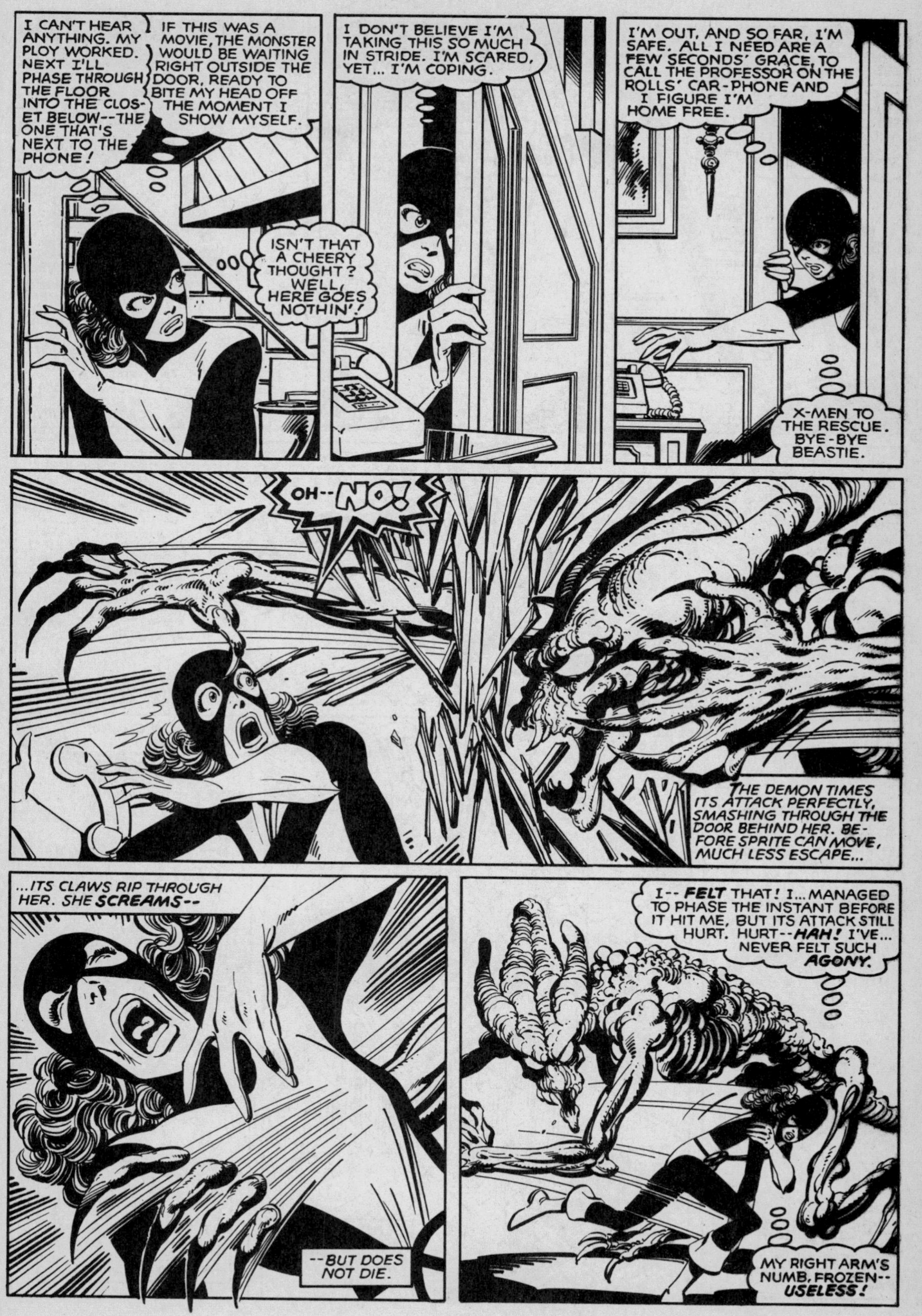
I CAN'T HEAR ANYTHING. MY PLOY WORKED. NEXT I'LL PHASE THROUGH THE FLOOR INTO THE CLOSET BELOW--THE ONE THAT'S NEXT TO THE PHONE!
IF THIS WAS A MOVIE, THE MONSTER WOULD BE WAITING RIGHT OUTSIDE THE DOOR, READY TO BITE MY HEAD OFF THE MOMENT I SHOW MYSELF.
I DON'T BELIEVE I'M TAKING THIS SO MUCH IN STRIDE. I'M SCARED, YET... I'M COPING.
ISN'T THAT A CHEERY THOUGHT? WELL, HERE GOES NOTHIN'!
I'M OUT, AND SO FAR, I'M SAFE. ALL I NEED ARE A FEW SECONDS' GRACE, TO CALL THE PROFESSOR ON THE ROLLS' CAR-PHONE AND I FIGURE I'M HOME FREE.
X-MEN TO THE RESCUE. BYE-BYE BEASTIE.
OH--NO!
THE DEMON TIMES ITS ATTACK PERFECTLY, SMASHING THROUGH THE DOOR BEHIND HER. BEFORE SPRITE CAN MOVE, MUCH LESS ESCAPE...
...ITS CLAWS RIP THROUGH HER. SHE SCREAMS--
--BUT DOES NOT DIE.
I--FELT THAT! I...MANAGED TO PHASE THE INSTANT BEFORE IT HIT ME, BUT ITS ATTACK STILL HURT. HURT--HAH! I'VE... NEVER FELT SUCH AGONY.
MY RIGHT ARM'S NUMB, FROZEN--USELESS!

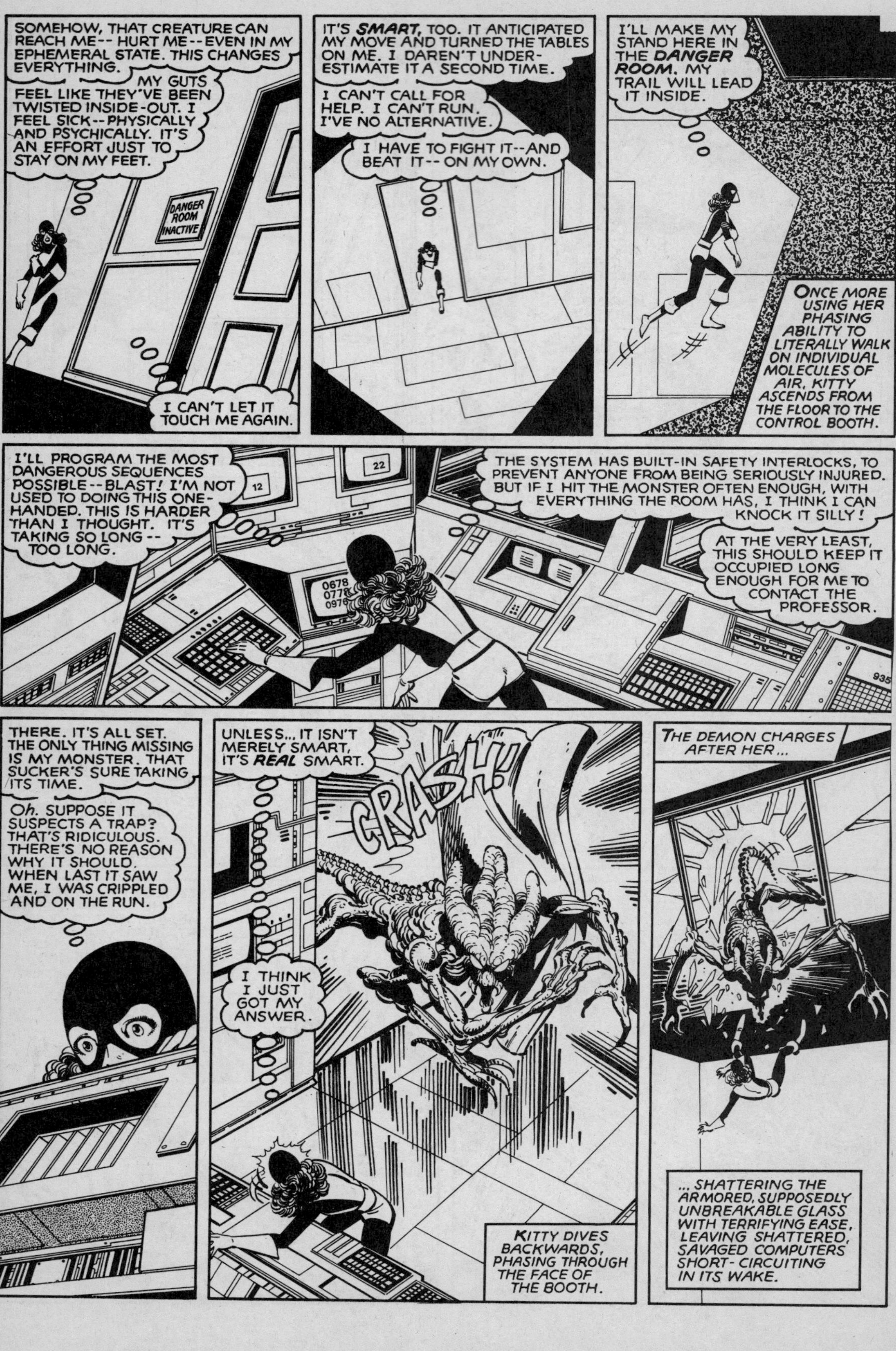

SOMEHOW, THAT CREATURE CAN REACH ME-- HURT ME-- EVEN IN MY EPHEMERAL STATE. THIS CHANGES EVERYTHING.
MY GUTS FEEL LIKE THEY'VE BEEN TWISTED INSIDE-OUT. I FEEL SICK-- PHYSICALLY AND PSYCHICALLY. IT'S AN EFFORT JUST TO STAY ON MY FEET.
DANGER ROOM INACTIVE
I CAN'T LET IT TOUCH ME AGAIN.
IT'S SMART, TOO. IT ANTICIPATED MY MOVE AND TURNED THE TABLES ON ME. I DAREN'T UNDER-ESTIMATE IT A SECOND TIME.
I CAN'T CALL FOR HELP. I CAN'T RUN. I'VE NO ALTERNATIVE.
I HAVE TO FIGHT IT--AND BEAT IT-- ON MY OWN.
I'LL MAKE MY STAND HERE IN THE DANGER ROOM. MY TRAIL WILL LEAD IT INSIDE.
ONCE MORE USING HER PHASING ABILITY TO LITERALLY WALK ON INDIVIDUAL MOLECULES OF AIR, KITTY ASCENDS FROM THE FLOOR TO THE CONTROL BOOTH.
I'LL PROGRAM THE MOST DANGEROUS SEQUENCES POSSIBLE--BLAST! I'M NOT USED TO DOING THIS ONE-HANDED. THIS IS HARDER THAN I THOUGHT. IT'S TAKING SO LONG-- TOO LONG.
THE SYSTEM HAS BUILT-IN SAFETY INTERLOCKS, TO PREVENT ANYONE FROM BEING SERIOUSLY INJURED. BUT IF I HIT THE MONSTER OFTEN ENOUGH, WITH EVERYTHING THE ROOM HAS, I THINK I CAN KNOCK IT SILLY!
AT THE VERY LEAST, THIS SHOULD KEEP IT OCCUPIED LONG ENOUGH FOR ME TO CONTACT THE PROFESSOR.
THERE. IT'S ALL SET. THE ONLY THING MISSING IS MY MONSTER. THAT SUCKER'S SURE TAKING ITS TIME.
Oh. SUPPOSE IT SUSPECTS A TRAP? THAT'S RIDICULOUS. THERE'S NO REASON WHY IT SHOULD. WHEN LAST IT SAW ME, I WAS CRIPPLED AND ON THE RUN.
UNLESS... IT ISN'T MERELY SMART, IT'S REAL SMART.
CRASH!
I THINK I JUST GOT MY ANSWER.
KITTY DIVES BACKWARDS, PHASING THROUGH THE FACE OF THE BOOTH.
THE DEMON CHARGES AFTER HER...
... SHATTERING THE ARMORED, SUPPOSEDLY UNBREAKABLE GLASS WITH TERRIFYING EASE, LEAVING SHATTERED, SAVAGED COMPUTERS SHORT-CIRCUITING IN ITS WAKE.

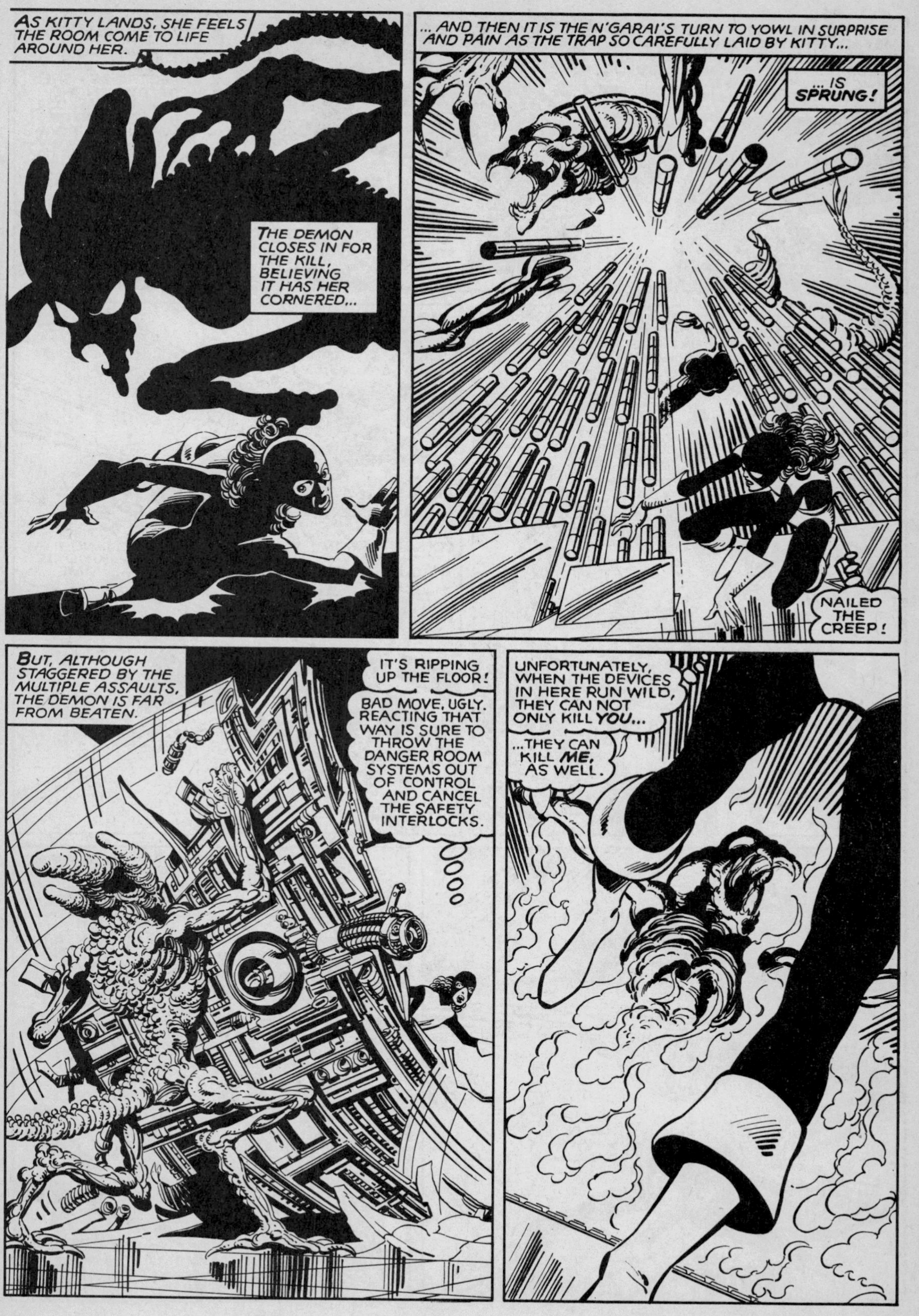
AS KITTY LANDS, SHE FEELS THE ROOM COME TO LIFE AROUND HER.
THE DEMON CLOSES IN FOR THE KILL, BELIEVING IT HAS HER CORNERED...
... AND THEN IT IS THE N'GARAI'S TURN TO YOWL IN SURPRISE AND PAIN AS THE TRAP SO CAREFULLY LAID BY KITTY...
... IS SPRUNG!
NAILED THE CREEP!
BUT, ALTHOUGH STAGGERED BY THE MULTIPLE ASSAULTS, THE DEMON IS FAR FROM BEATEN.
IT'S RIPPING UP THE FLOOR!
BAD MOVE, UGLY. REACTING THAT WAY IS SURE TO THROW THE DANGER ROOM SYSTEMS OUT OF CONTROL AND CANCEL THE SAFETY INTERLOCKS.
UNFORTUNATELY, WHEN THE DEVICES IN HERE RUN WILD, THEY CAN NOT ONLY KILL YOU...
...THEY CAN KILL ME, AS WELL.

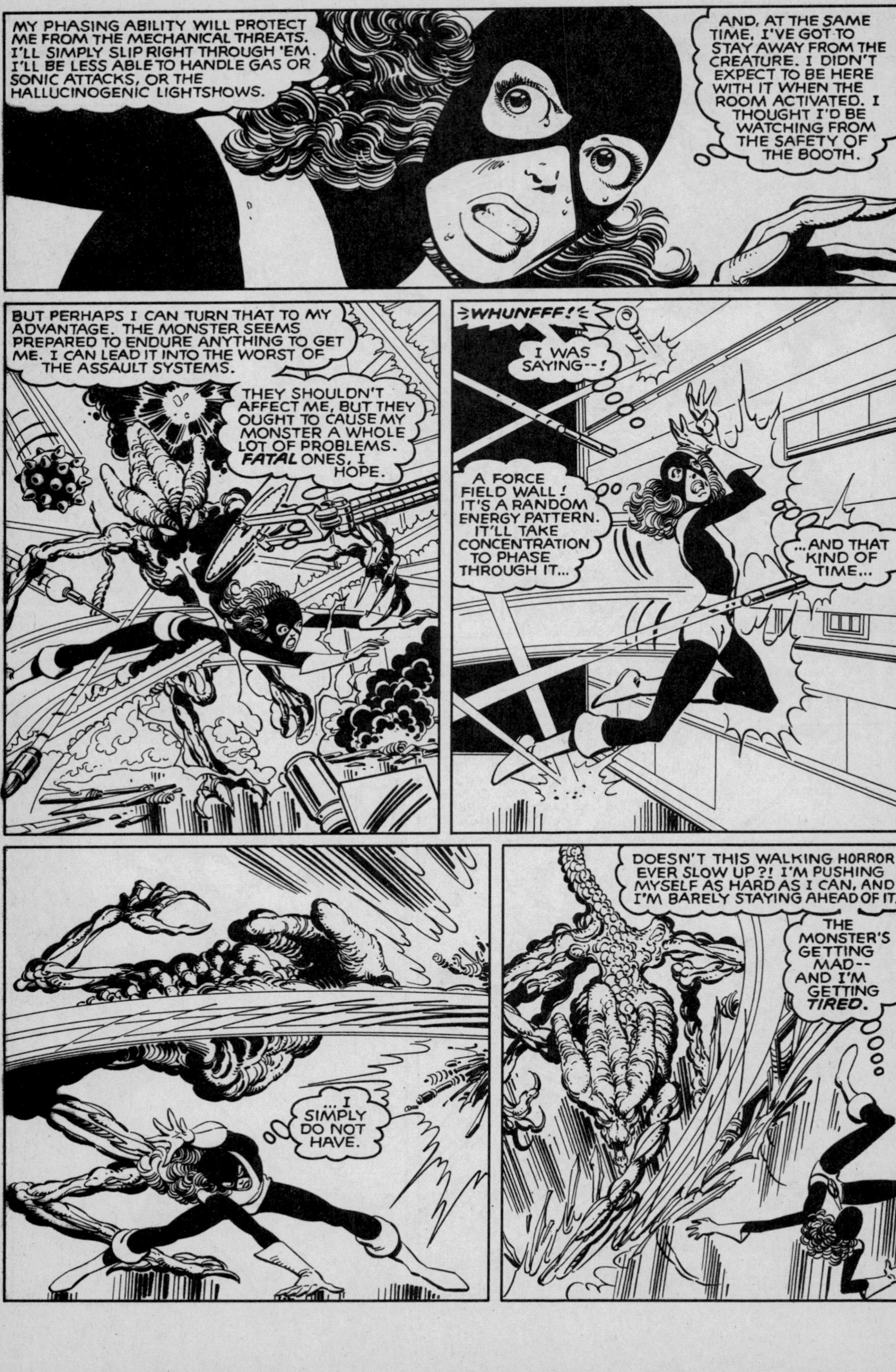
MY PHASING ABILITY WILL PROTECT ME FROM THE MECHANICAL THREATS. I'LL SIMPLY SLIP RIGHT THROUGH 'EM. I'LL BE LESS ABLE TO HANDLE GAS OR SONIC ATTACKS, OR THE HALLUCINOGENIC LIGHTSHOWS.
AND, AT THE SAME TIME, I'VE GOT TO STAY AWAY FROM THE CREATURE. I DIDN'T EXPECT TO BE HERE WITH IT WHEN THE ROOM ACTIVATED. I THOUGHT I'D BE WATCHING FROM THE SAFETY OF THE BOOTH.
BUT PERHAPS I CAN TURN THAT TO MY ADVANTAGE. THE MONSTER SEEMS PREPARED TO ENDURE ANYTHING TO GET ME. I CAN LEAD IT INTO THE WORST OF THE ASSAULT SYSTEMS.
THEY SHOULDN'T AFFECT ME, BUT THEY OUGHT TO CAUSE MY MONSTER A WHOLE LOT OF PROBLEMS. FATAL ONES, I HOPE.
WHUNFFF!
I WAS SAYING--!
A FORCE FIELD WALL! IT'S A RANDOM ENERGY PATTERN. IT'LL TAKE CONCENTRATION TO PHASE THROUGH IT...
...AND THAT KIND OF TIME...
... I SIMPLY DO NOT HAVE.
DOESN'T THIS WALKING HORROR EVER SLOW UP?! I'M PUSHING MYSELF AS HARD AS I CAN, AND I'M BARELY STAYING AHEAD OF IT.
THE MONSTER'S GETTING MAD-- AND I'M GETTING TIRED.

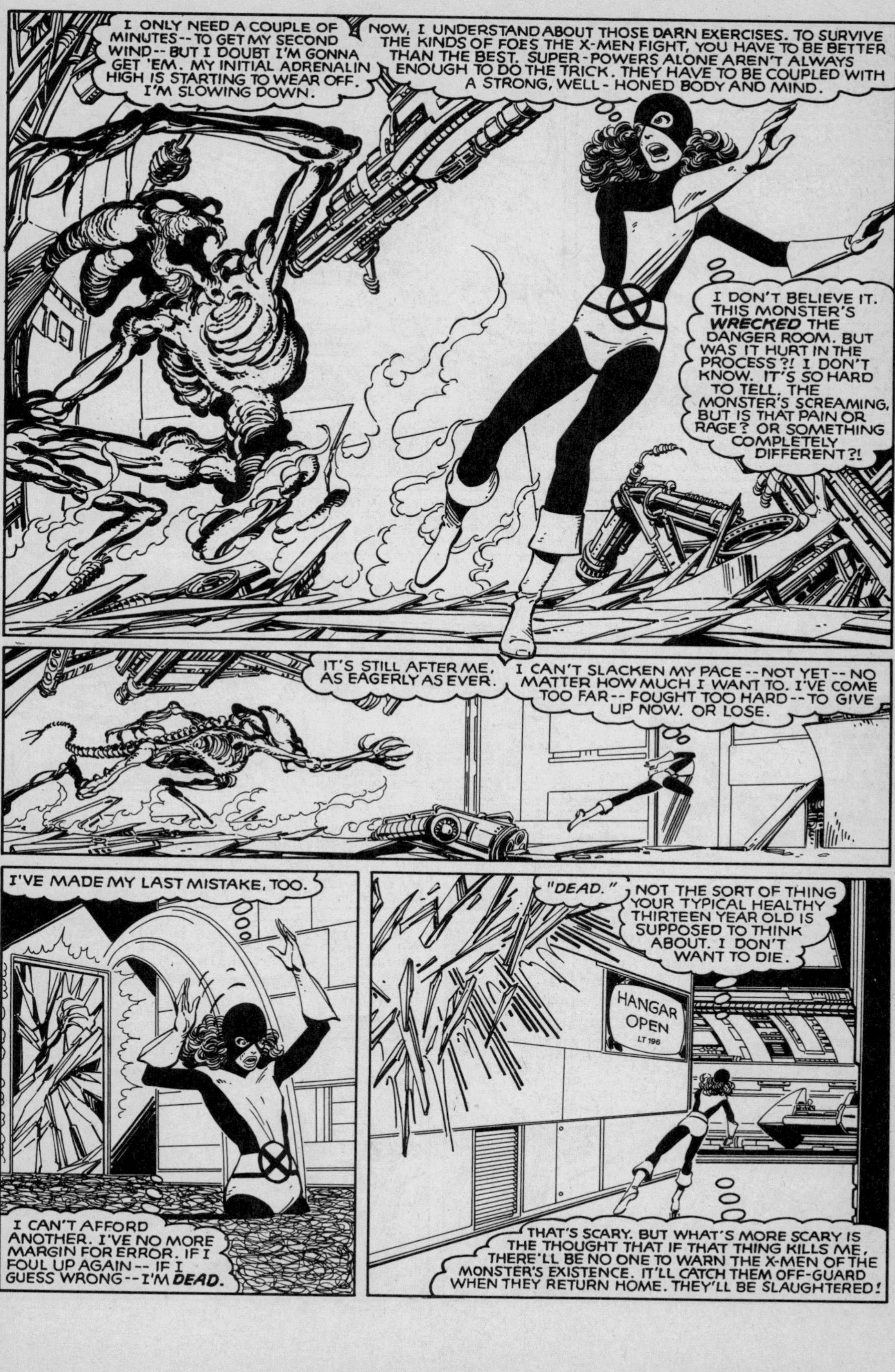
I ONLY NEED A COUPLE OF MINUTES-- TO GET MY SECOND WIND-- BUT I DOUBT I'M GONNA GET 'EM. MY INITIAL ADRENALIN HIGH IS STARTING TO WEAR OFF. I'M SLOWING DOWN.
NOW, I UNDERSTAND ABOUT THOSE DARN EXERCISES. TO SURVIVE THE KINDS OF FOES THE X-MEN FIGHT, YOU HAVE TO BE BETTER THAN THE BEST. SUPER-POWERS ALONE AREN'T ALWAYS ENOUGH TO DO THE TRICK. THEY HAVE TO BE COUPLED WITH A STRONG, WELL-HONED BODY AND MIND.
I DON'T BELIEVE IT. THIS MONSTER'S WRECKED THE DANGER ROOM. BUT WAS IT HURT IN THE PROCESS?! I DON'T KNOW. IT'S SO HARD TO TELL. THE MONSTER'S SCREAMING, BUT IS THAT PAIN OR RAGE? OR SOMETHING COMPLETELY DIFFERENT?!
IT'S STILL AFTER ME, AS EAGERLY AS EVER.
I CAN'T SLACKEN MY PACE--NOT YET--NO MATTER HOW MUCH I WANT TO. I'VE COME TOO FAR-- FOUGHT TOO HARD--TO GIVE UP NOW. OR LOSE.
I'VE MADE MY LAST MISTAKE, TOO.
I CAN'T AFFORD ANOTHER. I'VE NO MORE MARGIN FOR ERROR. IF I FOUL UP AGAIN-- IF I GUESS WRONG--I'M DEAD.
"DEAD."
NOT THE SORT OF THING YOUR TYPICAL HEALTHY THIRTEEN YEAR OLD IS SUPPOSED TO THINK ABOUT. I DON'T WANT TO DIE.
HANGAR OPEN
LT 196
THAT'S SCARY. BUT WHAT'S MORE SCARY IS THE THOUGHT THAT IF THAT THING KILLS ME, THERE'LL BE NO ONE TO WARN THE X-MEN OF THE MONSTER'S EXISTENCE. IT'LL CATCH THEM OFF-GUARD WHEN THEY RETURN HOME. THEY'LL BE SLAUGHTERED!

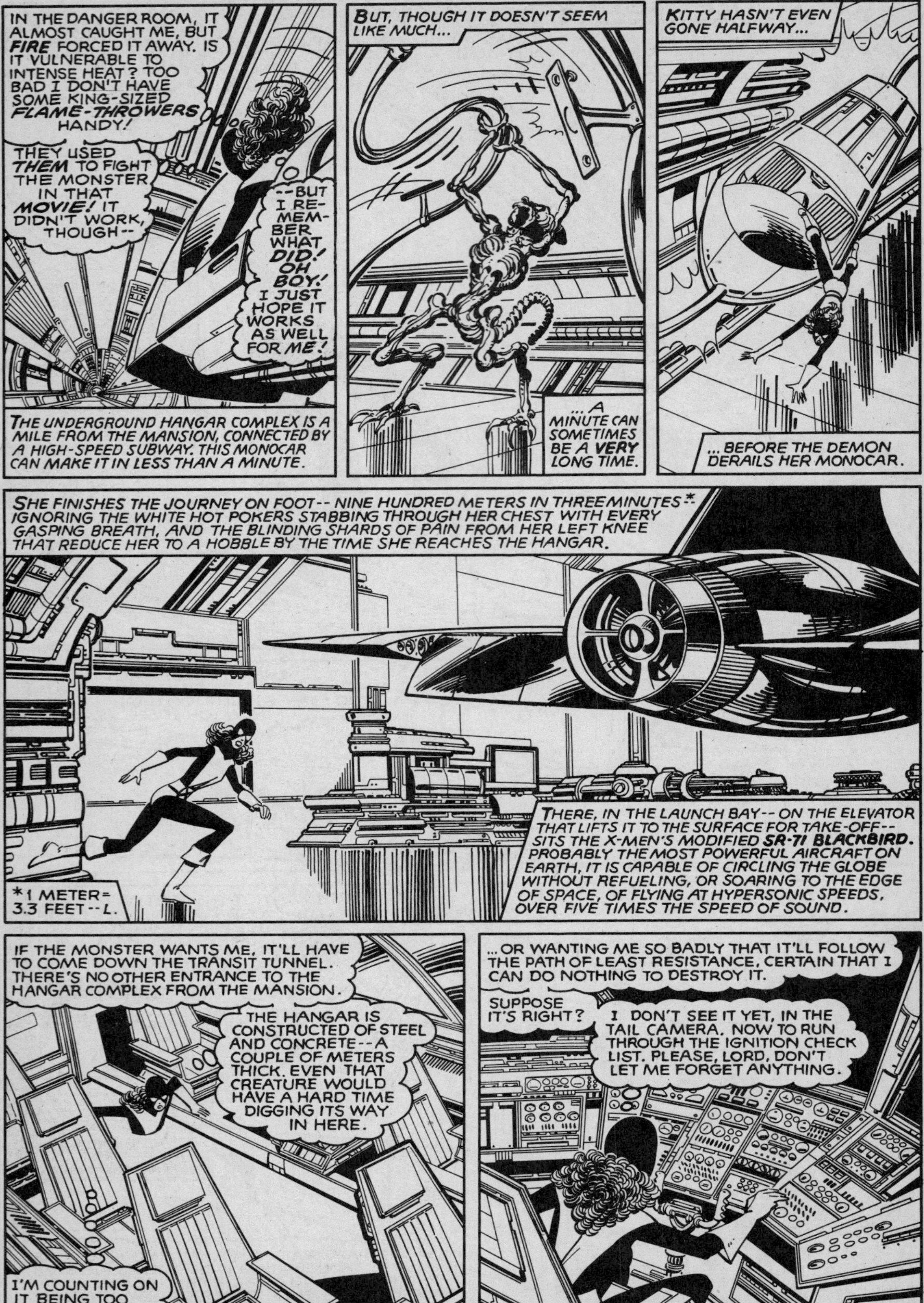
IN THE DANGER ROOM, IT ALMOST CAUGHT ME, BUT FIRE FORCED IT AWAY. IS IT VULNERABLE TO INTENSE HEAT? TOO BAD I DON'T HAVE SOME KING-SIZED FLAME-THROWERS HANDY!
THEY USED THEM TO FIGHT THE MONSTER IN THAT MOVIE! IT DIDN'T WORK, THOUGH--
--BUT I REMEMBER WHAT DID! OH BOY! I JUST HOPE IT WORKS AS WELL FOR ME!
THE UNDERGROUND HANGAR COMPLEX IS A MILE FROM THE MANSION, CONNECTED BY A HIGH-SPEED SUBWAY. THIS MONOCAR CAN MAKE IT IN LESS THAN A MINUTE.
BUT, THOUGH IT DOESN'T SEEM LIKE MUCH...
...A MINUTE CAN SOMETIMES BE A VERY LONG TIME.
KITTY HASN'T EVEN GONE HALFWAY...
...BEFORE THE DEMON DERAILS HER MONOCAR.
SHE FINISHES THE JOURNEY ON FOOT-- NINE HUNDRED METERS IN THREE MINUTES* IGNORING THE WHITE HOT POKERS STABBING THROUGH HER CHEST WITH EVERY GASPING BREATH, AND THE BLINDING SHARDS OF PAIN FROM HER LEFT KNEE THAT REDUCE HER TO A HOBBLE BY THE TIME SHE REACHES THE HANGAR.
THERE, IN THE LAUNCH BAY-- ON THE ELEVATOR THAT LIFTS IT TO THE SURFACE FOR TAKE-OFF-- SITS THE X-MEN'S MODIFIED SR-71 BLACKBIRD. PROBABLY THE MOST POWERFUL AIRCRAFT ON EARTH, IT IS CAPABLE OF CIRCLING THE GLOBE WITHOUT REFUELING, OR SOARING TO THE EDGE OF SPACE, OF FLYING AT HYPERSONIC SPEEDS, OVER FIVE TIMES THE SPEED OF SOUND.
*1 METER= 3.3 FEET--L.
IF THE MONSTER WANTS ME, IT'LL HAVE TO COME DOWN THE TRANSIT TUNNEL. THERE'S NO OTHER ENTRANCE TO THE HANGAR COMPLEX FROM THE MANSION.
THE HANGAR IS CONSTRUCTED OF STEEL AND CONCRETE--A COUPLE OF METERS THICK. EVEN THAT CREATURE WOULD HAVE A HARD TIME DIGGING ITS WAY IN HERE.
I'M COUNTING ON IT BEING TOO ANGRY TO TRY...
...OR WANTING ME SO BADLY THAT IT'LL FOLLOW THE PATH OF LEAST RESISTANCE, CERTAIN THAT I CAN DO NOTHING TO DESTROY IT.
SUPPOSE IT'S RIGHT?
I DON'T SEE IT YET, IN THE TAIL CAMERA. NOW TO RUN THROUGH THE IGNITION CHECK LIST. PLEASE, LORD, DON'T LET ME FORGET ANYTHING.

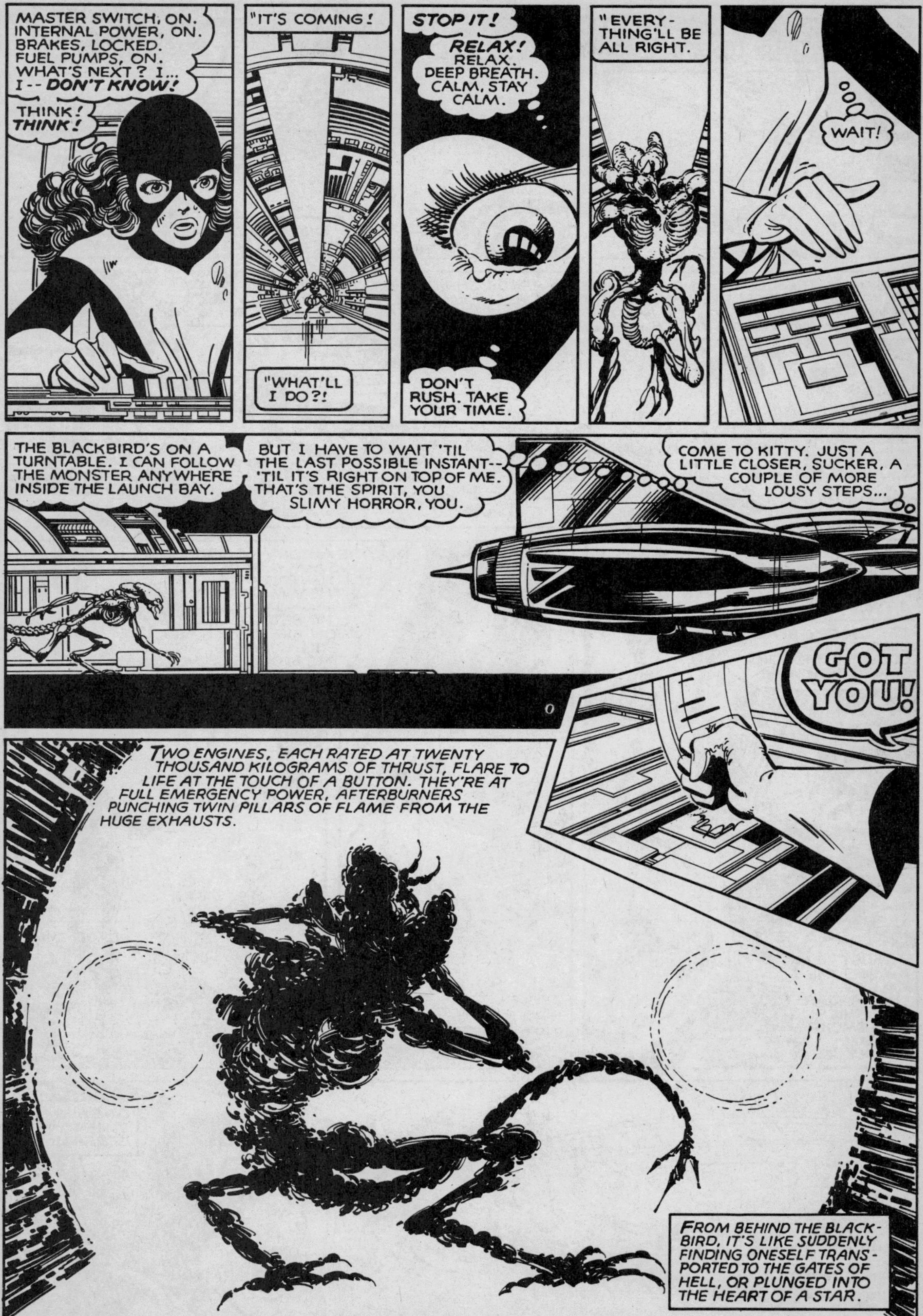
MASTER SWITCH, ON. INTERNAL POWER, ON. BRAKES, LOCKED. FUEL PUMPS, ON. WHAT'S NEXT? I... I-- DON'T KNOW!
THINK! THINK!
"IT'S COMING!
"WHAT'LL I DO?!
STOP IT!
RELAX! RELAX. DEEP BREATH. CALM, STAY CALM.
DON'T RUSH. TAKE YOUR TIME.
"EVERY-THING'LL BE ALL RIGHT.
WAIT!
THE BLACKBIRD'S ON A TURNTABLE. I CAN FOLLOW THE MONSTER ANYWHERE INSIDE THE LAUNCH BAY.
BUT I HAVE TO WAIT 'TIL THE LAST POSSIBLE INSTANT-- 'TIL IT'S RIGHT ON TOP OF ME. THAT'S THE SPIRIT, YOU SLIMY HORROR, YOU.
COME TO KITTY. JUST A LITTLE CLOSER, SUCKER, A COUPLE OF MORE LOUSY STEPS...
GOT YOU!
TWO ENGINES, EACH RATED AT TWENTY THOUSAND KILOGRAMS OF THRUST, FLARE TO LIFE AT THE TOUCH OF A BUTTON. THEY'RE AT FULL EMERGENCY POWER, AFTERBURNERS PUNCHING TWIN PILLARS OF FLAME FROM THE HUGE EXHAUSTS.
FROM BEHIND THE BLACKBIRD, IT'S LIKE SUDDENLY FINDING ONESELF TRANSPORTED TO THE GATES OF HELL, OR PLUNGED INTO THE HEART OF A STAR.

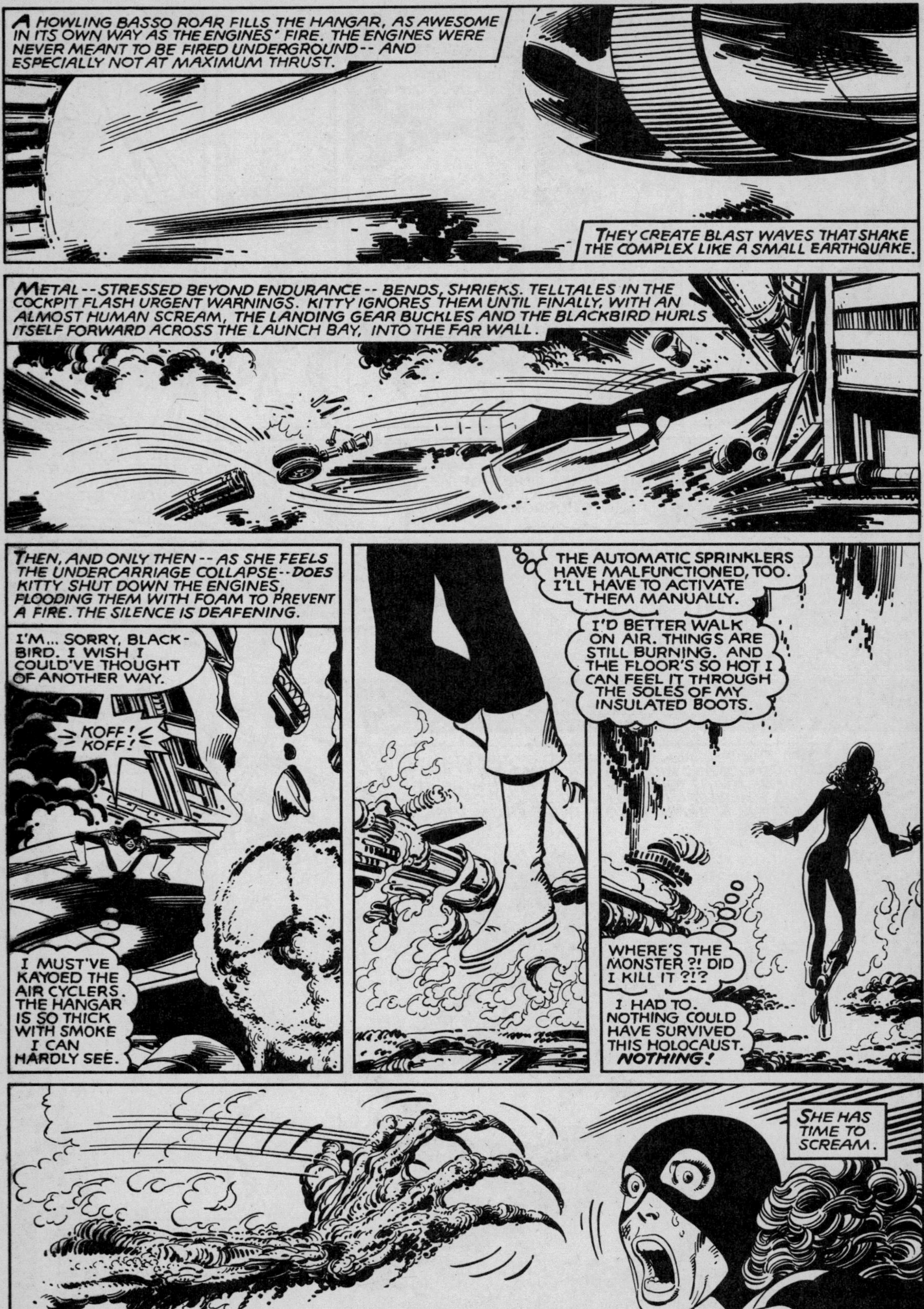

A HOWLING BASSO ROAR FILLS THE HANGAR, AS AWESOME IN ITS OWN WAY AS THE ENGINES' FIRE. THE ENGINES WERE NEVER MEANT TO BE FIRED UNDERGROUND -- AND ESPECIALLY NOT AT MAXIMUM THRUST.
THEY CREATE BLAST WAVES THAT SHAKE THE COMPLEX LIKE A SMALL EARTHQUAKE.
METAL -- STRESSED BEYOND ENDURANCE -- BENDS, SHRIEKS. TELLTALES IN THE COCKPIT FLASH URGENT WARNINGS. KITTY IGNORES THEM UNTIL FINALLY, WITH AN ALMOST HUMAN SCREAM, THE LANDING GEAR BUCKLES AND THE BLACKBIRD HURLS ITSELF FORWARD ACROSS THE LAUNCH BAY, INTO THE FAR WALL.
THEN, AND ONLY THEN -- AS SHE FEELS THE UNDERCARRIAGE COLLAPSE -- DOES KITTY SHUT DOWN THE ENGINES, FLOODING THEM WITH FOAM TO PREVENT A FIRE. THE SILENCE IS DEAFENING.
I'M... SORRY, BLACKBIRD. I WISH I COULD'VE THOUGHT OF ANOTHER WAY.
KOFF! KOFF!
I MUST'VE KAYOED THE AIR CYCLERS. THE HANGAR IS SO THICK WITH SMOKE I CAN HARDLY SEE.
THE AUTOMATIC SPRINKLERS HAVE MALFUNCTIONED, TOO. I'LL HAVE TO ACTIVATE THEM MANUALLY.
I'D BETTER WALK ON AIR. THINGS ARE STILL BURNING. AND THE FLOOR'S SO HOT I CAN FEEL IT THROUGH THE SOLES OF MY INSULATED BOOTS.
WHERE'S THE MONSTER ?! DID I KILL IT ?!?
I HAD TO. NOTHING COULD HAVE SURVIVED THIS HOLOCAUST. NOTHING!
SHE HAS TIME TO SCREAM.

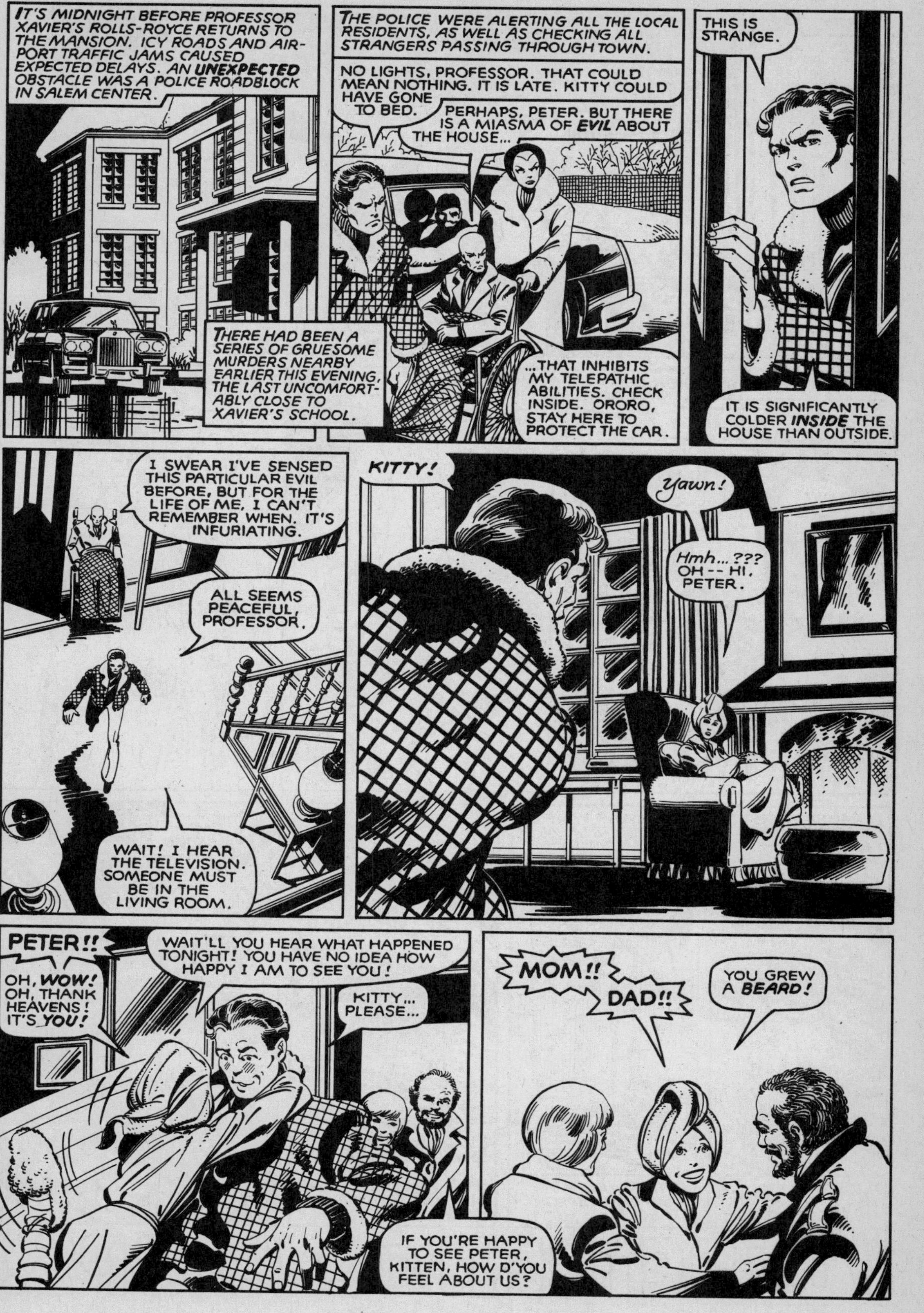
IT'S MIDNIGHT BEFORE PROFESSOR XAVIER'S ROLLS-ROYCE RETURNS TO THE MANSION. ICY ROADS AND AIR-PORT TRAFFIC JAMS CAUSED EXPECTED DELAYS. AN UNEXPECTED OBSTACLE WAS A POLICE ROADBLOCK IN SALEM CENTER.
THE POLICE WERE ALERTING ALL THE LOCAL RESIDENTS, AS WELL AS CHECKING ALL STRANGERS PASSING THROUGH TOWN.
NO LIGHTS, PROFESSOR. THAT COULD MEAN NOTHING. IT IS LATE. KITTY COULD HAVE GONE TO BED.
PERHAPS, PETER. BUT THERE IS A MIASMA OF EVIL ABOUT THE HOUSE...
THERE HAD BEEN A SERIES OF GRUESOME MURDERS NEARBY EARLIER THIS EVENING, THE LAST UNCOMFORT-ABLY CLOSE TO XAVIER'S SCHOOL.
...THAT INHIBITS MY TELEPATHIC ABILITIES. CHECK INSIDE. ORORO, STAY HERE TO PROTECT THE CAR.
THIS IS STRANGE.
IT IS SIGNIFICANTLY COLDER INSIDE THE HOUSE THAN OUTSIDE.
I SWEAR I'VE SENSED THIS PARTICULAR EVIL BEFORE, BUT FOR THE LIFE OF ME, I CAN'T REMEMBER WHEN. IT'S INFURIATING.
ALL SEEMS PEACEFUL, PROFESSOR.
WAIT! I HEAR THE TELEVISION. SOMEONE MUST BE IN THE LIVING ROOM.
KITTY!
Yawn!
Hmh...??? OH -- HI, PETER.
PETER!!
OH, WOW! OH, THANK HEAVENS! IT'S YOU!
WAIT'LL YOU HEAR WHAT HAPPENED TONIGHT! YOU HAVE NO IDEA HOW HAPPY I AM TO SEE YOU!
KITTY... PLEASE...
IF YOU'RE HAPPY TO SEE PETER, KITTEN, HOW D'YOU FEEL ABOUT US?
MOM!!
DAD!!
YOU GREW A BEARD!

SHORTLY...

I'M SO GLAD YOU BOTH COULD MAKE THE TRIP, CARMEN. YOUR PRESENCE HAS DONE WONDERS FOR KITTY'S MORALE.

CHARLES, TO BE HONEST, YOU COULDN'T HAVE KEPT US AWAY. I DIDN'T REALIZE I'D-- *WE'D*--MISS OUR KITTEN SO MUCH. OUR VISIT--YOUR SPECIAL CHANUKAH SURPRISE--IS AS MUCH A GIFT TO US AS TO HER.

KITTY, I'VE JUST BEEN UPSTAIRS TO MY ATTIC.

UH-OH.

WHAT PRECISELY *HAPPENED* WHILE WE WERE GONE?!

I WAS ATTACKED BY A BIG, UGLY MONSTER.

A -- MONSTER?!

ORORO, YOU HAD TO SEE IT TO BELIEVE IT. WE FOUGHT. I GOT LUCKY. I WON.

BUT, IN THE PROCESS, WE KIND'A WRECKED THE DANGER ROOM.

"WRECKED...THE *DANGER ROOM?!*"

AND THE BLACKBIRD. AND THE HANGAR. AND A LOT OF THE HOUSE.

OH. MY.

ARE YOU ANGRY?

I'M NOT QUITE SURE. BUT FROM THE SOUND OF THINGS, I'M FAIRLY CERTAIN I SHOULD FEEL TERRIBLY *PROUD* OF YOU.

GEE.

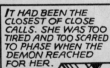

IT HAD BEEN THE CLOSEST OF CLOSE CALLS. SHE WAS TOO TIRED AND TOO SCARED TO PHASE WHEN THE DEMON REACHED FOR HER.

IT COULD HAVE KILLED HER, HAD IT GOT ITS HANDS ON HER.

BUT IT WAS DYING ON ITS FEET, ITS UNEARTHLY FORM CRUMBLING INTO DUST WITH EVERY STEP.

IT TRIED. IT MADE A SUPREME EFFORT. IT FAILED.

ALONE, ON CHRISTMAS EVE, KITTY PRYDE UNDERWENT A RITE OF PASSAGE--

-- A SUPREME TEST OF HER ABILITIES, HER INTELLECT, HER COURAGE, HER... SELF.

SHE PASSED.

NEXT: THE RETURN OF CYCLOPS!

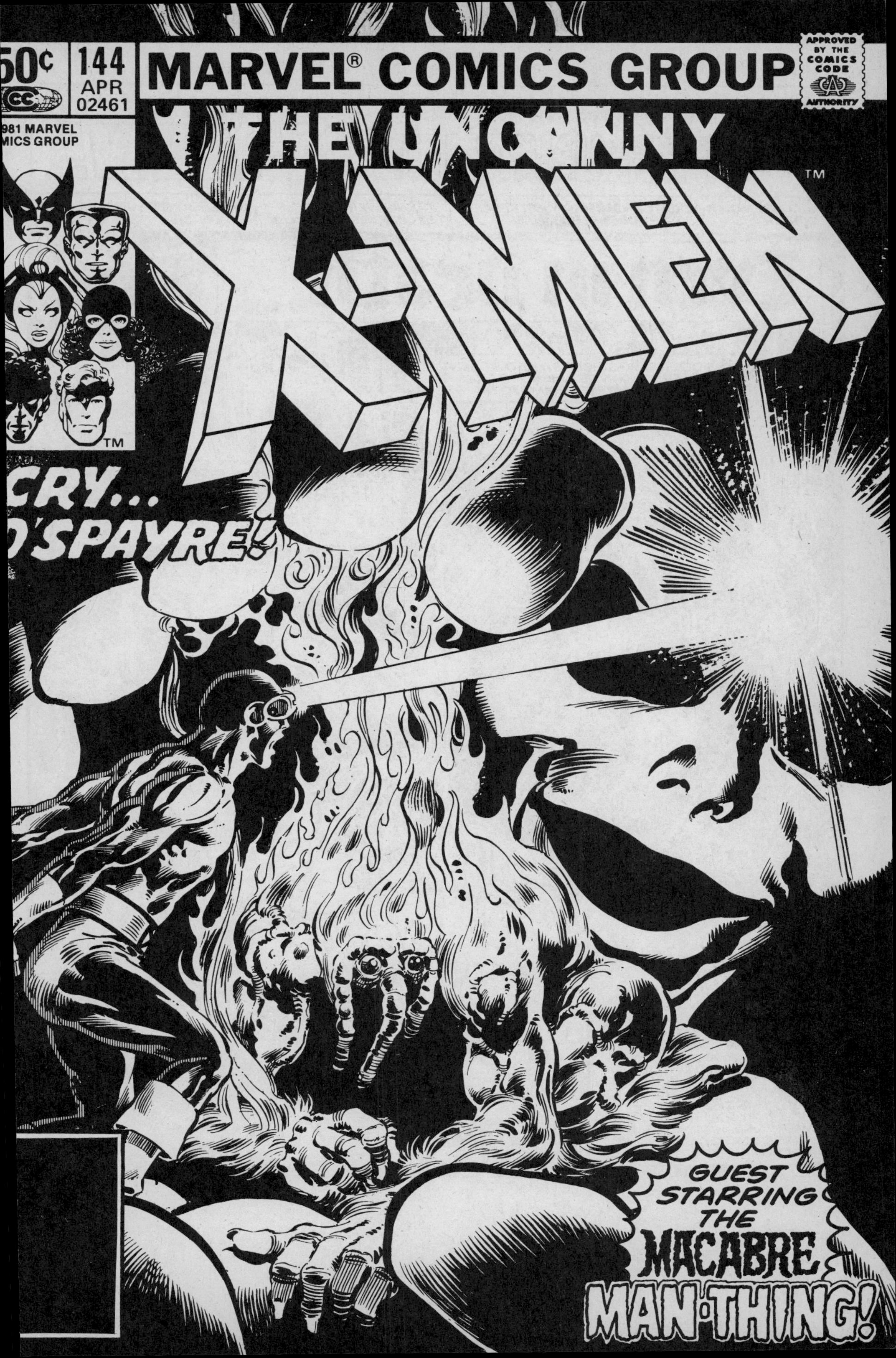

50¢
144
APR
02461
MARVEL® COMICS GROUP
APPROVED BY THE COMICS CODE AUTHORITY
981 MARVEL
MICS GROUP
THE UNCANNY
X-MEN™
CRY...
D'SPAYRE!
GUEST STARRING THE MACABRE MAN-THING!

Cyclops. Storm. Nightcrawler. Wolverine. Colossus. Children of the atom, students of Charles Xavier, MUTANTS — feared and hated by the world they have sworn to protect. These are the STRANGEST heroes of all!

STAN LEE PRESENTS: THE UNCANNY X-MEN!™

CHRIS CLAREMONT WRITER | BRENT ANDERSON, GUEST PENCILER JOSEF RUBENSTEIN, INKER | GLYNIS WEIN, colorist TOM ORZECHOWSKI, letterer | LOUISE JONES EDITOR | JIM SHOOTER Ed.-IN-CHIEF

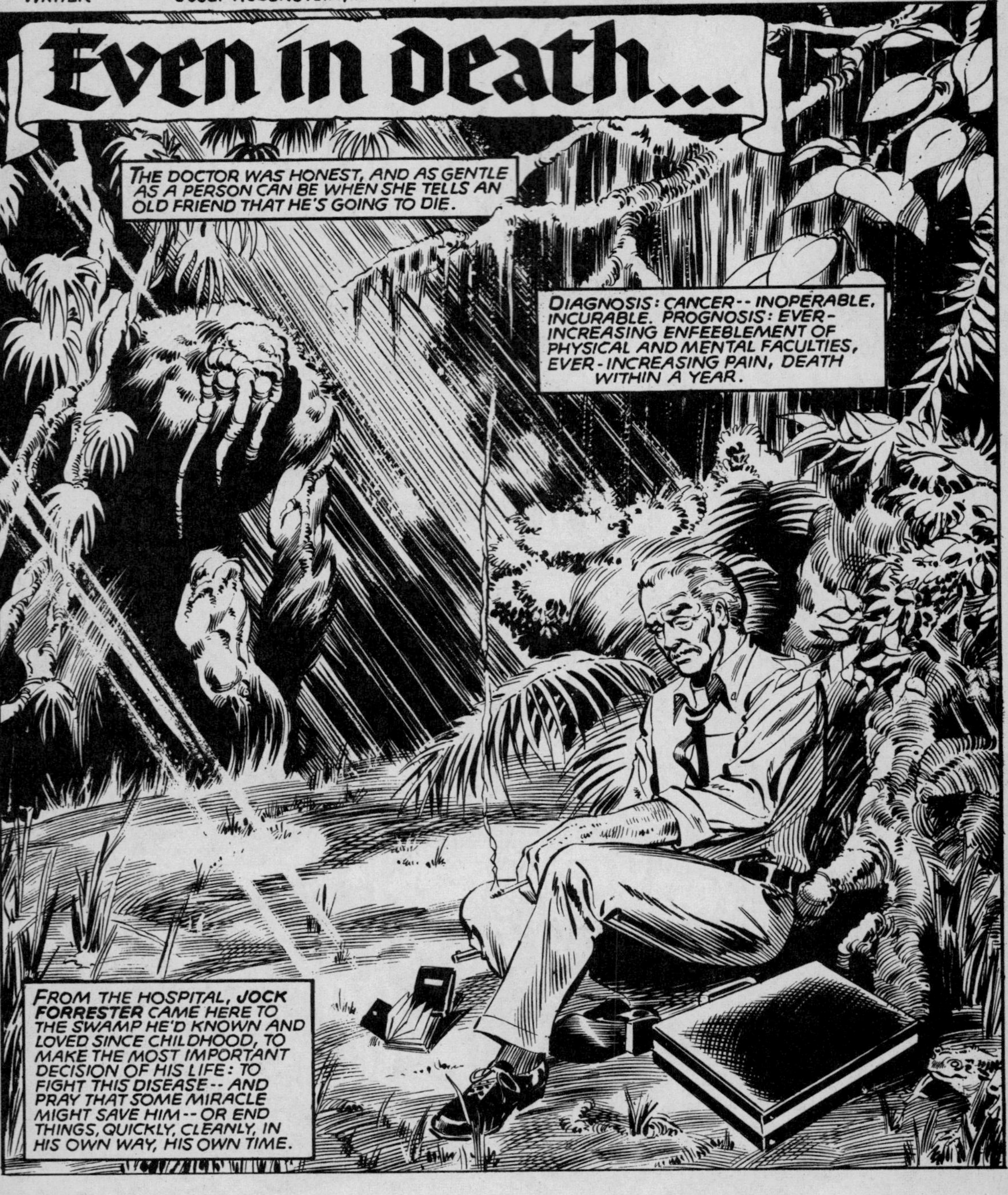

Even in death...
THE DOCTOR WAS HONEST, AND AS GENTLE AS A PERSON CAN BE WHEN SHE TELLS AN OLD FRIEND THAT HE'S GOING TO DIE.
DIAGNOSIS: CANCER -- INOPERABLE, INCURABLE. PROGNOSIS: EVER-INCREASING ENFEEBLEMENT OF PHYSICAL AND MENTAL FACULTIES, EVER-INCREASING PAIN, DEATH WITHIN A YEAR.
FROM THE HOSPITAL, JOCK FORRESTER CAME HERE TO THE SWAMP HE'D KNOWN AND LOVED SINCE CHILDHOOD, TO MAKE THE MOST IMPORTANT DECISION OF HIS LIFE: TO FIGHT THIS DISEASE -- AND PRAY THAT SOME MIRACLE MIGHT SAVE HIM -- OR END THINGS, QUICKLY, CLEANLY, IN HIS OWN WAY, HIS OWN TIME.

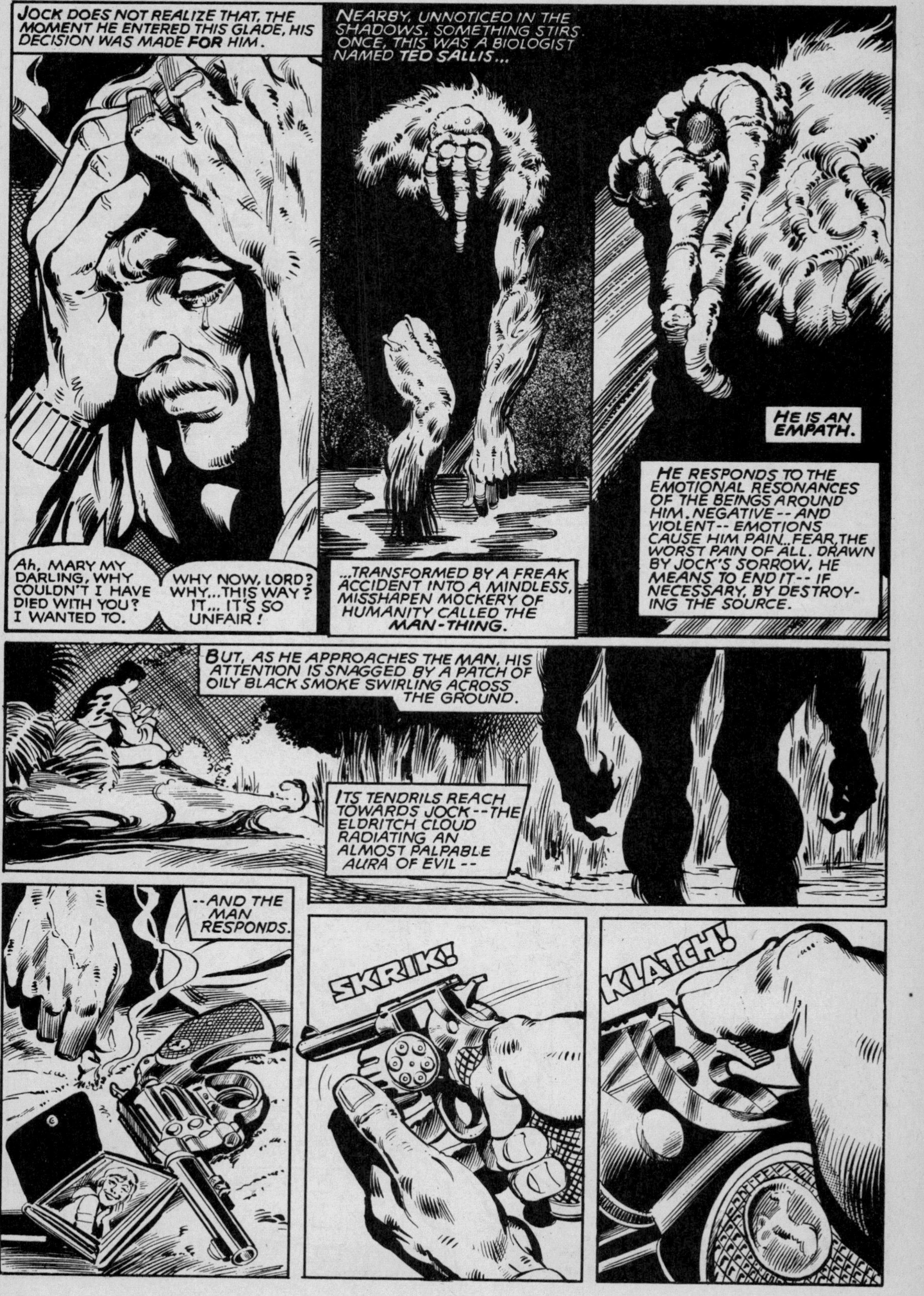
JOCK DOES NOT REALIZE THAT, THE MOMENT HE ENTERED THIS GLADE, HIS DECISION WAS MADE FOR HIM.
Ah, MARY MY DARLING, WHY COULDN'T I HAVE DIED WITH YOU? I WANTED TO.
WHY NOW, LORD? WHY... THIS WAY? IT... IT'S SO UNFAIR!
NEARBY, UNNOTICED IN THE SHADOWS, SOMETHING STIRS. ONCE, THIS WAS A BIOLOGIST NAMED TED SALLIS...
...TRANSFORMED BY A FREAK ACCIDENT INTO A MINDLESS, MISSHAPEN MOCKERY OF HUMANITY CALLED THE MAN-THING.
HE IS AN EMPATH.
HE RESPONDS TO THE EMOTIONAL RESONANCES OF THE BEINGS AROUND HIM. NEGATIVE -- AND VIOLENT -- EMOTIONS CAUSE HIM PAIN... FEAR, THE WORST PAIN OF ALL. DRAWN BY JOCK'S SORROW, HE MEANS TO END IT -- IF NECESSARY, BY DESTROYING THE SOURCE.
BUT, AS HE APPROACHES THE MAN, HIS ATTENTION IS SNAGGED BY A PATCH OF OILY BLACK SMOKE SWIRLING ACROSS THE GROUND.
ITS TENDRILS REACH TOWARDS JOCK -- THE ELDRITCH CLOUD RADIATING AN ALMOST PALPABLE AURA OF EVIL --
-- AND THE MAN RESPONDS.
SKRIK!
KLATCH!

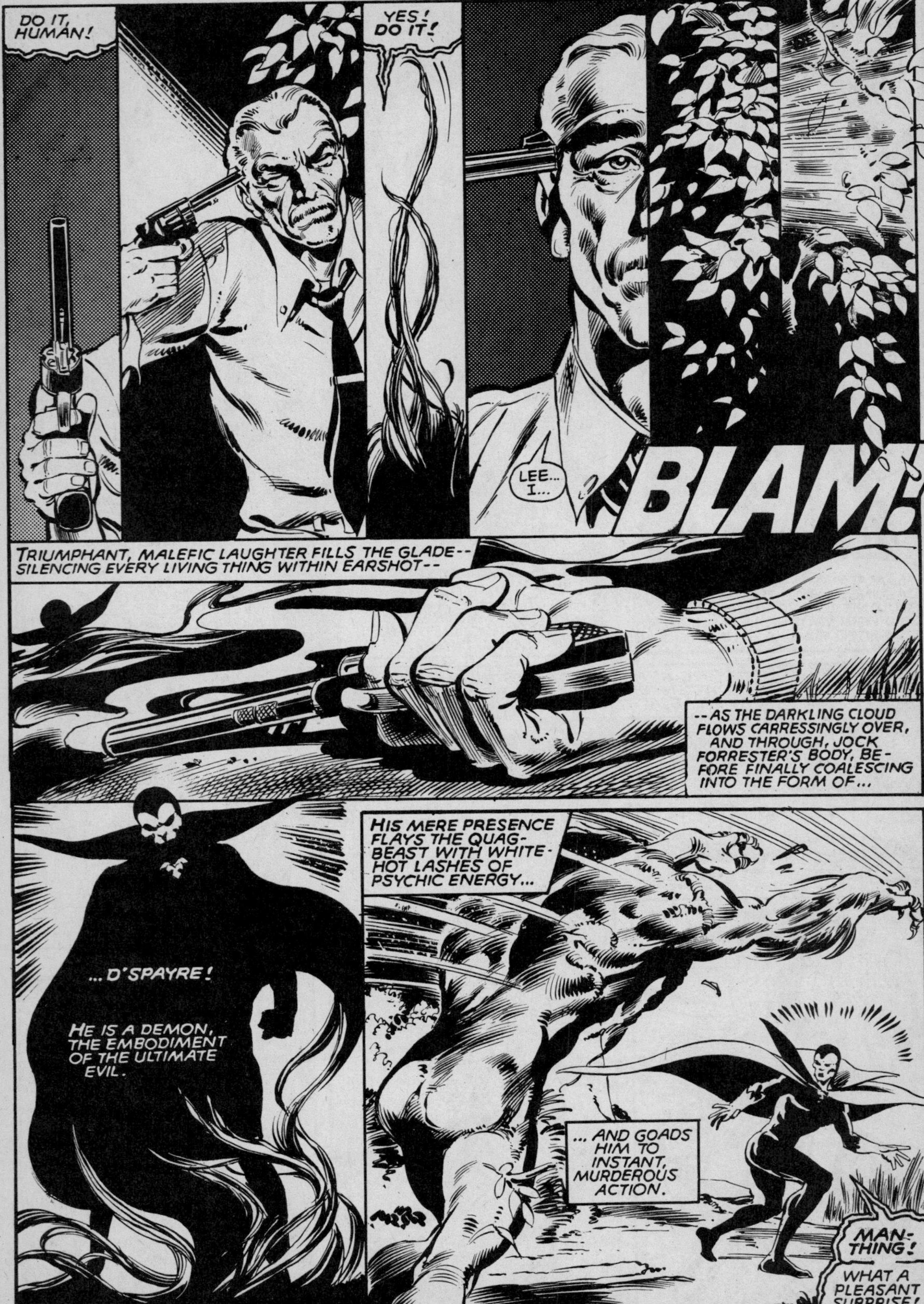
DO IT, HUMAN!
YES! DO IT!
LEE... I...
BLAM!
TRIUMPHANT, MALEFIC LAUGHTER FILLS THE GLADE-- SILENCING EVERY LIVING THING WITHIN EARSHOT--
--AS THE DARKLING CLOUD FLOWS CARRESSINGLY OVER, AND THROUGH, JOCK FORRESTER'S BODY, BEFORE FINALLY COALESCING INTO THE FORM OF...
...D'SPAYRE!
HE IS A DEMON, THE EMBODIMENT OF THE ULTIMATE EVIL.
HIS MERE PRESENCE FLAYS THE QUAG-BEAST WITH WHITE-HOT LASHES OF PSYCHIC ENERGY...
...AND GOADS HIM TO INSTANT, MURDEROUS ACTION.
MAN-THING!
WHAT A PLEASANT SURPRISE!

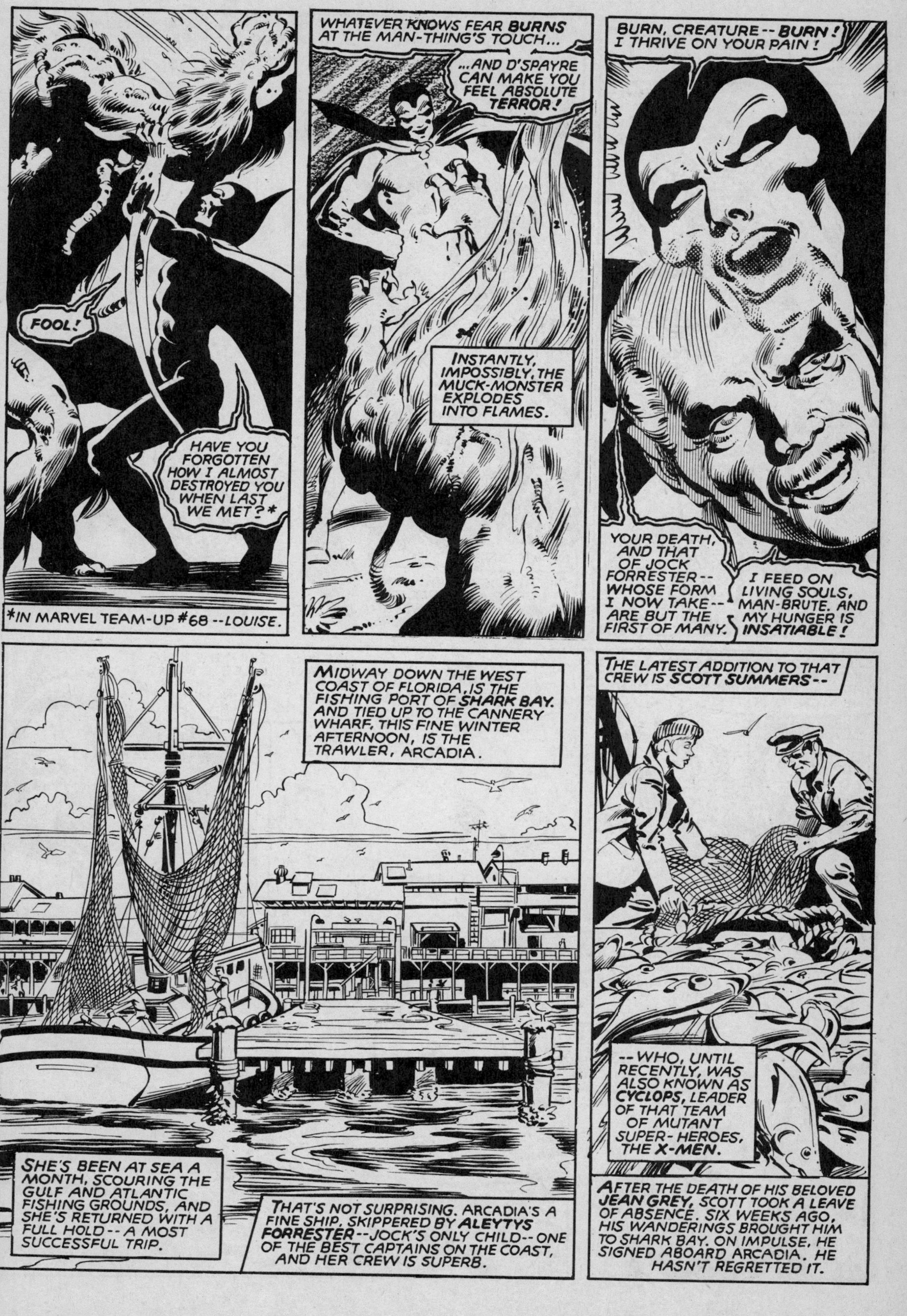
FOOL!
HAVE YOU FORGOTTEN HOW I ALMOST DESTROYED YOU WHEN LAST WE MET?*
*IN MARVEL TEAM-UP #68 --LOUISE.
WHATEVER KNOWS FEAR BURNS AT THE MAN-THING'S TOUCH...
...AND D'SPAYRE CAN MAKE YOU FEEL ABSOLUTE TERROR!
INSTANTLY, IMPOSSIBLY, THE MUCK-MONSTER EXPLODES INTO FLAMES.
BURN, CREATURE -- BURN! I THRIVE ON YOUR PAIN!
YOUR DEATH, AND THAT OF JOCK FORRESTER -- WHOSE FORM I NOW TAKE -- ARE BUT THE FIRST OF MANY.
I FEED ON LIVING SOULS, MAN-BRUTE, AND MY HUNGER IS INSATIABLE!
MIDWAY DOWN THE WEST COAST OF FLORIDA, IS THE FISHING PORT OF SHARK BAY. AND TIED UP TO THE CANNERY WHARF, THIS FINE WINTER AFTERNOON, IS THE TRAWLER, ARCADIA.
SHE'S BEEN AT SEA A MONTH, SCOURING THE GULF AND ATLANTIC FISHING GROUNDS, AND SHE'S RETURNED WITH A FULL HOLD -- A MOST SUCCESSFUL TRIP.
THAT'S NOT SURPRISING. ARCADIA'S A FINE SHIP, SKIPPERED BY ALEYTYS FORRESTER -- JOCK'S ONLY CHILD -- ONE OF THE BEST CAPTAINS ON THE COAST, AND HER CREW IS SUPERB.
THE LATEST ADDITION TO THAT CREW IS SCOTT SUMMERS --
-- WHO, UNTIL RECENTLY, WAS ALSO KNOWN AS CYCLOPS, LEADER OF THAT TEAM OF MUTANT SUPER-HEROES, THE X-MEN.
AFTER THE DEATH OF HIS BELOVED JEAN GREY, SCOTT TOOK A LEAVE OF ABSENCE. SIX WEEKS AGO, HIS WANDERINGS BROUGHT HIM TO SHARK BAY. ON IMPULSE, HE SIGNED ABOARD ARCADIA. HE HASN'T REGRETTED IT.

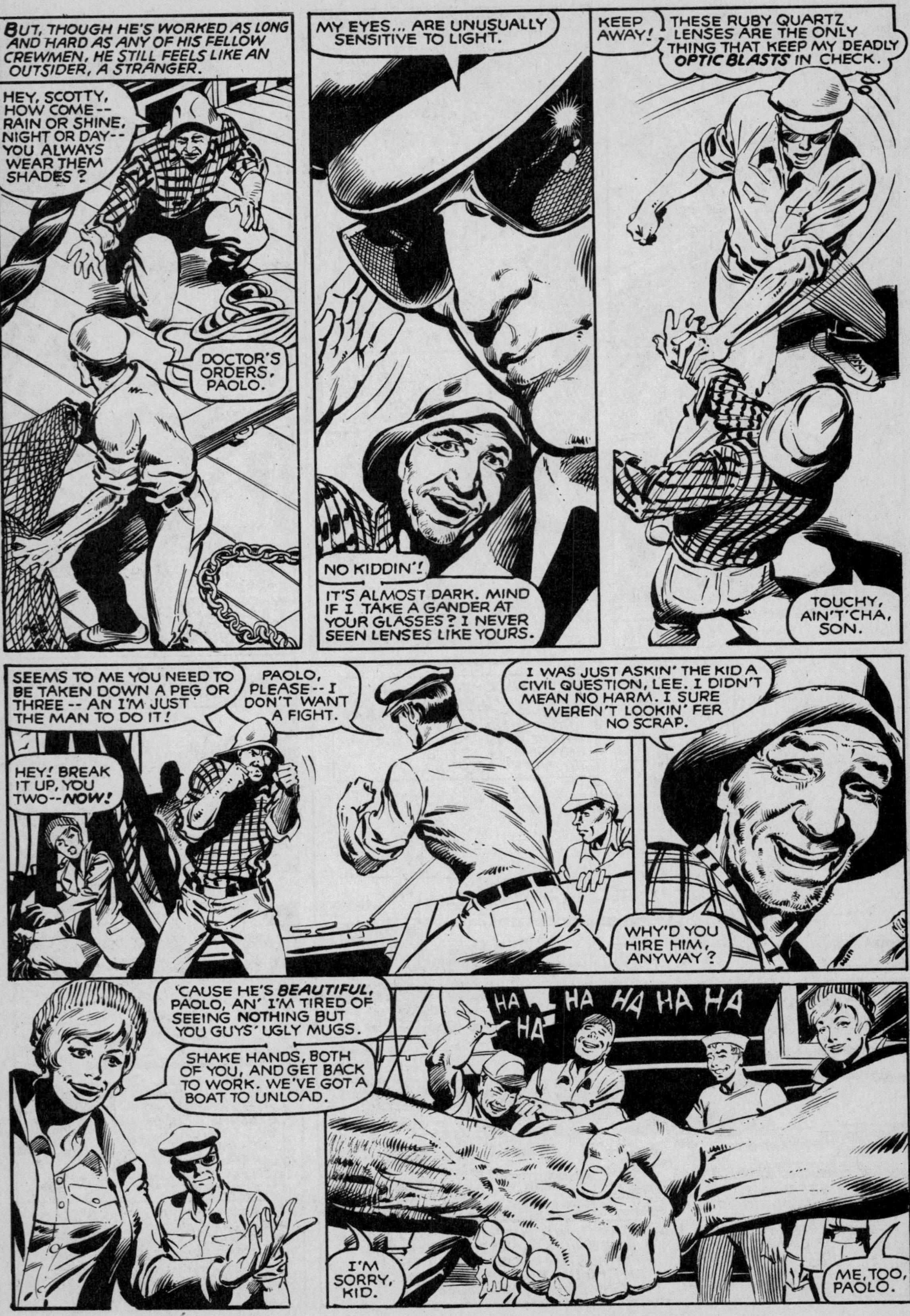
BUT, THOUGH HE'S WORKED AS LONG AND HARD AS ANY OF HIS FELLOW CREWMEN, HE STILL FEELS LIKE AN OUTSIDER, A STRANGER.
HEY, SCOTTY, HOW COME-- RAIN OR SHINE, NIGHT OR DAY-- YOU ALWAYS WEAR THEM SHADES?
DOCTOR'S ORDERS, PAOLO.
MY EYES... ARE UNUSUALLY SENSITIVE TO LIGHT.
NO KIDDIN'!
IT'S ALMOST DARK. MIND IF I TAKE A GANDER AT YOUR GLASSES? I NEVER SEEN LENSES LIKE YOURS.
KEEP AWAY!
THESE RUBY QUARTZ LENSES ARE THE ONLY THING THAT KEEP MY DEADLY OPTIC BLASTS IN CHECK.
TOUCHY, AIN'T'CHA, SON.
SEEMS TO ME YOU NEED TO BE TAKEN DOWN A PEG OR THREE -- AN I'M JUST THE MAN TO DO IT!
PAOLO, PLEASE -- I DON'T WANT A FIGHT.
HEY! BREAK IT UP, YOU TWO--NOW!
I WAS JUST ASKIN' THE KID A CIVIL QUESTION, LEE. I DIDN'T MEAN NO HARM. I SURE WEREN'T LOOKIN' FER NO SCRAP.
WHY'D YOU HIRE HIM, ANYWAY?
'CAUSE HE'S BEAUTIFUL, PAOLO, AN' I'M TIRED OF SEEING NOTHING BUT YOU GUYS' UGLY MUGS.
SHAKE HANDS, BOTH OF YOU, AND GET BACK TO WORK. WE'VE GOT A BOAT TO UNLOAD.
HA HA HA HA HA HA
HA
I'M SORRY, KID.
ME, TOO, PAOLO.

Panel (top left):

LATER... WE'RE HEADING FOR THE "SHANTY" FOR FOOD AND BEER. INTERESTED?

WELL...

CONSIDER IT AN ORDER, SCOTT, CAPTAIN TO CREW. IT'LL DO YOU SOME GOOD TO UNWIND.

Panel (top right):

AND SO, SCOTT MAKES HIS RELUCTANT WAY TO THE LOCAL TAVERN, WHERE HE AND HIS CREWMATES CONSUME ONE OF THE FINEST SEAFOOD DINNERS HE'S EVER TASTED.

LEE? YER DAD PHONED, SAID TO CALL HIM BACK, PRONTO.

THANKS, EARL.

I WASN'T KIDDING--SCOTT *IS* BEAUTIFUL. STRONG, GENTLE--YET HURTING DEEP INSIDE. I LIKE HIM A LOT--MAYBE TOO MUCH.

BUT THEN, I ALWAYS WAS A SUCKER FOR A BIRD WITH A BROKEN WING.

LETTERS FROM HOME. SUCH PROSAIC THINGS, YET SO IMPORTANT TO ME. THE X-MEN ARE MY FAMILY. NO MATTER WHERE I GO, WHAT I DO, I'LL NEVER BREAK THE TIES THAT BIND US.

THEY HAD AN EVENTFUL CHRISTMAS, I SEE. *KITTY PRYDE* --SPRITE-- SINGLE-HANDEDLY DEFEATED SOME SORT OF HORRIBLE MONSTER. AND IN THE PROCESS, DARN NEAR TOTALED THE MANSION.*

OUCH!

*FOR DETAILS, SEE LAST ISH --LOUISE.

Panel (bottom left):

ON THAT NOTE, LET'S SEGUE UP THE COAST TO *PROFESSOR CHARLES XAVIER'S* SCHOOL FOR GIFTED YOUNGSTERS, JUST OUTSIDE NEW YORK CITY...

...WHERE THE X-MEN...

Panel (bottom right):

... ARE DOING THEIR BEST TO REPAIR THE DAMAGE DONE BY SPRITE'S EPIC BATTLE. *STORM* -- CYCLOPS' REPLACEMENT AS TEAM LEADER-- USES HER ELEMENTAL WEATHER POWERS TO MANIFEST A WIND THAT SWEEPS A LOAD OF DEBRIS INTO A DUMPSTER...

...WHILE *WOLVERINE* USES HIS RETRACTABLE ADAMANTIUM CLAWS...

....TO CUT A RUINED PIECE OF EQUIPMENT DOWN TO SIZE.

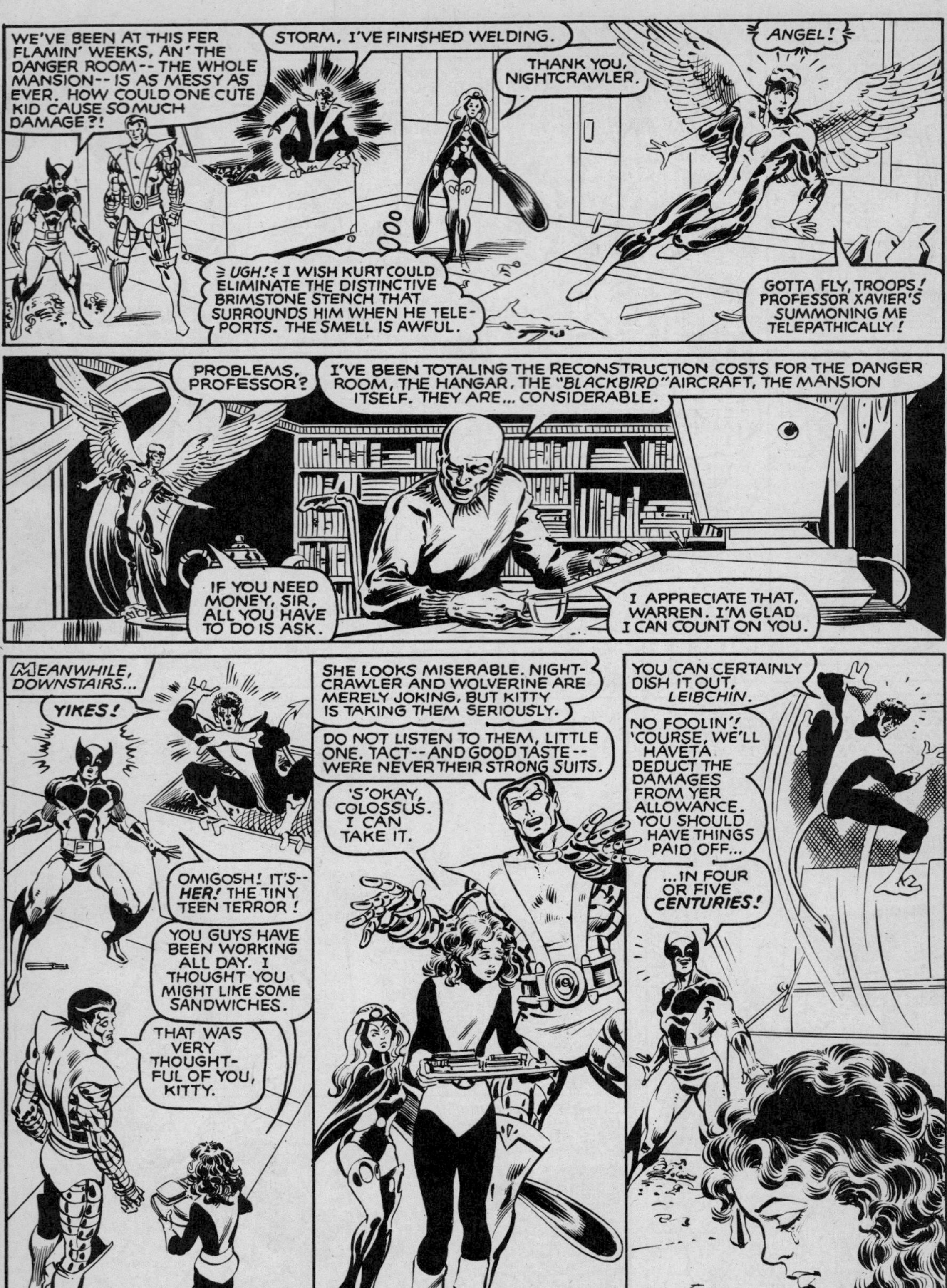

WE'VE BEEN AT THIS FER FLAMIN' WEEKS, AN' THE DANGER ROOM -- THE WHOLE MANSION -- IS AS MESSY AS EVER. HOW COULD ONE CUTE KID CAUSE SO MUCH DAMAGE?!
STORM, I'VE FINISHED WELDING.
THANK YOU, NIGHTCRAWLER.
ANGEL!
UGH! I WISH KURT COULD ELIMINATE THE DISTINCTIVE BRIMSTONE STENCH THAT SURROUNDS HIM WHEN HE TELEPORTS. THE SMELL IS AWFUL.
GOTTA FLY, TROOPS! PROFESSOR XAVIER'S SUMMONING ME TELEPATHICALLY!
PROBLEMS, PROFESSOR?
I'VE BEEN TOTALING THE RECONSTRUCTION COSTS FOR THE DANGER ROOM, THE HANGAR, THE "BLACKBIRD" AIRCRAFT, THE MANSION ITSELF. THEY ARE... CONSIDERABLE.
IF YOU NEED MONEY, SIR, ALL YOU HAVE TO DO IS ASK.
I APPRECIATE THAT, WARREN. I'M GLAD I CAN COUNT ON YOU.
MEANWHILE, DOWNSTAIRS...
YIKES!
OMIGOSH! IT'S-- HER! THE TINY TEEN TERROR!
YOU GUYS HAVE BEEN WORKING ALL DAY. I THOUGHT YOU MIGHT LIKE SOME SANDWICHES.
THAT WAS VERY THOUGHTFUL OF YOU, KITTY.
SHE LOOKS MISERABLE. NIGHTCRAWLER AND WOLVERINE ARE MERELY JOKING, BUT KITTY IS TAKING THEM SERIOUSLY.
DO NOT LISTEN TO THEM, LITTLE ONE. TACT--AND GOOD TASTE--WERE NEVER THEIR STRONG SUITS.
'S'OKAY, COLOSSUS. I CAN TAKE IT.
YOU CAN CERTAINLY DISH IT OUT, LEIBCHIN.
NO FOOLIN'! 'COURSE, WE'LL HAVETA DEDUCT THE DAMAGES FROM YER ALLOWANCE. YOU SHOULD HAVE THINGS PAID OFF...
...IN FOUR OR FIVE CENTURIES!

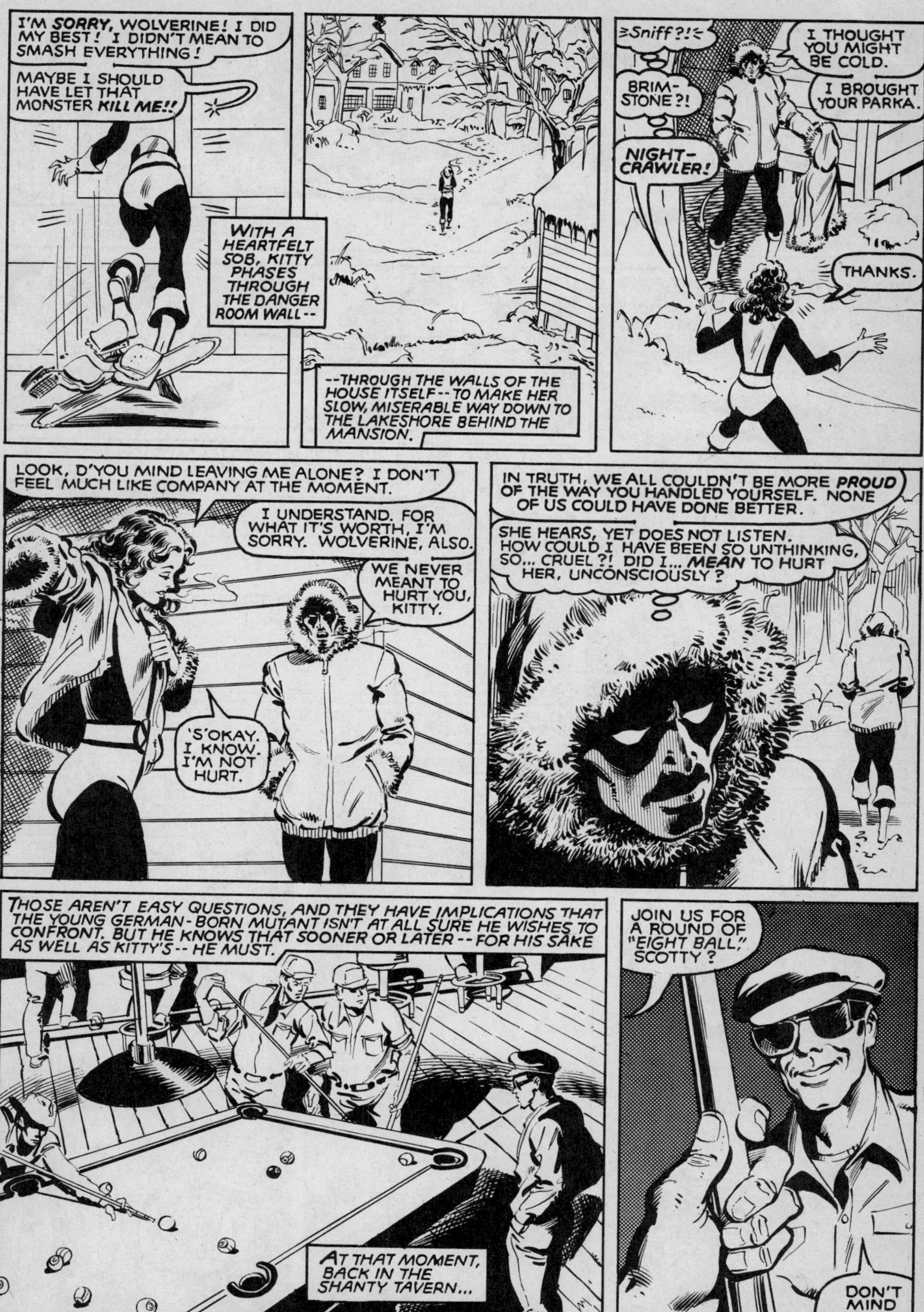
I'M SORRY, WOLVERINE! I DID MY BEST! I DIDN'T MEAN TO SMASH EVERYTHING!
MAYBE I SHOULD HAVE LET THAT MONSTER KILL ME!!
WITH A HEARTFELT SOB, KITTY PHASES THROUGH THE DANGER ROOM WALL--
--THROUGH THE WALLS OF THE HOUSE ITSELF--TO MAKE HER SLOW, MISERABLE WAY DOWN TO THE LAKESHORE BEHIND THE MANSION.
=Sniff?!=
BRIM-STONE?!
NIGHT-CRAWLER!
I THOUGHT YOU MIGHT BE COLD.
I BROUGHT YOUR PARKA.
THANKS.
LOOK, D'YOU MIND LEAVING ME ALONE? I DON'T FEEL MUCH LIKE COMPANY AT THE MOMENT.
I UNDERSTAND. FOR WHAT IT'S WORTH, I'M SORRY. WOLVERINE, ALSO.
WE NEVER MEANT TO HURT YOU, KITTY.
'S'OKAY. I KNOW. I'M NOT HURT.
IN TRUTH, WE ALL COULDN'T BE MORE PROUD OF THE WAY YOU HANDLED YOURSELF. NONE OF US COULD HAVE DONE BETTER.
SHE HEARS, YET DOES NOT LISTEN. HOW COULD I HAVE BEEN SO UNTHINKING, SO... CRUEL?! DID I... MEAN TO HURT HER, UNCONSCIOUSLY?
THOSE AREN'T EASY QUESTIONS, AND THEY HAVE IMPLICATIONS THAT THE YOUNG GERMAN-BORN MUTANT ISN'T AT ALL SURE HE WISHES TO CONFRONT. BUT HE KNOWS THAT SOONER OR LATER--FOR HIS SAKE AS WELL AS KITTY'S--HE MUST.
AT THAT MOMENT, BACK IN THE SHANTY TAVERN...
JOIN US FOR A ROUND OF "EIGHT BALL," SCOTTY?
DON'T MIND IF I DO, FRANK.

BUT, AS SCOTT SETS HIMSELF FOR SOME PRACTICE SHOTS...

WAY TO GO!

TAMPA BAY JUS' TIED THE STEELERS!

ALL EYES IMMEDIATELY GO TO THE BAR TV.

Hmmm -- SINCE NO ONE'S LOOKING MY WAY, I THINK I'LL USE THIS OPPORTUNITY TO GIVE MY *OPTIC BLASTS* A QUICK WORKOUT.

I HAVE TO BE CAREFUL ABOUT REMOVING MY GLASSES. IF I OPEN MY EYES EVEN THE MINUTEST FRACTION, THE BEAMS WILL FIRE -- WITH DEVASTATING EFFECT.

GENTLY.

TOO MUCH POWER WILL SMASH THE TABLE.

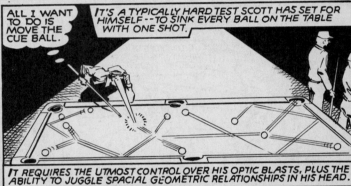

ALL I WANT TO DO IS MOVE THE CUE BALL.

IT'S A TYPICALLY HARD TEST SCOTT HAS SET FOR HIMSELF -- TO SINK EVERY BALL ON THE TABLE WITH ONE SHOT.

IT REQUIRES THE UTMOST CONTROL OVER HIS OPTIC BLASTS, PLUS THE ABILITY TO JUGGLE SPATIAL GEOMETRIC RELATIONSHIPS IN HIS HEAD.

CYCLOPS DOES BOTH SUPREMELY WELL.

Huh --?!?

8

PLOP

I'M WARMED UP, GUYS. SHALL WE BEGIN?

SCOTT, I HATE TO INTERRUPT, BUT MY DAD WANTS ME TO COME OVER TO HIS PLACE IN CITRUSVILLE. I THINK SOMETHING'S WRONG.

IT'LL BE AN OVERNIGHT TRIP. MIND KEEPING ME COMPANY?

UH, NO, LEE. OF COURSE NOT.

I'M OBLIGED. LET'S GET GOING.

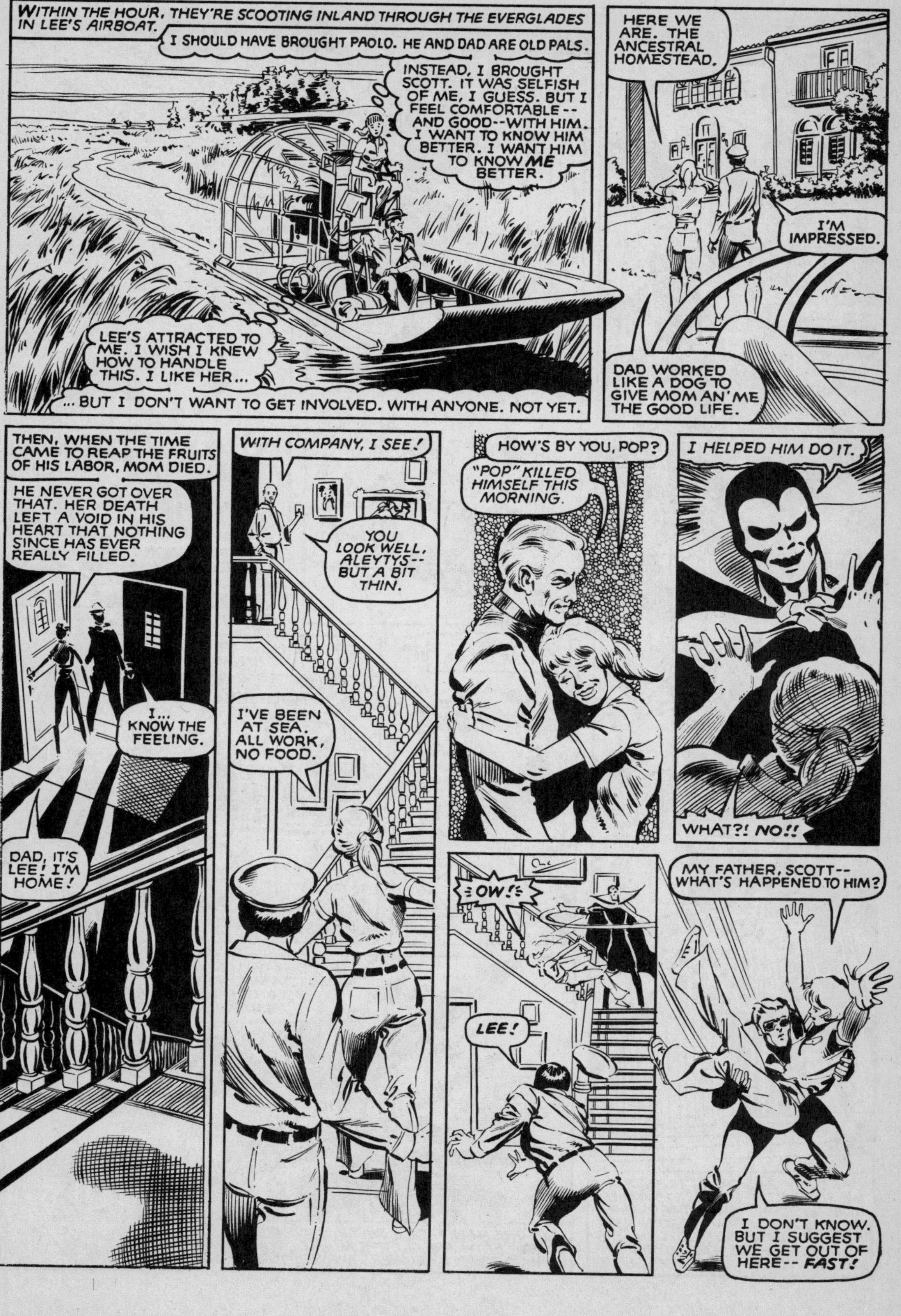
WITHIN THE HOUR, THEY'RE SCOOTING INLAND THROUGH THE EVERGLADES IN LEE'S AIRBOAT.
I SHOULD HAVE BROUGHT PAOLO. HE AND DAD ARE OLD PALS.
INSTEAD, I BROUGHT SCOTT. IT WAS SELFISH OF ME, I GUESS. BUT I FEEL COMFORTABLE -- AND GOOD--WITH HIM. I WANT TO KNOW HIM BETTER. I WANT HIM TO KNOW ME BETTER.
LEE'S ATTRACTED TO ME. I WISH I KNEW HOW TO HANDLE THIS. I LIKE HER...
... BUT I DON'T WANT TO GET INVOLVED. WITH ANYONE. NOT YET.
HERE WE ARE. THE ANCESTRAL HOMESTEAD.
I'M IMPRESSED.
DAD WORKED LIKE A DOG TO GIVE MOM AN' ME THE GOOD LIFE.
THEN, WHEN THE TIME CAME TO REAP THE FRUITS OF HIS LABOR, MOM DIED.
HE NEVER GOT OVER THAT. HER DEATH LEFT A VOID IN HIS HEART THAT NOTHING SINCE HAS EVER REALLY FILLED.
I... KNOW THE FEELING.
DAD, IT'S LEE! I'M HOME!
WITH COMPANY, I SEE!
YOU LOOK WELL, ALEYTYS-- BUT A BIT THIN.
I'VE BEEN AT SEA. ALL WORK, NO FOOD.
HOW'S BY YOU, POP?
"POP" KILLED HIMSELF THIS MORNING.
I HELPED HIM DO IT.
WHAT?! NO!!
OW!
LEE!
MY FATHER, SCOTT-- WHAT'S HAPPENED TO HIM?
I DON'T KNOW. BUT I SUGGEST WE GET OUT OF HERE-- FAST!

YOU ARE IN MY DOMAIN, HUMANS! YOU WILL LEAVE WHEN I AM DONE WITH YOU, NOT BEFORE!

AROUND THEM, REALITY WARPS INSIDE-OUT...

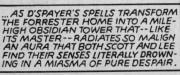

...AS D'SPAYRE'S SPELLS TRANSFORM THE FORRESTER HOME INTO A MILE-HIGH OBSIDIAN TOWER THAT--LIKE ITS MASTER--RADIATES SO MALIGN AN AURA THAT BOTH SCOTT AND LEE FIND THEIR SENSES LITERALLY DROWNING IN A MIASMA OF PURE DESPAIR.

NOW, CHILDREN, THE FUN BEGINS.

WHO-- WHAT-- ARE YOU?!

WHAT DO YOU WANT WITH US?!!

WHEN HIS SENSES CLEAR...

...HE DOES NOT BELIEVE WHERE HE IS...

I AM D'SPAYRE!

AND I WANT ALL YOU ARE CAPABLE OF GIVING!

HE LAUGHS.

AND SCOTT FINDS HIMSELF...

...STRUCK BLIND, DEAF, AND DUMB.

...OR WHO HE IS, OR WHAT IS HAPPENING TO HIM. YET, HE KNOWS THIS IS TRUTH.

ANN, GET THE KIDS INTO THEIR 'CHUTES!

THIS DEHAVILLAND MOSQUITO--LOVINGLY, PAINSTAKINGLY REMODELED AND MAINTAINED BY SCOTT'S FATHER, MAJOR CHRISTOPHER SUMMERS, USAF-- IS A SUPERB AIR-CRAFT...

...IN THE HANDS OF A SUPERLATIVE PILOT. BUT TODAY, BOTH ARE QUITE SIMPLY OUT-MATCHED AND STRUCK DOWN BY POWERS FAR BEYOND HUMAN KEN.

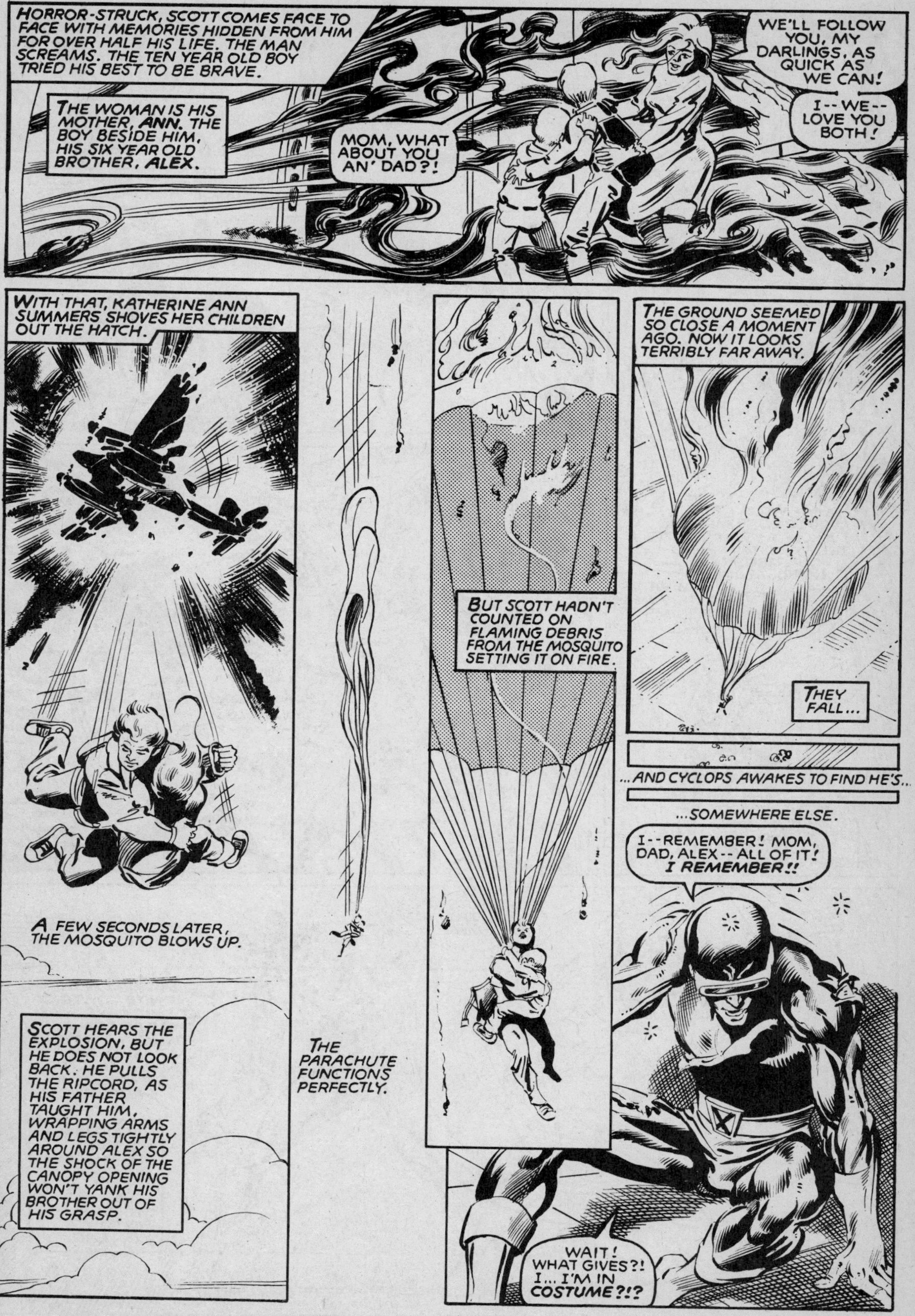
HORROR-STRUCK, SCOTT COMES FACE TO FACE WITH MEMORIES HIDDEN FROM HIM FOR OVER HALF HIS LIFE. THE MAN SCREAMS. THE TEN YEAR OLD BOY TRIED HIS BEST TO BE BRAVE.
THE WOMAN IS HIS MOTHER, ANN. THE BOY BESIDE HIM, HIS SIX YEAR OLD BROTHER, ALEX.
MOM, WHAT ABOUT YOU AN' DAD?!
WE'LL FOLLOW YOU, MY DARLINGS, AS QUICK AS WE CAN!
I--WE--LOVE YOU BOTH!
WITH THAT, KATHERINE ANN SUMMERS SHOVES HER CHILDREN OUT THE HATCH.
A FEW SECONDS LATER, THE MOSQUITO BLOWS UP.
SCOTT HEARS THE EXPLOSION, BUT HE DOES NOT LOOK BACK. HE PULLS THE RIPCORD, AS HIS FATHER TAUGHT HIM, WRAPPING ARMS AND LEGS TIGHTLY AROUND ALEX SO THE SHOCK OF THE CANOPY OPENING WON'T YANK HIS BROTHER OUT OF HIS GRASP.
THE PARACHUTE FUNCTIONS PERFECTLY.
BUT SCOTT HADN'T COUNTED ON FLAMING DEBRIS FROM THE MOSQUITO SETTING IT ON FIRE.
THE GROUND SEEMED SO CLOSE A MOMENT AGO. NOW IT LOOKS TERRIBLY FAR AWAY.
THEY FALL...
...AND CYCLOPS AWAKES TO FIND HE'S...
...SOMEWHERE ELSE.
I--REMEMBER! MOM, DAD, ALEX--ALL OF IT! I REMEMBER!!
WAIT! WHAT GIVES?! I... I'M IN COSTUME?!?

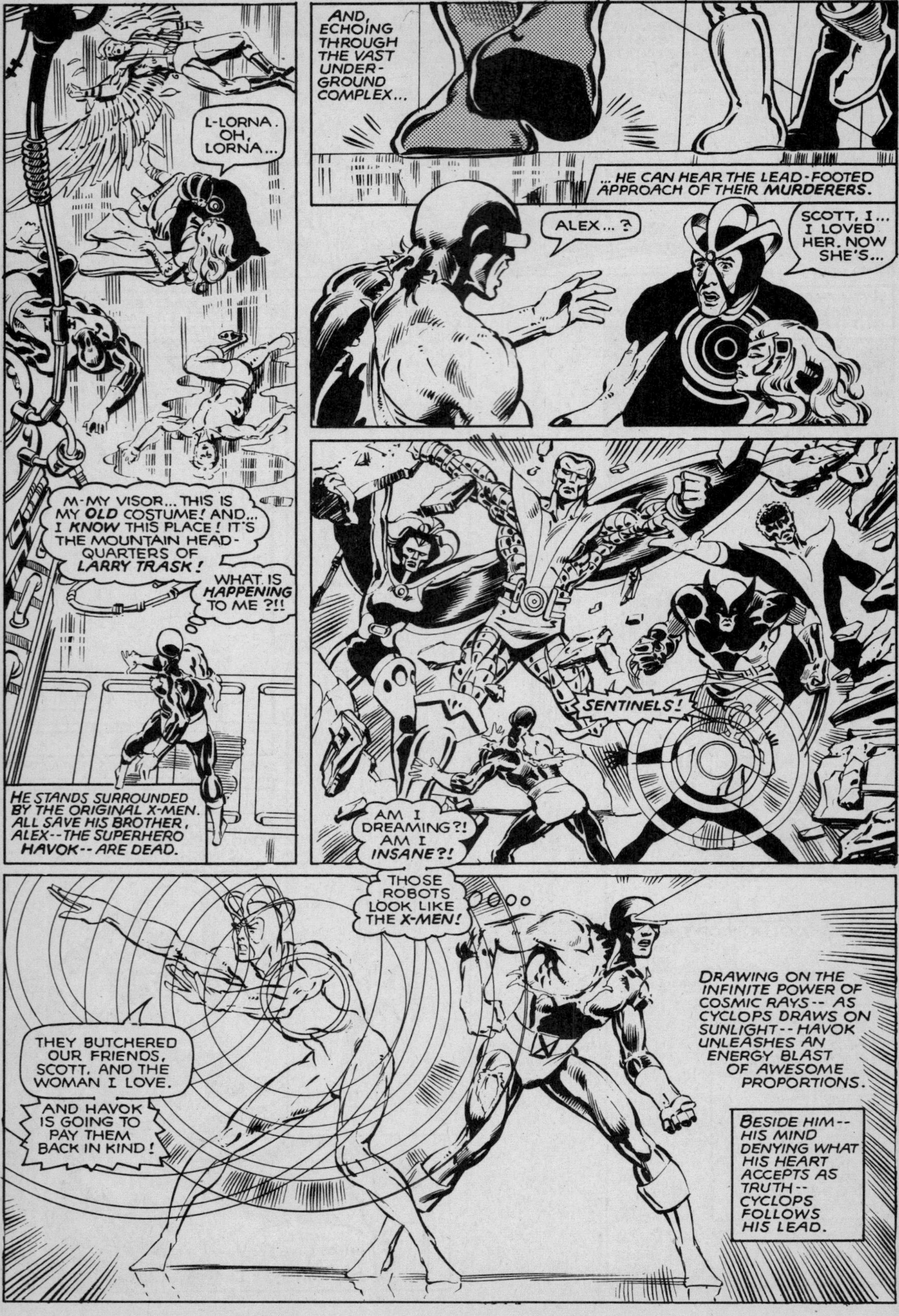

L-LORNA. OH, LORNA...
M-MY VISOR... THIS IS MY OLD COSTUME! AND... I KNOW THIS PLACE! IT'S THE MOUNTAIN HEAD-QUARTERS OF LARRY TRASK!
WHAT IS HAPPENING TO ME ?!!
HE STANDS SURROUNDED BY THE ORIGINAL X-MEN. ALL SAVE HIS BROTHER, ALEX--THE SUPERHERO HAVOK--ARE DEAD.
AND, ECHOING THROUGH THE VAST UNDER-GROUND COMPLEX...
...HE CAN HEAR THE LEAD-FOOTED APPROACH OF THEIR MURDERERS.
ALEX...?
SCOTT, I... I LOVED HER. NOW SHE'S...
SENTINELS!
AM I DREAMING?! AM I INSANE?!
THOSE ROBOTS LOOK LIKE THE X-MEN!
THEY BUTCHERED OUR FRIENDS, SCOTT, AND THE WOMAN I LOVE.
AND HAVOK IS GOING TO PAY THEM BACK IN KIND!
DRAWING ON THE INFINITE POWER OF COSMIC RAYS-- AS CYCLOPS DRAWS ON SUNLIGHT--HAVOK UNLEASHES AN ENERGY BLAST OF AWESOME PROPORTIONS.
BESIDE HIM-- HIS MIND DENYING WHAT HIS HEART ACCEPTS AS TRUTH-- CYCLOPS FOLLOWS HIS LEAD.

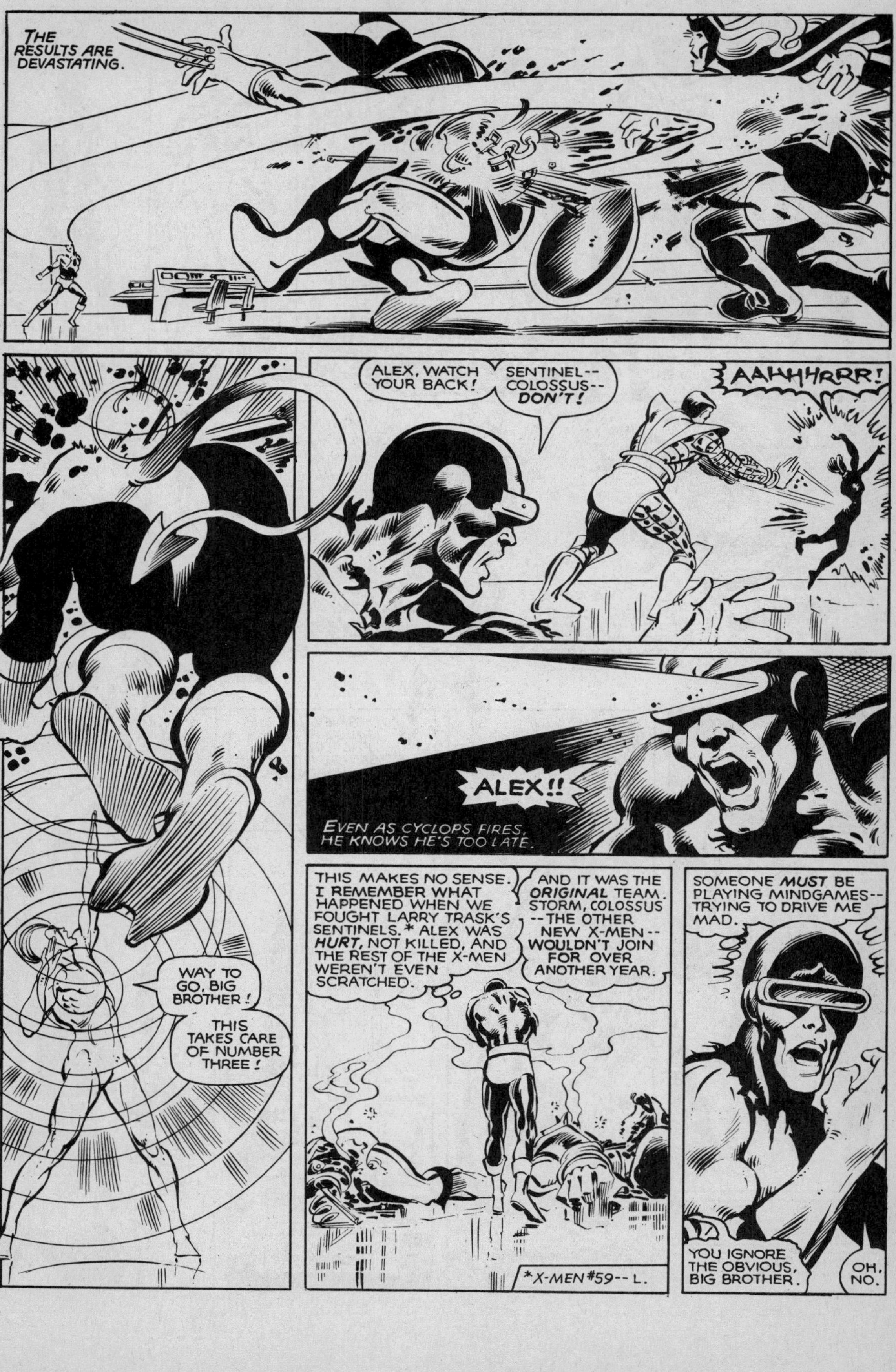
THE RESULTS ARE DEVASTATING.
ALEX, WATCH YOUR BACK!
SENTINEL-- COLOSSUS-- DON'T!
AAHHHRRR!
WAY TO GO, BIG BROTHER!
THIS TAKES CARE OF NUMBER THREE!
ALEX!!
EVEN AS CYCLOPS FIRES, HE KNOWS HE'S TOO LATE.
THIS MAKES NO SENSE. I REMEMBER WHAT HAPPENED WHEN WE FOUGHT LARRY TRASK'S SENTINELS.* ALEX WAS HURT, NOT KILLED, AND THE REST OF THE X-MEN WEREN'T EVEN SCRATCHED.
AND IT WAS THE ORIGINAL TEAM. STORM, COLOSSUS --THE OTHER NEW X-MEN-- WOULDN'T JOIN FOR OVER ANOTHER YEAR.
*X-MEN #59-- L.
SOMEONE MUST BE PLAYING MINDGAMES-- TRYING TO DRIVE ME MAD.
YOU IGNORE THE OBVIOUS, BIG BROTHER.
OH, NO.

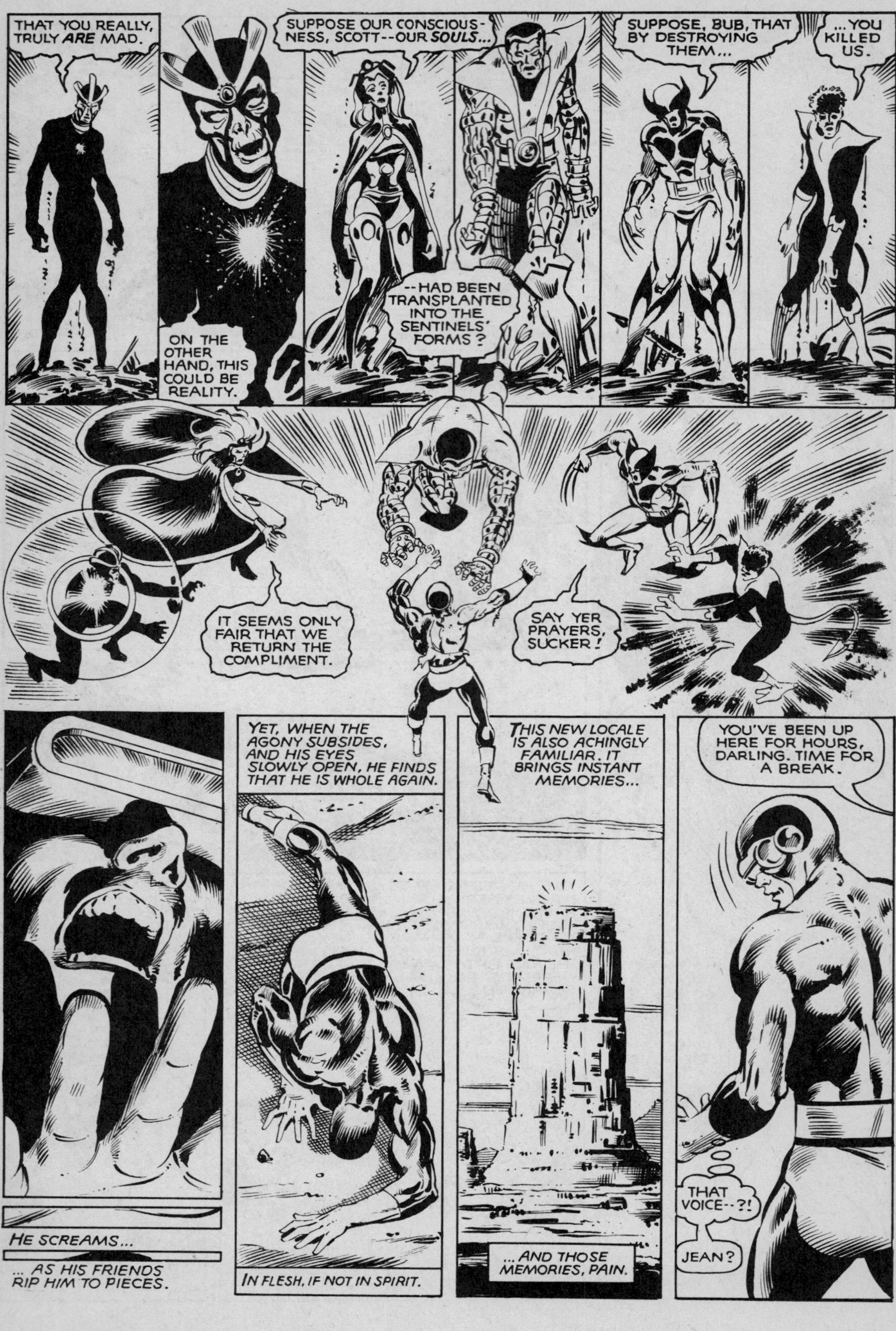
THAT YOU REALLY, TRULY *ARE* MAD.
ON THE OTHER HAND, THIS COULD BE REALITY.
SUPPOSE OUR CONSCIOUSNESS, SCOTT--OUR *SOULS*...
--HAD BEEN TRANSPLANTED INTO THE SENTINELS' FORMS?
SUPPOSE, BUB, THAT BY DESTROYING THEM...
...YOU KILLED US.
IT SEEMS ONLY FAIR THAT WE RETURN THE COMPLIMENT.
SAY YER PRAYERS, SUCKER!
HE SCREAMS...
...AS HIS FRIENDS RIP HIM TO PIECES.
YET, WHEN THE AGONY SUBSIDES, AND HIS EYES SLOWLY OPEN, HE FINDS THAT HE IS WHOLE AGAIN.
IN FLESH, IF NOT IN SPIRIT.
THIS NEW LOCALE IS ALSO ACHINGLY FAMILIAR. IT BRINGS INSTANT MEMORIES...
...AND THOSE MEMORIES, PAIN.
YOU'VE BEEN UP HERE FOR HOURS, DARLING. TIME FOR A BREAK.
THAT VOICE--?!
JEAN?

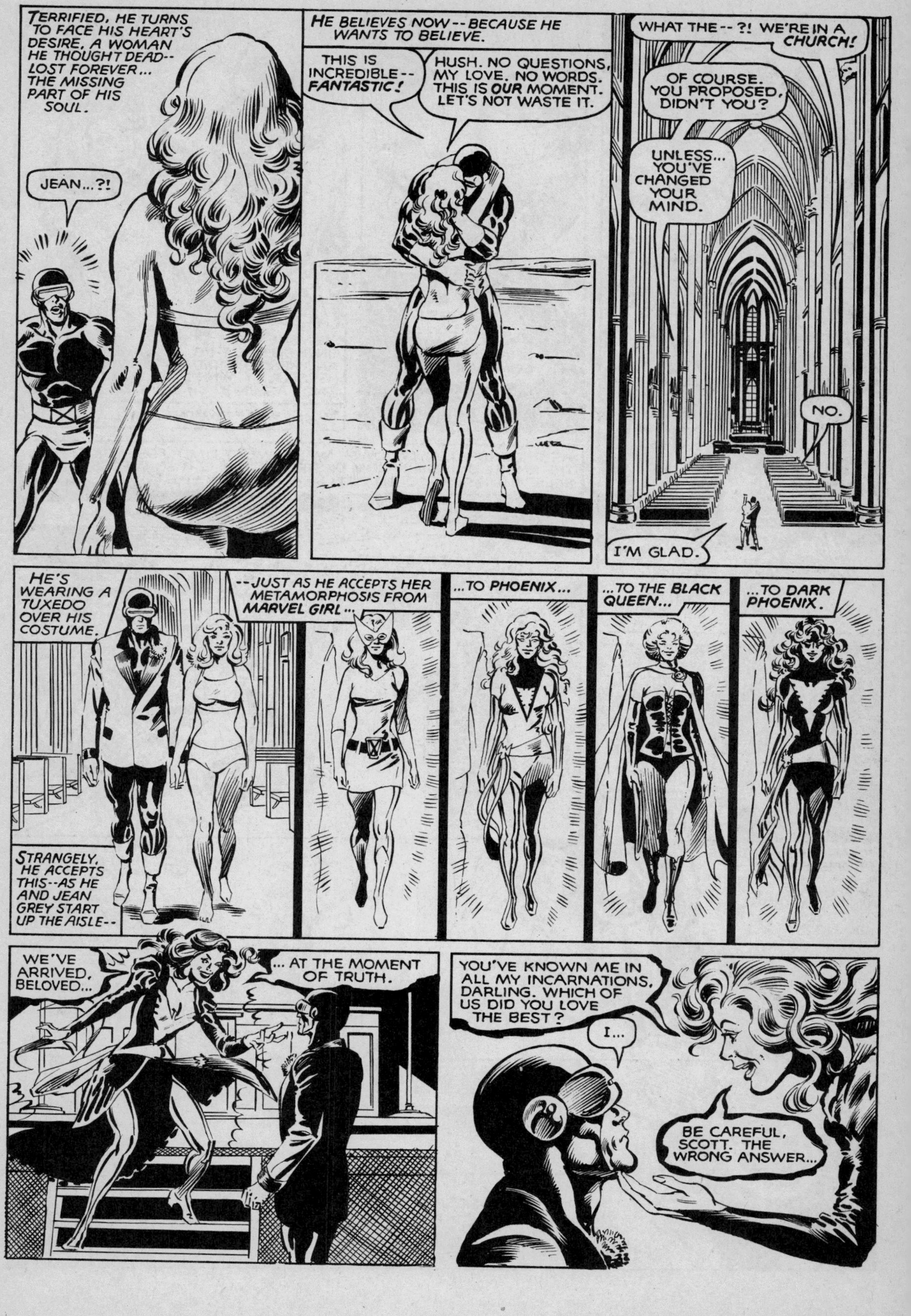
TERRIFIED, HE TURNS TO FACE HIS HEART'S DESIRE, A WOMAN HE THOUGHT DEAD-- LOST FOREVER... THE MISSING PART OF HIS SOUL.
JEAN...?!
HE BELIEVES NOW -- BECAUSE HE WANTS TO BELIEVE.
THIS IS INCREDIBLE -- FANTASTIC!
HUSH. NO QUESTIONS, MY LOVE. NO WORDS. THIS IS OUR MOMENT. LET'S NOT WASTE IT.
WHAT THE -- ?! WE'RE IN A CHURCH!
OF COURSE. YOU PROPOSED, DIDN'T YOU?
UNLESS... YOU'VE CHANGED YOUR MIND.
NO.
I'M GLAD.
HE'S WEARING A TUXEDO OVER HIS COSTUME.
STRANGELY, HE ACCEPTS THIS--AS HE AND JEAN GREY START UP THE AISLE--
--JUST AS HE ACCEPTS HER METAMORPHOSIS FROM MARVEL GIRL...
...TO PHOENIX...
...TO THE BLACK QUEEN...
...TO DARK PHOENIX.
WE'VE ARRIVED, BELOVED...
... AT THE MOMENT OF TRUTH.
YOU'VE KNOWN ME IN ALL MY INCARNATIONS, DARLING. WHICH OF US DID YOU LOVE THE BEST?
I...
BE CAREFUL, SCOTT. THE WRONG ANSWER...

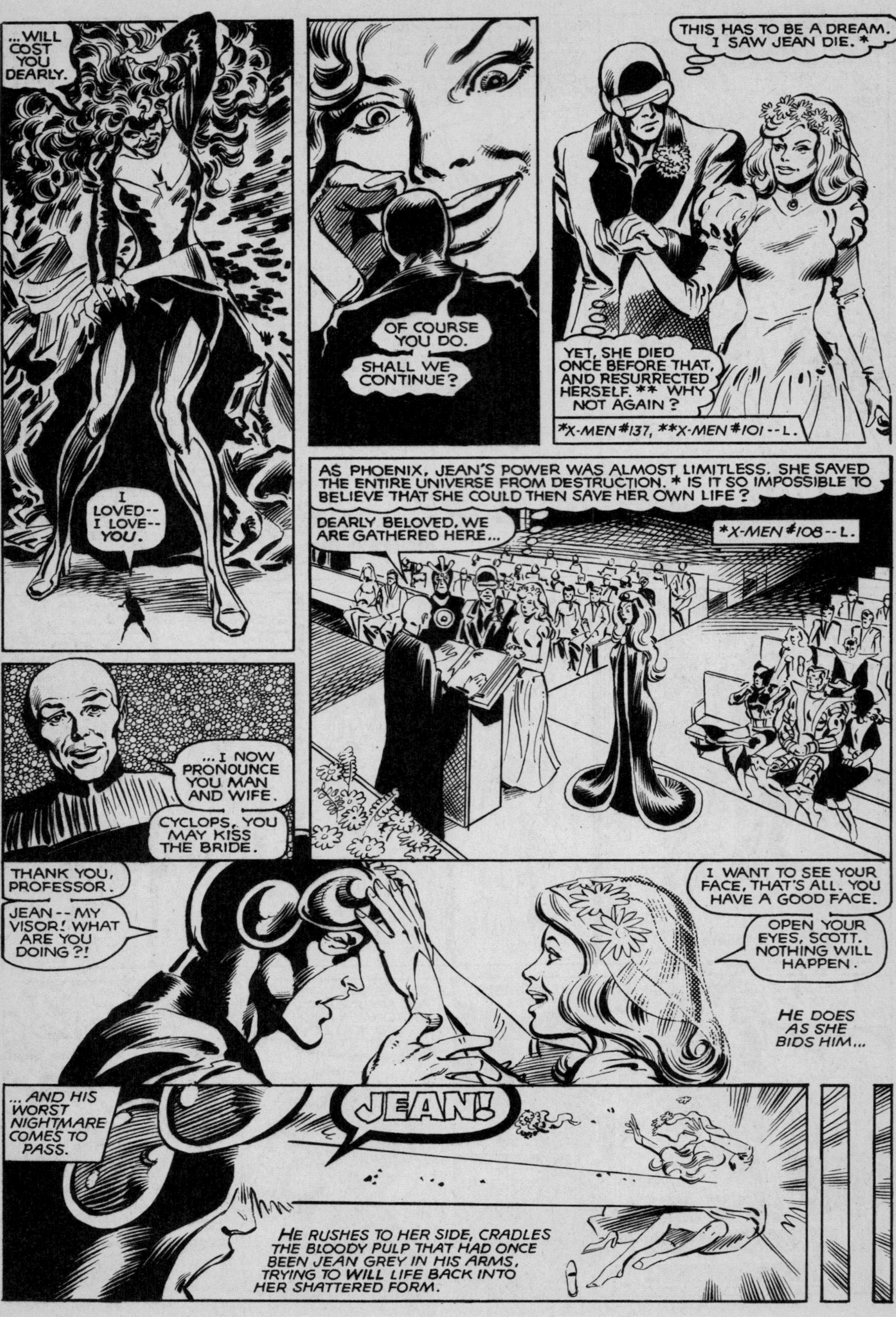
...WILL COST YOU DEARLY.
I LOVED-- I LOVE-- YOU.
OF COURSE YOU DO.
SHALL WE CONTINUE?
THIS HAS TO BE A DREAM. I SAW JEAN DIE.*
YET, SHE DIED ONCE BEFORE THAT, AND RESURRECTED HERSELF.** WHY NOT AGAIN?
*X-MEN #137, **X-MEN #101 --L.
AS PHOENIX, JEAN'S POWER WAS ALMOST LIMITLESS. SHE SAVED THE ENTIRE UNIVERSE FROM DESTRUCTION.* IS IT SO IMPOSSIBLE TO BELIEVE THAT SHE COULD THEN SAVE HER OWN LIFE?
DEARLY BELOVED, WE ARE GATHERED HERE...
*X-MEN #108 --L.
...I NOW PRONOUNCE YOU MAN AND WIFE.
CYCLOPS, YOU MAY KISS THE BRIDE.
THANK YOU, PROFESSOR.
JEAN -- MY VISOR! WHAT ARE YOU DOING?!
I WANT TO SEE YOUR FACE, THAT'S ALL. YOU HAVE A GOOD FACE.
OPEN YOUR EYES, SCOTT. NOTHING WILL HAPPEN.
HE DOES AS SHE BIDS HIM...
...AND HIS WORST NIGHTMARE COMES TO PASS.
JEAN!
HE RUSHES TO HER SIDE, CRADLES THE BLOODY PULP THAT HAD ONCE BEEN JEAN GREY IN HIS ARMS, TRYING TO WILL LIFE BACK INTO HER SHATTERED FORM.

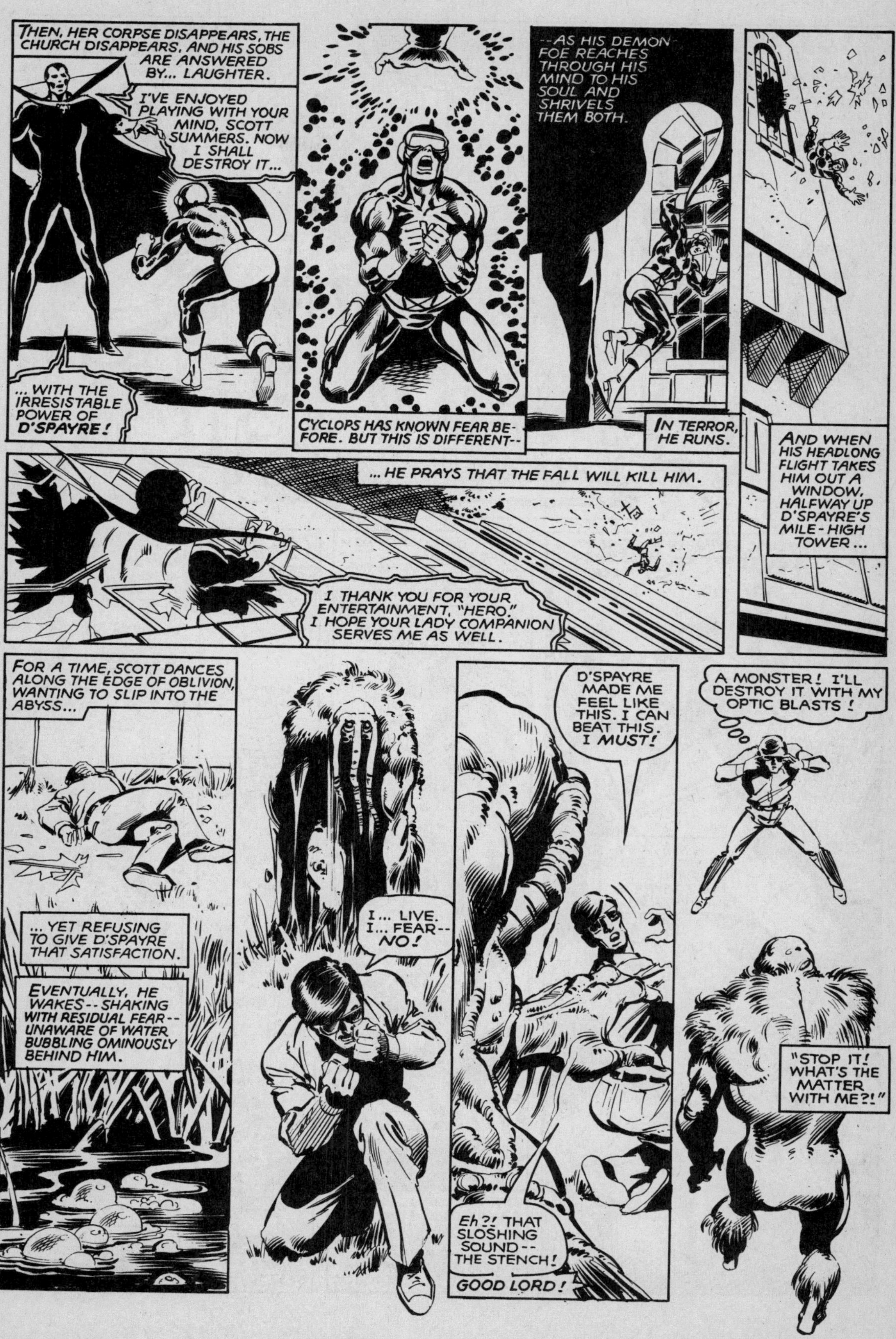
THEN, HER CORPSE DISAPPEARS, THE CHURCH DISAPPEARS, AND HIS SOBS ARE ANSWERED BY... LAUGHTER.
I'VE ENJOYED PLAYING WITH YOUR MIND, SCOTT SUMMERS. NOW I SHALL DESTROY IT...
...WITH THE IRRESISTABLE POWER OF D'SPAYRE!
CYCLOPS HAS KNOWN FEAR BEFORE. BUT THIS IS DIFFERENT--
--AS HIS DEMON FOE REACHES THROUGH HIS MIND TO HIS SOUL AND SHRIVELS THEM BOTH.
IN TERROR, HE RUNS.
AND WHEN HIS HEADLONG FLIGHT TAKES HIM OUT A WINDOW, HALFWAY UP D'SPAYRE'S MILE-HIGH TOWER...
...HE PRAYS THAT THE FALL WILL KILL HIM.
I THANK YOU FOR YOUR ENTERTAINMENT, "HERO." I HOPE YOUR LADY COMPANION SERVES ME AS WELL.
FOR A TIME, SCOTT DANCES ALONG THE EDGE OF OBLIVION, WANTING TO SLIP INTO THE ABYSS...
...YET REFUSING TO GIVE D'SPAYRE THAT SATISFACTION.
EVENTUALLY, HE WAKES--SHAKING WITH RESIDUAL FEAR--UNAWARE OF WATER BUBBLING OMINOUSLY BEHIND HIM.
I... LIVE. I... FEAR--NO!
D'SPAYRE MADE ME FEEL LIKE THIS. I CAN BEAT THIS. I MUST!
Eh?! THAT SLOSHING SOUND--THE STENCH!
GOOD LORD!
A MONSTER! I'LL DESTROY IT WITH MY OPTIC BLASTS!
"STOP IT! WHAT'S THE MATTER WITH ME?!"

AM I SO PANICKED THAT I'VE FORGOTTEN MY TRAINING? I *NEVER* UNLEASH MY BEAMS AGAINST ANY LESS THAN A DEFINATE FOE, A DEFINATE ATTACK.

THIS CREATURE ISN'T AFTER ME.

IT'S HEADING FOR D'SPAYRE'S TEMPLE.

BUT-- IS IT AFTER THE DEMON, OR LEE?!

JUST THINKING ABOUT GOING BACK IN THERE SCARES ME SILLY, BUT I HAVE TO DO IT.

FIRST, THOUGH, I'VE GOT TO CHANGE INTO COSTUME.

I NEED THE ABSOLUTE CONTROL OVER MY OPTIC BLASTS THAT MY RUBY QUARTZ VISOR AFFORDS ME.

THAT SCREAM-- *LEE!*

WITH A CASUAL SWEEP OF HIS GREAT MOSSY ARMS...

...THE MAN-THING CLEARS A PATH INTO D'SPAYRE'S SANCTUM.

Ah, MUCK-BEAST, WILL YOU *NEVER* LEARN?

LIGHT EXPLODES FROM D'SPAYRE'S HAND, TO INSTANTLY SEATHE THE SWAMP DWELLER IN ACID FLAMES.

IT'S A SIMPLE, AWFUL PROGRESSION. A TINY PART OF MAN-THING IS STILL HUMAN ENOUGH TO KNOW FEAR--AND WHATEVER KNOWS FEAR, *BURNS* AT THE MAN-THING'S TOUCH.

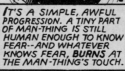

THUS DOES D'SPAYRE...

...MAKE HIS EMPATHIC FOE DESTROY HIMSELF. CYCLOPS, SEEING THE BEAST IN AGONY...

...TRIES HIS BEST TO HELP...

...ONLY TO SEE THE DEMON APPEAR TO TELE-PORT--LIKE NIGHT-CRAWLER ALL AROUND THE ROOM...

...LAUGHING SADISTIC-ALLY AS HE BLASTS THE QUAG-BEAST AGAIN AND AGAIN.

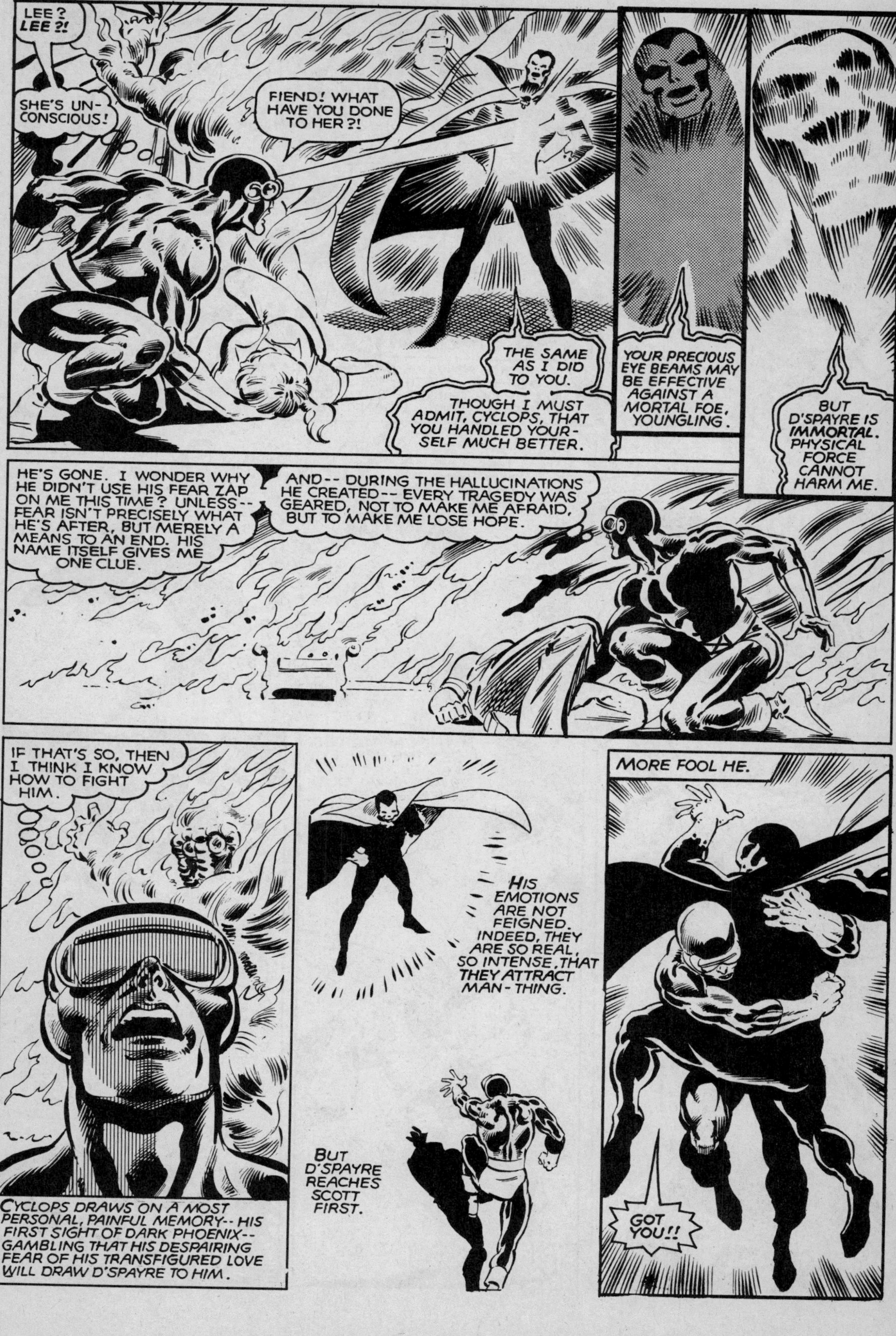
LEE? LEE?!
SHE'S UN-CONSCIOUS!
FIEND! WHAT HAVE YOU DONE TO HER?!
THE SAME AS I DID TO YOU.
THOUGH I MUST ADMIT, CYCLOPS, THAT YOU HANDLED YOUR-SELF MUCH BETTER.
YOUR PRECIOUS EYE BEAMS MAY BE EFFECTIVE AGAINST A MORTAL FOE, YOUNGLING.
BUT D'SPAYRE IS IMMORTAL. PHYSICAL FORCE CANNOT HARM ME.
HE'S GONE. I WONDER WHY HE DIDN'T USE HIS FEAR ZAP ON ME THIS TIME? UNLESS-- FEAR ISN'T PRECISELY WHAT HE'S AFTER, BUT MERELY A MEANS TO AN END. HIS NAME ITSELF GIVES ME ONE CLUE.
AND-- DURING THE HALLUCINATIONS HE CREATED-- EVERY TRAGEDY WAS GEARED, NOT TO MAKE ME AFRAID, BUT TO MAKE ME LOSE HOPE.
IF THAT'S SO, THEN I THINK I KNOW HOW TO FIGHT HIM.
CYCLOPS DRAWS ON A MOST PERSONAL, PAINFUL MEMORY-- HIS FIRST SIGHT OF DARK PHOENIX-- GAMBLING THAT HIS DESPAIRING FEAR OF HIS TRANSFIGURED LOVE WILL DRAW D'SPAYRE TO HIM.
HIS EMOTIONS ARE NOT FEIGNED. INDEED, THEY ARE SO REAL, SO INTENSE, THAT THEY ATTRACT MAN-THING.
BUT D'SPAYRE REACHES SCOTT FIRST.
MORE FOOL HE.
GOT YOU!!

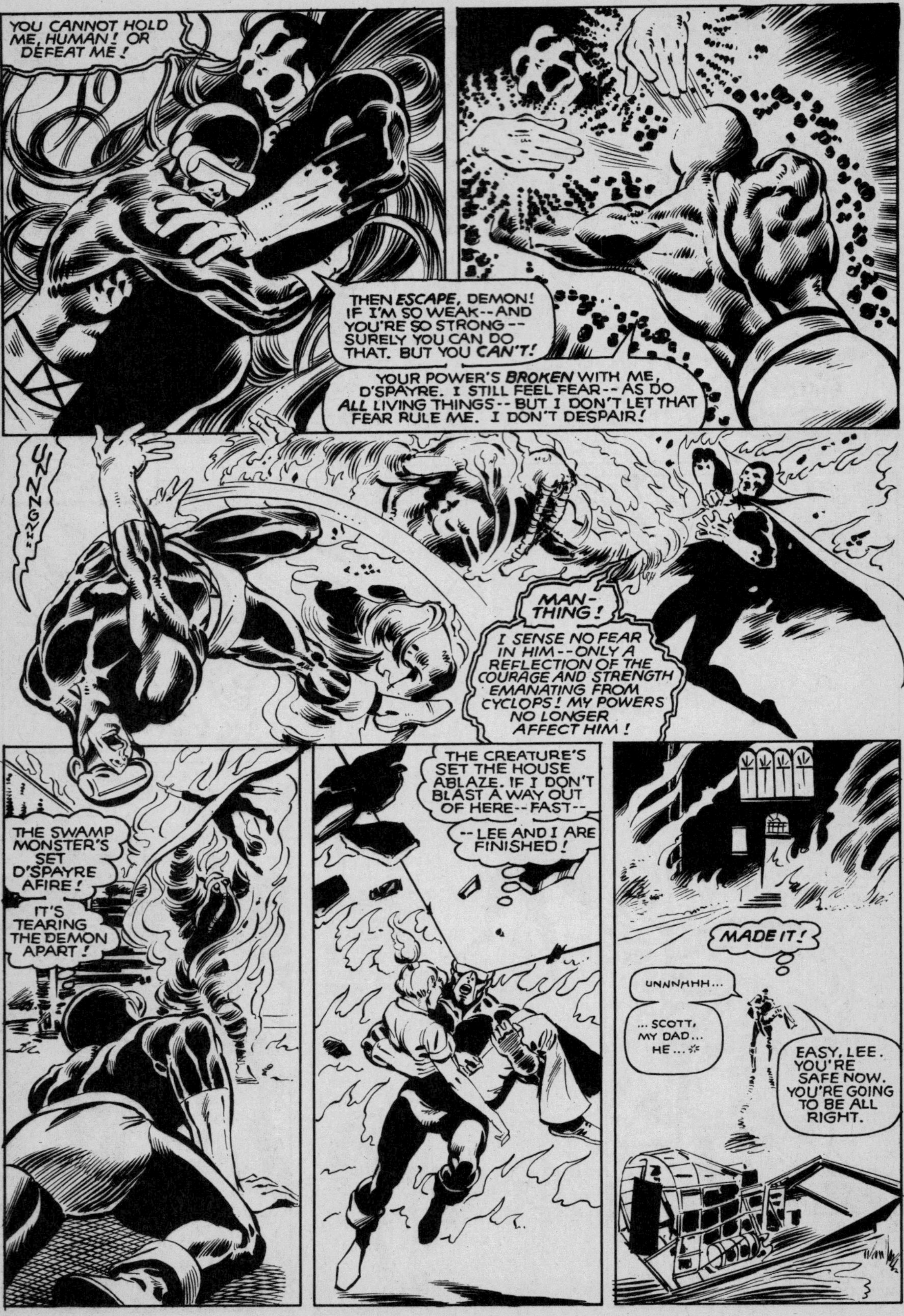

YOU CANNOT HOLD ME, HUMAN! OR DEFEAT ME!
THEN ESCAPE, DEMON! IF I'M SO WEAK--AND YOU'RE SO STRONG--SURELY YOU CAN DO THAT. BUT YOU CAN'T!
YOUR POWER'S BROKEN WITH ME, D'SPAYRE. I STILL FEEL FEAR--AS DO ALL LIVING THINGS--BUT I DON'T LET THAT FEAR RULE ME. I DON'T DESPAIR!
UNNNGHH
MAN-THING!
I SENSE NO FEAR IN HIM--ONLY A REFLECTION OF THE COURAGE AND STRENGTH EMANATING FROM CYCLOPS! MY POWERS NO LONGER AFFECT HIM!
THE SWAMP MONSTER'S SET D'SPAYRE AFIRE!
IT'S TEARING THE DEMON APART!
THE CREATURE'S SET THE HOUSE ABLAZE. IF I DON'T BLAST A WAY OUT OF HERE--FAST--
--LEE AND I ARE FINISHED!
MADE IT!
UNNNHHH...
...SCOTT, MY DAD... HE...
EASY, LEE. YOU'RE SAFE NOW. YOU'RE GOING TO BE ALL RIGHT.

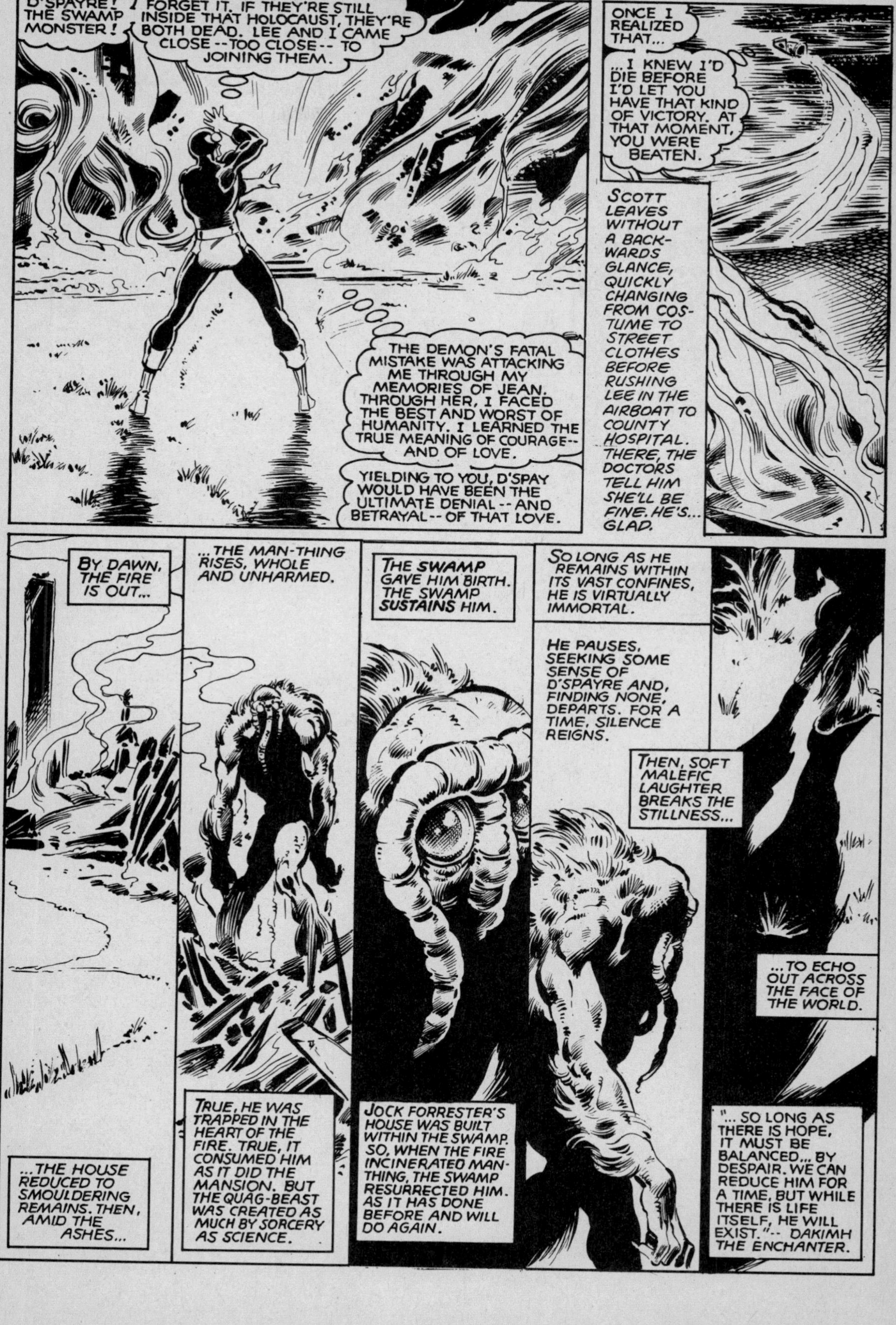
D'SPAYRE! THE SWAMP MONSTER!
FORGET IT. IF THEY'RE STILL INSIDE THAT HOLOCAUST, THEY'RE BOTH DEAD. LEE AND I CAME CLOSE -- TOO CLOSE -- TO JOINING THEM.
THE DEMON'S FATAL MISTAKE WAS ATTACKING ME THROUGH MY MEMORIES OF JEAN. THROUGH HER, I FACED THE BEST AND WORST OF HUMANITY. I LEARNED THE TRUE MEANING OF COURAGE -- AND OF LOVE.
YIELDING TO YOU, D'SPAY WOULD HAVE BEEN THE ULTIMATE DENIAL -- AND BETRAYAL -- OF THAT LOVE.
ONCE I REALIZED THAT...
...I KNEW I'D DIE BEFORE I'D LET YOU HAVE THAT KIND OF VICTORY. AT THAT MOMENT, YOU WERE BEATEN.
SCOTT LEAVES WITHOUT A BACK-WARDS GLANCE, QUICKLY CHANGING FROM COS-TUME TO STREET CLOTHES BEFORE RUSHING LEE IN THE AIRBOAT TO COUNTY HOSPITAL. THERE, THE DOCTORS TELL HIM SHE'LL BE FINE. HE'S... GLAD.
BY DAWN, THE FIRE IS OUT...
...THE HOUSE REDUCED TO SMOULDERING REMAINS. THEN, AMID THE ASHES...
...THE MAN-THING RISES, WHOLE AND UNHARMED.
TRUE, HE WAS TRAPPED IN THE HEART OF THE FIRE. TRUE, IT CONSUMED HIM AS IT DID THE MANSION. BUT THE QUAG-BEAST WAS CREATED AS MUCH BY SORCERY AS SCIENCE.
THE SWAMP GAVE HIM BIRTH. THE SWAMP SUSTAINS HIM.
JOCK FORRESTER'S HOUSE WAS BUILT WITHIN THE SWAMP. SO, WHEN THE FIRE INCINERATED MAN-THING, THE SWAMP RESURRECTED HIM. AS IT HAS DONE BEFORE AND WILL DO AGAIN.
SO LONG AS HE REMAINS WITHIN ITS VAST CONFINES, HE IS VIRTUALLY IMMORTAL.
HE PAUSES, SEEKING SOME SENSE OF D'SPAYRE AND, FINDING NONE, DEPARTS. FOR A TIME, SILENCE REIGNS.
THEN, SOFT MALEFIC LAUGHTER BREAKS THE STILLNESS...
...TO ECHO OUT ACROSS THE FACE OF THE WORLD.
"... SO LONG AS THERE IS HOPE, IT MUST BE BALANCED... BY DESPAIR. WE CAN REDUCE HIM FOR A TIME, BUT WHILE THERE IS LIFE ITSELF, HE WILL EXIST." -- DAKIMH THE ENCHANTER.

PROFESSOR X

Real Name: Charles Xavier
Occupation: Geneticist, teacher
Identity: Not publicly known to be mentor of the X-Men and "New Mutants."
Legal status: Citizen of the United States with no criminal record
Former aliases: None
Place of birth: New York City
Marital status: Single
Known relatives: Brian (father, deceased), Sharon (mother, deceased), Kurt Marko (stepfather, deceased), Cain Marko (stepbrother)
Group affiliation: Founder and mentor of the X-Men and "New Mutants"
Base of operations: Professor Xavier's School for Gifted Youngsters, Salem Center, Westchester County, New York
First appearance: X-MEN #1

Origin: Charles Xavier is the mutant son of nuclear researcher Brian Xavier and his wife Sharon. Even as a pre-adolescent, Xavier could use his powers to sense other people's intentions and emotions. Upon reaching puberty, Xavier's telepathic powers began to fully emerge. As a side effect, he began losing his hair until by high school graduation he was entirely bald. Xavier entered Bard College in Annendale-on-Hudson, New York, at 16 years of age, and earned his bachelor's degree in biology within 2 years. He was then accepted as a graduate student by England's Oxford University, where he earned degrees in genetics and biophysics at the same time. While at Oxford, Xavier met the daughter of Lord Kinross of Scotland, a college student named Moira, who was also a brilliant scholar in the field of genetics. Pending the annulment of her marriage, Moira agreed to marry Xavier. But immediately after finishing work at Oxford, Xavier was drafted and sent to Asia.

Wounded in battle, Xavier was recovering in a M.A.S.H. (Mobile Army Surgical Hospital) unit when he befriended psychiatrist Daniel Shomron. While he was there Xavier also received a letter from Moira putting an end to their engagement without explanation. Crushed, Xavier attempted to return to academic study after leaving the army, but he could not maintain his interest. Instead, he began aimlessly travelling about the Mediterranean, finally coming to terms with himself. Going to Cairo, he successfully defeated in battle the powerful criminal telepath Amahl Farouk, the first evil mutant he had ever met. He decided to make his life's work the protection of humanity from mutants like Farouk, and the protection of mutants from the prejudices of humanity.

From Egypt he went to Israel, where Shomron introduced him to one of his patients, Gabrielle Haller, and a mutant calling himself Magnus, who would later become Magneto, the foremost enemy of Xavier and the X-Men (see *Magneto*). Together Xavier and Magnus rescued Gabrielle from Baron Wolfgang von Strucker and his HYDRA agents (see *HYDRA*). Xavier then visited India and came to Tibet, where he found a walled city controlled by Lucifer, an alien plotting the conquest of Earth. Xavier led a successful rebellion against Lucifer, who took his revenge by dropping a heavy stone block on Xavier, permanently crippling his legs.

Xavier returned to Salem Center, again deeply depressed, and resumed his graduate work at Columbia University, New York, but spent most of his time as a recluse in his mansion. Eventually a friend of Xavier's from Bard, Prof. John Grey, brought his 10-year old daughter Jean to him for help. Xavier discovered that Jean was a mutant whose telepathic powers had emerged prematurely through the trauma of telepathically experiencing a close friend's death. Xavier helped Jean recover from her trauma, and maintained contact with her over the following years. After receiving a Ph. D. in anthropology at Columbia, Xavier spent the next several years earning an M.D. in psychiatry in London. While he was in England, Xavier crossed professional paths with his ex-fiancee Moira MacTaggert, now a renowned geneticist. Xavier and Moira discussed the possiblity of establishing a school for young mutants. However, after Xavier received his M.D., professional commitments forced him to put the idea of such a school aside. At Columbia, Xavier, now a visiting professor, continued his studies of mutation in what he called "Project Mutant."

When the F.B.I. launched an investigation of mutants, spurred by an incident involving the adolescent Scott Summers (see *Cyclops*), Xavier went to Washington, D.C. and met with Fred Duncan, the F.B.I. agent in charge of the investigation. Xavier proposed that he himself track down the superhumanly powered mutants in the United States, train young ones to use their powers for humanity's welfare, and report on his progress to

Investigator Duncan, who would keep Xavier's involvement entirely secret. Duncan fully agreed. (Xavier severed this connection with the government later, when anti-mutant prejudice grew evident in later presidential administrations, and all prior F.B.I. records on Xavier and the X-Men have been destroyed.) Xavier then found and befriended Scott Summers, who became the first of his students, or "X-Men," at his "School for Gifted Youngsters." Over the next several months Xavier also recruited the Iceman, Angel, the Beast, as well as Jean Grey, now several years older, who took the code-name of Marvel Girl. Xavier himself was given the nickname Professor X.

Sometime later Xavier decided that he had to spend months in solitary preparation of his psionic powers in order to deal with the forthcoming invasion by the alien Z'nox. He therefore allowed the Changeling, a mutant shape-changer with psionic powers, to impersonate him. When the Changeling died posing as Xavier, Xavier allowed everyone except Marvel Girl to believe that it was he himself who had died. Months later, he reemerged and helped defeat the Z'nox. In an as yet unexplained way, Xavier's massive use of psionic power in fighting the Z'nox forged a telepathic bond between him and Princess Lilandra of the Shi'ar Empire (see *Shi'ar*). She and Xavier later became romantically involved and engaged to marry.

Xavier recruited a number of new X-Men, including the Banshee, Colossus, Nightcrawler, Storm, and Wolverine, to help the others battle a "living island" called Krakoa. After this adventure, the Angel, Iceman, and Marvel Girl left the X-Men (the Beast had already left), leaving Xavier and Cyclops with the aforementioned "new X-Men" to train. After the second team of X-Men disappeared while in outer space, Xavier, believing them dead, vowed never again to train young mutants for combat. Moira, however, persuaded him to continue to run the school to train young mutants simply how to deal with their powers. Xavier agreed and founded the "New Mutants." In part he did so because he was under the influence of a member of the alien Brood who had been implanted as an egg within his body, and was seeking superhuman victims. However, Xavier reaffirmed his decision to have a "New Mutants" team even after he was freed from Brood influence and after the X-Men had returned alive. (See *Alien Races: Brood*.)

The growing Brood alien implanted within Xavier eventually took full control of his mind and transformed his body into that of a Brood member. The Xavier-alien was defeated and captured by the X-Men and Binary. Using cell samples taken from the human Xavier and Shi'ar science, Moira and "Sikorsky" of the Starjammers (see *Alien Races: Chr'ylites*) cloned a new body for Xavier that was slightly younger than his original, and

transferred his mind, now free from Brood control, into it. Xavier's new body theoretically should be able to walk; for some as yet unexplained reason he cannot.

Height: 6'
Weight: 190 lbs
Eyes: Blue
Hair: Bald

Powers: Professor X possesses numerous psionic powers making him the world's most powerful telepath. He can read minds and project his own thoughts into the minds of others within a radius of 250 miles. With extreme effort he can extend that radius to about 500 miles. (In past years, Professor X could use his telepathic powers over even greater distances, but Magneto has since altered the Earth's magnetic fields, thus creating long range "psychic static".) Xavier can psionically manipulate the minds of others; for example, to make himself seem to be invisible or look like someone else. He can also induce temporary mental or physical paralysis, and partial or total amnesia. Xavier can manipulate almost innumerable minds at close range for such simple feats. However, he can only take full possession of another person's mind one at a time, and he can only do so if he is within that person's presence.

Professor X can project powerful "mental bolts" of psionic energy enabling him to stun the mind of another person into unconsciousness. These bolts only apply force upon other minds, and thus have no effect on non-living creatures.

Professor X can sense the presence of another mutant within a small but as yet undefined radius of himself by perceiving the distinctive mental radiations emitted by such a being. In order to detect the presence of a superhuman mutant beyond this radius, he must use his powers in tandem with his invention called Cerebro (see *X-Men*), a device which is sensitive to that portion of the electromagnetic spectrum which contains the mental frequencies.

Professor X can project his astral form (the sheath of the life essense) onto astral planes (abstract dimensions congruent to our own), where he can use his powers to create "ectoplasmic" objects. He cannot engage in long-range astral projection on the earthly plane. (When he appeared to do so in the past, he was actually engaging in long-range telepathic communication involving the projection of a mental image of himself into another's mind.)

Professor X is unable to control matter psychokinetically to create psionic force fields, to project physical force bolts, or to mentally probe buildings, machines, or chemical substances. Examples of his performing any of these feats were either freak occurrences or were actions accomplished with the aid of artificial devices.

Charles Xavier is a genius in genetics and various other sciences. He is also talented at creating devices like Cerebro which enhance his psionic abilities.

CYCLOPS

Real Name: Scott Summers
Occupation: Adventurer
Legal status: American citizen with no criminal record
Identity: Secret
Former nicknames: Slim
Place of birth: Anchorage, Alaska
Marital status: Single
Known relatives: Major Christopher Summers/Corsair (father), Katherine Anne Summers (mother, deceased), Alexander Summers/Havok (brother)
Group affiliation: X-Men
Base of operations: Professor Xavier's School for Gifted Youngsters, Salem Center, New York
First appearance: X-MEN #1
Origin: Scott Summers was the oldest of two sons born to an Air Force Major and his wife. When he was still a youth, the plane flown by his father and carrying his mother and younger brother became engaged in an aerial skirmish with a Shi'Ar scoutship, and crashed. Before it crashed, Scott Summers and his brother Alex were pushed out of the craft by their father, with but one parachute between them. The two boys were hospitalized for injuries sustained during the high-speed landing of the over-burdened parachute. Scott himself was comatose for a year and was diagnosed as having brain damage. Scott had amnesia about the incident; Alex was too young to remember it. Leaving the hospital, Scott was placed in an orphanage in Omaha, Nebraska. When he was in his mid-teens, he began to get severe headaches and eyestrain, and was taken to an eye specialist in Washington, D.C. Through trial and error, the optometrist discovered that eyeglasses whose lenses were made out of ruby quartz seemed to alleviate the boy's vision problems. While en route to a second check-up, Summers' mutant metabolism reached a critical point and an uncontrolled optic force-blast was released for the first time. This demonstration occured in public and provoked the anger of a mob of witnesses. Summers managed to escape by hopping aboard a moving freight train. Afraid to go back to the orphanage because of his destructive power, he eventually fell into an unwilling partnership with a mutant named Jack Winters. In the meantime, Professor Charles Xavier had come out of self-imposed solitude to locate and help other mutants like himself. Meeting with special agent Fred Duncan of the Federal Bureau of Investigation, Xavier learned that Summers' eye doctor reported to the FBI that the boy may be a mutant. Eventually Xavier tracked dwon Summers and helped free him from Winters' criminal scheme. Xavier offered Scott Summers to be the first student at his School for Gifted Youngsters. Summers enthusiastically agreed and was given an identity-disguising school uniform and the codename Cyclops.
Height: 6' 3" **Weight:** 175 lbs
Eyes: Black **Hair:** Brown
Powers: Cyclops possesses the mutant ability to project a beam of concussive, ruby-colored force from his eyes. Cyclops's eyes are no longer the complex organic jelly that utilize the visible spectrum of light to see the world around it. Instead, they are interdimensional apertures between this universe and another, non-Einsteinian universe, where physical laws as we know them do not pertain. This non-Einsteinian universe is filled with particles which resemble photons, yet they interact with this universe's particles by transferring kinetic energy in the form of gravitons (the particle of gravitation). These particles generate great, directional concussive forces when they interact with the objects of this universe.

Cyclops's mind has a particular psionic field that is attuned to the forces which maintain the apertures which have taken the place of his eyes. Because his mind's psionic field envelops his body, it automatically shunts the other-dimensional particles back into their point of origin when they collide with his body. Thus, his body is protected from the effects of the particles, and even the thin membrane of his eyelids are sufficient to block the emission of energy. The synthetic ruby quartz crystal used to fashion the lenses of

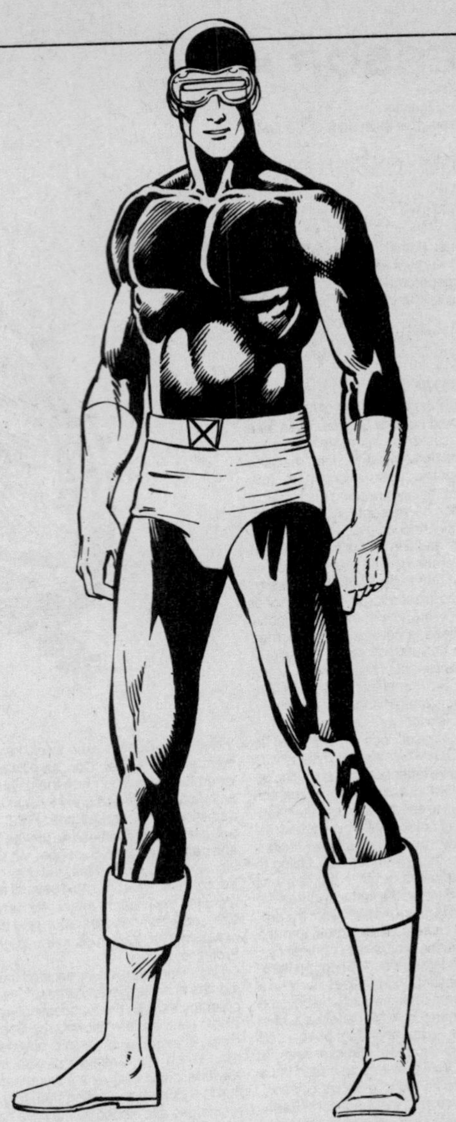

Cyclops's eyeglasses and visor is resonant to his minds' psionic field and is similarly protected.

The width of Cyclops's eye-blast seems to be focused by his mind's psionic field with the same autonomic function that regulated his original eyes' ability to focus. As Cyclops focuses, the size of the aperture changes and thus acts as a valve to control the flow of particles and the beam's relative power. The height of Cyclops's eye-blast is controlled by his visor's adjustable slit (see Equipment). His narrowest beam, about the diameter of a pencil at a distance of 4 feet has a force of about 2 pounds per square inch. His broadest beam, about 90 feet across at a distance of 50 feet, has a force of about 10 pounds per square inch. His most powerful eye-blast is a beam 4 feet across which, at a distance of 50 feet, has a force of 500 pounds per square inch. The maximum angular measurement of Cyclops's eye-blast is equivalent to a wide-angle 35mm camera lens field of view (90° measured diagonally, or the angle subtended by holding this magazine's pages spread open, upright at 9.5 inches from your eyes). The minimum angular measurement is equivalent to the angle that the thickness of a pencil would subtend at 4 feet (3.5°, about a quarter of an inch viewed at 4 feet). The beam's effective range is about 2,000 feet, at which point a 1-inch beam has spread out to 10 feet square, and then has a pressure of .38 pounds per square inch. Cyclops's maximum force is sufficient to tip over a filled 5,000 gallon tank truck at a distance of 20 feet, or puncture a 1-inch carbon-steel plate at a distance of 2 feet.

The extradimensional supply of energy for Cyclops's eye-blast is practically infinite. Thus, so long as Cyclops's psionic field is active (which is constantly), there is the potential to emit energy. The only limit to the eye-blast is the mental fatigue of focusing constantly. After about 15 minutes of constant usage, the psionic field subsides and allows only a slight leakage of energy to pass through the aperture. Cyclops's metabolism will recover sufficiently for him to continue in about an additional 15 minutes.
Equipment: The mask Cyclops wears to prevent random discharge is lined with powdered ruby quartz crystal. It incorporates two longitudinally mounted flat lenses which can lever inwards providing a constantly variable exit slot of 0 inches to .79 inches in height and a constant width of 5.7 inches. The inverted clamshell mechanism is operated by a twin system of miniature electric motors. As a safety factor there is a constant positive closing pressure provided by springs. The mask itself is made of high-impact cycolac plastic. There is an overriding finger-operated control mechanism on either side of the mask, and normal operation is through a flat micro-switch installed in the thumb of either glove.

WOLVERINE

Real name: Logan
Occupation: Adventurer; captain in the Canadian armed forces, assigned to intelligence (retired)
Identity: Secret, known to certain members of the Canadian government
Legal status: Citizen of Canada, now permanent resident in the United States; no criminal record
Former aliases: Weapon X
Place of birth: Unknown
Marital status: Single
Known relatives: None known
Group affiliation: X-Men
Base of operations: Professor Xavier's School for Gifted Youngsters, Salem Center, Westchester County, New York
First appearance: INCREDIBLE HULK #180
Origin: (partial) ALPHA FLIGHT #33–34
History: Wolverine's past is shrouded in mystery. There is no known record of his birth, and since his mutant healing ability causes him to age at a considerably slower rate than that of ordinary human beings, his age cannot be estimated. Wolverine has known the assassin Sabretooth for many years, but the nature of their past relationship is unknown (see *Sabretooth*). Before Wolverine's skeleton was laced with Adamantium, he served in a war with a group called the Devil's Brigade, and later worked as a freelance intelligence operative.

Wolverine's skeleton has been laced with the artificial, virtually indestructible metal called Adamantium, and he has been given artificial Adamantium claws (see *Adamantium*). Adamantium was first developed by the American scientist Dr. Myron MacLain (see *Appendix: MacLain, Dr. Myron*). After World War II a Japanese scientist known as Lord Dark Wind developed a process for bonding Adamantium to human bone (see *Appendix: Lord Dark Wind*). Lord Dark Wind thus hoped to create an army of invincible warriors, each with an Adamantium-reinforced skeleton. However, Lord Dark Wind's notes on the process were stolen by an unknown party, and it took him decades to reinvent the process.

It is known that within the last decade James MacDonald Hudson, then the head of Department H, a division of the Canadian government that would eventually form the team of superhuman agents known as Alpha Flight, possessed a report on the process of bonding Adamantium to the human skeleton, that was translated from Japanese (see *Alpha Flight, Deceased: Guardian*).

Hudson and his wife Heather took a delayed honeymoon in Canada's Wood Buffalo National Park (see *Vindicator*). There they were attacked by Logan, who had become savage and animalistic, and seemingly incapable of speech. Heather wounded Logan with gunfire and the Hudsons brought him to their cabin. James Hudson noticed Logan's fast healing ability and said that he would prove valuable to Department H. James Hudson skiied away, saying he was going to get medical help for Logan, and leaving Heather in the cabin with the unconscious "wild man," whom he had tied to a bed. But a blizzard prevented James Hudson from returning to the cabin, Logan regained consciousness and unwittingly extended his claws, severing his bounds, and then, again unwittingly, retracted the claws. Furious at being trapped in the cabin, Heather Hudson began berating Logan,

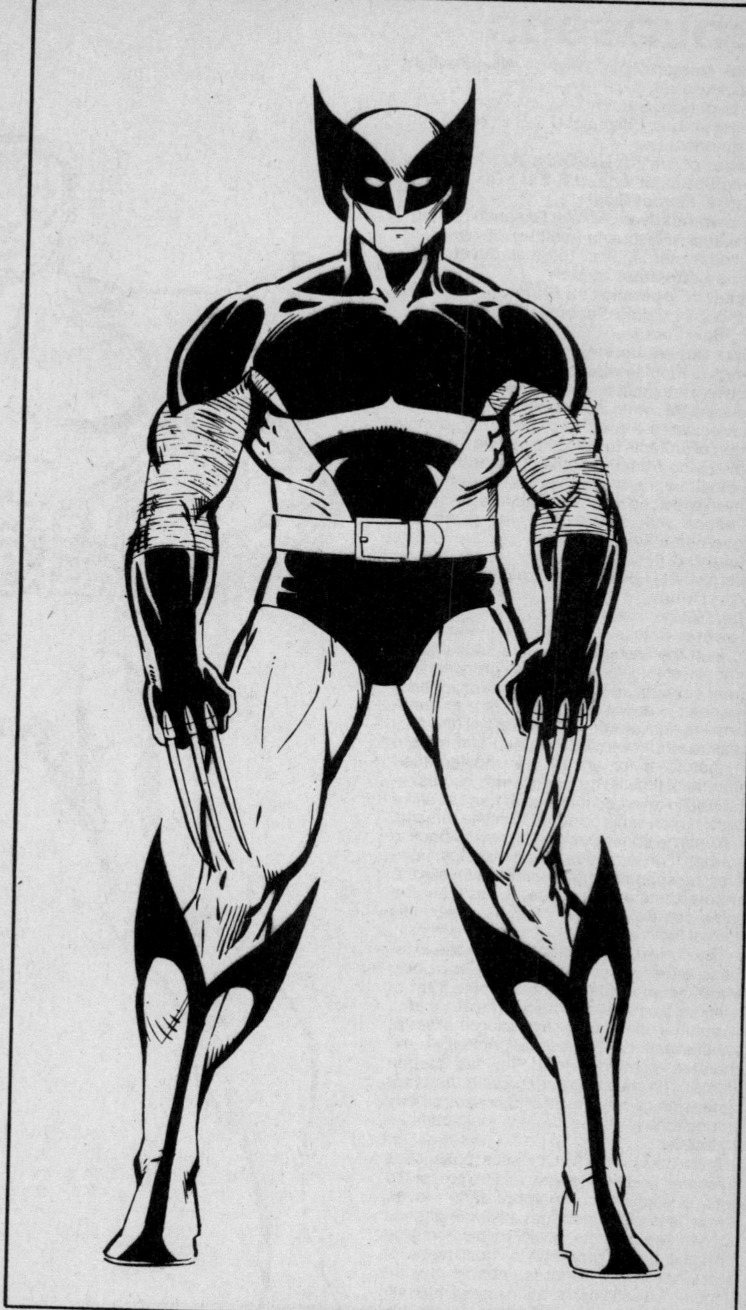

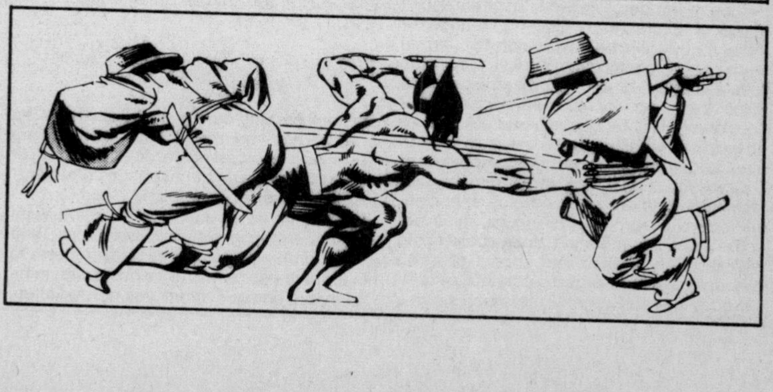

COLOSSUS

Real Name: Piotr ("Peter") Nikolaievitch Rasputin
Occupation: Student
Legal status: Citizen of U.S.S.R. now living in America
Place of birth: Ust-Ordynski Collective, Lake Baikal, Siberia, U.S.S.R.
Marital status: Single
Known relatives: Nikolai Rasputin (father), Alexandra Rasputina (mother), Illyana Rasputina (sister), Mikhail (brother, deceased)
Group affiliation: X-Men
Base of operations: Professor Xavier's School for Gifted Youngsters, Salem Center, New York
First appearance: GIANT-SIZE X-MEN #1
Origin: Piotr Rasputin is a mutant whose power manifested itself while in adolescence. He was contacted by Professor Xavier when Xavier was organizing a new team of mutants to help him rescue the original X-Men from the sentient island Krakoa. Rasputin agreed to leave the farm community in which he was born and raised to go to America with Xavier. He was given the code-name Colossus.
Height: 6' 6" (7' 5" armored)
Weight: 250 lbs (500 lbs armored)
Eyes: Blue
Hair: Black
Powers: Colossus possesses the ability to convert the tissue of his entire body into an organic steel-like substance, granting him great strength and a high degree of imperviousness to bodily harm. He is able to transform into this armor-like state at will (the process is virtually instantaneous) and remain in that form for an as yet undetermined amount of time. (The longest time he has remained in armored form so far has been five days.) Once in his armored form, he remains in it until he consciously wills himself back to normal. If he is rendered unconscious, however, he spontaneously reverts. While in the armored state, Colossus possesses the same degree of mobility that he does in his normal form.

The conversion from flesh and bone to organic steel is accomplished by a psionic whole-brain interface with an ionic form of osmium, an extremely dense metal, located in another dimension. In willing the act of transformation, Colossus actually exchanges osmium atoms for his carbon atoms. The psionic interface with the other dimension re-creates all of Colossus's body in functionally similar organic ionic-osmium materials.

In his metal form, Colossus possesses sufficient bodily strength to lift (press) 70 tons, equivalent to an empty earth mover. Since he is still a teenager, his strength has not yet reached its peak. In his armored form, he is invulnerable to most types of bodily harm. His armor is capable of withstanding ballistic penetration up to a 110 millimeter Howitzer shell. He can survive extremes of temperature from 70° Fahrenheit above absolute zero (–390° F) to approximately 9,000° F (the boiling point of normal osmium). Colossus could survive a collision with a loaded, 1 ton flatbed truck at 100 miles per hour, or an explosion of 450 pounds of TNT. Colossus could not survive an nuclear weapon blast nor a sustained blast from a molecular disintegration beam.

Colossus cannot become partially or selectively armored; his body is either entirely converted or not. Even his eyes become steel-like, meaning his eyeballs could withstand and deflect the impact of a .45 caliber bullet. The organic-osmium cells of his body die and regenerate much like his ordinary organic-carbon cells, so that if he were injured, he would heal at much the same rate. Ionic osmium does not oxidize under normal Earth atmospheric conditions; hence Colossus cannot rust.

Colossus is in unusually fine physical health permitting the transition back and forth from his normal organic flesh state to his organic-osmium state to occur with minimal stress on his system. His normal lungs are capable of holding his breath for 3.6 minutes, and in his hardier, armored state he is able to hold his breath for 15.7 minutes, even in space's hard vacuum. His endurance is somewhat greater in his armored form, but his practical exertions are not too dissimilar, for example, while armored he can run at about 26 miles per hour for short sprints, but while un-armored he can run at about 23 mph.

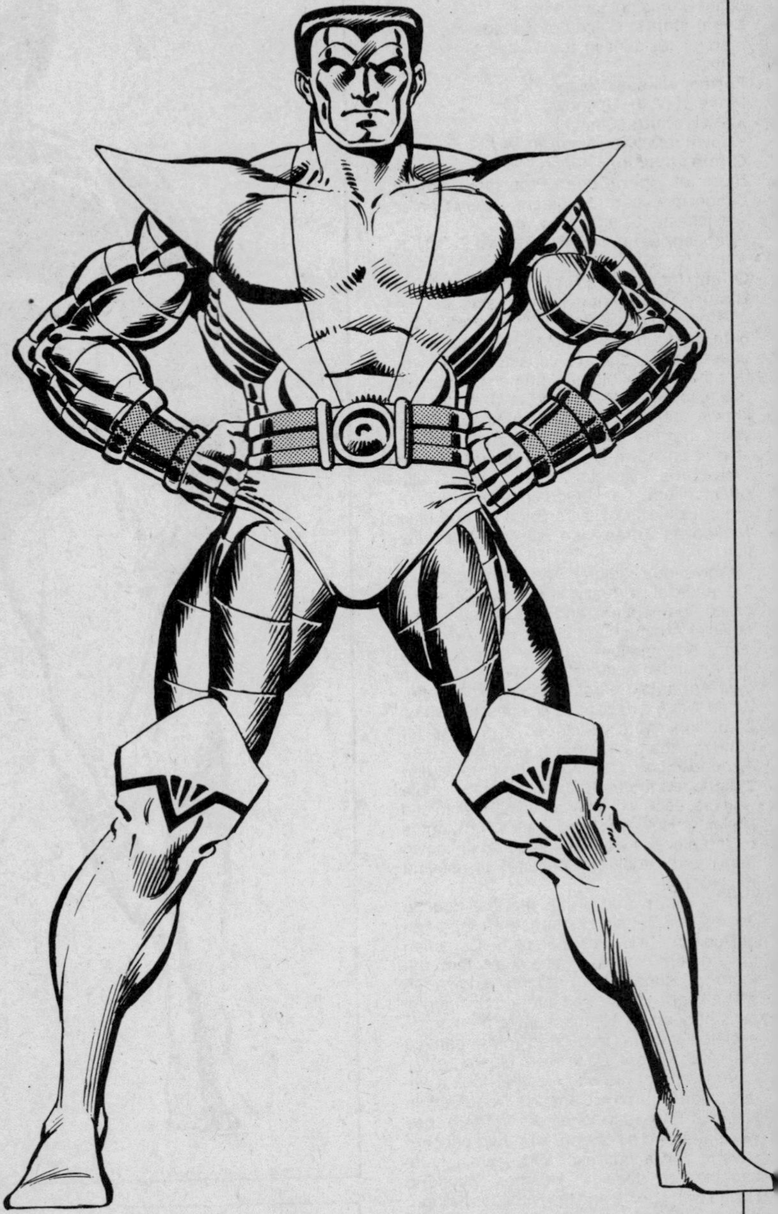

NIGHTCRAWLER

Real name: Kurt Wagner
Occupation: Adventurer, student
Identity: Secret
Legal status: Citizen of West Germany with no criminal record
Former aliases: None
Place of birth: Somewhere in the Bavarian Alps
Marital status: Single
Known relatives: Eric Wagner (father, deceased), Margali Szardos (foster mother), Jemaine Szardos (alias Amanda Sefton, foster sister), Stefan Szardos (foster brother, deceased). The name of Wagner's mother, who is presumed to be deceased, is not known
Group affiliation: X-Men
Base of operations: Professor Xavier's School for Gifted Youngsters, Salem Center, Westchester County, New York
First appearance: GIANT-SIZE X-MEN #1
History: Kurt Wagner was born with certain unusual physical characteristics, but his power of self-teleportation did not emerge until puberty. Less than an hour after his birth, Wagner was found in a small roadside shelter in the Bavarian Alps by Margali Szardos, a sorceress and gypsy queen (see *Appendix: Szardos, Margali*). She found his father, Eric Wagner, dead of a heart attack on the road outside. Margali is said to have found Wagner's mother lying next to the baby and dying, but this assertion has been called into question, and not even Kurt Wagner knows the truth. Margali took the baby to the small Bavarian circus where she worked as a fortuneteller as a "cover" for her activities as a sorceress. Wagner was never legally adopted by anyone, but was raised by all the members of the circus, who had no prejudices against "freaks." Margali acted as Wagner's unofficial foster mother.

Wagner grew up happily in the circus, and his two closest friends were Margali's natural children Stefan and Jemaine. Long before his teleportation power emerged, Wagner had tremendous natural agility, and by his adolescence he had become the circus's star acrobat and aerial artist. Circus audiences assumed that he was a normal-looking human being wearing a demon-like costume.

Years later, the Texas millionaire Amos Jardine, who ran a large circus based in Florida, heard of the circus Wagner worked for and bought it. Jardine intended to move its best acts into his American circus. However, he demanded that Wagner be placed in the circus's freak show. Appalled, Wagner quit and made his way towards Winzeldorf, Germany, where Stefan was. He discovered that Stefan had gone mad and had brutally slain several children. Two nights after leaving the circus, Wagner found Stefan and fought him, hoping to stop his rampage. In the course of the struggle Wagner unintentionally broke Stefan's neck. Then Wagner was discovered by the villagers of Winzeldorf, who assumed him to be a demon who was responsible for the child killings. They were about to kill him when they were all psionically paralyzed by Professor Charles Xavier, who had come to recruit Wagner into the X-Men (see *Professor X, X-Men*). Wagner agreed to join the group, but before they left for America, he and Xavier went to the Bavarian circus so that Wagner could explain to Margali about Stefan's death. However, Margali was not there. She held Wagner responsible for murdering Stefan, but years later, she learned the truth and she and Wagner were recon-

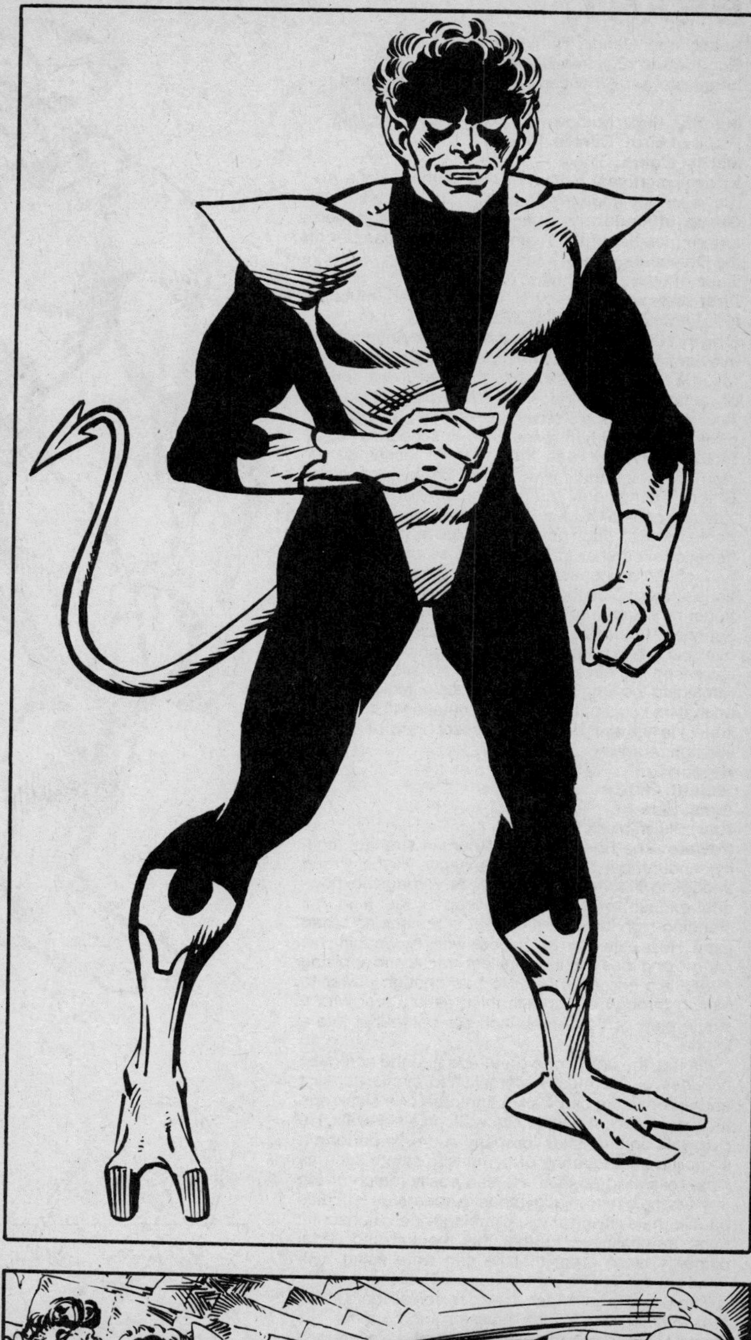

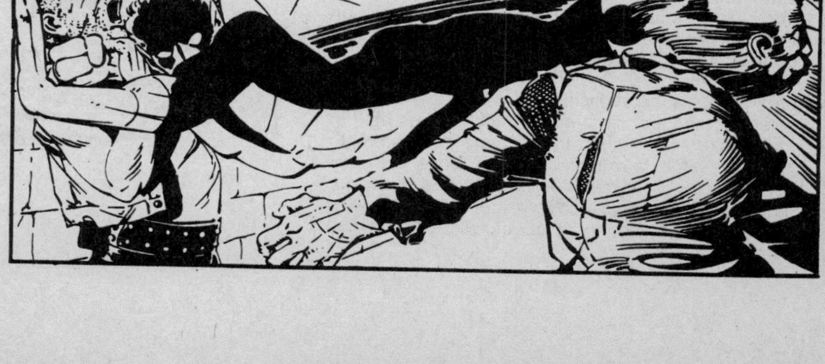

BEAST

Real Name: Henry ("Hank") McCoy
Occupation: Biochemist, adventurer
Legal status: American citizen with no criminal record
Identity: Publicly known
Place of birth: Dunfee, Illinois
Marital status: Single
Known relatives: Norton McCoy (father), Edna Andrews McCoy (mother), Robert McCoy (uncle)
Group affiliation: Former member of the X-Men, former member of the Avengers, current member of the Defenders
Base of operations: New York area
First appearance: X-MEN #1, (in current mutated form) AMAZING ADVENTURES #11
Origin: Henry McCoy is a mutant whose powers were in evidence since birth. The probable cause of his mutation was his father's exposure to massive amounts of radiation during a nuclear power plant "incident." As a youth, McCoy's superhuman agility and athletic prowess earned him recognition in school as a star football player. It was then that Professor Xavier learned of him and invited him to join his School for Gifted Youngsters. As a member of Professor Xavier's original X-Men, McCoy was given the code name "Beast." Upon graduation, McCoy got a job as a genetic researcher at the Brand Corporation. There he isolated a chemical catalyst that triggered mutations and sampled the serum in hopes of changing his appearance enough so he could ferret out enemy agents at the facility. The serum caused fur to grow over his entire body, enlarged his canine teeth, and increased his already prodigious athletic ability. By remaining too long in this altered state, McCoy learned that he could not reverse the mutation to its former state. He has since learned to accept his rather beast-like appearance.
Height: 5' 9"
Weight: 250 lbs
Eyes: Blue
Hair: Bluish black
Powers: The Beast has superhuman strength, agility, endurance, speed and dexterity. He is strong enough to lift (press) 2,000 pounds. His legs are powerful enough to enable him to leap 14 feet high in a standing high jump, and 22 feet in a standing broad jump. He is able to crawl up brick walls by wedging his fingers and toes into the smallest cracks and applying a vise-like grip on them. He has enough power to smash through a four-inch thick oaken door with a single blow or tie a three-inch solid steel bar into a knot.

He has the agility of a great ape and the acrobatic prowess of the most accomplished circus aerialist and acrobat. He can walk a tightrope or a slackrope as easily as most people can walk on a sidewalk. He can walk on his hands for many hours, or perform a complicated sequence of gymnastic stunts such as flips, rolls, and springs. He can easily match or top any Olympic record at gymnastic apparatus (such as parallel bars, flying rings, climbing ropes, horizontal bars, trampolines). Further, his manual and pedal dexterity is so great that he can write using both hands at once or tie knots in rope with his toes.

The Beast is quite fast, able to run on all fours at approximately 40 miles per hour for short sprints. His stamina is approximately triple that of a well-trained athlete in his prime. His physiology is durable enough to permit him to take a three story fall without a broken bone or sprain (providing he lands on his feet).

At the time of his further mutation into his present furry form, his metabolism underwent a period of accelerated change. As a side effect, he was able to metabolize and recover from penetration wounds to his body within a matter of hours. Since then, his body's metabolism has stabilized and he no longer has quite such a rapid recovery rate. He is still able to recover from a wound at about twice the normal human rate.

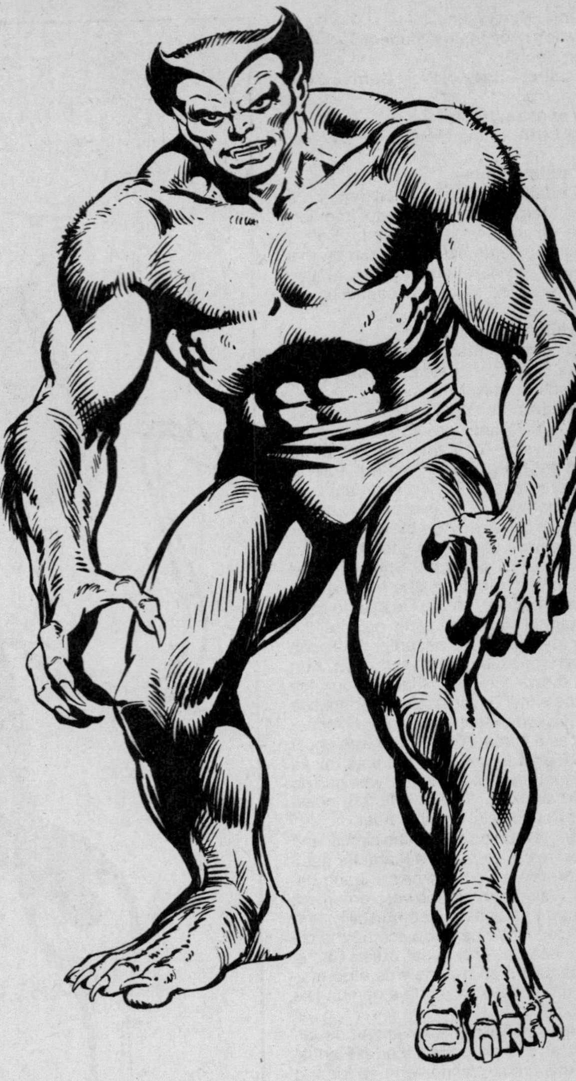

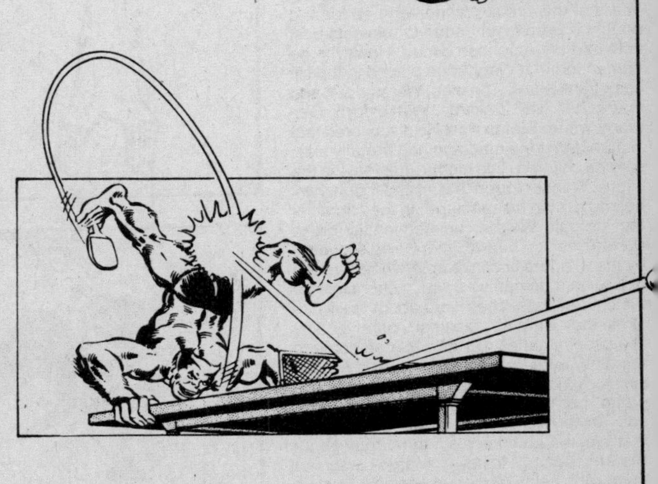